Controlling with SAP® ERP: Business User Guide

SAP PRESS

SAP PRESS is a joint initiative of SAP and Rheinwerk Publishing. The know-how offered by SAP specialists combined with the expertise of Rheinwerk Publishing offers the reader expert books in the field. SAP PRESS features first-hand information and expert advice, and provides useful skills for professional decision-making.

SAP PRESS offers a variety of books on technical and business-related topics for the SAP user. For further information, please visit our website: *www.sap-press.com*.

John Jordan
Product Cost Controlling with SAP (3rd Edition)
2016, 700 pages, hardcover and e-book
www.sap-press.com/3920

Vanda Reis
Actual Costing with the SAP Material Ledger (2nd Edition)
2015, 547 pages, hardcover and e-book
www.sap-press.com/3882

Kathrin Schmalzing
Configuring Controlling in SAP ERP
2016, 526 pages, hardcover and e-book
www.sap-press.com/3887

Marco Sisfontes-Monge
Controlling-Profitability Analysis with SAP (2nd Edition)
2012, 550 pages, hardcover and e-book
www.sap-press.com/2834

Janet Salmon

Controlling with SAP® ERP: Business User Guide

Rheinwerk Publishing

Editor Will Jobst
Acquisitions Editor Emily Nicholls
Copyeditor Melinda Rankin
Cover Design Graham Geary
Photo Credit Shutterstock.com: 92012588/© sodafish; 372864847/© Kaspars Grinvalds, 124638133/© Bugtiger
Layout Design Vera Brauner
Production Graham Geary
Typesetting SatzPro, Krefeld (Germany)
Printed and bound in the United States of America, on paper from sustainable sources

ISBN 978-1-4932-1736-6

3rd edition 2018

Library of Congress Cataloging-in-Publication Data
Names: Salmon, Janet, author.
Title: Controlling with SAP ERP : business user guide / Janet Salmon.
Description: 3rd Edition. | Boston : Rheinwerk Publishing, [2018] | Revised edition of the author's Controlling with SAP, [2014] | Includes index.
Identifiers: LCCN 2018021616 (print) | LCCN 2018025323 (ebook) | ISBN 9781493217373 (ebook) | ISBN 9781493217366 (alk. paper)
Subjects: LCSH: SAP ERP--Handbooks, manuals, etc. | Corporations--Accounting--Handbooks, manuals, etc. | Controllership--Handbooks, manuals, etc.
Classification: LCC HF5686.C7 (ebook) | LCC HF5686.C7 S266 2018 (print) | DDC 658.15--dc23
LC record available at https://lccn.loc.gov/2018021616

Contents at a Glance

Dear Reader,

Products should be designed for users.

We see this maxim in practice everywhere we look. For example, once cell phones and the internet went mainstream, drivers' on-the-go requirements evolved, and car manufacturers rolled out Bluetooth-enabled audio systems. Voilà! Hands-free phone calls and voice-controlled music.

But even the best products require some hints to align the settings with your expectations. (If only I could find my car stereo's user guide!) And when it comes to financial software, the systems are exponentially more complex—and for users, the stakes are even higher. If SAP ERP is your system and you have a question, Janet Salmon has the answer.

As a recognized Controlling specialist, Janet Salmon's mission with this book is to provide a day-to-day guide for SAP ERP Controlling. Janet knows the system inside and out, and years working with accountants and controllers have kept her perfectly attuned to business users' concerns. What does that mean for you? Access to the best practices and hot tips for running your Controlling processes, straight from the expert.

What did you think about *Controlling with SAP ERP: Business User Guide*? Your comments and suggestions are the most useful tools to help us make our books the best they can be. Please feel free to contact me and share any praise or criticism you may have.

Thank you for purchasing a book from SAP PRESS!

Will Jobst
Editor, SAP PRESS

willj@rheinwerk-publishing.com
www.sap-press.com
Rheinwerk Publishing · Boston, MA

Contents

Preface

In this chapter, I'll discuss my own roots in the Controlling component of SAP ERP Financials (CO), how I came to write this book, and what I am trying to achieve as I introduce the individual chapters.

When I joined SAP back in 1992, the documentation available in English was minimal, and what there was came in blue binders. My job was to translate some of these binders into English. The short form was a series of cardboard quick reference guides that listed the transaction codes needed to perform the tasks and the tables required to configure the system in each module. I spent my early weeks in Germany in the training center working my way through cost accounting (RK), materials management (RM), and financial accounting (RF) courses (in those days we were still on SAP R/2). Each week, I would add another German binder and quick reference guide to my pile. In theory, I was learning lots, but I was frustrated because I couldn't see the big picture and couldn't relate what I found in my heap of English accounting books with what I was learning about SAP. It was soon clear that translating CO was going to require more than a good dictionary.

The breakthrough came when a colleague suggested that I read Wolfgang Kilger's cost accounting bible, *Flexible Plankostenrechnung und Deckungsbeitragsrechnung*. Given my level of business German at that time, I sometimes wonder how much I actually took in. In retrospect, it hardly matters. Kilger's book told me how the pieces fit together and how my ever-growing list of transactions related to the business world. It allowed me to ask the right questions of the consultants who would spend time in our office testing the new software. When SAP R/3 came along, I stopped translating and started writing documentation.

For most English speakers, the breakthrough came with the publication of *Product Costing Made Easy* in 1998. This book walked users through every posting performed in product costing, giving the T-accounts for each step in the process. I still meet controllers and consultants who go misty eyed at the mention of this book and confess to a terror of losing their copy. This book was the ultimate reference, and I still pull it out when I'm testing new functions and trying to remember how they should work.

In 2009, I gave a presentation at SAP Financials in Prague that was based on the postings described in *Product Costing Made Easy* to a full house. It showed me that 10 years on, people were still struggling to relate the business processes in sales, production, and purchasing with the T-accounts in Financials and the various cost objects used to provide information to management. There were still people searching for the big picture, as I had been back in 1992. The germ of this book you're reading was contained in that presentation.

However, things have moved on in the last 10 years—not least in the fact that SAP R/3 has become SAP ERP. In this book, I'll give you the same menu paths and transaction codes that I would have given 10 years ago. I loved the menus when we moved from transaction codes in SAP R/2 to menus in SAP R/3, but the sheer number of transactions means that the menus are now becoming as unwieldy as my quick reference guides for SAP R/2, so I'll also show you how to use roles to present those transactions in a more user-friendly manner.

I'll show you where to find the reports you'll need in SAP ERP, but I'll also tell you where SAP Business Warehouse (SAP BW) fits into the picture. I'll introduce the reporting options available with SAP BusinessObjects. I'll show you how to plan in SAP ERP, but I'll also show you how to use the newer planning options. I'll tell you how to set up your master data in SAP ERP but also how to use a change request to document why you need to make changes to your master data at all and introduce the newer solutions for managing master data in a multisystem or shared service environment. I'll talk about allocations in SAP ERP but also about when to consider SAP Profitability and Cost Management. I'll walk you through the period-close activities, but I'll also show you how to use the SAP Financial Closing cockpit to provide a framework for the close.

Moving forward in time, I'll introduce SAP HANA, SAP's in-memory database, and explain its impact on Controlling. Finally, I'll show you the major changes that SAP S/4HANA will bring to Controlling and show where we're planning to take the solution going forward.

In 2010, I took over the role of chief product owner for management accounting and now manage new developments that are taking place in CO. This book will explain the basics for a reader new to CO, but it will also look at the enhancements that affect CO in all releases up to EHP 8 for SAP ERP 6.0, so it should provide information relevant for more experienced controllers and consultants. When I wrote the first edition, things didn't seem to be changing as fast as they had in the 1990s, but there were still changes that affected CO, such as International Financial Reporting Standards

(IFRS) becoming more prevalent or corporate controlling attempts to take a group view that would have been pure fantasy back in the early 1990s. By the time I finished the first edition, SAP HANA, SAP's new platform for in-memory computing, was redefining what was possible in Controlling, and my team was involved in radical changes. These are covered in Chapter 13, which introduces many new options only available with SAP HANA. With the third edition, I've added another chapter to cover changes introduced with SAP's new product, SAP S/4HANA.

However, this book is not a configuration guide. I spent the mid-1990s writing implementation guides, so it didn't seem fair to write about configuring cost components and costing variants now when there are others better qualified than me to do so. I'll generally assume that you have a configured system before you, though I might show you things that were not available or that your implementation didn't know about when it was carried out. When this happens, I'll try to include enough information to enable you to find what you need in the SAP documentation.

This book also is not a white paper, though I've written plenty of those, too. I wanted to fill the space between the high-level white paper and the detailed implementation guide because for me this is where the most interesting questions lie. If you understand how the pieces fit together, then you should be able to ask the right questions, whether these are general questions, such as where to plan or report, or specific questions about the handling of an individual business process from a controlling perspective.

Over the last several years, I have had the pleasure of working with controllers at many customer sites, and these conversations are reflected in the pages of this book. I may not be a controller, but I am in constant discussions with controllers working with SAP ERP. I hear where they are struggling, whether in conversations with user groups, answering a customer message asking for help on a specific issue, or when we are developing new functions in collaboration with some of our key customers. It is these conversations that make this a practical guide.

As for the examples in this book, I've tried to take my screenshots from the standard demo system, IDES, whenever possible so that anybody with access to that demo landscape can follow the examples for themselves. In most cases, I was using EHP 7 for SAP ERP 6.0 and the demo system was running on the SAP HANA Enterprise Cloud. In Chapter 13 I was using various test systems, and in Chapter 14 I was using SAP S/4HANA 1709.

This may mean that the examples I show are not specific to your industry, though I do try to mention industry variants when I consider them relevant. Some of the examples are a little simplistic, because I wanted them to be easy to understand, unlike some of the real-life examples I see at customer sites. If there are issues surrounding more complex examples, such as performance or locking, I've tried to mention them, though clearly I can't know every detail of your organization's particular implementation.

SAP S/4HANA brings significant architectural changes to Controlling. I've added boxes throughout the book that introduce the changes so that you will be prepared for the future whenever your organization feels ready to make the move. If your organization intends to stay exactly where it is in the near future, feel free to ignore these boxes.

A Practical Guide to Controlling with SAP

Let's briefly look at what's covered in each chapter. I've tried to make it easy for a new controller with basic accounting experience to start at the beginning and work from front to back. Experienced controllers may prefer to use the index to find the key features that interest them or use the downloadable appendix on new business functions to find out about areas they haven't yet explored.

Introduction

In **Chapter 1**, we'll explain basic concepts such as cost elements, fixed and variable costs, standard costs, and actual costs as they apply to CO. We'll introduce the roots of CO, explaining where there are differences with respect to typical cost accounting practices in the United States and where there is common ground. We'll introduce record keeping by cost center, order, and project and introduce the main tasks to be performed at period close. We'll also look at planning and budgeting as a key element of CO and introduce the internal controls necessary for the business processes involved in CO.

Reporting

In **Chapter 2**, we'll introduce cost center line items, order line items, and line items in Profitability Analysis not only in terms of the information they offer but also as an introduction to the way controllers work with such data. We'll look at the key functions in SAP List Viewer, so you'll learn how to use existing layouts and create new layouts for your particular purposes. We'll also look at your reporting options for Product Cost Controlling and the various tree reports that allow you to view the structure of bills of material (BOMs), both for standard costs and actual costs. Finally, we'll introduce the data flows to Profitability Analysis, explain the difference between costing-based and account-based Profitability Analysis, and look at the record types available for reporting.

Master Data Owned by Controlling

In **Chapter 3**, we'll look at the master data for which the controlling department is responsible, showing how to create cost centers, internal orders and settlement rules, statistical key figures, activity types, secondary cost elements, product cost collectors, and cost object hierarchies. We'll look at how to group this master data to ease selection for reporting and allocations and how to handle time-dependent master data. We'll look at statuses of internal orders and discuss how to create change requests to initiate a master data change. We'll also introduce new user interfaces for this master data, first delivered with EHP 6 for SAP ERP 6.0.

Master Data for Which Controlling Is a Stakeholder

In **Chapter 4**, we'll look at the master data for which the controlling department is one of several stakeholders, showing the relevant fields in the material master, customer master, BOM, routing, and work center. We'll look at different types of BOMs, including BOMs for joint production, BOMs for configurable materials, and recursive BOMs, and different types of routings, including master recipes and rate routings. We'll also look at production alternatives and how to mix them for product costing. We'll then look at the master data for projects and investment programs and discuss the fields that matter to the controlling department. We'll explain the link between the operational chart of accounts and the primary cost elements used in CO. Finally, we'll look at the price information in the material master and purchasing info records for the raw materials; this key information has to be in place before we start planning in Chapter 5 or performing goods movements in Chapter 6.

Planning and Budgeting

In **Chapter 5**, we'll look at a complete planning cycle, starting with the sales plan in Profitability Analysis, transferring the results to sales and operational planning in logistics, bringing a scheduled activity from the production plan back to the cost center plan, and then planning cost center expenses for both operational and supporting cost centers and taking account of activity-dependent and activity-independent costs. We'll then calculate the activity price for those cost centers and look at how to generate a primary cost component split for that activity price before looking at how to create a costing run to calculate the standard costs for all the materials we plan to manufacture. We'll then mark and release the cost estimates to transfer the results to the material master and use valuation to pull the results of the cost estimate into Profitability Analysis. We'll also look at investment planning, starting with an investment program and planning values for the projects assigned to that program, preparing budgets for these projects, and learning how to initiate a change request to change or transfer a budget. We'll also introduce the new user interfaces delivered for planning with EHP 6 for SAP ERP 6.0.

Actual Postings

In **Chapter 6**, we'll walk through the typical steps in a procure-to-pay, plan-to-manufacture, and order-to-cash process to show you what a controller typically monitors in each step and where variances can potentially occur. We'll then look at how to handle differences identified during a physical inventory and assign them to the work orders or product cost collectors processed during the time between inventory counts. Next, we'll look at how to handle coproducts, perform an order split or rework, handle outsourced manufacturing processes, work with product cost collectors, use configurable materials and sales order stock, work with Work Breakdown Structure (WBS) elements as account assignments, and work with maintenance and service orders. We'll discuss how to make correction postings, and we'll end the chapter by looking at a cross-company stock transfer from both a legal and group perspective.

Period Close

In **Chapter 7**, we'll look at the main tasks that take place at period close, including allocations both between cost centers and to Profitability Analysis, and explain the differences between real-time direct activity allocations and the typical period-close allocations. We'll look at the different forms of allocation, including assessment cycles, distribution cycles, reposting cycles, and indirect activity allocation cycles. We'll then look at target costs and variances on cost centers and how to calculate an activity price based on actual costs. Having completed the close steps in Cost Center Accounting, we'll look at the close activities in Cost Object Controlling, including calculating work in process (WIP), variances, and settlement. If you're using the Material Ledger, we'll also look at the periodic costing run and the alternative valuation run as a means of calculating actual product costs once the period is complete. Finally, we'll look at the revaluation and top-down distribution tasks in Profitability Analysis.

Reporting in SAP BW and SAP BusinessObjects

In **Chapter 8**, we'll look at how to analyze large volumes of data in SAP ERP, explaining the use of extracts and variation in Report Writer, summarization levels in Profitability Analysis, and summarization objects in Cost Object Controlling. We'll look at some of the criteria that might affect a decision to move to SAP Business Warehouse (SAP BW), including performance issues, multidimensionality, and a need to mix data from multiple systems. This chapter won't have the depth of a book dedicated to reporting in SAP BW, but it will show you how to find the delivered DataSources, InfoProviders, and queries for CO and bring data from an existing operating concern into SAP BW. We'll explore examples of querying data in cost center reporting and using physical, virtual, and transient InfoProviders and will wrap up with an introduction to SAP Analysis for Office, SAP Crystal Reports, and SAP BusinessObjects Dashboards.

Master Data in a Multisystem/Shared Service Environment

In **Chapter 9**, we'll return to the internal service request we introduced in Chapter 3 and look at the configuration required to prepare the form, workflow, and notification to document the requested change and the proper execution. We'll then introduce a solution for master data maintenance in a multisystem environment, available from EHP 4. We'll look at the data model, editions, change requests, and distribution services delivered with SAP Master Data Governance for Financials. Finally, we'll look at master data maintenance in the context of a shared service scenario delivered through the SAP Shared Service Framework.

Planning Using SAP BW Technologies

In **Chapter 10**, we'll return to the planning layouts we looked at in Chapter 5 and discuss how they are used to structure the data available for planning in SAP ERP before moving on to discuss your options for planning in SAP BW or SAP Strategic Enterprise Management (SAP SEM), where we'll look at examples of investment planning using SAP BW. We'll then look at new solutions in EHP 6 that combine the flexibility of an input-enabled query in SAP BW with the ability to write the planned data directly to the SAP ERP tables, where there is no business requirement for full data modeling.

Allocations Using SAP Profitability and Cost Management

In **Chapter 11**, we'll look at more sophisticated ways of allocating overhead, using either template allocation—if most of your allocations can be made using drivers in SAP ERP—or SAP Profitability and Cost Management, which allows you to load the relevant data into a dedicated environment and perform allocations and what-if simulations with the goal of understanding the cost to serve a customer segment or the true profitability of an individual customer.

Period Close Using the SAP Financial Closing Cockpit

In **Chapter 12**, we'll pick up where we left off in Chapter 7 and look at ways to document which steps are performed as part of your period close, automate the close steps by using executable programs and workflows, handle errors that occur during the period close, and handle a close process that crosses multiple systems. We'll also look at new options for reporting on the progress of your period close.

Controlling with New Technologies

In **Chapter 13**, we'll revisit Chapter 2 and Chapter 8 to introduce new options for reporting that are available through SAP's in-memory database, SAP HANA. We'll also return to the period-close tasks we looked at in Chapter 7 to understand which of these have been accelerated by moving to the new database. We'll introduce SAP Fiori as the umbrella term for a series of initiatives to improve the user interface and allow you to run SAP applications on smartphones and tablet devices as well as on the standard desktop.

SAP S/4HANA and Controlling

In **Chapter 14**, we'll walk you through the key changes that affect Controlling in SAP S/4HANA, SAP's new product. These include the introduction of the Universal Journal, which brings together the transactional tables for Financial Accounting and Controlling; use of the Material Ledger to handle all forms of inventory valuation; changes to Profitability Analysis; and changes to reporting and planning in the new environment.

Appendices

The appendices for this book are available for you to download at *www.sap-press.com/4691*.

In **Appendix A**, we'll look at how to use SAP Business Client or SAP Enterprise Portal to display transactions, reports, and web applications, so your administrator will be able to make your system look like the examples shown in the book.

In **Appendix B**, we'll look at how to configure a report launchpad to make it easier for your users to find the reports relevant to their roles, so your administrator can recreate some of the screens shown in Chapter 2.

In **Appendix C**, we'll discuss how to activate the enterprise extensions and business functions needed for the newer functions described in this book.

Acknowledgments

The first edition of this book wouldn't have been possible without the help and support of many colleagues. Hendrik Ahlgrimm, Michael Alexander, Dirk Degrell, Mario Franz, Johannes Gierse, Markus Königstein, Hartmut Körner, Ralf Ille, Stefan-Claudius Müller, Stephan Rehmann, Thomas Pike, Alfred Schaller, Sadaf Shakil, Stefan Tex, Marco Valentin, and Klaus Weiss answered many of the questions that came up during the writing process and corrected the manuscript. To them, I extend my sincerest thanks. I'm delighted to be able to thank many of the same colleagues for their help with the second and third editions.

For all editions, I'd also like to thank Dondogmaa Lkhamdondog for her help and support when I needed changes to the SAP ERP demo systems, Thomas Schultze for his support when working with the SAP BusinessObjects demo systems, and Birgit Starmanns for preparing the original T-account presentation shown at SAP Financials in

Las Vegas. While writing the first edition, I was helping to train our China team, and their questions inevitably flowed into the text. In this context, I'd like to thank Alex Hu, Emily Li, Bill Liu, Alex Ouyang, Zhiqiang Wu, and Ivan Zhang from the Shanghai office.

Next I'd like to thank Michael Franz for his help on the Material Ledger, Ilona Massong for her help on master data governance, Richard Gu and Jack Li for their help on SAP HANA, Phong Huynh and Fernando Rodriguez for their help on SAP Fiori, Steffen Vollmert for his help with the new planning applications, and Stefan Walz for his help on the new approach to controlling for professional services.

I'd also like to thank Meg Dunkerley, Emily Nicholls, Will Jobst, and the SAP PRESS team for their help in guiding me through all three books.

And finally, the biggest thank-you to my family: my husband, Nick, and my children, Martin and Lucy. As usual, Nick's biggest contribution was helping me to keep cycling while the book was in progress, since my creative thoughts tend to happen on the bike.

Chapter 1
Introduction

This chapter discusses the roots of Controlling with SAP ERP Financials and introduces the basic Controlling functions. You'll learn what might be different from other systems you've encountered and where there is common ground.

People taking their first class on Controlling with SAP ERP Financials (which we'll refer to as CO moving forward) are often daunted by the sheer range of functions, because CO is several costing systems rolled into one, covering responsibility accounting, planning, activity-based costing, product cost accounting, and profitability management, whereas most other systems handle each of these areas separately. A quick glance at the SAP menu (see Figure 1.1) shows a series of folders that you may not instantly be able to map to your current approach to cost accounting.

Let's start with the top menu folder: **Cost Element Accounting.** This can sound like an alien concept if you're used to seeing cost centers and orders simply as account assignments in the General Ledger, with postings made to an account and a "center." You may only be familiar with the term *account* and never have encountered the term *cost element* at all. The cost element provides the link to the General Ledger accounts, so typical cost elements are wages and salaries (for recording the costs associated with your workforce), materials and services (for recording the costs associated with the goods you buy and sell), depreciation (for recording the costs associated with your assets), utility costs, and so on. In some countries, you'll hear this transformation discussed in terms of *costs by nature*. These are really just words, so if it helps to carry on thinking of a cost element as an account, by all means do, at least for *primary cost elements*. Cost elements are also used to store the results of any allocation, so you'll also use several additional cost elements to define how costs flow through your organization. These cost elements are known as *secondary cost elements*, and we'll look at how to define the two types in Chapter 3 and Chapter 4. When defining your cost elements, it's also important to understand how the costs behave. Energy costs are *variable*, rising as the output of the cost center rises, but rent costs are *fixed*, remaining constant irrespective of how much work the cost center performs.

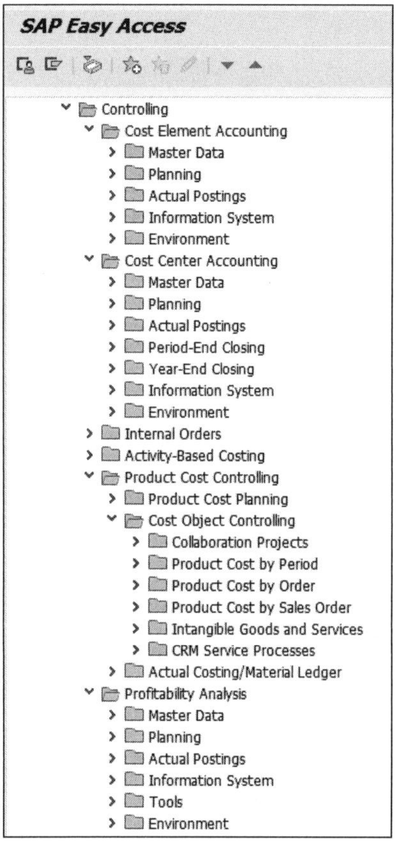

Figure 1.1 Controlling in SAP Easy Access Menu

If the cost element answers the question of the *type* (or nature) of costs incurred, the question of *why* such costs were incurred is answered in the next folders: **Cost Center Accounting** and, to a lesser extent, **Internal Orders**. Every posting in the SAP General Ledger recorded under an account with a sister cost element (the primary cost element) also requires you to enter the following:

- The *cost center* for which the costs were incurred (e.g., in the example of wages and salaries, for which department the employees were working)
- The *order or project* for which the costs were incurred (e.g., in the example of goods and services, which project required the purchase to be made)

Within this type of posting, there is an idea of *responsibility accounting*—that is, making the cost center manager responsible for the costs incurred for his cost center and the project manager responsible for the costs incurred for his project. For small projects, you may not even need a project in SAP ERP but will find that an internal order is adequate for your needs. The word *accounting* is related to *accountability*. It's the controller's task to ensure the accountability of the relevant managers for their spending on each cost center, order, or project. Another term you'll sometimes hear in this context is *stewardship*, associated with the idea that the cost center manager is safeguarding the assets in his responsibility.

With Cost Center Accounting and internal orders, we are essentially looking at cost or expense accounting. If we now look at how to capture sales *revenue*, we move into the realm of Profitability Analysis (often shortened to CO-PA; see the bottom folder in Figure 1.1). If you're new to SAP, you need to understand that Profitability Analysis is essentially a data warehouse within SAP ERP in which you can capture the costs and revenue associated with each customer and product and analyze your profitability by region, sales organization, business area, company code, and so on. Profitability Analysis is a very powerful tool but may provide a degree of granularity that differs from what you're used to if you currently capture costs and revenue mainly in your General Ledger. It offers two alternative taxonomies for viewing the relevant values: by cost element (account-based) and by value field (costing-based). Although most people can imagine costs and revenue accounts, the value fields represent a different view that can be more or less detailed than the account view, depending on business requirements.

Cost Center Accounting and **Internal Orders** are represented as separate folders but provide base data for **Profitability Analysis**. Rent, payroll, and insurance costs are assigned initially to a cost center but are later assigned to the parts of the business that this cost center serves by means of an *allocation*. Similarly, costs assigned to a research and development order can later be *settled* to the product lines supported by the research activities. This effectively *transforms* such costs into period expenses for the income statement. In some countries, you'll hear this transformation explained as the shift from costs by nature (wages, operating supplies, depreciation, and so on) to costs by function (production, sales, marketing, administration, and so on) with the idea that all costs will ultimately become costs of sales.

If you now look more closely at the menus for **Cost Center Accounting**, **Internal Orders**, and **Profitability Analysis**, you'll see that each one contains a folder called **Planning**. The idea of planning and setting standards is central to CO, and we'll talk later about how to plan and why a plan is necessary in SAP ERP. This is especially important, because it's usually the controller who drives the creation of the plan, establishing the framework and collaborating with all the involved parties until agreement is reached.

If you're performing any kind of manufacturing, then the process of turning the materials you buy into products you can sell is covered in Product Cost Controlling. Again, if you're used to managing work orders in a separate system, the idea that every work order in SAP ERP is a cost object in CO may be new. In this book, we'll discuss the different levels of detail you can use to capture the information on work orders. We'll compare the classic approach to standard costing with newer approaches, including *lean accounting*, which rejects the work order as the sole focus of cost accounting. Just as we saw for Profitability Analysis, Product Cost Controlling is not used in isolation. The costs we captured for the production cost centers will be charged to the production process and flow into the cost of goods manufactured in Profitability Analysis and into the inventory values for the goods manufactured, undergoing a transformation from expense to inventory value and finally cost of goods sold. Product Cost Controlling includes options for make-to-stock, make-to-order, and engineer-to-order manufacturing.

There is also a folder for **Activity-Based Costing**, allowing you to capture costs for business processes such as quality control or product configuration that cannot be described in routings and master recipes. We'll return to this in more detail in Chapter 11.

Figure 1.2 may help you visualize the value flows through CO, with the cost centers and internal orders capturing expenses from the SAP General Ledger at the top; the business process as an optional account assignment for Activity-Based Costing below; the production orders, sales orders, and projects that are used to handle the organization's operations in the middle; and the multidimensional cube that is Profitability Analysis at the bottom. The boxes on the left represent the inputs to CO from the other components, and the boxes on the right represent the way costs flow from Cost Center Accounting to production orders, sales orders, and projects and via order settlement to Profitability Analysis.

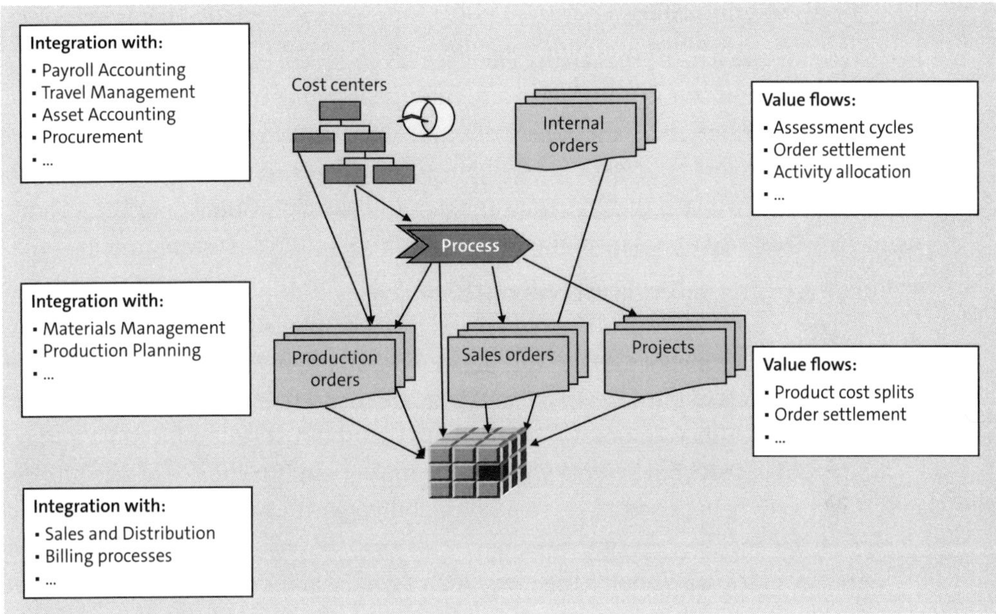

Figure 1.2 Value Flows in Controlling

1.1 Basic Controlling Functions

To understand how CO started, we need to look at the work of Hans-Georg Plaut, an automotive engineer who became involved in management accounting in the late 1940s. His legacy is the system of *Grenzplankostenrechnung* (GPK), translated into English as either "marginal planned cost accounting" or "flexible analysis cost planning and accounting," which has been the mainstay of German cost accounting for nearly 80 years. This approach shaped what we now know as CO when he and his consultants worked with the SAP developers to build the RK components in SAP R/2 and the early CO components in SAP R/3. That said, you certainly don't need to have studied cost accounting (i.e., controlling) in Germany to understand Controlling in SAP, but it's worth taking a few minutes to look at the basic principles of cost accounting before we look at the software in detail.

1.1.1 Goals of Controlling

In this section, we'll take Hans-Georg Plaut's ideas about cost accounting as a starting point. The goal of controlling is to provide meaningful insight and analysis of accounting information for the benefit of internal users, such as controllers, cost center managers, project managers, plant managers, and so on. It's the controller's job to put a structure in place that provides meaningful cost information to the various managers. This is achieved by doing the following:

- **Building clearly defined cost center structures**
  Each *cost center* represents the cost of resources employed; a resource could be a machine, a building, or people working in a department. Each cost center should be homogenous in purpose. In general, a single cost center is the responsibility of one manager. This is important in the sense that the cost center is not an anonymous pool of costs but an entity for which one person is responsible. Accounting is effectively being used to drive accountability, with each manager being held responsible for the cost of the resources his cost center uses and what that cost center provides, whether it's the provision of goods and services or the support of other cost centers. It's the controller's job to ensure that a workable structure is in place that supports both the reporting needs of each cost center manager and the business needs of corporate reporting.
- **Separating fixed and proportional costs**
  Costs behave differently depending on their type. For example, costs such as rent and insurance generally remain the same (*fixed*), whereas costs such as energy (*proportional*) rise if the production line runs for longer or the department has to handle more orders. The goal is to understand how costs behave under changing output levels and to explore capacity limitations and the utilization of available capacity. This is important because it's the reason that CO is separated from Financial Accounting. The rent payments or energy payments are recorded in the financial accounts, but the explanation of what drives changes to the level of payments is in CO. The notion of fixed and variable costs is an area of endless debate among cost accountants who have to balance the practicality of their approach against absolute accuracy. In recent years, there has been a trend toward unraveling and simplifying some of these assignments to make it easier for cost center managers and project managers to understand their costs and take effective action.
- **Establishing clearly defined activities and drivers**
  The aim is to define at least one representative output measure for each cost center and to ensure a linear relationship between the product and the output

measure (e.g., machine hours) and between the output measure and the cost pool (costs incurred by the production cost center to provide machine hours). This approach focuses on outputs or drivers—whether the quantity of goods to be sold or produced in a given period or the quantity of work to be performed by a cost center—as a way of determining whether resources are being used efficiently. This approach applies to both the actual outputs and to planning, which is output-driven in the SAP approach. It's the controller's job to work with the cost center managers in this area. Some cost centers are easy; for example, it's quite clear that a production line provides work in the form of machine hours. Whether an energy cost center is merely an expense that should be allocated to the operational cost centers or carries an output in the form of kilowatt hours of energy used will be a subject for discussion, and you'll find that there are no hard-and-fast rules governing how to determine the output of a cost center.

- **Using analytical cost planning**
  The goal is to prepare a plan for each cost center that reflects realistic expectations for budget setting and operational performance. This plan is based on the output of the cost center (i.e., the machine hours required to perform the work) as a realistic expectation modeled during planning. The cost center output is driven in turn by the demand from production and sales for output (goods to be sold). This planning approach involves more work but provides greater insight than the "last year plus X%" approach that prevails in some organizations. It's the controller's job to coordinate and manage this plan in a collaborative effort, involving the sales managers, cost center managers, project managers, and so on, because the plan is not just about gathering the numbers but is also about reaching an agreement on realistic goals for the next planning period.
- **Setting standards**
  The aim is to set stable standards for the period that allow users to understand variances, and it's the controller's job to ensure that such a standard is in place. Standard-setting is an important part of the cost accounting approach, providing a standard for the provision of a given level of activity by a cost center or a standard for producing a given lot size of a product. In both cases, variances with respect to this standard are analyzed at period close to explain the source of the variance (price change, quantity change, etc.). Variance analysis is initially the controller's task, but for high variances or scrap it typically involves discussions with the relevant plant managers to understand the underlying cause of the variance and where it indicates problems on the shop floor. Variance analysis should be

treated not as an academic exercise but as a need to ask why. Was the standard wrong, or do we need to make some changes to reduce rework or scrap?

- **Correctly allocating internal service costs**
  The goal is to reflect the true supply-and-demand conditions for the use of each resource. This applies not only to production cost centers but also potentially to all cost centers for which output measures can reasonably be established, so you'll find cost centers for IT services, human resources, finance, and so on being modeled as service providers alongside more obviously measurable cost centers. It's the controller's job to set up a model that supports the proper allocation of all internal services.

1.1.2 Cost Accounting in the United States

Although the notion of standard cost accounting and variance analysis is well-established in the United States, there are some fundamental differences between the processes in Germany and the United States:

- US organizations typically have fewer cost centers than their German counterparts, making it sometimes difficult to establish a single output for each cost center.
- US organizations often separate fixed and variable accounts, rather than separating the idea of the account from the idea of the cost element. In CO, costs are categorized in terms of how they respond to the changing output of the cost center and to the changing production output. Indeed, it's often clearer to use the word *proportional* rather than *variable* to represent the way this relationship works. To understand this, think of how the energy costs for the cost center will rise if the number of machine hours produced in the period rises and how the number of machine hours needed in the period will rise if more units are produced.
- US organizations often plan by using software that is not integrated with their cost accounting system rather than seeing planning as an integral part of controlling and the basis for all variance analysis.

Nevertheless, since the introduction of segment reporting with IFRS 8, many European organizations have found themselves trying to harmonize the values in their internal accounting systems with those reported externally, and the two worlds have moved substantially closer together.

1.1.3 Standard Costs and Actual Costs

The central importance of planning and standard-setting brings us to one of the first myths about CO—namely, that it's only possible to work with *standard costs*. When we discuss the material master in Chapter 4, we'll cover how setting a standard price for the manufacture of a unit of the product is an option and that it makes sense to apply a standard price to goods movements, in which case finished goods are received to stock and issued to sales before all actual costs (invoices, time recording, etc.) have been recorded. However, since SAP Release 4.6C, it has been possible to use the Material Ledger to calculate true actual costs at period close that take into account all purchase price variances and production variances. This approach has gained massively in popularity in recent years due to fluctuations in commodity prices and in the foreign exchange markets and the general distrust of standard costs that comes with highly volatile business conditions. We'll look at the process of capturing data at standard costs and reconciling with actual costs at period close in Chapter 6 and Chapter 7. The wording on some of the screens only adds to the confusion, because many of the delivered reports use the term *actual costs* simply to mean the actual quantity multiplied by a standard price, whereas the *true* actual costs are only calculated at period close when the periodic costing run is executed. We'll look at this whole process when we consider the period close in Chapter 7.

1.1.4 Investment and Project Controlling

Alongside production controlling, sales controlling, and so on, we'll also explore investment controlling as a way of getting to grips with your *capital expenses*. You'll find the functions for Investment Management in a separate part of the menu (see Figure 1.3), but there is so much overlap in the assignment of costs to internal orders and projects that no book on CO can afford to leave out the subject of Investment Management. If you're completely new to the subject, think of the investment program simply as a reporting layer that structures the investment portfolio and provides budgeting functions over and above a simple plan/actual comparison at the project or order level. This area is of interest for the controller whenever there is significant expense involved in bringing a new product to market or building a new production line that is not captured if you only look at sales or production controlling, which is essentially period-based.

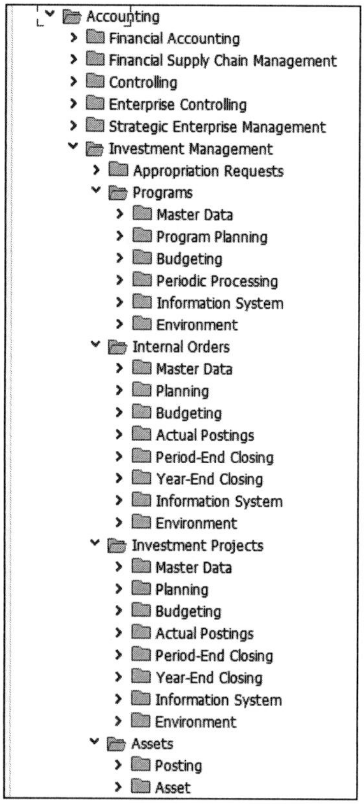

Figure 1.3 Investment Management in SAP Easy Access Menu

If you compare the CO menu and the Investment Management menu, you'll notice that the **Internal Orders** folder for **Investment Management** contains the same entries as the **Internal Orders** folder for **Controlling**. The difference is in the definition of investment programs to which the investment orders and projects are assigned and the use of appropriation requests to initiate an investment proposal.

1.1.5 Lean Accounting

One function that you won't find in the SAP Easy Access Menu but you will find discussed throughout this book is lean accounting. The practice of lean accounting can provide a useful guide for many implementation questions, encouraging the use of clean master data, simple reporting structures, and data that everyone (not just the controller) can understand and act upon.

Now that we've introduced the main elements, let's look at CO as a bookkeeping function and discuss how expenses move from the SAP General Ledger into CO.

1.2 Essential Record-Keeping Functions

Apart from the general ideas that underpin Controlling, it's also important to understand that CO is not standalone software that takes feeds from financial and operational logistics systems. It's embedded in SAP ERP and is essentially the glue that links operational logistics to finance. What a financial accountant sees as essential bookkeeping the controller sees as a dialog between purchasing and finance or between production and finance.

To understand what we mean, think about the nature of a cost center. In a standalone system, a cost center describes a pool of costs that are incurred by a department, a group of workers, or a machine. The assignment to the cost center may be made in the general ledger as an extension of the account assignment, or it may involve mapping certain accounts to that cost pool.

In SAP ERP, the cost center is part of the SAP General Ledger posting, but it's also part of the Logistics transaction that initiates the cost posting. A purchase request is created and approved with reference to the cost center under which the costs for the purchased goods will ultimately be posted. The purchase order and invoice from the supplier carry the information that the purchase relates to a specific cost center. The purchase costs are captured in Logistics and recorded in both the SAP General Ledger and Cost Center Accounting. This means you can't design your cost center structure without also looking at how purchases will be initiated with reference to the cost center. The cost center thus becomes more than just an account assignment, affecting the way you design your approval processes, so that the cost center manager can authorize all purchases carried out with reference to the cost center.

Figure 1.4 shows a posting for insurance expenses to a cost center. This posting will be passed from the SAP General Ledger into Cost Center Accounting under the cost element associated with the profit and loss (P&L) account for the insurance expenses. You'll also notice that the expenses have been assigned to the profit center and segment in the cost center master to provide the basis for enterprise reporting. What you need to remember is that in a fully integrated SAP ERP implementation, most postings coming into CO originate not in the General Ledger but in purchasing, production, human resources, and so on and that the account assignment is automatically populated based on the cost center in the relevant application (the purchase order in purchasing, the organizational unit for payroll, etc.).

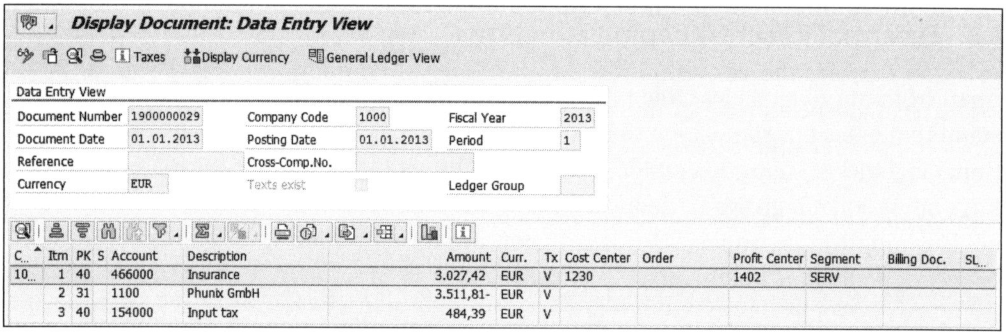

Figure 1.4 Expense Posting to Cost Center

The same basic principle applies to orders and projects:

- A standalone system can also capture order or project costs as an extension of the general ledger posting and even support basic time recording.
- What makes CO unique is the way the order is embedded in Logistics and in Time Recording in human resources. A cost allocation takes place automatically when an order confirmation is recorded in Logistics to record that an operation has been completed, a quantity of product finished, or even a quantity scrapped. The same thing happens when an employee records his working time with reference to the order or project in human resources. This cost assignment uses the planned activity rate for the machine or labor hours confirmed to the production order or the hourly rate for the employee charging time to a project to make an immediate charge to the order or project. This may be corrected at period close when the actual costs for the period are known.
- This tight integration has its challenges in the sense that you have to make sure that the master data in production and the organizational units in human resources tie in with the cost center master data. On the other hand, the basis for many of the allocations is being collected not in finance but where the activity is carried out on the shop floor or an employee's time sheet. Bills of material (BOMs), routings, master recipes, maintenance plans, and so on provide the basis for cost calculations and require only basic monitoring work from the controlling department. By comparison, most organizations' attempts to capture activity drivers in

activity-based costing systems have been quite difficult, with frequent reliance on spreadsheets and slightly unreliable data integration.

1.2.1 Record Keeping by Cost Center

As we discussed, the cost center represents the cost of resources employed; a resource might be a machine, a building, or people working in a department. This helps you answer simple questions, such as the amount of travel expenses incurred by a given department or the level of rent and maintenance costs for a building, but also the level of efficiency of a production line or an oven.

It's best to design cost centers so that a single manager is responsible for each. This may simply be a management view for reporting purposes, but it's also relevant in operational processes because the cost center manager approves purchase requests, travel expenses, and working time.

When you're designing your cost center structures, also think about how they will flow into the other dimensions that you will want to consider in your financial reports. You'll want to understand the functional area to which the cost center belongs and how this will change as the cost center charges its costs to different functions in the business. You'll want to understand how the cost center relates to your profit center structure and again how this will change as the costs flow through the business.

Cost Center Expenses

Let's look first at the types of costs that might be assigned to a cost center. We already mentioned that purchase costs are assigned to the cost center via the purchase order. Travel expenses are captured in a similar way, with all travel requests containing the assignment to the employee's cost center. When the travel expense is paid out, it's automatically assigned to the employee's cost center.

Cost centers can also represent production resources, including machines and equipment. In production, the machine is represented as a work center or resource, and in plant maintenance, the machine is represented as equipment. In general, the machine is also a fixed asset, the costs of which have to be depreciated according to whichever generally accepted accounting principle (GAAP) applies in the relevant company code. The amount of depreciation according to each accounting principle is calculated in fixed asset accounting and transferred to the cost center during the depreciation run that takes place once a month.

Payroll is another significant cost input. The costs of employing staff and workers are captured in SAP ERP Human Capital Management and paid out based on the organizational unit to which the employee is assigned. In SAP ERP, the organizational unit is linked with a cost center, and all payroll expenses are transferred to the General Ledger with the correct cost center assignment.

Cost centers can also receive costs from other cost centers. This might be in the form of general expenses (i.e., rent and insurance that are captured centrally and then allocated) or work performed by other cost centers (i.e., maintenance work, quality checks, or the cost of hiring or training new workers).

Cost Center Outputs

In CO, cost centers represent both where the costs were incurred in the organization and what was done with these costs. For a machine, this may seem obvious. The production cost center receives depreciation expenses, payroll costs, energy costs, maintenance costs, and so on, and provides machine hours. Assuming you have established routings or master recipes to describe the production steps, confirmations in Logistics record how many hours of machine time are required for each order. Even if you don't have detailed routings yet, there are ways to capture machine time, which we'll discuss in Chapter 6.

For a maintenance department, the same principle applies. The cost center receives payroll costs, operating supplies, and so on and provides maintenance hours. Assuming you have established maintenance plans, the costs of each maintenance task are assigned to the maintenance order when you make a confirmation.

For a sales department, the question of output may be more difficult. The Plaut approach advocates having an output measure for all cost centers, so you may find an activity such as sales hours being captured—but how can this be charged? What typically happens in these circumstances is that some form of allocation takes place. Either the expenses incurred by the sales department or the sum of the sales hours worked in the period are allocated to the customers served. We'll discuss the various forms of allocation in more detail when we look at the master data for activity types in Chapter 3, how to perform allocations in Chapter 7, and new options for allocations in Chapter 11.

For other departments, it may be possible to establish time recording in human resources, in which time worked is charged to orders or projects. These might be research departments, development departments, consulting departments, or so on.

Handling Inventory

One source of confusion if you're moving from a US legacy system is that the cost center output is always machine time, labor time, setup time, and so on (i.e., work provided), but not inventory (i.e., material produced). This is important in a manufacturing scenario because although the costs of operating supplies might be assigned to a cost center, the inventories of raw materials and semifinished and finished products don't flow through the cost center but are recorded on production orders, sales orders, projects, and the like. The inventories, however, are considered part of profit center accounting, and all sales orders, production orders, and so on are automatically assigned to a profit center. We'll look at this process in more detail in Chapter 6.

1.2.2 Record-Keeping by Order

We've already examined production orders for manufacturing a product and maintenance orders for repairing an asset, but there are many more types of orders in SAP ERP, from investment orders for capital expenses to service orders for performing external maintenance work and internal orders that represent activities outside of SAP ERP. There are also internal orders that the controlling department creates as cost collectors, for which more detail is required than is possible on a single cost center (such as for each vehicle assigned to a car pool).

When you are thinking about the type of orders that you intend to use, again think about how they will flow into the other dimensions that you will want to consider in your financial reports. As we discussed for the cost centers, think about the functional areas and profit centers to which each order type should belong.

Order Expenses

Regarding expense postings, all these orders behave the same way. You can assign purchasing costs, travel costs, and payroll costs to an order instead of a cost center by adjusting the account assignment. The underlying business question is simply why the purchase is necessary—for example:

- Will the purchase provide equipment, such as a laptop or cell phone, for an employee assigned to the cost center, or operating supplies, such as oil or grease, that are needed for the work of the cost center? If this is the case, the costs should be assigned to the cost center.
- Will the purchase provide goods or services that are specific to the order, such as buying consulting services to deliver on a project or order, buying materials for a

building that is under construction for which costs will later be capitalized as assets under construction, or buying materials for a special project? If this is the case, the costs should be assigned to an order.

For production orders and maintenance orders, it's also common to issue goods from stock to the order, whether as raw materials for use in a production order or as service parts for use in a maintenance or service order.

Other Postings to an Order

In addition to general overhead costs, you'll also find orders used in a *time-and-materials* approach, in which the time part can be as significant as the materials. The SAP approach records time from external contractors as a primary cost via the purchase order, but time worked by people in the same organization is captured using the Time Recording functionality in SAP ERP HCM or Direct Activity Allocation in CO. In both cases, the employee enters working time in the form of the number of hours worked for the order, and a standard rate for one unit of this time is applied to the order. Now, let's go back to the output measure for each cost center. The activities of the employees are represented in the cost center as research tasks, development tasks, maintenance tasks, and so on. When the employee charges his development time to the order or project, his cost center is credited and the order debited for his work.

Order Settlement

Once costs have been accumulated on an order, they are *settled*, or charged to another object. There are as many settlement options as there are types of orders. Maintenance orders and quality orders generally settle their costs back to the "parent" cost center. Production orders generally settle their production variances to Profitability Analysis. Investment orders generally settle their costs to assets under construction or fixed assets. Internal orders that represent a detailing of the cost center's activities, such as attending trade fairs, may settle either to the parent cost center (here, the marketing cost center) or to the regions and customer groups attending the trade fairs. You'll also find mixed assignments, in which some of the construction costs are assigned to a fixed asset and others to a cost center. We'll look at settlement in more detail in Chapter 3 and Chapter 7.

1.2.3 Record-Keeping by Project

Sometimes an order does not provide adequate detail for the activity to be undertaken. A complex research project or construction project may need to be broken down into separate phases and activities for transparency. It can also be the case that parts of the project are being handled by different parts of the organization and in extreme cases by different companies in the organization. This breakdown of the project activities is known as a *Work Breakdown Structure* (WBS), with each element represented as a WBS element.

In complex engineering environments, you may find the WBS being used in conjunction with networks. In this case, the WBS elements represent the organizational view of the project, whereas the networks represent the logistics view that provides scheduling tools for handling different work dependencies. WBS elements, networks, and network activities are all cost objects and can carry costs just like an internal order. WBS elements can also carry budgets, because it's common in these scenarios to set an upper limit on spending in a given time frame.

With *commercial projects*, alongside the expense postings and time-and-materials postings, it's common also to capture revenue because the customer is invoiced when certain milestones are reached. The billing process differs from the billing process for a make-to-stock product in that the delivery of the finished product is not the trigger. Instead, billing has to be triggered based either on an invoice plan or on the resources spent on the project. In this situation, it's usual for the project costs to be settled to the sales order item.

Although cost collection by cost center, order, or project essentially takes place in real time whenever a goods movement is posted and Controlling is largely in a *monitoring* role, the controller is in the front seat at period close when the time comes to handle the close and the valuation of work in process and assets under construction. If we consider *capital expense projects* rather than commercial projects, the point is to move those costs that have been captured by project to the balance sheet at period close, a process we'll cover in the next section.

1.3 Managing Close and Valuation Processes

We've looked so far at many of the transactions that result in costs being assigned to cost centers and orders. Something that makes CO confusing if you're coming from a standalone costing system is that some transactions, such as goods movements, asset acquisitions, invoice receipts, and so on, result in postings in the SAP General Ledger in *real time*, whereas other postings take place at *period close*, such as allocations and order settlement. This is perhaps the most difficult part of the SAP approach to Controlling. Inventory movements are valued immediately at standard costs but may be adjusted to account for variances later. Work in process, on the other hand, is moved to the balance sheet at period close and then reversed when the order is complete.

1.3.1 Valuation of Goods Movements

SAP recommends that you value finished and semifinished products at standard costs. This is because the delivery of these goods to stock and removal for sale can take place before all cost information relating to the production order has been posted. The standard cost thus represents the best guess for valuation purposes—even though, as we said earlier, the inventory value can be adjusted later if you use Actual Costing. This approach also takes away the danger of inconsistencies during settlement because goods are only revalued if there are still goods in stock.

1.3.2 Work in Process

In most US systems, the movement of raw materials to the shop floor and on completion from the shop floor to finished goods inventory is treated as a reclassification of the balance sheet from raw materials inventory to *work in process* (WIP) and from there to finished goods inventory.

In CO, although the issue of the raw materials to the shop floor and the delivery of the finished product to the stores are *immediately* visible in the balance sheet, work in process is only calculated once per period. The raw materials issued to the production order therefore are treated as an expense on the P&L statement during the period. Any work performed to convert the raw materials into a product is also expensed to the production order.

If the order is not complete at period close, the difference between the actual costs on the order and the value of any deliveries of the finished goods to stock is captured as work in process. On settlement, the value of the work in process is moved to the balance sheet. If work continues in the next period, then the value of the work in process increases. The difference from the previous period is moved to the balance sheet using settlement. Finally, when the order is complete, the value of the work in process is reversed and the balance sheet value is zero.

1.3.3 Scrap

In most US systems, *scrap* is treated as a balance sheet item. In CO, the value of scrap is calculated during variance calculation. In the SAP approach, a distinction is made between normal and abnormal spoilage. *Normal spoilage* arises under efficient operation conditions and is an inherent result of the production process. The costs of normal spoilage are viewed as part of the costs of good units manufactured and included in the standard costs as *planned scrap*. *Abnormal spoilage* is not expected to arise under efficient operation conditions, and most abnormal spoilage is regarded as avoidable and controllable. The costs of abnormal spoilage are written off as losses of the accounting period in which the detection of the spoiled units occurs. In the SAP approach, abnormal spoilage is treated as a *scrap variance*.

1.3.4 Work in Process for Projects

In large-scale projects, the costs and revenues may not be representative of the actual stage of completion. At the beginning of the project, high costs may be incurred to procure the correct components and begin work. On the revenue side, the billing schedule to the customer may not correspond with the amount of work completed or the costs incurred.

In this case, *results analysis* is used to smooth the pattern of the postings. There are two main approaches:

- **Percentage of completion (POC)**
  The POC method involves looking at the costs incurred compared to the planned costs to determine the percentage of completion. The revenue to be recognized in the period is then calculated based on the percentage of completion. In general, the actual revenue is lower than the revenue calculated according to the POC method, and a posting is prepared for revenues in excess of billings.
- **Revenue-based results analysis**
  The revenue-based results analysis method involves comparing the revenues to the planned revenues and planned costs to calculate the cost of goods sold that relate to these revenues. Normally, the actual costs are higher than the calculated cost of goods sold, because expenses have been incurred that have yet to be billed for, so work in process is calculated for the difference. Occasionally, the actual costs are lower than the calculated costs, because time recording and invoices from contractors are missing, so reserves for missing costs are calculated for the difference.

Your implementation team defines which methods of results analysis are active in your system, but it's the controller's job to execute the valuation tasks at period close. We'll come back to results analysis when we look at period-close activities in Chapter 7.

If period close has the controller in the hot seat for several days each month, then the other area in which the controller is active is preparing budgets and planning, as described in the next section.

1.4 Preparing Budgets and Planning

As we noted earlier, analytical cost planning is a key element of a good costing system and an area in which the integration between the different plans in SAP ERP makes the approach feasible. People are often confused by this in the English-speaking world, because the terms *planning* and *budgeting* tend to be used synonymously. In SAP systems, the *cost plan* refers to the exercise of valuating a sales plan or preparing a plan for individual cost centers or orders. A plan is just a plan—a set of assumptions about future business performance. A *budget* is something else. A budget may be derived from a plan, but it refers to the fixed budget to complete the order or project. The budget is checked whenever postings are made that will affect costs, whether these are expense postings in the General Ledger or purchase orders that will result in costs in the future. Once these purchase orders have been created, there is a *commitment* to pay for the goods ordered. This commitment to pay is also recorded and treated as if the expense had already occurred when budgets are checked. One option to consider in this context is the use of mobile applications such as My Spend to provide managers with details of their cost center plan and how costs compare against this plan. We'll look at these applications in more detail in Chapter 13.

1.4.1 Driver-Based Cost Planning

The driver-based planning approach is considered a best practice in the manufacturing industry, in which the sales plan or the production plan defines the expected output. Companies in the service industries also use driver-based planning, but instead of a physical quantity of goods to make and sell, a bank, for instance, might plan the clerical hours required to handle the loan applications it hopes to process in a given region or the clerical hours required to issue the new credit cards it hopes to issue in the next planning period.

The objective of planning is to provide a more accurate picture of expected future business performance by planning and monitoring the key operational activities that drive these results. This sounds easy enough but can mean completely rethinking the way you approach planning. With the SAP approach, you start the planning process not with the monetary values for the period, such as dollars per line of business, but with the sales quantities and production quantities. You then use these to calculate how much work you'll need to put in to meet your targets. Ultimately, the amount of work required takes you to the capacity per resource, whether this is a cost center supplying machine time or a call center providing clerical hours. You then plan your expenses against these drivers to calculate the resources you'll consume on each cost center to execute your plan.

We'll walk through the whole process in Chapter 5, but to get an idea of the scope of the plan, consider the following steps:

1. Create a sales plan. In this plan, you can enter the quantities of product to sell to each customer and check the planned revenue (sales managers).
2. Create a production plan. You can transfer the sales quantities to production and adjust them if necessary (production planners).
3. Transfer production requirements to a cost center plan. You can use the production quantities to calculate the number of production activities required to complete the necessary work and transfer these quantities to the cost center plan as the *scheduled activity* (administrator).
4. Match cost center capacities against scheduled activity from production. You can check the capacities for each cost center and activity against scheduled activity to provide a reality check regarding the amount of activity requested by production (controllers).
5. Plan activity-dependent costs per cost center and activity type. This is probably the most fundamental difference between the way many organizations plan monetary values per cost center and the way the SAP approach distinguishes between costs such as rent and insurance that are fixed and costs such as energy that vary with the amount of activity provided in each period. The two are planned in separate *planning layouts* (cost center managers).
6. Plan expenses for supporting cost centers and orders and define how these allocate to production cost centers or profitability segments (controllers).
7. Calculate standard rates for activity types. For a cost center with a single output, or one activity type, this activity price calculation divides the expenses by the activ-

ity type to provide a rate per hour. If the cost center provides more than one activity, then activity price calculation first splits the expenses to the activity types using the relative activity quantities or equivalence numbers. The result is a rate per hour for each of the activities (controllers).

8. Calculate standard costs for products to be manufactured. From here, you can calculate standard costs for all the finished products in the original sales plan. This uses the bill of material to determine the material usage and the routing to determine the number of machine hours and so on needed. The activity rate per hour is then applied to these machine hours (controllers).
9. Transfer standard costs to a sales plan to determine planned profitability. You can use the valuation function in the sales plan to pull the standard costs for the materials into the sales plan to determine profitability (controllers).

1.4.2 Driver-Based Cost Planning among Cost Centers

Although the preceding approach to sales planning is widely used in the United States, the business of planning activities among cost centers is not very common outside of the German-speaking world. Most organizations plan expenses by cost center and then compare the actual costs with the planned costs for the period and analyze the variance. However, such an approach has its limitations in that it doesn't account for whether the cost center did more or less work in the period.

In CO, if you've captured an output quantity for the cost center, then the planned costs will be adjusted to reflect the actual output for the period. The adjusted costs are known as *target costs*. Although production cost centers usually have a planned output in terms of the number of machine hours, labor hours, and so on, service cost centers often don't. The SAP approach is to plan activities for most cost centers. This involves planning the following:

- **What the cost center output is**
  The activity types to be performed and the quantities of that activity (output) to be provided.
- **What the cost center will spend to perform this activity**
  SAP differentiates here between activity-dependent costs and activity-independent costs.
- **How the output of this cost center is to be used**
  How much of each activity will flow to other cost centers and orders during the planning period.

This is a much more detailed form of cost center planning than many organizations currently perform, but it provides a very powerful way of establishing the targets for the cost center and measuring whether these targets have been achieved. This form of planning also presupposes that the activity flow is *reconciled*—supply reflects demand—and that the flow of activities will be valued with a price that is calculated by dividing the planned costs by either the planned activity or (more rarely) the planned capacity for the cost center. In theory, this reconciliation is technical in nature, but the controller provides the human element, negotiating with both the supplying and the requesting cost center to determine whether the plan is reasonable. We'll walk through this process in detail in Chapter 5.

1.4.3 Budgeting

It's also common to perform very detailed cost planning for projects prior to approval, and it's the controller's job to coordinate the planning process with the individual project managers and ensure that their demands are reconciled with the goals set by corporate controlling. This may start with a rough plan, called the *overall plan*, which provides rough values per WBS element and year. The work breakdown structure is hierarchical. Values can be entered for the top WBS elements and distributed down to lower WBS elements or can be entered for lower WBS elements and aggregated up to the higher-level WBS elements. The process thus involves both *top-down* and *bottom-up planning*. Figure 1.5 illustrates the flow in both directions, with the budget for Europe being distributed down to the individual projects on the left and the order and project plans for the United States being rolled up to the corporate level on the right.

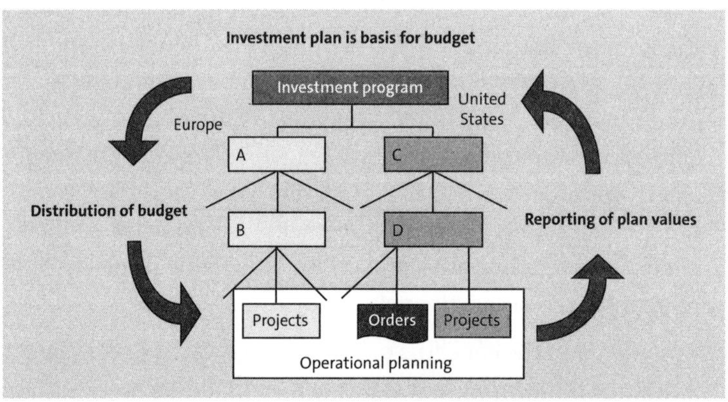

Figure 1.5 Value Flow in Top-Down and Bottom-Up Planning of Investments

This plan is often created more than a year before execution is expected to begin in order to provide supporting information for the investment decision. This may be supplemented by detailed cost element planning when sufficient information exists to support this type of planning.

Once the plan is approved, it's often copied to the *budget*. This represents a binding plan that is used to determine how resources can be spent on the project. There are two types of budgeting:

- Passive budgeting involves the use of reports to monitor spending and commitments and to alert managers to potential budget overruns.
- Active budgeting or *active availability control* is used to set a ceiling on spending. If the ceiling is reached, then you won't be allowed to create another purchase order or post costs to the project. This may take the form of a warning message or an error message that effectively blocks spending.

Because the budget is so critical, processes exist in Controlling to document the level of the original budget and to allow you to assign additional budget to the project (a *supplement*), return unused budget (a *return*), and request a budget transfer from another project. These processes are handled as separate transactions and can involve the use of a workflow to handle the necessary approvals.

Now that you understand budgets and planning, let's move on to process analysis and internal controls.

1.5 Process Analysis and Internal Controls

The material we've covered up to this point could have been written at any point since SAP R/3 Release 4.6C. What changed at the turn of the century was the massive failure in financial reporting, governance practices, and risk prevention that created a need for sustainable improvement in these areas, leading to the Sarbanes-Oxley Act (SOX) in the United States and similar mandates and regulations in other countries. In terms of financial compliance, Section 302 of SOX states that CEOs and CFOs must personally sign off on their company's financial statements. Section 404 mandates that well-defined and documented processes and controls must be in place for all aspects of company operations that affect financial reports.

A whole industry has risen around the concerns of governance, risk, and compliance, and this guide cannot cover all the internal and external risks that organizations face.

What is important in this context is to understand where you need to look at your Controlling processes to achieve compliance.

1.5.1 Master Data Controls

The obvious place to start is the area of master data controls. The master data underlies all business processes, and poor master data quality can lead to significant risks. There needs to be a clear process in place to govern who can create or change any object to which costs can be assigned. This includes the creation of cost elements, cost centers, orders, projects, and so on. We'll return to this in Chapter 3 and Chapter 4. We'll also look at a new solution, SAP Master Data Governance for Financials, in Chapter 9.

1.5.2 Workflow

Once the master data is correctly in place, it makes sense to review all workflows and approval procedures to understand who is authorized to approve purchases, travel expenses, time recording, and anything else that can result in costs. Normally, this sort of procedure applies mainly to incidental expenses, such as the purchase of a new laptop for a cost center; the purchase of goods for use in production is not handled via a single workflow item. Here it's important to ensure that system controls are in place to check the three-way match required for logistics invoice verification (purchase order, goods receipt, and invoice receipt) and how price variances are handled in Purchasing.

For budget approval, SAP has its own transactions for releasing budgets and documenting the issue of budget supplements, budget returns, budget transfers, and so on. We'll look at these in Chapter 5.

1.5.3 Process Controls

Because of the huge impact of the standard costs in determining how goods movements are valuated, it's important to properly document the planning process, including how activity rates are calculated and checked, how standard costs are calculated and checked, and who can mark and release the standard cost estimate and thus trigger a balance sheet adjustment for the inventory of that material currently in stock.

Similarly, if you have commercial projects or investment projects, it's important to understand how planning for these projects is performed, who signs off on the plan, and which planning values are used in results analysis to calculate work in process or put a value on assets under construction so that your projects are correctly represented in the balance sheet at period close.

It's also important to review every step of the period close and to understand who signs off on each step and what checks are performed. This is especially important in the area of order settlement, in which expenses are capitalized as work in process, assets under construction, and so on. If you're using Actual Costing, it's also important to document carefully which checks are performed after each stage of the costing run to ensure that the values are correct, how manual changes are performed and documented, and who can create the inventory adjustment postings to take account of the newly calculated actual costs.

1.6 Summary

In this chapter, we introduced the roots of the SAP approach to Controlling and explained how it differs in certain respects from common practices in the United States and other countries. We looked at recommendations for cost center design, a subject we'll return to, along with what output measures to use and how to create internal orders, in Chapter 3. We looked at how cost centers, orders, and projects provide the link between operational processes, such as purchasing and production, and the General Ledger, a subject we'll return to in Chapter 4. We introduced some of the actual postings that result in costs being applied to a cost center and order, which we'll return to in Chapter 6, and some of the period-end close processes, which we'll return to in Chapter 7. We also looked at the underlying assumptions behind planning and budgeting, a subject we'll return to in Chapter 5. Finally, we looked at the type of process controls that may be needed when working with CO.

The next step is to look a little closer at the software and introduce the reports available to support you in these tasks.

2

Chapter 2
Reporting

In this chapter, we'll discuss the basic reports that every organization needs to run its core business, including coverage of general Controlling, Product Cost Controlling, and Profitability Analysis reports.

Almost all SAP documentation and training materials cover reporting at the end, as something of an afterthought, once the main topics surrounding the business processes and underlying master data have been explained. However, if you're a controller, the need to analyze business performance each month is at the heart of your job, the very reason for doing controlling in the first place, so it makes sense to start by looking at some of the standard reports that controllers use every day. This way, you'll get a sense of what information is available in each area of the Controlling component of SAP ERP Financials (CO) and what you can expect from the chapters to follow.

The other reason to start with reporting is that it means we'll have covered the basic functions, such as changing the column structure or downloading the report contents to a spreadsheet, when we walk through how to post expenses to a cost center or production order later.

In this chapter, we'll focus on the line item that records expense postings, allocations, and so on, looking at reports that allow you to search for the relevant line items in each application area. Controllers also like to bring these line items into *context* to understand whether cost center spending is going according to plan, whether project spending is about to exceed a budget limit, or whether production lines are executing to target. While we're looking at the line items for each area, we'll try to bring these line items into their Controlling context.

This chapter will look at your reporting options in SAP ERP. If your organization is already using a data warehouse for reporting, you'll find a discussion on when to use SAP Business Warehouse (BW) in Chapter 8. However, even controllers whose organizations have implemented SAP BW still tend to use the line item reports in SAP ERP for detailed cost tracking and analysis. In Chapter 13, we'll look at the newer options available with SAP HANA. Because these newer options build directly on the line items, it's more important than ever to understand what information is being captured at the source.

Note

Wherever possible in this book, we'll use the new-look user interfaces that are available from EHPs 5 and 6 for SAP ERP 6.0. For readers not yet using this version of the software, we'll also provide the menu path and transaction so that you can follow the instructions no matter which version of SAP ERP you're running. You'll find information about how to install the SAP NetWeaver Business Client in SAP Note 1029940 and information about how to implement the user interfaces in Appendix A, which you can download at *www.sap-press.com/4691*. If you're concerned about the continued availability of the SAP NetWeaver Business Client, check the details of the maintenance strategy in SAP Note 2302074.

2.1 Cost Center Line Items

Let's start our journey in Cost Center Accounting. The cost center line item report that helps you monitor expense postings to a cost center and allocations from the cost center is one of the most widely used transactions in SAP ERP Financials. If you know how to use it properly, you'll already be well on the way to being an expert in CO with SAP ERP Financials.

2.1.1 Classic Cost Center Line Item Report

In the **SAP Easy Access** menu, all transactions and reports are grouped into folders for the main application areas, such as **Cost Center Accounting**, **Internal Orders**, **Product Cost Controlling**, **Profitability Analysis**, and so on. These *application areas* are delivered as *roles* in EHP 5 for SAP ERP 6.0. When you log on, you'll see all the roles assigned to your user. We'll start each section of this chapter by looking at the relevant role structure. Figure 2.1 shows the entries in the **Cost Center Accounting** role. You'll find all the reports available for this role under **Information System**.

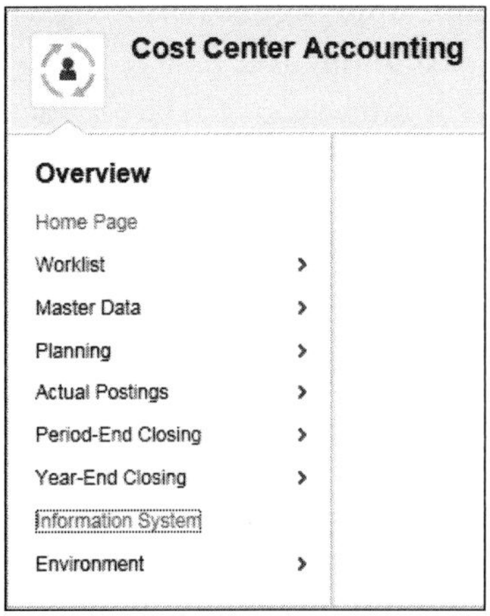

Figure 2.1 Cost Center Accounting within SAP NetWeaver Business Client

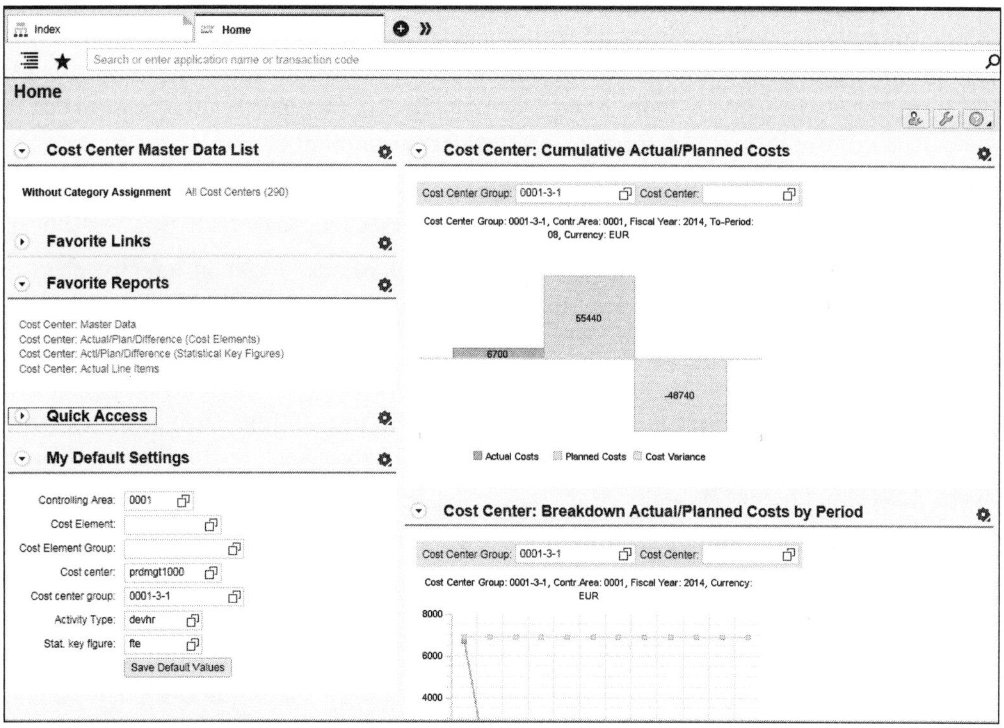

Figure 2.2 Home Page for Cost Center Accounting

Before we explore the reports on offer, let's look at the **Home** page shown in Figure 2.2. This page is delivered as part of the **Cost Center Accounting** role (SAP_EP_RW_CO_KSMN) if you're on EHP 6 for SAP ERP 6.0. As a controller, it can be good to start the day with a quick overview of the plan/actual costs on your cost centers before you delve into the details. To make sure that this report can run without you entering any selection parameters, you need to set certain defaults for your user. To do this, select **System • User Profile • Own Data**, choose the **Parameters** tab, and enter the parameter CAC for the controlling area. You'll notice an area called **My Default Settings** in the lower left of the screen. As you enter a cost center and/or cost center group, you'll be updating your user parameters with the parameter KOS for the cost center and your chosen cost center.

The **Information System** link shown in Figure 2.1 will take you to a screen that shows the reports available for **Cost Center Accounting**. This is the equivalent of choosing the menu path **Financials • Controlling • Cost Center Accounting • Information System • Reports for Cost Center Accounting** in earlier versions of the software. If you compare the links in Figure 2.3 with the entries in the classic menu, you'll find that more reports are shown here. This is because we've included newer reports in the list that were delivered in EHPs 3 and 5 for SAP ERP 6.0. All reports with the word **List** in the title can be run directly in your SAP ERP environment.

Activating New Reports via the Enhancement Packages

To find out how to make the new reports work in your organization, refer to Appendix B, which you can download at *www.sap-press.com/4691*.

In the **Line Items** folder, select the **Cost Centers: Actual Line Items** link. The *actual line items* document every posting taking place to CO in real time (such as the expense posting we looked at in Chapter 1) and at period close (such as the allocations we'll look at in Chapter 7).

The selection screen for the cost center line item report now appears (see Figure 2.4). Experienced controllers will recognize this as Transaction KSB1. From this point onward, all functions will be the same as in the classic transaction. The new user interface simply changes the way the transaction is accessed, replacing a menu or transaction call with a role-based approach.

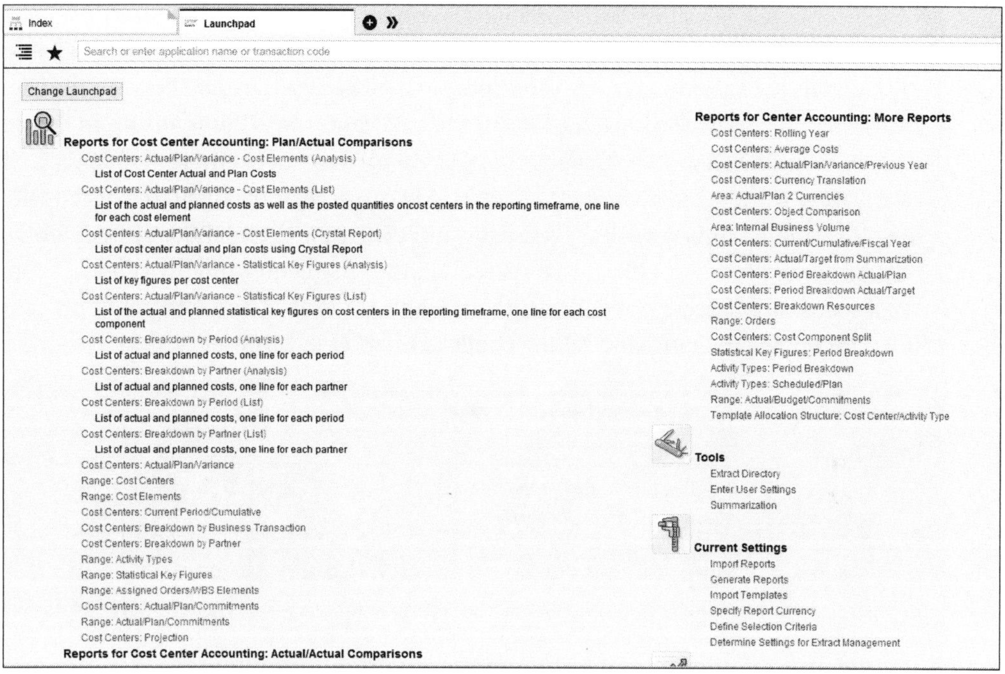

Figure 2.3 Reports for Cost Center Accounting

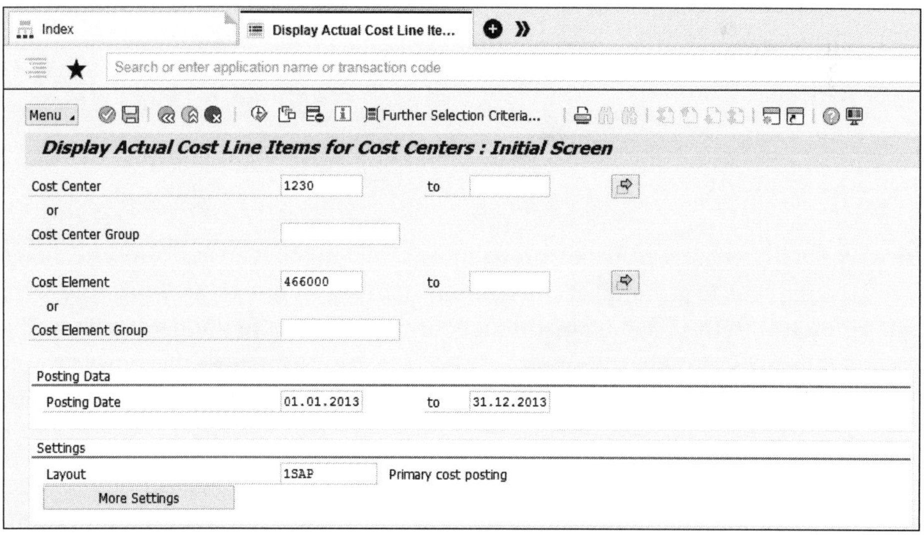

Figure 2.4 Cost Center Line Items: Selection Screen

To select the relevant line items for analysis, enter cost center 1230 (Power), cost element 466000 (Insurance Expenses), and posting dates between 01.01.2013 and 31.12.2013 in the selection screen, then click on the **Execute** button. The result is a list of all postings for insurance expenses to the cost center in 2013, as shown in Figure 2.5. This is the CO view of the expense posting we used as our example in Chapter 1. Of course, if you know the document number, you can access the line items of the relevant documents directly using Transaction KSB5 (Display Actual Cost Documents), but it's generally more efficient to search via the cost center or cost center group. We'll see how to access the CO document when we look at the integrated process flows for buying, making, and selling goods in Chapter 6.

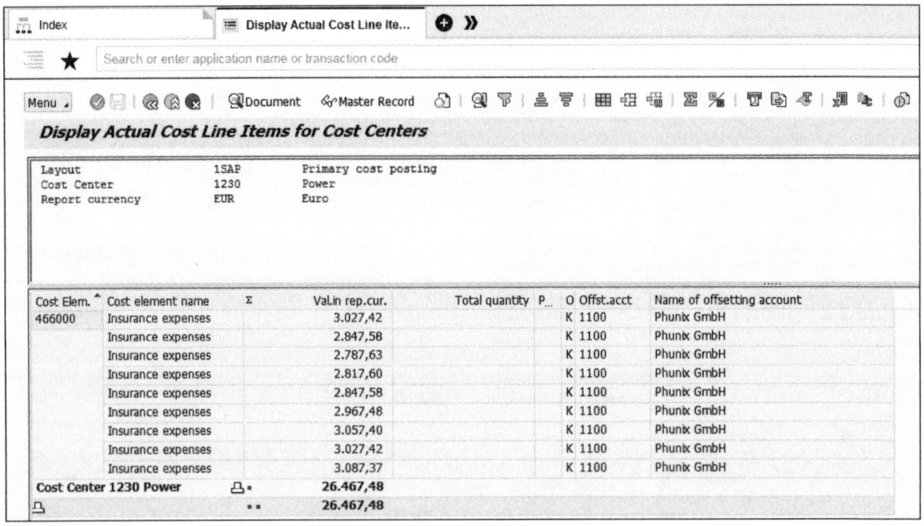

Figure 2.5 Result List

This type of *list report* is available throughout CO and in other areas of SAP ERP, so it's worth taking time to get familiar with the standard report functions. You'll recognize reports built with this technology throughout the book by the standard toolbar. The technical term for this kind of report is *SAP List Viewer*. To explore this type of result list, some controllers immediately reach for the **Export to Excel** button to start exploring their data in a spreadsheet.

You should know, however, that SAP List Viewer has its own spreadsheet-like functions. You can sort columns, include totals and subtotals, and so on in any list. To remove unnecessary columns, position the cursor on the column, right-click, and select **Hide**.

In general, you are more likely to add fields to such reports than remove them because the line item includes far more fields than can reasonably be displayed on a single screen. The group of fields displayed in SAP List Viewer at any point is called the *layout*. SAP delivers several layouts for use with cost centers. You can change these with the **Change Layout** dialog, which you can reach by clicking on the **Choose Layout** button; the **Choose Layout** screen is shown in Figure 2.6.

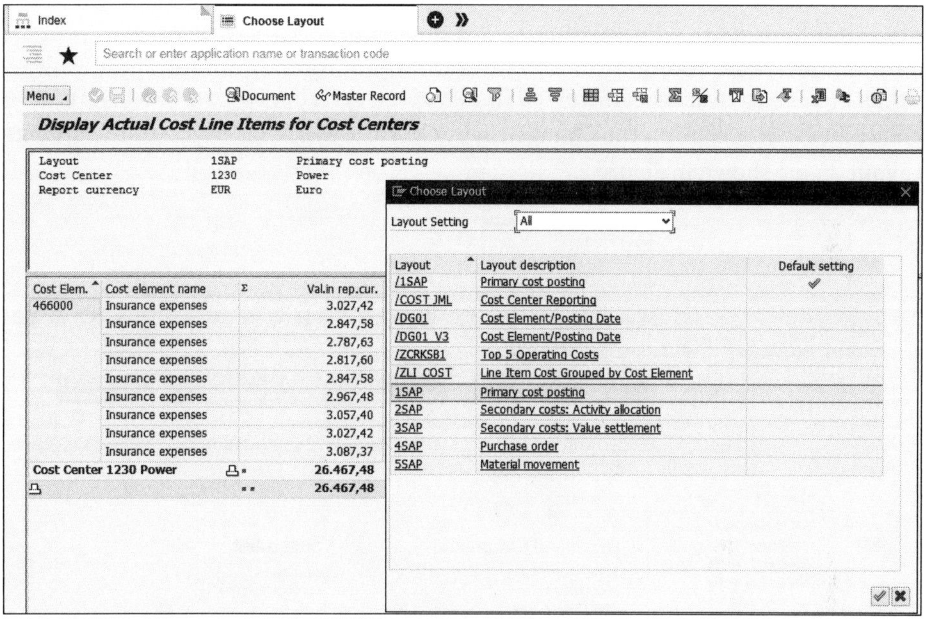

Figure 2.6 Change Layout in SAP List Viewer

The cost center line item includes layouts for the following:

- **Primary Cost Posting**
  Use this layout to analyze expense postings from the General Ledger.
- **Secondary Costs: Activity Allocation**
  Use this layout to analyze direct activity allocations charged from another cost center (see Chapter 6).
- **Secondary Costs: Value Settlement**
  Use this layout to analyze order values that have been settled to the cost center (see Chapter 7).

- **Purchase Order**
  Use this layout to analyze purchase orders for which the account assignment is the cost center (see Chapter 6).
- **Material Movement**
  Use this layout to analyze goods movements charged to the cost center (see Chapter 6).

These layouts will get you started, but you'll almost certainly want to create more layouts to organize the data in the list the way you want to see it (you'll notice that additional layouts have also been created in this demo system). To change a layout or to create a new one, click on the **Change Layout** button, which takes you to the **Change Layout** dialog shown in Figure 2.7.

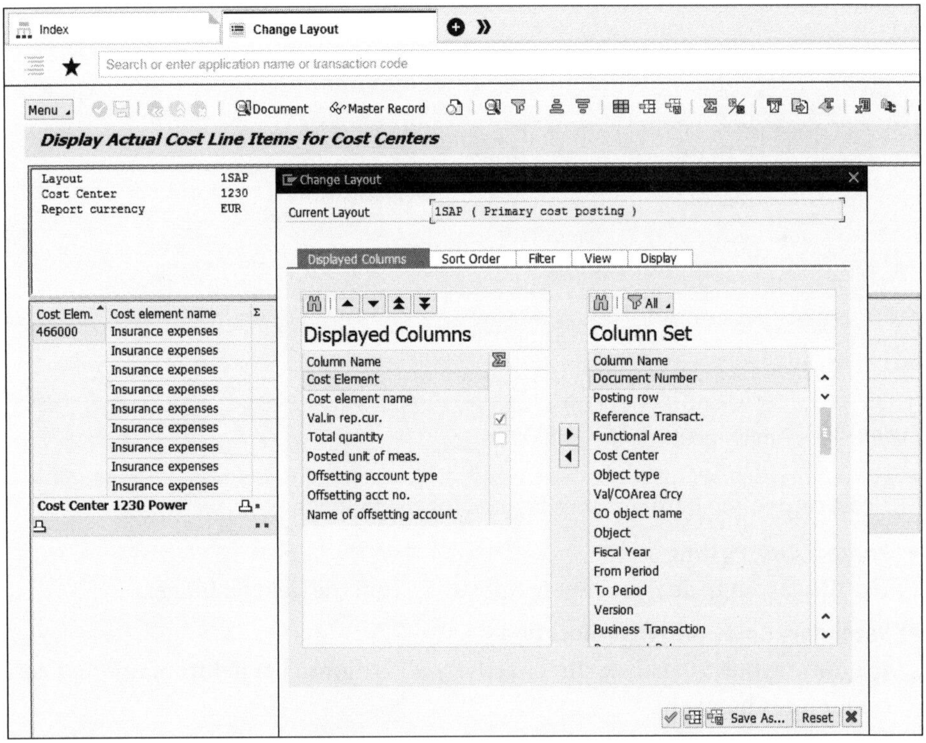

Figure 2.7 Adding Fields Using SAP ABAP List Viewer

To add fields, move them to the left by marking the relevant field in the right-hand column (**Column Set**) and selecting the left-facing arrow button in the center. To hide columns, move them to the right by marking the relevant fields in the left-hand column (**Displayed Columns**) and selecting the right-facing arrow button in the center. If the result is a layout that you want to use regularly, it's worth saving the layout under a meaningful name by clicking on the **Save** button. The new layout is assigned to your user, so nobody else will see your layout. To help you explore the potential of this list, let's consider the data available in the line item report.

Primary Cost Postings

The layout shown in Figure 2.6 and Figure 2.7 is for primary cost postings. It explains expense postings that originated in the General Ledger and shows the cost element in CO that mirrors the profit and loss account in the General Ledger and the offsetting reconciliation account for the vendor in Accounts Payable. We'll look at cost elements and accounts in more detail in Chapter 3 and Chapter 4. The layout also includes details of the offsetting account type—the insurance company whose services have been purchased—so the layout includes account type K for vendors and the offset account for the vendor invoice in our example.

If you want to reconcile your cost center documents against the data in the General Ledger, you can extend this layout to include the following fields, all of which are defaulted from the cost center master record:

- **Company Code**
  If you're looking at cross-company postings, you may want to know in which company code each posting was made.
- **Business Area**
  This is the main way of segmenting your business activities in the General Ledger.
- **Functional Area**
  This is used to segment activities for cost-of-goods-sold (COGS) reporting and in Public Sector Accounting.
- **Segment**
  This is used for segment reporting according to International Financial Reporting Standards (IFRS). The segment is derived from the profit center in the cost center.

One field you won't find in the layout is the controlling area. Every posting in CO takes place in a controlling area. Depending on your configuration, the controlling area may cover one or more company codes. In recent years, there has been a trend in global organizations toward a global controlling area. Whatever your settings, the golden rule is that all postings in CO and all reporting activities take place in a single controlling area. The only way to show data in multiple controlling areas is to report in SAP BW.

Secondary Postings or Allocations

If we assume that the cost center allocates the insurance expenses to several other cost centers, you might want to explain these postings by creating a new layout to show the *partners* participating in the allocation. This layout still includes the cost element and the cost center as the sender of the allocation, but you can extend it to include the following fields for the *sender*:

- **Object Type**
  The type of object against which the posting was made. In our example, the cost center is CTR. For the order line item that we'll look at later, the object type is ORD, for example.
- **Object**
  The object against which the posting was made. In our example, this is cost center number 1230.
- **Debit/Credit Indicator**
  Whether the posting was a debit (D) or a credit (C).

To explain the other side of the *partner relationship,* include the following fields:

- **Partner Type**
  The type of object to which you made the allocation. This might be CTR if you are using assessment cycles or distribution cycles or ORD (order) if you are charging a department's costs to an order using time recording.
- **Partner Object**
  The key of the other cost center or the order that received the allocation.
- **Partner Object Name**
  The name of the other cost center or the order that received the allocation.
- **Business Transaction**
  This enables us to distinguish between different types of postings and allocations for auditing purposes. We'll see examples of the different codes for the business transactions when we look at sample expense postings in Chapter 6 and the various forms of allocations that take place at period close in Chapter 7. It's worth

familiarizing yourself with the business transactions used in your organization as the locking mechanisms at period close will lock, for example, the assessment postings (RKIU) or the settlement postings (KOAO).

Multiple Currencies

If you work with several currencies, it's is also a good idea to create a separate version of your chosen layouts for each of the relevant currencies and another layout that shows relevant combinations:

- **CO Area Currency**
  This is usually the group reporting currency and is set for the controlling area. In general, this is the same as the group currency in the General Ledger.
- **Object Currency**
  This is the currency of the object (in our case, the cost center) and is set in the cost center master record. For example, a cost center based in the United States would have US dollars as the object currency. In general, this is the same as the company code currency in the General Ledger.
- **Transaction Currency**
  This is the local currency in which the transaction was performed. For example, if the US cost center purchases goods in Canada, the Canadian supplier would invoice in Canadian dollars (transaction currency).
- **Report Currency**
  This is set centrally for reporting purposes.

The other fields in the line item report are of two types. Some are specific to the business process (such as supplier, material, or employee) and make sense in that context but will not be filled by other transactions. Others are fairly technical and tend to be used for troubleshooting or when extracting data to another system, such as SAP BW.

2.1.2 Simplified Cost Center Line Item Report

In EHP 3 for SAP ERP 6.0, SAP modernized the user interface for the cost center line item report so that the whole user interface is on the web. From EHP 5 for SAP ERP 6.0, you'll find the new reports in the list we showed in Figure 2.3. In earlier enhancement packages, you'll find them in a separate list that you'll have to copy into your existing roles. All reports labeled List behave the same way as the cost center line item report. There are also reports labeled Analysis and SAP Crystal Reports. We'll come back to these reports when we look at alternative reporting options using SAP BW (for the analysis reports) and SAP BusinessObjects (for SAP Crystal Reports) in Chapter 8.

Clicking on **Cost Centers: Actual Line Item (List)** takes you to the new report. Enter the same search criteria as before. Figure 2.8 shows the resulting layout. Without getting too technical, notice that the screen rendering of an application built specifically for the web looks "cleaner" than a transaction that was built in preweb days and has simply been called via the role. However, the costs displayed are identical, because both reports read the same underlying data from SAP ERP. You might also consider making this report available to cost center managers and keeping the classic line item report for use in Controlling.

This report looks slightly different, in that the selection screen can be toggled on and off with the **Search Criteria** button rather than being left behind once the report is executed. The basic principles for list reporting that we just discussed are the same. To create layouts and change the fields displayed, click on the **Settings** button. Be aware, however, that this time the hidden columns are on the left and the displayed columns on the right (see Figure 2.8).

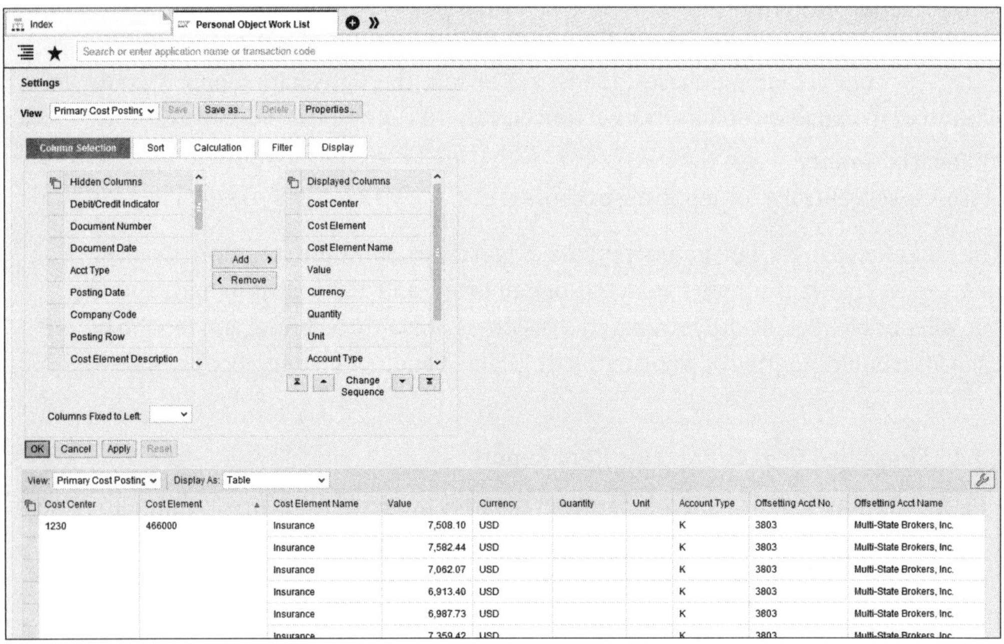

Figure 2.8 Simplified Cost Center Line Item Report

Simplified Reporting and the SAP Easy Access Menu

Although the first enhancements for simplified reporting were introduced in EHP 3 for SAP ERP 6.0, activating the business function FIN_REP_SIMPL_1 does not activate new transaction codes or bring these reports into your SAP Easy Access menu. The way to work with the list reports delivered for simplified reporting is to make them part of a report launchpad that is included in the user's role. To find out how to configure a report launchpad like the one shown in Figure 2.3, refer to Appendix B (found at *www.sap-press.com/4691*).

2.1.3 Totals Records for Cost Centers

The line item is by far the most commonly used data record for reporting. Similar data records exist to document what happened during the planning process (Transaction KSBP) and how commitments are created and used (Transaction KSB2). However, to put the entries in the line items into context, most controllers will want to look at how the costs compare with their plan. The plan data is generally at a higher level of aggregation than the line item (it's rare to plan by supplier, employee, and so on). Every line item has its sister *totals record* that stores a subset of the data available in the line item in each accounting period. Most of the period-close reports that we will look at in Chapter 7 read the totals records rather than the line items because performance is better if you select from a handful of fields organized in period blocks rather than from all 80 fields in the line item table. You'll find that most of the other reports in **Cost Center Accounting**, including the plan/actual comparison, target/actual comparison, and so on (see Figure 2.3), also work with totals records. In essence, the reports are bringing the detailed line item data up to the level at which you planned (cost center/account/period) so that you can make a line-by-line comparison. We'll look at planning in more detail in Chapter 5.

In general, you can display the line items from these reports by selecting the line you're interested in and double-clicking. The selection parameters (cost center, cost element, time frame, etc.) are passed to the line item report through the *report-to-report interface*. As an example, select **Plan/Actual Comparison Report** (shown in Figure 2.3) and enter the cost center 1230 and the periods January to December 2013 in the selection list. The result is a formatted report (see Figure 2.9) designed to show the cost center manager the state of spending on his cost center in that time frame (the total **Debit** line), together with how these costs have been charged to other cost centers (the total **Credit** line). To display the line item, double-click on the line for insurance expenses, then select **Cost Center: Actual Line Items** from the pop-up. This passes the parameters from your selection, and you then see the line item report we used as our initial example.

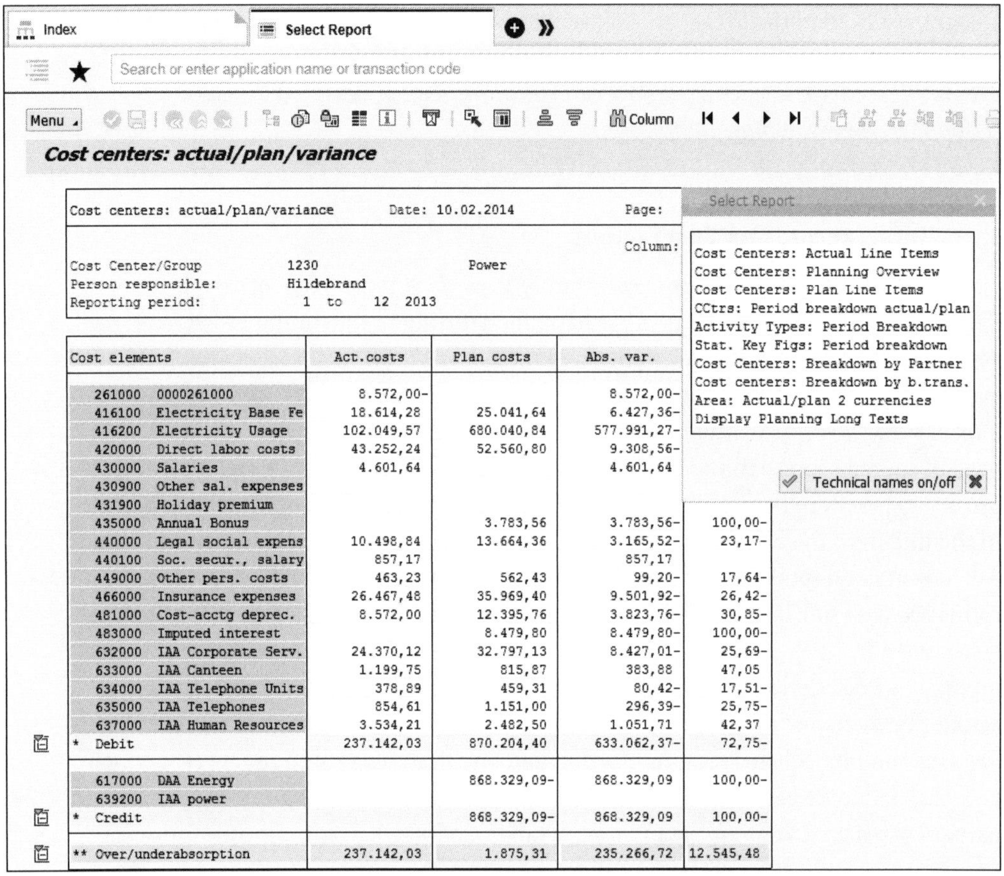

Figure 2.9 Cost Center Plan/Actual Variance and Link to Line Item Report

It's unlikely that you'll work with cost centers alone, so let's now look at the reports for internal orders.

2.2 Order Line Items

Let's continue our journey by looking at internal orders. Orders have many uses in SAP ERP, either detailing the activities on a cost center or representing activities going on completely separate from the cost center, such as capital investments. Others are purely statistical and are entered as an additional account assignment alongside the real cost center or order. There are also many orders that don't originate in CO but are created in Logistics (production orders, process orders, maintenance orders, QM orders, networks, and so on).

The costs for these orders can be analyzed using the same report, which probably explains why the order line item report is one of the most widely used transactions in SAP ERP Financials.

Order line item reports follow the same basic principles as cost center line item reports. In Figure 2.10, we've selected the **Internal Orders** role (SAP_EP_RW_CO_KAMN). You'll find all the reports available for this role under **Information System**. This corresponds to the menu path **Financials • Controlling • Internal Orders • Information System • Reports for Internal Orders** in earlier versions of the software.

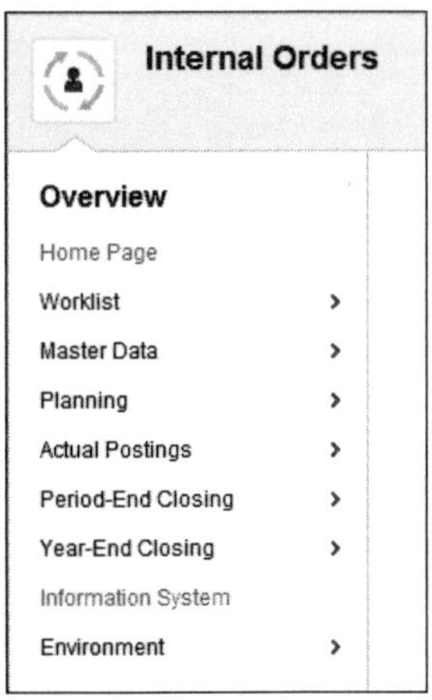

Figure 2.10 Internal Order Accounting within SAP NetWeaver Business Client

Again, let's look at the **Home** page (see Figure 2.11) before looking at the reports in detail. This time, consider setting defaults for the order type AAT and the order number ANR to ensure that the report can start with a default setting.

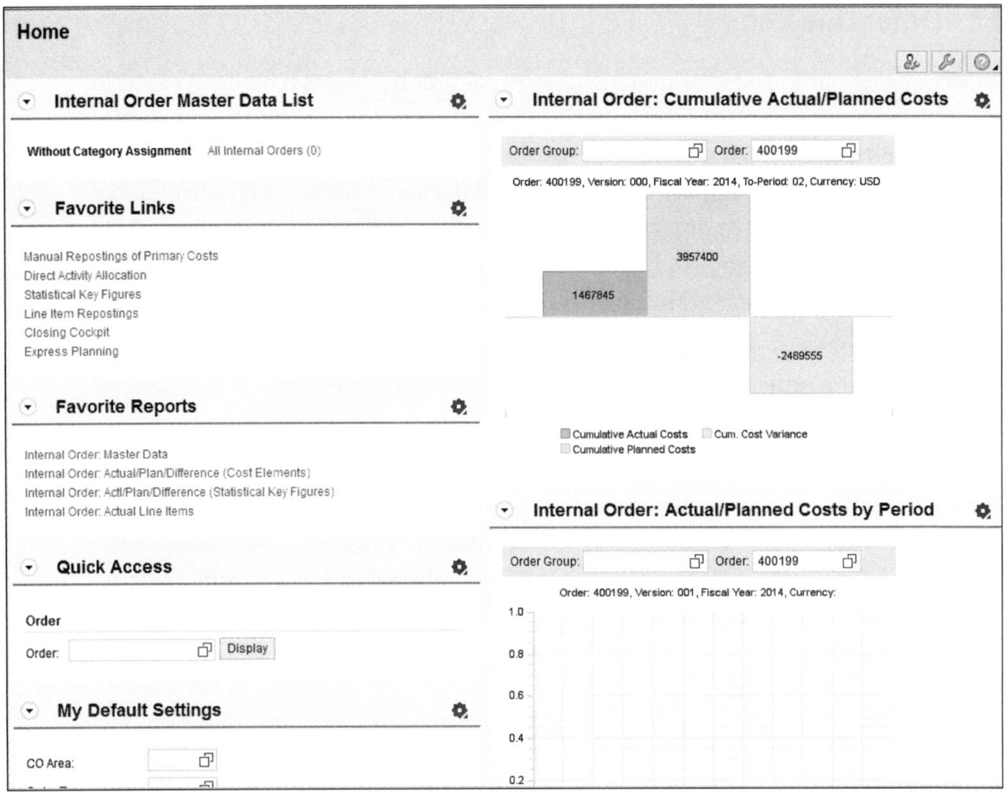

Figure 2.11 Home Page for Order Accounting

Figure 2.12 shows the list of reports for the internal orders. Again, this includes classic reports in all releases of SAP ERP and further reports that can be activated through the simplified reporting business functions.

Now, select the **Line Items** folder and then **Orders: Actual Line Items**. Experienced controllers will recognize this as Transaction KOB1. To select the relevant line items for analysis, enter order 400199, leave the cost element group blank, and enter posting dates between 01.01.2013 and 31.12.2013 in the selection screen. Then click on the **Execute** button. The result is a list of all postings for order 400199 in 2013, as shown in Figure 2.13.

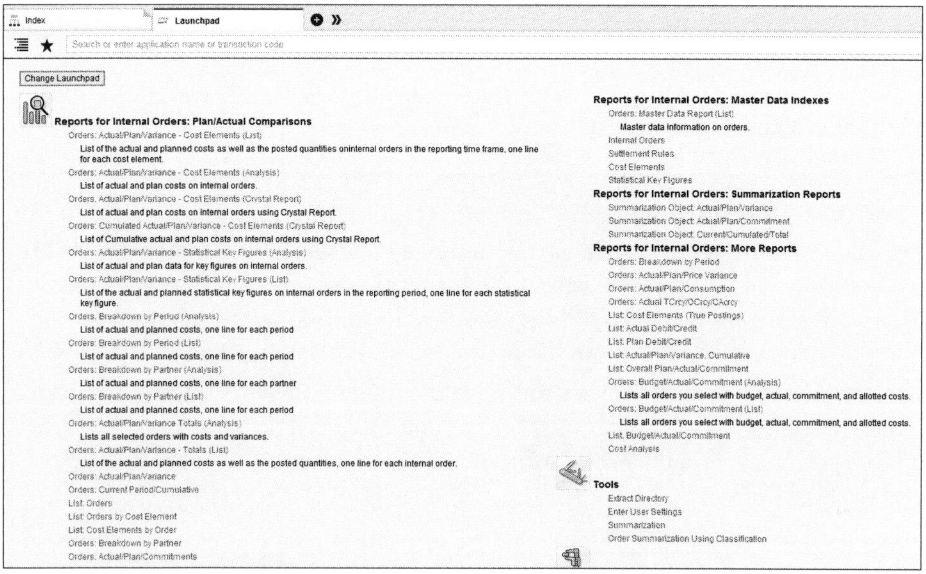

Figure 2.12 Reports for Order Accounting

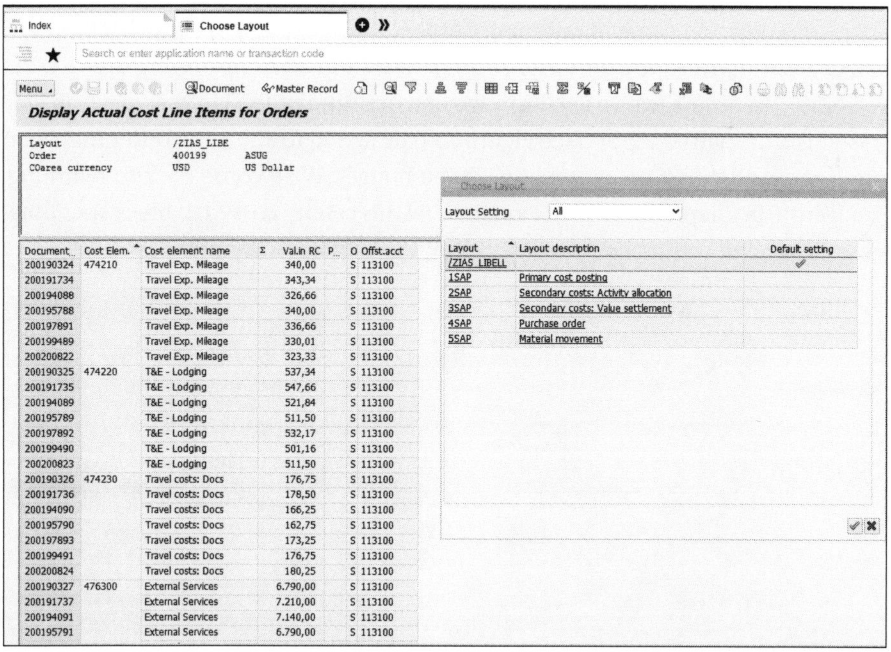

Figure 2.13 Order Line Item Results

The same layouts are available as for the cost center line item report except that this time the account assignment is the internal order. Additional line item reports document what happened during order planning (Transaction KABP) and how commitments are created and used (Transaction KAB2).

User-Specific Layouts

Once order managers understand how to create their own layouts, you are likely to find that layouts for this transaction proliferate. These same managers will tend to set their own layouts as default for all users. Encourage users to set the **User-specific** flag when they save their layouts, especially if they are creating a default. If you need to clean up your layouts at any point, choose **Settings • Layout • Manage**. You can then toggle between your personal layouts and those belonging to your organization, checking them and if necessary deleting ones that are no longer needed.

When it comes to putting order-spending in context, you can of course compare planned costs against actual costs just as we did for the cost center, but it's also possible to set a budget for internal orders—in other words, a ceiling on spending for that order. You won't use this for all order types, but it's common to set budgets for investment orders and some maintenance orders. As an example, select **List: Budget/ Actual/Commitments** (shown in Figure 2.12) and enter the controlling area and a range of internal orders (we've used a range of marketing orders) in the selection list. The result is a formatted report (see Figure 2.14) designed to show the order manager the state of spending by comparison with the budget. We'll come back to planning and budgeting in Chapter 5 and will explain how this ceiling is used to block spending on the order and how the **Commitment** column gets filled in Chapter 6.

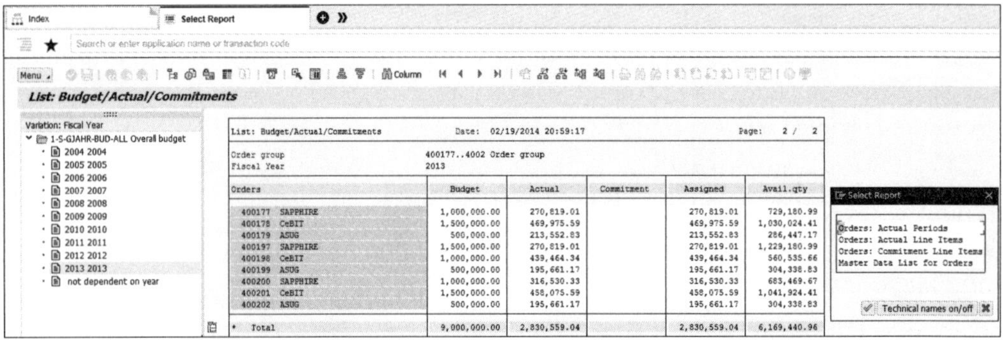

Figure 2.14 Budget/Actual Report for Marketing Orders

Although cost centers and internal orders are the simplest account assignments, if you work for a manufacturing company you'll also want to understand how to report on product costs, which we cover in the next section.

2.3 Product Costs: Itemization

The concept of cost center line items and order line items is easy for most accountants to grasp because of the affinity between a line item and a document in the General Ledger. When we come to product costing, the data structures change as the document takes something of a back seat and the focus moves to multilevel production structures, a familiar view for engineers but a new world for some accountants.

The *standard costs* for each manufactured product are calculated using a product cost estimate. The first step in costing is to read the bill of material (BOM) in Logistics to determine the materials to be used. The BOM is a multilevel structure that describes which raw materials are used to make a quantity of semifinished product and which semifinished products are used to make a quantity of finished product. The costs of converting the raw materials into semifinished products and then into finished products is described in *routings*. This focus on the production master data is also apparent in the reports, with the multilevel costed BOM being by far the most commonly used report, followed by the itemization that displays a line for each input to the production process (i.e., for each material and each internal activity from the routing).

If the product can be manufactured on different production lines or manufactured in-house and purchased, then you'll find each approach represented in the reports as a procurement alternative. If such alternatives have been defined for a product, the system creates a cost estimate for each alternative and then mixes them according to a percentage (such as 60% make, 40% buy). Depending on the implementation, you may also see items for purchasing info records, subcontracting, external activities, coproducts, planned scrap, and so on in the product cost reports.

Every costing item is automatically assigned to a cost element that represents the account under which actual goods movements are posted. The cost elements are then assigned to *cost components* that represent the major cost blocks in production. There are several ways of looking at product costs:

- **Cost of goods manufactured**
  This method sees the product costs as material costs, internal activities, external

activities, overhead, and so on. There can be up to 40 cost components, and the assignment is based on the cost elements under which the actual postings are captured in the system.

- **Primary cost component split**
  This split looks at what is behind the internal activity. In other words, to provide an internal activity, a cost center uses energy, wages, depreciation, operating supplies, and so on.
- **Partner cost component split**
  This split looks at the value added by each plant, company code, or business area involved in the manufacturing process.

2.4 Classic Reports for Product Cost Reporting

We'll start as we did for the cost centers and internal orders, with the role for Product Cost Planning (SAP_EP_RW_CO_CKOO).

To access the relevant reports, select **Information System**, shown in Figure 2.15. Figure 2.16 shows a list of reports for product cost planning. In earlier versions of the software, follow the menu path **Controlling • Product Cost Controlling • Product Cost Planning • Information System • Reports for Product Cost Planning**. You may find that these reports are used not just by controllers but also by the engineers responsible for designing new products and the supply chain people responsible for cost assignment on the production line.

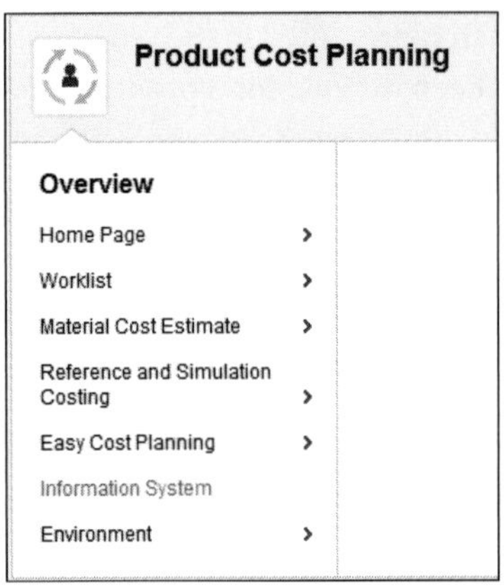

Figure 2.15 Product Cost Planning within SAP NetWeaver Business Client

Let's start with the **Detail Reports** folder and select **Costed Multilevel BOM** (see Figure 2.16). Enter the following and execute the report:

- **Material number and plant**
  This identifies the product you're interested in. The plant is always part of the key in these reports.
- **Costing variant**
  This provides the link to the configuration settings, telling you the purpose of the cost estimate (setting standard costs, determining the accuracy of current standard costs, balance sheet valuation for annual close, etc.), how the bill of material and routing should be selected, and what prices will be used in this calculation.
- **Costing version**
  Normally, this is 1, unless you're using mixed costing (for which multiple cost estimates are weighted) or group costing (for which the same BOM and routing are costed first using the local prices and again using the group costs).
- **Costing lot size**
  The reference quantity for the cost estimate against which all variable costs will be adjusted.

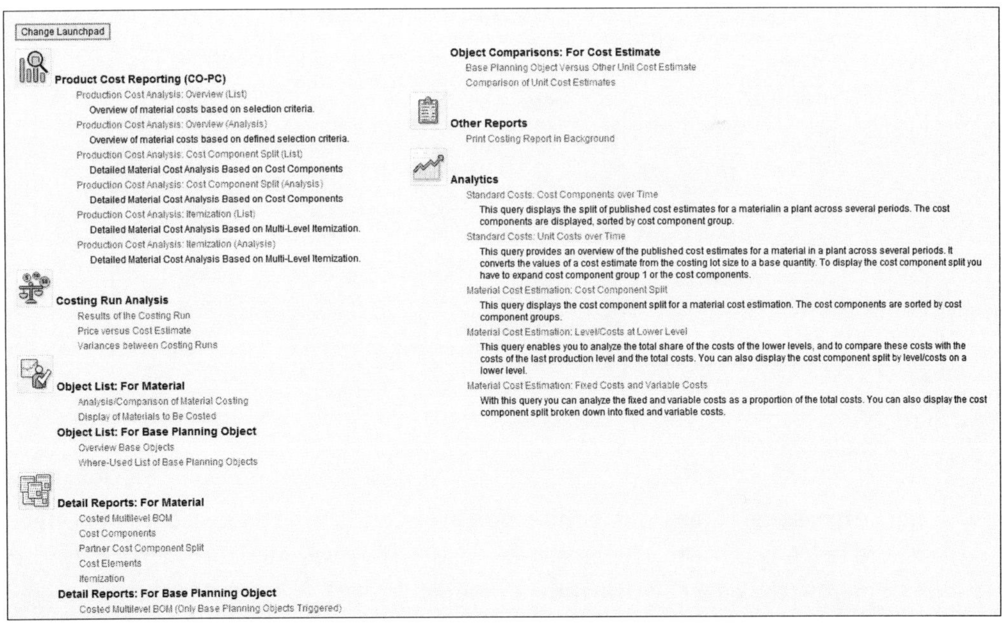

Figure 2.16 Reports for Product Cost Planning

Figure 2.17 shows the BOM together with the cost per item. You'll see the same report integrated in the cost estimate itself when we calculate the standard costs in Chapter 5.

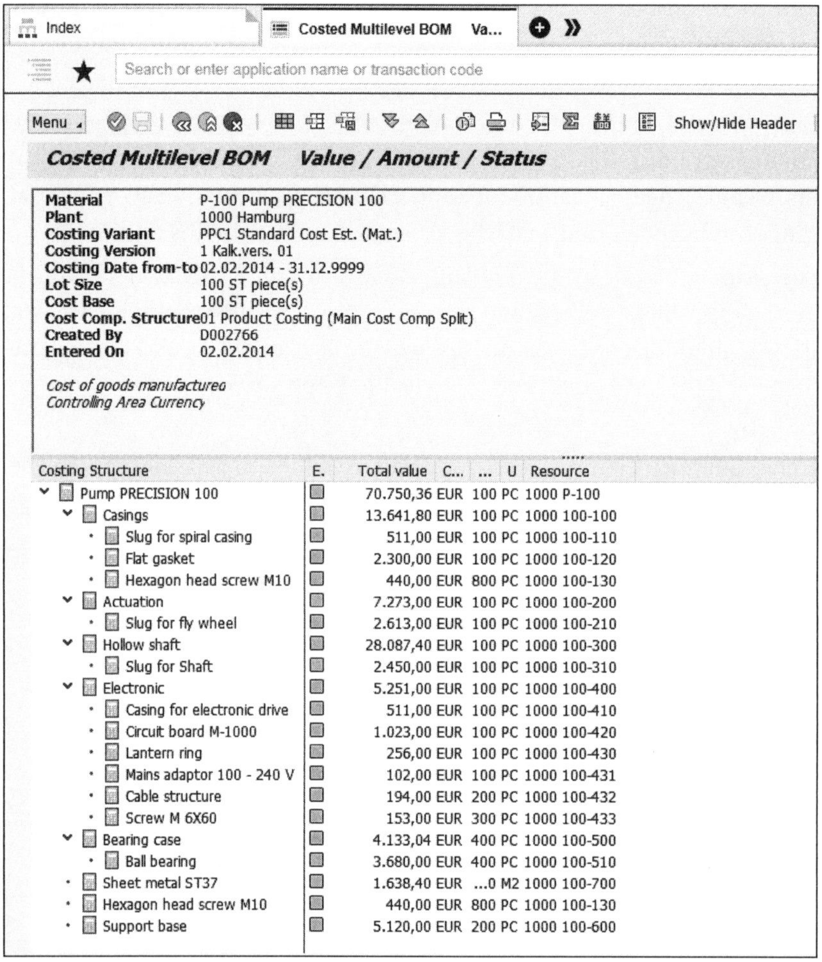

Figure 2.17 Costed Multilevel BOM

Notice that some of the icons in this report are familiar from the cost center line item report. This is because this report also uses SAP List Viewer, but it uses a tree structure to represent the quantity structure in production, with each level in the tree representing an assembly with its own bill of material.

To display the costs per operation in the routing, select the **Itemization** report in the **Detailed Reports** folder. Because of the sheer number of ways of looking at data for a cost estimate (by item category, by operation, by cost element, by cost component, etc.), SAP delivers many layouts. To view the operations in the routing, select the **Operations** layout before executing the report.

Figure 2.18 shows the items by operation, together with the delivered layouts:

- **Item Categories**
  Groups the items of the cost estimate by the internal categories **Material**, **Internal Activity**, **Overhead**, and so on.
- **Costing Items**
  Lists the items of the cost estimate by their technical IDs.
- **Cost Components**
  Shows the assignment of each costing item to one of up to 40 cost components.
- **Assemblies/Raw Materials**
  Shows the raw materials (materials without BOMs—i.e., purchased materials) and assemblies (materials with their own BOMs—i.e., manufactured materials) used in the final product.
- **Cost Components/Cost Elements**
  Used to check the assignment of the items to cost elements and from there to cost components.

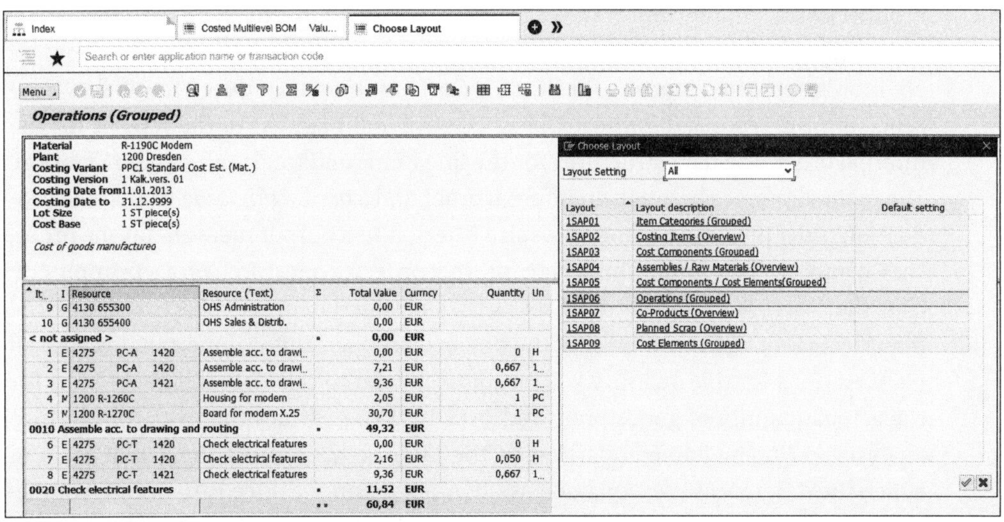

Figure 2.18 Itemization with Layouts

- **Operations**
  Shows the assignment of the costing items to the operations in the routing.
- **Coproducts**
  In the case that multiple products are manufactured in a single process (joint production), each coproduct is shown with item category A. We'll discuss coproducts in more detail in Chapter 4 and Chapter 6.
- **Planned Scrap**
  Normal spoilage is planned in the BOM, routing, and material master for the assembly. We'll discuss planned scrap in more detail in Chapter 4.
- **Cost Elements**
  Shows the assignment of the costing items to the accounts/primary cost elements and the secondary cost elements.

The product cost reports we've looked at so far help us analyze the *standard costs* for the product and support us mainly during the planning process (see Chapter 5). We'll now look at the reports available during the manufacturing process to explain how the costs are captured for production orders and similar objects. These are later compared against the standard costs for the product during variance analysis.

2.5 Product Costs: Cost Objects

Product Cost Planning almost never exists in isolation but exists as a preparation for Cost Object Controlling, in which the costs of executing the individual work orders are monitored. The reporting for Product Cost Planning introduced many new concepts, but the reporting for Cost Object Controlling is similar to the reports for the internal order. The data structures for the line items and totals records are identical. The main difference between an internal order and a *production order* is that the production order includes a planned lot size (the planned output measure for the order; see Chapter 1). Therefore, although an internal order for a research project simply collects the costs associated with the research, a production order collects costs for the manufacture of a given *quantity* of the finished product. This is important because all planned costs for this quantity will be adjusted later to calculate the *target costs* for the actual quantity of goods produced. This in turn provides the basis for variance analysis—a line-by-line comparison of the target costs against the actual costs in which the differences are explained as quantity variances, price variances, resource-usage variances, and so on. We'll look at the calculation of target costs and variances in more detail in Chapter 7.

Probably the biggest initial challenge is gaining an understanding of which cost objects your organization has chosen to work with because several approaches exist in Cost Object Controlling, depending on the nature of the chosen manufacturing process and your organization's approach to management accounting.

2.5.1 Product Cost by Order

The product cost by order approach is used when the individual production order or process order is the focus for cost management and the production costs for each individual lot are regularly monitored. The idea of the work order as the key element is an approach that has been around since the 1930s. The business goal is to monitor how each order gradually accumulates costs as goods are issued to the shop floor, operations confirmed, scrap reported, and so on. This approach makes sense when setup costs are significant and full cost traceability for each order is a business requirement and is widely used. It's also common when batch traceability is required in certain industries. However, practitioners of lean accounting argue that focusing on the work order in isolation encourages a "push" approach that potentially results in excessive inventory for which there is not necessarily a demand. Cost collection by order is also necessary for *joint production*—in other words, cases in which multiple products are produced in the same manufacturing process and the order costs have to be split to the coproducts. The **Product Cost by Order** menu offers several reports for tracking the costs of *production campaigns*, in which a series of production orders are manufactured in sequence because of the high costs of initial setup and cleanup on completion. This is particularly common in the chemical and pharmaceutical industries. More recently, developments for cost collection in outsourced manufacturing have brought the CO production order back into favor. We'll explore this in Chapter 6.

In Controlling terms, this approach is characterized by the delivery of the finished product to stock, the calculation of variances on completion of the order, and the calculation of work in process if the production or process order happens to be open at the time of the period close. We'll look at this process in detail in Chapter 7.

Figure 2.19 shows the role for **Order-Related Controlling** (SAP_EP_RW_CO_KKSM). To see the reports, select the **Information System** link. This is the equivalent of following the menu path **Financials • Controlling • Product Cost Controlling • Cost Object Controlling • Product Cost by Order • Information System • Reports for Product Cost by Order**.

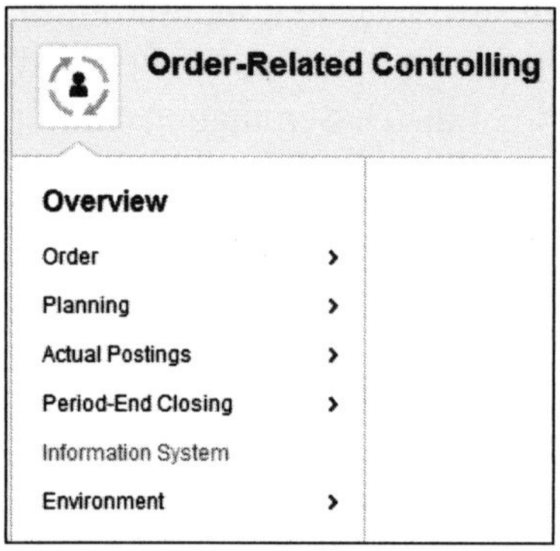

Figure 2.19 Order-Related Controlling in SAP NetWeaver Business Client

Figure 2.20 shows all reports for product cost by order. Because of the number of production orders being processed at any given time, the detailed reports we looked at for the internal orders are supplemented by various mass reports that select, for example, all materials in a given plant or for a given product group.

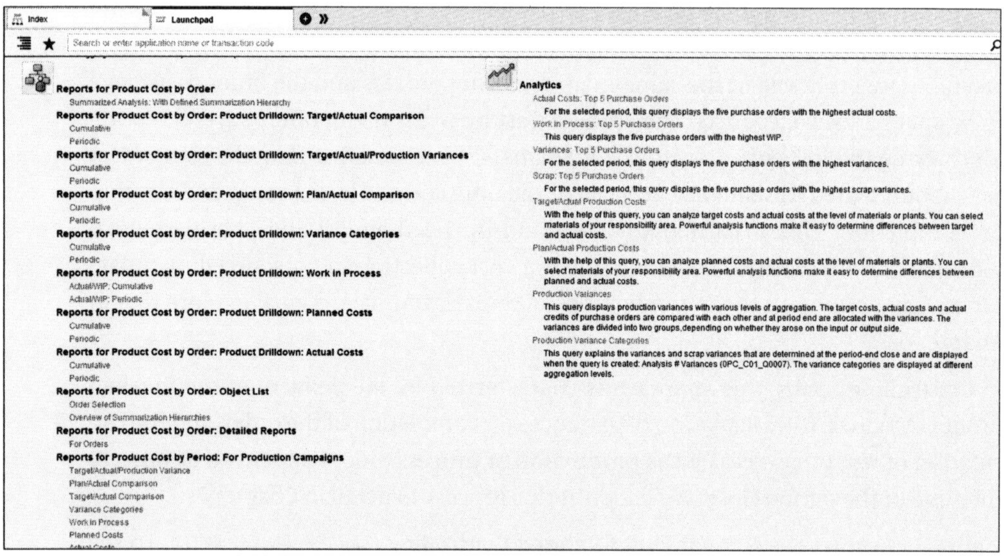

Figure 2.20 Reports for Production Order Reporting

Figure 2.21 shows the various production orders we created for the manufacture of material ACT-DCD in plant 6000 in February 2014 (you'll see how we created these postings in Chapter 6). To view this report, choose **Reports for Product Cost by Order** •

Object List • Order Selection or Transaction S_ALR_87013127. From here, you can select an order and navigate to the detailed reports that show the actual costs in context.

Order Selection: Results List

Values in Company Code Currency/Object Currency

Current Data

Order	Material Number	Plan cost debit	Actual cost debit	Crcy	Plan qty	Actual qty	O...
701644	ACT-DCD	0,00	0,00	MXN			
60003867	ACT-DCD	265,85	265,85	MXN	5	5	PC
60003868	ACT-DCD	188,35	188,35	MXN	5	5	PC
60003872	ACT-DCD	1.063,42	853,42	MXN	20	20	PC
60003873	ACT-DCD	531,71	426,71	MXN	10	10	PC
60003874	ACT-DCD	531,71	426,71	MXN	10	10	PC

Figure 2.21 List of Production Orders

In Figure 2.22, we've selected one of these production orders for detailed analysis. The target costs have been adjusted in line with the delivered quantity (five pieces). You'll immediately notice some significant variances. This is because we posted additional inventory to the order after an inventory count and additional activity costs to demonstrate the distribution of variances.

Target/Actual - Comparison

Order 60003867 ACT-DCD
Order Type PP01 Standard Production Order (int. number)
Plant 6000 Mexico City
Material ACT-DCD Demo CD

Planned Quantity 5 ST piece(s)
Actual Quantity 5 ST piece(s)

Target Cost Version 0 IDES Mexico

Period 002.2014 February

Legal Valuation
Company Code Currency/Object Currency

Cost Elem.	Cost Element (Text)	Origin	Σ	Total target costs	Σ	Total act.costs	Σ	Target/actual var.	T/I var(%)	Currency
895000	Factory output production orders	6000/ACT-DCD		108,00-		108,00-		0,00		MXN
895000	Factory output production orders			0,00		157,85-		157,85-		MXN
Credit/Reporting			▪	**108,00-**	▪	**265,85-**	▪	**157,85-**		**MXN**
400000	Consumption, raw material 1	6000/ACT-LCD		25,00		25,00		0,00		MXN
890000	Consumption of semifinished product	6000/ACT-BCD		0,00		50,00		50,00		MXN
890000	Consumption of semifinished product	6000/ACT-BCD		50,00		0,00		50,00-	100,00-	MXN
Material Components			▪	**75,00**	▪	**75,00**	▪	**0,00**		**MXN**
655100	Overhead Surcharge - Raw Material	1000		0,00		2,50		2,50		MXN
Material Overhead			▪	**0,00**	▪	**2,50**	▪	**2,50**		**MXN**
619100	Machine	CC530-00/ATR-00		14,58		96,27		81,69	560,29	MXN
619200	Labor	CC530-00/ATL-00		6,25		92,08		85,83	1.373,28	MXN
Other Costs			▪	**20,83**	▪	**188,35**	▪	**167,52**		**MXN**
			▪▪	**12,17-**	▪▪	**0,00**	▪▪	**12,17**		**MXN**

Figure 2.22 Actual Costs, Target Costs, and Variances for Production Order

We'll look at the reports to aggregate production orders en masse when we look at mass reporting in Chapter 8. It's also common to move such orders to a data warehouse for reporting due to the huge data volumes involved. Some organizations choose the **Product Cost by Period** option simply because they believe this is the only way they'll be able to handle the data volumes in question.

2.5.2 Product Cost by Period

At some sites, the volume of production orders is so high that it's nearly impossible for CO to monitor the costs successfully. This can be the case in the food industry, in which the production orders can be very short-lived (less than a day). It can also be the case with continuous, repetitive production with minimal setup that there is simply no requirement for individual lot-oriented controlling and that storing each production order as a separate order in CO represents an unnecessary burden for reporting and at period close. In this case, costs can be assigned to product cost collectors that represent each production alternative, and you might report on each production version, where the production version represents a production line or a set of manufacturing cells, rather than on the individual work orders. We'll create a product cost collector for cost collection in Chapter 3. These provide lean controlling by period, in which the goods movements and confirmations in Logistics are made by production or process order, but the costs are automatically routed to the product cost collector. The output measure is then not the lot size on the individual order but the sum of all delivered quantities in the period. Variance calculation and work-in-process calculation take place for each product cost collector at the end of the period. This approach is mostly used in a make-to-stock environment but is occasionally found in simple make-to-order scenarios. A typical example might be a manufacturer of car tires, for which there is little variability in the specification for each product.

Lean Accounting

Lean accounting encourages organizations to move away from the collection of costs by work order and toward a value-stream-based view of the organization. The product cost collector fits nicely into this concept, capturing the costs for each production version by period. If the value stream involves multiple products, then such costs can be rolled up to the value-stream level in reporting, where the value stream is typically represented by a product group or material group.

Figure 2.23 shows the role for **Product Cost by Period** (SAP_EP_RW_CO_KKPM). To see the reports, select the **Information System** link. This is the equivalent of following the menu path **Financials • Controlling • Product Cost Controlling • Cost Object Controlling • Product Cost by Period • Information System • Reports for Product Cost by Period** (see Figure 2.24).

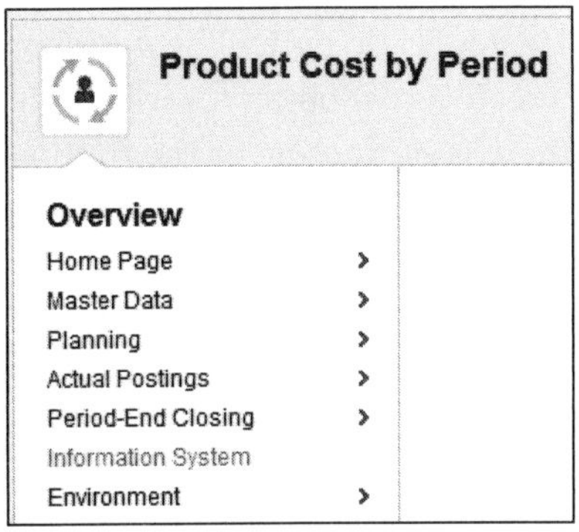

Figure 2.23 Product Cost by Period in SAP NetWeaver Business Client

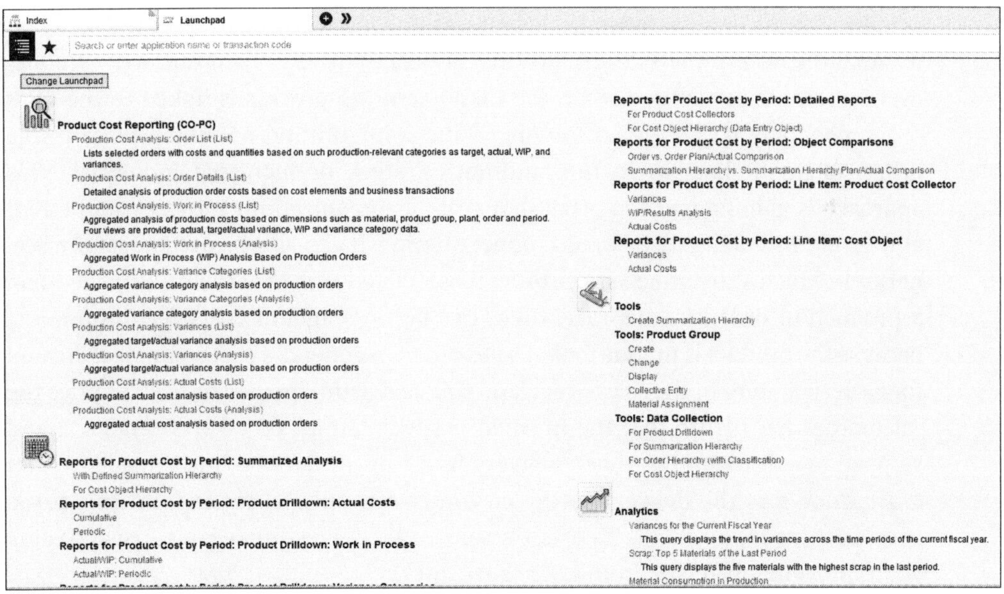

Figure 2.24 Reports for Product Cost by Period

The main difference between the product cost by period approach and product cost by order is that the status of the production order plays no role in the period close. At the end of every period, the confirmations to the product cost collector are analyzed to determine which operation quantities are work in process (i.e., have been started but not completed), which operation quantities are complete and can be analyzed for variances, and for which operations scrap has been confirmed. Although most of the reports are similar to those for product cost by order, you'll also notice line items for a cost object. The cost object hierarchy is used to create a cost object for which the cost of internal activities can be captured when there is no routing or the routing does not capture all manufacturing activities. These costs can then be distributed to the assigned product cost collectors or production orders at period close. Alternatively, the costs on the production orders or product cost collectors can be summarized to the cost objects and then settled. We'll look at how to create cost object hierarchies in Chapter 3.

2.5.3 Product Costs by Sales Order

The product cost by order and product cost by period approaches are mainly used in a make-to-stock environment. In this case, sales controlling takes place in Profitability Analysis, where the sales orders and associated invoices are captured. Product cost by sales order is used when the manufacturing process is linked to the sales order, generally because a customer-specific configuration has taken place in the order, as might happen in the automotive, steel, or high-tech industries. This approach is gaining favor in other industries as organizations move to adopt a lot size of one with a highly tailored product offering. It can also be used in service scenarios in which a customer service order is associated with the sales order rather than a production order. In this case, there can be no standard costs for the product because the product is unique to that sales order. In general, a cost estimate is created for each such item in the sales order, and this cost estimate may be used to price the sales order. To ensure that the finished product cannot be taken from stock and shipped to a different customer, delivery from the production line is made to *sales order stock*, and the delivery to the customer can only be made from this stock. Because there are no standard costs, the sales order cost estimate is also used to value goods movements to and from sales order stock.

Lean Accounting

Lean accounting encourages the use of make-to-order, where the sales order initiates, or "pulls," the manufacturing process in its wake. This is the opposite of the classic work order approach, where work orders "push" their goods into inventory in the hope that sales will then be able to sell the product in stock.

Figure 2.25 shows the role for **Sales Order Controlling** (SAP_EP_RW_CO_KKAM). To view the reports, select **Information System**. Figure 2.26 shows the standard reports delivered for sales order reporting. You can find this by following the menu path **Financials • Controlling • Product Cost Controlling • Cost Object Controlling • Product Cost by Sales Order • Information System • Reports for Product Cost by Sales Order**.

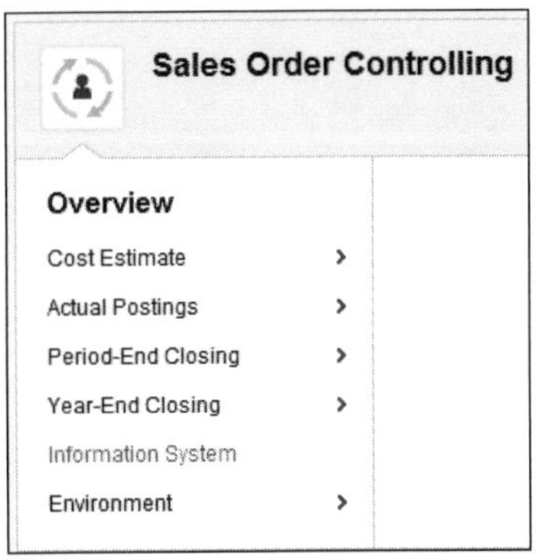

Figure 2.25 Sales Order Controlling in SAP NetWeaver Business Client

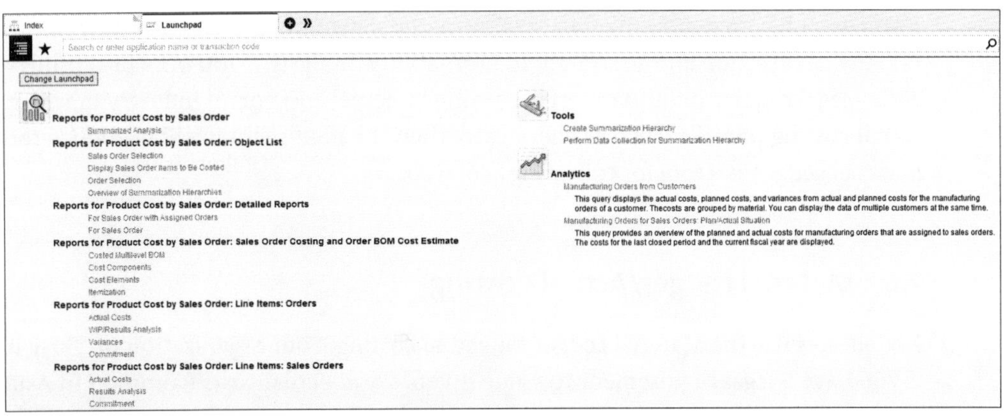

Figure 2.26 Reports for Sales Order Reporting

The line items and total records are similar to those you would see for any order, but you also have reports for sales order costing that are more like those we discussed for Product Cost Planning in that the quantity structure (BOM and routing) is very prominent. It's also important to be able to select sales orders the way we selected production orders, as shown in Figure 2.27. Be aware here that these aren't all the sales order items in your organization, but only those that are make-to-order items.

Sales Order Selection: Results List

CurrncyEUR Euro (EMU currency as of 01/01/1999)

Current Data

Sales Doc.	Item	Material	S...	SOff.	Planned Costs	Total plan costs	Planned Costs O	Actual Costs	Plan Revenue	Actual Revenue	Planned Profit	Actual Profit	Cur.
15710	10	IM0001	101	1000	0,00	0,00	0,00	0,00	2.520,00	0,00	2.520,00	0,00	EUR
15714	10	LOW_1AND2			0,00	0,00	0,00	0,00	673,89	0,00	673,89	0,00	EUR
15715	10	LOW_1AND2			0,00	0,00	0,00	0,00	1.010,84	0,00	1.010,84	0,00	EUR
15717	10	LOW_1AND2			0,00	0,00	0,00	0,00	1.186,05	0,00	1.186,05	0,00	EUR
15718	10	LOW_1AND2			0,00	0,00	0,00	0,00	12.558,24	0,00	12.558,24	0,00	EUR
15722	10	IM0001	101	1000	0,00	0,00	0,00	0,00	1.890,00	0,00	1.890,00	0,00	EUR
15733	10	LOW_1AND2			0,00	0,00	0,00	0,00	219.504,59	0,00	219.504,59	0,00	EUR
15757	30	C-1100	110	1010	0,00	0,00	0,00	0,00	1.124,80	0,00	1.124,80	0,00	EUR
15975	10	M-777	110	1010	0,00	0,00	0,00	0,00	5.200,00	0,00	5.200,00	0,00	EUR
15976	10	M-777	110	1010	0,00	0,00	0,00	0,00	1.040,00	0,00	1.040,00	0,00	EUR
15976	20	M-444	110	1010	0,00	0,00	0,00	0,00	2.120,00	0,00	2.120,00	0,00	EUR
15977	10	M-777	110	1010	0,00	0,00	0,00	0,00	520,00	0,00	520,00	0,00	EUR
15980	10	M-111	110	1010	0,00	0,00	0,00	0,00	1.000,00	0,00	1.000,00	0,00	EUR
15980	20	M-444	110	1010	0,00	0,00	0,00	0,00	2.120,00	0,00	2.120,00	0,00	EUR
16033	10	PROD319			0,00	0,00	0,00	0,00	10,00	0,00	10,00	0,00	EUR
16038	10	PROD319			0,00	0,00	0,00	0,00	10,00	0,00	10,00	0,00	EUR
16040	10	PROD319			0,00	0,00	0,00	0,00	10,00	0,00	10,00	0,00	EUR
16042	10	PROD319			0,00	0,00	0,00	0,00	0,00	0,00	0,00	0,00	EUR
5002301	1200	HT-1010			0,00	0,00	0,00	0,00	0,00	0,00	0,00	0,00	EUR
30000058	10	104844-15			0,00	0,00	0,00	0,00	1.226,05	0,00	1.226,05	0,00	EUR
30000059	10	104844-15			0,00	0,00	0,00	0,00	1.226,05	0,00	1.226,05	0,00	EUR
40000073	10	PC_SERVICE_CONF	130	1030	0,00	0,00	0,00	0,00	0,00	0,00	0,00	0,00	EUR
40000074	10	PC_SERVICE_CONF	130	1030	0,00	0,00	0,00	0,00	0,00	0,00	0,00	0,00	EUR
40000075	10	PC_SERVICE_A	110	1010	0,00	0,00	0,00	0,00	0,00	0,00	0,00	0,00	EUR
40000076	10	REPAIR_SERVICE	101	1000	0,00	0,00	0,00	0,00	0,00	0,00	0,00	0,00	EUR
40000083	10	PC_SERVICE_A	110	1010	0,00	0,00	0,00	0,00	0,00	0,00	0,00	0,00	EUR
40000094	10	PC_SERVICE_A	110	1010	0,00	0,00	0,00	0,00	0,00	0,00	0,00	0,00	EUR
40000095	10	REPAIR_SERVICE	101	1000	0,00	0,00	0,00	0,00	0,00	0,00	0,00	0,00	EUR
					0,00	**0,00**	**0,00**	**0,00**	**517.195,68**	**0,00**	**517.195,68**	**0,00**	**EUR**

Figure 2.27 Sales Order Results List

If you don't have a requirement to revalue material inventory at actual costs, you can skip the next section and go straight to Profitability Analysis. If you work in a country with a legal requirement to report according to actual costs or an industry in which actual costing prevails (such as chemicals), then the next section will introduce the Material Ledger as a tool for collecting actual costs.

2.6 Material Ledger/Actual Costing

Not all sites use the Material Ledger for actual costing. Your organization may use it if you have a legal requirement to value inventory at actual costs (common in Asia and South America), if you have highly volatile raw material prices or unstable production structures that make standard costing with detailed variance analysis impractical, or if you use it to provide a second inventory valuation approach for legal reporting.

From a reporting point of view, the Material Ledger differs from cost center and order reporting in that the reports display the *inputs and outputs* in each procurement, production, and sales process. The Material Ledger has its own documents for every goods movement, every business transaction that affects material prices (invoices, order settlement, etc.), and its own calculations at period close. Call up a report for a raw material, and you'll see the goods receipt and invoice from the supplier in the **Receipts** line and the goods issue to production in the **Consumption** line along with details of any stock currently in inventory. Call up the same report for a finished material, and you'll see the goods receipt from raw material inventory in the **Receipts** line and the goods issue to sales and the invoice to the final customer in the **Consumption** line. Chapter 6 will walk you through a complete manufacturing process from procurement to sales, showing you the Material Ledger postings for each goods movement that will provide the basis for Actual Costing at period close.

Figure 2.28 shows the role for **Actual Costing/Material Ledger** (SAP_EP_RW_CO_CKML). To access the list shown in Figure 2.29, select **Information System**. You can find this by following the menu path **Financials • Controlling • Product Cost Controlling • Material Ledger/Actual Costing • Information System**. Two reports are used frequently: **Material Price Analysis** (Transaction CKM3N) and the **Valuated Material Quantity Structure** (Transaction CKMLQS). Note that the standard reports focus on the reporting of a single material. SAP recently introduced new drill-down reports for reporting on multiple materials. We'll show how to work with these in Chapter 13, because they were originally introduced in the context of SAP HANA.

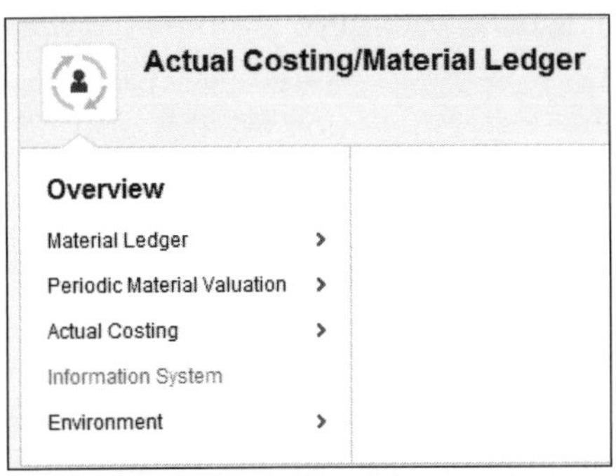

Figure 2.28 Material Ledger in SAP NetWeaver Business Client

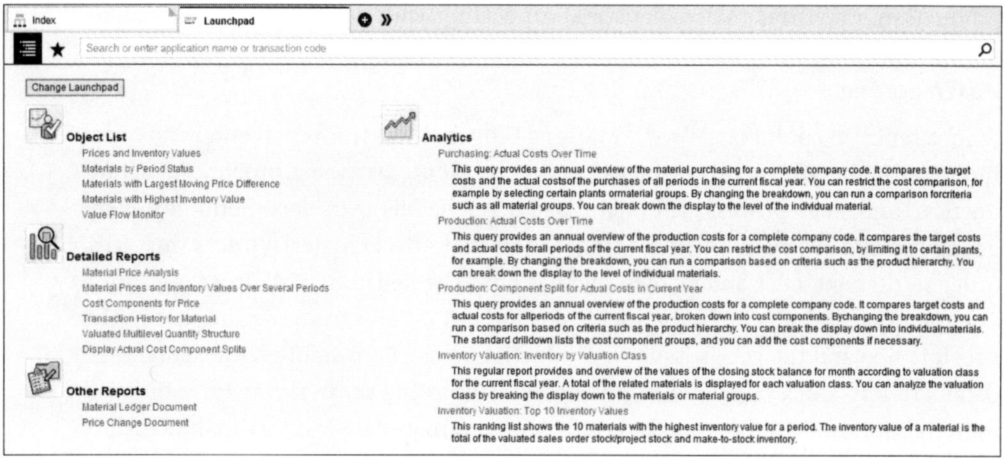

Figure 2.29 Reports for Material Ledger Reporting

Figure 2.30 shows the Material Ledger postings for a raw material that has been purchased from an external supplier and then issued to an internal production process for conversion into a finished product. Technically, this is a list viewer tree report like the one we saw for the multilevel costed BOM in Product Cost Planning.

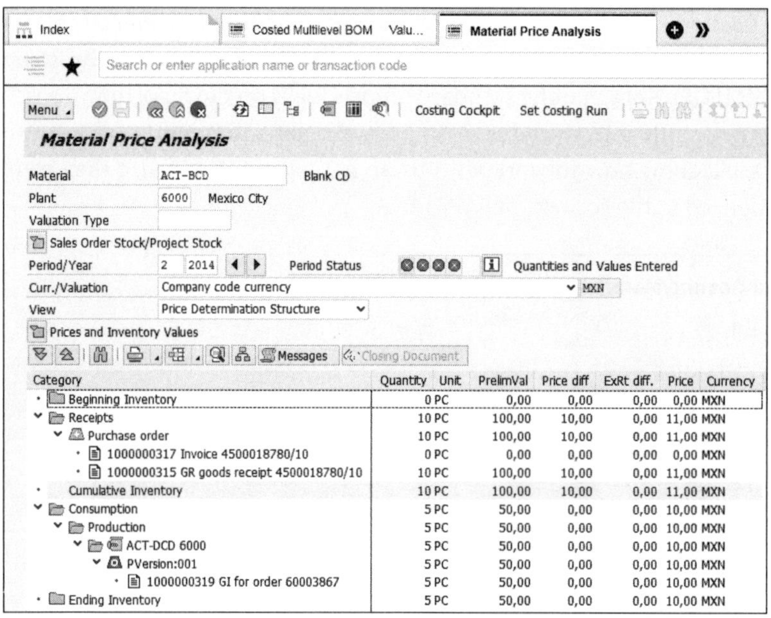

Figure 2.30 Material Price Analysis for Raw Material

Figure 2.31 shows the quantity structure for a finished product (PCG-FERT-01) that has required three semifinished products (PCG Barrel Head, PCG Construction Kit, and PCG Motor Housing) in its manufacture. Manufacturing activities were performed to convert the three semifinished products into PCG-FERT-01. This report first became available in Release 4.7 of SAP R/3 (see Appendix C at *www.sap-press.com/4691*).

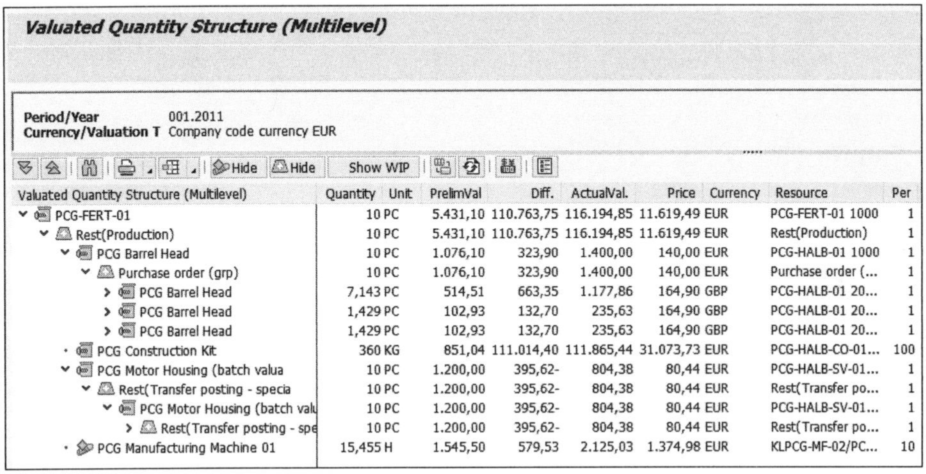

Valuated Quantity Structure (Multilevel)

Period/Year 001.2011
Currency/Valuation T Company code currency EUR

Valuated Quantity Structure (Multilevel)	Quantity	Unit	PrelimVal	Diff.	ActualVal.	Price	Currency	Resource	Per
PCG-FERT-01	10	PC	5.431,10	110.763,75	116.194,85	11.619,49	EUR	PCG-FERT-01 1000	1
Rest(Production)	10	PC	5.431,10	110.763,75	116.194,85	11.619,49	EUR	Rest(Production)	1
PCG Barrel Head	10	PC	1.076,10	323,90	1.400,00	140,00	EUR	PCG-HALB-01 1000	1
Purchase order (grp)	10	PC	1.076,10	323,90	1.400,00	140,00	EUR	Purchase order (...	1
PCG Barrel Head	7,143	PC	514,51	663,35	1.177,86	164,90	GBP	PCG-HALB-01 20...	1
PCG Barrel Head	1,429	PC	102,93	132,70	235,63	164,90	GBP	PCG-HALB-01 20...	1
PCG Barrel Head	1,429	PC	102,93	132,70	235,63	164,90	GBP	PCG-HALB-01 20...	1
PCG Construction Kit	360	KG	851,04	111.014,40	111.865,44	31.073,73	EUR	PCG-HALB-CO-01...	100
PCG Motor Housing (batch valua	10	PC	1.200,00	395,62-	804,38	80,44	EUR	PCG-HALB-SV-01...	1
Rest(Transfer posting - specia	10	PC	1.200,00	395,62-	804,38	80,44	EUR	Rest(Transfer po...	1
PCG Motor Housing (batch valu	10	PC	1.200,00	395,62-	804,38	80,44	EUR	PCG-HALB-SV-01...	1
Rest(Transfer posting - spe	10	PC	1.200,00	395,62-	804,38	80,44	EUR	Rest(Transfer po...	1
PCG Manufacturing Machine 01	15,455	H	1.545,50	579,53	2.125,03	1.374,98	EUR	KLPCG-MF-02/PC...	10

Figure 2.31 Valuated Quantity Structure

In addition to these two detailed reports for the material and the quantity structure, much reporting in the Material Ledger is performed in the context of the period close (see Chapter 7), in which each step in the periodic costing run (used to calculate the weighted average costs per material at the end of each period) and each step in the alternative valuation run (used to provide actual costs in a wider time frame or according to a second accounting approach) has its own supporting report that allows you to check the values calculated in that step.

The Material Ledger collects all costs from the first purchase of the raw material through all conversion steps to the final delivery of the finished product to the customer. We'll walk through all the steps in this process when we look at actual postings in Chapter 6. However, as the name implies, the Material Ledger gathers costs by material. It keeps track of the cost of goods sold for these materials, but it does not capture revenue, and it provides no information about the customer who bought the finished product, the sales organization that performed the sale, and so on. For such information, we must move to Profitability Analysis (or CO-PA).

2.7 Profitability Analysis Reports

The Profitability Analysis reports differ from the other reports we've looked at so far in that there are virtually no standard reports because the structure of the operating concern is determined during implementation. Figure 2.32 shows the **Profitability Analysis** role (SAP_EP_RW_CO_KEMN). Choose **Information System** to access the reports.

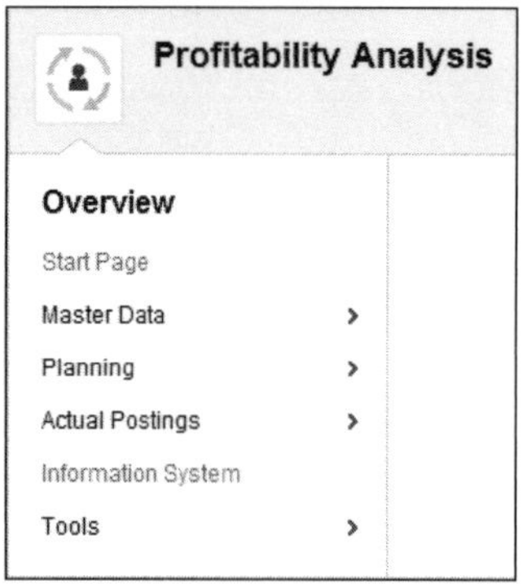

Figure 2.32 Profitability Analysis within SAP NetWeaver Business Client

The only commonality in Profitability Analysis reports is that certain standard events write data into the Profitability Analysis application. In costing-based Profitability Analysis, these are distinguished by the *record type*. The following transactions transfer data to Profitability Analysis:

- Incoming sales orders (record type A)
- Direct postings from Financial Accounting (record type B)
- Order and project settlement (record type C)
- Cost center allocations (record type D)
- Single-transaction costing (record type E); industry specific, so you might not use it
- Billing documents from Sales and Distribution (record type F)
- Customer agreements (record type G); used in some industries
- Statistical key figures (record type H)
- Transfer of sales orders from projects (record type I); used for commercial projects that are linked with sales orders for billing

If this list sounds fairly technical, consider instead the different levels of detail captured for the main record types in Profitability Analysis:

- Let's start with an *incoming sales order* (record type A). We'll see in Chapter 6 that an incoming sales order includes the name of the customer, the product or products purchased, the sales organization making the sale, the distribution channel, the division, the sales office, the sales group, and so on. This is the lowest level of granularity available in Profitability Analysis.
- Usually, the same characteristics are captured when the customer is *billed* for his purchase (record type F). Again, this is extremely detailed information.
- A *direct posting* from Financial Accounting (record type B) may be made at this level of detail if the person making the posting has all the listed information. However, as you'll see in Chapter 6, it may be possible to know only the affected material at the time of the posting and not the customer who will ultimately purchase the finished product. In this case, the record includes the product as a characteristic but not the customer.
- *Production variances* (carried in the settlement document, record type C) always apply to the product produced, but only apply to the customer if it's a make-to-order scenario and the production process is triggered by the sales order.
- *Cost center allocations* (record type D) offer the most options. In Chapter 7, you'll learn how to set up assessment cycles that can be very granular, breaking all expenses down to individual customers or products. You'll also see that it's possible to do an allocation to a much higher-level characteristic, such as a region or a country. This might be key for marketing expenses (e.g., if it's clear that a trade fair took place in the northwestern region of the United States but unclear which customers participated).

We'll look at some of these different record types by selecting the line item report (Transaction KE24). Figure 2.33 shows the selection screen for the CO-PA line items. We've selected all documents created by this user in company code currency.

Figure 2.34 shows all line items that we posted while creating the examples in Chapter 6. You'll see that we created invoices (record type F), sales orders (record type A), direct postings to FI (record type B), and production variances (record type C). You'll also notice that although the lines for the invoices and sales orders contain most of the dimensions, there are blank entries for the direct postings from FI and production variances, because these could only be assigned to the material-related dimensions and not to the customer-related dimensions.

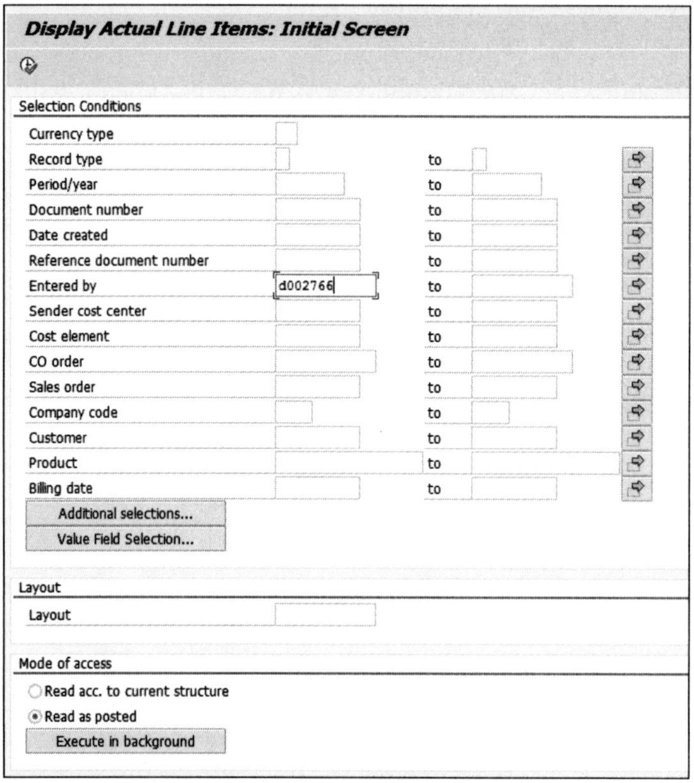

Figure 2.33 CO-PA Line Items Selection Screen

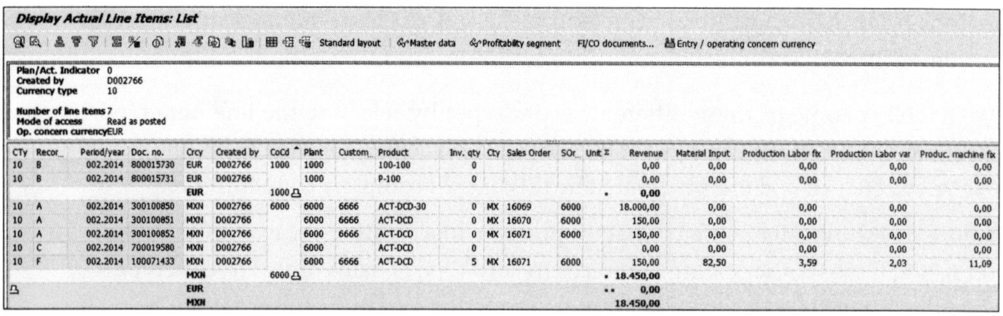

Figure 2.34 Line Item Report Showing CO-PA Documents

The structure of the operating concern and with it of the CO-PA tables is the business of the implementation team. Figure 2.35 illustrates one approach to designing the relationships among the entities for Profitability Reporting.

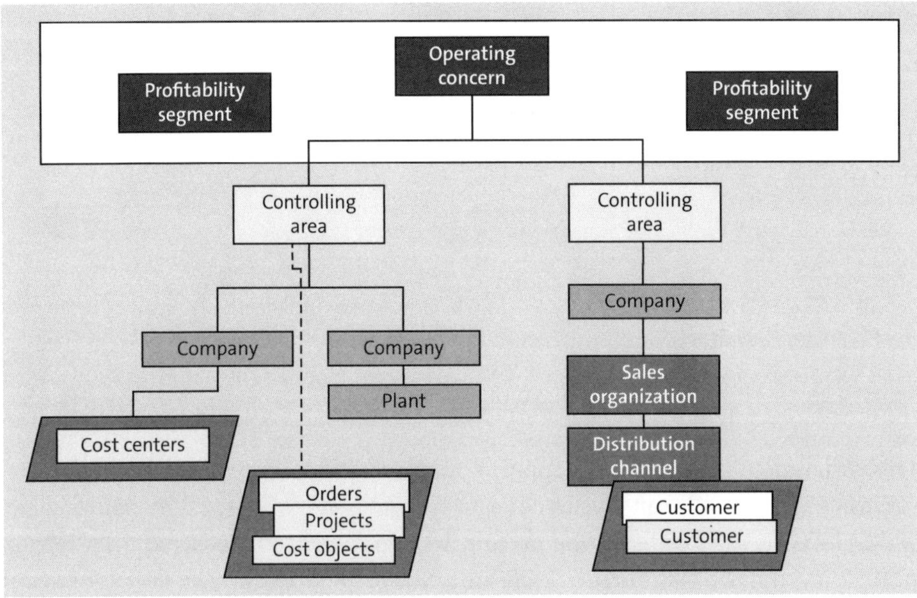

Figure 2.35 Organizational Structures in CO-PA

> **Note**
>
> The implementation team determines all other fields when they configure your system. Because the focus is on sales reporting, most organizations have the product, customer, and sales region dimensions and other dimensions that can be derived from these entities (product group, customer group, division, sales office, etc.). You'll find details of the recommended size of the operating concern (generally the maximum number of characteristics is 50 and the maximum number of value fields is 120, but this can be extended) in SAP Note 1029391.

The combination of dimensions is known as the *profitability segment*. You can display the profitability segment for any of the line items in Figure 2.34 by selecting a line and clicking on the **Profitability Segment** button; you'll see the report shown in Figure 2.36. We've picked a line item that refers to a sales order, so most of the dimensions (material-based and customer-based) are filled. You'll notice additional dimensions, such as those for WBS elements, that are not filled. We would see entries here if the costs for a WBS element had been settled.

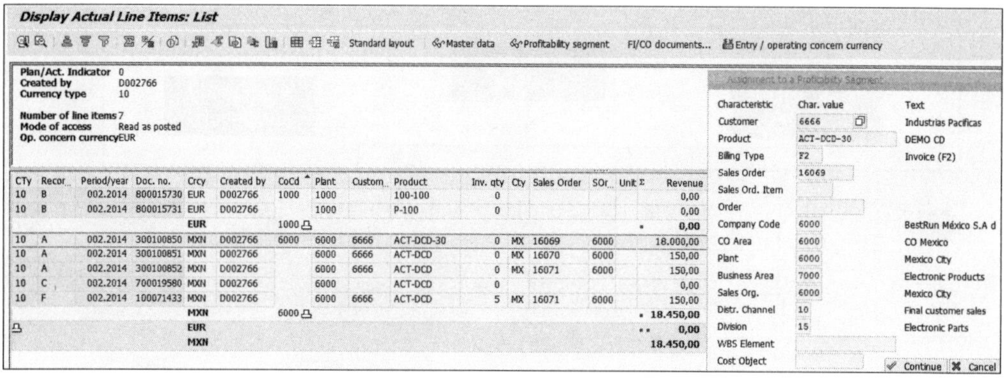

Figure 2.36 Line Item Report Showing Profitability Segment

This assignment of costs at the appropriate level of detail is essential to an understanding of CO-PA. We can fill customer-based and material-based dimensions when we capture the sales order or the invoice, we can fill material-based dimensions in purchasing and production; for overhead, we have to make our own decisions about whether to fully load the products and customers or to assign the costs at a higher level. We'll return to this process when we look at how to create *assessment cycles* in Chapter 7.

If you are new to Controlling, use the line item report to draw up your own list of the characteristics used in your organization and to understand which are derived from the product, which are derived from the customer, and which are derived from the sales organization. Then look in turn at the different record types to understand which characteristics are filled from the invoice, which are filled during settlement, and which are filled as the result of an allocation.

Because the assignments within this schema are fairly dynamic, with the assignments to sales organizations, distribution channels, divisions, and so on changing on a regular basis, CO-PA reports allow you to report either on the dimensions as posted (see Figure 2.33) or according to the current structure (i.e., following a realignment).

There are two types of fact tables, depending on whether you use account-based CO-PA or costing-based CO-PA or both. You'll find a full description of the difference between the two approaches in SAP Note 69384, but some key points are summarized here:

- Costing-based CO-PA assigns all postings to *value fields* that capture the individual elements of a contribution margin (sales, cost of goods sold, general overhead, etc.). This approach provides the ability to break down account-level information into further detail, such as fixed and variable costs for the same cost element, and separate the components of the standard cost into different value fields.

In costing-based CO-PA, the value fields are determined during implementation, so some teams break out the price conditions for the sales deductions into many separate value fields, whereas others lump them into one field. Most implementations distinguish between fixed and variable costs for their product cost estimate, but some implementations keep a lot of detail from their cost components, and others lump the cost components together. The same variability applies to allocations, order settlement, and the settlement of production variances and to the transfer of cost components from the Material Ledger.

- Account-based CO-PA records data to a cost element that represents the account used to post the data originally. This makes it much easier to reconcile the cost elements and the accounts by company code, business area, and so on. But you should be aware that low-level characteristics such as customers and products are generally summarized and therefore not captured in the General Ledger, so they won't be available for reconciliation.

  In account-based CO-PA all allocations and settlements are posted under the secondary cost elements created to document the value flows in CO. We'll look at secondary cost elements in detail in Chapter 3.

The characteristics apply to both costing-based and account-based CO-PA. However, different fact tables are used. The transaction or fact tables for costing-based CO-PA are delivered with a placeholder for the operating concern (CE1XXXX) and are generated on-site. The transaction tables for account-based CO-PA are the same as those used for cost centers, orders, projects, and so on. If you use both approaches in the same operating concern, be careful to check which approach you select when calling reports or running transactions, because the results can look dramatically different. Figure 2.37 shows a line item report for account-based CO-PA. Again, we've selected the profitability segment, but you can see that the columns are completely different. This is because instead of assigning costs to value fields we're looking at them by account/cost element.

If you are using only costing-based CO-PA and not account-based CO-PA, you may still discover records that appear to be posting to account-based CO-PA. These postings are made under a cost element but are assigned to what is known as a *reconciliation object* (object type REO) rather than genuine CO-PA characteristics. As the name implies, they are used for reconciliation purposes rather than for genuine profitability analysis and simply ensure that when a cost center allocates its costs to multiple lines in costing-based CO-PA, the credits and debits balance in CO.

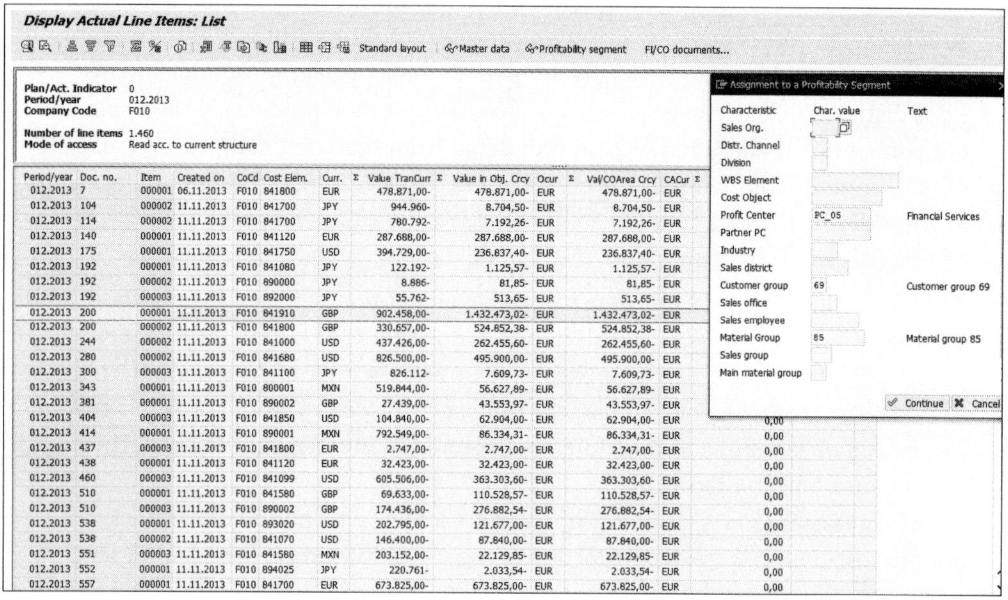

Figure 2.37 Line Item Report for Account-Based CO-PA

The only reports that are standard in CO-PA are the actual line items (Transaction KE24) and the plan line items (Transaction KE25). If the underlying tables are different at every site, so are the drill-down reports. Creating reports is part of the implementation effort for Profitability Analysis, because Transaction KE30 (Execute Report) only shows data if you've properly configured your operating concern and built the appropriate reports first. The drill-down potential of CO-PA is almost unlimited, with organizations slicing and dicing their data by customer, by product, by distribution channel, and so on to try to understand where and with whom they are making or losing money. Many also move the entire operating concern to SAP BW for analysis. We'll return to this in Chapter 8. Others are starting to use SAP HANA (see Chapter 13) to explore their CO-PA data. If your organization is making a move to SAP S/4HANA (see Chapter 14), you'll need to understand what it means to move to account-based CO-PA even as costing-based CO-PA continues to run.

2.8 Summary

In this chapter, you learned about the line item reports for Cost Center Accounting, Internal Orders, Cost Object Controlling, and Profitability Analysis and looked at how to compare the actual costs captured in these line items with planned costs, budgets, and target costs as appropriate. We also looked at some tree reports for Product Cost Planning and Material Ledger/Actual Costing and saw how an operating concern is defined for Profitability Analysis.

As we work through the chapters that follow, we'll refer to any reports that support the process, so you'll find the master data reports in Chapter 3 and the line items for planning in Chapter 5. All reports shown in Chapter 1 through Chapter 7 are based on reporting capabilities inherent in the SAP ERP system and don't require an additional data warehouse.

We'll return to the subject of reporting in Chapter 8 to look at SAP BW and the case for moving data to a dedicated data warehouse. There, we'll also discuss some of the newer options made possible using the SAP BusinessObjects tools and specifically how to use a generic function in SAP List Viewer to call SAP Crystal Reports. We'll make another visit in Chapter 13 when we look at how to work with reports in SAP HANA. But first, we'll look at the master data that needs to be in place before you can run any of these reports.

Chapter 3
Master Data Owned by Controlling

The master data defines the resources in your organization, the output measures for these resources, and other measures needed for allocations. In this chapter, we'll look at how to group your master data to ease selection and discover some new account assignments.

In Chapter 1, you learned about the process controls needed for master data management following the passage of the Sarbanes-Oxley Act (SOX). In this context, it makes sense to distinguish between master data for which the controlling department is the main stakeholder (such as cost centers and activity types) and master data for which the controlling department is one of several stakeholders, as is the case for the material master record or a customer master record.

In this chapter, we'll discuss the master data for which the controlling department is in the lead—namely, cost centers, cost center hierarchies (standard and alternative), internal orders, order groups, statistical key figures, activity types, secondary cost elements, product cost collectors, and cost object hierarchies. We'll look not only at the master data but also at the issues you need to consider during maintenance (i.e., time-dependent fields and status management). We'll also review the concept of change requests for providing a SOX-compliant master data process.

After reviewing the principles in Chapter 1, we need to set up proper master data in the form of a cost center structure that represents the resources in the organization, such as a department, group of people, machine, or building. Wherever possible, we'll define output measures for these cost centers in the form of *activity types* that represent work time, machine time, and so on. In some cases, this will not be practical. There can also be cost centers that are simply used for general cost collection, such as paying the bills for rent or power, and for which costs are then charged to the operational cost centers via a simple resource driver, such as square footage of floor space or number of employees at each operational cost center. Such resource drivers are defined as *statistical key figures*.

For reporting, the cost centers are grouped into hierarchies, which enables you to select a whole hierarchy or simply a group of related cost centers. This can aid selection, allowing you to report on the costs for all production cost centers or all sales cost centers or plan on these cost centers. The groups are also the basis for setting up allocation structures, in which a cost center may charge its costs to all production cost centers or all sales cost centers, or you may choose the cost groups that will take part in such an allocation.

We'll also look at some of the other *account assignments* that we covered briefly in Chapter 2—namely, the internal order, the product cost collector, and the cost object hierarchy—and we'll learn how to create cost elements in the Controlling component of SAP ERP Financials (which we'll refer to as CO throughout the rest of this chapter) to document the different sorts of allocation being performed.

Note

In this chapter, we'll also introduce the new-look user interfaces for the master data that are available from EHP 6 for SAP ERP 6.0. Again, we'll show the menu paths and transaction codes for the original transactions so that you can follow the instructions, whichever version of SAP ERP you're running. You'll find information about how to activate the new user interfaces in SAP Note 1836149.

3.1 How to Set Up Cost Centers

For most organizations, Cost Center Accounting is the first phase of an SAP ERP implementation, along with setting up the General Ledger. If establishing the chart of accounts is the first challenge of Financial Accounting, then establishing the proper cost center structure is the first challenge of CO, because the cost center represents the first contact between operational processes such as purchasing and reporting on such processes in finance. If you're unsure what constitutes a cost center, then you need to understand that in SAP ERP a cost center represents a stable, manageable unit, such as a department or business unit, whereas orders and projects exist only for the duration of their execution.

Master Data and Customizing

Setting up master data and reporting structures can either be considered part of the initial implementation effort or an ongoing task. To ensure consistency, some organizations maintain their master data in the same client as their configuration settings and then transfer them to their productive systems. Others see maintenance of such master data as an ongoing part of running their business and make changes directly in the productive system. Make sure you know which approach your organization has chosen before making critical master data changes.

To set up your cost centers, use the Cost Center Accounting role and select the **Cost Center** folder, as shown in Figure 3.1. Alternatively, you can go to **Accounting • Controlling • Cost Center Accounting • Master Data • Cost Center • Create** or use Transaction KS01.

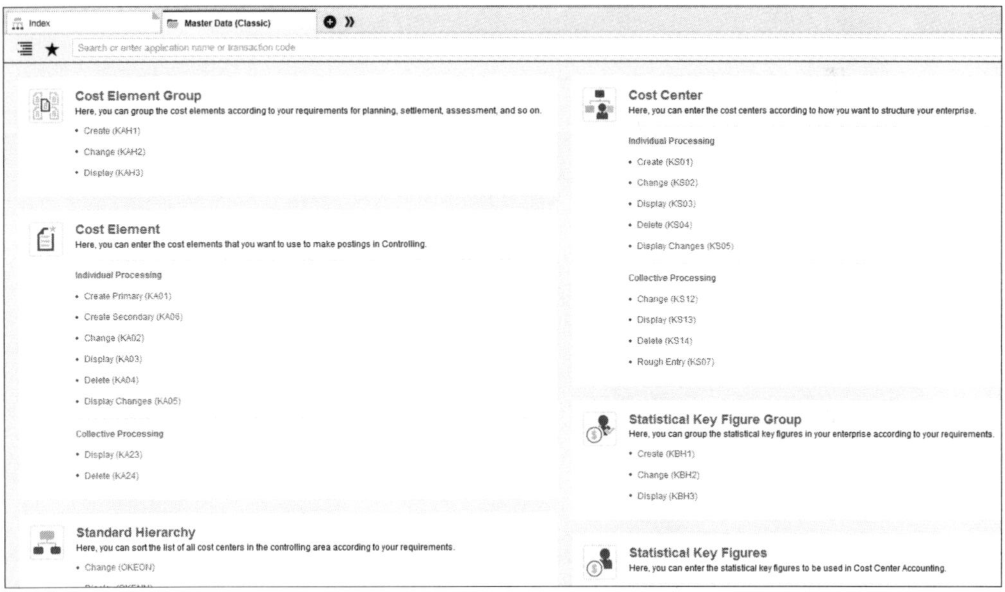

Figure 3.1 Master Data for Cost Center Accounting

The cost center represents the resources employed by the organization. A resource could be a machine, a building, or people working in a department. Sometimes it's easier just to look at the departments you have (i.e., research, sales, or corporate services). At other times, it may be better to represent the production department as a whole production line or split it to cover each of a group of machines on a factory floor. When establishing your cost center design, it also can be helpful to distinguish between operational cost centers and supporting cost centers:

- *Operational cost centers* are those that provide work to production, maintenance, and so on. We'll link these cost centers with work centers in Chapter 4 and use them to charge work to a production order, to a project, or to a maintenance order in Chapter 6.
- *Supporting cost centers* provide general services, such as energy or telecommunications. We'll explore the various ways of allocating costs from the supporting cost centers to the operational cost centers in Chapter 7. At this stage, it's important to decide whether the cost center will be used to capture *expenses* (such as rent or telephone costs) that will later be split to the operational cost centers using an *assessment cycle* or whether there is a *quantity* in play, such as the kilowatt hours supplied by an energy cost center. In the latter case, you'll be able to use an *indirect activity allocation cycle* to assign the kilowatt hours to your operational cost centers.

Cost Center Design

When drawing up the design, it's important to ensure that the cost centers are homogenous in purpose. It's not a good idea to lump teams performing different types of work or machines of hugely different efficiencies into one cost center. The first test of your cost center design will be whether you can easily select a cost center category, such as administration or production, for each cost center (see Figure 3.2). If the category is unclear, then the purpose of the cost center is potentially unclear, and you'll struggle to define outputs for such a cost center.

3.1.1 Responsibility for a Cost Center

Another guiding principle of good cost center design is that a single cost center should be the responsibility of one manager. If the number of cost centers starts to approach the number of employees in the organization, the question of who "owns" each cost center can be a good way of pruning the list of potential cost centers and ensuring that each cost center has an owner. Figure 3.2 shows the master data for a corporate services cost center. As you can see, there are two fields to hold the name of the manager:

- The **Person Responsible** field has been in the cost center master from the very beginning and allowed organizations to document the name of the cost center manager at a time when the manager was likely to receive paper reports on the performance of his cost center prepared by the controlling department. The **Address** and **Communication** tabs date from the same era and are rapidly becoming redundant, because organizations employ new mechanisms to notify their managers about the spending on their cost centers online.

- The **User Responsible** field was added in SAP ERP 6.0 and illustrates how cost center management has evolved. With more recent developments, such as Manager Self-Service (a web application for managers, available with SAP ERP 6.0) and My Spend (an application for desktop, mobile, and tablet devices), it's now commonly assumed that the cost center manager is an SAP user, accessing his reports and entering his own planning data online. The **User Responsible** field is used in Manager Self-Service and My Spend to prefill the selection screens in various reports and to ensure that managers see data for only their cost centers (a process known as *personalization*).

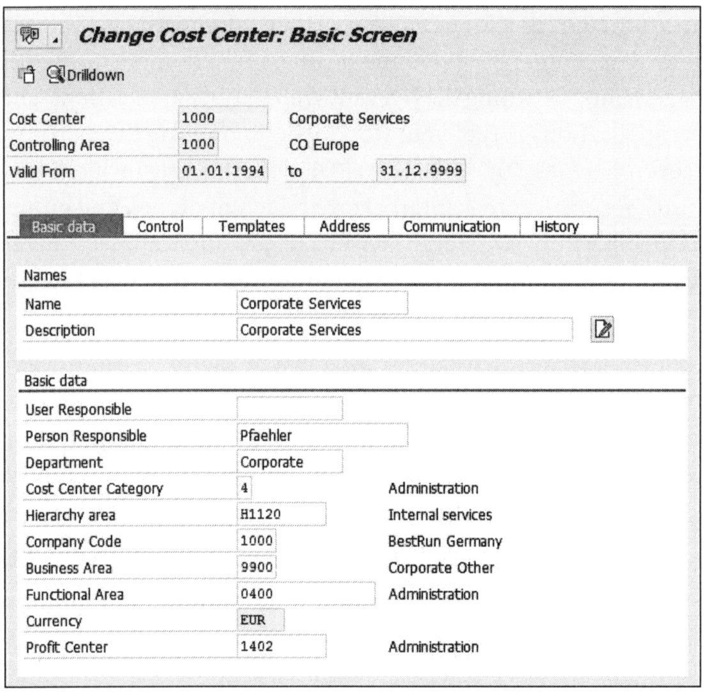

Figure 3.2 Cost Center Master Record (SAP GUI)

Extending the Cost Center Master Data

One of the most commonly asked questions about the cost center master data is whether it's possible to add extra fields, usually to make additional attributes available for reporting. If you find yourself involved in this kind of discussion, talk with your IT department about the possibility of activating user exit COOMKS01 (Cost Center: Customer-Specific Additional Fields in the Master Record). This allows you to extend the structure of the cost center master record and include whatever attributes you feel would help with your reporting. Most organizations will use exit COOMKS02 (Cost Center: Checks during Saving) to ensure that these fields are filled appropriately. You'll find further details about recent enhancements in this area in SAP Note 2420186 (Customer Connect CO: Customer-Defined Additional Fields in Cost Center Master Data).

If your organization is running EHP 6 for SAP ERP 6.0, then you might also want to update the look of your cost centers by activating business function FIN_CO_CCMGMT (CO, Cost Center Management), activating the relevant Web Dynpro applications, and either making the new applications part of your working roles or using the delivered role for the internal controller (SAP_CO_INTERNAL_CONTROLLER). This role includes new Web Dynpro applications for cost centers, internal orders, activity types, and groupings of these objects. One tip before you start: the Web Dynpro applications read the controlling area from your user parameters, so be sure to select **System • User Profile • Own Data** and enter the parameter CAC and your controlling area.

The new applications begin with a search screen, as shown in Figure 3.3. Here, we've searched for all cost centers named Corporate Services. To select a cost center, click the line and choose the **Edit** or **Copy** button above the result list, or double-click on the line to display the cost center. Alternatively, you can use the list to do the following:

- To select multiple cost centers, select the plus button (+) to create a new line in the search screen and enter a second cost center.
- To select according to different criteria, select the plus button to create a new line in the search screen, right-click on **Person Responsible**, and choose one of the other options.
- If this is a selection that you will be using regularly, consider saving the search by entering a name in **Save Search As**.

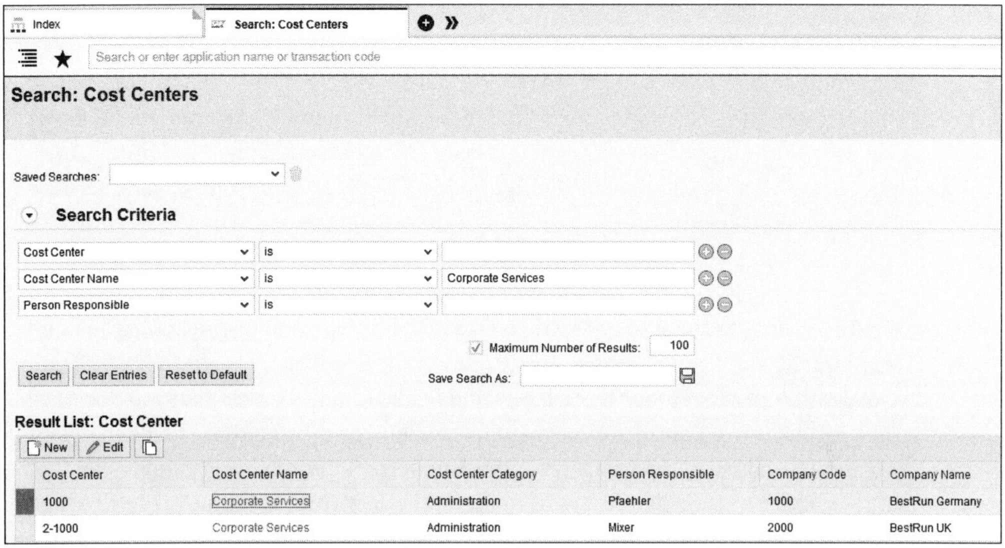

Figure 3.3 Cost Center Search (Web Dynpro)

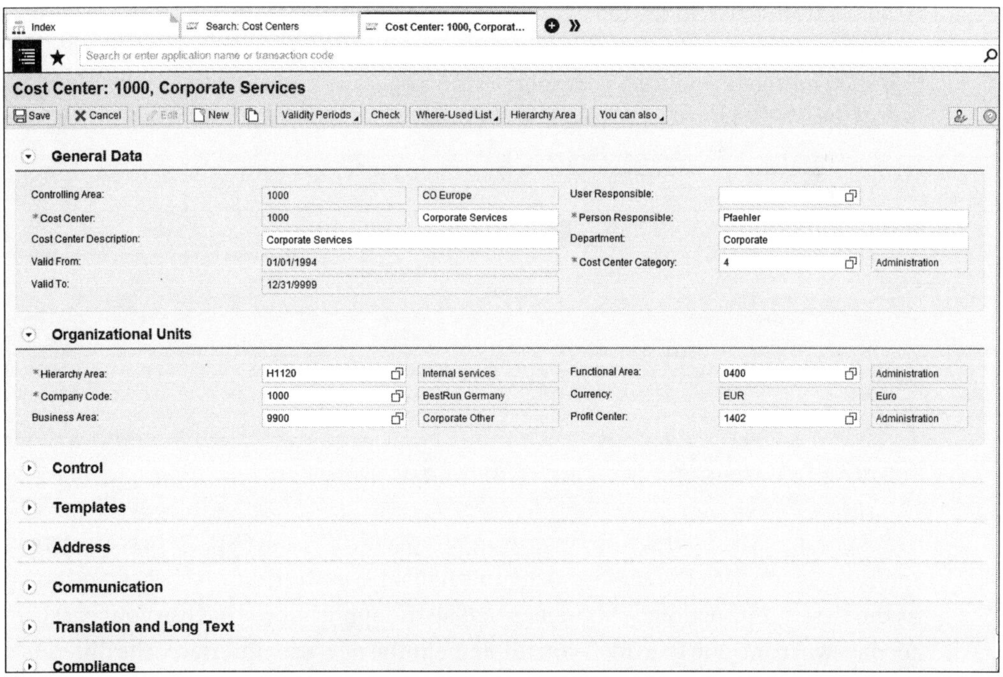

Figure 3.4 Cost Center Master Record (Web Dynpro)

New User Interfaces

One thing to be aware of here is that if you have been given the appropriate role you will also see this search list as a Web Dynpro application in your user menu. Resist the temptation to access it from here, because the buttons shown in Figure 3.3 will not work. You need to access it through the SAP NetWeaver Business Client because the parameters needed to navigate to the detail applications are only read when the application is called from SAP NetWeaver Business Client. Figure 3.4 shows the new cost center master record. This might not look like a huge step forward compared to Figure 3.2, but the thing to understand is that this application is simply a default and your organization can configure this screen to include exactly those fields that you work with. You can remove those boxes and fields from the screen that you don't use on a regular basis. Consider removing unused fields or moving those fields that your organization uses as reporting attributes into a more prominent position. Plenty of organizations use fields like **Telex** to store key reporting attributes, even though telex machines haven't been used since the 1980s. Figure 3.5 shows an example of a much-reduced UI for the cost center. We've right-clicked on unused fields and removed them from the UI, and we've removed whole blocks using the **Personalization** button shown in the top right of Figure 3.4 to create a leaner application. These blocks are merely hidden; if you need to display the relevant fields, use the **Personalization** button to make the relevant tab visible again.

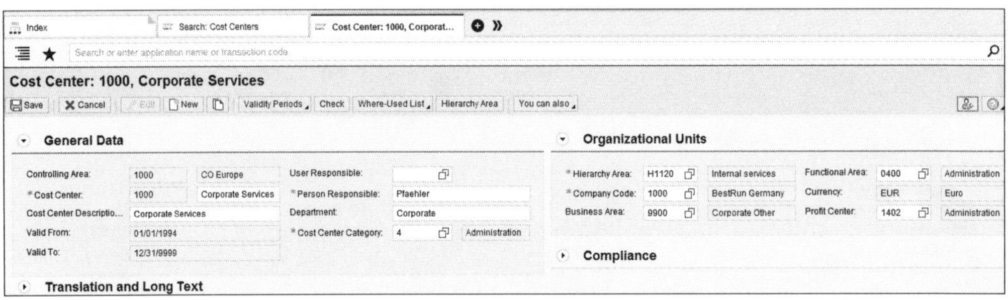

Figure 3.5 Cost Center Master Data Following Personalization

Transaction KS01 and the Web Dynpro application FCOM_COSTCENTER access the data in table CSKS and share the same locking mechanisms, authorization checks, and so on as the classic transactions. This means that all the applications that use your cost center data will continue to work if you implement the new user interface. The difference is that changing the screens in Transaction KS01 counts as a modification, whereas your organization can easily change the fields shown in `FCOM_COSTCENTER` and create a cost center master record that meets your organization's needs.

3.1.2 Embedding the Cost Center Design in SAP ERP

The cost center design can't be undertaken in isolation. Because all employees who perform the work of the cost center are also assigned to an organizational unit in human resources, you'll need to ensure that your cost center design harmonizes with your organizational structure. Entering the name of the relevant cost center in the master data of the relevant organizational unit ensures that the costs for payroll, benefits, travel, and so on can be successfully transferred to the cost center. This cost center is also credited when the employee posts work time to an order or project using a time sheet. In Chapter 6, we'll show how an employee posts his work time to a project and how this credits the cost center and debits the WBS element.

Lean Accounting

If you're considering lean accounting, it's a good idea to make sure that your cost center design meshes with your value stream design and that all employee-related costs are being assigned to the correct value stream. This is usually easy for shop floor employees who operate or maintain one or more machines but can be tricky for employees on supporting cost centers. If you can't assign such employees to one value stream, then use an allocation to split the costs between the production cost centers supported by these employees. Sometimes it's the nature of the business to have such cost centers. IT departments and shared service centers that serve many parts of the business are examples of cost centers that will never assign neatly to value streams.

Likewise, the machines on the production line are likely to be managed as *fixed assets* in Asset Accounting. Linking the cost centers with the assets ensures that the depreciation expenses can be successfully transferred to the cost center at period close. This cost center assignment also determines the profit center and the segment to which the asset is assigned. From EHP 5 for SAP ERP 6.0, the link between fixed assets and the cost center has been extended to include the profit center and the segment in the asset master record. This is done to ensure that the profit center for the asset is not derived on the fly during the relevant cost center-related postings but is permanently available in the asset master record, allowing asset reporting by segment and profit center. To see the new fields in the asset master record, check whether your organization has activated business function FIN_GL_REORG_1. Note also that the link between the cost center and the fixed asset is *time-dependent* because the assignments can change over time and a new data slice will be created for each assignment. Refer to Section 3.8 for more information on this concept.

The same linkage to the cost center is made for equipment in Plant Maintenance in SAP ERP. This ensures that the costs of equipment are correctly captured on the cost center. This assignment is used to display the assigned assets and equipment in Manager Self-Service.

If the machines perform work during production, they'll normally be defined as *work centers* in production or *resources* in the process industries. Linking the cost centers with the work centers ensures that the costs performed at the work center can be charged to the production orders correctly during order confirmation. We'll return to this assignment in Chapter 4.

3.1.3 Ensuring that Cost Center Expenses Are Handled Correctly

Figure 3.2 and Figure 3.4 show the assignment of the cost center to organizational entities, such as the company code, business area, functional area, and profit center. These are important, because they determine how expenses assigned to this cost center are treated in the General Ledger and related ledgers. By making these assignments, you ensure that your cost centers are assigned to the proper legal and management reporting entities.

Company Code

If the controlling area (the main organizational unit for CO) contains multiple company codes (which is usually the case), then you need to assign each cost center to a company code. This determines the object currency of the cost center (Euros in our example). The object currency is usually the local currency for the company code and may be different from the controlling area currency, which is usually the group currency.

The company code assignment is important not only for capturing expenses but also for allocations. If a cost center allocates costs to another cost center and the partner cost center is in a different company code, then two things may happen:

1. If you use the classic General Ledger (available in all releases prior to SAP ERP 5.0), this cross-company allocation is stored in a reconciliation ledger. At period close, these values are moved to the other company code, via Transaction KALC or the

menu path **Accounting • Controlling • Cost Element Accounting • Actual Postings • Reconciliation with FI.**

2. If you use the SAP ERP General Ledger (also known as the new General Ledger), this cross-company allocation results in a transfer to the cost center in the other company code being made immediately. The configuration settings are described in the implementation guide under scenario FIN_CCA (Cost Center Update) and the Real-Time Integration of Controlling with Financial Accounting entry.

Business Area

The *business area* represents one way of segmenting your business within the General Ledger. Any posting to the Corporate Services cost center, for example, is automatically assigned to business area 9900 (see Figure 3.2) in the General Ledger, and any allocation also updates the business area.

If you use the SAP ERP General Ledger, it's worth checking whether scenario FIN_GSBER (business area) is active, because this determines whether the business area and the partner business area are updated in the General Ledger during an allocation. If you've activated Real-Time Integration of Controlling with Financial Accounting, then allocations between different business areas will also be updated in real-time.

Functional Area

The most common use of the functional area is in the context of cost of sales accounting, which is a legal requirement in many countries. This ensures that the costs of sales are broken down by function (administration, research and development, sales, etc.) in the income statement. The field is used differently in Public Sector Accounting. The functional area is then used to classify expenses by economic purpose, so any posting to the Corporate Services cost center is automatically assigned to functional area 0400 (Administration). Depending on the age of your system, there are two options:

1. If you use the classic General Ledger, cost of sales accounting is handled in the Special Ledger, and a substitution rule is used to derive the correct functional area from the CO postings and update it to the Special Ledger (sometimes called the cost of sales [COS] ledger).
2. If you use the SAP ERP General Ledger, you can capture this assignment immediately, provided that scenario FIN_UKV (Cost of Sales Accounting) is active. This means you can obtain financial statements according to cost of sales accounting by using the standard balance sheet report and drilling down by functional area.

Profit Center

The *profit center* represents another way of segmenting your business. In principle, it supersedes the business area, but in many organizations the two continue to be used in parallel. SAP Note 321190 explains SAP's strategy about how the two approaches will be supported going forward. The profit center began as a management way of viewing revenue and costs but was subsequently extended to include payables and liabilities. From SAP ERP 5.0 on, the profit center was linked with the *segment* to support the legal requirements for segment reporting according to International Financial Reporting Standards (IFRS) 8 or International Accounting Standards (IAS) 14. Depending on the age of your system, there are two options:

1. If you use the classic General Ledger, the assignment to the profit center results in expense postings to the cost center being assigned to the Profit Center Ledger (technically, this is ledger 8A).
2. If you use the SAP ERP General Ledger, the assignment to the profit center results in expense postings to the cost center updating both the profit center and the segment, provided you have activated scenarios FIN_PCA (Profit Center Accounting) and FIN_SEGM (Segmentation).

Document Splitting for Profit Centers

When assigning profit centers to your cost centers, you should also consider the use of splitting in the SAP ERP General Ledger. When goods are purchased for the cost center, the expense items are automatically posted to cost center 1000 and profit center 1402. However, the vendor payable item and the tax item are normally stored at the company code level. Document splitting allows the system to use rules to automatically assign the vendor item and the tax item to the correct profit center (usually the profit center assigned to the cost center).

Cost Centers and the Universal Journal in SAP S/4HANA

With the introduction of SAP S/4HANA, all financial transactions are stored in the *Universal Journal*. Journal entries for cost accounting assign costs to a cost center and to all the reporting dimensions we saw under the **Basic Data** tab in Figure 3.2 and Figure 3.4. There is no longer any need to choose scenarios because these reporting dimensions always will be filled automatically if the master data is maintained correctly.

3.1.4 Cost Center Hierarchies

All cost centers are assigned to a hierarchy area, as shown in Figure 3.2 and Figure 3.4. The hierarchy area is a node in the *standard cost center hierarchy*. This assignment ensures that it's possible to report across all cost centers in a single controlling area because the top node of the standard cost center hierarchy is linked to the controlling area and all cost centers are assigned to one of the nodes in this hierarchy. In general, organizations use both the standard cost center hierarchy and alternative cost center hierarchies to aggregate their cost centers for reporting.

Standard Cost Center Hierarchies

All cost centers have to be assigned to a node of the standard cost center hierarchy (the **Hierarchy Area** field in the cost center master). To check the structure of your cost center hierarchy, you can take the following steps:

1. Use the Cost Center Accounting role (see Figure 3.1).
2. Select **Standard Hierarchy** or go to **Accounting • Controlling • Cost Center Accounting • Master Data • Standard Hierarchy • Change** (or Transaction OKEON). You cannot create a new hierarchy; you can only change the existing one. This is because the root node of the cost center hierarchy is already assigned to the controlling area in Customizing.

What makes the standard cost center hierarchy special is that it's *complete*: it shows every cost center in a given controlling area. Just to make sure you haven't created cyclical relationships when defining your hierarchy nodes, select **Extras • Ambiguity Check** and check that your tree is correctly defined.

Some organizations use the standard cost center hierarchy as their only reporting structure and ensure that the nodes are detailed to the extent required for corporate reporting. Other organizations treat the standard cost center hierarchy as something of a formality, with only a few nodes, and then create alternative cost center hierarchies for different reporting purposes. The assignment to the alternative cost center hierarchy is made not in the cost center master but in a separate transaction.

Figure 3.6 shows a sample cost center hierarchy from the IDES demo system.

> **Note**
>
> Since Release 4.6C, you can maintain the nodes that make up the tree structure and the cost centers in a single transaction. In earlier releases, the maintenance transaction is identical to the user interface for the alternative cost center hierarchy we'll

show next. If you have an extremely large standard cost center hierarchy, SAP recommends that you continue to use the old transaction (Transaction OKEO) for hierarchy maintenance. You'll find more information and links to other SAP Notes associated with system performance for the hierarchies in SAP Note 402088.

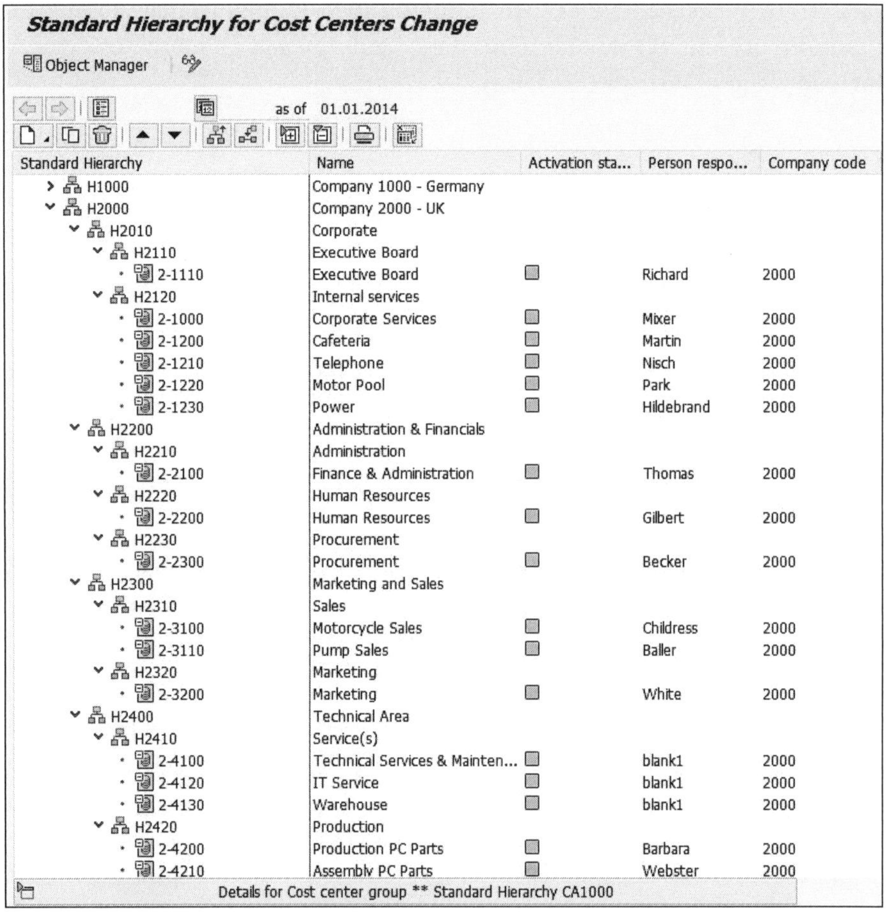

Figure 3.6 Standard Cost Center Hierarchy in IDES Demo System

Alongside reporting, the other use of the cost center hierarchy is as a basis for allocations. The nodes of the hierarchy can be the senders or, more commonly, the receivers of an allocation. Figure 3.7 shows an assessment cycle in which the costs for cost center MFC_1040 are to be allocated to all cost centers in group MFC_A_4000. You can view assessment cycles like this one by following the menu path **Accounting • Controlling • Cost Center Accounting • Period-End Closing • Single Functions • Allocations • Assessment** and then **Extras • Cycle • Change** or by using Transaction KSU2. We'll return to allocation cycles in Chapter 7. For now, it's sufficient to know that cost center groups can be both the senders and the receivers of an allocation. In the real world, the receivers of an allocation are almost always cost center groups—all production cost centers, all maintenance cost centers, all sales cost centers, and so on. With the senders, it depends on how different the cost centers themselves are. Sometimes you'll want to handle each sender cost center in a separate segment of an assessment cycle (as we'll see in the examples in Chapter 7), but if the cost centers are very similar you can put them into a group and handle them in a single segment.

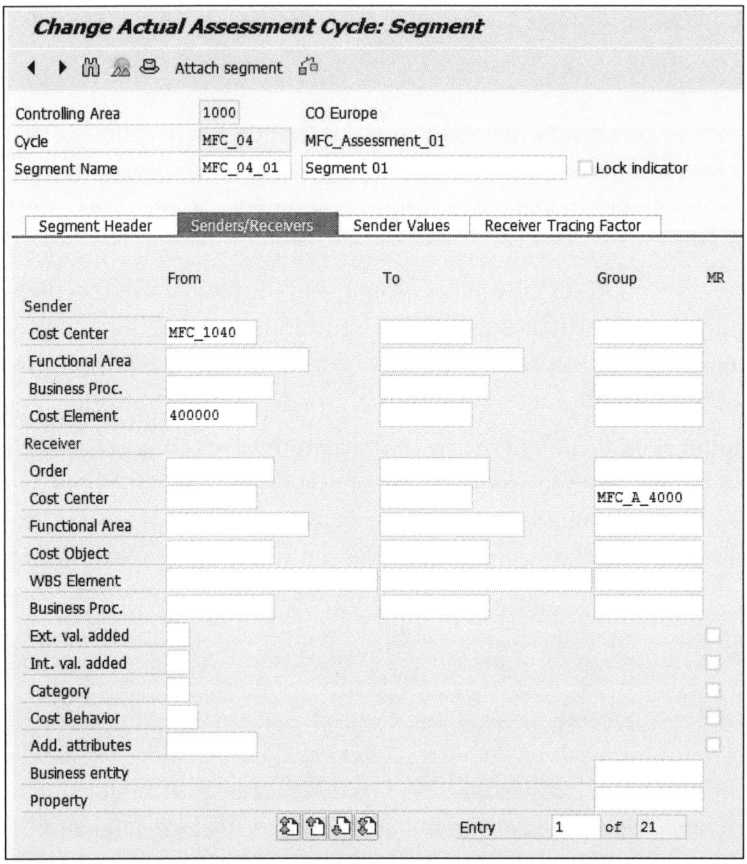

Figure 3.7 Sample Assessment Cycle

Alternative Cost Center Hierarchies

Many organizations find that a single cost center hierarchy cannot meet all the requirements placed upon such a structure. Some define cost center groups for use in allocation cycles that differ radically from those in the standard hierarchy. Others use the alternative hierarchies to establish multiple ways of rolling expenses up through the organization for reporting. There's no limit to the number of alternative cost center hierarchies you can create.

Lean Accounting

One obvious use for an alternative cost center hierarchy is to construct nodes that represent the main value streams in your organization. This allows you to report along these lines and along the more traditional reporting lines of your departmental structure.

To create an alternative cost center hierarchy, use the Cost Center Accounting role and select **Cost Center Groups** as shown in Figure 3.1. You can also use Transaction KSH1 or go to **Accounting • Controlling • Cost Center Accounting • Master Data • Cost Center Group • Create**.

Alternative cost center hierarchies are built as *groups*, and the toolbar used to maintain cost center groups within an alternative cost center hierarchy is the same for order groups, cost element groups, activity type groups, statistical key figure groups, and so on.

During group maintenance, you build up the tree structure by entering nodes with texts either on the same level as the root node or on the lower level until you have built up a tree structure that meets your requirements. You can use nodes in an alternative hierarchy as receivers of an allocation in the same way as we illustrated in Figure 3.8.

Tip

You then assign the cost centers to these nodes. If you have labeled your cost centers with meaningful codes (such as 1XXX for internal services, 2XXX for administration, 3XXX for production, and so on), it will save time if you enter intervals or ranges, such as 3000–3999. Assuming you follow the naming convention that any cost center beginning with a 3 is assigned to production, then all new cost centers will automatically be assigned to the production node.

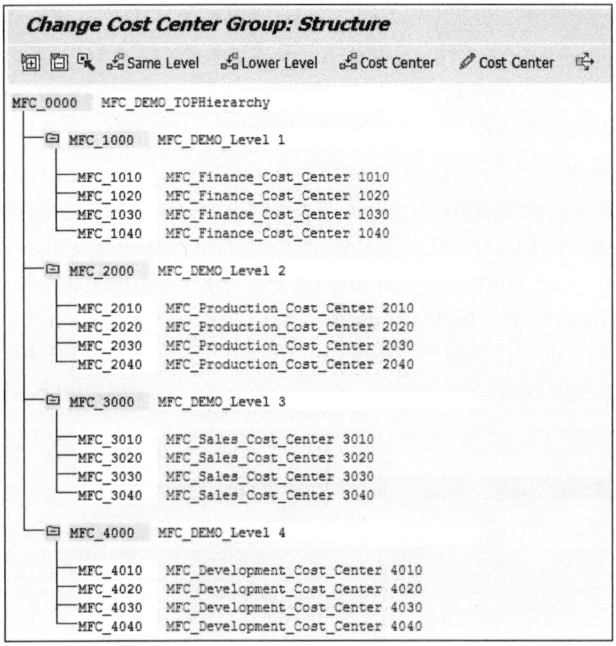

Figure 3.8 Alternative Cost Center Hierarchy

If your organization works with a single controlling area, it can be difficult to tell at a glance which cost centers belong to which company code, especially when you are creating allocation cycles. If this is the case, consider including the company code key in the codes for your cost centers.

You can also include a suffix in the cost center hierarchy to represent the year in which it's valid or the purpose of the reorganization. Some organizations create copies of their hierarchies each year and then adjust them to take account of changing operational requirements. To copy a cost center hierarchy with a suffix, use Transaction KSH1, go to **Group • Copy**, and enter a four-digit suffix.

Once you have copied your hierarchy and started to change it, it makes sense to run the ambiguity check we showed in the standard cost center hierarchy. If you're building an alternative cost center hierarchy that aims to provide a complete view of all the cost centers in a controlling area, you should make sure you have included every cost center in the controlling area by selecting **Extras • Check and Help Functions • Check Completeness**. Once you've pruned your structure, you can also remove groups that are now empty by selecting **Extras • Check and Help Functions • Delete Unused Groups**.

While you're building your hierarchies, it also makes sense to consider how you'll use the groups within your hierarchies for reporting. With this in mind, refer to Chapter 8, Section 8.1 for information on how to create extracts for each cost center group to speed up the response time of reports that use large cost center groups.

As we noted for the cost centers, EHP 6 for SAP ERP 6.0 also includes new applications to maintain both the standard cost center hierarchy and alternative cost center hierarchies. Figure 3.9 shows the same hierarchy you saw in Figure 3.6, but we've used Web Dynpro application FCOM_GROUP_COSTCENTER to display it in the new look. Again, to see this screen you'll need to activate the business function FIN_CO_CCMGMT and be assigned to the role SAP_CO_INTERNAL_CONTROLLER. Build up the nodes of the hierarchy using the **New, Add**, and **Edit** buttons. As your hierarchy gets larger, use the **Find** box to find cost centers that are offscreen.

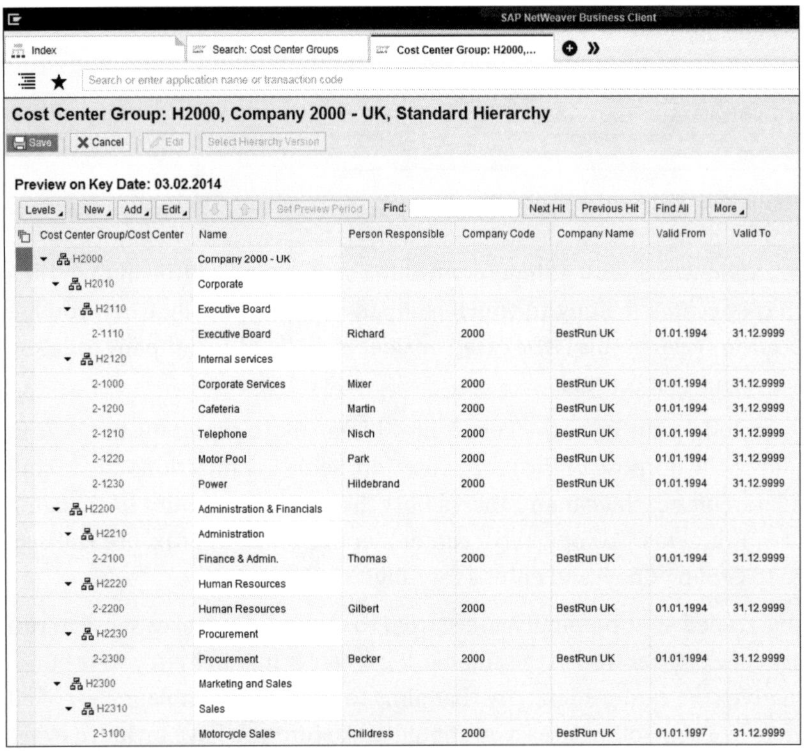

Figure 3.9 Cost Center Hierarchy (Web Dynpro)

In addition to finding your cost center groups, you can also use the new search screen to copy an existing group to create a new group with a suffix, as shown in Figure 3.10.

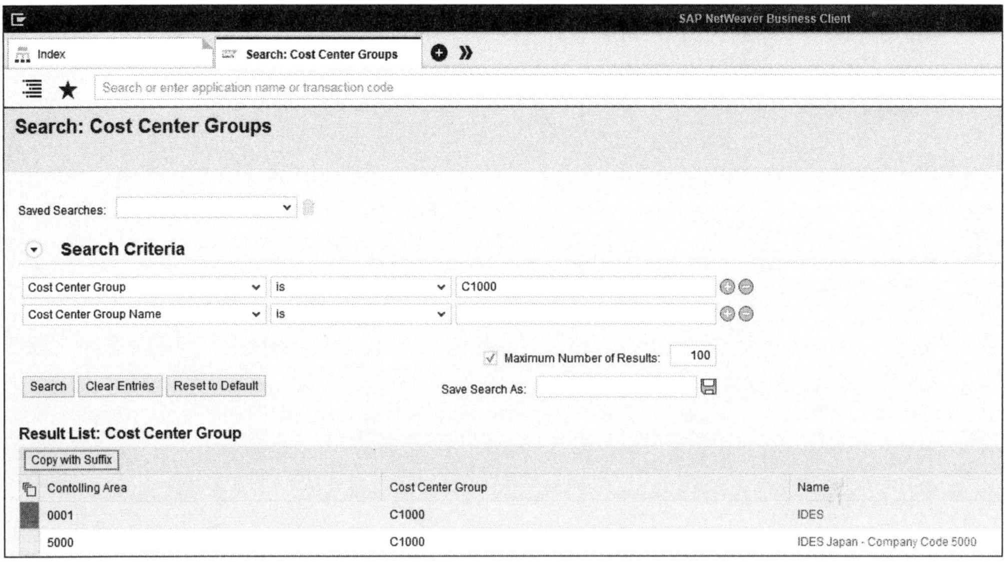

Figure 3.10 Search and Copy Cost Center Group

> **Enterprise Organization**
>
> You'll also find an entry in the SAP Easy Access menu to link your cost center hierarchy with the organizational hierarchy in human resources. In general, this is not widely used and can be ignored.

3.1.5 Reporting of Cost Center Master Data

When the cost center structure is complete, you can check the consistency of your cost centers with the help of the cost center master data report. The traditional report is Transaction KS13. You'll find this in the **Master Data Indexes** folder shown in Chapter 2, Figure 2.1. You can also use the simplified report **Cost Centers: Master Data Report (List)**, shown in Figure 3.11.

If you need to create several new cost centers, consider using Transaction KS01N instead of creating lots of cost centers separately. If it's not available in your system, refer your administrator to the instructions in SAP Note 2350462 (Customer Connect CO: Transaction KS01N Mass Creation of Cost Center Masters). On a similar note, if you need to make mass changes to a group of cost centers, consider using Transaction KS12N. Refer your administrator to SAP Note 2068063 (Customer Connect CO: Transaction KS12N for Mass Maintenance of Cost Center Master Data).

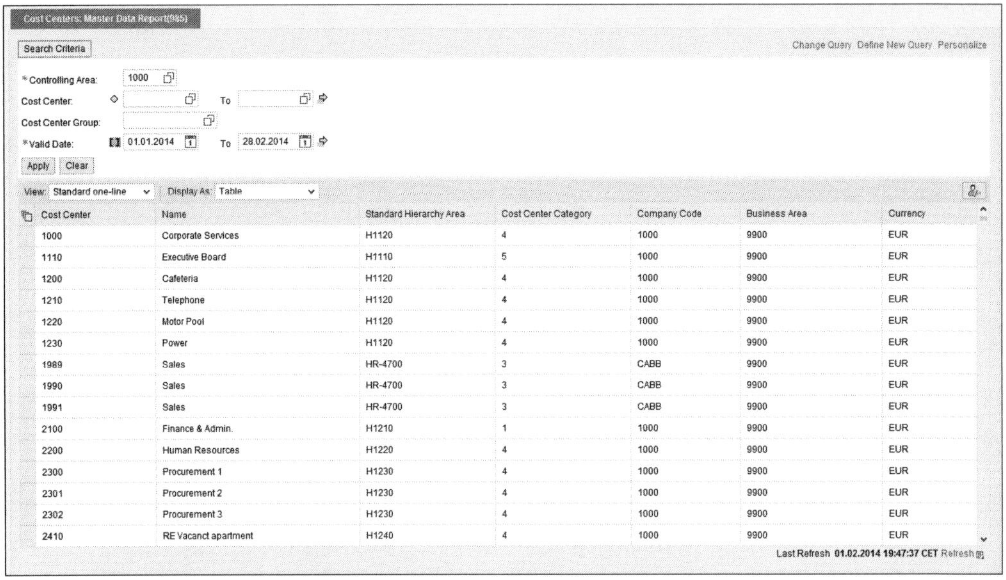

Cost Center	Name	Standard Hierarchy Area	Cost Center Category	Company Code	Business Area	Currency
1000	Corporate Services	H1120	4	1000	9900	EUR
1110	Executive Board	H1110	5	1000	9900	EUR
1200	Cafeteria	H1120	4	1000	9900	EUR
1210	Telephone	H1120	4	1000	9900	EUR
1220	Motor Pool	H1120	4	1000	9900	EUR
1230	Power	H1120	4	1000	9900	EUR
1989	Sales	HR-4700	3	CABB	9900	EUR
1990	Sales	HR-4700	3	CABB	9900	EUR
1991	Sales	HR-4700	3	CABB	9900	EUR
2100	Finance & Admin.	H1210	1	1000	9900	EUR
2200	Human Resources	H1220	4	1000	9900	EUR
2300	Procurement 1	H1230	4	1000	9900	EUR
2301	Procurement 2	H1230	4	1000	9900	EUR
2302	Procurement 3	H1230	4	1000	9900	EUR
2410	RE Vacanct apartment	H1240	4	1000	9900	EUR

Figure 3.11 Simplified Master Data Report for Cost Centers

We've discussed how intertwined the cost centers are with other master data in SAP ERP. This means that before executing any kind of change, it's worth looking at the *where-used lists*. You can find these in the cost center master record under **Extras • Where-Used Lists** (see Figure 3.2) or click the **Where-Used Lists** button shown in Figure 3.4. Figure 3.12 shows the fixed assets that are linked with cost center 1000, which is just one of the delivered where-used lists. We'll find the same links used in the fact sheets that we'll look at in Chapter 13.

Where-used lists are also available to display the following:

- Activity types assigned to the cost center (e.g., machine hours)
- Splitting structure to display how the costs from a single cost center are split to multiple activity types
- Activity types used in time recording in human resources (CATS)
- Assessment cycles, distribution cycles, and reposting cycles that include the cost center
- Assessment cycles to Profitability Analysis that include the cost center

- Settlement rules that include the cost center
- Internal orders for which the cost center is defined as the responsible cost center
- WBS elements for Project Management where the cost center is defined as the responsible cost center

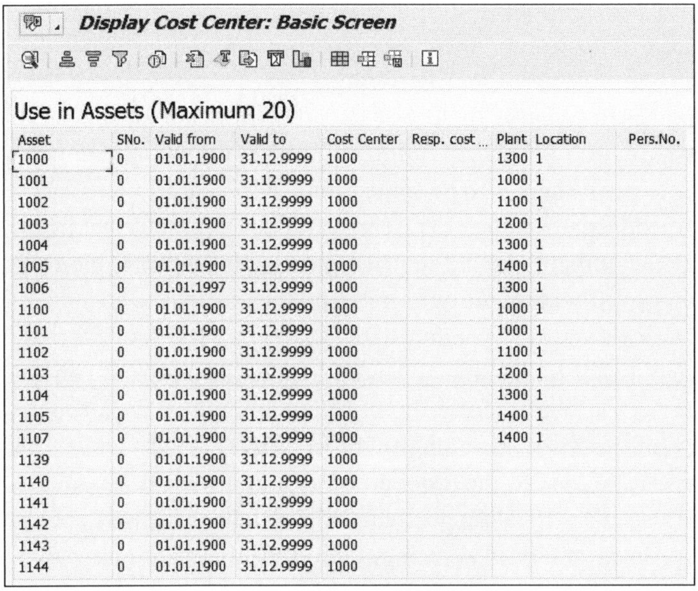

Asset	SNo.	Valid from	Valid to	Cost Center	Resp. cost...	Plant	Location	Pers.No.
1000	0	01.01.1900	31.12.9999	1000		1300	1	
1001	0	01.01.1900	31.12.9999	1000		1000	1	
1002	0	01.01.1900	31.12.9999	1000		1100	1	
1003	0	01.01.1900	31.12.9999	1000		1200	1	
1004	0	01.01.1900	31.12.9999	1000		1300	1	
1005	0	01.01.1900	31.12.9999	1000		1400	1	
1006	0	01.01.1997	31.12.9999	1000		1300	1	
1100	0	01.01.1900	31.12.9999	1000		1000	1	
1101	0	01.01.1900	31.12.9999	1000		1000	1	
1102	0	01.01.1900	31.12.9999	1000		1100	1	
1103	0	01.01.1900	31.12.9999	1000		1200	1	
1104	0	01.01.1900	31.12.9999	1000		1300	1	
1105	0	01.01.1900	31.12.9999	1000		1400	1	
1107	0	01.01.1900	31.12.9999	1000		1400	1	
1139	0	01.01.1900	31.12.9999	1000				
1140	0	01.01.1900	31.12.9999	1000				
1141	0	01.01.1900	31.12.9999	1000				
1142	0	01.01.1900	31.12.9999	1000				
1143	0	01.01.1900	31.12.9999	1000				
1144	0	01.01.1900	31.12.9999	1000				

Figure 3.12 Where-Used List for Cost Center 1000 Showing Assigned Assets

Using Where-Used Lists

Where-used lists are the controller's primary checklist for master data management. Before any change is made to the cost center master data, Controlling checks what other areas will be affected by the change. The most common use case is a reorganization in which two cost centers are merged or one is split. Before implementing any such change, Controlling checks which assets are currently assigned to the cost center and notifies the accountant that these assets need to be moved to another cost center before locking the cost center.

On a smaller scale, if an employee changes a cost center, they checks which assets and equipment (such as his mobile phone and laptop) they are taking with them and ensures that such equipment is transferred to the new cost center. In the run up to the period close, these lists are used to check that the allocation cycles relating to each cost center are up-to-date.

The cost center is the backbone of any CO implementation and meshes tightly with the organizational structure of the company in terms of the assigned employees and assets. Whenever you need to capture costs for items that exist for a shorter time frame, you should look at internal orders as a way to capture costs.

3.2 Internal Orders

Some organizations manage to assign all their costs to cost centers, but most need an alternative account assignment in the form of internal orders (or sometimes projects). This is typically the case if there is to be some capital expenditure to replace a production line or overhead expense, such as research and development that needs to be captured in more detail than simply the R&D cost center. Depending on the design, an internal order can either provide more detail on the postings to an individual cost center, such as a single vehicle belonging to the cost center Car Pool or a trade fair belonging to the cost center Marketing, or can be considered a separate entity, such as a research order or an investment order on which individual departments work. You can distinguish orders by assigning them to different *order types*. This determines how expenses assigned to the order are settled and what fields are displayed in the user interface. It's generally a good idea to distinguish capital expense orders from general overhead orders. Bear in mind also that there are many additional order types in Logistics that are used to capture production costs, maintenance costs, and so on. You'll see many examples in Chapter 6.

To create an internal order, use the Internal Orders role, select the **Master Data** folder, and then select **Order Manager**, as shown in Figure 3.13. You can also use Transaction KO04 or go to **Accounting • Controlling • Internal Orders • Master Data • Orders • Order Manager**.

The Order Manager is an early example of a work list that allows you to select and store a list of orders that you work on regularly. The work list appears on the left side of the screen; selecting an item in the list takes you to the master data for that object on the right side of the screen (see Figure 3.14). Note the **Reference Order** field in this list. If you have to create a lot of similar orders for which most of the master data will be similar and only a few fields change, then it's worth working with references or setting up a dedicated order type to serve as a reference or model order.

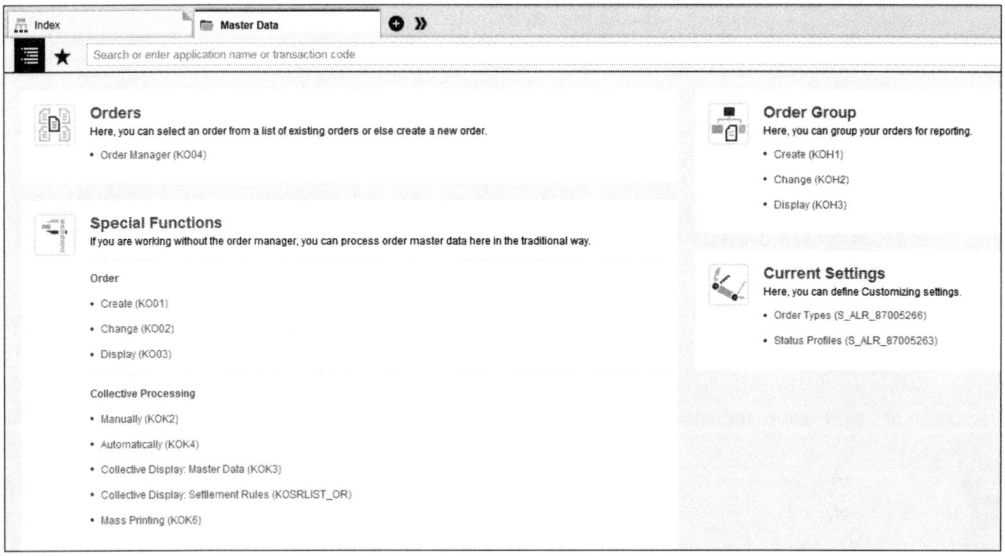

Figure 3.13 Internal Order Master Data

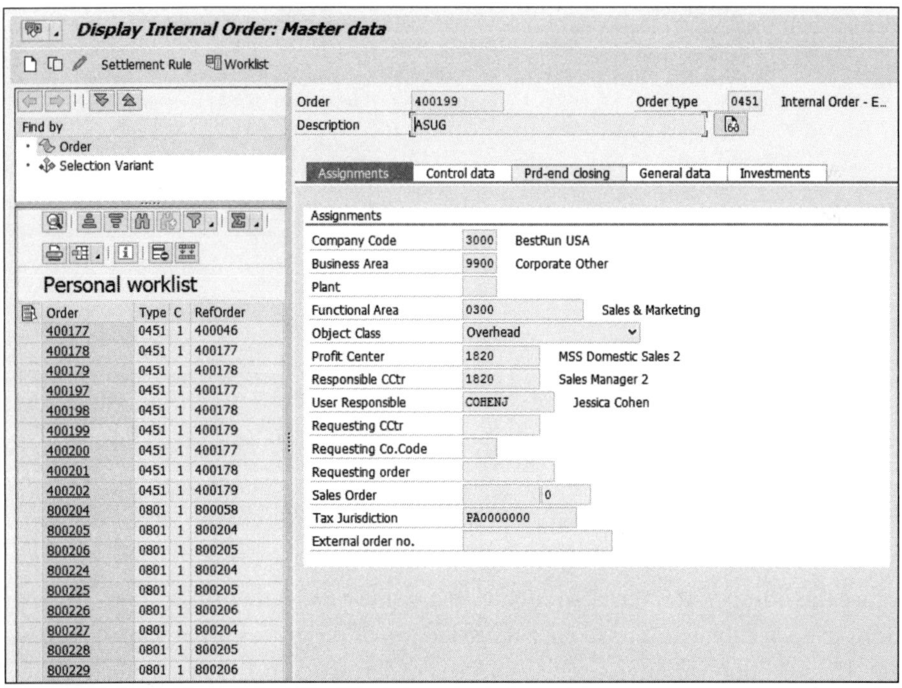

Figure 3.14 Internal Order with Work List (SAP GUI)

As we saw for the cost centers, EHP 6 for SAP ERP 6.0 also includes new applications to maintain internal orders. Figure 3.15 shows the same order as Figure 3.14, but we've used Web Dynpro application `FCOM_INTERNALORDER_ADAPTATION` to display it in the new look. The prerequisites are as before, but because internal orders are used for so many different purposes it's worth considering whether to create not one UI configuration, but several. There are around 200 fields in the internal order, but typically only around 20 are used in any one order, and the active fields will vary by order type. Use Floorplan Manager to create a different configuration for each order type (or whatever other criterion is useful to distinguish your orders) and enter the Web Dynpro application along with each configuration setting in your roles. We've removed some tabs in Figure 3.15, but we could be substantially more radical in removing those fields that are not commonly used for marketing orders of this kind.

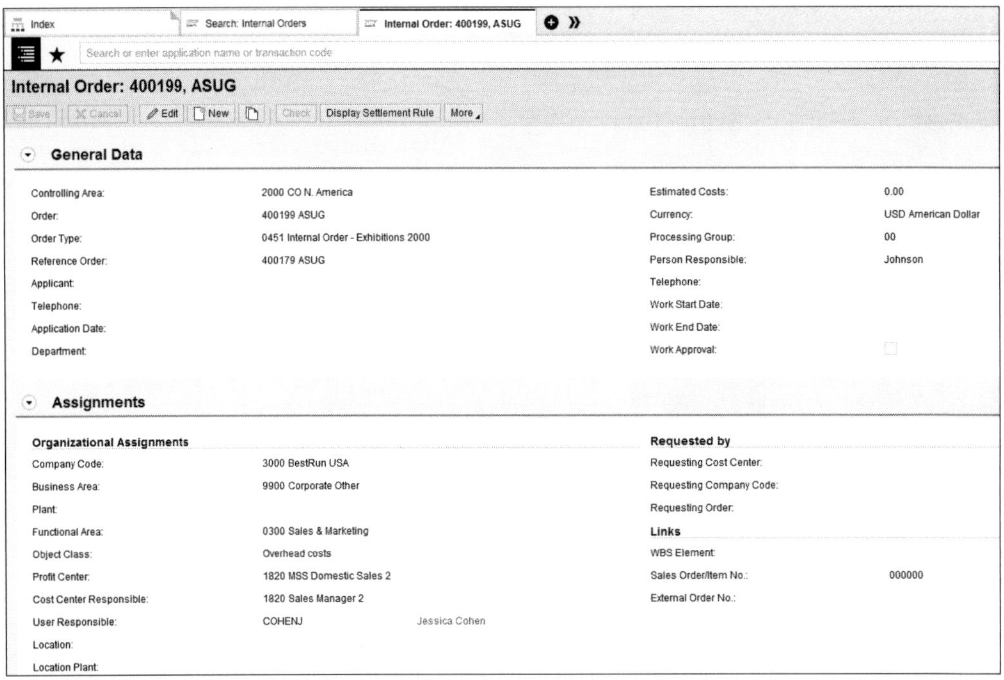

Figure 3.15 Internal Order Master Data (Web Dynpro)

Because the number of internal orders in an organization can be huge, many organizations use *selection variants* to ease the selection of orders for reporting and settlement. The selection variant is used to select all orders with entries in particular fields, such as all internal orders of order type 0100 that have the status **Created** and the status **Released**. Figure 3.16 shows the fields available to create a selection variant. We'll cover other options for selecting orders as work lists when we look at optimizing close activities in Chapter 12.

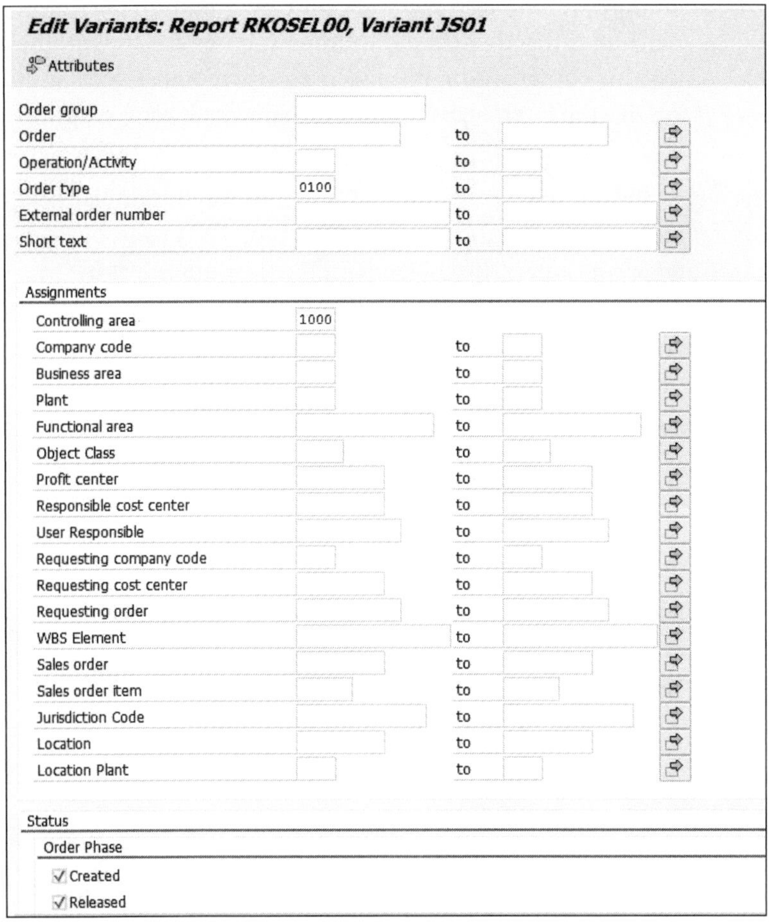

Figure 3.16 Selection Variant for Internal Orders

Selection Variants

Once you understand how selection variants work, you can use them for all the master data in CO. You'll find an option to use selection variants in all the master data reports.

3.2.1 Internal Orders and Cost Centers

You can connect internal orders with their parent cost centers by entering the cost center in the **Responsible Cost Center** field. This link was evaluated in the where-used lists that we discussed for the cost centers. If you work with SAP BW, InfoCube `0COOM_C02` (Costs and Allocations) brings together the cost center expenses and the internal order expenses based on this combination. It's also used when you're setting up Manager Self-Service to derive the internal orders for which the manager is responsible.

As you look at the rest of the internal order, many of the fields will be familiar from the cost center master record, including the assignment to a company code, business area, functional area, and profit center. This assignment has the same effect in terms of how an expense posting to an internal order is updated in the General Ledger (or the Universal Journal in SAP S/4HANA). Internal orders are also assigned to a plant (unlike cost centers). There are also additional fields, maintained in the **General Data** tab, that show who requested the order. Internal orders that are part of a larger investment initiative can also be assigned to investment programs using the fields in the **Investments** tab. We'll look at investment programs in more detail in Chapter 4.

Certain standard tasks are performed for an internal order at period close. The main tasks are the calculation of overhead, based on a costing sheet that's configured in the IMG and, sometimes, an overhead key. Interest can be calculated based on an interest profile. You'll find these settings in the **Period-End Closing** tab. We'll look at these options in more detail using the example of a production order in Chapter 7, but the options for an internal order are the same.

3.2.2 Settlement Rules for Internal Orders

When we looked at the cost center design, we noted that cost centers frequently charge their costs to other cost centers using assessment cycles. Internal orders, on the other hand, charge their costs to other account assignments using the entries in a *settlement rule*. Figure 3.17 shows a very simple settlement rule, in which all the costs for an internal order for attending ASUG events are charged back to the parent cost center, 1820. The user interface for the settlement rule is highly dynamic depending on the approaches allowed and potential receivers as defined in the *settlement profile*, so you may find that your settlement rules look slightly different, showing fewer fields or a different number of potential distribution rules. Depending on your configuration, each order type can have a different settlement profile. When we look at production orders in Chapter 6, we'll see settlement rules that look similar to this one but assign costs to materials and profitability segments, and when we look at settlement rules for sales orders, we'll see settlement rules that assign costs to profitability segments.

Figure 3.17 shows several empty lines, allowing you to create more than one **Distribution Rule** in a single settlement rule. This can allow you to create a first distribution rule, in which 80% of the investment costs for an order are assigned to a fixed asset, and a second distribution rule, in which 20% of the investment costs are assigned to a cost center. To make sure all costs on your internal order are cleared during settlement, ensure that the sum of the percentages for the distribution rules is 100%.

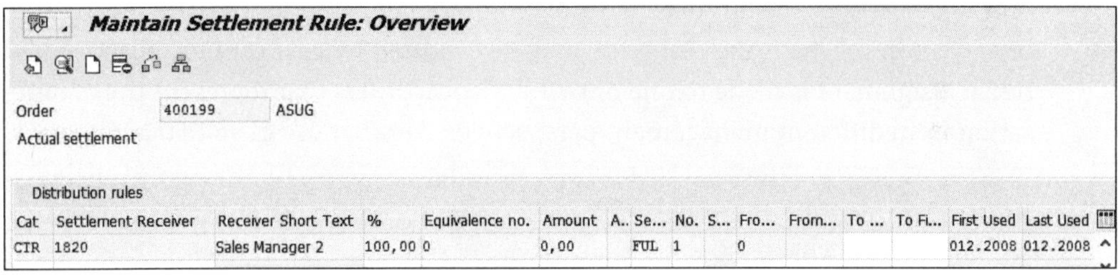

Figure 3.17 Settlement Rule for Internal Order

You can also see that there is a validity period for each distribution rule. This allows you to settle to an asset under construction until order completion and then create a new distribution rule with a new validity period that settles all costs to the final fixed asset on order completion. You do this by creating a first distribution rule that was valid until the date when the asset was taken into productive use. You then define a second distribution rule valid from the same date for which the settlement receiver would be the relevant asset.

Also note the **Hierarchy** icon. If the order is assigned to a project or other order, it can be useful to visualize where your order is in the settlement hierarchy to understand how the costs will flow from one order to another or from an order to a project.

Generating Settlement Rules Automatically

If you're worried about errors in your settlement rules, it's also possible to configure the system to generate settlement rules automatically (in this case, there's an entry in the **Strategy** column). This is essential if orders are generated for objects in other systems, such as CRM service orders that are initiated in SAP Customer Relationship

Management (SAP CRM) and cProjects that are initiated in SAP Product Lifecycle Management (SAP PLM). For internal orders, you might consider automatically generating a settlement rule to the requesting cost center or the responsible cost center based on the fields in the order.

3.2.3 Statistical Internal Orders

Statistical orders are used to provide an additional statistical posting when expenses are posted to a cost center or real internal order. These costs are purely statistical and don't have to be settled, so statistical orders don't have a settlement rule. Statistical orders are used for various reasons, most commonly to provide a matrix view of the organization in which the real costs may be captured by cost centers, but an additional assignment is made to one or two statistical orders that represent the organization from different management perspectives. Another use of statistical orders is to act as a shadow of the real cost center, allowing you to perform active availability control for the order representing the cost center. Full details of this approach are provided in SAP Note 68366.

Figure 3.18 shows an example of a statistical internal order. In this example, several vehicles have been defined as statistical orders, and the actual costs are posted to the cost center for motor pool 1220 (in the **Actual Posted CCtr** field).

Statistical Orders in SAP S/4HANA

The Universal Journal in SAP S/4HANA includes postings to cost centers, internal orders, projects, and so on in one common table. With this merge, it becomes important to identify which account assignment is the genuine cost carrier and which is statistical. SAP therefore added the new fields **Account Assignment** (ACCASS) and **Object Type** (ACCASSTY) to the Universal Journal to identify the genuine account assignment. A posting made to the order shown in Figure 3.18 would have KS (for cost center) as the **Object Type** and 1220 as the **Account Assignment**. The internal order number A-3100 would be updated in the same posting line but without the update to the object type. Order reports include an **Is Statistical** flag to allow you to identify statistical postings.

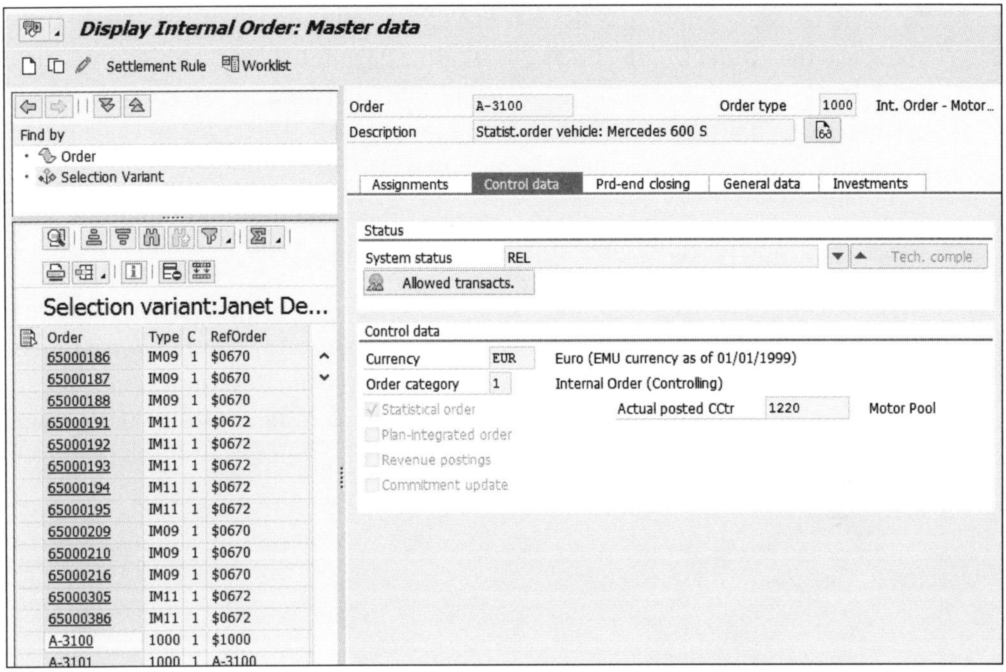

Figure 3.18 Statistical Internal Order

3.2.4 Order Groups

Because organizations typically have many orders, it also makes sense to consider how you are going to select them later:

- *Order groups* are used for reporting and for selecting orders during an allocation (the same procedure applies that you saw for cost centers). When we look at allocations in Chapter 7, you'll see many examples of order groups being used to group orders as potential receivers of an allocation. We'll also see them during cost center and order planning in Chapter 5, in which they're used to select the orders for which planned costs can be entered. They're typically used for long-living orders that tend to be treated as one unit.
- *Selection variants* can be easier to use for selecting internal orders for settlement rather than manually assigning orders to an order group, because the selection variants offer more dynamic selection. If you want to assign the selection variants that you use regularly to your user, refer to the instructions in SAP Note 2082795 (Customer Connect CO—Internal Order Master Data List).

To create an order group, use the Internal Orders role and select the **Master Data** folder and then **Order Group • Create**, as shown in Figure 3.13. You can also use Transaction KOH1 or go to **Accounting • Controlling • Internal Orders • Master Data • Order Group • Create**. The procedure is then the same as for cost center groups. There is also a new user interface for creating order groups in EHP 6.

3.2.5 Reporting Order Master Data

When you've created your internal orders, you can check their consistency with the help of the internal order master data reports. You can access the traditional report by using Transaction KOK5 (available under the **Master Data Indexes** folder in Reporting). Alternatively, use the simplified **Internal Orders: Master Data Index** report, shown in Figure 3.19.

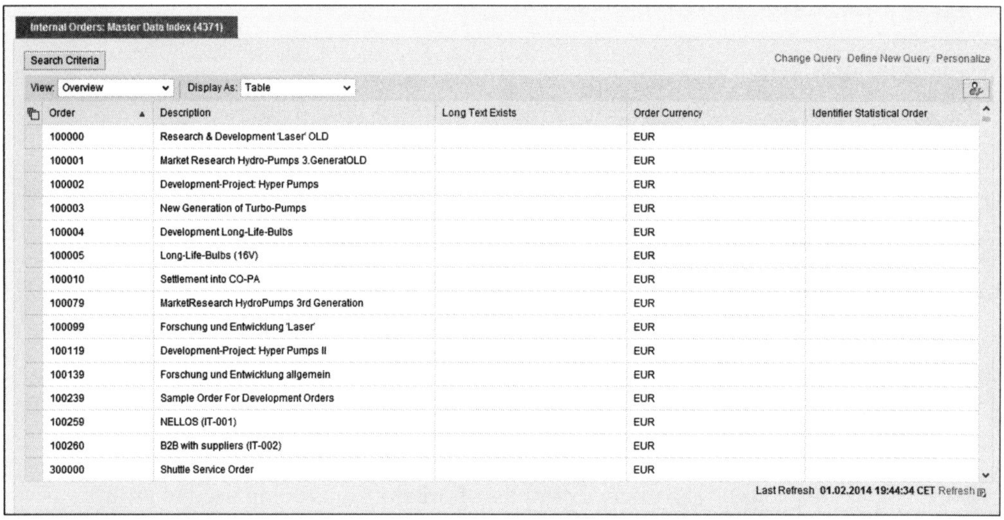

Order	Description	Long Text Exists	Order Currency	Identifier Statistical Order
100000	Research & Development 'Laser' OLD		EUR	
100001	Market Research Hydro-Pumps 3.GeneratOLD		EUR	
100002	Development-Project: Hyper Pumps		EUR	
100003	New Generation of Turbo-Pumps		EUR	
100004	Development Long-Life-Bulbs		EUR	
100005	Long-Life-Bulbs (16V)		EUR	
100010	Settlement into CO-PA		EUR	
100079	MarketResearch HydroPumps 3rd Generation		EUR	
100099	Forschung und Entwicklung 'Laser'		EUR	
100119	Development-Project: Hyper Pumps II		EUR	
100139	Forschung und Entwicklung allgemein		EUR	
100239	Sample Order For Development Orders		EUR	
100259	NELLOS (IT-001)		EUR	
100260	B2B with suppliers (IT-002)		EUR	
300000	Shuttle Service Order		EUR	

Figure 3.19 Internal Orders: Master Data Index

In addition, you can display a list of the settlement rules by using Transaction KOSR_LIST_OR. This is also available under the **Master Data Indexes** folder in Reporting and is especially useful in the run up to the period close, when you want to make sure the correct settlement parameters have been maintained for all internal orders. The list in Figure 3.20 shows how all the internal orders for marketing events settle their costs back to the parent cost center.

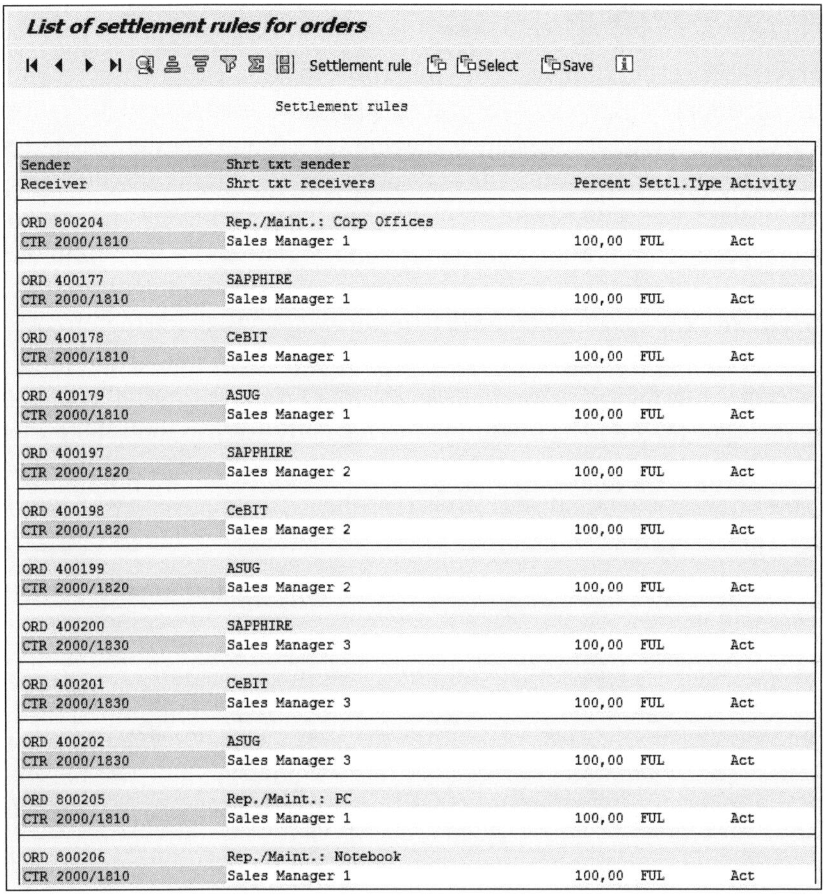

List of settlement rules for orders

Settlement rule Select Save

Settlement rules

Sender / Receiver	Shrt txt sender / Shrt txt receivers	Percent	Settl.Type	Activity
ORD 800204	Rep./Maint.: Corp Offices			
CTR 2000/1810	Sales Manager 1	100,00	FUL	Act
ORD 400177	SAPPHIRE			
CTR 2000/1810	Sales Manager 1	100,00	FUL	Act
ORD 400178	CeBIT			
CTR 2000/1810	Sales Manager 1	100,00	FUL	Act
ORD 400179	ASUG			
CTR 2000/1810	Sales Manager 1	100,00	FUL	Act
ORD 400197	SAPPHIRE			
CTR 2000/1820	Sales Manager 2	100,00	FUL	Act
ORD 400198	CeBIT			
CTR 2000/1820	Sales Manager 2	100,00	FUL	Act
ORD 400199	ASUG			
CTR 2000/1820	Sales Manager 2	100,00	FUL	Act
ORD 400200	SAPPHIRE			
CTR 2000/1830	Sales Manager 3	100,00	FUL	Act
ORD 400201	CeBIT			
CTR 2000/1830	Sales Manager 3	100,00	FUL	Act
ORD 400202	ASUG			
CTR 2000/1830	Sales Manager 3	100,00	FUL	Act
ORD 800205	Rep./Maint.: PC			
CTR 2000/1810	Sales Manager 1	100,00	FUL	Act
ORD 800206	Rep./Maint.: Notebook			
CTR 2000/1810	Sales Manager 1	100,00	FUL	Act

Figure 3.20 List of Settlement Rules

Cost centers and internal orders are both account assignments; in other words, you can charge costs to these objects. For a Controlling implementation, it's rarely enough to draw up a list of cost centers and a list of internal orders. You also need a way to define the nature of the cost center: the number of employees that work there, the number of square feet it occupies, the number of telephones it has, and so on. This type of information is captured as a *statistical key figure*.

3.3 Statistical Key Figures

The cost center design is not complete until you define the resource drivers that you need to perform simple allocations. Statistical key figures are used to establish ratios between cost centers. A typical key figure is the number of employees assigned to a cost center, and this is used to allocate the costs of the cafeteria from the sender cost center to all receiver cost centers with employees. Another example is the area in square feet occupied by a cost center, which is used to allocate utility costs from the sender cost center to all receiver cost centers in accordance with the amount of floor space occupied. We'll use square footage as a basis for assigning administration costs to a group of cost centers in Chapter 7. It's good business practice to establish *measurable* drivers as the basis for such allocations and to make it the responsibility of the cost center manager to check such information regularly so that controlling can update the statistical key figures as required. We'll look at statistical key figures in combination with cost centers, but you can also use them in combination with internal orders and projects.

Lean Accounting

Lean accounting generally strives to avoid allocations and to assign costs directly to the value stream wherever possible. If an allocation has to be used, a measure such as square footage is considered preferable, because it's easily understood by the cost center manager, easy to check, and encourages the cost center manager to try to reduce his square footage by clearing up his "patch."

There are two types of statistical key figures:

1. *Fixed values* are used for key figures that remain constant in each period (such as square footage of floor space).
2. *Total values* are used for key figures that vary in each period (such as number of telephone units).

Note

There is sometimes confusion between the use of statistical key figures and the use of activity types, because they both act as "resource drivers" and have a unit of measure (such as pieces). Statistical key figures can be used only to establish ratios or equivalences for allocations. If you want to charge work time to a project or operation time to a production order, you need to define activity types, which we'll discuss in the next section.

If you need to use data that is already being captured somewhere in Logistics for your allocations, it's possible to link statistical key figures with key figures in the Logistics Information System (LIS). This saves you from having to manually enter, for example, the number of telephone units used each month.

You'll find the master data for the statistical key figures in the **Statistical Key Figures** folder, as shown in Figure 3.1. You can also use Transaction KK01 or go to **Accounting • Controlling • Cost Center Accounting • Master Data • Statistical key Figure • Create**. Figure 3.21 shows a statistical key figure for the square footage of office space occupied by each cost center.

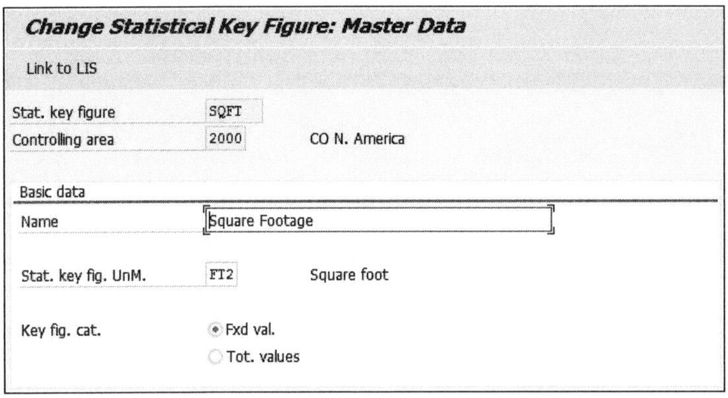

Figure 3.21 Statistical Key Figure

To link this statistical key figure with a cost center, you can take the following steps:

1. Go to **Accounting • Controlling • Cost Center Accounting • Actual Postings • Statistical Key Figure • Enter** or use Transaction KB31N. This takes you to the screen shown in Figure 3.22.
2. Enter cost center 1000.
3. Enter the statistical key figure (SQFT) and the relevant square footage for the cost center (100 square feet in our example).
4. Save your entries.

If you set up your assessment cycles to read the statistical key figures by cost center, this can be the starting point for the allocation, as you'll see in Chapter 7.

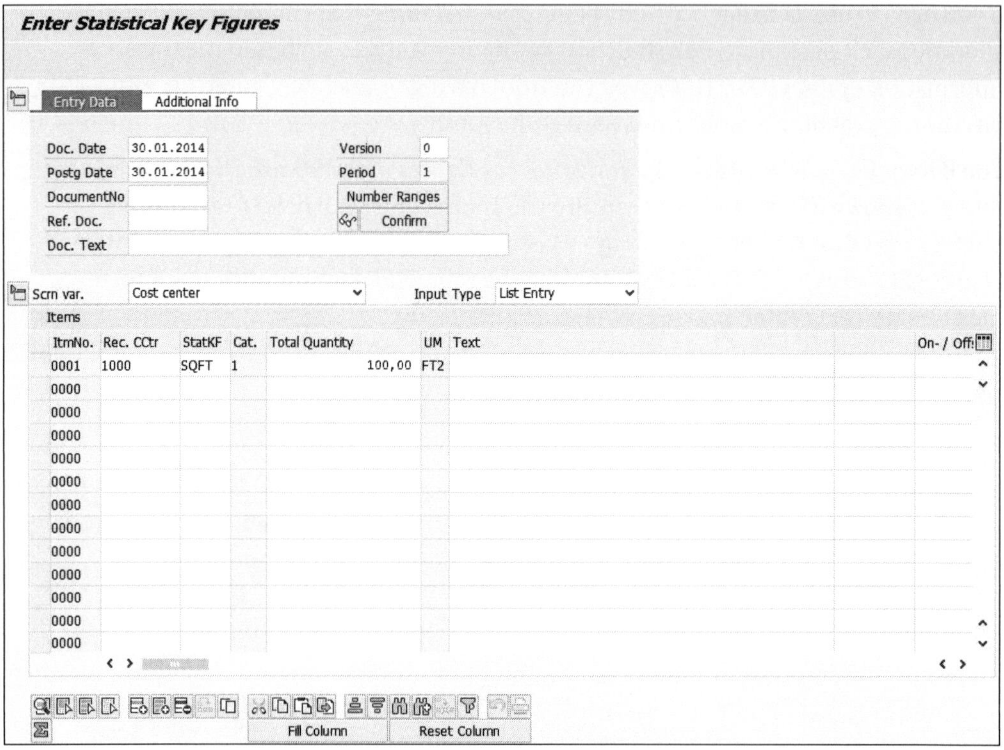

Figure 3.22 Recording Square Footage as Statistical Key Figure

Fixed Values and Total Values

When you record a statistical key figure, make sure you know whether it's a fixed value or a totals value (see Figure 3.21):

- If the square footage is a *fixed value*, updating the value means the new value applies from the date of posting onward. If you change the value, you *overwrite* the old value. This would be the case if we changed the square footage from 100 to 120 square feet.
- You need to enter *totals values* (such as number of telephone units) in every period. If you post the totals values twice, each record counts as a separate entry, and you may have double the number of telephone units. Before you start, check whether somebody else has already recorded the values in that period.

Statistical Key Figure Groups

Statistical key figure groups are much less commonly used than cost center groups and orders groups, but you can use them to help with selection in all allocation cycles. They're mainly useful if you want to plan several statistical key figures on one cost center or set up assessment cycles to read several statistical key figures as the basis for the equivalences in the allocation. The example shown in Figure 3.23 is used to select all relevant statistical key figures for planning equipment-related costs on a cost center. During planning, the manager enters how many units of each item he has on his cost center, and Controlling uses this information to calculate the manager's equipment costs.

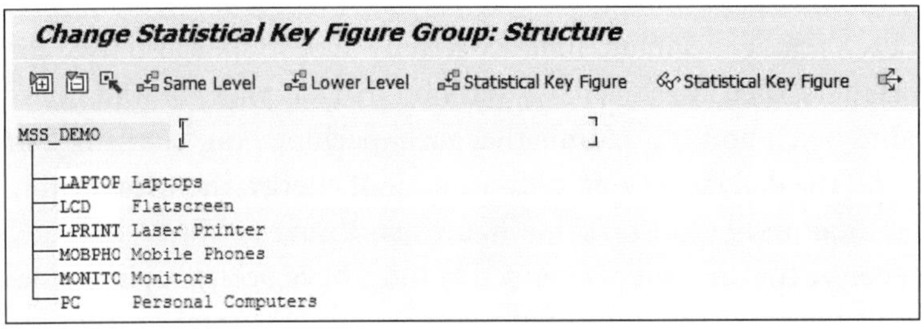

Figure 3.23 Statistical Key Figure Groups

Now that we've established the statistical key figures for the cost center—in other words, the number of employees that work there, the number of square feet it occupies, the number of telephones it has, and so on—it's time to establish the output of the cost center. This means defining activity types for the work performed by the cost center. This might take the form of machine hours, labor hours, kilowatt hours, or so on. Technically, these are all activity types, as explained next.

3.4 Activity Types

The cost center design is not complete until you define output measures for all operational cost centers in the form of *activity types*. SAP ERP distinguishes between direct activity allocation and indirect activity allocation:

- *Direct activity allocation* is used whenever a direct activity allocation is posted in CO using Transaction KB21N, working time is recorded in a time sheet in human resources, and operations are confirmed in Logistics. We'll present many examples of this kind of allocation, in which manufacturing work is performed for a production order or an employee's work time is posted to a project, in Chapter 6. This type of allocation is always performed in real time as the work is recorded. Think of this type of allocation as the equivalent of entering paper time sheets. It's usually possible to assign most of the work performed by blue-collar workers this way. For white-collar workers, it depends on whether their work lends itself to being recorded in a time sheet (such as consulting hours) or whether it's essentially overhead, because employees are unwilling or unable to record it in such detail (you'll often find that this is the case for administrative tasks).

- *Indirect activity allocation* is used for two reasons. It can be used when a direct activity allocation is unfeasible but it's possible to split, for example, the total hours worked by the sales department into several receivers based, say, on the revenue earned by each market segment. Indirect activity allocation is also used for supporting cost centers, such as an energy cost center that supplies kilowatt hours of power to production. If you can assume that each machine hour confirmed in production requires the delivery of one kilowatt hour of energy, then you simply have to read the total number of machine hours confirmed in production and have the system derive the amount of energy that must have been supplied if the machine ran for so long. Use this type of allocation when time recording is not possible and Controlling has to start making business assumptions about how much work is being performed or how much energy is being supplied.

Activity types are first created without reference to a cost center but can only be used for direct activity allocations, time recording, order confirmations, or indirect activity allocations once they have been linked with the relevant cost center and an activity rate has been defined for the combination. The combination is created with reference to a fiscal year and contains control data for the activity allocation. We'll cover this combination and the calculation of the activity rate in more detail in Chapter 5.

You'll find the master data for the activity types using Transaction KL01 or by going to **Cost Center Master Data** and **Activity Types**, by scrolling lower in Figure 3.1. Alternatively, follow the menu path **Accounting • Controlling • Cost Center Accounting • Master Data • Activity Type • Individual Processing • Create**. Figure 3.24 shows the master data for the activity type **Wage Hours**. In Chapter 4, we'll link this activity type with a work center to plan the number of wage hours needed to manufacture a product.

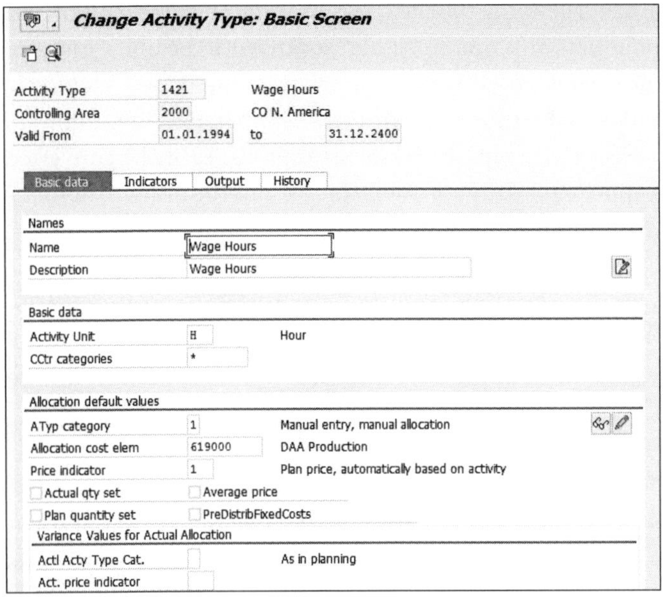

Figure 3.24 Activity Type Master Record (SAP GUI)

Just as you saw for cost centers and internal orders, if you prefer you can use the new, leaner user interface for the activity type, shown in Figure 3.25. We've taken the delivered Web Dynpro application FCOM_ACTIVITYTYPE and removed unused fields for a cleaner look.

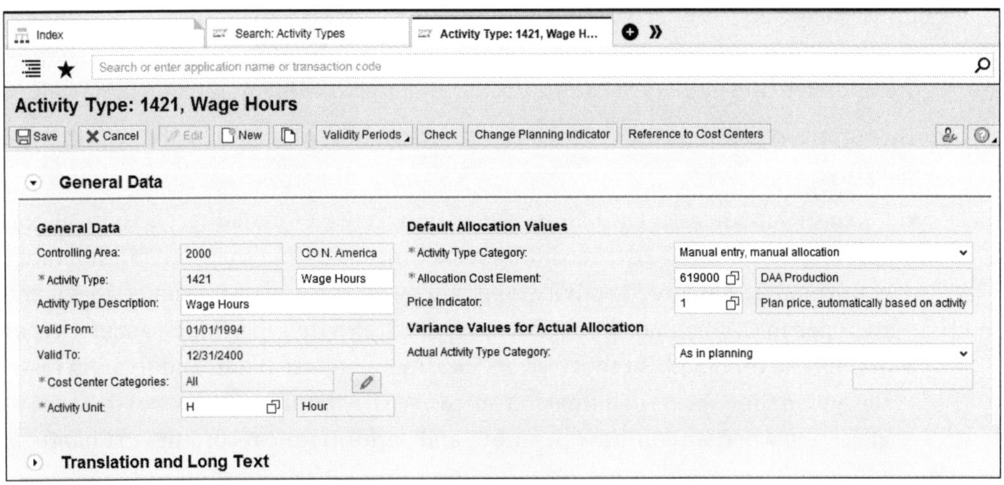

Figure 3.25 Activity Type Master Record (Web Dynpro)

The first decision to make when defining the activity type is the choice of unit (in our example, we've used H for hours). This unit must harmonize with the units you plan to use to capture the *standard values* in your routings, recipes, and so on. It's perfectly acceptable to express standard values for machine time per operation in minutes in the routing and hours in the activity type, because one unit can easily be converted into the other. It's not acceptable to maintain one in pieces and the other in hours.

The next decision is under which cost element the posting for the activity values will be recorded. The cost element will be visible in all cost center reports and provide the assignment to the cost component split, which is one of the major elements for reporting product cost estimates. We'll look at the cost element in more detail in Section 3.6.

3.4.1 Direct and Indirect Activity Allocations

As already mentioned, there are two main types of activity: activities involved in *direct* activity allocations and those involved in *indirect* activity allocations. Some organizations use only direct activity allocations, and all other allocations take the form of assessments or distribution, for which no activity quantity is recorded, but only the value of, for example, rent expenses are allocated. In Chapter 7, we'll look at an example of an administrative cost center that charges its costs based on the square footage of office space occupied by the cost centers it supports and a cost center used to capture telephone costs that charges its costs using percentages. These cost centers do *not* require you to define an activity type, because no quantities are involved and only the *costs* are allocated. As an example of an indirect activity allocation, we'll look at an energy cost center that supplies power in kilowatt hours to production. Here the *number of kilowatt hours* is charged to the production cost centers.

The various types of quantity-based allocation are differentiated by the activity type category:

- *Category 1* (Manual Entry, Manual Allocation) is used for all direct activity allocations (Transaction KB21N), recording work time via a time sheet (CATS), and order confirmation. Category 1 activity types are by far the most commonly used activity types in CO. You need to create category 1 activity types for all activity types you intend to include in routings, recipes, maintenance plans, and so on in logistics and in time sheets in human resources. We'll examine examples of this type of allocation when we confirm operations and perform time recordings in Chapter 6.

Note that it doesn't matter whether you confirm your operations individually or backflush in Logistics; both are considered Activity 1 activity types.

- *Category 2* (Indirect Determination, Indirect Allocation) is used when a direct activity allocation is not feasible, but the total activity usage can be inferred from the activity requested by other cost centers (sometimes called *backflushing* or *pull allocation*). In this scenario, the receiver cost centers record the amount of activity they need from the sender cost center (activity input planning). This request is treated as the scheduled activity for the sender cost center, and it plans its costs and calculates the activity rate to supply the requested activity. We'll look at an example in Chapter 7 in which the total kilowatt hours provided by an energy cost center are calculated by checking the machine time on the production cost centers served by this cost center.
- *Category 3* (Manual Entry, Indirect Allocation) is used when a direct activity allocation is not feasible, but a total activity can be manually entered based on experience from the previous period. Therefore, a quality cost center might record the total time worked by the quality staff and then allocate this quantity to the production cost centers based on a statistical key figure such as number of units produced.
- *Category 4* (Manual Entry, No Allocation) is rarely used but records the activity quantity against the cost center without performing an allocation.

Note the second field in Figure 3.24 for the **Actual Activity Type Category**. This is used when the method chosen for actual price calculation at period close is different from the method chosen to establish the standard rate. This might be the case for an energy cost center, for which the actual activity is calculated as if the plan applies (this method is called *target = actual calculation*).

Activity Types in SAP S/4HANA

SAP S/4HANA 1610 includes a new approach to direct activity allocation for workers in professional service and similar industries. The activity type we looked at in Figure 3.24 and Figure 3.25 is typically performed for a receiver order in the same legal entity as the cost center providing the activity. With increased globalization, it's becoming ever more common for the cost center providing the service and the project receiving the service to be in different legal entities. For this reason, SAP introduced a new service pricing approach that can include intercompany markups when the sender and receiver of the activity are in different company codes. We'll look at this in more detail in Chapter 14.

3.4.2 Settings for Activity Price Calculation

We'll calculate the activity price in Chapter 5, but it's important to choose the correct method of calculating the activity price when you define your activity types. This acts as a default but can be adjusted when you enter the settings for the activity rate during planning.

As organizations start to use activity prices, they typically start with a manual rate that is calculated by spreadsheet and manually updated to the price tables. This approach is easy enough for the controllers to follow but has the disadvantage that you cannot then break the activity price into its cost components (wages, salaries, depreciation, energy, etc.) and show these components in Product Costing and Profitability Analysis.

If your organization wants to have an activity rate with this level of detail, the choice is between calculating the planned rate based on the *activity* or on the *capacity*. If the activity type chosen is a fair representation of the cost center's output, it makes sense to calculate the rate based on the activity provided. Normally, this is the best option, provided that the cost center output is fairly stable. But if the cost center output fluctuates wildly, it may be fairer to calculate the rate based on the output that the cost center has the capacity to produce rather than the output it's currently required to produce. This does mean, however, that the costs of the idle capacity, needed only at periods of peak demand, are passed on to the other cost centers. Bear in mind also that these flags can be overwritten during planning per version and year, so you can have a planning version based on activity and another based on capacity. We'll come back to this topic in Chapter 5.

The following price indicators exist:

- **1 (Plan Price, Automatic Based on Activity)**
  Use the activity as the basis when activity output is relatively stable and the rate can be calculated by dividing the cost of the resources used by the quantity of activity delivered.
- **2 (Plan Price, Automatic Based on Capacity)**
  Use the capacity as the basis when activity output is radically different from the cost center's capacity and the rate is best calculated by dividing the cost of the resources used by the quantity of activity that the cost center has the capacity to deliver.
- **3 (Determined Manually)**
  Use manual prices in the early days, when an externally set price is the best way to get the project started.

Again, note the second field for the actual **Price Indicator**. Use this when the approach used for the standard rate calculated during planning is different from the approach used for the actual rate calculated at period close.

3.4.3 Activity Type Groups

Just as we created cost center groups and order groups, we can group activity types hierarchically. The activity type groups are much less commonly used than the other groups, because activity types are selected for reporting via the associated cost center. However, as you'll see when we look at planning in Chapter 5, it can be useful to group similar activity types to aid selection for planning. Maintenance uses the same set maintenance transactions, but the hierarchies are rarely as complex as the cost center hierarchy.

To create an activity type group, use the Cost Center Accounting role and select the **Activity Type Group** folder, as shown in Figure 3.1. Alternatively, follow the menu path **Accounting • Controlling • Cost Center Accounting • Master Data • Activity Type Group • Create** or use Transaction KLH1. There is also a new user interface for the creation of activity type groups in EHP 6.

3.4.4 Reporting Activity Type Master Data

Although the grouping of the activity type groups is generally little more than an aid to selection, a list of the existing activity types can be useful if you want to make a quick check of existing activity types and their main settings. You can access such a list in the **Master Data Indexes** folder in Cost Center Reporting or by using Transaction KL13. Figure 3.26 shows a sample list of the activity types used in an engineering project. These are referenced during planning and when the activities for the project are confirmed.

We've now covered the master data required for planning and operational use, but we won't be able to perform a single allocation until we've created the cost elements under which these allocations will be recorded. You saw our first cost element of this type in Figure 3.24, when we had to assign our activity type to a cost element.

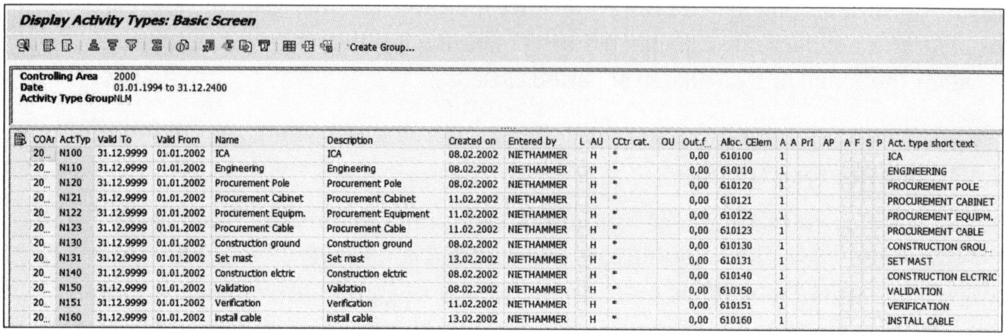
Display Activity Types: Basic Screen

Create Group...

Controlling Area 2000
Date 01.01.1994 to 31.12.2400
Activity Type GroupNLM

COAr	ActTyp	Valid To	Valid From	Name	Description	Created on	Entered by	L	AU	CCtr cat.	OU	Out.f...	Alloc. CElem	A	A	PrI	AP	A	F	S	P	Act. type short text
20...	N100	31.12.9999	01.01.2002	ICA	ICA	08.02.2002	NIETHAMMER		H	*		0,00	610100	1								ICA
20...	N110	31.12.9999	01.01.2002	Engineering	Engineering	08.02.2002	NIETHAMMER		H	*		0,00	610110	1								ENGINEERING
20...	N120	31.12.9999	01.01.2002	Procurement Pole	Procurement Pole	08.02.2002	NIETHAMMER		H	*		0,00	610120	1								PROCUREMENT POLE
20...	N121	31.12.9999	01.01.2002	Procurement Cabinet	Procurement Cabinet	11.02.2002	NIETHAMMER		H	*		0,00	610121	1								PROCUREMENT CABINET
20...	N122	31.12.9999	01.01.2002	Procurement Equipm.	Procurement Equipment	11.02.2002	NIETHAMMER		H	*		0,00	610122	1								PROCUREMENT EQUIPM.
20...	N123	31.12.9999	01.01.2002	Procurement Cable	Procurement Cable	11.02.2002	NIETHAMMER		H	*		0,00	610123	1								PROCUREMENT CABLE
20...	N130	31.12.9999	01.01.2002	Construction ground	Construction ground	08.02.2002	NIETHAMMER		H	*		0,00	610130	1								CONSTRUCTION GROU...
20...	N131	31.12.9999	01.01.2002	Set mast	Set mast	13.02.2002	NIETHAMMER		H	*		0,00	610131	1								SET MAST
20...	N140	31.12.9999	01.01.2002	Construction elctric	Construction elctric	08.02.2002	NIETHAMMER		H	*		0,00	610140	1								CONSTRUCTION ELCTRIC
20...	N150	31.12.9999	01.01.2002	Validation	Validation	08.02.2002	NIETHAMMER		H	*		0,00	610150	1								VALIDATION
20...	N151	31.12.9999	01.01.2002	Verification	Verification	11.02.2002	NIETHAMMER		H	*		0,00	610151	1								VERIFICATION
20...	N160	31.12.9999	01.01.2002	install cable	install cable	13.02.2002	NIETHAMMER		H	*		0,00	610160	1								INSTALL CABLE

Figure 3.26 List of Activity Types

3.5 Secondary Cost Elements

Cost elements are used to record transactions in CO. They can either replicate a profit and loss (P&L) account (e.g., wages, salaries, depreciation, and material usage) or be used to record allocations in CO (e.g., assessments, activity allocations, and overhead). They're also used to record work in process on a production order or results analysis on a sales order or project as a basis for the balance sheet posting for work in process made during order settlement. You'll see many examples of such cost elements when we look at the postings that take place at period close in Chapter 7. You'll also need to ensure that they're in place before we embark on the planning process in Chapter 5, because the secondary cost elements record the flow of costs from sender to receiver within CO. There are two types of cost element in SAP Controlling:

- The cost elements that represent P&L accounts are known as *primary cost elements* and are created using Transaction KA01. They can be created only if the P&L account they represent already exists. We'll explore this relationship in more detail in Chapter 4, Section 4.9.
- The cost elements for allocations in CO are known as *secondary cost elements* and are created using Transaction KA06. They can be created independently of the general ledger accounts and are a prerequisite for the creation of activity types, assessment cycles, indirect activity cycles, and so on. They're also used to charge overhead and to post work in process to production orders.

To update your cost elements, use the Cost Center Accounting role shown in Figure 3.1 or follow the menu path **Accounting • Controlling • Cost Element Accounting**. This role includes fewer transactions than the roles for Cost Center Accounting and internal orders, because the cost element is used not in isolation but in combination with the account assignment (i.e., the cost center or order to which the costs are charged). The main exception is the use of the reconciliation ledger, which we discussed in the section on cost centers, but even this is redundant if you use the SAP ERP General Ledger. In general, cost elements change much less frequently than cost centers and orders, because the chart of accounts is normally more stable. You are most likely to use this role or menu folder when your organization decides to revisit the structure of its chart of accounts. In some situations, all that changes is the text for the cost element, but more often there's a major rethinking of the way costs flow in CO and how these flows are recorded. This puts the Controlling department in the thick of the action.

The cost elements are a prerequisite for many of the steps performed in Customizing in preparation for the period close:

- **Overhead calculation**
  Ensures that the correct cost elements are selected as the starting point for overhead calculation. You'll see this in Chapter 7, Section 7.2.1.
- **Order settlement**
  Ensures that the correct cost elements are selected for the sender object. You'll see this in Chapter 7, Section 7.2.4.
- **Cost component split for activity rate**
  Ensures that the cost elements are correctly assigned to components of the activity price, such as wages, salaries, depreciation, and so on, so that they can then be mapped to the primary cost component split for the product cost estimate. You'll see this in Chapter 5, Section 5.1.2.
- **Cost component split for product cost estimate**
  Ensures that the cost elements are correctly assigned to the components of the cost of goods manufactured, such as material input, setup, labor, machine time, overhead, and so on. You'll see this in Chapter 5, Section 5.1.3.
- **Work-in-process calculation**
  Ensures that the costs are categorized properly during work-in-process (WIP) calculation—in other words, for which cost elements WIP should be capitalized, for which cost elements there is an option to capitalize WIP, and so on. You'll see this in Chapter 7, Section 7.2.2.

- **Assets under construction**
  Ensures that the costs are categorized properly for capitalization during AUC calculation.
- **Value fields for Profitability Analysis**
  Ensures that the costs are categorized properly for profitability reporting. You'll see this in Chapter 6, Section 6.1.3.

Many of the secondary cost elements will already have been defined in Customizing:

- **Overhead calculation**
  Used to document the assignment of overhead (category 41)
- **WIP calculation**
  Used to store the results analysis values before they're settled to FI (category 31)
- **Settlement**
  Used to store the offsetting entry for the settlement on the sender object (category 21)

For this reason, you may find that most of the cost elements you need have already been defined by the people who configured your system initially. However, you may need to create new cost elements in the following cases:

- To define how the costs for new activity types will be allocated (category 43). Usually, you assign the costs of each activity type to a separate cost element, so you'll find yourself adding cost elements whenever you create new activity types.
- To define how the costs will be allocated in assessment cycles (category 42). Usually, you assign the costs of each assessment cycle to a separate cost element, so you'll find yourself adding cost elements whenever you create new assessment cycles. You'll learn about this in Chapter 7, Section 7.1.3.

Figure 3.27 shows the cost element for the allocation of production activities. You can access this data by going to **Accounting • Cost Element Accounting • Master Data • Cost Element • Individual Processing • Change** or Transaction KA02. To see how this cost element is used, go back to Figure 3.24, where you can see how it's assigned to the activity type for wage hours.

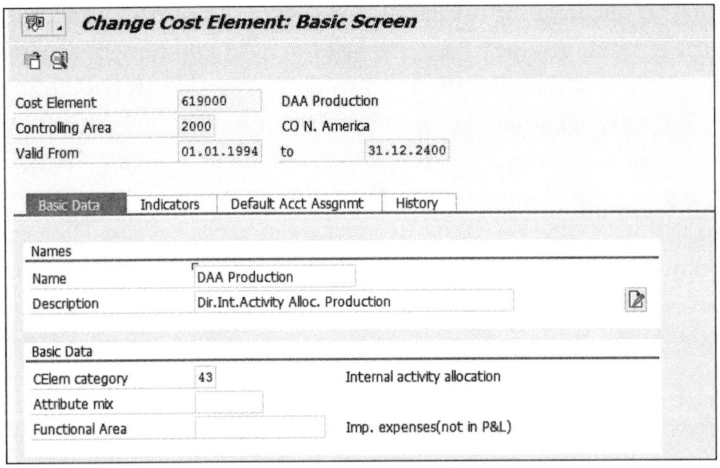

Figure 3.27 Cost Element Master Record

Secondary Cost Elements in SAP S/4HANA

In SAP S/4HANA, the Universal Journal contains one field account, which covers both accounts and cost elements. Transactions KA01, KA02, KA03, and KA06 are no longer available; users are redirected to Transaction FS00 for account maintenance instead. This is one of the most fundamental changes to Controlling in SAP S/4HANA. However, though the separate transactions vanish, the idea of the cost element remains. The basic design rational for assessments, activity allocations, and so on remains unchanged, and the **CElem Category** (cost element category) shown in Figure 3.27 becomes part of Transaction FS00 (Account Maintenance) in the new environment.

3.5.1 Cost Element Groups

Cost element groups have two uses. One is as a mirror of the P&L statement and focuses mainly on the primary cost elements, though the structure can be extended to give a complete picture of all cost elements used. You're asked to enter the chart of accounts when you create your cost element group to ensure the link. This is something that tends to be handled centrally along with the chart of accounts, so Controlling merely uses such a structure for reporting.

The other use is as a grouping to aid selection for planning and for allocations. Here Controlling is in the lead, and you'll see examples of such cost element groups in use in all the allocation cycles we discuss in Chapter 7, Section 7.1.3. You'll also see them in use as selection parameters in planning in Chapter 5, Section 5.1.2. Controlling defines hundreds of such cost element groups to provide just the right grouping in general for each planning requirement and allocation. Don't get too carried away defining cost element groups for every eventuality or you'll find that they aren't much help. If you have a standard numbering convention for your cost elements, you can often get away with entering appropriate number ranges. For example, if all your assessment cost elements begin with 63XXXX, you don't need to create a special cost element group, provided you make sure that everybody follows the numbering convention when they create new cost elements. You can access this data by selecting **Accounting • Cost Center Accounting • Master Data • Cost element Group • Change** or using Transaction KAH2.

Figure 3.28 shows the structure of a sample cost element group. By now, the button bar for creating tree nodes and adding cost elements to the groups will be familiar from the cost center groups. Normally, controllers check the cost element groups just before the period close to make sure that all relevant cost elements are included in each group from which they intend to allocate.

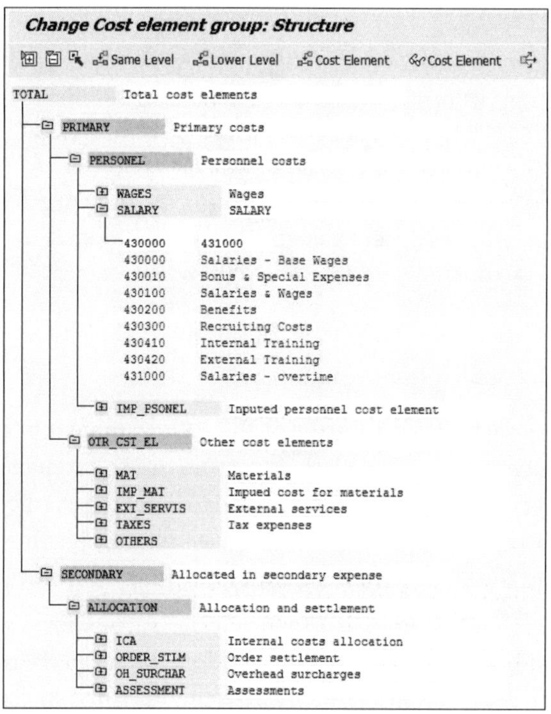

Figure 3.28 Cost Element Set Maintenance

3.5.2 Reporting on Cost Element Master Data

Whenever an organizational change occurs and allocation structures need to be revisited or there are changes to the chart of accounts, it can be useful to use the master data report of Transaction KA23 to list all cost elements, as shown in Figure 3.29. Notice that a **Cost Center** field and an **Order** field are shown for the cost elements. These provide a default account assignment when costs are posted under a particular General Ledger account; you might assign all price differences to one cost center, rather than assigning them to Profitability Analysis, as you'll see in Chapter 6, Section 6.1.1. Other organizations leave these fields blank and instead set up this relationship in Customizing using Transaction OKB9 (this will be the only approach offered in SAP S/4HANA). The selection options for the cost element are fairly straightforward because the cost element does not include a huge number of fields. You'll most likely use the **Cost Element Category** option because it defines what sort of posting will be recorded under that cost element.

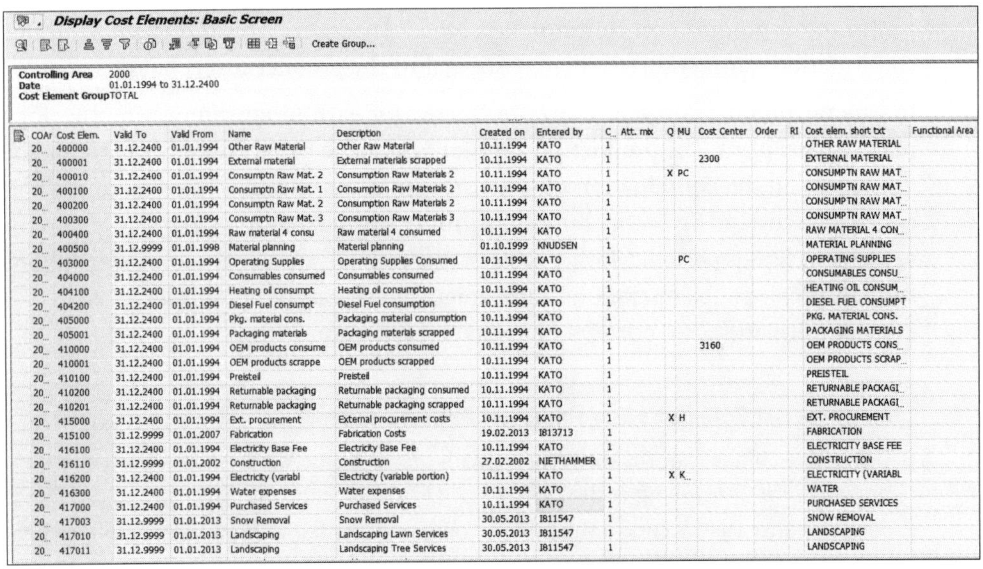
Display Cost Elements: Basic Screen

Create Group...

Controlling Area 2000
Date 01.01.1994 to 31.12.2400
Cost Element Group TOTAL

COAr	Cost Elem.	Valid To	Valid From	Name	Description	Created on	Entered by	C...	Att. mix	Q	MU	Cost Center	Order	RI	Cost elem. short txt	Functional Area
20...	400000	31.12.2400	01.01.1994	Other Raw Material	Other Raw Material	10.11.1994	KATO	1							OTHER RAW MATERIAL	
20...	400001	31.12.2400	01.01.1994	External material	External materials scrapped	10.11.1994	KATO	1				2300			EXTERNAL MATERIAL	
20...	400010	31.12.2400	01.01.1994	Consumptn Raw Mat. 2	Consumption Raw Materials 2	10.11.1994	KATO	1		X	PC				CONSUMPTN RAW MAT...	
20...	400100	31.12.2400	01.01.1994	Consumptn Raw Mat. 1	Consumption Raw Materials 2	10.11.1994	KATO	1							CONSUMPTN RAW MAT...	
20...	400200	31.12.2400	01.01.1994	Consumptn Raw Mat. 2	Consumption Raw Materials 2	10.11.1994	KATO	1							CONSUMPTN RAW MAT...	
20...	400300	31.12.2400	01.01.1994	Consumptn Raw Mat. 3	Consumption Raw Materials 3	10.11.1994	KATO	1							CONSUMPTN RAW MAT...	
20...	400400	31.12.2400	01.01.1994	Raw material 4 consu	Raw material 4 consumed	10.11.1994	KATO	1							RAW MATERIAL 4 CON...	
20...	400500	31.12.9999	01.01.1998	Material planning	Material planning	01.10.1999	KNUDSEN	1							MATERIAL PLANNING	
20...	403000	31.12.2400	01.01.1994	Operating Supplies	Operating Supplies Consumed	10.11.1994	KATO	1			PC				OPERATING SUPPLIES	
20...	404000	31.12.2400	01.01.1994	Consumables consumed	Consumables consumed	10.11.1994	KATO	1							CONSUMABLES CONSU...	
20...	404100	31.12.2400	01.01.1994	Heating oil consumpt	Heating oil consumption	10.11.1994	KATO	1							HEATING OIL CONSUM...	
20...	404200	31.12.2400	01.01.1994	Diesel Fuel consumpt	Diesel Fuel consumption	10.11.1994	KATO	1							DIESEL FUEL CONSUMPT	
20...	405000	31.12.2400	01.01.1994	Pkg. material cons.	Packaging material consumption	10.11.1994	KATO	1							PKG. MATERIAL CONS.	
20...	405001	31.12.2400	01.01.1994	Packaging materials	Packaging materials scrapped	10.11.1994	KATO	1							PACKAGING MATERIALS	
20...	410000	31.12.2400	01.01.1994	OEM products consume	OEM products consumed	10.11.1994	KATO	1				3160			OEM PRODUCTS CONS...	
20...	410001	31.12.2400	01.01.1994	OEM products scrappe	OEM products scrapped	10.11.1994	KATO	1							OEM PRODUCTS SCRAP...	
20...	410100	31.12.2400	01.01.1994	Preisteil	Preisteil	10.11.1994	KATO	1							PREISTEIL	
20...	410200	31.12.2400	01.01.1994	Returnable packaging	Returnable packaging consumed	10.11.1994	KATO	1							RETURNABLE PACKAGI...	
20...	410201	31.12.2400	01.01.1994	Returnable packaging	Returnable packaging scrapped	10.11.1994	KATO	1							RETURNABLE PACKAGI...	
20...	415000	31.12.2400	01.01.1994	Ext. procurement	External procurement costs	10.11.1994	KATO	1		X	H				EXT. PROCUREMENT	
20...	415100	31.12.9999	01.01.2007	Fabrication	Fabrication Costs	19.02.2013	I813713	1							FABRICATION	
20...	416100	31.12.2400	01.01.1994	Electricity Base Fee	Electricity Base Fee	10.11.1994	KATO	1							ELECTRICITY BASE FEE	
20...	416110	31.12.9999	01.01.2002	Construction	Construction	27.02.2002	NIETHAMMER	1							CONSTRUCTION	
20...	416200	31.12.2400	01.01.1994	Electricity (variabl	Electricity (variable portion)	10.11.1994	KATO	1		X	K...				ELECTRICITY (VARIABL	
20...	416300	31.12.2400	01.01.1994	Water expenses	Water expenses	10.11.1994	KATO	1							WATER	
20...	417000	31.12.2400	01.01.1994	Purchased Services	Purchased Services	10.11.1994	KATO	1							PURCHASED SERVICES	
20...	417003	31.12.9999	01.01.2013	Snow Removal	Snow Removal	30.05.2013	I811547	1							SNOW REMOVAL	
20...	417010	31.12.9999	01.01.2013	Landscaping	Landscaping Lawn Services	30.05.2013	I811547	1							LANDSCAPING	
20...	417011	31.12.9999	01.01.2013	Landscaping	Landscaping Tree Services	30.05.2013	I811547	1							LANDSCAPING	

Figure 3.29 Cost Element Master Data List

If you work for a public-sector organization or a financial services company, you can skip from here to Section 3.8, because you'll have no use for product cost collectors or cost object hierarchies. If you work for a manufacturing company and want to look at options other than the classic work order approach to Controlling, the next section will introduce the product cost collector.

3.6 Product Cost Collectors

We introduced product cost collectors in Chapter 2 as a special kind of order used for capturing the costs of production orders, process orders, or run schedule headers and settling them to stock. From a Controlling point of view, they really are master data, because they're created once (when the material master and associated BOM and routing are created) and can then be left alone. They were introduced in release 4.5 and are generally used for managing product costs by period, when the individual production orders are not considered relevant for cost management because they're too short-lived or too similar to require detailed variance analysis. It's also common to use product cost collectors in lean accounting, in which there is a move away from reporting by individual work order to a view of the value stream in each period.

The associated production or process orders have a special order type (PP08 in the standard settings) that determines that the costs that would normally be posted to the work orders during goods movements, and confirmations are automatically posted to the product cost collector. Run schedule headers have their own dedicated confirmation transaction to record costs against the product cost collector.

In general, product cost collectors are created for each *production alternative* for a material and plant. The production alternatives can be based either on a production version or on the combination of bill of material and routing. The settlement rule assigns the costs to inventory but differs from a normal production order in that the settlement type is periodic. Target costs, scrap, and WIP are calculated in every period to analyze completed operations, incomplete operations (WIP), and scrap. We'll look at these calculations in more detail in Chapter 7, Section 7.2.2.

Product Cost Collectors and the Fiscal Period

One of the things that makes working with production orders and process orders a challenge for Controlling is that they rarely fit neatly into the fiscal period, and an input variance that occurs in the first period is only settled to FI and CO-PA when the order is completed in the subsequent period. Using product cost collectors can make it easier to reconcile FI and CO if you have production orders that extend over several periods, because the variance is always recognized in the period in which it occurs.

In general, the **Cost Object Controlling** menus don't support the creation of master data, because the assumption is that production orders, process orders, and so on are created on the shop floor in Logistics. The **Product Cost by Period** menu is the exception, as the master data for product cost collectors and cost object hierarchies is maintained by the Controlling department in collaboration with production. Figure 3.30 shows the master data for **Product Cost by Period** (discussed in Chapter 2). Notice that you can create a product cost collector to collect the costs of the individual work orders and a cost object hierarchy to collect any costs that cannot be easily assigned to the work orders but belong to production (such as inventory variances).

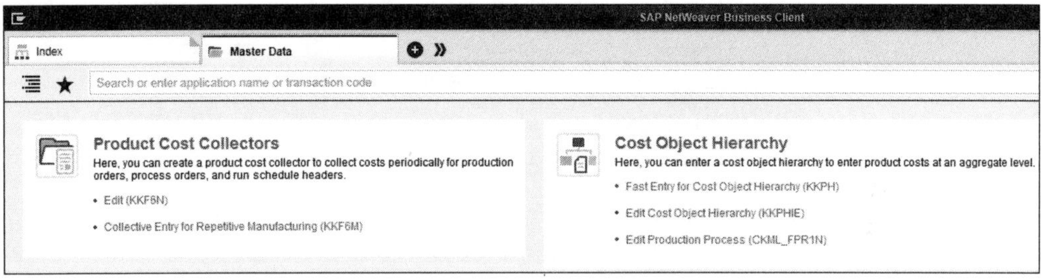

Figure 3.30 Master Data for Product Cost Controlling by Period

To create a product cost collector, go to **Accounting • Controlling • Product Cost Controlling • Product Cost by Period • Master Data • Product Cost Collector • Edit** or Transaction KKF6N.

Figure 3.31 shows the master data for a product cost collector. Two production versions exist for the manufacture of material T-B400, on lines T-C00 and T-D00, and we've created a product cost collector for each version. The **Header** tab shows the link to the order number for each product cost collector (702645, in our example), and the link to the cost estimate, settlement rule, and production orders associated with the product cost collector are provided as buttons. We'll look at how to capture costs for a product cost collector in Chapter 6, Section 6.3.2 and how to calculate work in process, scrap, and variances in Chapter 7, Section 7.2.2 and Section 7.2.3.

The product cost collector stores the costs associated with all the work orders created for a particular production alternative. If you're at a stage of the implementation in which your routings are still in flux or it's not practical to track cost-relevant information by work order or product cost collector, then cost object hierarchies can represent a way of recording data for a production line or a part of the factory. We'll explore that next.

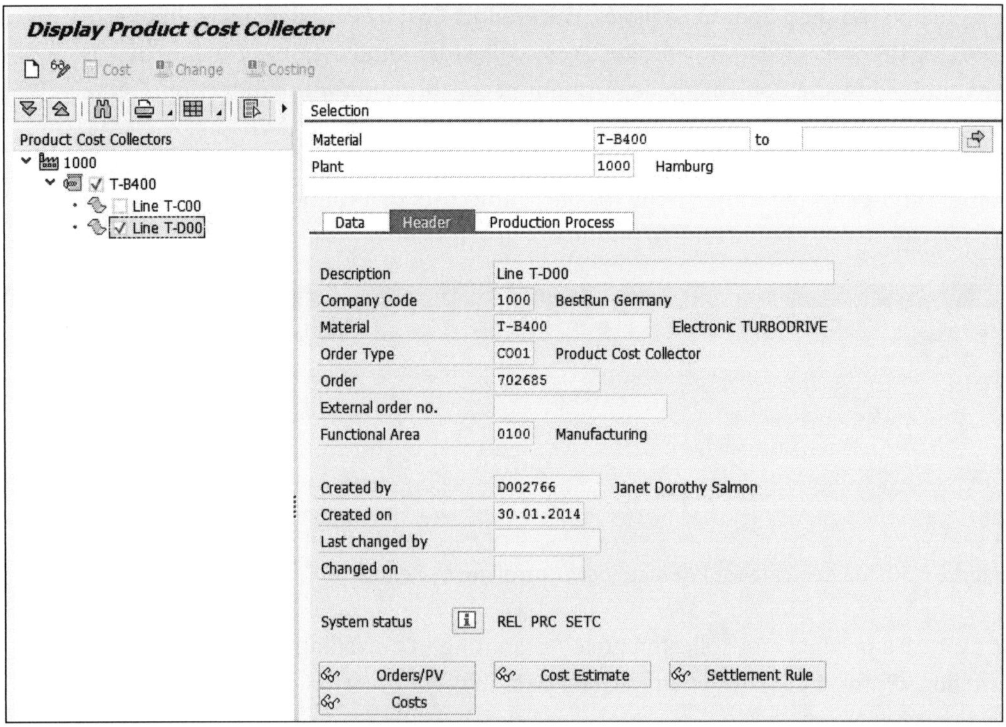

Figure 3.31 Master Data for Product Cost Collector

3.7 Cost Object Hierarchies

Cost object hierarchies are used when costs exist that cannot easily be assigned to production orders, process orders, or product cost collectors. This can be the case when organizations have yet to define routings for their operations and only assign activity costs in total. They can also be used to capture certain types of costs, such as inventory differences or energy. Since the arrival of the distribution of usage variances function (see Chapter 6), the cost object hierarchy is no longer used for assigning inventory differences but can still be useful for capturing activity costs if your organization has yet to maintain accurate routings for all materials or to assign energy and other supporting costs to production.

The cost objects are account assignments to which actual costs can be assigned and typically represent plants and production lines. The bottom level of the hierarchy is the materials being manufactured on those lines. The costs for these materials are captured using production orders or product cost collectors.

To create a cost object hierarchy, go to **Accounting • Controlling • Product Cost Controlling • Product Cost by Period • Master Data • Cost Object Hierarchy • Edit Cost Object Hierarchy** or Transaction KKPHIE.

Figure 3.32 shows an example of a cost object hierarchy built to represent two production lines:

1. This allows Controlling to use a direct activity allocation (Transaction KB21N) to assign costs to the production line to capture, for example, the total machine time provided by that production line or the total hours worked by employees assigned to that production line if the routings are incomplete. We'll look at how to perform a direct activity allocation in Chapter 6, Section 6.3.4. The important thing to know when working with cost object hierarchies is that you have to switch the screen variant from **Cost Center** to **SAP: Cost Center/Cost Object** to be able to enter the relevant node of the cost object hierarchy as a receiver of the allocation.
2. It also allows Controlling to use an indirect activity allocation (Transaction KSC5) to assign energy costs in kilowatt hours directly to the production line. We'll look at how to perform an indirect activity allocation in Chapter 7, Section 7.1.4. Here you'll proceed as described but enter the names of the cost object nodes rather than the operational cost centers as receivers of the allocation.

The master data includes the same assignments to the organizational entities as you saw for the cost center in Figure 3.2. In addition, you see the assignment to a variance key. This is important for variance calculation at period close. There are two ways of handling variances on a cost object hierarchy:

1. You can *distribute* the costs collected on the hierarchy nodes to the associated product cost collectors or work orders. In this case, you don't need to enter a variance key, because all period-close activities take place with reference to the product cost collector or attached work orders.
2. You can *summarize* the costs collected on the assigned work orders or product cost collectors. In this case, you need the variance key, because the period-close activities take place using the cost object hierarchy.

Now that we've discussed the master data elements in general that the Controlling department is charged with keeping up to date, we'll discuss some of the more generic issues associated with master data maintenance.

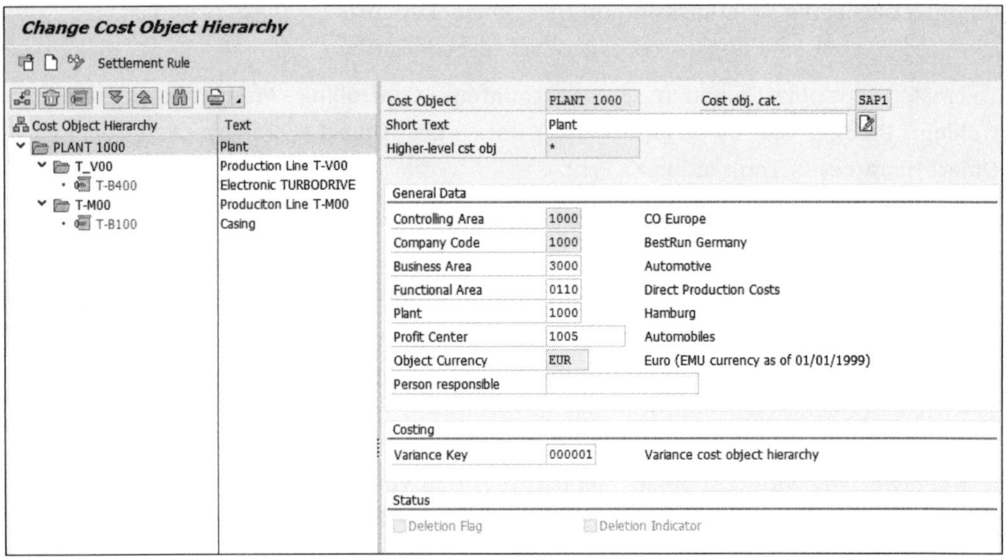

Figure 3.32 Cost Object Hierarchy

> **Cost Object Hierarchies in SAP S/4HANA**
>
> If you are in the early stages of an implementation project, note that the use of cost object hierarchies is no longer supported in SAP S/4HANA. SAP Note 2270411 (S4TWL General Cost Objects and Cost Object Hierarchies) explains alternative options.

3.8 Maintenance Issues

As we discussed at the start of the chapter, compliance requirements affect the master data used in CO. Long before the Sarbanes-Oxley Act, any changes to the master data for cost centers, orders, cost elements, and activity types were documented in *change documents*. These are displayed in the **History** tab of each of these master data elements. This could document the assignment of the cost center to a new profit center or that the name of the cost center manager has changed. You need this information for retrospective reporting. Normally, you analyze the situation for your cost centers at the current time, but for auditing purposes you need to be able to view the situation on your cost centers in years past. When the organization has undergone major restructuring, it's important to be able to document for the auditors when and why the change took place. Figure 3.33 shows the documents for all changes that have taken place on cost center 1000 (the Corporate Services cost center we used earlier).

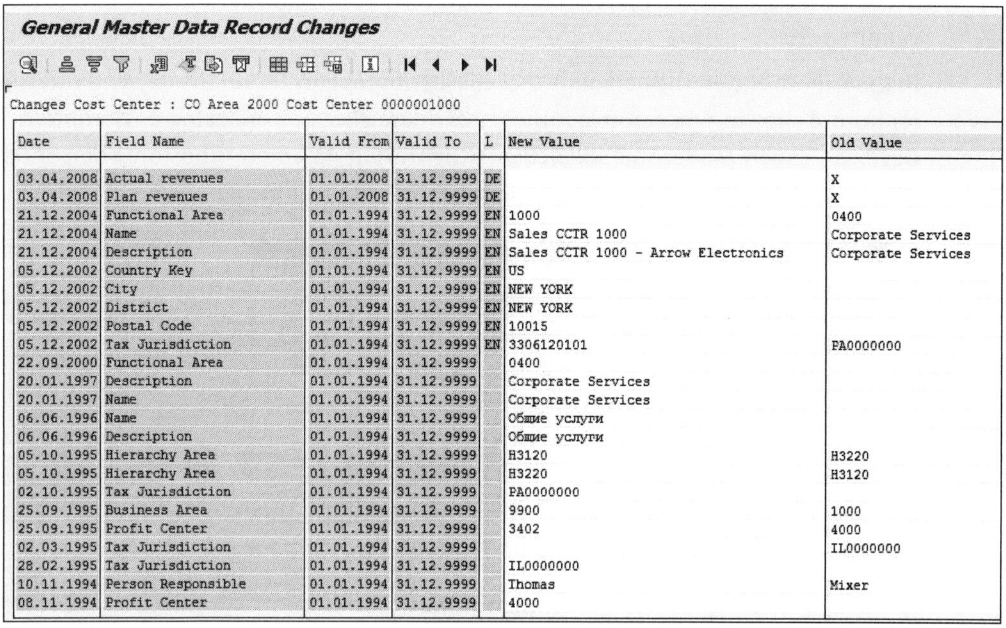
General Master Data Record Changes

Changes Cost Center : CO Area 2000 Cost Center 0000001000

Date	Field Name	Valid From	Valid To	L	New Value	Old Value
03.04.2008	Actual revenues	01.01.2008	31.12.9999	DE		X
03.04.2008	Plan revenues	01.01.2008	31.12.9999	DE		X
21.12.2004	Functional Area	01.01.1994	31.12.9999	EN	1000	0400
21.12.2004	Name	01.01.1994	31.12.9999	EN	Sales CCTR 1000	Corporate Services
21.12.2004	Description	01.01.1994	31.12.9999	EN	Sales CCTR 1000 - Arrow Electronics	Corporate Services
05.12.2002	Country Key	01.01.1994	31.12.9999	EN	US	
05.12.2002	City	01.01.1994	31.12.9999	EN	NEW YORK	
05.12.2002	District	01.01.1994	31.12.9999	EN	NEW YORK	
05.12.2002	Postal Code	01.01.1994	31.12.9999	EN	10015	
05.12.2002	Tax Jurisdiction	01.01.1994	31.12.9999	EN	3306120101	PA0000000
22.09.2000	Functional Area	01.01.1994	31.12.9999		0400	
20.01.1997	Description	01.01.1994	31.12.9999		Corporate Services	
20.01.1997	Name	01.01.1994	31.12.9999		Corporate Services	
06.06.1996	Name	01.01.1994	31.12.9999		Общие услуги	
06.06.1996	Description	01.01.1994	31.12.9999		Общие услуги	
05.10.1995	Hierarchy Area	01.01.1994	31.12.9999		H3120	H3220
05.10.1995	Hierarchy Area	01.01.1994	31.12.9999		H3220	H3120
02.10.1995	Tax Jurisdiction	01.01.1994	31.12.9999		PA0000000	
25.09.1995	Business Area	01.01.1994	31.12.9999		9900	1000
25.09.1995	Profit Center	01.01.1994	31.12.9999		3402	4000
02.03.1995	Tax Jurisdiction	01.01.1994	31.12.9999			IL0000000
28.02.1995	Tax Jurisdiction	01.01.1994	31.12.9999		IL0000000	
10.11.1994	Person Responsible	01.01.1994	31.12.9999		Thomas	Mixer
08.11.1994	Profit Center	01.01.1994	31.12.9999		4000	

Figure 3.33 Change Documents for Cost Center

3.8.1 Time-Dependent Fields

In our initial discussion of the different types of master data, we mentioned time-dependent fields for the asset but didn't mention the validity periods in the cost center header. If the master data never changes, the cost center validity will remain constant. However, for cost centers, cost elements, and activity types there is a concept of *data slices* in SAP ERP. You determine for which fields data slices can be created during configuration.

For a cost center, this might translate into the following data slices:

- From 01.01.2009 to 31.12.2013, assigned to profit center 1000
- From 01.01.2014 to 31.12.2014, assigned to profit center 1001
- From 01.01.2014 to 31.12.9999, new manager

Each time a major change is made, a new data slice is created to record the change. These slices are reflected in reporting, so calling up a report for the cost center in 2013 would show the assignment to profit center 1000 and in 2014 the assignment to profit center 1001. You see the slices when you display a cost center if you click on the **Drill-Down** button (see Figure 3.2) and then select the data slice for the appropriate validity period.

In the Report Writer, the default is that the attributes current on the day you run the report are shown. You can select the earlier data slices by choosing **Environment • Options • Expert Mode**. This will activate the **Output Parameters** button. Then enter your chosen date in the **Fixed Value** field, as shown in Figure 3.34.

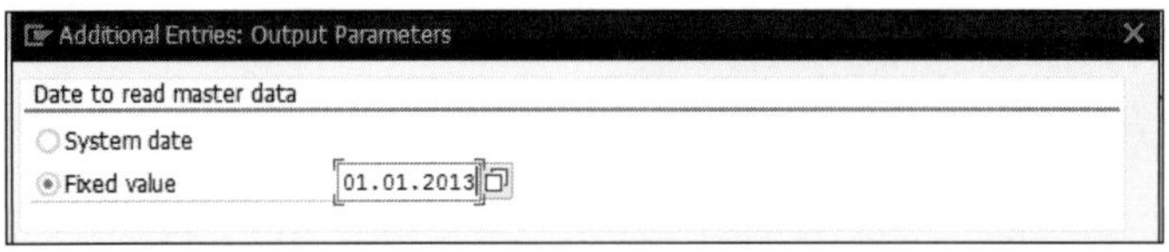

Figure 3.34 Switching Key Date to Read Time-Dependent Master Data

This is also important if you're loading data into SAP BW as it's important to ensure that the attributes are up to date for reporting. Normally, they will be selected on the current date, but you can build queries that select on earlier dates.

Caution

Because the cost center master records are time-dependent but the cost center hierarchies are not, there are sometimes strange effects in reporting. If the cost center hierarchy is selected for a time frame that stretches over several years, cost centers that are not valid for the full time frame will be shown with the message **No Valid Master Record**. In EHP 6, by contrast, if several data slices exist within this time frame, in the new user interface they will be shown separately, as if they were separate cost centers.

3.8.2 Creating Hierarchies for a Specific Time Frame

Aside from the visual benefits of moving to the new cost center hierarchies offered in EHP 6, a practical benefit is that you can build new cost center hierarchies in anticipation of a future change. Let's take a closer look at the search screen for the cost center groups. To prepare a cost center group for an upcoming change, select a cost center group from the results list, as shown in Figure 3.35, and click on the **Copy to Inactive Version** button. Note that this function is only available for alternative hierarchies, not for the standard hierarchy.

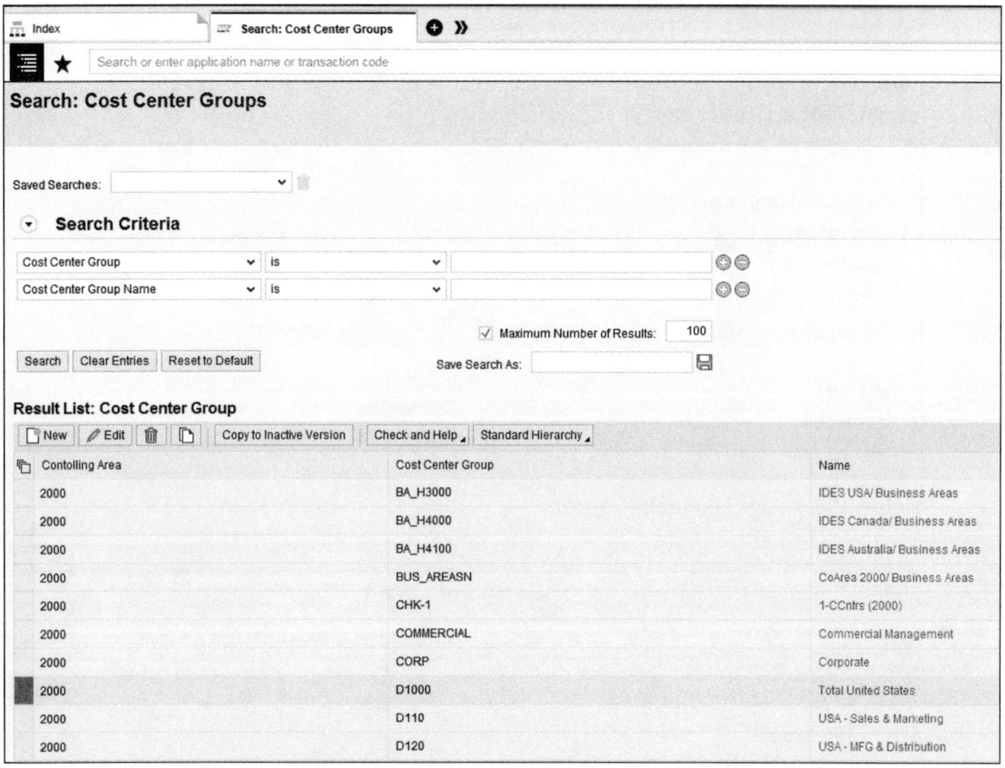

Figure 3.35 Search Screen for Cost Center Groups

The wrapper around your change is a *hierarchy version*, so before you start you'll need to create a configuration entry in the IMG under **Controlling • Cost Center Accounting • Master Data • Cost Centers • Define Hierarchy Versions**. Now assign the selected hierarchy node to an inactive version (JS01 in our example), as shown in Figure 3.36.

Once in the cost center group, you can restructure as described for Figure 3.9. To swap between the active hierarchy and the hierarchy in preparation, use the **Select Hierarchy Version** button, as shown in Figure 3.37. Here you'll see that the hierarchy node D100 is still in active use but that there is an alternative version (JS01) that is awaiting release. If others try to change D100 in the meantime, they will receive the message **Group Contains an Inactive Version** and will know that changes are afoot. As soon as you are ready to activate the new hierarchy, choose Transaction FCOM_AIH or **Activate Inactive Hierarchy**. This will copy the inactive hierarchy into the standard tables for active hierarchies.

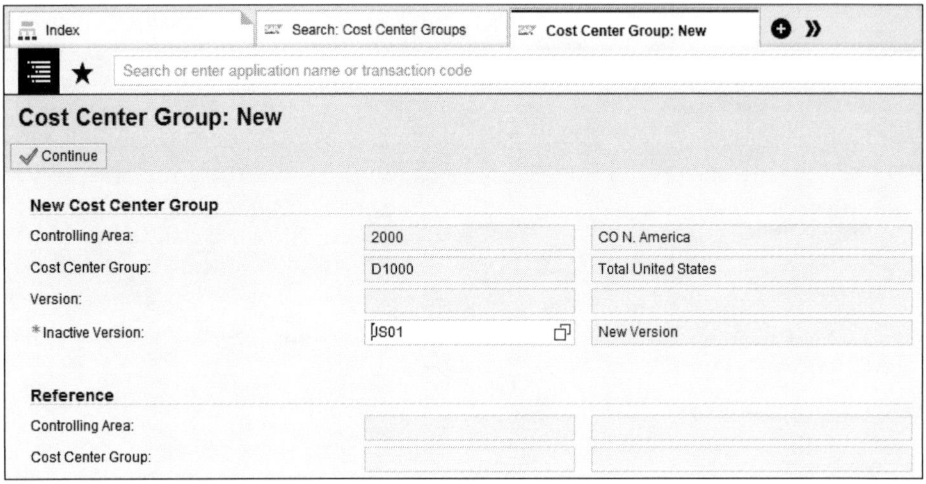

Figure 3.36 Assign Hierarchy Version

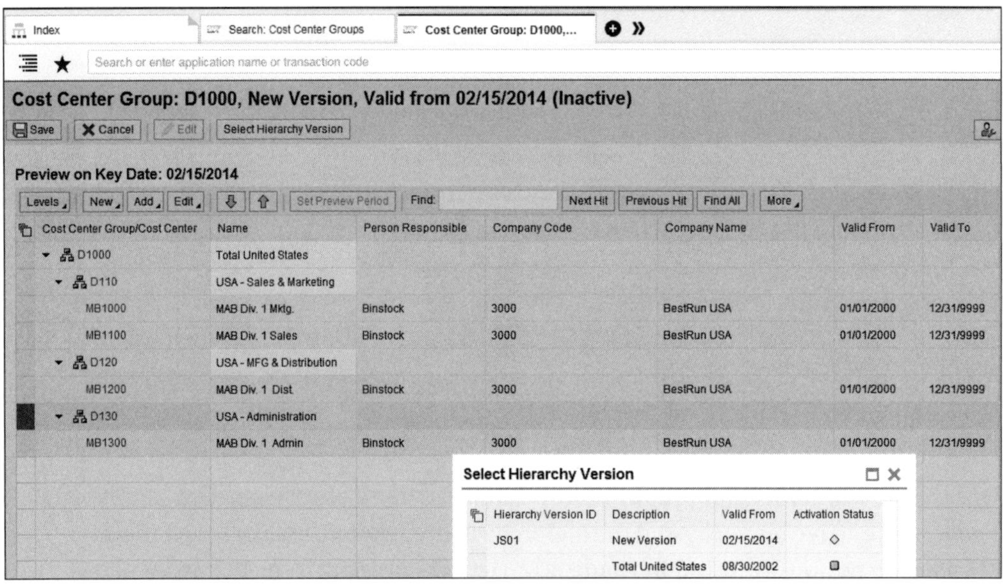

Figure 3.37 Hierarchy Versions for Hierarchy D1000

Again, the default is that the current active hierarchy is displayed in Report Writer. If you want to display an earlier hierarchy that is no longer active, then choose an earlier key date, as shown in Figure 3.34.

3.8.3 Status Management

Internal orders, product cost collectors, and cost object hierarchies don't use the concept of time dependency. This is because they live for the duration of the task and are then completed and archived. Instead, *status management* is used to determine what transactions are allowed for an order at any point in time. The key statuses of an order are as follows, though many others are possible:

- **Created**
  Planned costs can be entered, but it's not possible to perform transactions that result in actual costs.
- **Released**
  Actual costs can be assigned. Usually, this status covers the main lifespan of the order.
- **Technically Closed**
  This status implies that the order is complete and no more costs should be assigned to it. Any WIP or reserves created with respect to the order will be cancelled.
- **Closed**
  This status is required before an order can be deleted or archived.

For production and process orders, the other important status is **Final Delivery**. This status is a prerequisite for the calculation of variances and determines that any work in process for the orders is cancelled. We'll return to these statuses when we look at the period-close activities for orders in Chapter 7.

Although the functions we've just looked at have been around for many years, the business requirements concerning the documentation of organizational change have become considerably stricter since the Sarbanes-Oxley Act. For this reason, many organizations now have some kind of formal change request process in place for all master data changes.

3.9 Change Requests for a SOX-Compliant Master Data Process

In this chapter, we've discussed at length the need for consistent master data in CO. In practice, this often translates to authorization for the master data transactions being assigned to a few super users within an organization who are responsible for performing all the necessary data checks prior to changing a cost center or creating a new activity type.

Since the advent of the Sarbanes-Oxley Act, most organizations have some form of process in place to document why and on whose behalf a change has been made to master data, but this is often a matter of an email or phone call to initiate the request and a spreadsheet to document the nature of the change. Others use their own forms and web services to document what changes need to be executed. We'll come back to this topic in Chapter 9, but let's first look at your options within SAP ERP.

If you use the new cost center master data available from EHP 6, then you can initiate the creation of a new cost center or request a change to an existing cost center from within the Web Dynpro application. To initiate a change request, click on the **You Can Also** button shown in Figure 3.4. This takes you into the dialog to create a change request. As shown in Figure 3.38, you can define a **Request Description** and a **Priority**. To access the form proper, click on **Continue**.

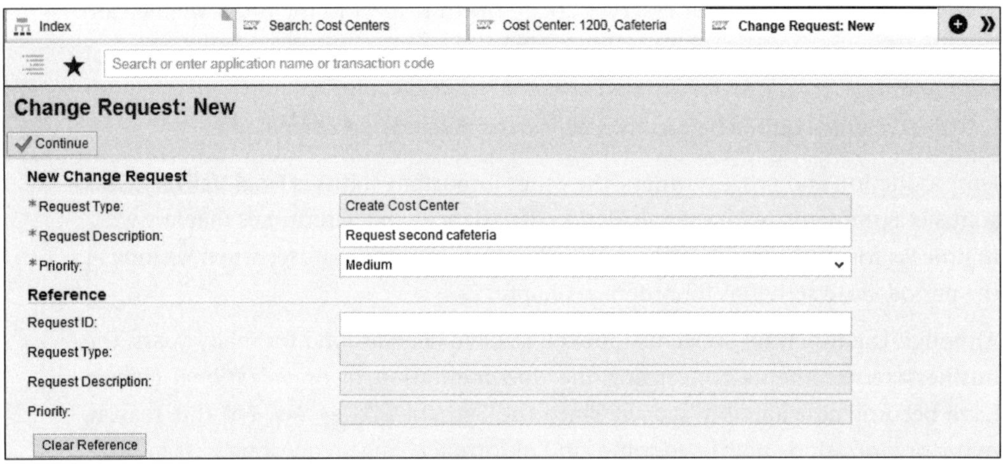

Figure 3.38 Request for New Cost Center

Figure 3.39 shows the main form. In this example, we're logged on as Melissa Adams, and the request will be submitted in her name.

Figure 3.40 shows the complete form. Here you can see that the fields in the form map to fields in the cost center master. When you request the creation of a new cost center, the existing fields are checked, and the system will issue an error message if you try to create a cost center that already exists or assign the cost center to master data that is not valid.

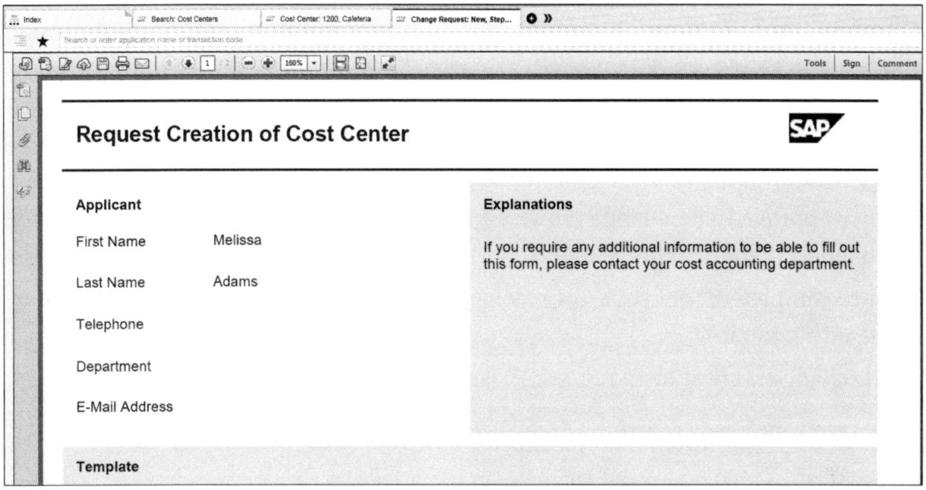

Figure 3.39 Adobe Interactive Form for Cost Center Creation

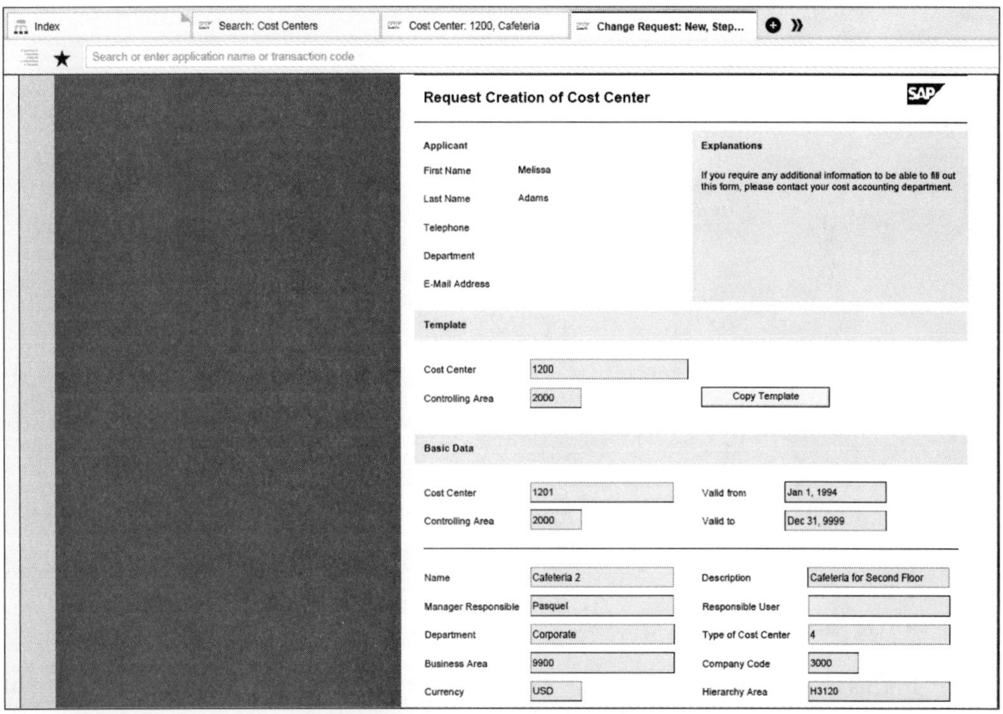

Figure 3.40 Adobe Interactive Form for Cost Center Creation with Fields

You can support your request with additional notes and attachments, as shown in Figure 3.41. Once submitted, the process is as follows:

1. The request is submitted to the manager for approval. The delivered cost center manager role (see Chapter 2) includes a worklist for change requests pending approval.
2. Once approved, the change request appears in the worklist for the internal controller for update in the system.
3. Once completed, the requestor receives a notification of completion in the worklist within her role.
4. The change request has a request ID (see Figure 3.38) that can be used by auditors.

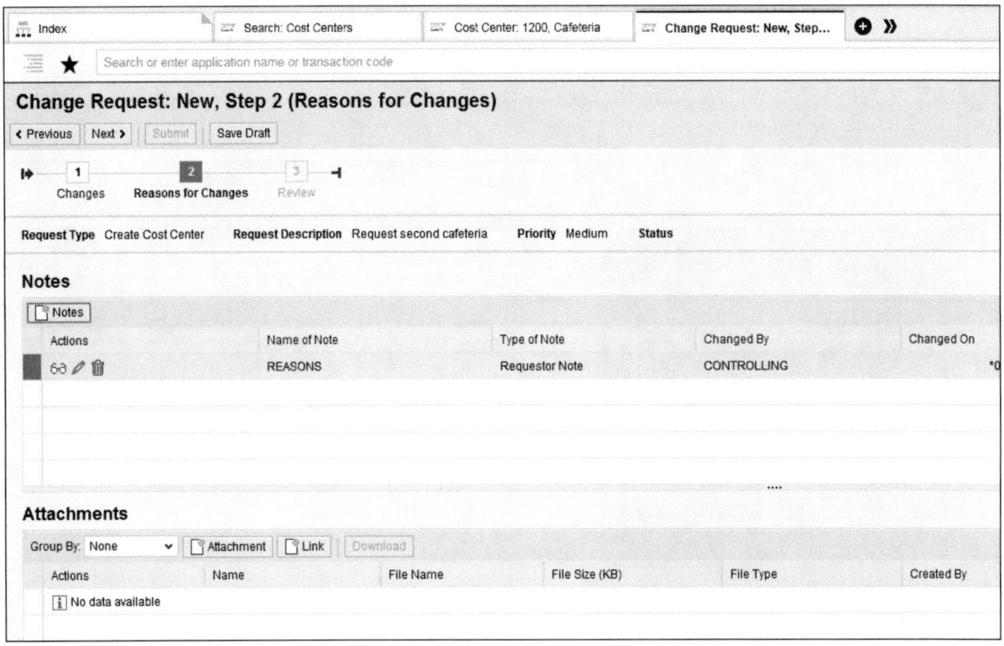

Figure 3.41 Supporting Notes and Attachments

3.10 Summary

In this chapter, we looked at the key elements of cost center design and the use of activity types and statistical key figures. We looked at the use of internal orders, product cost collectors, and cost object hierarchies and discussed the various groupings that exist in the system for reporting and allocations. You should now feel confident when you create and change this master data and understand the implications of any change in CO on other master data in SAP ERP. We also discussed compliance in this area and introduced the change request as a way of promoting compliance for master data control. We'll return to the subject of compliance in Chapter 9. But first, we'll look at master data that isn't owned by Controlling, but in which you have a custodial interest in ensuring its accuracy because wrong prices in SAP ERP Materials Management lead to wrong values in SAP ERP Controlling.

4

Chapter 4
Master Data for Which Controlling Is a Stakeholder

In this chapter, we'll discuss the relevant fields for Product Costing and Profitability Analysis in the material master, customer master, work center, project, and investment program and how they relate to the Controlling processes, such as setting standard costs, calculating actual costs, cross-company costing, and so on.

In Chapter 3, we discussed the master data for which the Controlling department is in the lead, including cost centers and activity types. These are used in conjunction with work centers and routings in production to put a value on the activities performed during the manufacturing process. To create an estimate of the costs to manufacture a product, this master data is combined with information in the bill of material (BOM) to determine the quantities of materials used. Because the quantities in the BOM and routing affect the standard costs, Controlling has a shared responsibility with engineering and production for ensuring the accuracy of this master data. Technically, it's possible to store two or even three sets of BOMs and routings: one for Controlling, one for engineering, and one for production. Using a costing BOM can be a good way to get the Controlling implementation off the ground while the engineering and production implementations are still in their infancy. In the long term, however, keeping separate structures in Controlling is dangerous, because they can cease to reflect the reality on the shop floor. Once the engineering process is complete, it's much better to work with production to have a single, accurate set of master data to determine what the material and activity input for each product is.

A material master must exist for all materials that are purchased, manufactured, or sold. The material master is the key element for which the logistics requirements (size, weight, manufacturing approach, etc.) meet the requirements of the financials processes (standard price, future price, account determination, etc.). The material master is the single version of the truth. There can be only one material master for each material in each plant. Controlling must work with all the other stakeholders to ensure the accuracy of the master data. Because the same material may be acquired from multiple sources, we'll also look at how to set up procurement alternatives and establish mix relationships for Product Costing.

A customer master must exist before a sales order or an invoice can be created. Again, the requirements for the sales processes and for the handling of accounts receivable meet the Controlling requirements in terms of key data for segmenting customers for Profitability Analysis. It's important to consider at an early stage to what extent customer-specific costs are relevant for Controlling, because this will determine whether sales controlling takes place in Profitability Analysis alone or whether you have a requirement for sales order controlling, as we saw in Chapter 2.

Likewise, a vendor master must exist before a purchase order or an invoice can be created. Pricing information for the goods to be purchased is typically stored in a purchasing info record; it makes sense to understand how your organization manages its purchasing negotiations, because this can have a significant impact on product costs and on project costs. It's also important to understand whether you procure to stock (typical in make-to-stock environments) or whether you make project- or even order-specific purchases for which the goods will be delivered as sales order or project stock rather than to a warehouse that supplies the whole factory.

We'll also look at projects and investment programs, for which Controlling is clearly a major stakeholder but project or program management is in the lead. Here the role of Controlling is to provide a basic structure for the projects (perhaps distinguishing investment projects from cost projects) and determine at what level the budget is set (for example, only for the top nodes of the project), for which Work Breakdown Structure (WBS) elements actual costs can be captured (it may not make sense to capture costs for every WBS element in the structure), and for which WBS elements plan costs will be captured (it's common practice to plan at a much finer level of detail than actual costs are calculated at). Finally, we'll look at the profit and loss (P&L) accounts and their relationship with the cost elements in the Controlling component (CO) of SAP ERP Financials. Normally, the role of controlling there is merely as a custodian of the data, ensuring that all follow-up processes are handled correctly. Controlling tasks might include the classification of these cost elements for overhead calculation, work-in-process (WIP) calculation, or settlement.

As we discussed in Chapter 1, CO is highly reliant on the existence of standards in the form of standard prices. You might feel that the standard prices are not obviously master data, in the way that the weight and dimensions of a product clearly are, but they have to be in place before any of the goods movements can begin or planning can commence. Therefore, we'll look at the different methods of price setting in SAP ERP before we look at the planning process in the next chapter.

4.1 Material Masters

The material master is arguably the most important master record in Logistics. You'll need to create a material master for any material that is bought or sold on a commercial basis or is used, consumed, or created in production. Materials are distinguished by *material type*. Common material types include raw materials and trading goods for purchased materials and finished and semifinished materials for manufactured materials, though there are many industry-specific variants.

The material master is also the best example of shared master data, with each department having its own *view* of the material master:

- The *basic* view assigns the material to a *division*, a *material group*, and a *product hierarchy*, all of which are important for selecting the material for reporting. Most organizations have so many materials that controlling almost always makes a preliminary selection of the data using the material group or product hierarchy or another form of classification.
- The *accounting* view contains the valuation class that determines how the material costs are assigned to accounts and the price control indicator that determines whether the material is valued at a *standard price* or at a *moving* or *weighted average price*. Controlling has its part to play in recommending the price strategy for each type of material and whether Actual Costing is required or not.
- The *costing* view contains the base data required for Product Costing, including the costing lot size (the standard output on which all targets are based) and key data affecting the costing process, such as the default production version or whether the material is a coproduct. From a reporting point of view, the costing view defines the default profit center that will be included in any production orders. It also contains *planned prices* that can be used to set a standard price for the material in the future. Controlling "owns" these views, and it's their job to ensure that the correct prices and lot sizes are stored here.
- The *MRP* view contains additional data that's important for the costing process, including whether the material is make to stock or make to order, and settings that affect the allowance for planned scrap. Production owns these views, but it's important for controlling to understand which type of manufacturing is being

performed because this determines which will be the most appropriate form of Cost Object Controlling (product cost by order, product cost by period, or sales order controlling), as you saw in Chapter 2.

- The *sales* view contains key data for the sales process, including the assignment of the material to a division, which determines the business area to which the material is assigned. Probably the most important link from a controlling point of view is to the price conditions used to create the sales order, because these determine the degree of detail that's available for analyzing sales deductions in Profitability Analysis.

To access the material master, you can use Transaction MM03 or go to **Logistics • Materials Management • Material Master • Material • Display • Display Current** and select the appropriate view(s). To display some of the views, you'll have to enter the appropriate organizational unit(s). The costing, accounting, and MRP views also require you to enter a plant, and the sales view requires you to enter a sales organization and a distribution channel.

> **Key Dates in the Material Master**
>
> It's possible to schedule changes to the material master for a key date in the future, but this doesn't apply to some data affecting costing, including configuration data, production versions, and coproducts for which changes cannot be scheduled.

4.1.1 Basic View

Let's start with the basic view. For controlling purposes, the assignment to a division, a material group, and a product hierarchy are important for reporting, and we'll see these fields showing up later as characteristics in CO-PA. For product costing, the assignment of a base *unit of measure* is critical, because this determines the unit for the costing lot size. For a material like a pump, choosing the unit of measure is something of a nonevent because it's easy to count units of such products. In other industries, the unit of measure presents more challenges. For foods, the physical quantity, such as a liter of milk or a pound of cheese, tells you the volume but little about the value of the goods. In these industries, SAP Catch Weight Management is used to store two separate units of measure for each material—one referring to the physical quantity and the other to the valuation-relevant quantity. There has been significant development effort in this area in EHPs 4 and 5, so if you're in the food industry it's probably worth looking at the latest developments because they allow you to use the double quantity units within core SAP ERP. It's also common for Profitability Analysis to work with multiple units of measure. Typically, the base unit of measure might be a case, but you might want to perform sales reporting in units that are comparable across multiple divisions and product lines, such as pounds, kilograms, or gallons. You can check the link between cases and kilograms by clicking on the **Additional Data** button and looking at the conversion factor between the two units.

Also notice that the basic view is not assigned to an organizational unit. This is *master* data in the true sense of the word: it applies to everybody. The same data is repeated in the sales view (product hierarchy, material group) and the purchasing view (material group). Figure 4.1 shows the basic data for a pump, material number P-100. Later you'll be able to enter a lot size for the pump in pieces and select it for reporting via the product hierarchy, the material group, or the division shown here.

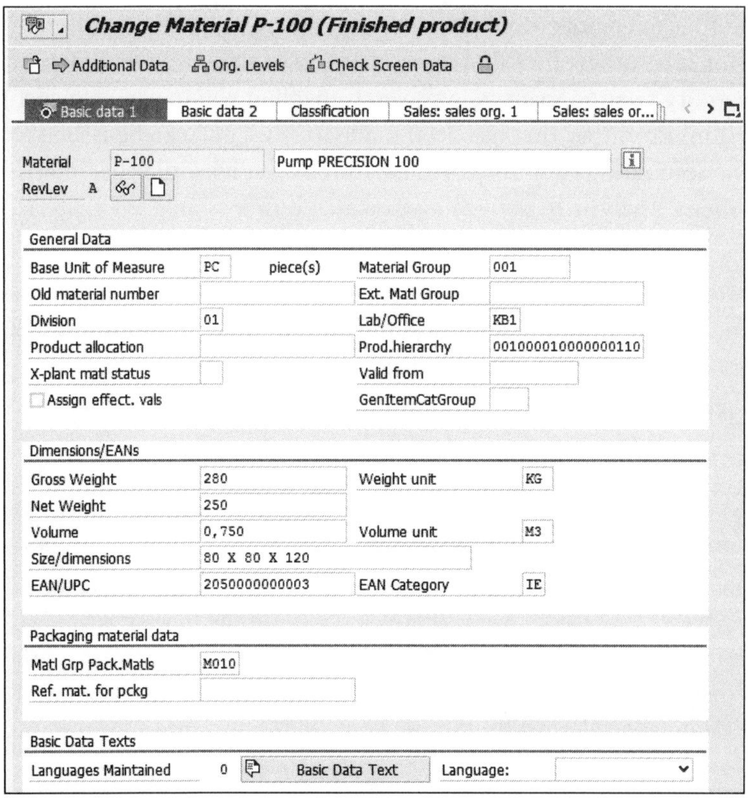

Figure 4.1 Material Master: Basic View

Material Masters in SAP S/4HANA

Unless you are using an industry solution, the key for the material master can contain up to 18 characters in SAP ERP. From SAP S/4HANA 1511 on, the key is extended to 40 characters. To find out more about the implications, refer to SAP Note 2270396 (S4TWL—Long Material Number).

4.1.2 Accounting View

The accounting view assigns the material to a particular *valuation class*, which in turn determines to which *material account* the product costs will be assigned. The valuation class is derived from the material type, so it's possible to assign raw material costs to a different account from finished goods inventory. If your manufacturing involves make-to-order or engineer-to-order products, you can also set up different valuation classes for sales order stock (inventory relating to a single sales order) or project stock (inventory relating to a single project), enabling you to separate such inventory values from inventory that has been made to stock and can be issued to any sales order. The accounting view assigns the material to a division, a characteristic used in Profitability Analysis to determine to which business area the material belongs.

The accounting view records the quantity of goods in stock and their value. It's updated every time a goods movement takes place. The value of the goods in stock depends on the price control for the material. In general, there are two options:

1. Standard price (S)
2. Moving average price (V)

Choosing the Correct Price Control Indicator

The moving average price is usually used for raw materials and the standard price for manufactured materials. SAP recommends that you don't use the moving average for manufactured materials, because the moving average can become distorted due to the timing of cost postings, settlements, and the number of orders in progress for the same material (for more information, see SAP Note 81682).

From Release 4.6C, the moving average price, which changes in response to every goods movement and invoice receipt, can be replaced by a *weighted average price*, which is calculated at period close using values stored in the Material Ledger. The accounting view looks different depending on whether the material is assigned to a plant in which the Material Ledger is active or not. Figure 4.2 shows the accounting view for a material in a plant *without* the Material Ledger. The material is valued at standard costs (price control S), and a link is provided to the *standard cost estimate* that was used to calculate the standard costs. We'll look at how to set the initial standard price later in Section 4.10 and how to calculate and update the standard price as part of the planning process in Chapter 5.

If you want to use a weighted average price rather than a moving average price, you should activate **Actual Costing** for the relevant plants. This is a switch that's set in the configuration for each plant.

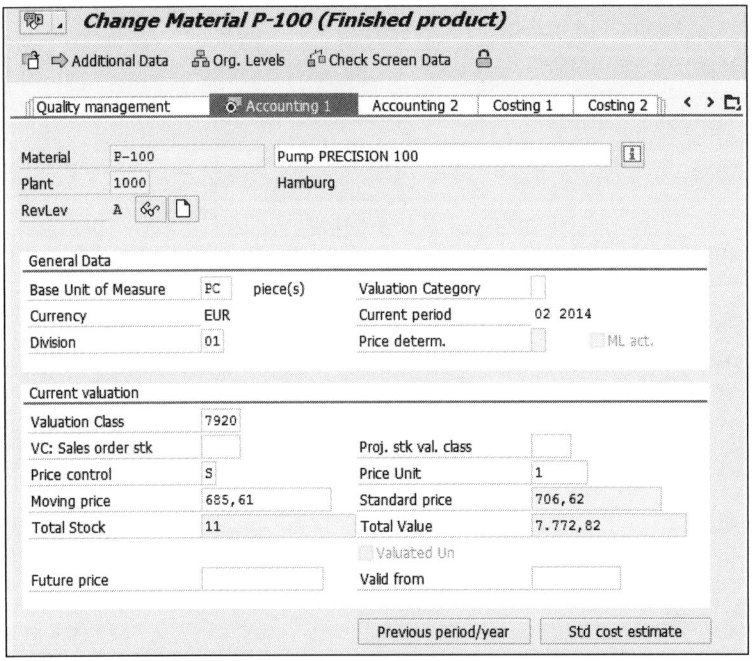

Figure 4.2 Material Master: Accounting View in Plant without Material Ledger

> **Activating Material Ledger/Actual Costing**
>
> Activating Material Ledger/Actual Costing has a considerable impact on your SAP ERP system. Before you embark on such a journey, read the detailed explanation in SAP Note 398949.

Activating the Material Ledger for the plant changes the look of the accounting view, creating additional tables to store the inventory values in multiple currencies and requiring an additional process at period close to calculate the periodic unit price for each material. Figure 4.3 shows the accounting view for a material in a plant *with* the Material Ledger.

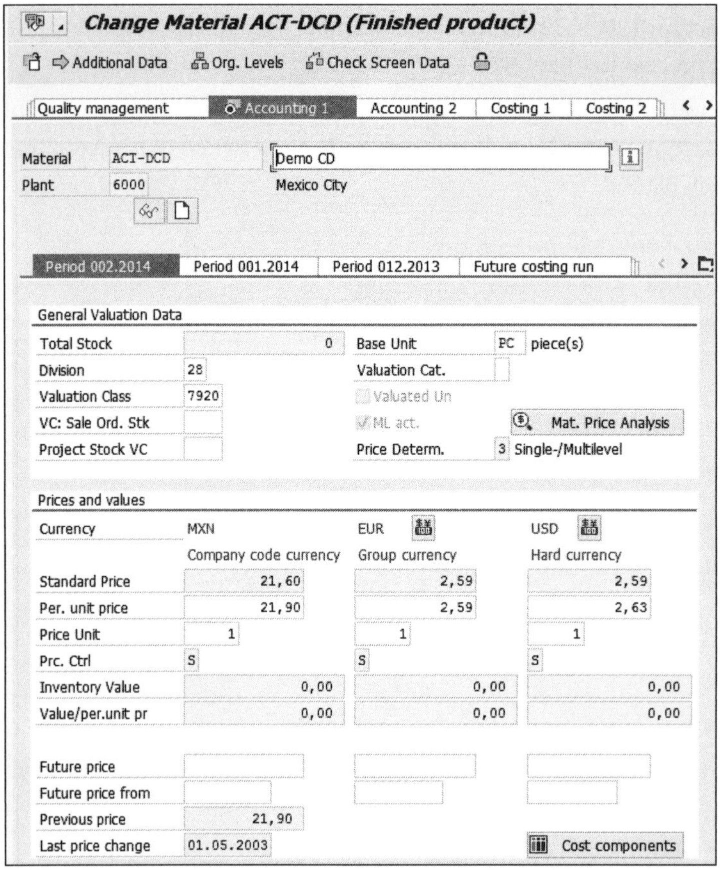

Figure 4.3 Material Master: Accounting View in Plant with Material Ledger

You reach this screen by the same route you take to get to the screen shown in Figure 4.2. The difference is that material ACT-DCD is in plant 6000, where we've activated the Material Ledger for demo purposes, whereas the pump was in plant 1000, where the Material Ledger isn't active. All material masters will look like this in SAP S/4HANA, where the use of the Material Ledger becomes compulsory from 1511. The

Price Determ. box determines which form of Material Ledger postings you use for the material:

- **Transaction-based**
  Transaction-based price determination simply means that a moving average price is created automatically in the currencies you've activated in the Material Ledger. It behaves exactly like the normal moving average price but in multiple currencies. This is the default in SAP S/4HANA.
- **Single-/Multilevel**
  Single-/multilevel price determination means that a weighted average price (or periodic unit price) is calculated using a costing run at period close. This is optional in SAP S/4HANA.

We'll look at this process in more detail in Chapter 7.

In addition to storing the prices that are used for valuing goods movements, the accounting view includes a second set of prices that are used for balance sheet valuation at period close. There are various methods for valuing inventory, including last in, first out (LIFO); first in, first out (FIFO); and lowest of cost or market. German law also distinguishes between commercial law and tax law, so you'll see both commercial prices and tax prices on this screen. In the United States, it's becoming common to distinguish between IFRS (which uses FIFO) and local GAAP (where LIFO is allowed). At the time of writing, it's not yet a legal requirement for US companies to store both, but there's undeniably a global trend toward IFRS reporting. We'll look at the options for balance sheet valuation later in Section 4.10.

4.1.3 Costing Views

The costing view (see Figure 4.4) contains control data for Product Costing, such as the costing lot size (the default quantity on which any cost estimate is based) and data to build up the quantity structure for Product Costing.

General Data

The **General Data** section in the top area of the costing view has a control function:

- The **With Qty Structure** checkbox determines that the costs for the material are usually calculated using its BOM and routing (its quantity structure). This is the default for all manufactured materials.

- The **Material Origin** checkbox determines that the material costs include details of the material used and the assignment to the cost element. This is particularly important for *variance analysis* because it determines the level of detail stored on the production order (only the account information or details of the individual materials assigned to that account). If the checkbox is not already selected in your master data, use Report RKHKMATO to prepare your data. However, be aware that setting the flag significantly increases the amount of data written to the database during each transaction. This will no longer be a concern in SAP S/4HANA, in which costs will always be updated by material.
- The **Origin Group** field serves a similar purpose as and predates the **Material Origin** checkbox. In general, if you work with the **Material Origin** checkbox, you don't need to enter an origin group, unless you specifically need to distinguish between different groups of material assigned to one cost element when you're setting up your cost components for Product Costing. This can be useful if you want a simple way of classifying different types of material for costing or reporting.

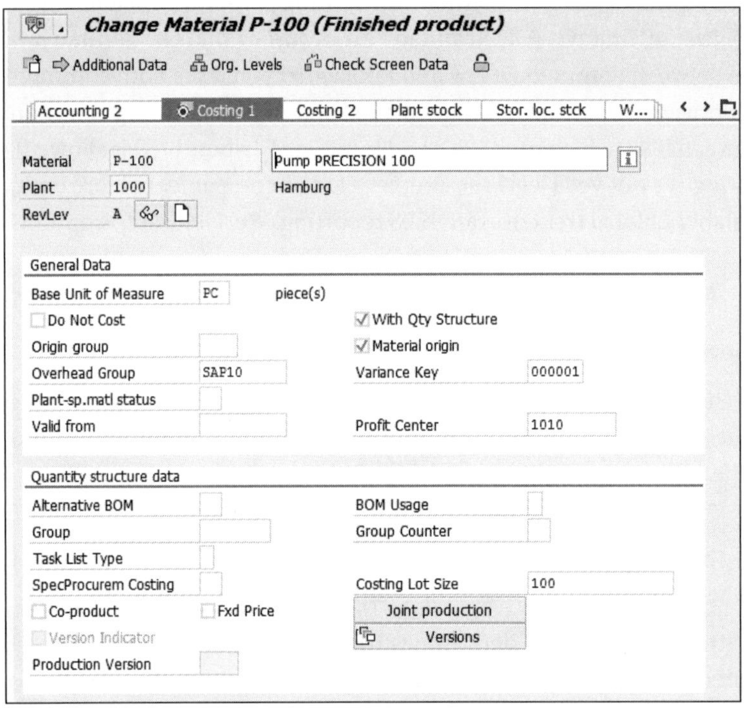

Figure 4.4 Material Master: Costing View

- You use the **Overhead Group** field if you need to calculate overhead percentages that are specific to certain groups of materials. In our example, the overhead group is SAP10. We'll use this overhead group in Chapter 7 to determine the percentage of overhead to be applied for all materials assigned to overhead group SAP10.
- The **Profit Center** field assigns the material to a profit center for Profit Center Accounting. It's copied into all purchase order items, production orders, sales order items, and so on created for this material, unless you define a substitution rule to invoke a different logic. As you saw when we looked at the cost center in the previous chapter, the profit center is one of the key ways of segmenting your business, so it's worth giving a lot of thought to how you want each material to be reflected in your Segment Reporting if you report according to IFRS 8 or IAS 14.
- The variance key determines how variances are calculated and is copied into the production orders, process orders, and so on. We'll copy this variance key into a production order and then use it to calculate the variances for our production order in Chapter 7.

Quantity Determination

The costing view contains the costing lot size—the standard output quantity for the material and the basis for the standard costs. All other fields in this block are optional. You can specify that a particular BOM and routing should be used as a basis for costing, though most customer sites use the configuration settings for quantity structure determination in the costing variant to determine which BOM and routing are used.

There are also several fields that overlap with fields in the MRP views, which include the following (also shown in Figure 4.4):

- The production versions are defined centrally and determine the BOM and routing used in each version. You saw these used when we looked at product cost collectors in Chapter 3 because you generally define a separate product cost collector for each production version. You'll also see them later in Section 4.6, when we define procurement alternatives for costing. Note that the use of production versions becomes compulsory with SAP S/4HANA. To find out more, refer to SAP Note 2267880 (S4TWL BOM, Routing, Production Version)
- The **Coproduct** and **Fxd Price** checkboxes determine the handling of coproducts (multiple outputs from the same production process). The **Joint Production** button determines how costs are split to the products. We'll return to these checkboxes when we look at the BOMs for such products. Selecting the **Coproduct** checkbox also affects how you perform Cost Object Controlling because, as we noted in Chapter 2, only product cost by order is possible for joint production.

- If your manufacturing process involves multiple plants, don't overlook the special procurement key (labeled **SpecProcurem. Costing** in Figure 4.4); this field can provide a link to the other plants for costing. For example, you can establish in Customizing that a special procurement key links an input material in plant A with an output material in plant B. When costing the input material in plant A, the system then reads or calculates the product costs for the output material in plant B and rolls them up through the costing structure. You can use transfer control in Customizing to determine whether a new cost estimate is created in the other plant or an existing cost estimate is copied from the other plant.

4.1.4 MRP Views

Although not owned by the controlling department, the MRP views contain several fields that influence Product Costing.

When we talked about Cost Object Controlling in Chapter 2, we discussed the options for make to order and make to stock. The procurement type in the MRP 2 view controls whether the material is made in-house, procured externally, or both. Depending on your configuration, the strategy group or the MRP class controls how the requirements category for the sales order item is determined. The requirements category determines whether the material is made to order or made to stock. The settings in the MRP 4 view control whether all dependent items are made to order (individual requirements) or whether standard items are made to stock (collective requirements).

The options for setting planned scrap are also covered here. You can enter component scrap when you know that a given percentage of additional components is usually wasted during manufacture. Entering scrap results in the component requirements being raised accordingly when the material usage is calculated. You can also enter assembly scrap when you know that problems at individual operations usually result in the assembly being damaged. This results in the order lot size or the costing lot size being raised accordingly to end up with the desired lot size.

4.1.5 Sales View

The sales view shown in Figure 4.5 is created by sales organization and distribution channels, organizational units that you'll find in the sales order. It's generally worth clicking on the **Conditions** button to check the price conditions here, because these affect the revenues and sales deductions in Profitability Analysis. Normally, controlling has no control over the negotiation of price conditions but analyzes them and makes recommendations as part of sales controlling. Notice the assignment to a division and to a material group here. We'll see these characteristics when we create a sales order item in Chapter 6 and look at how the product is reflected in Profitability Analysis.

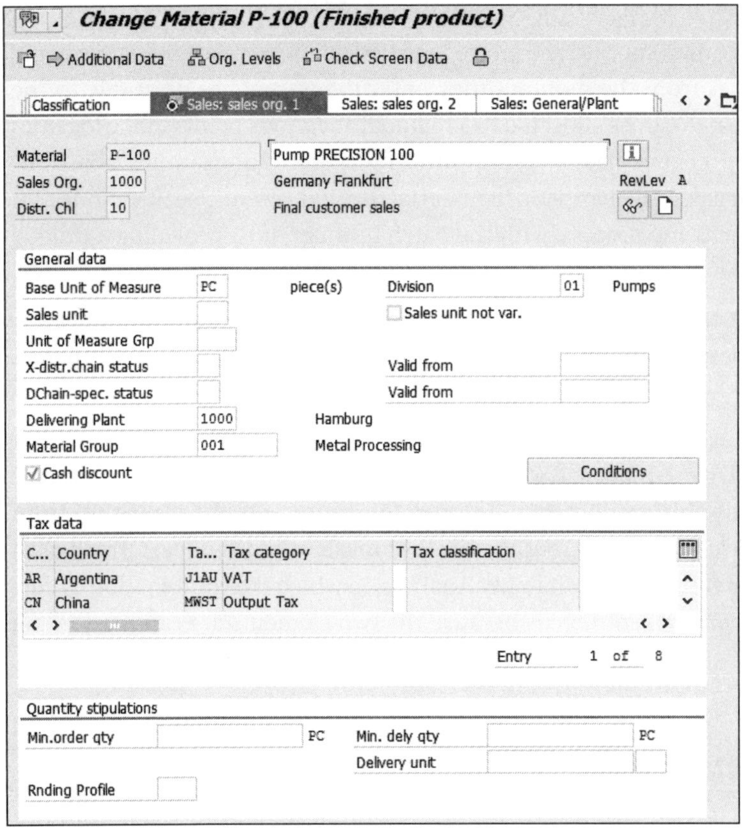

Figure 4.5 Material Master: Sales View

4.1.6 Batches

In the chemical, pharmaceutical, and food industries, materials have to be managed in *batches* to ensure traceability and ensure that each batch meets the specifications of the process (often determined via a quality control process). The batch quantity represents a nonreproducible unit with unique specifications. The batch is a subset of the material, and batches of a material are managed separately in stock. The specifications for the batch are set up using classification, so a batch might be identified, for example, by its viscosity and its color.

For accounting, the batch can be valued separately, especially if it includes active ingredients or other elements that significantly affect the value of a volume of material (e.g., the fat content in a liter of milk or a kilogram of cheese). This is achieved by setting the value category to allow split valuation in the **Accounting 1** view.

Batch management may apply to the entire logistics chain, with raw materials being managed as batches from the moment they enter the warehouse until sale to the final customer. A batch can be allocated to a material at various points in the logistics process by creating a batch master record with a specific ID. For example, a batch ID may be created for a partial quantity of a material that has certain specifications as it leaves the manufacturing process, with the batch number or ID providing a unique identification of the quantity produced.

In Product Costing, the costs of individual batches are mixed to provide the value per material. In the Material Ledger, each batch can be handled as if it were a separate material.

We've now looked at the master data for each material that we might make or sell, but we cannot sell such a product until we've also created a customer master for the customer who will buy this product. In CO terms, this represents the transition from Product Costing—in which all activities, whether make or buy, are performed with reference to the material—to Profitability Analysis, in which the combination of customer and product comes into focus because the two elements are captured in the sales order.

4.2 Customer Masters

In Chapter 2, we looked at an example of a report for Profitability Analysis. The key information for any kind of customer-based analysis is set up in the customer master, which is shared between the sales department and accounts receivable. For controlling, there is significantly less information in the customer master than in the material master (which controls the whole procurement and production process). The main points of interest are the code for the customer (which is used to select the customer for analysis or as a receiver of an allocation) and the company code (which determines which company will carry the revenue for any sales to this customer).

The customer master also includes the reconciliation account used to store details of the open item in the General Ledger. This reconciliation account stores the revenue earned with the customer and appears in both account-based Profitability Analysis and Material Ledger Reporting. This account is also linked with a value field for cost-based Profitability Analysis.

To create a customer master, you can use Transaction XD01 or go to **Logistics • Sales and Distribution • Master Data • Business Partner • Customer • Create • Complete.** Figure 4.6 shows a sample customer and the assignment to the customer account. We'll see this account when we deliver goods to our customer in Chapter 6, Section 6.1.3. To understand the significance of the customer account, you need to understand how accounts receivable links with the General Ledger. The General Ledger stores the totals for this account so that customer receivables in total can be displayed in the balance sheet. Accounts Receivable, on the other hand, stores details of the payments owed by every customer so that each open item can be cleared when the customer makes the payment. The information shown here is sufficient to monitor any customer outside of your organization. We'll look at the fields relevant for monitoring sales between affiliated companies in Section 4.10.4.

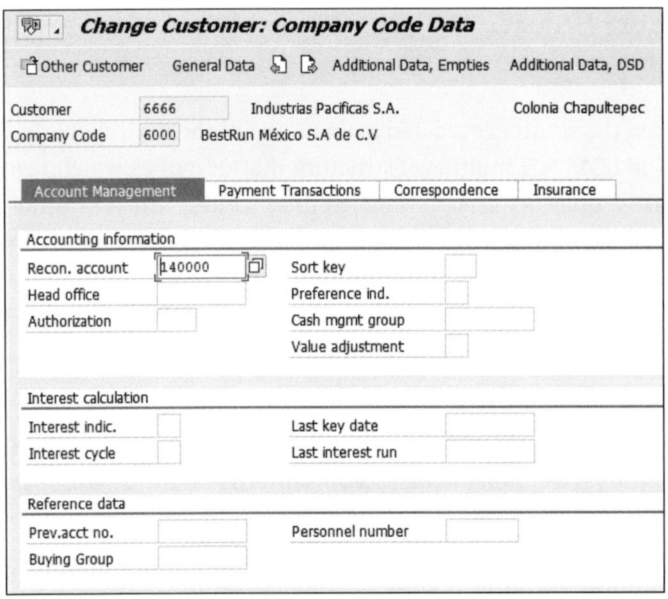

Figure 4.6 Customer Master Record

Business Partners in SAP S/4HANA

Transaction XD01 is no longer supported as of SAP S/4HANA 1511, in which the use of the business partner to represent both customers and vendors becomes compulsory (see SAP Note 2265093 [S4TWL—Business Partner Approach]). You'll sometimes find this referred to as customer vendor integration (CVI). However, table KNA1 continues to exist, as do the fields for customer (KUNNR), ship-to party (KUNWE), bill-to party (KUNRE), and so on that are used to fill the CO-PA characteristics.

Because of the central nature of both the material master and the customer master, there has been a trend in recent years to take maintenance out of the hands of the individual departments and perform it centrally. You might want to refer to Chapter 9 to find out how to handle material and customer masters centrally before moving on to the more local production master data, for which it's still much more common for local plants to perform master data maintenance. We'll now look at the master data that needs to be in place before the product can be manufactured—namely, the BOM, the routing, and the work centers where the operation is performed.

4.3 Bills of Material

In Chapter 2, we introduced the multilevel costed BOM as one of the key reports for Product Cost Planning. The BOM is a multilevel structure that describes which raw materials are used to make a quantity of semifinished product and which semifinished products are used to make a quantity of finished product. Before a material can be included in a BOM, it must exist as a material master. The levels of the BOM are then built up in stages, with a BOM existing for each finished and semifinished material.

There are two approaches to ownership of the BOM for Product Cost Planning.

1. The first is simply to use the same BOM for costing as is used in production. This has the advantage that the production planners work with the same structures as the cost accountants, but it requires you to set up clear rules for collaboration so that any errors discovered during costing can quickly be corrected.
2. The other approach is to create dedicated BOMs for costing. This can be useful at the start of an implementation, when production may not yet be up to speed. The approach has the advantage that the cost accountants are in the lead, but it risks

inaccuracies if the costing BOM drifts away from the production BOM. This is handled by setting the appropriate BOM usage in the BOM header and then configuring the quantity structure determination in the costing variant to select the most appropriate BOM for product costing.

It's also worth considering how you handle engineering BOMs. These exist in the early stages of a product's lifecycle and often have a different granularity from production BOMs because many decisions that will affect the final BOM have yet to be made. SAP recently introduced a new approach in this area, SAP Product Lifecycle Costing (SAP PLC), which supports the costing process in the early stages of product development during which the master data required for costing is still evolving.

Lean Accounting

Lean accounting encourages the use of accurate BOMs and routings to allow you to backflush using the standard material and production costs. Having more than one BOM for any given product is wasteful. It's better to have one accurate set of BOMs than to have two different ones and spend time arguing about which BOM represents the true material usage.

To display a BOM, use Transaction CS03 or go to **Logistics • Production Planning • Master Data • Bills of Material • Bill of Material • Material BOM • Display**, and enter the material number, plant, and appropriate BOM usage.

Figure 4.7 shows a sample BOM for the manufacture of pump P-100. It consists mostly of materials of item category L for materials kept in stock. Items of category R have to be cut to size first, and the BOM contains directions for this process. Other BOMs may contain materials of category N for materials that have to be procured specially and text items. Figure 4.8 shows how this BOM is used in costing. The left side of the screen shows the eight materials used to make the pump. Because the top five materials are assemblies, they have their own BOMs, which are also evaluated during costing. Clicking on the arrow icon takes you to the costed BOM for each item. The process of rolling up the costs through the multilevel BOM structure is called *product roll-up*.

If you're unsure which BOM has been used for costing, check the details on the **Quantity Structure** tab, as shown in Figure 4.8. It's worth noting that BOM structures are time-dependent, and costing selects the BOM items on a specific key date (entered in the costing run). If you're unsure, use the **Dates** tab shown in Figure 4.8 to check the quantity structure date used to read the BOM. Notice that in our example the production version field is blank. In SAP S/4HANA, the use of the production version becomes compulsory, and all BOMs must be part of a production version. You'll find details of how to make the transition in SAP Note 2267880 (S4TWL—BOM, Routing, Production Version).

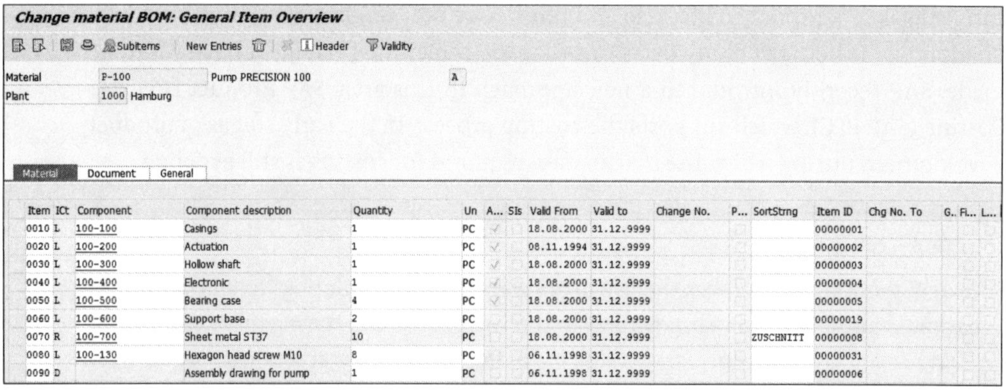

Figure 4.7 Sample BOM

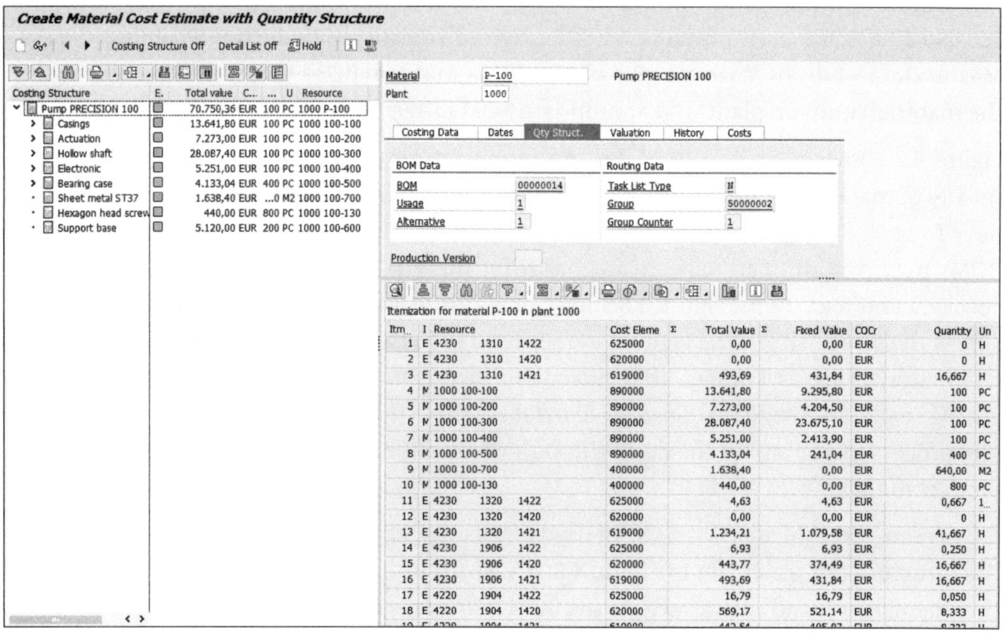

Figure 4.8 Cost Estimate for BOM

Lean Bills of Material

One trend you may want to be aware of here is the move toward simpler BOMs (the so-called pile of parts) rather than multilevel BOMs. For production, each arrow in Figure 4.8 represents a semifinished product that will be manufactured and delivered to stock. Each issue to and receipt from inventory interrupts the flow of production and can lead to piles of inventory building up, waiting for a sales order to request their usage. One way of getting around this is to use *order networks*, in which each production order immediately picks up from the previous production order without waiting for the material to be delivered to and issued from stock. For controlling, however, this posting to and from stock is needed to ensure proper variance analysis. Therefore, if you work with order networks you should ensure that your configuration team sets the flag in the order type for the plant that specifies that a goods receipt, and a simultaneous goods issue should be generated when each production order hands over to the next.

4.3.1 Quantity Definition

In general, the quantities given in the BOM determine the quantities needed to manufacture a given lot size of the finished product. One exception is when spoilage is anticipated. Sometimes the manufacturing process is such that it's *never* possible to achieve the full output quantity in the order (computer chips are an obvious example). In other cases, experience tells that there will be some loss along the way. In either case, a planned scrap percentage can be defined in the BOM. Entering 5% scrap for a component means that if 100 units are normally required to manufacture 100 units of the finished product, then 105 units are included in Product Costing to account for the anticipated loss. This planned scrap is included in the scrap layout for the itemization (one of the layouts you saw when we looked at the product cost itemization in Chapter 2).

Another exception is the handling of components for inventory costing. In this case, you can flag material costs as relevant, partially relevant, or not relevant. Partially relevant items are linked with a percentage in Customizing, allowing you to specify that, for example, only 60% of the packaging costs should be included in inventory costing for balance sheet purposes.

4.3.2 Coproducts and Byproducts

In our pump example, multiple components were used to manufacture *one* finished product. In some industries, the BOM is turned on its head, and *several* finished products may result from one production process (known as *joint production*). Meat production is an extreme example, in which a single side of beef is processed to provide many different forms of meat product, but joint production is also common in the chemical and pharmaceutical industries, in which several products may result from the same manufacturing process, some more valuable than others. SAP distinguishes between *coproducts* and *byproducts*. Both are included in the BOM with a negative quantity (see Figure 4.9), but coproducts are flagged as such in the costing and MRP view of the material master. The key differences are as follows:

- *Coproducts* are considered equally valid outputs of the production process when manufacture is intentional (planned). During Product Costing, they're shown in the itemization with item category A and negative costs. During order costing, an order item is created for each coproduct. Each item is delivered to stock and has its own status. The order costs split to the order items in accordance with equivalence numbers during settlement. Variances can be calculated for each order item following settlement. The costs for the order items are then settled to stock. During reporting of the production or process order, you can view the details for the coproducts by selecting **Extras • Order items • On/Off**.
- *Byproducts* are considered incidental outputs of the production process; their manufacture is incidental (unplanned). They differ from coproducts in that a fixed price is set in the material master. They reduce the costs of the production process.

A *fixed-price coproduct* (see Figure 4.4) is a mixture of coproduct and byproduct. The order contains an order item for this coproduct, but it's treated with a fixed price like a byproduct. Figure 4.9 shows the BOM for the manufacture of paint.

The manufacture of the paint also results in the manufacture of paste (a coproduct). Contaminated water occurs as a byproduct, and there's a catalyst that can be recovered from the process. All of these are shown with negative quantities in the BOM. Every material in this list is linked with the operation to which it will be issued. This assignment is important for the calculation of WIP and scrap per operation, a subject we'll return to in Chapter 7.

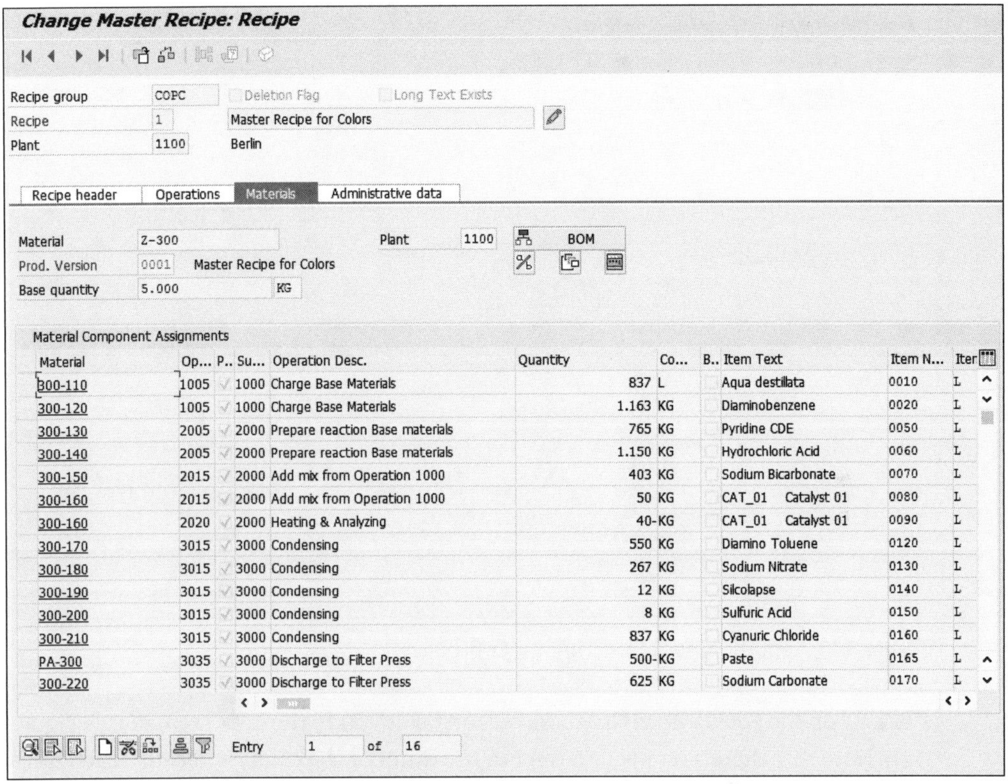

Figure 4.9 Sample BOM for Joint Production

If you create a process order for material Z-300, order items are automatically created for each of the coproducts. You'll see this in Chapter 6. Costs captured at the order level are then split to the order items based on equivalence numbers in the settlement rule. The equivalence numbers for the splitting are defined in the material master in the form of an apportionment structure. The simplest option is to split all the costs in the same way, such as 80% to the first coproduct and 20% to the second product. But if the split is different depending on the type of costs incurred, then you can use a *source structure* to separate the material costs, production costs, and so on and then define a different percentage split for each of the elements in the source structure. Figure 4.10 shows the apportionment structure used for material Z-300. To see this, select the **Costing 1** view of the material master and then click on the **Joint Production** button.

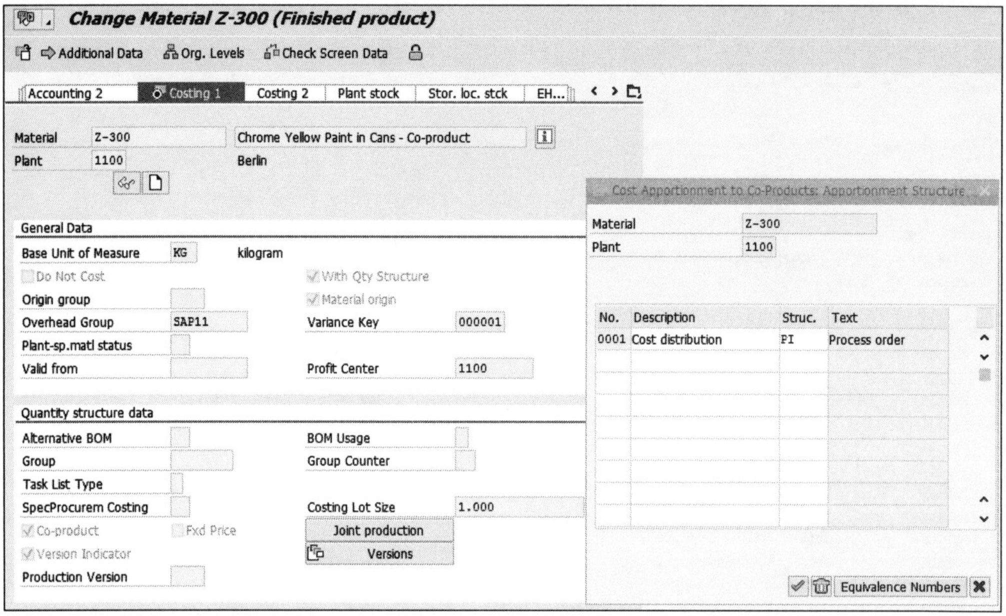

Figure 4.10 Apportionment Structure for Coproducts

Clicking on the **Equivalence Numbers** button takes you to the detail screen (see Figure 4.11). Note that there's no need to refer to the water or the catalyst because each has a fixed price, entered in the material master. Only the materials to which the order costs must be split are referred to in the apportionment structure. One of the challenges for the controller here is to keep these equivalence numbers up to date. Especially in the chemical industry, the relative output of the coproducts is rarely completely stable, and these equivalence numbers need to be adjusted regularly in the material master—and in some cases for every order. For the food industry, there has been some extra development in the context of SAP Catch Weight Management to allow you to define quantity-based equivalence numbers to account for the relative weights of different meat products.

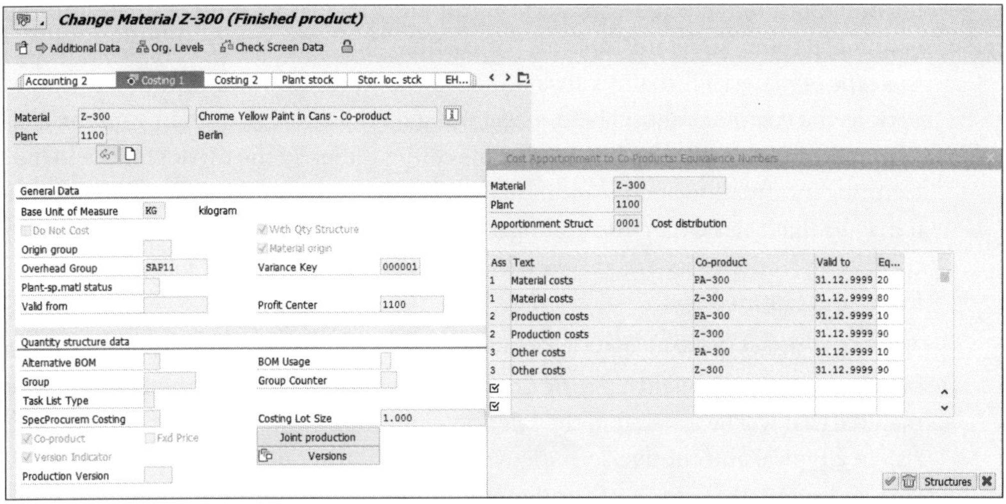

Figure 4.11 Apportionment Structure for Coproducts

4.3.3 Recursive BOMs

In some industries, it's also common for BOM structures to be recursive (or circular). A familiar household example might be the production of yogurt, for which the BOM might include milk, sugar, and a small amount of yogurt cultures. This BOM structure is therefore a cycle, because yogurt is both an input and an output. During Product Costing, each cycle has to be calculated separately before the next costing level is handled. The materials within a cycle are costed iteratively until they converge. Only then is the next costing level in the BOM costed.

4.3.4 Configurable BOMs

In the automotive industry, it's common for the final product to be heavily configurable, with the customer selecting the paint color, engine size, wheels, seats, stereo system, and so on as he places his order. To handle this variability, the BOM for the vehicle includes all the possible options, together with certain rules that determine which combinations are technically feasible. Such materials that include all options are known as *configurable materials*. For the controlling department, it's not possible to set a standard price for the configurable material, because it contains all possible options that a customer might choose. The cost estimate is generally created in the sales order once the customer has selected his options and is in the process of placing his order. But for selected variants you can prepare a cost estimate in advance by defining certain "standard" options for costing. The other thing that characterizes this type of material is that it's always made to order (because we have to know what options the customer chose) before beginning manufacture. Depending on the configuration, however, it may be that the sales order is merely the carrier for the manufacturing information and no additional costs will be captured for the sales order, or it may be that Sales Order Controlling (see Chapter 2) is required, because additional costs, such as the costs associated with discussing the configuration with the customer, are captured on the sales order.

Figure 4.12 shows the MRP view for a material master for a configurable material. The important section is **Plant-Specific Configuration**, which provides the link from the material that will be entered in the sales order and all possible variants of that material. In a typical automotive scenario, you might find about 2,000 "standard" products and many thousands of configurations, because every car sold is potentially unique.

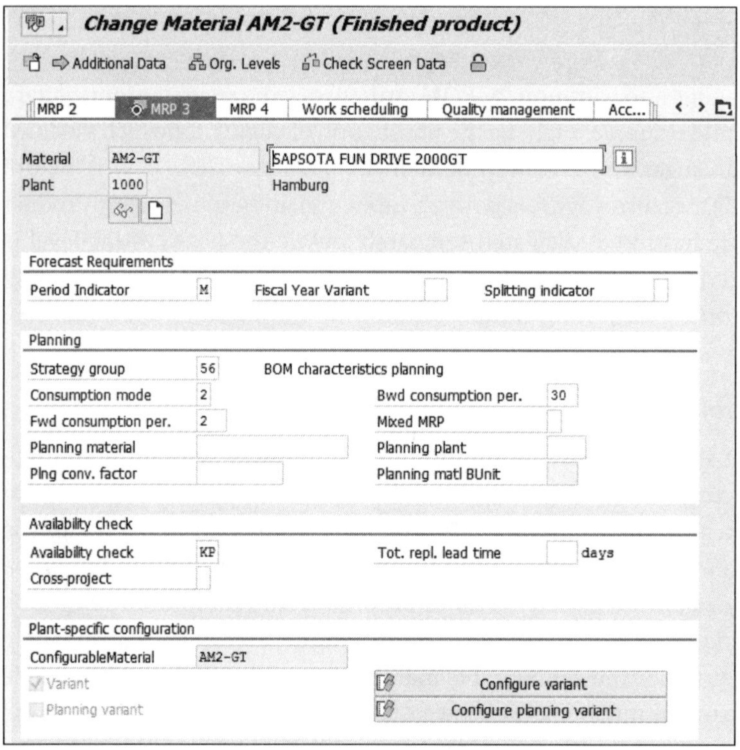

Figure 4.12 Material Master for Configurable Material

The BOM for this assembly contains all possible options, as shown in Figure 4.13. Compared to the normal BOM that is simply a list of the parts to be used, there's an extra tab, **Class**. The BOM itself contains several similar components (such as multiple choices of paint finishes). At the point of sale, the customer selects his chosen options, and the BOM is reduced to contain only those components that will be used in production. The technical variants that the customer is allowed are defined in the classification system, which is why the important data for a configurable BOM is in the **Class** tab.

4

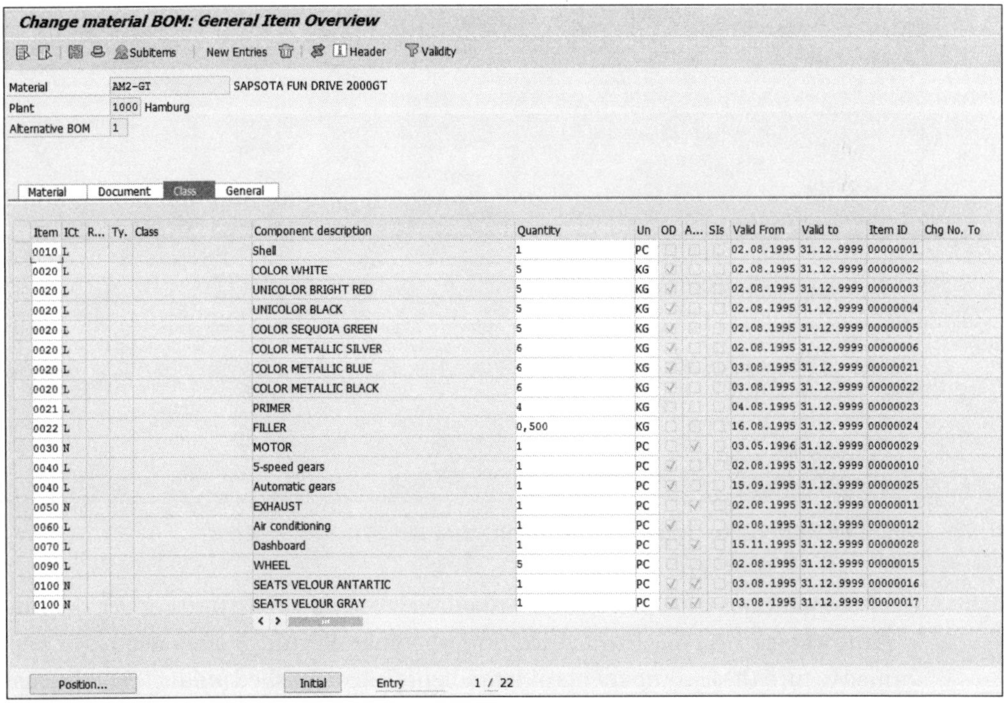

Figure 4.13 BOM for Configurable Material

For planning, it's also possible to define certain standard configurations from within the material master and to use these for planning. Such a configuration is shown in Figure 4.14. Here items with variants are represented as characteristics. Normally, the process of picking the relevant characteristics doesn't take place until the customer places the order, but you can define certain plan variants in advance and store them in the MRP view of the material master. This information can then be used to set the standard costs for the standard product variant. Here you can see the characteristic value **Paint**, which determines the color picked from the BOM in Figure 4.13.

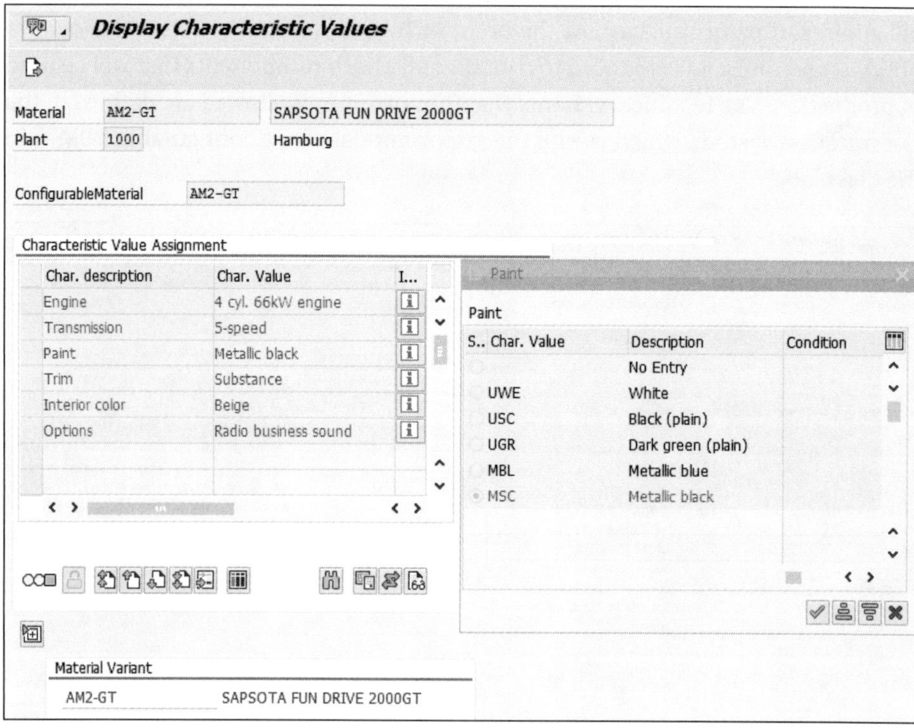

Figure 4.14 Choosing Options for Planning Variant

The BOM indicates what materials are required to manufacture the product, but this isn't the whole story. We also have to know what manufacturing steps need to be performed to turn these components or ingredients into a finished product that the customer will buy. These steps are defined in the routing.

4.4 Routings

In Chapter 2, we introduced itemization as one of the key reports for Product Cost Planning that shows the manufacturing operations performed according to the *routing*, which determines the processing steps to be performed in the manufacture of the material, the material components assigned to that step, and any planned scrap anticipated in the step.

We described how to set up activity types such as machine time, labor time, and so on in Chapter 3. These activity types must be linked with the operations in the routing or recipe for Product Costing.

4.4.1 Types of Routing

There are several types of routing, including standard routings, rate routings, and master recipes. Further task lists exist for use in maintenance and customer service, but they all have the same basic structure:

- The standard routing is the most commonly used type of routing and describes the quantities of work required to create a given number of units of the finished products. You'll find such routings wherever there is batch-oriented production, describing the steps to create each finished product or semifinished product. Our pump example provides a classic use case for this kind of routing. To display a standard routing, you can use Transaction CA03 or go to **Logistics • Production • Master Data • Routings • Standard Routings • Display**. If you're selecting them for use in Product Costing, the standard routings have type N.
- The rate routing describes the throughput of the process volume in a given time frame. Rate routings emerged with lean manufacturing and attempts to describe production as a more or less constant flow rather than as a series of disjointed batches with deliveries to inventory for each semifinished product. To display a rate routing, you can use Transaction CA23 or go to **Logistics • Production • Master Data • Routings • Rate Routings • Display**. If you're selecting them for use in Product Costing, the standard routings have type R.
- The master recipe is used in the pharmaceutical and chemical industries and describes the production of one or more materials in one production run. From a costing point of view, master recipes are essentially a combination of a standard routing and a BOM but include additional functions for material quantity calculation that are specific to these industries. Our paint example uses a recipe rather than a routing, so we saw that all items in the material list were linked with an operation. Operations may be broken down into phases. To display a master recipe, you can use Transaction C203 or go to **Logistics • Production—Process • Master Data • Master Recipes • Recipes and Material List • Display**. If you're selecting them for use in Product Costing, the standard routings have type 2.

One thing to be aware of is that, as you saw for the BOM, it's possible to have routings and recipes that belong to production and routings and recipes that belong to controlling. Again, this may be a good way of getting started, but in the long term it's better to strive for one accurate set of recipes rather than multiple versions of the truth. Figure 4.15 shows a sample master recipe for the manufacture of paints, showing the operations and suboperations performed to manufacture the paint and the resources at which each operation is performed. On the far right of the screen are the base quantity (5,000 kg) and the standard values—the number of minutes taken to perform the task to deliver the base quantity. This is needed to calculate the standard times for Product Costing.

If you go back to Figure 2.18 in Chapter 2, you'll see the costs per operation in the cost estimate.

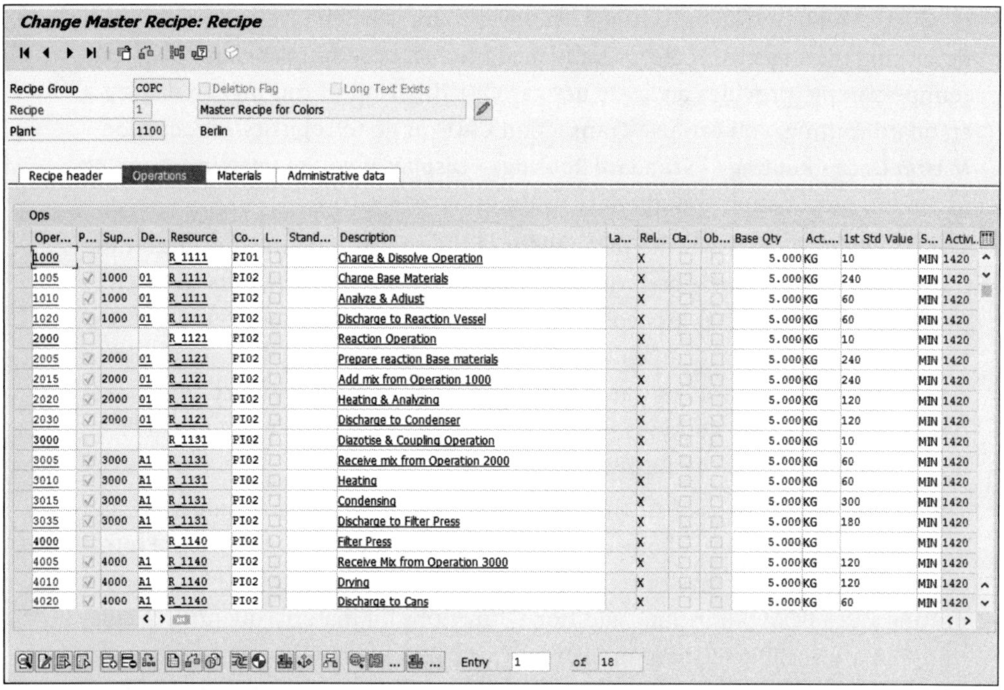

Figure 4.15 Sample Recipe

Although the controlling department does not own the recipes and routings, it must work with production to ensure that the values per operation are correct and that the correct materials are assigned to each operation. You'll see how important this is when we look at the calculation of WIP and scrap in Chapter 7. When considering how to value scrap and WIP bear the following points in mind:

- If the product has to be scrapped at the first operation, it's important that only those materials are included in the scrap value that have genuinely been issued from stock for this operation.
- If some of your components are very expensive, make sure they're issued at the correct operation to ensure that the WIP capitalized for each operation is correct.

4.4.2 Operation Values

Each operation in a routing or recipe contains a control key, which determines whether the operation is performed in-house or externally and whether costs are calculated for the operation. Figure 4.16 shows a sample operation with control key PI02. You can reach this screen by double-clicking on the correct line for the operation, shown in Figure 4.15.

Each operation includes standard values for the manufacture of a particular base quantity of the product. As you learned for the BOM, it's also possible to flag operations as relevant for costing, partially relevant, or not relevant. In our example, to manufacture 5,000 kg of the base quantity, 240 minutes (or four hours) of activity type 1420 would be required. The activity type is linked with the resource (because this is a process industry example) or a work center to determine the cost center supplying the activity and the activity price.

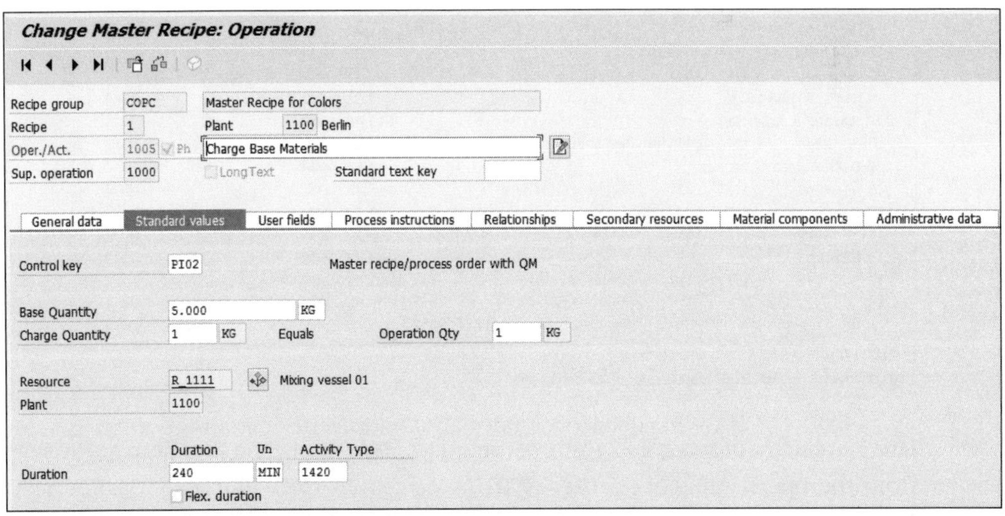

Figure 4.16 Sample Operation

If we now look at the cost estimate for material Z-300, we can display the itemization (i.e., the list of costing items from the BOM and routing) and the assignment of the items to the operations by selecting the **Operations** layout (see Chapter 2). Figure 4.17 shows the cost estimate for material Z-300. We looked at Operation 1005 (Charge Base Materials) in Figure 4.16.

Create Material Cost Estimate with Quantity Structure

Costing Structure On   Detail List Off   Hold

Itemization for material Z-300 in plant 1100

It...	I...	Resource	Resource (Text)	Σ	Total Value	Currncy	Quantity	Un
31	G	4130 655100	OHS Raw Material		151,62	EUR		
32	G	4130 655300	OHS Administration		0,00	EUR		
33	G	4130 655400	OHS Sales & Distrib.		0,00	EUR		
< not assigned >				▪	**151,62**	**EUR**		
1	E	4240 R_1111 1420	Charge Base Materials		395,07	EUR	4	H
2	M	1100 300-110	Aqua destillata		0,86	EUR	167,400	L
3	M	1100 300-120	Diaminobenzene		179,10	EUR	232,600	KG
1005 Charge Base Materials				▪	**575,03**	**EUR**		
4	E	4240 R_1111 1420	Analyze & Adjust		98,77	EUR	1	H
1010 Analyze & Adjust				▪	**98,77**	**EUR**		
5	E	4240 R_1111 1420	Discharge to Reaction V...		98,77	EUR	1	H
1020 Discharge to Reaction Vessel				▪	**98,77**	**EUR**		
6	E	4240 R_1121 1420	Prepare reaction Base ...		395,07	EUR	4	H
7	M	1100 300-130	Pyridine CDE		163,71	EUR	153	KG
8	M	1100 300-140	Hydrochloric Acid		540,50	EUR	230	KG
2005 Prepare reaction Base materials				▪	**1.099,28**	**EUR**		
9	E	4240 R_1121 1420	Add mix from Operation...		395,07	EUR	4	H
10	M	1100 300-150	Sodium Bicarbonate		51,58	EUR	80,600	KG
11	M	1100 300-160	CAT_01 Catalyst 01		2,60	EUR	10	KG
2015 Add mix from Operation 1000				▪	**449,25**	**EUR**		
12	E	4240 R_1121 1420	Heating & Analyzing		197,54	EUR	2	H
13	M	1100 300-160	CAT_01 Catalyst 01		2,08-	EUR	8-	KG
2020 Heating & Analyzing				▪	**195,46**	**EUR**		
14	E	4240 R_1121 1420	Discharge to Condenser		197,54	EUR	2	H
2030 Discharge to Condenser				▪	**197,54**	**EUR**		
15	E	4240 R_1131 1420	Receive mix from Opera...		98,77	EUR	1	H
3005 Receive mix from Operation 2000				▪	**98,77**	**EUR**		
16	E	4240 R_1131 1420	Heating		98,77	EUR	1	H
3010 Heating				▪	**98,77**	**EUR**		
17	E	4240 R_1131 1420	Condensing		493,84	EUR	5	H
18	M	1100 300-170	Diamino Toluene		28,60	EUR	110	KG
19	M	1100 300-180	Sodium Nitrate		125,49	EUR	53,400	KG

Figure 4.17 Operations in Cost Estimate

Line 1 is an item of category E (internal activity). Here we see the four hours of activity from the operation, work center R_1111, cost center 4240, and activity type 1420. Notice that two raw materials—aqua destillata (300-110) and diaminobenzene (300-120)—are assigned to this operation (these costing items are shown above the totals line for the operation). This is important for when we calculate WIP and scrap in Chapter 7, because we want to be sure the material usage is recorded at the correct operation. Also notice that three costing items haven't been assigned to an operation. These are the percentage overheads applied to the cost estimate as a whole rather than to individual operations. We'll look at how to set up the percentages for this allocation in Chapter 7, Section 7.2.

It's also possible to define planned scrap for an operation. This can be used to set the assembly scrap in the material master. You can see this in the cost estimate by selecting the layout for the scrap view.

4.4.3 Operation-Level Costing

When you look at the reports in the standard cost estimate, you'll see the costs of each operation or suboperation. However, if you look at the costs for an individual production order or process order, you'll see the costs and quantities for each cost center/activity type combination but no mention of the operation. This is because order costs are assigned at the order header level, and the operation doesn't exist as an account assignment object in Controlling.

The only exceptions to this rule in SAP ERP are the operations for a maintenance or service order. The option to use the operation as an account assignment for a maintenance or service order was introduced in EHP 5 for SAP ERP 6.0 with the business function LOG_EAM_OLC. Logistics, Controlling, and financial transactions were enhanced to allow the use of the operation as an account assignment object. We'll look at how this works in more detail in Chapter 6, Section 6.3.5. In SAP ERP, it's not possible to capture costs for production orders by operation. However, this situation changes with SAP S/4HANA, as we will discuss in Chapter 14.

The routings, recipes, and rate routings describe the steps required to manufacture a product, but they don't tell you *where* each step takes place. We need to know where the operation is performed to establish the link with the cost centers and activity types we defined in Chapter 3 and determine the value of the internal activity being supplied to production. In this way, we'll prepare the charge for the four hours of activity we saw in Figure 4.17.

4.5 Work Centers and Resources

Work centers and resources are used for capacity requirements planning and scheduling in Logistics. Every operation in a routing must be assigned to a work center (the place where the operation is performed). The work center includes formulas that determine how each standard value in the operation is interpreted (fixed in the case of setup time and varying with the lot size in the case of machine time and labor time). You can also include an efficiency rate to take account of different efficiencies in the operation:

- To display a work center, use Transaction CR03 or go to **Logistics • Production • Master Data • Work Centers • Work Center • Display**.
- To display a resource, use Transaction CRC3 or go to **Logistics • Production—Process • Master Data • Resources • Resource • Display**.

For costing, every work center and resource must be assigned to a single cost center. This link is defined for a specified validity period. Figure 4.18 shows the resource used in the operation to manufacture the paint we showed earlier. You may recall that the activity type was 1420. The activity includes a formula key that determines how the activity quantities are calculated. For example, a setup operation may require a fixed effort of 15 minutes regardless of what lot size is in the order or cost estimate. The example shown in Figure 4.16 referred to a base quantity that's referenced in the formula.

The costing view in the work center determines the cost center that is linked with the work center and the activity types that can be performed at that work center. When you create a cost estimate, the quantity determination date will determine the timing of the selection.

Activity Types per Work Center

Confusion frequently arises about the limit of only six activity types at any work center. Why only six? The reason lies in SAP's understanding of the activity type as the *output measure* for the work center. The output measure is typically expressed in terms of drilling hours, welding hours, and so on. In other words, these are the outputs that are measured when order confirmation takes place.

When people want to use more than six activity types, they're often confusing inputs and outputs. A work center may supply welding hours, but it often uses energy hours, maintenance hours, and so on. If what you're really trying to do by using more than six activity types is see the impact of increases in energy prices, higher wage costs, or changes in depreciation on product profitability, then you should consider activating the *primary cost component* split for your activity rates. Without the primary cost component split, energy costs, wage costs, and so on are subsumed in the activity price for the welding hours. With the primary cost component split, you can break out the activity rate into its cost components, which might be wages, salaries, operating supplies, depreciation, energy, maintenance, and so on. We'll look at this process in more detail in Chapter 5.

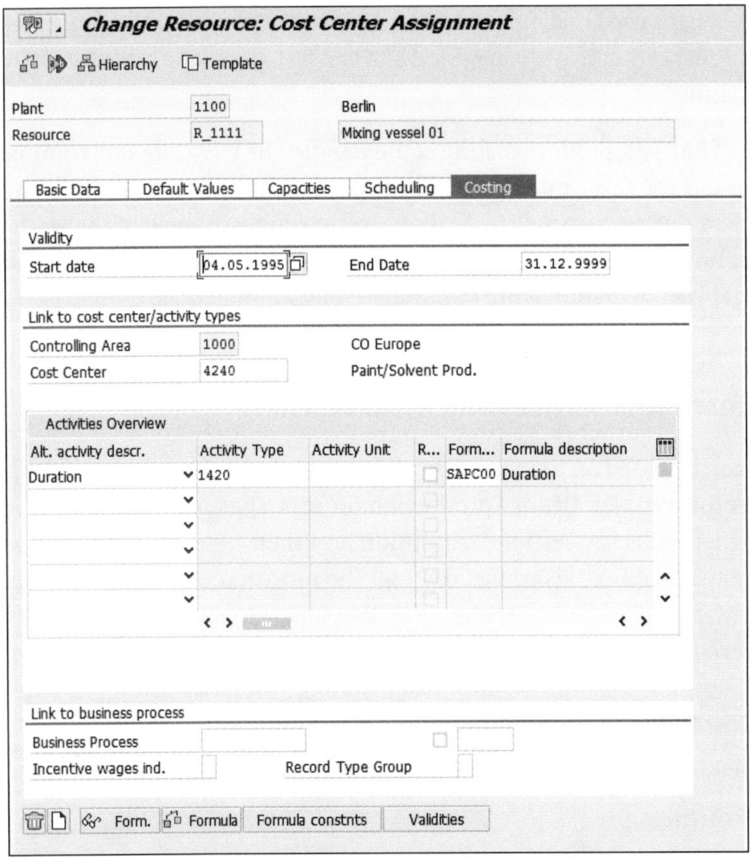

Figure 4.18 Sample Work Center/Resource

Looking at Figure 4.18, note the **Capacities** tab in the resource. This is used during capacity requirements planning to determine how many units can be handled in each operation. When we look at Cost Center Planning in Chapter 5, you'll see that you can also enter a *capacity* for each cost center and activity type in a given period. This is sometimes a source of confusion, but the two are quite different:

- The *work center* capacity refers to the ability of a single machine to perform a given operation. It affects the activity quantity calculations in Product Costing because to produce a given lot size the operation has to be performed a given number of times. For example, if the capacity of an oven is 100 units, to deliver a lot size of 200 units the operation has to be performed twice.
- The *cost center/activity type* capacity refers to the whole period and can cover multiple work centers. It's used to define a standard quantity output over all machines assigned to the cost center in a given period and can be used as the basis for activity price calculation.

In the early days of SAP R/3, product costing could handle one BOM and one routing, and it was the task of the Customizing settings to ensure that the correct BOM and routing were picked during costing. This was an overly simplistic view of the world. We'll now look at how to set up procurement alternatives to represent the different ways you can organize the manufacture or purchase of your materials.

4.6 Procurement Alternatives and Mixed Costing

Product costing can be based on a single BOM and routing for each material, but this does not consider the complexities of a production process. These can be reflected by creating procurement alternatives for each option and then weighting the relative use of each alternative within the product costing. The procurement alternatives are also used in the Material Ledger to separate the data for each alternative. To create procurement alternatives, you can use Transaction CK91N or go to **Accounting • Controlling • Product Cost Controlling • Product Cost Planning • Material Costing • Master Data for Mixed Cost Estimate • Edit Procurement Alternatives.**

4.6.1 Internal Processing

Procurement alternatives for internal processing are needed when several BOMs or routings exist for the manufacture of the same material or when the product can be manufactured externally when there is insufficient capacity to manufacture the required volume in-house. This may be the case if several production lines can manufacture the same product and capacity decisions determine which line is used.

Figure 4.19 shows a sample procurement alternative for in-house production of ACT-DCD. This simply references the production version that stores the BOM and routing used to manufacture material ACT-DCD in-house. We'll create a production order and manufacture this material according to this production version when we look at actual postings in Chapter 6.

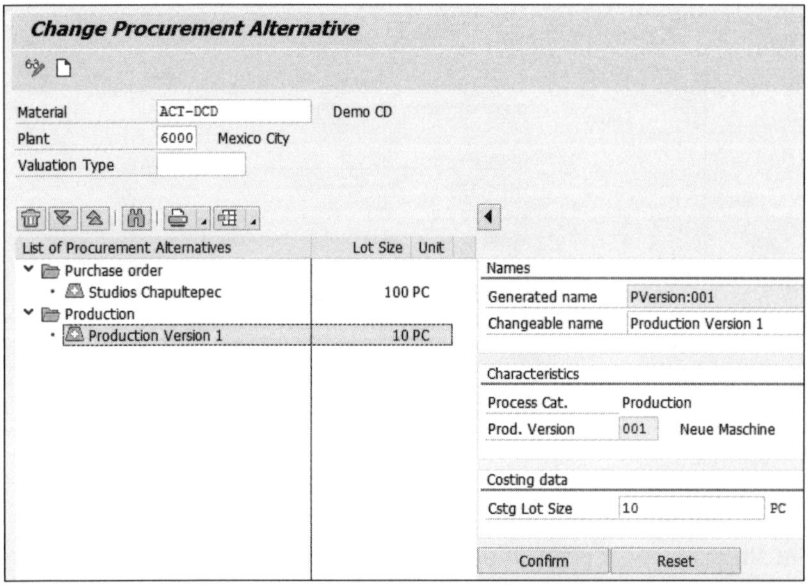

Figure 4.19 Procurement Alternative for Internal Processing

4.6.2 External Procurement

A procurement alternative by vendor is needed if the same material can be procured from several vendors or to support make-or-buy decisions for this material. A purchasing info record is maintained for each vendor. Figure 4.20 shows a procurement alternative for external procurement. Here we see the purchasing organization responsible for procurement and the vendor from whom material ACT-DCD is usually purchased. Instead of using a BOM and routing to perform costing, the information from the purchasing info record is read to determine the price conditions agreed upon with this vendor.

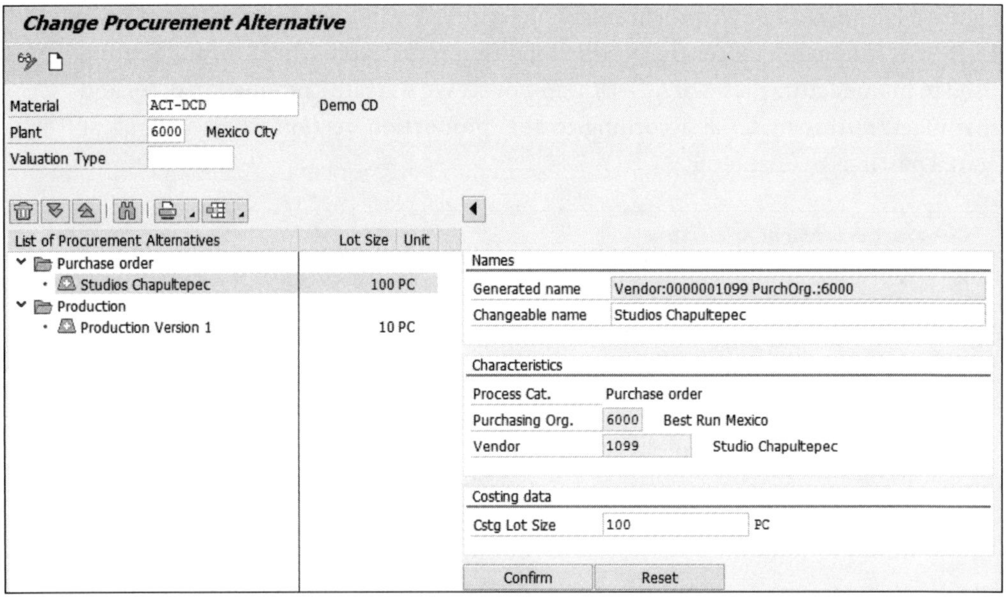

Figure 4.20 Procurement Alternative for External Procurement

4.6.3 Plant-to-Plant Transfer

Procurement alternatives for plant-to-plant transfer are needed if you manufacture the same material at multiple plants and transfer the semifinished products to a different plant for final assembly. In this case, you enter the name of the plant that will provide the stocks to be transferred. This corresponds to the use of the special procurement key in the costing view of the material master that we discussed earlier.

4.6.4 Subcontracting

Procurement alternatives are needed for *subcontracting*, in which several vendors can take your material components and complete the finished product for you. For costing, the BOM is used to determine the material components to be sent to the vendor(s) and a purchasing info record that defines the price charged for the work by each vendor. We'll come back to the subcontracting process in Chapter 6, Section 6.3.1 when we'll look at new options to give you more cost transparency for subcontracting.

4.6.5 Mixing Ratios

Before you can use any of these procurement alternatives to calculate standard costs, you must define mixing ratios that state what percentage of production is performed in-house and what percentage is performed externally. Although the procurement alternatives are largely in the hands of production and procurement, maintaining the mixing ratios is typically a controlling task because they are only needed for Product Costing. During material requirements planning, different mix factors may be used.

To create a mixing ratio or update an existing one, go to Transaction CK94 or **Accounting • Controlling • Product Cost Controlling • Product Cost Planning • Material Costing • Master Data for Mixed Cost Estimate • Mixing Ratios • Create/Change** and enter the material and plant. Because mixing ratios are not constant, the quantity structure type defines how long the ratio is valid. (Depending on the timescale of your standard costing, choose either a month or a year.) Then enter the relevant period and fiscal year. Figure 4.21 shows the mixing ratio for material ACT-DCD in plant 6000, where 90% is manufactured in-house using production version 1 and 10% is procured externally. We'll see this material again in Chapter 5 when we look at how to calculate standard costs and how the two cost estimates are weighted against one another.

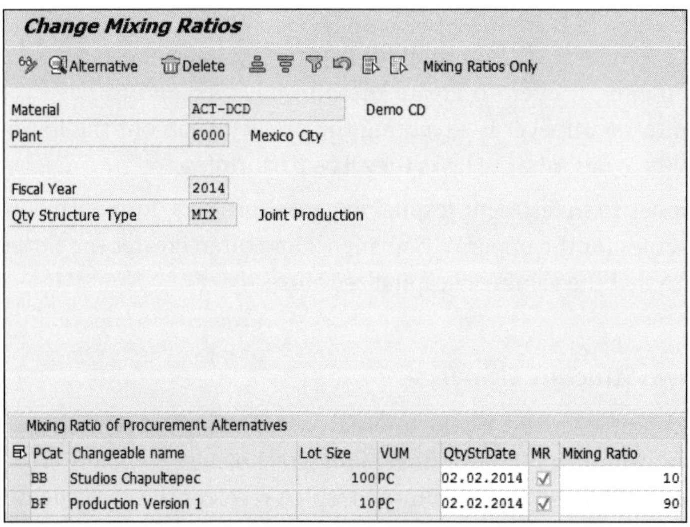

Figure 4.21 Mixing Ratio for Multiple Procurement Alternatives

We have now looked at the main master data required to describe how to manufacture a product and can proceed to create sales orders or production orders. In addition to this master data, many organizations also use projects, either for complex make-to-order production or to manage internal investments, such as building a new production line.

4.7 Projects

In Chapter 3, we looked at internal orders as a means of capturing marketing costs, research costs, and so on. From a controlling point of view, a project is in essence an internal order with a hierarchical structure. A project definition defines the header data for the entire project. The activities to be performed within the project are defined as WBS elements. In an engineer-to-order scenario, it's also common to assign networks and network activities to the WBS elements. Responsibility for project master data varies depending on the organization:

- For engineer-to-order scenarios, the engineering department is generally in the lead, because its members work with the customer to specify the technical details of each element of the project. Similarly, it's unusual for controlling to be in the lead for professional service projects, though this time it will be the manager of the consulting engagement who negotiates the details of the project with the client.
- For internal projects, however, it's common for controlling to establish rules for the upper WBS elements or even to create these in advance and to have the research departments, or whoever is executing the project, flesh out the lower-level detail of the WBS to describe the tasks they'll be performing.
- The same often applies to investment (capital expense) projects, for which controlling establishes rules for the upper WBS elements and often creates the settlement rules to ensure that the values are capitalized correctly.

4.7.1 Work Breakdown Structure Elements

WBS elements have a certain overlap with the internal orders we looked at in Chapter 3. They also have a status (open, released, final billing, technically complete, complete, etc.) and a settlement rule that determines to which receiver the project costs are charged. The type of receiver is affected by the project type (investment, overhead, engineer to order, etc.). To access any element in a project, use the project builder that shows WBS elements, networks, network activities, and so on. To display a project, use Transaction CJ20N or go to **Logistics • Project System • Projects • Project Builder** and then select the project definition that represents the header for the project as whole.

Figure 4.22 shows a WBS comprising several WBS elements for the steps required to obtain approval of a new drug. To see the basic data for each WBS element in the structure, click on the **Overview** icon (triangle). This takes you to a list of the control settings for each WBS element.

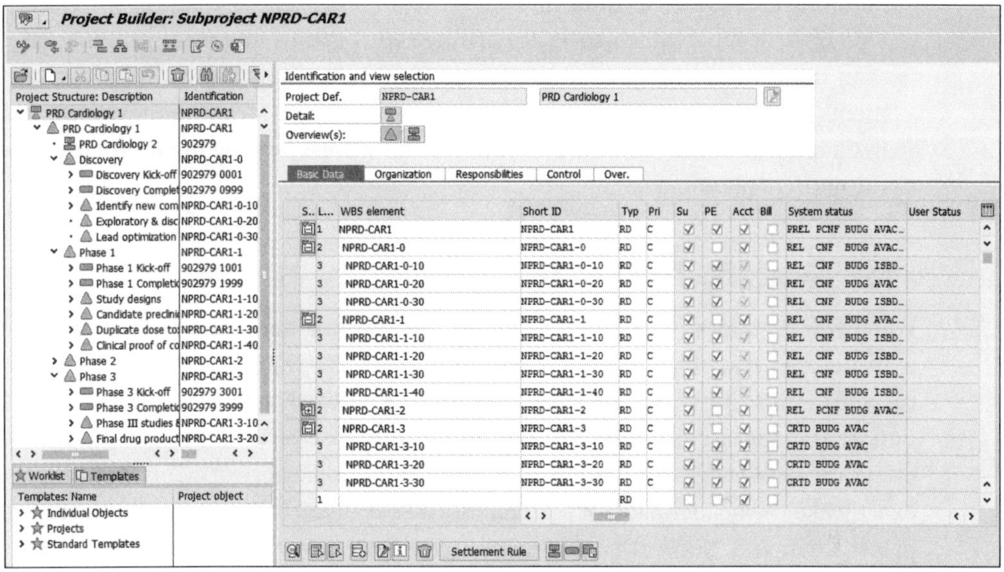

Figure 4.22 WBS Elements

You can issue materials to a WBS element, charge time to them, assign overheads, and so on, provided that the WBS element has the status **REL** (released). We'll look at examples of these postings in Chapter 6. The main difference with respect to an internal order is the hierarchical nature of the project, which becomes especially relevant when you assign the budget, because you may assign the budget at a much higher level than that at which you plan or capture actual costs.

When looking at how a project is handled from a controlling point of view, three checkboxes are important:

- **Billing elements (Bill column)**
  This defines the level at which revenue is captured (this mainly applies for commercial or customer projects to which the services are billed). The **Bill** checkbox is

unselected in our example because the example uses an internal research project for which costs are not charged to a customer. We're simply using the project to provide cost transparency.

- **Account assignment elements (Acct column)**
  This is the level at which costs are captured. In this example, you can assign costs to any of the WBS elements in the structure. We'll look at how to assign costs to a WBS element in Chapter 6, Section 6.3.4.
- **Planning elements (PE column)**
  This is the level at which costs are planned (this can be at a more granular level than the account assignment elements). In this example, only level-3 WBS elements are flagged as planning elements. We'll look at how to plan these elements in Chapter 5, Section 5.2, in which you'll see how these WBS elements are open for the entry of planning data.

4.7.2 Networks and Network Activities

When you need more accurate scheduling and deadline management, the WBS also may include networks and network activities. These also capture costs and have a status and settlement rule. To display networks or network activities, use the Project Builder as in the last example, but click on the **Network Overview** icon and then select one of the networks in the list. Figure 4.23 shows a sample network. This looks almost exactly like the header data for a production order if you compare it with the examples in Chapter 6. Networks and network activities carry status information and are assigned to the organizational units in SAP ERP just like any other orders. The work they carry out is executed at work centers, so in this sense they are costed just like production orders.

> **Project Size**
>
> As you can imagine, the project structure in Transaction CJ20N can easily include a huge number of WBS elements, network activities, and activities if the project has any degree of complexity. If you're concerned that your projects will fall into this category (generally the problems start when you approach 10,000 WBS elements), look at the recommendations in SAP Note 206264. If you have very large projects and are on the appropriate enhancement package, consider using the Project System, Handling Large Projects 2 business function (OPS_PS_HLP_2).

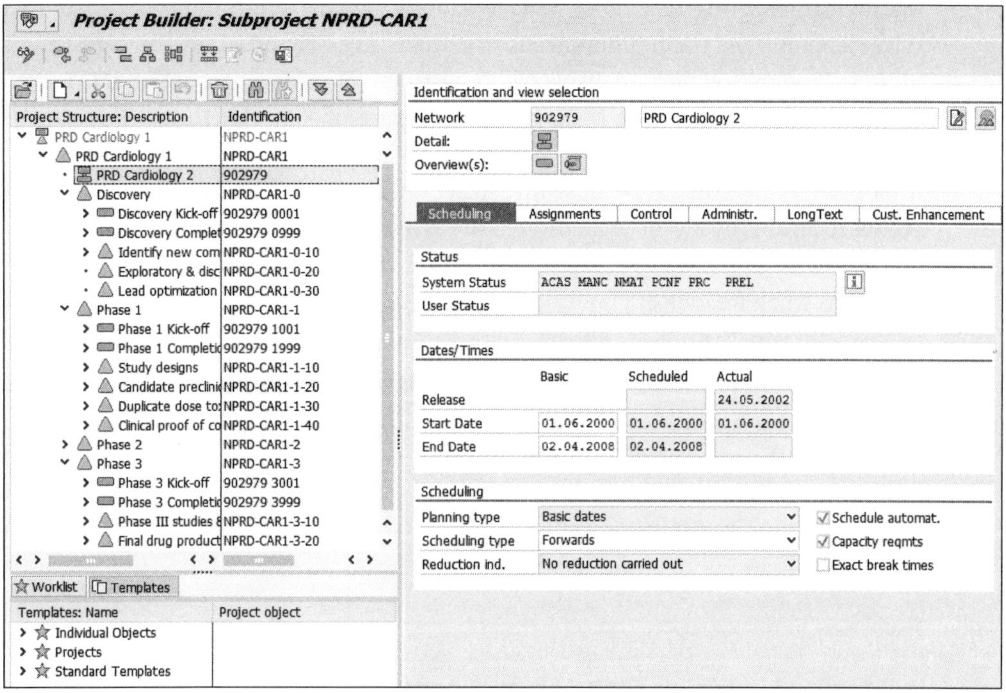

Figure 4.23 Network Assigned to WBS Structure

If your organization only has a handful of investment projects running at any time, what you've just seen will meet your purposes. But if you want to take a more structured approach to project management, then you may want to link your projects with an investment program.

4.8 Investment Programs

In Chapter 3, we looked at investment orders as a type of internal order. If there are many investment orders to be handled, more structure is often needed. If this is the case, you can create an investment program to structure the undertaking. This is particularly useful during planning and when assigning a budget to the individual nodes. Once approved, investment orders or investment projects may be created for the execution of the investment. The investment program itself can't carry costs, so you won't find any transactions that include the investment program as an account assignment. Instead costs are assigned to the orders and WBS elements assigned to the investment program. These behave exactly like any other internal orders and WBS elements. The main difference is that they can be reported via the investment program and in isolation. To display an investment plan, use Transaction IM34 or go to **Accounting • Investment Management • Programs • Master Data • Investment Structure • Display** and enter the program and approval year. The approval year is important in this context because investment programs are always created with reference to an approval year, even though the assigned projects or orders may take several years to complete. We'll look at how to move orders and projects between programs when we look at planning and budgeting in Chapter 5.

Figure 4.24 shows a sample investment program for 2013. You may recognize the structure from the cost center hierarchy we looked at in Chapter 3. This is just one way of structuring an investment program, with the investment taking place with reference to the associated cost centers.

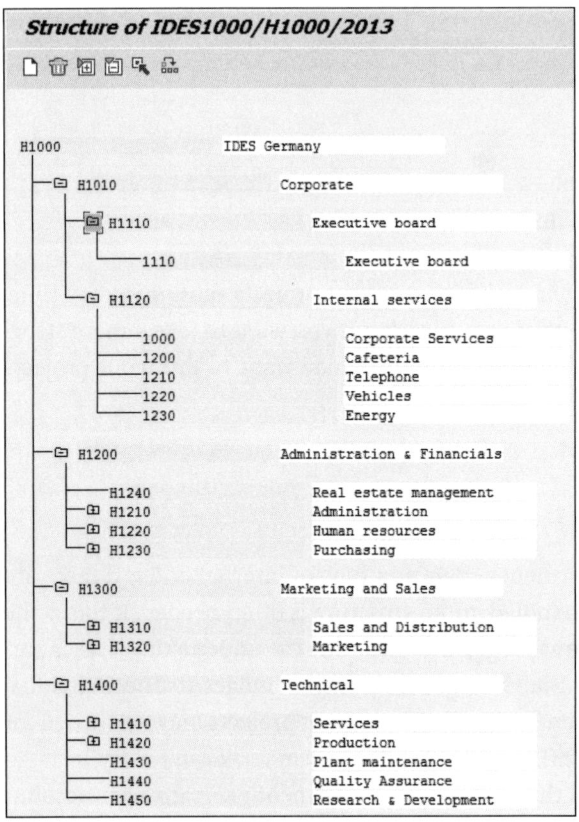

Figure 4.24 Investment Program

If we now return to our project, we can display the link to the investment program by selecting the detail of a WBS element and selecting the **Investments** tab. Figure 4.25 shows that WBS element I/1000-1 is linked to the Corporate Services item of our investment program. You'll see how this assignment affects the budget in Chapter 5, Section 5.2.4. The same link can be made for internal orders if you don't need quite as much structure as a project provides.

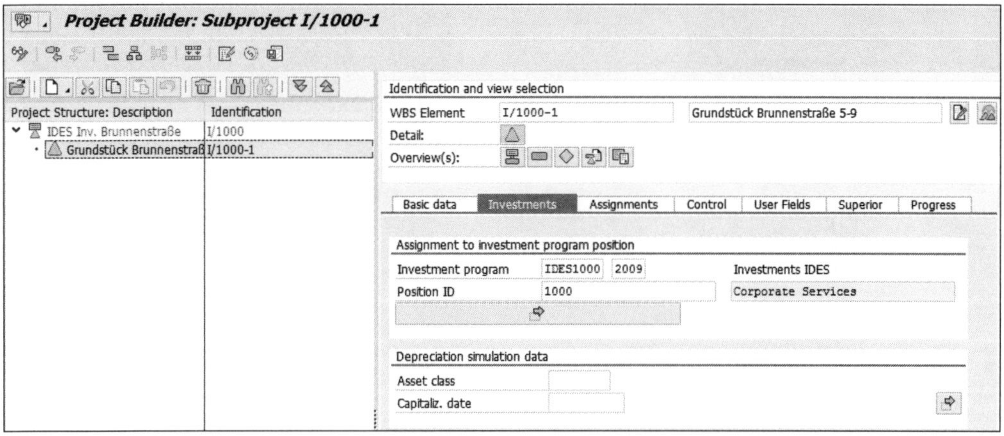

Figure 4.25 Link to Investment Program Item

Appropriation requests are used to request investment as part of the investment program. The appropriation request contains details of the plan required to complete the investment. Several variants can be created that show the planning values along with return on investment (ROI) values. Figure 4.26 shows a sample appropriation request along with the estimate of the investment costs, overhead, and revenue submitted by the requester to support his request. To display the appropriation request, go to Transaction IMA11 or **Accounting • Investment Management • Appropriation Request • Edit Appropriation Request • Individual Processing**. To display the planned values, select the **Variants** tab at the top and the **Plan Values** tab at the bottom.

So far, we've looked at the master data in logistics and master data such as projects and investment programs that sit in logistics and SAP ERP Financials. To complete the picture, we also need to look at the key master data for Controlling in Financial Accounting. We need this to document the flow of costs from the financial accounts to Controlling and from Controlling back to the financial accounts.

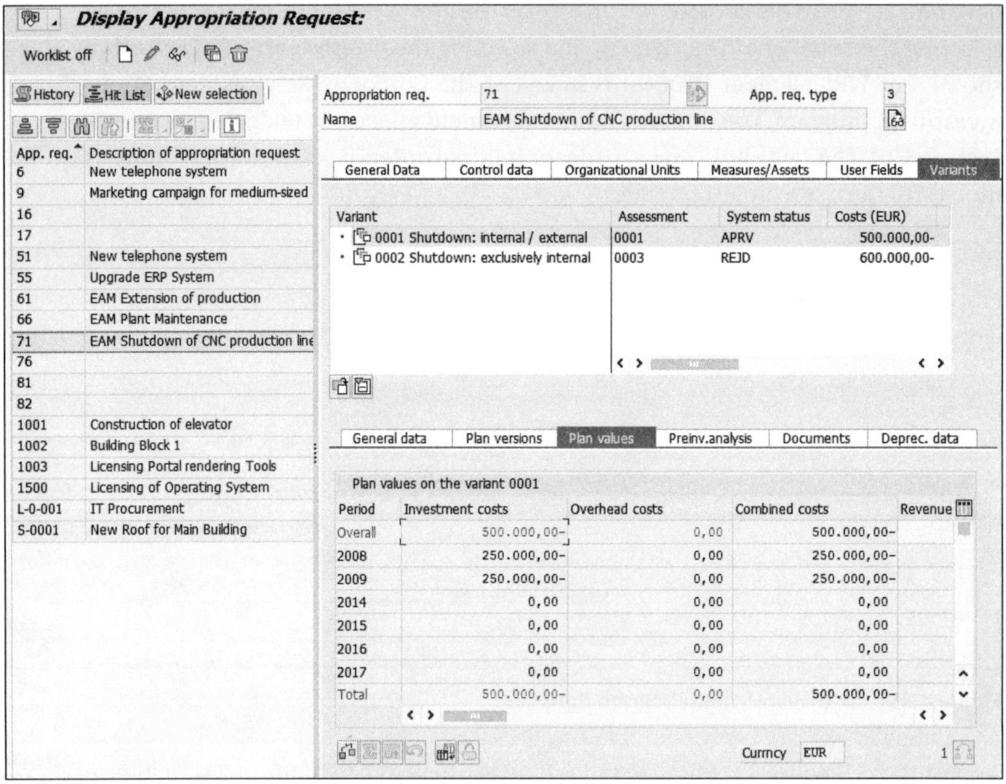

Figure 4.26 Appropriation Request

4.9 Primary Cost Elements and Profit and Loss Accounts

In this chapter, we've focused on the integration between CO and the master data in logistics, touching on account assignment in terms of the material accounts to be updated during a goods movement or the reconciliation account to be used for a customer. As we discussed in Chapter 1, CO sits between Logistics and Financial Accounting, so it's also important to understand how the master data in Financial Accounting impacts CO.

The *chart of accounts* is arguably the most important master data element in SAP ERP Financials. In recent years, there's been a move in large organizations toward unifying the chart of accounts to provide a consistent account definition and consistent account usage across the whole enterprise. This has gone hand in hand with a move toward a global controlling area with common cost elements across all company codes. This increases data integrity across systems and makes it easier to compare performance across units. Implicitly, this has also resulted in changes to the way organizations handle the definition of their cost elements.

Organizations used to create the accounts in Financial Accounting and then notify CO that a cost element was needed for the new account. Now it's more common to have one team create the P&L account and then generate the associated cost element automatically. A setting in the global parameters for the chart of accounts determines whether the associated cost elements are created automatically or continue to be created manually. Your team will find the setting for Controlling integration in the global settings for the chart of accounts in Customizing. Cost elements are generated automatically if the **Automatic Creation of Cost Elements** flag is set here. Because there's also a trend toward having this kind of central master data maintained by a shared service center, you may want to refer to Chapter 9, in which we'll look at the tasks of a shared service center and how other departments can raise requests to initiate the creation of a new account and its sister cost elements centrally.

4.9.1 Chart of Accounts

Let's consider the different types of charts of accounts. SAP ERP includes three charts of accounts:

1. **Operational chart of accounts**
   The *operational* chart of accounts contains the *operational accounts* used for recording financial transactions within a company code. The chart of accounts is included in the global parameters for the company code. These are the accounts we talked about in the context of material account assignment and the customer master, and it's these accounts that are linked with the primary cost elements for controlling purposes.
   - **Group chart of accounts**
     The *group* chart of accounts contains all *group accounts* companies in the group use for consolidated financial reporting. The operational accounts are linked to the group chart of accounts in the account master record. Normally, they're not relevant for CO, unless you're part of the team preparing group data for consolidation.
   - **Country chart of accounts**
     Some countries have specific legislative requirements concerning the chart of

accounts to be used to submit financial statements. The *country* chart of accounts is also included in the global parameters for the company code. These are defined as *alternative accounts* and are mapped to the operational accounts in the account master data at the chart-of-account level. They're not relevant for controlling unless they're used in isolation. In this case, the country chart of accounts is effectively the operational chart of accounts. This can be the case if you operate only in one country and that country prescribes the accounts to be used.

To display the accounts, use Transaction FS00 or go to **Accounting • Financial Accounting • General Ledger • Master Records • GL Accounts • Individual Processing • Centrally**. Figure 4.27 shows the master data definition for an inventory account. The main checkbox for our purposes is the **P&L Statmt Acct Type** checkbox, because only postings to P&L accounts are transferred to CO. You can also see the assignment to the group account, which is used for consolidation and group controlling. The **Edit Cost Element** button at the top right takes you to the master data for the associated cost element.

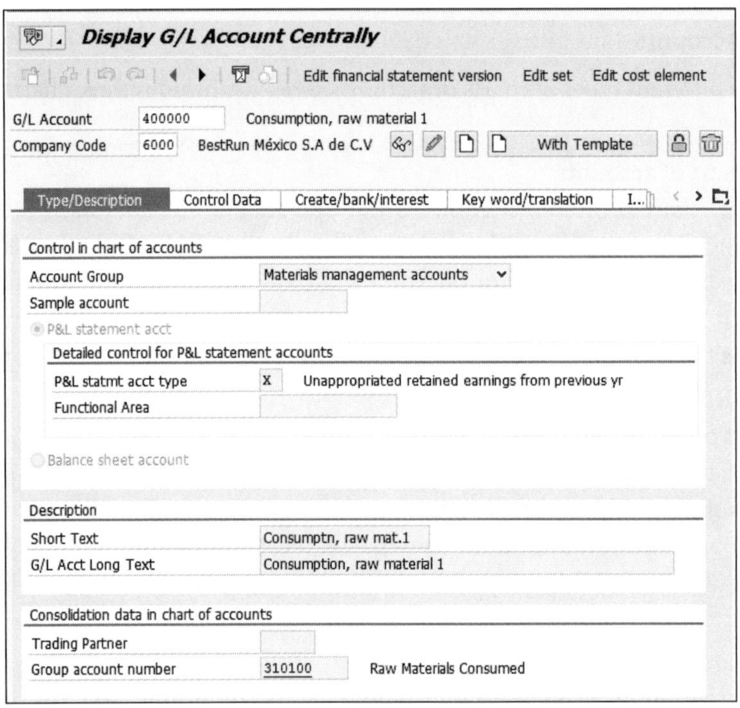

Figure 4.27 General Ledger Account Master Data Definition

> **Cost Elements and Accounts in SAP S/4HANA**
>
> In SAP S/4HANA, the General Ledger accounts and cost elements merge; there is no longer a separate transaction, Transaction KA01, to create the cost element associated with the account. Instead, you will be able to identify accounts that act as cost elements by the General Ledger account type **Primary costs or Revenues**. We'll look at the merge in more detail in Chapter 14.

Figure 4.28 shows the associated cost element (which you can also reach using Transaction KA03). The definition is relatively simple (which is why the process can be automated). The important setting is the **Cost Element Category**:

- For costs, the cost element category is 1 (primary costs). You need cost elements of category 1 for all material accounts, asset accounts, wages, salaries, or for any P&L account for which you want to capture costs in CO. In account-based Profitability Analysis, you will also need cost elements of category 1 for your cost-of-goods-sold accounts.
- For revenues, the cost element category is 11 (revenue). You only need to create cost elements of category 11 for revenues that are assigned to projects or for make-to-order production with sales order controlling (see Chapter 2). All other revenues are captured as value fields in CO-PA and do not need to be recorded as cost elements, unless you are using account-based CO-PA, in which case you will need to define cost elements for your revenues.

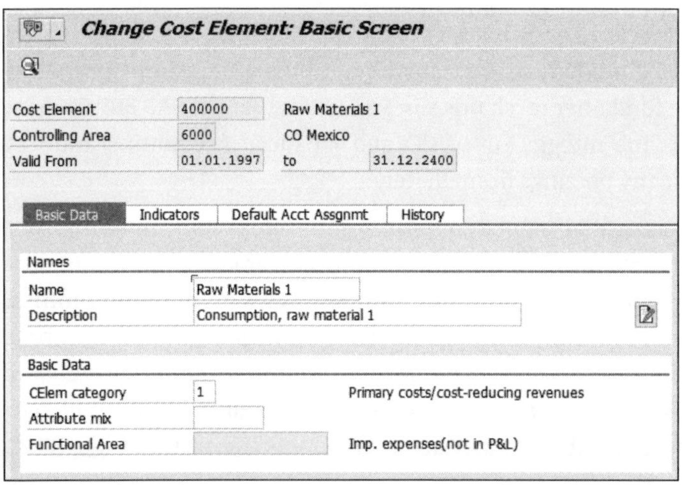

Figure 4.28 Primary Cost Element

- For sales deductions, the cost elements category is 12. Again, you will only need cost elements if you are working with account-based CO-PA. If you are working with cost-based CO-PA, you can capture these as value fields in CO-PA.

Once a cost element has been created, it's important to ensure that it's properly assigned for overhead calculation, settlement, inclusion in WIP, and so on, as discussed in Chapter 3. You'll see this linkage again in Chapter 9 when we look at how to set up a dedicated system for master data governance, which is usually installed on the same client as the master Customizing client so that this kind of data can be maintained in one go.

4.9.2 Controlling and the Financial Accounts

The normal value flow is from the General Ledger account to the cost element. For example, whenever a goods movement is recorded, material account determination selects the correct accounts to be posted in the General Ledger for that business transaction, and a posting to CO is made under the appropriate cost element. We'll see lots of examples of this when we post goods movements in Chapter 6. Occasionally, the flow is in the other direction.

Cross-Company Allocations

There is a flow of costs from CO to FI during allocations that cross the boundary of the company code. An example of this might be a shared service center for Controlling that works for multiple companies in a group and allocates its costs to these companies using an allocation cycle. In early releases of SAP ERP and SAP R/3, such postings were stored in a reconciliation ledger and transferred to the other company code at period close. One of the fundamental changes in SAP ERP is that the SAP ERP General Ledger allows the real-time integration of CO and Financial Accounting and can update such cross-company postings immediately.

The SAP ERP update process affects not only postings that cross company codes, but also postings that cross business areas, profit centers, segments, and functional areas. Cross-company postings are generally quite rare, but it's much more common for allocations to take place between cost centers that are assigned to different profit centers or different business areas, so it's important to define *reconciliation accounts* in Financial Accounting to capture the results of each type of allocation you plan to use. You can define a separate account for each CO business transaction. Figure 4.29

shows an example of such a reconciliation account. It looks much like any other P&L account. The important thing is to include such accounts in your thinking, because it's easy to imagine that the data flow from Financial Accounting to CO is a one-way street with nothing flowing in the other direction.

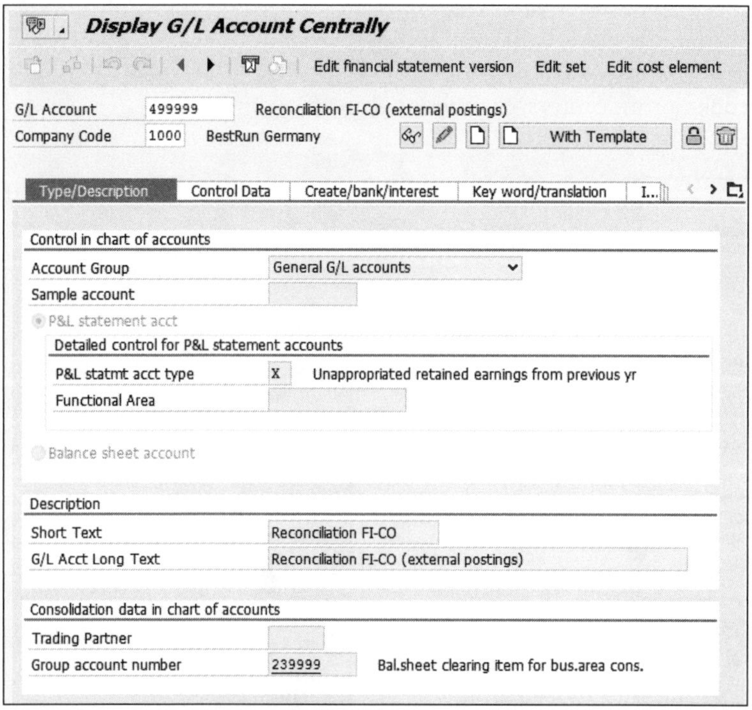

Figure 4.29 Reconciliation Account

Figure 4.30 illustrates the relationship between the General Ledger accounts and the cost elements:

- Postings made to the General Ledger for payroll, material expenses, depreciation, and so on flow from left to right and are recorded as *primary cost elements*. You'll recognize these postings in your cost center and order/project reporting by the business Transaction COIN, which means that they have been transferred from Financial Accounting to CO via the CO interface. If you've activated account-based CO-PA, you'll also find postings for revenue and cost of goods sold being transferred using the same method.

- Postings that originate in Controlling, such as time recording, order confirmation, and so on, are recorded under *secondary cost elements* (see Chapter 3). They will be updated in Financial Accounting only if the senders and receivers are in different company codes, profit centers, functional areas, and so on. Thus an allocation from a shared service cost center to cost centers in different company codes will always result in an FI posting, but an allocation from an administration cost center to a production cost center will only result in an FI posting if the two are in different company codes, profit centers, or functional areas.

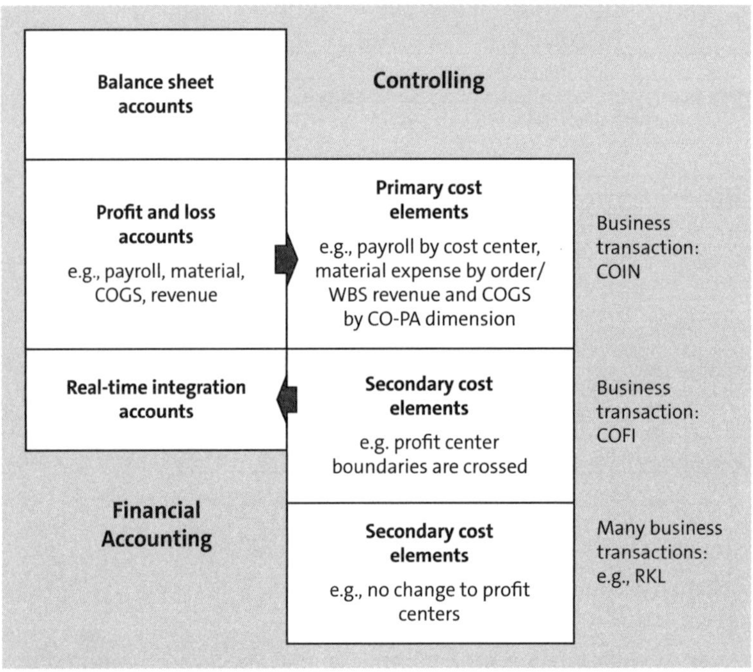

Figure 4.30 Relationship between Accounts and Cost Elements

Accounts for Secondary Postings in SAP S/4HANA

With the merge of the cost elements and accounts in SAP S/4HANA, you will no longer need a separate reconciliation account for each business transaction in CO. Instead the cost flow will be recorded under the secondary cost element for the allocation in question, with the sender and receiver costs balancing to zero from a Financial Accounting perspective.

Balance Sheet Postings

It's common to think of Controlling simply as a way of bringing more detail into the P&L statement. However, there are business transactions, such as order settlement, that move expenses into the balance sheet.

If you calculate WIP, you must set up posting rules in Customizing that determine the balance sheet and P&L account to which the WIP is assigned. The P&L accounts used in this context are unusual in that you're not allowed to create cost elements for them to stop WIP flowing back into CO, where they would run the risk of being counted twice. Typical postings in this context are for the following:

- Work in process (WIPR)
- Reserves for unrealized costs (RUCR)
- Revenue in excess of billings (POCI)
- Revenue surplus (POCS)

If you have orders or projects for *assets under construction*, then you will use similar mechanisms to create postings that capitalize these costs. When you settle production variances, you will create postings that impact the price difference account.

Now that we've defined the accounts to be used to record the goods movements in Logistics and the cost elements to record the postings in CO, we're almost ready to start planning. The last step is to make sure the material masters contain the correct prices for costing.

4.10 Setting Prices for Product Costing

In Chapter 1, we introduced the concept of standard setting as a key element of CO. We already discussed the two fundamentally different approaches to cost accounting—standard costs and actual costs—but we have yet to look at how prices get to the material master in the first place. One of the controlling department's most important jobs is to ensure that the material masters contain the correct standard costs at all times; the planning process that we'll look at in Chapter 5 and the actual postings that we'll discuss in Chapter 6 rely on this data being accurate.

4.10.1 Setting Standard Costs for Raw Materials

Let's look first at how to determine the costs of the raw materials used to manufacture a product. Several options exist that go beyond the methods used for the real-time valuation of goods movements.

If you use the *moving average price* for your raw materials, you can simply have the system include the latest moving average price for each raw material in costing (this is configured in the valuation variant). The challenge for the controller in this case is to ensure that the purchasing department is doing a reliable job when maintaining the purchase orders.

If you use *standard costs* for your raw materials, then you need to configure the valuation variant to determine what constitutes the standard costs in the context of your business. The options include the following:

- Price from a purchasing info record (set up for the relevant vendor)
- **Planned Price 1** (field in **Accounting 2** view of material master)
- Standard price
- Moving average price

The logic of the valuation variant (configuration for Product Costing) means that the system first searches for a purchasing info record for that material. If the system is unable to find a purchasing info record with a price agreement with a specific vendor for that material, then it reads the planned price for the material, and so on.

Enhancements for Material Valuation

Although the material valuation options available in Customizing will take you a long way, many organizations have requested the ability to apply their own logic to select material prices. If you find yourself involved in this kind of discussion, consider having your IT department implement one or more of the following SAP Notes:

- SAP Note 1306588 (Costing: BAdI for Valuation of Subcontracting)
- SAP Note 1326416 (Costing: BAdI for Valuation of External Processing)
- SAP Note 1445940 (Raw Material Cost Estimate: Origin Group for Delivery Costs)

Whatever price you choose, marking and releasing the cost estimate (see Chapter 5) results in the cost estimate (either a material price or a purchasing info record) being updated to the material master as the new standard price. Figure 4.31 shows a sample purchasing info record. This contains the pricing agreement for the material negotiated by your purchasing department. To display a purchasing info record, you can use Transaction ME13 or go to **Logistics • Materials Management • Purchasing • Master Data • Info Record • Display**, and then enter the relevant vendor, material, purchasing organization, and plant.

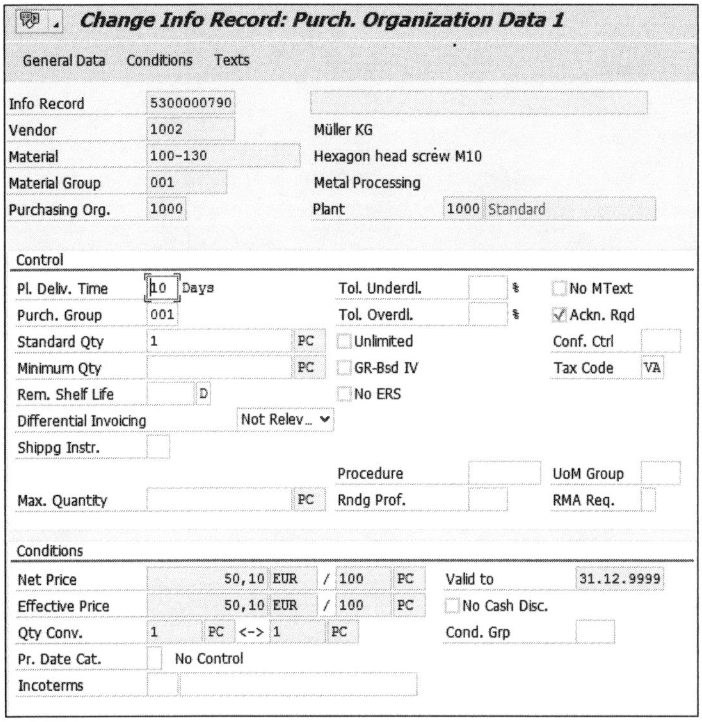

Figure 4.31 Conditions in Purchasing Info Record

You use the **Costing 2** view in the material master, shown in Figure 4.32, to set planned prices that will become the standard price in the future as part of the costing process. Many organizations automate the process of updating values to these fields with their own ABAP code. Note the link to the existing standard costs shown here, which enables you to check how realistic the new prices will be.

During Product Costing, you can always check which price has been used for a raw material by selecting the **Valuation** tab in Transaction CK13N (see Figure 4.33). In this example, a value has been read from the purchasing info record. We've changed the layout (see Chapter 2) to show the vendor, as well to make it easier to check the conditions used in the purchasing info record.

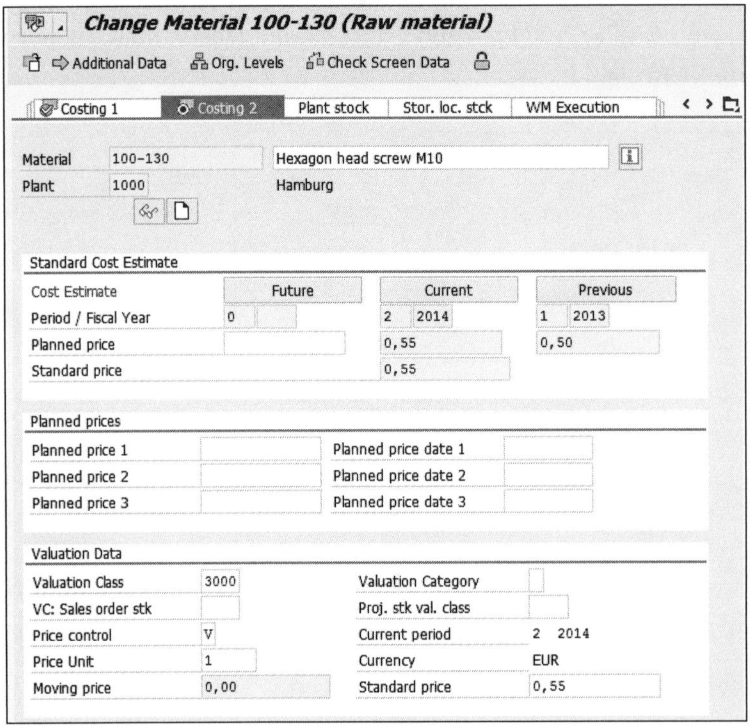

Figure 4.32 Material Master: Costing 2 View

The **Valuation** tab in Figure 4.33 shows that a substrategy for reading the info record has been used that reads the contents of a condition table. The purchasing info record in Figure 4.32 is fairly simple in that it only reads a material price, but it's common to include additional conditions for freight, duty, insurance, and other related costs in the info record. You can pull these conditions into the product cost estimate as well by mapping them to the origin groups we saw in the costing view of the material master. Because these conditions are not relevant for inventory valuation, you should flag them as not part of the cost roll-up and not relevant for inventory valuation during configuration of the cost components.

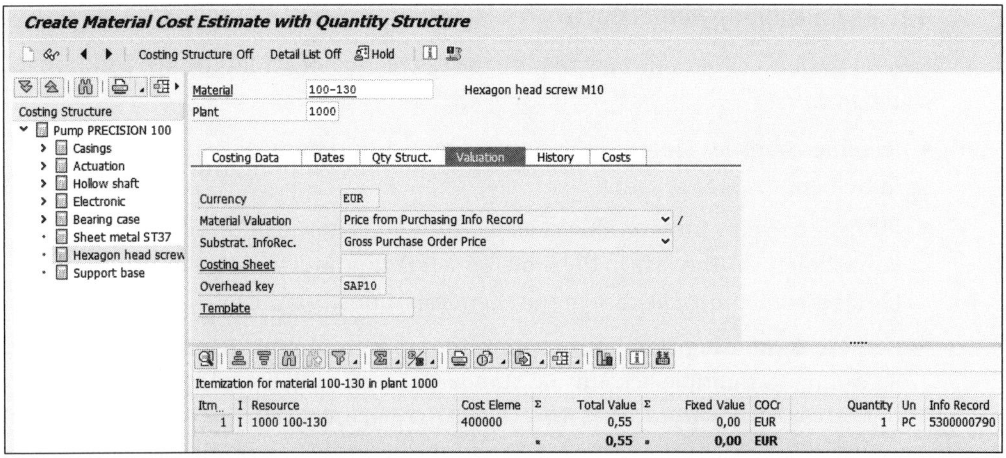

Figure 4.33 Valuation Tab in Product Cost Estimate

4.10.2 Balance Sheet Valuation

For balance sheet valuation, you can define tax and commercial prices in the **Accounting 2** view of the material master. The same principle applies as for the calculation of standard costs. You can configure a valuation variant for inventory costing to select one of the commercial prices or one of the tax prices, as shown in Figure 4.34. You can then transfer the results of this cost estimate to the material master for the finished product.

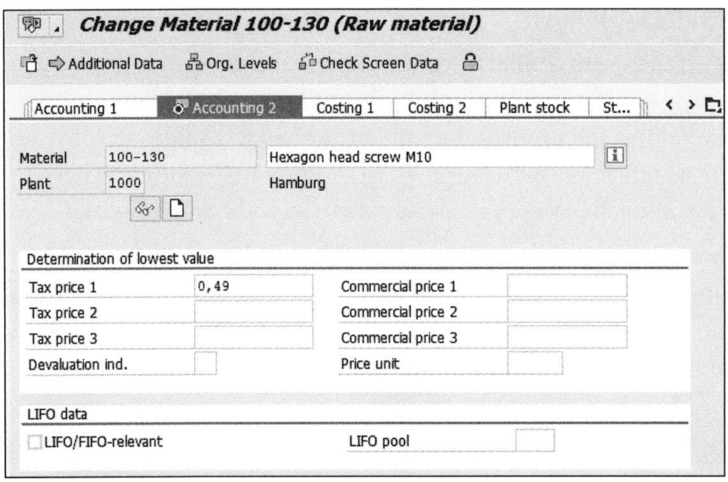

Figure 4.34 Material Master: Accounting 2 View

4.10.3 Calculating Actual Costs

Several business situations may require the calculation of actual costs in addition to standard costs:

- In some countries (common in South America and parts of Asia), it's a legal requirement to value at actual costs.
- It can also make sense to value at actual costs when raw material costs are volatile (as is sometimes the case in the food industry) or production structures are unstable (as is sometimes the case in the chemicals industry).
- Because accounting standards change, there's a requirement to value inventory according to multiple accounting standards (such as IFRS and local GAAP). This option is available from EHP 5 for SAP ERP 6.0 and involves using the Material Ledger to calculate actual costs according to the alternative accounting principle. To use this function, you need to have your IT department activate business function `FIN_CO_COGM` (Parallel Valuation of Cost of Goods Manufactured).

In such a case, all goods movements and transactions affecting prices (including invoice receipts and order settlement) are updated to the Material Ledger. At period close, this information is used to calculate a weighted average price for the goods in stock. Because changes in the raw material costs also affect the costs of the products manufactured, any differences are then assigned to the manufactured products and to cost of sales. We'll come back to this process in more detail in Chapter 7.

4.10.4 Cross-Company Costing

If your organization trades with affiliated companies within the same group, you may also consider using the Material Ledger for group costing. The example we presented at in Figure 4.3 stores the group values in Euros, the local values in Mexican pesos, and the American dollar as a hard currency. In addition to the different currencies, it's possible to distinguish between the legal valuation and group valuation:

- In the *legal valuation*, trade between companies in the same group is treated as if the affiliated companies are external partners, with a profit mark-up being charged according to the price conditions. This is required to accommodate local tax regulations and is often known as *arm's length trading*.

- In the *group valuation*, trade between companies in the same group is treated as if the movement is simply a stock transfer, with the cost of goods manufactured being passed between the affiliated companies. This uses a special price condition, KW00, which selects the cost component split rather than a selling price.

Affiliated companies are identified by the **Trading Partner** field in the vendor and customer masters, as shown in Figure 4.35.

To create a vendor master, you can use Transaction XK01 or go to **Logistics • Materials Management • Purchasing • Master Data • Vendor • Central • Create**. Enter the name of the vendor (e.g., VEND2820) and the company code for the supplying plant in China. In the **General Data** section, click on the **Control** checkbox. Figure 4.35 shows the vendor master for the supplying plant. The control data links the supplying plant to the receiving plant in the United States via the entry in the **Customer** field (e.g., CUST2821). The entry in the **Trading Partner** field (e.g., 1000) identifies the company ID to which the plant belongs for consolidation purposes.

Figure 4.35 Vendor Master Showing Intercompany Customer and Trading Partner

To create a customer master, use Transaction XD01 or go to **Logistics • Sales and Distribution • Master Data • Business Partner • Customer • Create • Complete**. Enter the name of the customer (e.g., CUST2821) and the company code for the receiving plant, then click on the **Control Data** tab. Figure 4.36 shows the customer master for the receiving plant. The control data links the receiving plant to the supplying plant via the entry in the **Vendor** field (VEND2820 here). The entry in the **Trading Partner** field (2000 in this example) identifies the company ID to which the plant belongs for consolidation.

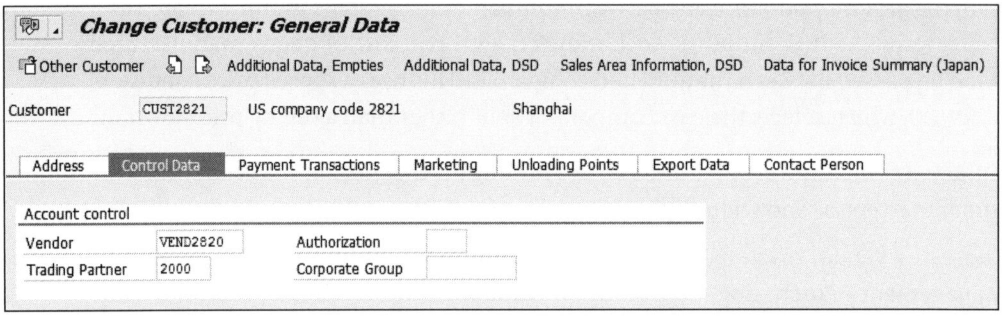

Figure 4.36 Customer Master Showing Intercompany Vendor and Trading Partner

> **Business Partners in SAP S/4HANA**
>
> As we discussed earlier, Transactions XK01 and XD01 are no longer supported from SAP S/4HANA 1511, in which the use of the business partner to represent both customers and vendors becomes compulsory.

4.11 Summary

In this chapter, we looked at the master data that affects costing (material master, BOM, routing, and work center) and profitability analysis (material master, customer master), together with the master data for projects and investment programs. We also looked at the links to the financial accounts and showed how to establish the initial prices for raw materials in the material master. This means we have pretty much all the information we need to embark on the planning process. This will pull together the assumptions documented in the master data throughout SAP ERP to tell us what it will cost to deliver on a given sales plan. We'll look at how to use this data in planning in the next chapter. We'll also return to our investment program and look at how to plan and budget for projects and orders assigned to an investment program.

Chapter 5
Planning and Budgeting

This chapter discusses two forms of planning: one for a complete sales plan in a manufacturing environment and the other for the planning and budgeting of investment projects.

In Chapter 1, we discussed the importance of cost planning and standard setting in the SAP approach to controlling. We also raised the terminology issue that SAP applications tend to refer to a *sales plan* and a *production plan*, whereas others might refer to a *sales budget* or a *production budget*. What is meant is the process of estimating future sales or production volumes and then determining the cost of delivering on this plan in terms of the *resources* to be used. Only when we look at projects and internal orders do we find SAP referring to a *project budget*. The term *budget* refers to the *approved plan* that will act as a ceiling for spending on the project and not to the process of arriving at that figure by estimating the labor, time, materials, and so on required to complete the project.

Terminology issues aside, why is planning so important for the controller? Beyond the need to establish targets and the resources required to achieve these targets, there's the business requirement to set *standard costs* for the materials to be manufactured. The standard costs are used to provide the initial valuation every time a goods movement is posted and as a basis for variance analysis at period close. The correct standard costs need to be in place before goods movements can take place, and ensuring that the standard costs are correct is one of the key responsibilities of controllers in any manufacturing organization. Similarly, because every shop floor worker who records a confirmation in Logistics and every employee who charges his work time to a project triggers a *direct activity allocation* in Controlling, an *activity price* needs to be in place before time can be charged this way; ensuring that the activity price is correct is another key responsibility of the controller.

Both the standard costs and the activity price represent a "best guess" by the organization as to the cost to produce a given volume of product or supply a given amount of activity. These standards can be corrected as the actual costs for the period are known; we'll look at that process in Chapter 7. Because of the importance of planning and standards, we're sometimes asked if it's even possible to use the Controlling (CO) component of SAP ERP Financials without planning. You do need standard costs that remain fixed during the period even if you have the Material Ledger calculate the actual costs at period close. However, this "standard" can be set by selecting the actual costs from the previous period. The challenge here is the timing. The period close needs to have reached the stage when the actual costs for all materials are calculated and updated to inventory before the first goods movement is posted in the next period.

The other fundamental question a controller has to answer is the degree of variance analysis that's required or even relevant for the organization. The planning process is about setting targets in terms of what it should cost to manufacture a product or provide a service. There are arguments against using standard costs and variance analysis—mainly that doing so drives the wrong behavior in terms of encouraging large lot sizes and overproduction—but most organizations continue to use variances against plan to measure the efficiency of their organization, and the level of detail in your plan determines the level of variance analysis you can perform later.

These days, there's also the question of where to plan, and we'll explore the relationship between planning in SAP ERP and planning in SAP BW or SAP Strategic Enterprise Management (SAP SEM) in Chapter 10. For the moment, we'll focus on what determines the planning model in two cases:

1. In SAP ERP, it's the *output* of the sales plan, the production plan, or the activity requirements that drive the planning model. It's against these *volume or quantity assumptions* that the planning cycle in SAP ERP works, establishing the relationships among the proportional costs, which vary depending on the amount of goods sold or the amount of activity to be provided. The planning cycle uses the volumes and master data in SAP ERP and simulates the "pull" of the business transactions that ultimately execute the sales orders. In its most extreme form, it can try to capture the impact of all these business transactions, simulating allocations, order settlements, and all transfers of activities between units.
2. In SAP BW and SAP SEM, the model is not so closely tied to the underlying business processes. It can be *freely modeled* in terms of the entities against which planning data is captured and the granularity of the plan. This can lead to benefits in the sense that planning data isn't forced into the cost center/cost element/period straightjacket, but additional administrative costs as master data and transactional data from previous years also has to be extracted from SAP ERP for use in SAP BW or SAP SEM.

The idea of a quantity- or output-driven plan is at the heart of planning in SAP ERP, but we'll find the same approach when we look at activity-based budgeting in the context of SAP Profitability and Cost Management (SAP PCM) in Chapter 11.

5.1 Complete Sales Plan in a Manufacturing Environment

In this section, we'll look at how to prepare the annual operating plan (AOP) or annual budget. This involves planning all aspects of the business—revenue, production, procurement, capacity, and product/overhead costs—and is an exercise typically started in the last quarter of each fiscal year. It's a process driven by the controller in collaboration with sales managers, production managers, cost center managers, plant controllers, and finance.

Figure 5.1 provides an overview of the process. It's a highly collaborative process with a tacit assumption that the departments at each interface are prepared to share data and assumptions. We've drawn it as a linear process, but in practice there are iterations and changes at every intersection as each department revisits its assumptions and adjusts its proposal.

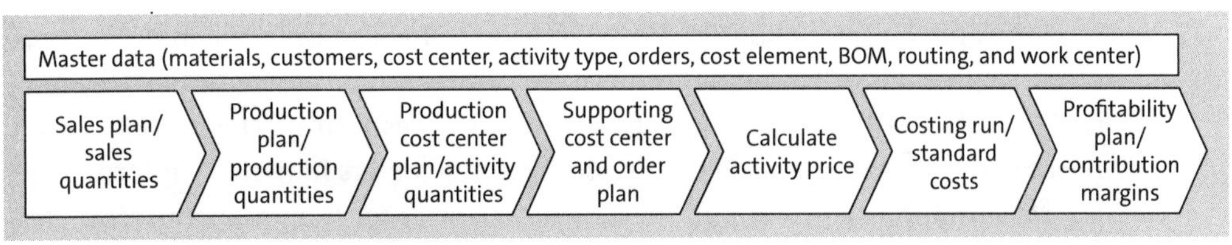

Figure 5.1 Planning Process Overview

The same basic flow can be used with some simplification to plan for a shorter time frame. It's possible to perform the same exercise on a quarterly or even a monthly basis, allowing you to provide a forecast or simply to develop standards that are more in keeping with the changing business conditions.

The different assumptions behind this process are usually modeled as *versions*. Normally, there's an agreement about which version is the working version and which is the final approved version. Various copy functions allow the controller to copy data between different versions as required. When planning is complete, it makes sense to lock the version to prevent anybody from accidentally changing the plan. Don't let the term *version* fool you into thinking that you can save a version of your personal planning data as easily as you would save a new copy of a spreadsheet. Versions are created centrally and have a specific business purpose (annual plan, monthly forecast, etc.). As you save, you need to be clear whether you're saving data to the working version of the company plan or the final version. Once the data is saved, it's there for everyone with appropriate authorization to see. There's no "Janet's version" outside of test systems.

Because the planned volume or output drives the process, it also makes sense to reflect on the meaning of the three main quantities we'll be planning for:

1. **Sales quantity**
   This is the basis for the sales plan and the profit plan and represents the volumes that each sales manager believes he can sell within the target time frame. This is sometimes called the *commercial plan* and can be linked with marketing plans and product placement plans depending on industry specifics. The volume in this plan will pull the production quantity and often be used as a driver in allocations for which sales costs are allocated proportionally to products and customers.
2. **Production quantity**
   This is the basis for the production plan and is derived from the sales plan but expanded to cover all semifinished products and raw materials and to account for any materials in stock. To understand the difference between the production quantity and the sales quantity, think of the extreme example of a manufacturer of ice cream. Sales will be highest during the summer months, but production may well take place all year round, with much of the ice cream simply being stored until needed. This quantity is used by the production planners in their long-term planning assumptions and will pull the activity quantity for the production cost centers.

   For the standard costs, the production quantity is the costing lot size in the material master, which is adjusted to reflect the planned sales volumes when the cost estimate is transferred to the profitability plan. Ensuring that these "ideal" lot sizes are in line with the typical lot sizes used in production is the controller's job.
3. **Activity quantity**
   This can either be the capacity of the cost center that's set by the cost center manager or a dynamic quantity that responds to the pull of the production plan and the requests for activity from other cost centers. It's the controller's job to ensure that the capacity is a fair representation of the cost center's typical output.

Before you start, it's worth looking at your cost center hierarchy (see Chapter 3) to decide which cost centers have an output or activity quantity and which do not and what drives usage of this activity. Production cost centers always have an output quantity in terms of machine hours, labor hours, and so on, and their output is driven by the production plan. Cost centers for maintenance, quality control, and the like typically also have an output quantity in terms of repair hours, testing hours, and so on. Sometimes there will be a maintenance plan in place to determine how much work they will provide. For others there may be a relationship between the production quantity and the amount of quality control required, which will also affect planning. For cost centers such as energy, it's a matter of taste whether you plan in dollars or kilowatt hours and whether the kilowatt hours vary in proportion to the production quantities. For other cost centers, planning an output quantity is nonsense. The costs for these cost centers are simply allocated either to the operational cost centers or to the relevant CO-PA dimensions depending on whether they are considered part of the cost of goods manufactured or not.

5.1.1 Sales and Operations Planning

The planning exercise generally begins with forecasting the sales quantities and revenue for the coming fiscal year.

Figure 5.2 shows the planning folder for **Profitability Analysis**. This corresponds to following the menu path **Accounting • Controlling • Profitability Analysis • Planning**. In general, it's the sales managers who enter their sales quantities and revenues under **Plan Data • Edit Planned Data** (Transaction KEPM), but controlling always checks and sometimes adjusts these figures to ensure that they're in line with company guidelines. These adjustments represent both the technical exercise of ensuring that the correct figures are entered and a business dialog in which the controller questions the underlying planning assumptions and verifies the figures against historical actual data, and the sales manager explains and justifies his decisions.

An additional folder, **Integrated Planning**, provides many functions to transfer the plan to other applications, such as production and the General Ledger, and to pull data from order planning, project planning, or cost center planning to get a complete picture of the likely profitability of the entire plan. We'll use functions in this folder to transfer the sales plan from CO-PA to the sales and operational plan in Logistics, where it will act as the starting point for requirements planning and to run assessment cycles to transfer overhead costs for marketing, sales and distribution, and so on to the CO-PA characteristics. These transactions are the domain of the controller because they simulate the mass allocations and settlements that normally take place at period close. The data volumes can be similarly large, so you may have to schedule the planned allocations and calculations as carefully as those performed at period close (see Chapter 7 and Chapter 12). Note also the **Schedule Manager** folder. This allows you to define how any allocations, settlements, and so on required for the plan are to be carried out and to automate the process of performing these tasks. We'll look at the Schedule Manager functions in more detail in Chapter 12.

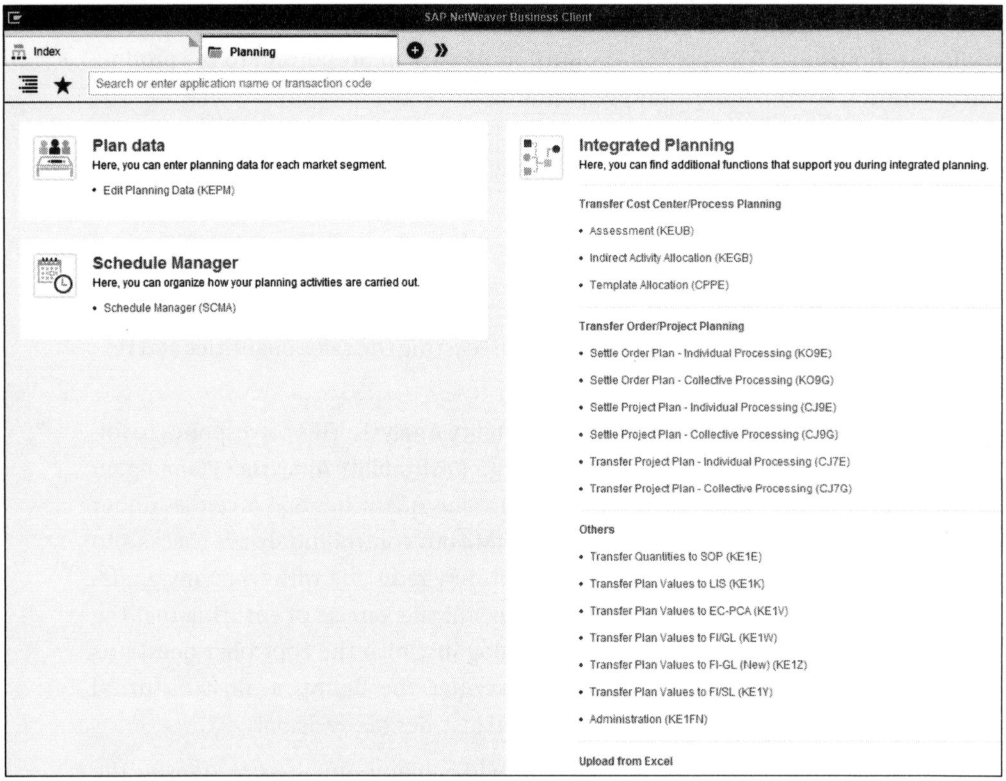

Figure 5.2 Planning Applications in Profitability Analysis

Owing to the large data volumes involved, some of the transactions a controller uses during planning lock all related objects to ensure that other applications cannot make changes while the planning application is running. For details of the locking procedure, refer to SAP Note 79634.

Create Sales Plan

There are many approaches to sales planning:

- One question is what level of detail will be captured in the plan. Does it make sense to capture data at the level of the product/customer, or does it make more sense to capture it at a higher level, such as by product line, and then have the system break down the plan to the product/customer level using top-down distribution, a planning function in Profitability Analysis? If you have highly configurable products, then the chances are that you can't plan by product, because you have to wait for the sales order before configuring the exact product specification. In this situation, it's common to plan by product group and then break down the planned values using the actuals from the previous year if data is needed at this granularity. We'll come back to top-down distribution in Chapter 7.
- Another question is whether to start from zero or refer to the past. Some organizations copy actual sales quantities from previous periods into a new planning version and have the sales managers adjust them. Others have the sales managers enter their data from scratch, believing this to provide a more rigorous basis for planning.

Clearly, the first technical requirement of a planning application is *flexibility*, in terms of the granularity of the planning, the time frame for which data can be entered, and the sources from which data can be copied. Just like the reporting functions in Profitability Analysis, the planning applications are completely configurable. You can plan against any entity that exists in the operating concern, and part of the configuration effort is then to restrict what can be planned: the version to be used, the organizational units, the time frame, the level of detail, and so on. This is done by creating planning levels that group together the CO-PA characteristics that are relevant for planning and determine the key figures that you will plan (volumes, costs, etc.).

Figure 5.3 shows the characteristics that we'll be using to create our sales plan. To access this screen, choose **Edit Planning Data** (shown in Figure 5.2) or enter Transaction KEPM. We're using the sample operating concern S_GO, delivered to illustrate one approach to the implementation of Profitability Analysis in SAP ERP. This contains four sample planning levels for the planning of contribution margins, sales and marketing expenses, and other overhead and for the distribution of costs from higher-level to lower-level characteristics.

Let's first look at the planning level for the contribution margins by selecting the planning level **1VOLREV** on the left of the screen and the **Characteristics** tab on the right of the screen. Here you can see that we can plan by customer group, distribution channel, material group, period, and version. You'll also notice a distinction by record type. Planning, just like reporting (see Chapter 2), distinguishes between the revenue stream represented by planning lines of record type F (billing) and the expenses represented by planning lines of record type C (settlement) and D (allocation). We'll plan sales volume with reference to record type F, sales and marketing costs, research and development costs, administration costs, and other overhead with reference to record type D (allocations).

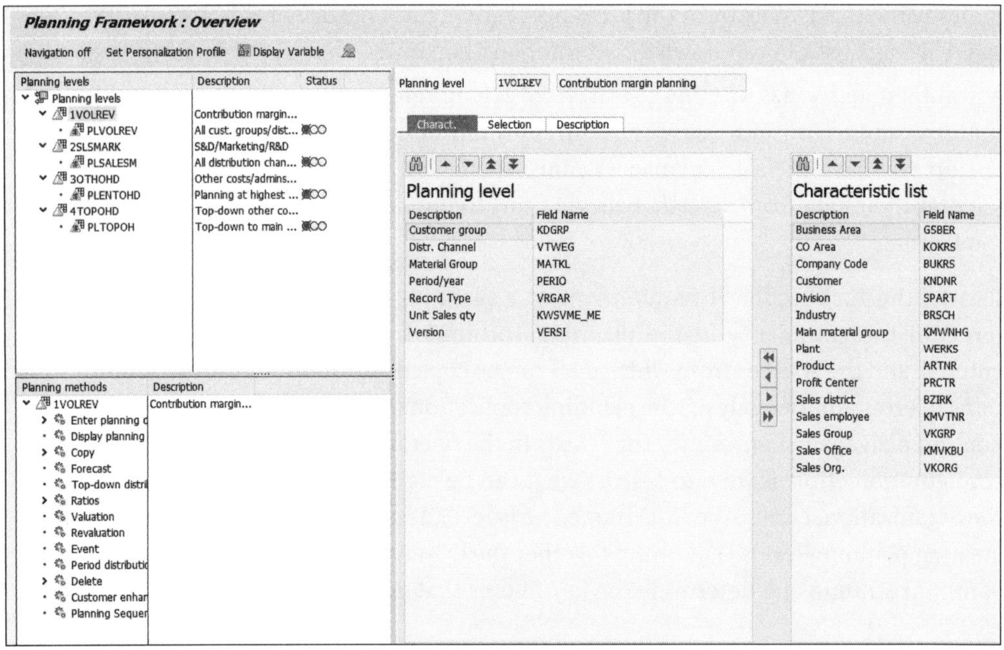

Figure 5.3 Planning Level: Market Segment Planning

Figure 5.4 shows the planning package for contribution margin planning. Here you can see how we've restricted the characteristics to a specific year, a specific version, and to record type F (billing documents). The version provides the framework for the plan. You need to know the version when transferring data to the other applications. In this example, quantity data can be entered for the customer group, distribution channel, and material group. Notice also that we've restricted the quantity entry to a particular unit of measure—**PC** (pieces) in this example.

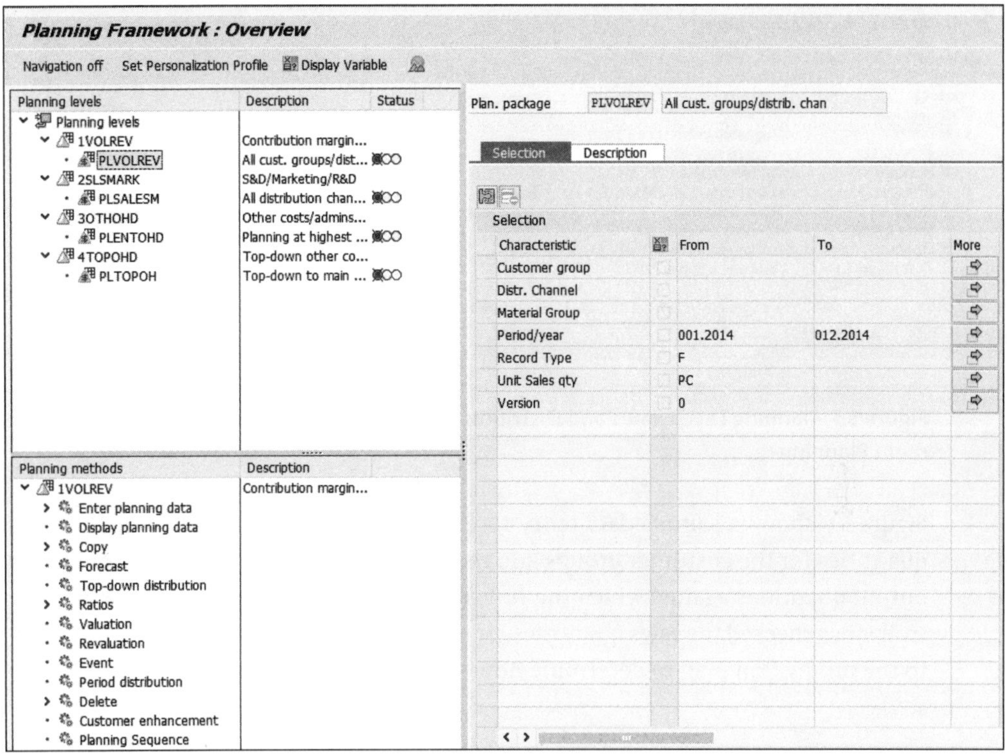

Figure 5.4 Planning Package: Contribution Margin Planning

Figure 5.5 shows the planning package for the various costs associated with these revenues. You'll notice that these are collected as record type D, which represents the result of an allocation. We won't enter them directly for the distribution channel and material group, but will plan them for the sales, marketing, and R&D cost centers and then allocate them to the relevant distribution channels and material groups using assessment cycles. There is a relationship between this planning package and the previous planning package in the sense that the allocations are based on the quantities planned per distribution channel and material group. This simple example gives us the idea that the controller's job also involves orchestrating who should be planning what in which sequence to ensure that all the necessary facts are in place for each planning step.

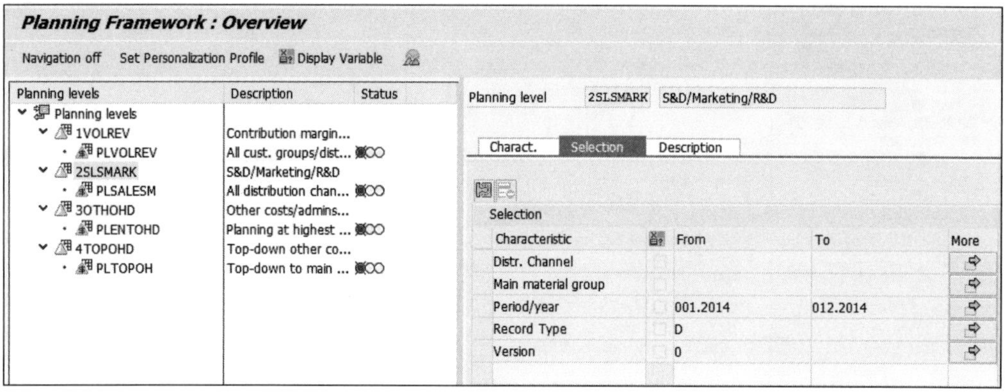

Figure 5.5 Planning Level: Sales and Distribution, Marketing, and Research and Development Planning

Figure 5.6 shows a sample data-entry screen for the sales and profit plan. The sales quantities for the customer groups and material groups on the far right provide the output quantities against which the rest of the plan will be executed. Once the controller has checked the sales quantities for accuracy, the next stage is to transfer them to the production plan to determine how to manufacture the quantities that will be sold.

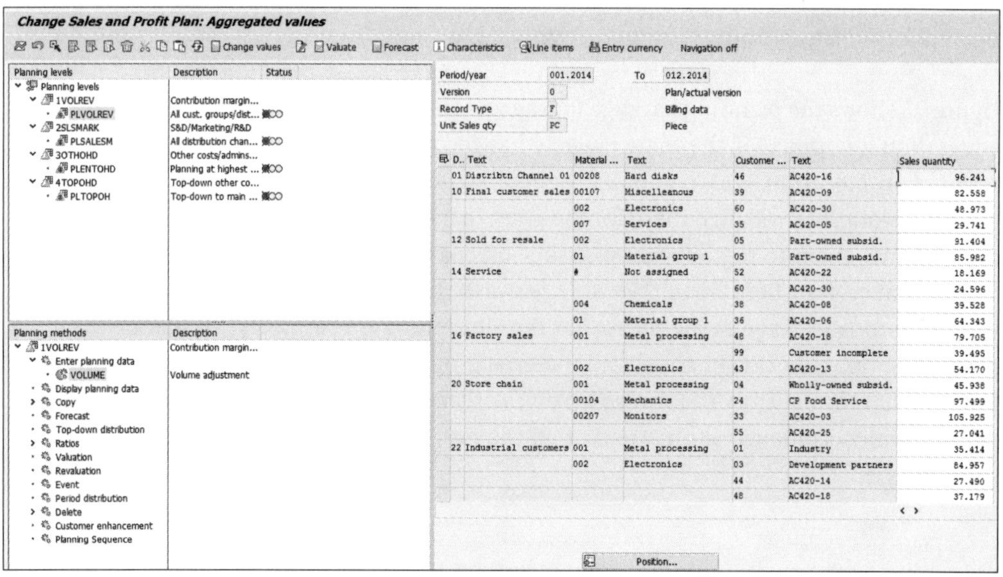

Figure 5.6 Planning Layout for Sales and Profit Plan

The cycle will complete when we use the *valuation* function to associate these quantities with the product costs. If the sales manager enters sales of 100 units of a particular product as a planning assumption, the valuation function will select the product cost estimate and the cost components for that product and adjust the costs to reflect the lot size of 100 units. The valuation functions are set up in configuration and executed when the controller clicks on the appropriate button in the planning layout. However, before we can usefully execute this function, we need to complete the cost center plan and calculate the standard costs for the products. We'll use the same function at the end of the period close to pull the actual costs from the periodic costing run into Profitability Analysis.

Sales Planning in SAP S/4HANA

The mention of record types as the basis for planning tells you that this example is using costing-based CO-PA. In SAP S/4HANA we switch to an account-based planning model, but the system still supports the planning of sales quantities, prices, and the valuation of these sales quantities using a cost estimate. We'll explain how to undertake this form of planning in Chapter 14.

The controller initiates the transfer of the planning quantities from the sales and profit plan to the sales and operations plan by using the **Transfer Quantities to SOP** function (Transaction KE1E) in the **Integrated Planning • Others** folder (shown in Figure 5.2). Figure 5.7 shows the parameters for the transfer, particularly the version used to plan in Profitability Analysis and the receiving version in Long-Term Planning.

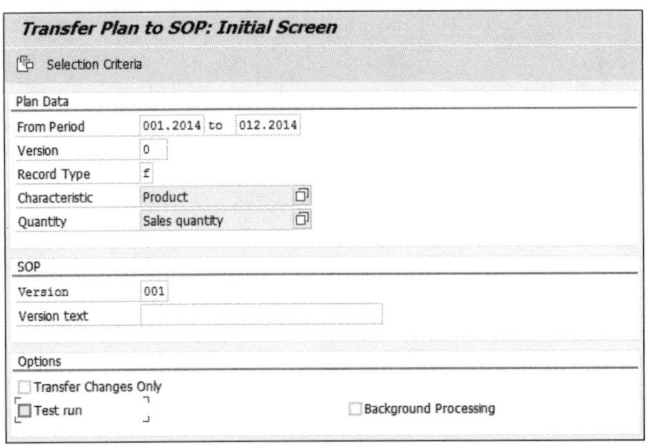

Figure 5.7 Transfer Sales and Profit Plan to Sales and Operations Plan

You might wonder why you have to enter the sales quantity at all, but depending on the configuration of your operating concern it's possible to plan multiple quantities in CO-PA, so you'll want to transfer a quantity that can be converted into the unit of measure used in production.

Create Production Plan

Once the controller has transferred the sales quantities to the sales and operations plan, the next step is for the production department to plan the semifinished products needed as intermediates and the raw materials that need to be purchased to enable delivery on the sales plan, using the bills of material (BOMs) for the finished products as a starting point.

Whereas the *plan version* provides the framework for the sales plan, the *planning scenario* provides the framework for the production plan. To define the planning scenario, go to Transaction MS31 or **Logistics • Production • Production • Planning • Long Term Planning • Planning scenario • Create** and give your scenario a name.

To bring the requirements from Profitability Analysis into the production plan, you need to link the plan version to the planning scenario by clicking on the **Planned Independent Requirements** button (see Figure 5.8). You also need to determine which plant(s) are affected by clicking on the **Plants** button before releasing and saving the scenario by clicking on the **Release and Save** button.

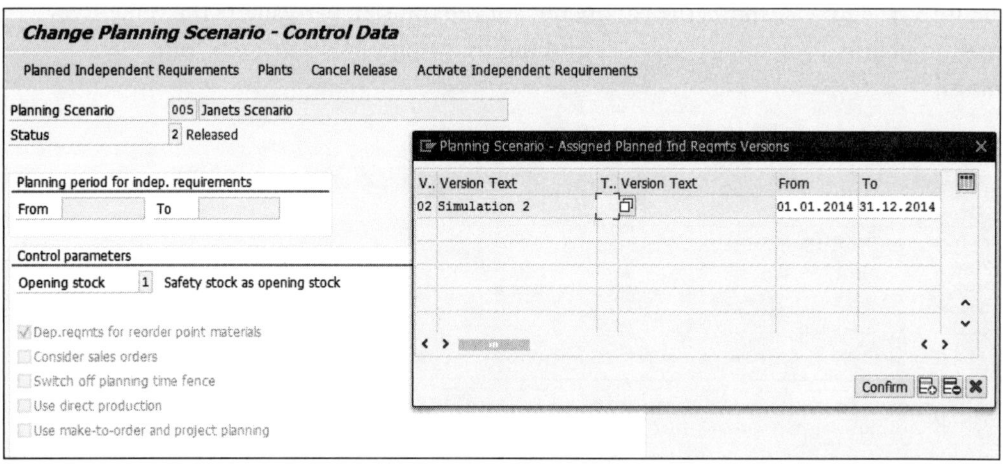

Figure 5.8 Planning Scenario with Link to Sales and Profit Plan

To create a long-term planning run, go to **Logistics • Production • Production Planning • Long Term Planning • Long-Term Planning • Planning Run** or Transaction MS01. Enter the planning scenario and plant and click on **Execute**. This triggers the following steps:

- Executing the long-term planning run reads the BOM for each finished product to determine the dependent requirements (semifinished products and raw materials needed for the finished products).
- The long-term planning run also reads the routings for each of the materials to be manufactured to determine the machine time, labor time, and so on required. In controlling terms, this represents the scheduled activity that the production cost centers are required to produce. This is the quantity against which controlling is required to plan the cost center expenses.

Figure 5.9 shows the result of the long-term planning run.

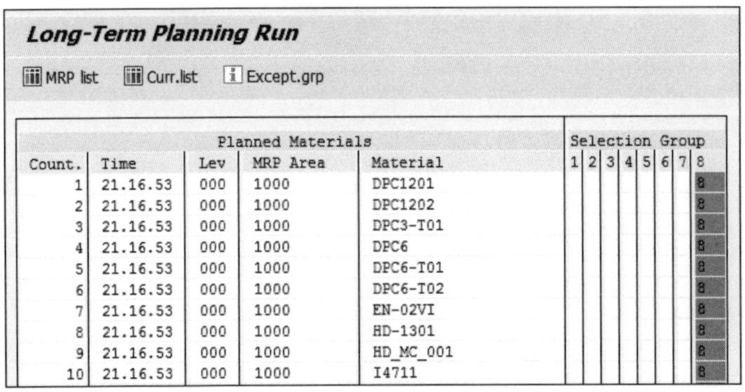

Planned Materials					Selection Group							
Count.	Time	Lev	MRP Area	Material	1	2	3	4	5	6	7	8
1	21.16.53	000	1000	DPC1201								8
2	21.16.53	000	1000	DPC1202								8
3	21.16.53	000	1000	DPC3-T01								8
4	21.16.53	000	1000	DPC6								8
5	21.16.53	000	1000	DPC6-T01								8
6	21.16.53	000	1000	DPC6-T02								8
7	21.16.53	000	1000	EN-02VI								8
8	21.16.53	000	1000	HD-1301								8
9	21.16.53	000	1000	HD_MC_001								8
10	21.16.53	000	1000	I4711								8

Figure 5.9 Result of Long-Term Planning Run

Once the production quantities have been checked, the next stage is to transfer them to the cost center plan—a task the controller performs.

5.1.2 Cost Center Planning

The next stage of the planning exercise involves the cost centers and their managers. Figure 5.10 shows the planning folder for **Cost Center Accounting**. This corresponds to following the menu path **Accounting • Controlling • Cost Center Accounting • Planning**. Again, we see the planning applications used mainly by cost center managers and then checked by controlling under **Cost and Activity Inputs**, **Activity Outputs/**

Prices, and **Statistical Key Figures** and the transactions used only by controlling under **Planning Aids** for copying data and transferring relevant data from other applications. The applications in this list illustrate how planning in SAP ERP mirrors the data flows during actual postings, with planned data being brought in from SAP ERP Human Capital Management (wages and salaries), Fixed Asset Accounting (depreciation), and Sales and Operations Planning (our production plan).

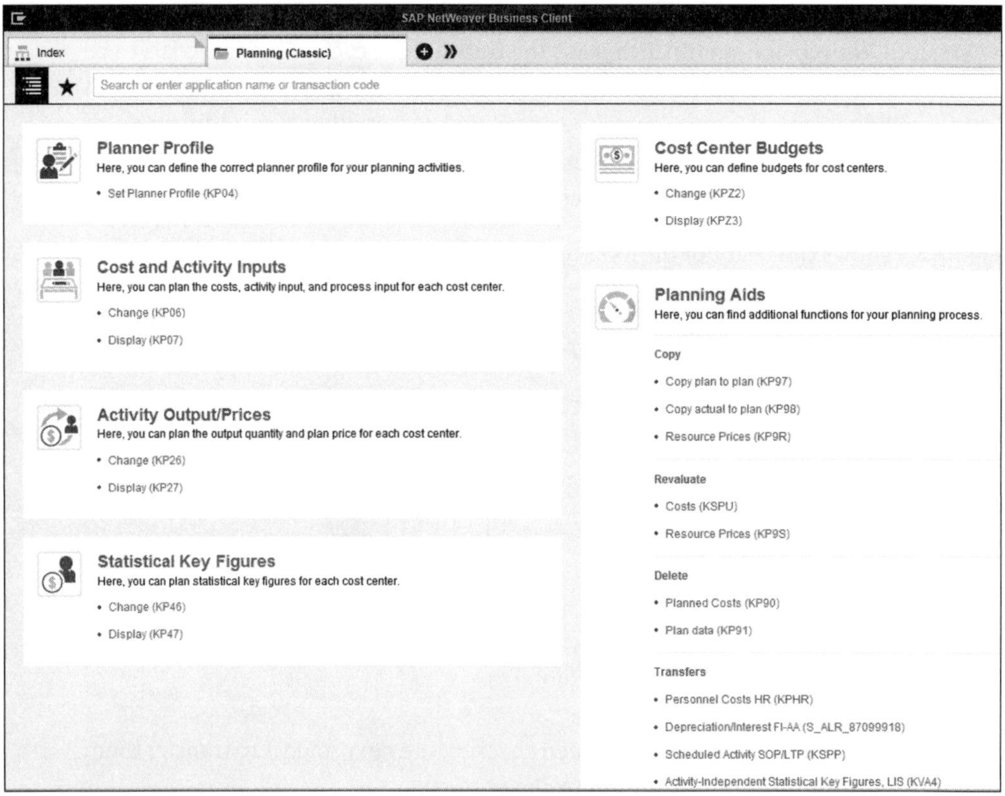

Figure 5.10 Planning Applications in Cost Center Accounting

Plan integration ensures that any data you enter for one object or sender (such as a maintenance cost center) that affects another object or receiver (such as a production cost center) is updated on both the sender cost center and the receiver cost center. Before you start planning, it's worth checking whether the **Integrated Planning** checkbox has been selected for the version and fiscal year you intend to use for your plan. To do this, select **Controlling • Cost Center Accounting • Planning • Current Settings • Maintain Versions**. Select your controlling area, then select the relevant version and the **Settings for the Fiscal Year** folder. Ensure that the **Integrated Planning** checkbox is selected for the year in question.

Activity Quantities

As we said at the beginning of this section, cost center planning in the SAP approach is driven by the activity quantities for the cost center. When we talked about the activity types in Chapter 3, we discussed the difference between calculating an activity price using the *capacity* or the *activity quantity*. The capacity behaves much like a costing lot size: it's set by the cost center manager or the controller as an "ideal" for the cost center. This can be the right approach if you have large seasonal variations or your planning process is still fairly raw. You can either enter the planned activity for each cost center manually or pull it from the requesting cost centers and production. However, the decision whether to plan by capacity or activity quantity isn't necessarily an either/or decision because you can create two planning versions: one that uses the capacity as its starting point and the other that uses the activity quantity as its starting point.

To check the settings for your activity types, select **Activity/Output Prices** and **Change**, shown in Figure 5.10. Alternatively, go to Transaction KP26 or **Accounting • Controlling • Cost Center Accounting • Planning • Activity Output/Prices • Change**, tab to layout **1-202 (Activity Types: Indicators)**, and enter the cost center, the activity types, the version, and the planning time frame.

Figure 5.11 shows the settings for cost center **4230** in version **0**. We'll plan all three activity types using price indicator 1 (**Plan Price Automatically Based on Activity**), because this is what we assume will be a realistic performance for our cost center. We could create a second version to plan the same activities on this cost center using price indicator 2 (**Plan Price Automatically Based on Capacity**). This might represent what the industrial engineers believe could be achieved under ideal conditions with none of the usual planning contingencies in place.

The **Act. sched.** (scheduled activity) column in Figure 5.12 represents this pull or demand captured in other plans. If this pull is considered realistic, you can use the plan reconciliation function to transfer the scheduled activity into the **Planned Activity** column so that it can be used to calculate the activity price.

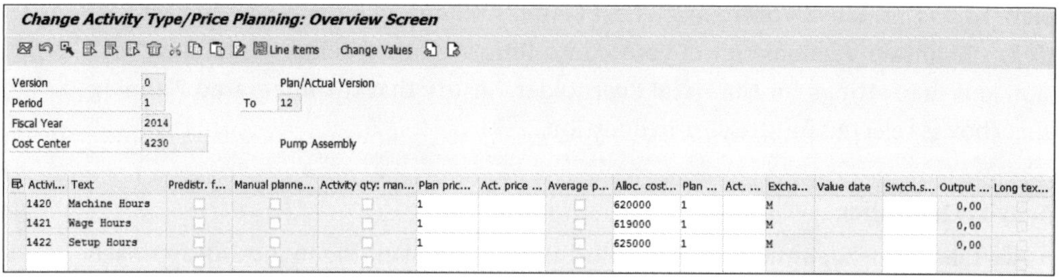

Figure 5.11 Settings for Price Calculation

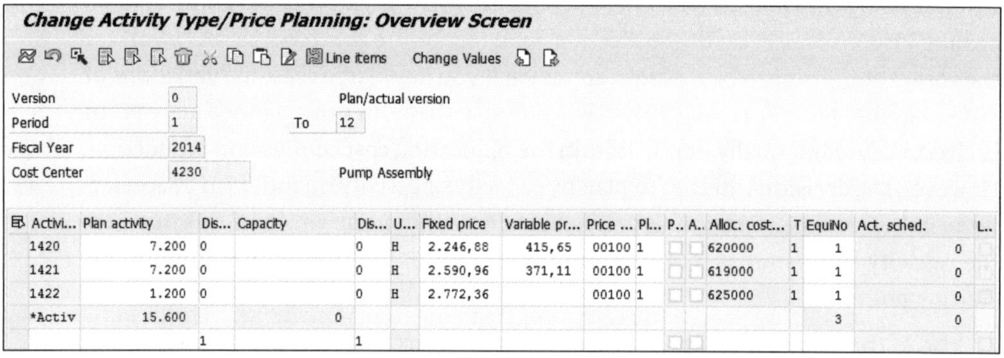

Figure 5.12 Capacities and Activity Quantities for Cost Center (SAP GUI)

To enter the capacities and output quantities, select **Activity/Output Prices** and **Change**, shown in Figure 5.10. Alternatively, go to Transaction KP26 or **Accounting • Controlling • Cost Center Accounting • Planning • Activity Output/Prices • Change**, choose layout **1-201 (Activity types with prices: standard)**, and enter the cost center, the activity types, the version, and the planning time frame. To keep the data entry in this transaction manageable, it makes sense to revisit the section on activity type groups in Chapter 3. If you try to plan too many activity types in one session, it's easy to put the wrong figures in the wrong line.

Figure 5.12 shows the planned activity for the activity types used in **Pump Assembly**, but the **Act. sched.** column reads zero. Before we look at how to fill this column, let's look at an alternative to this transaction.

As we saw for the master data in Chapter 3, EHP 6 for SAP ERP 6.0 includes new user interfaces for cost center planning. These reference the same master data and use the same tables to store their data as Transaction KP26. They also use the same authorizations and locking mechanisms, meaning that you can even choose by user role who accesses the new applications and who continues to work with the classic transactions.

To use the user interface shown in Figure 5.13, activate the business function FIN_CO_CCPLAN, the relevant Web Dynpro applications, and the BI Content bundle, and then make the new applications part of your working roles. For testing, you can use the delivered roles either for the cost center manager (SAP_CO_COST_CENTER_MANAGER) or for the internal controller (SAP_CO_INTERNAL_CONTROLLER). You'll find a general introduction to these applications at *https://scn.sap.com/docs/DOC-32680*, and SAP Note 1836149 contains a how-to guide that will walk your system administrator through the process of setting up these planning applications. If you use these roles, you'll find the new application under **Cost Center Planning • Activity Output and Price Planning • Cost Center: Activity Output and Price Planning**. The selection screen will look familiar from Chapter 3. You can easily add further cost centers and activity types by using the plus (+) button to add extra lines to the selection screen.

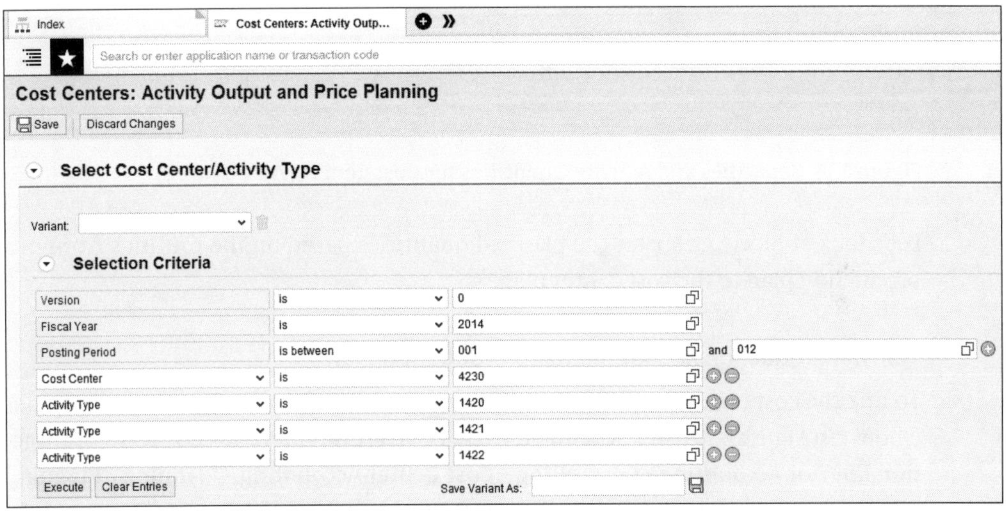

Figure 5.13 Selection Screen for Cost Center and Activity Planning (Web Dynpro)

Figure 5.14 shows the data entry screen for the activity quantities. You'll notice minor differences compared to Figure 5.12: whereas there you can access the periods by double-clicking on the relevant line, in the new application the period values are in a separate query. As you save a value with reference to a year, these values are automatically distributed to the period. If you prefer to enter the values by period (perhaps because you have seasonal variations in output), the values will be automatically aggregated to the year view as you save. You'll also notice a dedicated planning function to copy data between versions or fiscal years and planning functions to revalue the quantities entered with the latest activity price. Notice also that there are further queries for planning activity prices if you opt not to have the system calculate your activity prices, preferring to enter them manually. Just like the master data applications we looked at in Chapter 3, these user interfaces are configurable. More important, you can extend the queries used for data entry to include further columns. We'll look at how to configure these planning queries in Chapter 10.

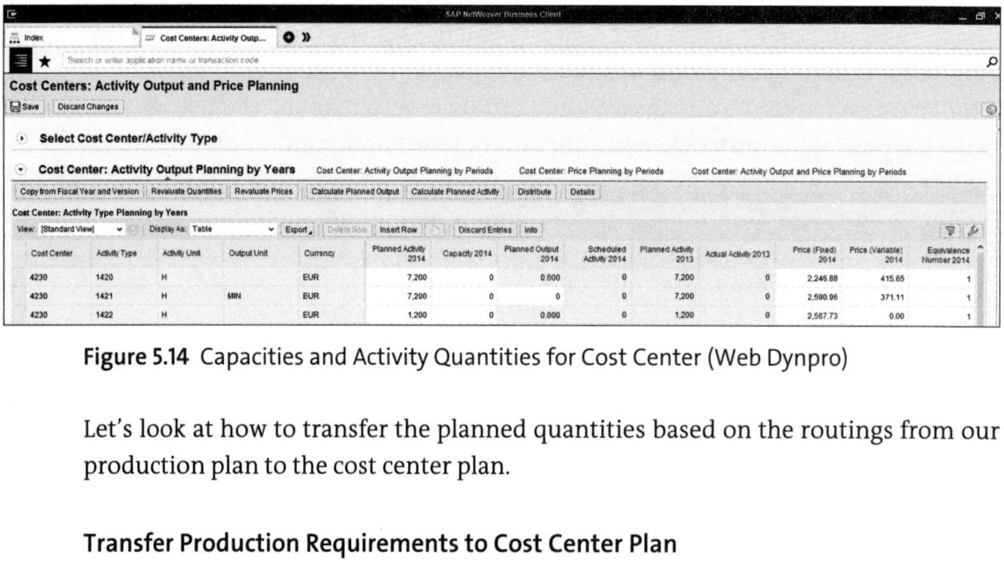

Figure 5.14 Capacities and Activity Quantities for Cost Center (Web Dynpro)

Let's look at how to transfer the planned quantities based on the routings from our production plan to the cost center plan.

Transfer Production Requirements to Cost Center Plan

To link the cost center plan with the production plan, select the **Planning Aids** folder (shown in Figure 5.10) and **Scheduled Activity SOP/LTP**. Alternatively, go to Transaction KSPP or **Accounting • Controlling • Cost Center Accounting • Planning • Planning Aids • Transfers • Scheduled Activity SOP/LTP** and click on the **Transfer Control** button. Figure 5.15 shows the link between the CO version and the planning scenario from the previous step. Remember that we fed data via a CO version from the sales plan to production, and now we're receiving data back from production via this same version. The result of this transaction will be that the **Act. sched.** column in Figure 5.12 will be filled for all production cost centers that are referenced in the routings used to prepare the long-term plan.

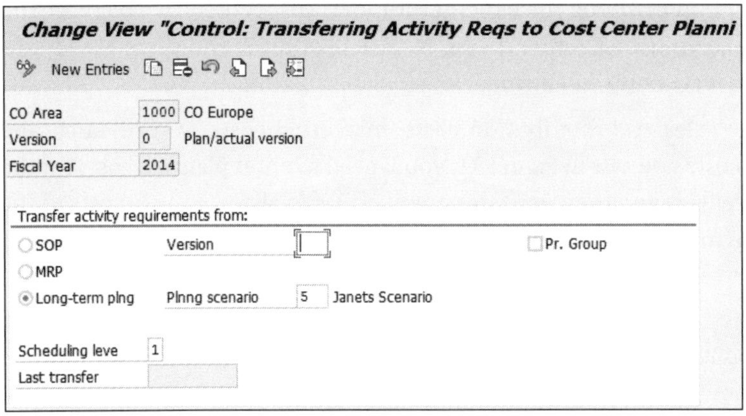

Figure 5.15 Transfer Planned Activity Requirements from Production

If you're only looking at production cost centers, you can now transfer the scheduled activity quantity to the **Planned Activity** column in Figure 5.12. To do this, select the **Planning Aids** folder and **Plan Reconciliation** (shown in Figure 5.10) or go to Transaction KPSI or **Accounting • Controlling • Cost Center Accounting • Planning • Planning Aids • Plan Reconciliation**. Enter the version, the time frame, and whether you want to reconcile for all cost centers or just for a selection. If you also want to include the activities from other cost centers (e.g., energy, repair, and quality cost centers) in this plan, you should *wait* until you've planned the activities required by the production cost centers from these cost centers before running plan reconciliation. We'll do that when we look at how to plan activity usage from supporting cost centers.

Plan Cost Center Costs

The controller now needs to work with the cost center managers to plan the costs required by each cost center to provide this level of output. There are various ways of working here:

- Some controllers sit down with their cost center managers and enter these values together.
- Others send out spreadsheets and have their cost center managers prepare the data for them to enter.
- Still others have the cost center managers enter this data. If you are using the user interfaces we looked at in Figure 5.14, you can also use SAP Analysis for Microsoft Office to provide an Excel frontend. We'll look at this in more detail in Chapter 10.

Before you embark on planning the expenses for your cost centers, we recommend that you go back to your cost center hierarchy (see Chapter 3) and understand how the costs for each cost center will be included in planning:

- To capture the sales and distribution costs, marketing costs, and research and development costs you saw in Figure 5.5, you'll need to enter planned costs for the relevant cost centers and then use assessment cycles to allocate these costs to the distribution channels and product groups, replicating the allocations that run at period close.
- To capture the costs for the production activities we've just planned, you'll need to plan your production cost centers. For these cost centers, it's worth being absolutely clear about which cost elements are activity-dependent (such as external procurement and direct labor) and which are activity-independent (such as rent and facility costs); you should also make sure that you've set up cost element groups for each task that contain exactly these cost elements (see Chapter 3). If your cost elements were created using a standard numbering convention, you can dispense with cost element groups to a large extent and simply make you selection by entering cost elements 400000–415000 or whichever number ranges correspond to the type of cost elements for which you want to enter costs.
- You'll also want to capture the costs for other cost centers that provide work to these production cost centers, such as maintenance cost centers, quality cost centers, and so on. You'll then need to plan activity output for these cost centers and activity input on the receiving cost centers.
- You'll have several other cost centers for administration and general overhead that either have no output, the costs of which are best allocated using an assessment cycle, or that have an output such as KWH of energy, the costs of which can be allocated using an indirect activity allocation cycle.

To enter the planned costs for the cost center, select **Cost and Activity Inputs** and **Change** (shown in Figure 5.10). Alternatively, go to Transaction KP06 or **Accounting • Controlling • Cost Center Accounting • Planning • Cost and Activity Inputs • Change**. The fields available for data entry in cost center planning are controlled by planning layouts configured in Customizing (we'll look at these settings in more detail in Chapter 10). Again, if your organization is using EHP 6, consider using the new user interfaces, because the planning queries will give you more options than the planning layouts.

The default planning layout for this type of planning is 1-101, but check that your organization has not configured its own. If you can't find planning layout 1-101, check whether it's been assigned to your planner profile. In the standard settings, it's assigned to planner profile SAP101 rather than SAPALL. Refer to Figure 10.1 in Chapter 10 if you're not sure how to do this.

The selection screen in Transaction KP06 is the same for activity-independent and activity-dependent costs. For administrative cost centers, sales cost centers, and so on, you will probably plan cost elements only. For production, maintenance, and similar cost centers or anything with an output, you'll have to access the same transaction twice—once to plan the activity-independent (fixed) costs and once to plan the activity-dependent costs:

- Leave the activity type fields blank for activity-independent (or fixed) costs.
- Enter an activity type group for activity-dependent costs. It will make life easier if you set up suitable activity type groups so that you aren't handling too many activity types at one time.

We'll first enter *activity-independent* costs to cover the fixed costs, such as rent and facilities costs. Select Transaction KP06 and enter the version, time frame, cost center, and your chosen cost element group, but leave the **Activity Type** field blank.

Before pressing [Enter], choose between **Free** and **Form-Based planning** (the default is **Free**):

- If you select **Form-based planning**, you'll see a line for every cost element entered in the initial screen. This can be cumbersome if you have a large chart of accounts and aren't careful with your initial cost element selection. However, you may find it easier to start with a form-based plan and a small cost element group or interval and then switch to free planning once you've captured your initial planning data. Because the form-based planning approach generates a line for every cost element in the interval or group for which active master data exists, this saves you from having to know exactly which cost element you want to plan for.
- If you select **Free planning**, you'll see a line for every line of planned data already entered. You can add new rows for additional cost elements as required. Once you've entered some data and are mainly adjusting the figures, free planning gives you a better overview of what has already been entered. However, to add data you have to manually enter the number of each relevant cost element. If you choose free planning before any data has been entered, you'll see the message **No Data**

Has Been Entered Yet. How easy you find entering your cost elements in free planning depends on how well you know your own chart of accounts.

Figure 5.16 shows the data entry screen, with form-based planning selected. Here you see an empty line for each of the cost elements entered in the selection screen (and why it's worth creating lots of small, specific cost element groups).

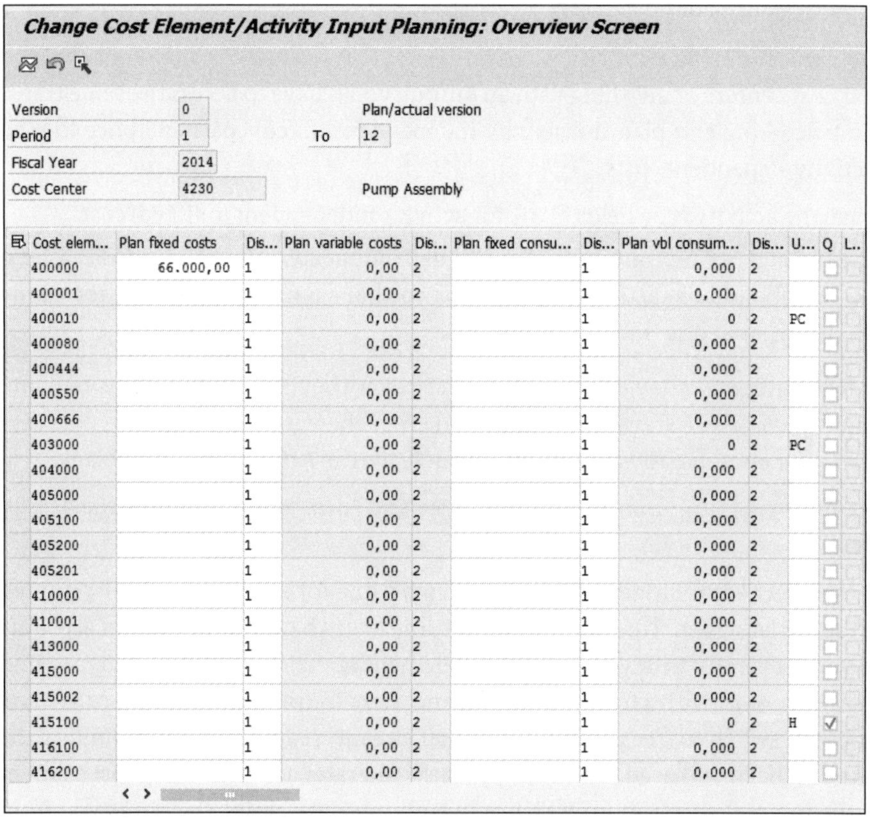

Figure 5.16 Activity-Independent Cost Planning (Form-Based)

You can go down this list and enter a figure for each relevant cost element. Also notice the distribution key 1 (equal distribution) that will be used to spread the figures you enter equally to the twelve periods of the fiscal year. For costs such as rent and insurance that are essentially fixed, it generally is appropriate to spread the costs equally across the periods.

By comparison, in Figure 5.17 we chose **Free Planning** in the selection screen. Now we see only those lines for which data has been entered. Notice here that we used equal distribution (distribution key 1) for the first line, but for the other lines we're using distribution key 2, which uses any existing values as a guide for the distribution. You can check the result of the distribution by choosing the **Periods** button. The controller can adjust the distribution key to select the method that best suits the business requirements in terms of seasonal variations and spikes in spending.

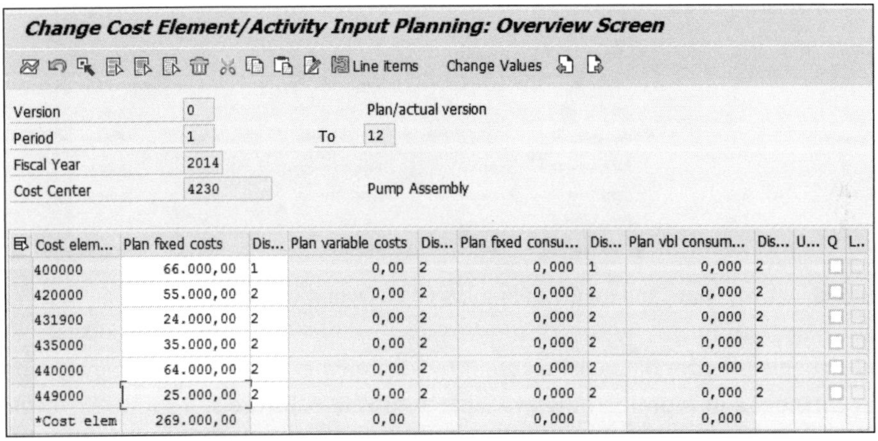

Figure 5.17 Activity-Independent Cost Planning (Free)

Just as you saw for the activity prices, if you are using EHP 6 you have a second option for collecting your activity-independent costs. Figure 5.18 shows the planning query for **Primary Cost Planning by Year**. From a usability perspective, the most obvious difference is that the new query shows the cost center and cost element texts. You can use the **Personalize** button (on the far right) to add or remove columns. You'll notice a second tab, **Primary Cost Planning by Period**. If you enter a value by year, it will be automatically distributed to the periods as you navigate to the other tab or save the query. The same happens in reverse if you enter your values by period. If you know that you will have spikes in your expenses, enter the values period by period, and the values will be automatically aggregated to the year when you navigate to the other query or save. Note that the mechanism used here is not the distribution keys we just discussed but a planning function. We'll look at how to configure these planning functions—and indeed the planning queries in general—in Chapter 10.

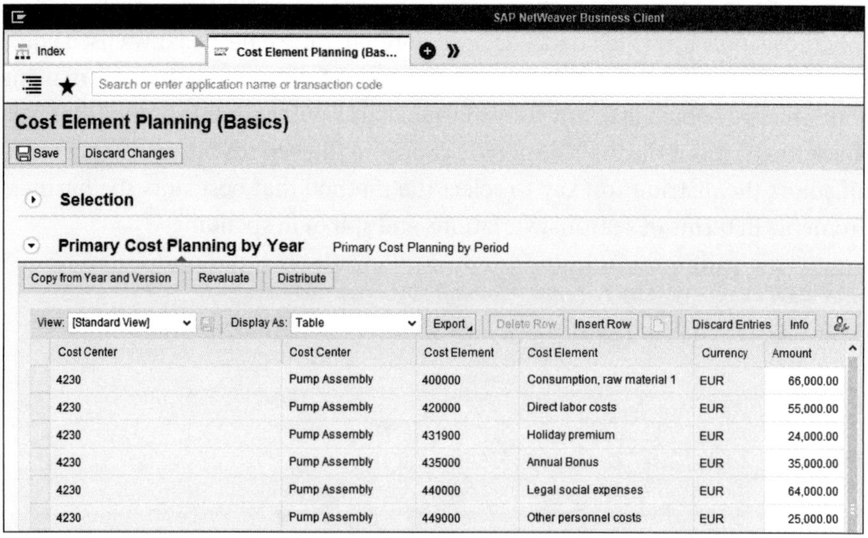

Figure 5.18 Activity-Independent Cost Planning (Web Dynpro)

If you struggle to enter data cost element by cost element for each cost center, you might consider a new option only available with EHP 6. Figure 5.19 shows the same cost center and cost elements as Figure 5.18. The difference is that this time you can enter costs for each **Cost Element Group**, so you can enter costs for the **Wages** group or the **Personnel Cost Element** groups rather than entering them for the cost elements line by line.

We talked about the way distribution is used to break down a figure entered for the fiscal year into periods. Figures entered for **Wages** are treated the same way and distributed to the *underlying* cost elements using a planning function. Using cost element groups instead of cost elements can really speed up planning, because most cost center managers think in terms of cost blocks rather than lines in the chart of accounts, especially when they are planning primary costs.

We'll now enter *activity-dependent* costs to cover those costs, such as direct labor and external procurement that vary with the output of the cost center. Again, go to Transaction KP06 and enter the version, time frame, cost center, and your chosen cost element group or interval, but this time enter an activity type group (see Chapter 3) that contains your chosen activity types. Figure 5.20 shows an example of activity-dependent planning. If you compare this with Figure 5.16, you'll notice that there's now a lead column containing the activity type. Proceed as before, this time entering the cost elements that refer to the delivery of a specific activity type.

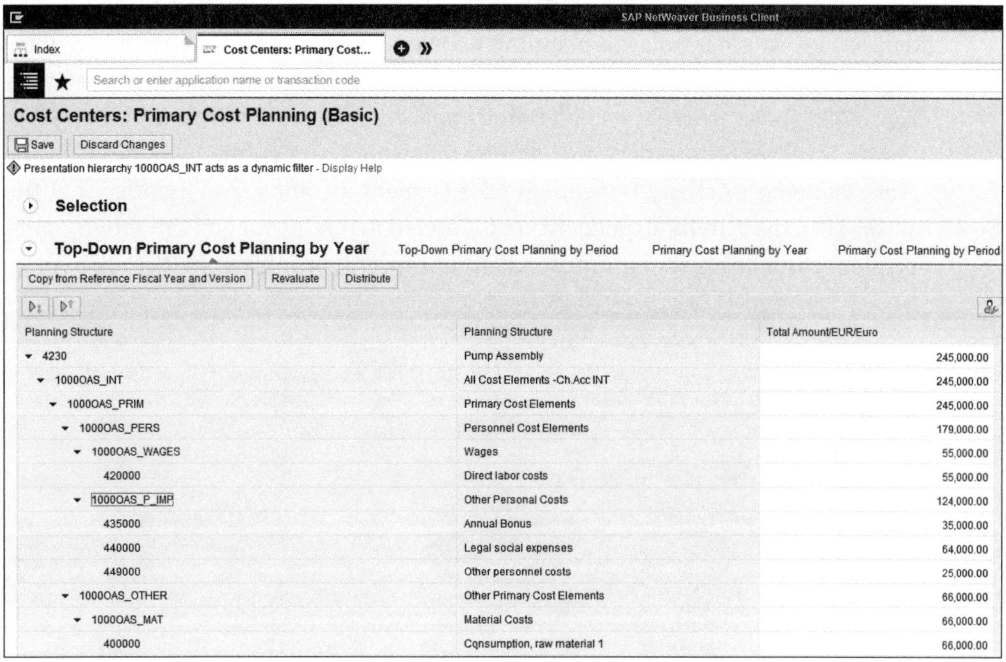

Figure 5.19 Top-Down Primary Cost Planning by Year (Web Dynpro)

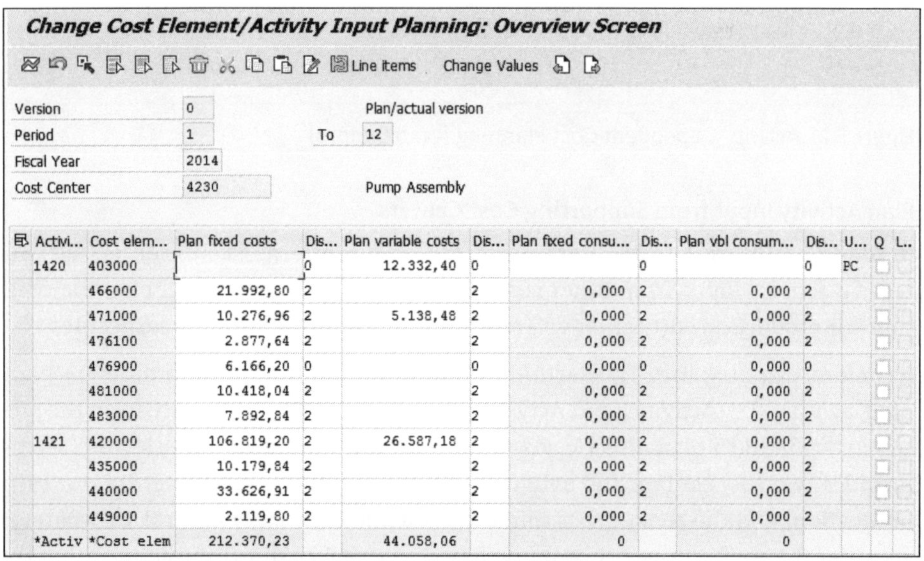

Figure 5.20 Activity-Dependent Cost Planning (SAP GUI)

Whereas in Transaction KP06 your entry of the activity type in the entry screen determines whether you are planning activity-dependent or activity-independent costs, in EHP 6 there is a separate application for planning activity-dependent costs. Figure 5.21 shows the new web planning application. You'll find this in the role Cost Center Manager or Internal Controller by following **Cost Center Planning • Cost Element Planning • Activity-Dependent Cost Element Planning.** You'll notice that this shows both the activity-dependent costs entered in this layout and the activity-independent costs we entered in Figure 5.19 (the activity type is blank in these lines).

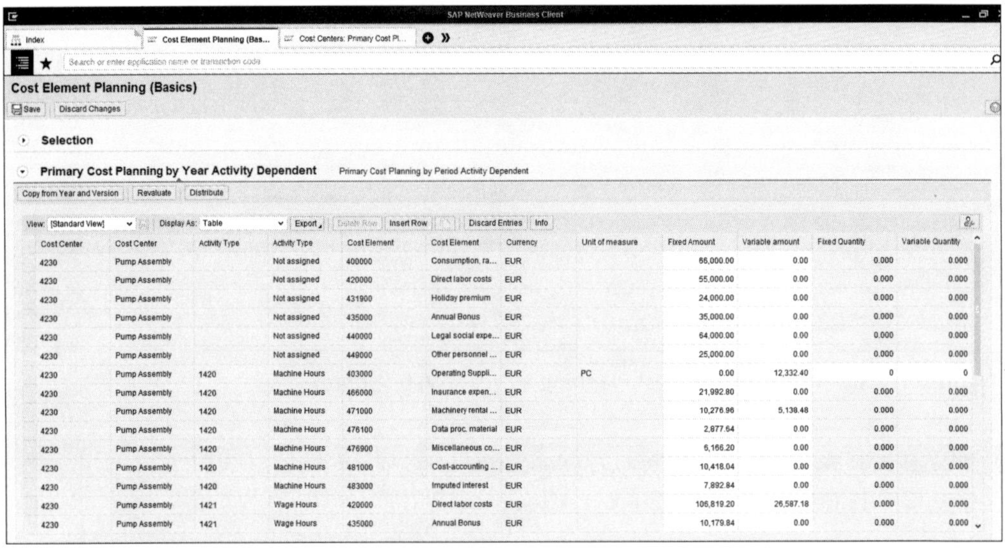

Figure 5.21 Activity-Dependent Cost Planning (Web Dynpro)

Plan Activity Input from Supporting Cost Centers

In addition to planning direct expenses for the cost center, most cost centers also will receive activity input from other cost centers. In our example, we'll plan the costs that our production cost center will receive from the quality control cost center.

As before, planning uses Transaction KP06, but this time we'll use a different planning layout, 1-102 (**Activity Input Acty-Indep./Acty-Dep.**). The difference from the procedure we used to plan direct costs for the cost center is that the selection screen includes two cost centers and activity types: the receiver cost center (in our case, production) and the sender cost center (maintenance, quality control, or whatever activities the production cost center will use). Figure 5.22 shows the activity that the production cost center (shown in the header) will receive from quality control (the sender cost center shown in the planning layout).

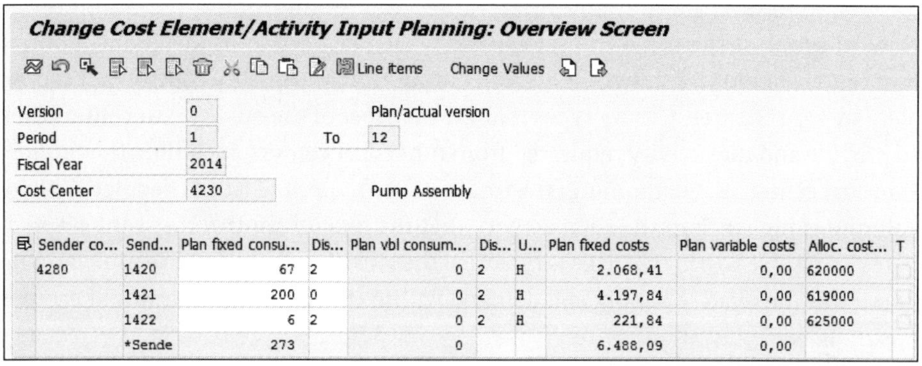

Figure 5.22 Activity Input Planning (SAP GUI)

Again, in EHP 6 there is an option to create the same plan using a new user interface, as shown in Figure 5.23. You can access this screen from the roles Internal Controller and Cost Center Manager by using **Cost Center Planning • Activity Input Planning • Cost Element Planning with Activity Input**. Notice that what you enter are the quantities of quality control activities required and that the system converts these into a monetary value when you save or when you select **Apply Prices**. You can continue in this way, planning all the other activity inputs that the production cost center will need.

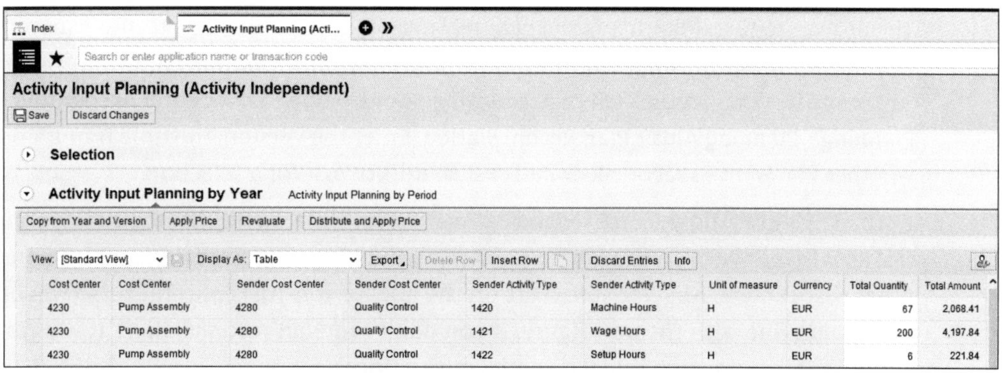

Figure 5.23 Activity Input Planning (Web Dynpro)

As you build up this network of activities, the concept of *scheduled activity* that we talked about at the start of the section comes into play. The production cost center has effectively requested activity from the quality control cost center.

Now let's look at the same transaction from the perspective of the quality control cost center. Figure 5.24 shows the activity output from the quality control cost center. Here we see the three activity types that the manager of the quality cost center plans to provide and the activity requested from other cost centers, including the production cost center. At the moment, the total activity requested (see **Scheduled Activity** column) is higher than the total activity that the quality control cost center anticipates being able to provide. This is typical of the situation that will arise in a planning process as the relative supply and demand within the cost center network becomes apparent.

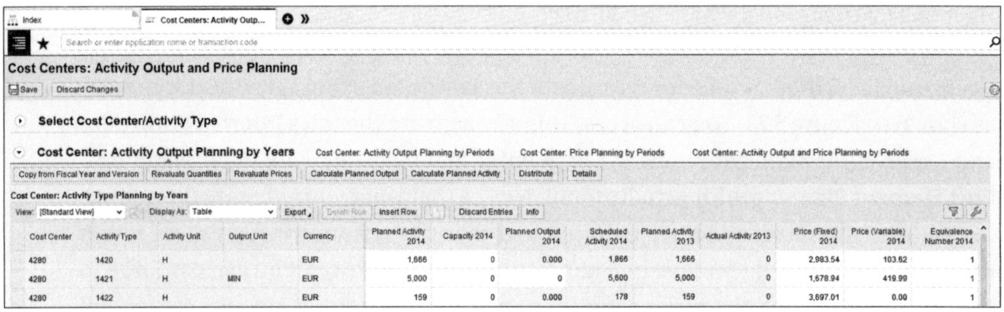

Figure 5.24 Output of Quality Control Cost Center (Web Dynpro)

The answer to this dilemma is the *plan reconciliation* function. To execute plan reconciliation, select the **Planning Aids** folder and **Plan Reconciliation** (shown in Figure 5.10) or go to Transaction KPSI or **Accounting • Controlling • Cost Center Accounting • Planning • Planning Aids • Plan Reconciliation**. Enter the version, the time frame, and whether you want to reconcile for all cost centers or just for a selection.

Figure 5.25 shows the result of reconciliation. The first line shows that the quality control activities have been adjusted by 200, 600, and 19 to reflect the demand from the other cost centers. Any variable costs on the quality control cost center also will be adjusted in line with the new figure. If you don't run plan reconciliation, it will run automatically when you calculate your activity prices.

Plan Reconciliation: List

Messages Choose Save

Controlling Area	1000	CO Europe		
Version	0	Plan/actual version		
Fiscal Year	2014			
Period	001	to	012	
Processing status	TestRun			
Number of messages	2			
Maximum Categ.	Warning			

Processing completed with warnings

Display status Total for all per.

OTy	Object	Name	AUn	Total plan activity	New plan activity	Activity difference
ATY	4280/1420	Quality Control	H	1.666	1.866	200
ATY	4280/1421	Quality Control	H	5.000	5.600	600
ATY	4280/1422	Quality Control	H	159	178	19
ATY	4290/1420	Prod. Elevators/Turb	H	9.600	9.600	0
ATY	4290/1421	Prod. Elevators/Turb	H	9.600	9.600	0
ATY	4290/1426	Prod. Elevators/Turb	H	11.000	11.000	0
ATY	4290/1428	Prod. Elevators/Turb	H	3.000	3.000	0
ATY	4290/1429	Prod. Elevators/Turb	H	6.000	6.000	0
ATY	4290/1430	Prod. Elevators/Turb	H	3.000	3.000	0
ATY	4290/1463	Prod. Elevators/Turb	H	500	500	0
ATY	4295/1420	Elevator Assembly	H	300	300	0
ATY	4295/1421	Elevator Assembly	H	3.600	3.600	0
ATY	4295/1426	Elevator Assembly	H	11.000	11.000	0
ATY	4295/1428	Elevator Assembly	H	3.000	3.000	0
ATY	4295/1429	Elevator Assembly	H	6.000	6.000	0
ATY	4295/1430	Elevator Assembly	H	3.000	3.000	0
ATY	4295/1463	Elevator Assembly	H	500	500	0
ATY	4296/1420	Turbine preassembly	H	10.000	10.000	0
ATY	4296/1421	Turbine preassembly	H	3.000	3.000	0
ATY	4296/1426	Turbine preassembly	H	11.000	11.000	0
ATY	4296/1428	Turbine preassembly	H	3.000	3.000	0
ATY	4296/1429	Turbine preassembly	H	6.000	6.000	0
ATY	4296/1430	Turbine preassembly	H	3.000	3.000	0
ATY	4296/1463	Turbine preassembly	H	500	500	0
ATY	4297/1420	Turbine fin. assmbly	H	10.000	10.000	0
ATY	4297/1421	Turbine fin. assmbly	H	12.000	12.000	0

Figure 5.25 Result of Plan Reconciliation

Splitting Cost Center Costs

If the cost center provides more than one activity, such as machine hours, wage hours, and setup hours, as in our example, then the expenses captured at the cost center level (shown in Figure 5.16) have to be "split" across the activity types before an activity price can be calculated. The split can use either equivalence numbers or a splitting schema. You define the approach in Customizing using a *splitting structure* and then assign it to the relevant cost centers. To perform splitting, go to Transaction KSS4 or **Accounting • Controlling • Cost Center Accounting • Planning • Allocations • Splitting**. Enter the relevant version, periods, and fiscal year. Figure 5.26 shows the result of splitting; each line in the cost element plan is broken down into three lines—one for each of the activities that the cost center plans to provide.

Plan Cost Splitting: List

Display status Total for all periods

Cost Object	Cost Elem.	Name	Partner object	Resource	Planned (COArCurr)	Crcy	Plan quantity	UM
CTR 4230	400000	Raw Materials 1				EUR		
ATY 4230/1420	400000	Raw Materials 1			21.999,97	EUR	0,000	
ATY 4230/1421	400000	Raw Materials 1			22.000,01	EUR	0,000	
ATY 4230/1422	400000	Raw Materials 1			22.000,02	EUR	0,000	
CTR 4230	420000	Direct labor costs				EUR		
ATY 4230/1420	420000	Direct labor costs			18.333,35	EUR	0,000	
ATY 4230/1421	420000	Direct labor costs			18.333,33	EUR	0,000	
ATY 4230/1422	420000	Direct labor costs			18.333,32	EUR	0,000	
CTR 4230	431900	Holiday premium				EUR		
ATY 4230/1420	431900	Holiday premium			8.000,03	EUR	0,000	
ATY 4230/1421	431900	Holiday premium			7.999,99	EUR	0,000	
ATY 4230/1422	431900	Holiday premium			7.999,98	EUR	0,000	
CTR 4230	435000	Annual Bonus				EUR		
ATY 4230/1420	435000	Annual Bonus			11.666,65	EUR	0,000	
ATY 4230/1421	435000	Annual Bonus			11.666,67	EUR	0,000	
ATY 4230/1422	435000	Annual Bonus			11.666,68	EUR	0,000	
CTR 4230	440000	Legal social expense				EUR		
ATY 4230/1420	440000	Legal social expense			21.333,35	EUR	0,000	
ATY 4230/1421	440000	Legal social expense			21.333,33	EUR	0,000	
ATY 4230/1422	440000	Legal social expense			21.333,32	EUR	0,000	
CTR 4230	449000	Other pers. costs				EUR		
ATY 4230/1420	449000	Other pers. costs			8.333,33	EUR	0,000	
ATY 4230/1421	449000	Other pers. costs			8.333,33	EUR	0,000	
ATY 4230/1422	449000	Other pers. costs			8.333,34	EUR	0,000	
CTR 4230	619000	DAA Production	ATY 4280/1421			EUR		H
ATY 4230/1420	619000	DAA Production	ATY 4280/1421		1.878,23	EUR	66,667	H
ATY 4230/1421	619000	DAA Production	ATY 4280/1421		1.878,26	EUR	66,671	H
ATY 4230/1422	619000	DAA Production	ATY 4280/1421		1.878,25	EUR	66,662	H
CTR 4230	620000	DAA Machine Costs	ATY 4280/1420			EUR		H
ATY 4230/1420	620000	DAA Machine Costs	ATY 4280/1420		1.196,53	EUR	22,332	H
ATY 4230/1421	620000	DAA Machine Costs	ATY 4280/1420		1.196,56	EUR	22,332	H
ATY 4230/1422	620000	DAA Machine Costs	ATY 4280/1420		1.196,53	EUR	22,336	H
CTR 4230	625000	DAA Setup	ATY 4280/1422			EUR		H
ATY 4230/1420	625000	DAA Setup	ATY 4280/1422		370,97	EUR	2,003	H
ATY 4230/1421	625000	DAA Setup	ATY 4280/1422		370,95	EUR	1,999	H
ATY 4230/1422	625000	DAA Setup	ATY 4280/1422		370,97	EUR	1,998	H
**					279.337,25	EUR	273,000	

Figure 5.26 Result of Plan Price Splitting

Plan Indirect Activity Allocation from Supporting Cost Centers

As well as planning direct activity allocations for quality control, maintenance, and so on, you can consider using *indirect activity allocation cycles* to plan other activities. You may remember the term from when we discussed the master data for the activity types in Chapter 3. Indirect activity allocations work on certain assumptions:

- One assumption might be that every hour of machine time provided by a production cost center requires one kilowatt hour from the energy cost center. To model this, define kilowatt hours as a category 2 activity type (**Indirect Determination, Indirect Allocation**). Then create an indirect activity allocation cycle that contains the energy cost center as a sender and the production cost centers as the receivers.

The receiver tracing factor for the cycle would be the machine hours on the production cost center (planned using Transaction KP26). When you execute the allocation cycle, the system reads the machine hours planned for each production cost center and calculates the total kilowatt hours that need to be provided to ensure this number of machine hours. It's worth knowing that this does not need to be a one-to-one relationship. You can also use a weighting factor to allocate one kilowatt hour of energy for every 10 hours of machine time—or whatever factor makes sense in your business.

- Another approach might be to manually enter the total kilowatt hours supplied for the period. This makes sense if there's some kind of counter in place that records the energy supplied and you can use these historical figures in your plan. To model this, define kilowatt hours as a category 3 activity type (**Manual Entry, Indirect Allocation**). The sender, receivers, and receiver tracing factor in the cycle would be the same as previously discussed. However, in this approach the manually planned total energy would be split to the production cost centers in proportion to the machine hours supplied by each cost center.

Because the same mechanisms are used to calculate planned costs as are used to allocate actual costs at period close, you'll find a more detailed description of how to set up indirect allocation cycles in Chapter 7. The only difference is the menu path (you'll find planned allocations in the **Allocations** folder shown in Figure 5.10) and the fact that you have to include your plan version in the cycle.

Plan General Overhead and Sales-Related Overhead by Cost Centers

Make sure that you plan the costs for all cost centers that aren't involved in the production process. You'll use the same transactions/applications as we used to plan the production and quality cost centers. The difference is that you'll need to decide how to allocate these costs. For general overhead, it's common to use statistical key figures (see Chapter 3). Figure 5.27 shows the planned headcount for the Corporate Service cost center we looked at in Chapter 3. To access statistical key figure planning, refer to Figure 5.10 or follow **Accounting • Controlling • Cost Center Accounting • Planning • Statistical Key Figures • Change** or use Transaction KP46. Enter the version, time frame, cost center, statistical key figure, and the appropriate figure. A new planning application for statistical key figure planning is available with SAP_APPL 606, SP14.

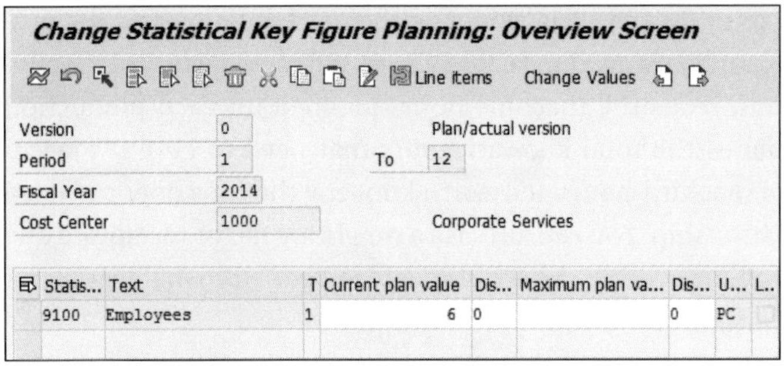

Figure 5.27 Statistical Key Figure Planning by Cost Center

For sales, marketing, and research and development cost centers, among others, it's common to look to the sales quantities as the drivers for an allocation, so you'll either access the sales plan quantities that we planned at the beginning of the chapter or the planned revenues for these products.

Cost Center Planning in SAP S/4HANA

SAP S/4HANA offers a multidimensional approach to planning, in which cost center planning is automatically combined with profit center planning and profit and loss planning in a single planning model. We'll explain how the planning model works and where you may still need to use the traditional model in Chapter 14. SAP Note 2270407 (Profit and Loss Planning, Profit Center Planning, Cost Center Planning, Order Planning, and Project Planning) explains what issues to consider during a conversion.

Calculate and Settle Order Costs

If orders are assigned to the cost centers to provide additional detailing (such as orders for marketing events assigned to the marketing cost center), you should also include these order costs in the cost center plan. Clearly, this plan only applies to a subset of the available orders—namely, those that exist for the whole planning period. Planning such orders can be the job of the individual manager (e.g., the person responsible for a particular marketing event), the cost center manager (if a research and development cost center performs many different R&D tasks), or even controlling (for which the orders are for general administrative tasks).

The costs for production orders, process orders, and so on are captured when we calculate the standard costs for the manufactured materials, so we can ignore them here; we'll capture them in the next section. The costs of other logistics orders for maintenance activities and on the like are usually planned via the cost center to which they settle their costs. We'll look at how to plan investment orders and projects Section 5.2.

Figure 5.28 shows the **Planning** folder for order planning. Unlike the **Profitability Planning** and **Cost Center Planning** folders, only expenses and activity input are planned for the internal order, but there's no output quantity. Instead, order costs are settled or charged either to the parent cost center or to the relevant market segment. If you aren't able to link the long-term production plan into cost center planning (Section 5.1.1), you can also use shadow internal orders to represent demand for each production activity and plan this activity input just as we did for the usage of quality control effort by the production cost center.

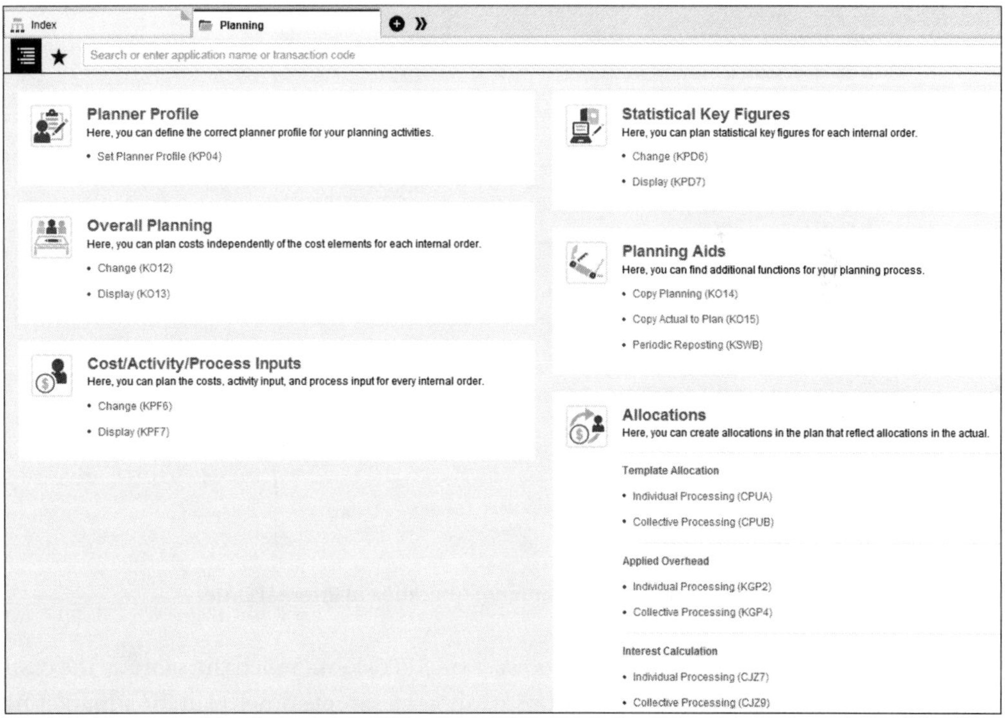

Figure 5.28 Planning Applications for Internal Orders

Plan Integration for Orders

The Customizing settings for the version and order type include selecting the **Plan Integration** checkbox. This checkbox is transferred to the **Control Data** tab of the internal order (see Chapter 3) and determines how the planned costs on the order (or Work Breakdown Structure [WBS] elements) are handled and whether a demand for activities from an order or project is treated the same way as a demand from another cost center.

Figure 5.29 shows the order master data (Transaction KO01) and an order for which the **Plan-Integrated Order** checkbox has been selected. The value in the version is merely a default. It's the flag in the order itself that determines whether values planned for the order will be transferred or not, so make sure you're consistent in selecting this checkbox for order types whose values you want to include in planning. These will typically be those order types that exist for the full duration of the planning period rather than short-lived production and maintenance orders.

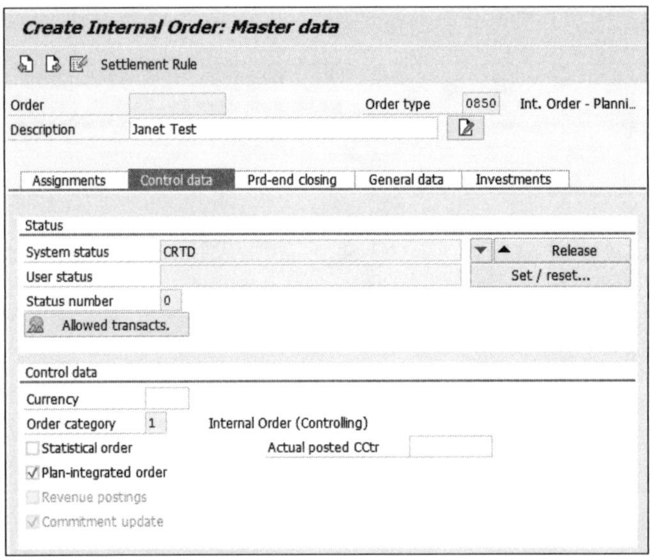

Figure 5.29 Plan-Integrated Order Planning: Checkbox in Internal Order

The order-planning application (Transaction KPF6) looks much the same as the cost-center-planning application. Figure 5.30 shows a sample order plan for a marketing event that will ultimately settle to the marketing cost center. This data is normally entered either by the manager of the SAPPHIRE event or the cost center manager for the marketing cost center and then checked by controlling.

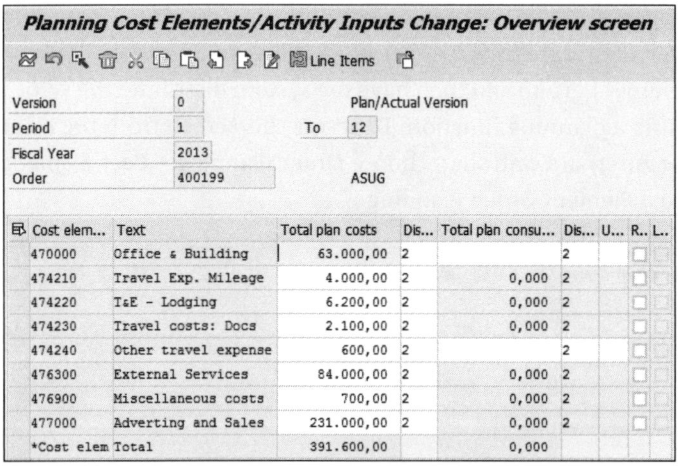

Figure 5.30 Order Cost Planning for Marketing Order (SAP GUI)

Again, as we saw for cost center planning, EHP 6 includes new user interfaces for order planning. Figure 5.31 shows the costs for the same order in the Web Dynpro application. To access this application, use the role Internal Controller or Cost Center Manager and choose **Order Planning • Cost Element Planning • Cost Element Planning (Basic)**, fill out the selection screen, and click on **Execute**. These applications are delivered via the business function FIN_CO_ORPLAN.

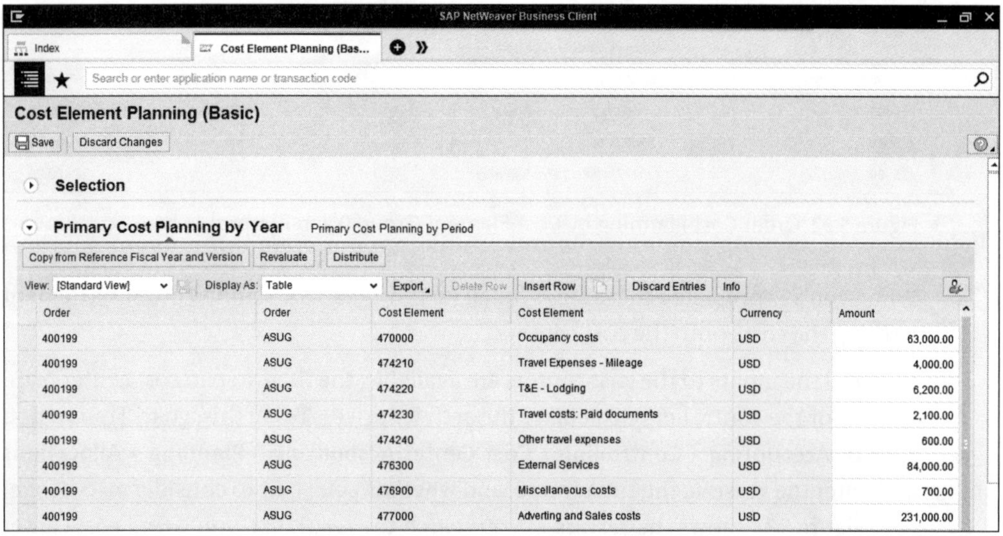

Figure 5.31 Order Cost Planning for Marketing Order (Web Dynpro)

Just as cost center managers struggle to enter expenses line by line, order managers may also prefer to enter their expenses by cost block. Figure 5.32 shows the new option to plan by cost element group and then have the system distribute the values to the cost elements using a planning function. To access this screen from the roles Cost Center Manager or Internal Controller, choose **Order Planning • Cost Element Planning • Top-Down Cost Element Group Planning**.

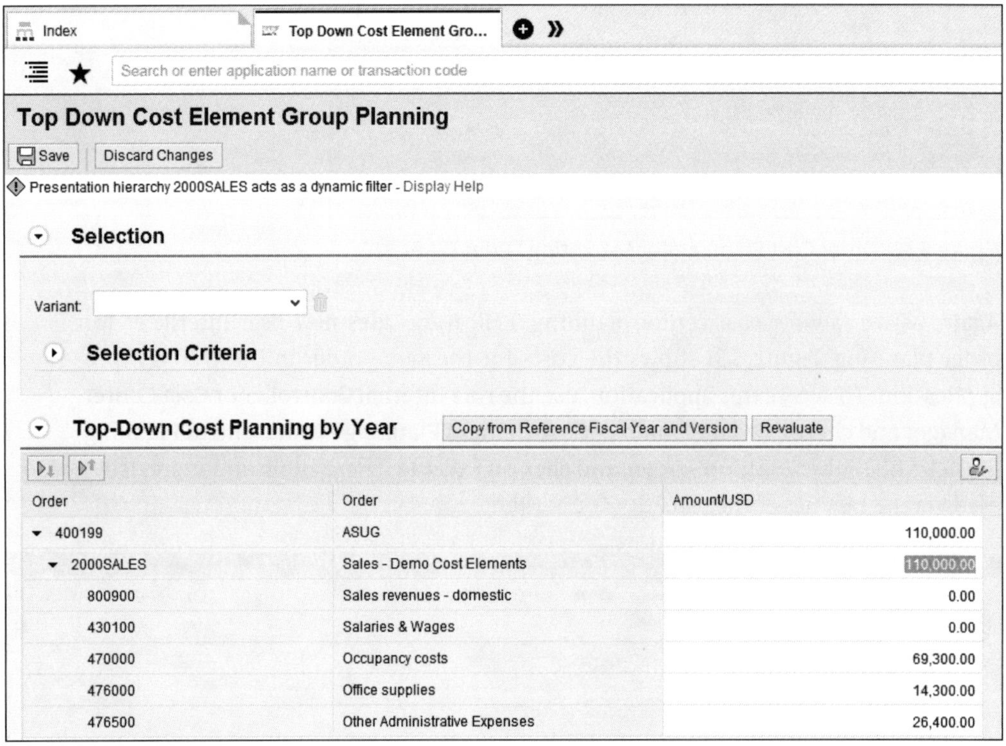

Figure 5.32 Order Cost Planning by Cost Element Group (Web Dynpro)

When you've completed these steps for all your orders, run planned order settlement to bring the costs onto the cost centers.

When all the inputs to the cost centers are available, the final step in cost center planning is for the controller to calculate the activity prices. To do this, go to Transaction KSPI or **Accounting • Controlling • Cost Center Accounting • Planning • Allocations** and enter the version, the time frame, and whether you want to consider all cost centers. Figure 5.33 shows the results. If you search the result list, you'll find cost center

4230, which has been our sample cost center for much of this section, along with three activity types: 1420, 1421, and 1422. We'll use these activity prices to calculate the cost of manufacturing the pumps in the next section.

Price Calculation Results - Plan

Messages | Activity Analysis

```
Controlling Area      1000          CO Europe
Version               0             Plan/actual version
Fiscal Year           2014
Period                001           to          012
Cost center group     H1420
Plan price calc.      1             Periodic price
Cost Comp Struct. (M  IE            IDES Europe
Currency              EUR           Euro (EMU currency as of 01/01/1999)
Exchange Rate Type    M             Standard translation at average rate
Value Date            01.01.2014

Processing status     UpdateRun
Number of messages    144
Maximum Categ.        Error

Update performed despite errors

Document number from  32373
                      32372
                      32371

Period                001
```

OTy	Object	Name	AUn	Activity Quantity	Total price	Price (Fixed)	PUnit
ATY	4230/1420	Pump Assembly	H	600	3.403,96	2.988,31	100
ATY	4230/1421	Pump Assembly	H	600	3.765,96	3.396,69	100
ATY	4230/1422	Pump Assembly	H	100	7.651,35	7.651,35	100
ATY	4240/1420	Paint/Solvent Prod.	H	300	8.397,60	5.687,67	100
ATY	4240/1421	Paint/Solvent Prod.	H	300	3.272,63	2.846,56	100
ATY	4250/1420	Chem.Products Prod.	H	150	13.243,73	8.012,86	100
ATY	4250/1421	Chem.Products Prod.	H	150	3.204,35	2.636,25	100
ATY	4258/1420	Prod. Pharmac./Cosm.	H	350	4.335,95	3.589,85	100
ATY	4258/1421	Prod. Pharmac./Cosm.	H	350	3.459,33	2.789,78	100
ATY	4258/1422	Prod. Pharmac./Cosm.	H	25	1.228,32	1.228,32	10
ATY	4260/1420	Bulb Production I	H	600	2.091,73	1.602,50	100
ATY	4260/1421	Bulb Production I	H	600	3.329,14	2.711,33	100
ATY	4270/1420	Bulb Production II	H	150	6.148,00	4.150,81	100
ATY	4270/1421	Bulb Production II	H	150	3.742,03	3.031,90	100
ATY	4271/1420	Foodstuffs Prod.	H	200	6.192,96	5.020,59	100

Figure 5.33 Result of Activity Price Calculation

Calculating activity prices with Transaction KSPI sets the prices used to value production activities and work time throughout SAP ERP. If you run the calculation in test mode, you'll receive a message asking whether you want to save the results as you leave the transaction. Think before you save, especially if your plan data refers to the current year, because you don't want to overwrite your operative valuation.

One trick to use if you aren't sure your activity price calculation will be completely accurate is to copy all the relevant input data into a version other than 0 using Transaction KP97 (in the **Planning Aids** folder) and run activity price calculation in a version that isn't going to be used for active valuation until you're satisfied with the results.

Only save results in version 0 that you really want to release for productive use. To ensure consistency, consider locking the plan version (under **Current Settings**) as soon as planning is complete.

As you come to the end of your planning activities, it makes sense to check the results. The easiest way to do this is to go to **Accounting • Controlling • Cost Center Accounting • Information System • Reports for Cost Center Accounting • Planning Reports • Cost Centers: Planning Overview** or Transaction KSBL, as shown in Figure 5.34.

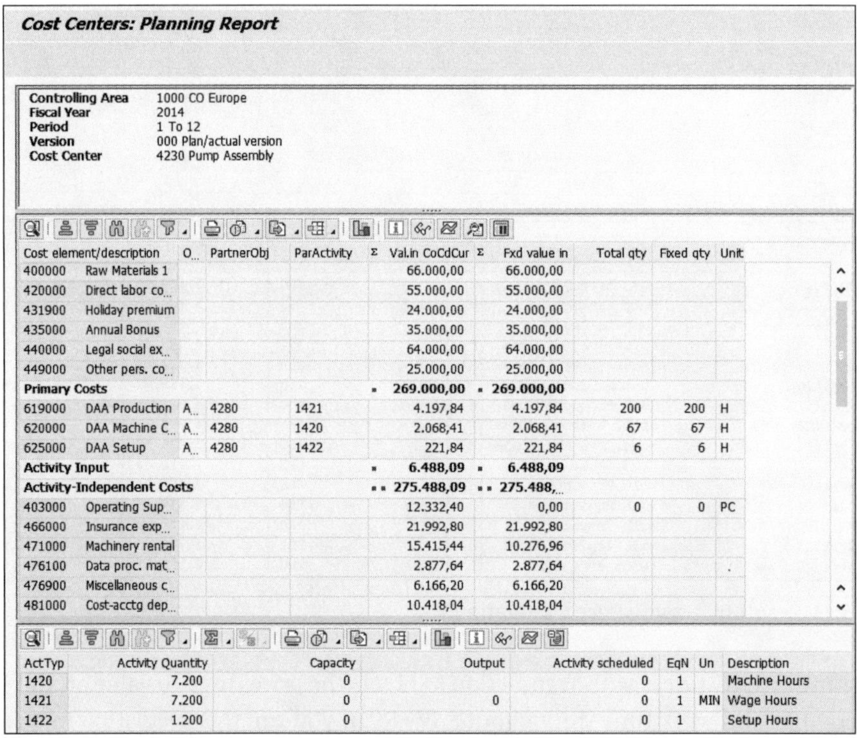

Cost Centers: Planning Report

Controlling Area	1000 CO Europe
Fiscal Year	2014
Period	1 To 12
Version	000 Plan/actual version
Cost Center	4230 Pump Assembly

Cost element/description		O...	PartnerObj	ParActivity	Σ Val.in CoCdCur	Σ Fxd value in	Total qty	Fixed qty	Unit
400000	Raw Materials 1				66.000,00	66.000,00			
420000	Direct labor co...				55.000,00	55.000,00			
431900	Holiday premium				24.000,00	24.000,00			
435000	Annual Bonus				35.000,00	35.000,00			
440000	Legal social ex...				64.000,00	64.000,00			
449000	Other pers. co...				25.000,00	25.000,00			
Primary Costs					▪ 269.000,00	▪ 269.000,00			
619000	DAA Production	A...	4280	1421	4.197,84	4.197,84	200	200	H
620000	DAA Machine C...	A...	4280	1420	2.068,41	2.068,41	67	67	H
625000	DAA Setup	A...	4280	1422	221,84	221,84	6	6	H
Activity Input					▪ 6.488,09	▪ 6.488,09			
Activity-Independent Costs					▪▪ 275.488,09	▪▪ 275.488,...			
403000	Operating Sup...				12.332,40	0,00	0	0	PC
466000	Insurance exp...				21.992,80	21.992,80			
471000	Machinery rental				15.415,44	10.276,96			
476100	Data proc. mat...				2.877,64	2.877,64			
476900	Miscellaneous c...				6.166,20	6.166,20			
481000	Cost-acctg dep...				10.418,04	10.418,04			

ActTyp	Activity Quantity	Capacity	Output	Activity scheduled	EqN	Un	Description
1420	7.200	0		0	1		Machine Hours
1421	7.200	0	0	0	1	MIN	Wage Hours
1422	1.200	0		0	1		Setup Hours

Figure 5.34 Cost Center Planning: Overview Report

You'll see the activity-independent expenses (layout 1-101), the activity input (layout 1-102), the activity-dependent costs (layout 1-101), and the total. In the boxes below, you'll see the planned activity output and any statistical key figures planned for the cost center. You'll notice also that the concept of *partner object* that we discussed first in Chapter 2 returns here as you see the activity provided to the production cost center by the quality control cost center showing in the **PartnerObj** (partner object) column.

Customer Connect Enhancements for Forecasting

So far, we've described the planning of cost center costs as if we are starting the process from scratch for the fiscal year that follows. Many organizations also produce a forecast for their cost centers, with the plan copied to a different version and adjusted to reflect the latest forecast figures. A new function is now offered that offers various projection methods to adjust the planned data automatically during copy. You'll find details of the new solution in SAP Note 2419549 (Customer Connect CO: Plan Copy Based on Projection Values).

Primary Cost Component Split for the Activity Price

When we discussed work centers in Chapter 4, we said there's often confusion about the fact that the maximum output of a work center is six activity types and that many people feel that they need more. We argued that they're missing the distinction between inputs (wages, depreciation, energy, etc.) and outputs (machine hours, wage hours, etc.). Once your activity rates start to become stable, it's worth considering activating a primary cost component split for your activity types by defining a cost component structure and entering this in the planning version (these are Customizing activities).

The cost component structure takes the input cost elements (wages, depreciation, energy, etc.) from cost center planning and assigns them to cost components (these are configured the same way as the cost components we encountered when reporting on the product costs in Chapter 2). The same limit of 40 cost components applies as for the product cost component split.

Figure 5.35 shows an activity rate that has been broken out this way to show wages, salaries, employee benefits, material costs, imputed benefits, and external processing (primary cost elements) and energy and maintenance (secondary cost elements). You can get to this view by selecting the result line for cost center 4230 and activity type 1420 shown in Figure 5.33 and choosing **Goto • Components**.

It's then possible to map the cost component split for the activity rate into the product cost estimate as a primary cost component split and to map these costs to value fields in Profitability Analysis to allow you to include these costs in your product and customer profitability reporting. We'll see how this works in Section 5.1.3.

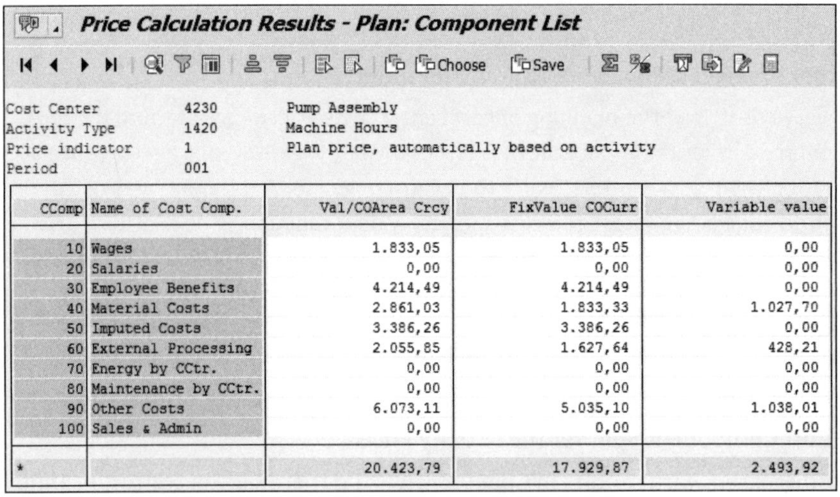

Figure 5.35 Primary Cost Component Split for Activity Rate

The activity price calculation is the final step in cost center planning—but not the last step in planning. We can now use this rate per hour, broken down into its cost components, to calculate the standard costs for each of the materials we'll manufacture and apply these figures to the sales plan to calculate the contribution margin for the sales plan.

5.1.3 Calculating Standard Costs for Products to Be Manufactured

When we created the production plan, we used the BOMs and routings for each material to determine the *scheduled activity* required for production. We'll now use the same master data from production to determine the standard costs for all our products. Figure 5.36 shows the planning applications for product cost planning.

You use a *costing run* to calculate standard costs for all the materials in a plant or plants. This is a very different planning application from the sales and cost center planning applications in that it's largely automated and always performed by either central controlling or plant controlling, though individual managers may be called in to verify the results. The results of costing flow into profitability planning but are also used to set the standard costs in the material master (see Chapter 4). It's also possible to calculate the costs of individual materials using the Cost Estimate with Quantity Structure applications (Transaction CK11N), but this is mostly used for testing and for setting a standard price for new products rather than for the mass calculation of standard prices for all materials as part of the AOP. Be aware also that the quality of the costing run is largely driven by the quality of the master data we looked at in Chapter 4. You are relying on high-quality BOMs, routings, and work centers as the basis for your standard costs.

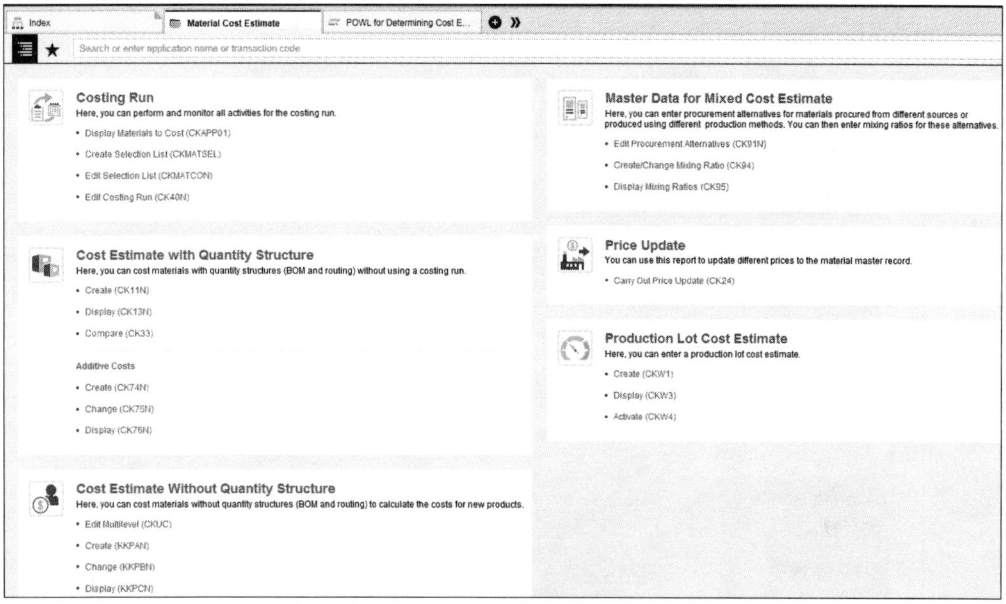

Figure 5.36 Planning Applications for Product Cost Planning

Create Costing Run

To create a costing run, select **Edit Costing Run**, shown in Figure 5.36; use Transaction CK40N; or follow the menu path **Accounting • Controlling • Product Cost Controlling • Product Cost Planning • Material Costing • Costing Run • Edit Costing Run**. Figure 5.37 shows the initial screen for a costing run on a specific key date. The costing run acts as the framework around the costing steps (selection, structure explosion, costing, analysis, marking, and release) that are performed during costing. Technically the costing steps are ABAP jobs that can be scheduled in the background because of the high data volumes involved. The **Flow Step** column shows a line for each step. To perform the steps, proceed as follows:

1. To determine what information is used in each step, enter the selection parameters in the **Parameter** column (e.g., the parameters for the **Selection** step are the finished products to be included in costing). You need to check the parameters before you enter each job.
2. To schedule the job (set it to start at a given time), click on the icon in the **Execute** column. This icon is activated after you maintain the selection parameters.
3. As each step is completed, you can monitor the status and the error logs in the other columns.

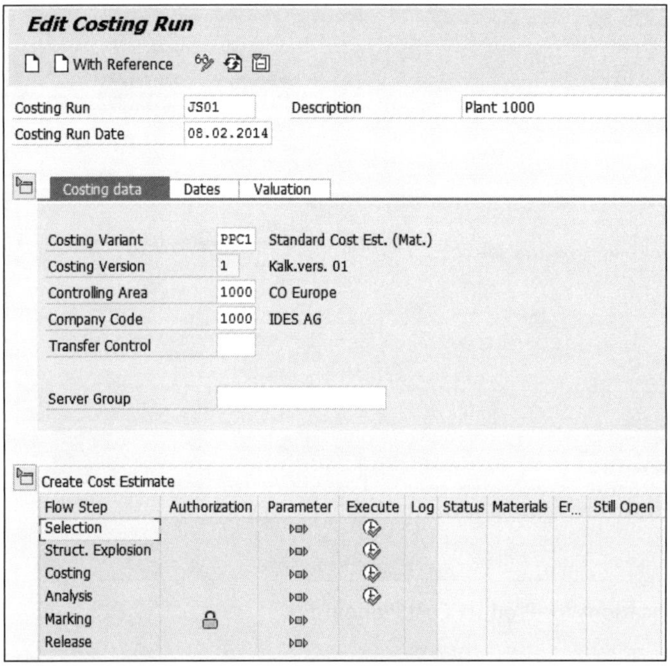

Figure 5.37 Create Costing Run: Initial Screen

As we discussed in Chapter 4, the underlying master data for the costing run is predominantly managed by the production department, so fixing the errors listed in the logs frequently requires collaboration between controlling and the other departments, especially if the cost estimates are based on shared master data.

Once each costing step has been completed, the costing results are shown in the bottom part of the screen. This allows you to view a list showing the details of what was selected or calculated in each step and to navigate from there to the individual cost estimate (the equivalent of calling Transaction CK13N for each material cost estimate). Because of the danger of errors, it's rare to schedule all costing jobs in one flow. Make sure that you have made a manual check on the data before the mark and release steps, which initiate the inventory revaluation and thus can have a significant impact on the balance sheet.

If you select more than 500 materials in your costing run, the material masters for all materials in the relevant plant will be locked while the costing step is performed. You'll find more information about this in SAP Note 1415153. Because of this, most organizations perform their costing runs overnight. You should also be careful if you have costing runs that cross several company codes that you don't encounter a deadlock. During the marking and releasing steps, the locks are set for the materials being updated in turn. If you have many tasks running in parallel, this can lead to an overrun of the lock tables.

The **Costing Data** tab contains the main organizational settings for the costing run. The *costing variant* provides the link to the configuration settings for Product Cost Planning and establishes the following:

- The purpose of costing, such as the calculation of standard costs for inventory valuation or the calculation of inventory costs based on methods such as FIFO and LIFO for balance sheet valuation. We're interested in calculating standard costs here, so select **Costing Variant** PPC1, which has the correct costing type for standard costing.
- How the BOMs and routings/recipes for each material are selected. The relevant settings are combined in the quantity structure determination settings for the costing variant. If you create multiple costing runs for different purposes, such as group costing and inventory valuation, make sure that you read the quantity structures only once, and then for the second costing run set up a *reference variant* that points to the costing variant and version as the key of the original costing run.
- Which activity prices are selected. Remember that we discussed the possibility of calculating one activity price based on the activity quantities and one based on capacity. You can create two costing variants—one that uses the activity-based price and another that uses the capacity-based price—to compare the cost impact of the two planning assumptions.
- Which prices are selected to value the raw materials and how overhead costs are applied. You may remember the purchasing info records and raw material prices that we looked at in Chapter 4. During costing, these prices will be selected for each of the raw materials included in the costing run and added to the activity prices to

determine the costs of the semifinished and finished products in the costing run. The settings are combined in a valuation variant assigned to the costing variant.

- Proposals for the selection dates for selecting the items in the BOMs and routings and the material and activity prices. You can overwrite these in the **Dates** tab of the costing run. You may remember from Chapter 4 that BOMs and routings are time-dependent, so be sure to select the correct key date.

Usually, it's sufficient to enter costing version 1. You should enter a different version only in the following cases:

- If you're performing mixed costing to weigh several cost estimates for different procurement alternatives (see Chapter 4).
- If you're performing group costing to reference the data in the first costing run. In this case, the quantity structure used as a basis for the standard costs in legal valuation is reused by the group valuation and profit center valuation to ensure that only the values and not the quantities change.

The **Controlling Area** and **Company Code** fields determine the framework within which the costing run takes place. Depending on the degree of centralization in the organization, a costing run may be performed by each plant in isolation, or a single costing run can cover all the materials in every plant in the world. As the use of a single controlling area becomes more widespread, the trend is toward a single, global costing run.

If you create a costing run at a time other than during the AOP, you can use the **Transfer Control** field to have the system copy existing cost estimates for materials that have already been costed and only create new ones for materials that have been created since the last annual plan. This can significantly reduce the time it takes to perform a costing run. This can also be used when plants procure materials from one another to ensure that the receiving plant copies the cost estimate from the supplying plant rather than creating a new cost estimate in the other plant.

Because the volumes of materials in the costing run can lock up system resources, you may also want to build packages of materials and run them on different server groups to spread the load.

Select Materials

If you want to make a fairly general selection, you can select the materials you want to include in the costing run by entering the appropriate plant and material type directly in the costing run. However, if you want to make a more specific selection, perhaps to exclude materials for which you have already created cost estimates, then you should consider using the separate selection list that was introduced in Release 4.7. You'll find the new transactions in the **Costing Run** folder under **Create Selection List** (Transaction CKMATSEL) and **Edit Selection List** (Transaction CKMATCON), as shown in Figure 5.36.

Figure 5.38 shows the selection screen for such a selection list. This includes the same selections as in the costing run but also includes fields from the material master, such as **BOM Usage** and the **Special Procurement Key**, making it easier to be specific about the materials to be included and not waste system resources creating new cost estimates for materials that already have cost estimates.

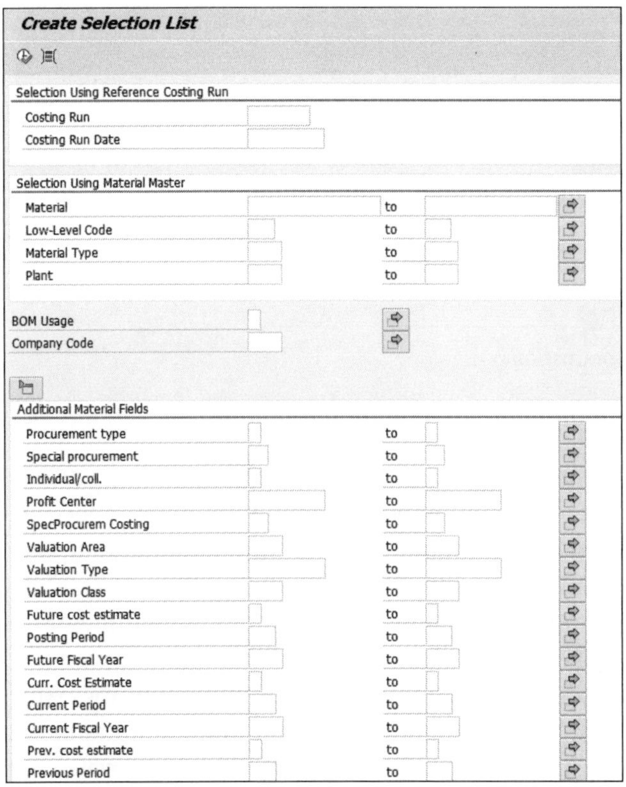

Figure 5.38 Create Selection List for Costing

Some customers require even more sophisticated logic for selecting the relevant materials for costing. SAP Note 1019389 describes how to activate the `MAT_SELECTION_CK` BAdI to enable you to define your own logic for material selection.

Once you have a list, you may want to edit it further to add additional materials manually or remove others by marking the lines and using the icons shown in Figure 5.39. When you're satisfied with your selection list, you can move on to the next costing steps.

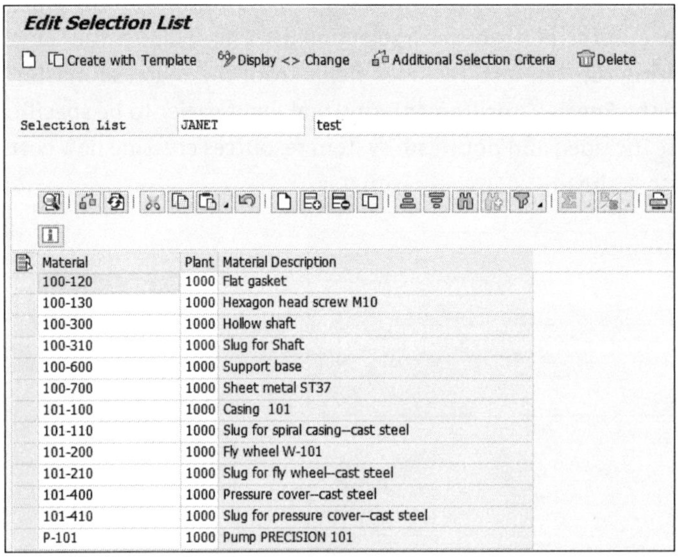

Figure 5.39 Edit Selection List for Costing

Structure Explosion

The next costing step does the same thing as the production plan—namely, explode the BOMs to determine which semifinished products and raw materials are needed in the manufacture of each material. The difference is that the production plan takes the sales plan as its starting point and calculates all material quantities and activity quantities, using the sales quantities (with minor adjustments) as its starting point. The standard costs, however, have to account for the cost behavior of the underlying cost elements (fixed or variable). Each cost estimate is created independently, taking the costing lot size as the "ideal" output and adjusting the input quantities in the BOM in line with this output quantity. This process is repeated for each level of the BOM.

Costing

The costing step creates a cost estimate for each material in the BOM structure. For raw materials, it uses the valuation variant to determine how the initial costs will be calculated (the price from the purchasing info record or one of the prices in the material master; see Chapter 4) and creates a cost estimate that contains the new price. For the semifinished products, it reads the routing and work center in combination to determine the activity usage and roll up the prices for the individual raw materials in the BOM to form a cost estimate for the semifinished product. Figure 5.40 shows a list of the materials costed as part of the costing run.

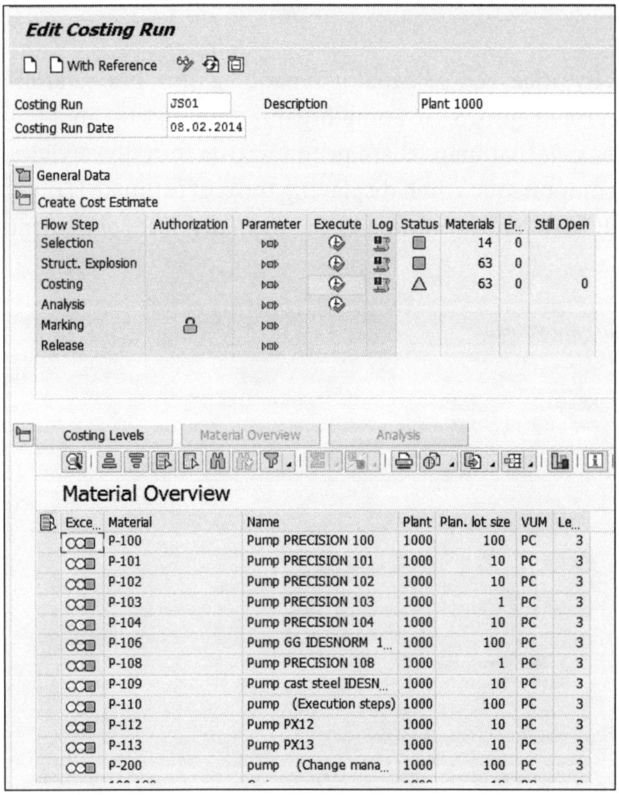

Figure 5.40 Edit Costing Run: Results List

You'll also notice a log for each costing step that documents any errors encountered during costing. The errors determine whether the status of the run is successful or not. Many of the errors used in costing are configurable, so once you've gone beyond your first couple of costing runs, consider analyzing the errors that are still occurring and decide whether some of these messages really belong in the error list or could be removed via configuration. To display the cost estimate for each material, click on the material in the list.

All cost estimates have the same basic structure: the cost component split that we introduced in Chapter 2. Figure 5.41 shows the cost component split for material P-100, comprising raw materials, purchased parts, production labor, production setup, production machine, material overhead, and production processes in this configuration. These are split into their fixed and variable parts based on the activity rates (for the labor, setup, and machine cost components) and the business process rates (for the Logistics processes cost component). All cost estimates are saved in this form: the *main cost component split*.

When you looked at the activity price, you saw that it's made up of wages, salaries, employee benefits, and so on (see Figure 5.35). Some organizations set up an additional *primary cost component split* that maps these primary costs from the activity rate into a second set of cost components. When displaying the cost estimate (Transaction CK13N), you can switch between the *main* and the *auxiliary cost component split*, as shown in Figure 5.41.

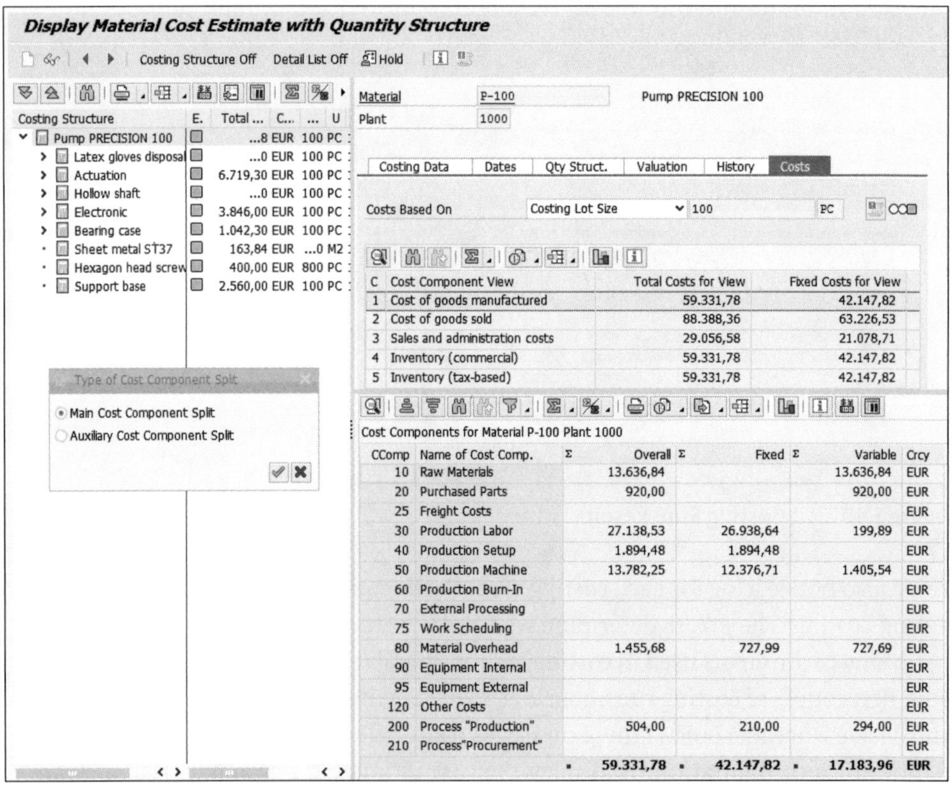

Figure 5.41 Cost of Goods Manufactured (Main Cost Component Split)

Figure 5.42 shows the primary cost component split for the material, comprising material components, wages and salaries, energy, depreciation, and other costs in this configuration. Comparing the two screens, you'll see that the total product costs are the same, but in Figure 5.41 the cost elements in the activity rates from the routing determine to which cost components the costs are assigned (setup, labor, and machine), whereas in Figure 5.42 the underlying cost center costs determine the cost components (personnel, employee benefits, and depreciation). This configuration thus allows you to look at your product costs from two different perspectives. In one view, you're seeing the activity costs simply as items consumed from the cost center; in the second, you're seeing the activity costs in terms of the costs that drive them (people costs, machine costs, etc.).

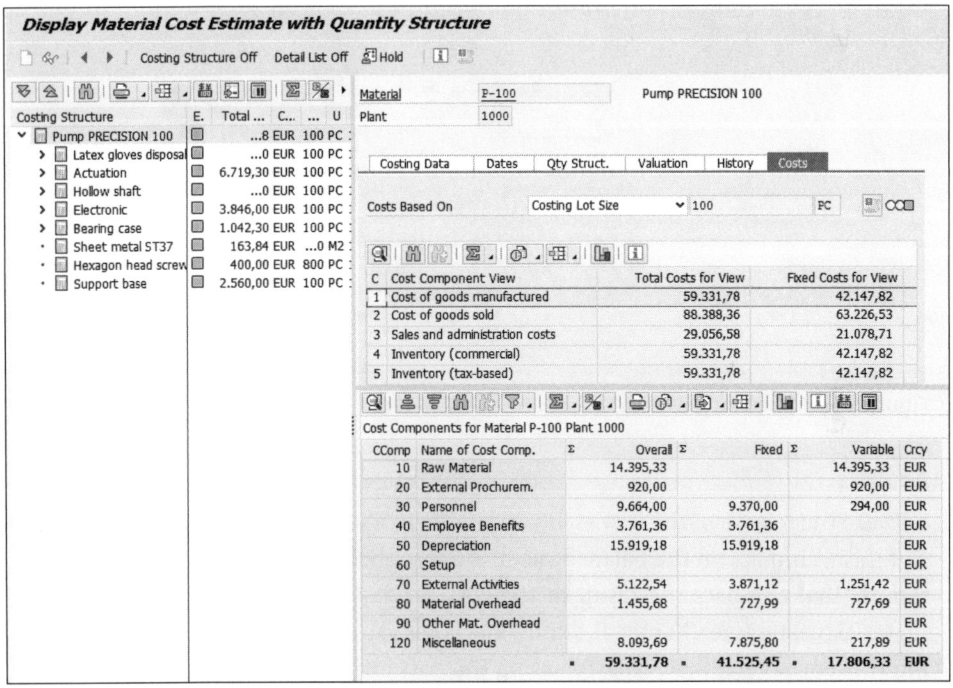

Figure 5.42 Primary Cost Component Split (Auxiliary Cost Component Split)

If multiple procurement alternatives exist for a single material (see Chapter 4), the costing step creates a separate cost estimate for each procurement alternative (manufacture according to production version 1, purchase from supplier A, etc.) and then reads the mixing ratios defined as master data for a mixed cost estimate and creates a mixed cost estimate.

Figure 5.43 shows a sample cost estimate in which 10% is externally procured (first line) and 90% is manufactured in house (second line). The first cost estimate is based on the purchasing info record with the appropriate supplier, whereas the second cost estimate is based on the BOM and routing. Notice that the itemization shows the cost estimate for each item. To see the info record for the supplier, click on the line for the first procurement alternative. To see the results of costing the BOM and routing for internal manufacturing, click on the line for the second procurement alternative.

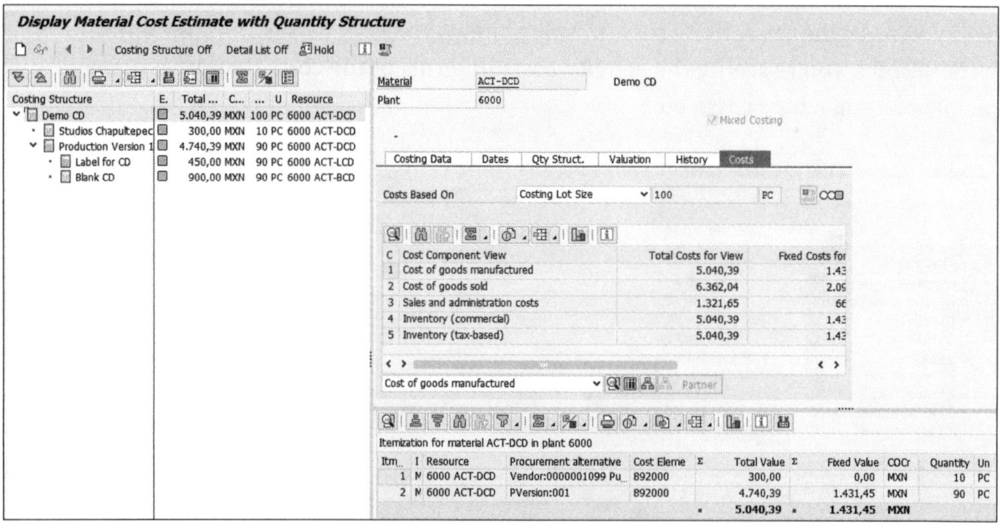

Figure 5.43 Mixed Cost Estimate Showing Two Procurement Alternatives

Analysis

Because the release of the cost estimate results in a stock revaluation that can have a significant impact on the balance sheet, it's essential for the controller to run check reports that compare the result of the cost estimate with the current price in the material master (see Chapter 4). Figure 5.44 shows such a report from within the costing run. For several materials, releasing the cost estimates would result in a significant revaluation, and the controller must work to determine whether these changes are justified before moving on to the next steps in costing.

In such a situation, the controller repeats individual steps in the costing run using the selection list we discussed earlier to select exactly those materials that are causing errors and leaving untouched the materials that were costed successfully until the results are satisfactory.

Only when all the signal lights for the anticipated revaluation in Figure 5.44 are within an acceptable range should you move on to the next step because the marking and releasing steps lead to every costing result prepared during the costing run being used to revaluate inventory. In our examples, you'll see that we've done some significant revaluations to the inventory in our demo system.

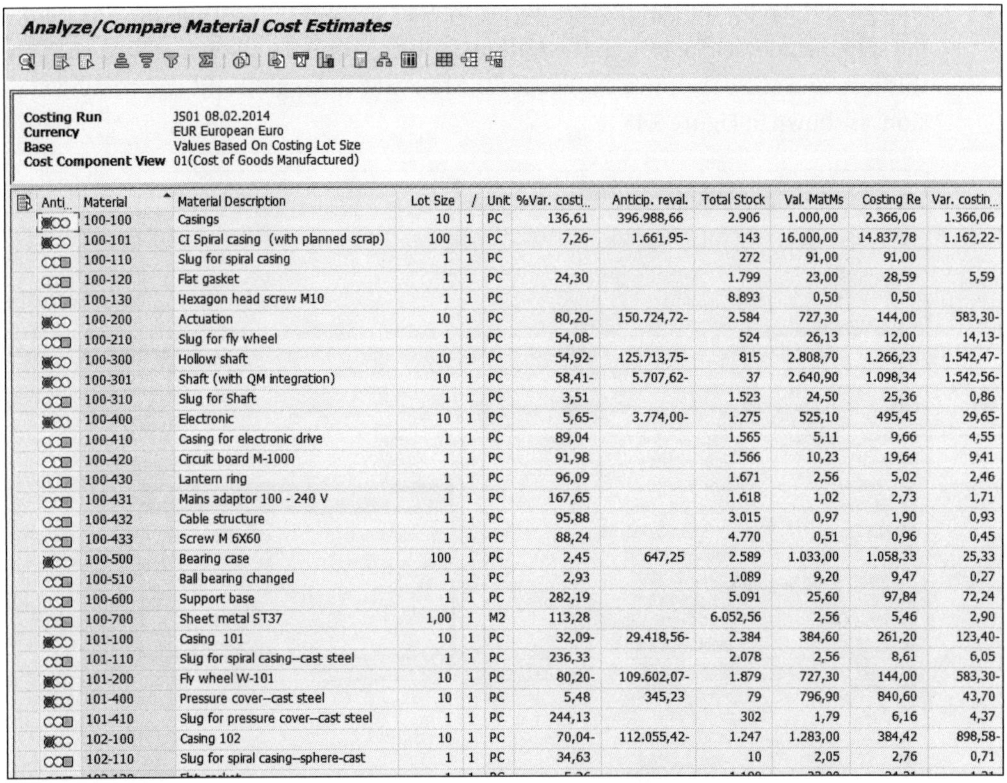

Analyze/Compare Material Cost Estimates

Costing Run JS01 08.02.2014
Currency EUR European Euro
Base Values Based On Costing Lot Size
Cost Component View 01(Cost of Goods Manufactured)

Anti...	Material	Material Description	Lot Size	/	Unit	%Var. costi...	Anticip. reval.	Total Stock	Val. MatMs	Costing Re	Var. costin...
	100-100	Casings	10	1	PC	136,61	396.988,66	2.906	1.000,00	2.366,06	1.366,06
	100-101	CI Spiral casing (with planned scrap)	100	1	PC	7,26-	1.661,95-	143	16.000,00	14.837,78	1.162,22-
	100-110	Slug for spiral casing	1	1	PC			272	91,00	91,00	
	100-120	Flat gasket	1	1	PC	24,30		1.799	23,00	28,59	5,59
	100-130	Hexagon head screw M10	1	1	PC			8.893	0,50	0,50	
	100-200	Actuation	10	1	PC	80,20-	150.724,72-	2.584	727,30	144,00	583,30-
	100-210	Slug for fly wheel	1	1	PC	54,08-		524	26,13	12,00	14,13-
	100-300	Hollow shaft	10	1	PC	54,92-	125.713,75-	815	2.808,70	1.266,23	1.542,47-
	100-301	Shaft (with QM integration)	10	1	PC	58,41-	5.707,62-	37	2.640,90	1.098,34	1.542,56-
	100-310	Slug for Shaft	1	1	PC	3,51		1.523	24,50	25,36	0,86
	100-400	Electronic	10	1	PC	5,65-	3.774,00-	1.275	525,10	495,45	29,65-
	100-410	Casing for electronic drive	1	1	PC	89,04		1.565	5,11	9,66	4,55
	100-420	Circuit board M-1000	1	1	PC	91,98		1.566	10,23	19,64	9,41
	100-430	Lantern ring	1	1	PC	96,09		1.671	2,56	5,02	2,46
	100-431	Mains adaptor 100 - 240 V	1	1	PC	167,65		1.618	1,02	2,73	1,71
	100-432	Cable structure	1	1	PC	95,88		3.015	0,97	1,90	0,93
	100-433	Screw M 6X60	1	1	PC	88,24		4.770	0,51	0,96	0,45
	100-500	Bearing case	100	1	PC	2,45	647,25	2.589	1.033,00	1.058,33	25,33
	100-510	Ball bearing changed	1	1	PC	2,93		1.089	9,20	9,47	0,27
	100-600	Support base	1	1	PC	282,19		5.091	25,60	97,84	72,24
	100-700	Sheet metal ST37	1,00	1	M2	113,28		6.052,56	2,56	5,46	2,90
	101-100	Casing 101	10	1	PC	32,09-	29.418,56-	2.384	384,60	261,20	123,40-
	101-110	Slug for spiral casing--cast steel	1	1	PC	236,33		2.078	2,56	8,61	6,05
	101-200	Fly wheel W-101	10	1	PC	80,20-	109.602,07-	1.879	727,30	144,00	583,30-
	101-400	Pressure cover--cast steel	10	1	PC	5,48	345,23	79	796,90	840,60	43,70
	101-410	Slug for pressure cover--cast steel	1	1	PC	244,13		302	1,79	6,16	4,37
	102-100	Casing 102	10	1	PC	70,04-	112.055,42-	1.247	1.283,00	384,42	898,58-
	102-110	Slug for spiral casing--sphere-cast	1	1	PC	34,63		10	2,05	2,76	0,71

Figure 5.44 Effect of Releasing Cost Estimates on Material Valuation

Marking

Because the release results in a *revaluation* of all materials in stock and can cause a significant difference in the balance sheet, the revaluation step is split into two steps:

- Marking the cost estimate takes the value in the cost estimate and updates it to the value in the **Future Standard Price** field in the **Costing 2** view of the material master (see Chapter 4). You can still mark again if you discover that you have marked an incorrect cost estimate.

- Releasing the cost estimate takes the future standard price and supporting cost estimate and uses them to create a new standard price. Once this has happened, you can't change the standard price until the next period—another reason to be sure to check the results before releasing.

Before you can perform either of these steps, you have to explicitly allow the price change in the relevant company code. Figure 5.40 showed the costing run. The marking step includes a lock icon in the **Authorization** column. To allow marking, click on this icon and allow the price change for the relevant costing variant and costing version, as shown in Figure 5.45.

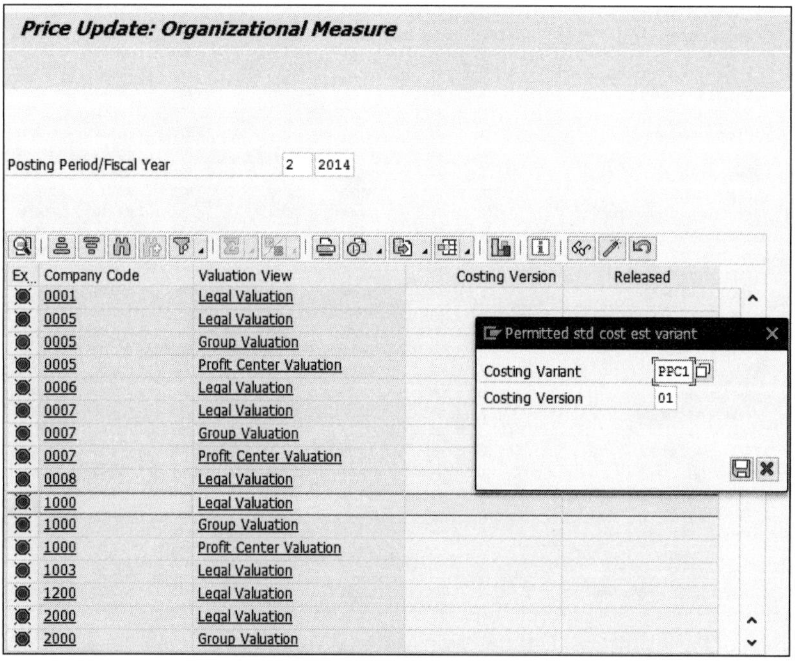

Figure 5.45 Allow Price Update for Company Code

Be careful to enter the correct version (usually 1). Organizations are usually very restrictive about who has authorization to perform this step. Figure 5.46 shows the result of marking the materials contained in the costing run. Once marking has taken place, the cost estimates have the status **VO** (marked).

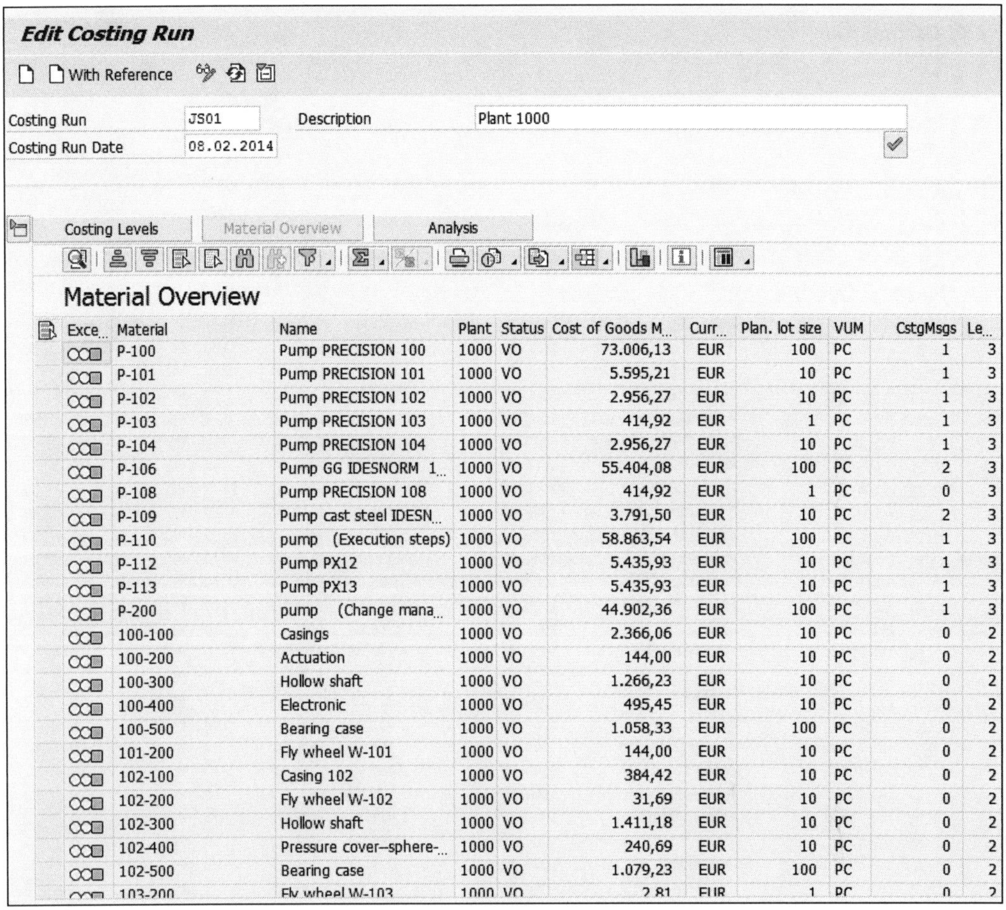

Figure 5.46 Using Marking to Create Future Standard Price

Release

Figure 5.47 shows the result of completing the release step. Once release has taken place, the cost estimates have the status **FR** (released).

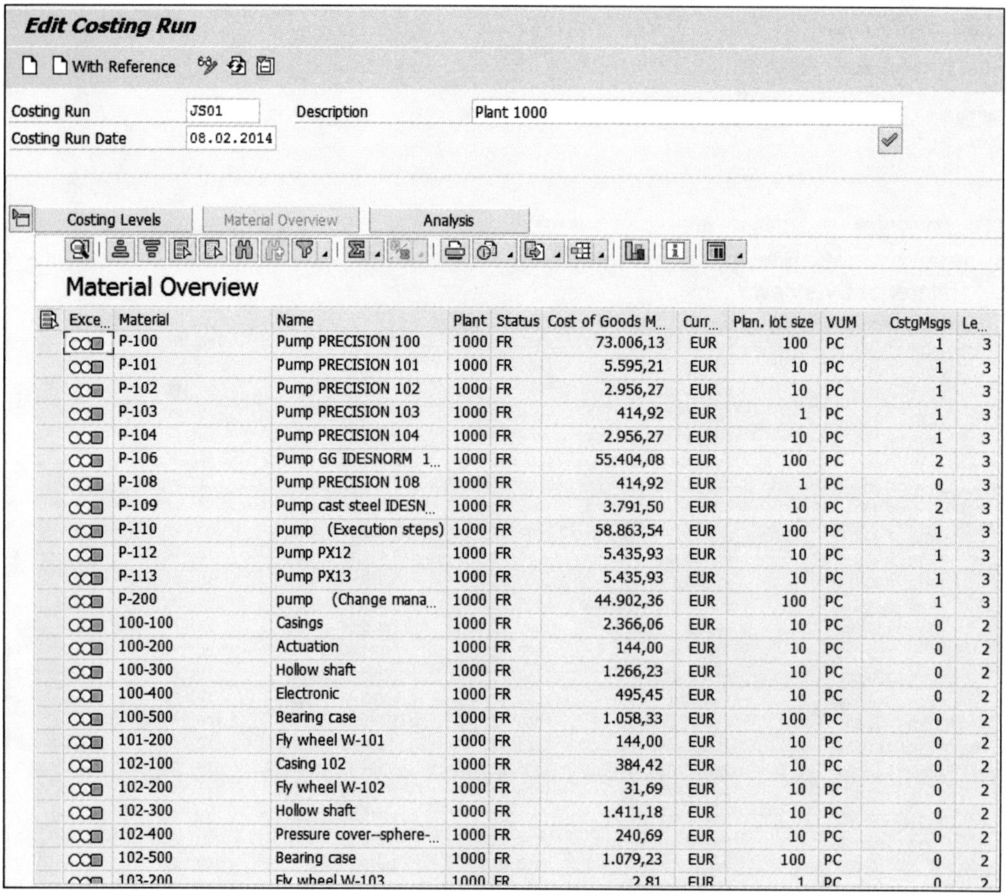

Exce...	Material	Name	Plant	Status	Cost of Goods M...	Curr...	Plan. lot size	VUM	CstgMsgs	Le...
	P-100	Pump PRECISION 100	1000	FR	73.006,13	EUR	100	PC	1	3
	P-101	Pump PRECISION 101	1000	FR	5.595,21	EUR	10	PC	1	3
	P-102	Pump PRECISION 102	1000	FR	2.956,27	EUR	10	PC	1	3
	P-103	Pump PRECISION 103	1000	FR	414,92	EUR	1	PC	1	3
	P-104	Pump PRECISION 104	1000	FR	2.956,27	EUR	10	PC	1	3
	P-106	Pump GG IDESNORM 1...	1000	FR	55.404,08	EUR	100	PC	2	3
	P-108	Pump PRECISION 108	1000	FR	414,92	EUR	1	PC	0	3
	P-109	Pump cast steel IDESN...	1000	FR	3.791,50	EUR	10	PC	2	3
	P-110	pump (Execution steps)	1000	FR	58.863,54	EUR	100	PC	1	3
	P-112	Pump PX12	1000	FR	5.435,93	EUR	10	PC	1	3
	P-113	Pump PX13	1000	FR	5.435,93	EUR	10	PC	1	3
	P-200	pump (Change mana...	1000	FR	44.902,36	EUR	100	PC	1	3
	100-100	Casings	1000	FR	2.366,06	EUR	10	PC	0	2
	100-200	Actuation	1000	FR	144,00	EUR	10	PC	0	2
	100-300	Hollow shaft	1000	FR	1.266,23	EUR	10	PC	0	2
	100-400	Electronic	1000	FR	495,45	EUR	10	PC	0	2
	100-500	Bearing case	1000	FR	1.058,33	EUR	100	PC	0	2
	101-200	Fly wheel W-101	1000	FR	144,00	EUR	10	PC	0	2
	102-100	Casing 102	1000	FR	384,42	EUR	10	PC	0	2
	102-200	Fly wheel W-102	1000	FR	31,69	EUR	10	PC	0	2
	102-300	Hollow shaft	1000	FR	1.411,18	EUR	10	PC	0	2
	102-400	Pressure cover--sphere-...	1000	FR	240,69	EUR	10	PC	0	2
	102-500	Bearing case	1000	FR	1.079,23	EUR	100	PC	0	2
	103-200	Fly wheel W-103	1000	FR	2,81	EUR	1	PC	0	2

Figure 5.47 Using Release Step to Create New Standard Price

This process revalues inventory and results in price change documents being written that document the change. For auditing, you can always view the supporting cost estimate from the material master using Transaction MM03 (see Figure 5.48). Here you'll see that the standard price was created using a cost estimate created in February 2014.

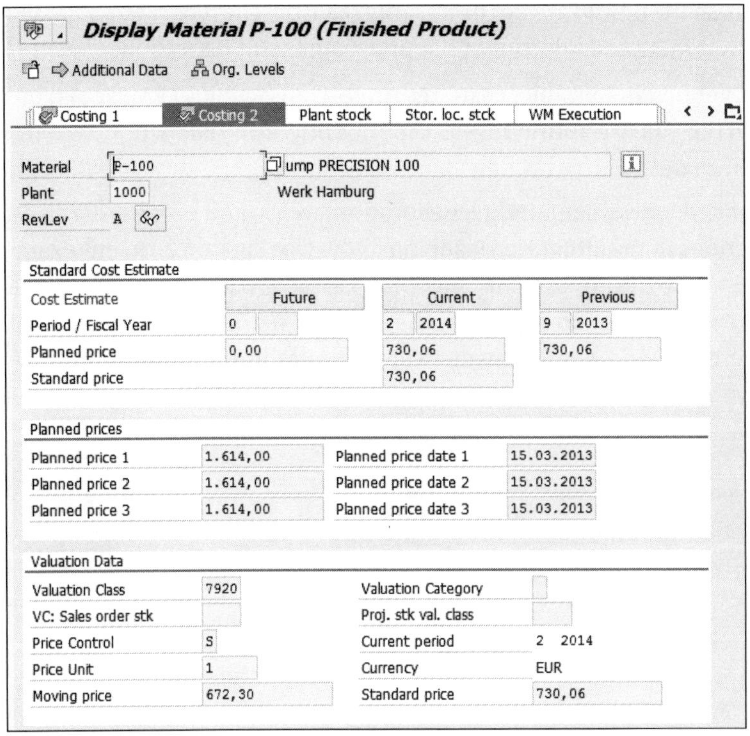

Figure 5.48 Results of Releasing Cost Estimate

5.1.4 Profitability Planning

Once the standard costs have been calculated and the cost centers and internal orders planned, the final stage of planning is to pull all the values together in Profitability Analysis. There are two parts to the completion of the plan:

1. Click on the **Valuate** button in the planning layouts to select the sales prices and deductions and the product cost estimates we just created. This allows you to forecast net revenue and the first and second contribution margin.
2. Run assessment cycles, indirect activity allocation cycles, and order settlement to include the overhead. This allows you to forecast the final profit and contribution margin.

Figure 5.49 shows a sample profitability report, including the planned data that will be used to assess the success of the actual data. This is based on the sample S_GO operating concern, so the figures are not necessarily realistic. The report was accessed by using Transaction KE30 and selecting the appropriate report definition:

- To select the revenues and product costs, return to Transaction KEPM (see Figure 5.2) and click on the **Valuate** button to read the sales prices and deductions and the product cost estimates.
- To run the planned assessment, indirect allocation cycles, and order settlement, use the transactions in the **Integrated Planning** folder (see Figure 5.2). In our example, you'll need to use the assessment function (Transaction KEUB) to allocate the planned sales and distribution expenses, the planned marketing expenses, and the planned research and development expenses for the relevant market segments. If you've also planned costs on orders or projects, use the settlement functions to settle costs such as planned research activities.

Execute Drilldown Report Analysis of Operating Profit: Detail List

Analysis of Operating Profit

001.2014 012.2014

Navigation
Distr. Channel
Sales Org.
Main material group

.	Actual	Plan	Prev. year	Actual vs. pla	%ActvsPlan	Act. vs. prev.	%ActvsPrev
Net sales	45.106.511	45.766.920	0	660.409-	1,44-	45.106.511	•/0
Sales commission	725.951	737.201	0	11.250-	1,53-	725.951	•/0
SalesSpecDirectCosts	781.865	794.671	0	12.806-	1,61-	781.865	•/0
Accrued shipmt costs	948.878	961.787	0	12.909-	1,34-	948.878	•/0
Total S&D dir. costs	2.456.694	2.493.659	0	36.965-	1,48-	2.456.694	•/0
Net revenue	42.649.816	43.273.261	0	623.445-	1,44-	42.649.816	•/0
Direct MaterialCosts	7.429.035	7.541.099	0	112.064-	1,49-	7.429.035	•/0
Var.Production costs	4.573.981	4.646.207	0	72.226-	1,55-	4.573.981	•/0
Total var. COGM	12.003.016	12.187.306	0	184.290-	1,51-	12.003.016	•/0
Contrib. margin I	30.646.800	31.085.955	0	439.155-	1,41-	30.646.800	•/0
Mat. overhead costs	4.247.728	4.300.644	0	52.916-	1,23-	4.247.728	•/0
Fixed prod. costs	3.629.220	3.663.393	0	34.173-	0,93-	3.629.220	•/0
Total fixed COGM	7.876.947	7.964.036	0	87.089-	1,09-	7.876.947	•/0
Contrib. margin II	22.769.853	23.121.919	0	352.066-	1,52-	22.769.853	•/0
Material variances	1.945.047-	1.724.025-	0	221.023-	12,82	1.945.047-	•/0
Price variances	1.064.813	944.458	0	120.355	12,74	1.064.813	•/0
Other variances	685.422	610.903	0	74.519	12,20	685.422	•/0
Total variances	194.812-	168.664-	0	26.149-	15,50	194.812-	•/0
Contribn margin III	22.964.666	23.290.583	0	325.917-	1,40-	22.964.666	•/0
Sales overhead costs	2.379.826	2.422.856	0	43.030-	1,78-	2.379.826	•/0
Admin overhead costs	1.843.333	1.881.281	0	37.948-	2,02-	1.843.333	•/0
Marketing	2.139.523	2.181.240	0	41.717-	1,91-	2.139.523	•/0

Figure 5.49 Sample Profitability Report

Once the plan is satisfactory to all parties, lock the plan version against changes to freeze it for future analysis. To do so, select **Current Settings • Maintain Plan Versions**.

Although that wraps up the AOP for the sales-driven processes and the operating expenses incurred in delivering on such plans, it doesn't cover investment plans or project plans, which many organizations, including manufacturing companies, plan to a greater or lesser extent. We'll now look at how investment plans fit in to the planning environment.

5.2 Planning and Budgeting for Investment Programs

In this section, we'll look at investment planning. Investment programs describe the organization's targets in terms of capital investment projects to replace production equipment and prepare new products for launch, as you saw in Chapter 4. There's a link to the cost center plan in the sense that the same organizational structure (generally the cost center hierarchy) is often used to structure the investment program. In this type of plan, however, the controller plans the investment needed to ensure the cost center output in the longer term rather than the costs of providing the output in the immediate future.

This plan is subject to much greater variability than the AOP. Although the costs incurred by a cost center in any period should be relatively stable, building a new production line is an inherently different undertaking. SAP introduced the notion of a budget as a ceiling for such spending, a subject we'll return to in Chapter 6. Because the plan includes so much variability, it can't be considered to represent a standard, so the variance analysis available for investment projects and orders is limited to a line-by-line comparison of plan and budget against actual costs and commitments. You'll sometimes hear the process of preparing such a plan referred to as *budget formulation*, and you will find the approach in both the private and the public sector.

5.2.1 Investment Program

Investment planning generally starts with the items of the investment program that we looked at in Chapter 4. These items provide the framework for the planning activities. However, if you don't use Investment Management, you can simply track your planning progress against a list of investment projects and orders and perform the same planning tasks on the individual objects. Before you start, check the budget settings for your program by going to Transaction IM03 or **Accounting • Investment**

Management • Programs • Master Data • Investment Program Definition • Display and entering the program and approval year.

In the context of investment budget planning, we recommend that you select the **Budget Distribution Annual** checkbox so that any orders or projects assigned to the program position do not receive more annual budget for the fiscal year than is available for the program position to which they're assigned. This makes it easy to ensure that each project manager keeps to his allotted budget during the planning process.

5.2.2 Overall Plan

The high-level goals for investment planning are not determined by the sales, production, and cost center output but by the ability of the organization to make the investment at all. The overall plan exists as a form of planning for orders and projects but not for cost centers. This plan is used to document the progress from the high-level goal, such as the planned spending for a single project, to a level of detail appropriate for project approval. This documents the progress toward the final project structure, breaking down the total values to the individual WBS elements, and toward an understanding of the timing of the expenses: the years in which the costs will be incurred. To create an overall plan for a project, use Transaction CJ40 or follow the menu path **Accounting • Investment Management • Investment Projects • Planning • Total Costs • Change** or **Accounting • Project System • Financials • Planning • Costs in WBS • Overall Values • Change**. Enter the project definition, the currency, and the version. If you already know which level of the project hierarchy interests you in a large project, you can also enter a WBS element.

Figure 5.50 shows a sample overall plan. You can toggle between this view (the element view), in which the leading column shows the WBS elements, and the annual view, in which the leading column shows the year, by clicking on the **Annual Overview** button. Project planning generally works in two directions:

- The process of breaking down the project plan structurally and across the time dimension is generally known as *top-down planning*. The **Distributable** column gives an overview of the costs awaiting distribution to the lower levels. The costs that have been distributed are shown in the **Distributed** column.
- Alongside this process, we often find planned data being entered for individual WBS elements when details are known (contracts with a supplier, agreements on the level of work required to perform the task, etc.). These are shown in the

Planned Total column and aggregated in a process known as *bottom-up planning*. At some point, the two value flows should meet, but the essence of the planning application is in matching the detail against the target and understanding where compromises will be needed.

We'll use this overall plan later to prepare the budget for the project.

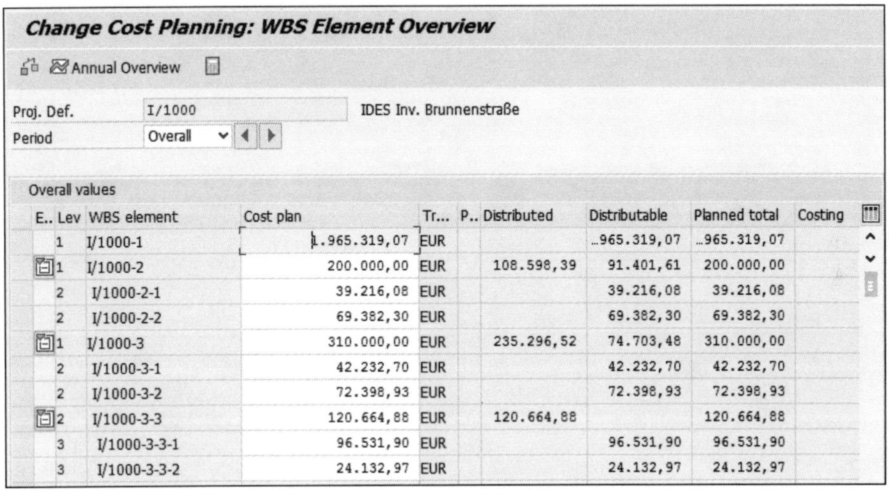

E..	Lev	WBS element	Cost plan	Tr...	P..	Distributed	Distributable	Planned total	Costing
	1	I/1000-1	1.965.319,07	EUR			...965.319,07	...965.319,07	
	1	I/1000-2	200.000,00	EUR		108.598,39	91.401,61	200.000,00	
	2	I/1000-2-1	39.216,08	EUR			39.216,08	39.216,08	
	2	I/1000-2-2	69.382,30	EUR			69.382,30	69.382,30	
	1	I/1000-3	310.000,00	EUR		235.296,52	74.703,48	310.000,00	
	2	I/1000-3-1	42.232,70	EUR			42.232,70	42.232,70	
	2	I/1000-3-2	72.398,93	EUR			72.398,93	72.398,93	
	2	I/1000-3-3	120.664,88	EUR		120.664,88		120.664,88	
	3	I/1000-3-3-1	96.531,90	EUR			96.531,90	96.531,90	
	3	I/1000-3-3-2	24.132,97	EUR			24.132,97	24.132,97	

Figure 5.50 Overall Plan for Project (SAP GUI)

Just as you saw for cost center and order planning, EHP 6 includes new applications for overall planning on projects. You'll find these in the standard roles Project Planner and Estimator and Internal Controller. Figure 5.51 shows a sample project. To access this application, choose **Project Planning and Cost Estimation • Overall Planning • Overall Planning (Basic)** and complete the selection screen. Note that you can plan for multiple projects using the same screen by entering more than one project in the selection screen. If you compare the two screens, you'll notice a difference in the way the WBS elements are presented. If you compare the hierarchies in the two screens, you'll see two lines for some of the WBS elements, one open for entry and one locked in the newer screen. The WBS element line that is locked against data entry represents the aggregation of costs planned for WBS elements that are below this one in the hierarchy. Notice finally that this screen uses the same analytics as you saw in the home pages for cost centers and orders that we looked at in Chapter 2.

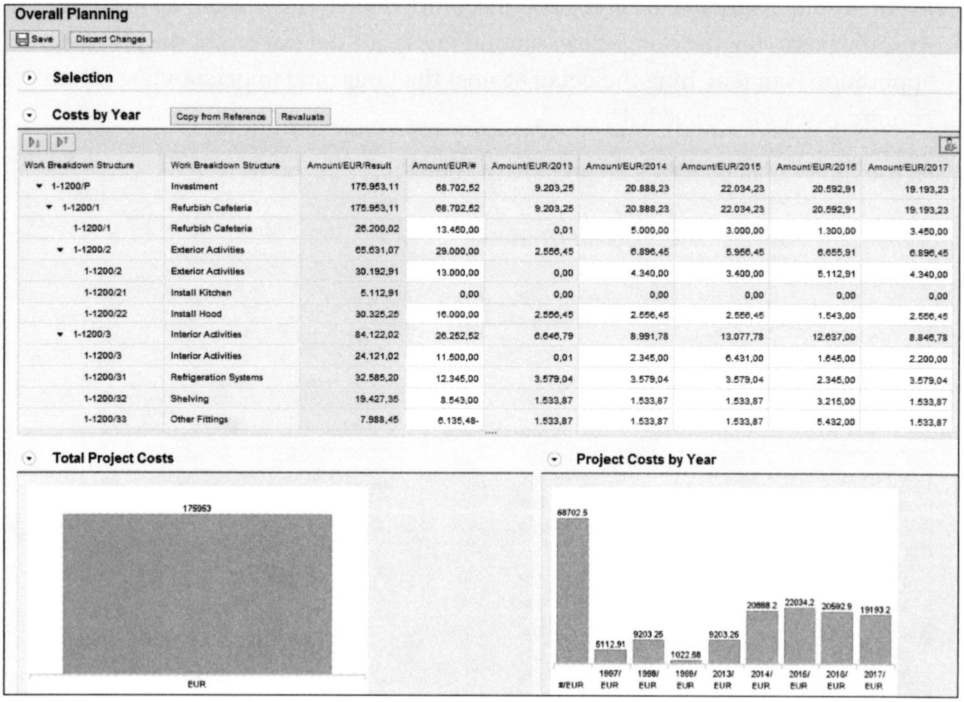

Figure 5.51 Overall Plan for Project (Web Dynpro)

5.2.3 Cost Element Planning

The overall plan also aggregates any other known planning data available for the project. If assets under construction have to be capitalized for the project, it's is important to distinguish the type of costs in the project (direct, indirect, material, etc.). This forces the controller to plan at the same level of detail as the inputs in the cost center. To access the planning application shown in Figure 5.52, choose the **Annual Overview** button shown in Figure 5.50 and then click on the **Primary Costs** button. This takes you into the form-based cost element plan, where you'll see a line for every cost element in your chart of accounts.

If you click on the **Primary Costs** button, a standard planning layout will be used that cannot be switched once you're in the planning transaction. If you want planners to be able to jump to the primary costs from the overall plan but use a different planning layout, refer to the instructions in SAP Note 47207 for details of how to change the planning layout. Alternatively, use Transaction CJR2 with layout 1-701 or follow the menu path **Accounting • Investment Management • Investment Projects •**

Planning • Cost and Activity Inputs • Change or **Accounting • Project System • Financials • Planning • Costs in WBS • Cost and Activity Inputs • Change**. Enter the project definition, the currency, the version, and the cost element group or interval. If you choose this route, you can choose between free planning (where you'll only see data for the cost elements you've already captured) and form-based planning (where you'll see an empty line for every cost element in the group or interval you entered in the initial screen). Figure 5.52 shows the planning screen. This behaves the same way as cost element planning on cost centers or on internal orders.

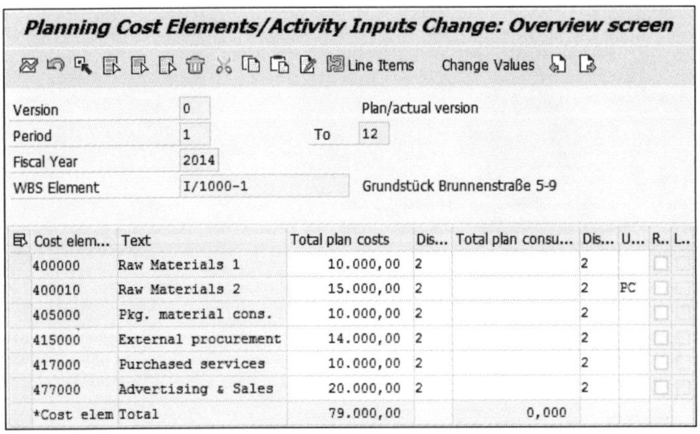

Figure 5.52 Cost Element Plan for Project (SAP GUI)

You'll also find new applications for cost element planning in the standard roles Project Planner and Estimator and Internal Controller. Figure 5.53 shows the cost element plan for a sample project. To access this application, choose **Project Planning and Cost Estimation • Cost Element Planning • Cost Element Planning (Basic)** and complete the selection screen.

Although the cost center/cost element combination can be irritating for cost center planning, it can make data entry almost impossible for project planning, because the number of cost elements that can be potential inputs for a WBS element can be even greater. If you choose form-based planning for a project, you can easily have hundreds of cost elements in each layout. For this reason, there's also a new query that allows you to enter data for a cost element group and have the system distribute the costs to the underlying cost elements. To use the planning application shown in Figure 5.54, choose **Project Planning and Cost Estimation • Cost Element Planning • Top-Down Cost Element Group Planning** and enter the relevant cost element group along with your project.

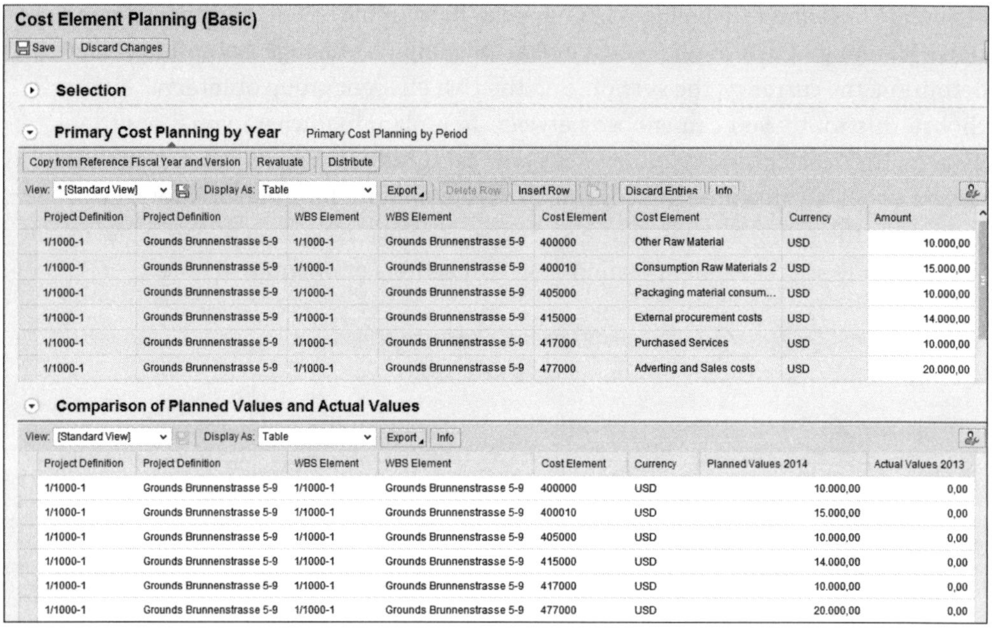

Figure 5.53 Cost Element Plan for Project (Web Dynpro)

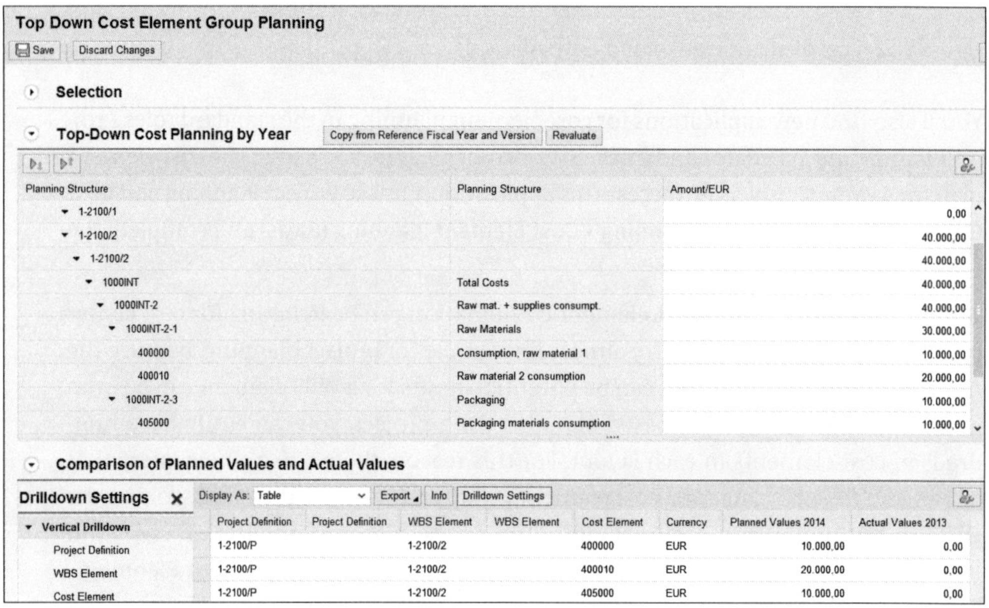

Figure 5.54 Top-Down Cost Element Planning for Project

Alongside the primary costs (the purchased materials and contract work) that are required to complete the project, you can also plan the work required to complete the project in the form of activity input.

If these projects are assigned to an investment program, when you finish the detailed planning you can roll up the values captured on the assigned orders and projects by going to Transaction IM34 or **Accounting • Investment Manage-ment • Program Planning • Default Plan Values**. Figure 5.55 shows the result of rolling the plan values captured for the project assigned to the research and development node into the investment program.

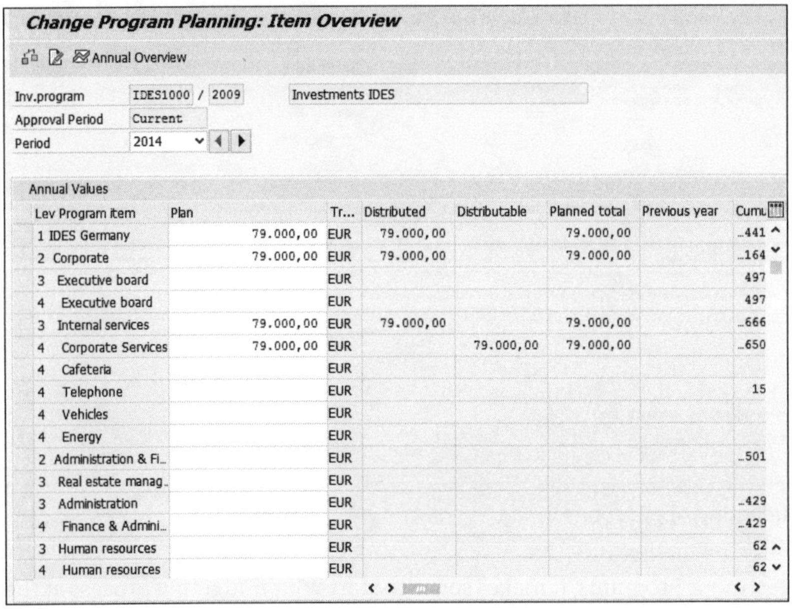

Figure 5.55 Investment Program Planning

Normally, we would continue planning for each item in the investment program, but for now we'll go straight to budgeting.

5.2.4 Budgeting

If we now assume that the project plan has been approved, the next task is the creation of the budget. Figure 5.56 shows the budgeting applications for an internal order, but the same applications are available for projects. If you refer to Figure 5.10, you'll see that it is also possible to create a budget for a cost center and report against this budget. The difference is that a cost center budget doesn't actually block spending on the cost center. For this reason, some organizations create shadow internal orders for those cost centers and have the system perform checks against the order budget. The *original budget* for an order or project is created using the approved plan as a guide. This budget is more than just a plan: it's an agreement with the organization about proposed spending levels, and any budget movements will be documented accordingly. Changing circumstances can render this ceiling inappropriate. At this stage, you can either create a *return* to give back some of the original budget or a *supplement* to document the assignment of an additional budget.

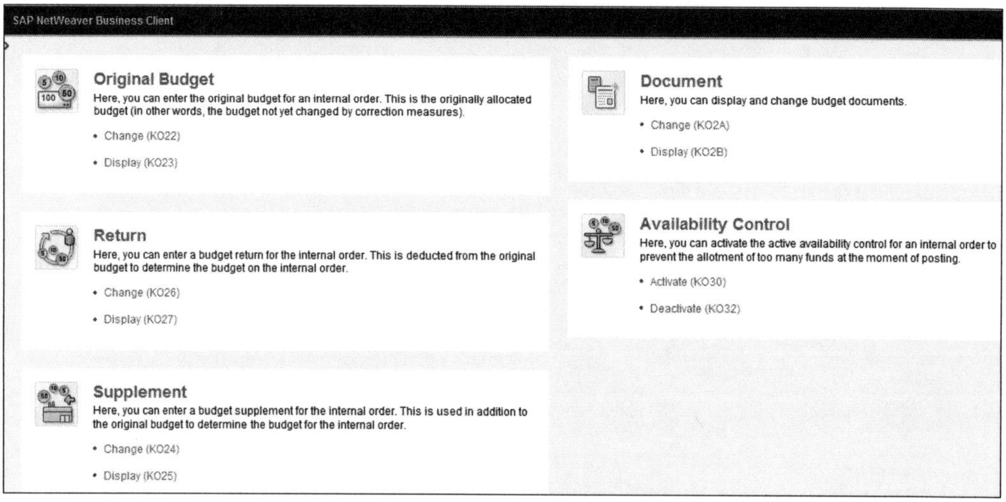

Figure 5.56 Budgeting Applications

If you use investment programs, it makes sense to start your budgeting process at the highest level—namely, in the investment program. You can prepare the budget using Transaction IM32 or by following the menu path **Accounting • Investment Management • Programs • Budgeting • Edit Original** and entering data in much the same way as for the overall plan. If you've already prepared plan data for the investment program, you can copy this data by selecting **Edit • Copy View** as shown in Figure 5.57. Once you have the rough values for the items, adjust them to meet your needs by selecting **Edit • Revaluate.** When you're satisfied with your budget at the program level, you can ensure that the budget set can't be exceeded on the associated WBS elements, orders, and appropriation requests using Transaction IM52 or by following the menu path **Accounting • Investment Management • Programs • Budgeting • Budget Distribution • Edit.**

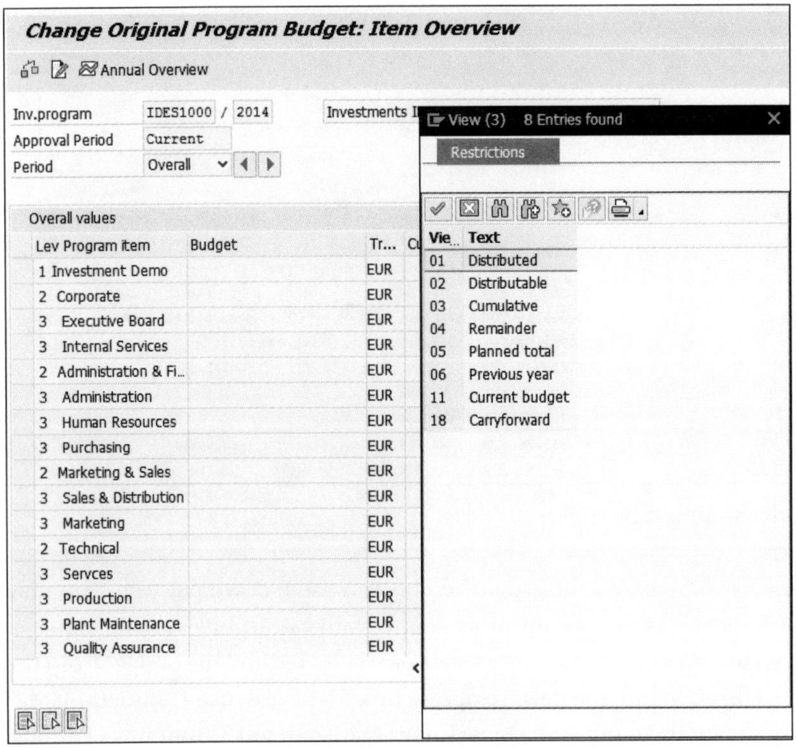

Figure 5.57 Change Investment Program

Figure 5.58 shows the original budget for a WBS element. You can enter the budget for a project using Transaction CJ30 or by selecting **Project System • Financials • Budgeting • Original Budget • Change**. Notice that some of the lines in the **Budget** column don't allow entry. This is because we assigned the WBS elements to an investment program position in Chapter 4, and we specified that the budget for the investment program should not receive more annual budget for the fiscal year than is available for the program position by selecting the **Budget Distribution Annual** checkbox for the investment program. If you want to check the connection between the WBS element and the investment program during budgeting, simply select **Extras • Investment Program**.

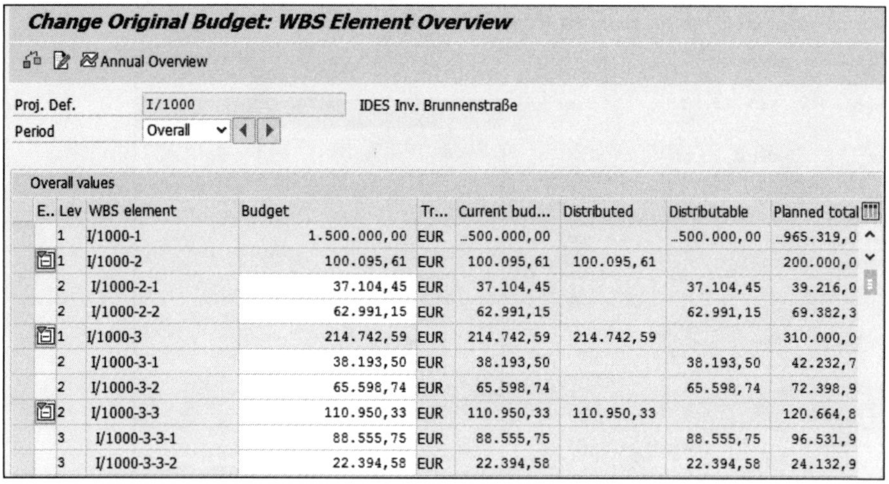

E..	Lev	WBS element	Budget	Tr...	Current bud...	Distributed	Distributable	Planned total
	1	I/1000-1	1.500.000,00	EUR	..500.000,00		..500.000,00	..965.319,0
	1	I/1000-2	100.095,61	EUR	100.095,61	100.095,61		200.000,0
	2	I/1000-2-1	37.104,45	EUR	37.104,45		37.104,45	39.216,0
	2	I/1000-2-2	62.991,15	EUR	62.991,15		62.991,15	69.382,3
	1	I/1000-3	214.742,59	EUR	214.742,59	214.742,59		310.000,0
	2	I/1000-3-1	38.193,50	EUR	38.193,50		38.193,50	42.232,7
	2	I/1000-3-2	65.598,74	EUR	65.598,74		65.598,74	72.398,9
	2	I/1000-3-3	110.950,33	EUR	110.950,33	110.950,33		120.664,8
	3	I/1000-3-3-1	88.555,75	EUR	88.555,75		88.555,75	96.531,9
	3	I/1000-3-3-2	22.394,58	EUR	22.394,58		22.394,58	24.132,9

Figure 5.58 Original Budget by Project

Having planned your overall values and then broken them down per year, you may wonder what happens as you go into the next fiscal year. In Investment Management, you need to ensure that a new approval year is created and the budget from the old year carried through into the new. To open a new fiscal year, use Transaction IM27 or follow the menu path **Accounting • Investment Management • Programs • Periodic Processing • Fiscal Year Change • Open New Approval Year**. You can then copy the existing program structure and carry forward the planned values, budget values, and measures (orders and projects).

Remembering what you need to do to correctly move an investment program into the next fiscal year can be tricky. SAP Note 444444 tells you exactly how to proceed and avoid any pitfalls.

5.2.5 Displaying and Changing a Budget

The management of these budgets is usually in the hands of controlling or a dedicated investment management department. However, it's equally important that project managers have the details of their available budget at their fingertips. For this reason, budget availability reports are also delivered as part of Manager Self-Service (see the accompanying downloadable appendices at *www.sap-press.com/4691*) so that the responsible managers can monitor the budget they still have at their disposal. Figure 5.59 shows the budget availability report delivered with Manager Self-Service and the Project Planner and Cost Estimator role to allow managers to monitor the available budget for the WBS elements for which they're responsible.

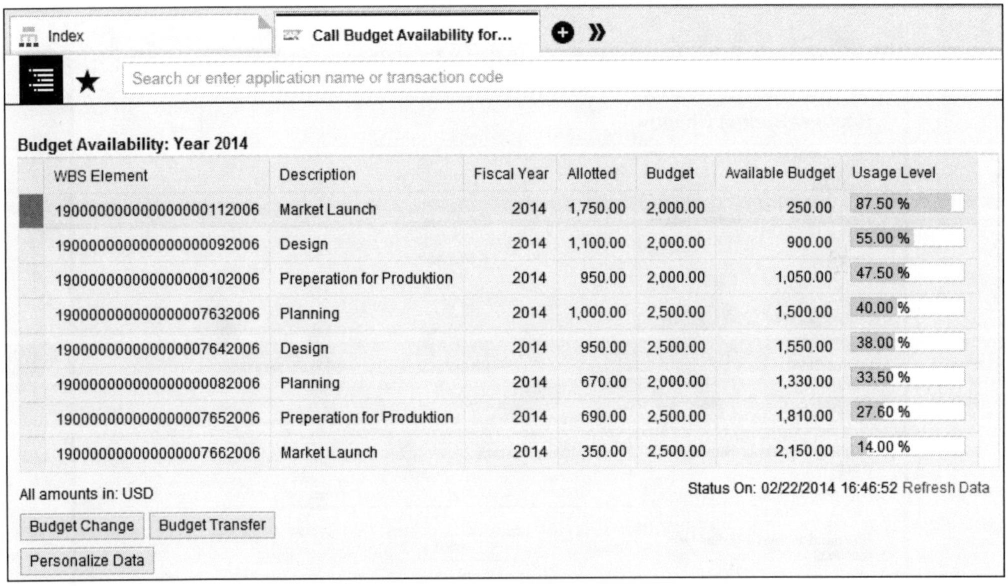

WBS Element	Description	Fiscal Year	Allotted	Budget	Available Budget	Usage Level
190000000000000000112006	Market Launch	2014	1,750.00	2,000.00	250.00	87.50 %
190000000000000000092006	Design	2014	1,100.00	2,000.00	900.00	55.00 %
190000000000000000102006	Preperation for Produktion	2014	950.00	2,000.00	1,050.00	47.50 %
190000000000000007632006	Planning	2014	1,000.00	2,500.00	1,500.00	40.00 %
190000000000000007642006	Design	2014	950.00	2,500.00	1,550.00	38.00 %
190000000000000000082006	Planning	2014	670.00	2,000.00	1,330.00	33.50 %
190000000000000007652006	Preperation for Produktion	2014	690.00	2,500.00	1,810.00	27.60 %
190000000000000007662006	Market Launch	2014	350.00	2,500.00	2,150.00	14.00 %

Figure 5.59 Budget Availability in Manager Self-Service

We looked at the subject of change requests for cost centers in Chapter 3. Because the need for a budget change normally arises in the field, the same mechanisms can be used to allow project managers to request budget changes and supplements and make returns. Figure 5.60 shows a sample budget transfer request form. To launch this form, click on the **Budget Change** button in the budget availability report in Manager Self-Service (shown in Figure 5.59).

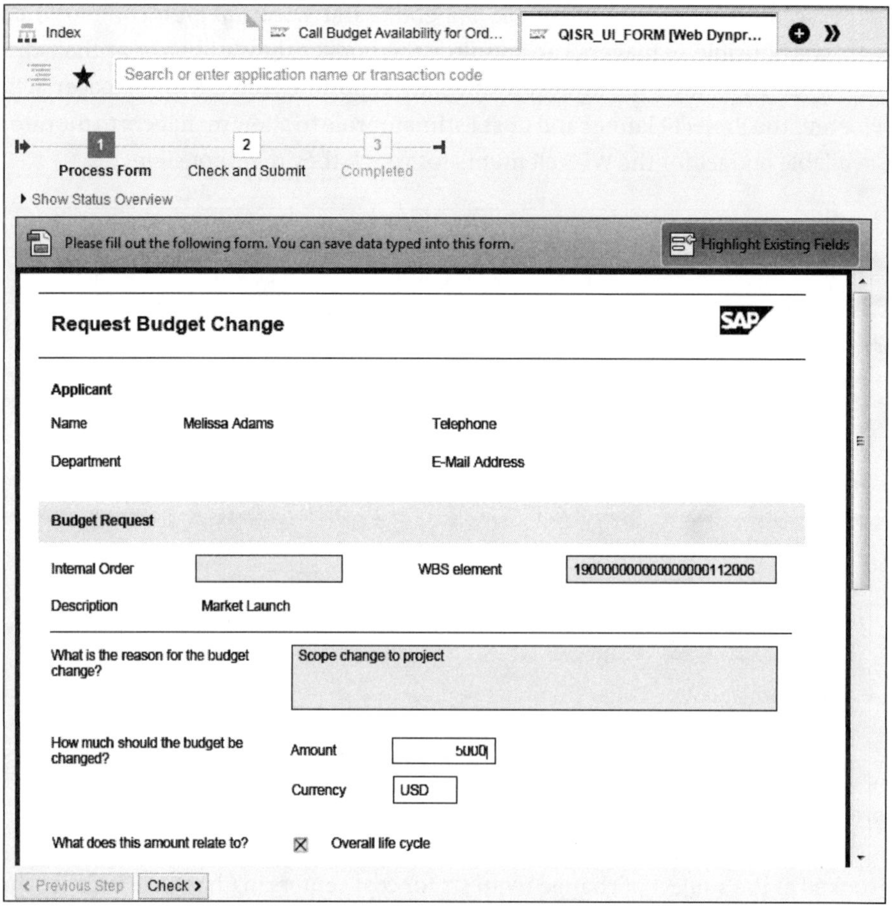

Figure 5.60 Budget Change Request as SAP Interactive Form

The form is linked with the fields in the project, so it can determine whether budget values refer to the whole lifecycle of the project or individual years and the currency used for budgeting. To enter the type of change required from Controlling, scroll down the form and choose from the dropdown box shown in Figure 5.61. The controller can initiate these changes without a form by choosing the appropriate transactions under **Project System • Financials • Budgeting**, but the change request provides a good way of documenting the rationale behind a change in a budget and including a workflow so that the budget change can be approved properly. To find out whether using the forms will have license implications for your organization, refer to SAP Note 750784.

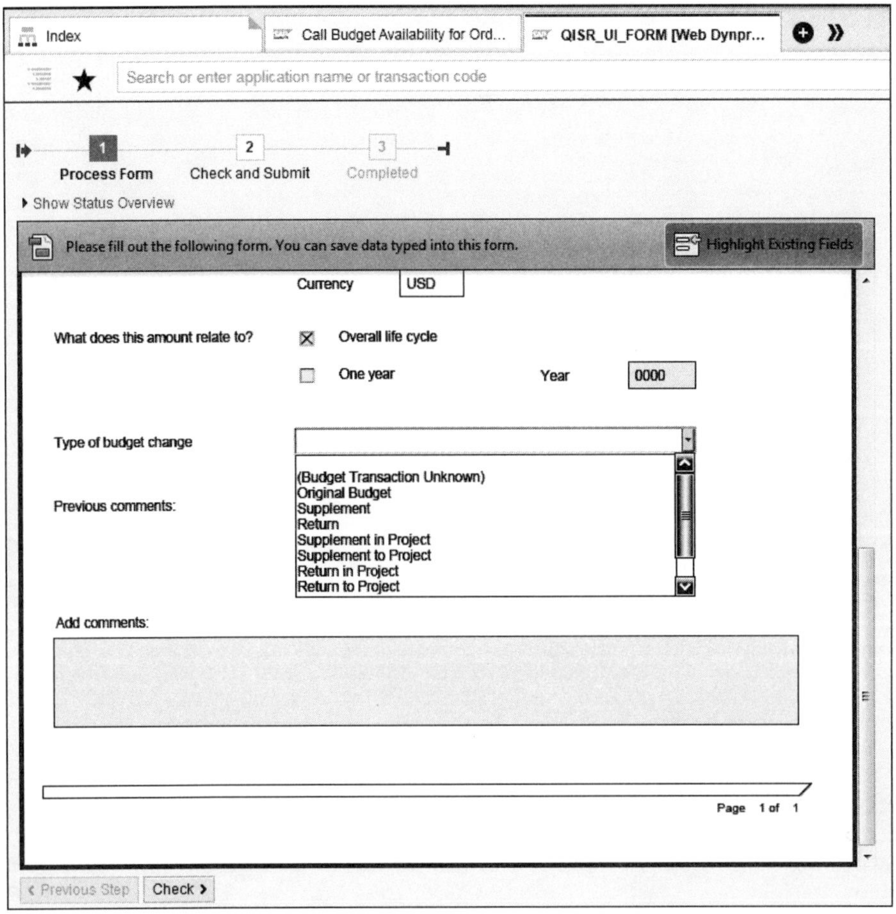

Figure 5.61 Types of Budget Change Requests in SAP Interactive Form

5.3 Summary

You've seen that planning in SAP ERP relies heavily on the existing master data we created in Chapter 3 and Chapter 4. It's also a prerequisite for most of the actual postings you'll see in Chapter 6 because it's needed to set standard costs as an initial valuation for all goods movements and standard activity rates for all confirmations in production and time recording in SAP ERP Human Capital Management. We'll now look at how our plan is used during the posting of actual costs. To find out how to set up forms like those we just displayed for a budget change request, see Chapter 9.

Chapter 6
Actual Postings

This chapter looks at actual postings by following the costs incurred during procurement, production, and sales in various situations, including intercompany goods movements. It explains what to do if you find differences during an inventory count or need to make corrections.

Because of the integrated nature of SAP ERP, it's rare for a controller to make a manual posting. In many cases, the controller simply monitors the postings created in Logistics and Human Capital Management and anticipates their impact on the Controlling (CO) component of SAP ERP Financials.

The best way to get a feel for the nature of the actual postings is to follow a business process from end to end, showing what transactions initiate the postings and what data is then available for you to monitor in CO. In the first section of this chapter, we'll follow two raw materials from their initial purchase through the manufacturing process, where they are converted into a finished product for final sale to the customer, and discuss the issues that a controller monitors at each stage. When we looked at the master data in Chapter 4, we discussed how to backflush the goods movements and confirmations based on the information in the BOM and routing for our finished product. We'll do this here too and then look at how to handle any differences discovered during a physical inventory check. After that, we'll return to the scenarios we discussed in Chapter 2 and look at the typical postings for product cost by order, product cost by period, product cost by sales order, and project controlling. We'll then discover how to make corrections and adjustment postings. Finally, we'll look at how to post values in a logistics scenario involving two affiliated companies.

6.1 Integrated Process Flows: Buy, Make, and Sell

A controller in a manufacturing environment monitors the following key logistics processes:

- The *procurement process* and the impact of the price his buyers can negotiate on the product costs
- The *manufacturing process* and the impact of the value added during production on the product costs
- The *sales process* and the impact of the product costs on profitability

This section is based on a very simple example involving the sale of a finished product (ACT-DCD) to the final customer, looking at how the raw materials ACT-BCD and ACT-LCD are procured for use in the manufacture of this finished product and how these raw materials are issued to production and delivered to stock as the finished product for sale. In each step, we'll look at the logistics steps and then explain their impact on CO.

6.1.1 Procure to Pay

Let's start by looking at how CO works for a material purchased to stock for use in a manufacturing process. Figure 6.1 shows the basic flow of the procure-to-pay process.

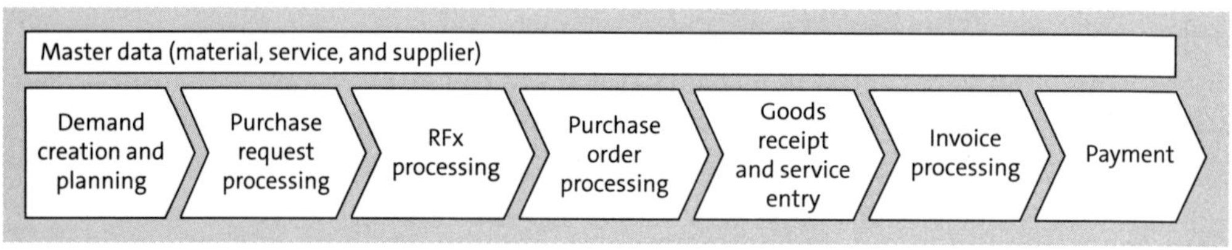

Figure 6.1 Procure-to-Pay Process

Usually, a materials requirements planning (MRP) run, as discussed in Chapter 5, and the creation of a purchase request precedes the creation of the purchase order, but we'll start here with the purchase order (the purchase order processing step) because this is where the choice of account assignment (cost center, project, neutral stock, etc.) impacts how the values will be transferred to CO.

The purchase order is an agreement with a vendor to supply materials at a given price. As you saw in Chapter 4, this price is established in a purchasing info record that defines the agreement between the supplier/vendor and the buyer. This price can be used to set the standard price in the material master, but it may change depending on the business climate. The receipt of the materials into stock (the goods receipt step) and the invoice (the invoice processing step) reference this purchase order (you'll hear this process referred to as a *three-way match*). The goods receipt is valued initially using the price in the purchase order, and the invoice may adjust this price. The controller's concern in this process is *purchase price variances*.

Purchase Order Processing

The first step is to create a purchase order to request the supply of two raw materials from a vendor. To create a purchase order, use Transaction ME21N or follow the menu path **Logistics • Materials Management • Purchasing • Purchase Order • Create • Vendor/Supplying Plant Known**. Then enter the vendor, purchasing organization, and company code in the header and, below, the material, plant, and quantity for each item (see Figure 6.2).

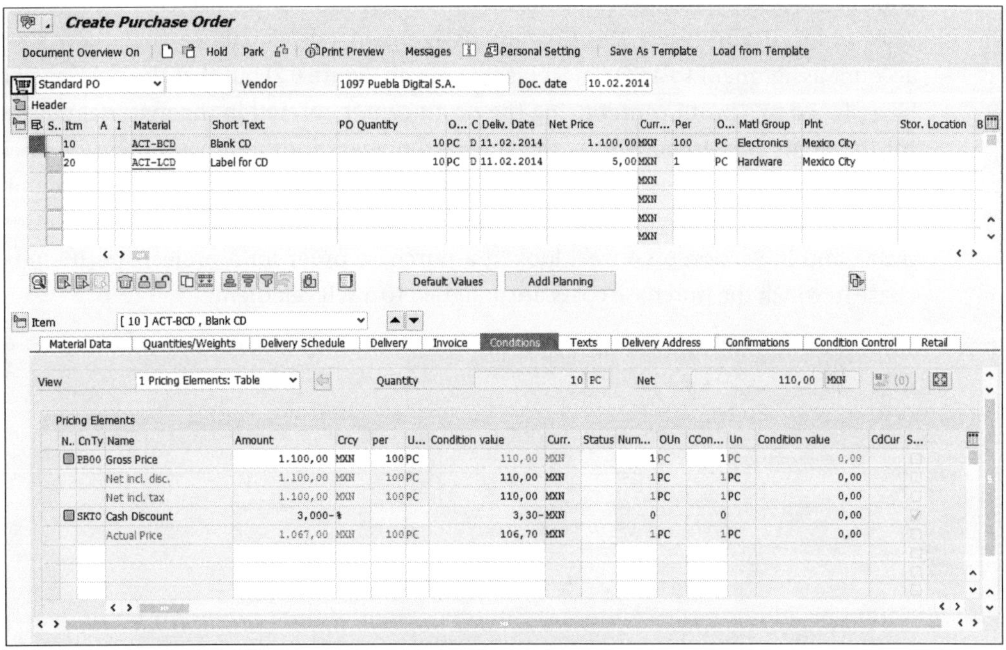

Figure 6.2 Creating Purchase Order (Purchase Order Processing Step)

To view the *price* of each item, select the item and then select the **Conditions** tab. Here we see that the first item for the blank CD costs 1,100 Mexican pesos per 100 units. This may already be the source of a purchase price variance if the agreement with the vendor is based on a different price than that currently in the material master. The controller might also check the *account assignment*. In our example, column **A**

(**Account Assignment** category) is blank, meaning the purchase order will be delivered to regular inventory and can be used by any production order that reserves it. The next step is to record the arrival of the goods into stock.

Posting a Goods Receipt

Now we'll create the goods receipt for the purchase order by referencing the purchase order and the prices contained in it. The easiest way to do this is to stay in the **Purchasing** menu and select **Follow-On Functions • Goods Receipt** or Transaction MIGO. Enter the purchase order from Figure 6.2 as a reference.

Figure 6.3 shows the two items we ordered and indicates that they're to be delivered into unrestricted stock. By comparison, in Section 6.3.3 we'll look at what happens if goods are delivered to sales order stock, where they can only be used for the relevant sales order. If you select the **Account Assignment** tab, you'll see that there's no account assignment to a CO object (as you saw in Figure 6.2) but that the posting will be assigned to a profit center using the profit center entered in the material master for the items concerned. This is the standard process for the procurement of stock materials. By comparison, in Section 6.3.1 we'll look at a purchase order for outsourced manufacturing in which the purchase costs are assigned to a CO production order, and in Section 6.3.4 we'll look at a purchase order for a project-specific purchase in which the purchase costs are assigned to a WBS element.

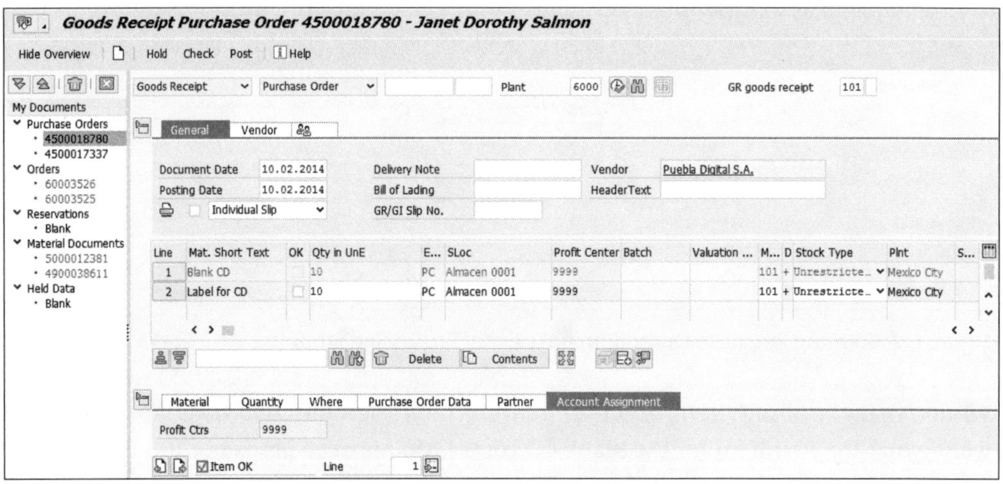

Figure 6.3 Creating Goods Receipt (Goods Receipt Step)

Goods receipts for stock materials don't show up as actual costs on a cost center or order until the material is issued to production later. However, if the **Material Ledger** is active in the plant concerned, the goods receipt is recorded in the Material Ledger, where it can be used as the starting point for actual costing. To display the postings for the goods receipt, use Transaction CKM3N or go to **Controlling • Product Cost Controlling • Actual Costing/Material Ledger • Information System • Detailed Reports • Material Price Analysis**. Enter the material number for the blank CD, the plant, and the current period. Figure 6.4 shows that the price in the purchase order differs from the standard price for the raw material in the material master. The preliminary valuation is based on the standard price for the material (10 pesos per unit), whereas the price conditions in the purchase order item were 11 pesos per unit. This difference of 10 pesos for 10 units is recorded in the Material Ledger and will be included in the actual costs for the material when we use the *periodic costing run* to calculate the periodic unit price for the material as part of the period close in Chapter 7.

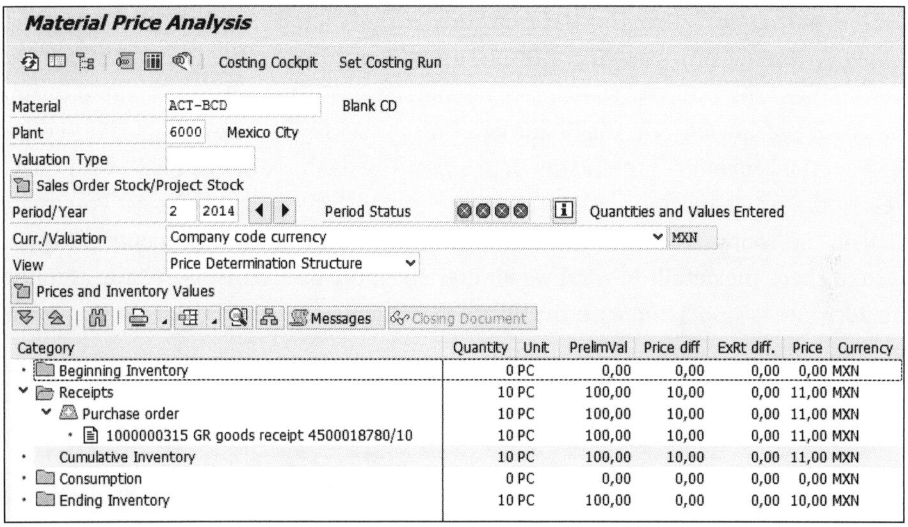

Figure 6.4 Material Price Analysis following Goods Receipt

System Performance with the Material Ledger

When people first hear that the Material Ledger stores an extra document for each goods movement, invoice, and so on, they tend to worry that this will put an unnecessary burden on their system. The act of writing a Material Ledger document adds a couple of percent to the time it takes to post the goods receipt. If you want to find more information about system performance metrics, check the information in SAP Note 668170.

Use of Material Ledger in SAP S/4HANA

The use of the Material Ledger becomes compulsory with SAP S/4HANA 1511. This means that all material inventories can be stored in multiple currencies (the local currency, the group currency, and another currency, as required). The use of the Material Ledger to provide multiple valuations (legal valuation, group valuation, and profit center valuation) or as a basis for actual costing remains optional. You'll find full details in SAP Note 2267834 (S4TWL—Material Ledger Obligatory for Inventory Valuation). We'll explain the implications of the changes in the data model in Chapter 14.

The **Purchase Order** line in the **Material Price Analysis** screen shows both the Material Ledger document number (1000000315) and the purchase order item (4500018780) that initiated the posting. To display the Material Ledger document created during the goods receipt, click on the document line shown in Figure 6.4. This takes you to the Material Ledger document shown in Figure 6.5. As the controller, you won't have created the goods receipt as we just did, so normally on checking this list you might click on the **Source Document** button to display the goods receipt document if you need to check the details of what we entered in Figure 6.3. To display all the accounting documents associated with the goods movement, click on the **Accounting Documents...** button, as shown in Figure 6.5.

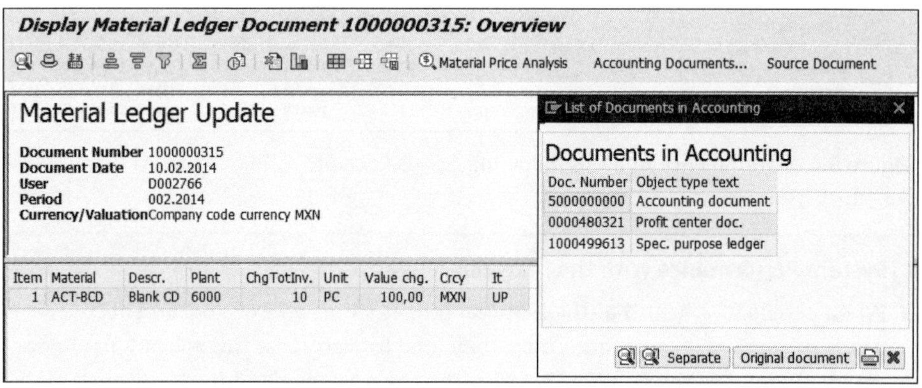

Figure 6.5 Material Ledger Document and Links to Accounting Documents

The goods receipt has been recorded as an accounting document in the General Ledger. We can display this accounting document by selecting it from the list. Figure 6.6 shows the goods valuation (100 pesos) and the variance (10 pesos) for ACT-BCD. Our example predates the ability to include the profit center and the functional area in the General Ledger (see Chapter 3), so there are separate documents for Profit Center Accounting and the Special Ledger.

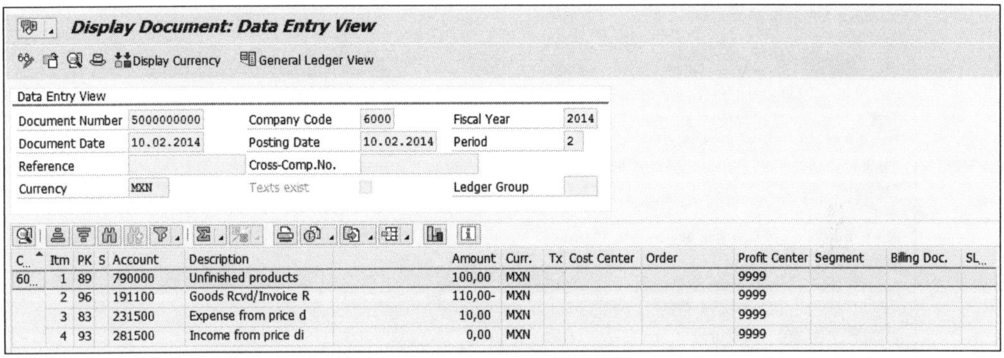

Figure 6.6 Accounting Document for Goods Receipt

The next step is to record the invoice from the vendor for these goods.

Entering an Incoming Invoice (Invoice Processing Step)

Now we'll record the receipt of the invoice from the vendor for the delivery of the materials. To record the invoice, return to the **Purchasing** menu and select **Follow-On Functions • Logistics Invoice Verification** or Transaction MIRO. For invoices to be captured in the Material Ledger, it's important to use the Logistics Invoice Verification transaction (Transaction MIRO) rather than the Invoice Entry transaction (FB60) in Accounts Payable, because you need to ensure that the invoice is linked to the *material* purchased for the Material Ledger. Just as you saw for the goods receipt, the invoice also is created with reference to the initial purchase order (see Figure 6.7).

Again, the controller's task is to monitor the values of such invoices in the Material Ledger. The Material Price Analysis report shown in Figure 6.8 now includes a second line for the invoice (Material Ledger document 1000000317, again with reference to the purchase order 4500018780). In our example, the values are zero because the supplier invoiced for the amount in the initial purchase order. However, there are situations in which a supplier invoices for a different amount. For example, it's common in the food industry for milk to be delivered by volume but for the invoice to be based on the fat content (the higher the cream content, the higher the price). This results in a purchase price variance that most manufacturers want to pass on to the cheese products made using that milk.

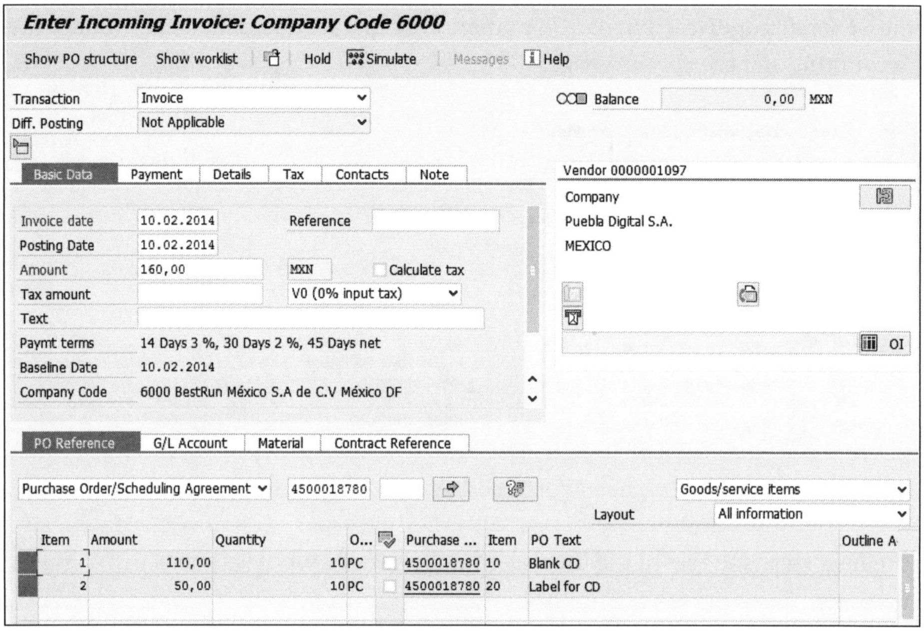

Figure 6.7 Entering Incoming Invoice (Invoice Processing Step)

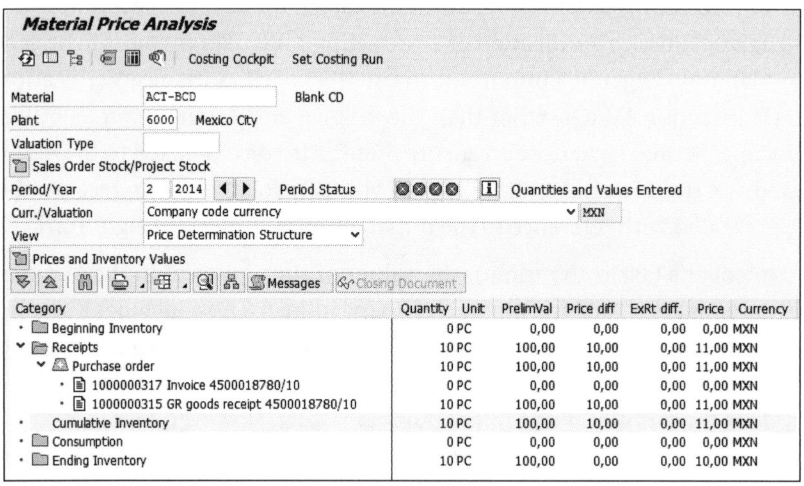

Figure 6.8 Material Price Analysis following Invoicing

Again, we can display the Material Ledger document by clicking on the invoice line. We can display all the accounting documents associated with this invoice by clicking on the Material Ledger document, as shown in Figure 6.9.

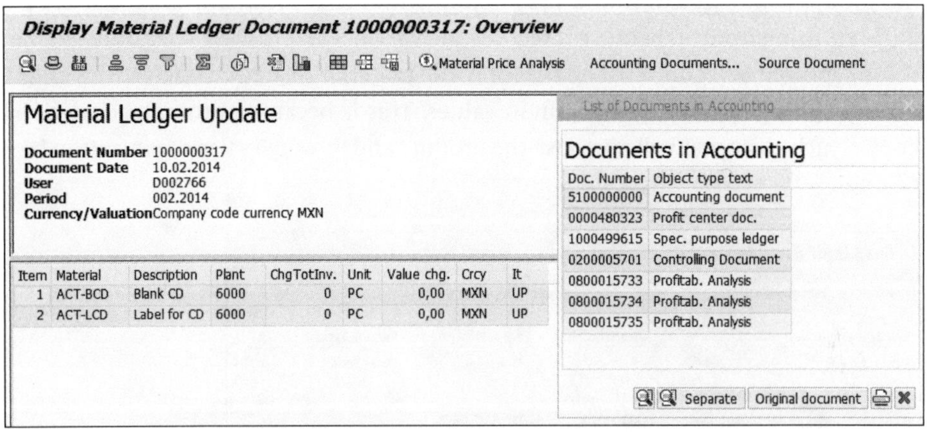

Figure 6.9 Material Ledger Document and Links to Accounting Documents

To check the General Ledger document, select **Accounting Document** from the list. Figure 6.10 shows that the vendor (1097) has invoiced us for the supply of the two materials. You'll also notice additional lines for the variances.

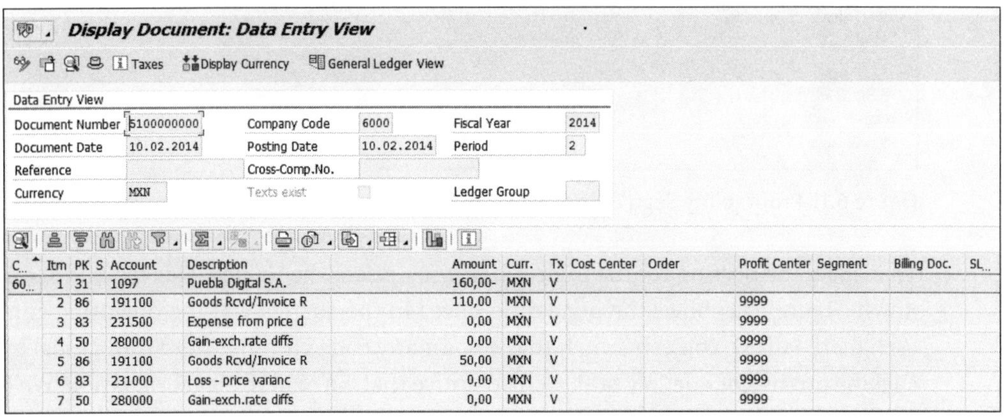

Figure 6.10 Vendor Invoice in General Ledger

Now return to the list of accounting documents, where we see a CO document that records all postings to CO-PA and three CO-PA documents. To display this document, select one of the **Profitability Analysis** documents listed in Figure 6.5. We chose the first document, 800015733.

Figure 6.11 shows the characteristics for the purchased material, including the material group, company code, and plant. Notice that the document is record type B (direct posting from FI) because it records the variances from the General Ledger (i.e., those captured in Figure 6.9) and that only the material-related characteristics (plant, material group, division, etc.) contain values. This is because at this stage we don't know which customer will purchase the product and to which sales organization he'll belong.

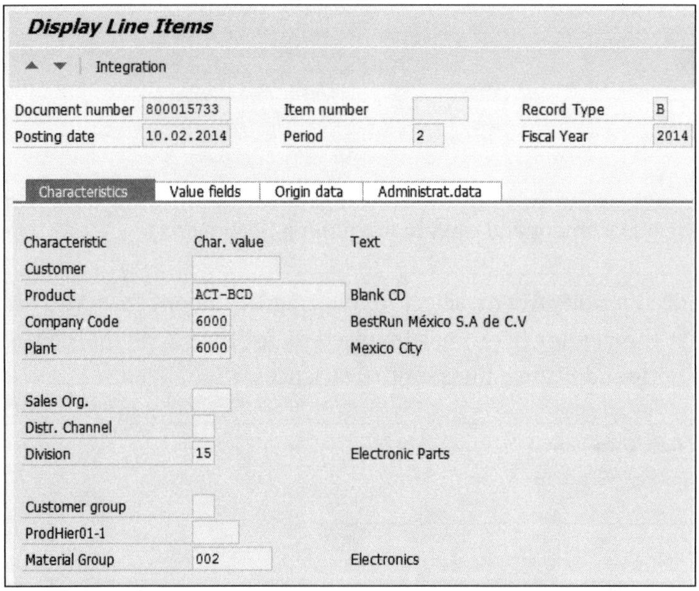

Figure 6.11 Profitability Segment for Raw Material

To display the posting for the price differences, select the **Value Fields** tab and scroll down. Figure 6.12 shows the price differences in the currency of the operating concern (here Euros). You can switch to the company code currency (Mexican pesos) by clicking on the **CoCodeCrcy** button. Also notice that we're in the legal valuation. We'll look at the difference between *legal* and *group valuation* in Section 6.5.

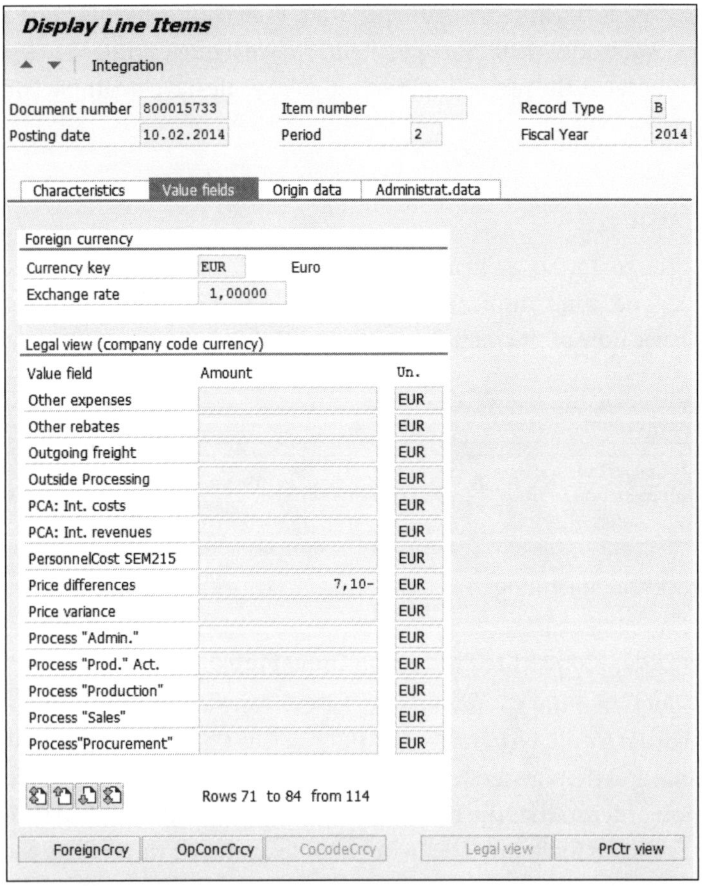

Figure 6.12 Value Fields Showing Price Differences for Raw Materials

Assignment of Purchase Price Variances to CO-PA in SAP S/4HANA

Figure 6.11 and Figure 6.12 show the line item for the purchase price variances in costing-based CO-PA. The document header shows that this line item is of **Record Type B** (direct postings from Financial Accounting). In account-based CO-PA, we would assign the purchase price variances to the product-related characteristics shown in Figure 6.11 but wouldn't make the transformation to value fields shown in Figure 6.12 and instead would see the variances directly on the account/cost element in Figure 6.10.

Normally, the process would continue with an open item in Accounts Payable and a payment to the vendor that would clear that open item, but we'll move straight to the manufacturing process because the processes in accounts payable have no impact on CO.

6.1.2 Plan to Manufacture

Now we'll look at how the materials we just purchased to stock are consumed in the manufacturing process and what information is available to CO in this process. Figure 6.13 shows the basic flow of the manufacturing process.

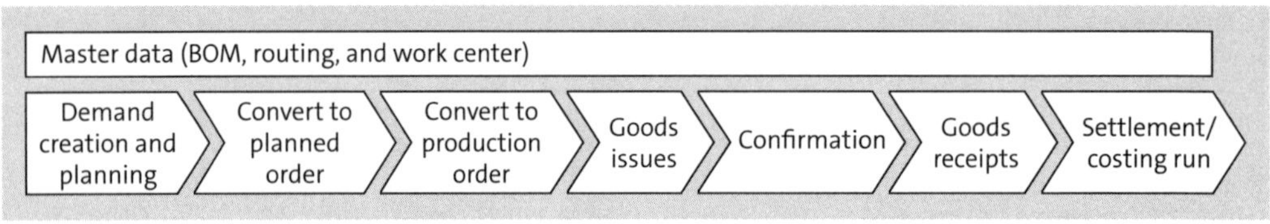

Figure 6.13 Make-to-Stock Manufacturing

Creating a Production Order (Convert to Production Order Step)

First we'll create a production order for material ACT-DCD. Normally, the procedure to create a production order would be to have the MRP run (see Chapter 5) determine demand for the material and then generate a planned order that would then be converted into a production order so that the production activities would be linked with the production plan, as shown in Figure 6.13. In our simple example, we'll create the production order directly by using Transaction CO01 or following the menu path **Logistics • Production • Shop Floor Control • Order • Create with Material**. Enter the material to be manufactured (ACT-DCD), the plant (6000), and the order type (this controls many of the configuration settings). Then enter the order lot size (this may differ from the costing lot size used in planning, giving rise to MRP variances) and the key dates for the order. Based on the quantities and the key dates, the system selects the relevant bill of material (BOM) to determine the material components required and the relevant routing to determine the operations required. This is almost exactly what happened when we created the standard cost estimate for this material in Chapter 5, but production may have made minor changes to the BOM and routing in the meantime, or the changed lot size may give rise to lot-size variances. Figure 6.14 shows the production order header. Given the potential for lot-size variances, our major concern here is whether the lot size (here five units) is standard or not.

To understand where the material usage costs for the order will come from, let's display the material components copied from the BOM by clicking on the **Material Components** icon shown in Figure 6.14. Figure 6.15 shows the component overview and the two materials (ACT-BCD and ACT-LCD) required to manufacture material ACT-DCD. When the production order is released, a reservation will be created for these materials. Notice also that the **Backflush** flag is set in that column for both materials. This means that instead of being issued to the line prior to production, their usage will be recorded automatically during confirmation.

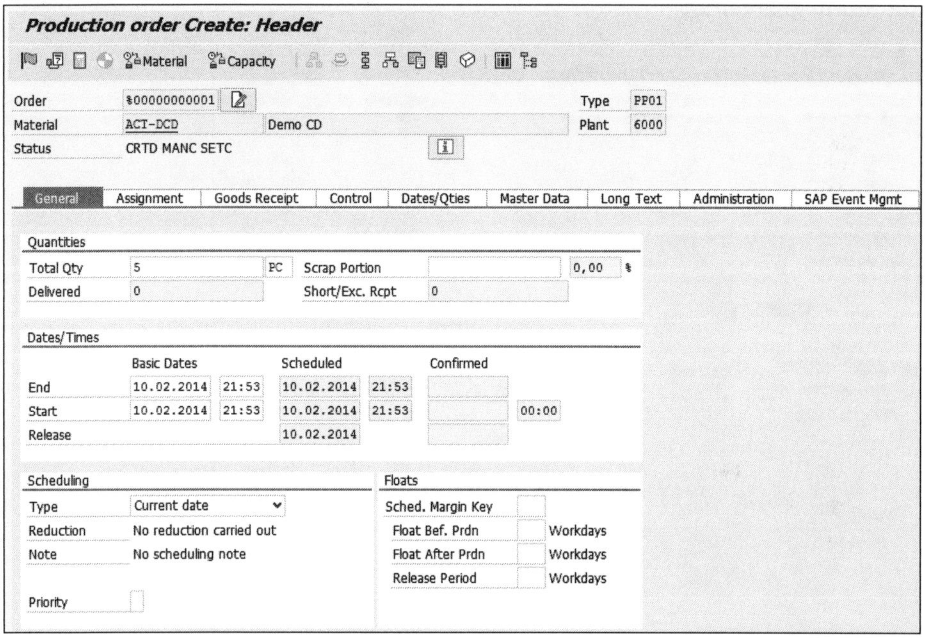

Figure 6.14 Creating Production Order

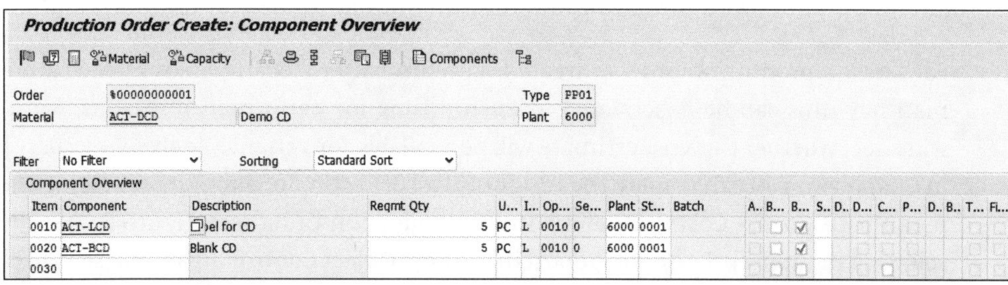

Figure 6.15 Material Components in Production Order

To understand where the labor and machine costs for the order will come from, let's display the operations copied from the routing by clicking on the **Operations** icon shown in Figure 6.15 and then selecting the first operation.

Figure 6.16 shows this first operation. Operation 0010 is being performed at work center WP530-00. According to the standard times for the operation, one hour of labor and one hour of machine time will be required to produce five units of the finished product. These standard values are linked with the activity types for labor and machine time in Cost Center Accounting, as you saw when we looked at the planning process in Chapter 5.

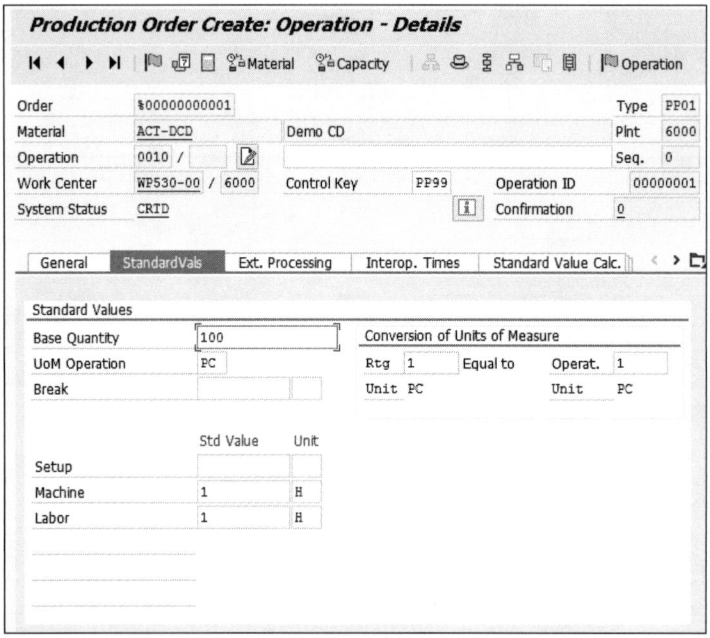

Figure 6.16 Operation in Production Order

Each time a production order is created, a preliminary cost estimate is created automatically (this can be deactivated in Customizing for performance reasons, which will affect whether this cost estimate will be available for variance analysis, discussed in Chapter 7). You can display the result of the cost estimate either by following the menu path **GoTo • Costs • Analysis** in the production order (see Figure 6.17) or by selecting the appropriate detail report in the **Cost Object Controlling** menu (see Chapter 2, Section 2.4). Notice at this stage that the actual costs are zero because we haven't yet released the order for posting.

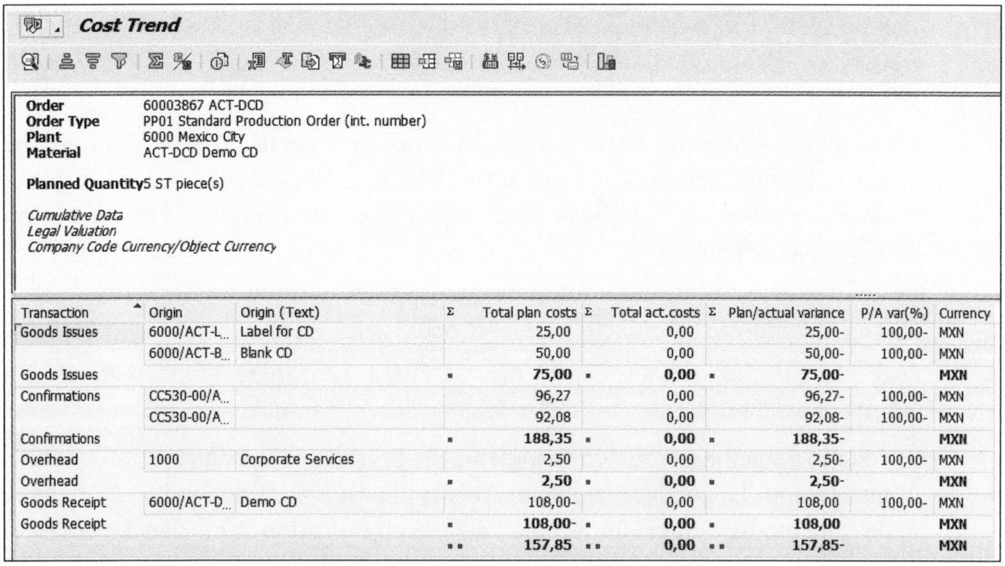

Cost Trend

Order 60003867 ACT-DCD
Order Type PP01 Standard Production Order (int. number)
Plant 6000 Mexico City
Material ACT-DCD Demo CD

Planned Quantity5 ST piece(s)

Cumulative Data
Legal Valuation
Company Code Currency/Object Currency

Transaction	Origin	Origin (Text)	Σ	Total plan costs	Σ	Total act.costs	Σ	Plan/actual variance	P/A var(%)	Currency
Goods Issues	6000/ACT-L...	Label for CD		25,00		0,00		25,00-	100,00-	MXN
	6000/ACT-B...	Blank CD		50,00		0,00		50,00-	100,00-	MXN
Goods Issues			▪	**75,00**	▪	**0,00**	▪	**75,00-**		**MXN**
Confirmations	CC530-00/A...			96,27		0,00		96,27-	100,00-	MXN
	CC530-00/A...			92,08		0,00		92,08-	100,00-	MXN
Confirmations			▪	**188,35**	▪	**0,00**	▪	**188,35-**		**MXN**
Overhead	1000	Corporate Services		2,50		0,00		2,50-	100,00-	MXN
Overhead			▪	**2,50**	▪	**0,00**	▪	**2,50-**		**MXN**
Goods Receipt	6000/ACT-D...	Demo CD		108,00-		0,00		108,00	100,00-	MXN
Goods Receipt			▪	**108,00-**	▪	**0,00**	▪	**108,00**		**MXN**
			▪▪	**157,85**	▪▪	**0,00**	▪▪	**157,85-**		**MXN**

Figure 6.17 Planned Costs for Production Order

The goods issue line in the cost analysis report shows the two raw materials together with their standard costs. The confirmation line shows the standard values for the activities at each operation. A percentage overhead has been applied. You may also want to include additional costing items for one-off costs (such as work scheduling or quality checks) in your order costs. If this is the case, refer to Chapter 11 to discover how to set up a template allocation to include these costs in your estimate.

In addition, the value of the goods receipt has been calculated, again using the standard price. This makes the preliminary cost estimate look slightly different from the standard cost estimate, because it simulates the effect of delivering the finished goods to stock, whereas the standard cost estimate only shows the inputs. Notice that there's already a variance, because the planned costs for the order are not identical to the standard costs for the material. Such variances are considered MRP variances because it's MRP that has resulted in a change, for example, to the lot size.

Data Model Changes in SAP S/4HANA

You'll notice in Figure 6.17 that although Figure 6.16 showed the information needed to calculate the costs for operation 0010 at work center WP530-00, the result has been aggregated by cost center and activity type, with the result that the costs for the work center and operation are effectively lost. In SAP S/4HANA, SAP added the

Work Center and **Operation** fields to the Universal Journal, allowing you to report your production costs by work center and operation.

We'll now show how the costs of the goods issues and operations are assigned to the production order. Before you can perform these steps, you need to release the order by selecting **Functions • Release** (see Chapter 3) or choosing the **Release** button shown in Figure 6.14.

Issuing Materials to a Production Order (Goods Issues Step)

For posting the goods issues for the raw materials, there are two fundamentally different approaches:

1. You can issue the raw materials individually to the shop floor and post the confirmation and the goods receipt later. This approach is common in batch-oriented, discrete production in which there's a focus on capturing as much detailed information as possible on the work order (in this case, the production order). Use the pump example (material P-100) to follow this approach in the demo system.
2. You can *backflush* the goods issue, the goods receipt, and the confirmation in a single step. Backflushing is easier in the sense that all the transactions happen in one go, but it can mean compromising accuracy because of the tacit assumption that the BOM and the routing are accurate representations of the amount of material to be issued and the amount of time to be worked for a given lot size.

Backflushing is common in the chemical and pharmaceutical industries, in which it's often physically impossible to issue goods to individual operations or measure exactly how much of the component is being issued. It's also considered good practice in lean manufacturing, in which there's an emphasis on removing unnecessary transactions. We'll work with this approach.

To create the confirmation at the header level, follow the menu path **Logistics • Production • Shop Floor Control • Confirmation • Enter • For Order** or use Transaction CO15 and enter the order number (you'll find the transactions for confirmations at the operation level in the same folder). We confirmed the completion of five units of the finished product, resulting in the creation of a goods issue and a goods receipt (to see these, click on the **Goods Movements** button). Figure 6.18 shows the materials issued (movement type 261) and the goods received (movement type 101). The costs for these materials will be assigned automatically to the production order, in contrast to the situation we had in purchasing.

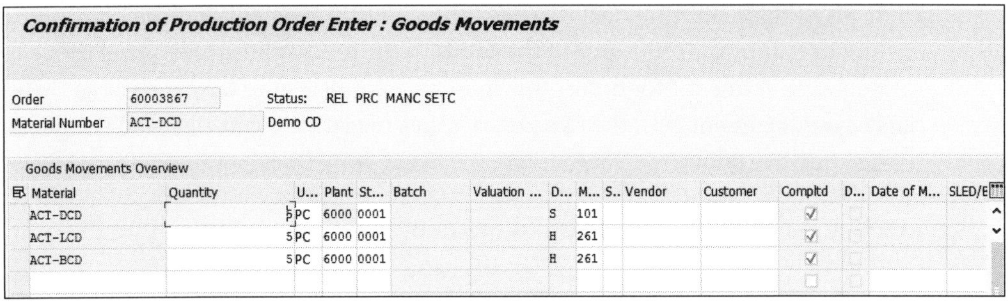

Figure 6.18 Goods Movements Associated with Confirmation

If we now display one of the raw materials (ACT-BCD) we purchased previously in the Material Ledger using material price analysis (Transaction CKM3N), we can see that of the ten units we delivered to stock five have been issued to the production order (see Figure 6.19). If the period close were to occur now, we would need to apply any purchase price variances to the five units in inventory and the five units that have been issued to production, and each would receive the price difference of five Mexican pesos.

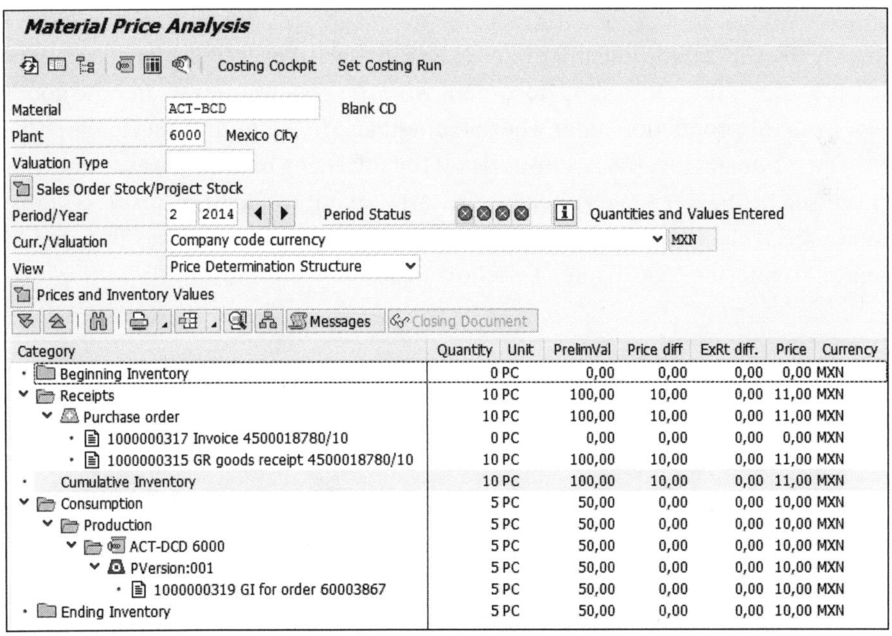

Figure 6.19 Material Price Analysis following Goods Issue

To display the accounting document for the goods movement and the controlling document that records the issue of the goods to the production order, select the relevant document line (GI for order) shown in Figure 6.19. Figure 6.20 shows the Material Ledger document with the two goods issues (negative quantities) and the goods receipt (positive quantity). Now click on the **Accounting Documents...** button.

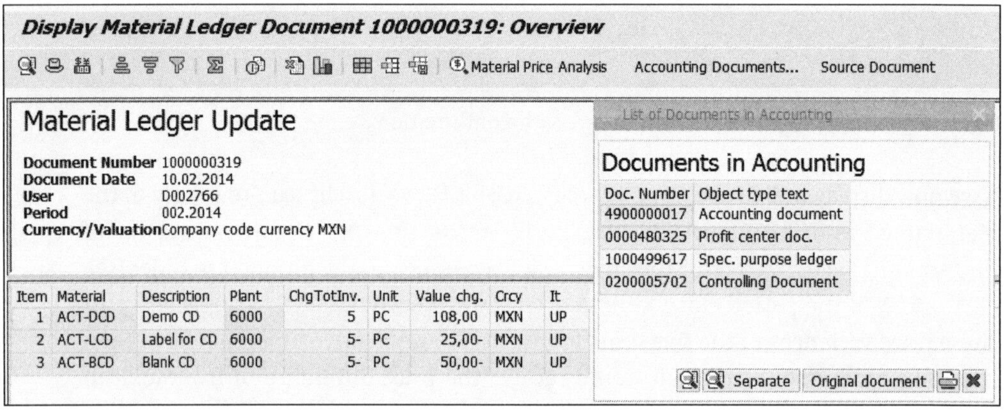

Figure 6.20 Accounting Documents for Goods Issues and Receipts

To display the controlling document, select it from the list of accounting documents. Figure 6.21 shows the controlling document with the goods issues to and the goods receipt from the production order. The document also includes the cost element (the link to the profit and loss [P&L] account) and the offsetting balance sheet account, as we discussed in Chapter 4. We've adjusted the ALV layout to show the business Transaction COIN in the header. This identifies the posting as one that was initiated in Financial Accounting (see Chapter 4, Section 4.9.2).

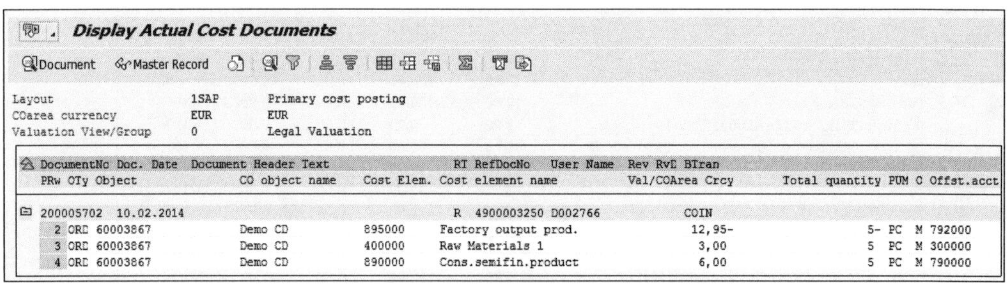

Figure 6.21 Controlling Document for Goods Issues and Receipts

Controlling Documents in SAP S/4HANA

Figure 6.21 shows the controlling document with the postings for the goods issues and goods receipt to the production order. The controlling document is subsumed in the Universal Journal in SAP S/4HANA, but for compatibility reasons you will still see a document number that looks at first glance exactly like this one. On closer inspection, you will notice that it does not contain a real document number (**200005702** in this example) but rather a technical alphanumeric number beginning with A that is stored in the `CO_BELNR` (CO document number) field of the Universal Journal but has no business meaning.

Confirming a Production Order (Confirmation Step)

Now let's return to the confirmation document from the **Goods Movements** tab, under **Environment • Source Document**, as shown in Figure 6.18. This will take us to the confirmation document shown in Figure 6.22.

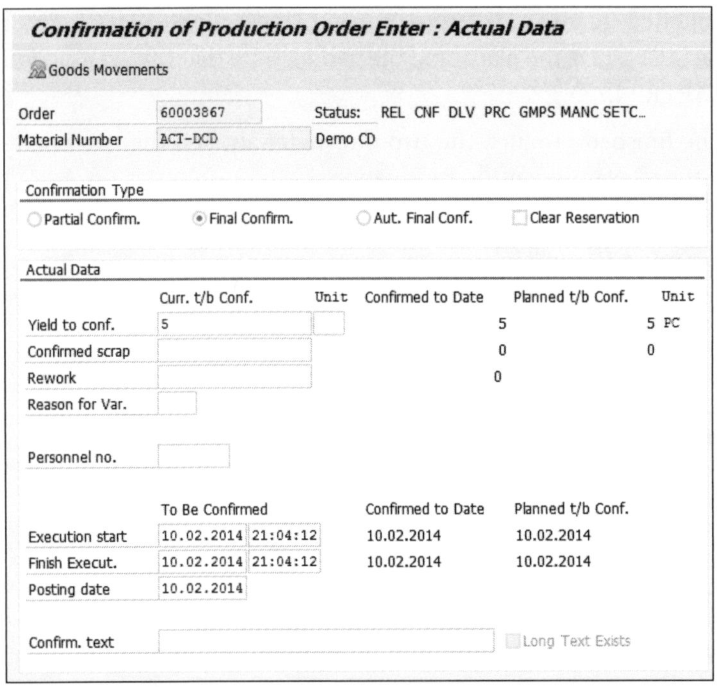

Figure 6.22 Confirming Production Order

Again, it's possible either to post the finished quantity and have the system calculate the actual hours based on the standard values in the routing or to record the hours worked on each operation as separate transactions. The industry tends to determine which approach is more common. In the discrete industry, operation-based confirmation prevails. In the chemical industry, such detail can be virtually impossible to achieve, and the assumptions in the routing must be assumed to apply. In our case, you can see that five units of finished product have been confirmed. The confirmation results in a charge to the production order for the production activities performed.

When we discuss scrap calculation in Chapter 7, note that the confirmation is also used to record scrap either by operation or for the whole order (as shown here). Also notice the field for entering rework. We'll look at the impact of rework in Section 6.3.1.

Because the activity confirmation is not material-related, you won't find it in the Material Price Analysis report. To display the activity usage for the finished product, use the Valuated Quantity Structure report by following the menu path **Controlling • Product Cost Controlling • Actual Costing/Material Ledger • Information System • Detailed Report • Valuated Quantity Structure** or using Transaction CKMLQS. Enter the finished material (ACT-DCD), the plant, and the period. Note that this transaction was introduced in SAP ERP 4.7.

Figure 6.23 shows the finished product, the two raw materials, and the two operations, together with the relevant quantity information.

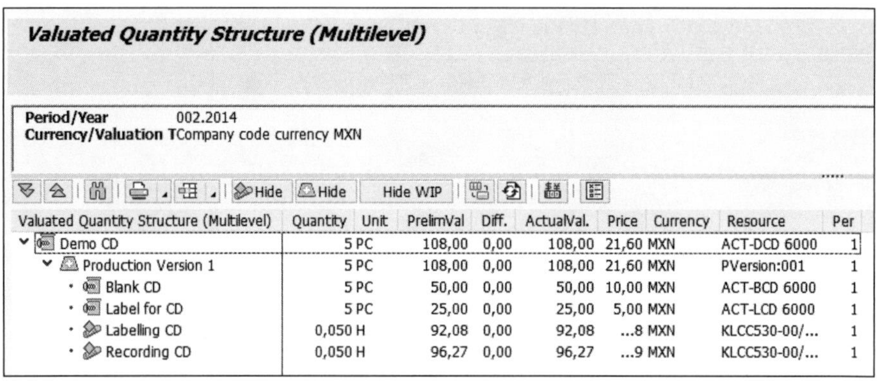
Valuated Quantity Structure (Multilevel)

Period/Year 002.2014
Currency/Valuation TCompany code currency MXN

Hide Hide Hide WIP

Valuated Quantity Structure (Multilevel)	Quantity	Unit	PrelimVal	Diff.	ActualVal.	Price	Currency	Resource	Per
Demo CD	5	PC	108,00	0,00	108,00	21,60	MXN	ACT-DCD 6000	1
Production Version 1	5	PC	108,00	0,00	108,00	21,60	MXN	PVersion:001	1
Blank CD	5	PC	50,00	0,00	50,00	10,00	MXN	ACT-BCD 6000	1
Label for CD	5	PC	25,00	0,00	25,00	5,00	MXN	ACT-LCD 6000	1
Labelling CD	0,050	H	92,08	0,00	92,08	...8	MXN	KLCC530-00/...	1
Recording CD	0,050	H	96,27	0,00	96,27	...9	MXN	KLCC530-00/...	1

Figure 6.23 Valuated Quantity Structure for Finished Product

To display the actual costs in the production order, follow the menu path **GoTo • Costs • Analysis**. Figure 6.24 shows that all quantities have been recorded to plan (see the **Total Actual Costs** column) because we backflushed the materials and activities. However, you can see significant variances in the activity prices. All that's missing is the overhead calculation, which is normally applied at period close (see Chapter 7, Section 7.2). When working with a report like this one, the goal of the controller is to monitor *production variances*.

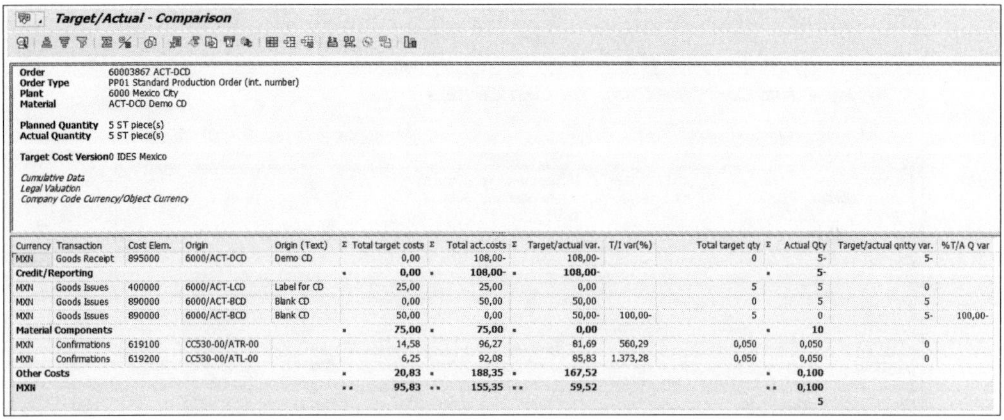
Target/Actual - Comparison

Order 60003867 ACT-DCD
Order Type PP01 Standard Production Order (int. number)
Plant 6000 Mexico City
Material ACT-DCD Demo CD

Planned Quantity 5 ST piece(s)
Actual Quantity 5 ST piece(s)

Target Cost Version0 IDES Mexico

Cumulative Data
Legal Valuation
Company Code Currency/Object Currency

Currency	Transaction	Cost Elem.	Origin	Origin (Text)	Σ	Total target costs	Σ	Total act.costs	Σ	Target/actual var.	T/I var(%)	Total target qty	Σ	Actual Qty	Target/actual qntty var.	%T/A Q var
MXN	Goods Receipt	895000	6000/ACT-DCD	Demo CD		0,00		108,00-		108,00-		0		5-	5-	
Credit/Reporting					•	**0,00**	•	**108,00-**	•	**108,00-**			•	**5-**		
MXN	Goods Issues	400000	6000/ACT-LCD	Label for CD		25,00		25,00		0,00		5		5	0	
MXN	Goods Issues	890000	6000/ACT-BCD	Blank CD		0,00		50,00		50,00		0		5	5	
MXN	Goods Issues	890000	6000/ACT-BCD	Blank CD		50,00		0,00		50,00-	100,00-	5		0	5-	100,00-
Material Components					•	**75,00**	•	**75,00**	•	**0,00**			•	**10**		
MXN	Confirmations	619100	CC530-00/ATR-00			14,58		96,27		81,69	560,29	0,050		0,050	0	
MXN	Confirmations	619200	CC530-00/ATL-00			6,25		92,08		85,83	1.373,28	0,050		0,050	0	
Other Costs					•	**20,83**	•	**188,35**	•	**167,52**			•	**0,100**		
MXN					••	**95,83**	••	**155,35**	••	**59,52**			••	**0,100**		
														5		

Figure 6.24 Actual Costs for Production Order

One source of confusion is the term *actual costs* in a report like the one shown in Figure 6.24. These costs are not actual costs in the full sense of the term because they are determined by multiplying the *actual quantities* recorded during backflushing by the *standard costs* for the materials and activities. At this point, any purchase price variances may not be known because the vendor may not have submitted his invoice. We saw in the first section that the values in the purchasing info record differed from the standard price for one of the raw materials. The real *actual costs* for the material will only be calculated when we use the *periodic costing run* to transfer any purchase price variances for the raw materials to production as part of the period close in Chapter 7.

The cost posting to the production order has also credited the cost center that provided the machine time and labor time to production. You can display this activity by going to Transaction KSB1 or **Accounting • Controlling • Cost Center Accounting • Information System • Reports for Cost Center Accounting • Line Item Reports • Display**

Line Items and entering the name of the cost center (CC530-00), the cost elements under which the confirmation posting was made, and the relevant time frame. Figure 6.25 shows the line item for the posting to the cost center. Notice that whereas the goods movements were posted under business Transaction COIN, we've extended the ALV layout to show that activity allocations are posted under business Transaction RKL. Again, this allocation is based on a *standard* activity rate, because we don't yet know how much energy the cost center used to supply this activity, how much overhead it absorbed, and so on. At period close, we'll be able to calculate the *actual* activity price and adjust the values on the production order to account for this.

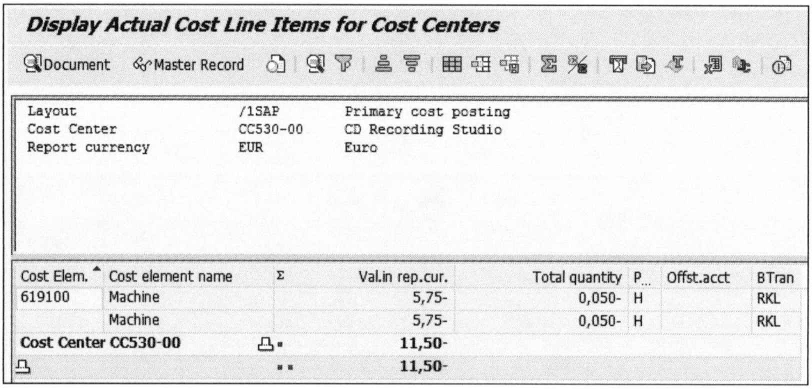

Figure 6.25 Line Items for Activity Posting

Viewing the Goods Receipt (Goods Receipt Step)

Finally, we can display the goods receipt by looking at the finished product in the Material Ledger. Figure 6.26 shows that the goods receipt for the finished material has been captured at the standard cost because the value in the **Price Diff.** column is zero.

To display the Material Ledger document, click on the goods receipt line and then the **Accounting Documents...** button, as shown in Figure 6.27.

From here, we can display the accounting document that documents the goods movement in the General Ledger and the controlling document that documents the goods movements on the production order that we looked at in Figure 6.21.

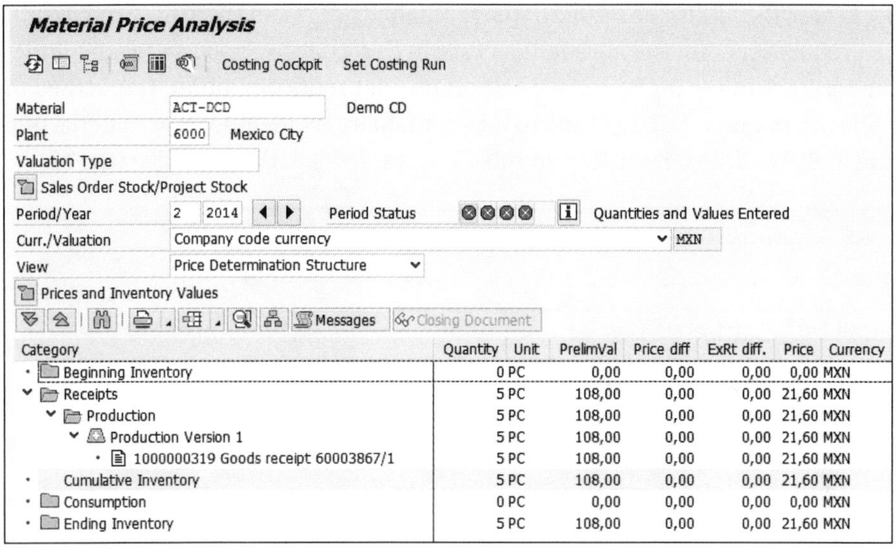

Figure 6.26 Material Price Analysis following Goods Receipt for Finished Product

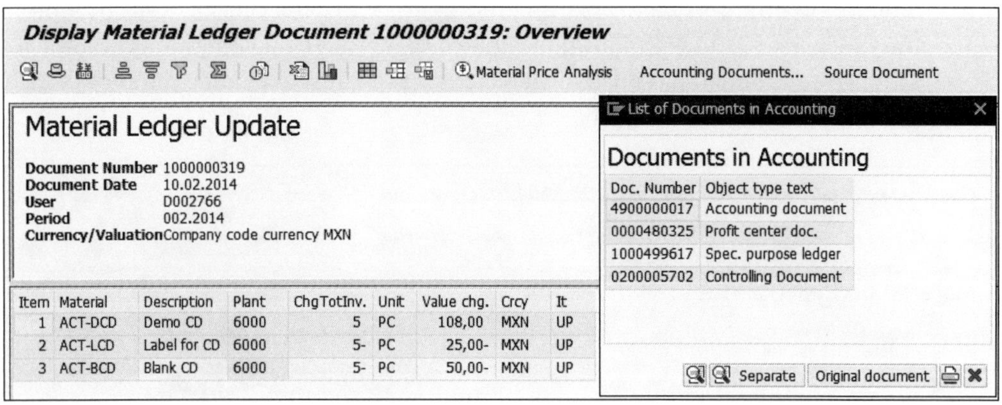

Figure 6.27 Documents for Goods Receipt

Settling the Production Order (Settlement Step)

The final step in our process usually takes place at period close, when overhead is applied to the production order and any variances are settled. Variances are always settled to a stock account, from which, depending on the price control for the material (see Chapter 4), they may either affect the material price (moving average price) or be assigned to a variance or price difference account (standard price). If you're using CO-PA, they'll also be settled to the profitability segment there so that the complete product costs are available for analysis. In this example, you can see the settlement document showing how the variances on our production order were settled to the finished material ACT-DCD and to the profitability segment for that material (see Figure 6.28). We'll look at settlement rules in more detail in Chapter 7, Section 7.2.

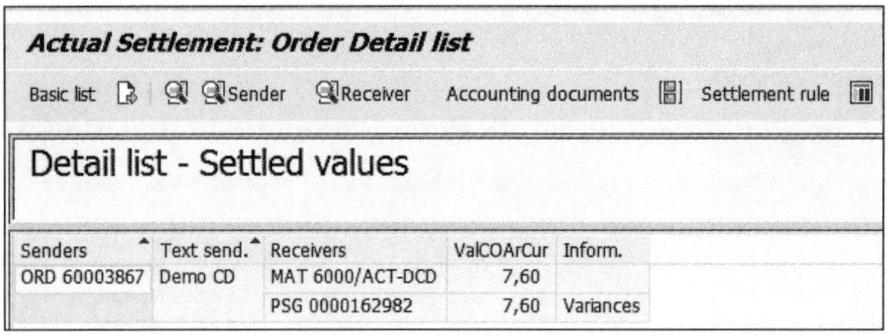

Figure 6.28 Details of Values Included in Settlement

We can also use material price analysis to display the settlement document in the Material Ledger and can again use the document links to display the settlement document in CO, the posting to price differences in the General Ledger, or the posting of the variances to CO-PA, as shown in Figure 6.29. Again, the postings to CO-PA will be assigned to the material-related characteristics, because we don't yet know which customer will purchase the product.

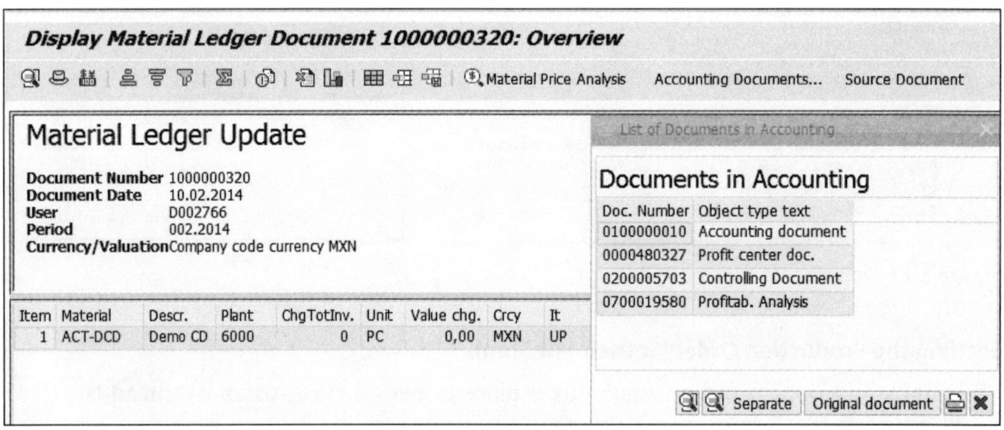

Figure 6.29 Accounting Documents for Settlement

Of course, the production process doesn't have to be single-level only. Another production process could now consume the semifinished product and perform further activities to manufacture a finished product, but the process would be identical from a Controlling point of view, so we'll now look at how to sell our finished product.

6.1.3 Order to Cash

Now we'll look at how the material we just delivered to stock is issued to the sales process and what information is available to CO in this process. Figure 6.30 shows the basic flow of the sales process.

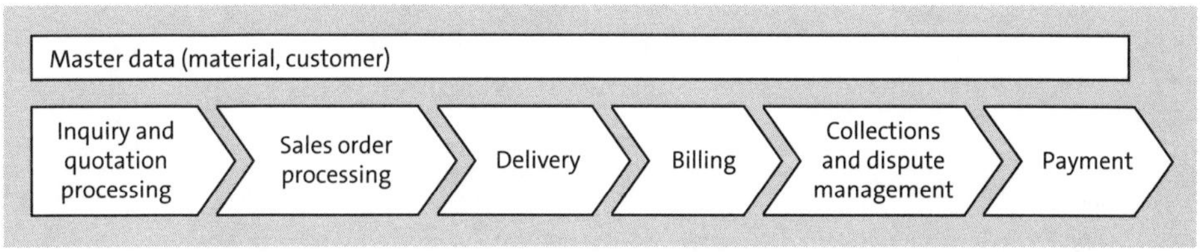

Figure 6.30 Order-to-Cash Process

Creating a Sales Order (Sales Order Processing Step)

Sometimes an inquiry or quotation precedes the sale, but we'll start by creating a sales order for the product ACT-DCD that we manufactured in the previous step. The sales order records the agreement by the organization to supply the customer with a particular product. The focus from a controlling perspective is on the price conditions and the assignment to CO-PA. This is because, as we discussed in Chapter 2, every sales order item generates a preliminary valuation in costing-based CO-PA. The profitability segment is derived from the customer, product, and other organizational information in the sales order.

To create a sales order, go to Transaction VA01 or **Logistics • Sales and Distribution • Sales • Order • Create** and enter the order type, the sales organization, the distribution channel, the division, the sales office, and the sales group. Then enter the name of the sold-to party (customer) in the order header and the material and quantity in the order item. From a controlling perspective, these are the characteristics that will form the basis of your sales controlling activities in Profitability Analysis. Figure 6.31 shows the characteristics that will be recorded in Profitability Analysis for the sales order. Notice that you now can see both product-related and customer-related characteristics.

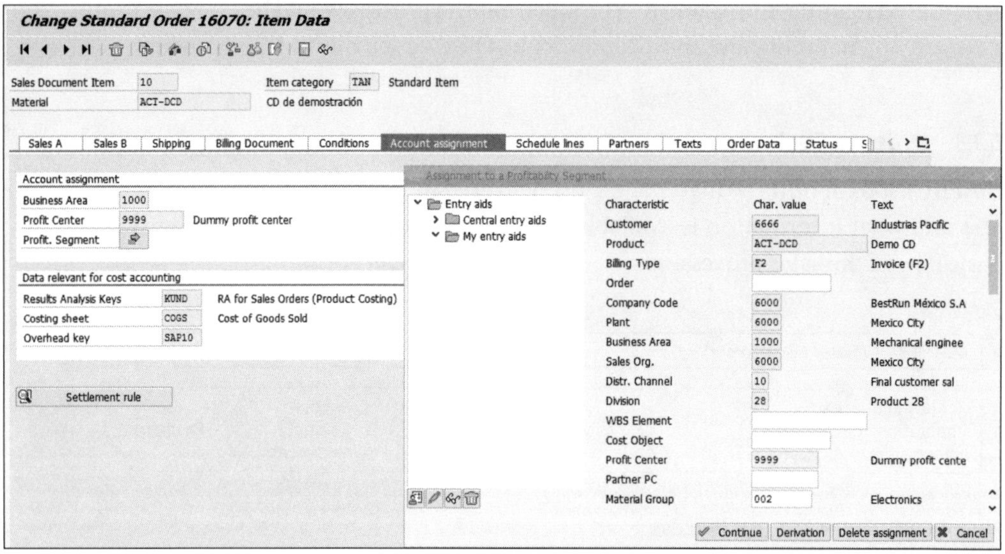

Figure 6.31 Sales Order Item and Associated Profitability Segment

To check these characteristics, once you've created your sales order select **Item Details** on the initial entry screen and then the **Account Assignment** tab. Now click on the **Profitability Segment** button. Here you can see that in addition to the information we entered when we created the order (order type, sales organization, distribution channel, division, sales office, sales group, customer, and product), the system has selected additional characteristics, including billing type, business area, company code, material group, plant, and profit center, using a process known as *derivation*. To simulate this step, when you're creating an order, click on the **Derivation** button shown in Figure 6.31 to check the assignments. The program logic for performing such a derivation is set up in Customizing with the goal of deriving additional data about the product, such as the material group, the division, or the product hierarchy from the fields in the material master, and additional data about the customer, such as the billing type from the customer master.

When you've saved the sales order, display the line item in CO-PA by following the menu path **Controlling • Profitability Analysis • Information System • Display Line Item List • Actual** or using Transaction KE24. Line items derived from the sales order are recorded as record type A (sales order entry). Figure 6.32 shows the characteristics for the sales order. Here you can see many more characteristics than were shown in the previous screen, including the customer group, country, region, and so on.

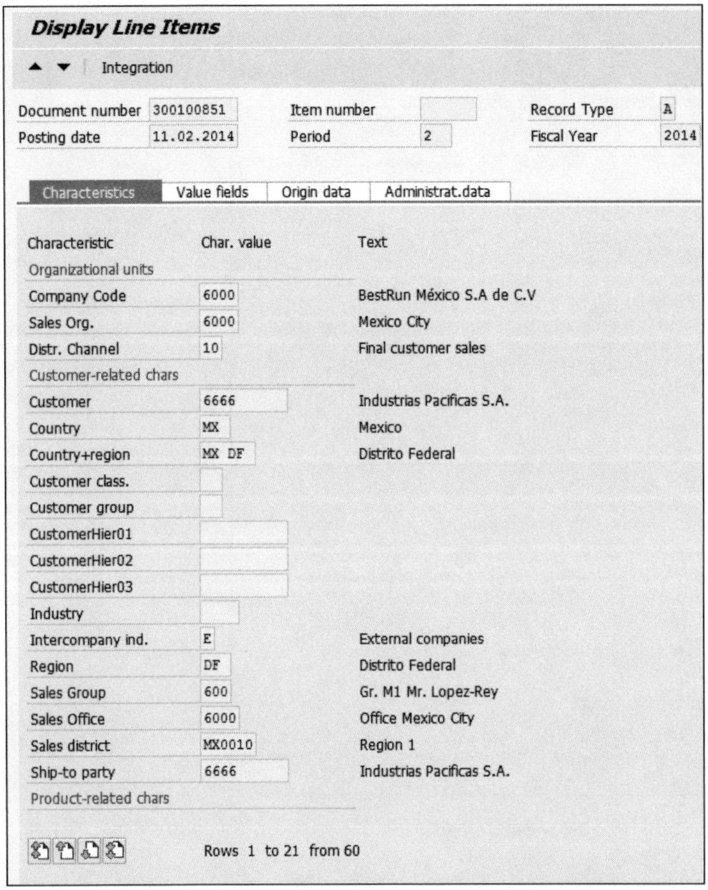

Figure 6.32 CO-PA Line Item for Sales Order Item: Characteristics

Figure 6.33 shows the value fields for the sales order item. In this case, revenue (8.25 Euros) and cost of goods manufactured (5.94 Euros) have been transferred to Profitability Analysis to provide an initial contribution margin for the order. It's also common for the price conditions to be transferred in more detail; this is a matter for configuration, as we discussed in Chapter 2.

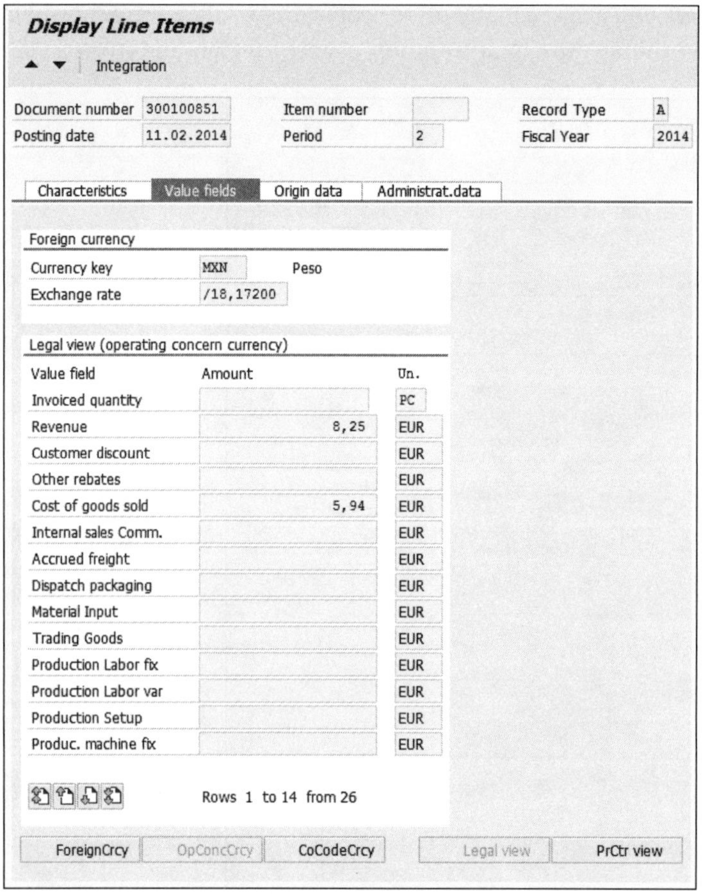

Figure 6.33 CO-PA Line Item for Sales Order: Value Fields

Sales Order Entry in SAP S/4HANA

As we discussed in Chapter 2, costing-based CO-PA stores separate documents for the sales order entry (record type A) and the invoice (record type F). In account-based CO-PA, only the invoice results in a revenue posting and the delivery in a posting for cost of goods sold, since the sales order is not considered GAAP-relevant. From SAP S/4HANA 1809, the revenue and cost of goods sold for the sales order will be recorded in accordance with the predictive accounting approach. We'll explain how these postings work and how they differ from a traditional one-sided posting in costing-based CO-PA in Chapter 14.

Delivering the Sales Order (Delivery Step)

We'll now record the delivery of the finished product to the customer. In the **Sales Order** menu, select **Subsequent Functions • Outbound Delivery** and enter your sales order number. Then enter the quantity to be delivered as the picking quantity and post the goods issue as shown in Figure 6.34. Note that, depending on your configuration, you might need to create a stock transfer order as part of this step.

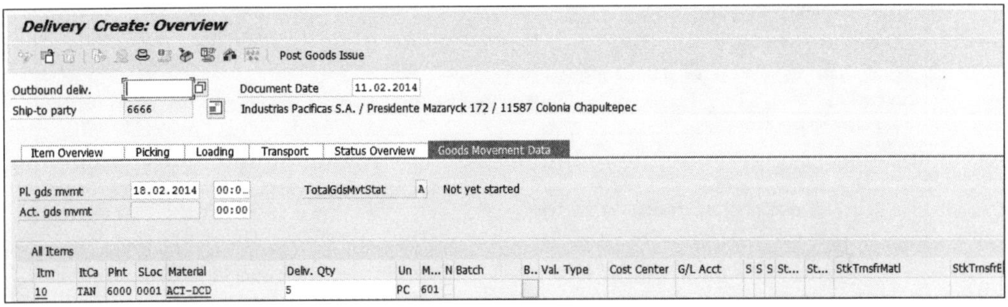

Figure 6.34 Delivery with Goods Issue

Figure 6.35 shows the goods movement in the Material Price Analysis report following the delivery. Here you can see the goods issue of five units to the customer account. What is shown here is not the customer number you saw in the profitability segment but the reconciliation account for the customer (entered in the customer master) that records the goods movement in the General Ledger.

Figure 6.36 shows the accounting documents again, with a posting to the General Ledger and a controlling document. Notice that there's no **Profitability Analysis** document. The delivery is recorded in the financial accounts as the goods movement is posted. If we were using account-based Profitability Analysis, then the delivery would result in a cost of goods sold posting in CO-PA. In costing-based CO-PA, however, the revenue is recorded when the invoice is posted. If there is a long time lag between delivery and invoicing, then it's important to defer the goods issue postings in the General Ledger to ensure that the cost of goods sold postings in CO-PA match the values in the General Ledger. The cost of sales is determined using condition type VPRS and reading the price from the goods receipt on the date of the goods receipt. However, if the delivery takes place in one period and the invoice in the next, the values in the P&L statement won't reconcile with the values in costing-based CO-PA. In this case, you'll want to use the reports listed under **Accounting • Controlling • Profitability Analysis • Tools • Analyze Value Flows** to find such differences.

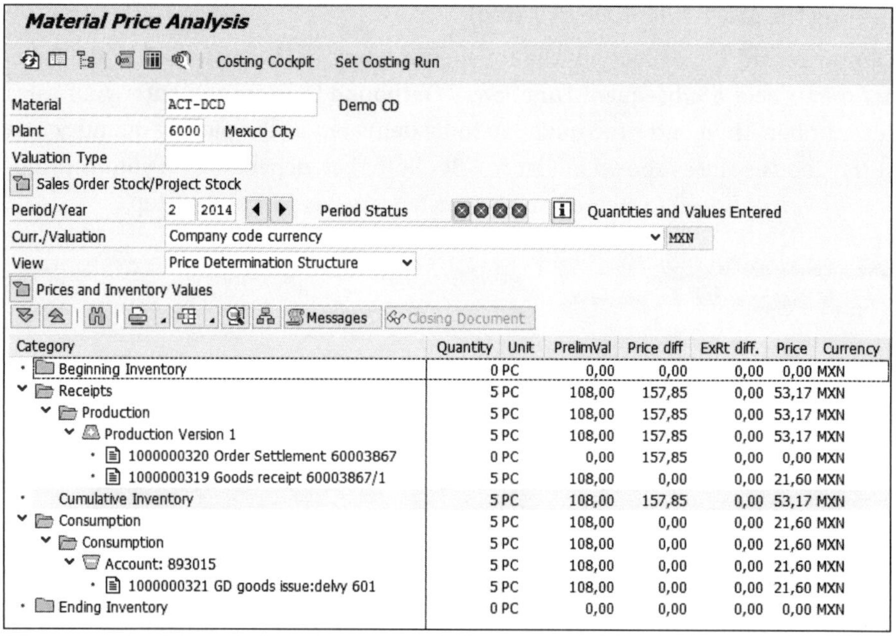

Figure 6.35 Material Price Analysis for Goods Issue to Sales

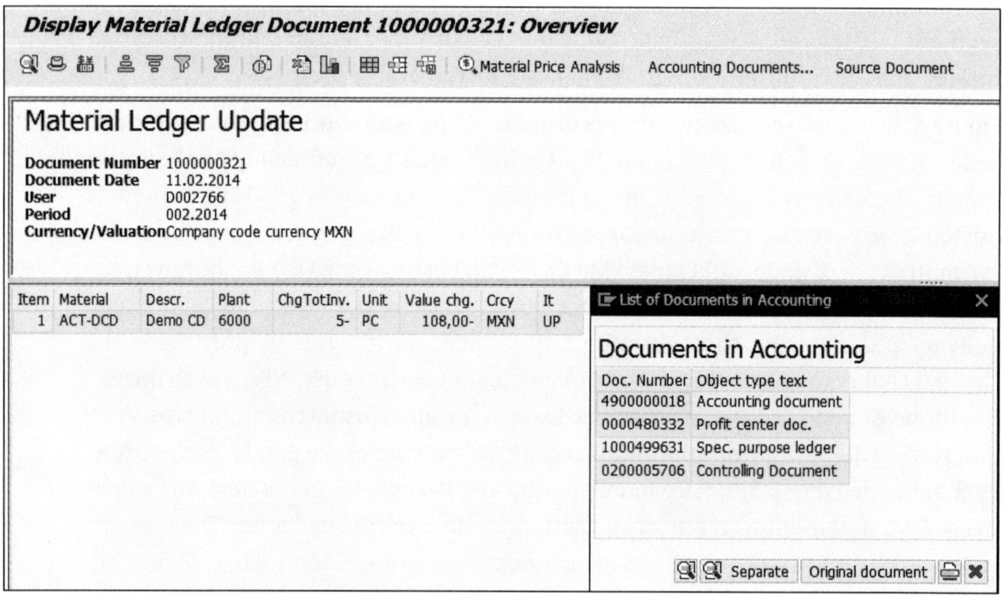

Figure 6.36 Accounting Documents for Delivery

Sales Order Delivery in SAP S/4HANA

In Figure 6.36, you'll notice an accounting document and a controlling document, but no profitability analysis document. This is because the delivery is not captured in costing-based CO-PA until the invoice is recorded. In account-based CO-PA, the cost of goods sold posting is linked with the profitability characteristics that you will see in Figure 6.38; the 108 Mexican pesos are assigned to a cost element and, of course, to the relevant profit center. In a make-to-stock environment, the cost of goods sold accounts are not usually considered cost elements for the purposes of costing-based CO-PA, but in SAP S/4HANA you will need to ensure that these accounts are flagged as cost elements of type 01 (primary cost elements).

Billing the Customer (Billing Step)

Finally, the customer is invoiced for receipt of the goods, again triggering a posting to Profitability Analysis, this time as a record of type F. To trigger the invoice, select **Subsequent Functions • Billing Document** in the **Sales Order** menu and enter the delivery document number. Figure 6.37 shows the customer invoice document for the demo CD.

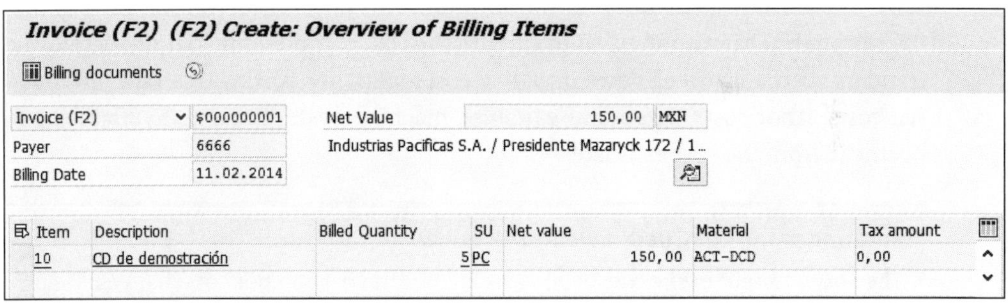

Figure 6.37 Billing Document

Again, we can display the line item in Profitability Analysis using Transaction KE24 and selecting record type F for billing. Figure 6.38 shows the characteristics for the invoicing document.

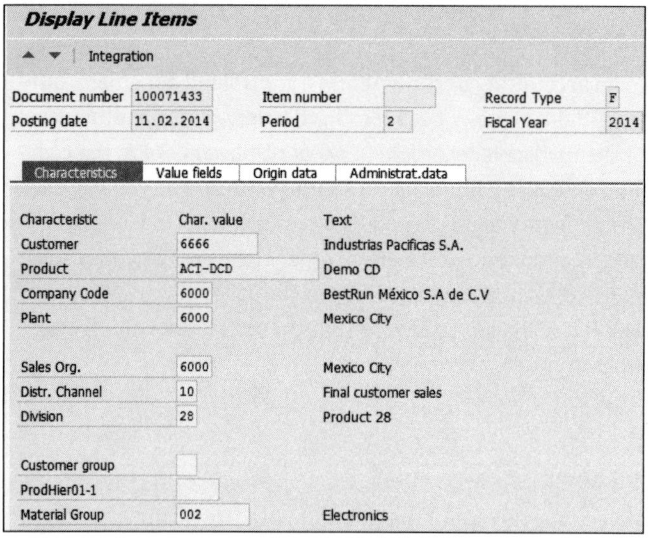

Figure 6.38 CO-PA Line Item for Billing: Characteristics

To show the value fields, select the **Value Fields** tab, as shown in Figure 6.39. The revenue (150 Mexican pesos) and the cost of goods sold (108 Mexican pesos) are the same as you saw for the sales order document. This time, however, you can see that the system has been configured to capture the cost components in more detail. The standard costs are broken down into their cost components, so you can see raw material costs, labor costs (fixed and variable), machine costs (fixed and variable), and overhead from the cost estimate.

Splitting of Cost of Goods Sold in SAP S/4HANA

The ability to split of the cost of goods sold into the cost components that you see in Figure 6.39 is one of the reasons that many controllers choose to work with costing-based CO-PA. In SAP S/4HANA, you can use the same logic to split the 108 Mexican pesos used to value the delivery and thus post to separate accounts for each of the cost components. We'll explain how this works in Chapter 14.

In Figure 6.37, you'll also notice the invoice quantity of five pieces. Many organizations create multiple invoice quantities in costing-based CO-PA to be able to convert from the unit of measure used in sales (here pieces) into a unit of measure that can be aggregated across the whole organization (e.g., kilograms or pounds). The Universal Journal includes three new quantity fields that you can fill via a BAdI implementation if you need to see multiple quantities in your sales reporting.

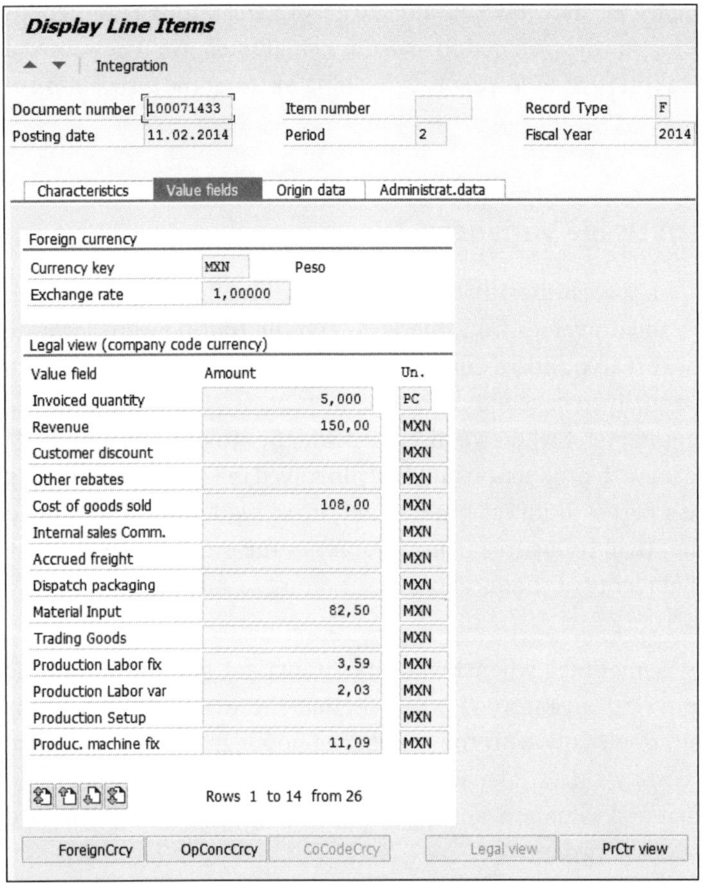

Figure 6.39 CO-PA Line Item for Billing: Value Fields

The process would normally continue with the open item being monitored in accounts receivable and then in receipt of payment or collection activities. At period close, the cycle would be closed by settling the production variances to Profitability Analysis and running allocations to transfer cost center expenses to Profitability Analysis. Because we've been collecting all the relevant data in the Material Ledger, it's also possible to calculate the periodic unit price for each of the raw materials and include the variances in the raw materials inventory at period close. We can then roll the variances up to the finished goods inventory and finally to the cost of sales to provide a complete picture of the cost impact of the whole process. We'll also be able to use the revaluation function to pull the actual cost component split for the material into CO-PA. We'll walk through this whole process in Chapter 7.

In the previous example, we used *backflushing* to record the goods issue, goods receipt, and confirmation for the production order in a single step. We'll now look at how to correct any data concerns following backflushing by using the *distribution of usage variances* function.

6.2 Distribution of Usage Variances

One of the concerns of organizations that consider using backflushing is the tacit assumption that the standard values from the BOM and the routing were accurate and thus a fair basis for cost accounting. Controllers instinctively believe it's better to confirm operations manually to have full control of the process. Here we're covering the same ground as in Chapter 4 when we discussed whether to use a costing BOM and routing or share data with production. Anybody involved in lean manufacturing will advise you that it's better to invest time and effort in high-quality BOMs and routings up front rather than trying to ensure accuracy as the orders are processed. Let's also not forget that plenty of chemical processes refuse to submit to operation-based confirmations.

Whatever your views, sometimes when inventory counts are performed for the goods in stock, the physical inventory (PI) reveals that the material movements recorded in the system don't tally with the number of goods in stock. Controllers working with actual costs want to take account of the inventory differences and include them in the material valuation, and even controllers working with standard costs want to be aware of the variances.

There was a time when plants stopped work to perform a PI, but now regular cycle counts are the order of the day for reasons of efficiency, and PI can be performed daily, weekly, or monthly. More importantly for controllers, you can distribute the inventory differences recorded using a function called *distribution of usage variances*, which you'll find in the **Material Ledger** menu, although it does not require use of the Material Ledger. This function was introduced in SAP ERP Release 4.7. If you can't find the relevant entries in your menu, check with your IT department to see whether the Enterprise Extension `EA_FIN` is activated (see Appendix C at *www.sap-press.com/4691*).

6.2.1 Capturing Physical Inventory Documents

A physical inventory requires whoever performs the check to create a PI document to act as the header for all activities associated with the count for the auditors. To create a PI document, use Transaction MI01 or follow the menu path **Logistics • Materials Management • Physical Inventory • Physical Inventory • Document • Create**. Enter the document date, plant, and storage location and the materials you intend to include in the count, which takes place per storage location. For controlling purposes, it's important to ensure that all relevant materials in the PI documents are flagged as relevant for the distribution of PI differences (**DD** field). Figure 6.40 shows a PI document for a count of material ACT-LCD (one of the raw materials we used in the previous example).

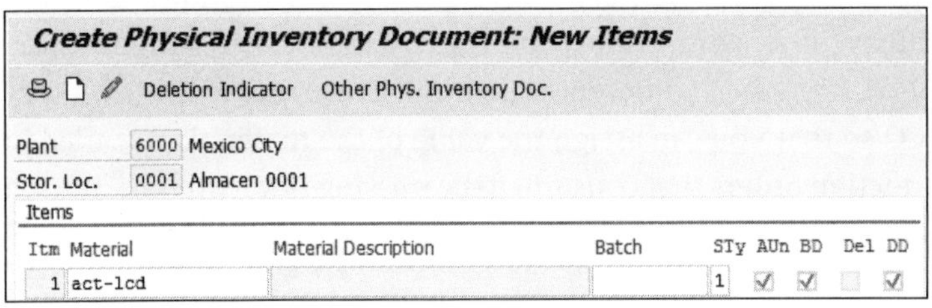

Figure 6.40 Physical Inventory Document

The next step is to enter the difference in the inventory counts for the material in question. This extends the PI document to record exactly how much material is missing or in excess. To do this, go to Transaction MI04 or **Logistics • Materials Management • Physical Inventory • Inventory Count • Enter**. Enter the number of the PI document from the previous step and then the inventory count for each of the materials in the PI document. Note that this document does not impact the financial accounts. Again, make sure that whoever records the inventory count sets the **DD** flag for material ACT-LCD, as shown in Figure 6.41.

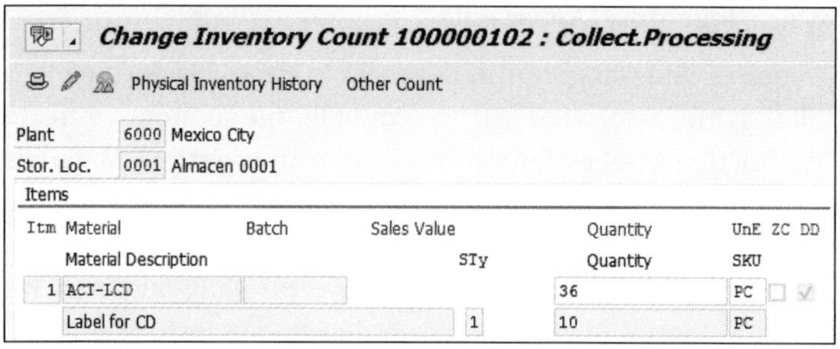

Figure 6.41 Recording Inventory Differences

Finally, to post the inventory differences to FI, go to Transaction MI07 or **Logistics • Materials Management • Physical Inventory • Differences • Post**, as shown in Figure 6.42. This posting adjusts the stock level and posts the costs associated with the missing materials to the P&L from the PI differences account. It also makes the inventory count available for CO so that you can assign the value of the materials recorded in the count to the production orders that consumed the missing raw materials. We will be assigning the costs for 36 missing pieces to the production orders that used material ACT-LCD since the last inventory count.

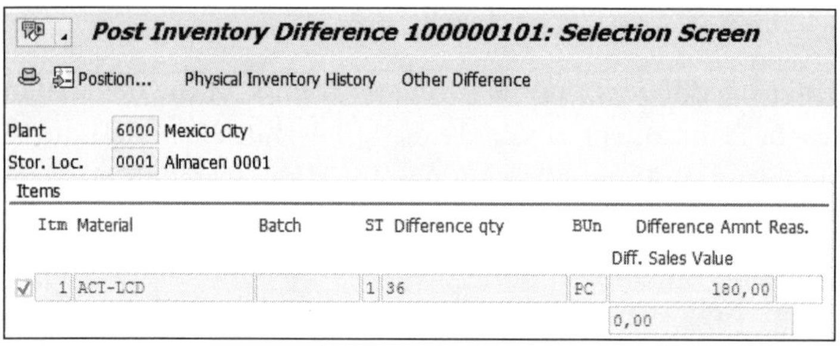

Figure 6.42 Posting Inventory Differences

6.2.2 Distribution of Usage Variances

Once the PI differences have been captured for the storage location, the controller distributes them to the production orders that used that material in the period. To do this, use Transaction CKMATDUV or follow the menu path **Accounting • Controlling • Product Cost Controlling • Actual Costing/Material Ledger • Actual Costing • Distribution of Usage Variances • Distribution of Inventory Differences**. To perform the distribution, proceed as follows:

1. Enter either the range of PI documents (if you know them) or the materials for which you want to select differences, as shown in Figure 6.43. You can see a list of the PI documents selected (only one in our example), the quantity (36 pieces), and the status **New**.

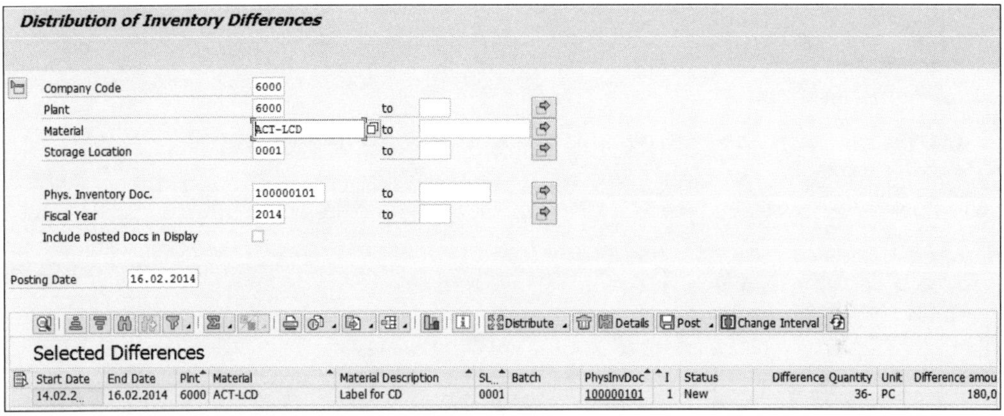

Figure 6.43 Selection of PI Document for Distribution

2. Now click on the **Distribute** button, located in the button bar above the selected document(s).
3. This results in the status **New** shown in Figure 6.43 changing to the status **Distribution Completed**, as shown in Figure 6.44. To understand how the system distributed that value to the orders that used the component in that period, click on the line containing the PI document and then click on the **Details** button. The quantities of material issued to the orders were 20, 10, and 10 (shown in the **Withdrawn Quantity** column), and the system proposal for the distribution of the 36 units is 18, 9, and 9 (shown in the **Default Quantity** column). In general, you accept the system's proposal and click on **Post**. However, if you know that one order has caused particularly high variances you can correct the proposal by overwriting the figure proposed and entering a different figure in the **Quantity** column.

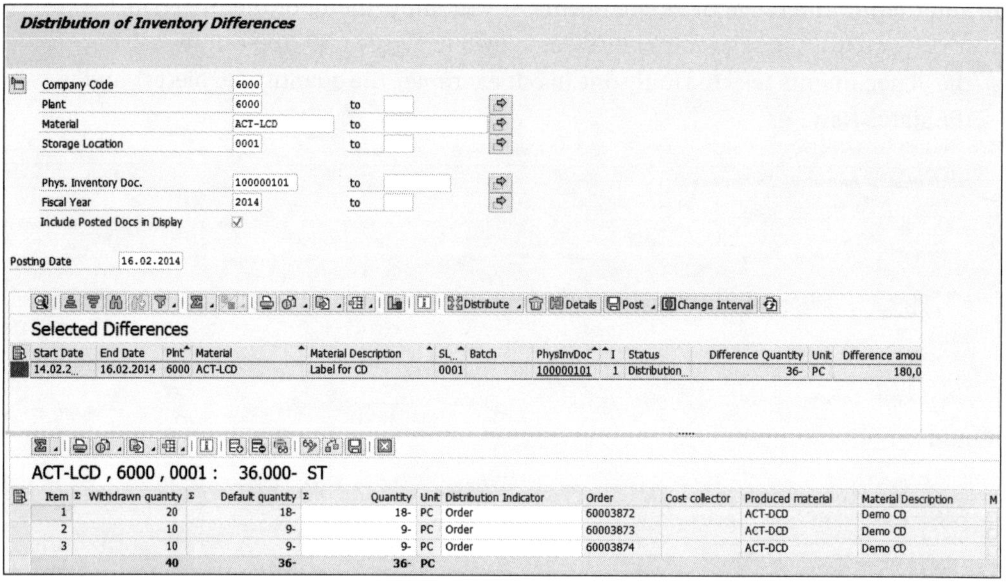

Figure 6.44 Distribution of Inventory Differences

6.2.3 Distribution of Activities

If you want to correct the machine or labor time from the routing, you can use the same mechanism to assign differences to the production orders. This might be the case if you're posting standard time to your orders but have found that the machine ran for more hours than the sum of the standard values suggests. This information might come from workers' time sheets, machine hour counters, or electricity consumption meters. To record the initial differences, use Transaction CKMDUVREC or follow the menu path **Accounting • Controlling • Product Cost Controlling • Actual Costing/Material Ledger • Actual Costing • Distribution of Usage Variances • Enter Actual Activity Quantities**. Enter values for cost center CC530-00 and activity types ATL-00 and ATR-00, as shown in Figure 6.45. Note that the system only saves the data if you select the **Item OK** checkbox on the far left.

To assign the times to the production orders using that activity, go to Transaction **CKMDUVACT** or **Accounting • Controlling • Product Cost Controlling • Actual Costing/ Material Ledger • Actual Costing • Distribution of Usage Variances • Distribution of Activity Differences**. Enter the cost center and the relevant activity types. Figure 6.46

shows the actual activity quantities being distributed instead of the quantities from the PI documents we saw in the previous example. The proportions are the same, because the split on the relevant orders was identical.

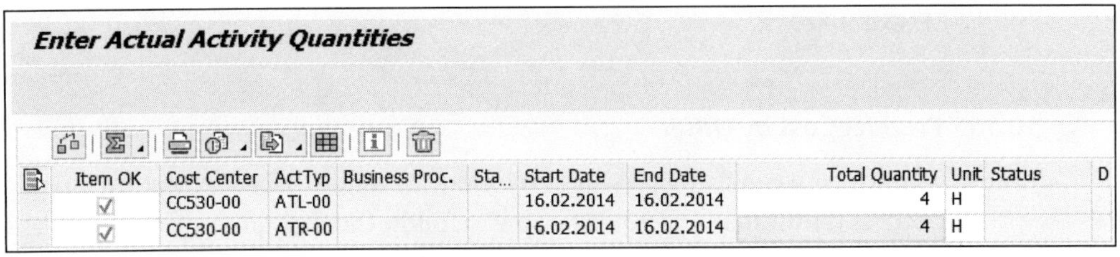

Figure 6.45 Correcting Activity Quantities

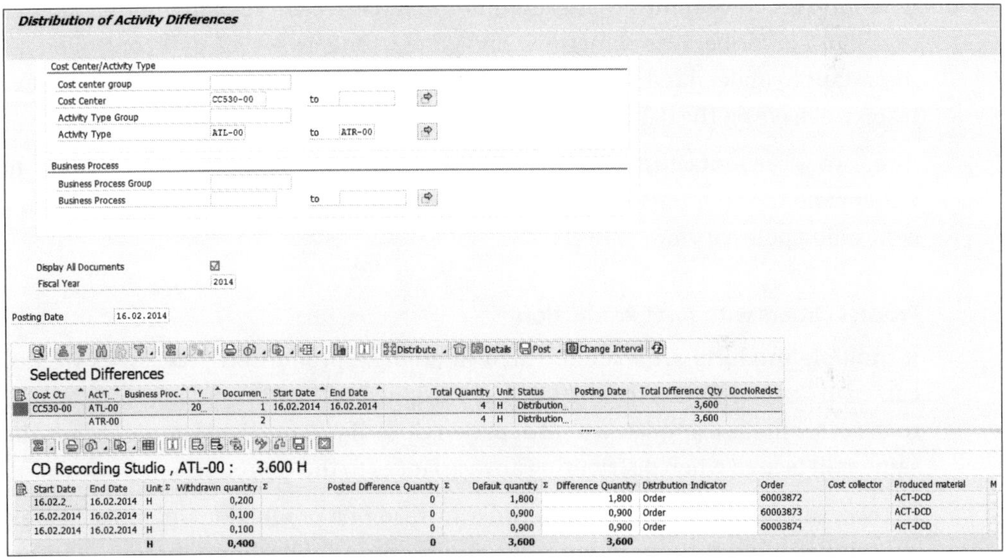

Figure 6.46 Distribution of Activity Differences

If we worked as manufacturers of demo CDs, we could now move on to the period close in Chapter 7, having captured all relevant data. Before we do that, however, we'll look at some of the process variants you might find for each of the cost object controlling approaches we discussed in Chapter 2.

6.3 Integrated Process Flows: Other Logistics Scenarios

In this section, we'll look at product cost by order, product cost by period, product cost by sales order, and project controlling to take us a little deeper than the simple demo CD example.

6.3.1 Product Cost by Order

The difference between using production orders (as we described in Section 6.1) and process orders is minimal, and you'll be able to follow the flow quite successfully. The process looks slightly different if you have coproducts, as we discussed when we looked at master data in Chapter 4.

In Section 6.1, we assumed that everything went perfectly; we didn't initiate rework or split an order because something had gone wrong. However, as a controller, it's important to understand what can happen in Logistics and what effect the measures taken will have on the data you analyze.

Also, not all manufacturing takes place in house these days, so it's important to understand how the outsourced manufacturing process has been enhanced from a controlling point of view.

Process Orders with Joint Production

If multiple products are manufactured in a single production process, as we discussed in Chapter 4, then the costs that are assigned to the work order have to be split to the order items using settlement at period close. If you use the Material Ledger, the same split is used when distributing any variances to the coproducts.

In this example, we'll use a process order instead of a production order. To create a process order, go to Transaction COR1 or **Logistics • Production—Process • Process Order • Process Order • Create**. Enter material Z-300, the plant, the order type, and the quantity for the leading product. The material list selected for Z-300 includes coproduct PA-300. To display the material list, click on the **Materials** button. Figure 6.47 shows the material list for Z-300, which includes the input materials and the output materials. Both the leading product and the other coproduct are flagged as coproducts. Notice the small amounts of catalyst and contaminated water being recovered from the process.

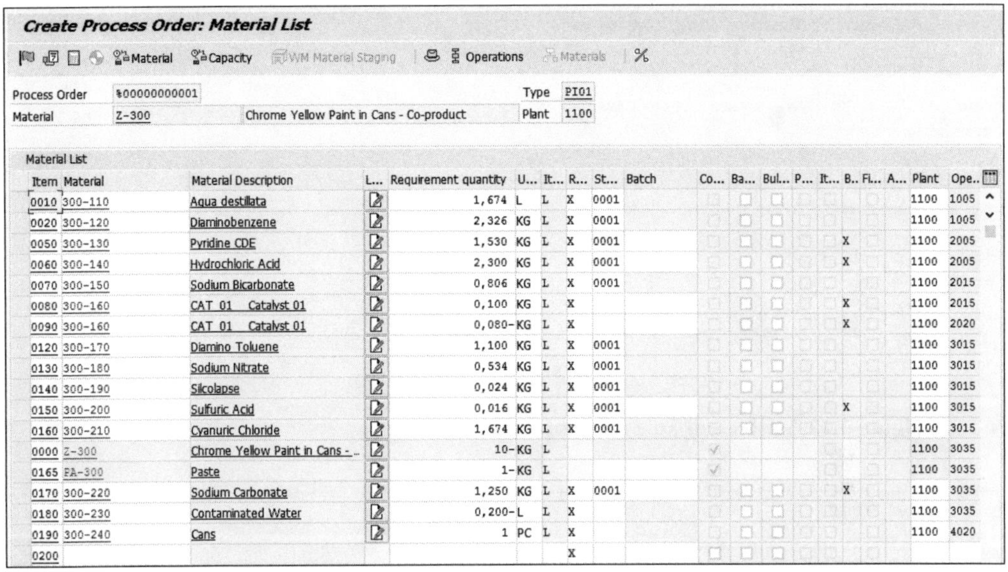

Figure 6.47 Material List Showing Coproducts

The structure of the process order includes a header to which all costs are posted and order items for each coproduct. We discussed the assignment of the order costs to the order items in Chapter 4, Section 4.3.2. To display the cost split in the settlement rule, select **Header • Settlement Rule**. Figure 6.48 shows the settlement rule for the process order with two settlement receivers, item 0001 (material Z-300) and item 0002 (material PA-300). The apportionment structure in the material master specifies that when splitting the costs to the order items, the different cost elements are treated differently. The values in the **Equivalence Numbers** column have been derived from the apportionment structure and can be adjusted manually in the order.

Figure 6.49 shows the cost report for the process order. You can display this by selecting **GoTo • Costs • Analysis** in the order. This shows two planned goods receipts: one for Z-300 and one for PA-300. It also includes negative costs for the contaminated water and the part of the catalyst that can be recovered from the process because they are byproducts.

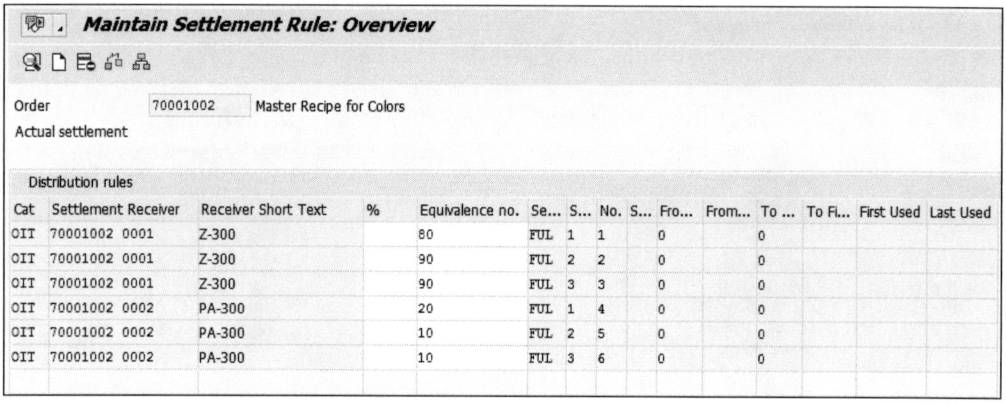

Maintain Settlement Rule: Overview

Order 70001002 Master Recipe for Colors

Actual settlement

Distribution rules

Cat	Settlement Receiver	Receiver Short Text	%	Equivalence no.	Se...	S...	No.	S...	Fro...	From...	To ...	To Fi...	First Used	Last Used
OIT	70001002 0001	Z-300		80	FUL	1	1		0		0			
OIT	70001002 0001	Z-300		90	FUL	2	2		0		0			
OIT	70001002 0001	Z-300		90	FUL	3	3		0		0			
OIT	70001002 0002	PA-300		20	FUL	1	4		0		0			
OIT	70001002 0002	PA-300		10	FUL	2	5		0		0			
OIT	70001002 0002	PA-300		10	FUL	3	6		0		0			

Figure 6.48 Settlement Rule for Joint Production

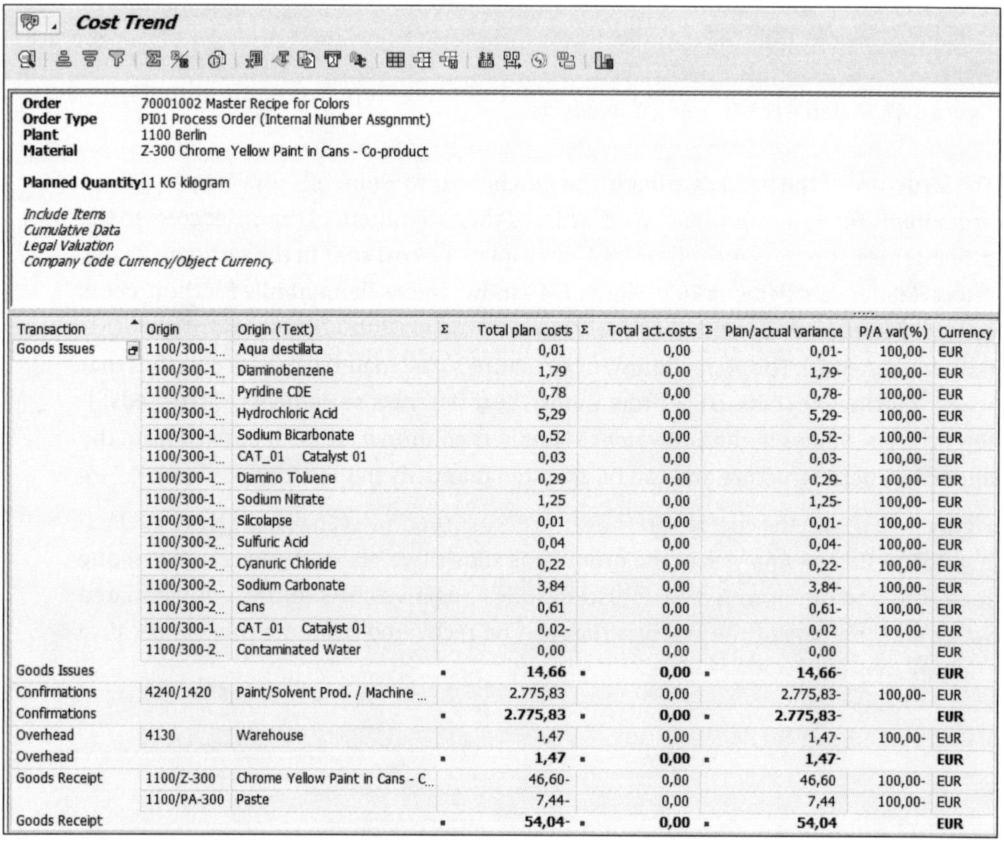

Cost Trend

Order 70001002 Master Recipe for Colors
Order Type PI01 Process Order (Internal Number Assgnmnt)
Plant 1100 Berlin
Material Z-300 Chrome Yellow Paint in Cans - Co-product

Planned Quantity 11 KG kilogram

Include Items
Cumulative Data
Legal Valuation
Company Code Currency/Object Currency

Transaction	Origin	Origin (Text)	Σ	Total plan costs	Σ	Total act.costs	Σ	Plan/actual variance	P/A var(%)	Currency
Goods Issues	1100/300-1...	Aqua destillata		0,01		0,00		0,01-	100,00-	EUR
	1100/300-1...	Diaminobenzene		1,79		0,00		1,79-	100,00-	EUR
	1100/300-1...	Pyridine CDE		0,78		0,00		0,78-	100,00-	EUR
	1100/300-1...	Hydrochloric Acid		5,29		0,00		5,29-	100,00-	EUR
	1100/300-1...	Sodium Bicarbonate		0,52		0,00		0,52-	100,00-	EUR
	1100/300-1...	CAT_01 Catalyst 01		0,03		0,00		0,03-	100,00-	EUR
	1100/300-1...	Diamino Toluene		0,29		0,00		0,29-	100,00-	EUR
	1100/300-1...	Sodium Nitrate		1,25		0,00		1,25-	100,00-	EUR
	1100/300-1...	Silcolapse		0,01		0,00		0,01-	100,00-	EUR
	1100/300-2...	Sulfuric Acid		0,04		0,00		0,04-	100,00-	EUR
	1100/300-2...	Cyanuric Chloride		0,22		0,00		0,22-	100,00-	EUR
	1100/300-2...	Sodium Carbonate		3,84		0,00		3,84-	100,00-	EUR
	1100/300-2...	Cans		0,61		0,00		0,61-	100,00-	EUR
	1100/300-1...	CAT_01 Catalyst 01		0,02-		0,00		0,02	100,00-	EUR
	1100/300-2...	Contaminated Water		0,00		0,00		0,00		EUR
Goods Issues			▪	**14,66**	▪	**0,00**	▪	**14,66-**		**EUR**
Confirmations	4240/1420	Paint/Solvent Prod. / Machine ...		2.775,83		0,00		2.775,83-	100,00-	EUR
Confirmations			▪	**2.775,83**	▪	**0,00**	▪	**2.775,83-**		**EUR**
Overhead	4130	Warehouse		1,47		0,00		1,47-	100,00-	EUR
Overhead			▪	**1,47**	▪	**0,00**	▪	**1,47-**		**EUR**
Goods Receipt	1100/Z-300	Chrome Yellow Paint in Cans - C...		46,60-		0,00		46,60	100,00-	EUR
	1100/PA-300	Paste		7,44-		0,00		7,44	100,00-	EUR
Goods Receipt			▪	**54,04-**	▪	**0,00**	▪	**54,04**		**EUR**

Figure 6.49 Order Report for Joint Production

When setting up the period close for joint production, bear in mind that order settlement is a two-stage process. The order costs are first split into the order items and then settled to stock for the relevant coproduct. You'll find this extra closing step by following the menu path **Accounting • Controlling • Product Cost Controlling • Cost Object Controlling • Product Cost by Order • Period-End Closing • Single Functions • Preliminary Settlement for Coproducts/Rework • Single Processing** or via Transaction CO8B.

Order Rework and Order Split

When looking at production orders, we've emphasized the importance of the order lot size as the basis for variance analysis. However, things don't always go completely to plan, and during manufacture it sometimes becomes clear that the order cannot be completed in the form intended. Sometimes it's impossible to save the order, and the entire quantity has to be scrapped. In this case, all costs are considered scrap when variances are calculated.

Two other situations are potentially interesting to the controller:

- **The order has to be reworked.**
  In this case, the order can be saved and the final product delivered, but additional effort in the form of rework is required to resolve the issues. This can take the form of additional operations that are added to the original order when rework is confirmed or the creation of a completely new order. In the first case, the costs for the additional operations are recorded on the production order as variances. In the second case, the settlement rule in the rework order assigns the costs to the original production order. When preparing to settle your production orders (see Chapter 7), you should ensure that rework orders are settled before the main production order is settled to stock. Again, as we saw for coproducts, use Transaction CO8B.
- **The order has to be split.**
  The ability to split production and process orders was introduced with the business function enhancements for splitting of production orders (LOG_PP_PROD_ORDER_SPLIT) in EHP 4 for SAP ERP 6.0.

  Several business situations can make an order split necessary:

  - The customer changes his requirements, and the production order has to be adjusted to reflect this.

- Part of the quantity manufactured is faulty and has to be reworked or used to manufacture a different product.
- The priorities of the production plan are changed, and production orders have to be postponed.
- The necessary machines or tools are defective.

The order split means that a child order is created either for the new materials (if the customer changes his order or the product specifications change) or for the original material (if the dates or production resources change significantly). It can also mean that the part of the semifinished product completed to date is delivered to stock.

For the controller, what matters is how the planned costs are apportioned between the parent and child orders. This is based on the proportion of the quantities up to the operation at which the split took place, so a meaningful comparison of planned and actual costs is still possible.

Outsourced Manufacturing

Alongside production orders and process orders, you'll also find that the **Product Cost by Order** menu references something called a *CO production order*. This is a more like an internal order than a production order in that it's created in CO to capture manufacturing costs (goods issues, goods receipts, etc.) when production planning isn't implemented in SAP ERP. Although the original CO production order dates back to the early days of SAP R/3, it's come back into focus as a means of collecting costs in external manufacturing scenarios with the introduction of business function `LOG_MM_OM_1` (Outsourced Manufacturing in SAP ERP Operations) in EHP 4 for SAP ERP 6.0.

Outsourced manufacturing involves the subcontracting of the manufacturing work to an external supplier, who takes delivery of the material components, performs the necessary work, and then ships the finished product back to the requesting organization and bills for his services. The purchase order that requests the subcontracting work creates a CO production order automatically. Figure 6.50 shows a standard purchase order for outsourced manufacturing. If you compare it with the purchase order we created for the raw materials at the start of the chapter, you'll notice that the **Account Assignment** tab assigns the subcontracting costs to an order (order number 7000282 in our example).

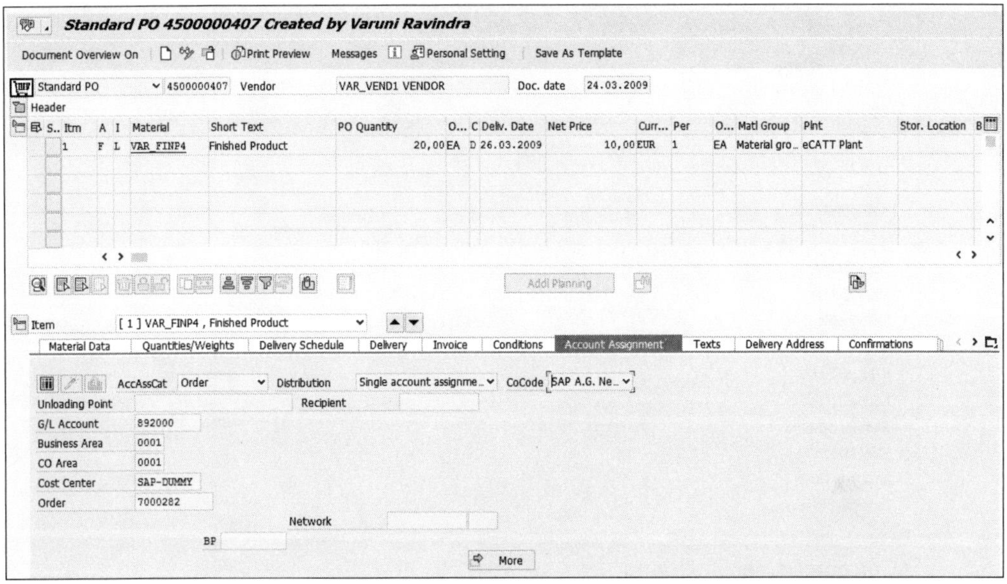

Figure 6.50 Purchase Order for Outsourced Manufacturing

You can't create confirmations for these orders (because the assumption is that the work is being performed by a subcontractor), but you can apply overhead and calculate work in process (WIP), meaning that the costs associated with these orders can be included in the financial statements earlier. It's also possible to transfer status information from the external supplier to these orders. Figure 6.51 shows the CO production order associated with this purchase order. To display the CO production order, use Transaction KKF3 or follow the path **Accounting • Controlling • Product Cost Controlling • Cost Object Controlling • Product Cost by Order • Master Data • CO Production Order • Display** and select the order number. To search for outsourced manufacturing orders in your own system, press F4 while on the order field and choose the **CO Production Orders Created from OM** matchcode. Notice that the CO production order has all the fields that you would associate with a regular internal order (table AUFK) but also has additional characteristics for reporting that have been transferred from the purchase order that initiated outsourced manufacturing.

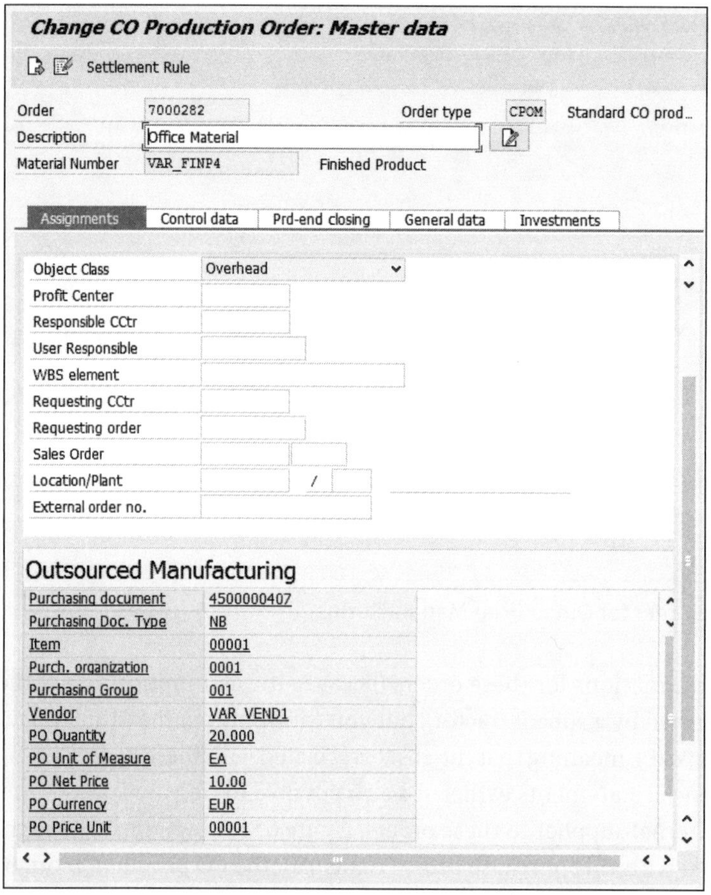

Figure 6.51 Production Order for Outsourced Manufacturing

6.3.2 Product Cost by Period

In Chapter 3, we showed how to create a product cost collector to collect costs by period rather than on the individual production orders. This is a way of moving away from the strong work order focus of traditional accounting systems and toward a lean accounting approach, in which the focus is on the direct costs incurred for the value stream in a period.

Before manufacturing begins, you must ensure that you create product cost collectors for all relevant materials and production versions (see Chapter 3). You then can create the production orders as described in Section 6.1 but using an order type that supports working with product cost collectors (order type PP08 in the standard configuration). For people working on the shop floor, the production order looks completely normal, allowing scheduling, material reservations, and so on. The difference is that the order has no settlement rule, and the costing functions and cost reports are inactive. You'll recognize these production orders by the status PCC (**Product Cost Collector**) in the header.

To display a list of all associated production orders and the relevant production version, click on the **Orders/PV** button, as shown in Figure 6.52. You can use this list to navigate to the individual production orders if you need to check the details of what quantities were recorded on the order.

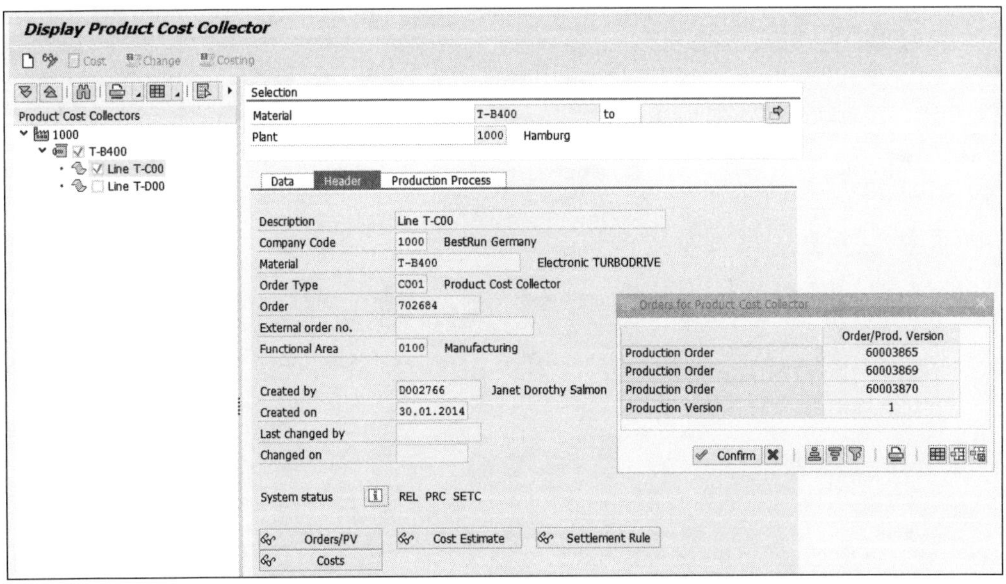

Figure 6.52 Production Orders Associated with Product Cost Collector

When you create the master data for a product cost collector, you're asked if you want to create a cost estimate for each production version. You don't have to create a cost estimate because you can use the standard cost estimate to determine the target costs for each operation to calculate the WIP and the scrap. However, if your production version includes a BOM or routing with a different structure than that used to set the standard costs, it makes sense to create a new cost estimate for the product cost collector using the BOM and routing in your production version as a starting point. Figure 6.53 shows the cost estimate for material T-B400. You can access it by clicking on the **Cost Estimate** button shown in Figure 6.52. If you compare this cost estimate with the cost estimates we looked at in Chapter 4 and Chapter 5, you'll notice that it's based on the BOM and the routing but also includes a link to the production version, the procurement alternative (because multiple production versions have been assigned to the product cost collector), and the special procurement key. The actual process of costing follows the same logic as the calculation of standard costs.

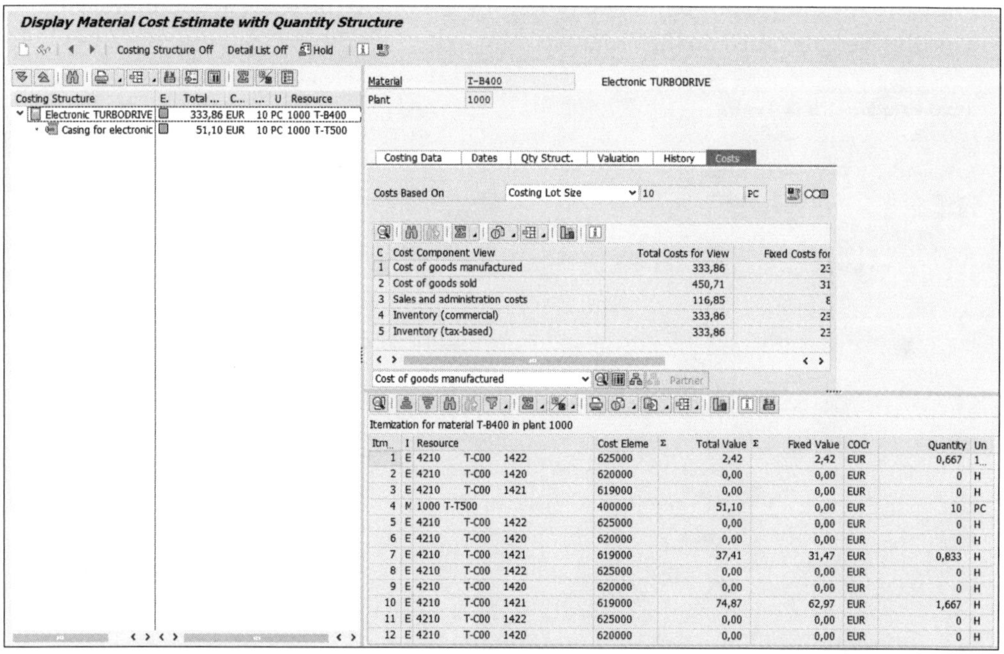

Figure 6.53 Cost Estimate for Product Cost Collector

As the production orders move through the production process and incur costs, you can display these costs by clicking on the **Costs** button shown in Figure 6.52. Doing so will take you to the report shown in Figure 6.54. Goods issues, goods receipts, order confirmations, and so on are treated the same way as for a normal production order. The difference is that instead of being recorded with reference to the production order, they're recorded by material and production version. In any given period, you'll have a mixture of completed operations (finished goods inventory), incomplete operations (WIP), and scrap (recorded at the operation). Any variances are settled to stock, and the product cost collector appears in the Material Ledger under the procurement alternative shown under the **Production Process** tab.

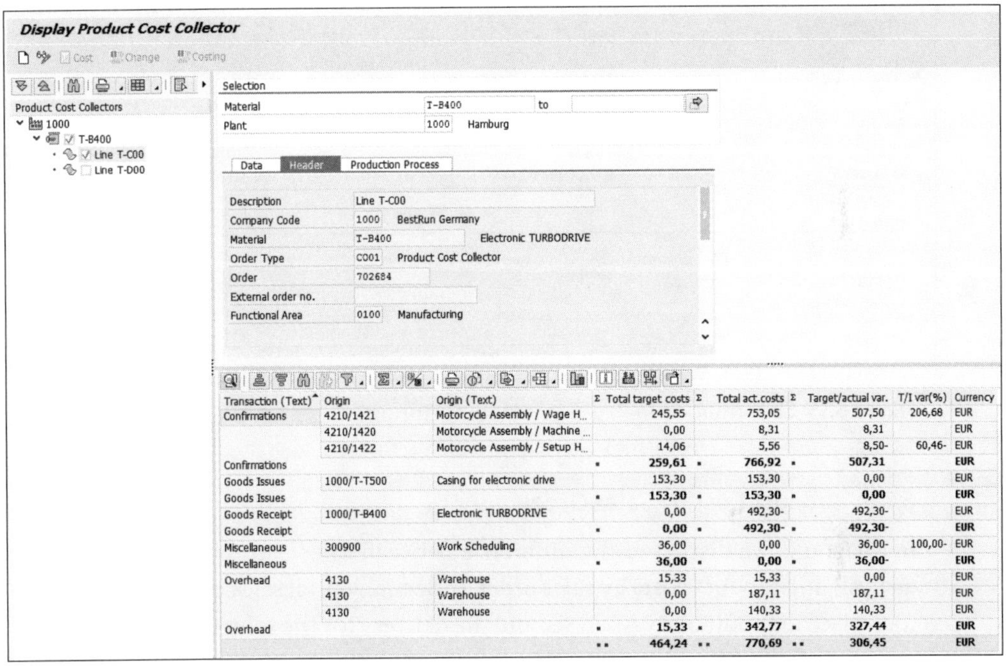

Figure 6.54 Product Cost Collector with Associated Costs

An even leaner approach dispenses with the production orders altogether and uses run schedule headers. To confirm run schedule headers, use Transaction MFBF or **Logistics • Production • Repetitive Manufacturing • Data Entry Repetitive Manufacturing Confirmation**, as shown in Figure 6.55. To identify the product cost collector, enter the relevant material, plant, and production version, then enter the quantity to be confirmed.

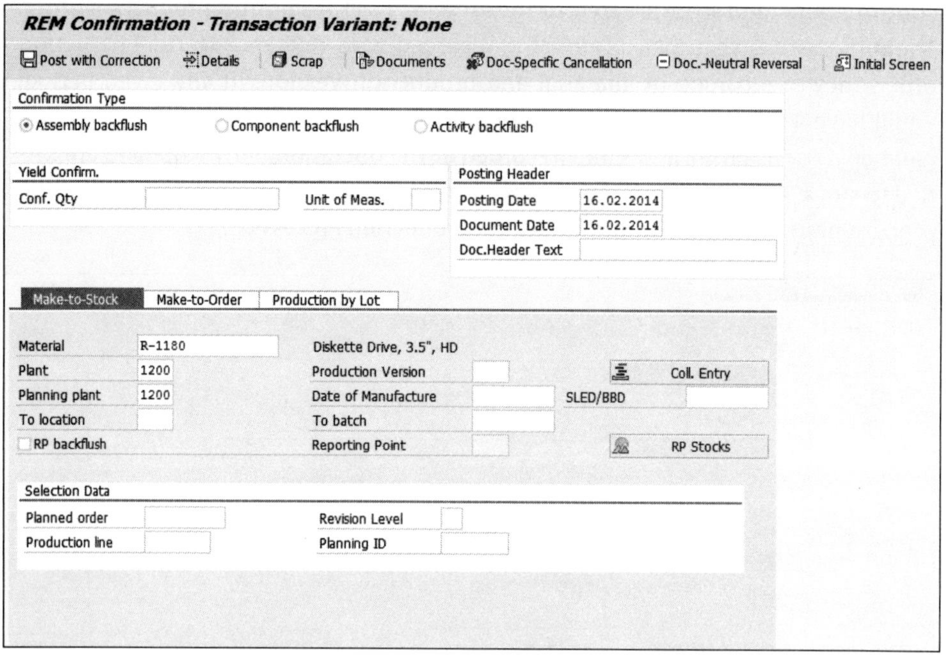

Figure 6.55 Confirmation in Repetitive Manufacturing

6.3.3 Product Cost by Sales Order

In Chapter 2, we discussed the difference between sales controlling in profitability analysis and product costs by sales order. In Section 6.1, all sales controlling activities took place in Profitability Analysis, and the delivery for the sales order involved picking goods from neutral stock to ship to the customer. It's also possible to configure your sales order process to initiate a production process to manufacture the goods to order (make to order).

The most common reason to initiate make-to-order production is that the product requested is configurable and the customer has made certain selections that will affect the parts needed in manufacturing and sometimes the operations to be performed. You have two options in a make-to-order scenario:

1. The production order is triggered from the sales order and delivers its completed product to sales order stock, from which it will be shipped to the customer. If there are no customer-specific costs for the delivery, then there's no need to configure the sales order item as an account assignment and set up revenue cost elements for the revenues.

The main difference compared to what we discussed in Section 6.1 is that the production order settles its costs to sales order stock. Reporting and variance analysis can still take place by production order as in Section 6.1. However, the sales order stock is *valued*, meaning the system is configured to pick a price for the sales order stock using a sales order cost estimate, the production order cost estimate, or occasionally the standard cost estimate (if one exists) rather than the standard price we used to value the receipt to stock in Section 6.1.

2. The sales order initiates make-to-order production, and production costs are collected on the production order. However, the cost of performing customer-specific configuration or the special delivery cost needs to be charged to the sales order. In this case, the sales order item needs to be configured as an account assignment, and sales revenue is captured as a cost element. You'll also have to perform results analysis at period close.

Let's look at the process flow for the first option. To illustrate this process, we'll create a sales order for configurable material DPC1. The procedure to create a sales order is the same as before, except that we entered a configurable material as the product. As soon as you create the sales item, the system directs you to the **Configuration** screen. Figure 6.56 shows the selection screen for the characteristics that represent the different configuration options. You may remember these from when we looked at the configuration settings in the material master in Chapter 4.

The sales manager maintains these in collaboration with the customer, or they can be transferred from an external application, such as a web order entry screen.

The sales order item for this material has a special requirements type (see Figure 6.57) that controls the fact that the production order will be created with reference to the sales orders so that the customers' requirements can be taken into account during production. To check the requirements type for a sales order, select the **Procurement** tab in the order overview. This requirements type also determines that the goods will be delivered to and issued from sales order stock—in other words, the inventory that belongs to the sales order—rather than the general finished goods inventory. This raises the issue of how the sales order item will be valued, because no standard cost estimate exists for the customer-specific configuration. Again, this is customizable. Usually, either a cost estimate is created for the sales order or the production order cost estimate is used to provide an initial valuation. The requirements type also determines whether the sales order item exists as an account assignment in CO or not. In both cases, the costs for the sales order item flow into Profitability Analysis.

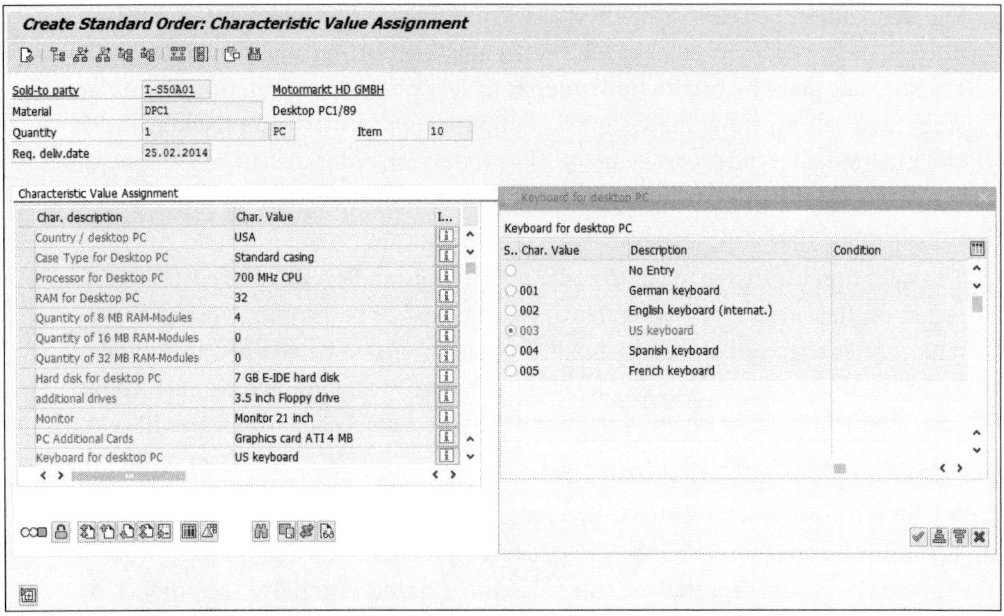

Figure 6.56 Configuration Settings for Product DPC1

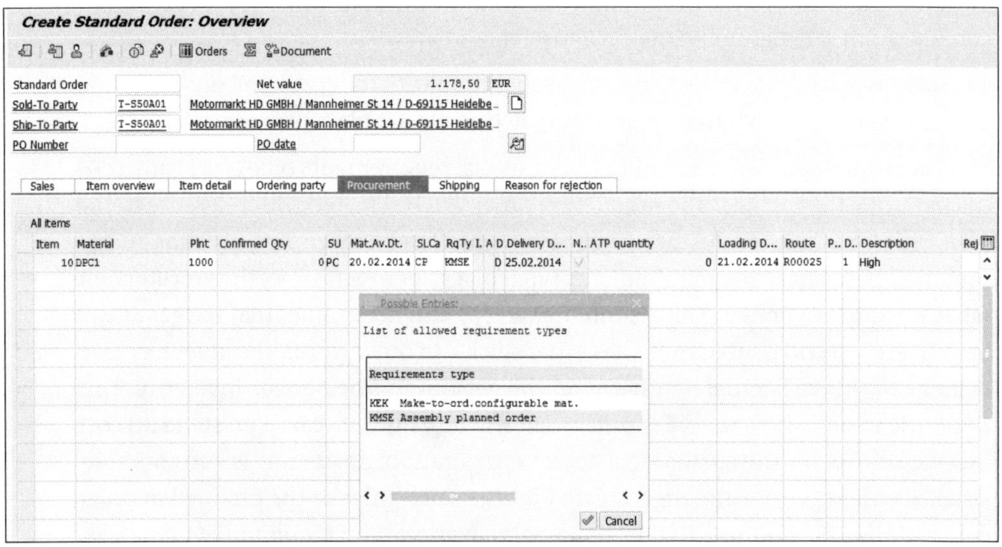

Figure 6.57 Requirements Type of Sales Order

The MRP run links the production order with the sales order item that triggered the order, or you can manually create a production order with reference to a sales order item. When we display a production order for make to order using Transaction CO03, we see a link to the sales order item and the ordering party in the **General** tab for the production order (see Figure 6.58).

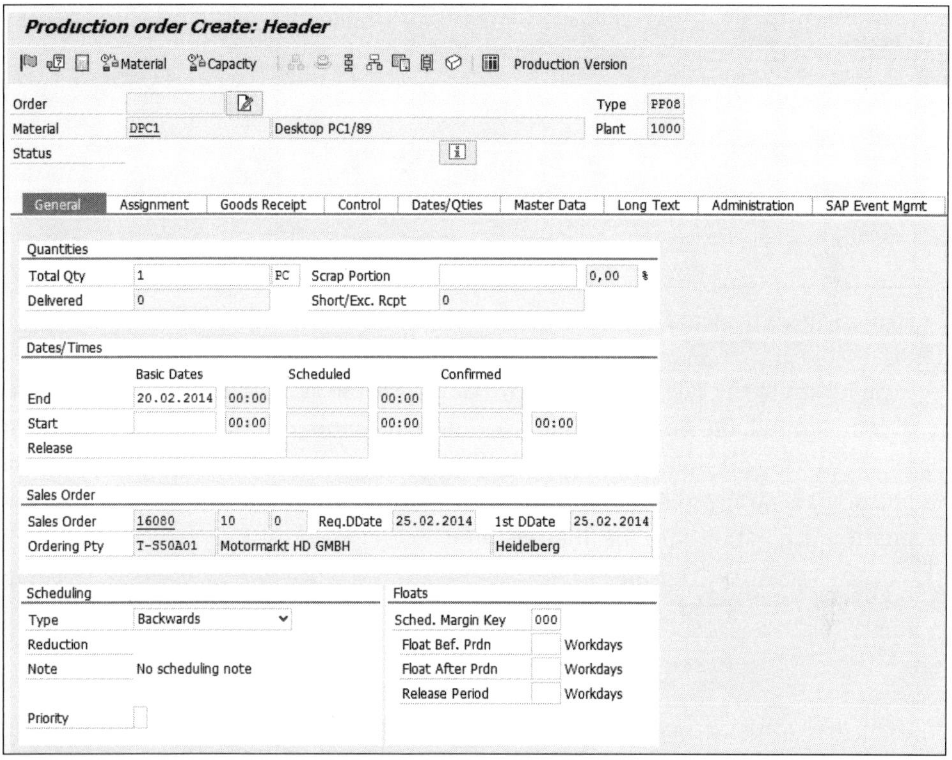

Figure 6.58 Production Order for Make to Order

The settlement rule for the production order settles to sales order stock (inventory that can only be delivered to the customer named in the sales order) rather than neutral material stock (which could be issued to any sales order). To display the settlement rule, select **Header • Settlement Rule**. Figure 6.59 shows the settlement rule with the receiver's material and sales order item. You may remember that the production order we settled in Section 6.1 only included the material as a receiver. As you saw in Chapter 4, you can set up a different valuation class in the material master to assign goods movements to sales order stock to a different set of accounts from normal goods movements.

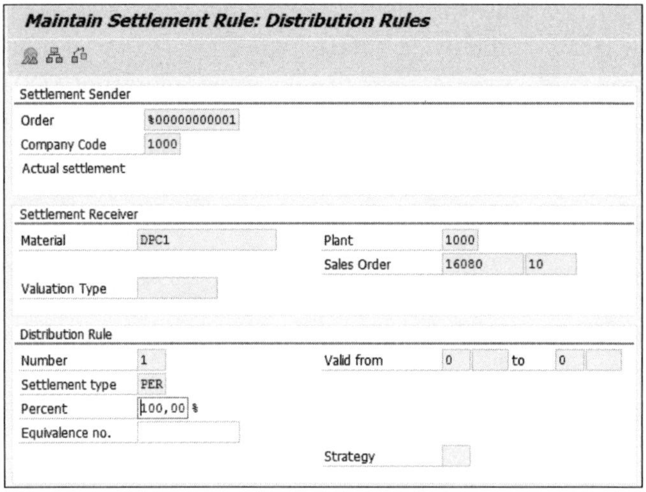

Figure 6.59 Settlement Rule for Production Order (Make to Order)

If we return to the sales order item, we can check the assignment of the sales order item to **Profitability Analysis** as before. Notice in Figure 6.60 that the material is still DPC1. This means that sales controlling will be based on the configurable material (encompassing all possible variants) rather than the individual configuration worked out in collaboration with the final customer.

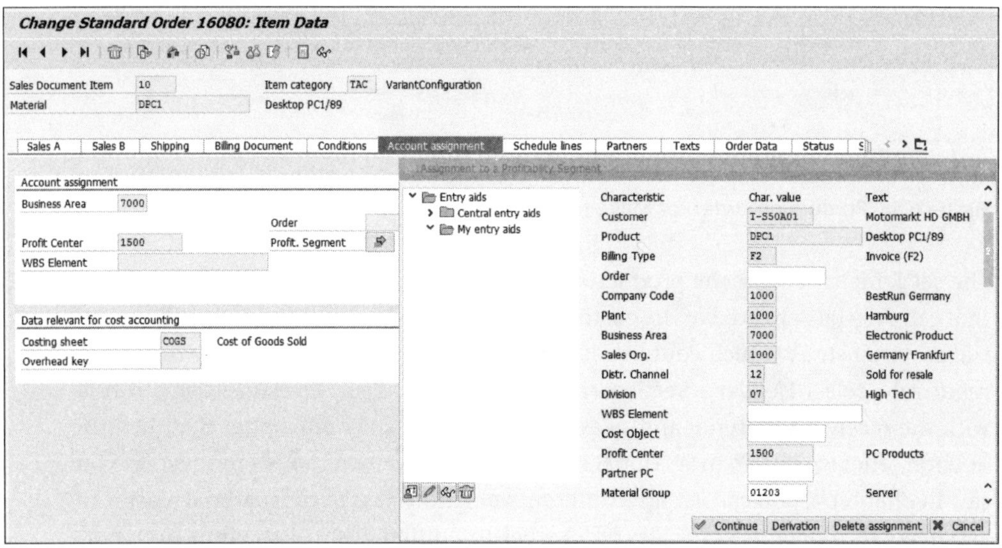

Figure 6.60 Profitability Segment for Make to Order

6.3.4 Project Controlling

Project controlling is similar to order controlling, with several notable exceptions:

- Whereas we procured the blank CDs and labels for production of our CDs with no reference to a cost center, order, or project, goods or services procured specifically for the project include the WBS element as an *account assignment* in the purchase order item. The costs are expensed to the WBS element immediately rather than when the goods are issued from raw materials inventory to the project/order.
- In addition to monitoring expenses on projects, it's also common to monitor future expenses that are known, because purchase orders have been created to buy materials or services for the project. Such known future expenses are called *commitments*.
- Projects that don't have networks or network activities associated with them (see Chapter 4) have no link to the confirmation step we saw for the production order. Instead, the cost of doing work for the project can either be assigned to the project in CO by using direct activity allocation (Transaction KB21N) or by using the cross-application time sheet (Transaction CATS). If you use the cross-application time sheet, the work time is recorded by the employees in human resources, but the value of that work is not transferred immediately. Instead, separate transactions are used to initiate the transfer to CO.

Let's dig into each of these a little deeper.

Project-Specific Purchasing

Goods and services that are purchased specifically for a project are handled using a purchase order as we saw before, but the account assignment (column A) in the purchase order item or **AccAssCat** field in the **Account Assignment** tab is P (project). This means you have to make an assignment to the WBS element that will carry the costs of the purchase. We discussed the use of budgets and active availability control to control spending in Chapter 2 and Chapter 5. Figure 6.61 shows a purchase order to buy materials for a project (WBS element T-20301). In this example, the system has been configured so that the availability check issues the message that the budget has been exceeded and spending is blocked for the WBS element. The project manager now has to request additional budget or transfer budget from another WBS element (see Chapter 5) before he can complete his purchase.

Scope of Availability Checks

It's only possible to activate availability checks for projects and internal orders. We're often asked whether such a function is also available for cost centers, but this is not possible as of the time of writing. SAP Note 68366 describes a workaround using statistical orders to represent each cost center.

The availability check is a hard check against the existing budget prior to making any expense or commitment posting to the project. The budget and spending to date is shown in several reports to enable managers to monitor where they stand prior to making a purchase.

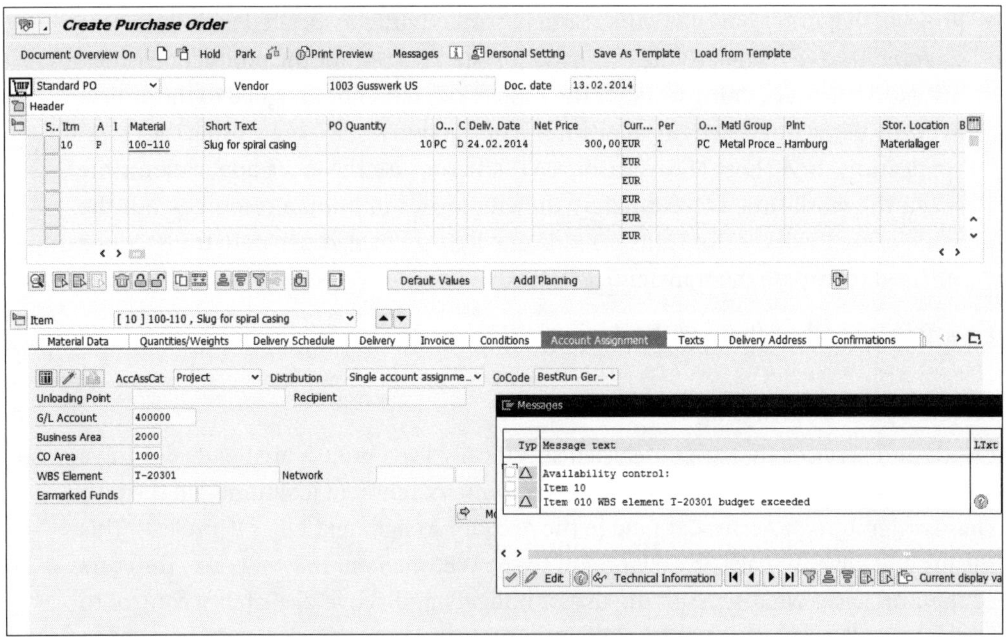

Figure 6.61 Purchase Order for Project with Availability Check

Commitment Management

Let's assume that in our previous example the manager now succeeds in requesting more budget and placing his purchase order. A commitment is created for the value of the purchase order. Figure 6.62 shows the commitment for the open purchase order. As each goods receipt is recorded, the commitment is reduced until the final goods receipt is completed.

To access this report, follow **Accounting • Project System • Information System • Financials • Costs • Plan-Based • By Cost Element • Actual/Commitment/Total/Plan in CO Area Currency** and enter the project number. There are various ways of displaying the commitments for investment programs, projects, and orders. Look for reports with the title "commitments" in the various report lists we showed in Chapter 2. These are particularly important if there are long lead times between placing the order (opening the commitment) and receiving the order (canceling the commitment).

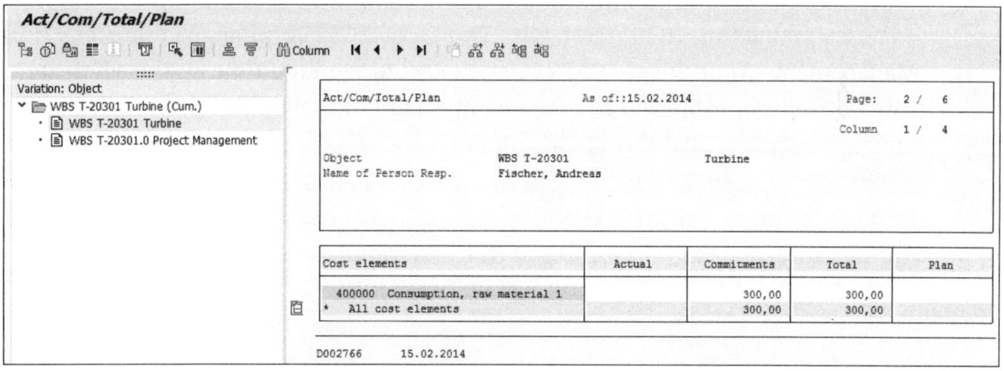

Figure 6.62 Commitments for Project-Related Purchases

Commitment Management in SAP S/4HANA

In SAP ERP, commitments can be created with respect to a WBS element, as you saw here; an order; a cost center; a sales order item; and so on, to reflect the impact of future spending. They are typically one-sided, showing only the spending planned for these objects, but not the cash impact. With SAP S/4HANA and the predictive accounting approach, the commitments become future accounting documents, with the double-entry approach capturing both the anticipated project costs and the liability to the vendor. As the accounting document is created, assignments will also be made to the relevant profit center, functional area, and so on, to support multidimensional commitment reporting. If you want to display commitments by profit center without waiting for SAP S/4HANA, consider implementing SAP Note 2414350 (Customer Connect CO: Commitment Report for Profit Center).

Time Recording

In Section 6.2, we looked at the activity allocation triggered by the order confirmation for our production order. The same process can be initiated in human resources to post working time to a project. The sending cost center in this case is the cost center in the employee's organizational unit. The activity types are defined as for production cost centers, and an activity rate is calculated the same way as you saw for production activities in Chapter 5. This activity rate is used to value the working time entered by the employee for his work on a particular project. Because there is often no real relationship between the amount of time worked and the organizational resources employed, it's also common to enter an activity rate manually to cover the different charges for a junior or senior consultant.

To post working time to a project, go to Transaction CAT2 or **Human Resources • Time Management • Time Sheet • CATS Classic • Record Working Time** and select the relevant data entry profile and a personnel number. The data entry profiles are configured to determine what account assignments the employee is allowed to record time against. Then enter the working times, as shown in Figure 6.63. The time sheet includes the employee's cost center and the activity type wage hours as the sender of the allocation and the WBS element as the receiver of the allocation.

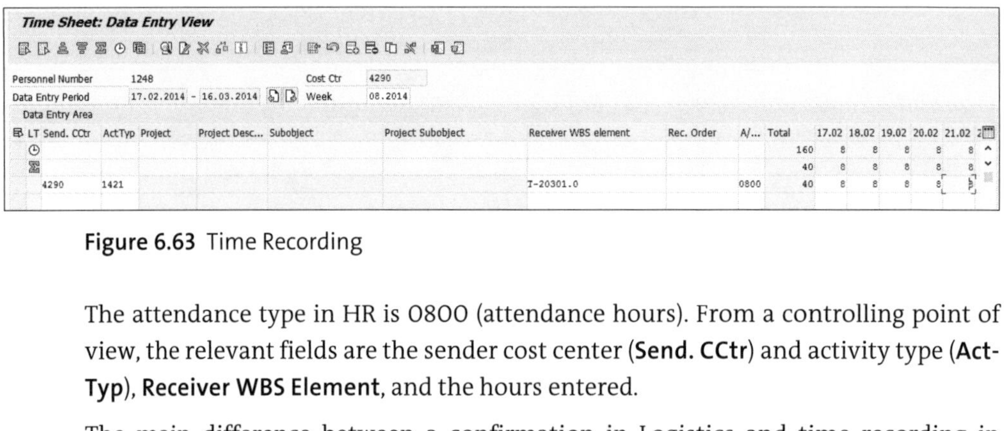

Figure 6.63 Time Recording

The attendance type in HR is 0800 (attendance hours). From a controlling point of view, the relevant fields are the sender cost center (**Send. CCtr**) and activity type (**ActTyp**), **Receiver WBS Element**, and the hours entered.

The main difference between a confirmation in Logistics and time recording in human resources is that the activity allocation doesn't take place immediately. Instead, a transfer has to be scheduled to transfer the working time recorded from human resources to CO, even when human resources and finance are on the same SAP ERP instance. To make the transfer, use Transaction CAT5 or follow the menu path **Human Resources • Time Management • Time Sheet • Transfer • Project System • Transfer** and enter the personnel number of the person whose work effort you want to transfer. Similar transactions exist for transfers to cost centers and plant maintenance or customer service orders. Figure 6.64 shows the transfer log with an item for each time record transferred.

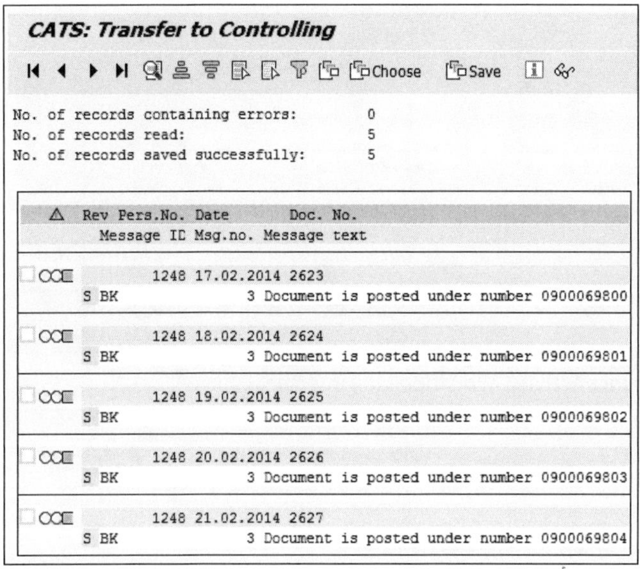

Figure 6.64 Transfer Work Times to Controlling

Figure 6.65 shows the line items for the activity allocation once the data transfer is complete. You can display the project line item by using Transaction CJ13 or following the menu path **Accounting • Project System • Information System • Financials • Line Items • Actual Costs/Revenues** and entering the relevant project, WBS number, cost element, and time frame. Notice again that we've adapted the ALV layout to show the business Transaction RKL, exactly as for the order confirmations in production. Just as you saw for the production activities, you can also see this work time on the cost center by using Transaction KSB1 (Section 6.1) to view the line items on the cost center.

If you don't use Time Recording in CATS, you can post an activity allocation to a WBS element directly by going to Transaction KB21N or **Accounting • Controlling • Cost Center Accounting • Actual Postings • Activity Allocation • Enter**. To enter the WBS element as a receiver, select the screen variant **WBS Element/Network**, then enter the cost center for which the employee works and the activity type as the sender, the WBS element as the receiver, and the appropriate quantities, as shown in Figure 6.66.

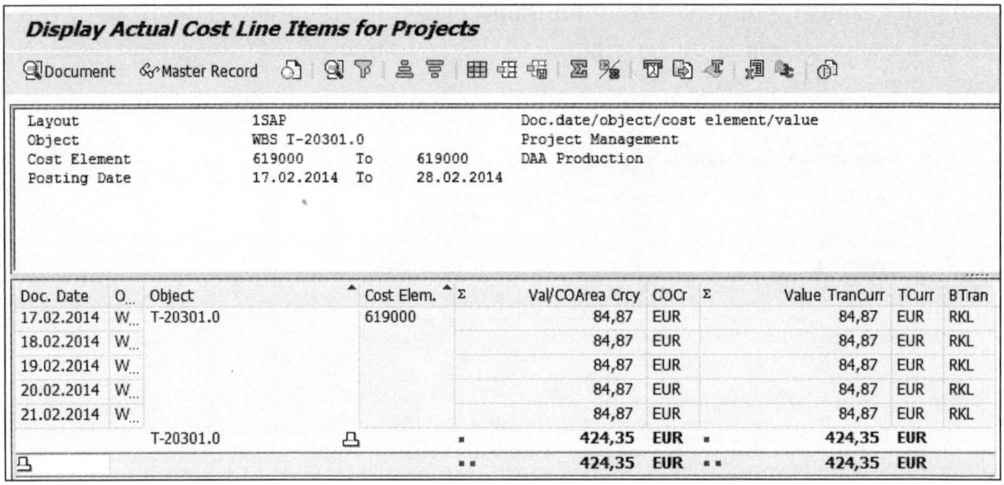

Figure 6.65 Line Items for Direct Activity Allocation via Time Sheet

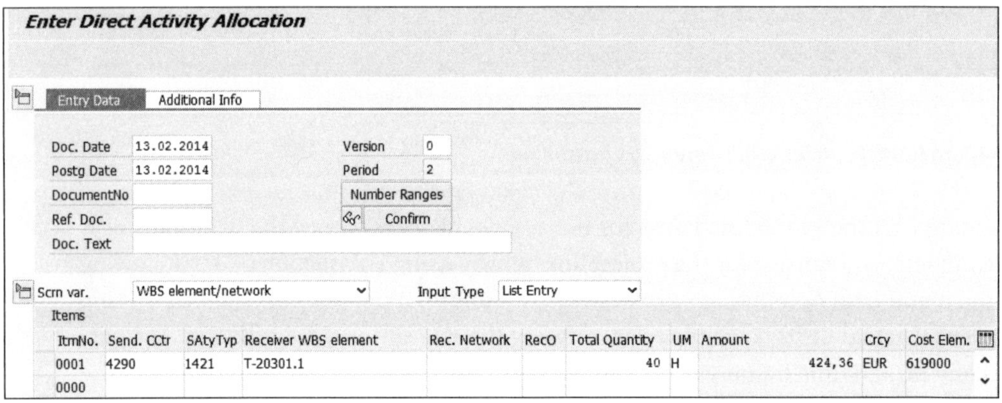

Figure 6.66 Direct Activity Allocation to WBS Element

Prior-Year Rates for Projects

A development for the public sector in EHP 4 for SAP ERP 6.0 may be of interest to controllers. Because federal agencies allow timesheet corrections in the 13 months preceding the document date, there was a need to value the changed working time not with the activity price valid on the key date for the change but when the work was originally performed. Follow-up functions, such as overhead calculation, also should be based on the values used for time recording. Although most industries don't allow such a long period for corrections to time recordings, many will be interested to learn that it's possible to calculate overhead in real time when the time sheet transfer from HR takes place or the activity allocation in CO is posted. You can activate this process using the business function CO_ALLOCATIONS.

Event-Based Revenue Recognition in SAP S/4HANA

SAP S/4HANA moves towards a continuous close by redesigning tasks that were traditionally performed as part of the period close. Business function `CO_ALLOCATIONS` is an early example of this approach as it triggers a posting for overhead with every time recording document. This approach was extended in SAP S/4HANA for professional service organizations, with the time recording triggering a posting for accrued revenue in anticipation of the work to be billed. Where the employee's cost center and the receiving project are in different legal entities, the time recording can also trigger an intercompany markup in anticipation of the intercompany billing. We'll look at this approach in more detail in Chapter 14.

6.3.5 Controlling for Maintenance and Service Orders

Maintenance and service orders use the same mechanisms to capture their costs as production orders. The main differences are that the task lists describe maintenance or service steps rather than manufacturing steps and that the orders are created with reference to a functional location instead of to a material number.

Although maintenance orders generally don't attract as much attention as production orders, largely because their costs don't impact the balance sheet, regulatory authorities have started to put them under increased scrutiny. One option to consider in this context is whether to use business function `LOG_EAM_OLC` (Operation Account Assignment), introduced in EHP 5 for SAP ERP 6.0. The classic maintenance order, like the production order, captures costs via the confirmations at the operation level but stores the costs at the header level. For the sort of maintenance orders that are completed in an afternoon, this can be perfectly adequate. For maintenance and service orders that are more complex and have hugely different operations, consider storing the costs at operation level instead. You can activate the operation as an account assignment by setting a flag in the order type. We've done this for order type POLC.

You can identify orders with operation-level costing by the activity account assignment status (status **ACAS**) in the order header. In this context, you might wonder where the term *activity* comes from. The same coding is used to assign maintenance costs to operations as is used to assign manufacturing costs to network activities, leading to confusion. Although the new function will allow you to show costs by operation, you don't have to change either your reporting or period-end close processes. You can continue to execute all your reports and period-close steps by order, but the system will automatically select costs for all the operations that are assigned to the order and display or process the costs for the multiple operations.

To create a maintenance order, choose **Logistics • Plant Maintenance • Maintenance Processing • Order • Create (General)** or Transaction IW31 and enter the order type and what is to be maintained (functional location, equipment). To see the operations, select the **Operations** tab and enter the work center (which will also provide the link to the cost center), the duration of the maintenance step, and the activity type to be used to charge the costs. Figure 6.67 shows a sample maintenance order together with the two operations that we'll use to capture costs. Note the status **ACAS** in the order header.

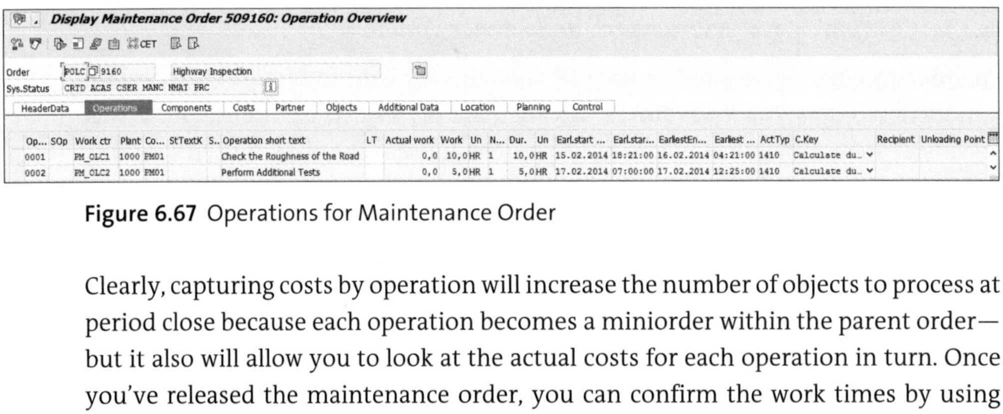

Figure 6.67 Operations for Maintenance Order

Clearly, capturing costs by operation will increase the number of objects to process at period close because each operation becomes a miniorder within the parent order—but it also will allow you to look at the actual costs for each operation in turn. Once you've released the maintenance order, you can confirm the work times by using Transaction IW41 or **Logistics • Plant Maintenance • Maintenance Processing • Completion Confirmation • Individual Time Confirmation** and entering the number of hours worked in each operation.

Figure 6.68 shows the costs for the two operations in the maintenance order. To reach this report, choose **Extras • Cost Reports • Operation Cost Overview** in the order header or access Transaction IW4ON (Operation Cost Overview) directly. You'll notice that we've been able to collect actual costs at the same level as planned costs. In maintenance, as in the project system, costs can be displayed not only by cost element but also by value category. This is simply a different way of structuring the costs and is part of the configuration effort of setting up the project system and maintenance orders.

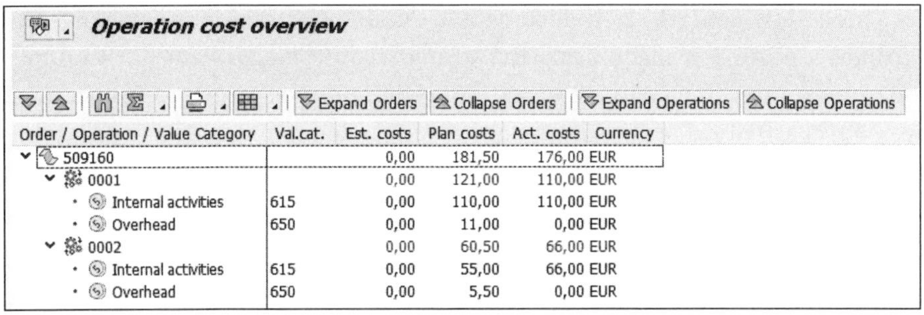

Figure 6.68 Maintenance Operations and Their Costs

Of course, you can also view maintenance orders just like internal orders or production orders, but you will need to adjust the ALV layouts to display the operation. Figure 6.69 shows the line items (Transaction KOB1) for our maintenance order, but we've extended the default ALV layout to include the operation field.

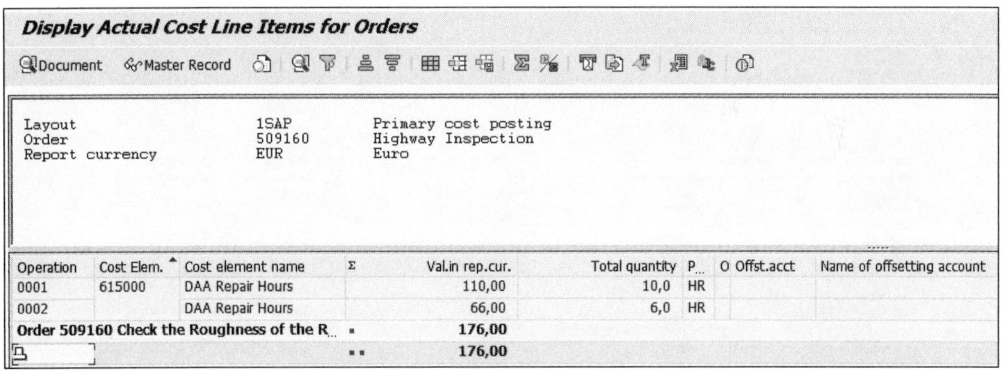

Figure 6.69 Line Items for Operations on Maintenance Order

We've looked at actual postings in many of the Logistics processes and in human resources and at how to make direct activity allocations in CO. If these are wrong for any reason, it's common to correct the working time in human resources or the confirmation in Logistics, but you should also know how to make correction postings in CO for when it's not possible or practical to reverse the original document. This can be the case in the heat of the period close.

6.4 Corrections or Adjustment Postings

Our examples showed complete flows that took place without a hitch, but the controller is occasionally called upon to make a correction. Sometimes a complete *reversal* is required, which acts as a documented "undo" of the original posting, and sometimes a posting is made using the wrong account assignment (for example, travel expenses are charged to the wrong cost center or order) or the controller must move a direct activity allocation from one account assignment to another (for example, work posted to one WBS element must be moved to a different WBS element).

Figure 6.70 shows the **Actual Postings** folder for Cost Center Accounting, but the same applications are available in the **Internal Orders**, **Product Cost by Order**, **Product Cost by Period**, **Sales Order Controlling**, and **Activity-Based Costing** folders. Here you'll see the transactions for time recording and direct activity allocation that we talked about in the previous section. We'll now look at the other actual posting transactions.

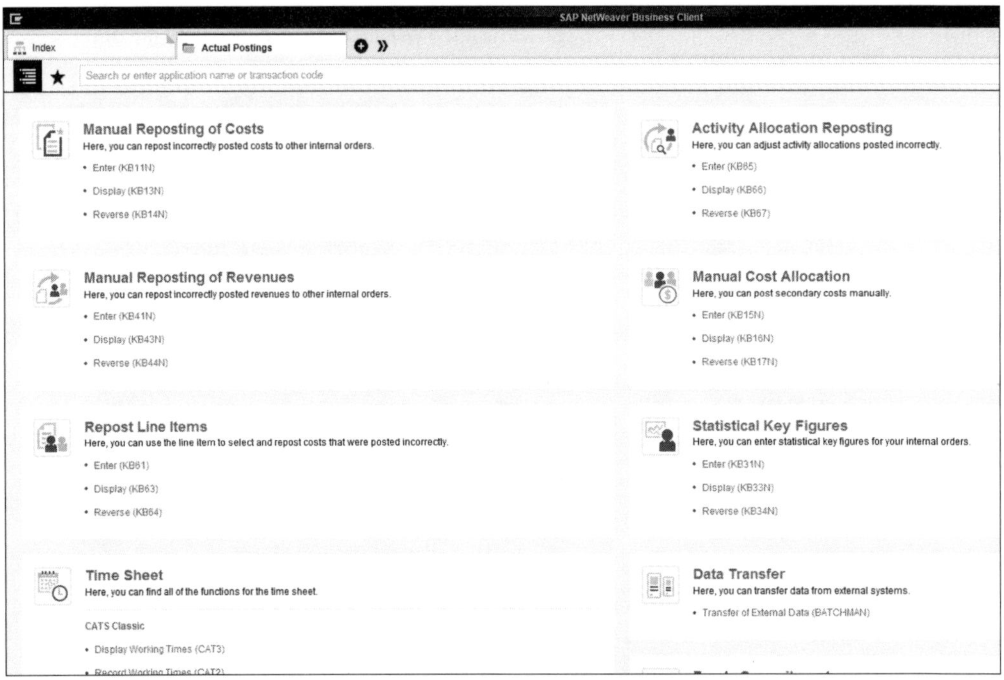

Figure 6.70 Actual Postings in Cost Center Accounting

6.4.1 Reposting Line Items

Let's assume that one of the employees on a cost center has just moved to another cost center, but his travel expenses from the previous period have been posted to the old cost center. To move these costs to the correct cost center, we need to *repost* the line item that recorded the original expense posting by using Transaction KB61 or following the menu path **Accounting • Controlling • Cost Center Accounting • Actual Postings • Repost Line Item • Enter**.

In an ideal world, you know the document number under which the travel expenses were posted and can enter it in the selection screen shown in Figure 6.71. Usually, however, the biggest challenge of reposting a line item is finding the document you want to repost in the first place. If you don't enter a document number in the selection screen, the system will select all documents that meet your selection criteria (all travel postings to the sales cost center in 2013 in our example). If this will result in too many documents being selected for reposting, click on the **Change Selection Parameters** button.

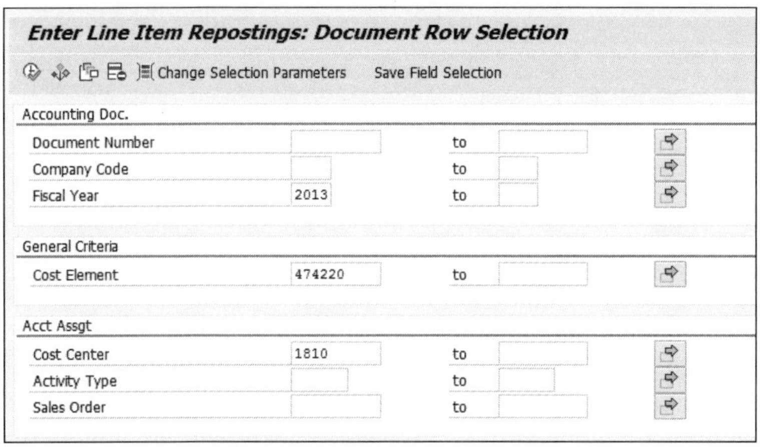

Figure 6.71 Selection Screen for Reposting

Figure 6.72 shows all selection parameters for a line item reposting; as you discovered in Chapter 2, the cost center line item includes a lot of fields. To include additional parameters on the selection screen, double-click on a field on the left, such as **Personnel Number**, to identify the employee who changed the cost center. This field then appears on the right as a dynamic selection parameter. When you save the dynamic selection, the personnel number appears as an additional selection parameter to help you locate the correct document to be reposted, as shown in Figure 6.71.

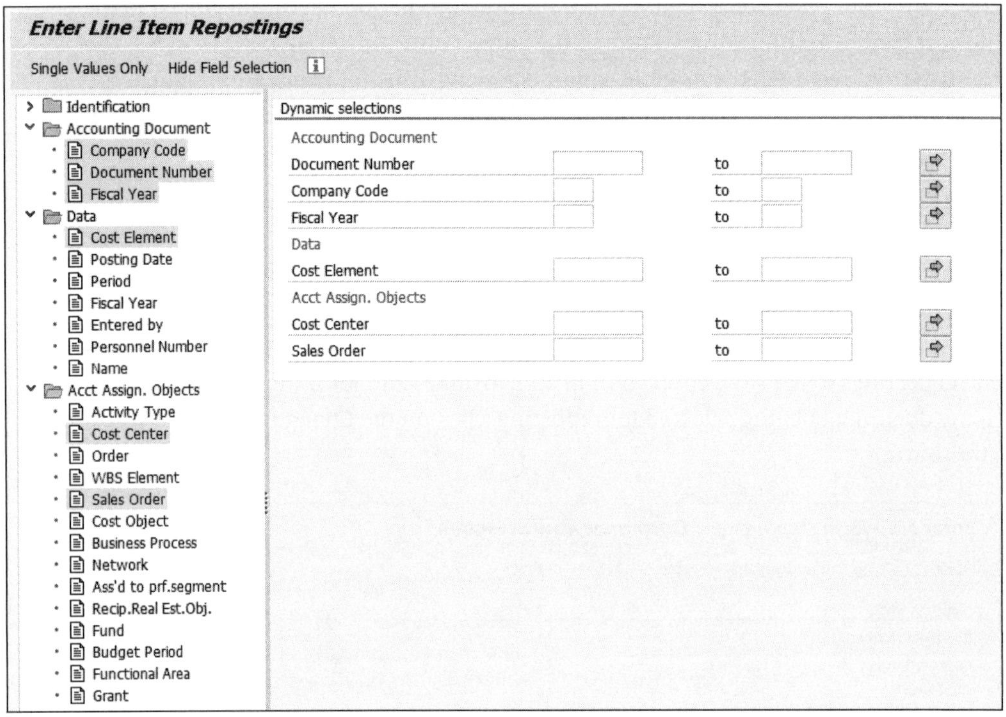

Figure 6.72 Selection Parameters for Line Item Reposting

Once you have made your selection, you have two options:

1. Figure 6.73 shows the list view, which is designed for mass entry of many items when mass corrections are needed (e.g., when the organization is being restructured and all postings for the period need to be moved to the new cost center). The list view requires you to choose the object type (**OType** column) for the account assignment using the F4 help and then to enter the new account assignment.
2. Figure 6.74 shows the row view, which is designed for entering details for a single item (e.g., an employee's travel expenses). The row view offers a separate field for each object type.

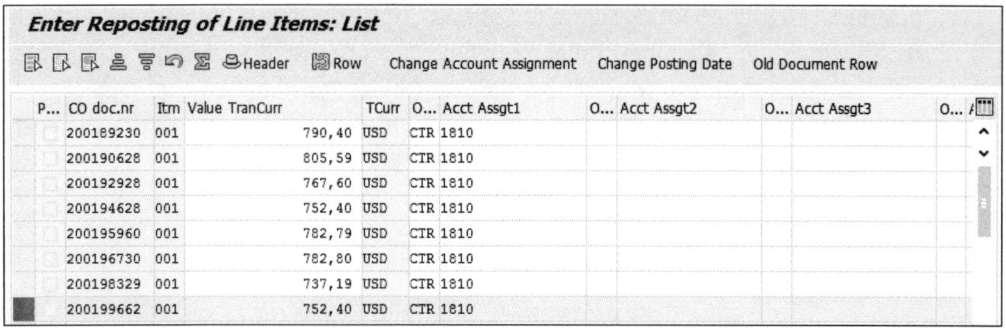

Figure 6.73 Reposting: List View

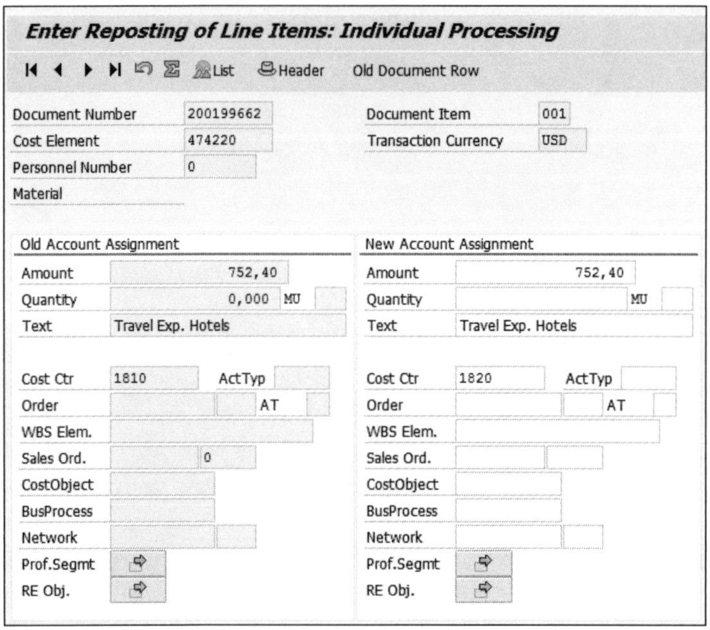

Figure 6.74 Reposting: Row View

You can switch to the row view by clicking on the **Row** button in the list view and to the list view by clicking on the **List** button in the row view.

In both cases, you can easily enter the correct cost center or another account assignment, such as a WBS element, for the document. You can identify the reposting documents for auditing by extending the ALV layout for the line item report to include business Transaction RKU3. Figure 6.75 shows a line item report for the sales cost center, in which the December travel costs have been reposted to another cost center and the fields **Business Transaction, Partner Object Type**, and **Partner Object** have been added to the report layout so that you can see to which cost center the costs have been reposted, as we explained in Chapter 2.

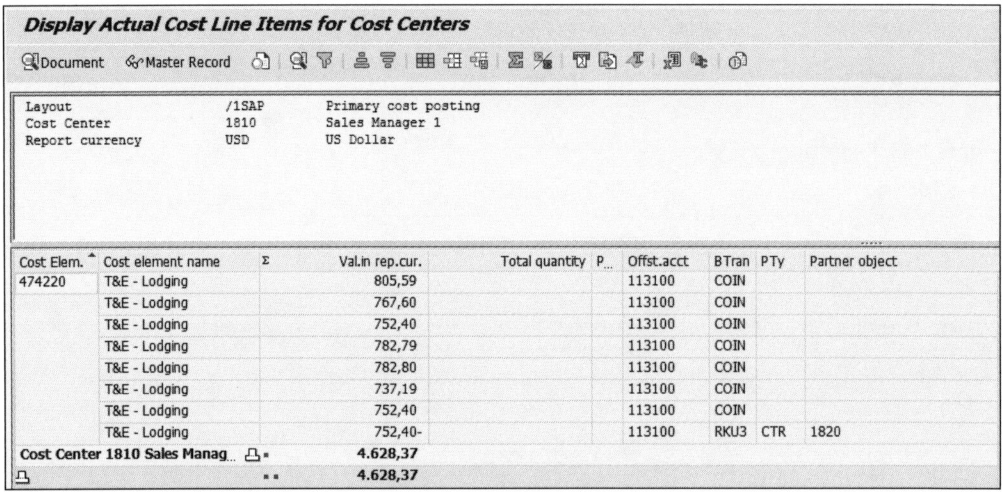

Figure 6.75 Line Item Report following Reposting

6.4.2 Correcting an Activity Allocation

If an employee has posted time to the wrong order or WBS element, you can correct the line item for the direct activity allocation in much the same way, by using Transaction KB65 or following the menu path **Accounting • Controlling • Cost Center Accounting • Actual Postings • Activity Allocation Reposting • Enter**. Figure 6.76 shows the row view for the correction. The difference is that the line item now contains the sender cost center and activity type rather than the cost center and the travel cost element. You'll effectively be posting time in the form of an activity type rather than expenses to the new cost object.

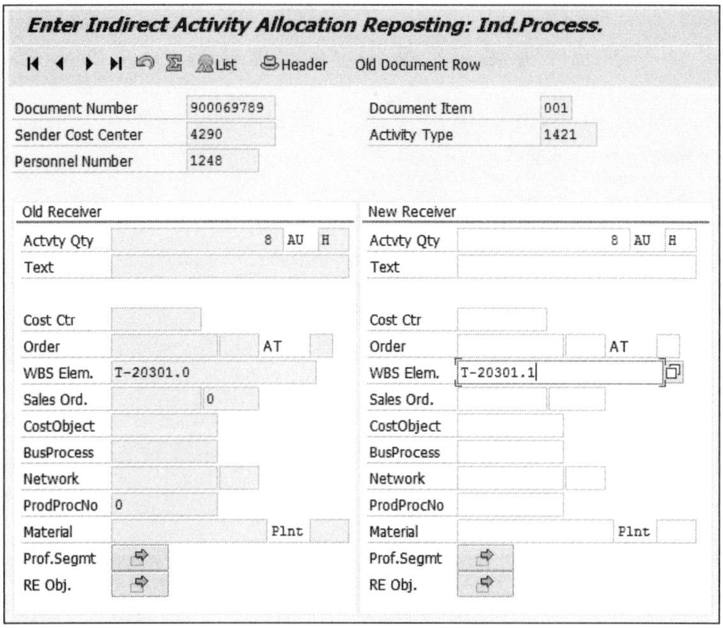

Figure 6.76 Repost Activity Allocation: Row View

6.4.3 Reposting Values

Although the two previous transactions involved selecting the original document as the basis for the reposting, it's also possible to move costs from one account assignment to another. This again can be used to handle organizational changes and moving costs from one cost center to another. To repost from one cost center to another, use Transaction KB11N or follow the menu path **Accounting • Controlling • Cost Center Accounting • Actual Postings • Manual Reposting of Costs • Enter**. To access the relevant account assignments in this transaction, select the appropriate screen variant (as we did for the direct activity allocation). Then enter the document date, the cost element, and the amount together with the old cost center and the new cost center (or whichever account assignment you're moving costs from and to), as shown in Figure 6.77.

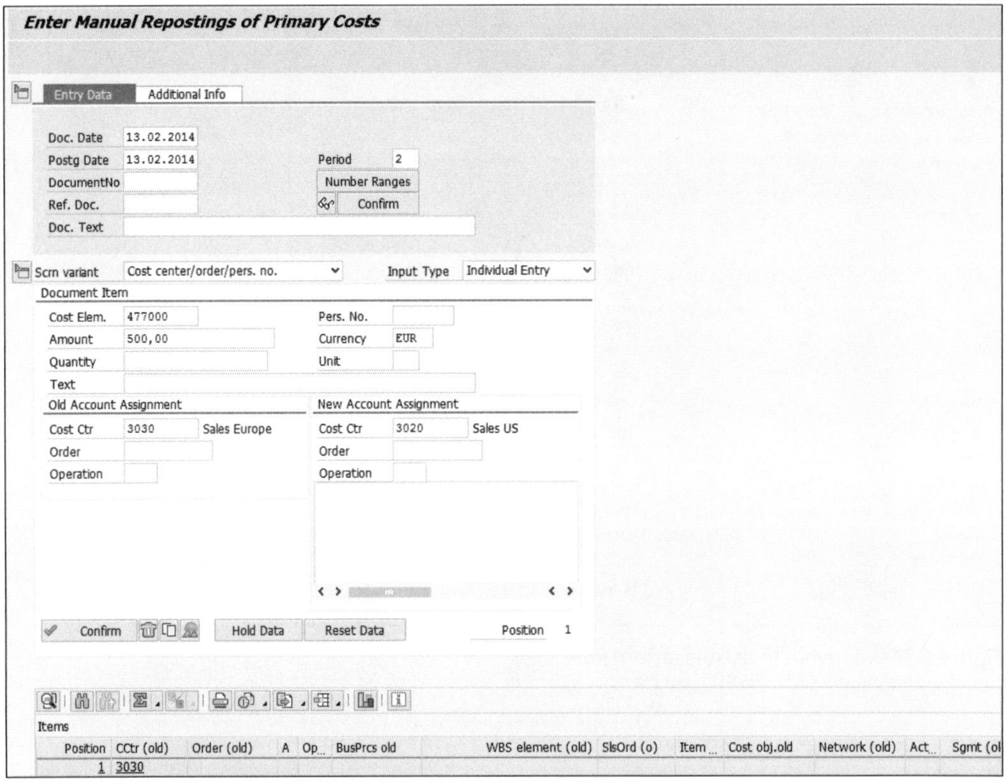

Figure 6.77 Manual Cost Reposting

In these examples, the actual postings were all within the same company code. However, if your controlling area covers multiple company codes, you can use these same transactions to move costs between cost centers, orders, and WBS elements in different company codes.

> **Customer Connect Enhancements for Authorizations**
>
> Although some controllers are authorized to move costs between affiliated companies, others are not. For this reason, a new authorization object, K_ORGUNIT, was introduced. Its purpose is to allow organizations to restrict posting access in certain company codes and provide a validation event to check whether the controller is authorized to post costs in that company code. You'll find details of the new solution in SAP Note 2445399 (Authorization Check for Company Code in Controlling).

We'll now look at what happens when goods move from one affiliated company to another in the same group and look at your options for cost accounting in such a situation.

6.5 Cross-Company Postings

We've looked at actual postings within a single company, but in today's global supply chains it's common for several plants to be involved in manufacturing a single product and for these plants to belong to different legal entities. It's also common for organizations to have a central distribution center that's supplied by multiple plants that belong to different legal entities. In this case, in addition to there being an initial purchase of the raw material from an external supplier and a final sale of the finished product to the end customer, there will be a sale and purchase of materials between affiliated companies along the way. One of the first challenges here is to make sure both affiliated companies are using the same code for the materials they're buying from and selling to each other. If this kind of harmonized master data is in place, you activate two separate value flows in CO to look at this type of goods movement from two perspectives. From a legal perspective, the sale and purchase of the materials are treated as if they took place with external customers/vendors, but from a group perspective, there has simply been a goods movement from one plant to another.

From a logistics point of view, the movement between the affiliated companies is handled using a stock transfer order. This results in the creation of a cross-company delivery and a goods issue from the supplying plant. There are several options for the transfer of goods ownership, as shown in Figure 6.78:

- There may be a one-step transfer, such that the goods receipt at the receiving plant is recorded *immediately*.
- If there is a significant *time lag* between goods issue and goods receipt, the material may be posted to stock in transit.
- Depending on the configuration, the stock in transit may remain in the ownership of the supplying company or move immediately to the ownership of the receiving company.
- The stock in transit may be transferred en route.

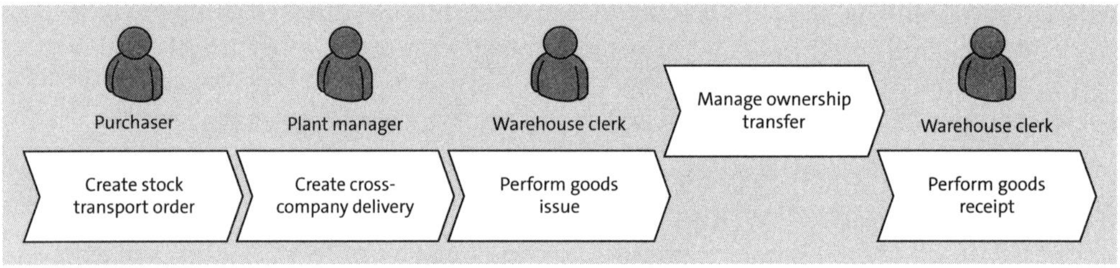

Figure 6.78 Cross-Company Stock Transport Order

From a financial point of view, there are two points to consider. One is the *legal transfer* of goods from one company to another. This takes place using pricing conditions just as if the materials were purchased from and sold to a nonaffiliated company (sometimes called *arm's-length trading*). The other point is the group controlling view, from which the intercompany markups can be eliminated and the flow treated as if it were taking place within the same company. This dual flow is enabled in the Material Ledger from EHP 5 for SAP ERP 6.0 by activating business function `LOG_MM_SIT` (Cross-Company Code Stock Transfer and Actual Costing).

We'll now look at an example of such a goods flow. Plant 2820 (Shanghai) in China has supplied material ACT-DCD to plant 2821 (US plant). Let's look first at the situation in the *supplying* plant, 2820 (Shanghai), by using Transaction CKM3N or following the menu path **Controlling • Product Cost Controlling • Actual Costing/Material Ledger • Information System • Detailed Reports • Material Price Analysis**. Figure 6.79 shows the legal valuation (company code currency). Here you'll see a folder, **Purchase Order (Grp)**, which shows three goods issues to the US plant. Make a note of the document numbers for these three lines; we'll need them later.

Now let's look at the stock situation for the same material in plant 2821 (US plant). Figure 6.80 shows that the same materials have been *received*. Here you'll see the same document numbers as in Figure 6.79, but this time they appear in the **Receipts** folder.

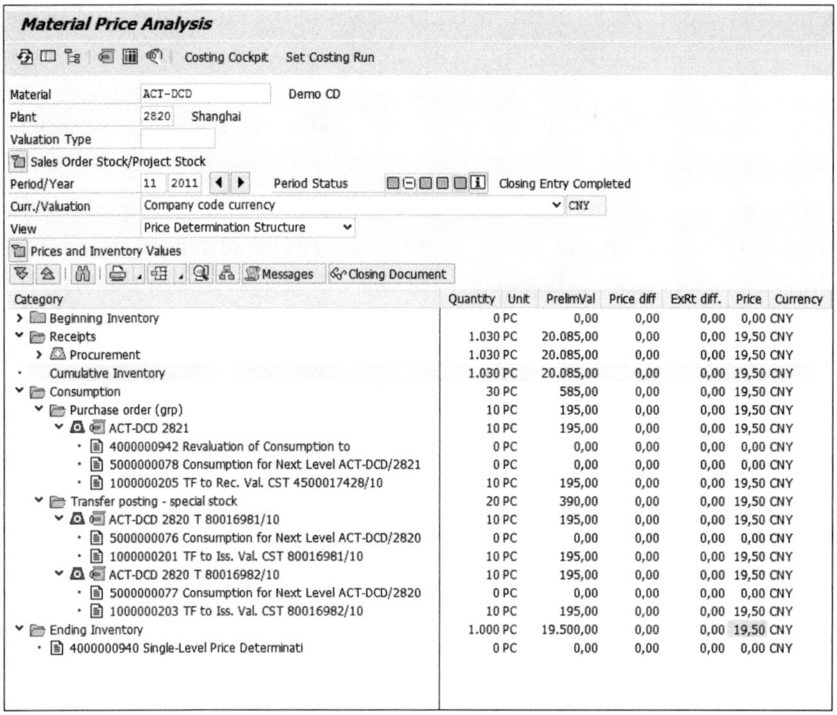

Figure 6.79 Material Price Analysis for Legal Valuation in Supplying Plant

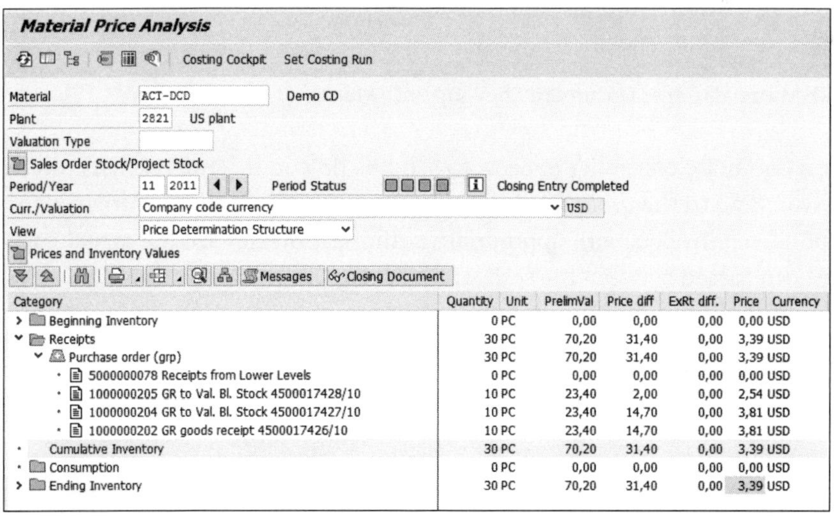

Figure 6.80 Material Price Analysis in Legal Valuation for Receiving Plant

The stock transfer order results in the material issue and the material receipt being recorded in the same document. You can see this by clicking on one of the lines. Figure 6.81 shows the issue recorded in Chinese yuan (the local currency for Shanghai, the supplying plant) and the receipt recorded in US dollars (the local currency in the receiving plant).

Return to the previous screens, and notice an additional line for each plant: **Consumption for Next Level** on the supplying plant in Figure 6.79 and **Receipt from Lower Levels** on the receiving plant in Figure 6.80. This is a posting created by the Material Ledger during the periodic costing run (something we'll cover in detail in Chapter 7). The costing run passes the actual costs from the supplying plant to the receiving plant. For Figure 6.79 and Figure 6.80, the value passed is zero, because we're looking at the legal valuation, which keeps the two companies at "arm's length." From a legal perspective, the US does not receive follow-on costs from China.

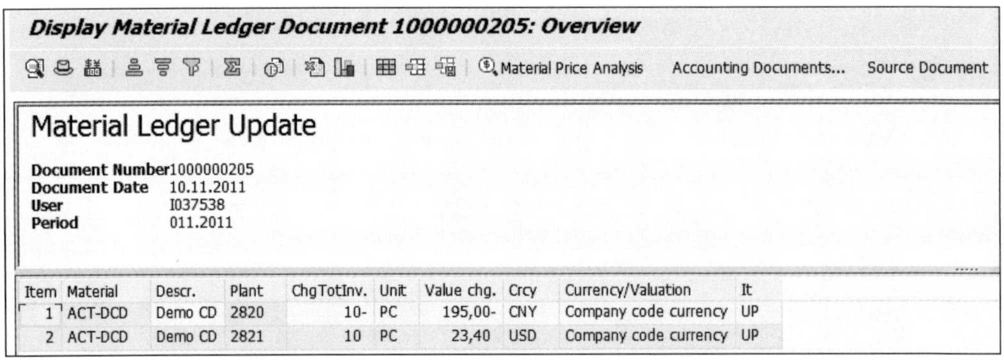
Display Material Ledger Document 1000000205: Overview

Material Price Analysis | Accounting Documents... | Source Document

Material Ledger Update

Document Number 1000000205
Document Date 10.11.2011
User I037538
Period 011.2011

Item	Material	Descr.	Plant	ChgTotInv.	Unit	Value chg.	Crcy	Currency/Valuation	It
1	ACT-DCD	Demo CD	2820	10-	PC	195,00-	CNY	Company code currency	UP
2	ACT-DCD	Demo CD	2821	10	PC	23,40	USD	Company code currency	UP

Figure 6.81 Material Ledger Document Showing Both Plants

However, a corporate controller expects to see this flow in its entirety. This can be done by switching to the *group view*. Usually, access to this view is restricted, and only corporate controllers with appropriate authorization can see the actual costs that have been passed between the companies during the costing run.

Figure 6.82 shows the same materials in group valuation. Both the US plant and the Chinese plant belong to a European group, so the group currency is Euros. In our example, there are no variances in the purchase line to be passed on, but if we had incurred purchase variances, we would see these price differences in the **Consumption for Next Level** line.

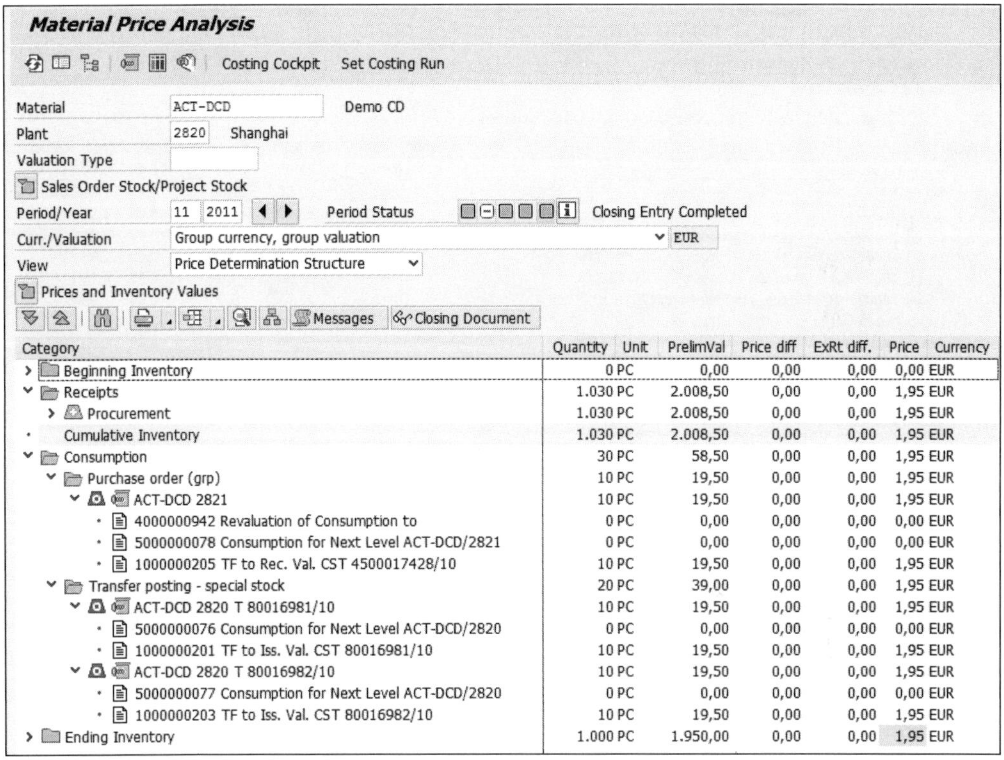

Figure 6.82 Material Price Analysis in Group Valuation in Supplying Plant

Figure 6.83 shows the mirror image of this posting in the line **Receipts from Lower Levels**, where we would see any differences being assigned to the receiving plant.

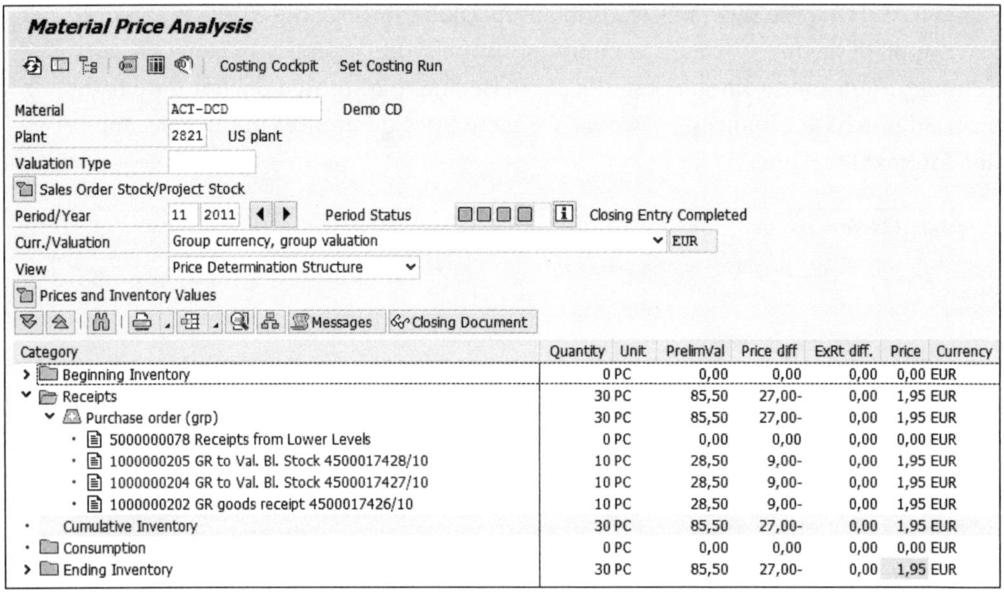

Figure 6.83 Material Price Analysis in Group Valuation in Receiving Plant

6.6 Summary

In this chapter, we walked through the full process of buying, making, and selling goods and how to assign inventory variances. We looked at several process variants, including joint production, rework, and order splits, and different forms of product cost controlling (by order, by period, and by sales order). We also looked at project controlling and integration with Time Management and at the costing of maintenance and service orders. Finally, we looked at the options to repost costs in CO and how cross-company flows are captured in the Material Ledger. We'll now look at how these postings are handled in the period close and what adjustments are made to reflect the actual costs for the period completed to have a complete view of the costs and revenues in the organization.

Chapter 7
Period Close

This chapter provides an overview of the main allocations and calculations that take place at period close. It also shows you the tasks that make up multilevel actual costing and how to bring all data into CO-PA.

In Chapter 1, we discussed the difference between postings that take place in *real time*, such as goods movements, and time recording and postings that take place at *period close*, such as allocations and order settlement. This is a significant change if you're moving from a legacy system in which all cost accounting effectively happens at period close after all relevant data has been loaded from the operational systems. The tasks themselves generally sound familiar enough, once you've mapped the SAP terminology to the terms you know. The other significant change is that in the SAP approach costs are not simply moved about within the Controlling component of SAP ERP Financials (CO); postings to Financial Accounting are generated for work in process (WIP), revaluation of inventory, cost of goods sold, and so on.

This is because during a period SAP ERP uses the *standards* that were established in the planning process (see Chapter 5) to value all goods movements, confirmations, and time recording, because these assumptions are the most reliable source of data *at the time of posting*. At the time when goods are issued from stock to production or sales, the supplier may not yet have submitted his invoice. As an operation is confirmed in production, the amount of energy used by the cost center in the period may not yet be known. The period close is the time to *adjust* these assumptions to reflect the reality of the business situation. You'll see the term *variance calculation* several times in the sections that follow. The difference between the original planning assumptions and reality is a *variance*, and it's the controlling department's job to work with the cost center managers and production managers to explain these variances and identify the root cause of any problems that have caused variances.

There are several approaches to variance analysis:

- If the raw material prices are stable and the production structures don't vary significantly, then the organization tends to use *standard costs* and analyze its variances by department (purchasing, production, sales, etc.) but not adjust the value of inventory or cost of goods sold. The rationale is that if the planning assumptions are reliable, then there's no need to make adjustments to the balance sheet.
- If the raw material prices are volatile or the production structures are constantly in flux, then the organization tends to use *actual costs* and to push the variances through the production process, adjusting inventory values, work in process, and cost of goods sold to reflect the variances.
- If the organization is presenting its financial statements according to multiple accounting principles, then you may find both approaches in the same organization, especially if the organization operates in countries such as Brazil and Russia where actual costing is common practice.

One frequently asked question is how often to close the books. For almost all CO processes, the close is identical in each fiscal period. For fast-moving orders, it's possible to run actual costing more frequently than once per period so that you can react quickly to changing cost situations. This function is available from EHP 4 for SAP ERP 6.0. However, inventory revaluation and other processes affecting Financial Accounting are only supported once per period.

The good news is that much of the closing process can be automated. We'll look at how to manage and automate the close in Chapter 12. In this chapter, we'll focus on what happens in each closing step to help you understand the implications of performing each step. We'll start by looking at the different forms of allocations.

7.1 Allocations

An allocation is simply a movement of costs from one cost center to another, from a cost center to an order or project, or from a cost center to the relevant market segment to allow profitability analysis. As you approach the period close it is important to understand the different types of allocation that can be used:

- In the SAP approach, some of the allocations have *already* happened. The costs to convert raw materials into products have already been assigned to the production orders when the orders or operations were confirmed or backflushed. The costs to perform maintenance operations have already been charged to the relevant receivers when the maintenance orders were confirmed. Any process with a time recording is already allocated. If you refer to the activity type master data in Chapter 3, any category 1 (manual entry, manual allocation) activity type has probably already been allocated. Here the question is whether an *adjustment* needs to be made because the standard activity rates were not accurate enough or if the difference will simply be treated as a cost center variance.

- In addition, allocations are used to move sales, administration, and marketing expenses from the departments in which the expenses were originally captured to the relevant market segments—in other words, from Cost Center Accounting to CO-PA.
- Other allocations are used to move the costs on supporting cost centers, such as rent and energy, to the operational cost centers. Here the critical distinction is between cost centers with an activity output (e.g., energy, quality, and repair) and those without an activity output.

This can require the creation of a complex network of allocation cycles to move costs around the organization. Although the controller could sit back and watch as the real-time allocations were posted, at period close he's in the driver's seat, ensuring that the allocation cycles are correctly prepared and that all relevant data is available. In this context, it's also worth bearing in mind that one of the guiding principles of lean accounting is that costs should be assigned directly to the value stream and not allocated in endless, wasteful iterations.

Figure 7.1 provides an overview of all tasks to be performed in Cost Center Accounting. This is the equivalent of following the menu path **Accounting • Controlling • Cost Center Accounting • Period-End Closing**. One folder contains the Schedule Manager, which can be used to manage the period close. We'll look at this tool in more detail in Chapter 12. Another folder includes tasks such as activity price calculation and variance calculation, which are used to calculate whether an adjustment is needed (activity price calculation) and to analyze the difference between the planning assumptions and the actual postings.

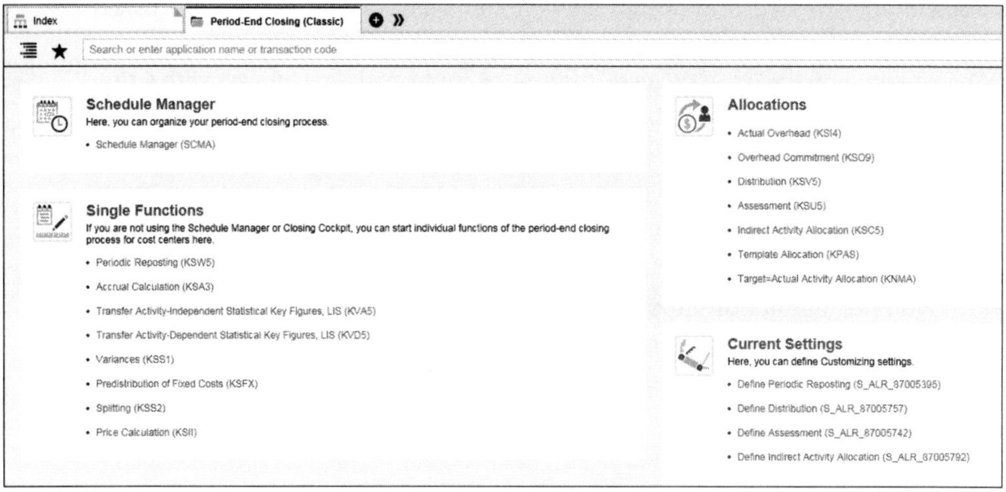

Figure 7.1 Period-Close Tasks in Cost Center Accounting

Before we look at the contents of the **Allocations** folder, you should be aware of the meaning of the **Current Settings** folder:

- For consistency, some organizations maintain their allocation cycles in their Customizing system and then transport them to the productive system, making only emergency changes in the productive system (the one in which you execute the close).
- Others maintain the allocation cycles only in the productive system.

Either way, if you need to make a change, use the **Current Settings** folder that contains a list of all allocation cycles.

7.1.1 Before the Start of the Period Close

Before we talk about the closing tasks in detail, it makes sense to ensure that all relevant data will be available before close can commence. Billing and payroll are typical tasks that take place in the days running up to the end of the month. Billing brings revenue into CO-PA and assigns revenue to commercial projects and orders. It's especially important in industries with contract accounting (such as utilities and telecommunications), in which most of the billing is done once a month. Payroll brings wage and salary costs to the relevant cost centers. It's not always a monthly process, but it makes sense to ensure that all payroll-related expenses are available in CO before embarking on the steps described ahead.

The costs of fixed assets (property, plant, and equipment) have to be matched against the revenues earned by their use. The asset is acquired at a given time via purchase or production. This one-off cost must be spread over the useful life of the asset. This spreading process is known as *depreciation* and is used to transfer the costs of the fixed assets to the periods in which the assets are used. All assets contain a link to the cost center, though they can be linked with an order or WBS element. Usually the asset depreciation run is executed by an asset accountant, but a controller often checks the asset-cost center assignment to ensure consistency. Figure 7.2 shows the master data for the property on which the cost center for pump assembly 4230 is located. To display the fixed asset, follow the menu path **Accounting • Financial Accounting • Fixed Assets • Asset • Display • Asset** or use Transaction AS03. Enter the name of the asset and the company code. The link between the asset and cost center is valid for a specified time period. To display the cost center assignment, select the **Time-Dependent** tab. There can be many methods of depreciation for the same asset, so it's a good idea to also check the entries on the **Depreciation Areas** tab.

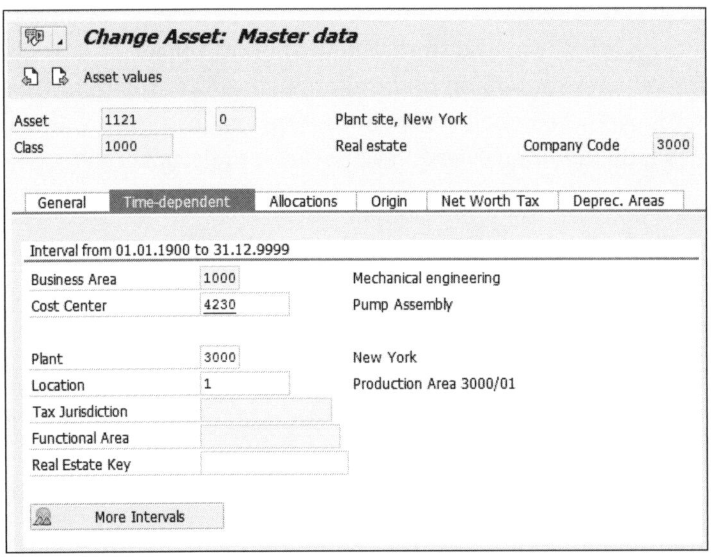

Figure 7.2 Asset Master Record

For cost accounting purposes, only one method of depreciation was reflected in **Cost Center Accounting** until recently. This transfer involved linking one depreciation area with the leading ledger. EHP 5 for SAP ERP 6.0 introduced business function FIN_CO_COGM (Parallel Valuation of Cost of Goods Manufactured). This allows you to link more than one depreciation area with Cost Center Accounting, taking each set of values into a different version. In this context, if you're using EHP 7 for SAP ERP 6.0, it's also worth looking at business function FIN_AA_PARALLEL_VAL (FI-AA, Parallel Valuation), which will allow you to assign your depreciation areas to the relevant ledgers and accounting principles, to make ledger-specific asset postings (e.g., if freight costs are to be treated differently depending on the GAAP), and to work with full postings rather than delta postings.

We'll see the term *version* time and time again in our discussions on the period close. Whereas the versions we encountered in planning represented different planning assumptions (optimistic, pessimistic, etc.), the versions for the actual values are used to separate value flows according to different accounting principles in CO. For example, one version might represent values under IFRS, and another could represent values under local GAAP. The term version is used in the period close as follows:

- Whenever you perform a step in the period close, you store the appropriate allocation, calculation, settlement, or whatever in version 0. In Customizing, version 0 is flagged as relevant for legal valuation.
- Some steps of the period close can also store data in another version so that the data is available for valuation according to the alternative GAAP. This version is flagged as relevant for parallel cost of goods manufactured in Customizing. Going forward, we'll mention this additional version whenever it's relevant.

7.1.2 Allocations between Cost Centers

As shown in Figure 7.1, there can be many forms of allocations between cost centers, depending on the design of the cost center structure:

- *Assessment cycles* are by far the most common form of allocation and move *amounts* from one or more cost centers to other cost centers or cost objects. A decision has to be made about whether the costs can be assigned to a *market segment* or from supporting cost centers to productive cost centers. The details of all cost elements on the sending cost center are rolled up under an assessment cost element (see Chapter 3), and the partner information (sender cost center and receiver cost center) is recorded.

- *Distribution cycles* can be used instead of assessment cycles if a small number of cost elements (such as telecommunications costs or rent costs) are initially posted to a single cost center and then charged to many cost centers. They work according to the same basic principle as assessment cycles but transfer the original primary cost element to the receiving cost center. Because of the data volumes, it makes sense to use them when the sender cost center only has a few cost elements.
- *Reposting cycles* provide a more compact way of allocating costs than distribution cycles, because they don't update the sender cost center as a partner in the totals record. This information can only be viewed in the line items.
- *Indirect activity allocation cycles* are used to move activity quantities between cost centers. They work in much the same way as assessment cycles, but a quantity (such as the total number of labor hours worked by a call center or the total number of kilowatt hours supplied to a group of production cost centers) is allocated rather than the costs of the call center or energy cost center. This quantity is valued with the activity price (calculated during planning).

Each type of allocation is considered a *business transaction* in SAP ERP and you'll find that business transaction in the document for each type of allocation. The business transaction is also used to determine whether the allocation can be performed or not, so it makes sense to lock each completed business transaction (assessment, distribution, reposting, etc.) as you complete the relevant steps to prevent accidental postings. You can do this by choosing **Accounting • Controlling • Cost Center Accounting • Environment • Period Lock • Change** or using Transaction OKP1, entering your **Controlling Area**, **Fiscal Year**, and **Version**, and choosing **Actual**. You can then lock each business transaction for the period once it's complete.

Before we compare the different types of allocation, you might want to check what's already active in your system. The overview is slightly hidden, but if you select any of the allocation types (e.g., **Accounting • Controlling • Cost Center Accounting • Period-End Closing • Current Settings • Define Assessment**) and then **Extras • Cycle • Display Overview**, or use Transaction KSOV, you can then choose the type of allocations you're interested in by selecting the relevant checkboxes under **Cycle Type** and then clicking on the **Execute** button to see all the cycles in your controlling area.

Figure 7.3 shows all the allocation cycles active in controlling area 2000 in our demo system. Many controllers keep a list like this in spreadsheets to remind them of the structure of the cycles they use.

One of the most useful functions in the overview is the **Find Object** function. There inevitably will be some cost center that has been locked and needs to be removed from the cycles in the run up to the period close. To select the sender or receiver that you're looking for, make a selection in the **Type of Object to Be Found** field and then select, for example, **Cost Center**, enter the cost center in question, and click on **Execute**. Once you've identified the cycle you're interested in, you can display the details of each segment by selecting the **Cycle Information** tab or the details of the previous allocations by selecting the **Previous Processing** tab.

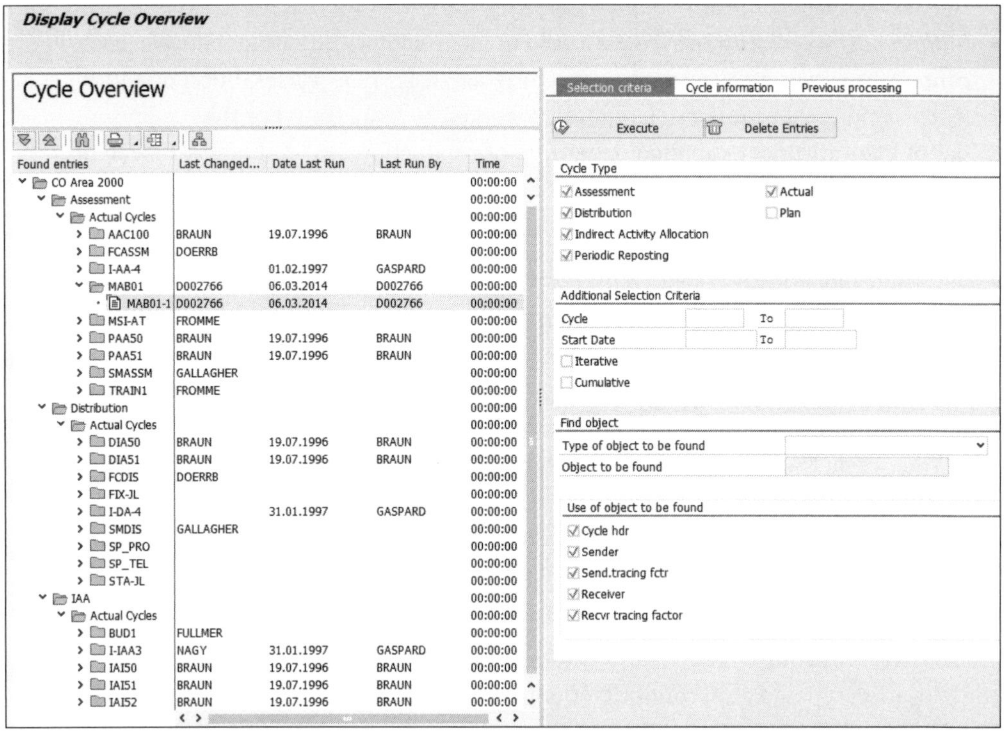

Figure 7.3 Cycle Overview

Real-Time Integration of CO with Financial Accounting

When you're building up allocation cycles, it's easy to become so focused on finding the right senders and receivers that you forget the impact of allocations on other areas. With this in mind, refer back to Chapter 3, Section 3.1.3, in which we discussed the impact of the assignment of the cost center to a company code, functional area, and profit center. When you perform an allocation, it's more than likely that in moving costs between cost centers you'll also move them between profit centers, functional areas, or even company codes. If you use the SAP ERP General Ledger, this means that you generate a posting in Financial Accounting at the same time. If you use the classic General Ledger, this posting is stored in the reconciliation ledger until you use Transaction KALC to move it to the other company code.

Cost Center Allocations in SAP S/4HANA

With SAP S/4HANA, there is no longer a separate document for Financial Accounting and Controlling. The process of creating and executing allocation cycles remains the same, but the resulting document will include not just the senders and receivers of the allocation but also the reporting dimensions affected by the allocation: profit centers and partner profit centers, functional areas and partner functional areas, and so on. In the case of an intercompany flow, an intercompany clearing account also will be updated, which you can use as a basis for your intercompany billing processes. We'll explain the changes in detail in Chapter 14.

Assessment Cycles

We introduced the assessment cycle when we looked at the cost center master data in Chapter 3. A common business requirement is the need to assign facilities costs that are usually captured on a supporting cost center for the operational cost centers. A good measure for the relative weighing of each cost center for this kind of charging process is the square footage occupied by each cost center, as we discussed when we looked at statistical key figures in Chapter 3.

You can view assessment cycles by following the menu path **Accounting • Controlling • Cost Center Accounting • Period-End Closing • Current Settings • Define Assessment** or using Transaction KSU2 and choosing a cycle and a start date. Each cycle has a header and one or more segments. Figure 7.4 shows the **Segment Header** tab for an assessment cycle that allocates rent to various other departments according to the square feet statistical key figure.

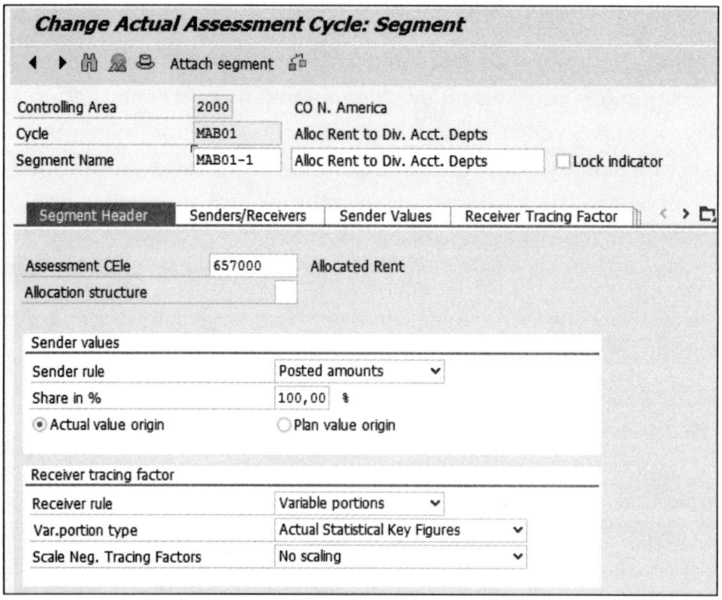

Figure 7.4 Segment Header for Assessment Cycle

One of the things that makes assessment cycles tricky at first is that the screen layout is highly dynamic. Changing the type of sender rule or receiver rule can result in new fields appearing on the screens and the tabs changing to reflect the different inputs needed:

- The **Sender Rule** field determines whether you're simply going to allocate all the costs on the cost center (**Posted Amounts**) or a fixed amount or fixed rate. Posted amounts is by far the most common approach and requires no work in preparation for the period close, because the costs on the sender cost centers are read during allocation. Fixed amounts and fixed rate require you to update the cycle prior to allocation but can be useful if you want to calculate the amounts for an allocation in an external system or spreadsheet and then load them to the assessment cycle. This might be the case if you want to calculate the work performed for different departments by a shared service center and then enter these manually as sender values in the segment.
- The **Receiver Rule** field determines the basis for the allocation. Selecting **Fixed Amounts, Fixed Percentages**, or **Fixed Portions** might seem like the easiest way to get started, because they're easy rules for everyone to understand. However, this type of rule forces you to revisit your assessment cycles each month to make sure

the percentages for each receiver are correct and check whether new cost centers have been added to a group and adjust the percentages accordingly.

If you select **Variable Portions**, you have to enter how these portions are to be determined. In our example, we're using the square footage statistical key figure, which we'll have to maintain once for each cost center (see Chapter 3, Section 3.3). In general, if you know that the relevant detail is being captured for the cost center, variable portions is the better way to allocate, because you're building on data being captured in the operational processes rather than creating unnecessary work for the controlling department.

- The assessment cost element (**Assessment CEle** field) determines the cost element under which the allocation posting will be recorded. If you require more detail than this, you can enter an allocation structure to group the costs according to their origins, allowing you to see, for example, wages and salary costs, material costs, and depreciation separately. This will give you more transparency but also increase the volume of data to be updated during the allocation.

The next step is to define the type of costs being allocated (facility costs in our example) and the partners in the allocation—in other words, which cost center is sending costs and which cost centers will be receiving costs—by navigating to the **Senders/ Receivers** tab. Figure 7.5 shows the sender cost center MB1300 (Administration) and the sender cost elements 470000 (Office and Building) to 471000 (Machinery Rental). Remember that the costs moved during one allocation can be moved themselves in the next allocation. In this example, the allocated rent will be posted to the receiving cost centers under cost element 657000 (see Figure 7.4). To move allocated rent from there to the next receiving cost centers, you will have to include this cost element as a sender for the next allocation. The receivers are all cost centers in group MGTACCTG. If you're not sure which cost centers are assigned to the receiver group, select the **Receiver Weighting Factors** tab on the far right, where you'll see all cost centers in group **MGTACCTG**. The entries in this cost center group will be expanded during the allocation. If new cost centers are added to the group, they'll automatically be included in the allocation, provided you ensure that the square footage statistical key figure is maintained for the new cost centers.

Before you can perform an allocation with the sender rule variable portions, you must define the key figure to be used to establish the ratio between the cost centers. To do this, select the **Receiver Tracing Factor** tab. Figure 7.6 shows that the rule type is **Actual Statistical Key Figures** (transferred from the screen shown in Figure 7.3), and the key figure is SQFT.

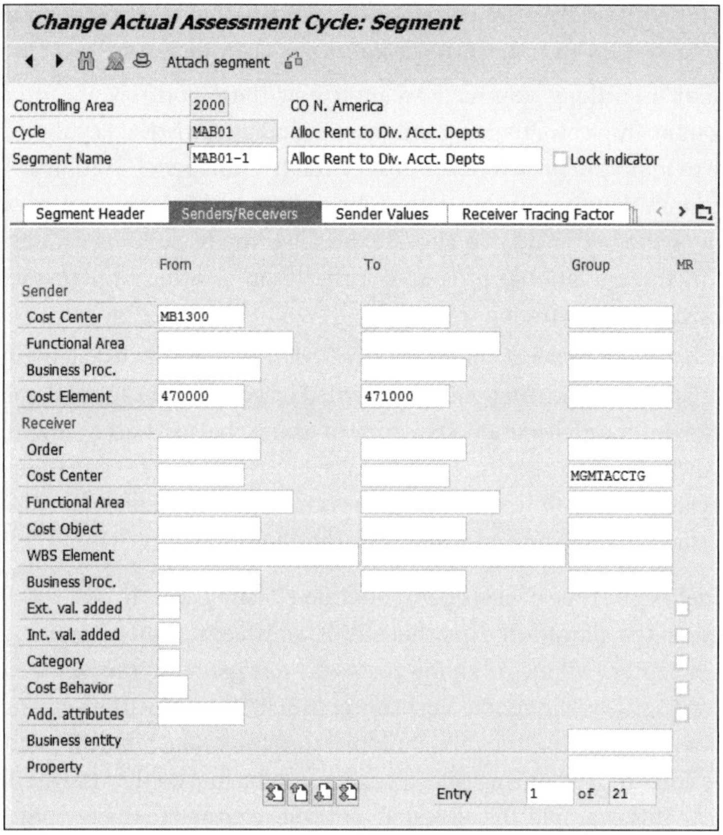

Figure 7.5 Sender/Receivers for Assessment Cycle

Once you've checked that the square footage figures have been maintained for each cost center (we explained how to do this in Chapter 3, Section 3.3), execute the allocation by following the menu path **Accounting • Controlling • Cost Center Accounting • Period-End Closing • Single Functions • Allocations • Assessment** or using Transaction KSU5. Enter the period and fiscal year and click on **Execute**. Figure 7.7 shows the results list for this assessment cycle. Cycle MAB01 contains one *sender* cost center and three *receiver* cost centers.

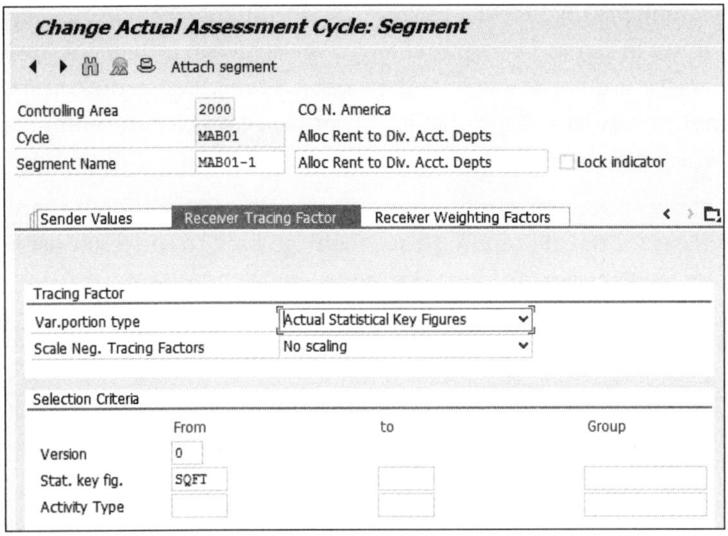

Figure 7.6 Receiver Tracing Factor for Assessment Cycle

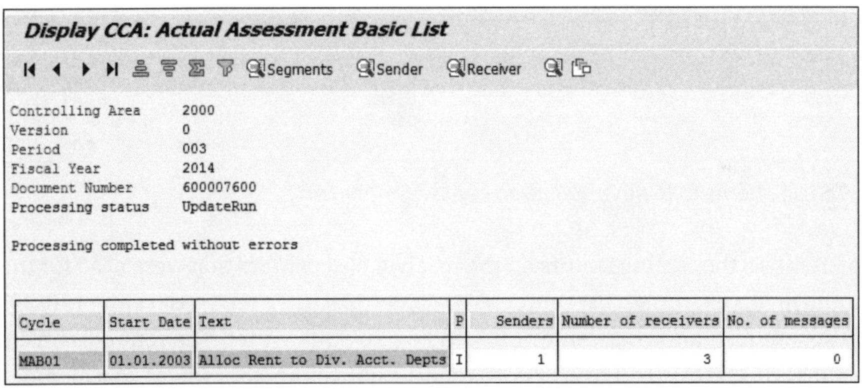

Figure 7.7 Result of Assessment Cycle

To display details of the posting, click on the **Cycle** line (MAB01) in the results list. This takes you to the line item report for the allocation, shown in Figure 7.8. You can see both the sender cost center (MB1300) and the receiver cost centers (MB1391, MB2391, and MB3391), as well as the assessment cost element (657000) we entered in the segment header. Notice that compared to an FI posting (for which there is generally a shift in account with each business transaction), in a CO allocation the cost element (account) stays the same but there is a shift from the sender to the receiver(s) objects.

You can identify assessments for auditing because the documents include business Transaction RKIU. Notice in Figure 7.8 that we changed the layout to include the **Business Transaction** in the column on the right and the **Debit/Credit** flags in the column on the left. We then sorted by this flag so that it's easier to see which cost center has been credited and which cost centers have been debited.

This report doesn't show what tracing factors (the statistical key figures in our example) were used as a basis for the allocation. To see them, go back to the result list in Figure 7.7 and click on the **Receiver** button in the menu bar.

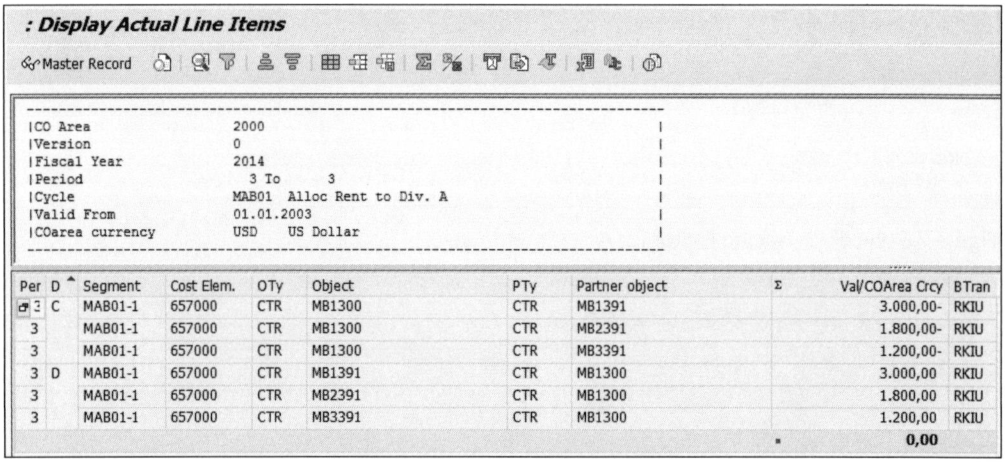

CO Area	2000
Version	0
Fiscal Year	2014
Period	3 To 3
Cycle	MAB01 Alloc Rent to Div. A
Valid From	01.01.2003
COarea currency	USD US Dollar

Per	D	Segment	Cost Elem.	OTy	Object	PTy	Partner object	Σ	Val/COArea Crcy	BTran
3	C	MAB01-1	657000	CTR	MB1300	CTR	MB1391		3.000,00-	RKIU
3		MAB01-1	657000	CTR	MB1300	CTR	MB2391		1.800,00-	RKIU
3		MAB01-1	657000	CTR	MB1300	CTR	MB3391		1.200,00-	RKIU
3	D	MAB01-1	657000	CTR	MB1391	CTR	MB1300		3.000,00	RKIU
3		MAB01-1	657000	CTR	MB2391	CTR	MB1300		1.800,00	RKIU
3		MAB01-1	657000	CTR	MB3391	CTR	MB1300		1.200,00	RKIU
								▪	**0,00**	

Figure 7.8 Line Items following Execution of Assessment Cycle

Figure 7.9 shows the tracing factors on the receiver cost centers that were used for the allocation. In our example, cost center MB1391 had 50 square feet, cost center MB2391 had 30 square feet, and cost center MB3391 had 20 square feet. The rent costs have been split in this ratio: 5 to 3 to 2. In both reports, notice the assessment cost element 657000 that we entered in the segment header. You'll see this as a line in your cost center reports, recording the credit to the sender and the debit to the receiver cost centers.

If instead of using an assessment cost element you had entered an **Allocation Structure** in the segment header (see Figure 7.4), you would see several lines for each sender/receiver, one for each of the cost groups you included in the allocation structure.

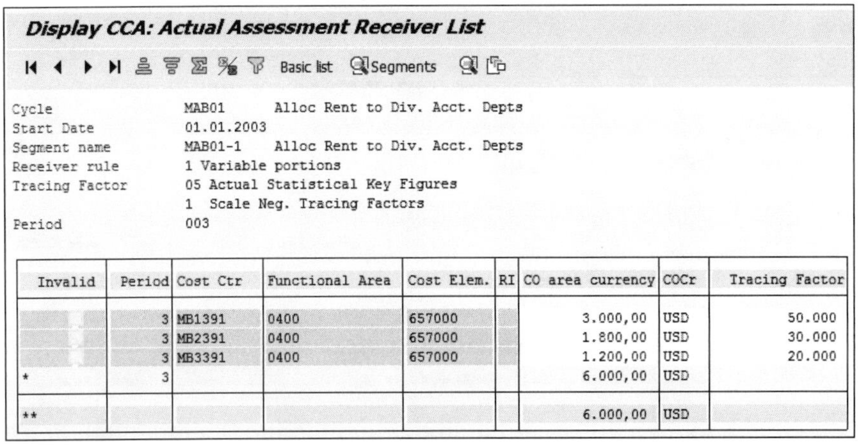
Display CCA: Actual Assessment Receiver List

Basic list Segments

```
Cycle            MAB01      Alloc Rent to Div. Acct. Depts
Start Date       01.01.2003
Segment name     MAB01-1    Alloc Rent to Div. Acct. Depts
Receiver rule    1 Variable portions
Tracing Factor   05 Actual Statistical Key Figures
                 1  Scale Neg. Tracing Factors
Period           003
```

Invalid	Period	Cost Ctr	Functional Area	Cost Elem.	RI	CO area currency	COCr	Tracing Factor
	3	MB1391	0400	657000		3.000,00	USD	50.000
	3	MB2391	0400	657000		1.800,00	USD	30.000
	3	MB3391	0400	657000		1.200,00	USD	20.000
*	3					6.000,00	USD	
**						6.000,00	USD	

Figure 7.9 Tracing Factors on Receiver Cost Centers

We've just stepped through an example in which we allocate and check in the same session, but of course you often also want to check what happened in a previous allocation. To do this, return to the screen shown in Figure 7.3 and choose the **Cycle Information** tab. Figure 7.10 shows the details of how our assessment cycle ran and the document number that records the transaction.

We looked at a very simple example here, in which the sender cost centers and the receiver cost centers were different. Assessment cycles often involve a cyclical relationship in which one cost center passes its costs to "all" cost centers and by definition receives a small portion of its own costs back. If you want to create this sort of cycle, you need to make sure your sender cost elements include not only the primary cost elements (470000–471000 in our example) but also the assessment cost element (657000 here) that you're using to record the allocation. If multiple segments exist in which each segment is sending costs to "all" cost centers, then the situation is more complicated still. In recent years, there has been a move in some organizations to unravel such iterative cycles because it can be difficult to trace their results reliably, but they are still relatively common. If you do use this approach in your organization, consider using Report RKALITER to trace exactly what is happening during these iterations.

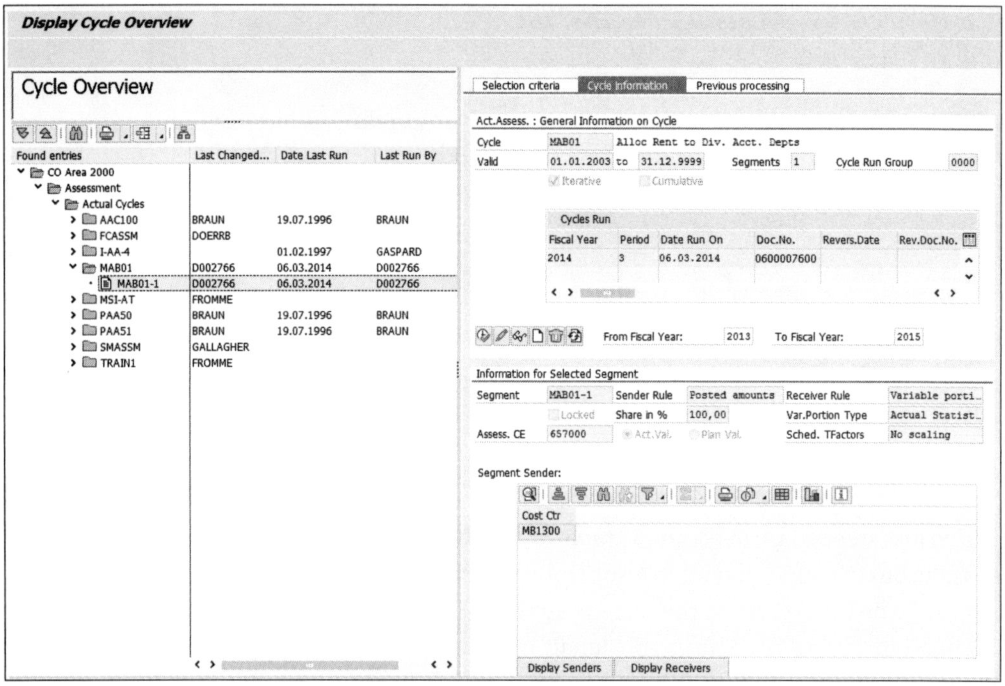

Figure 7.10 Results of Assessment from Cycle Overview

If you use other reports to analyze the result of this allocation, you'll find the data in version 0 (which represents the legal valuation). If you've activated an additional version for the parallel valuation of cost of goods manufactured, a second set of values will be used in the allocation. To view these values in reporting, you have to select the other version as you execute the report.

Using Cycle Run Groups for Allocations

All allocation cycles are defined at the controlling area level and automatically assigned to Cycle Run Group 0000. Because of the iterative nature of many cycles, only one assessment cycle can run at a time to ensure consistency. If you want to run assessment cycles in parallel—for example, because you want to allocate the costs from all cost centers in company code A and all cost centers in company code B at the same time—then create two cycle run groups, one for company code A and one for company code B. To create a cycle run group, select **Goto • Cycle Run Group** from within the cycle. If you use cycle run groups, be careful to ensure that the cycles really are independent of each other; the system will no longer check this.

Customer Connect Enhancements for Cycle Maintenance

Although the basic functions for maintaining cycles have changed only little in recent years, new functions were added recently to make it easier to copy individual segments or a whole cycle and then make mass changes to the attached segments. You can find details of how to implement this enhancement in SAP Note 2374063 (Allocations—Enhancements for Cycle Maintenance).

Distribution Cycles

Once you understand the basic principles of working with assessment cycles, you'll find that the other types of cycles are similar. The proper term for what happens during the execution of a distribution cycle is *primary cost distribution*. These cycles make sense when you use a supporting cost center to capture a few very specific primary costs (such as utility or telephone costs) and then want to distribute these over many cost centers. The main visual difference between an assessment and a distribution cycle is that you don't need to enter an assessment cost element. This is because the original cost element (whatever account was used to record the utility or telephone costs) will be used in the posting. You should also be careful when defining the senders to only include primary cost elements as senders when you choose the cost element group. Most organizations have a numbering scheme that makes it easy to identify cost elements tied to accounts (primary) and cost elements used to record allocations (secondary).

You can view distribution cycles by following the menu path **Accounting • Controlling • Cost Center Accounting • Period-End Closing • Current Settings • Define Distribution** or using Transaction KSV2 and entering the cycle. Figure 7.11 shows the segment header for a distribution cycle. This distributes telephone costs to several operational cost centers based on the square footage of office space entered for those cost centers (the same measure as we used during assessment).

To execute the distribution, follow the menu path **Accounting • Controlling • Cost Center Accounting • Period-End Closing • Single Functions • Allocations • Distribution** or use Transaction KSV5. Enter the period and fiscal year and click on **Execute**. Figure 7.12 shows the line items created during the distribution. If you compare this list with Figure 7.8, you'll see that the cost element is the primary cost element under which the telephone costs were captured. The sender cost center is 4-1210, and the receiver cost centers are 4-1000, 4-1110, and 4-1200. The business transaction is Transaction RKIV.

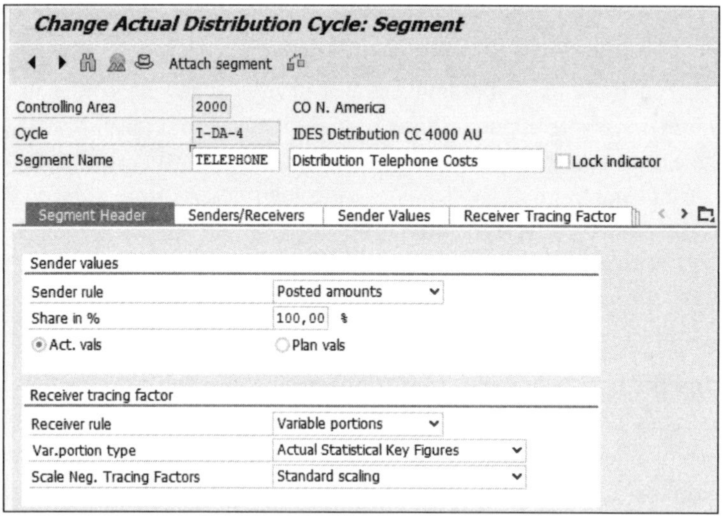

Figure 7.11 Segment Header for Distribution Cycle

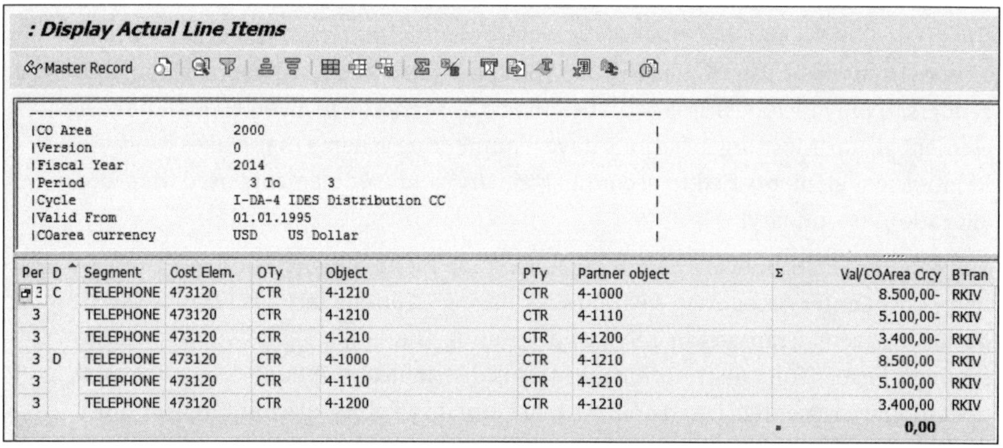

Figure 7.12 Line Items following Execution of Distribution Cycle

Reposting Cycles

Reposting cycles look exactly like distribution cycles but store the data in a more compact way. Figure 7.13 shows the line items that resulted from executing a reposting cycle. The line items also look similar, with the exception that the business transaction is Transaction RKIB. The main difference is that the partner type and partner object are not included in the totals record, which saves space if you won't be reporting on these.

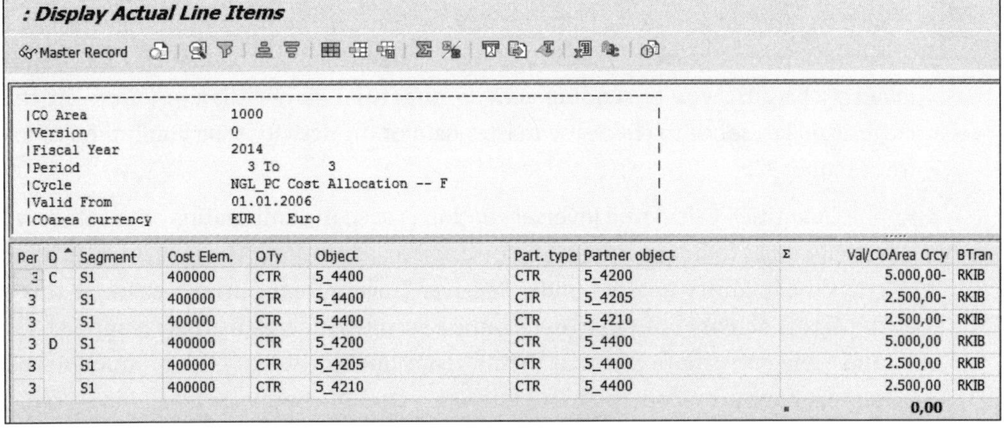

Figure 7.13 Line Items following Execution of Reposting Cycle

> **Reposting Cycles in SAP S/4HANA**
>
> Totals records are no longer created in SAP S/4HANA, so from a data storage point of view there is no real benefit in using reposting cycles rather than distribution cycles.

Indirect Activity Allocation Cycles

The main difference between an assessment and an indirect activity allocation cycle is that the sender is not a cost center but is the combination of a cost center and an activity type (see Chapter 3). You should use an indirect activity allocation cycle whenever the quantity (e.g., kilowatt hours) rather than the amount is important. A quality cost center might record the total *time in hours* worked by the quality staff and then allocate this quantity to the production cost centers based on a statistical key figure such as number of units produced, or an energy cost center might allocate the *kilowatt hours* provided to the production cost centers based on the machine hours confirmed by the production cost centers. Because it's the *quantity* rather than the amount that's allocated, you also need to define an activity price before you execute such allocations. You can view indirect activity allocation cycles by following the menu path **Accounting • Controlling • Cost Center Accounting • Period-End Closing •**

Current Settings Define Indirect Activity Allocation or using Transaction KSC2 and choosing a cycle.

Figure 7.14 shows the **Segment Header** tab for an indirect activity allocation cycle. The main difference compared to the assessment cycle is in the sender rule, for which you have the options **Posted Quantities, Fixed Quantities**, and **Quantities Calculated Inversely** because you're sending activity quantities rather than amounts. At this stage, it makes sense to check the master data of the activity type you intend to use (see Chapter 3):

- The **Quantities Calculated Inversely** option is used in combination with category 2 activity types (indirect determination, indirect allocation). The inverse calculation reads the quantity entered under **Receiver Tracing Factor** (in our example this is the **Actual Activity** option) to determine how much energy has been supplied. The underlying assumption is that the more production activity the production cost centers have provided, the more kilowatt hours of energy they will have used. If the relationship between machine time and kilowatt hours of energy is not 1:1, then you need to tab to the far right (see Figure 7.14) and change the receiver weighting factor from 100 (the default) to a factor that better reflects your business needs.
- The **Posted Quantities** option is used in combination with category 3 activity types (manual entry, indirect allocation). To use this option, every month you need to enter a quantity for the cost center and activity type entered in the **Senders/Receivers** tab. To enter quality hours for the cost center, go to **Accounting • Controlling • Cost Center Accounting • Actual Postings • Sender Activities • Enter** or Transaction KB51N and enter the sender cost center (quality cost center), the sender activity type (quality hours), and the number of hours performed in the period. The allocation then spreads the quantity entered to the selected receivers based on whatever receiver tracing factor has been entered.
- Fixed quantities are entered manually in the allocation cycle (like fixed amounts in an assessment cycle).

To execute an indirect activity allocation cycle, follow the menu path **Accounting • Controlling • Cost Center Accounting • Period-End Closing • Single Functions • Indirect Activity Allocation** or use Transaction KSC5. Enter the period and fiscal year and click on **Execute**. Figure 7.15 shows the line items created during the indirect activity allocation. This time, the sender is an activity (**OType** ATY) rather than a cost center, and the receivers are the production cost centers that have performed work in the period. The amounts are calculated by multiplying the number of kilowatt hours by the activity price for one kilowatt hour. The business transaction is Transaction RKIL.

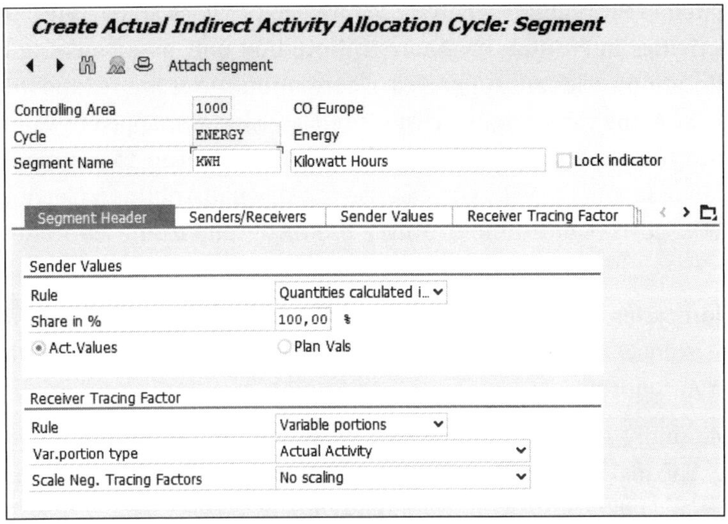

Figure 7.14 Segment Header for Indirect Activity Allocation Cycle

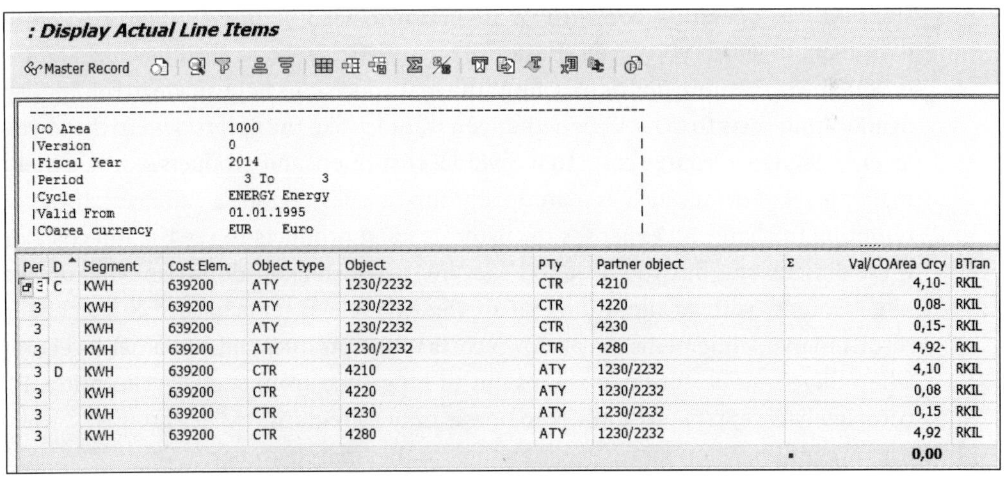

Figure 7.15 Line Items following Execution of Indirect Activity Cycle

7.1.3 Allocations to Profitability Analysis

The allocations we've discussed so far were all initiated in Cost Center Accounting. As you saw when we looked at the planning process in Chapter 5, there are also allocations that are initiated in Profitability Analysis. Figure 7.16 provides an overview of the period-close activities in **Profitability Analysis**. Note that only assessment and indirect activity allocation cycles are supported. Distribution cycles are redundant; for costing-based CO-PA, the values on the cost centers are always mapped to value fields. However, once you've passed costs from Cost Center Accounting to Profitability Analysis using an assessment cycle, you can use top-down distribution (Section 7.4.2) to distribute the costs—for example, from a product group to the associated products.

In general, allocation cycles in **Profitability Analysis** tend to be created in Customizing to ensure consistency, so you won't find a **Current Settings** folder here like the one for Cost Center Accounting.

Allocations to Profitability Analysis follow a pattern similar to allocations in Cost Center Accounting. The main difference is that the senders are the cost centers, but the receivers can be any characteristic in Profitability Analysis (see Chapter 2); also, the characteristics can be used in combination. You might use an allocation to perform a simple spreading of costs among one group of characteristics (e.g., all divisions in the operating concern) or to perform what is often called a *waterfall allocation*, in which you fill a series of characteristics, such as the divisions and the products within those divisions. One of the main decisions to be made in the context of allocating costs to CO-PA is whether you want to take the costs down to the lowest level of detail—to charge costs to individual customers and products—or whether a higher level of detail, such as a product group or sales region, is sufficient. It can be tempting to charge all expenses to customers and products to see the full costs on these dimensions, but you need to be aware that such allocations risk tying up system resources with an allocation that applies a couple of cents to each customer and results in many line items. Break down costs to the product and customer level only when there's sufficient business insight to be gained from such an allocation. It's completely acceptable to apply some costs only to regions or sales groups or whatever other dimension makes sense and not to the final customer.

To display an assessment cycle, follow the menu path **Accounting • Controlling • Profitability Analysis • Actual Postings • Period-End Closing • Assessment** and then **Extras • Cycle • Change** or use Transaction KEU2. Figure 7.17 shows the segment header for the allocation of research and development costs to the company's divisions.

Figure 7.16 Period-End Close Activities in Profitability Analysis

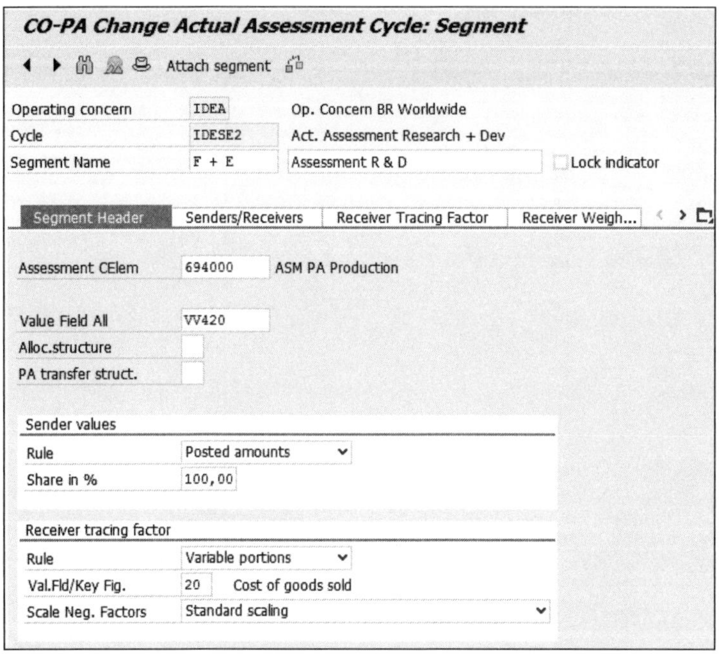

Figure 7.17 Segment Header with Receiver Rule Variable Portions

Again, it's important to consider the practicality of your cycles in terms of the receiver rules. If you select **Fixed Portions** as the receiver rule, you'll have to manually enter the split to each of the company's industries, customer groups, divisions, and sales organizations: a tedious manual effort each month. If, instead, you select the sender rule **Variable Portions**, you simply enter the value field to be used to determine the ratio for each characteristic. In our example, the allocation will be based on the cost of goods sold recorded for each division.

Performance Impact of SAP HANA

If you're concerned about the performance impact of reading and aggregating the cost of goods sold for each division at runtime, refer to new developments using SAP HANA in Chapter 13.

Figure 7.18 shows the **Senders/Receivers** tab for this segment. Because it's possible to allocate costs to any characteristic in Profitability Analysis (there can be up to 60 different characteristics), you almost always need to scroll down the receiver list to see all relevant receivers.

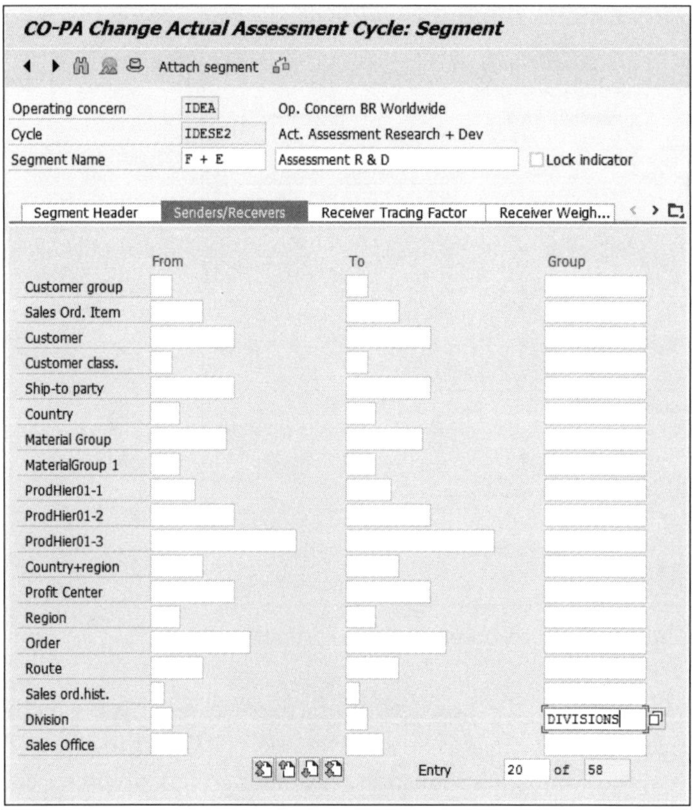

Figure 7.18 Senders/Receivers in Assessment Cycle to Profitability Analysis

Here the sender cost center is a research and development cost center (not on the screen), the costs of which are going to be charged to the divisions for which it works. You can also assign the values to more than one characteristic, so you might assign the research and development costs not just to the divisions supported, but also to other organizational units associated with those divisions. As we mentioned earlier, it makes sense to consider performance issues when defining which characteristics should be the receiver of an allocation and to stop at the level of detail that makes sense from a business perspective.

Now all you have to do is define which record types will be read from Profitability Analysis as a basis for the allocation. Figure 7.19 shows that we'll use record type F (for billing data) to determine the cost of goods sold. As we said for the cost center allocations, basing your allocations on data that the system records anyway is much preferred over fixed percentages, because it saves the preparatory work of checking the tracing factors in the run-up to the period close.

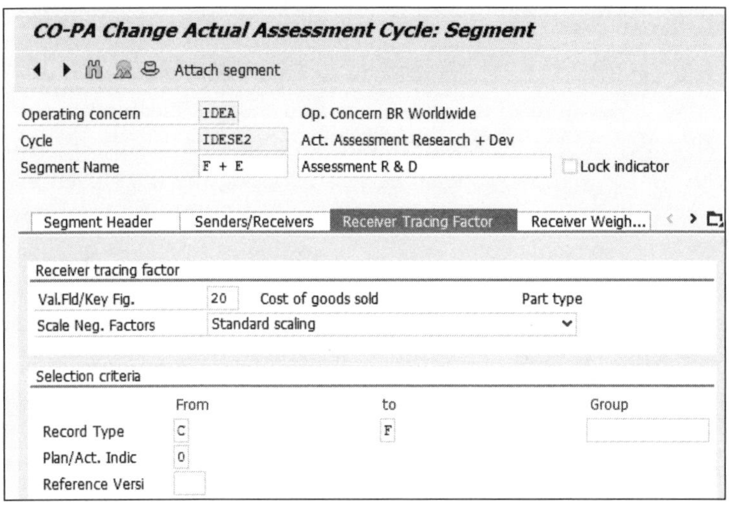

Figure 7.19 Receiver Tracing Factors for Cost of Goods Sold

To perform an allocation, follow the menu path **Accounting • Controlling • Profitability Analysis • Actual Postings • Period-End Closing • Assessment** or use Transaction KEU5.

Figure 7.20 shows the results of making this allocation. In this simple example, research and development costs have been assigned to two divisions in proportion to the relative cost of goods sold in each division (35:50).

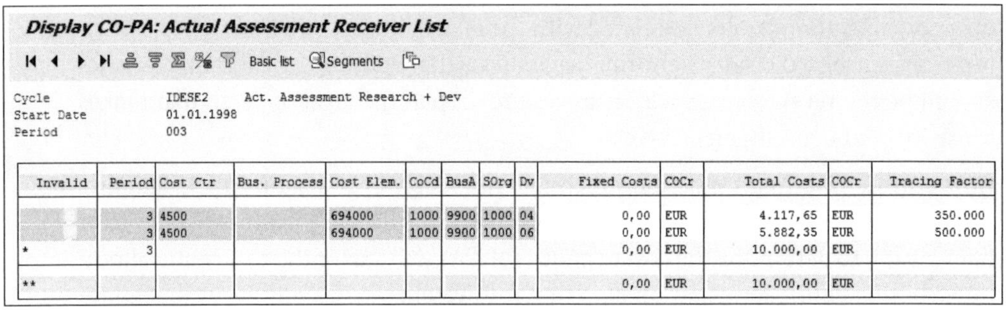
Display CO-PA: Actual Assessment Receiver List

Basic list Segments

Cycle IDESE2 Act. Assessment Research + Dev
Start Date 01.01.1998
Period 003

Invalid	Period	Cost Ctr	Bus. Process	Cost Elem.	CoCd	BusA	SOrg	Dv	Fixed Costs	COCr	Total Costs	COCr	Tracing Factor
	3	4500		694000	1000	9900	1000	04	0,00	EUR	4.117,65	EUR	350.000
	3	4500		694000	1000	9900	1000	06	0,00	EUR	5.882,35	EUR	500.000
*	3								0,00	EUR	10.000,00	EUR	
**									0,00	EUR	10.000,00	EUR	

Figure 7.20 Result of Assessment Cycle to CO-PA

CO-PA Allocations in SAP S/4HANA

If you activate account-based CO-PA in the move to SAP S/4HANA, the system will update the calculated values both to the value fields and the cost elements when you perform the allocation. If both approaches are active in your system, determine whether the drivers for the allocation should be selected using the value fields in costing-based CO-PA or the cost elements in account-based CO-PA, using the **TF Basis** flag in the cycle header, and choose either 1 for costing-based CO-PA or 2 for account-based CO-PA.

If account-based CO-PA isn't active in your current system, the credit to the cost center(s) will be offset against a single reconciliation object (object type RO) and the detail lines for the receivers of the allocated costs will only be available in costing-based CO-PA.

7.1.4 Target Costs and Variances on Cost Centers

When all the allocations for the period have been completed, the following tasks remain for the cost centers:

- For cost centers *without* activity types, check that the balance on the cost center is zero (all costs have been allocated) and analyze any variances between planned costs and actual costs.
- For cost centers *with* activity types, check the balance on the cost center. This is rarely zero, because the activity allocations were performed using a *standard rate* that does not include any variances that occurred during the period. However, this kind of cost center has an output quantity (the amount of machine hours supplied, the amount of kilowatt hours supplied, etc.). This quantity is used to adjust the plan to calculate the *target costs*—in other words, the costs that should have been incurred to provide that level of activity. In this case, variance calculation is not a line-by-line comparison of plan against actual but a system-supported process that suggests the source of the variance (price changes, quantity changes, etc.). Note that variance calculation only takes place in legal valuation (version 0), so it's worth being clear about which accounting approach you want to use for your management reporting when you prepare your design.
- If you want to include these variances in your production costs, calculate new activity rates and include these either in your production orders or in the Material Ledger. You can use the Material Ledger to include values in legal valuation and for the parallel valuation of cost of goods manufactured.

Target Costs

Before we look at what happens when we calculate target costs, let's look at the planned costs for a group of cost centers. In this example, the energy, quality, and repair cost centers provide activities to the two production cost centers. We'll focus on the quality cost center shown in Figure 7.21. Notice that the quality cost center *planned* to provide 150 hours of quality checks but *actually* provided 160 hours. The planned input costs to provide 150 hours of quality checks totaled 29,912 Euros. As you look at these costs, recall the distinction we made in Chapter 5: some of the costs are *activity-independent* and some are *activity-dependent*. The activity-dependent costs will be adjusted to reflect the higher level of output when we calculate the *target costs*.

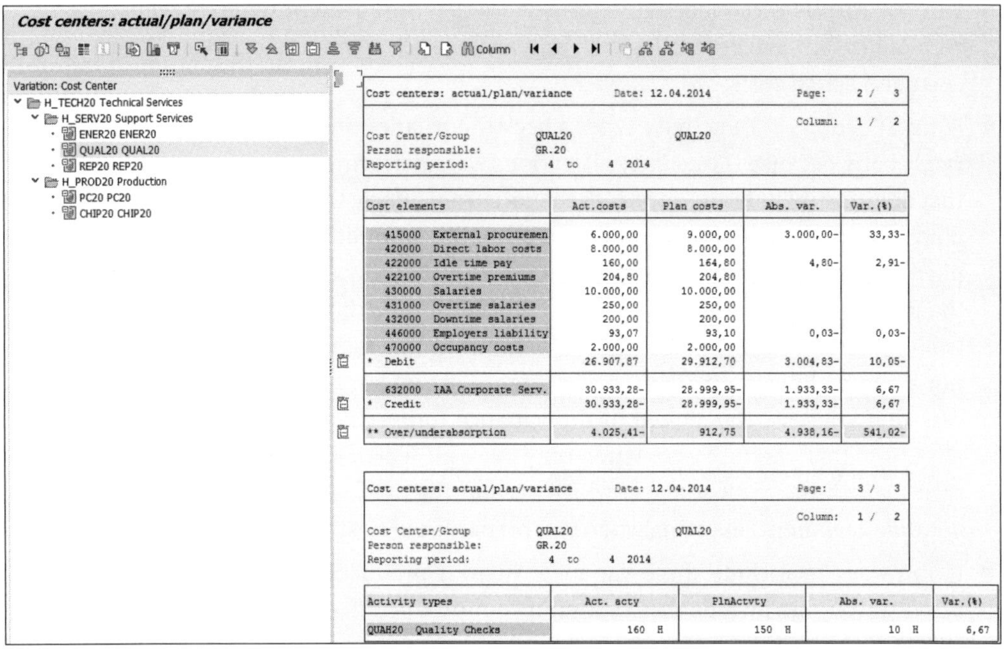

Figure 7.21 Plan/Actual Cost Report

Now compare these figures with those in Figure 7.22. If you look at the first line of the report for external processing, you'll recall that the planned costs were 9,000 Euros whereas the target costs are 9,600 Euros, reflecting the fact that an extra 10 activity hours were provided. You'll see the same situation for direct labor, with 8,000 Euros in planned costs and 8,200 Euros in target costs. The activity-independent costs, by contrast, remain the same regardless of the amount of activity provided. This kind of detailed analysis can help you understand the effect of the amount of work provided on the amount of resources used by your cost center.

Running variance analysis will provide an even more powerful explanation of the source of each variance. To run variance calculation, select Transaction KSS1 or **Accounting • Controlling • Cost Center Accounting • Period-End Closing • Single Functions • Variances**. Enter the cost center group, the version, the period, and the fiscal year and set the **Detailed Lists** flag. The results are shown in Figure 7.23. The critical column is **Operating Rate**. Notice that only the cost center for PC production (**PC20**) performed 100% to target. All the other cost centers performed either more or less work than planned for the period. To see more detail, choose one of the cost centers and click on the **Cost Elements** button.

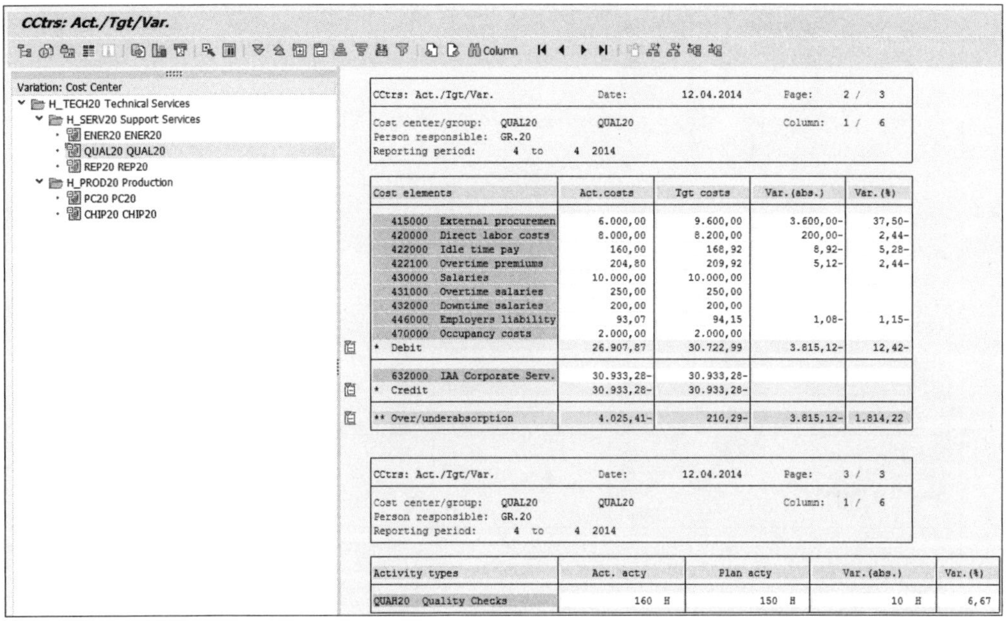

Figure 7.22 Target/Actual Cost Report

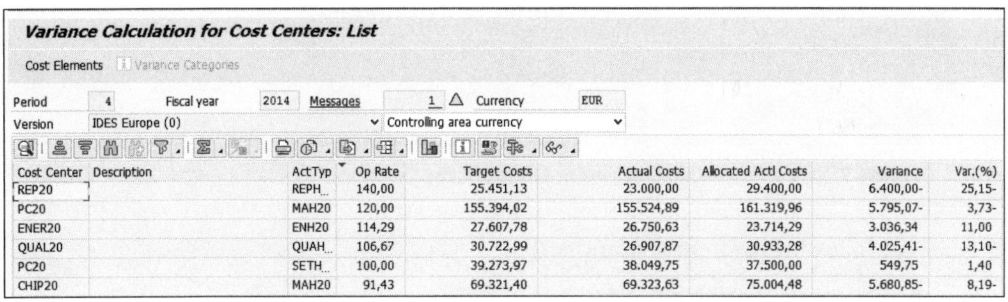

Figure 7.23 Variance Calculation with Operating Rate by Cost Center

To explore the details further, click on the **Variance Categories** button. The variance explanation is shown in Figure 7.24. In variance analysis, we distinguish between *input variances* (those resulting from changes in the costs coming on to the cost center) and *output variances* (those resulting from changes to the output of the cost center or the activity price).

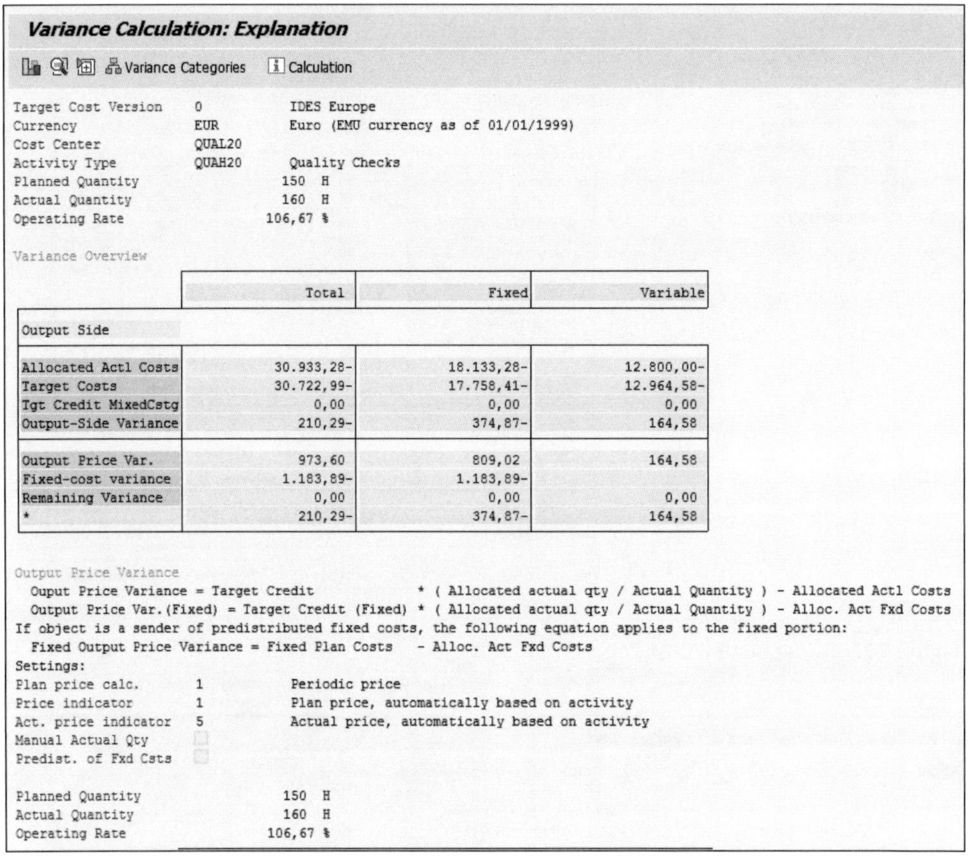

Variance Calculation: Explanation

Variance Categories | Calculation

```
Target Cost Version    0          IDES Europe
Currency               EUR        Euro (EMU currency as of 01/01/1999)
Cost Center            QUAL20
Activity Type          QUAH20     Quality Checks
Planned Quantity                150  H
Actual Quantity                 160  H
Operating Rate               106,67 %
```

Variance Overview

	Total	Fixed	Variable
Output Side			
Allocated Actl Costs	30.933,28-	18.133,28-	12.800,00-
Target Costs	30.722,99-	17.758,41-	12.964,58-
Tgt Credit MixedCstg	0,00	0,00	0,00
Output-Side Variance	210,29-	374,87-	164,58
Output Price Var.	973,60	809,02	164,58
Fixed-cost variance	1.183,89-	1.183,89-	
Remaining Variance	0,00	0,00	0,00
*	210,29-	374,87-	164,58

Output Price Variance

```
  Ouput Price Variance = Target Credit           * ( Allocated actual qty / Actual Quantity ) - Allocated Actl Costs
  Output Price Var.(Fixed) = Target Credit (Fixed) * ( Allocated actual qty / Actual Quantity ) - Alloc. Act Fxd Costs
If object is a sender of predistributed fixed costs, the following equation applies to the fixed portion:
  Fixed Output Price Variance = Fixed Plan Costs   - Alloc. Act Fxd Costs
Settings:
Plan price calc.        1      Periodic price
Price indicator         1      Plan price, automatically based on activity
Act. price indicator    5      Actual price, automatically based on activity
Manual Actual Qty
Predist. of Fxd Csts

Planned Quantity                150  H
Actual Quantity                 160  H
Operating Rate               106,67 %
```

Figure 7.24 Variance Calculation for Quality Cost Center

The following are input variances:

- **Input price variances**
  These occur because of changes to the activity prices for other cost centers or material price changes.
- **Input quantity variances**
  These occur when using a different quantity of activity from other cost centers.
- **Resource-usage variances**
  These occur if an activity is used from a different cost center than was originally planned. Some organizations call these substitution variances.
- **Remaining variances**
  This is a catchall for any unassigned variances.

The following are output variances:

- **Output price variances**
  These occur if the activity price changes for any reason.
- **Fixed cost variances**
  These occur if the operating rate changes, resulting in over- or undercharging for the fixed costs in the activity price. In our case, the production cost centers were overcharged for the fixed part of the activity price (salaries and building costs).
- **Remaining variances**
  This is a catchall for any unassigned variances.
- **Output side variances**
  These occur if the chosen activity price doesn't result in the cost center being credited, to give a final value of zero.

In Figure 7.24, we'll focus on the output side and look at the allocation line that shows that 30,933 Euros have been charged to the production cost centers. The target costs (30,722 Euros) are the planned costs adjusted to reflect the operating rate (106.67% in our case). As we explore the difference of 210 Euros, we see a high fixed-cost variance and an output price variance.

Activity Prices

The final step in the cost center close is to calculate a new activity price. This uses the same mechanisms as we saw during activity price planning in Chapter 5 and can also give you an actual cost component split. To execute activity price calculation, follow the menu path **Accounting • Controlling • Cost Center Accounting • Period-End Closing • Single Functions • Price Calculation** or use Transaction KSII. Figure 7.25 shows the activity prices for the cost centers we just saw.

If you use `FIN_CO_COGM` business function (Parallel Valuation of Cost of Goods Manufactured), available from EHP 5 for SAP ERP 6.0, two sets of input values are available in Cost Center Accounting to reflect the different accounting principles governing the approach to calculating depreciation in Asset Accounting and any other ledger-specific postings. These are used to calculate two activity prices, stored as separate versions.

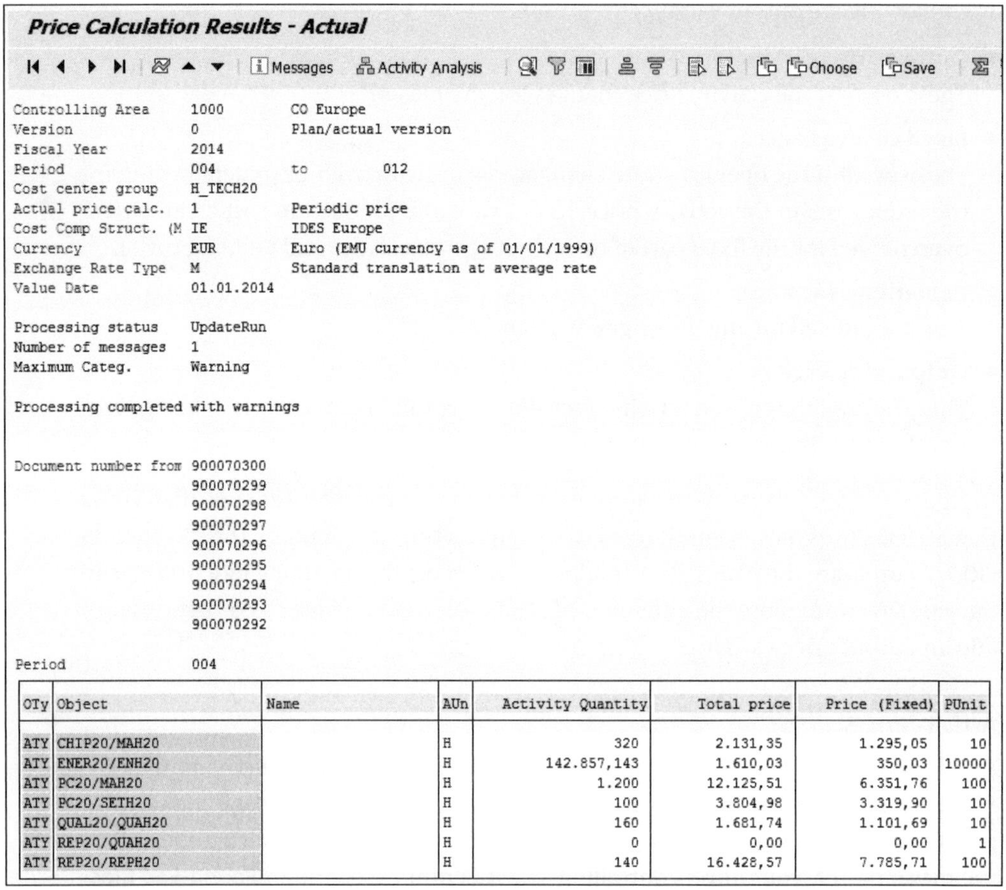
Price Calculation Results - Actual

Messages | Activity Analysis | Choose | Save

```
Controlling Area     1000        CO Europe
Version              0           Plan/actual version
Fiscal Year          2014
Period               004         to         012
Cost center group    H_TECH20
Actual price calc.   1           Periodic price
Cost Comp Struct. (M IE          IDES Europe
Currency             EUR         Euro (EMU currency as of 01/01/1999)
Exchange Rate Type   M           Standard translation at average rate
Value Date           01.01.2014

Processing status    UpdateRun
Number of messages   1
Maximum Categ.       Warning

Processing completed with warnings


Document number from 900070300
                     900070299
                     900070298
                     900070297
                     900070296
                     900070295
                     900070294
                     900070293
                     900070292

Period               004
```

OTy	Object	Name	AUn	Activity Quantity	Total price	Price (Fixed)	PUnit
ATY	CHIP20/MAH20		H	320	2.131,35	1.295,05	10
ATY	ENER20/ENH20		H	142.857,143	1.610,03	350,03	10000
ATY	PC20/MAH20		H	1.200	12.125,51	6.351,76	100
ATY	PC20/SETH20		H	100	3.804,98	3.319,90	10
ATY	QUAL20/QUAH20		H	160	1.681,74	1.101,69	10
ATY	REP20/QUAH20		H	0	0,00	0,00	1
ATY	REP20/REPH20		H	140	16.428,57	7.785,71	100

Figure 7.25 Result of Activity Price Calculation

To check the results of price calculation, follow the menu path **Accounting • Controlling • Cost Center Accounting • Information System • Reports for Cost Center Accounting • Prices • Cost Centers: Activity Prices** or use Transaction KSBT and enter the cost center, activity types, version, and time frame. Figure 7.26 shows two activity prices for each activity type on the cost center. The price indicator (**PrI**) column shows the following:

- **1**—planned activity price based on the planned quantity
- **2**—planned activity price based on planned capacity
- **5**—actual activity price based on the actual quantity
- **6**—actual activity price based on actual capacity

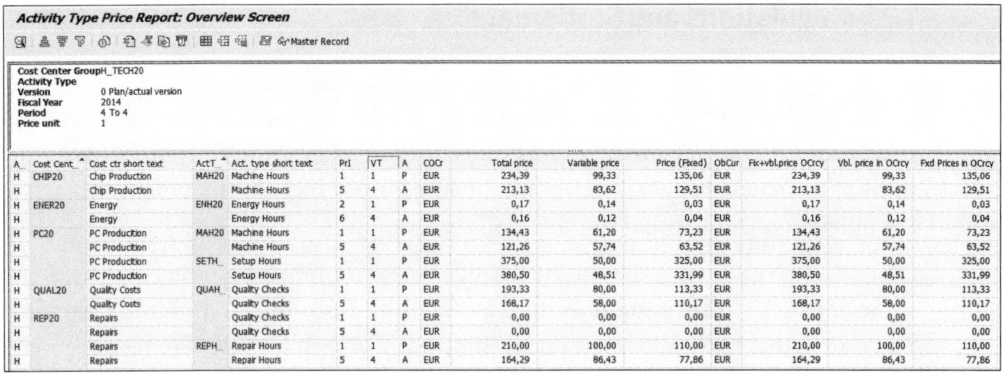

Activity Type Price Report: Overview Screen

Master Record

Cost Center Group H_TECH20
Activity Type
Version 0 Plan/actual version
Fiscal Year 2014
Period 4 To 4
Price unit 1

A...	Cost Cent...	Cost ctr short text	ActT...	Act. type short text	PrI	VT	A	COCr	Total price	Variable price	Price (Fixed)	ObCur	Fix+vbl.price OCrcy	Vbl. price in OCrcy	Fxd Prices in OCrcy
H	CHIP20	Chip Production	MAH20	Machine Hours	1	1	P	EUR	234,39	99,33	135,06	EUR	234,39	99,33	135,06
H		Chip Production		Machine Hours	5	4	A	EUR	213,13	83,62	129,51	EUR	213,13	83,62	129,51
H	ENER20	Energy	ENH20	Energy Hours	2	1	P	EUR	0,17	0,14	0,03	EUR	0,17	0,14	0,03
H		Energy		Energy Hours	6	4	A	EUR	0,16	0,12	0,04	EUR	0,16	0,12	0,04
H	PC20	PC Production	MAH20	Machine Hours	1	1	P	EUR	134,43	61,20	73,23	EUR	134,43	61,20	73,23
H		PC Production		Machine Hours	5	4	A	EUR	121,26	57,74	63,52	EUR	121,26	57,74	63,52
H		PC Production	SETH...	Setup Hours	1	1	P	EUR	375,00	50,00	325,00	EUR	375,00	50,00	325,00
H		PC Production		Setup Hours	5	4	A	EUR	380,50	48,51	331,99	EUR	380,50	48,51	331,99
H	QUAL20	Quality Costs	QUAH...	Quality Checks	1	1	P	EUR	193,33	80,00	113,33	EUR	193,33	80,00	113,33
H		Quality Costs		Quality Checks	5	4	A	EUR	168,17	58,00	110,17	EUR	168,17	58,00	110,17
H	REP20	Repairs		Quality Checks	1	1	P	EUR	0,00	0,00	0,00	EUR	0,00	0,00	0,00
H		Repairs		Quality Checks	5	4	A	EUR	0,00	0,00	0,00	EUR	0,00	0,00	0,00
H		Repairs	REPH...	Repair Hours	1	1	P	EUR	210,00	100,00	110,00	EUR	210,00	100,00	110,00
H		Repairs		Repair Hours	5	4	A	EUR	164,29	86,43	77,86	EUR	164,29	86,43	77,86

Figure 7.26 Actual Activity Prices

> **Customer Connect Enhancements for Activity Price Reporting**
>
> Customers working with Transaction KSBT missed the ability to compare versions, fiscal years, and different periods. There is now a new transaction, Transaction KSBTV, that allows you to make such comparisons. You can find details of how to implement this enhancement in SAP Note 2065880 (Customer Connect CO—New Transactions for Price Comparison).

If you want to assign the new activity prices to your production orders, process orders, and so on, every menu for the period close in Cost Object Controlling includes the step **Revaluate at Actual Prices** (Transaction CON2), which updates the orders with the newly calculated prices. If you use the Material Ledger, you can leave out this step and use the alternative valuation run to determine the activity rates for the materials and pass them on to the materials produced during the period. We'll look at this in Section 7.3. Alternatively, you can simply consider the difference as a cost center variance and use an assessment cycle to allocate it to **Profitability Analysis**.

With the calculation of the activity prices, we've completed all steps for Cost Center Accounting and are now ready to move on to Product Cost Controlling, where these activity prices can be included in the product costs. At this stage, the cost center reports should show a balance of zero, unless you're going to use the alternative valuation run in the Material Ledger to calculate your activity rates and clear the cost centers. If this is the case, your production cost centers still have a value awaiting clearing.

7.2 Calculations and Settlement

The period-close tasks for Product Cost Controlling are slightly different depending on whether you work with product cost by period, product cost by order, or Sales Order Controlling (see Chapter 2). Because there's a degree of overlap between the three approaches, we'll look at the whole flow for product cost by order and then at the differences in the other two approaches.

Figure 7.27 gives an overview of the period-close activities for product cost by order, some of which we encountered when we followed a production order in Chapter 6. You'll find the same activities under **Shop Floor Control** in the **Production** menu because some plants perform these tasks locally. In the menu, notice that all tasks have an entry for **Individual Processing** and **Collective Processing**. In this chapter, we'll discuss the individual processing of a single production order so that we can focus on the value flows and the details of what happens in an individual order. We'll come back to collective processing in Chapter 12, wherein we discuss your options for efficiently processing multiple orders.

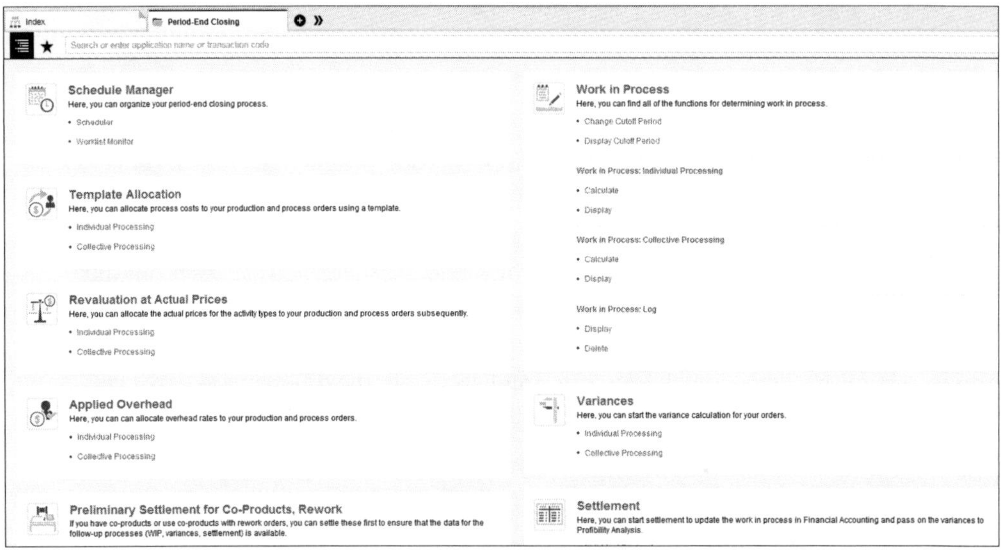

Figure 7.27 Period-Close Activities for Production Orders

The following tasks are included:

- Template allocation is used in the context of activity-based costing. We'll look at this in more detail in Chapter 11.
- Revaluation at actual costs allows you to update the production orders with the activity prices you calculated in the previous step.
- Applied overhead allows you to charge a percentage- or quantity-based overhead to your production orders.
- We discussed preliminary settlement for coproducts and rework when we looked at the handling of coproducts and rework orders in Chapter 6.
- WIP is required for all production orders that are open at the time of the period close. If you use product cost collectors (see Chapter 3), then you also need to calculate WIP for any operations that have been completed but not yet delivered to stock.
- The **Variances** folder allows you to calculate production variances and scrap for all completed production orders. If you use product cost collectors, it allows you to calculate production variances for all completed operations.

  Your use of the **Settlement** folder depends on your type of orders—in other words, on whether the expenses collected have to be capitalized (investment orders whose costs have to be capitalized as assets under construction, production orders carrying WIP, etc.) or are simply overhead (research and development orders, etc.).
- Overhead orders can settle either to a parent cost center or to profitability analysis depending on the entries in the settlement rule. You should settle overhead orders to their parent cost centers *before* you perform the allocations in the previous section. You can settle overhead orders to profitability analysis as soon as they have all relevant costs (usually this means after you've applied overhead).
- For orders that need to be *capitalized*, you use settlement to move the WIP to the balance sheet and the variances to profitability analysis. This means you can only settle once you have calculated WIP and variances.

Before you start to close the orders, you should check the parameters relevant to the period close in the order master data. Figure 7.28 shows the control parameters for a production order.

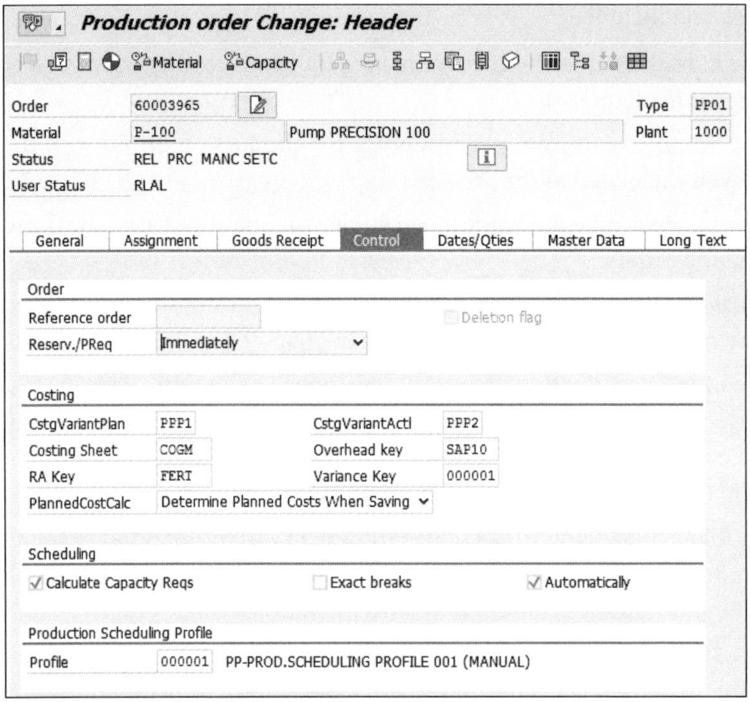

Figure 7.28 Control Parameters for Production Order

Before you execute your first close—and whenever you encounter errors during the close—you should check the entries in the following fields:

- **Costing Sheet**
  Contains all parameters relating to the calculation of overhead (Section 7.2.1).
- **Overhead Key**
  Used to calculate material-specific overheads. This is linked with the overhead group in the costing view of the material master (see Chapter 4).
- **RA Key (results analysis key)**
  Used to determine how WIP is calculated. The default is set by order type and plant (Section 7.2.2).
- **Variance Key**
  Used to determine how variances are calculated. The default is set in the costing view of the material master (Section 7.2.3).

7.2.1 Overhead Calculation

The purpose of overhead calculation is to charge the costs (e.g., of storing materials in the warehouse) to the production orders. The costing sheet links together several condition types that determine the following:

- The basis for the calculation (e.g., all relevant raw material costs)
- The conditions under which overhead is applied (e.g., within a particular plant or when manufacturing a certain material)
- The percentage to be applied (e.g., 10% on all raw material costs)
- The cost center that's the sender of the charge (e.g., the warehouse cost center)

Although you might calculate overhead for individual orders during testing, the normal procedure is to schedule a job that selects all relevant production orders in the plant and assigns overhead to each one in turn based on the conditions in the costing sheet. To calculate overhead, follow the menu path **Accounting • Controlling • Product Cost Controlling • Period-End Closing • Product Cost by Order • Overhead Calculation • Individual Processing** or use Transaction KGI2. Figure 7.29 shows the overheads for a single production order. Ten percent has been applied to the raw material costs to give an overhead of 55.22 Euros.

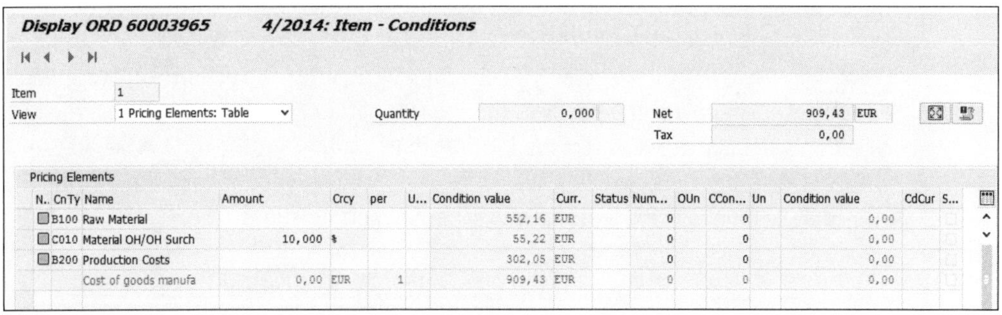

Figure 7.29 Overhead Calculation for Production Order

The costing sheets are set up in Customizing, so the controller's main task after implementation is to make sure the percentage rates are still correct. You'll find this activity under **Current Settings** (see Figure 7.27). Figure 7.30 shows the percentages used to calculate the overhead in our example. Our production order (see Figure 7.28) contained the costing sheet COGM, which applied overhead under condition type C010. Condition C010 calculates overhead by overhead type (planned or actual) and overhead key. Our production order included overhead key SAP10, so a 10% overhead was applied.

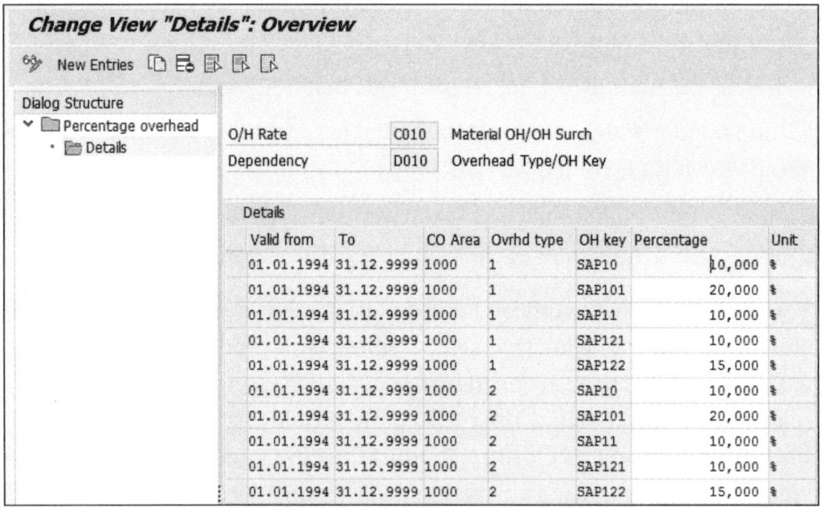

Valid from	To	CO Area	Ovrhd type	OH key	Percentage	Unit
01.01.1994	31.12.9999	1000	1	SAP10	10,000	%
01.01.1994	31.12.9999	1000	1	SAP101	20,000	%
01.01.1994	31.12.9999	1000	1	SAP11	10,000	%
01.01.1994	31.12.9999	1000	1	SAP121	10,000	%
01.01.1994	31.12.9999	1000	1	SAP122	15,000	%
01.01.1994	31.12.9999	1000	2	SAP10	10,000	%
01.01.1994	31.12.9999	1000	2	SAP101	20,000	%
01.01.1994	31.12.9999	1000	2	SAP11	10,000	%
01.01.1994	31.12.9999	1000	2	SAP121	10,000	%
01.01.1994	31.12.9999	1000	2	SAP122	15,000	%

Figure 7.30 Overhead Percentages in Costing Sheet

Event-Based Overhead Calculation

When we discussed direct activity allocations in Chapter 6, Section 6.4, we mentioned the ability to use the business function CO_ALLOCATIONS to calculate overhead as soon as the activity was recorded rather than waiting until period close. In SAP S/4HANA, this business function was extended to allow you to calculate overhead immediately for goods movements and other financial postings.

Template Allocation

If you think this type of percentage overhead is too simplistic for your business needs or you're having trouble calculating a percentage that will result in all costs being charged to the production orders, consider using template allocation for some of your overhead. This will allow you to calculate overhead using much more complex drivers and to clear all costs on the cost center at the end of the period. It's especially useful if you need to make sure that the outstanding balance on your cost centers is zero at the end of the period (a legal requirement in some parts of the world). We'll look at this in more detail in Chapter 11.

7.2.2 Work in Process

As we discussed in Chapter 1, WIP is a source of much confusion. In any multilevel bill of material, there are raw materials, semifinished products, and finished products. Production orders are created for each step that results in a product being delivered to *inventory*. Work in process occurs when an order to create a product has been started but not completed at period close. During production, all values on the production order are considered *expenses* until we move them to the balance sheet as *work in process* at period close. There are two basic ways of handling WIP:

1. **WIP at actual costs**
   WIP is calculated by subtracting the value of any deliveries to stock from the actual costs. Some organizations configure the WIP by cost element type and capitalize only part of the conversion costs. WIP is calculated afresh in each period until the order has the status **Final Delivery** or **Technically Completed** (see Chapter 3, Section 3.8.2). When you calculate the WIP in the next period, the last WIP is canceled.

   You have to use this method if you have coproducts, but you can't use it with product cost collectors or cost object hierarchies. If you have very long-running production orders, be aware that taking the actual costs as the basis means that variances are capitalized along with the WIP. If your variances are substantial and you use the Material Ledger, consider activating WIP revaluation via the material ledger to separate the initial valuation and the variance cleanly, as described in SAP Note 608162.

2. **WIP at target costs**
   WIP is calculated by taking the standard costs for each operation completed from the standard cost estimate, the cost estimate for the product cost collector, or another cost estimate created for this purpose. This approach relies on the existence of detailed values per operation, so you can't use this method with coproducts (because there's only a settlement of the amounts to the coproducts). Some organizations prefer this method because it avoids an overstatement of WIP. It can also be used in combination with WIP revaluation via the material ledger.

Before you calculate WIP for the first time, you should check that the production orders contain a results analysis key (see Figure 7.28). The settings are Customizing activities and can't be adjusted for reasons of consistency. When you calculate WIP, you'll be required to enter a results analysis version. Normally, you only need to enter version 0 for the legal valuation of your WIP. You may find that your organization has additional versions if you use group valuation or transfer price valuation or if you have activated parallel valuation of cost of goods manufactured. In such cases, it makes sense to calculate WIP for all results analysis versions.

To execute WIP, follow the menu path **Accounting • Controlling • Product Cost Controlling • Cost Object Controlling • Product Cost by Order • Period-End Closing • Single Functions • Work in Process • Individual Processing • Calculate** or use Transaction KKAX. Enter the order number, the period, the fiscal year, and the results analysis version(s) and click on **Execute**. Figure 7.31 shows the result of WIP calculation for a production order. The figure in the **WIP (Cumulated)** column is the WIP for the complete lifecycle of the order. The figure in the **WIP (Period)** column is the increase/decrease in WIP in that period. In our example, the production order was created in the same period as the WIP calculation, so the two figures are identical. This process of calculating the additional WIP in each period continues until the order is complete (in other words, has the status **Final Delivery** or **Technically Complete**). When you calculate WIP in the period that follows, the WIP is canceled.

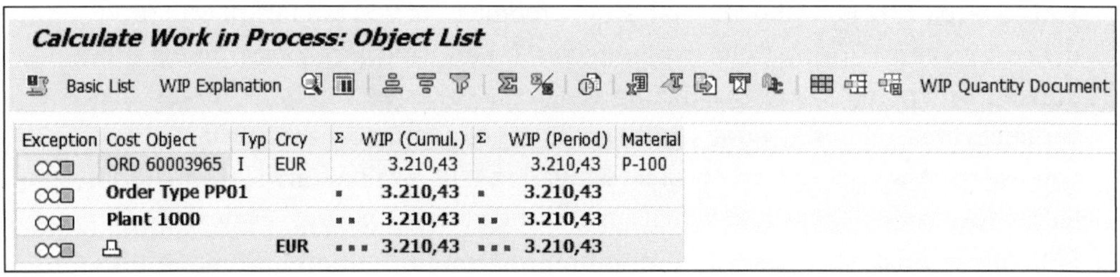

Figure 7.31 WIP Calculation for Production Order

Depending on your configuration, the WIP can be separated and stored under different results analysis cost elements depending on the underlying costs, such as raw material costs, production costs, and overhead. To check how your WIP has been stored, follow the menu path **Accounting • Controlling • Product Cost Controlling • Cost Object Controlling • Product Cost by Order • Information System • Reports for Product Cost by Order • Detailed Reports • For Orders** or use Transaction KKBC_ORD. Enter the order number and switch the layout to 1SAP03 (**Work in Process**). Figure 7.32 shows the results analysis cost elements that store these values in CO. Notice that they all begin with 672, distinct from the original cost elements under which the costs were first recorded in CO.

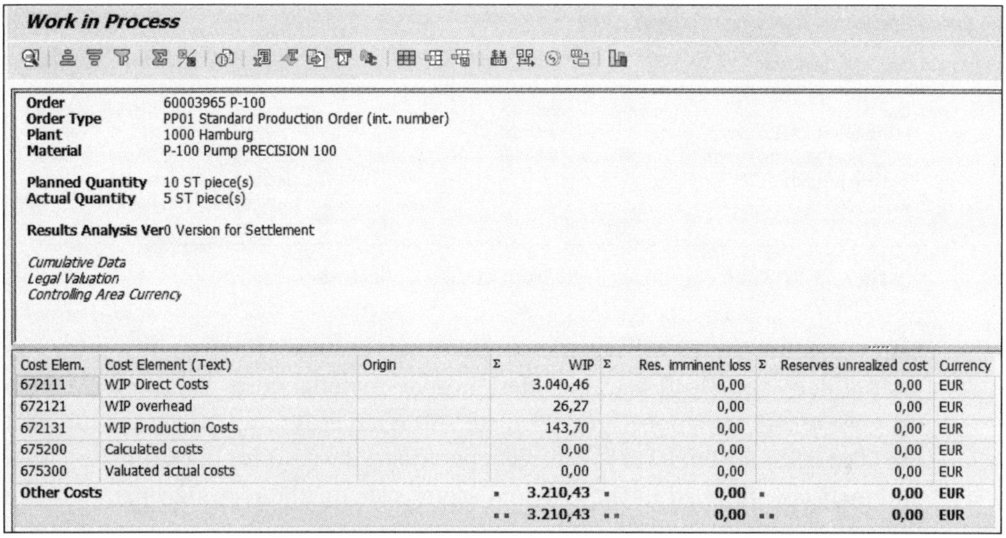

Cost Elem.	Cost Element (Text)	Origin	Σ	WIP	Σ	Res. imminent loss	Σ	Reserves unrealized cost	Currency
672111	WIP Direct Costs			3.040,46		0,00		0,00	EUR
672121	WIP overhead			26,27		0,00		0,00	EUR
672131	WIP Production Costs			143,70		0,00		0,00	EUR
675200	Calculated costs			0,00		0,00		0,00	EUR
675300	Valuated actual costs			0,00		0,00		0,00	EUR
Other Costs			•	**3.210,43**	•	**0,00**	•	**0,00**	**EUR**
			••	**3.210,43**	••	**0,00**	••	**0,00**	**EUR**

Figure 7.32 Work in Process: Detail Report

You can also access this report by selecting the order line and clicking on the **WIP Report** button shown in Figure 7.31 and then changing the layout to **Work in Process** once you get into the report. When you calculate WIP at actual costs, the **WIP Explanation** button doesn't work (you'll see it when we calculate WIP at target in the next section). The **WIP Quantity Document** button only works in conjunction with the Material Ledger. This shows the initial valuation of the work in process and creates items for all material issues and confirmations made during the period. Variances will be assigned to these WIP items when you execute the periodic costing run (Section 7.3.2).

But first, let's calculate WIP for production orders that don't carry their own costs but have been created with reference to a product cost collector (see Chapter 3 and Chapter 6). To calculate WIP, follow the menu path **Accounting • Controlling • Product Cost Controlling • Cost Object Controlling • Product Cost by Period • Period-End Closing • Single Functions • Work in Process • Individual Processing • Calculate** or use Transaction KKAS. Enter the material, plant, and, if multiple production versions exist for the material, the production process along with the period, fiscal year, and results analysis version(s) and click on **Execute**. Figure 7.33 shows the result of WIP calculation for the two product cost collectors that we originally created in Chapter 3, Section 3.6. To view the details by operation, select one of the product cost collector lines and click on the **WIP Explanation** button.

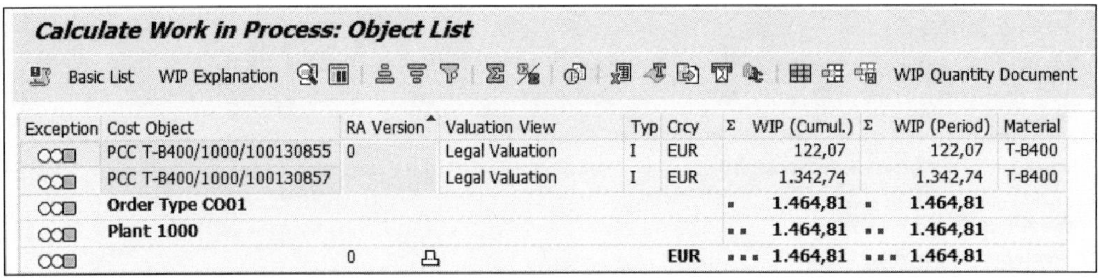

Calculate Work in Process: Object List

Basic List WIP Explanation WIP Quantity Document

Exception	Cost Object	RA Version	Valuation View	Typ	Crcy	Σ WIP (Cumul.)	Σ WIP (Period)	Material
OOO	PCC T-B400/1000/100130855	0	Legal Valuation	I	EUR	122,07	122,07	T-B400
OOO	PCC T-B400/1000/100130857		Legal Valuation	I	EUR	1.342,74	1.342,74	T-B400
OOO	**Order Type CO01**					▪ **1.464,81**	▪ **1.464,81**	
OOO	**Plant 1000**					▪▪ **1.464,81**	▪▪ **1.464,81**	
OOO		0			**EUR**	▪▪▪ **1.464,81**	▪▪▪ **1.464,81**	

Figure 7.33 WIP Calculation for Two Product Cost Collectors

Figure 7.34 shows the WIP by operation. Note that because of the way the routing was set up, operation 0010 also includes the raw material costs for the BOM item assigned to that operation. If you calculate WIP at target, it's important to ensure that the BOM items are linked to the correct operations: the costs for the raw material are automatically included in the WIP and scrap costs for the relevant operation (see Chapter 4).

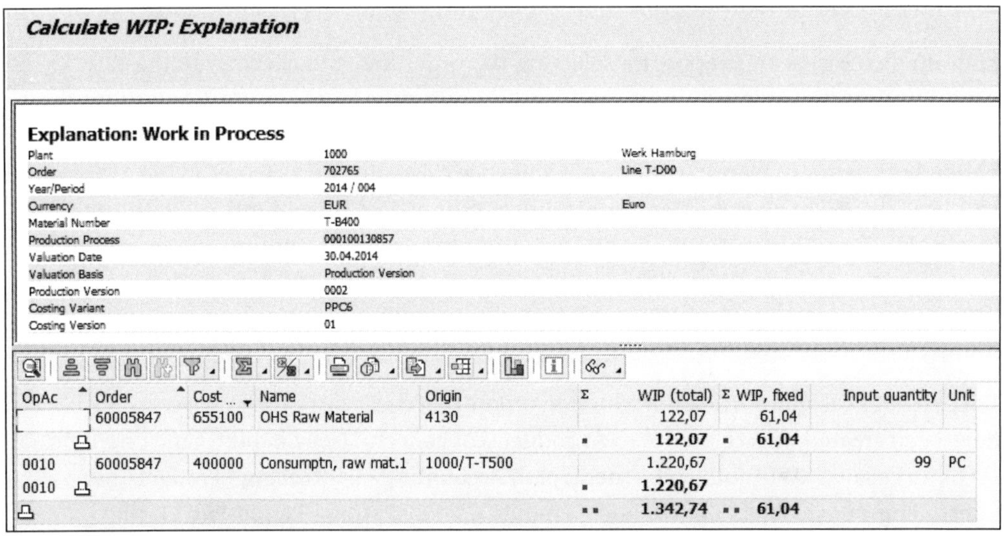

Calculate WIP: Explanation

Explanation: Work in Process

Plant	1000	Werk Hamburg
Order	702765	Line T-D00
Year/Period	2014 / 004	
Currency	EUR	Euro
Material Number	T-B400	
Production Process	000100130857	
Valuation Date	30.04.2014	
Valuation Basis	Production Version	
Production Version	0002	
Costing Variant	PPC6	
Costing Version	01	

OpAc	Order	Cost ...	Name	Origin	Σ	WIP (total)	Σ WIP, fixed	Input quantity	Unit
	60005847	655100	OHS Raw Material	4130		122,07	61,04		
					▪	**122,07**	▪ **61,04**		
0010	60005847	400000	Consumptn, raw mat.1	1000/T-T500		1.220,67		99	PC
0010					▪	**1.220,67**			
					▪▪	**1.342,74**	▪▪ **61,04**		

Figure 7.34 WIP by Operation

7.2.3 Target Costs and Variances in Production

We already discussed how to calculate target costs and variances for each activity type on the cost centers. You take the same approach for the production orders, but this time the *order quantity* provides the basis for the calculation of target costs. If you're working with product cost by order, you generally cancel the WIP and then calculate target costs and variances on completion of the order. You're also required to enter one or more target cost versions. These are configured in Customizing, and the usual settings are as follows:

- Version 0 compares the *actual costs* on the order with the *standard costs* in the standard cost estimate. This target cost version explains the difference between the standard costs used to valuate inventory when the goods are delivered to stock with the actual costs. These values will be settled, meaning they'll be included in the Material Ledger and CO-PA. The settlement profile for your production order ensures that the settlement rule automatically generates distribution rules to the correct senders.
- Version 1 compares the *actual costs* on the order with the *planned costs* calculated when the order is created. This target cost version explains the variances that occur during production.
- Version 2 compares the *planned costs* when the order is created with the *standard costs* in the standard cost estimate. This target cost version explains the variances that occur between the time of the standard cost estimate (planning) and order creation.

Note that these versions are not the same as the versions that store group valuation, profit center valuation, or parallel cost of goods manufactured. Production variances are only calculated in legal valuation.

Target Cost Calculation in SAP S/4HANA

From SAP S/4HANA 1610, you will be able to see the target costs in an SAP Fiori application called Production Cost Analysis. This app displays the target and actual costs per manufacturing order, together with any exceptions. It also displays the costs per work center and operation, information that is available during confirmation but isn't stored in the SAP ERP tables and therefore is difficult to report on. We'll look at the changes in detail in Chapter 14.

To calculate production variances, follow the menu path **Accounting • Controlling • Product Cost Controlling • Cost Object Controlling • Product Cost by Order • Period-End Closing • Single Functions • Variances • Individual Processing • Calculate** or use Transaction KKS2. Enter the order number, the period and fiscal year, and the target cost version(s) and click on **Execute**. Figure 7.35 shows the result of variance calculation on the production order in target cost version 0. To see the details, we selected the order line and clicked on the **Cost Elements** button. What we're looking at is a comparison of the actual costs for the order with the standard costs to produce the delivered quantity. Because the order is complete, there's no WIP.

Just as you saw earlier for the activity quantities on the cost center, the production variances are assigned to variance categories. To display the variance categories, switch the layout for the report in Figure 7.35 to **Variance Categories**. Figure 7.36 shows the variance categories for our production order.

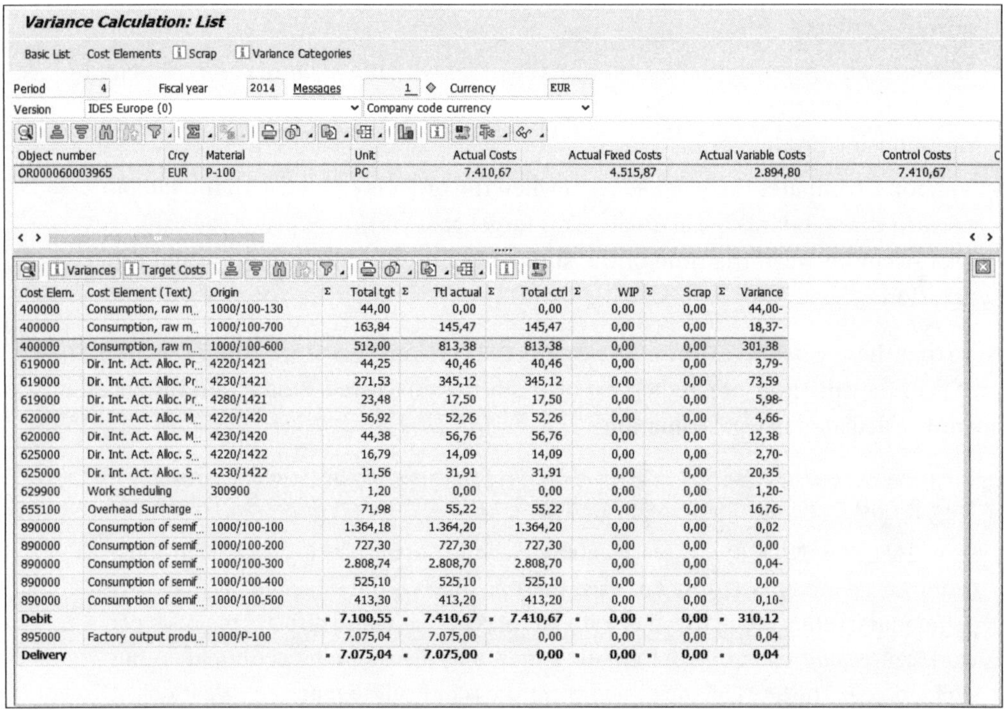

Object number	Crcy	Material	Unit	Actual Costs	Actual Fixed Costs	Actual Variable Costs	Control Costs
OR000060003965	EUR	P-100	PC	7.410,67	4.515,87	2.894,80	7.410,67

Cost Elem.	Cost Element (Text)	Origin	Σ Total tgt	Σ Ttl actual	Σ Total ctrl	Σ WIP	Σ Scrap	Σ Variance
400000	Consumption, raw m...	1000/100-130	44,00	0,00	0,00	0,00	0,00	44,00-
400000	Consumption, raw m...	1000/100-700	163,84	145,47	145,47	0,00	0,00	18,37-
400000	Consumption, raw m...	1000/100-600	512,00	813,38	813,38	0,00	0,00	301,38
619000	Dir. Int. Act. Alloc. Pr...	4220/1421	44,25	40,46	40,46	0,00	0,00	3,79-
619000	Dir. Int. Act. Alloc. Pr...	4230/1421	271,53	345,12	345,12	0,00	0,00	73,59
619000	Dir. Int. Act. Alloc. Pr...	4280/1421	23,48	17,50	17,50	0,00	0,00	5,98-
620000	Dir. Int. Act. Alloc. M...	4220/1420	56,92	52,26	52,26	0,00	0,00	4,66-
620000	Dir. Int. Act. Alloc. M...	4230/1420	44,38	56,76	56,76	0,00	0,00	12,38
625000	Dir. Int. Act. Alloc. S...	4220/1422	16,79	14,09	14,09	0,00	0,00	2,70-
625000	Dir. Int. Act. Alloc. S...	4230/1422	11,56	31,91	31,91	0,00	0,00	20,35
629900	Work scheduling	300900	1,20	0,00	0,00	0,00	0,00	1,20-
655100	Overhead Surcharge ...		71,98	55,22	55,22	0,00	0,00	16,76-
890000	Consumption of semif...	1000/100-100	1.364,18	1.364,20	1.364,20	0,00	0,00	0,02
890000	Consumption of semif...	1000/100-200	727,30	727,30	727,30	0,00	0,00	0,00
890000	Consumption of semif...	1000/100-300	2.808,74	2.808,70	2.808,70	0,00	0,00	0,04-
890000	Consumption of semif...	1000/100-400	525,10	525,10	525,10	0,00	0,00	0,00
890000	Consumption of semif...	1000/100-500	413,30	413,20	413,20	0,00	0,00	0,10-
Debit			**7.100,55**	**7.410,67**	**7.410,67**	**0,00**	**0,00**	**310,12**
895000	Factory output produ...	1000/P-100	7.075,04	7.075,00	0,00	0,00	0,00	0,04
Delivery			**7.075,04**	**7.075,00**	**0,00**	**0,00**	**0,00**	**0,04**

Figure 7.35 Total Variances on Production Order

The following are the input variances:

- **Input price variances**
  These occur because of changes to the material prices and activity prices.
- **Input quantity variances**
  These occur when using a different quantity of a material or activity.

- **Resource-usage variances**
  These occur if an operation has to be performed at a different work center or a material has to be replaced as a result of material shortages.
- **Remaining variances**
  This is a catchall for any unassigned variances.

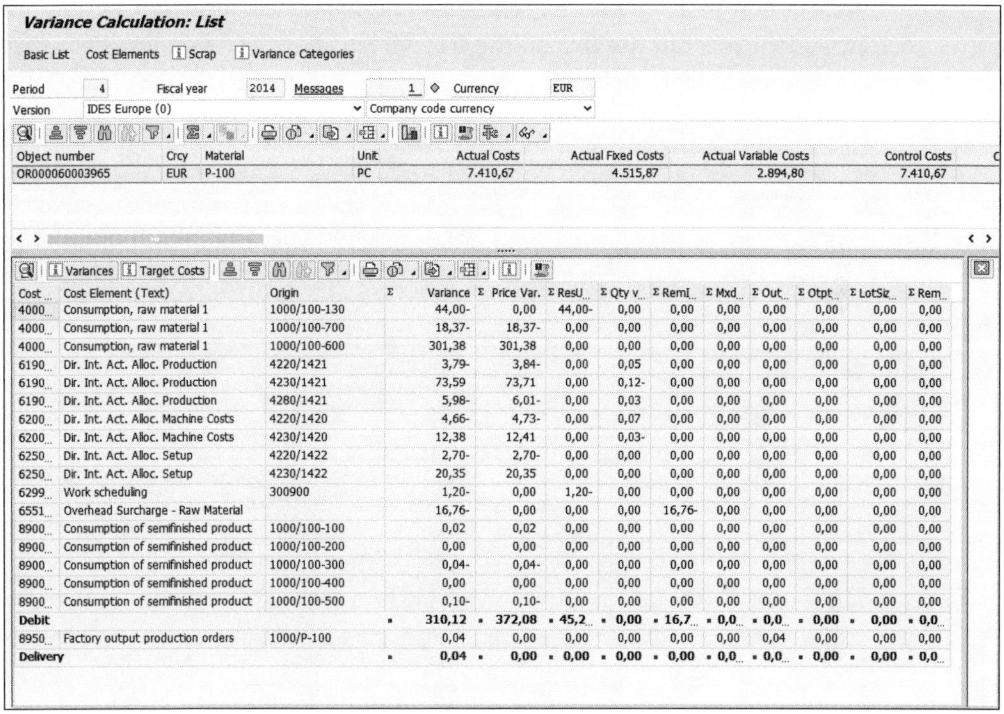

Variance Calculation: List

Basic List | Cost Elements | Scrap | Variance Categories

Period 4 | Fiscal year 2014 | Messages 1 | Currency EUR
Version IDES Europe (0) | Company code currency

Object number	Crcy	Material	Unit	Actual Costs	Actual Fixed Costs	Actual Variable Costs	Control Costs
OR000060003965	EUR	P-100	PC	7.410,67	4.515,87	2.894,80	7.410,67

Variances | Target Costs

Cost ...	Cost Element (Text)	Origin	Σ	Variance	Σ Price Var.	Σ ResU...	Σ Qty v...	Σ RemI...	Σ Mxd...	Σ Out...	Σ Otpt...	Σ LotSiz...	Σ Rem...
4000...	Consumption, raw material 1	1000/100-130		44,00-	0,00	44,00-	0,00	0,00	0,00	0,00	0,00	0,00	0,00
4000...	Consumption, raw material 1	1000/100-700		18,37-	18,37-	0,00	0,00	0,00	0,00	0,00	0,00	0,00	0,00
4000...	Consumption, raw material 1	1000/100-600		301,38	301,38	0,00	0,00	0,00	0,00	0,00	0,00	0,00	0,00
6190...	Dir. Int. Act. Alloc. Production	4220/1421		3,79-	3,84-	0,00	0,05	0,00	0,00	0,00	0,00	0,00	0,00
6190...	Dir. Int. Act. Alloc. Production	4230/1421		73,59	73,71	0,00	0,12-	0,00	0,00	0,00	0,00	0,00	0,00
6190...	Dir. Int. Act. Alloc. Production	4280/1421		5,98-	6,01-	0,00	0,03	0,00	0,00	0,00	0,00	0,00	0,00
6200...	Dir. Int. Act. Alloc. Machine Costs	4220/1420		4,66-	4,73-	0,00	0,07	0,00	0,00	0,00	0,00	0,00	0,00
6200...	Dir. Int. Act. Alloc. Machine Costs	4230/1420		12,38	12,41	0,00	0,03-	0,00	0,00	0,00	0,00	0,00	0,00
6250...	Dir. Int. Act. Alloc. Setup	4220/1422		2,70-	2,70-	0,00	0,00	0,00	0,00	0,00	0,00	0,00	0,00
6250...	Dir. Int. Act. Alloc. Setup	4230/1422		20,35	20,35	0,00	0,00	0,00	0,00	0,00	0,00	0,00	0,00
6299...	Work scheduling	300900		1,20-	0,00	1,20-	0,00	0,00	0,00	0,00	0,00	0,00	0,00
6551...	Overhead Surcharge - Raw Material			16,76-	0,00	0,00	0,00	16,76-	0,00	0,00	0,00	0,00	0,00
8900...	Consumption of semifinished product	1000/100-100		0,02	0,02	0,00	0,00	0,00	0,00	0,00	0,00	0,00	0,00
8900...	Consumption of semifinished product	1000/100-200		0,00	0,00	0,00	0,00	0,00	0,00	0,00	0,00	0,00	0,00
8900...	Consumption of semifinished product	1000/100-300		0,04-	0,04-	0,00	0,00	0,00	0,00	0,00	0,00	0,00	0,00
8900...	Consumption of semifinished product	1000/100-400		0,00	0,00	0,00	0,00	0,00	0,00	0,00	0,00	0,00	0,00
8900...	Consumption of semifinished product	1000/100-500		0,10-	0,10-	0,00	0,00	0,00	0,00	0,00	0,00	0,00	0,00
Debit			▪	**310,12**	**372,08**	**45,2...**	**0,00**	**16,7...**	**0,0...**	**0,0...**	**0,00**	**0,00**	**0,0...**
8950...	Factory output production orders	1000/P-100		0,04	0,00	0,00	0,00	0,00	0,00	0,04	0,00	0,00	0,00
Delivery			▪	**0,04**	**0,00**	**0,00**	**0,00**	**0,00**	**0,0...**	**0,0...**	**0,00**	**0,00**	**0,0...**

Figure 7.36 Variance Categories for Production Order

The following are the output variances:

- **Output price variances**
  These occur if the standard cost is not used for stock valuation.
- **Mixed price variances**
  These occur if the standard costs were calculated by weighting several cost estimates (see Chapter 5).
- **Lot size variances**
  These occur if the lot size for the order differs from the lot size in the standard cost estimate.

- **Remaining variances**
  This is a catchall for any unassigned variances.

The third line in the list (consumption of material 100-600) shows an exceptionally high variance. To analyze this in more detail, select the line and click on the **Variances** button. Figure 7.37 shows the details of this variance. Again, we see the input price variance, but now we have a full explanation of how variance calculation performed the calculation. You can use this button to perform spot checks on any lines that seem to be unreasonably high.

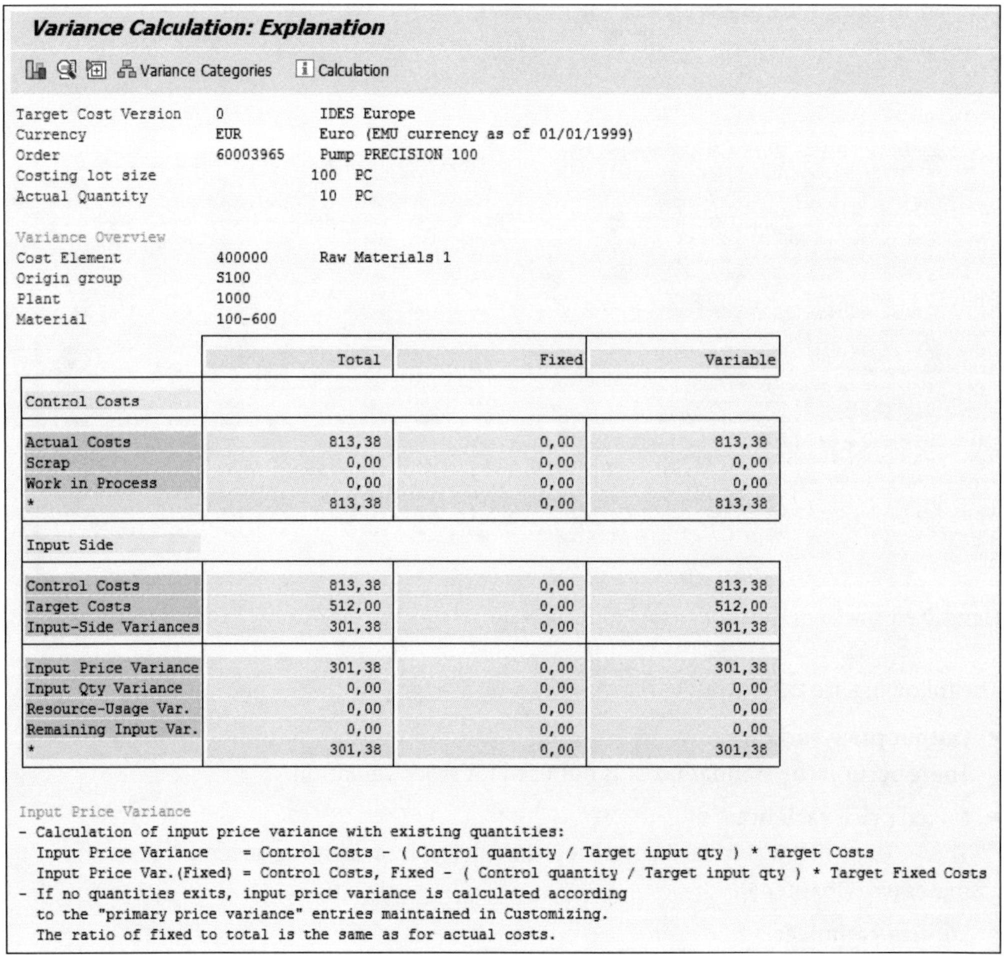

Figure 7.37 Explanation of Production Variances

If you're working with product cost collectors, you'll generally find work in process, variances, and scrap in the same period because for any given production version some orders are in process and some complete in that period. To calculate variances, follow the menu path **Accounting • Controlling • Product Cost Controlling • Cost Object Controlling • Product Cost by Period • Period-End Closing • Single Functions • Variances • Individual Processing • Calculate** or use Transaction KKS6. Enter the material, plant, and, if multiple production versions exist for the material, the production process, along with the period, fiscal year, and target cost version(s), and click on **Execute**. The only difference compared to product cost by order is that the planned costs are calculated for the product cost collector rather than the individual production order. Figure 7.38 shows the result of variance calculation for two product cost collectors. Again, we've selected the product cost collector line and clicked on the **Cost Elements** button. This time, we see the figure for WIP from the previous step, the variances, and the value of the scrap. The variances are split into variance categories, as for product cost by order.

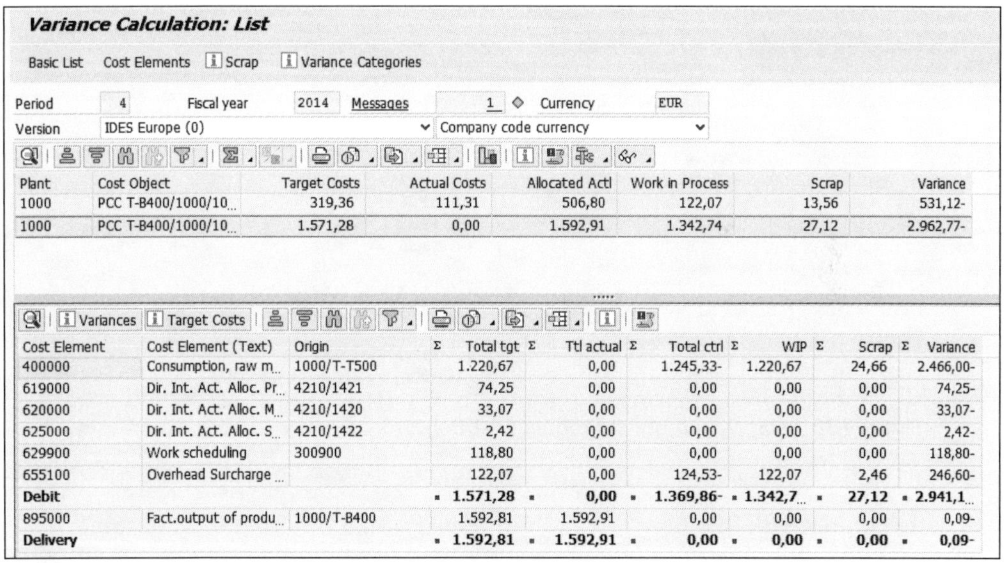

Figure 7.38 Variances on Product Cost Collectors

To see details of the value of the scrap, select the product cost collector line and click on the **Scrap** button. Figure 7.39 shows that scrap quantities were confirmed at operations 0040 and 0060. In our example, there was no planned scrap, so the whole scrap quantity is valued with the standard costs for that operation. However, sometimes a planned scrap quantity is included in the cost estimate. If this is the case, the planned scrap quantity is subtracted from the actual scrap quantity and the *difference* used to value the scrapped items. The scrap also will be updated to the balance sheet as a production variance when the product cost collector is settled.

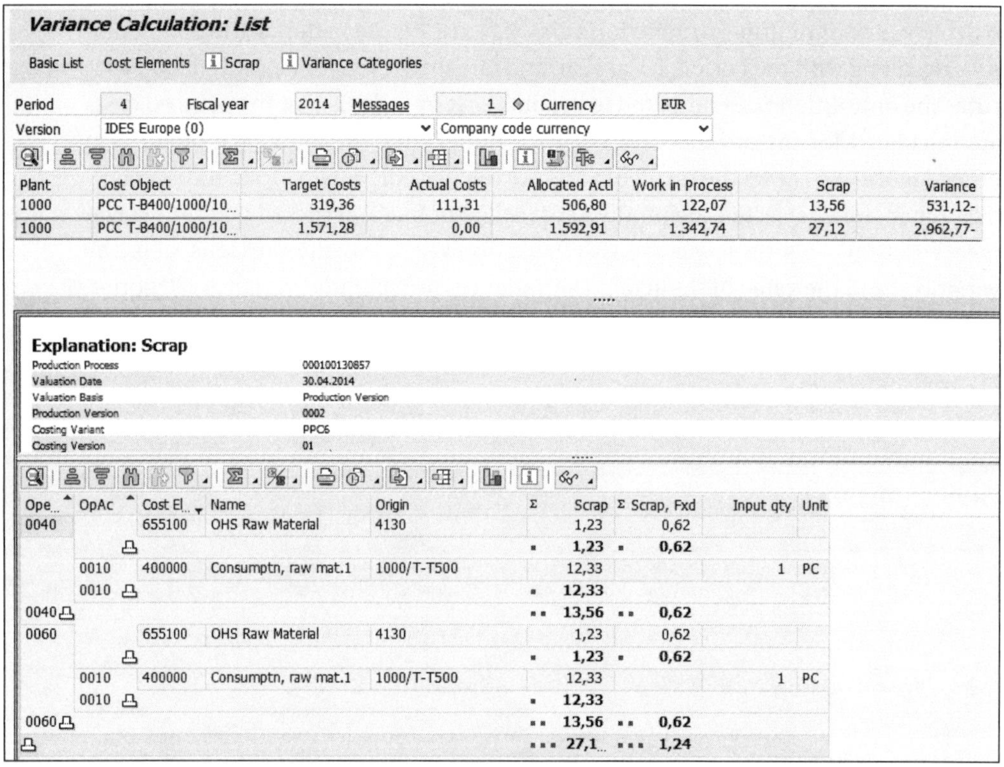

Figure 7.39 Scrap Valuation for Product Cost Collector

7.2.4 Settlement

The final step in cost object controlling is to settle the orders and product cost collectors. We looked at this process for production orders when we settled during the plan-to-manufacture process in Chapter 6. We'll now complete the process for our production cost collector and look at the postings in detail. To run settlement, follow the menu path **Accounting • Controlling • Product Cost Controlling • Cost Object Controlling • Product Cost by Period • Period-End Closing • Single Functions • Settlement •**

Individual Processing or use Transaction KK87. Enter the material, plant, and, if multiple production versions exist for the material, the production process, along with the period and fiscal year, and click on **Execute**. Figure 7.40 shows the result of settlement. The variances have been posted to stock as a total value and to **Profitability Analysis** split by the variance categories. To see the breakdown by variance category in more detail, select the profitability segment (**PSG**) line and click on the **Receiver** button.

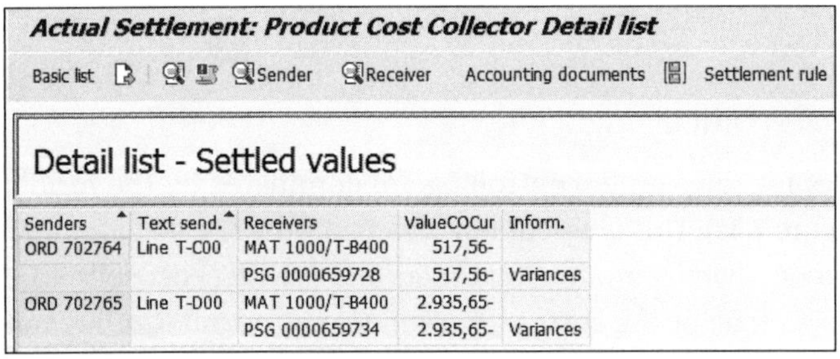
Actual Settlement: Product Cost Collector Detail list

Basic list | Sender | Receiver | Accounting documents | Settlement rule

Detail list - Settled values

Senders	Text send.	Receivers	ValueCOCur	Inform.
ORD 702764	Line T-C00	MAT 1000/T-B400	517,56-	
		PSG 0000659728	517,56-	Variances
ORD 702765	Line T-D00	MAT 1000/T-B400	2.935,65-	
		PSG 0000659734	2.935,65-	Variances

Figure 7.40 Settlement of the Product Cost Collector-Settled Values

Figure 7.41 shows the variance categories on our product cost collector. These correspond to the variance categories in Figure 7.36. Here we're settling input price variances (PRIV), input quantity variances (QTYV), resource usage variances (RSUV), remaining input variances (INPV), output price variances (OPPV), lot size variances (LSFV), remaining variances (REMV), and scrap (SCRP). Doing so will apply these variance categories to the relevant value fields in Profitability Analysis (the PSG receiver lines in Figure 7.41).

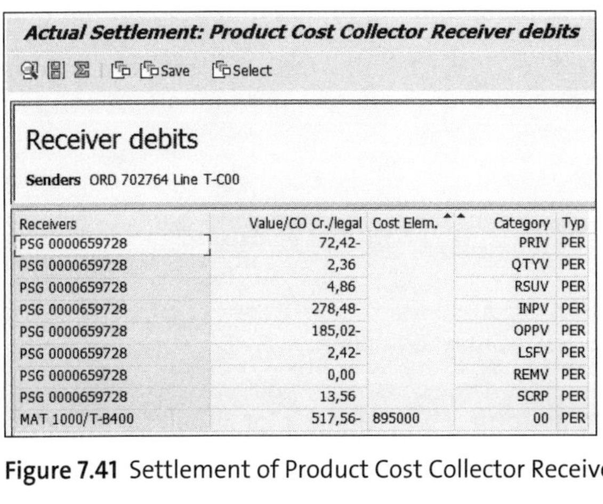
Actual Settlement: Product Cost Collector Receiver debits

Save | Select

Receiver debits

Senders ORD 702764 Line T-C00

Receivers	Value/CO Cr./legal	Cost Elem.	Category	Typ
PSG 0000659728	72,42-		PRIV	PER
PSG 0000659728	2,36		QTYV	PER
PSG 0000659728	4,86		RSUV	PER
PSG 0000659728	278,48-		INPV	PER
PSG 0000659728	185,02-		OPPV	PER
PSG 0000659728	2,42-		LSFV	PER
PSG 0000659728	0,00		REMV	PER
PSG 0000659728	13,56		SCRP	PER
MAT 1000/T-B400	517,56-	895000	00	PER

Figure 7.41 Settlement of Product Cost Collector Receiver Debits

Settlement of Variances in SAP S/4HANA

In SAP ERP, account-based CO-PA will only show the total variance (the material line in Figure 7.41); you will need to use costing-based CO-PA to see the detailed view of the variance categories (the PSG lines in Figure 7.41). In SAP S/4HANA, you can break out the total variance into separate accounts for each variance category to give you this level of detail in the income statement. We'll explain how this process works in Chapter 14.

7.2.5 Product Cost by Sales Order

The period-close activities for sales order controlling are dominated by the results analysis activities (see Figure 7.42). This is essentially a variant on WIP calculation for orders that also carry revenue (which production orders and product cost collectors do not). The basic idea is to look at the costs and revenues on the sales order and determine what part of that cost is WIP and what part is cost of goods sold.

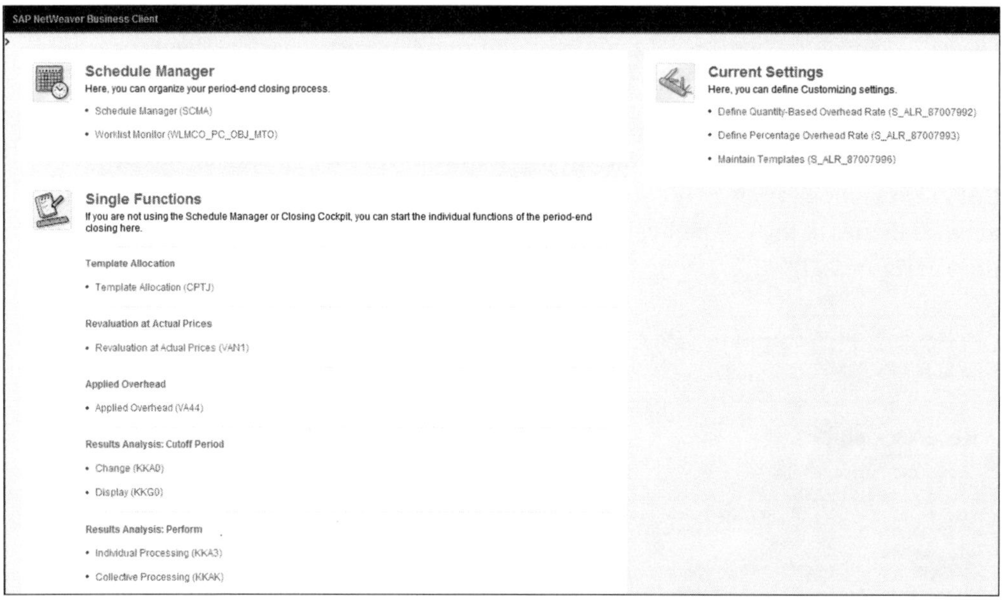

Figure 7.42 Period-Close Activities for Sales Order Controlling

In releases prior to 4.0, you had to perform results analysis for all sales orders with make-to-order production. From Release 4.0 onward, the approach varies depending on whether you're using sales order stock or not and whether the sales order carries costs over and above the manufacturing costs being captured on the assigned production orders (see Chapter 6). Currently, the following options exist:

- **Make to order without sales order controlling**
  Here the production order is created with reference to the sales order item, as you saw in Chapter 6, Section 6.3.3. All costs are captured on the production order, and WIP and variance calculation take place for the production order. Sales controlling takes place in Profitability Analysis. The only difference from the process described in Section 7.2.2 is that the final delivery is made to sales order stock rather than neutral stock.
- **Make to order with sales order controlling and valuated sales order stock**
  If there's a business requirement to capture special sales or marketing costs by sales order item or calculate reserves or the value of goods in transit, the requirements type for the sales order item can be configured to allow the sales order item to carry costs. In this case, you also need to define a revenue element for your revenue postings (see Chapter 3). The production orders still deliver to sales order stock and WIP, and variances are calculated for the production orders, but results analysis can be used to create reserves or value goods in transit.
- **Make to order with sales order controlling without valuated sales order stock**
  This was the only option prior to Release 4.0 and is still used by some companies even after an upgrade. It's still the only option for sales orders with no inventory, such as consulting projects. Because all costs on the production orders and sales order items are considered expenses (rather than inventory), there is a need to capitalize WIP. You perform results analysis by sales order item. This process selects all revenues and costs associated with the sales order item. Several approaches exist depending on your configuration, based on either the percentage of completion approach or the completed contract approach.

  In the *percentage of completion* approach, the costs incurred or the quantity completed is used to determine the degree of completion of the sales order item. The revenue appropriate to this degree of completion is then calculated and compared with the billing for the sales order item. If the calculated revenue is higher, a posting is made for *revenues in excess of billing*. If the calculated revenue is lower, a posting is made for *revenue surplus* (a type of reserve).

  In the *completed contract* approach, the revenue invoiced for is taken as the degree of completion for the sales order item. Some of the costs incurred are taken to be associated with that revenue and are treated as cost of goods sold, and the rest are treated as WIP. If costs appear to be missing in view of the revenue, *reserves for unrealized costs* are created.

Postings to Financial Accounting are made for revenues in excess of billing, revenue surplus and/or WIP, and reserves for unrealized costs. We discussed the posting rules and the accounts associated with these postings when we looked at the accounting master data for work in process in Chapter 4.

Event-Based Revenue Recognition in SAP S/4HANA

Although results analysis is always performed at period close, SAP S/4HANA provides new options for event-based revenue recognition. With this approach, each time an employee records time to a commercial project, the system will use the planned values to calculate the accrued revenue to be recorded for the project. At period close, these values will be trued up to reflect any changes to the project during the period. We'll look at this process in detail in Chapter 14.

Once you've settled all your production orders, product cost collectors, and sales orders, you've completed the closing steps in Cost Object Controlling. At this stage, there are still costs on your open production orders and sales orders, but you'll have created the necessary postings in your balance sheet to account for WIP. If your organization works with *standard costs*, you can skip the next section and go straight to the section on Profitability Analysis to complete your close. But if you use the Material Ledger, the next step is to perform your periodic costing run.

7.3 Multilevel Actual Costing in the Material Ledger

If your organization works with *actual costs*, the next stage is to pull together all the cost information gathered in the Material Ledger to provide the actual costs for all materials bought, manufactured, and sold in a period. Figure 7.43 shows the period-close activities for actual costing. We discussed distribution of usage variances in Chapter 6, Section 6.2. This does not need to be a period-close activity, especially if you perform cycle counts on a more regular basis, but if you haven't included inventory differences until now, the period close is the time to make sure that you've captured any known differences and assigned them to production. The costing run is always performed as part of the period close.

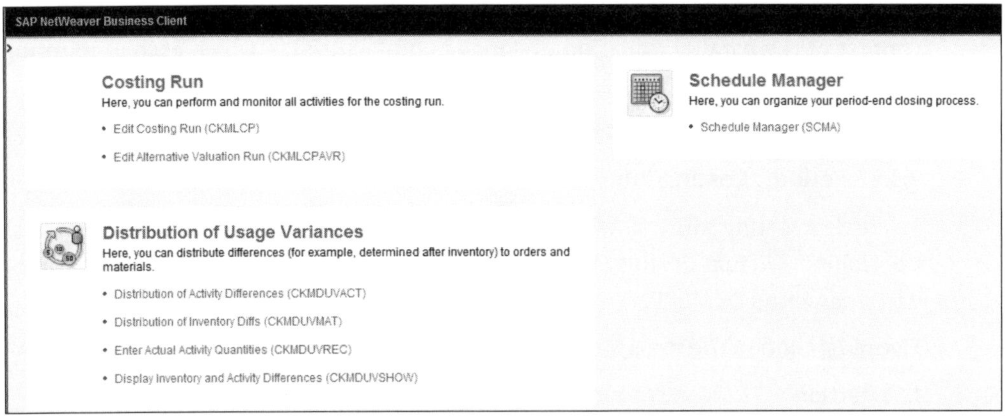

Figure 7.43 Actual Costing in Material Ledger

You may remember the term *costing run* from Chapter 5 when we looked at the process of calculating standard costs. There are a lot of similarities between the two costing runs. The main differences are that in planning you're working with planning data in the form of bills of material and routings, whereas at period close you're working with the actual goods movements and confirmations that took place during the period, all of which were stored in the Material Ledger, as you saw in Chapter 6. In planning, the prices are selected from the material master or purchasing info records, whereas at period close the values come from the invoices, goods movements, and settlements that were stored in the Material Ledger during the period.

7.3.1 Types of Costing Runs

There are two types of costing runs within the Material Ledger:

1. The *periodic costing run* is used to calculate the periodic unit price, sometimes known as a *weighted average price*. This run takes place once per period and is used to calculate the prices for the period just completed.
2. The *alternative valuation run* is used when material or activity prices are subject to seasonal variances that need to be smoothed, to reduce the effect of work in process and beginning and ending inventory on prices, or when material prices are subject to balance sheet adjustments (FIFO, LIFO, etc.). It's an *additional* costing run, taking as its starting point the quantity structure built based on goods movements during the periodic costing run.

More recently, a new form of alternative valuation run has been introduced in the context of the parallel valuation of goods manufactured in which each accounting principle is handled by a different run.

7.3.2 Periodic Costing Run

To create a costing run, follow the menu path **Accounting • Controlling • Product Cost Controlling • Actual Costing/Material Ledger • Actual Costing • Edit Costing Run** or use Transaction CKMLCP.

Figure 7.44 shows the steps in a periodic costing run:

1. **Selection**
   This step specifies which plants are to be included in the costing run. In general, it makes sense to include all plants in the same company code in one costing run. Because of the multilevel nature of the costing, it's not possible to exclude particular materials from a costing run as you can in standard costing. To perform actual costing for the cross-company example we looked at in Chapter 6, Section 6.5, you need to ensure that all relevant plants in the supply chain are included in the selection.
2. **Determine Sequence**
   This step checks the material inputs and outputs of each production process and determines the number of levels in the quantity structure. This step is needed to build the quantity structure for actual costing dynamically each period, especially for cyclical production structures and coproducts. It corresponds to the structure explosion step for standard costing and effectively determines the sequence that the multilevel price determination uses to roll actual costs through the structure.
3. **Single-Level Price Determination**
   This step calculates the periodic unit price for each material, accounting for price differences, revaluation differences, and exchange rate differences. It also determines the difference to be rolled through the quantity structure during the multilevel settlement. This step results in a new period status being set: **Single-Level Price Determination** (column **S** in Figure 7.44).
4. **Multilevel Price Determination**
   This step takes the difference calculated during the single-level settlement and passes it on to each material and procurement alternative in the quantity structure in turn. Note that this step handles goods movements arising from external procurement, subcontracting, and stock transfers, as well as in-house production.

After the multilevel settlement, you'll see a new material price and the cumulated price differences from the subordinate materials (multilevel price difference) for each material. In our cross-company example, this step also transfers the variance to the other company code, in which you'll see the difference in the group valuation and as a delta in the legal valuation. This step results in a new period status being set: **Multilevel Price Determination** (column **M** in Figure 7.44).

5. **Revaluation of Consumption**
   This step was added in Release 4.7 and is activated using the enterprise extension EA_FIN (see Appendix C at *www.sap-press.com/4691*). If you activate the appropriate movement type groups in configuration, it will update either the cost of goods sold account used to record the material movement or the sales order in a make-to-order scenario. This step results in a new period status being set: **Revaluation Of Consumption Completed** (column **R** in Figure 7.44).

6. **WIP Valuation**
   This step is offered if you have activated the WIP calculation described in SAP Note 608162. It makes sense to activate this option if you typically have large amounts of WIP at period close so that variances that really refer to the WIP are not mistakenly assigned to the goods that were finished in that period. If you have products for which no deliveries are made in a period, the values for the quantities that are still WIP will show up as unassigned variances unless you use this function to assign the variances to the WIP caught on the shop floor at period close.

7. **Post Closing**
   When you create closing entries, the system switches the price control in the material master from **S** (standard price) to **V** (periodic unit price) for the period closed, writes the price calculated to the material master as a new **V** price, and adjusts the balance sheet for the period closed. This step results in a new period status, **Closing Entry**, and must be completed before you start posting goods movements in the next period.

8. **Mark Material Prices**
   When we discussed the planning process in Chapter 5, we said that you can use the prices calculated in the Material Ledger as the standard costs for the next period, provided you can complete your closing activities quickly enough to have the new standard costs in place before the first goods movement was posted. The costing run can transfer the new prices to the material master (see Chapter 4) and set the status to **Marked**. The mechanism for picking these prices from the material master is then the same as for releasing the standard cost estimate.

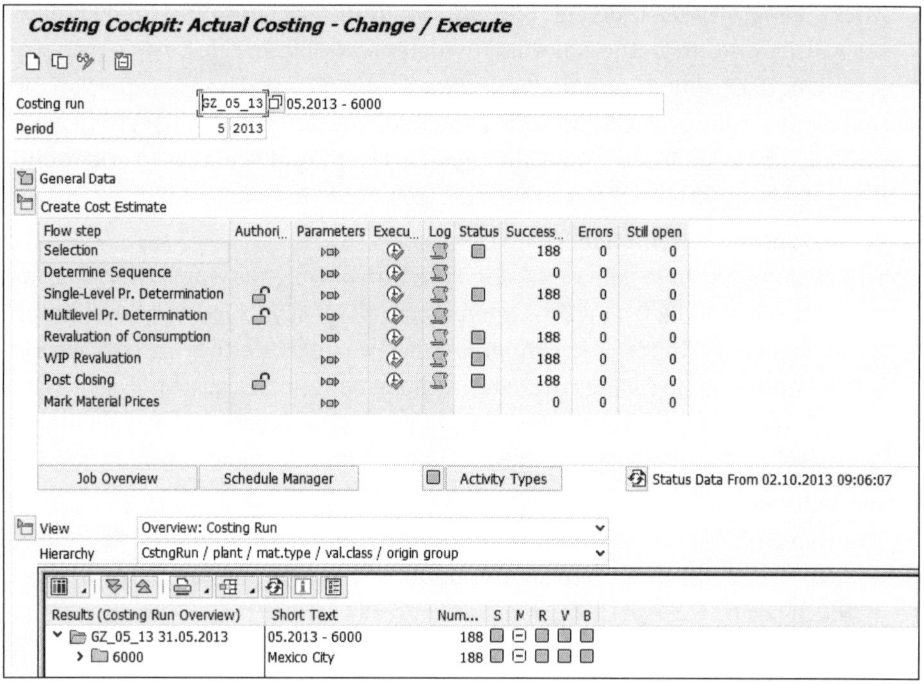

Figure 7.44 Steps in Periodic Costing Run

Also note the lock icons for the two **Price Determination** steps and the **Post Closing** step. Because these steps can have a significant impact on the balance sheet, you need to have rules in place about who can perform these steps and under what circumstances, as we discussed when we talked about process controls in Chapter 1.

As you saw for the standard costing run in Chapter 5, the **Execute** icon only appears when you've maintained the parameters for the step. On completion, you'll see an error log and a status for each step.

Costing Runs in SAP S/4HANA

In SAP S/4HANA, the same transaction is used to create periodic costing runs and alternative valuation runs. This costing run combines the **Single-Level Price Determination**, **Multi-Level Price Determination**, **Revaluation of Consumption**, and **WIP Revaluation** steps into a single step: **Settlement**. The **Determine Sequence** step in the periodic costing run and the **Cumulate** step in the alternative valuation run are combined and renamed to **Preparation**. We'll look at these changes in Chapter 14.

The name *Material Ledger* might lead you to think that only material movements are updated here, but there's also an **Activity Types** button in the costing run. Some countries have legal requirements for all production cost centers to be cleared at the end of each period, so the Material Ledger stores the activity prices for each cost center/ activity type combination in the period and can then clear the individual cost centers that have supplied production activities during a period.

To check the materials processed in each level, click on the line for the whole costing run or the line for one of the plants. A report, as shown in Figure 7.45, will appear. This report shows the current standard price for the material, the new periodic unit price, and the variance. The sum of the price variances tells you the impact of performing the **Post Closing** step on your balance sheet.

System Performance for a Costing Run

Because of the volume of materials handled in a periodic costing run, it's good to be aware of the sort of factors that affect the speed with which your costing run can execute. In general, it's the number of materials and not the number of Material Ledger documents that affect how long each step takes. In this context, a "material" is considered a material and plant (entry in table MBEW); a material, plant, sales order, and sales order item (entry in table EBEW); or a material, plant, and WBS element (entry in table QBEW). If you need to discuss system requirements with your IT department, you'll find details in SAP Note 668170.

Redesign of Data Model for Actual Costing in SAP S/4HANA

Improving performance was one of the drivers for the redesign of actual costing in SAP S/4HANA 1610. The data structure is simplified to store the required information in only two tables, one for the goods movements and their input/output relationships and another for the cost component split. The calculation logic is also vastly streamlined, taking substantial time out of the period-close process.

Occasionally, the controller discovers some errors in the costing run that need to be corrected before he makes the closing entries. He can correct these errors by making manual changes to the cost component split. To do so, select Transaction CKMCCD or **Accounting • Controlling • Product Cost Controlling • Actual Costing/Material Ledger • Material Ledger • Set Prices • Manual Change of Cost Component Split** (this transaction is only active if enterprise extension EA_FIN is active; see Appendix C at *www.sap-press.com/4691*). Figure 7.46 shows the initial screen once you've entered the relevant material, plant, and period. It looks almost identical to the material price analysis (or Transaction CKM3N), except that there are **Change** icons available. To change the base quantity, select **User Entry** in the **Base Quantity** field. To adjust the values for the beginning inventory or the receipts via purchase order, position the cursor on the relevant line and click on the **Change** icon.

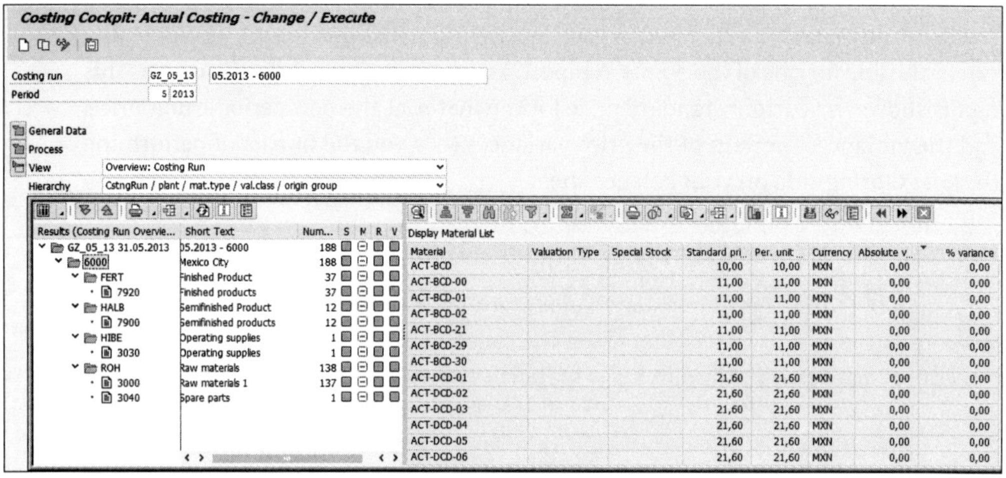

Figure 7.45 Material List for Costing Run

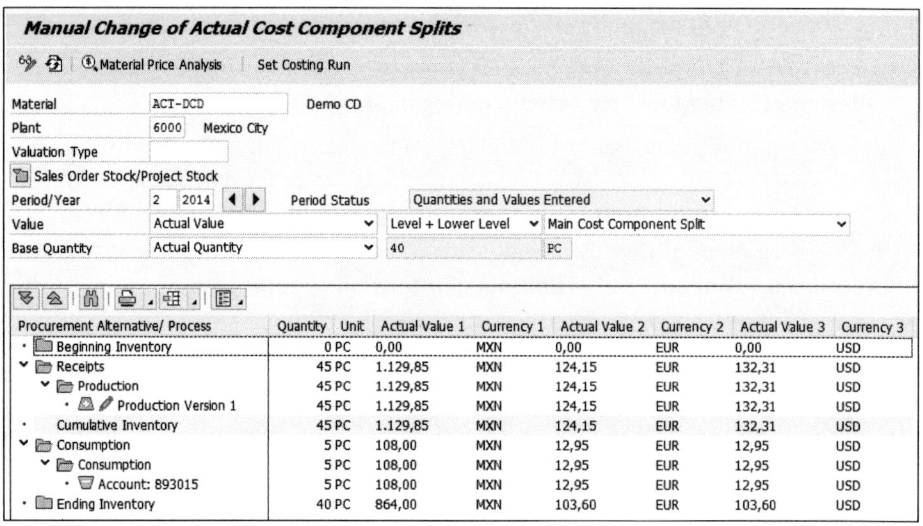

Figure 7.46 Cost Component Split for Material following Costing Run

Figure 7.47 shows a full cost component split for the chosen material. You can enter figures to correct data as required. Probably the most common change is not to change the totals but simply to shift the weighting between cost components. You can make corrections until the closing entries are made. To ensure consistency, after the status **Closing Entries Completed** has been set, the system won't allow you to make changes to the cost component split.

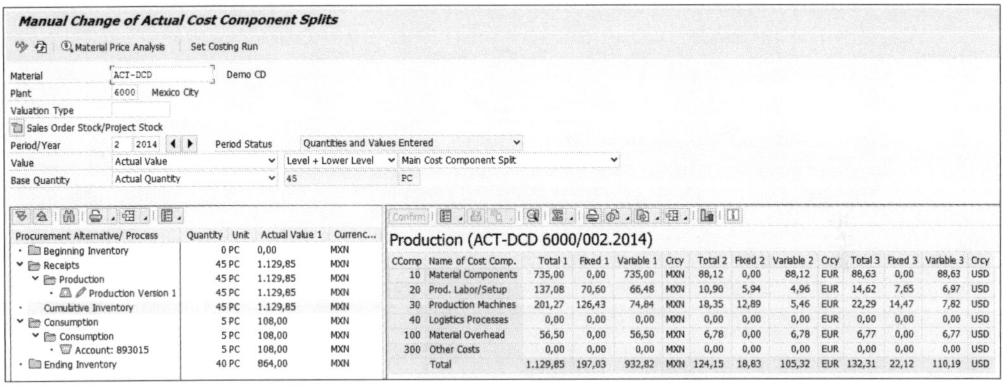

Figure 7.47 Adjusting Cost Component Split for Material

7.3.3 Alternative Valuation Run

To create an alternative valuation run, select Transaction CKMLCPAVR or **Accounting • Controlling • Product Cost Controlling • Actual Costing/Material Ledger • Actual Costing • Edit Alternative Valuation Run**.

Figure 7.48 shows the steps in an alternative valuation run. Some steps, such as **Selection**, are the same for both types of costing run, but the alternative valuation run includes several new steps:

1. **Cumulate Data**
   This step takes actual data from the original costing runs for the longer time frame, whether this is a quarter or year to date.
2. **Determine Actual Prices**
   This step cumulates activity prices, ensuring the full absorption of cost center costs even though the cost center activity output is zero in some periods (full absorption of cost center costs is a legal requirement in parts of South America). This step will only appear if the **Activity Update Relevant to Price Determination** checkbox was set when the Material Ledger was activated for the relevant plant

and replaces the use of Transaction CON2 to bring the activity prices into the inventory values.

3. **Determine Delta Postings**
   This step only applies if you flag the alternative valuation run as a posting run. The results of the alternative valuation run are compared with the current material valuation material by material. The difference is posted to a delta stock account that must be different from the normal stock to keep the new valuation separate from the operative valuation. The posting is automatically reversed with a key date in the next period.

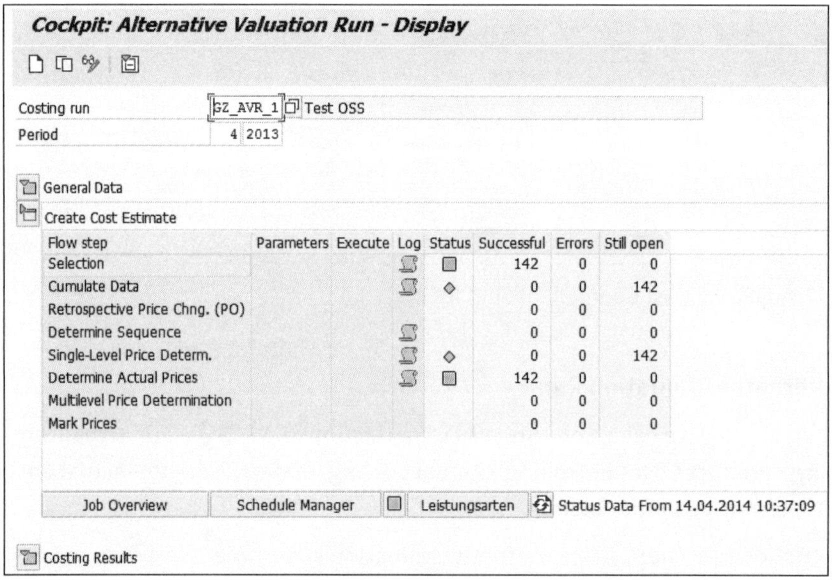

Figure 7.48 Steps in Alternative Valuation Run

Periodic Costing Runs and Alternative Valuation Runs

Before creating an alternative valuation run, it's a good idea to check that a periodic costing run has been performed for the periods you want to use before proceeding. Otherwise, the alternative valuation run won't find the beginning inventory, ending inventory, quantity structure, single-level price differences, and activity prices it needs as its starting point.

The next thing to be aware of is that you can create a chain of alternative valuation runs by entering the previous valuation run and clicking on the **Create Following Run** button. In a productive environment, this ensures that the ending inventory recorded by the first run is transferred to the follow-up run as the beginning inventory. If you don't enter a previous run, the system will take the beginning inventory for the first period you include in the valuation run as its starting point.

To create a new alternative valuation run, proceed as follows:

1. First, enter a name and description for the costing run together with the initial period (such as January if you're trying to cumulate values for the fiscal year) and the current period.
2. Select the **Plant Assignment** tab and enter the plants to be included in the calculations. If your aim is to smooth out price variances by taking a longer time frame, you should include the same plants here as you used in the original costing run. If your aim is to apply different valuation approaches, the company codes will probably be your guide. There may be legal obligations to apply alternative valuation approaches in only some of the countries in which the Material Ledger is active.
3. Select the **Settings** tab to enter the system settings for your alternative valuation run. You should only make entries in this tab after you've completed the entries under **Period Data** and **Plant Assignment** because the checks performed by the system are dependent on the plants and periods entered in these screens.

It may help to view the **Settings** screen (see Figure 7.49) as having three distinct parts:

1. The upper part of the **Settings** screen in Figure 7.49 determines what ultimately happens to the results of the costing run. If you select the **Posting Run** checkbox, you'll have to establish the link to the account assignment for the inventory accounts by making an appropriate entry in the **Acc. Modification** field. The system only allows you to update one inventory account per plant and period and issues an error if you try to update the same account twice with alternative valuation runs. If you're reporting according to multiple accounting principles, such as IFRS and local GAAP, you should also specify which accounting principle you're following. You can also update the cost of goods sold if you select the **Revaluate Consumption** checkbox. You can make the results available for use in the standard cost estimate (see Chapter 5) by selecting the **Relevant for Costing** checkbox. Whether the **Credit Cost Center** checkbox is selected depends on your configuration settings for the Material Ledger in each plant.

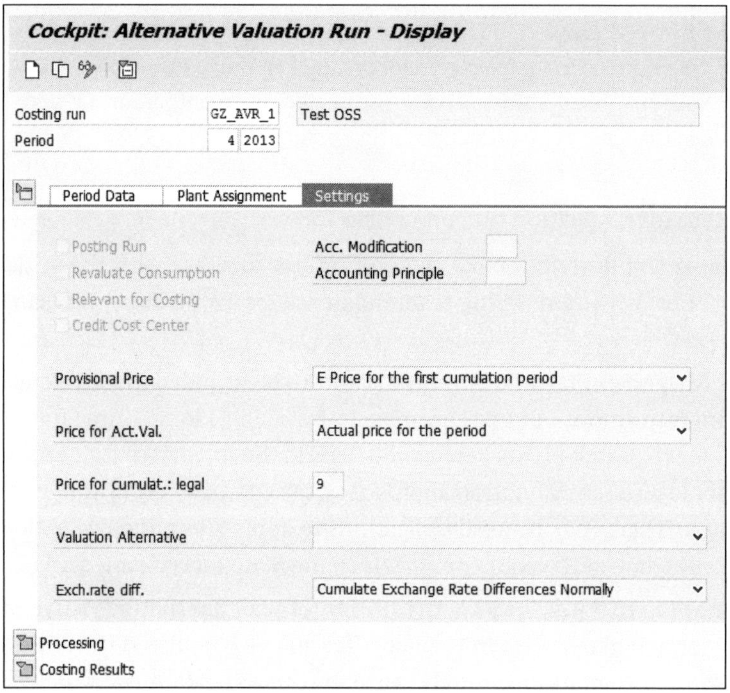

Figure 7.49 Settings for Alternative Valuation Run

2. The middle part of the screen (beginning with **Provisional Price**) determines which prices will be used for the valuation of the activities. The first field, **Provisional Price**, determines whether the initial activity price will be the standard activity price from the first period included in the alternative valuation run or the last period. This price is calculated in Cost Center Accounting using Transaction KSPI (see Chapter 5).

   The next field, **Price,** determines which price will be used to revalue the activities during the alternative valuation run. If you enter the actual price, this ensures that the actual price is calculated in the Material Ledger and not in Cost Center Accounting, so you should remove Transaction KSII (Actual Price Calculation) from your period-close activities. You should also enter the version under which this price will be updated in the **Price for Cumulat.: Legal** field. If your configuration settings also cover group and profit center valuation, the system will provide additional fields for the version used in group valuation and in the profit center valuation. By doing this, we're following the same principles as for the standard cost estimate, in which the quantity structure stays the same, but different prices are applied to the structure in each valuation approach.

3. The lower part of the screen determines which prices will be used to value the raw materials. Your entry in the **Valuation Alternative** field will determine which of the values from balance sheet valuation the system will apply to the quantity structure. The options include the FIFO valuation, the LIFO valuation, and the lowest value prices. These valuations are performed in Logistics via the menu path **Logistics • Materials Management • Valuation • Balance Sheet Valuation • Determination of Lowest Value/LIFO Valuation/FIFO Valuation**. You have to ensure that the appropriate balance sheet valuation has been performed and the data updated to the material master as physical inventory prices *before* you run the alternative valuation run.

Alternative Valuation Run for Parallel Valuation of Cost of Goods Manufactured

Since EHP 5 for SAP ERP 6.0, there's been a special form of alternative valuation run used specifically for inventory valuation. This is activated using the business function `FIN_CO_COGM` (Parallel Valuation of Cost of Goods Manufactured). The alternative valuation run looks slightly different in that it is flagged as being relevant for the calculation of the cost of goods manufactured in the **Period Data** tab, and the **Settings** tab is slightly different (see Figure 7.50). Notice that there's no account modification field because the inventory valuation can update to the same pair of accounts as the periodic costing run:

- The periodic costing run updates the accounting principle IFRS.
- The alternative valuation run updates the accounting principle local GAAP.

The version entered in the **Price** field is the version used to store the second set of activity prices in CO. There are no settings for group valuation or transfer price valuation because these are always updated in the leading ledger/leading valuation.

Figure 7.51 shows the steps included in an alternative valuation run for multiple valuations. This time there is no **Cumulate** step because we are working with the same period structure as in the periodic costing run. In fact, this is a key point for multiple valuations: you can vary the accounting approach but not the calendar.

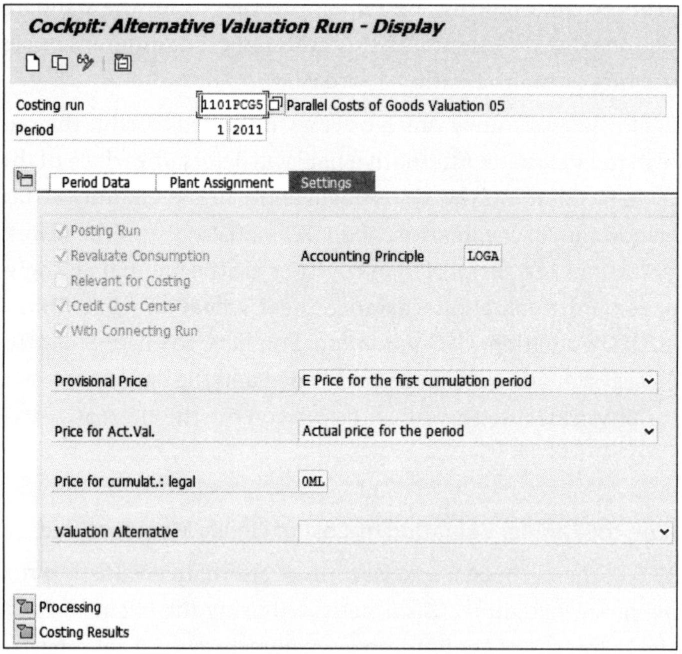

Figure 7.50 Settings Tab for Parallel Valuation of Cost of Goods Manufactured

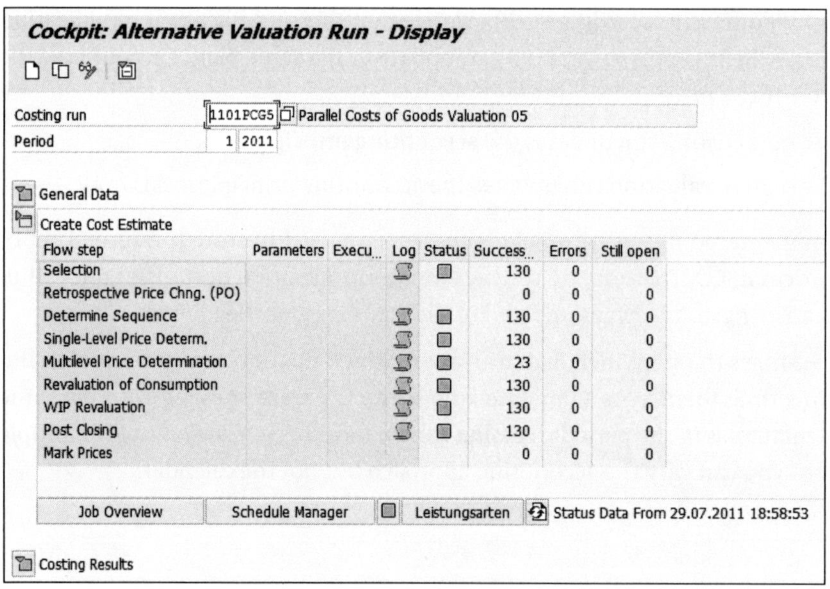

Figure 7.51 Steps in Alternative Valuation Run for Cost of Goods Manufactured

Figure 7.52 shows the effect of completing the alternative valuation run on a production cost center (we're using the cost center line item report we discussed extensively in Chapter 2, Section 2.1). Notice that this report shows the valuation view **Parallel Cost of Goods Manufactured** rather than the legal valuation, because we've cleared the activity costs in the second GAAP. Working through the report from top to bottom, you'll see the following:

- Primary cost postings for the depreciation of the fixed assets.
- Primary cost postings for pension reserves (from Payroll Accounting).
- Secondary costs for machine costs. There's one line for the posting made at the time of confirmation (10 hours) and an additional line for the correction made when the final activity rate was calculated and applied (business Transaction KSII in the report).
- Primary cost postings to clear the cost center made by the alternative valuation run.

Cost Elem.	Cost element name	Σ	Val.in rep.cur.	Total quantity	P...	Off...	Offst.acct	Name of offsetting account
211100	Deprec. Fixed Asset		1.250,00			A	1010	ADP - real estate
445000	Pension payments		1.000,00			S	92000	Pensio plan provisio
	Pension payments		2.000,00			S	92000	Pensio plan provisio
	Pension payments		2.000,00			S	92000	Pensio plan provisio
620000	DAA Machine Costs		45,50-	0,455-	H			
	DAA Machine Costs		1.500,00-	15-	H			
	DAA Machine Costs		1.455,31-	0	H			
	DAA Machine Costs		1.000,00-	10-	H			
694000	ASM PA Production		954,50-					
	ASM PA Production		954,50					
	ASM PA Production		0,01-					
895000	Fact.Output Prod.Ord		579,53-			S	231520	Pr.dif.loss low.lev.
	Fact.Output Prod.Ord		579,53			S	281520	Rev.pr.dif.lower.lev
	Fact.Output Prod.Ord		579,53-			S	231520	Pr.dif.loss low.lev.
	Fact.Output Prod.Ord		579,53			S	281520	Rev.pr.dif.lower.lev
	Fact.Output Prod.Ord		2.249,18-			S	231520	Pr.dif.loss low.lev.
	Fact.Output Prod.Ord		2.249,18			S	281520	Rev.pr.dif.lower.lev
	Fact.Output Prod.Ord		2.249,18-			S	231520	Pr.dif.loss low.lev.
	Fact.Output Prod.Ord		2.249,18			S	281520	Rev.pr.dif.lower.lev
	Fact.Output Prod.Ord		2.249,18-			S	231520	Pr.dif.loss low.lev.
	Fact.Output Prod.Ord		2.249,18			S	281520	Rev.pr.dif.lower.lev
	Fact.Output Prod.Ord		2.249,18-			S	231520	Pr.dif.loss low.lev.
Cost Center PCG-MF-02 PCG Manufacturin...		•	**0,00**					
		••	**0,00**					

Figure 7.52 Cost Center Line Items following Alternative Valuation Run

Now that we've calculated actual costs for all materials in the Material Ledger, we're ready to move to the final stage of the close and complete the valuations in Profitability Analysis.

7.4 CO-PA Processes

We looked at allocations from Cost Center Accounting to Profitability Analysis in Section 7.1.3. The other main processes in CO-PA are periodic valuation and top-down distribution:

- In Chapter 5, we used the valuation function to pull the results of the cost estimates into Profitability Planning. The periodic valuation works on the same principle. If you performed the revaluation of consumption step in the Material Ledger, you'll want to see these values not just on the COGS account in Financial Accounting but also in the value fields for cost of goods sold in Profitability Analysis. Once the controller has completed the periodic costing run, he can use the periodic revaluation function to update the value fields with the actual costs from the Material Ledger.
- Top-down distribution is also commonly used in planning but can be used to distribute actual data posted for higher-level characteristics (such as a region or branch) down to the lower-level characteristics (such as the customer or product). This process involves using reference data for the lower-level characteristics to determine how the high-level data should be spread. It's rather like an allocation in that you might use the revenue per customer to determine how expenses for a region should be distributed, but the value flow is entirely within CO-PA rather than between Cost Center Accounting and CO-PA. Another term for this kind of approach is *decomposition*.

Let's look at each process more closely.

7.4.1 Revaluation

The settings for revaluation are covered in Customizing. If you use the Material Ledger for actual costing, it makes sense to link the cost component split under which your actual product costs are stored with value fields in Profitability Analysis. The initial sales order and invoice will be valued with the standard cost component split during *real-time valuation*. You can then set up a second point of valuation for *periodic revaluation of actual data* to bring the latest actual costs into

Profitability Analysis from the revaluation of consumption step in the Material Ledger. To perform revaluation, select Transaction KE27 or **Accounting • Controlling • Profitability Analysis • Actual Postings • Period-End Closing • Periodic Adjustments • Periodic Valuation** and select the **Periodic Valuation** checkbox, as shown in Figure 7.53. The result will be an update of the value fields with the actual costs from the cost component split in the Material Ledger.

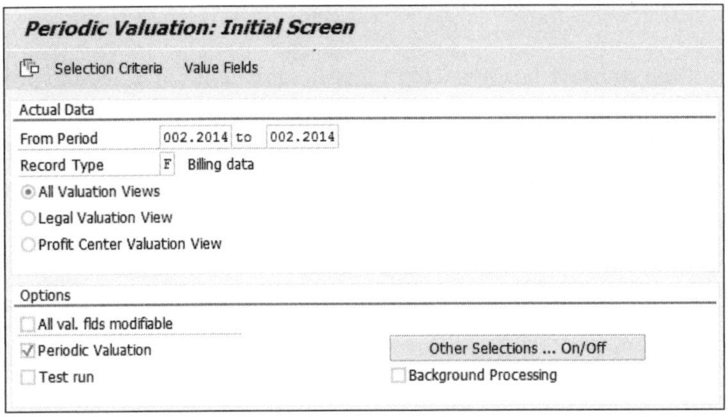

Figure 7.53 Periodic Revaluation in Profitability Analysis

> **Revaluation of Actual Costs in SAP S/4HANA**
>
> The revaluation of actual costs to account-based Profitability Analysis will be delivered with SAP S/4HANA 1809.

7.4.2 Top-Down Distribution

We've been exploring Profitability Analysis, in which one of the challenges is to understand what data is captured where. Typically, the sales order and the invoice have the most detailed data, with each line being assigned to both the customer-related dimensions and the product-related dimensions. As we walked through the manufacturing process in Chapter 6, we also had postings for variances that were only assigned to the product but not to the customer. In Section 7.1.3, we looked at assessments to CO-PA and discussed how we could choose whether to assign our costs to the most detailed product/customer level or keep them higher. We assigned ours to the division.

The purpose of top-down distribution is to take these product-related variances and assign them to the customer-related dimensions or to take the results of an allocation to the division and assign it to the products that are part of that division. This might sound like just another form of allocation, but with a top-down distribution there is no debit-credit posting as we saw in Sections Section 7.1.2 and Section 7.1.3. Instead the value initially assigned to the division remains on the division, but additional entries are created for the values on each product when you run top-down distribution.

In contrast to most of the steps we've looked at in this chapter, you don't need to prepare any Customizing to perform top-down distribution. To enter the relevant values for top-down distribution, select Transaction KE28 or **Accounting • Controlling • Profitability Analysis • Actual Postings • Period-End Closing • Periodic Adjustments • Top-Down Distribution**. Figure 7.54 shows the selection screen.

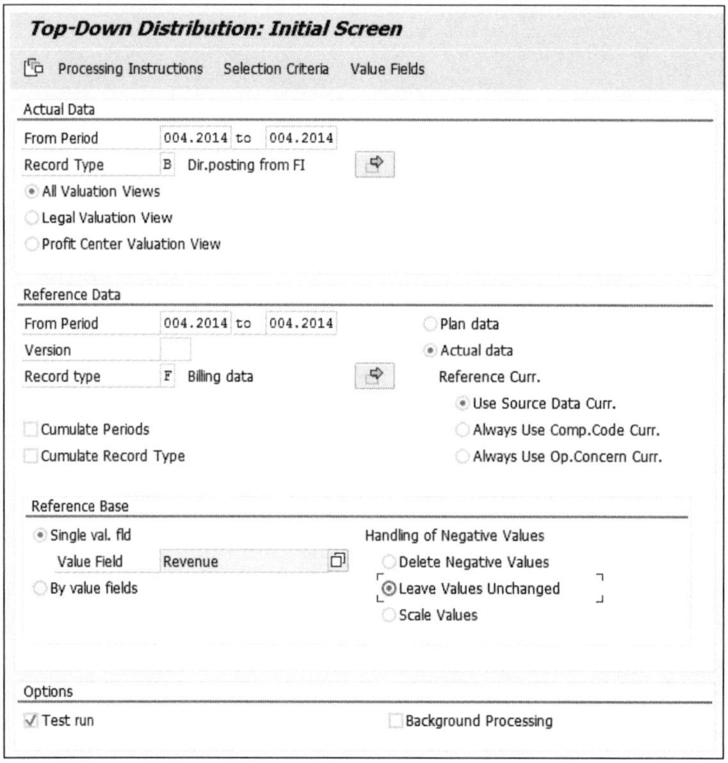

Figure 7.54 Initial Screen for Top-Down Distribution

The follow these steps:

1. The first decision to make is the type of actual data that you'd like to distribute. The price variances that we posted in Chapter 6 are stored as record type B, whereas the allocations we posted earlier in this chapter are stored as record type D. Enter this in the **Actual Data** section of the screen.
2. The second decision is the basis for the distribution. In our example, we're using the revenue that has been billed as the basis for our distribution. Enter this in the **Reference Data** part of the screen.

To enter the dimensions that you'd like to have the system assign values to, click on the **Processing Instructions** button. Figure 7.55 shows the processing instructions for assigning the production variances to the customer-related dimensions. The next two screens were significantly redesigned in EHP 5, so if your screens look different, refer to SAP Note 1695850.

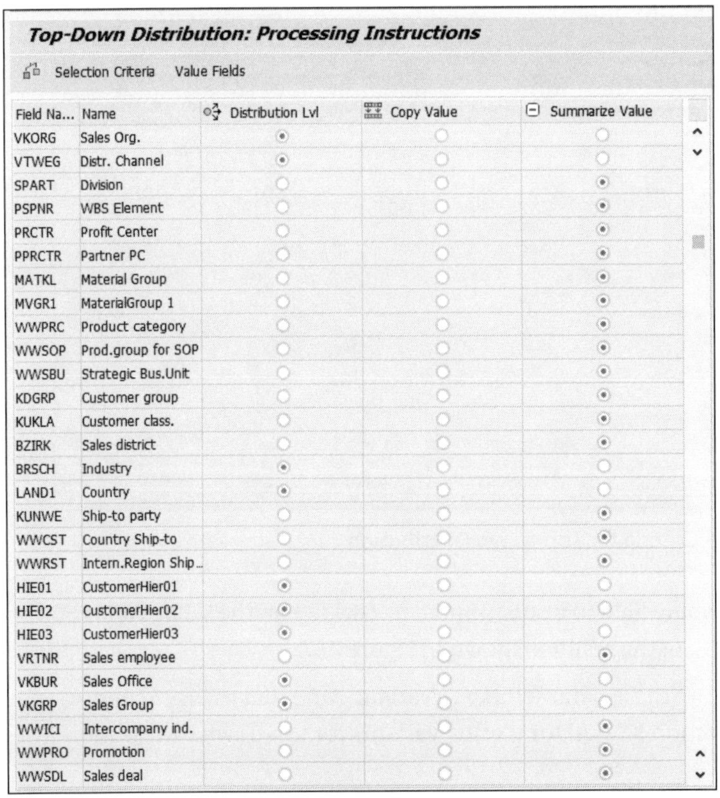
Top-Down Distribution: Processing Instructions

Selection Criteria Value Fields

Field Na...	Name	Distribution Lvl	Copy Value	Summarize Value
VKORG	Sales Org.	(•)	( )	( )
VTWEG	Distr. Channel	(•)	( )	( )
SPART	Division	( )	( )	(•)
PSPNR	WBS Element	( )	( )	(•)
PRCTR	Profit Center	( )	( )	(•)
PPRCTR	Partner PC	( )	( )	(•)
MATKL	Material Group	( )	( )	(•)
MVGR1	MaterialGroup 1	( )	( )	(•)
WWPRC	Product category	( )	( )	(•)
WWSOP	Prod.group for SOP	( )	( )	(•)
WWSBU	Strategic Bus.Unit	( )	( )	(•)
KDGRP	Customer group	( )	( )	(•)
KUKLA	Customer class.	( )	( )	(•)
BZIRK	Sales district	( )	( )	(•)
BRSCH	Industry	(•)	( )	( )
LAND1	Country	(•)	( )	( )
KUNWE	Ship-to party	( )	( )	(•)
WWCST	Country Ship-to	( )	( )	(•)
WWRST	Intern.Region Ship...	( )	( )	(•)
HIE01	CustomerHier01	(•)	( )	( )
HIE02	CustomerHier02	(•)	( )	( )
HIE03	CustomerHier03	(•)	( )	( )
VRTNR	Sales employee	( )	( )	(•)
VKBUR	Sales Office	(•)	( )	( )
VKGRP	Sales Group	(•)	( )	( )
WWICI	Intercompany ind.	( )	( )	(•)
WWPRO	Promotion	( )	( )	(•)
WWSDL	Sales deal	( )	( )	(•)

Figure 7.55 Processing Instructions for Top-Down Distribution

You'll then need to enter the selection criteria. We've used * to represent all characteristics with price differences, but you may need to enter the selection criteria to narrow down the characteristic values for the selection. Figure 7.56 shows the **Selection Criteria** for our top-down distribution. Notice that those characteristics we entered in the previous screen are locked here.

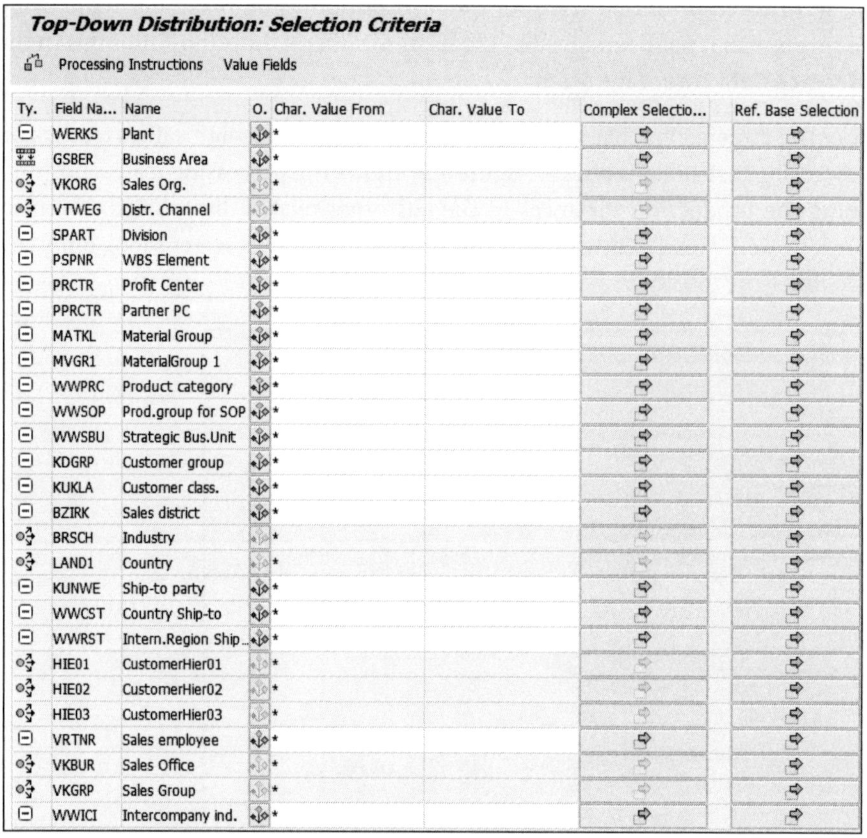

Figure 7.56 Selection Criteria for Top-Down Distribution

Finally, specify the value field to be distributed by clicking on the **Value Fields** button, as shown in Figure 7.56; the result is shown in Figure 7.57.

It makes sense to store these parameters as a variant. Note that in EHP 5 there is a new transaction (Transaction KE28A) for storing variants for top-down distribution.

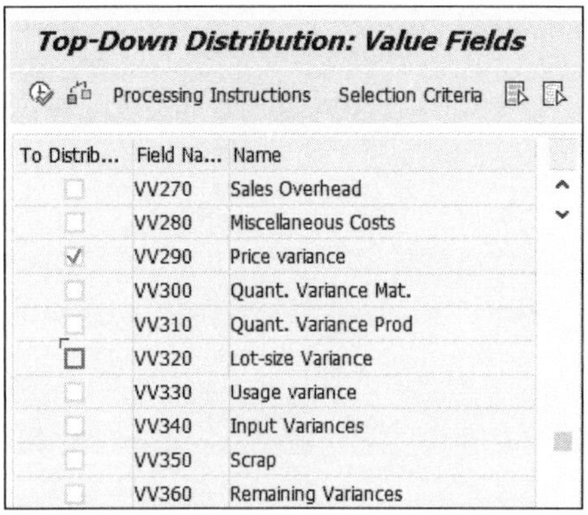

Figure 7.57 Value Fields for Inclusion in Top-Down Distribution

Top-Down Distribution in SAP S/4HANA

For several years, a myth circulated around Internet forums that top-down distribution was not available for account-based CO-PA, when in fact it has been available since Release 4.7. What can be challenging, however, is the fact that account-based CO-PA only stores data from financial accounting and allocations/settlement. This means that you will be able to distribute annual bonuses based on the relative revenues for individual product lines, but you will not be able to distribute the freight costs from your shipping agent to your products based on the statistical freight conditions in your sales order because the statistical freight conditions aren't available in accounting.

7.5 Summary

We've covered what happens during the main steps of the period close for controllers and in so doing completed our journey through the basic controlling functions. We'll now return to the reporting functions we discussed in Chapter 2 and discuss how to work with high volumes of data and the newer options for reporting. To find out more about managing and automating the period close, skip to Chapter 12.

Chapter 8

Reporting in SAP BW and SAP BusinessObjects

This chapter looks at how to handle large data volumes both in SAP ERP and in SAP Business Warehouse. It uses the requirements of cost center reporting as an example to show how the SAP BW Query is the basis for reporting in the SAP BusinessObjects tools.

When we discussed reporting in Chapter 2, we focused on list reporting for cost centers, internal orders, production orders, and so on and explained how to use SAP List Viewer to build your own layouts for the individual reports. This was partly because we wanted to introduce the data structures in SAP ERP before we looked at the operative processes in more detail, but it was also because list reporting is a task best performed in SAP ERP, because the data structures the controller uses for analysis are similar to the data structures in the underlying tables. For the most part, such reporting is simply a matter of selecting the data that interests you and then performing simple operations such as totaling and sorting on the results shown in your report. We also brought those values into context by comparing them with the planned values for each entity. However, most controllers will agree that there's more to reporting than neatly sorted lists. As we consider plan/actual comparisons, we find ourselves rolling up data from the very granular level at which it is captured to provide aggregations by profit center, plant, company code, and so on. It is this mass reporting that will be our focus in this chapter.

In Chapter 2, we assumed that our reports were being run *online*. Depending on your data volumes, such aggregations can be very performance-intensive. This chapter will introduce you to ways of handling these huge data selections. If it's not essential to have the very latest data in your reports, you can work with *extracts*, in which the data in the report is preselected and stored as an extract to accelerate access. This is especially useful when you're looking at large structures, such as the costs for an entire cost center hierarchy or all the items in a balance sheet and has the twofold effect of providing you with quicker access to the data in your report because it has been preselected and reducing strain on your system because the preparation of the extracts can be performed at night when system load is generally lower.

When we looked at the line items for CO-PA, we were looking at the characteristics and value fields recorded for each data record, which is clearly useful for performing a spot check on the integrity of the data. However, most controllers want to select all data records relating to a particular customer, customer group, product, product group, region, sales organization, and so on. Likewise, a report that shows an individual production order, as we saw in Chapter 6 and Chapter 7, is interesting once you've determined that there are issues with that production order, but you're unlikely to want to analyze thousands of production orders in turn. You'll want to select all production orders in a particular plant or in a particular product group and then drill down to the problem orders—so in this chapter we'll also look at your options for drilldown reporting and explain the use of summarization hierarchies in SAP ERP.

In case these options still aren't enough to meet your reporting requirements, we'll then discuss when to introduce SAP Business Warehouse (SAP BW) as a dedicated data warehouse and your reporting options with SAP BusinessObjects tools.

8.1 Reporting on Large Data Volumes in SAP ERP

In this section, we'll look at your options for accelerating Report Writer reports and your drilldown reports in SAP ERP.

8.1.1 Using Extracts to Accelerate Cost Center and Internal Order Reports

One way the controlling department can speed up cost center, internal order, and project reporting is to prepare extracts of the data and encourage cost center managers to work with these extracts rather than querying the live tables to speed up the selection and ease general system performance. This option works for any report built using Report Writer. If you refer to Figure 2.3 in Chapter 2, you'll see that this option covers reports such as Cost Centers: Actual/Plan Variance, Cost Centers: Actual/Target Variance, Cost Centers: Quarterly Comparison, and so on. The same applies to most of the reports shown for internal orders in Figure 2.12 in Chapter 2. You'll recognize these reports by the **Data Source** button in the selection screen, as shown in Figure 8.1. Clicking on this button allows you to switch between live data

(**New Selection**) and an extract (**Display Extract**). The result of executing the report is the same, but if you try it with your own data you should notice an improvement in response time.

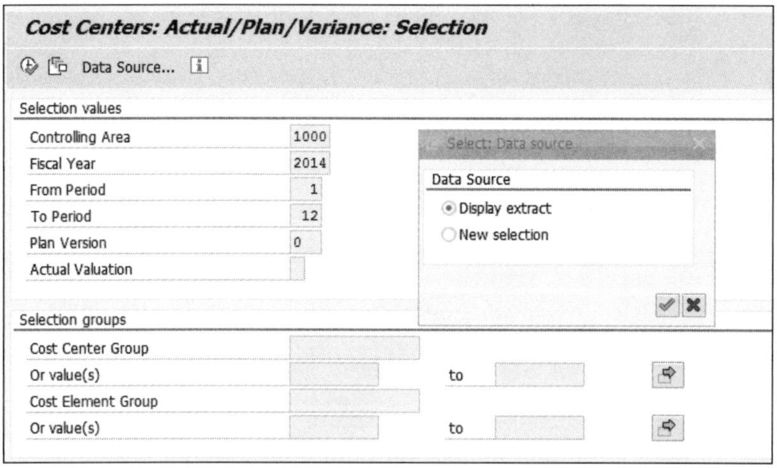

Figure 8.1 Using Extract for Cost Center Plan/Actual Report

If nobody has prepared an extract for you, you'll first need to create one. To find the settings for creating extracts, switch to expert mode by selecting **Environment • Options** and then selecting the **Expert Mode** checkbox. Several new buttons will appear on the selection screen, as shown in Figure 8.2. Let's go over the **Variation**, **Output Parameters**, and **Extract Parameters** buttons. To maintain the settings for your first extract, click on **Extract Parameters**, select **Create Extract**, give your extract a name, and enter an expiration date, as shown in Figure 8.2.

Caution: Use of Extracts

When you see the expiration dates in the extract parameters, it's easy to imagine that you've found the perfect solution for storing the contents of your report for safekeeping until the next audit. This only works if the structure of your report doesn't change. If your report structure changes, your extracts may become unusable. Don't rely on the extract for long-term auditing.

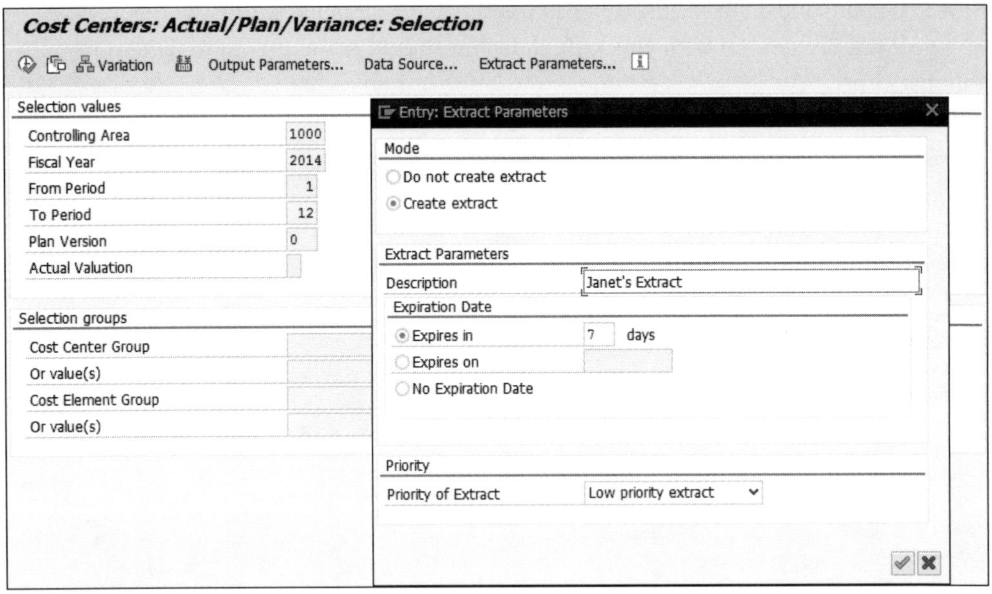

Figure 8.2 Setting Extract Parameters

If you're planning to execute the report for a large cost centelr group or even the whole cost center hierarchy, make sure that before you run the report you check the settings that appear when you click on the **Variation** button, as shown in Figure 8.3.

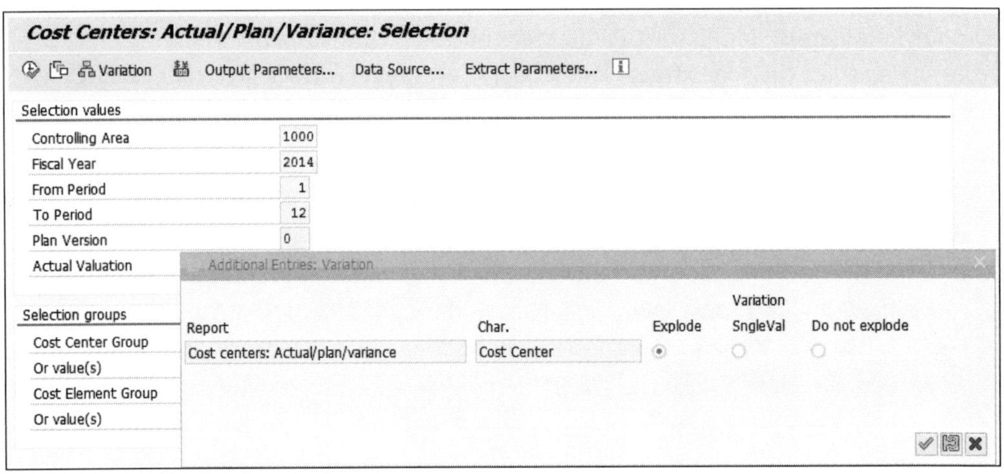

Figure 8.3 Setting Parameters for Variation in Large Hierarchy

Selecting the **Explode** radio button for the cost center means that when you execute the report for a large cost center group, the system will create a separate extract for each *variation*. This results in an extract for each cost center in the group and each node in the hierarchy, meaning that everybody who chooses the extract option as his data source is going to get faster report results. You may wonder why you need the other options at all. If you're only interested in the cumulative result of your balance sheet and profit and loss (P&L) statement rather than the individual accounts in your financial statement version, then it can make sense not to explode but only to view the totals. However, in the Controlling component of SAP ERP Financials (CO) you almost always want to explode for each cost center, each order, each project, and so on in your chosen group to provide a report for each cost center manager and project manager.

Before you execute a report in the background, you should also check the output parameters, as shown in Figure 8.4. It may seem at odds with common sense, but what you should do now is set the **Output Medium** to **No Output**. This means that instead of writing to a spool or a printer, the contents of the list are only written to the extracts. If you have no plans to use the spool list, this is another way to ease the load on your system. You're now ready to execute the report, either by selecting **Program • Execute** or, if you want to schedule it at night, by selecting **Program • Schedule Job**. It's good practice to execute this type of mass report in the background once all the relevant steps of the period close are complete. Many organizations include the preparation of these extracts in the SAP Financial Closing cockpit or Schedule Manager so that they can be scheduled automatically, as we'll discuss in Chapter 12.

Once the extract has been prepared, you'll see the extract when you select **Display Extract**, as shown in Figure 8.1, and you can then choose your extract, as shown in Figure 8.5.

Once you're working with the data in your report, you have the same options to navigate and drill down in the report as with live data. Only the initial selection is different, reading *extracted* rather than live data.

Creating Extracts for Line Items

If you're interested in creating extracts for line items for scheduled jobs, consider asking your IT department to implement SAP Note 1572806. This can also be used to prepare extracts for the line items you saw in the allocation cycles in Chapter 7.

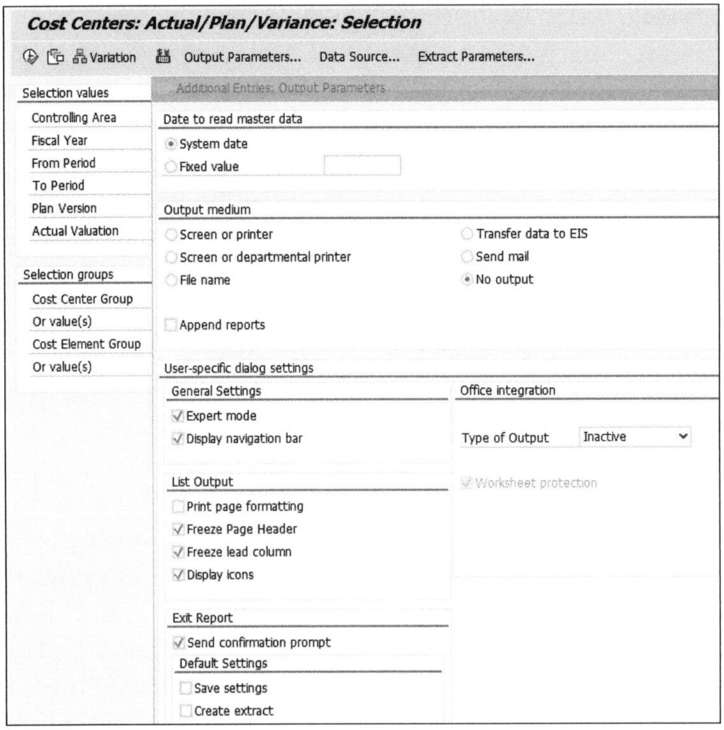

Figure 8.4 Setting Output Parameters for Report

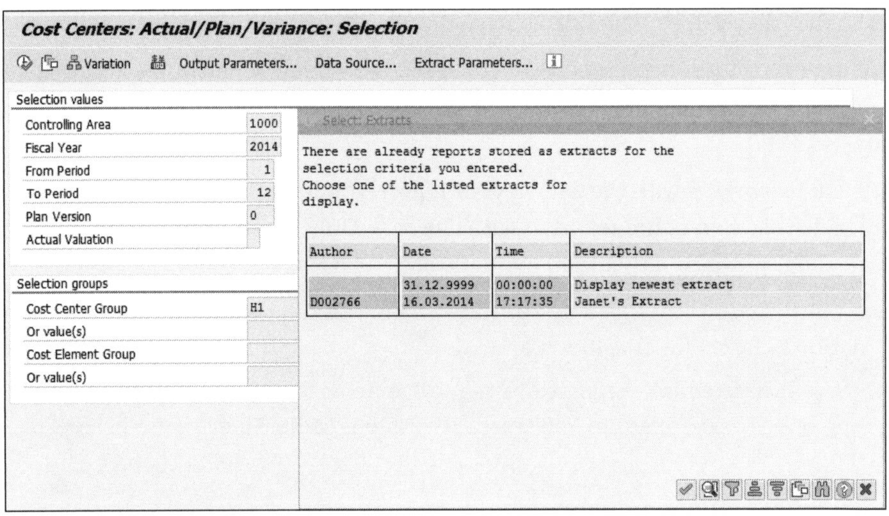

Figure 8.5 Choosing Prepared Extract

8.1.2 Using Summarization Levels to Accelerate CO-PA Reports

When we looked at profitability planning in Chapter 5, we showed an example of a drilldown report for CO-PA in SAP ERP. Figure 5.49 in Chapter 5 showed the results of planning for the whole operating concern presented in a drilldown report. Within this report, you could drill down to see the same key figures by distribution channel, sales organization, and material group. There are many different types of drilldown reports you can build to display the data in your operating concern. One way to ease performance concerns if you're working with huge sets of data is to use *summarization levels* to preselect and summarize data for dimensions you know you'll be reporting on regularly. Your implementation team will define the dimensions for which summarization levels are created when they configure your operating concern, but you should use the **Refresh** function to extract the latest data to these summarization levels on a regular basis. To prepare the summarization levels, follow the menu path **Accounting • Controlling • Profitability Analysis • Tools Summarization Levels • Refresh** and fill out the selection as shown in Figure 8.6. If you don't do this, the system has to select new data each time you drill down to a new characteristic, which can mean long wait times—because the system performs a new selection each time you click—and a lot of frustration. We'll return to these summarization options in Chapter 13, in which we look at new options using SAP HANA to accelerate CO-PA reporting.

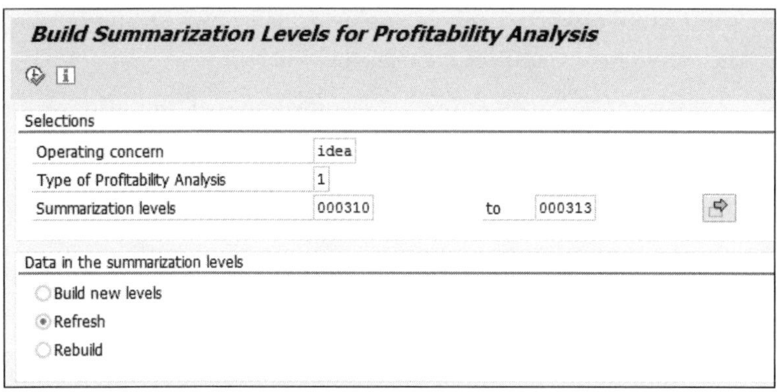

Figure 8.6 Building Summarization Levels for Profitability Analysis

8.1.3 Using Summarization in Product Cost Reports

You'll also find drilldown reports in Cost Object Controlling. These options are listed in Chapter 2, Figure 2.16, under **Summarized Analysis • With Product Drill-Down**. Technically, these are very similar to the CO-PA reports, though you don't have to build them from scratch when you implement. If you want to view a complete list of the product drilldown reports in your system, select Transaction KKOO. However, though not filling the summarization levels in CO-PA gives you a tedious wait when you run the report, in Cost Object Controlling you *must* run a special transaction (Transaction KKRV) to fill the summarization levels prior to executing the reports. If you don't, the report will indicate that no data is available.

To prepare the data for these reports, select Transaction KKRV or **Accounting • Controlling • Product Cost Controlling • Cost Object Controlling • Product Cost by Order • Information System • Tools • Data Collection • For Product Drilldown** and enter the relevant plant(s) and time frame. It's common to consider this transaction as part of the period close (see Chapter 7) because it requires you to have calculated work in process (WIP), variances, and so on prior to data collection. To display the report, follow the menu path **Financials • Controlling • Product Cost Controlling • Cost Object Controlling • Product Cost by Order • Information System • Reports for Product Cost by Order • Summarized Analysis • With Product Drilldown • Actual Costs • Cumulative** and enter the relevant plant and time frame.

Figure 8.7 shows the results of such a report. We've drilled down to the product groups to look at the cumulative variances for material R-B100.

If you explore the Investment Management reports, you'll find that they also use the drilldown techniques but don't require you to perform a preliminary collection run for the data.

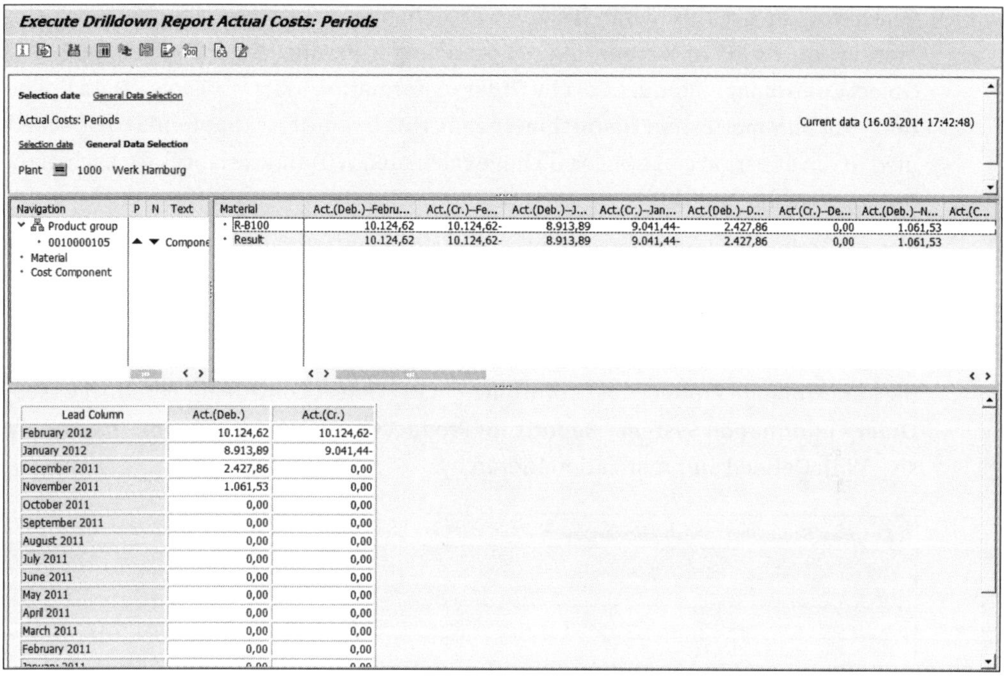

Figure 8.7 Sample Drilldown Report in Product Cost Controlling

8.1.4 Using Summarization Hierarchies for CO-PC Reporting

If you can't find all the dimensions that you need for product cost reporting in the drilldown reports, consider using a summarization hierarchy instead. Figure 8.8 shows a simple hierarchy containing three levels, but you can add any field from the order header to this hierarchy. To create a hierarchy, choose Transaction KKRO or **Accounting • Controlling • Product Cost Controlling • Cost Object Controlling • Product Cost by Order • Information System • Tools • Create Summarization Hierarchy** and select the fields that you want to use to build your hierarchy.

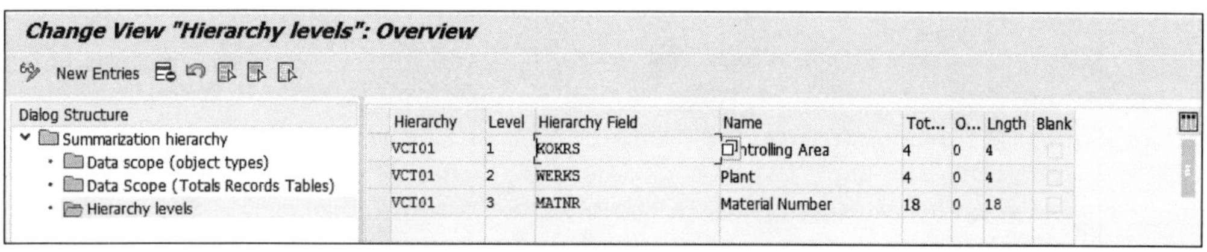

Figure 8.8 Levels within Summarization Hierarchy

Before you can use this hierarchy, you will again have to prepare data, this time using Transaction KKRC or **Accounting • Controlling • Product Cost Controlling • Cost Object Controlling • Product Cost by Order • Information System • Tools • Data Collection • For Summarization Hierarchies**. Again, this is a process that tends to be scheduled to run at period close once you have calculated WIP and variances for each of the orders in the hierarchy.

Figure 8.9 shows a sample hierarchy comprising plants and material numbers. If you click on any of the nodes in the structure, you will see an aggregation of the costs, either of all the orders in the selected plant or to manufacture the selected product. This summarization hierarchy is created using Transaction KKBC_HOE or **Accounting • Controlling • Product Cost Controlling • Cost Object Controlling • Product Cost by Order • Information System • Reports for Product Cost by Order • Summarized Analysis • With Defined Summarization Hierarchy**.

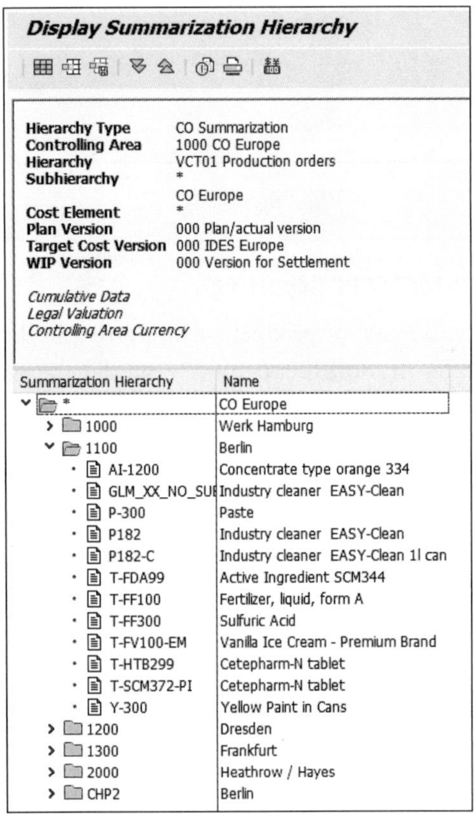

Figure 8.9 Sample Summarization Hierarchy Containing Nodes for Plants and Materials

Summarization Hierarchies in SAP S/4HANA

With SAP S/4HANA, you no longer need to use Transaction KKRC to preaggregate the data for each node of the summarization hierarchy but can execute Transaction KKBC_HOE_H (the new version of Transaction KKBC_HOE) immediately. Note however that the new transaction only aggregates data. It will not calculate target costs or variances for the assigned orders. You can find out more about these changes in SAP Note 2349282 (S4TWL—Summarization Hierarchies in Controlling).

Now that we've looked at the options for summarized reporting in SAP ERP, let's consider what might affect a decision to move your reporting tasks to SAP BW.

8.2 How to Decide Whether You Need SAP BW for Reporting

If your organization has yet to make the move to SAP BW or another data warehouse, you should ask several questions. It may be that the decision has been made for you or that you're already using SAP BW, but we'll look at some of the questions you might ask from a controlling perspective.

SAP BW for Controllers

The next 40 or so pages won't turn you into an SAP BW expert, but they *will* tell you where SAP BW provides options that don't exist in SAP ERP and help you understand what sort of reports you can build in SAP BW. As power users, controllers are frequently asked for their requirements in the early days of a reporting project, but they can find it difficult to provide an adequate answer because they don't know what can and can't be done in SAP BW, leading to frustration on both sides.

8.2.1 Performance Concerns

When we looked at the order-to-cash process in Chapter 6, you saw how CO-PA records sit behind every sales order and invoice. In Chapter 7, we allocated general expenses to CO-PA, settled production orders to CO-PA, and finally performed top-down allocations in CO-PA, generating yet more data records. It's easy to imagine just how huge the data volumes in the CO-PA tables can become and how the apparently simple act of selecting all the invoices in an operating concern can become a potential performance headache. The same applies to Cost Object Controlling. If you're capturing data for every production order and then aggregating this data for analysis by product group or plant, the data volumes can be large.

Moving data to a dedicated data warehouse is an extension of the extraction process we just discussed, but instead of simply preparing data extracts for analysis in SAP ERP, you move all relevant data to an environment designed specifically for reporting. As far as CO is concerned, SAP delivers a series of extractors that a system administrator can use to pull the data from the CO tables into SAP BW. These extractors select data from the CO tables and write them into a staging area within the data warehouse.

The process of moving data from SAP ERP to SAP BW is handled by setting up *InfoPackages* that parcel the data to be selected from SAP ERP and then schedule the data load. The load intervals can range from hourly to daily to once a month because the relevant data is only calculated as part of the period close. Think of it simply as an extension of the extraction process we discussed at the beginning of the chapter, in which you need to prepare your selection parameters and then schedule the timing of the load.

DataSources provide the link between the operational system and the reporting system. SAP delivers DataSources for all areas of CO and Investment Management. Your administrator can display and test the DataSources in your SAP ERP system using Transaction RSA3, provided that your SAP ERP system is on the correct release level (you can check the minimum release level for each DataSource in the SAP documentation for the BW content).

Once the SAP BW system is installed, the next step is for a system administrator to activate the relevant business content (the DataSources, InfoProviders, and so on that you plan to use). Once this infrastructure is installed, you can display the delivered InfoProviders by logging on to SAP BW and selecting **SAP Business Information Warehouse • Administration • Data Warehousing workbench Administration** and then **Modeling • InfoProvider**. To display the InfoProviders delivered for CO, select **Financial Management and Controlling • Controlling** and then **Overhead Cost Controlling** or **Product Cost Controlling** or **Profitability Analysis** in the right-hand part of the screen, as shown in Figure 8.10.

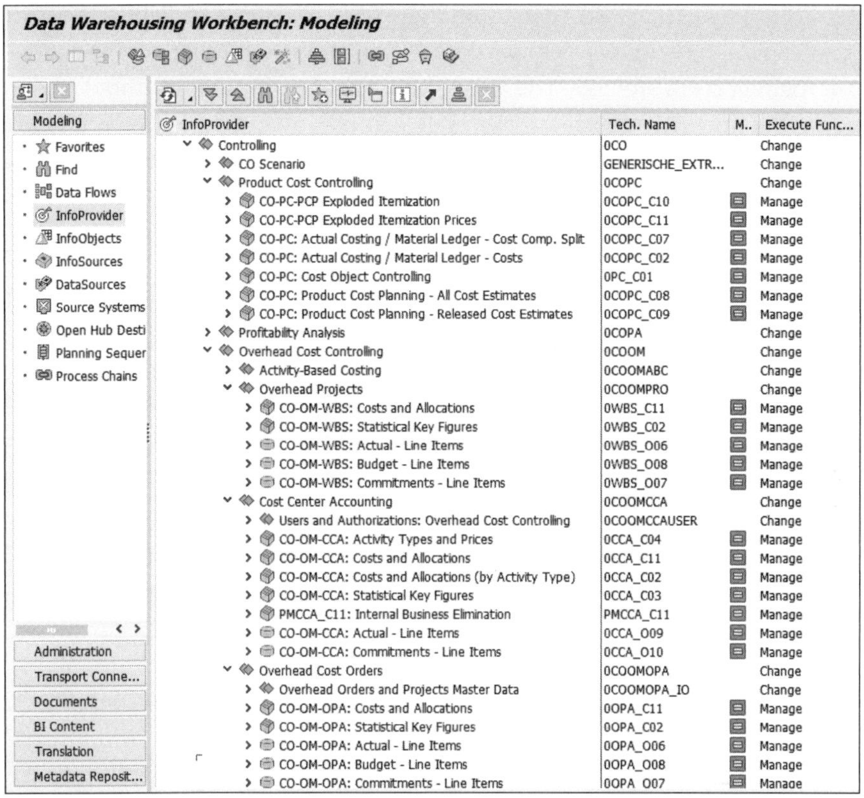

Figure 8.10 Delivered BW Content for Controlling (from Release 2.1C)

To work with the workbench, you need to understand three terms:

1. Each application menu in CO is mapped to an *InfoArea*. The InfoAreas are simply sets of folders that group the relevant applications, so the InfoArea for overhead cost controlling includes InfoAreas for activity-based costing, cost center accounting, overhead projects, and overhead cost orders.

2. If you select the Cost Center Accounting InfoArea, you'll see a series of *InfoProviders*. These InfoProviders, as the name implies, provide the data to be analyzed to the query when the user executes a report. You load data from the CO tables to the InfoProviders for activity types and prices, costs and allocations, statistical key figures, and so on. If you find the term *InfoProvider* off-putting, it may help to think of InfoProviders simply as the tables in which the transactional data is *stored* once it has been extracted from SAP ERP and from which it is read when you execute a query.

3. SAP delivers *queries* that select data from these InfoProviders and display the costs per cost center, the activity prices per cost center, and so on. These are the equivalent of the reports in SAP ERP. You will be able to execute queries without understanding the underlying data structures. If you plan to build your own queries, then it is important to understand the *data transformation* that takes place in the move from the SAP ERP tables that we looked at in Chapter 2 and SAP BW.

If you're using a newer version of SAP BW, you might want to consider using a newer set of InfoProviders that were delivered to take advantage of changes to the SAP BW architecture in Release 7.0. Your administrator will find the business content for Simplified Reporting by following the menu path above but selecting **Financial Management and Controlling • Reporting Financials (EhP3) • Cost Center Reporting • Overhead Cost Orders** or **Product Cost Controlling**, as shown in Figure 8.11. EHP 4 included additional new content for Profitability Analysis and Investment Management.

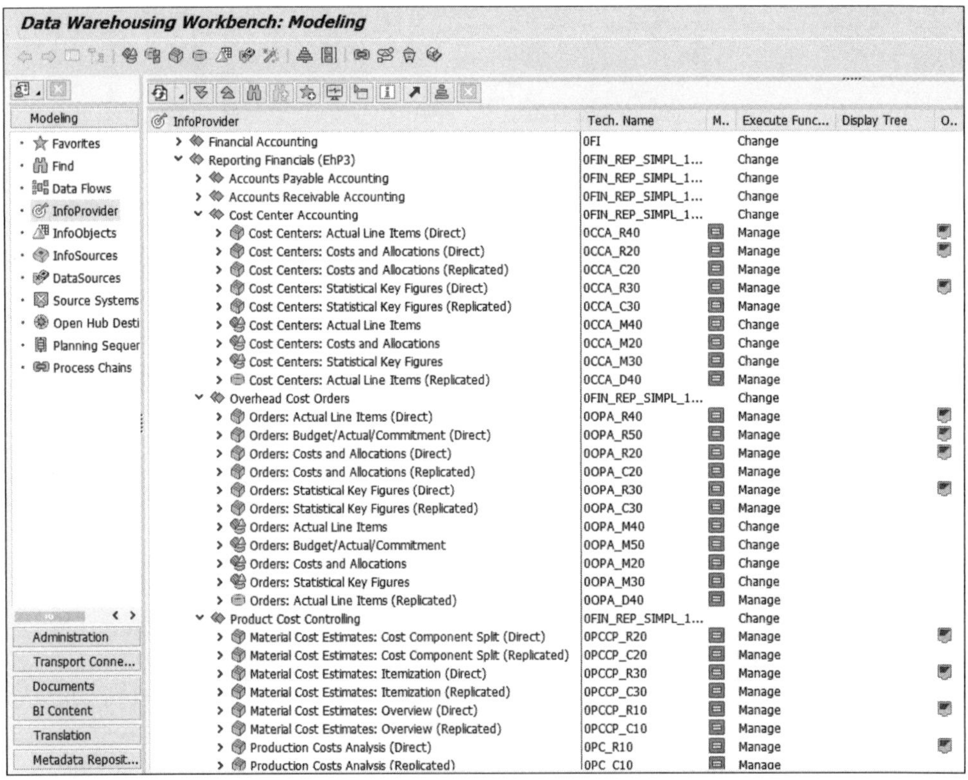

Figure 8.11 Delivered BW Content for Controlling (from Release 7.0)

At first glance, the two sets of business content look similar, but if you look closely you'll see that in the newer version a pair of InfoProviders is delivered for each application—one labeled **Replicated** and the other labeled **Direct**. This is because the new InfoProviders offer you a choice between working with *replicated* data (i.e., data that has been extracted or copied to SAP BW from SAP ERP and then stored redundantly in SAP BW) or working with live data in SAP ERP that is selected when the query is executed (*direct access* in SAP BW terms).

If your data volumes are not excessively large, direct access means you can dispense with the process of performing regular loads of data to the SAP BW tables but can enjoy the benefits of the modeling options to look at the data in ways that are not currently possible in SAP ERP alone. This is the data transformation process that involves taking raw data out of the SAP ERP tables and mapping it into new structures in SAP BW.

Whichever version of SAP BW you use, the link between the information in the SAP ERP tables and SAP BW is established using a DataSource. You can check this mapping by choosing any of the InfoProviders shown in Figure 8.11 and clicking on the **DataSource** icon, as shown in Figure 8.12.

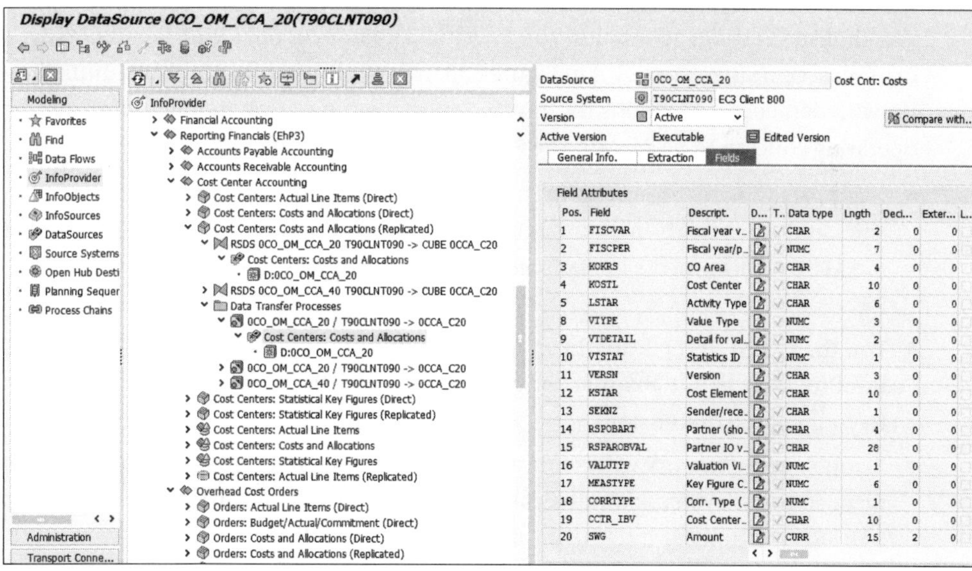

Figure 8.12 DataSource for Cost Center Accounting

This allows you to display the mapping of the fields from the SAP ERP tables that we used for our list reports in Chapter 2 and the DataSources that are the basis for SAP BW reporting.

As you explore, bear in mind that the delivered DataSources pull the data from the SAP ERP tables with very little transformation. If you're bringing data into SAP BW from multiple ERP systems, it's common to harmonize that data to bring it into a common structure. Typical changes that you might make during extraction include mapping of cost elements to a common chart of accounts or of cost centers to a common cost center structure if your master data is not harmonized.

Although you can easily move data from Cost Center Accounting, Internal Orders, and Product Cost Controlling into SAP BW because the underlying table structures are the same in all organizations, remember from Chapter 2 that Profitability Analysis is based on *generated* tables, so there's no standard BW content for CO-PA. Instead, your administrator will find an implementation guide in SAP ERP that will guide him through the process of creating DataSources that read the structure of the operating concern configured for your business and move this structure into SAP BW. Your administrator will find this implementation guide in SAP ERP by selecting **Integration with Other mySAP.com Components • Data Transfer to SAP Business Information Warehouse • Settings for Application-Specific DataSources (PI) • Profitability Analysis** or Transaction SBIW, as shown in Figure 8.13. This guide will provide your administrator with detailed instructions for how to set up the replication model to transfer the operating concern to SAP BW in the **Profitability Analysis** folder:

- This process involves setting up transactional data sources that read the characteristics and value fields in your operating concern and make them available for use in SAP BW. This process is available for both costing-based and account-based CO-PA.
- You then need to replicate these data sources from SAP ERP to SAP BW and build InfoProviders in SAP BW that assign the characteristics in your operating concern to your chosen dimensions.
- If you're going to work with replicated data, you need to establish the load mechanism so that a system administrator can schedule a data load to read the data in SAP ERP and transfer it to the InfoProviders in SAP BW.

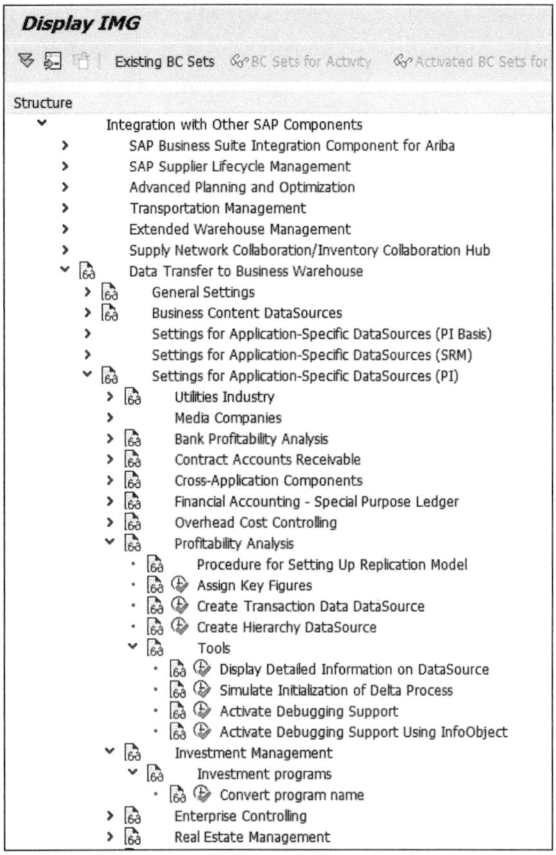

Figure 8.13 Implementation Guide for SAP BW in SAP ERP

If this process of moving data from SAP ERP to SAP BW appears cumbersome, you can also consider working with virtual InfoProviders within SAP ERP. We'll explain how to do this in Chapter 13, Section 13.1.

8.2.2 Multidimensionality

Simply moving the data out of SAP ERP and into SAP BW is not the whole answer to any performance issues you might be experiencing. When we talk about a *dedicated reporting environment*, what we often mean is one that is architected to support *multidimensional* analysis. The data in an operating concern is inherently multidimensional, meaning that any sales order or invoice can be queried to display the value fields by customer, by product, by sales organization, by region, and so on.

Profitability Analysis

In SAP ERP, the underlying data for a profitability report is stored in a single dimension, meaning that the characteristics (product, customer, sales organization, etc.) are stored in table CE4XXXX, and the value fields (sales quantity, gross sales, customer discount, etc.) are stored in table CE1XXXX (where XXXX stands for your operating concern). When you run a report in SAP ERP, the query accesses tables CE4XXXX and CE1XXXX to select the data required. To determine whether data exists for a specific customer or a specific product, every data record has to be read.

In SAP BW, CO-PA is modeled to provide a central fact table containing all the value fields and separate dimensions for the product, the customer, the sales organization, and time. This means that to determine whether data exists for a specific customer, the customer dimension is read. This subset of data is then read to determine whether a specific product was purchased. The use of a *star schema* (the technical term for this multidimensional model) is substantially more efficient than reading the CO-PA tables directly. Figure 8.14 shows the dimensions for the S_GO operating concern. You can access this view of the InfoCube by selecting the correct InfoProvider from the list shown in Figure 8.10 and Figure 8.11 and then clicking on the **InfoProvider** icon.

Notice that the material-related characteristics you saw when we looked at the material master in Chapter 4 (division, profit center, material group, etc.) are all assigned to the **Product** dimension, whereas the sales-related characteristics you saw when we created sales orders in Chapter 6 (distribution channel, sales organization, customer group, sales office, etc.) are all assigned to the **Customer** dimension. You'll find organizational units under **Organizational Structure** and general selection criteria, such as currency type and valuation view, under **Mandatory Characteristics**. The dimensions in S_GO are derived entirely from fields in SAP ERP, but it's also common to model additional reporting dimensions for the classification of products and customers that only exist in SAP BW. As you're building up a data model, be clear about which entities are needed for price determination and so on in SAP ERP and which are needed only for reporting purposes in SAP BW. If a standard operating concern includes up to 60 characteristics, it's not uncommon to find another 40 master-data-related attributes in SAP BW.

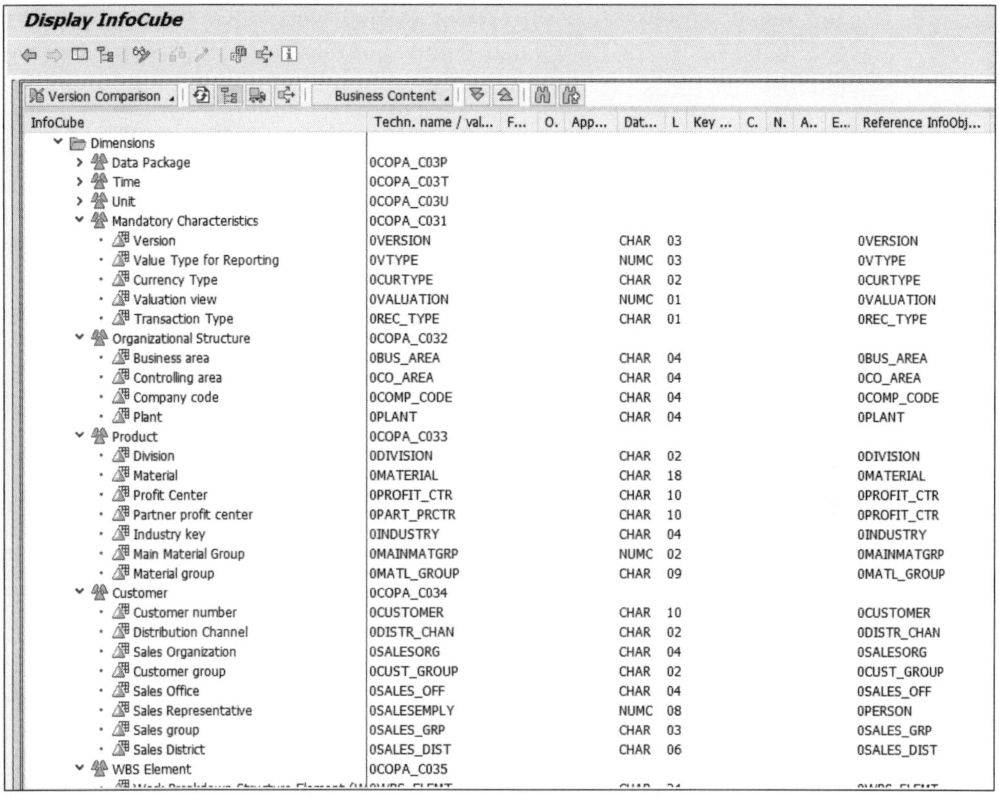

Figure 8.14 Dimensions of the S_GO InfoCube for CO-PA

This brings us to one of the most frequently asked questions since the advent of SAP BW—namely, whether you need Profitability Analysis in SAP ERP at all or whether all modeling can take place in SAP BW. In general, it still makes sense to configure and activate CO-PA even if you intend to do all your reporting in SAP BW because the purpose of CO-PA is not just to provide drilldown reporting on your sales orders and invoices: it's also to collect cost center costs during an allocation and order costs or production variances during settlement. If you refer to Chapter 7, you'll see that CO-PA is usually the final step for your period-close activities. In this context, the profitability segments behave as an account assignment, and you can always report on the partner relationship between the sender cost center and the receiver profitability segment, giving you a complete basis for an audit. You'll find that a properly configured CO-PA module gives you much for free that you would otherwise have to build rules for in SAP BW:

- You saw the *derivation* function when we created sales orders in Chapter 6 (see Figure 6.31 and Figure 6.32) and watched how the system used the information we entered to derive further characteristics for analysis.
- We used the *valuation* function to determine the product cost component split for the article we had just invoiced the customer for (see Figure 6.39).
- We used allocations, settlement, and top-down distribution in Chapter 7 to ensure that all costs ultimately ended up assigned to the appropriate profitability segment.

Cost Center Accounting

Although CO-PA is the obvious example of a multidimensional data structure, you'll also need multidimensional analysis in Cost Center Accounting. All the reports we looked at in Chapter 2 selected the relevant data set using the cost center (or cost center group) and then additional information such as the time frame, version, and (sometimes) a cost element group. This is because it's relatively easy to select data for all production cost centers, all sales cost centers, all marketing cost centers, and so on because the cost center is a *key field* in the underlying tables (tables COSP, COSS, etc.). If you need to turn the question around and determine salary and wage costs across all cost centers, it's a different story. To provide such a report, every data record has to be selected to determine whether salary and wage costs were incurred for the cost center in that time frame because the cost element under which the posting was recorded is not a key field. Moving the cost element data to a separate dimension from the cost center data when you set up your InfoProviders for SAP BW immediately resolves this issue by making it immaterial whether you query by cost center or by cost element from a performance point of view.

Figure 8.15 shows the InfoCube delivered for Cost Center Accounting, in which the cost center, cost element, and origin are modeled as separate dimensions to support just such reporting questions. Because the Cost Center Accounting tables (tables COSP, COSS, etc.) are also used to store the data for internal orders, production orders, WBS elements, sales order items, and so on, you'll find that the same benefits apply to the InfoCubes for Internal Orders, Projects, and Cost Object Controlling.

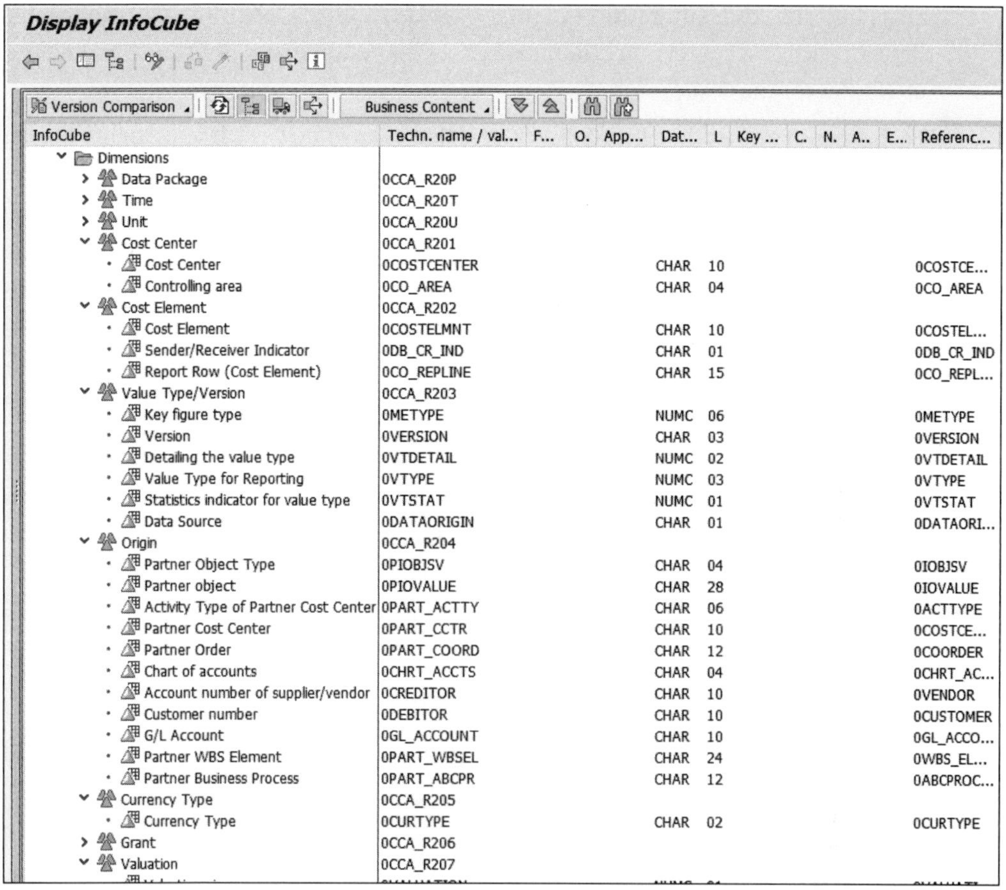

InfoCube	Techn. name / val...	F...	O.	App...	Dat...	L	Key ...	C.	N.	A..	E...	Referenc...
Dimensions												
Data Package	0CCA_R20P											
Time	0CCA_R20T											
Unit	0CCA_R20U											
Cost Center	0CCA_R201											
Cost Center	0COSTCENTER				CHAR	10						0COSTCE...
Controlling area	0CO_AREA				CHAR	04						0CO_AREA
Cost Element	0CCA_R202											
Cost Element	0COSTELMNT				CHAR	10						0COSTEL...
Sender/Receiver Indicator	0DB_CR_IND				CHAR	01						0DB_CR_IND
Report Row (Cost Element)	0CO_REPLINE				CHAR	15						0CO_REPL...
Value Type/Version	0CCA_R203											
Key figure type	0METYPE				NUMC	06						0METYPE
Version	0VERSION				CHAR	03						0VERSION
Detailing the value type	0VTDETAIL				NUMC	02						0VTDETAIL
Value Type for Reporting	0VTYPE				NUMC	03						0VTYPE
Statistics indicator for value type	0VTSTAT				NUMC	01						0VTSTAT
Data Source	0DATAORIGIN				CHAR	01						0DATAORI...
Origin	0CCA_R204											
Partner Object Type	0PIOBJSV				CHAR	04						0IOBJSV
Partner object	0PIOVALUE				CHAR	28						0IOVALUE
Activity Type of Partner Cost Center	0PART_ACTTY				CHAR	06						0ACTTYPE
Partner Cost Center	0PART_CCTR				CHAR	10						0COSTCE...
Partner Order	0PART_COORD				CHAR	12						0COORDER
Chart of accounts	0CHRT_ACCTS				CHAR	04						0CHRT_AC...
Account number of supplier/vendor	0CREDITOR				CHAR	10						0VENDOR
Customer number	0DEBITOR				CHAR	10						0CUSTOMER
G/L Account	0GL_ACCOUNT				CHAR	10						0GL_ACCO...
Partner WBS Element	0PART_WBSEL				CHAR	24						0WBS_EL...
Partner Business Process	0PART_ABCPR				CHAR	12						0ABCPROC...
Currency Type	0CCA_R205											
Currency Type	0CURTYPE				CHAR	02						0CURTYPE
Grant	0CCA_R206											
Valuation	0CCA_R207											

Figure 8.15 Dimensions of the InfoCube Cost Center: Cost and Allocations

8.2.3 Navigation Attributes

In addition to the data included in the operational tables, you'll often find yourself wanting to use additional data for drill down that wasn't included in the original table. An easy example is the drilldown in a cost center hierarchy that shows the person responsible for each cost center alongside the cost center key (see Chapter 3). In this case, you would create the cost center manager attribute for the cost center characteristic and use this to navigate within the query.

It's worth noting that though you never need to worry about the master data for reporting in SAP ERP, in SAP BW you have to make sure that you replicate not just the costs for each cost center (the contents of tables COSP, COSS, etc.), but also the master data for each cost center—in other words, the cost center hierarchy, the texts, and the attributes for the cost center.

Each piece of master data in SAP BW is modeled as an *InfoObject*. If you refer to Figure 8.15, you'll see InfoObjects for the cost center, the controlling area, the cost element, and so on.

If you double-click on InfoObject **0COSTCENTER**, you can check the master data for the cost center, as shown in Figure 8.16. One thing to be aware of is that though we talk about replicating master data to SAP BW, by no means do all the fields that we saw in the cost center master data in Chapter 3 need to be included in SAP BW. One challenge you'll face is to decide which attributes you want to report on for each master data element.

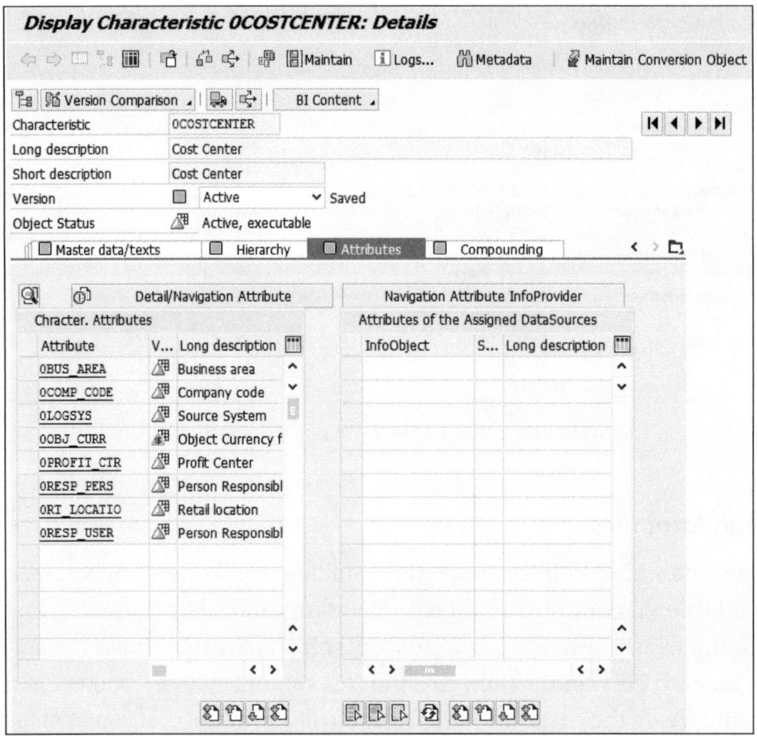

Figure 8.16 Master Data for Cost Center in SAP BW

Reading the tabs in Figure 8.16 from left to right, you'll see an extractor to read the cost center texts (**Master Data/Texts**), an extractor to read the cost center hierarchy

(**Hierarchy**), an extractor to read the attributes—in this case, business area, company code, and so on—and a tab called **Compounding** that ensures that the cost center is always read in combination with the controlling area. Remember that we saw in Chapter 2 that all data in CO is associated with a controlling area. Before you can run a cost center report, an administrator has to load the contents of each of these tabs to make sure you have the relevant cost center master data, cost element master data, and so on in your reports.

If you prefer, you can adjust your settings to determine that instead of preloading your *master data* from SAP ERP it should be read at run time. Figure 8.17 shows the **Master Data/Texts** tab for the cost center master data.

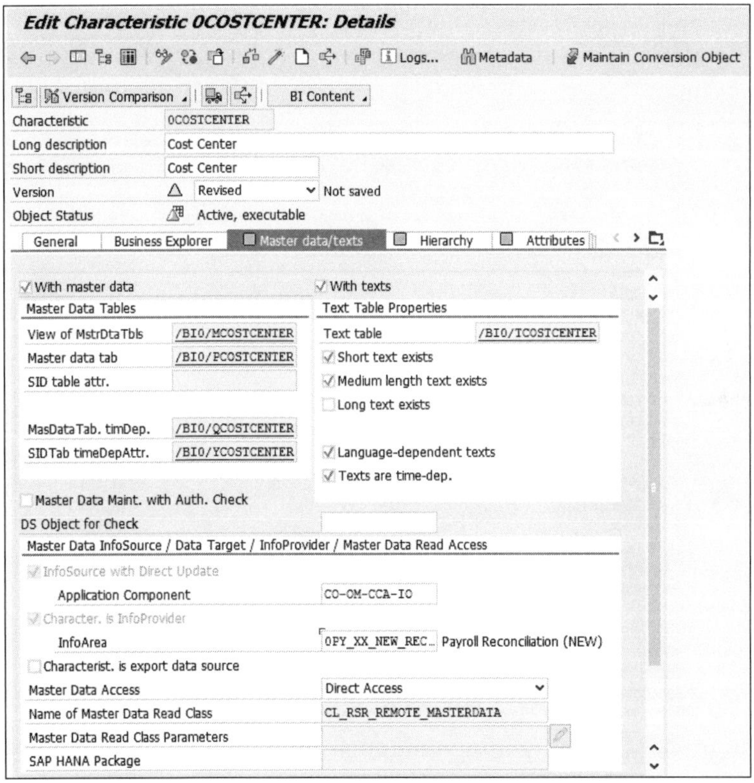

Figure 8.17 Master Data Access Options for Cost Center

The usual setting for the **Master Data Access** field is **Default** (which means access to replicated data), but in recent versions of SAP BW you can switch this to **Direct Access** to read data directly from the SAP ERP tables. Discuss with your system administrator whether this option makes sense in the context of your data volumes.

When we compare your options for reporting in Cost Object Controlling in SAP BW with those we just looked at in SAP ERP, the master data attributes provide the most powerful options for building new reports. Figure 8.18 shows the delivered InfoCube for Cost Object Controlling. You can flag any attribute of the **Material** InfoObject as a navigation attribute by clicking on the **Detail/Navigation Attribute** button (see Figure 8.18). Defining attributes such as division, material type, product hierarchy, profit center, and so on as navigation attributes allows you to build queries that select by these attributes, giving you substantially more options than we saw in the SAP ERP-based drilldown report in Figure 8.7.

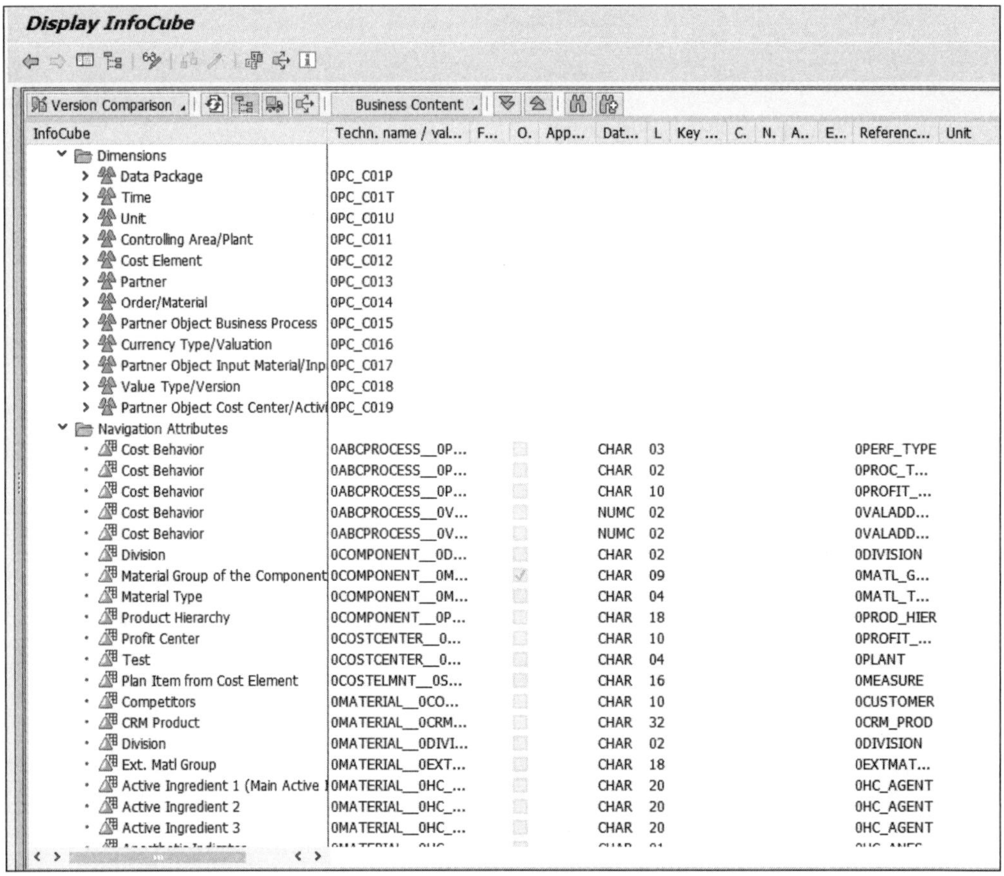

Figure 8.18 Navigation Attributes for Product Cost Controlling

If you refer to Chapter 4, it's clear that one of the reporting challenges you face is to decide what information you've entered in the material master that you're going to require for selection in your reports. You won't want most of the master data that controls the manufacturing process, but you will want all the dimensions by which you group materials for reporting. Remember also that material master records are often created using different naming conventions in each instance of SAP ERP. If you are bringing in material records from multiple SAP ERP instances, moving this data to SAP BW can involve a substantial mapping exercise.

8.2.4 Inclusion of Non-SAP Data

In general, SAP ERP reports show data from SAP ERP. However, there are countless cases in which you may need to mix data from SAP ERP and data from another system. One example is for reporting customer profitability. Profitability Analysis provides all the data you need to tell you the contribution margins per customer. However, if you're looking at retail customers, marketing people are likely to want to mix this information with demographic data about these customers to decide which customers to address in their next advertising campaign. Another example might be the use of data from a credit rating agency, such as Dun and Bradstreet, to include the customer's likelihood to pay alongside his profitability. To see an example of this, let's return to the CO-PA InfoCube and select the master data for the customer number. This includes attributes for the account group, city, and region that are being read from SAP ERP and additional attributes that are being selected from Dun and Bradstreet, as shown in Figure 8.19.

Not every organization runs all its business processes on SAP ERP. There are plenty of examples of mixed system landscapes in which only part of the relevant data is captured in SAP ERP and the rest is mapped from other systems—but because this book focuses on CO, we'll ignore those options. They're generally well covered in books dedicated to SAP BW reporting.

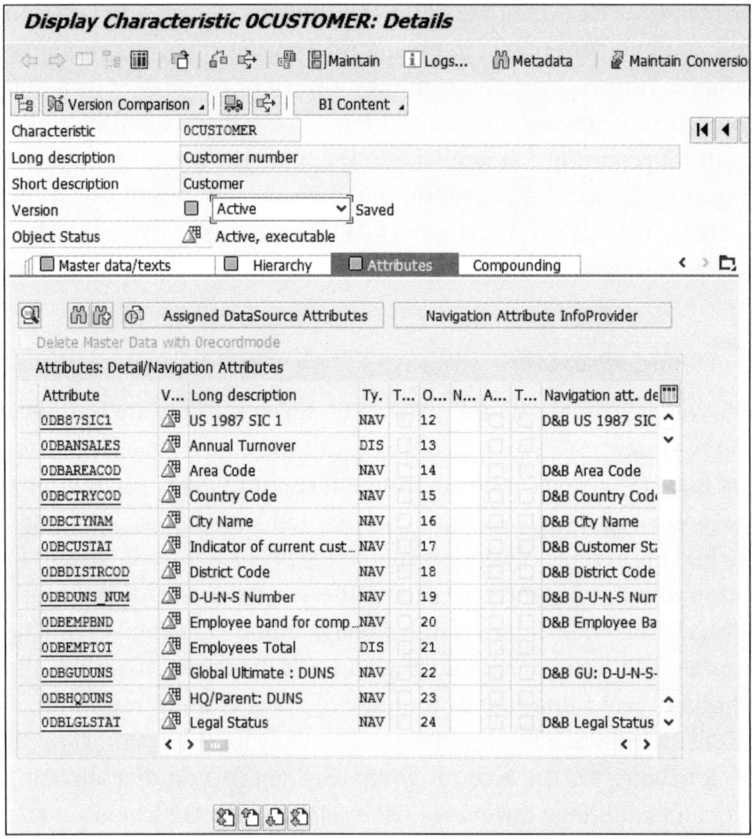

Figure 8.19 Master Data for Customer with Dun and Bradstreet Attributes

SAP BW and SAP S/4HANA

If your organization makes the move to SAP S/4HANA, the underlying data structure of the finance tables will change and totals records, such as tables COSP and COSS for controlling, will be replaced by views. The SAP BW extractors described here will continue to work by using *compatibility views* that select according to the old structures and ensure that the data loads to SAP BW can proceed as before. In Chapter 14, we'll introduce a new SAP BW extractor designed specifically to extract data from the Universal Journal.

8.2.5 Building Queries

Once you have your InfoProviders in place, you need queries to access the data. Although SAP delivers many queries for use in CO, it's worth knowing how to check the settings for an existing query and, if necessary, how to create a new one. You'll find the toolsets for query creation on your desktop, though some organizations are restrictive about providing access to the query building tools. If you have access, follow the menu path **Start • Programs • Business Explorer • Query Designer**, as shown in Figure 8.20. The system will then require you to log on to the required SAP BW system.

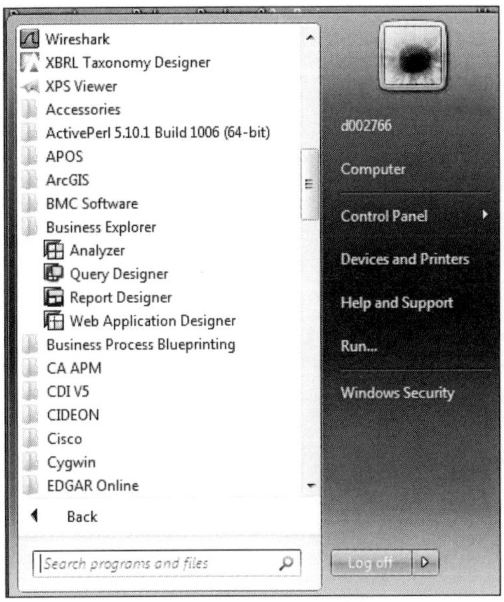

Figure 8.20 Finding Query Designer on Your Desktop

Once you've filled out the logon credentials, select either **Query • New** or **Query • Open.** In either case, you'll need to establish a link with the InfoProvider that contains the data you want to display in your query. Figure 8.21 shows the InfoAreas for Financial Management and CO. These correspond to the folders containing the BW content that you saw in Figure 8.11. Within this list, select the InfoArea that includes your InfoProvider. In our example, we'll select **Reporting Financials (EhP4)** and then **Profitability Analysis** to take us to a query to display data for the InfoCube we looked at in Figure 8.14.

All queries have the same basic structure regardless of the underlying InfoProvider. Figure 8.22 shows the initial screen for a query.

The area on the left provides the link to the InfoProvider. Here we're looking at the InfoProvider linked with the operating concern S_GO. In the case of our CO-PA cube, the structure of the InfoProvider gives a list of key figures and dimensions. The *key figures* are the value fields from SAP ERP plus several calculated key figures that are used to calculate the various contribution margins that characterize CO-PA reporting. The *dimensions* provide a grouping of the characteristics (product, customer, etc.). For each characteristic, you have two options. You can either use a variable to select, for example, the relevant customer group by choosing the relevant customer group as you run your report, or you can hard-code your query by selecting one of the customer groups that has been loaded to SAP BW from SAP ERP. You then will not be able to change this selection as you run the report.

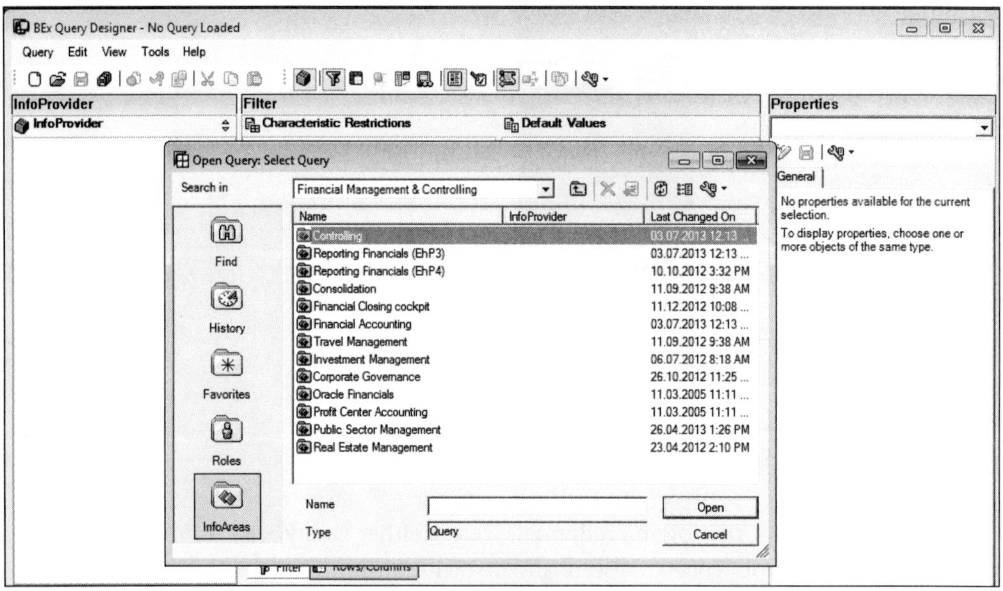

Figure 8.21 Choosing InfoProvider for Your Query

Figure 8.22 Building Queries (Filtering)

The area in the middle contains the *characteristic restrictions*—in other words, the filters that apply to the whole query. These are the fields in the selection screen that allow you to select the time frame, material group, sales organization, and distribution channel you're interested in by choosing a variable for these characteristics. Other restrictions can be hardwired for the query, such as the record types (transaction type) you want to view in this particular query. If you know you're only going to work with either live data or replicated data, then you can also hardwire the access method.

The next step is to define what should be shown in the lines of your report by clicking on the **Rows/Columns** button. Figure 8.23 shows a simple query comprising rows for each fiscal year and period and columns for revenues, costs, and the contribution margins. To execute this query in test mode, select **Query • Execute**. This will start the SAP BusinessObjects Explorer (SAP BEx) Web Analyzer tool, and a URL will appear that contains the selection screen for your query.

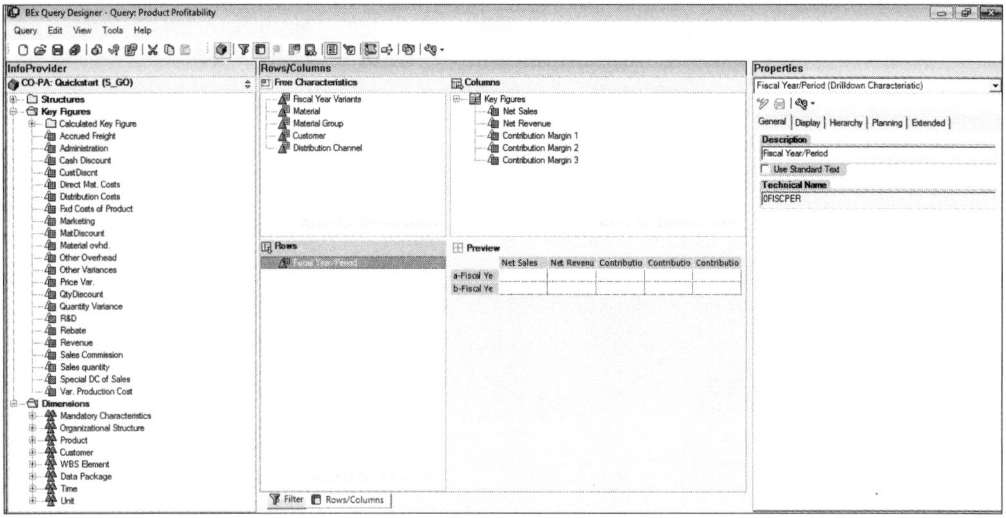

Figure 8.23 Building Queries (Rows and Columns)

So far, we've looked at the general architecture of SAP BW, how data is selected from the SAP ERP system (data provisioning is the technical term for this process), and how to build a query to display the data once it's in SAP BW. We'll now use the example of a cost center report to illustrate the options for displaying your data in SAP BW.

8.3 Cost Center Reporting in SAP BW

In this section, we'll look at different approaches to Cost Center Reporting to illustrate the different ways of using the latest version of SAP BW. We'll use the same basic report—cost center expenses with variances—to illustrate the different ways of accessing data from the cost center tables. You can access this report via the report launchpad we showed in Chapter 2, Figure 2.3 and selecting the line **Cost Centers: Actual/Plan/Variance – Cost Elements (Analysis).** This starts the SAP BEx Web Analyzer. To find out how to check the settings for this report and configure the launchpad to include your own reports, refer to Appendix B at *www.sap-press.com/4691*.

8.3.1 Reporting Using Virtual and Physical InfoProviders

Figure 8.24 shows the selection options for the Cost Centers: Actual/Plan/Variance—Cost Elements (Analysis) report. This contains all the InfoObjects that we identified as variables in the query. Most of the parameters will be familiar from SAP ERP reporting.

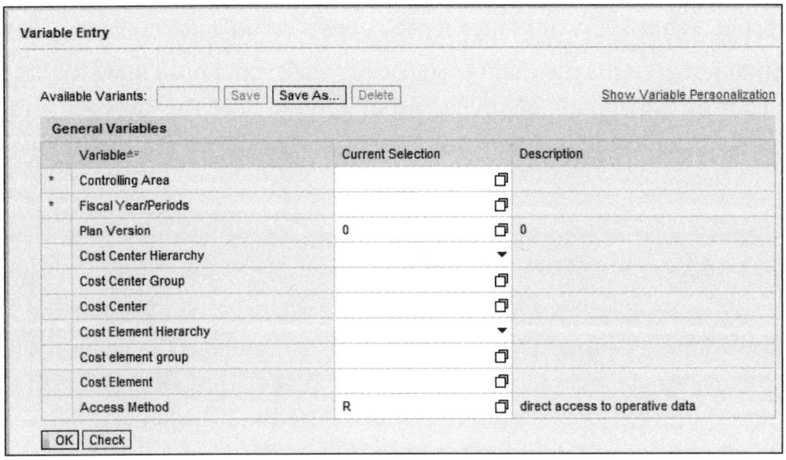

Figure 8.24 Selection Screen for Simplified Reporting

Hierarchies and Groups

In SAP ERP, it's easy enough to refer to cost center groups and cost center hierarchies as if they were synonyms for a cost center tree structure. In SAP BW, the cost center *hierarchy* is the root node that's entered in the controlling area (H1 in our examples), whereas a cost center *group* is any group that refers to this hierarchy. In SAP BW, the cost element *hierarchy* is the chart of accounts set for the controlling area (INT in our examples), whereas the cost element *group* is any group that refers to this hierarchy. In SAP ERP, you never need to enter the hierarchy in the selection screens because it can be derived from the settings for the controlling area in which you're working. In SAP BW, you need to include both fields in the selection parameters for your reports.

The other thing to notice is the **Access Method** option that's used in all queries built using the InfoProviders we saw in Figure 8.11. This allows you to switch between access method C (access to operative data) and access method R (direct access to replicated data):

- Access method C allows you to use the SAP BW data structures to select the data you need from SAP ERP when you execute the query. This uses the InfoProviders labeled **Direct** in Figure 8.11. Another term used here is *virtual InfoProviders*.
- Access method R represents the traditional use of a data warehouse in which data is first loaded from SAP ERP to SAP BW and then reported on. This uses the InfoProviders labeled **Replicated** in Figure 8.11. These are also known as *physical InfoProviders*.

Virtual InfoProviders

Virtual InfoProviders were introduced with SAP BW 7.0 to allow data modeling and transformation within a data warehouse environment but without the latency of waiting for overnight data replication. Further virtual InfoProviders were delivered with the support packages for SAP HANA. We'll introduce the virtual InfoProviders for Profitability Analysis and the Material Ledger in Chapter 13.

The result of executing the query is shown in Figure 8.25. If you compare this report with the cost center report we looked at in Chapter 2, Figure 2.8, the main difference you'll see is the block on the left, which allows you to drill down by selected dimensions. Choosing which dimensions you want to use for drilldown reporting is a key part of building your queries. You can then use these drilldown dimensions to create and save various *views* of the data contained in a single report.

Figure 8.26 shows the same report, but with a drilldown by partner, which we created by selecting the partner dimension in the free characteristics screen area on the left. This drilldown shows the cost centers and activity types that charged repair costs, energy costs, and on the like. You may remember that partner postings like this only exist for secondary costs occurring because of allocations and the like.

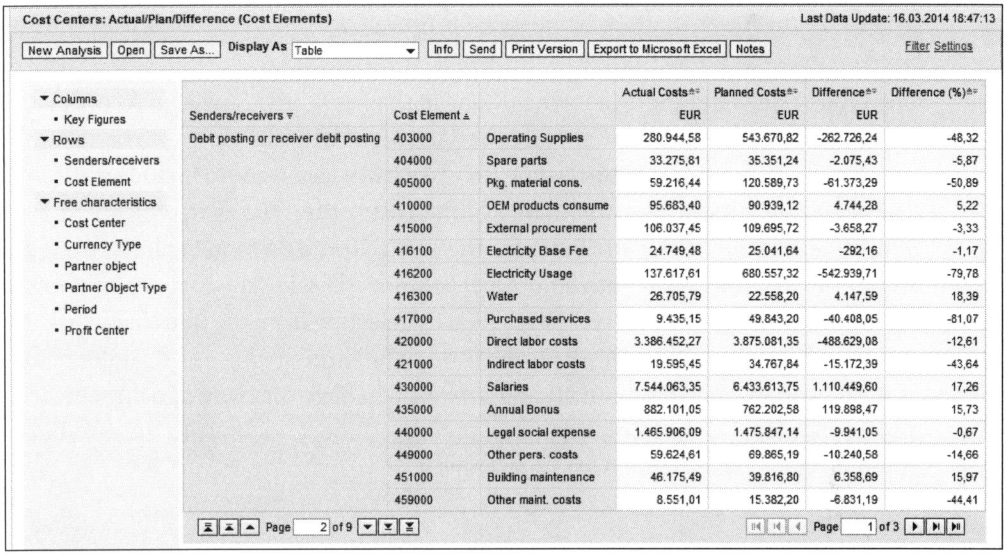

Figure 8.25 Sample Cost Center Report: Initial View

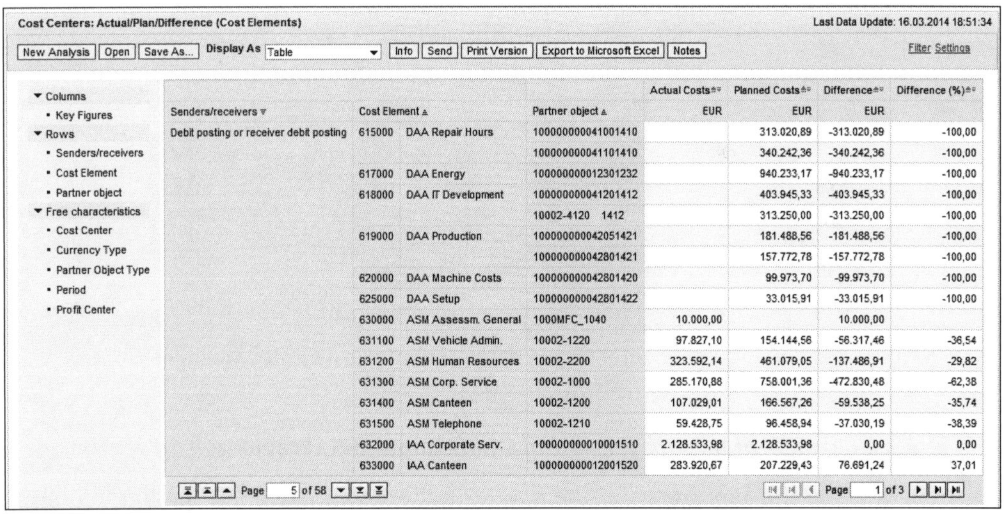

Figure 8.26 Sample Cost Center Report: Drilldown by Partner Object

One thing to get used to in SAP BW reporting is the use of the hash (#) symbol to mean "not assigned." Because the incoming electricity costs have been transferred from FI (primary costs), there's no partner dimension to be displayed for these lines, so SAP BW shows the hash symbol for these costs.

Once you understand the drilldown options in the query, you can begin to switch the dimensions around and really explore the data. Besides the drilldowns to be achieved by selecting elements from the DataSource, you may also want to include attributes for the master data, such as the name of the cost center manager, which you may remember was one of the *attributes* for the cost center we saw in Figure 8.16. Figure 8.27 shows the new report with additional columns showing the cost center and the person responsible. The cost center is added by selecting from the free characteristics shown on the left side of Figure 8.26 and then right-clicking on the cost center to add in the person responsible as an attribute. Once you have the hang of using the drilldown parameters and adding attributes, there are almost no limits to the number of potential views you can build for such a report.

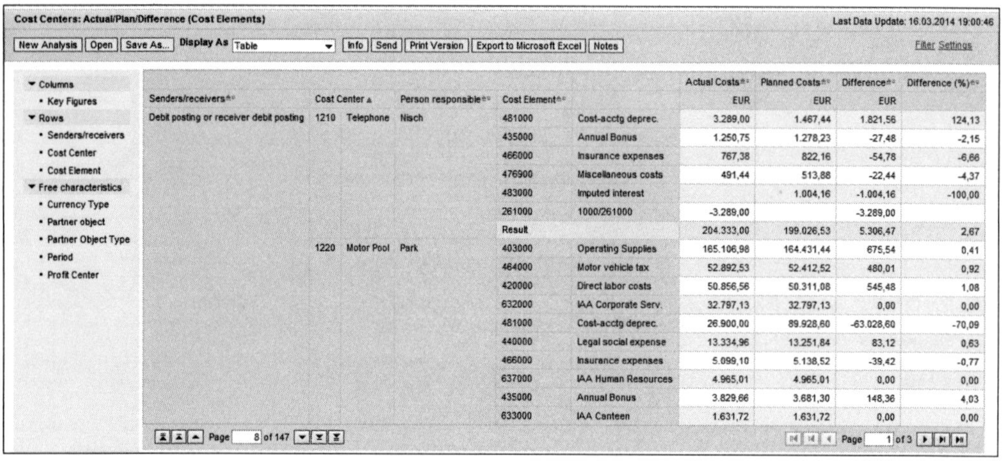

Senders/receivers	Cost Center		Person responsible	Cost Element		Actual Costs EUR	Planned Costs EUR	Difference EUR	Difference (%)
Debit posting or receiver debit posting	1210	Telephone	Nisch	481000	Cost-acctg deprec.	3.289,00	1.467,44	1.821,56	124,13
				435000	Annual Bonus	1.250,75	1.278,23	-27,48	-2,15
				466000	Insurance expenses	767,38	822,16	-54,78	-6,66
				476900	Miscellaneous costs	491,44	513,88	-22,44	-4,37
				483000	Imputed interest		1.004,16	-1.004,16	-100,00
				261000	1000/261000	-3.289,00		-3.289,00	
				Result		204.333,00	199.026,53	5.306,47	2,67
	1220	Motor Pool	Park	403000	Operating Supplies	165.106,98	164.431,44	675,54	0,41
				464000	Motor vehicle tax	52.892,53	52.412,52	480,01	0,92
				420000	Direct labor costs	50.856,56	50.311,08	545,48	1,08
				632000	IAA Corporate Serv.	32.797,13	32.797,13	0,00	0,00
				481000	Cost-acctg deprec.	26.900,00	89.928,60	-63.028,60	-70,09
				440000	Legal social expense	13.334,96	13.251,84	83,12	0,63
				466000	Insurance expenses	5.099,10	5.138,52	-39,42	-0,77
				637000	IAA Human Resources	4.965,01	4.965,01	0,00	0,00
				435000	Annual Bonus	3.829,66	3.681,30	148,36	4,03
				633000	IAA Canteen	1.631,72	1.631,72	0,00	0,00

Figure 8.27 Sample Cost Center Report with Attribute Cost Center Manager

8.3.2 Transient InfoProviders and Operational DataProviders

If you like the appearance of the queries but are worried about the burden of the infrastructure of InfoSources, InfoProviders, and so on, one option to consider from EHP 5 for SAP ERP 6.0 is *transient InfoProviders*. This allows you to have all the query options we just talked about, but there's no InfoProvider behind the query. The transient InfoProvider, as the name implies, only exists at runtime when you execute your query. Technically, the SAP BW query calls an InfoSet query in SAP ERP to perform the data selection. Let's look at these options.

To display the available InfoSet queries in SAP ERP, call up Transaction SQ01 and search for the InfoSet queries that include `CO_OM_CCA` in their key, as shown in Figure 8.28. Notice that there are also InfoSet queries for Product Cost Controlling in the same list.

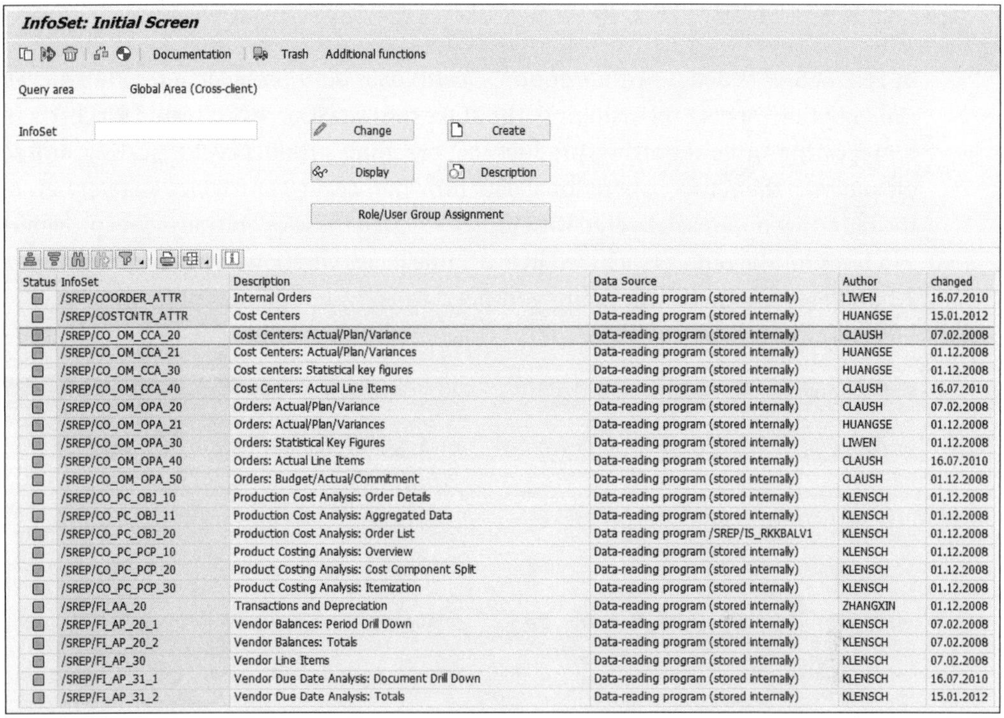

Status	InfoSet	Description	Data Source	Author	changed
	/SREP/COORDER_ATTR	Internal Orders	Data-reading program (stored internally)	LIWEN	16.07.2010
	/SREP/COSTCNTR_ATTR	Cost Centers	Data-reading program (stored internally)	HUANGSE	15.01.2012
	/SREP/CO_OM_CCA_20	Cost Centers: Actual/Plan/Variance	Data-reading program (stored internally)	CLAUSH	07.02.2008
	/SREP/CO_OM_CCA_21	Cost Centers: Actual/Plan/Variances	Data-reading program (stored internally)	HUANGSE	01.12.2008
	/SREP/CO_OM_CCA_30	Cost centers: Statistical key figures	Data-reading program (stored internally)	HUANGSE	01.12.2008
	/SREP/CO_OM_CCA_40	Cost Centers: Actual Line Items	Data-reading program (stored internally)	CLAUSH	16.07.2010
	/SREP/CO_OM_OPA_20	Orders: Actual/Plan/Variance	Data-reading program (stored internally)	CLAUSH	07.02.2008
	/SREP/CO_OM_OPA_21	Orders: Actual/Plan/Variances	Data-reading program (stored internally)	HUANGSE	01.12.2008
	/SREP/CO_OM_OPA_30	Orders: Statistical Key Figures	Data-reading program (stored internally)	LIWEN	01.12.2008
	/SREP/CO_OM_OPA_40	Orders: Actual Line Items	Data-reading program (stored internally)	CLAUSH	16.07.2010
	/SREP/CO_OM_OPA_50	Orders: Budget/Actual/Commitment	Data-reading program (stored internally)	CLAUSH	01.12.2008
	/SREP/CO_PC_OBJ_10	Production Cost Analysis: Order Details	Data-reading program (stored internally)	KLENSCH	01.12.2008
	/SREP/CO_PC_OBJ_11	Production Cost Analysis: Aggregated Data	Data-reading program (stored internally)	KLENSCH	01.12.2008
	/SREP/CO_PC_OBJ_20	Production Cost Analysis: Order List	Data reading program /SREP/IS_RKKBALV1	KLENSCH	01.12.2008
	/SREP/CO_PC_PCP_10	Product Costing Analysis: Overview	Data-reading program (stored internally)	KLENSCH	01.12.2008
	/SREP/CO_PC_PCP_20	Product Costing Analysis: Cost Component Split	Data-reading program (stored internally)	KLENSCH	01.12.2008
	/SREP/CO_PC_PCP_30	Product Costing Analysis: Itemization	Data-reading program (stored internally)	KLENSCH	01.12.2008
	/SREP/FI_AA_20	Transactions and Depreciation	Data-reading program (stored internally)	ZHANGXIN	01.12.2008
	/SREP/FI_AP_20_1	Vendor Balances: Period Drill Down	Data-reading program (stored internally)	KLENSCH	07.02.2008
	/SREP/FI_AP_20_2	Vendor Balances: Totals	Data-reading program (stored internally)	KLENSCH	07.02.2008
	/SREP/FI_AP_30	Vendor Line Items	Data-reading program (stored internally)	KLENSCH	07.02.2008
	/SREP/FI_AP_31_1	Vendor Due Date Analysis: Document Drill Down	Data-reading program (stored internally)	KLENSCH	16.07.2010
	/SREP/FI_AP_31_2	Vendor Due Date Analysis: Totals	Data-reading program (stored internally)	KLENSCH	15.01.2012

Figure 8.28 Delivered InfoSet Queries for Controlling

Right-click on **Cost Centers: Actual/Plan/Variance** and select **Queries for InfoSet**. This tells you the name of the SAP BW query for this InfoSet query. Armed with this knowledge, you can add the query to your report launchpad, as described in Appendix B (which you can download at *www.sap-press.com/4691*). Running this query will give you the same options in terms of building exceptions and storing views as you saw for a normal SAP BW query. The difference is that such a query can only include the data selected in the original InfoSet query. If you want to include the name of the responsible manager and the InfoSet query doesn't include this field, you can't add it because you don't have a modeled `0COSTCENTER` InfoObject behind the query (Figure 8.29).

Figure 8.29 Link from InfoSet Query to SAP BW Query

In EHP 6, SAP added a further option. *Operational data providers* provide an even leaner option for data provisioning. They take the DataSources delivered for cost center reporting, order reporting, product cost planning, product cost reporting, and so on and map them to an operational data provider. Table 8.1 provides an overview of the reporting options delivered with EHP 6. We used these operational data providers as a basis for the reports included in the home pages we showed in Chapter 2, Figure 2.2 and Figure 2.11. To use them, you need to activate business function `FIN_REP_SIMPL_4`.

DataSource	ODP Query	Description
0CO_OM_CCA_20	0FIN_CCA_T20_Q0001	Cost Centers: Actual/Plan/Variance—Cost Elements
0CO_OM_CCA_30	0FIN_CCA_T30_Q0001	Cost Centers: Actual/Plan/Variance—Statistical Key Figures
0CO_OM_CCA_40	0FIN_CCA_T40_Q0001	Cost Centers: Actual Line Items
0CO_OM_OPA_20	0FIN_OPA_T20_Q0001	Orders: Actual/Plan/Variance—Cost Elements
0CO_OM_OPA_30	0FIN_OPA_T30_Q0001	Orders: Actual/Plan/Variance—Statistical Key Figures
0CO_OM_OPA_40	0FIN_OPA_T40_Q0001	Orders: Actual Line Items
0CO_OM_OPA_50	0FIN_OPA_T50_Q0001	Orders: Budget/Actual/Commitment
0CO_PA_T10	0FIN_PA_T10_Q0001	Profitability Analysis: Net Sales (only for operating concern S_GO)
0CO_PC_10	0FIN_PC_T10_Q0001	Production Cost Analysis: Variances
0CO_PC_PCP_10	0FIN_PCP_T10_Q0001	Product Costing Analysis: Overview

Table 8.1 Operational Data Providers for Reporting

DataSource	ODP Query	Description
0CO_PC_PCP_20	0FIN_PCP_T20_Q0001	Product Costing Analysis: Cost Component Split
0CO_PC_PCP_30	0FIN_PCP_T30_Q0001	Product Costing Analysis: Itemization

Table 8.1 Operational Data Providers for Reporting (Cont.)

Now that we've looked at the data provisioning options for bringing data from SAP ERP to SAP BW and the options for querying this data in SAP BW, we'll look at your options for viewing the data provided by the SAP BusinessObjects tools.

8.4 Reporting with SAP BusinessObjects Tools

The first thing you need to know in the context of CO is that all the SAP BusinessObjects reporting tools use queries to access the data to be displayed. They can call an InfoSet query (the transient InfoProvider we just looked at), an SAP BW query that provides direct access to the SAP ERP data (sometimes called a virtual InfoProvider), or an SAP BW query that reads data that has been replicated to SAP BW (sometimes called a physical InfoProvider).

8.4.1 SAP Analysis for Microsoft Office

If you're familiar with SAP BEx Analyzer, it's easiest to move to SAP Analysis for Microsoft Office. This provides a spreadsheet frontend with all the drilldown options we discussed in the previous section.

Technically, the tool is an Excel add-in (you may have to activate it in your Excel options). When you call up your familiar spreadsheets, you'll see an extra tab, **Analysis,** on the far right. To connect your spreadsheets with the queries in SAP BW, choose **Insert • Select DataSource**. Figure 8.30 shows the InfoAreas delivered for simplified reporting (compare these against the folders shown in Figure 8.11). Choose the relevant query from the **Cost Center Accounting** folder.

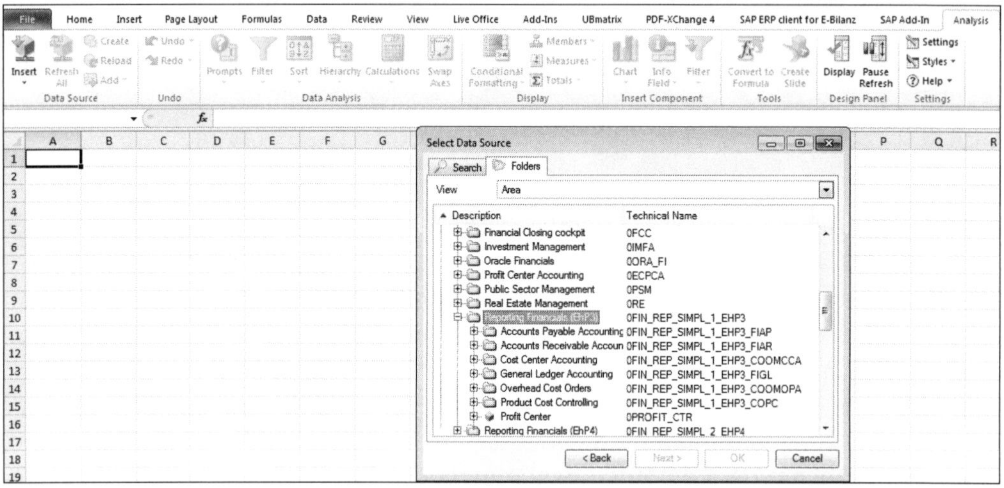

Figure 8.30 Selecting Query within SAP Analysis for Microsoft Office

Just as you saw in Figure 8.24, you will then be required to fill out a selection screen, as shown in Figure 8.31.

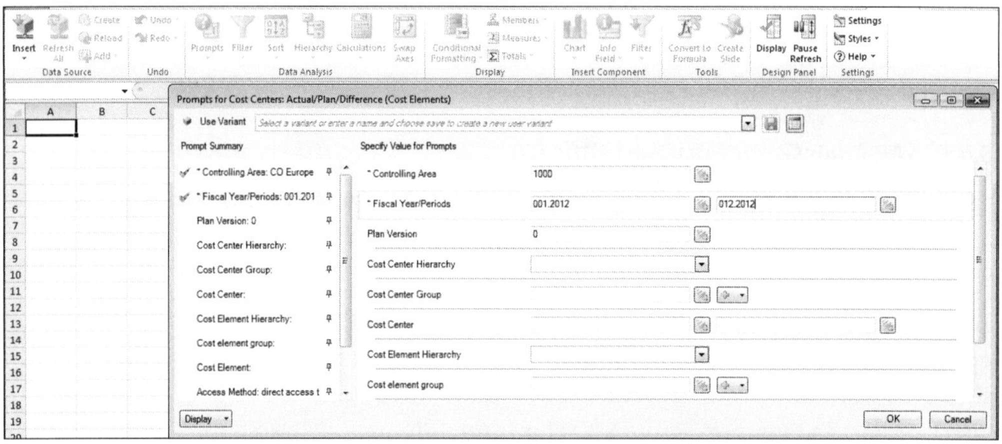

Figure 8.31 Selection Screen in SAP Analysis for Microsoft Office

Once you've completed the selection screen, you'll see the results in your spreadsheet. Figure 8.32 shows the result of executing the cost center query on the same dataset as we used earlier. To use the many drilldown options we discussed earlier, choose the **Display** option from the Excel ribbon. You can then pull dimensions into the rows and columns of your report as required.

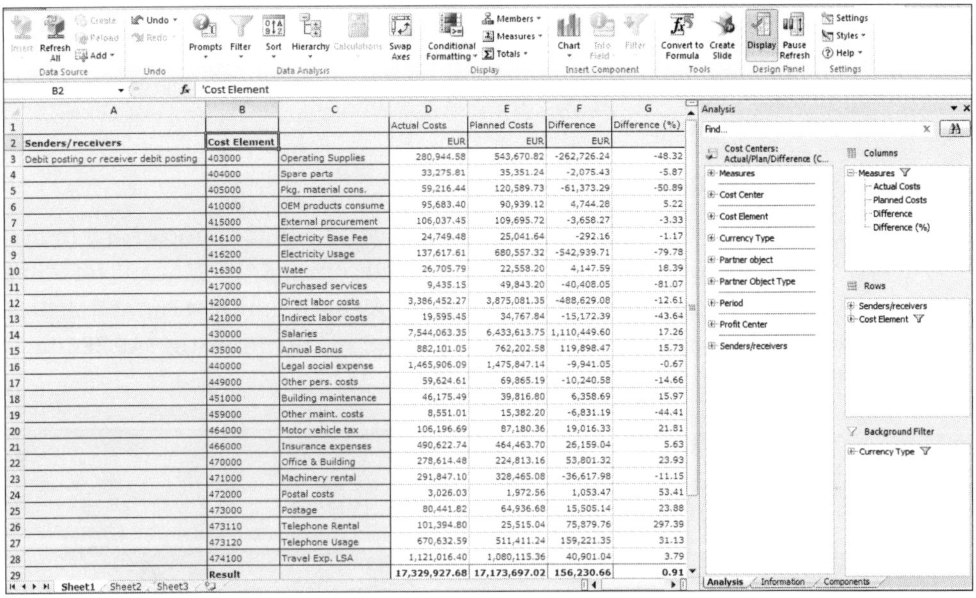

Figure 8.32 Cost Center Report in SAP Analysis for Microsoft Office

Figure 8.33 shows the result of adding the cost center and the name of the responsible manager as rows within the report. Again, after you start to explore you will soon get the hang of adding and removing dimensions and filtering on the members that interest you for further analysis.

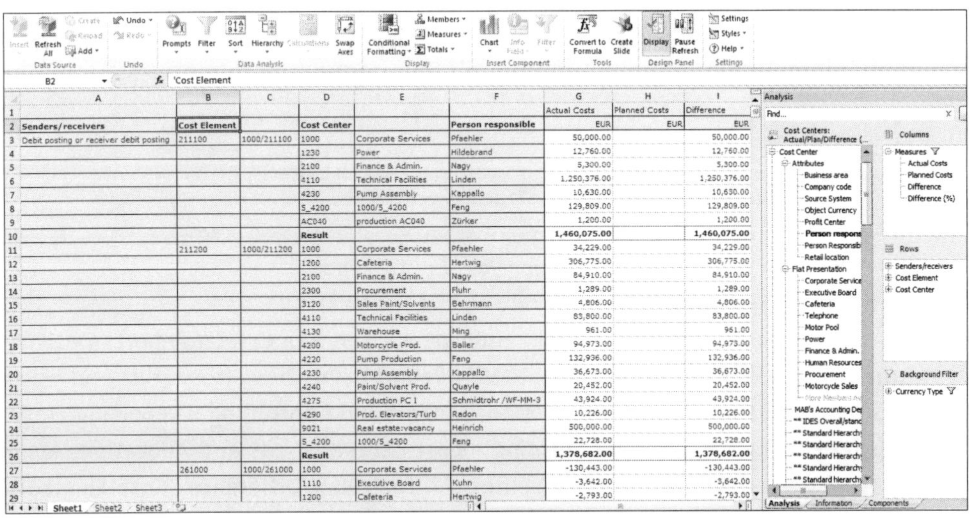

Figure 8.33 Cost Center Report with Additional Attributes

Although controllers tend to love the dynamic behavior of the spreadsheet approach, cost center managers often prefer to receive their cost center reports in a fixed format. In such a case, it's worth looking at SAP Crystal Reports.

8.4.2 SAP Crystal Reports for Controlling

You can use SAP Crystal Reports to build a formatted report on top of any InfoSet query, ABAP query, or transparent table in SAP ERP, or any SAP BW query, InfoCube, Virtual Cube, or operational DataStore (ODS) in SAP BW. Figure 8.34 shows SAP Crystal Reports (which is installed on the user's desktop) and the link to the SAP BEx query that will be used to select the data from SAP BW.

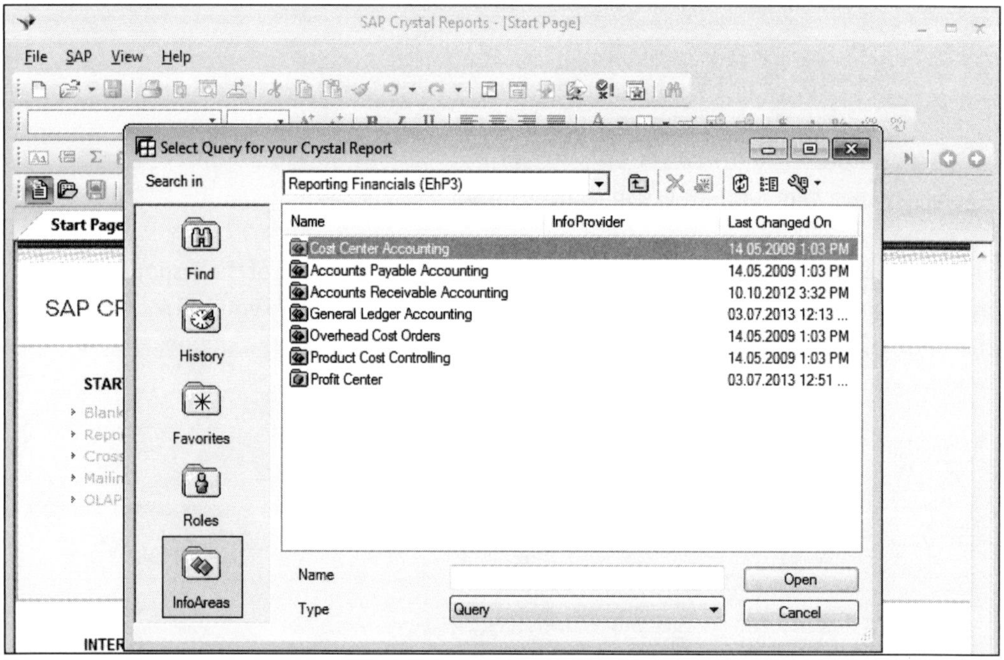

Figure 8.34 Choosing Query to Provision Your Crystal Report

To create a report that shows cost center data, open SAP Crystal Reports Designer from your desktop, select **SAP • Create New Report Using Query** (top right), and log on to SAP BW. Again, select **Financial Management and Controlling • Reporting Financials (EHP 3) • Cost Center Accounting • Cost Centers: Costs and Allocations** (as in Figure 8.11) and select the **Cost Centers: Actual/Plan/Difference (Cost Elements)** query. Then you can use SAP Crystal Reports Designer to format the data in this query to create a report like the sample report shown in Figure 8.35. This was built in one of the test systems to provide a taste of what the cost center reports we explored in Section 8.3 could look like with the improved formatting offered by SAP Crystal Reports.

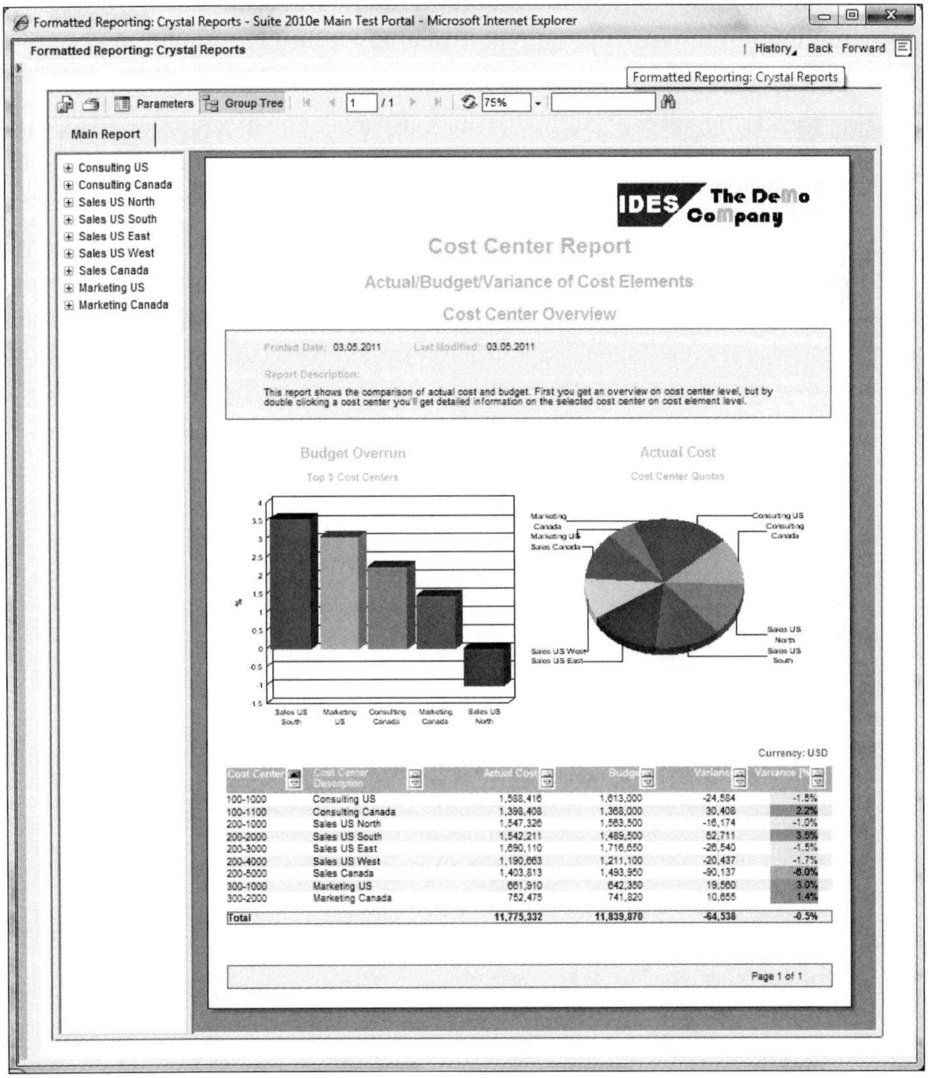

Figure 8.35 Sample Formatted Report for Cost Center Accounting

This approach requires you to license SAP Crystal Reports for the administrator who will build the reports. SAP Crystal Viewer is available for download according to a procedure described in SAP Note 1353044.

In addition, a handful of SAP Crystal Reports are delivered as part of EHP 5 for SAP ERP 6.0 and are covered by the SAP ERP license costs. These reports are listed in the report launchpads we showed in Chapter 2 (Figure 2.3 and Figure 2.12). You'll recognize them by the term *Crystal Report* in the report title. EHP 5 includes sample SAP Crystal Reports for Cost Center Accounting, Internal Orders, and CO-PA.

Starting with EHP 5 for SAP ERP 6.0, there's also a generic function for all SAP List Viewer reports that lets you use SAP Crystal Reports as an alternative to the table view.

Figure 8.36 shows the cost center line item report that we looked at in the first section of Chapter 2. To switch to the SAP Crystal Reports formatted version, click on **Change Layout** and select the **Display** tab shown in Figure 8.7. Switch to **Crystal Reports** and save the display settings for your layout. Every time you execute the report using this layout, SAP Crystal Reports will be used as a default. Notice that the SAP List Viewer toolbar is still shown in this view, meaning that all the functions we discussed in Chapter 2 are still available; we've simply changed the look of the report.

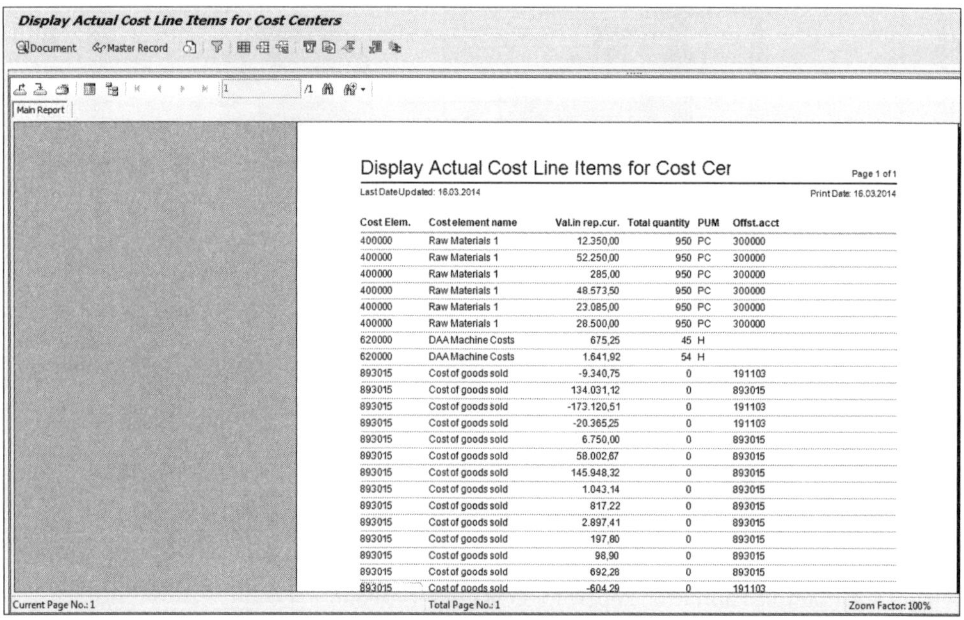

Cost Elem.	Cost element name	Val.in rep.cur.	Total quantity	PUM	Offst.acct
400000	Raw Materials 1	12.350,00	950	PC	300000
400000	Raw Materials 1	52.250,00	950	PC	300000
400000	Raw Materials 1	285,00	950	PC	300000
400000	Raw Materials 1	48.573,50	950	PC	300000
400000	Raw Materials 1	23.085,00	950	PC	300000
400000	Raw Materials 1	28.500,00	950	PC	300000
620000	DAA Machine Costs	675,25	45	H	
620000	DAA Machine Costs	1.641,92	54	H	
893015	Cost of goods sold	-9.340,75	0		191103
893015	Cost of goods sold	134.031,12	0		893015
893015	Cost of goods sold	-173.120,51	0		191103
893015	Cost of goods sold	-20.365,25	0		191103
893015	Cost of goods sold	6.750,00	0		893015
893015	Cost of goods sold	58.002,67	0		893015
893015	Cost of goods sold	145.948,32	0		893015
893015	Cost of goods sold	1.043,14	0		893015
893015	Cost of goods sold	817,22	0		893015
893015	Cost of goods sold	2.897,41	0		893015
893015	Cost of goods sold	197,80	0		893015
893015	Cost of goods sold	98,90	0		893015
893015	Cost of goods sold	692,28	0		893015
893015	Cost of goods sold	-604,29	0		191103

Figure 8.36 Cost Center Line Items as SAP Crystal Report

We can do the same if we return to the cost center master data report we showed in Chapter 3, Figure 3.11 and switch from **Show as Table** to **Show as Crystal Report**, as shown in Figure 8.37. If you then click on the icon in the top-right corner of the report, you can switch to full screen to show the whole report.

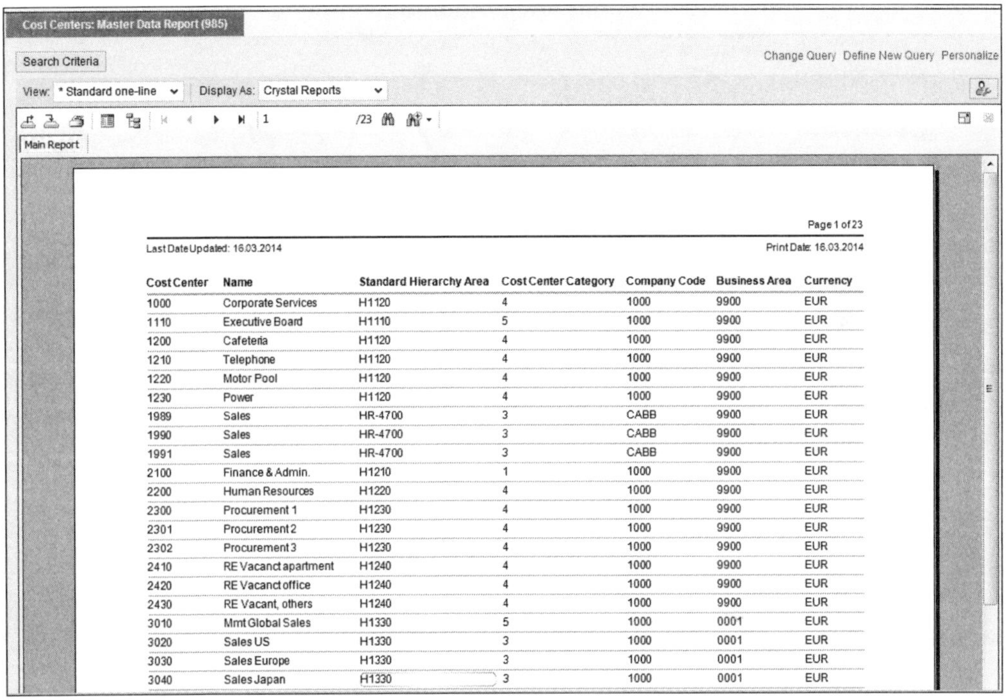

Cost Center	Name	Standard Hierarchy Area	Cost Center Category	Company Code	Business Area	Currency
1000	Corporate Services	H1120	4	1000	9900	EUR
1110	Executive Board	H1110	5	1000	9900	EUR
1200	Cafeteria	H1120	4	1000	9900	EUR
1210	Telephone	H1120	4	1000	9900	EUR
1220	Motor Pool	H1120	4	1000	9900	EUR
1230	Power	H1120	4	1000	9900	EUR
1989	Sales	HR-4700	3	CABB	9900	EUR
1990	Sales	HR-4700	3	CABB	9900	EUR
1991	Sales	HR-4700	3	CABB	9900	EUR
2100	Finance & Admin.	H1210	1	1000	9900	EUR
2200	Human Resources	H1220	4	1000	9900	EUR
2300	Procurement 1	H1230	4	1000	9900	EUR
2301	Procurement 2	H1230	4	1000	9900	EUR
2302	Procurement 3	H1230	4	1000	9900	EUR
2410	RE Vacanct apartment	H1240	4	1000	9900	EUR
2420	RE Vacanct office	H1240	4	1000	9900	EUR
2430	RE Vacant, others	H1240	4	1000	9900	EUR
3010	Mmt Global Sales	H1330	5	1000	0001	EUR
3020	Sales US	H1330	3	1000	0001	EUR
3030	Sales Europe	H1330	3	1000	0001	EUR
3040	Sales Japan	H1330	3	1000	0001	EUR

Figure 8.37 Cost Center Master Data as SAP Crystal Report

8.4.3 SAP BusinessObjects Dashboards for Controlling

Whereas the purpose of an SAP Crystal Report is to provide a standard format for a report that will be delivered in a familiar, stable form to every cost center manager, dashboards are meant to provide highly interactive interfaces that invite exploration. Here the focus is on a highly visual, intuitive representation of the data with lots of graphical elements, dials, and so on, as illustrated in the dashboard shown in Figure 8.38. This was built in one of the test systems to provide a taste of what the cost center reports we explored in Section 8.3 could look like if displayed as a dashboard.

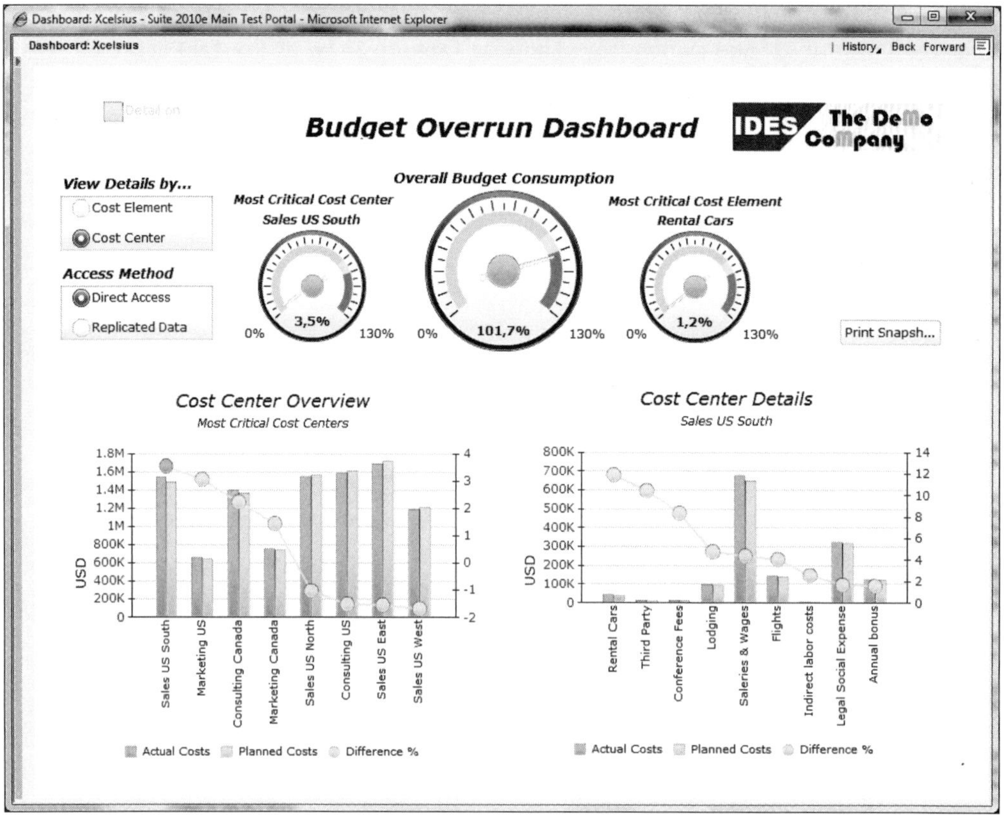

Figure 8.38 Dashboard for Cost Center Management

Although SAP Analysis for Microsoft Office, SAP Crystal Reports, and dashboards build on the queries available in SAP BW, whether transient, virtual, or replicated, SAP BusinessObjects Explorer uses a slightly different approach, as the name implies, to search and explore data.

8.4.4 SAP BusinessObjects Explorer for CO-PA Reporting

Because the data in profitability analysis lends itself better to exploration, let's look at how to use SAP BEx for profitability reporting. After logging on to SAP BEx, we entered the name of the query (ACT-IDES). The initial results are shown in Figure 8.39. The point of a report like this is to allow you to search and explore the data interactively.

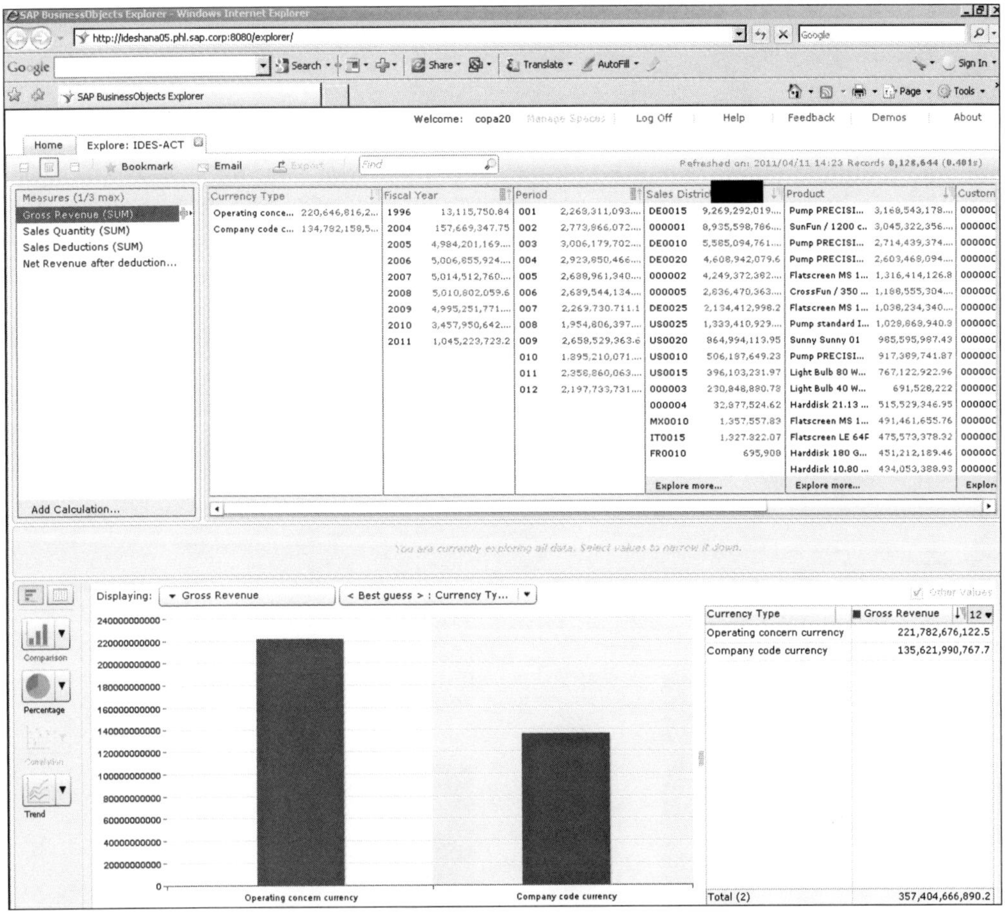

Figure 8.39 CO-PA Data in SAP BEx: Full Dataset

To drill down through this information, we'll select data from a single year (2010) and a single sales district. Figure 8.40 shows the result of setting this filter. You can see that a filter has been set by the two boxes for the filter conditions above the chart. You can continue like this, adding and removing filters until you have found the single record that interests you.

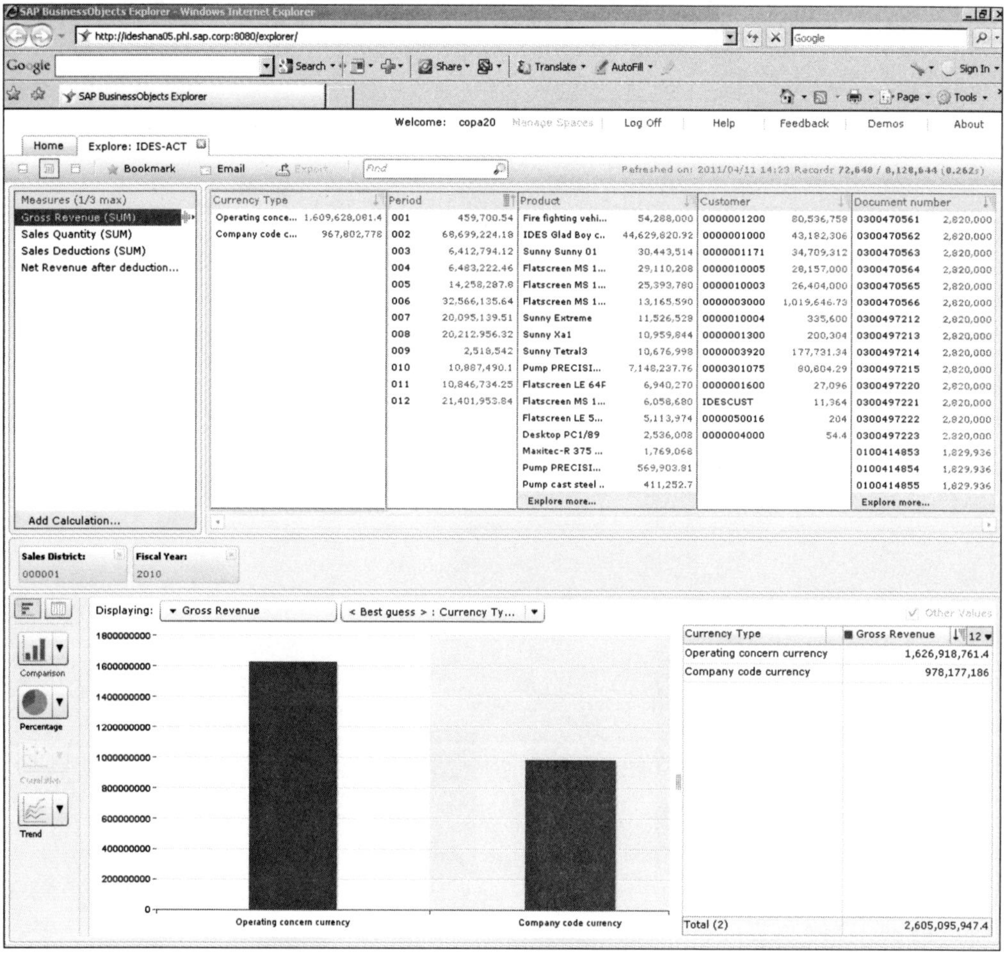

Figure 8.40 CO-PA Data in SAP BEx with Drilldown

8.5 Summary

In this chapter, we looked at your options for reporting on large volumes of data in SAP ERP and SAP BW. We showed how to build queries and to use these queries within SAP BEx and the various reporting tools from SAP BusinessObjects. We'll look at further options for reporting in Chapter 13, in which we'll explore the topic of SAP HANA in the context of reporting.

Chapter 9
Master Data in a Multisystem/ Shared Service Environment

This chapter covers change requests in SAP ERP. It introduces new solutions for handling master data in a multisystem environment with full governance requirements and in a shared service environment.

In Chapter 3 and Chapter 4, we discussed the need for consistent master data as a basis both for the planning and budgeting tasks we discussed in Chapter 5 and for the actual postings we performed in Chapter 6. Getting the master data right is essential if you are to have quality data in your ERP system, and agreeing on the master data can be one of the first challenges of an implementation. To prepare the material master, the purchasing, production, sales, accounting, and controlling departments have to come together and agree on a common code for each material. If several plants handle the material, then there needs to be a consensus on the common fields but also agreement about in what cases plants can go their own way and set parameters that make sense for them only.

As you start to think about cross-company goods movements of the kind we looked at in Chapter 6, you'll see that both companies have to use the same code for the material bought and sold to establish a stock-transfer process that moves materials from plant A to plant B. So long as everybody is working on the same SAP ERP system, the system enforces consistency because there's a single master record for each material. However, in larger implementations it's common to split production activities to several different SAP ERP instances. When we start to cross systems, this consistency becomes more important; it may only become clear that individual companies are using disparate codes for the same material when you report or consolidate. At the latest, when you start moving your costs into a data warehouse you'll need consistent master data; otherwise, your reports will be of little use. This can take place via consolidations as you move the data into the data warehouse, but many companies try to establish consistent rules for master data creation up front rather than trying to consolidate inconsistent data afterward. Ensuring that the master data is clean may sound like a technical challenge, but one of the most common causes of duplicate master data is the inconsistent use of abbreviations or special characters, so that two materials appear to be different when they aren't. It can also happen that the same material is sold on different markets under a different brand name. Effectively each country is speaking its own language for the material, but when the organization wants to report on the profitability of this product it needs to translate the variants into one common term.

The need for consistent master data is by no means limited to the material master. A consistent chart of accounts will make consolidating your General Ledger accounts for group reporting substantially easier. Business requirements often result in the separation of the SAP ERP Human Capital Management (SAP ERP HCM) system and the Financials and Logistics system. Here again if your payroll run is going to transfer data from HR to Financials, you have to make sure your cost center structure is consistent in both systems. The same applies to the time recording we discussed in Chapter 6. If you're going to assign time to a project or an order, your HR system is going to have to know which cost centers, activity types, projects, and orders have been created in your finance system.

Many organizations have already solved the technical side of master data management by establishing a separate master data server as a central hub in which they maintain their master data (and often Customizing settings as well) and then transfer the data from their master data server to the local ERP systems at regular intervals, usually using application link enabling (ALE) or similar technologies. It's also common to use SAP Solution Manager as a central repository for configuration settings and to replicate from there. Although this sounds sensible enough, there's still a challenge to decide which part of the master data is truly global and which is more local in nature and to set up your authorizations to support this division. Indeed, getting the right level of centralization and decentralization for your organization can be a key success factor in any project.

Along with the technical challenges of consistent data, recent years have seen changes in responsibility for executing a master data change and changes to the whole process of creating and changing master data. The main *business* reason for the change is the move toward treating the finance and controlling functions as a *shared service*. Once, every company in a large group had its own team of accountants and controllers, along with a group controlling function at headquarters, but quests for efficiency resulted in a split, with many of the more routine tasks (including some controlling tasks) being handled by a shared service center that can monitor receivables, collect payments, handle disputes, and so on—not just for a single company but for multiple companies in the same group.

For the controller, this means that new processes for requesting master data changes and new roles for approving and updating master data are defined. These processes usually include some kind of ticketing to initiate a change request and use workflow to move the ticket through approval and execution. In such an environment, the controller may initiate a request for a new cost element or cost center and comment on or approve such a change, but the creation of the master data as such is likely to be handled by an agent working in a shared service center, whereas the controller is only authorized to use the display transactions for the master data we discussed in Chapter 3 and Chapter 4.

In this chapter, we'll look at two solutions introduced to support these business requirements:

1. SAP introduced SAP Master Data Governance, Financials in EHP 4 for SAP ERP 6.0 to handle chart of accounts data, including the group chart of accounts, operational and local charts of accounts, and their hierarchies. We discussed these accounts when we looked at accounts and primary cost elements in Chapter 4. If you have global, operational, and country-specific charts of accounts, don't be afraid that a central hub means that headquarters makes all the rules. You can set up central workflows for the global and operational charts of accounts and local workflows for country-specific charts of accounts in the same environment. In EHP 5, the cost element, cost center, profit center, and group companies entities were added. In the enhancement packages that followed, SAP added further data models for materials, suppliers, customers, and business partners. From EHP 5, it's also possible to add your own master data entities if you decide that you want to use the same mechanisms to handle, for example, the creation of an activity type.
2. SAP introduced the SAP Shared Service Framework in EHP 5 for SAP ERP 6.0 to provide support for multiple business functions through one central shared service hub. In this solution, shared services for initiating master data changes and starting processes, such as a leave request in human resources, sit alongside business processes in the Financial Accounting (FI) and Controlling (CO) components of SAP ERP Financials. Because the focus here is on efficiency, the SAP Shared Service Framework supports the process of handling, for example, a payment dispute or a change to the vendor master, but also provides functions that allow you to monitor the level of service of the shared service center—tracking the time it takes from

receiving the request to the delivery of a solution. If you're the controller, you can then use these metrics to find out how long the shared service center took from the moment you requested a cost center change to the completion of your ticket.

Before we look at either of these solutions, let's return to the change request we discussed at the end of Chapter 3 as a simple way of providing a SOX-compliant ticketing solution if you're working with a single SAP ERP system.

9.1 Change Requests in SAP ERP

We ended Chapter 3 with a discussion of the use of change requests to initiate a cost center creation and described the approval workflow triggered by this request and how the notification provides a follow-up action to allow the controller to call the transaction and make the relevant change in SAP ERP. Let's now look behind the scenes to understand the mechanisms controlling such change requests.

To view the settings for change requests in the IMG, follow the menu path **Cross-Application Components • Internet/Intranet Services • Internal Service Request (ISR) • Scenario Definition • Define Scenario**. You might want to look at these settings with your system administrator to help you decide whether such a change request would meet your compliance needs or whether you need the more sophisticated options we'll cover later in the chapter.

Figure 9.1 shows some of the scenarios delivered in SAP ERP (there are too many to fit on one screen). To cover the master data we looked at in Chapter 3, you should explore the following scenarios:

- **Create Cost Center (SMC1)**
- **Change Cost Center (SMC2)**
- **Create Internal Order (SM01)**
- **Change Internal Order (SM02)**
- **Request to Change Project (SPS1)**
- **Request to Change WBS Element (SPS2)**
- **Create WBS Element (SPS3)**
- **Change WBS Element (extended) (SPS4)**
- **Notification About Missing Cost Center (SREA)**
- **Notification About Cost Center Change (SREB)**

- **Notification About Missing Internal Order (SREC)**
- **Notification About Change of Internal Order (SRED)**
- **Request to Create Cost Center (SRK1)**
- **Request to Change Cost Center (SRK2)**
- **Request to Lock Cost Center (SRK3)**

If you're interested in the change requests we discussed for budget changes in Chapter 5, you might also want to look at the following scenarios:

- **Budget Request (SRB1)**
- **Budget Request with Approval (SRB2)**
- **Budget Change (SRB3)**
- **Budget Change with Approval (SRB4)**
- **Budget Transfer (SRBA)**
- **Budget Transfer with Approval (SRBB)**

We'll now look at the scenario for requesting the creation of a cost center in more detail.

To view the scenario details, select scenario SMC1 (**Create Cost Center**) from the list shown in Figure 9.1. On the **Basic Data** screen (see Figure 9.2), notice that the scenario includes a version and characteristics. The characteristics provide the link to the data in SAP ERP by linking the request scenario with the underlying data structure of the cost center in SAP ERP.

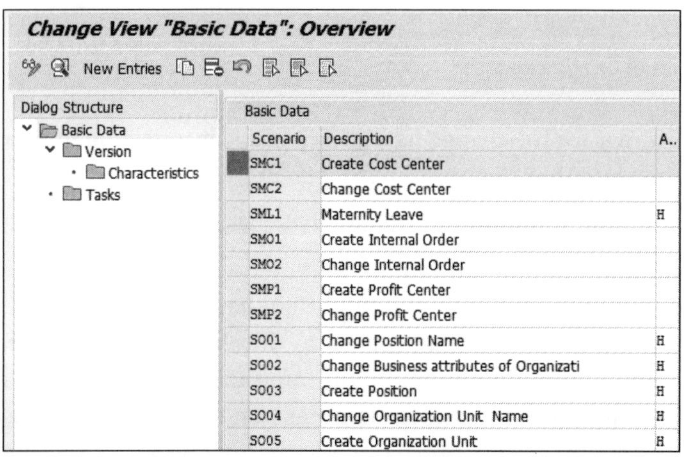

Figure 9.1 Change Request Scenarios in SAP ERP

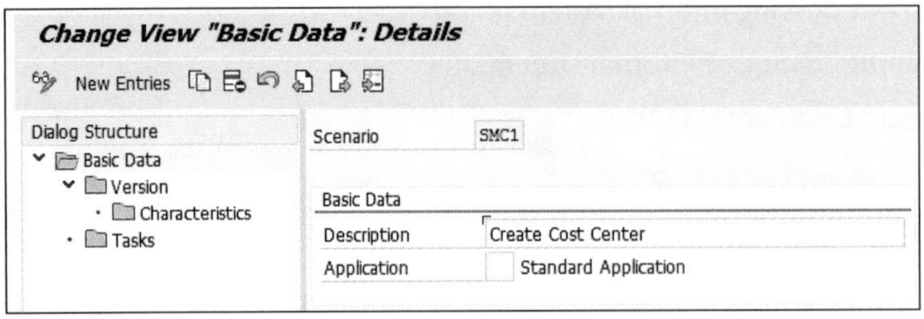

Figure 9.2 Basic Data for Change Request

To look at these fields, select the **Version** folder (on the left) and then the **Characteristics** folder. This takes you to the link between the characteristics in the change request and the data dictionary fields in SAP ERP, as shown in Figure 9.3. This ensures that each field in the form can display the correct master data in SAP ERP and perform checks and validations against this master data, ensuring that you can't accidentally request the creation of a cost center that already exists.

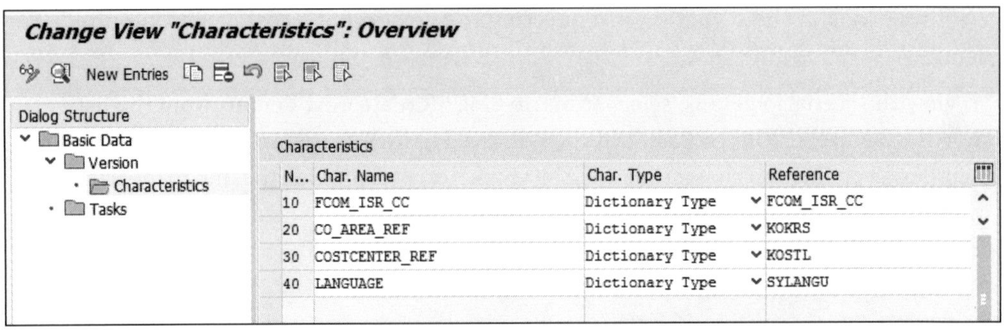

Figure 9.3 Characteristics of Change Request

Let's now look at the settings for the change request as a whole by selecting the **Version** folder. This takes you into the screen shown in Figure 9.4.

The version provides the link to the three elements that characterize a cost center change request:

1. The **Notification Type** indicates the type of notification that will be created with reference to the change request in SAP ERP. As far as the change request is concerned, its main feature is that it can record status information. Also notice that this scenario is flagged as requiring approval. In other words, the change request cannot be completed until the notification has the status **Approved**.

2. The form settings include a link to the Adobe form (ISR_FORM_SMC1) we saw the manager fill out in Figure 3.39 and Figure 3.40 in Chapter 3. This form is linked with fields in SAP ERP so that the relevant checks on the existence of the cost center and related fields can be performed as the manager fills out his form. You can use the icons beside the form field to access this form. We're using an SAP Interactive Forms by Adobe in this example, but you can use other form technologies instead.
3. The **Action Box** button provides a link to the transactions that the processor of the form will use to update the cost center information in SAP ERP.

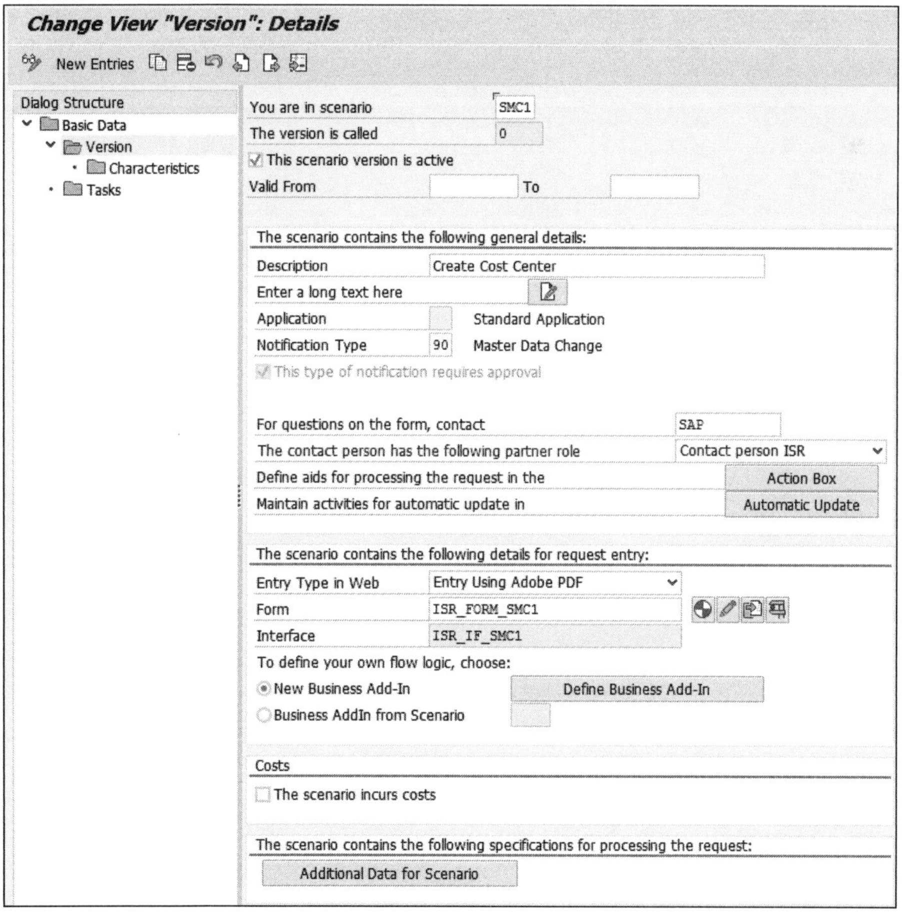

Figure 9.4 Details of Cost Center Change Scenario

Let's first look at the form (shown in Figure 9.5). If you don't have developer authorization, switch to **Display** mode and then click on the **Display** button next to the form field. Organizations can tailor these forms to include different data, formatting, and so on. You won't incur any additional license costs if you use the SAP Interactive Forms by Adobe as they are, but you'll need to change your license agreement if you want to build new forms (a similar agreement to the one we discussed for SAP Crystal Reports in Chapter 8).

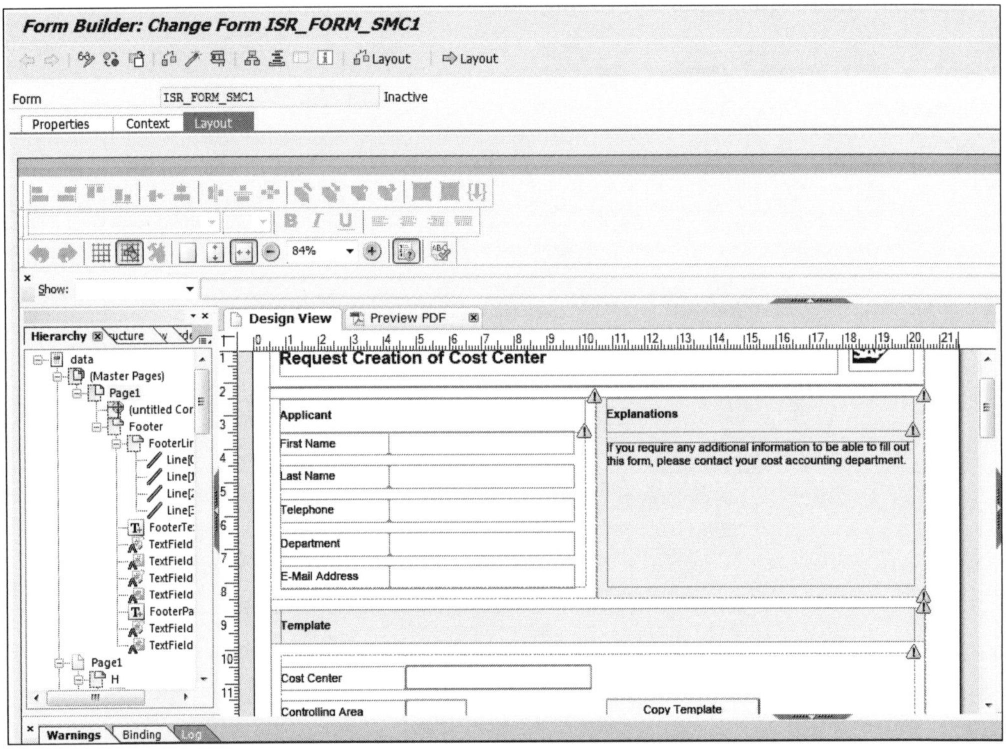

Figure 9.5 Sample Adobe Form for Cost Center Change

To display the related actions, click on the **Action Box** button shown in Figure 9.4. Figure 9.6 shows all the master data change actions. The context of the form tells the system to offer cost center change actions from the notification. There are two ways to implement your changes:

1. **Automatically**
   The data entered in the form is used to generate the master data automatically without the processor entering the master data transaction.

2. **Manually**
   The data from the form is passed to the master data change transaction, but the processor can make adjustments if necessary.

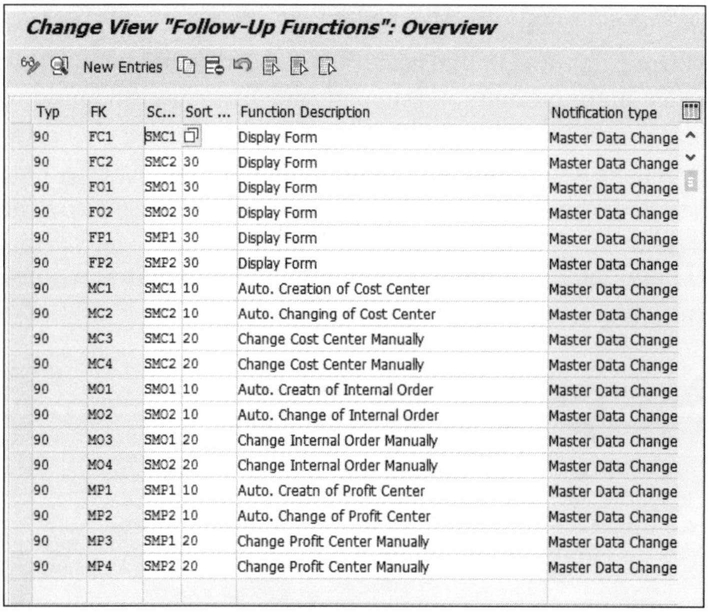

Change View "Follow-Up Functions": Overview

New Entries

Typ	FK	Sc...	Sort ...	Function Description	Notification type
90	FC1	SMC1		Display Form	Master Data Change
90	FC2	SMC2	30	Display Form	Master Data Change
90	FO1	SMO1	30	Display Form	Master Data Change
90	FO2	SMO2	30	Display Form	Master Data Change
90	FP1	SMP1	30	Display Form	Master Data Change
90	FP2	SMP2	30	Display Form	Master Data Change
90	MC1	SMC1	10	Auto. Creation of Cost Center	Master Data Change
90	MC2	SMC2	10	Auto. Changing of Cost Center	Master Data Change
90	MC3	SMC1	20	Change Cost Center Manually	Master Data Change
90	MC4	SMC2	20	Change Cost Center Manually	Master Data Change
90	MO1	SMO1	10	Auto. Creatn of Internal Order	Master Data Change
90	MO2	SMO2	10	Auto. Change of Internal Order	Master Data Change
90	MO3	SMO1	20	Change Internal Order Manually	Master Data Change
90	MO4	SMO2	20	Change Internal Order Manually	Master Data Change
90	MP1	SMP1	10	Auto. Creatn of Profit Center	Master Data Change
90	MP2	SMP2	10	Auto. Change of Profit Center	Master Data Change
90	MP3	SMP1	20	Change Profit Center Manually	Master Data Change
90	MP4	SMP2	20	Change Profit Center Manually	Master Data Change

Figure 9.6 Follow-Up Actions for Form

SAP Interactive Forms by Adobe

In this chapter we have barely scratched the surface of what you can do with interactive forms. If you want to learn more, refer to the book *SAP Interactive Forms by Adobe* by Hauser, Deutersfeld, Rehmann, and Szücs (SAP PRESS, 2011, *www.sap-press.com/2890*).

Now that we've looked at a simple change request that initiates a notification to approve a master data change in SAP ERP, let's look at a more complex scenario to introduce the new functions for SAP Master Data Governance in Financials.

9.2 New Solutions for Handling Master Data in a Multisystem Environment

The primary aim of SAP Master Data Governance, Financials is to ensure that consistent master data is prepared in a central hub and then made available across *multiple* systems. From a business point of view, the goal is to establish global standards to provide a consistent view of the business and support data-driven decision making. The software can be installed either on a dedicated hub or on top of one of your existing SAP ERP instances. Figure 9.7 shows one example of the use of SAP Master Data Governance, Financials with chart of account data being maintained centrally and then transferred to the SAP ERP systems and the consolidation system to ensure that the financial results from the entities performing their operations in SAP ERP can be submitted easily to the group system for consolidation.

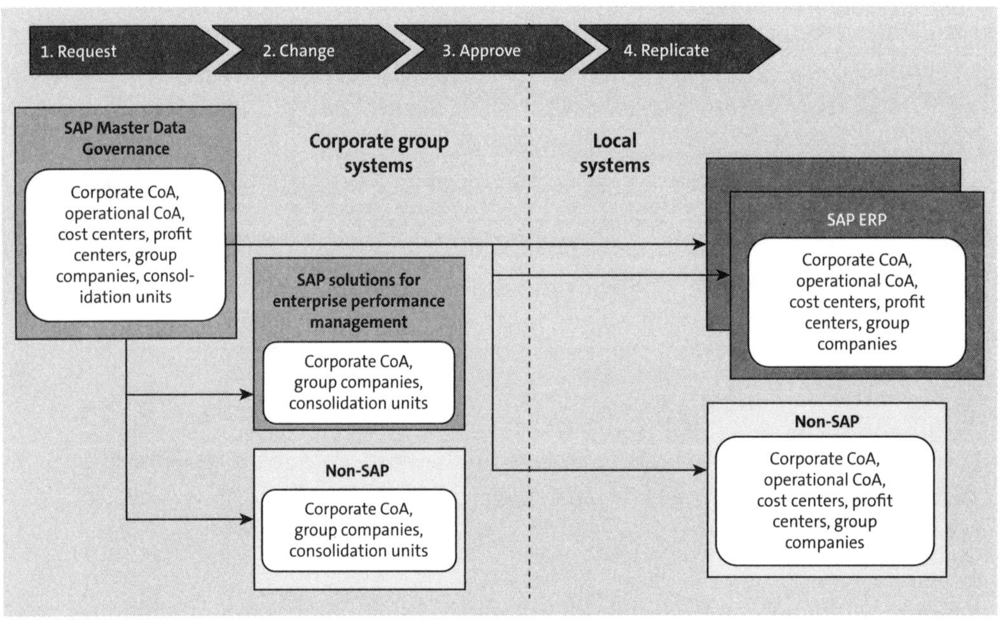

Figure 9.7 Overview of SAP Master Data Governance

With this approach, we are harmonizing the data model for Finance. This means that all companies will be using the same group and operational chart of accounts and ensures consistent mapping between the operational and corporate chart of accounts. Arrows indicate a change request process along the top because *governance* is a key part of the approach, with proper approvals of all changes being recorded in the system and providing documentation to auditors about when and why certain changes were made.

9.2.1 Data Modeling in SAP Master Data Governance for Financials

The data model for SAP Master Data Governance is not simply a copy of the master data tables in SAP ERP but a separate data model designed to stage the master data prior to replication and support harmonized reporting. The idea is that master data is defined once and used everywhere. Using a data model that is decoupled from the SAP ERP model makes it easier to identify master data defects early, before the master data has found its way into multiple systems.

In terms of data modeling, the master data governance requirements are similar to the requirements for master data reporting in SAP BW. Whereas in SAP BW we discussed a data model that included different InfoObjects for cost centers, customers, materials, and so on, in SAP Master Data Governance, Financials we find a data model that comprises multiple entity types and includes such information as their attributes, whether they can be viewed in a hierarchy, how groups are handled, and so on. It's important to understand that this model links related data, so the link between cost center and profit center is considered a part of such a model. From SAP Master Data Governance, Financials 7.0, you will also find a link between accounts and primary cost elements, as we discussed in Chapter 4. Figure 9.8 shows the relationships between the various entities in Financials.

SAP delivers several data models for master data governance, which your administrator can activate via the IMG. You'll find the settings under **Cross Application Components • Processes and Tools for Enterprise Applications • Master Data Governance • Central Governance • General Settings • Data Modeling • Edit Data Model.** The delivered data models include the following (again, look at these options with your administrator):

- **Chart of Accounts and Org. Units (OG)**
  This model was delivered in EHP 5 for use in combination with business function `FIN_MDM_ORG` (Master Data Governance for Financials, Organizational Units). The data model includes companies, profit centers, and cost centers, in addition to charts of accounts and cost elements. If you plan to implement EHP 5 or later, use this data model rather than OF. If you will be sending accounts and cost elements to both SAP ERP and SAP S/4HANA systems, refer to SAP Note 2021246 to see how the account/cost element transformation takes place in each case.

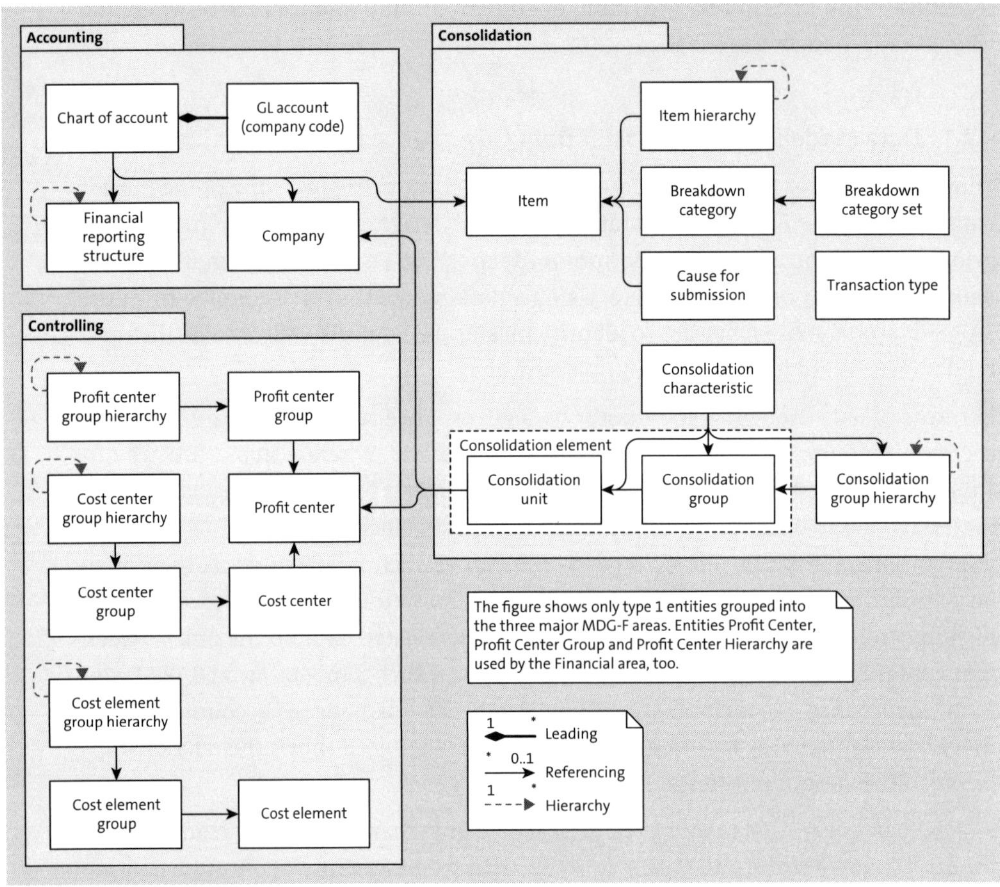

Figure 9.8 Data Model for Financial Entities in SAP Master Data Governance

- **Chart of Accounts (0F)**
  This model was delivered in EHP 4 for use in combination with the business function `FIN_MDM_ACC` (Financial Master Data Management: Charts of Accounts). The data model supports the central definition of global and local charts of accounts. This model has been superseded by data model 0G.
- **Business Partner (BP)**
  This covers the master data for the business partner, the supplier, and the customer. Delivery of the supplier model began with EHP 5 and continued over subsequent enhancement packages. Delivery of the vendor model began with EHP 6 and continued over subsequent enhancement packages. If you will be sending busi-

ness partners to SAP ERP, SAP CRM, and SAP S/4HANA systems, refer to SAP Note 2221398 to understand the variances in the associated data models.

- **Material Maintenance (MM)**
  This covers the master data for the material master. Delivery of the model began with EHP 5 and continued over subsequent enhancement packages. From a controlling point of view, you will find that the MDG-M model covers both general master data and valuation-specific data, making it compatible with the various views of the material master that we looked at in Chapter 4.

Figure 9.9 shows the entity types included in the master data model Chart of Accounts and Org. Units (OG). The entity types of most interest to the controller are the cost elements (CELEM), cost element groups (CELEMG), cost element hierarchies (CELEMH), cost centers (CCTR), cost center groups (CCTRG), and cost center hierarchies (CCTRH). If you're concerned about the difference between a group and a hierarchy, refer to the note in Chapter 8, Section 8.3.

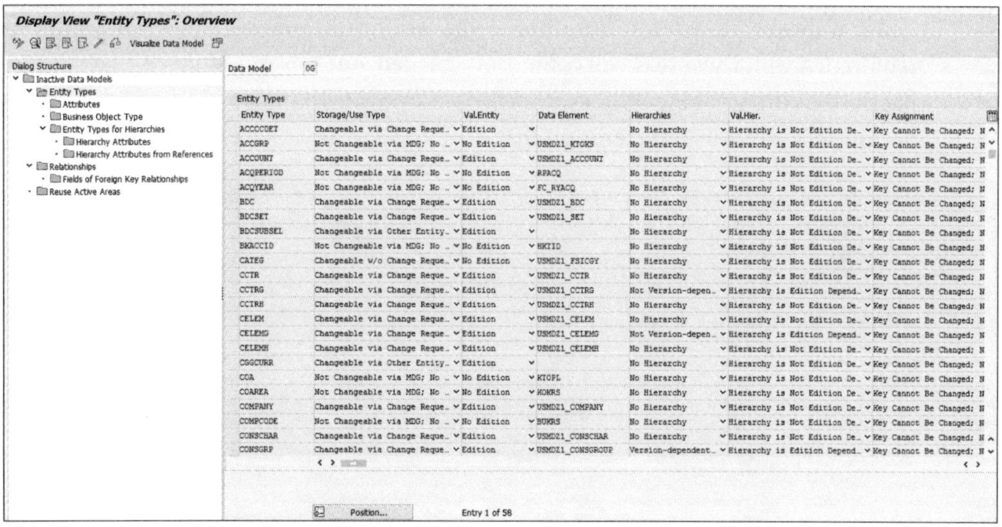

Figure 9.9 Entity Types in Data Model OG

In Figure 9.9, note two fundamental aspects of SAP Master Data Governance, Financials:

1. The controlling entity types are flagged as being changeable via a *change request*. This means that we'll find the change request used as both a ticketing mechanism to notify the relevant stakeholders that something is to be done and as a store for

the various approvals needed before the change can be executed. We'll look at the change process in more detail when we discuss governance requirements in Section 9.3.

2. The entity types are linked with an *edition*. An edition typically refers to a specific time frame, such as the second quarter of 2014, and groups together all changes to the master data requested within that time frame. Many change requests can be assigned to a single edition, and once all these requests have been processed the data in the edition can be replicated to the local systems.

If we compare this data model with the data model for material masters shown in Figure 9.10, we see that these entities are also linked with change requests but that there is no edition. The objects are simply maintained and then replicated to the associated systems via a change request. In Financials, it's common for headquarters to initiate changes to the account structures, profit center groupings, and cost center groupings and to issue an effective-from date for their usage to the subsidiaries. However, in Logistics, the creation of new materials, suppliers, or customers is rarely tied to a specific time frame but instead needs to be started as the new master data is required. A validity date is still commonly needed, but this might mean that if a supplier is moving to a new address from June 15 onward, then the address change must become effective in all systems on that date.

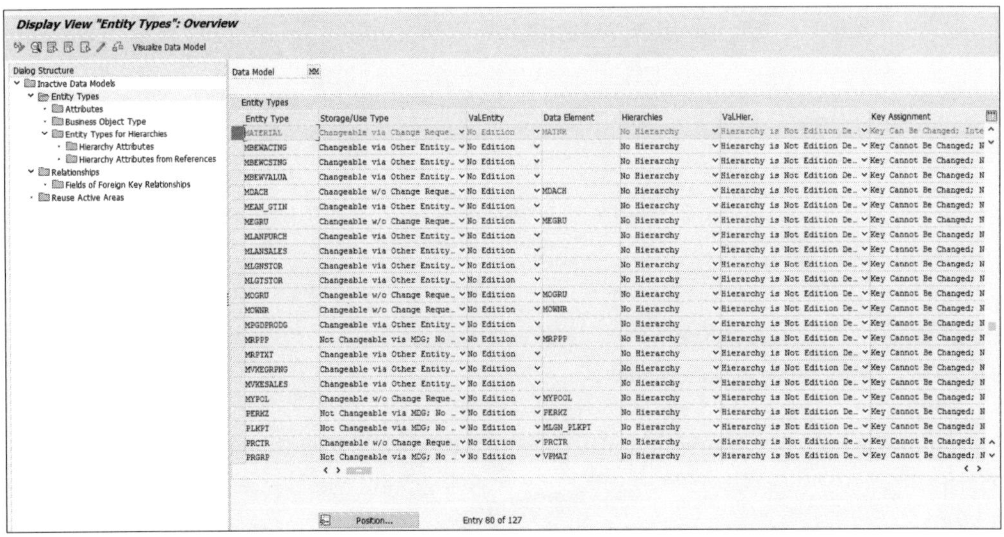

Figure 9.10 Entity Types in Data Model MM

Once you've established your model, you can load the relevant master data from your local systems using Transaction MDMGX. This is a generic tool for loading entities into your model. Other organizations use SAP Master Data Governance simply to create new clean master data going forward.

9.2.2 Roles for SAP Master Data Governance

Before you can create change requests in SAP Master Data Governance, you need to ask your administrator to assign your user to one or more of the following roles:

- SAP_MDGBP_MENU_04 (Master Data Governance for Business Partner: Menu)
- SAP_MDGC_MENU_04 (Master Data Governance for Customer: Menu)
- SAP_MDGF_ACC_MENU_04 (Master Data Governance for Financials: Accounting Menu)
- SAP_MDGF_CO_MENU_04 (Master Data Governance for Financials: Consolidation Menu)
- SAP_MDGF_CTR_MENU_04 (Master Data Governance for Financials: Controlling Menu)
- SAP_MDGM_MENU_04 (Master Data Governance for Material: Menu)
- SAP_MDGS_MENU_04 (Master Data Governance for Supplier: Menu)

Figure 9.11 shows the entry page for Financial Controlling Governance (part of the SAP Master Data Governance for Financials: Controlling Menu role).

The entry page offers three main areas:

- **Search**
  Here you can check whether the object you want to create already exists or is included in a pending change request. Effectively, this is the same approach as we saw in the Web Dynpro applications for master data maintenance in Chapter 3, all of which begin with a search screen.
- **Create**
  Once you're sure that the master data doesn't already exist, you can create a new object and include it in a change request.
- **Processing of Multiple Objects**
  Here you can create change requests that handle multiple objects if you're performing substantial reorganization.

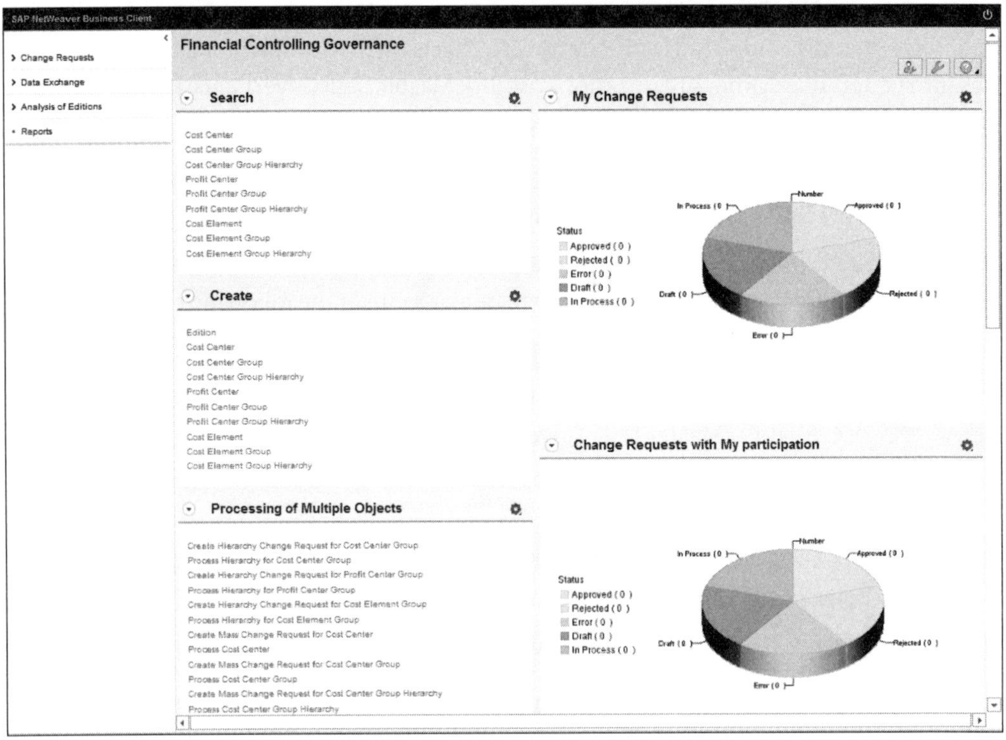

Figure 9.11 SAP Master Data Governance for Financials: Controlling

All roles have a similar structure. Figure 9.12 shows the entry page for Material Governance (part of the Master Data Governance for Material: Menu role). Again, you'll notice that you can search for individual materials, process multiple materials, and create change requests. The process reporting options and replication options that are hidden for the controlling data in Figure 9.11 are visible in Figure 9.12.

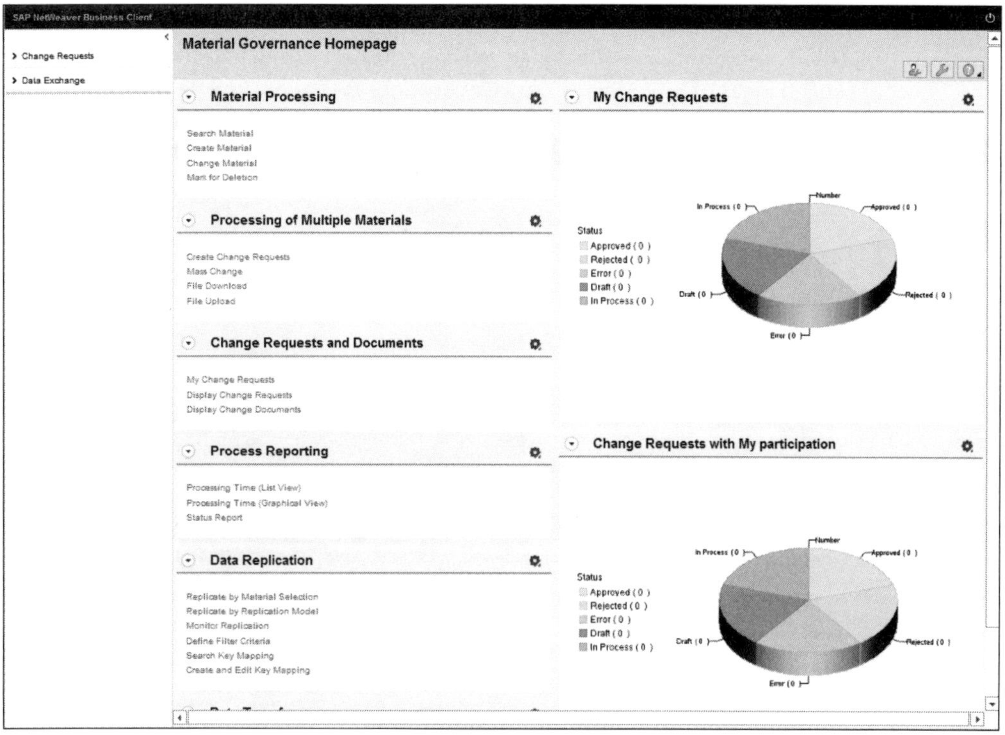

Figure 9.12 SAP Master Data Governance for Material: Menu

9.2.3 Editions in SAP Master Data Governance for Financials

Now that we've looked at the data model, let's look how data is replicated to the local systems. One of the central ideas of SAP Master Data Governance, Financials is the *edition*, which acts as a collector for all change requests raised within a given time frame. Whereas in earlier editions of SAP Master Data Governance, Financials the edition was the framework around all changes, in SAP Master Data Governance, Financials 7.0 you can choose to replicate single objects, individual change requests, or the whole edition, making the whole process of master data governance substantially more flexible. Nonetheless, you'll still technically need to assign your change request to an edition before you process it.

Figure 9.13 shows the cost center search screen. This looks very similar to the Web Dynpro application for cost center maintenance that we looked at in Chapter 3, Section 3.1.3. The difference is that some of the cost centers shown in the result list are included in a change request that has yet to be released (**Pending Change Request** column). You'll also notice that one of the search options is **Valid On**, because one of the other central ideas of SAP Master Data Governance is that of time dependency.

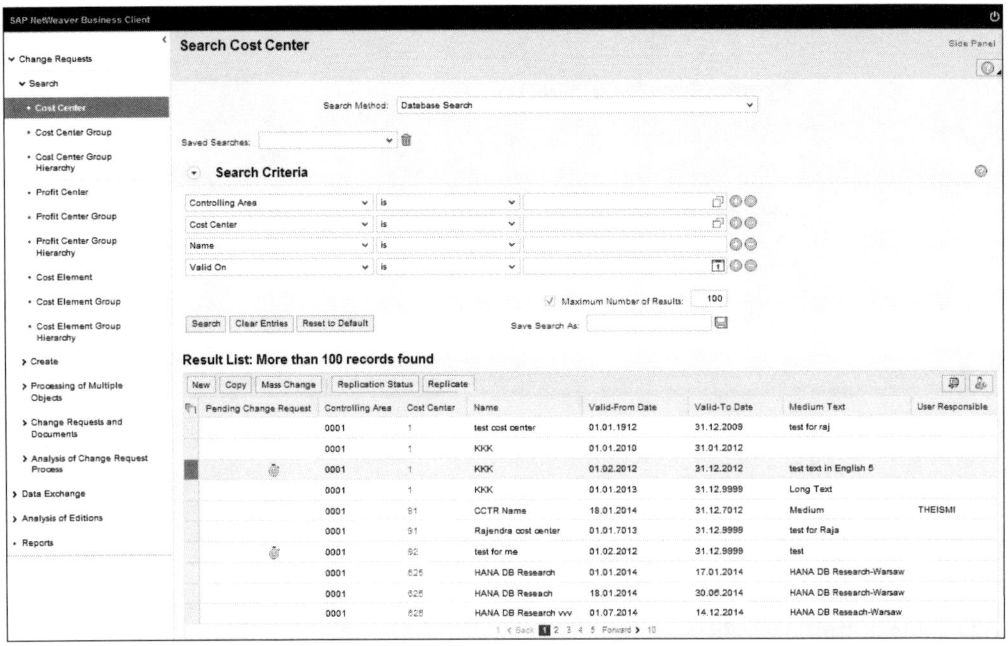

Figure 9.13 Search Screen for Cost Centers

If we navigate to the cost center selected in Figure 9.13, we see first the general details associated with the change request, including the notes and attachments used to document why the change is necessary, and then details of the edition and the validity of the change. Below that come the familiar master data details discussed in Chapter 3. You can expand the sections labeled **Cost Center Details**, **Cost Center Description**, and so on (see Figure 9.14).

One of the changes in SAP Master Data Governance, Financials 7.0 is that the **Address** and **Communication** tabs are included in the data model. Notice the way that the change request wraps itself around the master data—providing details of the status, who has initiated changes, and so on by comparison with the service request that we looked at in the first section of this chapter. Notice also the **Replication Timing** field: **On Final Approval of Change Request**. You will be able to replicate this cost center as soon as the change request is approved rather than waiting for all the objects in the edition to be completed.

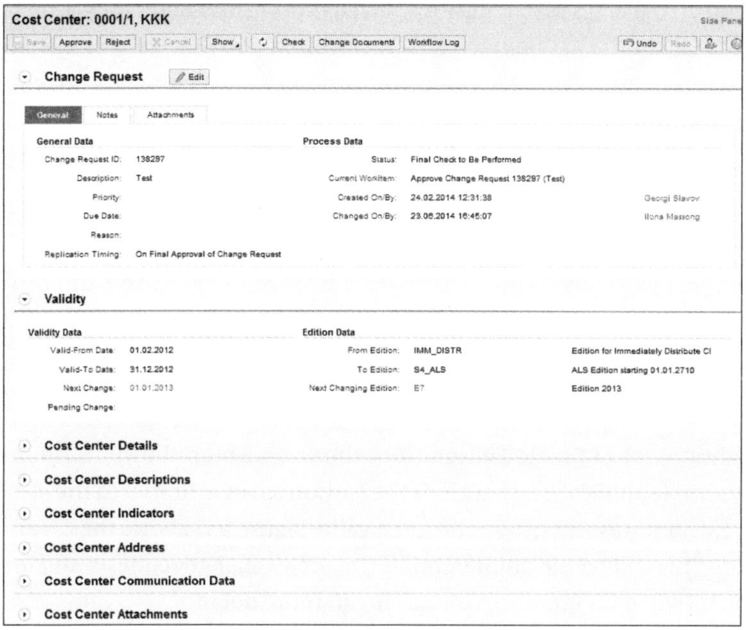

Figure 9.14 Change Request for Cost Center

Although you can now replicate individual objects or change requests, the edition continues to exist in the data model; if you want to create your own change request, you'll have to start by creating an edition:

- The edition provides the framework around the master data update (e.g., all changes for the first quarter).
- Change requests are created with respect to this edition to document in detail what has to be done (which cost centers are to be changed, how the groups are to be restructured, etc.). The change request is attached to a workflow that routes the request through the various approval steps until each request has been processed and is ready for transfer to the local systems.
- If only one object needs to be changed, it can be selected by searching and then included in a change request.
- The distribution monitor documents the replication to the local systems, providing an overview of what editions were used to transfer what data to the operational systems.
- The reports are used for audit purposes to document the state of the master data at a given time.

Going back to Figure 9.9, you'll see that entities such as cost center and cost element are assigned to editions in the data model. This means that you'll need to create an edition before you can request any changes to cost centers or cost elements. An edition can have one of three statuses:

1. Once created, an edition has the status **In Process**, meaning that change requests can be created and worked on for the edition.
2. As you approach release, set the status to **Marked for Release** to prevent the creation of further change requests that will in turn need to be approved and processed.
3. On completion, the edition has the status **Released**, meaning that the changes can be distributed to other systems.

To create a new edition, select **Create Edition** from the service map shown in Figure 9.11. This is a fairly simple application that gives the edition a name, links it to the data model via the type, and states when it will become valid. Figure 9.15 shows the **Create Edition** application. This will be the point of reference for all change requests and for all data replications. Two fields are worth discussing in more detail:

1. **Type** field
   The type is set up in Customizing and defines the entities that can be handled in a single change request. Because you can now distribute individual objects or change requests to the local systems, there's not quite the same onus to create separate types for cost centers, profit centers, and their groupings, another for accounts, cost elements, and their groupings, and so on. For this reason, we're using **Model 0G: All Entities**, which will allow us to replicate all entities covered in the data model shown in Figure 9.9.
2. **Replication Timing** field
   As we discussed earlier, the timing of replication is now more flexible than in earlier releases. You can stick with the old behavior by choosing **Manually Started after Release of Edition** to replicate, for example, a whole chart of accounts once you've collected all the necessary approvals. On the other hand, if you're in the middle of your period-close activities when you realize that you need a new account, you want a quick way to report and implement the change. You can release the contents of each change request separately by choosing **On Final Approval of Change Request**, as shown in Figure 9.14. Alternatively, you can choose **Selected in Each Change Request** to set the behavior within the change request.

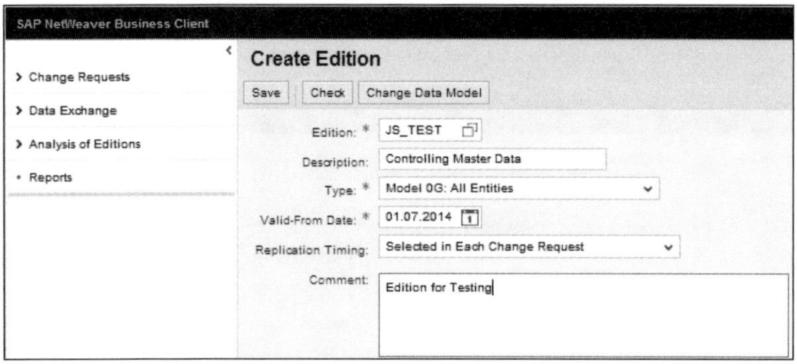

Figure 9.15 Create Edition

Once you've created your edition, it will appear in the list shown in Figure 9.16. Note the **Valid From** field in the context of time dependency. You have the following options to work using this list:

- To display this list, select **Overview of Editions** in the left-hand navigation panel. We've used the **Filter** icon to find our edition within the list.
- Initially, you'll see a series of inactive buttons above the list. If you select an entry, these buttons will become active and you'll be able to display any change requests created with respect to the edition. You can also run validations and change the status of the edition from **In Process** to **Released**.
- As always with lists like these, if you can't see your edition, click on the **Show Quick Criteria Maintenance** button to access the selection parameters for this list.

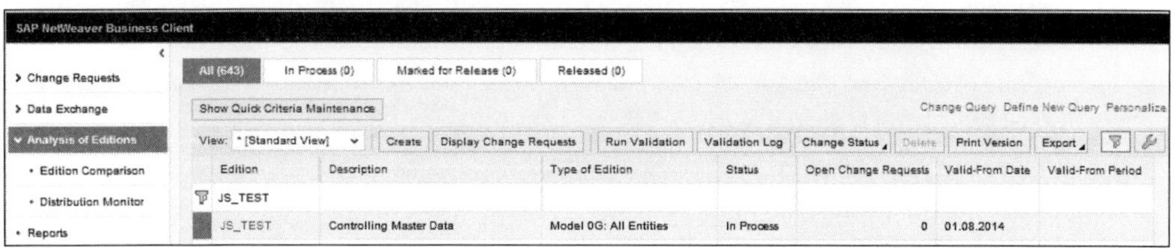

Figure 9.16 List of Editions

Once all change requests have been gathered and completed, you can release the edition. The edition provides the framework for the transfer of data to the underlying SAP ERP systems. This transfer takes place using SOA services or ALE. To activate these services, your administrator has to activate business functions FIN_MDM_SOA_CU and FIN_MDM_SOA_ORG in the receiving systems. Figure 9.17 shows the result of running a data transfer for the selected editions to the underlying SAP ERP system.

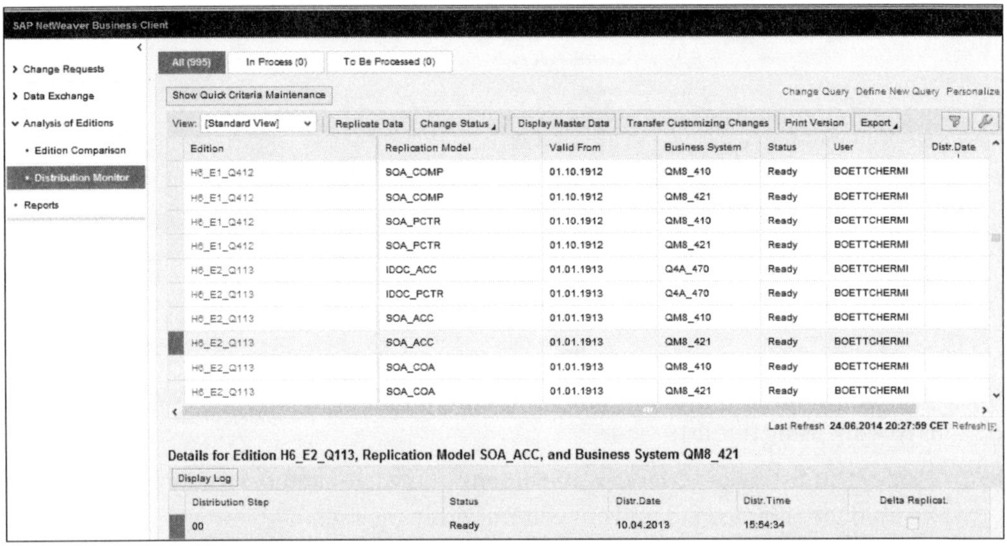

Figure 9.17 Distribution Monitor Showing Data Replication to Local Systems

---

Using SAP Master Data Governance with SAP S/4HANA

If you are distributing to both SAP ERP and SAP S/4HANA systems, you need to be aware of the data model changes in SAP S/4HANA. These include the merge of accounts and cost elements in Financials, the compulsory use of the business partner instead of customers and vendors, and the lengthening of the material field to 40 digits. You'll find details of how to handle the last change in SAP Note 2270396 (S4TWL—Long Material Number).

Except for terminology changes, most existing approaches to master data management that use a central master data server can handle the basic requirement to define the data centrally and then transfer it to the local systems. However, records of why and for whom a request was initiated are often stored as mail or in spreadsheets on local file servers, representing a potential compliance risk. What makes SAP Master Data Governance, Financials different is the use of change requests to handle all requirements relating to governance in this process, so let's now look at the options for handling change requests to ensure proper governance in the master data creation process.

9.3 Governance Requirements for Master Data

SAP Master Data Governance, Financials is essentially a more sophisticated version of the change request we looked at in Section 9.1, providing the ability to attach multiple objects to one request and link related requests via the edition. There's also the proviso that you have to license this solution, whereas the internal service request is covered by the normal SAP ERP license.

9.3.1 Creating a Change Request for a Single Object

Going back to Figure 9.11, you'll notice that your first option is simply to search among the relevant objects and then initiate a change request from the search screen. To do this, simply choose **New**, shown in Figure 9.13. The first thing you will be required to do is to link your change request with a request type and an edition, as shown in Figure 9.18. Alternatively, you can choose **Create • Cost Center**, shown in Figure 9.11. Again, you'll be asked to link your change request with an edition.

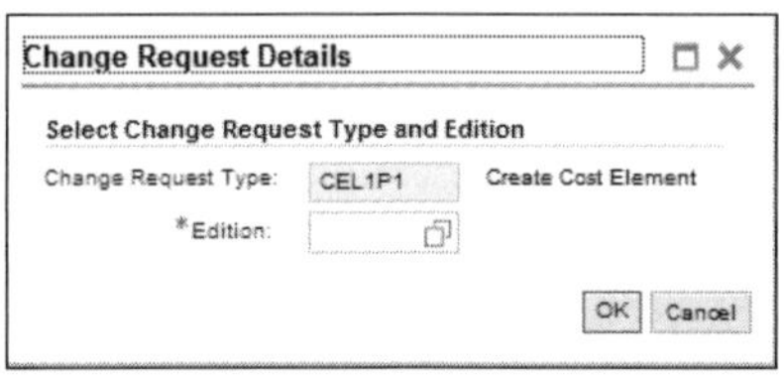

Figure 9.18 Link between Change Request and Edition

Once you've specified an edition, you'll be able to fill out the header details for your change request and then enter the details of your new cost center, as shown in Figure 9.19. Note that compared to the master data applications we looked at in Chapter 3 you will also be asked for an explanation of your change (**Notes** tab) and can update supporting documentation as required (**Attachments** tab). This is especially important for major changes for which there's large-scale restructuring.

There are some significant differences between this change request and the internal service request we looked at earlier:

- You can change *multiple* objects using a single change request.
- You can create hierarchies or groups by using the collective processing function and include them in your change request.
- You can perform mass changes—for example, to lock many cost centers in one go—and include them in your change request.

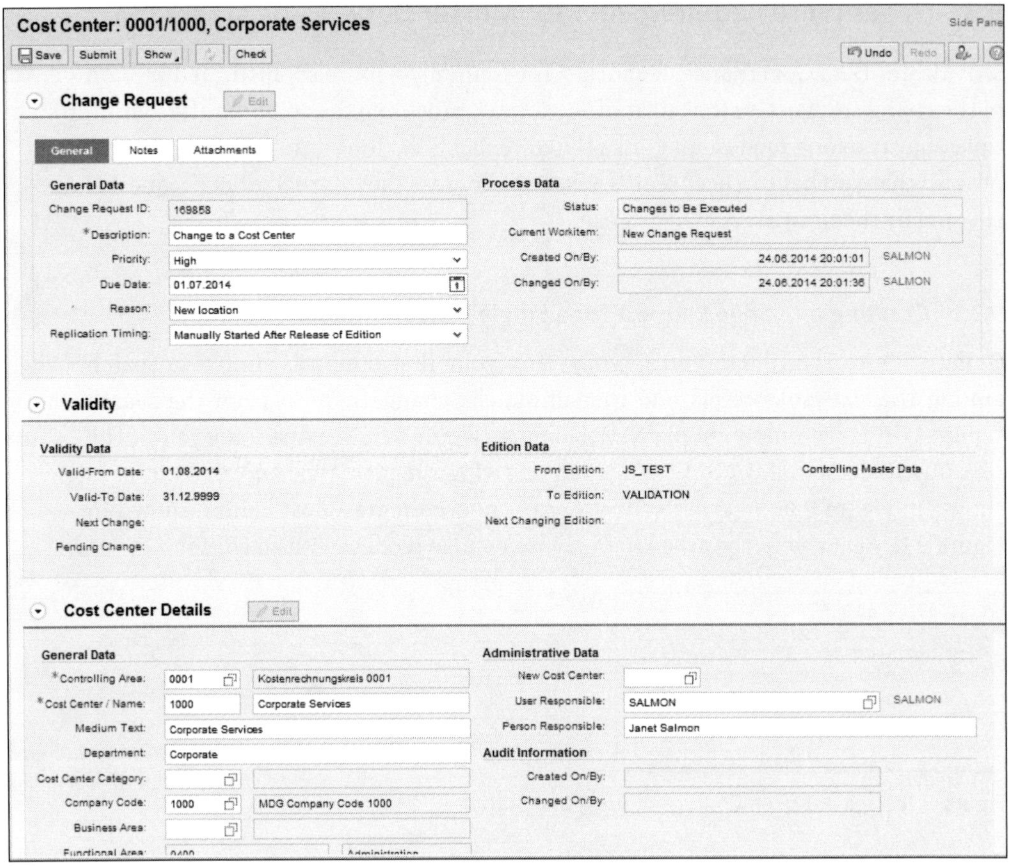

Figure 9.19 Create Change Request for Cost Center

To change multiple objects, choose **Change Request • Processing of Multiple Objects • Create Mass Change Request for Cost Center**. A roadmap will walk you through the main steps. Again, you'll be asked to document the reasons for your changes.

In **Step 3**, you'll be asked to list the relevant objects. Figure 9.20 shows a list of cost centers for which a change is being requested. You can add further objects by clicking on **Add Row**. If a major structural reorganization is in process, hundreds of cost centers may be affected, and there's a clear audit requirement. Finally, you'll be asked to specify the target system(s) to which your changes should be sent.

Another common requirement is to make the same change to multiple objects. To do this, choose **Change Request • Processing of Multiple Objects**. Figure 9.21 shows the cost center attributes that you can change in this way.

Figure 9.20 Create Change Request for Multiple Objects

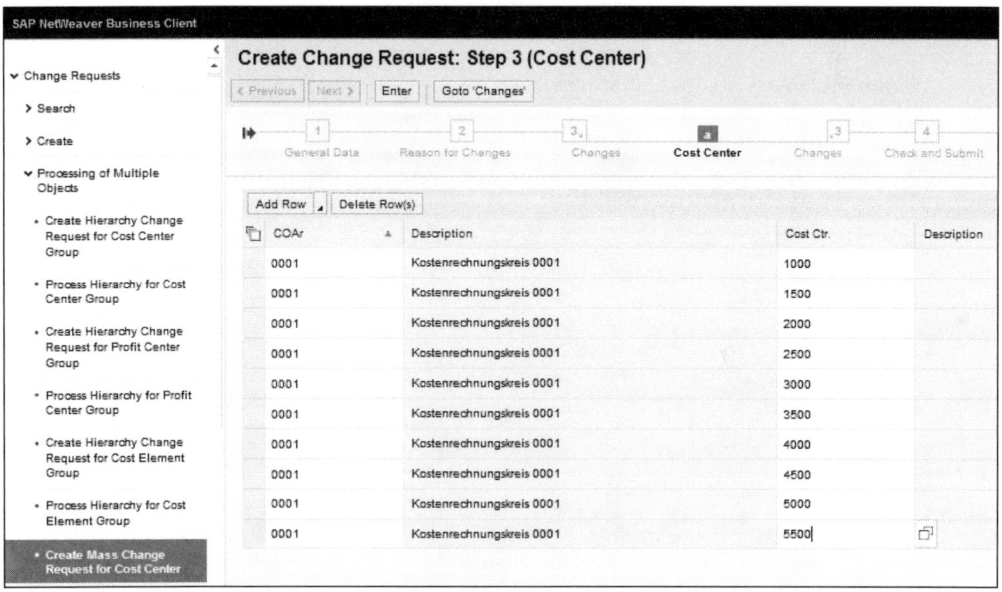

Figure 9.21 Including Multiple Cost Centers in Change Request

Of course, everything that we've done so far for a single cost center we can also do for cost center groups and hierarchies. Figure 9.22 shows the result of searching for cost center groups and the pending change requests for some of those groups.

From this result screen, you can maintain the structure of your cost center group, as shown in Figure 9.23.

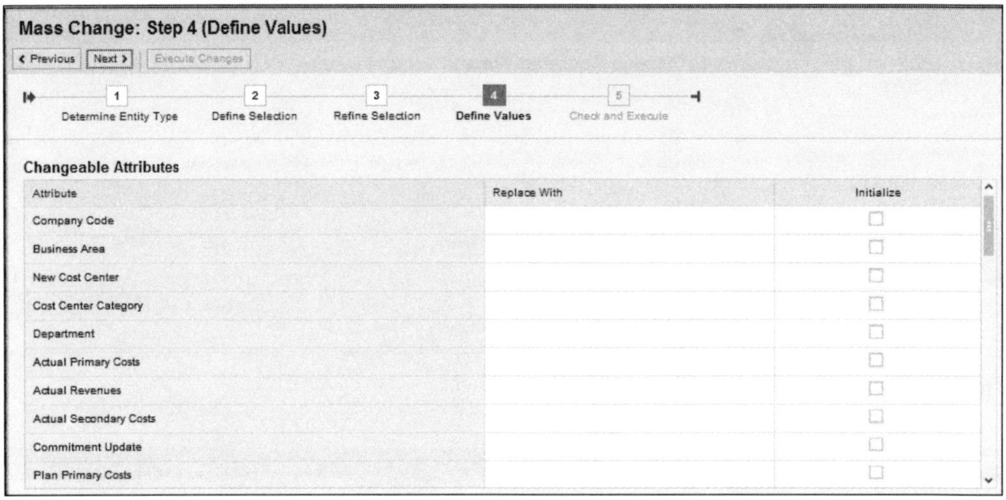

Figure 9.22 Mass Attribute Changes

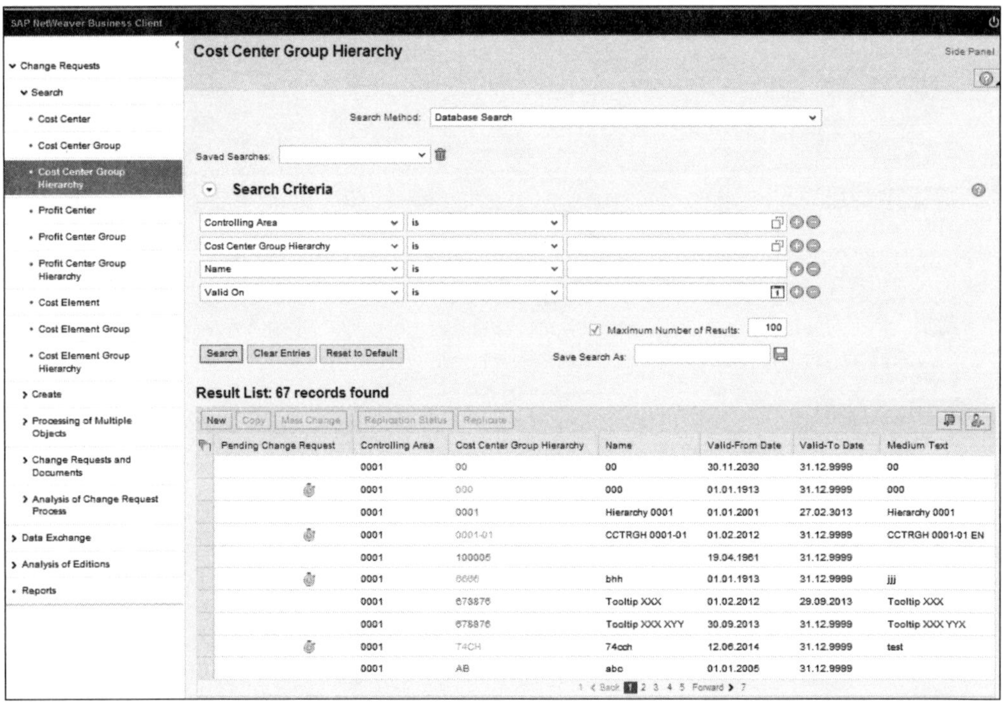

Figure 9.23 Search Cost Center Hierarchy

To create a new change request, choose **Change Requests • Create • Cost Center Group**. Figure 9.24 shows a change request for a cost center group. One of the nice features of SAP Master Data Governance, Financials 7.0 is that the system marks your changes in orange. When the next person in the workflow chain is required to approve these changes, they will see the changes marked in yellow. This makes it substantially easier to work through long lists of data with only a handful of changes.

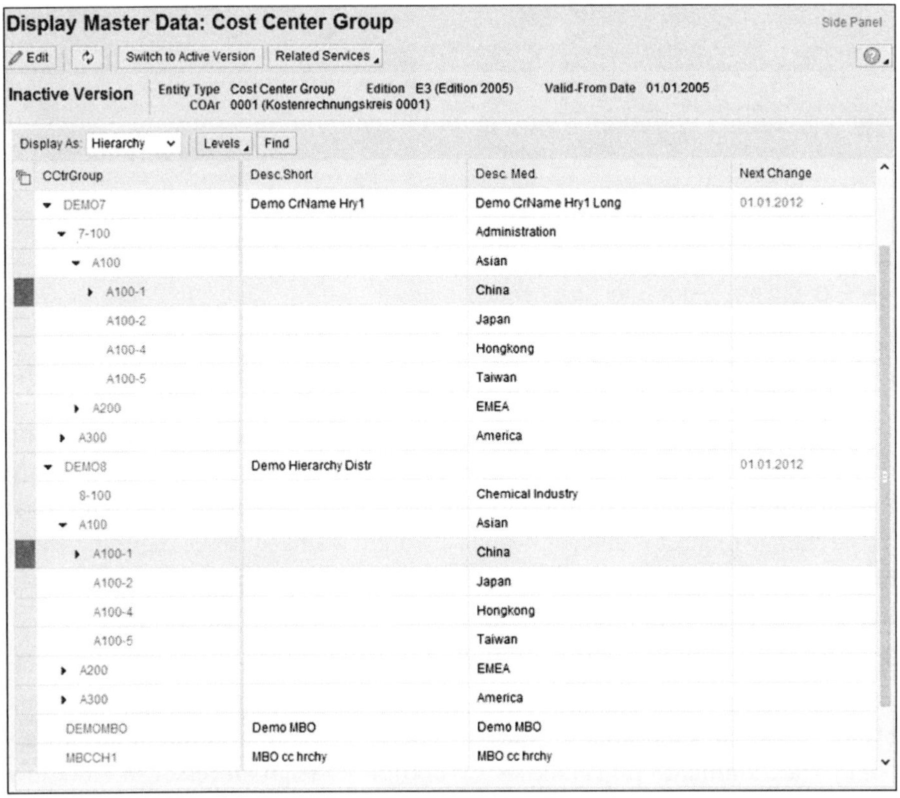

Figure 9.24 Maintenance of Cost Center Hierarchy

Once you've created a change request, you can find it by selecting **My Change Requests**, shown in Figure 9.11. Figure 9.25 shows a list of the change requests that we're currently working on.

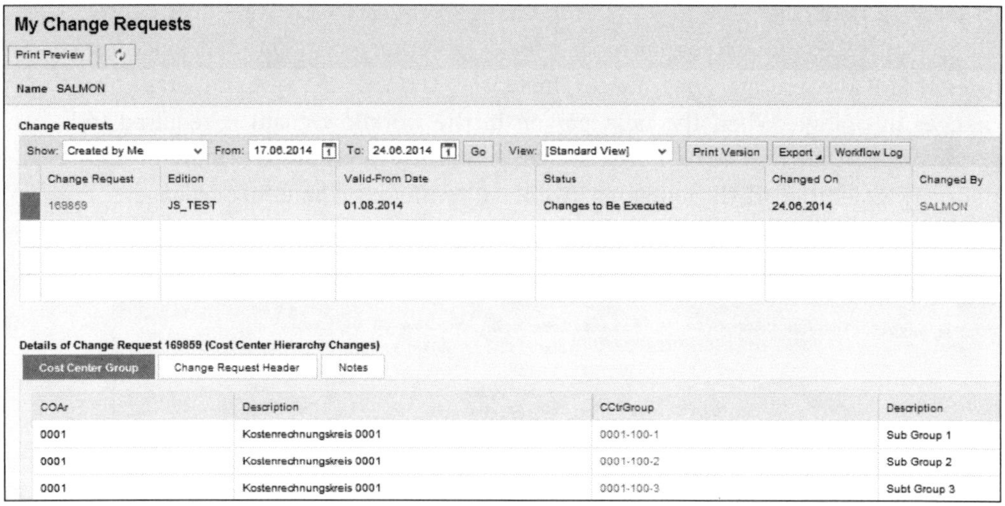

Figure 9.25 Change Request for Cost Center Group

9.3.2 Workflow Steps for a Change Request

In the change request we looked at initially, the approval is based on a notification and uses a classic SAP GUI user interface. In SAP Master Data Governance, Financials, the approvers, reviewers, and processors all see a web application. Who does what with the change request is determined via a workflow linked to the request. Clearly defined roles and responsibilities for creating and approving master data are the key to high master data quality.

Figure 9.26 shows some sample steps and processors. You can maintain these settings by following the menu path **Cross Application Components • Processes and Tools for Enterprise Applications • Master Data Governance • Central Governance • Master Data Governance for Financials • Workflow • Assign Processor to Workflow Step Number**. Figure 9.26 shows data model 0G, which has the following workflow steps:

- **Evaluation (1)**
- **Consideration and Approval (2)**
- **Processing (3)**
- **Final Check and Approval (4)**
- **Revision (5)**
- **Consider in Committee (80)**

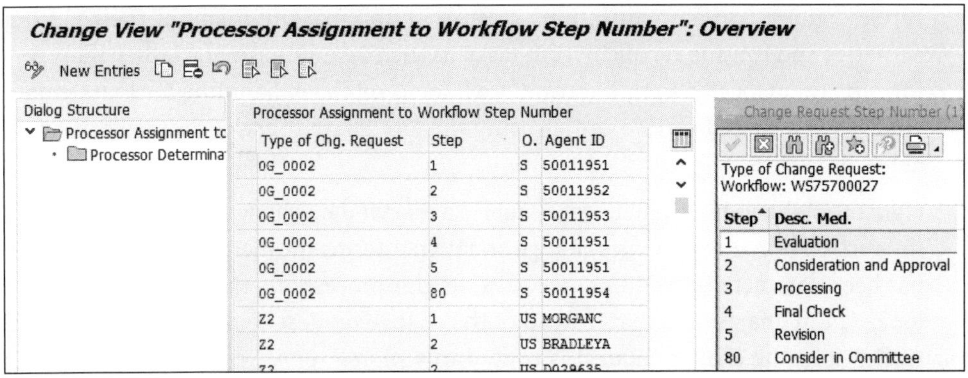

Figure 9.26 Assign Processors to Workflow Steps

Each of these workflow steps is assigned to an agent or processor. When the change request is first created, it has the status **To Be Evaluated**. The next person in the workflow chain considers the suggestion and approves (or rejects) the change. This results in the request being passed on to the next person in the workflow chain, who processes the request, maintaining the relevant entries in SAP Master Data Governance, Financials. On completion of this step, the request moves to another party, who makes a final check and again approves the change. This process continues until all steps are complete. When all change requests are complete, the edition can be released and an administrator can replicate the changes to the relevant systems. To stay up to date about changes to SAP Master Data Governance, use the following blog to access the latest information: *https://blogs.sap.com/2012/03/14/find-the-up-to-date-presentations-on-sap-master-data-governance/*.

Now that we've walked through a master data change process in a multisystem environment, we'll compare the process with the change requests in a shared service center.

9.4 Creating Change Requests in a Shared Service Center

One of the biggest business changes in recent years has been the move of parts of the finance functions to shared service centers. Many organizations embarked on their implementations of SAP ERP with a plan to standardize core processes, such as accounts payable, accounts receivable, and so on, to later shift the function from the local organization to a shared service center. As far as CO is concerned, it's fairly common to handle routine correction postings or master data changes in a shared service center. Some organizations go further and execute many of their closing activities and routine reconciliation tasks in such an environment rather than performing them locally. In this section, we'll focus on ticket handling for master data changes in a shared service center using the SAP Shared Service Framework, available from EHP 5.

Figure 9.27 shows how a manager requests a master data change and an agent in the interaction center handles the change and then informs the manager that the change has been completed. The difference between this process and the change request we looked at in Chapter 3 is that instead of the change request being routed to the controller, now the change request is routed to a *shared service center agent*. The SAP Shared Service Framework provides tools to enable the agent to complete the request and confirm completion. One goal is consistency, allowing the agent to work in multiple environments both technically (in terms of the SAP ERP system on which the change is performed) and in a business sense (so the agent might handle internal service requests but also calls from external suppliers questioning missing payments or calls from external customers querying invoices). The user interface for the request is similar, as is the connection to the underlying SAP ERP Financials system to perform the requested task.

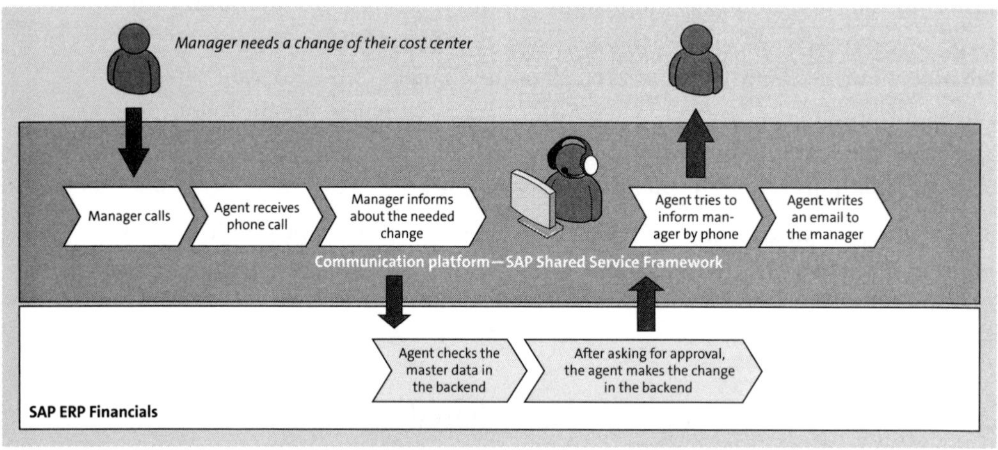

Figure 9.27 Internal Self-Services in Shared Service Center

SAP Shared Service Framework and SAP Master Data Governance, Financials

You might wonder why there appear to be two solutions for master data change requests in EHP 5, in addition to the internal service request, which is somewhat older. Technically, the self-services for master data changes offered in the SAP Shared Service Framework use the SAP Master Data Governance, Financials framework that we've just been looking at, even though approved changes are immediately updated in the corresponding backend system. This means that you have a central maintenance and governance process but are not initially forced to harmonize your master data. Later you can migrate to a central master data approach as described in Section 9.2 and Section 9.3 if your business so requires.

Before you can use an internal self-service, you have to activate business function FIN_SSC_ISS_1 (Internal Self Services, Enablement for Fin. Shared Services) and have your administrator assign the SAP_FIN_INT_SELF_SERVICE role to your user (see Appendix A, found at *www.sap-press.com/4691*). Figure 9.28 shows the internal self-services delivered in EHP 5. Whereas the assumption for SAP Master Data Governance, Financials was that the change request and master data model resided in a central master data system and data was replicated to *multiple* local systems when the change had been approved, the SAP Shared Service Framework assumes that the manager makes the request from his local system and the change is completed in that system (and only that system).

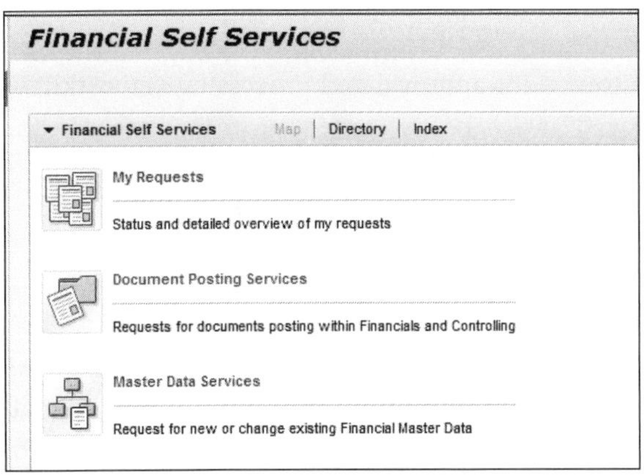

Figure 9.28 Financial Self-Services: List of Internal Services

Notice the **Master Data Services** folder and the **Document Posting Services** folder, which allow you to request a correction posting like you saw in Chapter 6. The framework itself is configurable, so you can extend the list of services included in this list if need be. To view all master data services, select the **Directory** tab. Figure 9.29 shows the result.

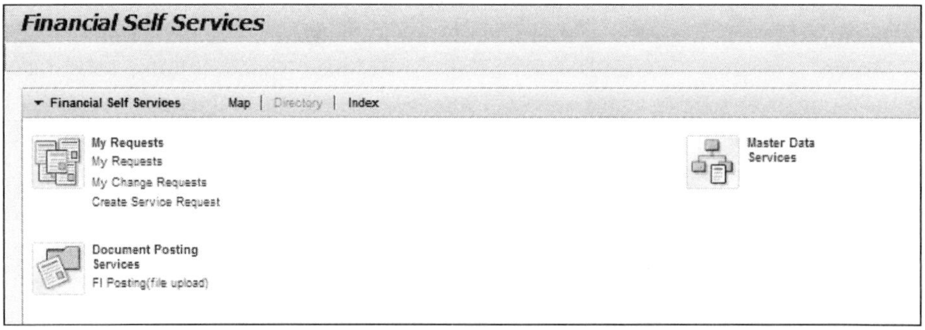

Figure 9.29 List of Financial Self-Services

To create a request for a new cost center, select the **Cost Center** link under **Master Data Services**. Compared to what we showed in Figure 9.14, where the cost center change request potentially triggered a major change affecting multiple systems, a shared service request will only affect the system in which the manager is working. The process of creating a change request is virtually the same as you saw for master data governance. The manager can add notes and attachments to support his request, and once the manager has placed the change request he can see it by selecting **My Requests**, shown in Figure 9.28. This takes him to the same screen as we saw for SAP Master Data Governance, Financials in Figure 9.25.

Again, the change request will be routed for approval and processing via workflow. Once the change has been approved, it can be implemented immediately in the underlying backend system because there's no replication process.

9.5 Summary

In this chapter, we looked at internal service requests for master data changes, SAP Master Data Governance, Financials, and the SAP Shared Service Framework. No matter how you handle your master data, it's clear that consistency is essential both for the operative processes we looked at in Chapter 6 and for planning. Now we'll return to planning to explore newer solutions for a modeled form of planning similar to those we previously discussed for reporting.

Chapter 10
Planning Using SAP BW Technologies

This chapter compares the planning options in SAP ERP with other options in SAP BW. It explains how to use SAP BW technology for planning both in a dedicated data warehouse and within SAP ERP.

When we looked at the subject of planning in Chapter 5, we focused on the flow of the planning process through the various applications. This sort of approach leverages the master data stored in SAP ERP, pulling together the information from the material masters, bills of material (BOMs), routings, work centers, cost centers, and activity types along with prices, capacities, existing inventory, and so on, to derive the annual operational plan based on the planning assumptions stored in SAP ERP.

Alongside this detailed annual operational plan, there are almost always other plans that look at the likely performance of the same operations over a longer time frame (up to five years) or under changing circumstances (e.g., accounting for increases or decreases in demand or capacity or changes to raw material prices). Such plans are rarely modeled in SAP ERP. They typically work not with individual products and customers but at a higher level, such as product groups and customer groups. There's a link with the master data in SAP ERP, but it's not a prerequisite that master records exist for every cost center and account included in the plan.

In the shorter term, there's usually another plan that allows the supply chain to react to fluctuations in customer demand or to prepare for changes in consumption patterns due to trade promotion campaigns. Often this plan is at a much finer level of detail—not by product and customer but by stock-keeping unit (SKU)—and covers a much shorter time frame. Make-to-order organizations generally can't plan by product at all because every product is uniquely configured to meet the customer's needs; they have to plan at an aggregate level until the customer's order is received. The short-term plan may then be the basis for material requirements planning (MRP), leading into the process of creating planned orders and production orders that we walked through in Chapter 6.

The two approaches to planning are most apparent when we look at the investment plan. If the organization plans to open a new plant or bring a new product to market, such a plan starts at a high level that has almost no relation to the master data in SAP ERP. It may also start at the corporate level and then be broken down to the local company codes, the controllers for which elaborate on the details of the local investment plan. Gradually, such a plan is broken down to the individual measures to be executed. At this stage, the project managers start to submit their plans by order and project. The bottom-up plan for the individual orders and projects supplied by the project managers is mapped against the top-down plan for the whole investment supplied by the corporate controllers. In the process of investment planning, we see the crossover between the detailed SAP ERP plan that we looked at in Chapter 5 and the higher-level corporate plan that's generally outside of SAP ERP.

It's common to talk about strategic plans, tactical plans, and operational plans in this context, but such terms are rarely helpful when deciding what form of plan is best created where. Some organizations have a single operational plan stored in one plan version to provide the basis for their variance analysis and budget control in SAP ERP and prepare all other plans outside of SAP ERP. Other organizations prepare multiple project plans that represent different planning assumptions and a complete investment plan in SAP ERP and only keep a corporate investment plan outside of SAP ERP.

"Outside of SAP ERP" generally means a plan based on SAP BW, though over the years there have been several planning tools based on SAP BW, including the following:

- SAP SEM, business and planning simulation
- SAP BW, business and planning simulation
- SAP BW, integrated planning
- SAP Business Planning and Consolidation, version for SAP NetWeaver

All these options use SAP BW as a standalone data warehouse to store both reference data to support planning and the data collected during the planning process. You'll remember that in Chapter 5 we also looked at the planning applications delivered in EHP 6 that use SAP BW queries, aggregation levels, planning functions, and so on but store the planned data in the SAP ERP tables. You'll also find several partner products on the market that allow you to create plans in spreadsheets that then use BAPIs to write data back to SAP ERP.

To understand the difference between a planning approach based on SAP ERP and a planning approach based on SAP BW, we'll look at the planning architecture in each case. This will help you understand what makes sense for you. We'll start by looking at the underlying architecture of the planning transactions in Chapter 5. We'll then look at how SAP BW can be used as a basis for planning and how to use virtual InfoProviders to leverage the SAP BW functions within SAP ERP.

SAP Planning Solutions for Controllers

Just as the reporting chapter merely scratched the surface, the next pages won't turn you into a planning expert in SAP BW. What we'll try to show you is where SAP BW provides options that don't exist in SAP ERP and to help you understand what sort of planning applications you can potentially build in SAP BW and how they differ from those available in SAP ERP.

10.1 Planning Applications in SAP ERP

To help us explore this topic, let's go back to some of the transactions we looked at in Chapter 5 and consider them from a more technical perspective. We'll look first at the classic planning transactions, such as Transactions KP06, KP26, and KP46.

The *planner profile* determines which planning applications you see when you select the planning transactions. In our example, we were using the planner profile SAPALL. This includes all standard planning applications delivered by SAP, but you may find that you use a different planner profile that includes a subset of the delivered applications and perhaps some others that your organization has configured for you:

- To find out which planner profile you've been using, select Transaction KP04 or **Accounting • Controlling • Cost Center Accounting • Planning • Set Planner Profile** in SAP ERP.
- To display the settings associated with your chosen planner profile, select **Accounting • Controlling • Cost Center Accounting • Planning • Current Settings • Create User-Defined Planner Profiles** or use Transaction S_ALR_87005852.

Figure 10.1 shows the planning areas associated with the planner profile SAPALL. We looked at the following elements in Chapter 5:

- Cost center plan (Transaction KP06) that uses the planning area **Cost ctrs: Cost Element/Activity Inputs**.
- Activity prices for the cost center (Transaction KP26) that uses the planning area **Cost Centers: Activities/prices**.

- The order plan (Transaction KPF6) that uses the planning area **Orders: Cost Element/Activity Inputs**.
- The statistical key figures plan (Transaction KP46) that uses the planning area **CCtr: Statistical key figures**.

In addition, in Chapter 5, Section 5.23 we looked at the project plan (Transaction CJR2) that uses the planning area **WBS Elements: Cost Element/Acty Inputs**.

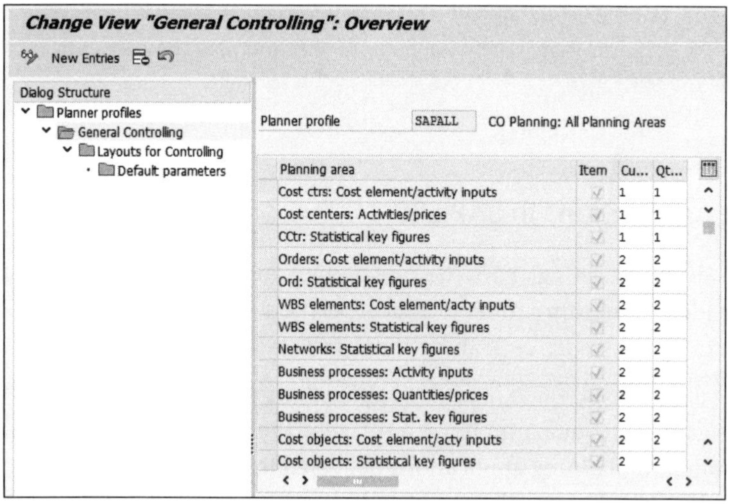

Figure 10.1 Planning Areas Assigned to Planner Profile

Each planning area contains a series of planning layouts that determine the data you can plan. Let's look at the first one in the list (used in Transaction KP06).

Figure 10.2 shows the five planning layouts offered for cost and activity input planning. You can scroll through these layouts from the selection screen when you first call up the transaction and in the overview and period screens when you're entering plan data (see Chapter 5, Figure 5.20 and Figure 5.22). We used the following layouts:

- Layout 1-101 to plan the activity-dependent and activity-independent costs on our production cost centers. Remember that in one we entered the activity type in the selection screen and in the other we left the **Activity Type** field blank.
- Layout 1-102 to plan the activities that the production cost center would use from the repair cost center.

The planning layouts are Customizing settings, so you may not have authorization to change them. You should be able to use Transaction KP67 to display the settings.

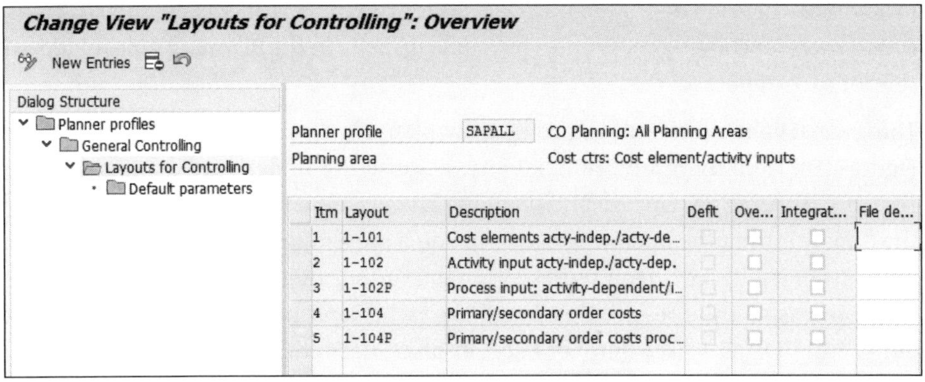

Figure 10.2 Planning Layouts in Planning Area

Figure 10.3 shows the settings for the first planning layout in our list (1-101). The layout determines the technical settings in the planning transaction, including the variables you're required to enter in the selection screen and the fields available for data entry.

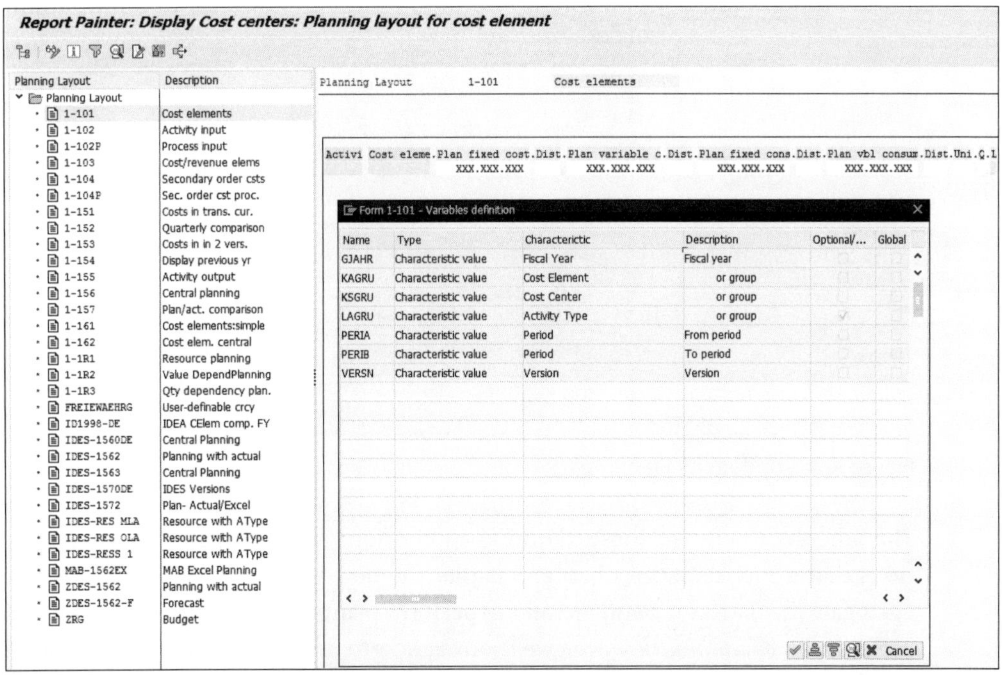

Figure 10.3 Settings for Planning Layout

In addition, there are dedicated transactions for copying planned data, such as Transaction KP97 for copying cost center plan data (usually in the **Planning Aids** folders we saw for each application).

Things are slightly different in profitability planning (Transaction KEPM), shown in Figure 10.4. Here there's more flexibility, because the underlying data structure is that of the operating concern and planning layouts are created that capture data for the dimensions in the operating concern. You'll see a range of planning methods on the bottom left of the screen representing the various methods possible in the planning processor. The presentation layer (the right-hand part of the screen) can use either SAP GUI (as we see here) or Excel-in-place, depending on the planning layout your configuration team has prepared for you.

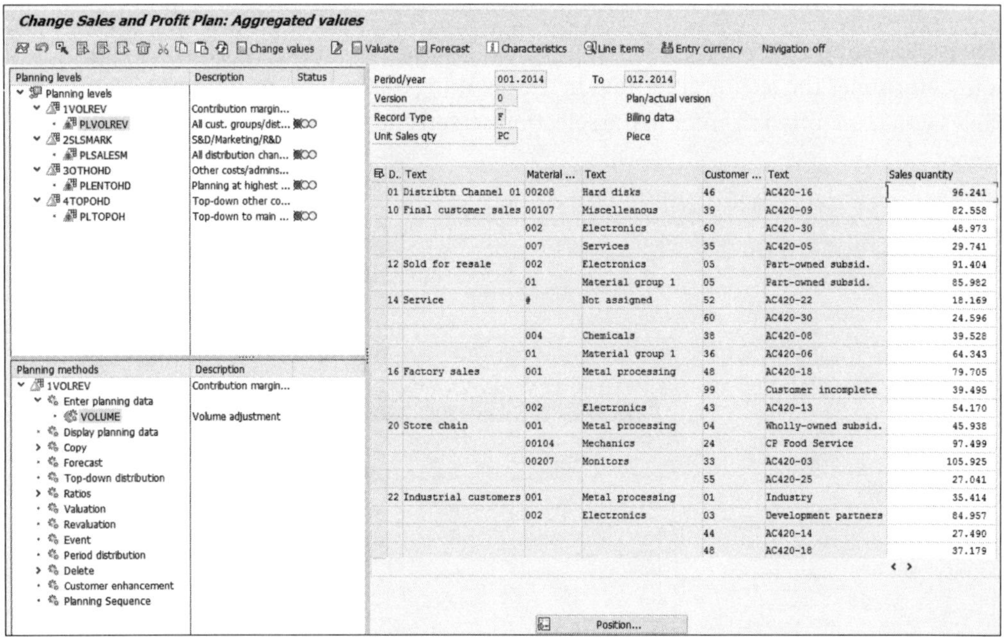

Figure 10.4 Profitability Planning

The difference between these planning applications and the Web Dynpro applications that we looked at in Chapter 5 is that the newer applications use SAP BW to aggregate the data as it's entered and to perform planning functions. Before we look at this type of planning, however, we'll look at how to use SAP BW as a *data warehouse* for planning purposes.

10.2 Planning Applications in SAP BW

To understand the difference between classic planning transactions, such as Transaction KP06, and a planning application built in SAP BW, you need to think about the three layers of a planning solution:

1. **The database layer**

   In SAP ERP, the planning data is stored in the same tables as the data from the operational processes. You can identify it for reporting by the value type (1 for planning) and business transaction (such as Transaction RKP1 for primary cost planning). The fixed structure of this database layer means that planning in SAP ERP can never be completely flexible because it wouldn't otherwise be possible to store data in the relevant tables. The same applies to any of the partner products that offer an update to SAP ERP. These use BAPIs to update the primary costs, activity inputs, activity outputs, and statistical key figures, and these BAPIs are subject to the same restrictions as the SAP ERP transactions.

   By contrast, in SAP BW the database layer is multidimensional, storing the data in logical cubes rather than in relational tables, just like you saw for reporting in Chapter 8. This layer stores not only the planning data but also any reference data that has been extracted from SAP ERP or other systems. The two types of cube look very similar; the difference is that the reporting InfoProviders are designed to display data extracted from SAP ERP or other systems, whereas the planning InfoProviders are designed to receive the data entered in the planning layouts (SAP SEM-BPS and SAP BW-BPS) or queries (SAP BW-IP or SAP Business Planning and Consolidation [SAP BPC]).

   From a controlling perspective, this gives you a degree of freedom. If you want to plan wage costs by cost element group, rather than by the 10 accounts coming over from payroll accounting, you can do that. Only if you want to retract data into SAP ERP do you have to make sure that the two data structures are in sync. If you want to plan by quarter rather than by period, you can set up your InfoProviders to include the quarter as a time dimension alongside periods and fiscal years. Again, if you want to retract to SAP ERP you'll have to build a planning function to split the figures for the quarter to the relevant periods. You can even plan by week if your business requires it, but this dimension must stay in SAP BW, because the CO tables do not include the week.

2. **The OLAP layer**

   In SAP ERP, the planning processor underlies all transactions used for cost center, order, project, and profitability planning. The exception is product costing, which stores cost estimates as a list of costing items. The planning processor provides generic planning functions, such as a distribution that spreads values entered for a fiscal year to the periods via a distribution key as you saw in Chapter 5 (see Figure 10.12).

In SAP BW, an *OLAP engine* supports these generic functions, allowing you to aggregate data entered by account and period or disaggregate data entered at a higher level, such as account group or fiscal year. You can build far more complex planning functions within this OLAP layer and link them to form planning sequences to automate various planning steps (e.g., copying the figures from last year and then applying a markup).

From a controlling perspective, this allows you to perform far more sophisticated planning functions than the "copy and adjust" functions available in SAP ERP. However, such functions come at a price. They require a level of expertise to build and have to be modeled and tested properly, but if you want to perform sophisticated calculations during planning, such functions are essential.

The planning applications available from EHP 6 offer a halfway house, allowing you to enter data by account group or fiscal year and then run planning functions to disaggregate such data. They provide a certain amount of flexibility in terms of the master data and reference data that they can include, but they are not totally flexible, because they must ultimately write data back to the SAP ERP tables.

The main situation in which to opt for a dedicated data warehouse for planning is when you want to merge heterogeneous data from different ERP systems and perform substantial transformations.

3. **The presentation layer**

   The presentation layer is what you see during planning. In SAP ERP, you select planning transactions, such as Transaction KP06, and then planning layouts, such as 1-101 or 1-102, in which to enter your data.

In SAP BW-IP, you enter your data either in web queries or in SAP BusinessObjects Explorer (SAP BEx) queries. You can also use SAP Analysis for Microsoft Office to make the planning functions available within a spreadsheet. Technically, these are like the queries you saw in Chapter 8 for reporting, except that they're *input-enabled*, meaning that you can enter and display data. This is the logical extension of the situation you saw in SAP ERP, in which the planning layouts use the same definition layer as Report Painter for reporting.

However, you cannot define a query by simply selecting an InfoProvider as we did for reporting purposes in Chapter 8. Instead, you have to define an *aggregation level* for your InfoProvider that tells the system which characteristics you intend to capture data for. In SAP ERP, we did this simply by either entering data in the activity type or leaving it blank during cost center planning.

In SAP SEM-BPS and SAP BW-BPS, you enter your data in planning layouts that use either SAP GUI or business server pages (BSPs; an early web technology) and report on it using SAP BEx queries. In this case, you need to define a *planning level* to tell the system which characteristics you intend to plan on.

Probably the most fundamental difference is that the new planning tools are designed to stand alone. They may share master data with SAP ERP, in the sense that you can extract cost center hierarchies, cost element hierarchies, and so on and use these as a basis for planning, but you are not bound by the same constraints, because the SAP ERP data and the SAP BW planning data are stored in separate databases.

10.2.1 Multidimensional Database Layer in SAP BW

To illustrate the difference between the tables used to store data in SAP ERP and in SAP BW, let's look at the sample InfoProviders for Corporate Investment Management.

To display the relevant InfoProviders, log on to SAP BW and select **SAP Business Information Warehouse • Administration • Data Warehousing Workbench Administration • Modeling • InfoProvider** (this menu path is the same as for reporting). From the list of InfoProviders, select **Financial Management and Controlling • Investment Management • Corporate Investment Management**. Figure 10.5 shows the InfoArea for **Corporate Investment Management** with a MultiProvider (a cube that combines data from several InfoProviders) for Corporate Investment Management that brings together a reporting InfoCube containing operative data (`0IMFA_C03`) and a planning InfoProvider that stores the data entered in the planning applications (`0SEM_C05`). Notice that InfoProvider `0SEM_C03` has a special icon on the far right that denotes that you can write data to it rather than merely reading data from it.

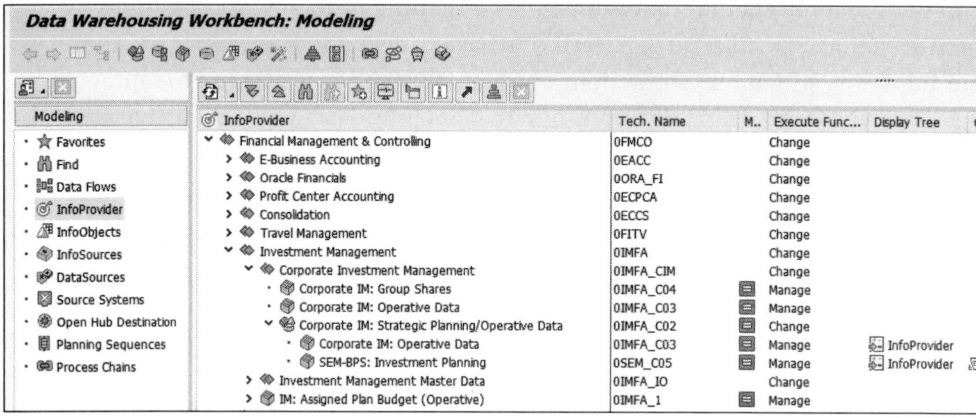

Figure 10.5 InfoProviders for Corporate Investment Management

You may wonder why you need the reporting InfoProvider (0IMFA_C03) at all. The purpose of this InfoProvider is to provide reference data for planning and information on spending for items started in previous years. This might allow you to perform a simple copy from the previous year and then add a certain percentage (typical planning functions) or merely to view the previous situation as a reference for planning.

To display the details of this InfoProvider, double-click on InfoProvider 0SEM_C05. Figure 10.6 shows the dimensions of the delivered planning InfoProvider. You'll recognize the items in the **Investment Dimension** as the same fields we saw in the investment program in Chapter 4. It's important to decide which attributes from your investment program are relevant in SAP BW. You'll want corporate reporting dimensions, such as the company code and profit center, but you might not need every detail in your appropriation requests. In the **Key Figures Dimension**, you'll recognize elements from Chapter 5, including the planning item and version. As you think through your key figures, it's important to decide whether your data will reside primarily in SAP BW or whether you need to retract your planned data to SAP ERP so that it can form the basis for budgeting (see Chapter 5) and availability checks (see Chapter 6).

What's important in SAP BW is that you can either stick closely to the structures in the investment program in SAP ERP or you can add new attributes for planning and reporting that only exist in SAP BW. This allows you to define new attributes for classifying the investment that go beyond the attributes such as reason for investment, priority, scale, and so on in the investment program item.

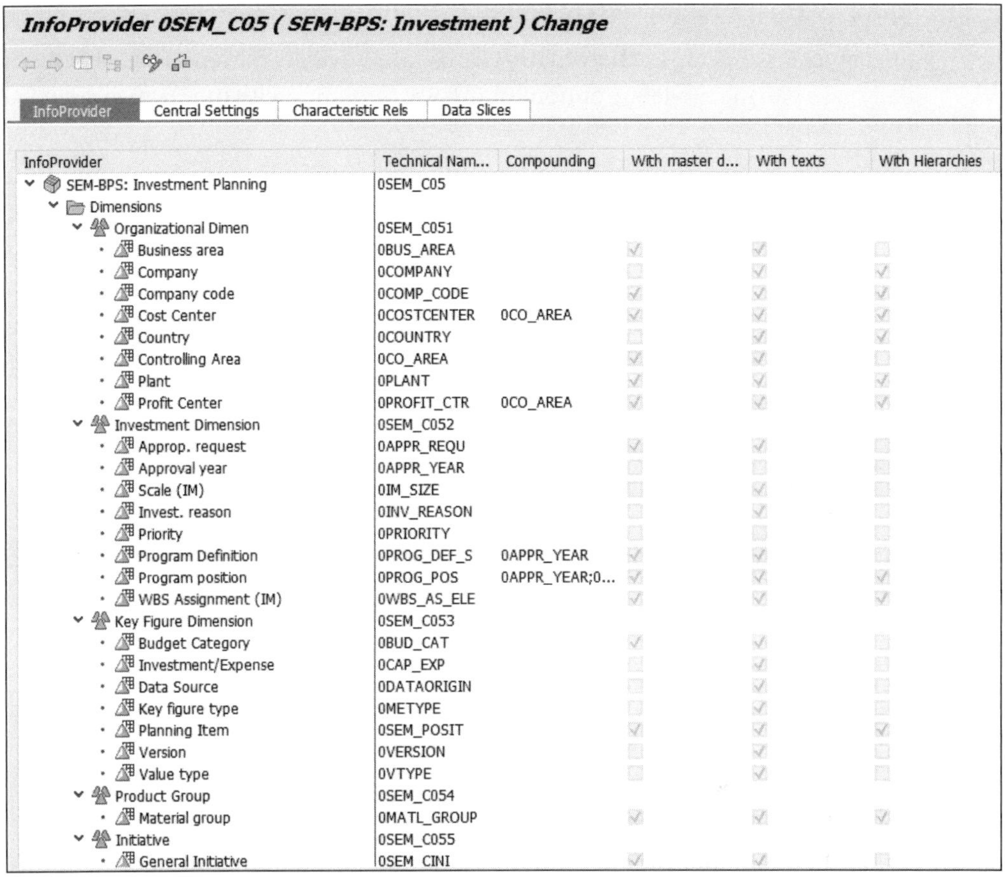

Figure 10.6 Dimensions of InfoProvider for Corporate Investment Planning

Working with a dedicated data warehouse makes sense in a corporate environment in which you are pulling data from disparate ERP systems and performing substantial transformations to harmonize your data prior to planning. If you do not need the full flexibility offered by SAP BW and you are running EHP 6 for SAP ERP 6.0 or later, you may want to consider a hybrid approach that uses SAP BW queries, aggregation levels, planning functions, and so on but stores the planned data in the SAP ERP tables so that you will not have to transfer data between systems. This approach provided the basis for the Web Dynpro planning applications we looked at in Chapter 5.

10.2.2 Virtual InfoProviders in SAP ERP

In Chapter 8, we discussed how to use virtual InfoProviders for reporting. This essentially gave you the modeling options of SAP BW combined with the DataStores in SAP ERP.

Figure 10.7 shows what appears to be the same **Administrator Workbench** as we looked at in Figure 10.5; it's accessed by following the same menu path in SAP ERP. You'll find the SAP BW objects for all the Web Dynpro planning applications that we looked at in Chapter 5 by choosing **InfoArea • Financial Management & Controlling • Controlling • Overhead Cost Management**. This covers cost center planning, order planning, and project planning. You'll notice that all the planning applications have an icon that denotes that they can write back to the SAP ERP tables.

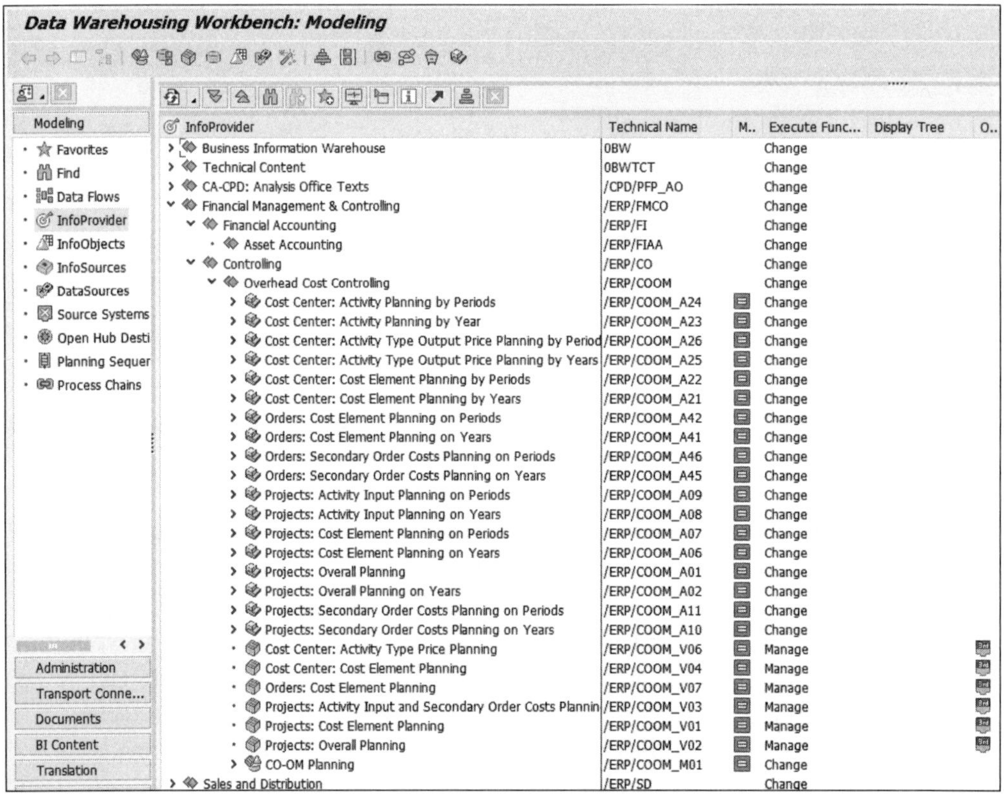

Figure 10.7 Virtual InfoProviders for Planning in SAP ERP

Activating the Business Content for Planning

Before you can use these planning applications, you'll need to follow the step-by-step instructions given as an attachment to SAP Note 1836149 (Business Functions FIN_CO_CCMGMT, FIN_CO_CCPLAN, FIN_CO_ORPLAN). This SAP Note will walk you through the process of activating embedded SAP BW in your SAP ERP system, making the basic configuration settings for operational analytics, switching on the relevant business functions, activating the BI content bundle for planning, and activating the relevant Web Dynpro applications. Activating the BI content bundle will allow you to see the list of queries shown in Figure 10.7.

Let's now look in more detail at one of the planning InfoProviders by selecting **Projects: Overall Planning** (/ERP/COOM_V02). This supports the planning application we looked at in Figure 5.51 of Chapter 5, in which we were able to enter an amount by WBS element and year. If you compare the entries in Figure 10.8 with the InfoProvider in Figure 10.6, you'll notice that the naming conventions are different.

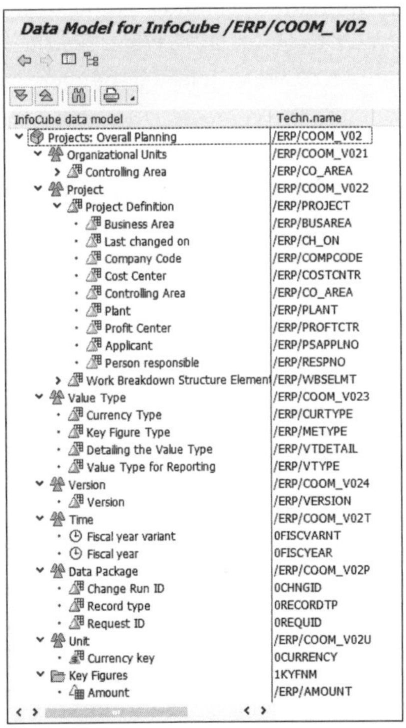

Figure 10.8 InfoProvider for Overall Project Planning

Although technically we're working with InfoObjects (an SAP BW concept), the namespace /ERP is reserved for InfoObjects used in combination with the SAP ERP tables. In this case, SAP BW is running on the same instance as SAP ERP. In other words, you can't install this SAP BW content on a dedicated data warehouse because instead of using extraction, transformation, and load (ETL) tools to extract data from SAP ERP to SAP BW, you're reading and writing directly from the SAP ERP tables. Nonetheless, you can extend this model to include other master data attributes, such as the status or start and end dates of the project, as required.

Although there are similarities between planning and reporting, one of the key differences is that in planning you will need to create *aggregation levels* (which determine the level at which you can capture data) and *planning functions* (which allow you to generate additional planning records). We'll now walk through these steps.

10.2.3 Aggregation Levels and Planning Functions

Whereas you can report by building a query that accesses an InfoProvider directly, for planning you need to decide which InfoObject combinations should be input-ready and which key figures you need to plan. If you refer to Figure 10.7, you'll see these aggregation levels above the InfoProviders. In Figure 10.9, we've selected the aggregation level for **Projects: Overall Planning**. This contains the characteristics that we'll need to select data or for which we wish to input data. Compare these entries with the columns in Chapter 5, Figure 5.51. When defining your aggregation levels, you need to think not just about the combinations for which you will want to enter data manually but also about the combinations for which you will want to copy or revalue data using planning functions.

The next step is to define *filters* for your aggregation levels that define which values can be entered. The aggregation levels, filters, and planning functions are defined using Transaction RSPLAN. Figure 10.10 shows the items you'll need in addition to your InfoProvider: the **Aggregation Level**, **Filters**, **Planning Function**, and sometimes **Planning Sequence** buttons.

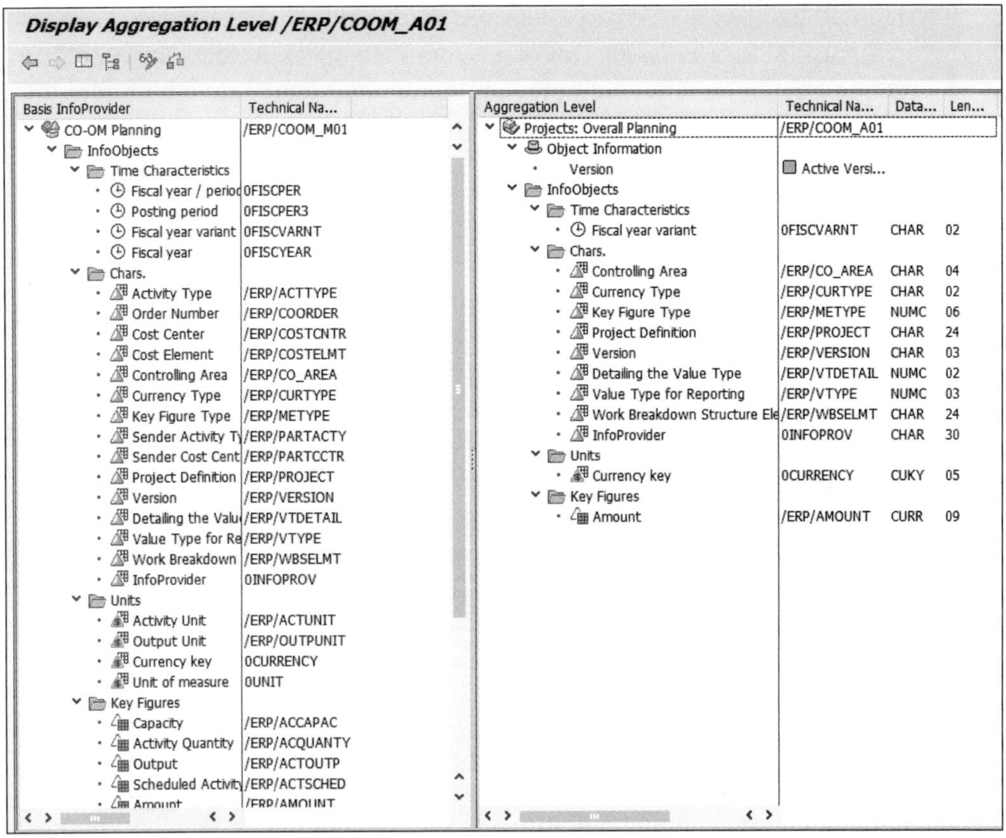

Figure 10.9 Aggregation Level for Overall Project Planning

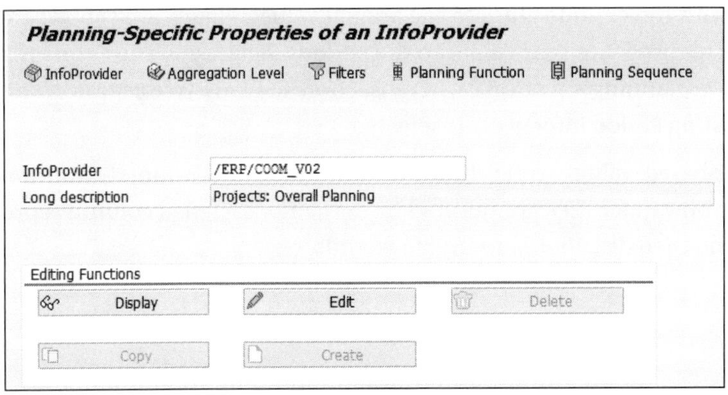

Figure 10.10 Planning Properties for InfoProvider

Figure 10.11 shows the variables delivered for overall project planning. Access this screen using Transaction RSPLAN (see Figure 10.10) and selecting the **/ERP/COOM_A02_FIL01** filter. This essentially provides the variables for the selection screen.

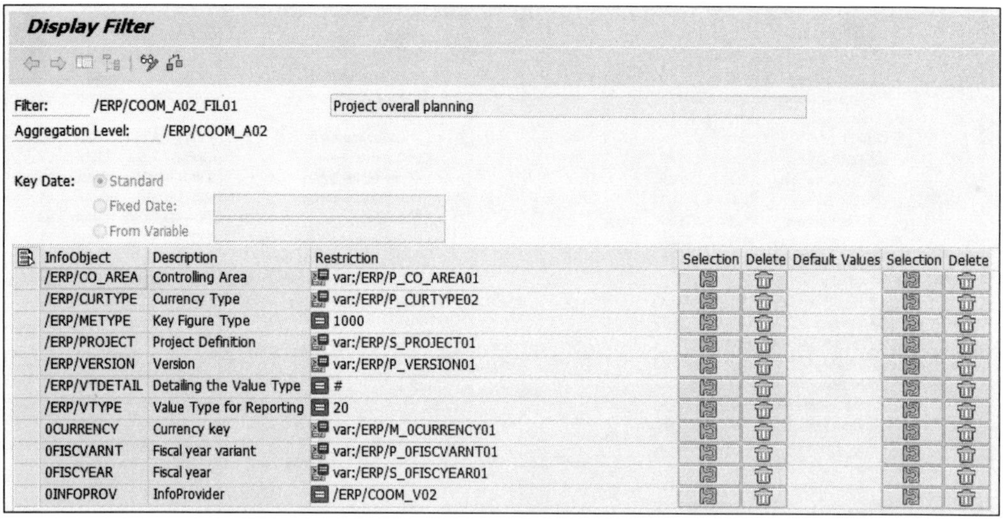

Figure 10.11 Variables for Overall Project Planning

Finally, to create the buttons that you saw in the Web Dynpro applications in Chapter 5, you'll need to create *planning functions* and potentially *planning sequences*. We used planning functions to copy data between planning functions and to revalue the planning data. We also used planning functions to distribute costs from the queries with the annual values to the queries with the period values and to aggregate values from the queries with the period values to the annual values. Figure 10.12 shows the planning function to distribute year values to the periods. Again, you can access this screen by choosing planning functions in Transaction RSPLAN (see Figure 10.10). Notice that the **Posting Period** InfoObject is selected.

To select the year-based values to be distributed, click on the **Parameter** button. Figure 10.13 shows how quantities are selected from the nonassigned column representing the year and then distributed to twelve periods.

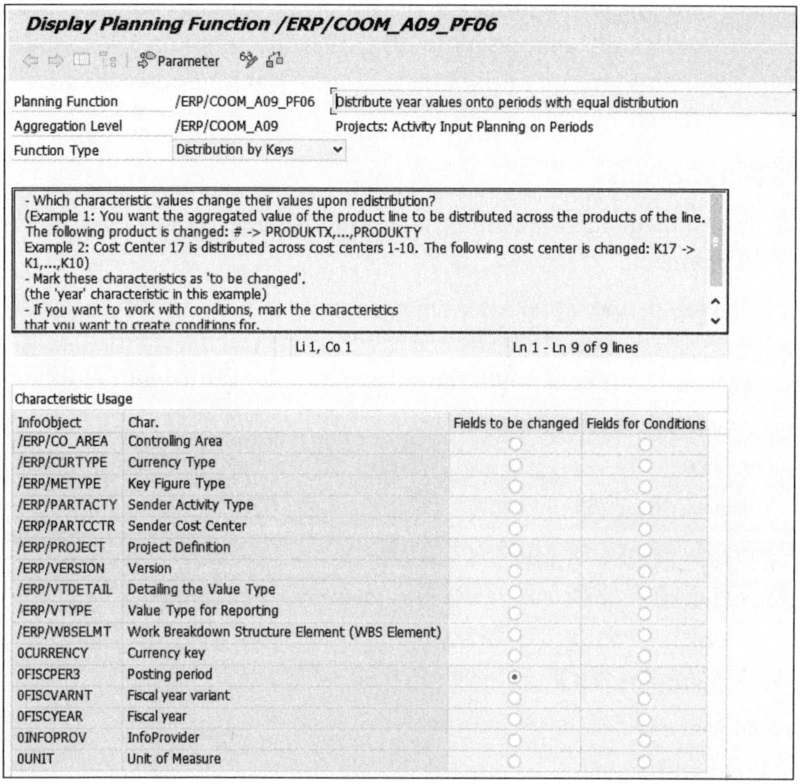

Figure 10.12 Planning Function for Distribution from Year to Periods

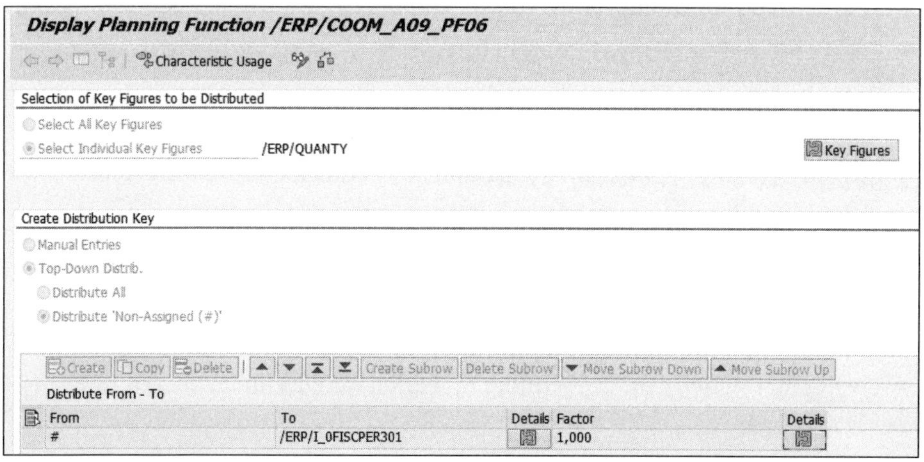

Figure 10.13 Distribution from Year to Period

Now that we have the basic infrastructure in place for the planning applications, we need to create queries to allow the users to enter their planning data. This is the equivalent of the planning layouts we used for the classic planning applications.

10.2.4 Data Entry Screens

The process of creating a query for planning is almost the same as the process of creating a query for reporting.

To find out which Web Dynpro applications refer to which queries, check the test catalogs for the FIN_CO_CCMGMT, FIN_CO_CCPLAN, and FIN_CO_ORPLAN business functions (see Appendix C at *www.sap-press.com/4691*). The following are standard queries for **Overall Planning**:

- Projects: Overview Plan (/ERP/COOM_A01_IRQ0001)
- Projects: Overview Chart (/ERP/COOM_A01_Q0001)
- Projects: Overview Chart (/ERP/COOM_A01_Q0002)
- Projects: Year Plan (/ERP/COOM_A02_IRQ0001)
- Projects: Year Plan (/ERP/COOM_A02_IRQ0002)
- Projects: Year Chart (/ERP/COOM_A02_Q0001)
- Projects: Year Analysis (/ERP/COOM_A02_Q0002)
- Projects: Year Chart (/ERP/COOM_A02_Q0003)

The following are standard queries for **Cost Center Planning**:

- Top-Down Cost Element Primary Cost Planning by Year (/ERP/COOM_A21_IRQ0013)
- Cost Centers: Cost Element Primary by Year (/ERP/COOM_A21_IRQ0002)
- Cost Center: Cost Element Secondary Cost Planning by Year (/ERP/COOM_A21_IRQ0003)
- Cost Centers: Top-Down Primary Planning by Period (/ERP/COOM_A22_IRQ0011)
- Cost Centers: Cost Element Planning by Period (/ERP/COOM_A22_IRQ0002)
- Cost Center: Cost Element Planning Primary by Period (/ERP/COOM_A22_IRQ0003)
- Cost Center Activity Input Planning by Year Activity Independent (/ERP/COOM_A23_IRQ0001)
- Cost Center Activity Input Planning by Period Activity Independent (/ERP/COOM_A24_IRQ0001)

In Figure 10.14, we've called up the **Query Designer** and navigated to the list of queries (we've activated the technical names to make it easier to identify the queries).

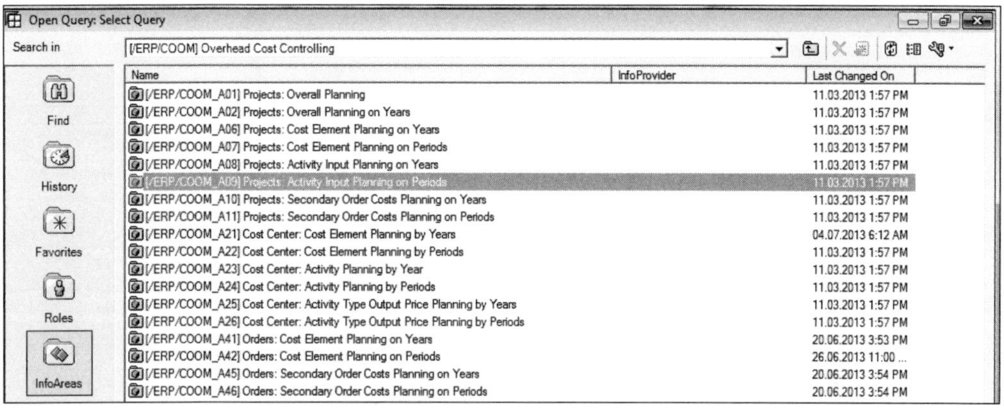

Figure 10.14 Selecting an Aggregation Level for Planning

Choose your query, as shown in Figure 10.15. The naming convention is that queries including IRQ are *input-ready* queries and queries only including the letter Q are *display* queries.

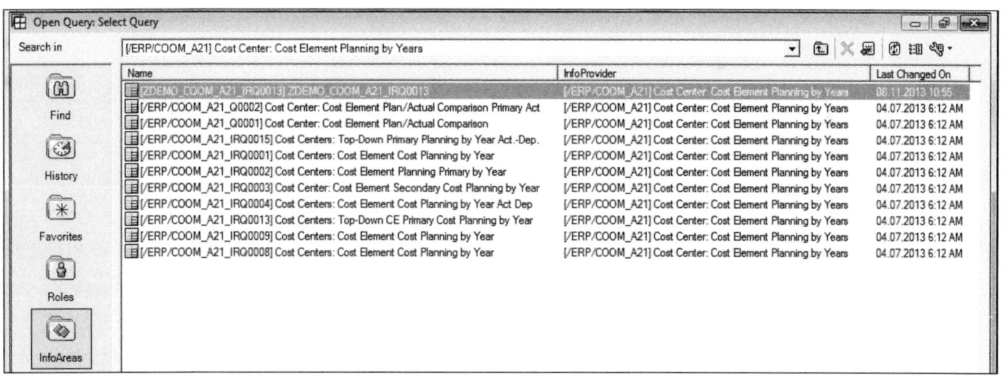

Figure 10.15 Selecting Query for Cost Center Planning

Figure 10.16 shows the settings for the delivered **Cost Element Planning by Year** query. Again, the business of maintaining the filter criteria and the rows and columns is the same as for reporting (see Chapter 8).

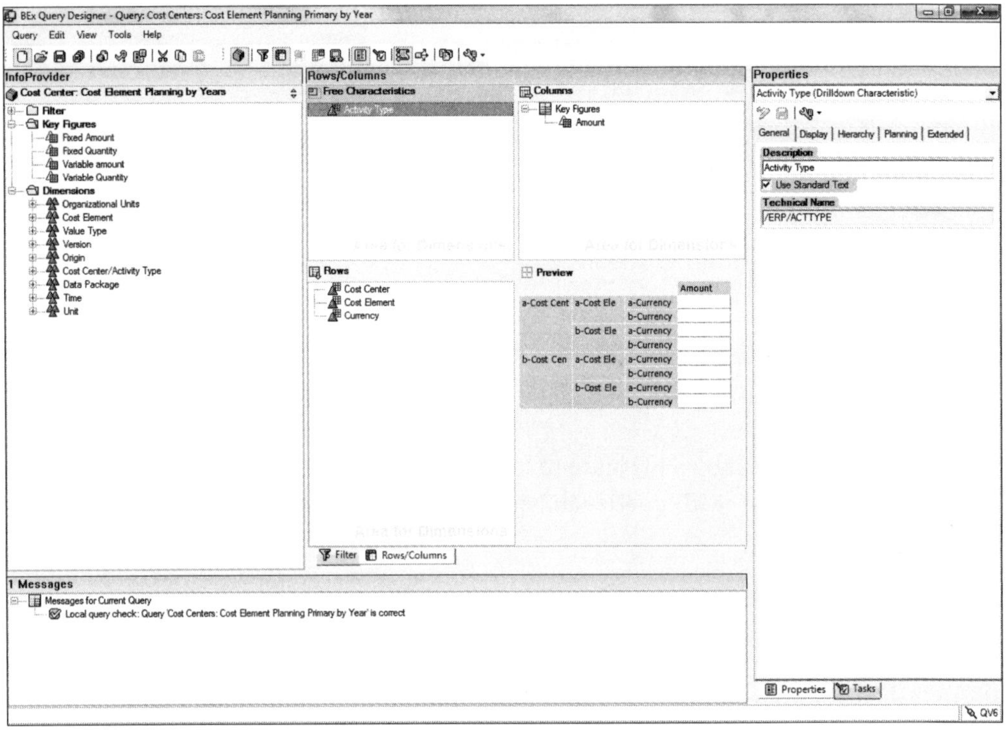

Figure 10.16 Settings within Planning Query

Although you probably won't change the data cells for which data is to be entered, you might copy the delivered queries and extend them to include additional columns for reporting. These are built in the same way as we described in Chapter 8, meaning that you can add additional columns to show other reference years, or commitments, or whatever data will help your planners to complete their tasks.

Figure 10.17 shows a sample cost center planning query running in SAP Analysis for Microsoft Office.

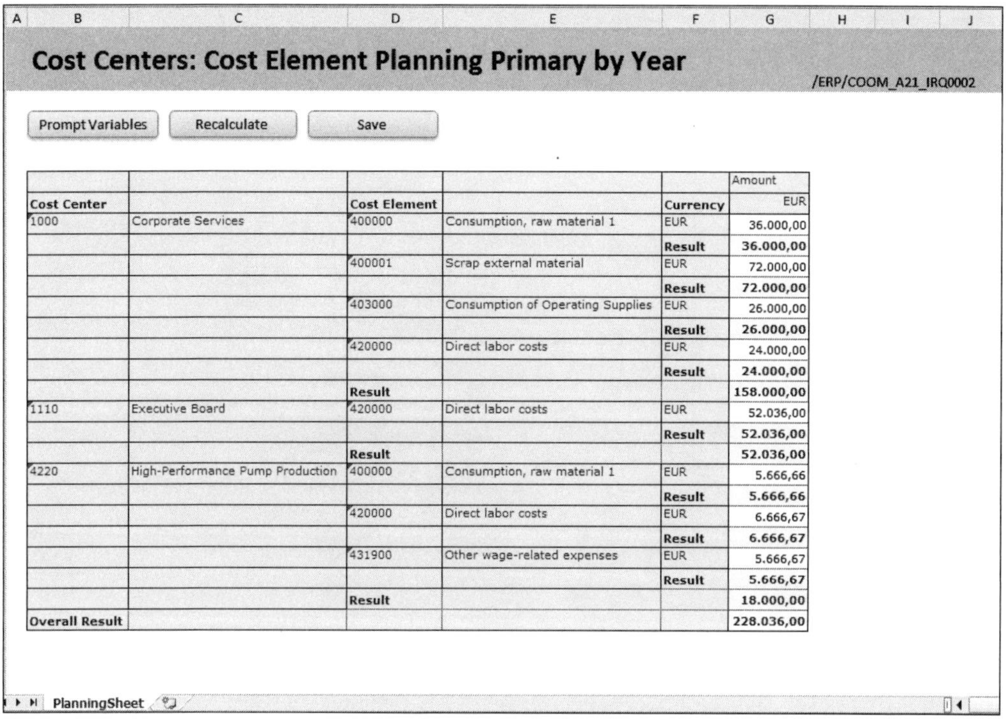

Cost Centers: Cost Element Planning Primary by Year

/ERP/COOM_A21_IRQ0002

Prompt Variables | Recalculate | Save

Cost Center		Cost Element		Currency	Amount EUR
1000	Corporate Services	400000	Consumption, raw material 1	EUR	36.000,00
				Result	**36.000,00**
		400001	Scrap external material	EUR	72.000,00
				Result	**72.000,00**
		403000	Consumption of Operating Supplies	EUR	26.000,00
				Result	**26.000,00**
		420000	Direct labor costs	EUR	24.000,00
				Result	**24.000,00**
		Result			**158.000,00**
1110	Executive Board	420000	Direct labor costs	EUR	52.036,00
				Result	**52.036,00**
		Result			**52.036,00**
4220	High-Performance Pump Production	400000	Consumption, raw material 1	EUR	5.666,66
				Result	**5.666,66**
		420000	Direct labor costs	EUR	6.666,67
				Result	**6.666,67**
		431900	Other wage-related expenses	EUR	5.666,67
				Result	**5.666,67**
		Result			**18.000,00**
Overall Result					**228.036,00**

PlanningSheet

Figure 10.17 Executing Planning Query in SAP Analysis for Microsoft Office

Let's now walk through the process of extending a query. Let's assume that we want to extend the cost center query to include a new column with further reference figures and a calculated column that shows the difference between these figures and the plan. Let's start by adding a new column to display additional data stored in the InfoProvider.

Figure 10.18 shows the query definition for our original query. To add a new column, right-click on **Columns** and choose **New Selection** to specify the data that you would like to display in this column.

Figure 10.19 shows the details of this selection. We want to see actual values in version 0 for the previous fiscal year. Instead of having users manually choose the fiscal year, we've entered a variable for the reference year.

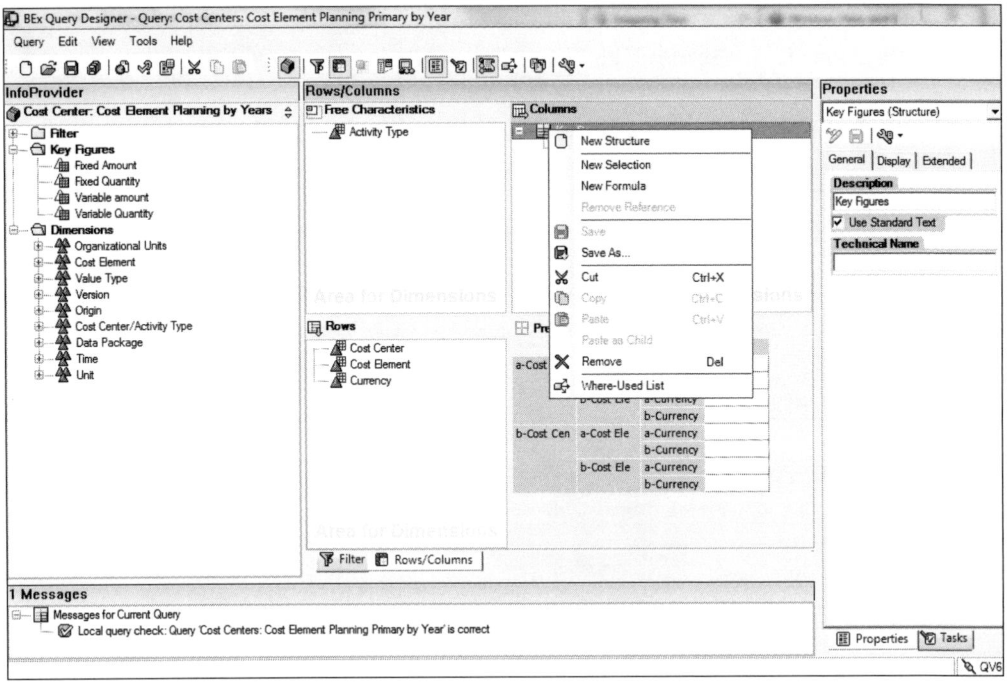

Figure 10.18 Adding Column to Query

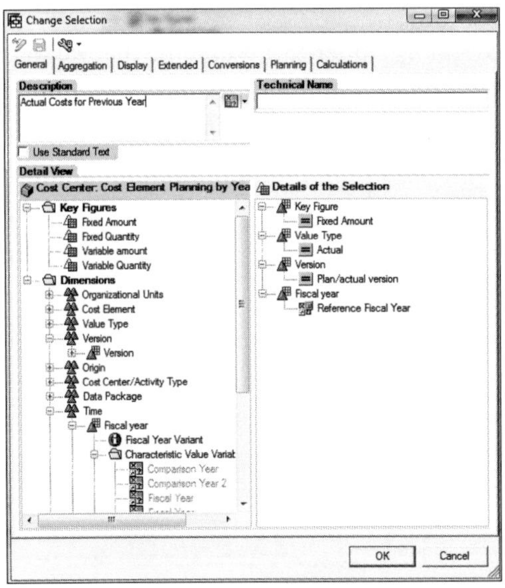

Figure 10.19 Changing Selection for Column

Now we want to create a further column in which we calculate the difference between the figures in the new column and in the original planned values column. To do this, right-click and select **New Formula**, as shown in Figure 10.18. Then use the Formula Editor to calculate the difference between the two columns, as shown in Figure 10.20.

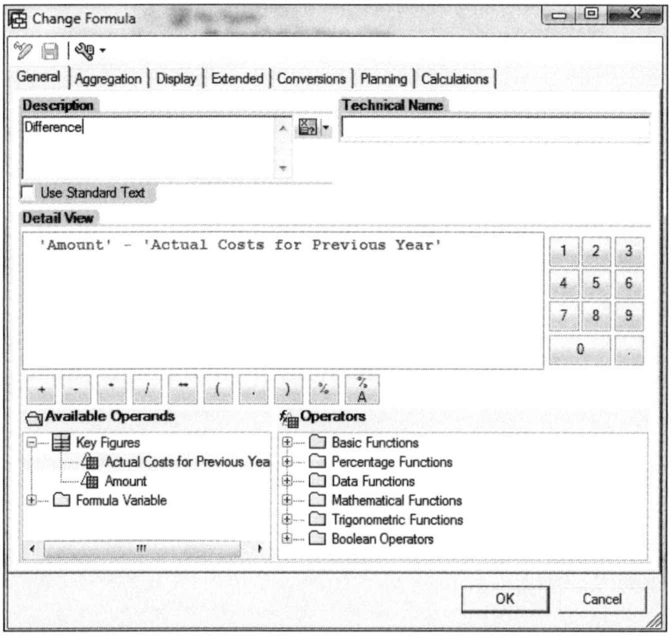

Figure 10.20 Changing Formula

The resulting query with its two new columns is shown in Figure 10.21.

Once you're happy with your queries, you have a choice:

- You can call the query in SAP BEx Analyzer or in SAP BusinessObjects Analysis, Edition for Microsoft Office, as we did here.
- You can embed the query in the Web Dynpro applications we looked at in Chapter 5. The link to the query is contained in the **Feeder Class Parameters** for the Web Dynpro application.

We've looked at the different DataStores for planning data (the SAP ERP tables and the InfoProviders in SAP BW) and the different planning layouts and queries. When we come to look at the options in SAP S/4HANA, we'll see that embedded SAP BW is used again for planning, this time in combination with SAP BPC.

Cost Centers: Cost Element Planning Primary by Year

Prompt Variables | Recalculate | Save

					Amount	Actuals Previous Year	Difference
Cost Center		**Cost Element**		**Currency**	EUR	EUR	EUR
1000	Corporate Services	400000	Consumption, raw material 1	EUR	36.000,00	38.000,00	
				Result	**36.000,00**	**38.000,00**	**0,00**
		400001	Scrap external material	EUR	72.000,00	72.000,00	
				Result	**72.000,00**	**72.000,00**	**0,00**
		403000	Consumption of Operating Supplies	EUR	26.000,00	26.000,00	
				Result	**26.000,00**	**26.000,00**	**0,00**
		420000	Direct labor costs	EUR	24.000,00	24.000,00	
				Result	**24.000,00**	**24.000,00**	**0,00**
		Result			**158.000,00**	**158.000,00**	**0,00**
1110	Executive Board	420000	Direct labor costs	EUR	52.036,00	52.036,00	
				Result	**52.036,00**	**52.036,00**	**0,00**
		Result			**52.036,00**	**52.036,00**	**0,00**
4220	High-Performance Pump Production	400000	Consumption, raw material 1	EUR	5.666,66	5.666,66	
				Result	**5.666,66**	**5.666,66**	**0,00**
		420000	Direct labor costs	EUR	6.666,67	6.666,67	
				Result	**6.666,67**	**6.666,67**	**0,00**
		431900	Other wage-related expenses	EUR	5.666,67	5.666,67	
				Result	**5.666,67**	**5.666,67**	**0,00**
		Result			**18.000,00**	**18.000,00**	**0,00**
Overall Result					**228.036,00**	**228.036,00**	**0,00**

PlanningSheet

Figure 10.21 Result of Extending Query

10.3 Summary

In this chapter, we revisited the planning transactions from a slightly more technical point of view and compared the planning transactions in SAP ERP with the newer planning applications available in SAP BW.

Chapter 11

Allocations Using SAP Profitability and Cost Management

The chapter looks at new ways of performing allocations to provide a full cost-to-serve model both in SAP ERP and in SAP Profitability and Cost Management and examines how these allocations can coexist with existing CO functions.

We've talked about allocations in various forms throughout this book. Just as a reminder, we need to perform allocations whenever we want to move primary costs, such as payroll, materials, depreciation, and so on, from the original cost center or order under which they were posted in the General Ledger to the final profitability segment for which we want to analyze costs. We looked at this value flow in detail when we discussed the use of *assessment cycles* to move costs from cost centers to profitability segments in Chapter 7. In addition, allocations are used to move costs between *supporting* and *operational* cost centers, as we discussed when setting up master data in Chapter 3, planning in Chapter 5, and performing allocations in Chapter 7. We also looked at direct activity allocations in Chapter 6 when we discussed what happens when we confirm a production order or record time to a Work Breakdown Structure (WBS) element.

You may remember from when we introduced the value flows used in the Controlling component of SAP ERP Financials (CO) in Chapter 1 that Figure 1.2 showed not only the cost centers, internal orders, sales orders, production orders, projects, and profitability segments that we've looked at until now, but also an additional account assignment object, the *business process*. SAP introduced the business process as part of its activity-based costing solution in Release 4.0 of SAP ERP to extend its existing cost-allocation capabilities. It makes sense to use a business process to capture costs for activities that can't easily be described in an employee time sheet or the routings, recipes, maintenance plans, networks, and so on that we find in Logistics.

When you consider the elements that make up product costs, a routing describes all the steps to make the product but doesn't necessarily cover the costs of the procurement, quality management, maintenance, transport, shipping, and so on associated with delivering that product. When we looked at make-to-order production in Chapter 6, for example, you saw that we could capture the costs of the raw materials needed to manufacture the configured material and associated manufacturing steps but did not capture the costs placed on the organization for handling complex configuration rather than a standard product. When we looked at this sales order in CO-PA, we ignored the costs of late changes to the order by the customer and the costs of chasing late payments and handling disputes if the customer was slow to pay. This is the domain of activity-based costing, in which you can create business processes to cover tasks such as configuring a sales order or chasing late payments and then set up a *template* to establish rules for when the costs for this extra task are to be charged.

More recently, SAP acquired SAP Profitability and Cost Management (SAP PCM), a tool designed from the start for building activity-based costing models. In this chapter, we'll look at template allocation in SAP ERP and then at how to build cost models in SAP PCM that can take the data you already have in SAP ERP as their starting point.

Let's consider in what context each tool makes sense and how they differ:

- Activity-based costing (CO-OM-ABC) is tightly integrated within the CO component, providing an extra "layer" between the cost center and the cost objects in Cost Object Controlling or the profitability segments in CO-PA and accessing information available in SAP ERP to determine when the costs for performing particular activities should be charged.
- SAP PCM is a dedicated allocation tool designed to take resource costs out of SAP ERP (or any other source system) and allocate them to activities and cost objects using rules that you establish in SAP PCM independently of whatever assessment cycles and direct activity allocations you may have built in SAP ERP.

One of the guiding principles of this book has been to leverage whatever data is available within SAP ERP to support cost accounting, whether it's the information in the bills of material (BOMs) and routings that tell us what needs to be done in manufacturing or the square footage of floor space that tells us the relative size of the different cost centers for cost allocation. This same understanding will help us as we consider the practicality of the different allocation options. Consider these three cases:

1. If we already have BOMs and routings in place and our main goal is to include the costs of a quality check performed once for each production order in our costing model, then we can use activity-based costing to extend the existing product costing process to include the costs of such a quality check. All we have to do is create a business process for the quality check and a template that will determine under what circumstances the costs of that quality check are to be charged to our production orders.
2. If we're only using Cost Center Accounting and basic allocations to move costs between cost centers, as might be the case for a bank or other financial service organization, then we often have almost no driver information for more complex cost allocations in SAP ERP because most of the information about the loans handled is in separate, industry-specific systems. If this is the case, you might find it more practical to create a costing model in SAP PCM to determine the costs of opening accounts, handling various insurance policies, and so on.
3. If we're capturing information on collections and disputes in SAP Financial Supply Chain Management and marketing activities in SAP Customer Relationship Management, then bringing this information into Profitability Analysis (CO-PA) is going to involve setting up extra value fields and data loads from external systems. Again, you might find it more practical to create a costing model for this purpose in SAP PCM that's not subject to the constraints in CO-PA.

Data Structures in CO-PA

For many years, the rule of thumb for an operating concern was that you should have no more than 60 characteristics as dimensions and no more than 120 value fields. This limit can be extended using SAP Note 1029391. The option of 200 value fields is standard in EHP 4.

Before we go into detail about the various costing models, it's worth addressing a few terminology issues up front. SAP PCM works with the terms *resources*, *activities*, and *cost objects*, but these terms are used differently in SAP ERP. You can map your SAP ERP model against this as follows:

- The *cost objects* in SAP PCM are equivalent to the market segments in CO-PA (product, customer, channel, region, etc.) rather than the more short-term production orders, process orders, maintenance orders, and so on. In general, the steps you perform in the Cost Object Controlling menus will be completely unaffected by any use of SAP PCM, because you aren't going to change how you assign material and labor to your products, update inventory, or charge time to a WBS element. If you do want to include the costs of a quality check in your product costs, then it's generally more practical to add an extra step in the form of a *template allocation* to the process you have in place in SAP ERP.

- The *resources* are generally your cost centers, though they can be individual items in the General Ledger or a different grouping of the cost centers. Normally, this isn't a one-to-one mapping exercise. It often makes sense to pull out the costs of certain service departments or supporting cost centers rather than your whole cost center hierarchy and allocate these costs using SAP PCM. This is perhaps a key difference between CO and SAP PCM. The assumption in CO is that *all* costs will ultimately be allocated to CO-PA or capitalized as investments. In SAP PCM, you decide how much of your organization the model will embrace. It can be a complete costing solution (and often is in the financial services or healthcare sectors), or it can be a partial model to answer a single business question (such as the cost impact of your receivables process on customer profitability).
- The *activities* might not exist in SAP ERP at all if you haven't been capturing marketing activities or collection activities in SAP ERP. If they do exist, it will be as a business process defined in the **Activity-Based Costing** menu or sometimes a cost center/activity type combination. In general, activity types associated with time sheets, routings, recipes, maintenance plans, and so on do not belong in SAP PCM.

We'll start by looking at template allocation to show how you can extend your CO implementation to include the costs of activities or business processes in your normal product costing approach.

11.1 Template Allocations in SAP ERP

Let's first look at how to represent the activity in SAP ERP. The most common way to do this is to create a business process for each activity. The business process has master data that combines the following elements:

- The assignment to a company code, business area, profit center, and so on works the same as for the cost center we looked at in Chapter 3, Section 3.1. Because you're going to be performing allocations that potentially cross company codes or profit centers, bear in mind that the General Ledger will also be affected (see Chapter 3, Section 3.1.3). The business process also has a responsible manager, which is important in the context of process management and the whole notion of process ownership.

- The assignment to a secondary cost element and the parameters for price calculation are the same as for an activity type (see Chapter 3, Section 3.5). The fact that you can calculate a price for a business process using the same mechanisms as for an activity price is often seen as an advantage over the percentage-based overheads we looked at in Chapter 7, Section 7.2; it's almost impossible to set the overhead percentage to completely clear the cost center at period close.

To create a business process, follow the menu path **Accounting • Controlling • Activity-Based Costing • Business Process • Individual Processing • Create** and enter the name of the business process, or use Transaction CP01. Figure 11.1 shows the basic data for business process 300900 (work scheduling). Notice the assignment to a company code, business area, and profit center, as you saw for the cost center, and to a hierarchy area. If you haven't worked with business processes in the past, ask your administrator to check whether activity-based costing is active in your controlling area. This will ensure that you can assign costs to a business process in the same way as you do for cost centers, internal orders, WBS elements, and so on. You can group business processes into hierarchies for reporting and to make it easy to select them as the senders or receivers of an allocation by using the same functions we used to group cost centers in Chapter 3.

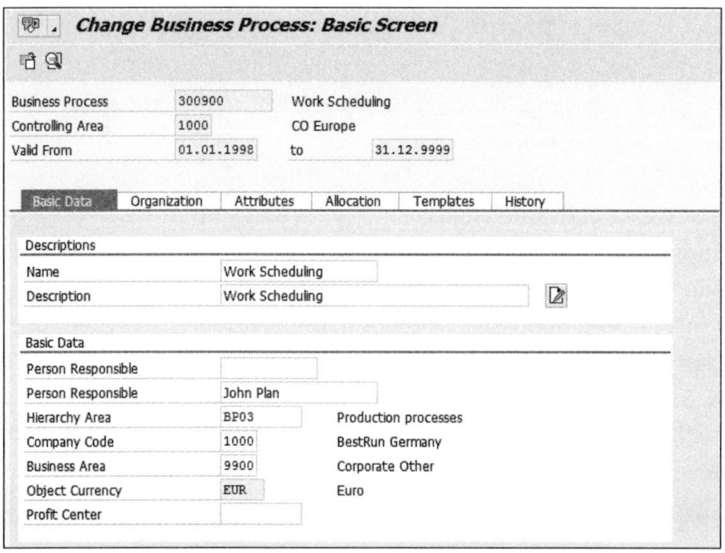

Figure 11.1 Business Process for Work Scheduling: Basic Data

If we return to the pump example that has accompanied us throughout this book (see Figure 11.2), you'll see that the cost estimate now contains two items of item category X in the itemization. These cover activities not described in the routing (these have category E). The costs for one unit of each activity have been applied to every subassembly in our BOM. In our example, this means that the costs of work scheduling (business process 300900) and sales order processing (business process 400900) have been included in the product costs, but this same approach also could be used for a quality check that has to be performed in every manufacturing order regardless of lot size, for example.

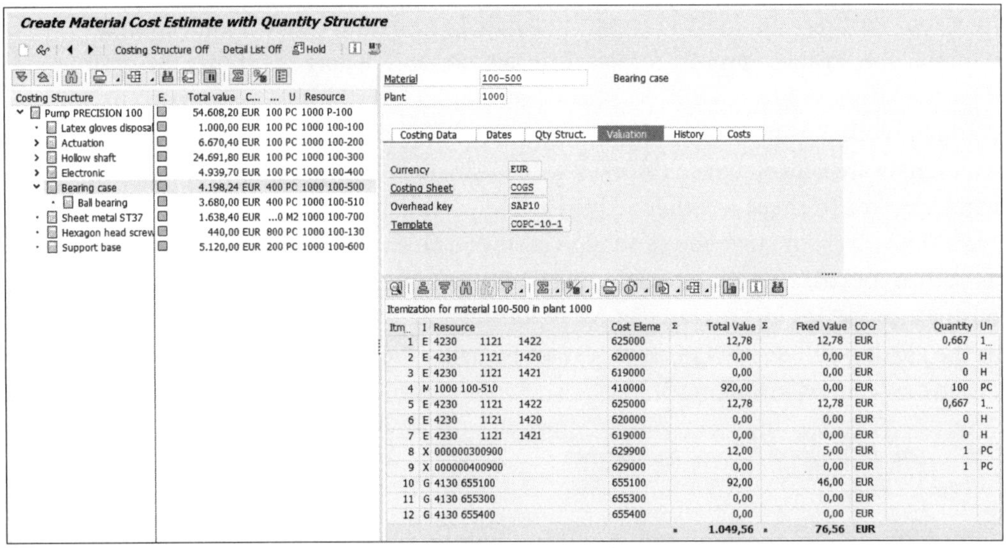

Figure 11.2 Cost Estimate: Business Processes

The business process costs are assigned to a cost element and from there to the cost components. This link is the same as those we discussed when we looked at Product Cost Planning in general in Chapter 2, meaning that you can distinguish between business processes that are part of the cost of goods manufactured (work scheduling) and those that are part of the cost of goods sold (sales order processing). In Figure 11.2, we're looking at the cost of goods manufactured view, so the value in item 9 is zero, because this value will only show up in the cost of goods sold view (you can switch between the two views using the **Costs** tab).

You create the link between the cost estimate and the business process by setting up a template in Customizing. If you're not sure which template has been used in your cost estimate, select the **Valuation** tab (see Figure 11.2). In our example, we used template CO-PC-10-1. The logic used to select the template is the same as the logic for overhead calculation that we looked at in Chapter 7, Section 7.2, with the template being selected based on the costing sheet (here COGS) and the overhead key in the material master during planning (here SAP10) and in the production order at period close. This link is created during configuration.

Figure 11.3 shows the template (CO-PC-10-1) that was used to apply the activity costs to our cost estimate. The easiest way to display this is to double-click on the **Template** field (shown in Figure 11.2). The template shown in Figure 11.3 comprises two calculation lines. The **Sales order proc.** line assigns a unit of one for our business process 400900. The **Order Processing** line refers to a subtemplate that in this example includes our other business process, 300900, and a unit of one. In this example, you don't need to stack the template, but you could have included both lines as business processes; however, this gives you a feel for the potential of the template.

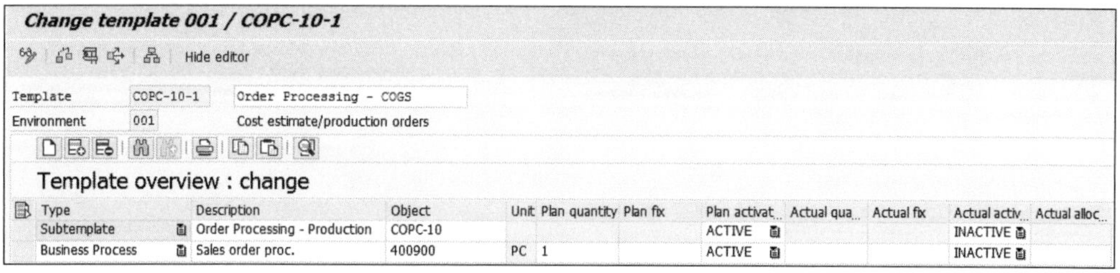

Figure 11.3 Template: Work Scheduling and Order Processing Costs

Having a unit of one is clearly the easiest way to work, but it won't get you beyond the simplest examples. If instead of entering a 1 in the **Plan Quantity** field you double-click on the field, the system will offer you a series of standard functions for calculating quantities in the context that your template is being used in. This context is stored as an environment in SAP ERP. Notice in Figure 11.3 that we're in **Environment 001**, which is used for both Product Cost Planning and production orders. This determines the functions that are relevant for the type of object you're working with. In the case of the production order, the quantities can be calculated using the following:

- The quantities available for the production order, such as order lot size, the scrap quantity, or the rework quantity (refer to Chapter 6 to learn how to post these in the first place)
- The quantities in the material master, such as weight, length, or volume (ideal for calculating volumes for transport processes)

- The quantities in the BOM, such as number of items in the BOM (ideal for calculating the costs of procurement processes)
- The quantities in the routing, such as number of items in the routing or number of work center changes (ideal for calculating internal transport costs)

You can extend these options almost indefinitely by writing your own functions to select other quantities to use as a basis for an allocation.

Figure 11.4 shows a template that reads the number of items in the BOM to determine the number of pallet movements required for each order. Notice that this time the **Plan Quantity** column includes a function name instead of a 1. You'll also see some of the other options you can use to calculate quantities on the right side of the screen.

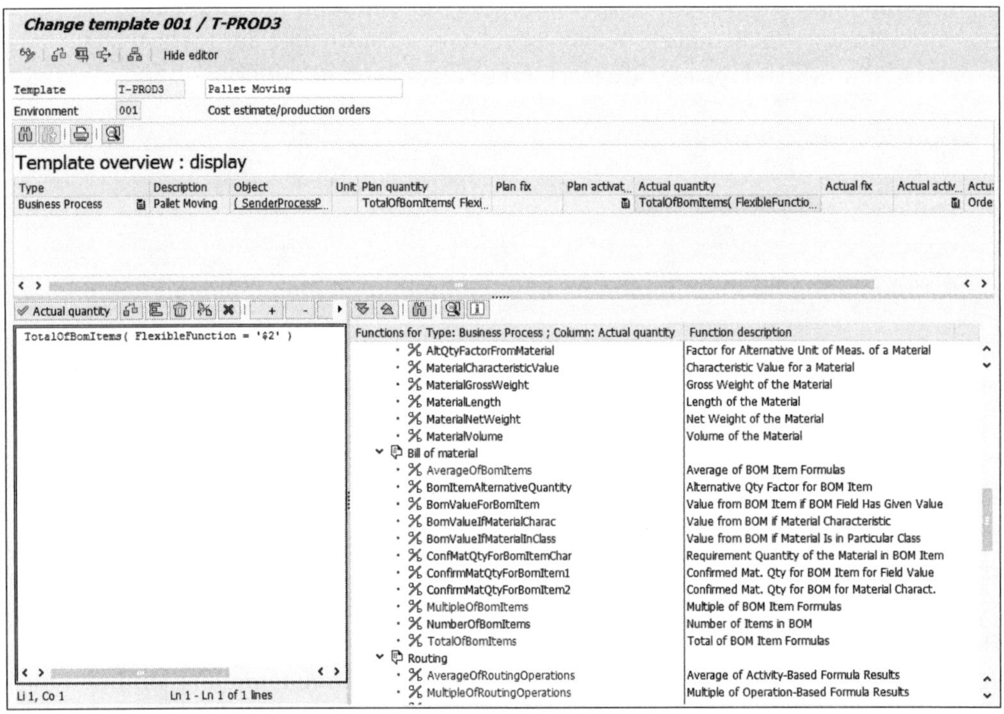

Figure 11.4 Template: Quantity Calculation Functions

Another option to consider is the **Plan Activation** column. If the business process is not sales order processing in general but sales order *configuration*, you might use this option to set up logic that specifies that order configuration is only applied if the material master is configurable. Figure 11.5 shows a template for the assignment of activity costs to CO-PA. In this example, the template reads the flag in the material master that determines whether the material is *configurable* (see Chapter 4, Section 4.3.4) to decide whether customer-specific configuration is necessary. The activity costs for order configuration will only be charged if the material is configurable.

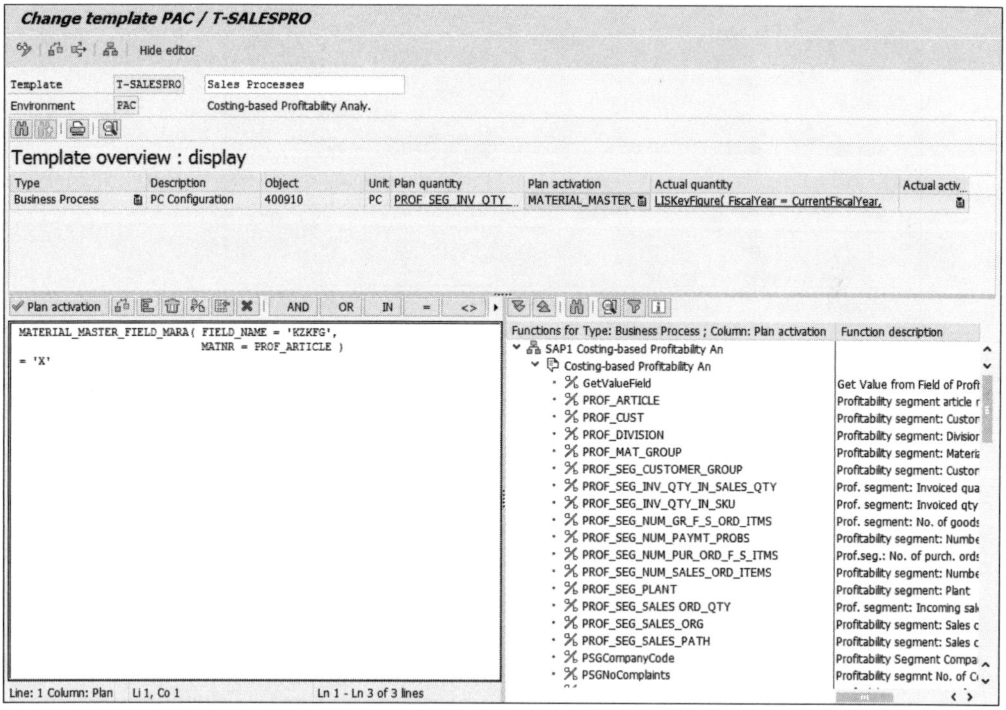

Figure 11.5 Template: Activation of Process

Whatever method of quantity calculation you choose, you won't be able to include your business process in your cost estimates until you have either manually set a price for it or had the system calculate a price, as we saw for the activity prices we planned in Chapter 5. One way to do this is to define another template that establishes what cost center resources your business process will use. Figure 11.6 shows the link between our work scheduling process and the template that determines which cost centers and activity types are providing work for this business process. You can access this screen by selecting the **Templates** tab shown in Figure 11.1. Another way of determining the costs of a business process is to make it part of an allocation. If you refer to the list of receivers for an allocation in Chapter 7, Figure 7.5, you'll see that the business process (**Business Proc.** field) is one of the potential receivers of an allocation.

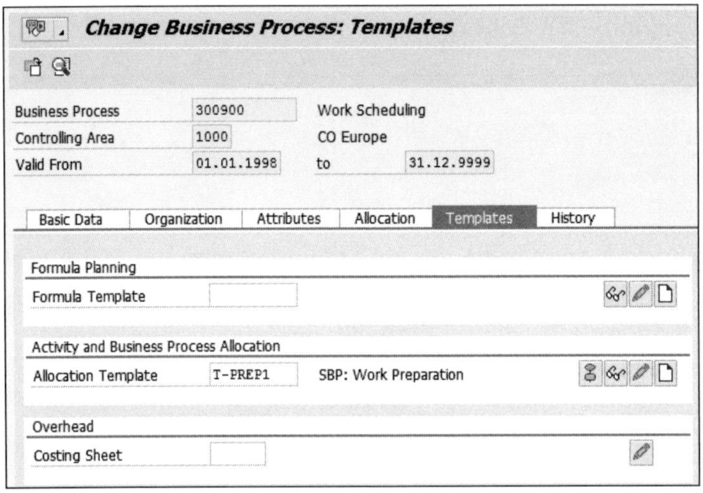

Figure 11.6 Resource Usage for Business Process

Because this template can refer to other templates, the best way to view the whole chain is to select the first icon (**Display Allocation Structure**) to the right of the **Allocation Template** field and click through the different levels. Figure 11.7 shows the allocation structure used to determine the costs for our work scheduling process. You'll see that it uses a fixed number of CPU minutes for the MRP run (an internal activity) and a unit of work from the order scheduling process. The order scheduling process in turn uses CPU minutes for order planning and wage hours (also internal activities). When you build up templates this way, the thing to remember is that you are building up a "pull" model, so you always start with the *receiver* and specify the *senders* from which it is receiving costs:

- You set up a template in CO-PA to define when order configuration is needed for a sales order.
- You set up a template for a production order or cost estimate to define when work scheduling or quality control is needed for the product.
- You set up a template for the business process to determine the amount of internal activity required to perform the work scheduling process.

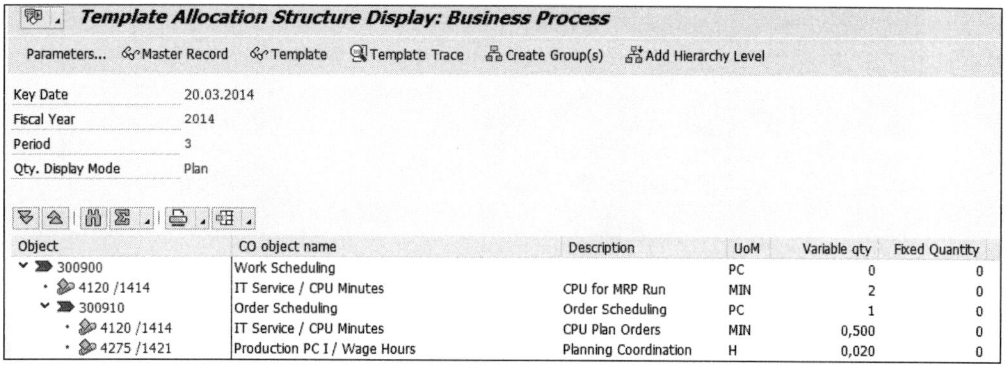

Template Allocation Structure Display: Business Process

Parameters... Master Record Template Template Trace Create Group(s) Add Hierarchy Level

Key Date	20.03.2014
Fiscal Year	2014
Period	3
Qty. Display Mode	Plan

Object	CO object name	Description	UoM	Variable qty	Fixed Quantity
300900	Work Scheduling		PC	0	0
4120 /1414	IT Service / CPU Minutes	CPU for MRP Run	MIN	2	0
300910	Order Scheduling	Order Scheduling	PC	1	0
4120 /1414	IT Service / CPU Minutes	CPU Plan Orders	MIN	0,500	0
4275 /1421	Production PC I / Wage Hours	Planning Coordination	H	0,020	0

Figure 11.7 Allocation Structure for Template Allocation

In our example, the template allocation took place during product costing (in either the costing run or Transaction CK11N). To assign *actual costs*, you'll find the functions to run template allocations in all the menus we used to demonstrate allocations as part of the period close in Chapter 7. To calculate the planned costs of performing work scheduling, refer to the menus we used for planning in Chapter 5. For example, Figure 11.2 shows the menu path for starting template allocation to CO-PA (Transaction CPTE).

In Figure 11.3 and the figures that followed, each template was created with reference to an *environment*. There are many environments for which you can create a template to apply process costs. The functions available within the environment will vary; for example, environment PAC for CO-PA allows you to reference any value field in the operating concern as a driver for template allocation, whereas environments 001 for production orders and 009 for process orders allow you to reference quantities referring to a production campaign (see Chapter 2, Section 2.4).

To create a template, go to any of the template allocation transactions (e.g., **Accounting • Controlling • Cost Center Accounting • Period-End Closing • Single Functions • Allocations • Template Allocation**) and then select **Extras • Template • Create** or go directly to Transaction CPT1. Then give your template a name and select the relevant environment. To decide which environments are potentially relevant for your organization, refer to the sections of this book listed in Table 11.1.

Environment	Object	Reference
PAC	Costing-based profitability analysis	Chapter 2, Section 2.6
SLI	Cost centers	Chapter 3, Section 3.1
SLD	Cost center/activity type	Chapter 3, Section 3.4
006	Cost object hierarchy	Chapter 3, Section 3.8
007	Internal orders	Chapter 3, Section 3.2
010	Product cost collector	Chapter 3, Section 3.7
004	Network	Chapter 4, Section 4.7
005	WBS element	Chapter 4, Section 4.7
SOP	Transfer sales and operations planning	Chapter 5, Section 5.1.1
CPD	Activity-dependent cost center planning	Chapter 5, Section 5.1.2
CPI	Activity-independent cost center planning	Chapter 5, Section 5.1.2
001	Cost estimate/production orders	Chapter 5, Section 5.1.3
001	Cost estimate/production orders	Chapter 6, Section 6.1
008	Sales order	Chapter 6, Section 6.3
009	Process order	Chapter 6, Section 6.3

Table 11.1 Template Environments for Master Data

Then proceed as follows:

1. Depending on whether you're allocating the costs of a business process or the combination cost center/activity type, choose either **Business Process** or **Cost Center/Activity Type** in the **Type** column. You can also build stacked templates as you saw in Figure 11.3 by entering the name of another template.
2. Enter the relevant business process or the combination cost center/activity type. The system will select the description from the relevant master data, as well as the unit of measure (usually pieces).
3. Enter the planned quantity either as an integer (one unit of work scheduling) or by choosing a quantity function. You can access the quantity functions by double-

clicking on the **Quantity** column. They'll vary depending on the environment you're working in.

4. If your costs will only apply under certain circumstances, choose an activation function by double-clicking on the **Plan Activation** column.

For the business process and the cost center, you can now include your template in the relevant master data (select the **Templates** tab for the business process or cost center). For the other objects, the selection is in Customizing, so you have to discuss with your configuration team how to ensure that the correct template is selected during product costing or in the period close.

Template Maintenance in a Productive System

Normally, template maintenance is a Customizing activity and can't be changed in a productive system. If you do want to maintain templates in a productive system, ask your IT department to use Transaction SOBJ to adjust the settings for object CPT2 (the template change transaction) to permit template maintenance as current settings. This will allow the same kind of maintenance as you saw for the allocation cycles in Chapter 7, Section 7.1.

Activity-Based Costing in SAP S/4HANA

There is some confusion on the various forums about whether activity-based costing is still available in SAP S/4HANA, but the topics described here *do* continue to be available in SAP S/4HANA. For confirmation, refer to SAP Note 2270408 (S4TWL—Activity-Based Costing).

Although template allocations can be a useful tool for performing allocations in SAP ERP, you may find that most of the driver quantities you want to use for allocations are outside of SAP ERP. In this case, it's worth looking at whether SAP PCM can help you.

11.2 Allocations in SAP PCM

The template allocation we just looked at makes perfect sense when the information we need for the allocations is already available in the material master, BOM, routing, or wherever. For CO-PA, we can set up templates that can read any value field in the operating concern. The tool discussions start when the *quantities* you need as a basis for your allocation aren't readily available in SAP ERP. The question of where most of the drivers reside that you want to use as a basis for your allocations can determine whether to perform allocations in SAP ERP, SAP PCM, or both:

- In SAP ERP, we've already looked at how to enter key figures, such as square footage, to use as a basis for an allocation or how to configure a template to pick up quantities available in Logistics. You can use any value field in your operating concern as the basis for an allocation. The issues start when you find yourself adding value fields for both drivers and the result of each allocation in CO-PA. If you have a complex model with a lot of drivers, you can easily find yourself running out of value fields in CO-PA.
- SAP PCM has its own data bridge to pull data out of an external system, or you can use SAP Financial Information Management to extract the relevant data from SAP BW, SAP ERP, SAP CRM, or any data warehouse. SAP PCM also includes a web-based data-collection tool to collect information from managers in the form of a survey.

Once you've collected the relevant data, the next stage is to think about your *model*. Before you start drawing out any details, think about the type of model you're interested in:

- If you're looking at *modeling* to understand the drivers for a single area of your business, then your corporate costing system—in which all allocations can impact the General Ledger—may not be the best place for experiments. In these circumstances, it's good to ask yourself how stable your model is. Even in SAP ERP, cost center structures change over time, but ask yourself whether the business process or activity you're describing refers to your core business or is something you're experimenting with. If you want to keep changing that model because of the lessons you've learned from your calculations, building in your corporate costing system where every change involves gaining the consensus of all involved parties may not actually be what you want.
- If you want to run different *simulations* based on your model, costing several plan versions as you saw in Chapter 5 may not give you sufficient flexibility to model the impact of different scenarios. One thing that makes simulations cumbersome in SAP ERP is that so many different applications are involved, as you saw when we followed the annual operating plan from start to finish. In these circumstances, it's good to ask yourself what the purpose of your simulation is. You saw how budget data is used in SAP ERP to limit spending on a project (see Chapter 6) and how

planned data is used as a basis for variance calculation (see Chapter 7), but as we discussed in Chapter 10, some plans are just plans—a modeled set of assumptions.

Further discussions typically start around the dimensions you use in your model. As we discussed in Chapter 2, setting up your operating concern for CO-PA is very much about deciding how to map the low-level detail, such as customers and products, and how these roll up via customer groups, material groups, product hierarchies, regions, and so on to provide a consistent profitability model for the whole organization. You may find, however, that for some parts of the organization you need more detail—going right down to the SKU level—and for others less. Another question is the product view versus the customer view. As we saw in Chapter 5, the product is very central to the planning process in SAP ERP. The customer dimension exists, but if you don't set up templates in CO-PA to handle questions about how much it costs to serve a particular customer, then all other customer-related costs are merely overhead and are applied using assessment cycles.

11.2.1 Mapping the Costing Model in SAP PCM with SAP ERP

You can build models in SAP PCM that have almost nothing to do with CO, but that isn't the focus of this book. We want to understand how to use the two models in *combination*. If you've installed SAP PCM, you can log on by selecting PCM—**Model Builder** on your desktop. Once you've filled in your login credentials, select the relevant model, as shown in Figure 11.8.

Notice that our demo system includes several types of model:

- Most of the models are used to demonstrate overhead allocation in an environment in which the use of CO is fairly limited. In such an example, there may be a link to a business process in SAP ERP, but it's more likely that the main purpose of CO is simply to capture the initial staff costs (from payroll), building costs (from asset accounting), and office costs (from the General Ledger) and bring these into Cost Center Accounting. All subsequent steps to assign these costs to the activities performed by the bank or telecommunications and understand their impact on customer profitability can take place in SAP PCM.
- We'll focus on the COPA_PCM model, which is used to demonstrate an alternative form of overhead allocation in which the relevant profitability segments in CO-PA are modeled as cost objects in SAP PCM and activity costs assigned to these cost objects. Here both the cost centers and the cost objects will be extracted to SAP PCM, but activities will be described in SAP PCM.

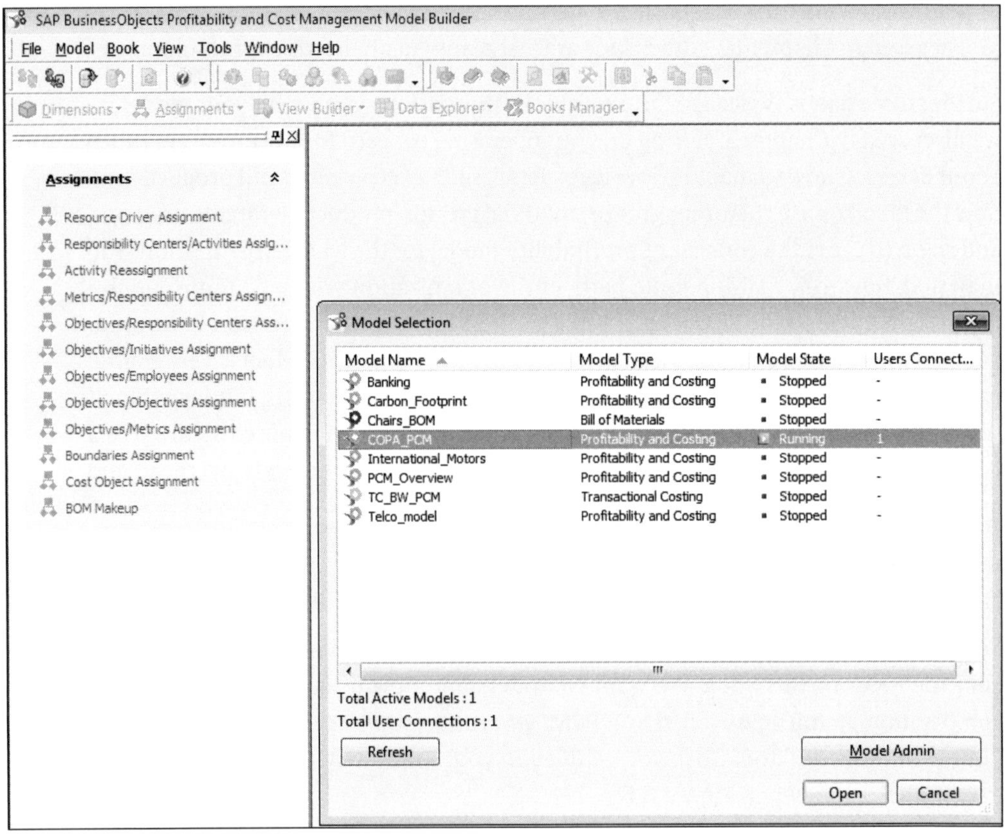

Figure 11.8 Select Model in SAP PCM

11.2.2 Dimensions of the Costing Model

Most models start with a series of *line items*. Don't be misled by the SAP term *line item* that we used in Chapter 2, which meant any document written to record the posting to a cost center, internal order, and so on. The line items in SAP PCM are not line items in the sense that they correspond to a document in table COEP that you would view using Transaction KSB1 or KOB1. They are as likely to be totals records if you're extracting data from CO because you're unlikely to need all the detail available in a CO line item. In SAP PCM, the term *line item* simply means the list of expense records that you're taking as the starting point for your model. Figure 11.9 shows the line items in SAP PCM. You'll find this view by following the menu path **Model • Dimensions • Line Item • Line Items** or selecting **Line Items** on the left.

In this example, we've loaded a list of accounts from SAP ERP. There may be a one-to-one relationship between these accounts and the cost elements in SAP ERP (see Chapter 3), or you may find yourself performing a mapping exercise to restructure your cost elements and cost element groups as you establish the data-transfer mechanisms.

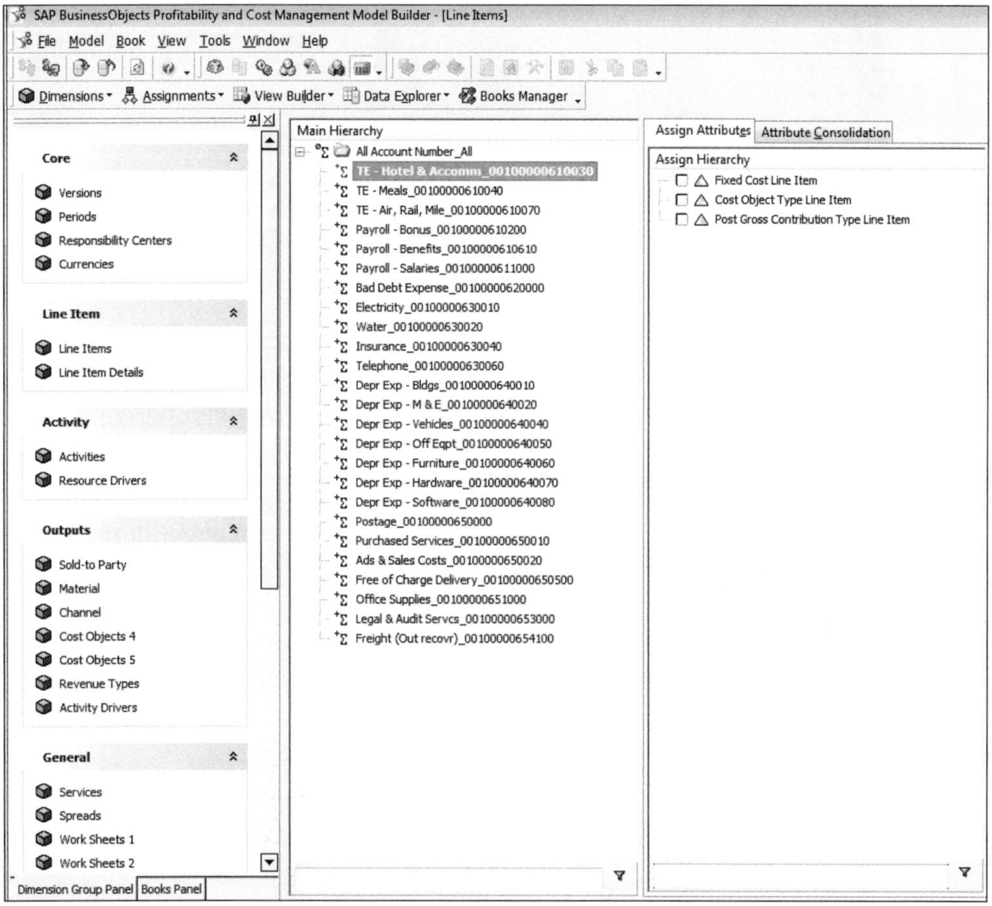

Figure 11.9 Line Items in SAP PCM

Just as in SAP ERP, the cost element information is always linked with the question of *where* the expense occurred, so SAP PCM includes information about the responsible center, as shown in Figure 11.10. You can access this view by following the menu path **Model • Dimensions • Core • Responsibility Centers** or selecting **Responsibility Centers** on the left.

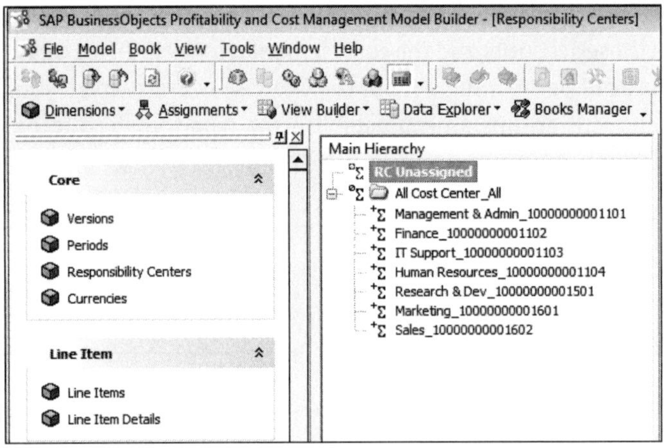

Figure 11.10 Responsibility Centers in SAP PCM

In this example, the **Responsibility Centers** are **Management & Admin**, **Finance**, **IT Support**, and so on. These usually link with the cost centers in SAP ERP, though occasionally you'll find a group of General Ledger accounts or even a profit center represented here depending on how you configure the data bridge.

You can perform a simple allocation from a marketing cost center to the cost objects, but you're more likely to add *activities* to your model. These might be business processes you've set up in CO, but they're more likely to be activities with no equivalent in CO: generating leads, managing key accounts, performing market trials on new products, and so on. Figure 11.11 shows the sample activities performed by our organization. You can access this view by following the menu path **Model • Dimensions • Activity • Activities** or selecting **Activities** on the bottom left.

In this example, you can see activities such as **Manage Key Accounts**, **Lead Generation**, **Sales Admin**, and so on. It's possible to perform an allocation that ends with the activities that simply helps you to understand the relative costs of each activity performed.

More often, however, the ultimate aim is to assign these expenses to *cost objects*. As we said earlier, these aren't the production orders and product cost collectors you'll find in SAP ERP but the characteristics you'll normally model in CO-PA (in our examples, the various retail outlets at which our pens are sold). Figure 11.12 shows how the sold-to party (or customer) is loaded into SAP PCM as a cost object. To display this dimension, follow the menu path **Model • Dimensions • Output • Sold-To Party** or select **Sold-to Party** on the bottom left.

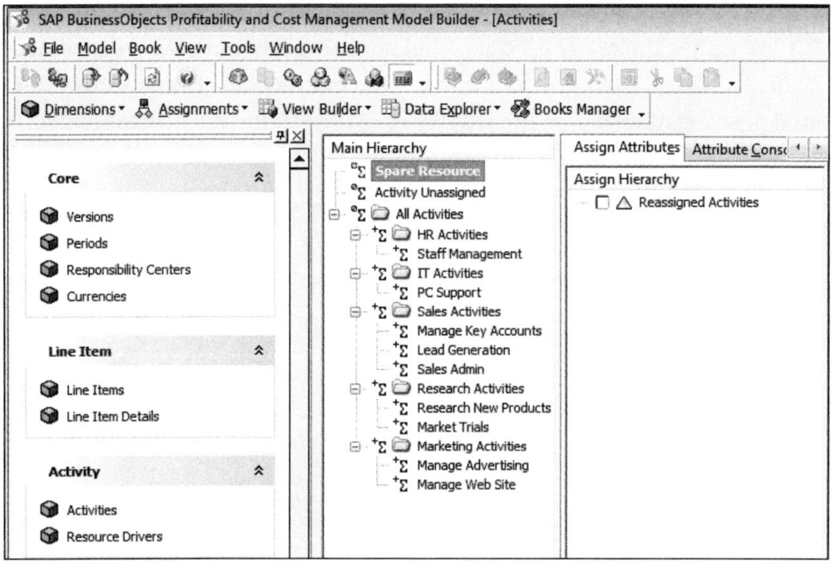

Figure 11.11 Activities in SAP PCM

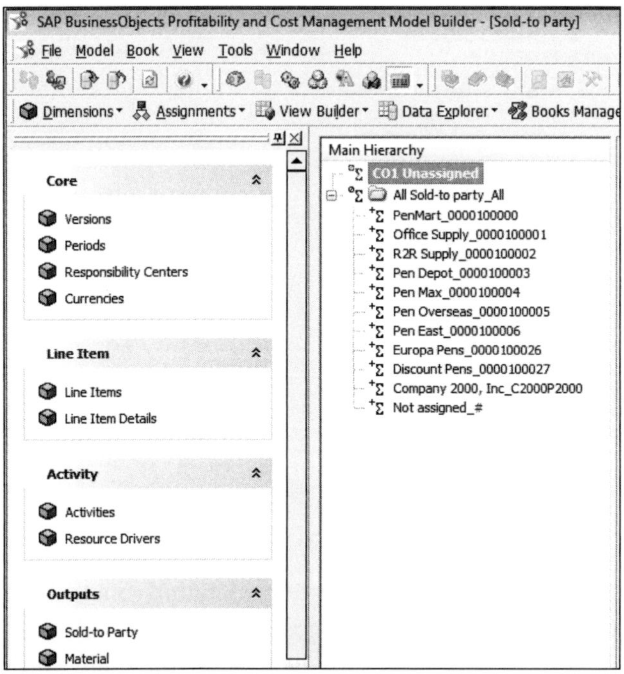

Figure 11.12 Sold-To Parties as Cost Objects in SAP PCM

Compare the sold-to party with the use of the material as a cost object as shown in Figure 11.13. Here we see the many products that our sample organization distributes and sells. To display this dimension, follow the menu path **Model • Dimensions • Output • Material** or select **Material** on the left. We could continue this process and look at channels in the same way.

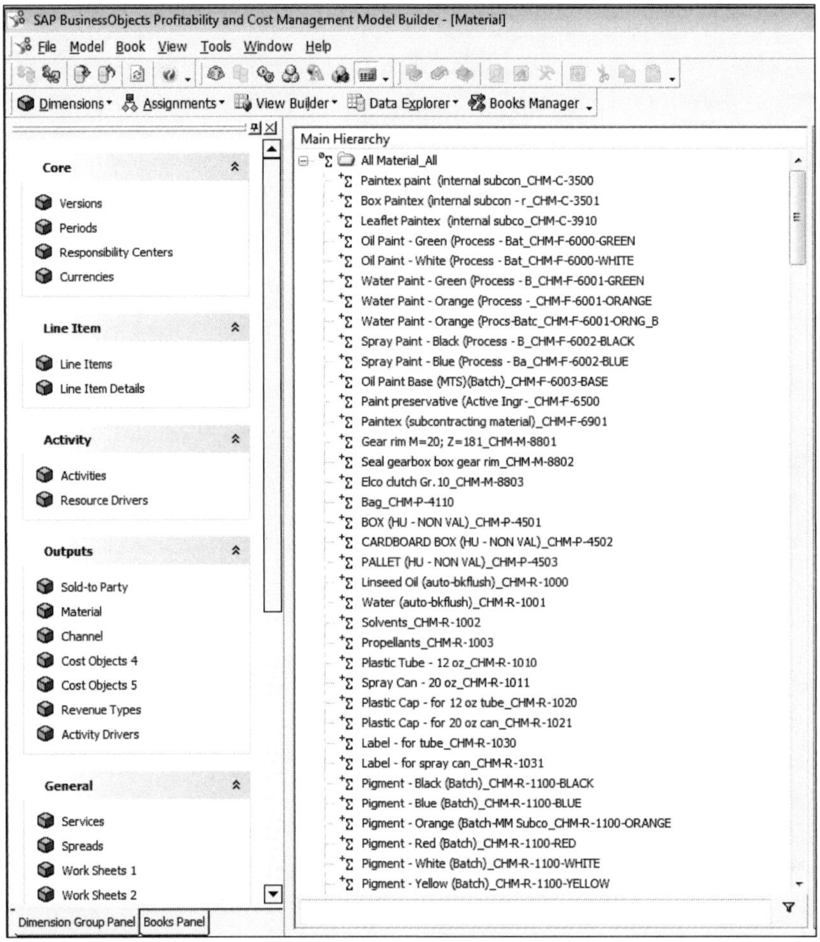

Figure 11.13 Materials as Cost Objects in SAP PCM

Controllers with almost 60 characteristics in their existing operating concerns are often concerned by the fact that SAP PCM has only five cost objects and wonder how characteristics in CO-PA can map to cost objects in SAP PCM. Two things are worth bearing in mind here:

- Organizational dimensions in CO-PA, such as versions, valuation views, and so on, don't count as cost objects. Entities such as versions and currencies are modeled as separate dimensions in SAP PCM, so you can ignore these in your characteristic count.
- Dependent dimensions, such as customer groups for customers or product groups for products, are considered as attributes of the main cost object, so you would model a Customer dimension with a Customer Group attribute in SAP PCM. Again, this will reduce the number of potential cost objects. If you have SAP BW in place, look at the dimensions you used to model your operating concern there or refer to Chapter 8, Figure 8.14 for an example. Your aim is to identify the *separate* dimensions that are relevant for profitability reporting and model them as cost objects.

In Figure 11.12 and Figure 11.13, we renamed the delivered dimensions **Cost Object 1**, **Cost Object 2**, and **Cost Object 3** to suit our purposes. You can do the same by selecting **Model • Rename Dimensions**, as shown in Figure 11.14. Here you'll also see that **Versions**, **Periods**, and **Currencies** are separate dimensions rather than one of the many characteristics included in the operating concern in CO-PA.

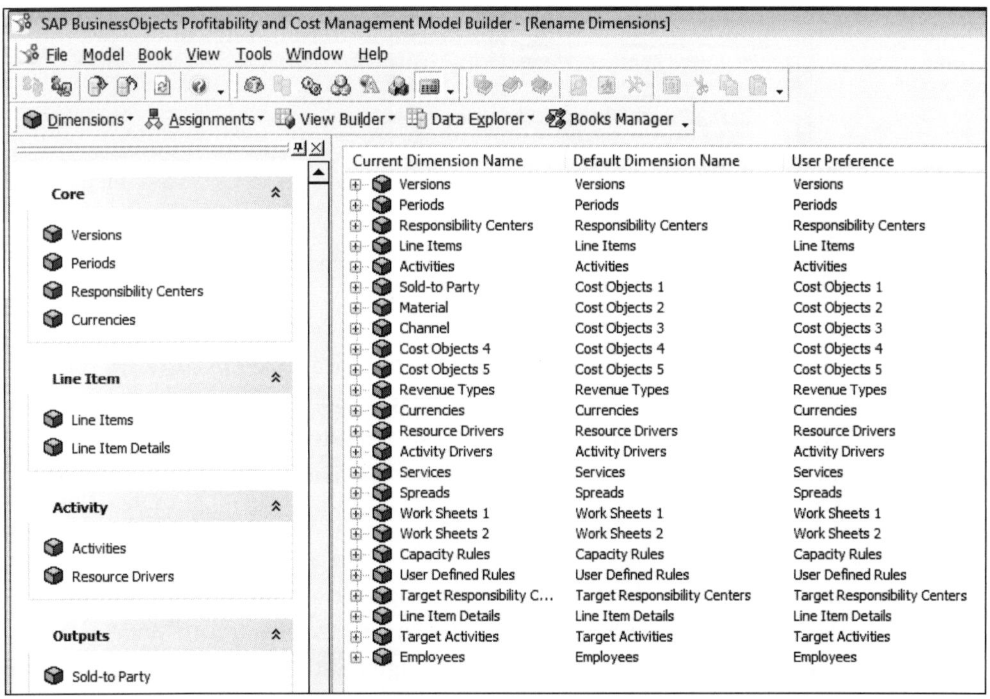

Figure 11.14 Dimensions Table in SAP PCM

11.2.3 Assignments in the Costing Model

Now that we have the three levels (resources, activities, and cost objects) in place, the next stage is to link these three levels. In SAP ERP, we did this by assigning statistical key figures, such as square footage of office space, to the cost center or by planning the activity types, such as machine hours, for the production cost center. Figure 11.15 shows the resource drivers to be used to allocate each type of cost. You can access this view by following the menu path **Model • Assignments • Resource Drivers Assignment** or selecting **Resource Drivers Assignment** in the bottom left.

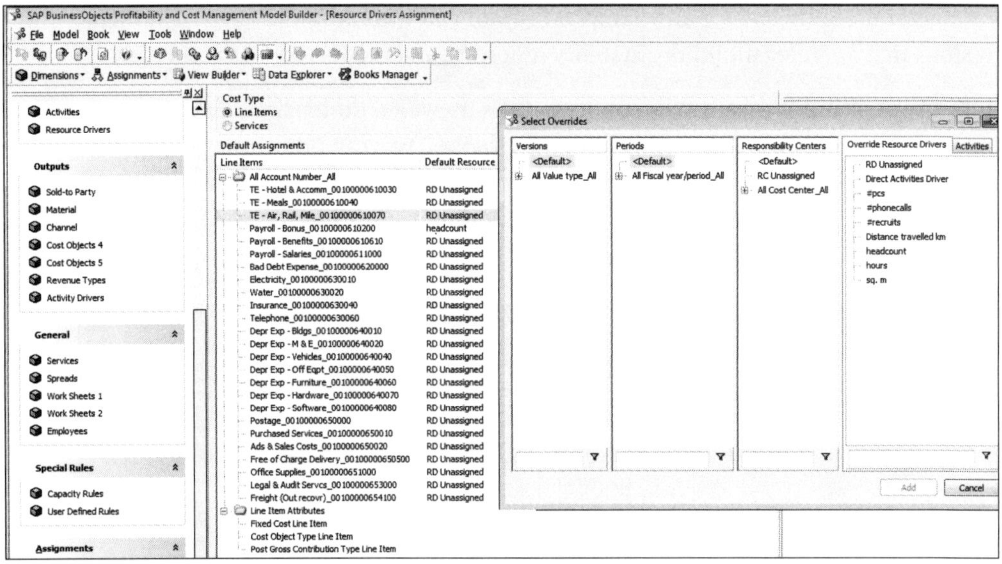

Figure 11.15 Resource Drivers Assignment in SAP PCM

In this example, you see **Headcount** being used to allocate payroll costs. We can then continue and use distance travelled in kilometers to allocate travel costs by right-clicking on the travel line and choosing **Assign Resource Driver**. You can create further resource drivers by selecting **Model • Resource Drivers** or **Resource Drivers** on the left. This is essentially the same as working with statistical key figures in SAP ERP.

We then need to map the responsibility centers to the activities they're performing. Figure 11.16 shows a sample assignment from the **Sales** department to the **Lead Generation** activity. You can access this view by following the menu path **Model • Assignments • Responsibility Centers/Activities Assignment** or selecting **Responsibility Centers/Activities Assignment** in the bottom left.

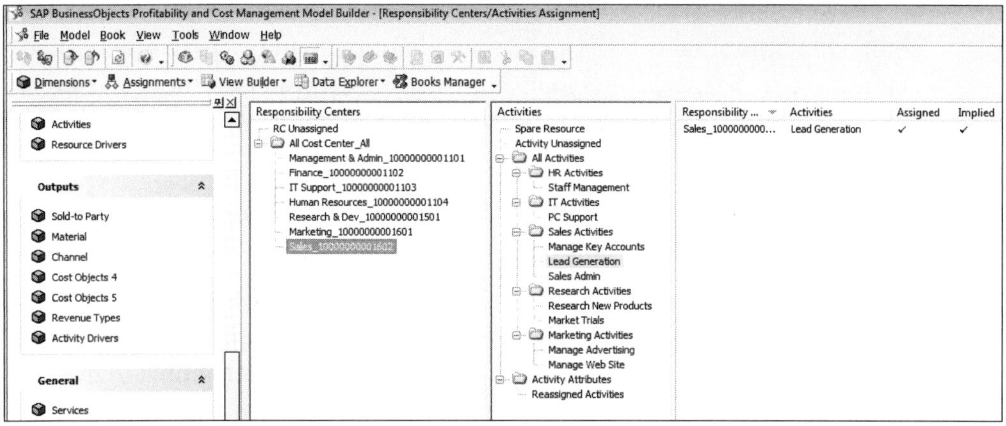

Figure 11.16 Responsibility Center Assignment in SAP PCM

Finally, the activities have to be assigned to cost objects, as shown in Figure 11.17. In our example, the lead generation activities are assigned to the products, customers, and channels served.

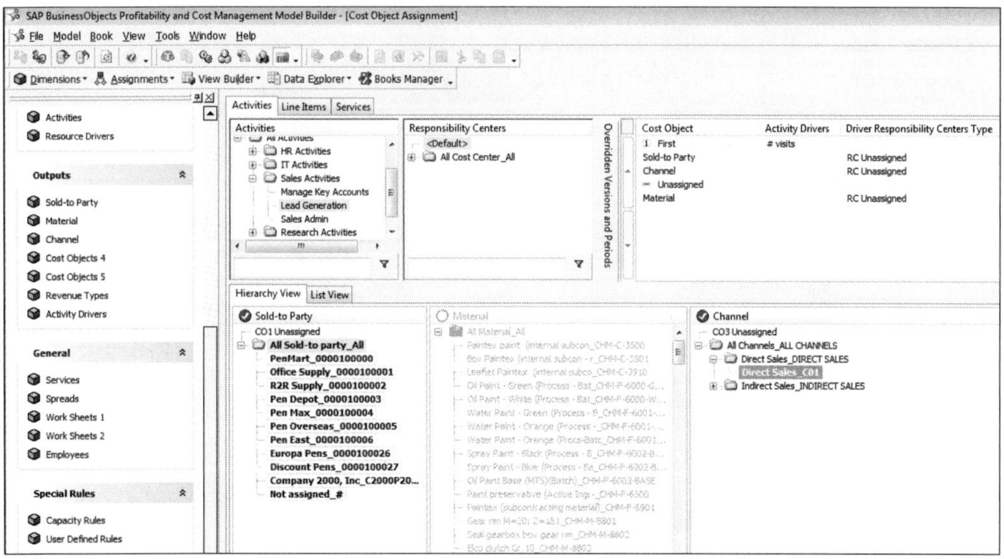

Figure 11.17 Cost Object Assignment

You can access this view by following the menu path **Model • Assignments • Cost Object Assignment** or selecting **Cost Object Assignment** in the bottom left. This assignment will behave much like the assessment cycles we looked at in Chapter 7, Section 7.1.4, with all costs being assigned to each activity and then charged to all cost objects. You can be much more sophisticated in SAP PCM and use the rules editor to build a template that provides options closer to those we discussed earlier when talking about building up templates in SAP ERP.

11.2.4 Loading Data into the Model

Once we've built our dimensions and established the links between them, we've effectively built the master data for our costing model. The next step is to load data into the model and run the allocations. To understand what's required in this step, look at Figure 11.18, which provides an overview of the SAP PCM architecture.

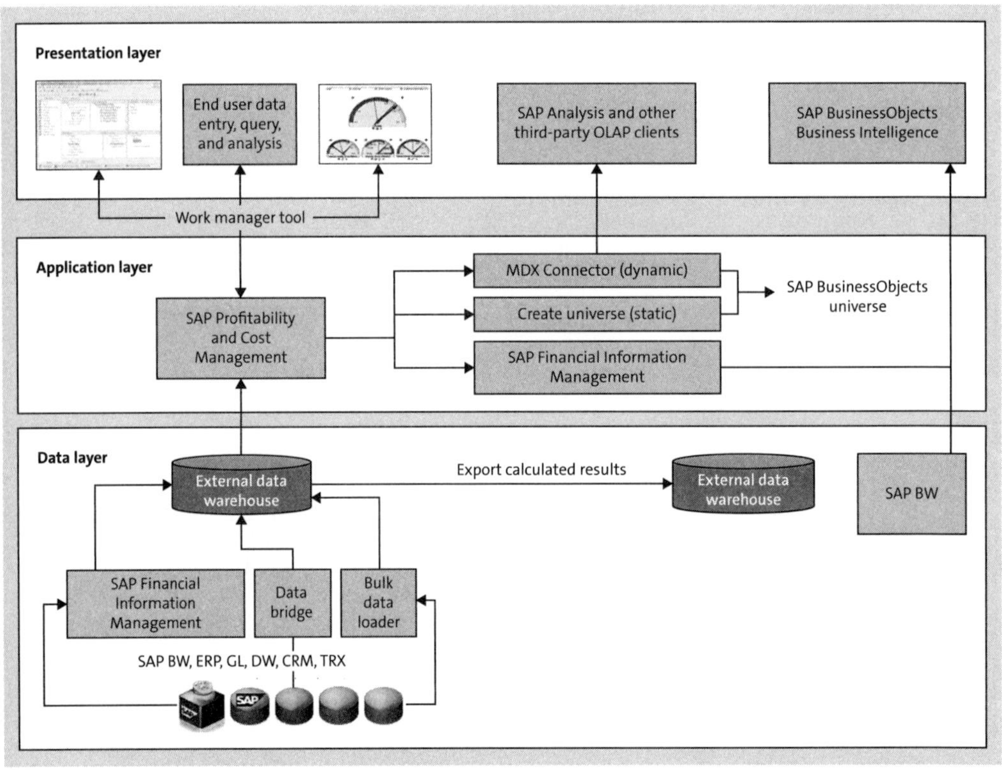

Figure 11.18 Solution Architecture for SAP PCM

At the bottom of the figure, you'll see the various options for bringing data out of SAP ERP or a data warehouse. For the data we've been looking at, the first decision to make is whether you're going to load data from the CO tables in SAP ERP or via an SAP BW query. As we mentioned earlier, SAP PCM has its own data bridge to pull data out of these systems, or you can use SAP Financial Information Management to extract the relevant data. Once the data is loaded, the data calculated can then be extracted to the reporting tool of your choice for analysis. This can mean extracting the results back to SAP BW, but there are several other options, as Figure 11.18 illustrates.

To explain exactly how this load process works is beyond the scope of this book because there are many options. The important thing at this stage is to understand how the CO component can integrate with SAP PCM and whether there are benefits for your organization in investigating the solution further. Now that we've looked at how to build models in SAP PCM, we'll finish by looking at the kind of insights into customer profitability that such calculations can provide.

11.3 Customer Value Analysis Using SAP PCM

The reason we've looked at how to build a costing model in SAP PCM is to understand how to extend our understanding of customer profitability in CO-PA with additional information calculated in SAP PCM. This brings us into the realm of customer value analysis. We'll therefore now look at some sample dashboards that were built with data determined using SAP PCM.

When we logon to PCM—Book Viewer and select the **PCM_Overview** model, as shown in Figure 11.19, we see trends in the net margin (upper line) and the cost to serve (lower line) by country. In the graph in Figure 11.19, we can choose an individual country (the United Kingdom, in our example) and see how the margin and cost to serve have been evolving over time. As the cost to serve (on the right) begins to exceed the net margin (on the left) in June, we have cause for concern and can dig deeper by selecting **Cost Breakdown**, on the right in Figure 11.19.

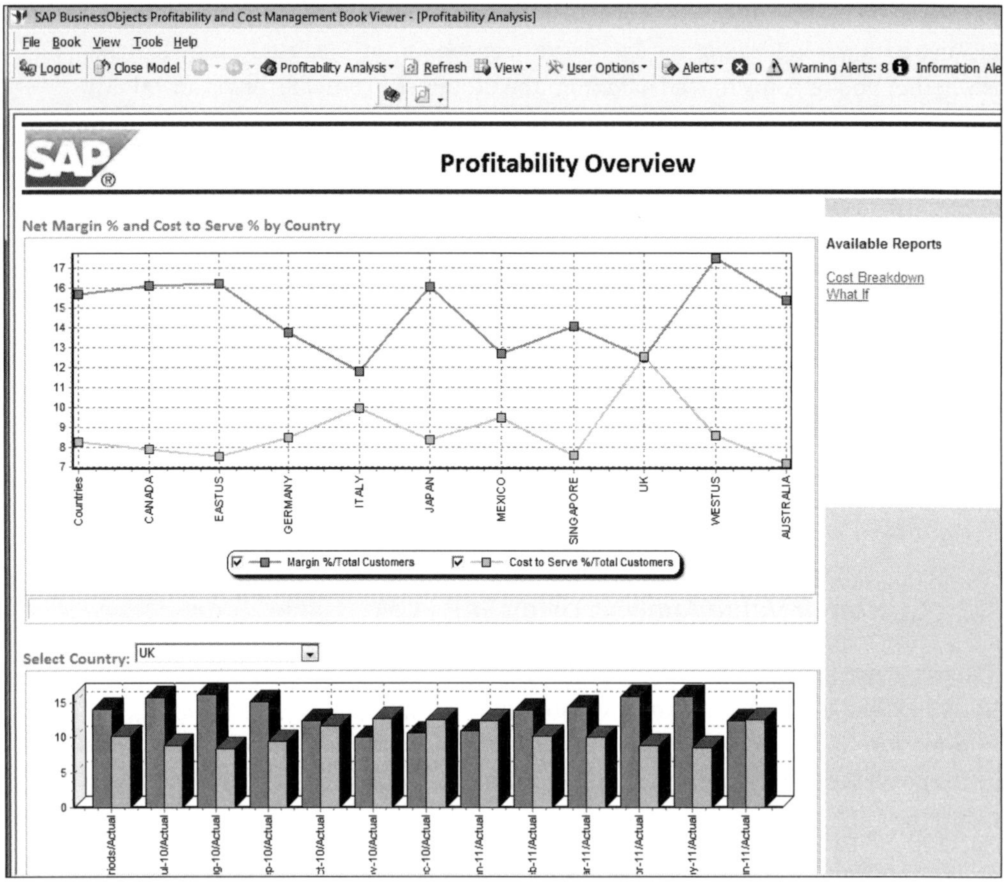

Figure 11.19 Profitability Analysis by Country

This takes us to the **Cost to Serve Analysis** screen shown in Figure 11.20. Here we can see that there are problems with **Grocery Stores** and **Hospitality**, which both have margins that are lower than our established threshold and high costs to serve. The graphic in the lower part of the screen explains what has been driving the high costs to serve. We can see that there are significant costs associated with shipping products and answering customer enquiries. To understand how best to improve the situation, we need to choose the **What If** link, shown on the right in Figure 11.20.

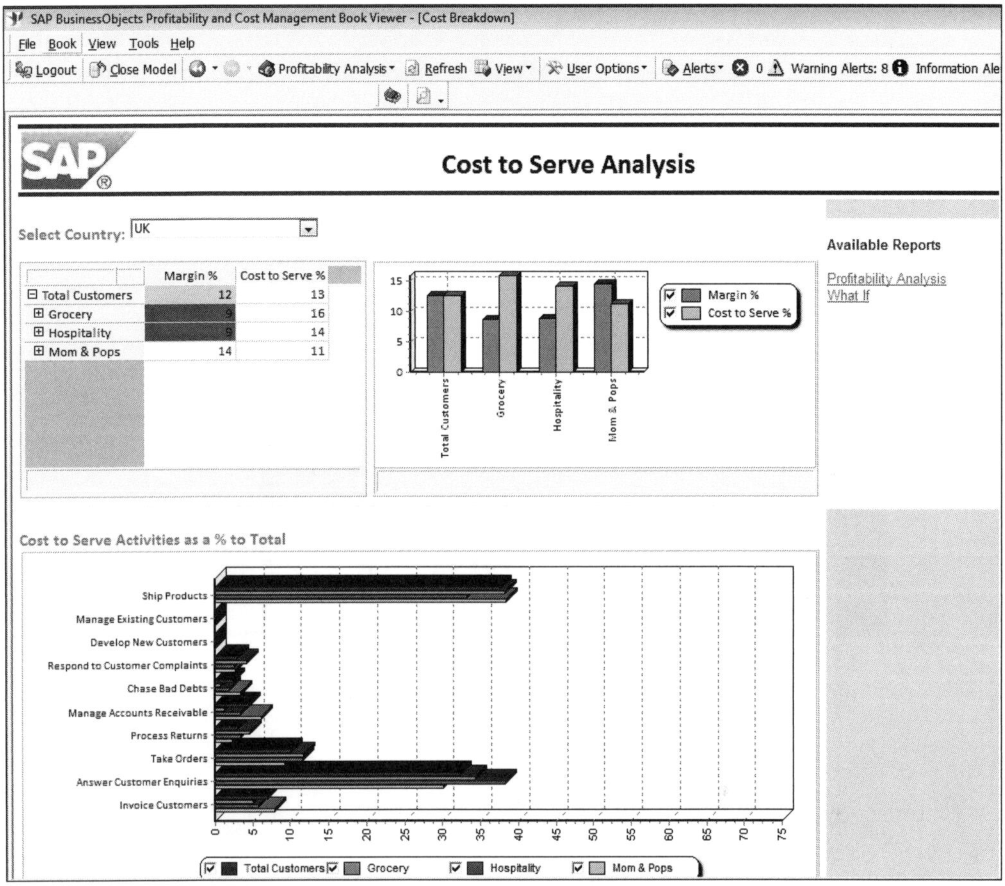

Figure 11.20 Cost to Serve Analysis

This takes us to the **What-If Analysis** shown in Figure 11.21. Here we can see that what has been driving the costs of shipping is how individual trucks have been used. Trucks have typically only been loaded to 60% capacity.

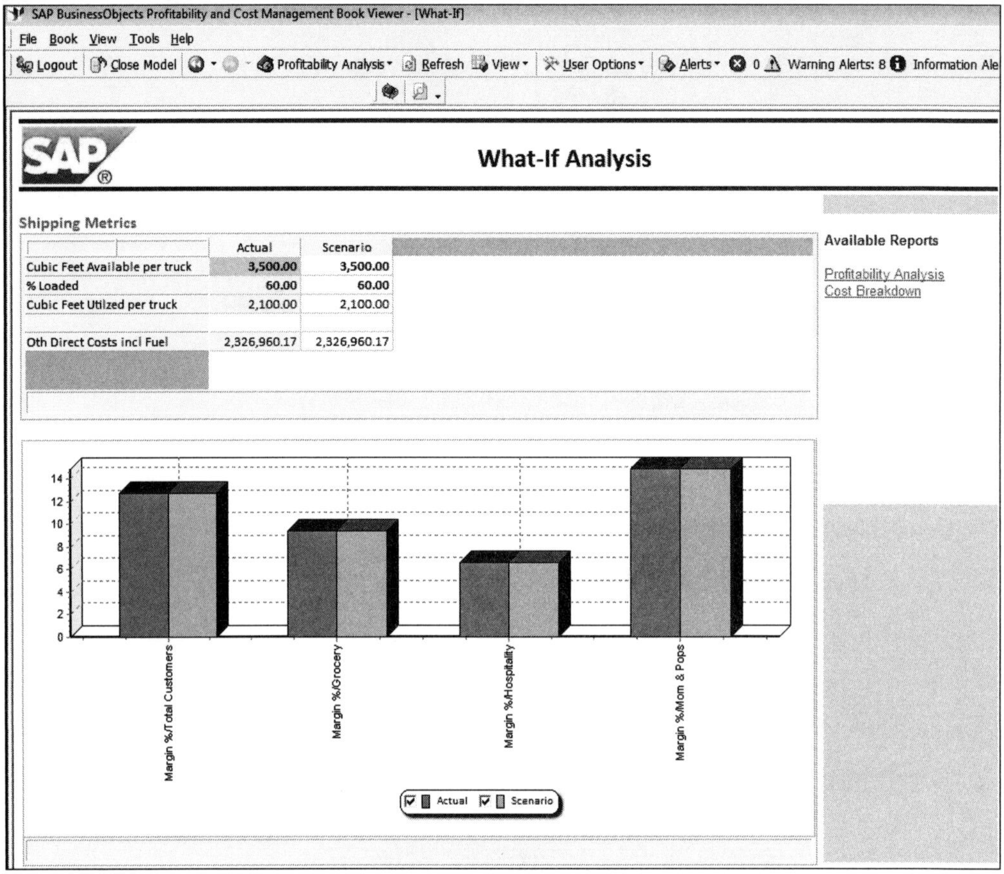

Figure 11.21 What-If Analysis (Initial Situation)

We want to understand the impact of changing this capacity, so in Figure 11.22 we've increased the capacity to 80% to see whether this change can potentially alleviate our cost-to-serve problem.

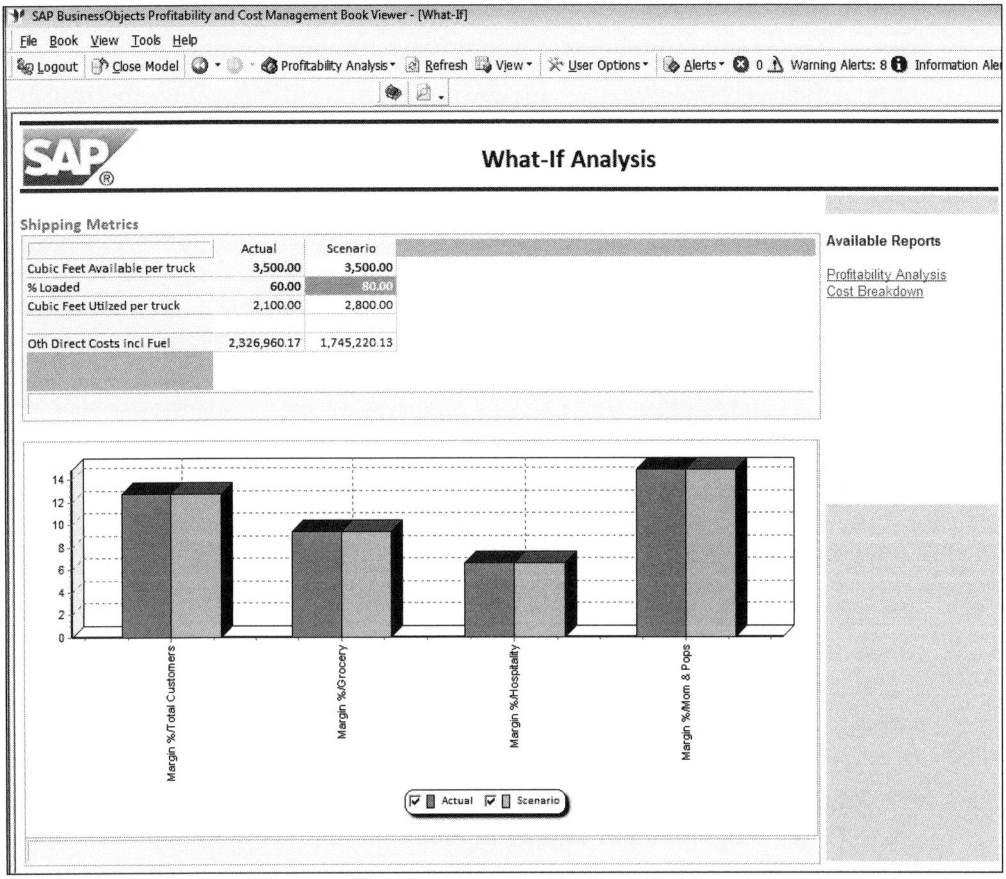

Figure 11.22 What-If Analysis (Scenario Modeling)

This example is simply an illustration of the kind of analysis an activity-based model can enable, but it should help you decide whether you want to embark on such a journey.

11.4 Summary

In this chapter, we looked at how to use template allocation to include the costs of certain business processes in our product costs and profitability analysis and how to use SAP PCM to build an alternative costing model that extends what you already have in SAP ERP to include other activities and cost drivers. We then looked at the type of insights into customer profitability that such allocations can enable.

Although such profitability calculations can be performed at any time, the availability of the relevant data means that they are typically part of the period-close process. In the next chapter, we'll therefore look at how to organize and automate your close process to free up more time for cost analysis and simulation, allowing you to act on the insights the costing model has provided.

Chapter 12
Period Close Using the SAP Financial Closing Cockpit

This chapter picks up where Chapter 7 left off: it looks at how to organize, schedule, and monitor the steps of the period close. It also shows you how to handle the huge volumes of data in a real period close and perform a close that crosses multiple systems.

When we looked at the details of the period close in Chapter 7, we focused on what was happening in the individual close steps rather than on how to optimize the close as a whole.

The most obvious difference between a real-life close and what we described in Chapter 7 was that in Section 7.2 we looked at individual production orders and product cost collectors and ignored the options for *collective processing*. Only when you're testing will you calculate work in process (WIP) or variances for an individual production order and then settle the order. In the real world, you'll use collective processing for all the steps in Section 7.2 to make sure that all relevant orders were selected and that all the steps were completed successfully. In this chapter, we'll focus on the close as a whole and how to perform tasks to make the best use of system resources because of the volumes of data to be processed.

If you skip through the various sections of Chapter 7, you'll get a sense of the flow of a close. We discussed the importance of not running the allocation cycles until you're sure that all the data from payroll, billing, and asset accounting is available. This represents a *dependency* between closing steps. There are many examples of dependencies in Chapter 7, in which one closing step builds on the result of a previous step:

- You can only run periodic revaluation in CO-PA when you've completed the revaluation of consumption step in the Material Ledger to calculate the actual costs for the finished materials for which sales were captured in CO-PA.
- You can only settle your production orders when you've finished calculating WIP, scrap, and variances for each of the orders.

The individual menus give a sense of this flow simply by the sequence in which they present the tasks, but you'll inevitably find yourself hopping between menus. Internal orders are a good example of where the menu is of only limited help:

- Internal orders that belong to their parent cost centers must first be settled to cost centers before you can allocate the cost center expenses and calculate activity prices.
- Once you've calculated the actual activity prices, you have to assign the new activity prices to a different set of orders (perhaps for research and development or investment) before settling these orders.

As you draw up your list of steps for the close, it's a good idea to look at the groupings you'll use for selection. You might want to refer to Chapter 3, in which we looked at how to define order groups and selection variants, to make sure that your objects are grouped in suitable blocks for processing. Refer to the settings shown in Figure 12.11 to remind yourself which selection parameters are available for use in closing.

12.1 New Options for Accelerating the Period Close

Fortunately, the first solutions to help you manage the closing process have been available since Release 4.6C. The menu screenshots throughout Chapter 7 show the Schedule Manager as the first step of the period-end closing menus for Cost Center Accounting, Internal Orders, Cost Object Controlling, and so on. The Schedule Manager is a generic tool that allows you to list your closing tasks, assign task owners, prepare a schedule for the tasks, and then execute each task in the correct sequence. We also saw the Schedule Manager in the planning menus in Chapter 5. You can use the mechanisms we describe for the period-closing tasks to execute the plan allocations and plan settlements in the same way.

The release of SAP ERP 5.0 coincided with demands from the Securities and Exchange Commission (SEC) for faster reporting. SAP's response was the SAP Financial Closing cockpit. This uses much of the same coding as had been used in the Schedule Manager but allows you to visualize the individual controlling areas and company codes participating in the close, flag closing tasks by *closing type* (month-end close, year-end close, etc.), and define *dependencies* between tasks. To access the SAP Financial Closing cockpit, select Transaction CLOCOC or **Accounting • Financial Accounting • General Ledger • Periodic Processing • Closing • Closing Cockpit (Manage Templates and Task Lists).** Don't be misled by the fact that the SAP Financial Closing cockpit is offered in the **General Ledger** menu. The idea is that it should cover tasks that cross the whole of SAP ERP Financials, including the Controlling component (CO). Because the initial release of the SAP Financial Closing cockpit coincided with the introduction of the SAP General Ledger, some people assume that they cannot use the SAP Financial Closing cockpit in combination with the classic General Ledger, but this isn't true. When you build up your templates, you simply have to make sure that you include the correct transactions for whichever General Ledger you are using.

Moving from Schedule Manager to SAP Financial Closing Cockpit

If you've already started using the Schedule Manager but are now on SAP ERP 5.0 or later, you can import your lists from one environment to another by selecting **Template/Task List • Import Template from Schedule Manager**. This also means you can start building task lists in Schedule Manager now and move them to the SAP Financial Closing cockpit without problems when you upgrade.

The SAP Financial Closing cockpit was released with EHP 3 for SAP ERP 6.0 and was further enhanced in EHPs 4 and 5. In this release, the name of the product was changed from Closing Cockpit to SAP Financial Closing cockpit, though menus and system documentation still refer to the Closing Cockpit. You can activate the enhancements using business functions `FIN_ACC_LOCAL_CLOSE` in EHP 3, `FIN_REP_SIMPL_2` in EHP 4, and `FIN_ACC_LOCAL_CLOSE_2` in EHP 5, and using the SAP Financial Closing cockpit add-ons. Before we discuss the details of these product iterations, let's look at what these solutions have in common—namely, the orchestration and automation of the close tasks.

The first step in accelerating your period close is to draw up a list of the period-closing steps that you already perform. While you're doing this, jot down the selection parameters that you use to start them; this will help you to understand how you bundle the various objects that you will process during the close. Let's use the tasks we discussed in Chapter 7 as a starting point:

- Section 7.1.3: Assessment cycles (Transaction KSU5 starts 1-N cycles)
- Section 7.1.3: Distribution cycles (Transaction KSV5 starts 1-N cycles)
- Section 7.1.3: Reposting cycles (Transaction KSW5 starts 1-N cycles)
- Section 7.1.3: Indirect activity cycles (Transaction KSC5 starts 1-N cycles)
- Section 7.1.4: Assessment cycles to CO-PA (Transaction KEU5 starts 1-N cycles)

- Section 7.1.5 : Activity price calculation (Transaction KSII selects all cost centers or a group of cost centers)
- Section 7.2.1: Revaluation at actual prices (Transaction CON2 selects orders per plant, but Transaction KON2 uses selection variants to select internal orders)
- Section 7.2.1: Overhead calculation (Transaction CO43 selects orders per plant, but Transaction KGI4 uses selection variants to select internal orders)
- Section 7.2.2: WIP calculation (Transaction KKAO selects orders per plant, but Transaction KKAI uses selection variants to select internal orders)
- Section 7.2.3: Variance calculation (Transactions KKS5 and KKS1 select orders per plant)
- Section 7.2.4: Settlement (Transaction CO88 selects orders per plant, but Transaction KO8G uses selection variants to select internal orders)
- Section 7.3.2: Periodic costing run (Transaction CKMLCP runs by plant[s])
- Section 7.3.3: Alternative valuation run (Transaction CKMLCPAVR runs by plant[s])
- Section 7.4.1: Periodic revaluation (Transaction KE27 runs by record type)
- Section 7.4.2: Top-down distribution (Transaction KE28 runs by record type)

Other Tasks in the Close

When you think of closing tasks, you tend to think of tasks that have to be executed to create the necessary postings before you close the books, but it is also important to include any reconciliation reports that check that the data in the various subledgers matches the General Ledger. Remember that we discussed scheduling Report Writer reports in the background and preparing extracts in Chapter 8, Section 8.1. Don't forget to add these tasks to your list if you haven't moved all your reporting to SAP BW. If you're using SAP BW, consider scheduling your loads to SAP BW in the same way.

In a new implementation, people typically keep a list with notes about task dependencies (like the one just shown) in a spreadsheet and check them off when they complete each task, making notes about any issues they encounter.

12.1.1 Orchestrating Your Closing Tasks

Figure 12.1 shows the same list of transactions as a list in the SAP Financial Closing cockpit, with folders that correspond to the sections to make it easier for you to refer to Chapter 7 for details of what happens in each step. To create a new template, select Transaction CLOCOC or **Accounting • Financial Accounting • General Ledger • Periodic Processing • Closing • Closing Cockpit (Manage Templates and Task Lists)**, switch to **Change** mode, and select **Template/Task List • Create Template**.

For this example, choose the **Controlling Area** organizational hierarchy. Because all close tasks in CO are performed either with reference to the controlling area or with reference to the plant(s), we've left out the other organizational units. The top node in Figure 12.1 represents the controlling area in our demo system. This makes the entries in the SAP Financial Closing cockpit look the same as in the Schedule Manager. We'll come back to how to add other organizational units in Section 12.1.8.

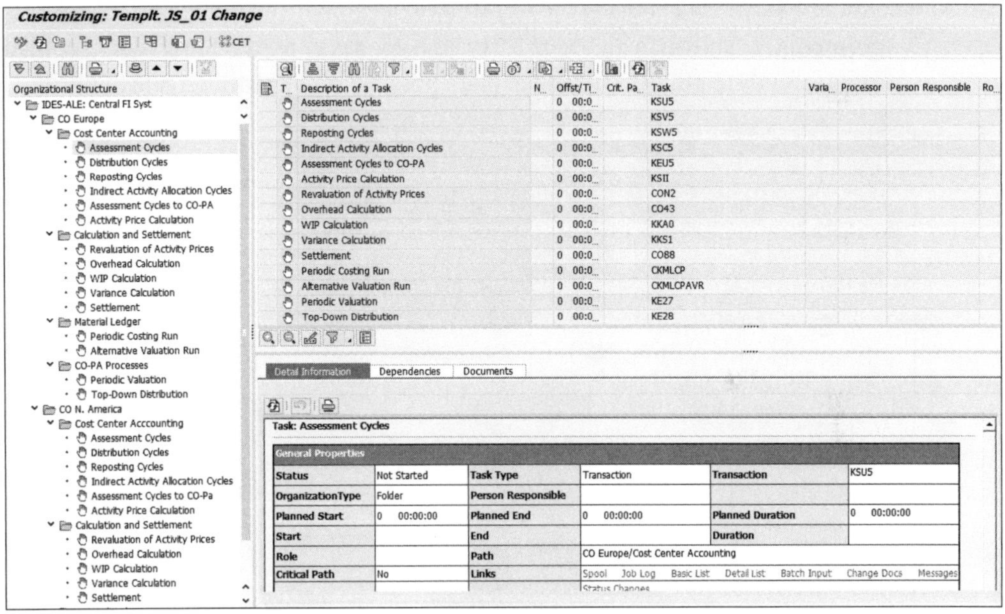

Figure 12.1 Period-Close Tasks Grouped in SAP Financial Closing Cockpit

To add transactions to the list, right-click on the tree on the left, select **Add Task**, and create a task for each of the transactions in the list. You can structure this list by adding folders for each section (right-click and select **Create Folder**). You can cut and paste folders to move tasks around in the list until you're happy with the sequence. Don't worry if your list isn't perfect in its first iteration. It's the nature of these lists to evolve over time.

If you're having trouble getting your tasks to fit neatly into folders, consider defining *global IDs*. A global ID is simply a way of classifying tasks across folders and is created in Customizing for the SAP Financial Closing cockpit add-on to provide a different way of structuring the close tasks across multiple folders.

Once you have the list in place, consider adding any other information that you've collected over the last few months. You have two options:

1. To add a note as a reminder, right-click on the task and select **Create Note.** This is a good way of including quick tips and simple instructions in your template.
2. To add a Microsoft document to explain a closing step in more detail, select the **Documents** tab shown in Figure 12.1. You can then upload your chosen document from the server by choosing **Create/Modify Document** and uploading the relevant document, as shown in Figure 12.2. This is a good way of providing more sophisticated job aids to guide users and explain possible pitfalls with screenshots.

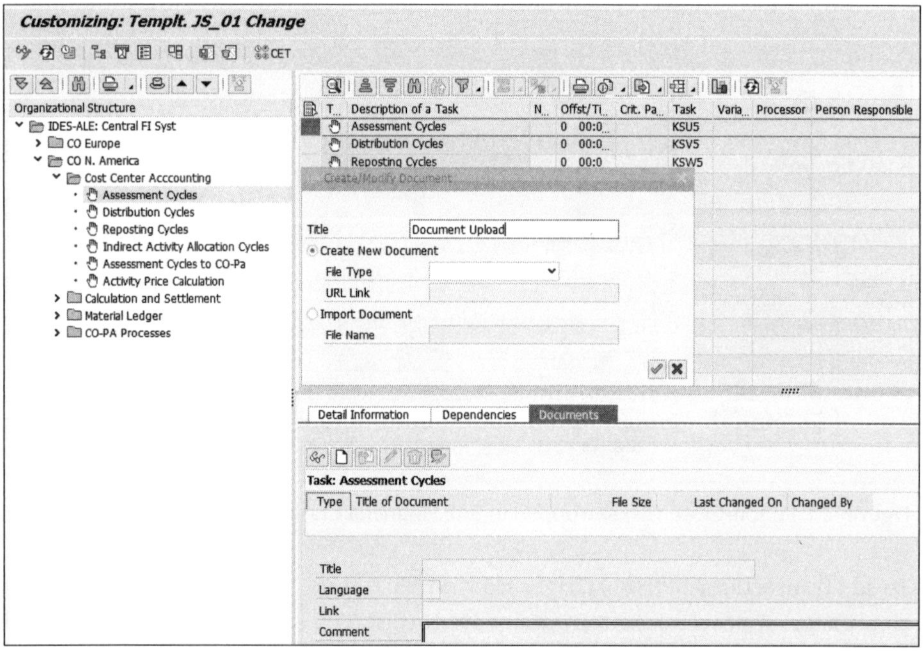

Figure 12.2 Adding Document for Close Task

Keeping these kinds of documents up to date can be a great way of ensuring that what you're learning is available to everyone who participates in the close and to help other people take over your tasks if you're unavailable at any time.

Where to Maintain Templates

As you can see from Figure 12.1, the template settings are Customizing settings by default, which means that you can transport them between systems. This is fine if you want to maintain a central template in your Customizing client and then transport it into your productive system. Many controllers feel that this will make them overly reliant on their IT department for quick changes to the template. If you want to take ownership of the closing process, ask your IT department to implement SAP Note 1179482 so that you can maintain the template settings in your productive system. Implementing this note will switch off the transport settings for your templates.

At this stage, it also makes sense to add *dependencies*. To create a dependency, you need to link the successor task with its predecessor. To do this, select the **Dependencies** block at the bottom right of the screen (see Figure 12.1). In our example, the periodic revaluation step in the **Profitability Analysis** folder uses data from the periodic costing run in the **Material Ledger** folder (i.e., there's a dependency between the tasks). Perform the following steps:

1. Click on the **Periodic Revaluation** step (the successor) to move it into the **Dependencies** part of the screen (lower right).
2. Mark the predecessor (**Periodic Costing Run**) on the left-hand part of the screen.
3. Go back to the **Dependencies** block, right-click on the follow-up task (periodic valuation), and select **Create Dependency**. The system will then show this dependency as a task hierarchy (see Figure 12.3).
4. Continue like this, working from the back of the close to the front, until you've identified all dependent tasks.

Maintaining Dependencies

It makes sense to think about dependencies immediately, because they're important to your understanding of the close as a whole. However, until EHP 5 for SAP ERP 6.0 the system only checked dependencies between jobs (programs with variants) prior to scheduling. Defining dependencies between other types of tasks merely serves as a reminder. In the latest release, the system checks all dependencies and issues a message if the predecessor doesn't have the correct status when the next task is started.

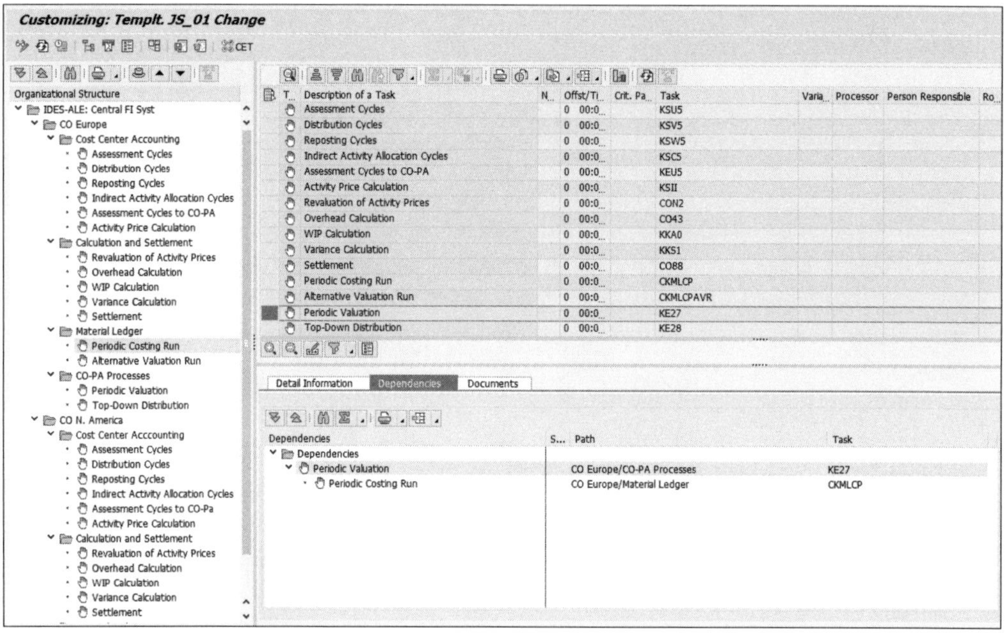

Figure 12.3 Maintaining Task Dependencies in SAP Financial Closing Cockpit

12.1.2 Executing Your Close Tasks

It's not yet possible to execute the transactions shown in Figure 12.3. To do this, we must first create a *task list* from our template by selecting **Template/Task List • Create Periodic Task List**. Then enter the key date, the period, and the fiscal year for that close in the task list header (see Figure 12.4). This will result in the creation of a task list with reference to your template for the next period close. When you're ready to start the closing activities, switch the status from **Not Released** to **Released**.

The procedure to create a task list changed in EHP 5 to allow organizations to separate the task of maintaining templates (generally the job of a select group of power users) from the task of creating a task list (usually more widely used). There's now a new transaction, Transaction CLOCOT, for the creation of task lists. This transaction calls up the same pop-up shown in Figure 12.4.

Schedule Manager does not have templates with separate task lists. To schedule a task in Schedule Manager, click on the task and move it into the appropriate slot on the calendar view. You can then monitor its progress by navigating to the Schedule Manager: Monitor.

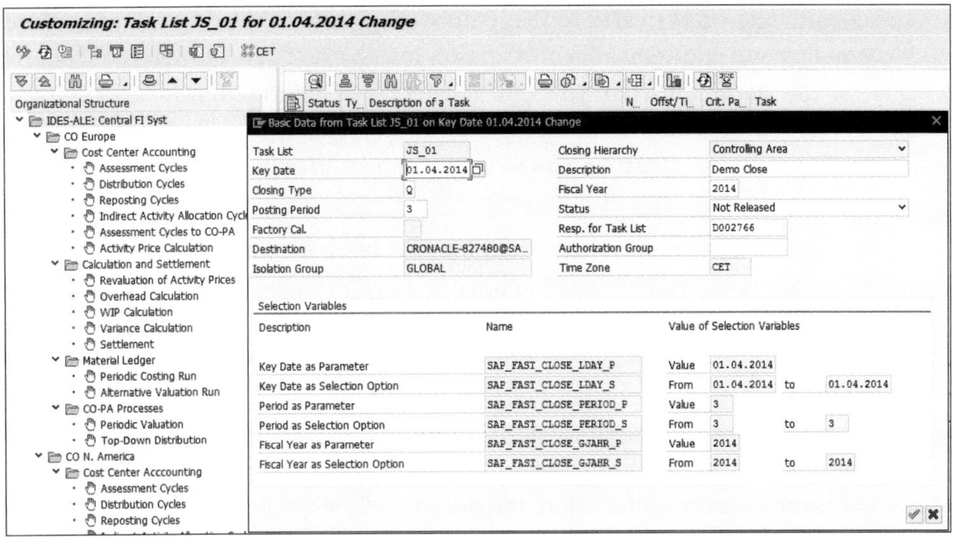

Figure 12.4 Task List Header for March Close

Once we've released the task list, we can perform any task by right-clicking on the task in the right-hand part of the screen (Figure 12.5) and selecting **Execute Transaction**.

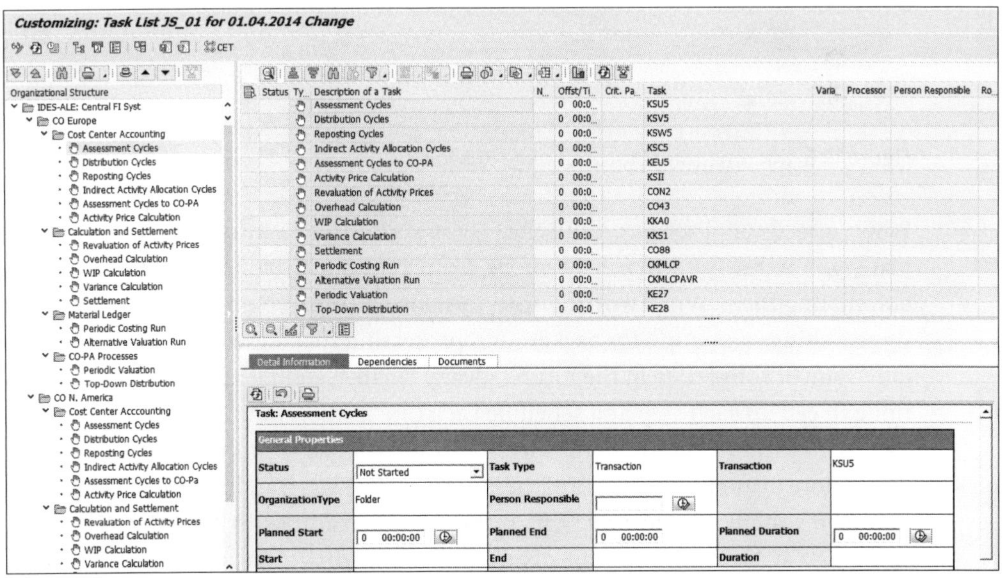

Figure 12.5 Task List for March Close

The documentation we added to the template supports us in performing the steps. We can also add additional documentation about events encountered during the close in the **Documents** tab. You can update status information for each task by switching the **Status** field from **Not Started** to **Completed without Errors** when you've successfully run the transaction. In so doing, you've effectively moved your spreadsheet and associated checklist online.

Executing your close tasks is important in itself, but compliance also plays a role in the move to a more system-based approach. As you change the status of your task, the system will ask you to enter a reason for the status change, as shown in Figure 12.6. This can be a very simple way of documenting the sign off that the assessment cycles have not only completed but also cleared all cost center costs correctly. If you're using the SAP Financial Closing cockpit add-on, you can formalize the internal controls that are part of the close process by documenting within the template the significance, degree of automation, and purpose of the closing task.

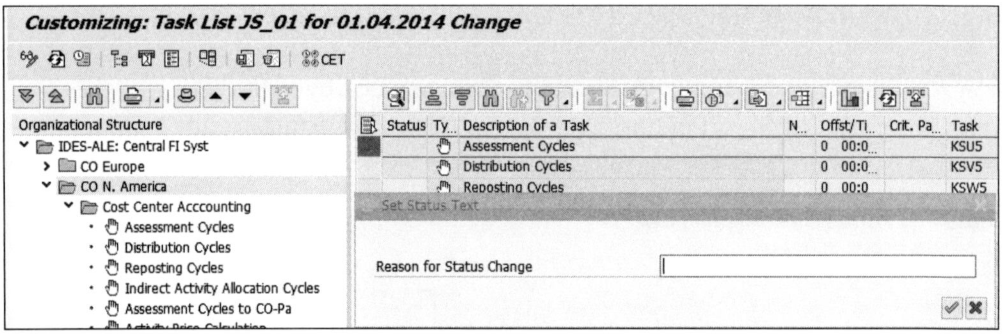

Figure 12.6 Documenting Status Change Reason

When, after a couple of successful closes, you start to feel comfortable with your template, you're ready to make the move from running these transactions online to automating them. When working with the closing steps, you may have noticed that there's always an option for background processing that allows you to schedule the job to run at some time in the future, ideally when system load is low. You can continue to call up each step and schedule each one in turn, but there's a more elegant way to do this, which is to enter the offset for each task (in other words, how many days before or after the key date of the close it should start) and the start time for each task. The system can then use this schedule, for example, to start the assessment cycles task at 8 a.m. on Day 1, the distribution cycles task at 9 a.m. on Day 1, and so on through the close.

12.1.3 Automating Closing Transactions

To allow the close steps to start at the scheduled time, you need to go back to your template (Figure 12.1) and enter a start time for each of the steps in turn (hopefully you've been keeping notes about how long each one takes to run). Initially, these times will merely serve as a reminder of when each action is due.

When we drew up our list of close steps, we also noted which selection parameters were used in each step. To automate the execution of the close step, you have to make sure that all the parameters that you've entered manually until now are in the system when your close step is scheduled to run:

- To do this, exchange the names of the transactions (designed to run with you present) with the names of the *executable programs* that are called when you run the transaction.
- To replace your manual entry of the fiscal period, fiscal year, controlling area, selection parameters, and so on, enter a *program variant* that will store these parameters and pass them to the program as it's scheduled. This will ensure that the program can run automatically at the scheduled start time without you being present.
- Although all program variants will include time variables (the fiscal period and fiscal year), you'll also have to store the appropriate selection variables, such as the relevant cycles for assessments and distributions and the relevant plants for order settlement.

Let's now translate our list of transactions from Chapter 7 into a list of executable programs:

- Section 7.1.3: Assessment cycles (Program RKGALKSU5)
- Section 7.1.3: Distribution cycles (Program RKGALKSV5)
- Section 7.1.3: Reposting cycles (Program RKGALKSW5)
- Section 7.1.3: Indirect activity cycles (Program RKGALKSC5)
- Section 7.1.4: Assessment cycles to CO-PA (Program RKGALKEU5)
- Section 7.1.5 : Activity price calculation (Program RKSPI_KSII)
- Section 7.2.1: Revaluation at actual prices (Program RKAZCON2 or RKAZKON2)
- Section 7.2.1: Overhead calculation (Program RKAZCO43 or RKAZKGI4)
- Section 7.2.2: WIP calculation (Program SAPKKA07)
- Section 7.2.3: Variance calculation (Program RKKKS000)

- Section 7.2.4: Settlement (Program RK07CO88 or RKO7KO8G)
- Section 7.3.2: Periodic costing run—separate programs for each step:
- Section 7.3.3: Alternative valuation run (AVR)—separate programs for each step:
- Section 7.4.1: Periodic revaluation (Program RKEBPBATCHGIPB)
- Section 7.4.2: Top-down distribution (Program RKEBPBATCHGITD)

To switch the first task in your list from a transaction to a program, return to the template (Transaction CLOCOC), switch to **Change** mode, right-click on the task, and select **Edit Task**, as shown in Figure 12.7. Because the assessment cycle is usually one of the first tasks of the close, we've scheduled it to run at 8:00 a.m. on the first day of the close. When we schedule the tasks, the offset of one day will be used to set the task start time as 8:00 a.m. on the key date (entered in Figure 12.7) plus one day.

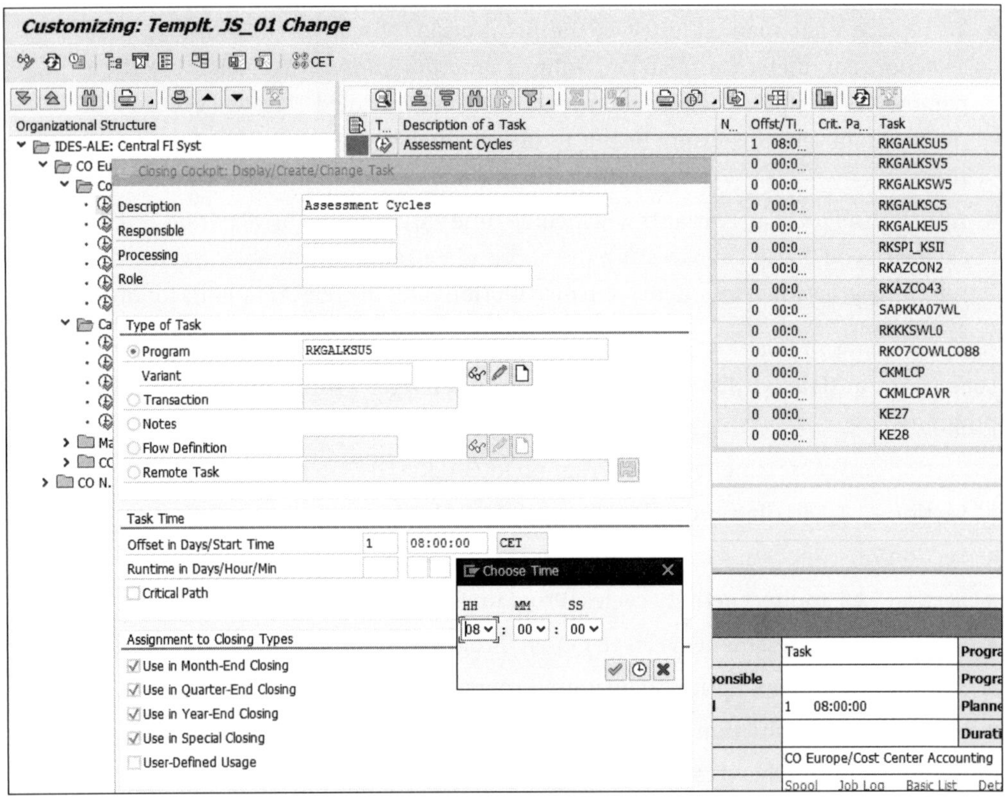

Figure 12.7 Timing Details for Assessment Cycle Task

Notice that the time shown in Figure 12.7 is in Central European Time (CET). If your close schedule crosses multiple time zones, it's also worth checking the settings for the relevant time zones. If you refer to Figure 12.4, you'll notice that we're on Central European Time (CET) there as well. To change your options, choose the **CET** button. Figure 12.8 shows the dialog screen for switching your time zone options.

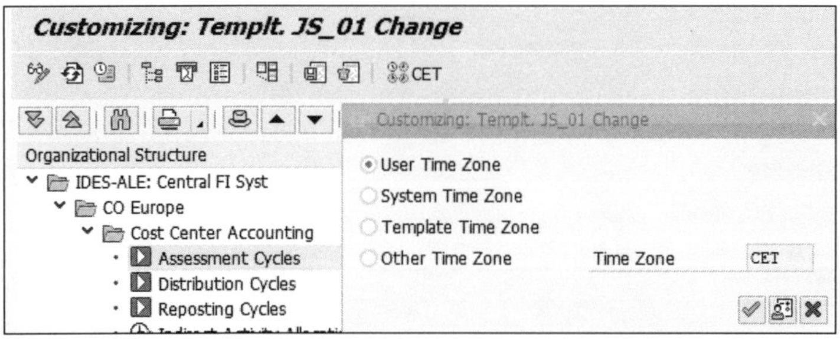

Figure 12.8 Time Zones within SAP Financial Closing Cockpit

You can cross-check your list and add any programs you might be missing by selecting Transaction CLOCOC and **Goto • Register Program for Closing Cockpit**. If you're working with the Schedule Manager, select Transaction SCMA (**Schedule Manager**) and **Environment • Closing SCMAPROGRAMS** instead.

Including Your Own ABAP Reports in the Template

If your organization has written its own ABAP reports for some tasks in the close, you can manually add these tasks to the list. To make sure that such programs will be able to send status information back to the SAP Financial Closing cockpit or Schedule Manager to confirm that they've been properly completed, have your IT department implement the code described in SAP Note 325118 for each of these reports.

Figure 12.9 shows the result of changing the tasks in the first folder of our template. We've replaced the transaction codes with the programs for executing the close in all six tasks. However, we've only maintained variants for four of the tasks. The system shows that these four tasks are executable (i.e., they have all the parameters they need to start immediately), whereas the other two tasks need the user to enter the parameters to be able to start. To completely automate the close, we need to create program variants for all the tasks, so let's look at how to maintain these program variants.

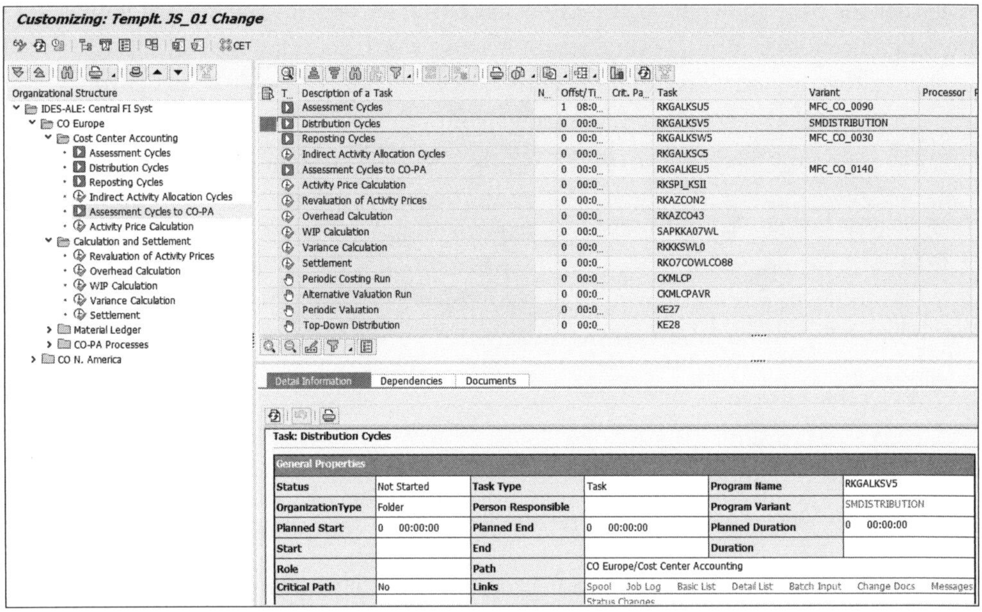

Figure 12.9 Executable and Nonexecutable Tasks in SAP Financial Closing Cockpit

Responsibility for Program Variants

In some organizations, the IT department is responsible for maintaining program variants, whereas in others the controlling department can create variants. Let's assume that you'll work with the IT department to complete the next section.

12.1.4 Creating Program Variants for Your Close Tasks

To maintain variants, for each of the above programs select Transaction SE38 or **Tools • ABAP Workbench • Development • ABAP Editor**. Enter the name of the relevant program, as shown in Figure 12.10, and select **GoTo • Variants**.

To create a new variant for the program, click on **Create**. If a variant already exists (you'll see it in the F4 help on the **Variant** field), select **Values** and click on the **Change** button. Figure 12.11 shows the selection parameters needed to execute an assessment cycle. Most of the parameters can be set once and will not change from close to close. Be sure to enter the cycle or cycles that you want to execute by clicking on the **Enter Cycles** button; otherwise, nothing will happen when you schedule the closing task.

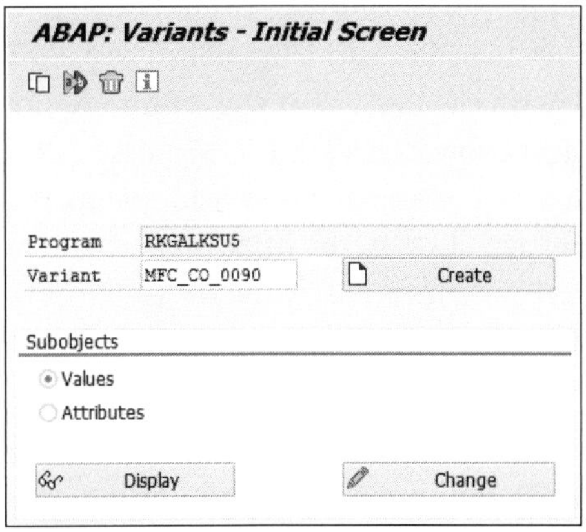

Figure 12.10 Program Variant for Assessment Cycles (Program RKGALKSU5)

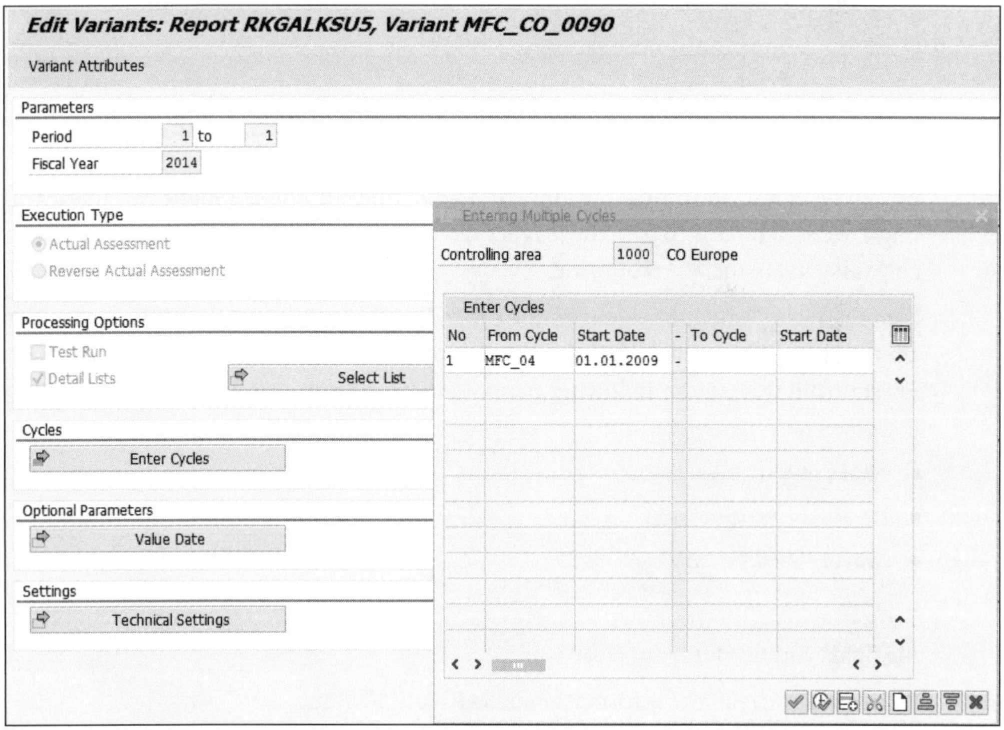

Figure 12.11 Variant for Executing Assessment Cycles

Once you've entered all the fixed parameters for your closing task, the next step is to ensure that the period and fiscal year don't have to be set manually but can be passed from the task list header when you schedule each closing task. If you refer to Figure 12.4, you'll see that the task list header contains two variables, SAP_FAST_CLOSE_PERIOD_P for the fiscal period and SAP_FAST_CLOSE_GJAHR_P for the fiscal year. To link the variants with the variables in the task list header, click on the **Attributes** button in Figure 12.11 or the **Variant Attributes** button in Figure 12.12. This will allow you to have the system set the period and fiscal year automatically based on the settings in the task list header (March 2014, in our example).

To have the system set the fiscal year and fiscal period during the close, enter "T" in the **Selection Variable** column (see Figure 12.12) and then make the following links using the F4 help.

If you're using the SAP Financial Closing cockpit, enter these parameters:

- FROM_P—SAP_FAST_CLOSE_PERIOD_P
- TO_P—SAP_FAST_CLOSE_PERIOD_P
- GJAHR—SAP_FAST_CLOSE_GJAHR_P (this is German for fiscal year)

If these standard variables aren't enough for the programs you have included in your list, you can add additional *custom variables* alongside the standard variables. You might want to do this to pass the ledger field to the close tasks, if you have ledger-specific tasks in Financial Accounting.

If you're using Schedule Manager, the procedure is similar, but the TVARV variables are not set in the task list header, so it's a good idea to define your own variables just for controlling. Use the following parameters as a reference, but *copy* them under your own naming convention:

- **FROM_P**: SAP_SCMA_PERIOD
- **TO_P**: SAP_SCMA_PERIOD
- **GJAHR**: SAP_FISC_YEAR

You can also define your own variables if a standard variable isn't available for one of the fields you need in your close task.

To learn more, read the information in SAP Note 502482.

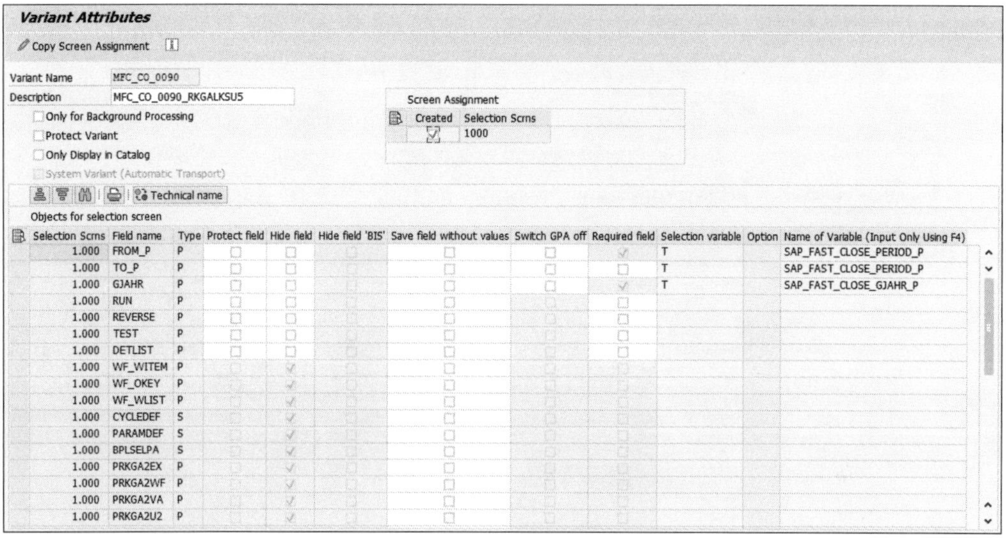

Figure 12.12 Variant Attributes for Executing Assessment Cycles

12.1.5 Scheduling Tasks

Once you've entered programs and variants for all relevant tasks, you can choose whether to execute each program separately from the SAP Financial Closing cockpit or establish your closing calendar using the start times shown in Figure 12.7 and then schedule the whole period close automatically:

- To start the tasks from the task list (see Figure 12.9), select one or more tasks and then select **Schedule Selected Tasks**.
- Because there may be dependencies between some of the tasks, select **Check Start Condition** for the task before you schedule if you're in doubt.

As the job completes, it will update the **Status** information (**Completed**, **Completed With Errors**, etc.) and any logs created to the task list for analysis by the task owner. Figure 12.13 shows the result of completing an assessment cycle. The **Status** of the task is **Completed without Errors**, the **Start** and **End** times have been recorded, and the **Selection Criteria** have been updated. We'll now look at the information in the **Links** section to display the information the system creates automatically while executing the close task. You might want to refer to Chapter 7, Section 7.1.3 to compare the results of running the transaction manually with scheduling it to run in the background.

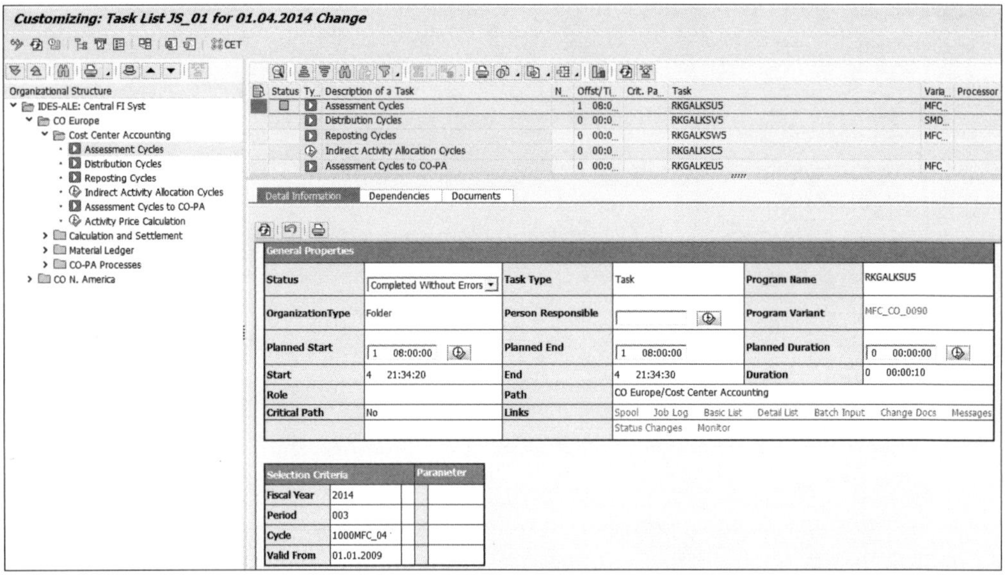

Figure 12.13 Status and Selection Criteria for Completed Close Task

Now, let's look at the job log by selecting **Job Log** in the **Links** section of the task details.

Figure 12.14 shows the entries in the job log for the assessment cycle. These are largely technical, though the document number is useful for audit purposes.

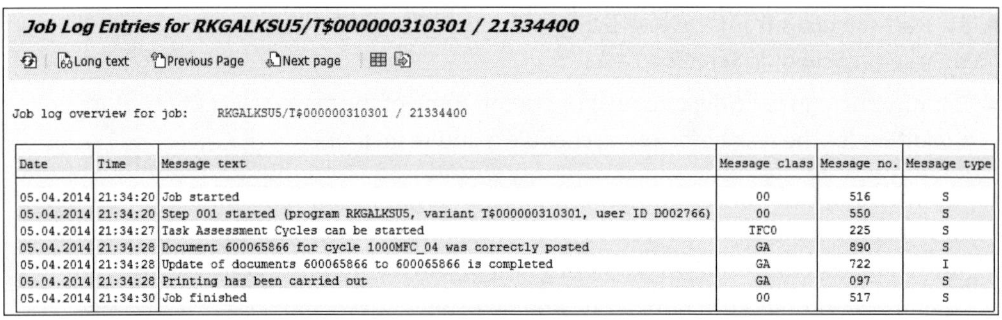

Figure 12.14 Job Log Entries for Completed Assessment Cycle

The main thing to notice is that although the program name is what we entered for the task (see Figure 12.9) the variant name has been switched to a technical name beginning with T$. This is because we used selection variables of type T for the time variables (see Figure 12.12). The generated program variant replaces the placeholders in the variant with the period and the fiscal year from the task list header and with the relevant organizational units (controlling area, company code, or plant) from the folders in the template.

Caution: Job Logs

The job log is potentially dangerous because error messages from the application will appear as information messages, implying that things went smoothly when you should really be stopping the close and fixing the issues before you move onto the next step.

The spool list will give you a better impression of what happened when the job was processed. To display the spool list, select **Spool List** in the **Links** section of the task details. You might want to compare the next two figures with Figure 7.7, Figure 7.8, and Figure 7.9 in Chapter 7.

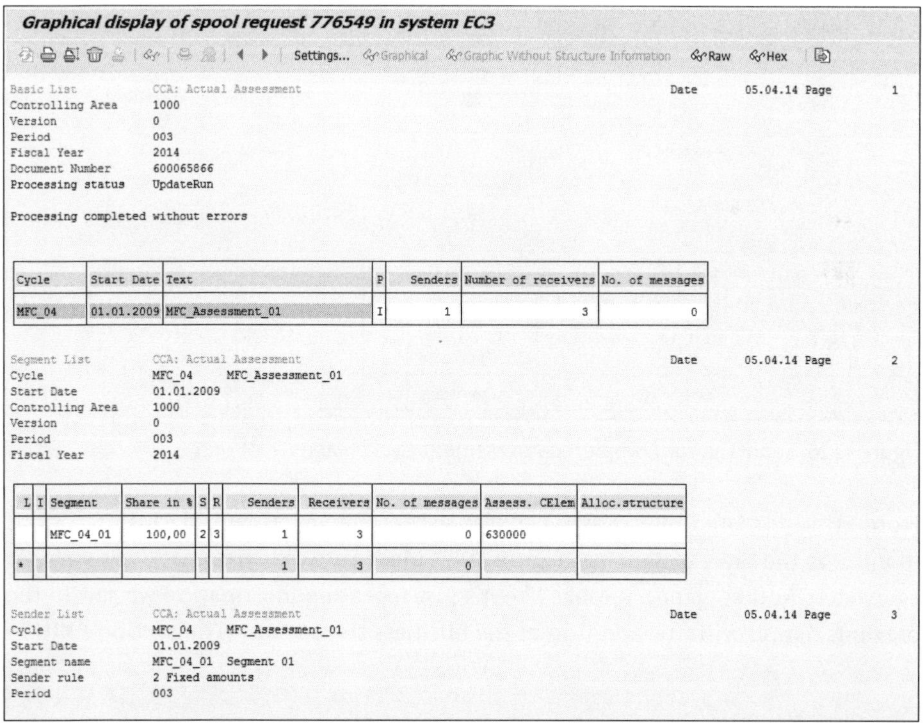

Graphical display of spool request 776549 in system EC3

Settings... Graphical Graphic Without Structure Information Raw Hex

Basic List CCA: Actual Assessment Date 05.04.14 Page 1
Controlling Area 1000
Version 0
Period 003
Fiscal Year 2014
Document Number 600065866
Processing status UpdateRun

Processing completed without errors

Cycle	Start Date	Text	P	Senders	Number of receivers	No. of messages
MFC_04	01.01.2009	MFC_Assessment_01	I	1	3	0

Segment List CCA: Actual Assessment Date 05.04.14 Page 2
Cycle MFC_04 MFC_Assessment_01
Start Date 01.01.2009
Controlling Area 1000
Version 0
Period 003
Fiscal Year 2014

L	I	Segment	Share in %	S	R	Senders	Receivers	No. of messages	Assess. CElem	Alloc.structure
		MFC_04_01	100,00	2	3	1	3	0	630000	
*						1	3	0		

Sender List CCA: Actual Assessment Date 05.04.14 Page 3
Cycle MFC_04 MFC_Assessment_01
Start Date 01.01.2009
Segment name MFC_04_01 Segment 01
Sender rule 2 Fixed amounts
Period 003

Figure 12.15 Spool List for Completed Assessment Cycle (Pages 1–2)

Figure 12.15 shows the result of executing a single cycle, MFC_04 (usually several cycles are scheduled at once). This cycle included one segment (MFC_04_01) with one sender cost center and three receiver cost centers. Scrolling down, Figure 12.16 shows the clearing posting to the sender cost center and the allocation to the receiver cost centers based on the fixed percentages 10, 30, and 60.

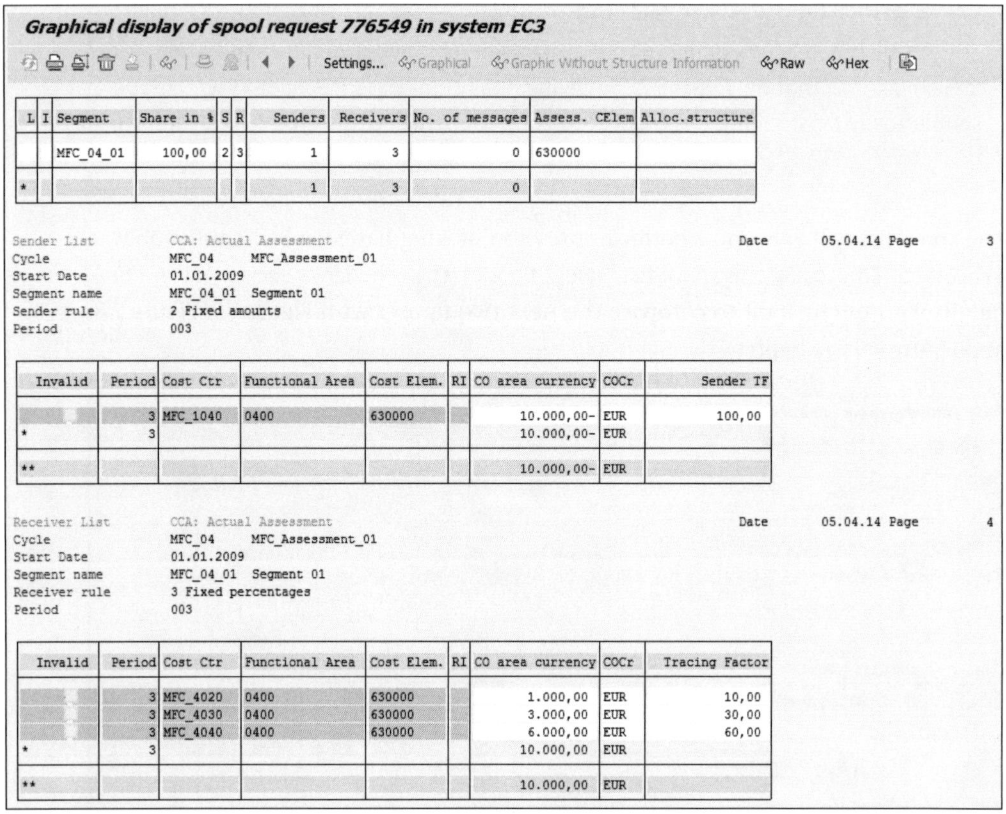

Figure 12.16 Spool List for Completed Assessment Cycle (Pages 3–4)

From EHP 5 for SAP ERP 6.0, you can also access the SAP Financial Closing cockpit monitor in the **Links** section (see Figure 12.17). Make sure that you check this view for every step. At first glance, it looks like it's just repeating information we saw in the previous figures with the addition of the business transaction (Transaction RKIU in this example), but it's here that you'll see whether errors really happened that should be corrected before you start the next step.

> **Schedule Manager Monitor**
>
> You might wonder why you had to go through all the effort of including the code described in SAP Note 325118 in all your own programs. The reason is that this code updates the Schedule Manager Monitor. It's this monitor that will tell you if errors occurred from an application perspective. Any external scheduler (there are several on the market) can only read the job log and the spool list. The truth of what happened during posting is set by the application and passed to the monitor using the code described in SAP Note 325118.

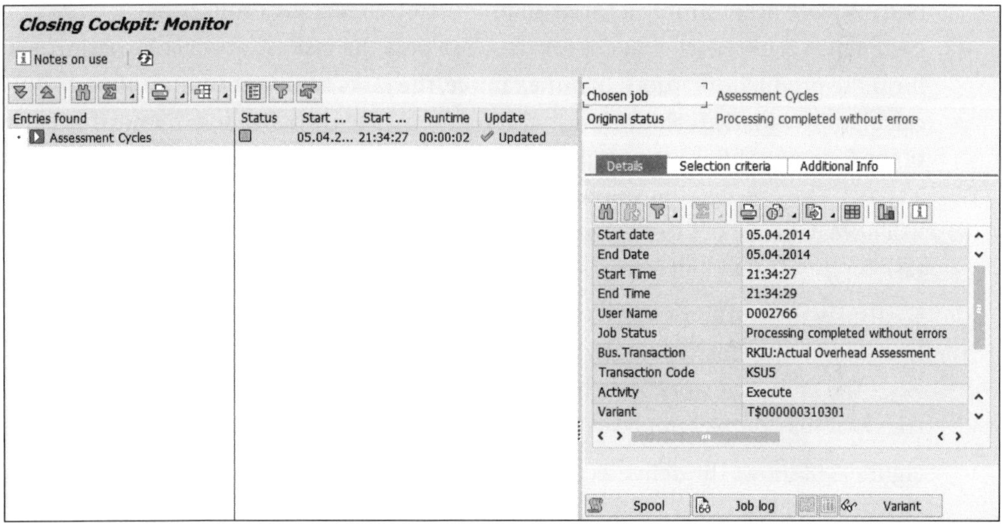

Figure 12.17 Monitor for SAP Financial Closing Cockpit

12.1.6 Using Workflows in the Close

Going back to Figure 12.9, you could carry on and define program variants for each of the closing steps in the calculation and settlement steps. There is, however, a key difference between running an allocation cycle and settling a group of orders. In an allocation cycle, the system works with a group of senders and receivers, typically several cost centers, passing the costs from the senders to the receivers and sometimes back to the senders again, iterating through this cycle until the task is complete. Only when the whole cycle is complete will the cost centers be released and the next task can be performed.

When handling orders, each order is essentially a separate object for which overhead can be calculated, then WIP, then variances, and so on. You'll be able to complete all the tasks for one production order even though the next might have errors. The only exceptions to this rule would be the rework orders that we discussed in Chapter 6 that must settle to their parent production order before they can be settled and coproducts for which the costs must be split out before the coproducts can be settled as miniorders in their own right. From this basic idea, the concept of a work list was born. A *work list* is simply a list of all production orders (or similar objects) that the system has selected as relevant for the close plus the tasks that must be performed for these production orders. In our example, the tasks are overhead calculation, WIP calculation, variance calculation, and settlement. The work list documents that each of the four steps has been completed or at what stage in the chain errors occurred. In a typical case, processing will be completed the first time for 95% of orders, and 5% will have to be parked in an error list for manual processing. You can then restart the task for the 5% that had errors, significantly reducing selection time.

To display the workflows delivered by SAP, return to the **Edit Task** screen (see Figure 12.9), switch the task type from **Transaction** or **Program** to **Flow Definition**, and press [F4]. The delivered workflows begin with 0 or 1 (there are some delivered by industries that may or may not be active in your system).

Figure 12.18 shows the delivered flow definitions for Cost Center Accounting (CO-OM-CCA), Cost Object Controlling (CO-PC-OBJ), Product Cost Planning (CO-PC-PCP), Internal Orders (CO-OM-OPA), and Project Systems (PS). For workflows that also include a work list, the **Work List** checkbox is selected. To display more details of the workflow, select one of the entries.

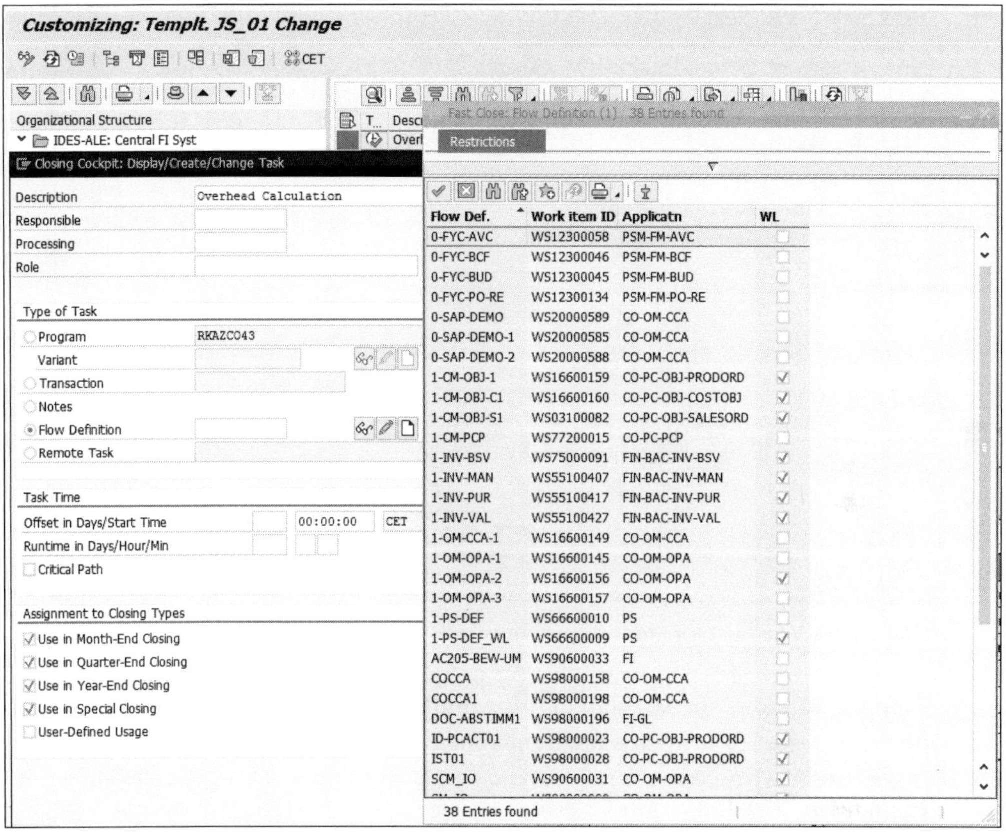

Figure 12.18 Sample Workflow Definitions for Use in Close

Figure 12.19 shows the details of workflow 1-CM-OBJ-1. You could copy this workflow and make minor adjustments to replace all the steps in the **Calculations and Settlement** folder. In the first close step, the system selects all production orders that are relevant for processing. This may sound obvious, but without this step each step would reselect the same group of production orders before processing them. Selecting the orders once and then passing the results to the next step saves time in the close because only production orders that have successfully completed each step will be passed on to the next step.

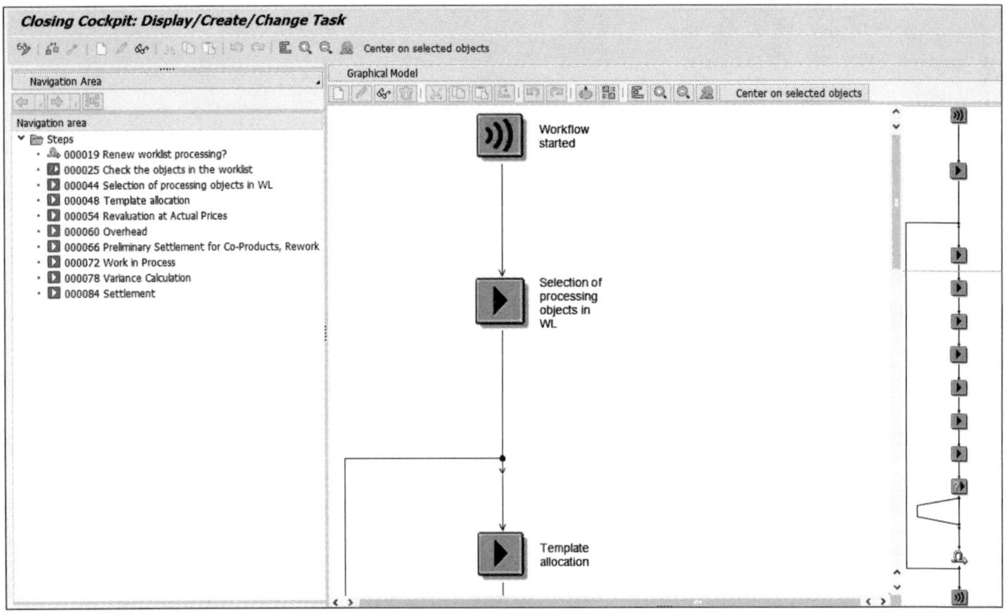

Figure 12.19 Work List for Production Orders

Figure 12.20 shows the key step in this workflow, in which the relevant production orders are selected using the program variant entered and stored as a work list. To make sure that you can use the workflow in each step, click on the tasks shown in Figure 12.20.

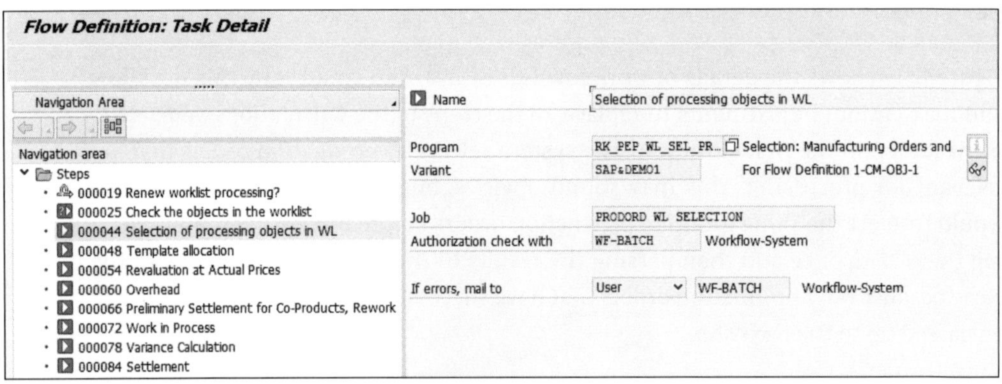

Figure 12.20 Selection of Objects for Processing

Once you're in the detail screen, check the program variant (Section 12.1.4). You should also decide who should be informed about errors (usually it's the user who scheduled the workflow, but you can use the full workflow functions if you want to be more sophisticated in your choice of processor) and how authority checks will be handled. Continue in this way, checking the parameters for all the relevant steps in the workflow.

We discussed template allocation in Chapter 11. Whether we need the template allocation step will depend on whether we're running activity-based costing in SAP ERP. Similarly, whether we need the preliminary settlement of coproducts and rework step will depend on whether we have coproducts or orders with rework (see Chapter 6). Assuming we choose *not* to use either step, we'd have to copy this workflow and remove these steps before we include the workflow in the template. To copy a delivered workflow, go to Transaction SCMA, select **Extras • Flow Definition • Administration of Flow Definition**, and copy your chosen workflow under a new name. Now mark the node you want to remove, then select **Cut Block**.

Responsibility for Workflows

In some organizations, the IT department is responsible for maintaining workflows, whereas in others the controlling department can create its own workflow definitions. The SAP Financial Closing cockpit and Schedule Manager use a subset of all workflow functions. The workflows shown can be maintained directly from the Schedule Manager transaction. To find out more about using workflows in the context of the Schedule Manager, refer to SAP Note 332149.

As you can see from Figure 12.20, one workflow can cover many programs. If we use workflows, we can drastically reduce the number of tasks in the list, as shown in Figure 12.21. We've removed the individual closing transactions from the **Calculations and Settlement** folder and replaced them with two workflows for production orders and sales orders. When you schedule the workflows, the main difference you'll see compared to the programs and variants is the result of the monitor shown in Figure 12.22.

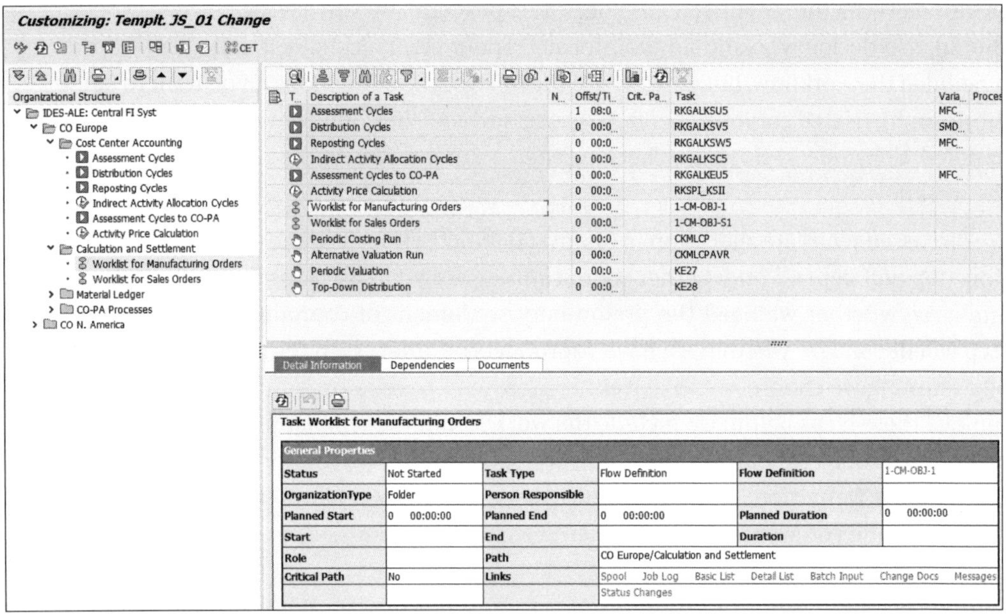

Figure 12.21 SAP Financial Closing Cockpit with Workflows

Figure 12.22 shows the results of scheduling a workflow. This looks similar to the single task shown in Figure 12.17, but we can see all the tasks in the workflow. In this case, we can see that the task encountered errors during the selection step. Once out of this step, the monitor will show which production orders have completed successfully and which have encountered errors. Normally, the controller would then check the details of the error, correct the affected orders using the information in the list, and then repeat the step for those objects that encountered errors. Only when the application status is green would he move on to the next step.

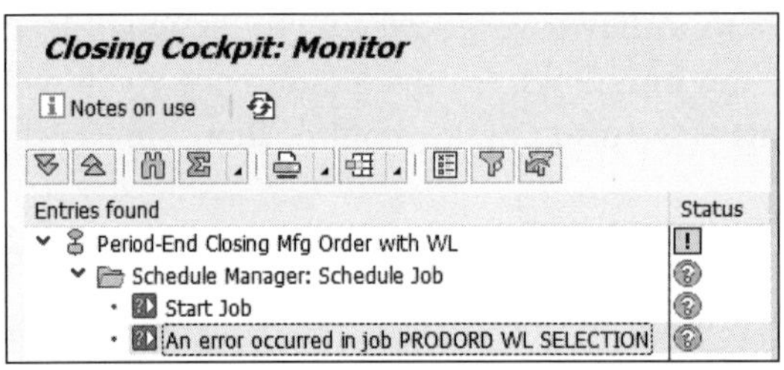

Figure 12.22 Monitor Showing Workflow Steps and Error List

12.1.7 Handling Costing Runs in Your Close

If you now go back to Chapter 7, Section 7.3 and look at the screenshots of the periodic costing run (Figure 7.44) and alternative valuation run (Figure 7.48), you'll notice that under the flow steps for each costing run there's a **Schedule Manager** button. Each flow step has its own program and variant (you're maintaining the program variant when you maintain the details in the **Parameters** column). As you execute the costing step, the system schedules the job and updates the Schedule Manager Monitor. If you click on the **Schedule Manager** button in the periodic costing run or the alternative valuation run, you'll see the same screen as if you clicked on the **Monitor** link in the SAP Financial Closing cockpit (see Figure 12.17). Figure 12.23 shows the monitor for the periodic costing run. Errors have occurred during the postclosing step. To display the errors, click on the line with the error status. This time, errors have been caused by the need to update the profit center split properly for the balance sheet.

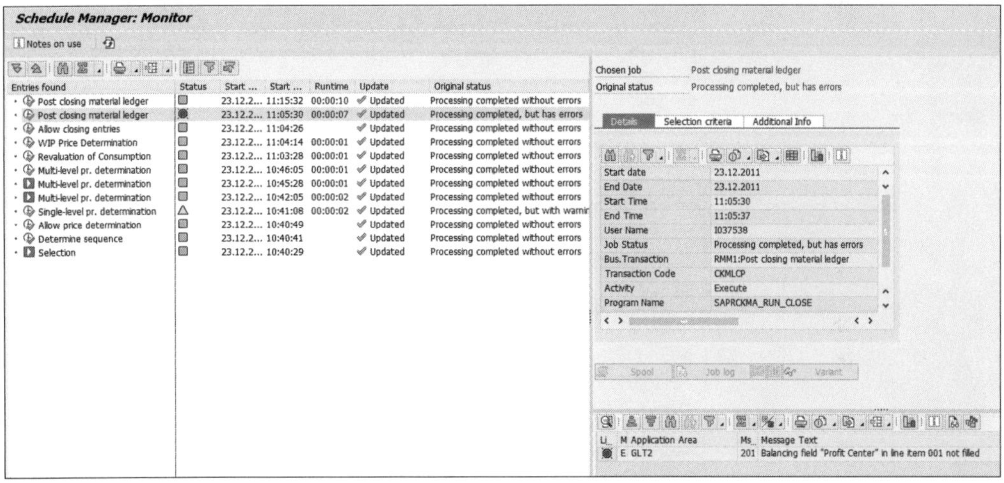

Figure 12.23 Monitor for Periodic Costing Run

Even though the approach for costing runs is slightly different from the previous steps, it makes sense to include the costing runs in the template as transactions. You can then call the costing run manually before executing the jobs and set a final complete status when you've completed each step in the costing run. This will prevent the periodic revaluation step in CO-PA from running before the closing run is flagged as complete.

12.1.8 Handling Organizational Units in the SAP Financial Closing Cockpit

So far, except for the dependency definition, everything we've looked at for the SAP Financial Closing cockpit could also have been handled in the Schedule Manager. Probably the most obvious difference between the two is the inclusion of a closing hierarchy in the SAP Financial Closing cockpit that organizes the closing steps according to the organizational unit responsible for performing the step.

When you create a new template in the SAP Financial Closing cockpit, the system asks you to select a closing hierarchy, as shown in Figure 12.24. Most organizations use the **Controlling Area/Company Code** option.

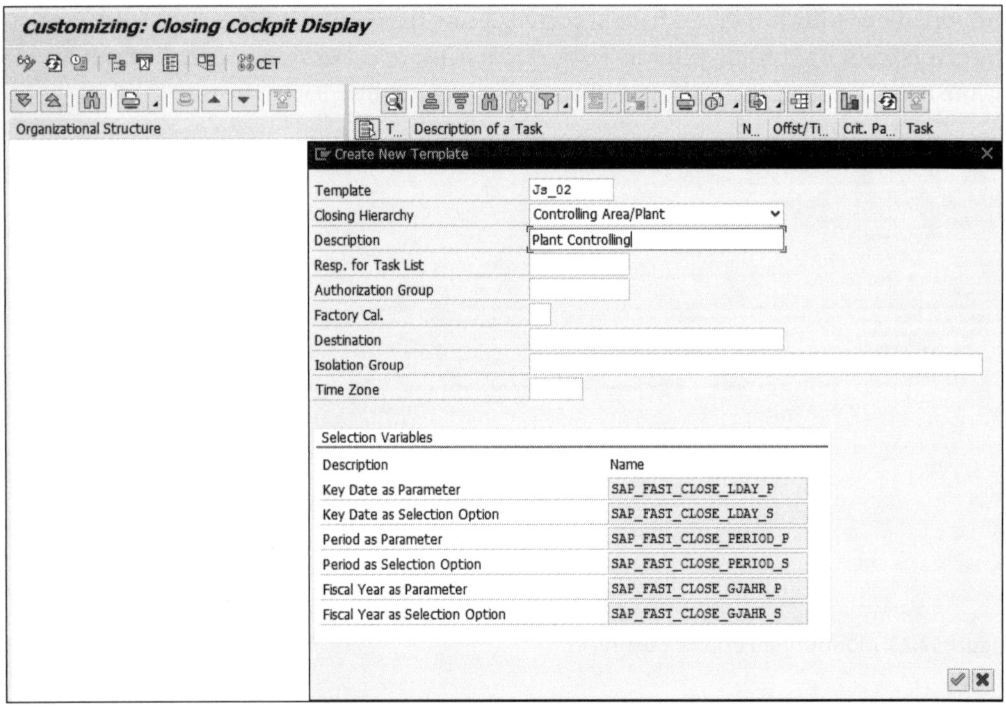

Figure 12.24 Choosing Organizational Hierarchy

If you choose this option, the template will automatically include a folder for every active controlling area and a folder for every active company code in your system. If you use Product Costing, your plants may perform their closing activities independently. If this is the case, choose the **Controlling Area/Plant** closing hierarchy (see

Figure 12.24) and the template will automatically include a folder for every active controlling area and a folder for every active plant.

Figure 12.25 shows all the controlling areas in our demo system and all the plants assigned to the North American controlling area.

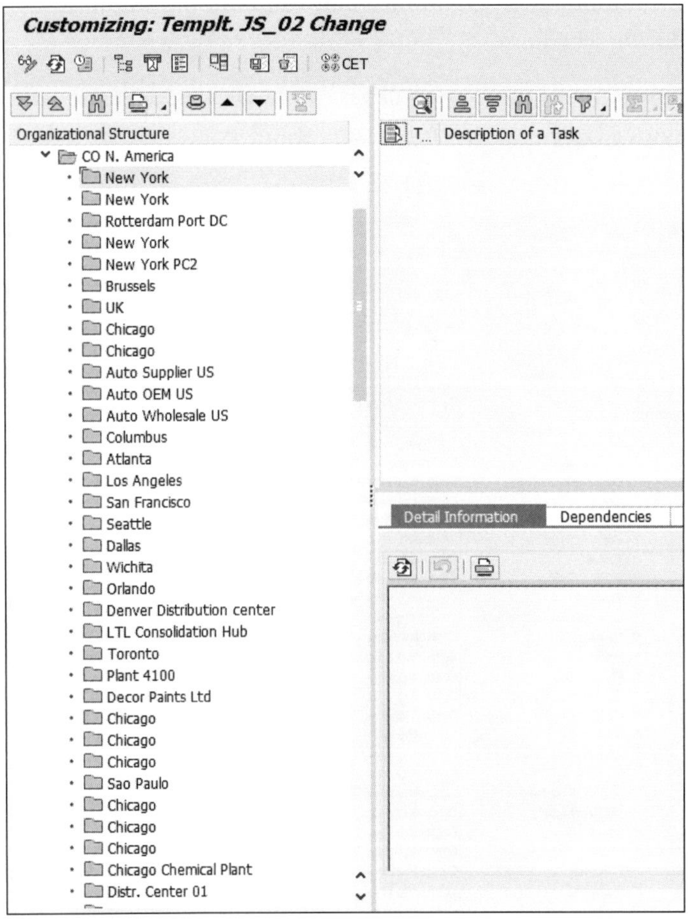

Figure 12.25 Controlling Areas and Plants in SAP Financial Closing Cockpit

Selecting the **New York** folder reveals that this folder is of organization type Plant (see lower right of screen). As we discussed with the time variables in Section 12.1.4, the organizational unit represented by the folder is passed to the jobs when they're scheduled:

- Folders that represent the organizational unit Controlling Area can pass the variable SAP_FAST_CLOSE_KOKRS_P during scheduling.
- Folders that represent the organizational unit Company Code can pass the variable SAP_FAST_CLOSE_BUKRS_P during scheduling.
- Folders that represent the organizational unit Plant can pass the variable SAP_FAST_CLOSE_WERKS_P during scheduling.

If you're not sure which parameters the folder will pass, right-click on the folder and select **Change Values**. Figure 12.26 shows controlling area 2000 assigned to the folder **CO North America**.

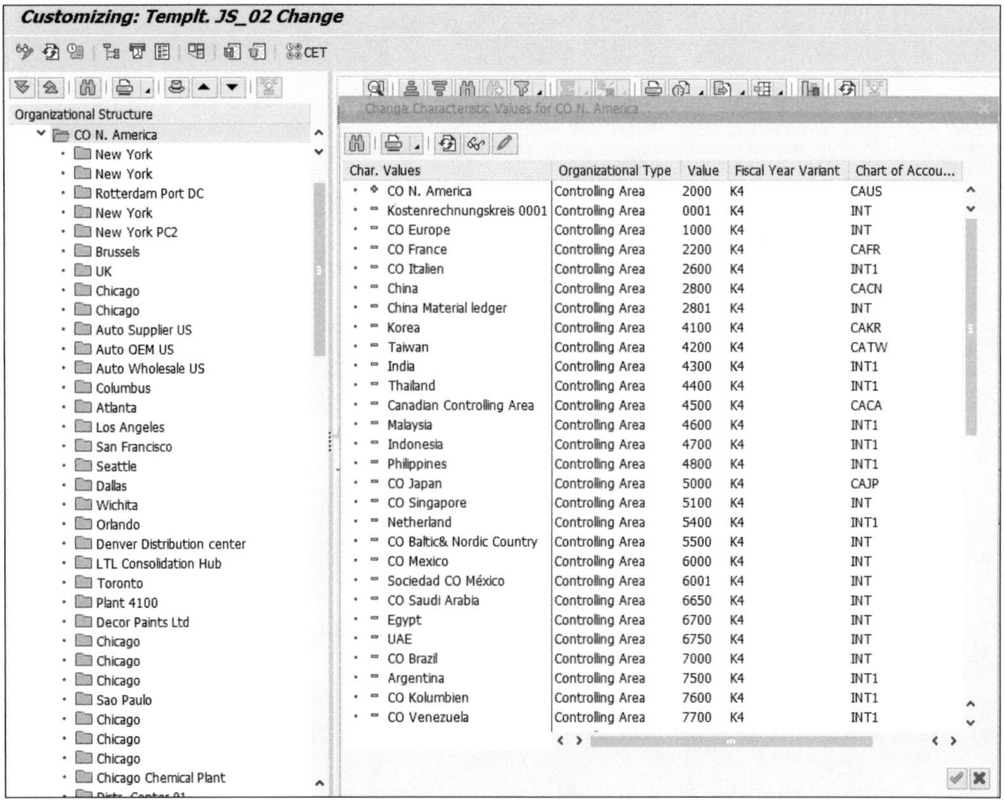

Figure 12.26 Controlling Area Assigned to Folder

The controlling area is needed to schedule all jobs in CO, so it makes sense to define the closing tasks under the controlling area by creating additional folders and subfolders under the **CO North America** folder. To add folders, position your cursor on the **CO North America** folder, right-click, and select **Create Folder** or **Create Sub Folder**.

If your plants are in different geographical locations, it can also make sense to include the relevant factory calendar. This means that when you schedule a task with respect to the key date of the close (such as on the key date plus one day) the system will first check whether that day is a working day for the plant. If the proposed day is not a working day, it will schedule the task on the next available working day. If tasks are scheduled for key date minus one day, as might be the case for a billing run or payroll run prior to the close, the system will schedule the task on the first working day before the proposed day. The folder also includes a field for the person responsible. You should consider entering the plant controller or similar person here (see Figure 12.27).

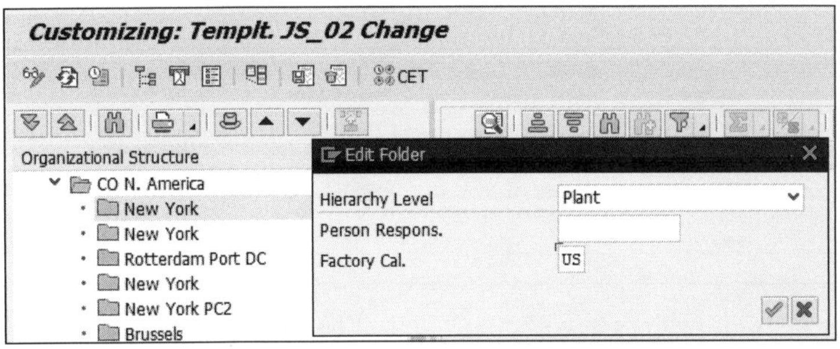

Figure 12.27 Assigning Factory Calendar to Plant Folder

If you find the hierarchy tree confusing and prefer the list view only, you can remove the tree by pressing F9 (Show/Hide Hierarchy Tree), as shown in Figure 12.28.

Notice the names of the processor, person responsible, and role in the list. If you're not going to perform all tasks yourself, you should maintain the proper user names here. As of EHP 3 for SAP ERP 6.0, there's a new authorization object, F_CLOCO, that your administrator can use to determine who can set statuses, change tasks, and so on in the SAP Financial Closing cockpit. Since EHP 5, you can also set authorizations by template. This is useful if different teams are responsible for individual templates.

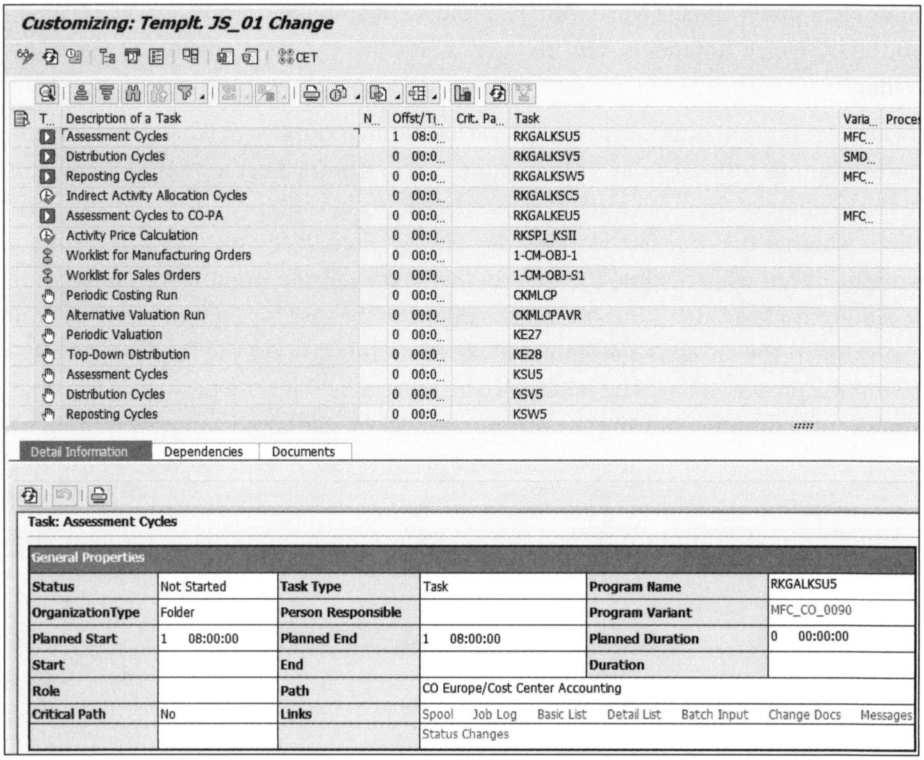

Figure 12.28 SAP Financial Closing Cockpit without Organizational Hierarchy

12.1.9 Closing Cockpit and SAP Financial Closing Cockpit

SAP Financial Closing cockpit covers all the enhancements of the Closing Cockpit from EHP 3 for SAP ERP 6.0 onward. From a visual point of view, the main difference is that there's an alternative user interface to replace Transaction CLOCO that is delivered using the role SAP_FAGL_CLOCO_WD_15 or the Closing Cockpit business package (see Appendix A at *www.sap-press.com/4691*). Figure 12.29 shows a list containing all the task lists in which the user is included (our two examples). In this example, we've selected all task lists that contain tasks assigned to our user ID.

To access details of the close tasks, select a line (**JS_01** in our example). Figure 12.30 shows the close tasks and task details. If several users are responsible for executing steps in the close, you can toggle between the two using **All Tasks** and **My Tasks** in the **Display** field. You can change the start and end time until the task has been scheduled.

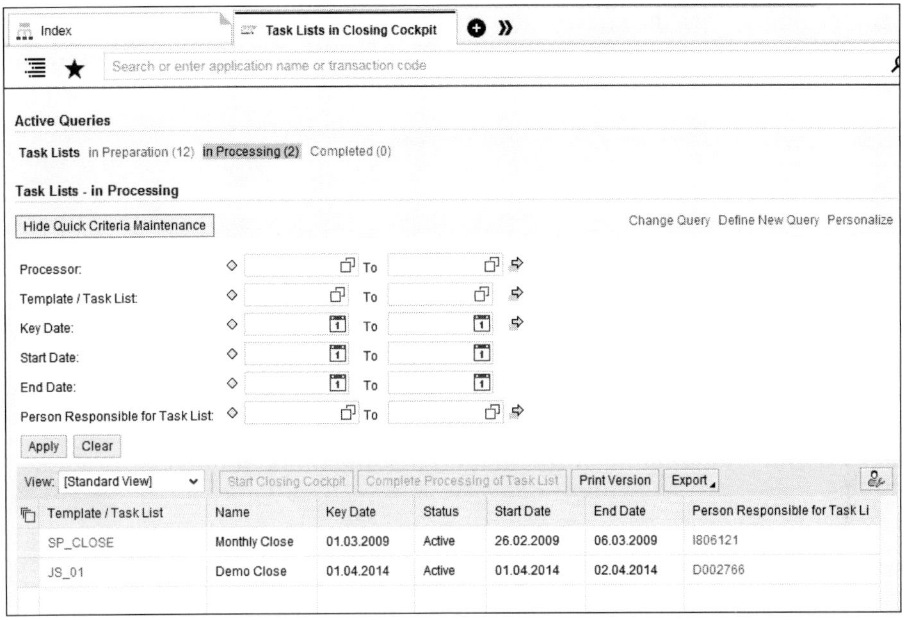

Figure 12.29 Finding Task Lists in Which User Is Active

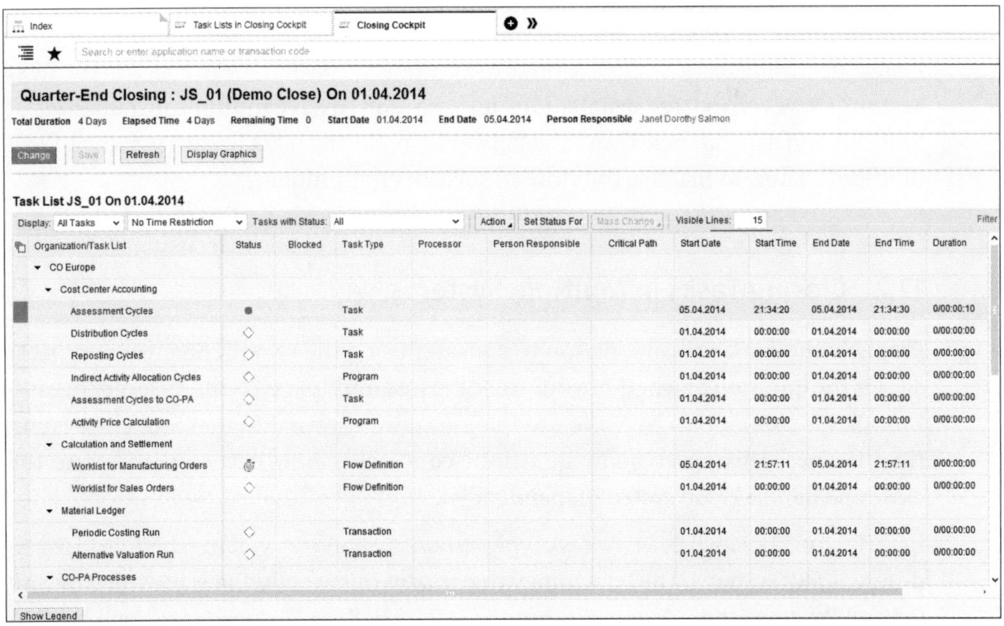

Figure 12.30 Task Details

On completion, all logs the system creates are attached to the **Task-Related Files** tab. Figure 12.31 shows the links to the spool list and job log created when our assessment cycle was scheduled.

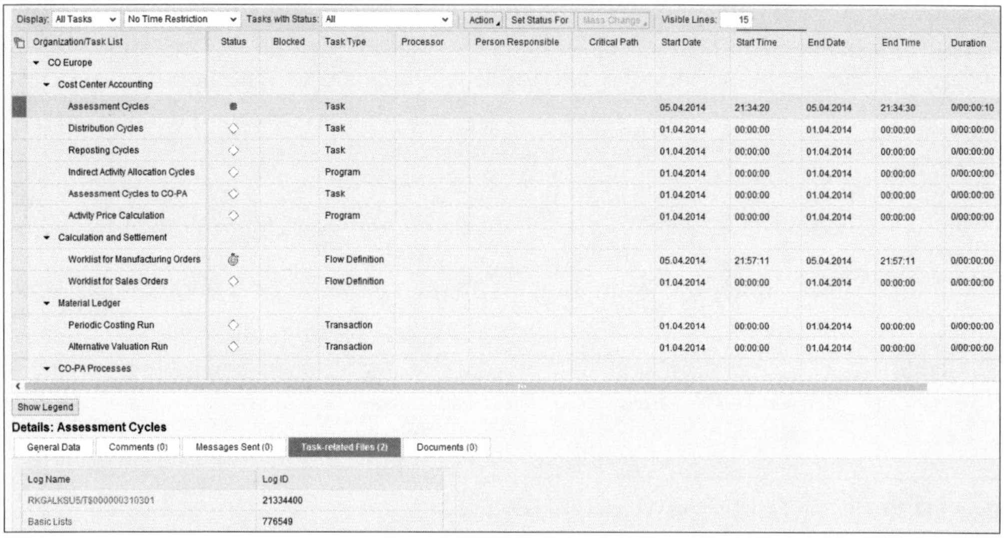

Figure 12.31 Link to Job Log and Job Spool

If all your closing tasks take place on the same SAP ERP system, you can skip the next section. However, in large installations it's common to have multiple installations of SAP ERP, and dependencies can exist between the closing tasks in each instance. We'll now look at how to manage the close in such an environment.

12.2 Closing Tasks in Multiple Systems

Probably the most pressing reason to consider using the newer enhancement packages is the question of whether your close crosses multiple systems. In larger organizations, it's common to have the production running on a different SAP ERP system than finance. This raises many questions concerning how best to orchestrate the close and handle cross-system dependencies.

In EHP 3 for SAP ERP 6.0, a new task type, *remote task*, allows you to schedule tasks on different ERP systems. The technology to perform this scheduling is provided by SAP Central Process Scheduling by Redwood (SAP CPS). Your IT department will have to install this dedicated scheduling software on SAP NetWeaver and set up a queue for each system on which closing tasks will run and jobs for each type of job that you'll want to schedule. People in the controlling department can complete the rest of the template in much the same way as we discussed earlier.

Figure 12.32 shows the **Display/Create/Change Task** screen again, this time with a remote task. In this scenario, the SAP ERP system on which the template has been created will call the remote system to schedule the distribution cycle. The SAP ERP system on which the template is defined must be on EHP 3 for SAP ERP 6.0 or higher because this release level is needed for delivery of the interfaces to call SAP CPS. The other SAP ERP system on which the remote task is performed can be on a lower release because the call that initiates the task is performed using a Remote Function Call (RFC). To display details of the job parameters, click on the **Detail View** icon to the right of the text field. Note that you will only be able to access this icon if your user also exists in SAP CPS.

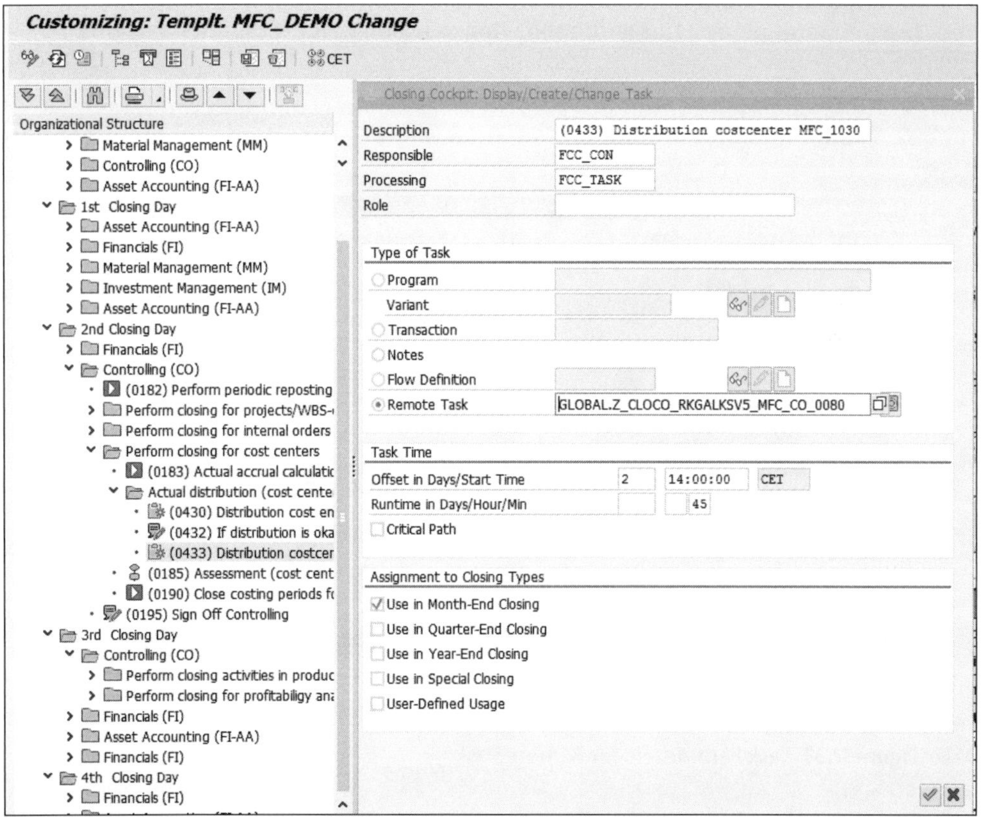

Figure 12.32 Remote Task in SAP Financial Closing Cockpit

Figure 12.33 shows the parameters for the remote job. In this example, we're scheduling a distribution cycle (see Chapter 7) on a different client of the demo system (SAP client 809 of SAP system EC3). The IT department generally creates the job definition (the shell) in SAP CPS and sometimes also the program variants (as we discussed earlier). However, once the template is complete both departments will have their own view of the closing task. The IT department will work with SAP CPS to ensure proper system performance and handle all technical issues relating to load balancing as the heavy lifting of the close begins, but the controlling department will see the tasks as usual and can display all related logs from the SAP Financial Closing cockpit add-on. Figure 12.34 shows a remote task that's currently being executed from the SAP Financial Closing cockpit in an additional tab, **Remote Task Data**.

On completion, the remote task attaches its job logs, spool list, and so on to the **Task-related Files** tab (see Figure 12.35), just as you saw for a locally executed task. Once SAP CPS has been set up, a central controlling department can schedule and monitor tasks on multiple systems without having to log on to the individual systems.

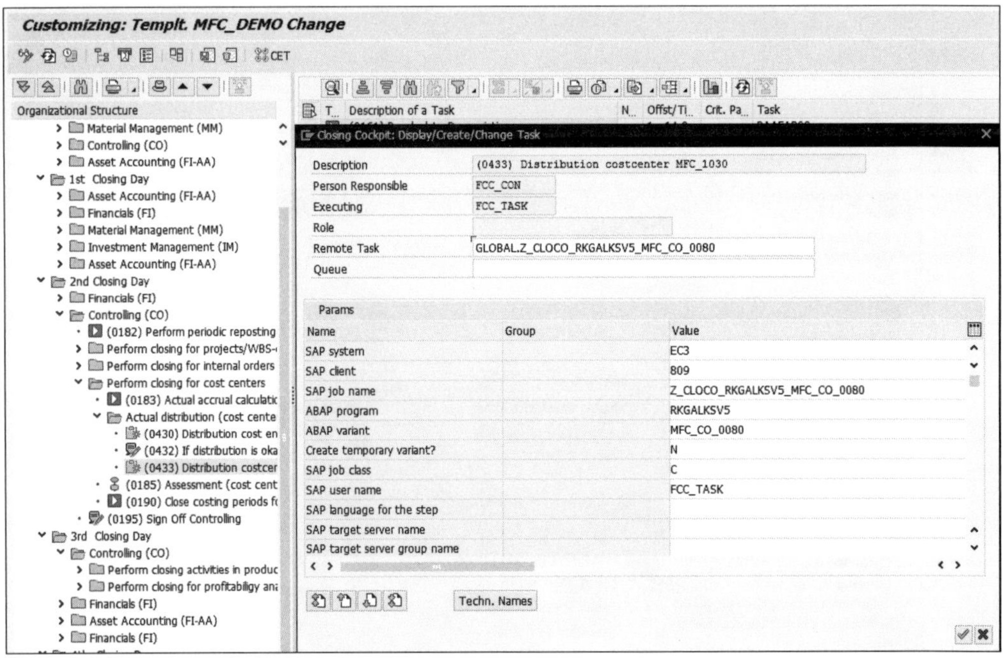

Figure 12.33 Task Parameters for Remote Task

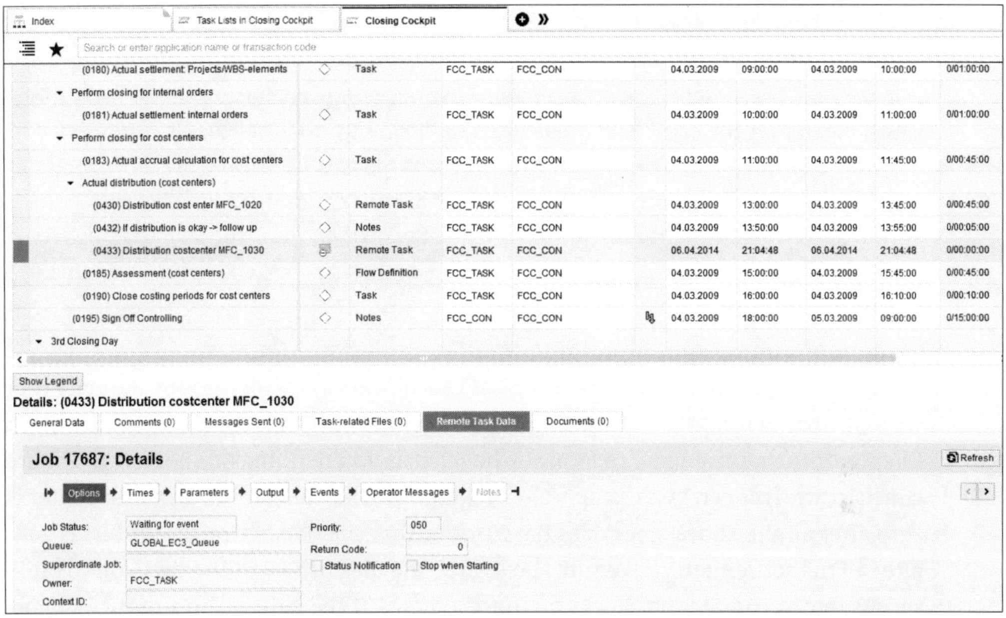

Figure 12.34 Remote Task Parameters

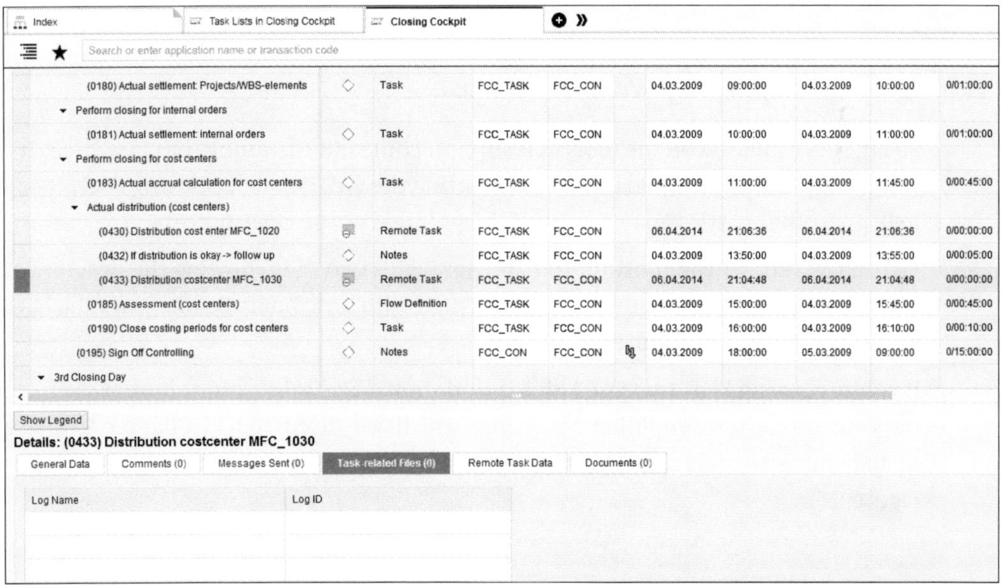

Figure 12.35 Logs from Remote Task

Storing Log Files

In general, the IT department is responsible for storing spool lists and job logs. This can mean that the spool lists are deleted fairly quickly and that the links in the SAP Financial Closing cockpit won't take you back to old spool lists. If you use SAP CPS, the lists and log files are stored there and the SAP Financial Closing cockpit links to them. Therefore, it makes sense to talk with your IT department to make sure that logs for jobs initiated from the SAP Financial Closing cockpit are stored longer to enable a proper audit.

Once you've automated the execution of the allocation cycles and settlements that we looked at in Chapter 7 and automated the creation of extracts as we discussed in Chapter 8, the next stage is to look at what checks you're doing on the data to ensure consistency. This can be as simple as checking that the balance on each cost center is zero after all the allocation cycles have run or that the balance on the orders is zero after all the settlements have run. Having the log files in SAP CPS allows you to build scripts that automate the checks on these log files. If the balance on a particular cost center is not zero, you can set up exceptions that send an email to notify you if the cost center still has a balance even though all assessment cycles have run.

12.3 Transparency within the Close

So far, we've focused on the tools that support controllers running the close steps. It's also worth bearing in mind that implementing the SAP Financial Closing cockpit can help give other parties an overview of the progress of the close process.

Figure 12.36 shows the most up-to-date view, with two tiles showing the progress of the 2012 close. These views were implemented with SAP Smart Business, a subject to which we'll return in Chapter 13.

If you're running EHP 4 for SAP ERP 6.0, you should also take a closer look at the business functions for simplified reporting, which we discussed in Chapter 8. These include InfoProviders and queries for checking the progress of the close, as shown in Figure 12.37.

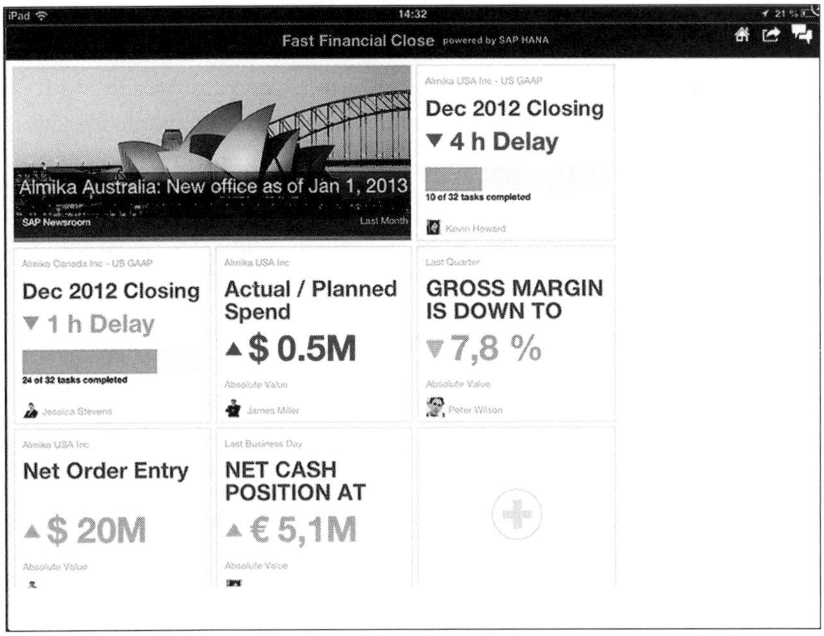

Figure 12.36 Progress of Financial Close in SAP Smart Business

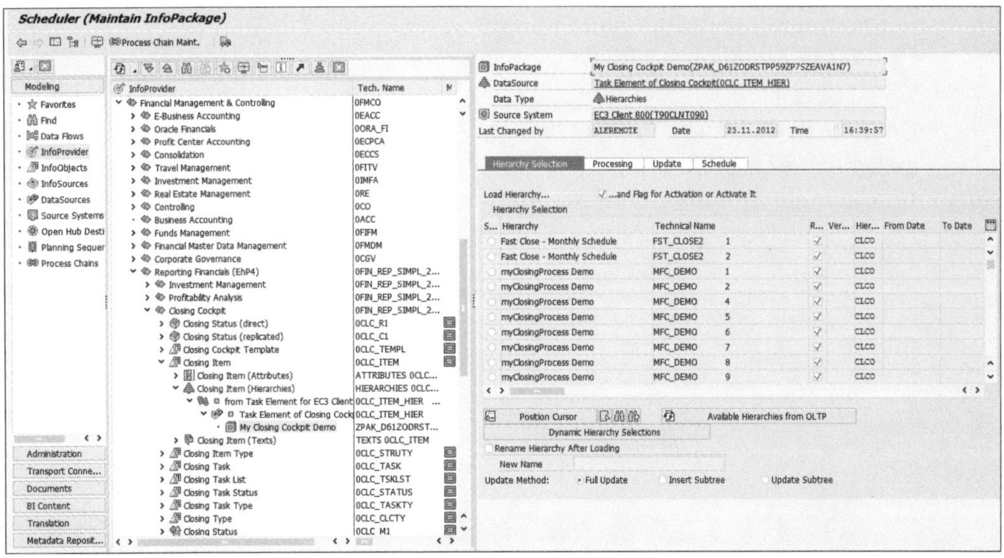

Figure 12.37 Business Content for Close Reporting in SAP BW

The important thing to understand is that the statuses for the closing items can all be read directly from your SAP ERP system, but you will need to load the hierarchy of tasks for the close to SAP BW. For this reason, it's worth checking the **Closing Item (Hierarchies)** InfoObject to see which task lists have already been loaded (see Figure 12.37).

The standard reports are available within SAP NetWeaver Business Client or SAP Enterprise Portal as part of a report **Launchpad**, as shown in Figure 12.38. To start the reports, click on one of the links.

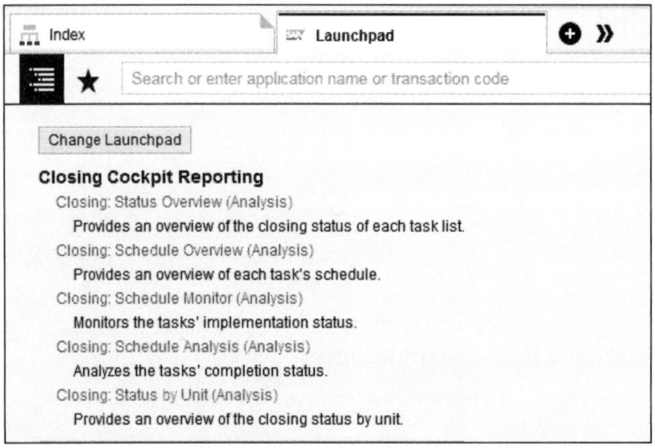

Figure 12.38 Report Launchpad for Close Reporting

Figure 12.39 shows a status overview in SAP BW for the close schedule we looked at earlier in the chapter.

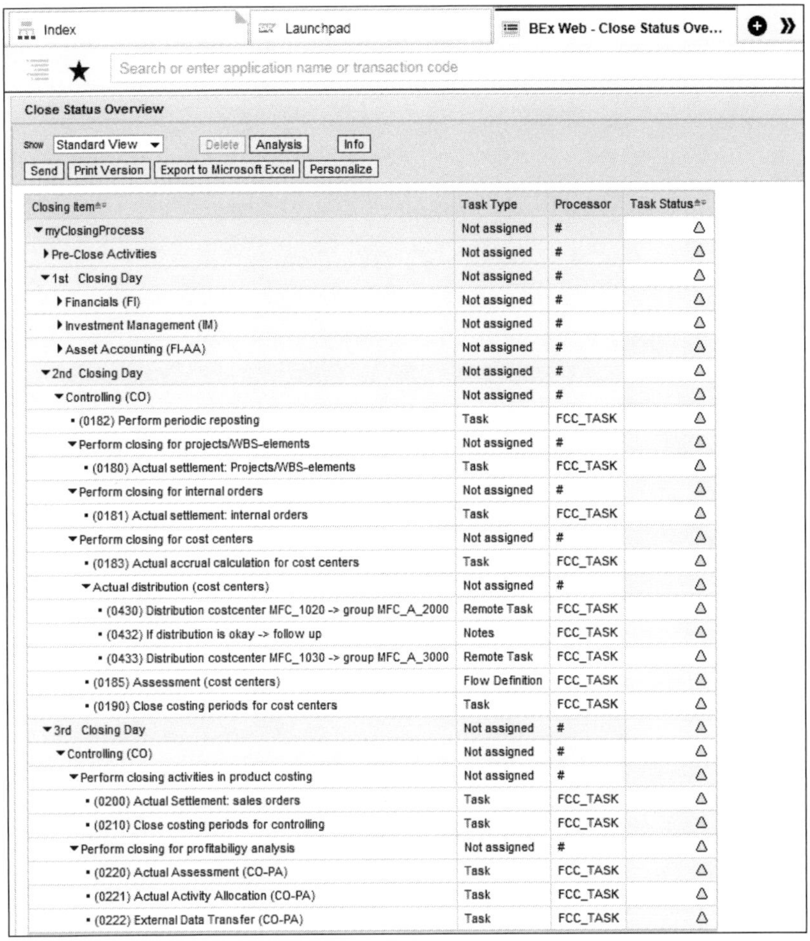

Figure 12.39 Overview of Status of Close Tasks

12.4 Summary

The SAP Financial Closing cockpit and Schedule Manager are tools that systematically support the application of your own best practices for the period close, documenting what has to be done, by whom, and when. You can add to your skeleton plan both technically, by including workflows and so on, and in a business sense, by including supporting documentation. You can start small, simply listing the transactions you use in the close, or go global with one master schedule for a multisystem close, depending on the nature of your requirements.

Chapter 13
Controlling with New Technologies

This chapter revisits Chapter 2 and Chapter 8 to explain how SAP HANA allows faster reporting with less redundant data and then revisits Chapter 7 and Chapter 12 to show which period-close tasks can be accelerated using SAP HANA. Finally, it introduces SAP Fiori and explains the impact of the new user interfaces.

We ended Chapter 8 by drilling down through the various characteristics in the CO-PA operating concern using SAP BusinessObjects Explorer and discussing the various options to prepare aggregated data for reporting, including extracts, summarization hierarchies, and summarization levels in SAP ERP and physical InfoProviders that store data in SAP BW. Since the first edition of this book was written, SAP introduced SAP HANA, an in-memory database. The goal of SAP HANA is to allow subsecond drilldown through the millions of records in a real operating concern using only the line item data collected as each transaction is posted. This means that you no longer have to worry about setting up summarization levels and which characteristics to keep in the segments and which to keep in the line items. You effectively have access to whatever information you're capturing in your line items.

This approach can radically change the way your period close works. Instead of waiting for nightly data loads to SAP BW, reports can be run in real time and the results delivered to mobile devices before the connection to the server times out. You'll also have less data in your system: only the original record of the business transaction, not the various aggregates in SAP ERP and SAP BW.

The CO-PA Accelerator was the first application released for SAP HANA and was quickly followed by other accelerators in Controlling. For a controller, the most important concept to understand is that with each navigation step you are not pulling data out of a pre-prepared extract or summarization level (and making sure that this data is kept up to date) but making a selection that collects and aggregates the data that meets your selection criteria in *real time*. This concept is known as *on-the-fly aggregation* and it means that you can select and aggregate freely from any of the fields in the CO-PA line items (see Chapter 2).

This works because SAP HANA stores all data in the main memory of the server instead of on the hard disk. SAP HANA allows developers to select directly from the line item data rather than selecting from the totals records that we looked at in Chapter 2 or using the summarization objects that we discussed in Chapter 8.

One of the reasons that this is possible is the switch in the structure of the database from a *row store* to a *column store*. Transactional data is organized in rows in traditional databases, so each invoice and sales order in Profitability Analysis and each material movement and order confirmation in the Material Ledger is recorded as a row on the database. When you run a report to show the revenues for a particular region in CO-PA, the system reads all the records in the database row by row, selects those that meet your selection criteria, and then aggregates the revenues for those invoices in the chosen region.

By contrast, in SAP HANA transactional data is organized in columns. To run the same report, the system reads only the region column and the revenue field. You get the most benefit from a column-based DataStore compared to a traditional DataStore when you have a high number of columns (such as the many dimensions in Profitability Analysis or the many material-related characteristics in the Material Ledger) and a low number of columns to be scanned for selection (only the region and revenue in our example).

What this effectively means is that we can query any field in the line item tables. If we want to select documents by trading partner or employee number, we can. To appreciate what this means, think about how your reports work today. Until recently it was virtually impossible to make dynamic selections on nonkey fields in the line item tables, so most of us have been in the habit of thinking in terms of the fields in the totals tables—in other words, the account assignment, the cost element, and the period—because this is what we've been used to reporting on and using in most of the period-close steps that we looked at in Chapter 7.

Of course, we won't just be using line items. We'll continue to use the master data tables to read cost center texts, material texts, and so on and the CO-PA dimension table CE4XXXX (where XXXX represents the operating concern) to read the characteristics in Profitability Analysis.

To get the most benefit out of SAP HANA, it makes sense to be very specific when you select fields from your line items. If you're working with ABAP list variants as discussed in Chapter 2, you'll be fastest when you have layouts that contain only a handful of fields. Remember that you can easily pull in an additional field if you need it, so if you need the document number and it isn't included in your layout, you can add the document number while you're in the report, and the field will be selected from the database.

Performance aside, as we discussed in Chapter 8, data modeling requirements will often take you toward a data warehouse. If you want your cost center plan/actual report to show the supplier for each purchase item, and this information isn't included in the underlying tables, you typically have a modeling requirement. SAP HANA Live is SAP's new solution for operational reporting. If you're using SAP HANA Live, you can copy SAP's delivered line item query that brings together the relevant transactional data from the line item tables and the relevant master data tables and extend it to link the purchase order document in the CO line item with the supplier master data.

It would be wrong to dismiss SAP HANA as only relevant for reporting. *SAP Fiori* is the new umbrella term for all UX innovations covering transactional applications (e.g., My Spend), analytical applications (e.g., Net Margin Results and Profit Analysis), and search engines with fact sheets. The search engines give the best idea of the changes driven by SAP HANA. Traditionally, search functions in SAP involve you navigating to the business object that interests you (e.g., the material master), pressing [F4] on the material field, and then choosing a matchcode (e.g., materials in a plant, materials with a bill of material [BOM], and so on). You're effectively searching within the data model that the developer designed when he built the application. If you search in SAP HANA, you search the way you search on the Internet. You enter your number/text, and the system lists all business objects that include the number/text you entered. These might be sales orders, cost centers, purchase orders, and so on. A fact sheet then shows the main fields for each of these objects, allowing you to find the business object based, for example, on your recollection that the supplier was based in Boston or the zip code was 02125.

Your organization can take two fundamentally different approaches to SAP HANA:

1. In this chapter, we'll look at how to use SAP HANA as a *secondary database* (sometimes called a *sidecar* approach) in which you copy the relevant tables to SAP HANA and then redirect all your reports and allocations to read from SAP HANA rather than from SAP ERP. In the CO-PA example, this would mean moving the CO

line table, table CE1XXXX (where XXXX represents the operating concern), to SAP HANA and then redirecting the drilldown reports and allocations to read from SAP HANA.

2. In the next chapter, we'll look at SAP S/4HANA, in which SAP HANA is the *primary database* and certain fundamental changes can be made to the underlying table structure because it's possible to assume a column store and use line items rather than totals records during the period close.

Let's start with the existing Controlling applications and go over how you can move selected tables to SAP HANA to accelerate your reporting and certain period-close processes.

13.1 Controlling with SAP HANA

The first application to take advantage of the new technology was costing-based CO-PA in 2011; it was followed by accelerators for cost center and order line items (CO-OM), availability control check on investment programs (IM), product cost drilldown (CO-PC), and Material Ledger reporting (CO-PC-ACT) in 2012 and finally by account-based CO-PA, project line item reports, Report Writer reports for CO-OM, and Public Sector Accounting. In each case, it's important to understand what changed and what potentially stays the same.

13.1.1 Profitability Analysis (CO-PA)

Profitability Analysis reports benefit massively from the move to SAP HANA, because the column store makes it much more efficient to select CO-PA dimensions and you can run most of your reports by selecting from live data rather than summarization levels. To find out whether your organization is running the CO-PA Accelerator, choose **Controlling • Profitability Analysis • Tools • SAP HANA Integration • Set Up SAP HANA Integration** in the IMG or use Transaction KEHC, enter the operating concern, and check whether the **CO-PA Accelerator Active** flag is set for your operating concern (see Figure 13.1). If it is, the dimension table (table CE4), the actual line items (table CE1), and the plan line items (table CE2) are being replicated to SAP HANA. If you're running SAP Business Suite powered by SAP HANA, SAP Accounting powered by SAP HANA, or SAP S/4HANA, you won't be allowed to access this transaction because SAP HANA is your primary database and all tables are on SAP HANA.

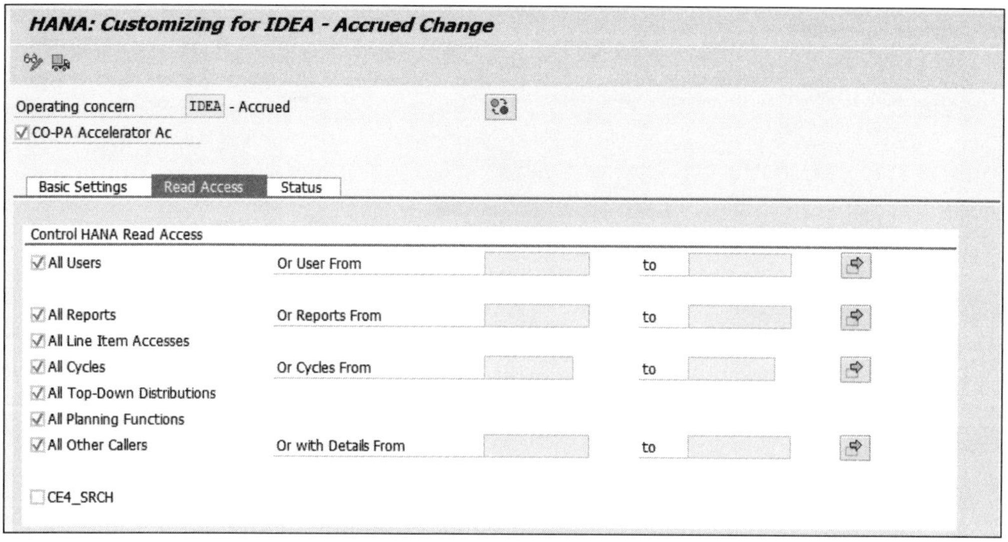

Figure 13.1 Settings for CO-PA Accelerator

To check exactly which processes are being accelerated, choose the **Read Access** tab. In our example, all profitability reports, all allocation cycles, all top-down distributions, and all planning functions are reading not from SAP ERP but from SAP HANA. Administrators can use the **Status** tab to check exactly how many data records have been transferred to SAP HANA. This means that, in general, when you run a transaction such as Transaction KEU5 (assessment to CO-PA) the system will read the assessment cycle and select the relevant driver data (such as the relative revenues per customer) from SAP HANA. If the connection is unavailable, the system will read the tables in SAP ERP and you will experience a loss of performance but not of functionality.

To get an understanding of how the data in the CO-PA tables is stored in SAP HANA, we'll now look at SAP HANA Studio. This is the design environment for those who build reports in your organization. Figure 13.2 shows a simple view of the operating concern. It includes an *analytical view* containing the transactional table (table CE1) and two *attribute views* for the customer and material master data. SAP HANA Studio is installed on your desktop and can be downloaded from the SAP Service Marketplace. Before proceeding, check the details in SAP Note 1514967 (SAP HANA—Central Note).

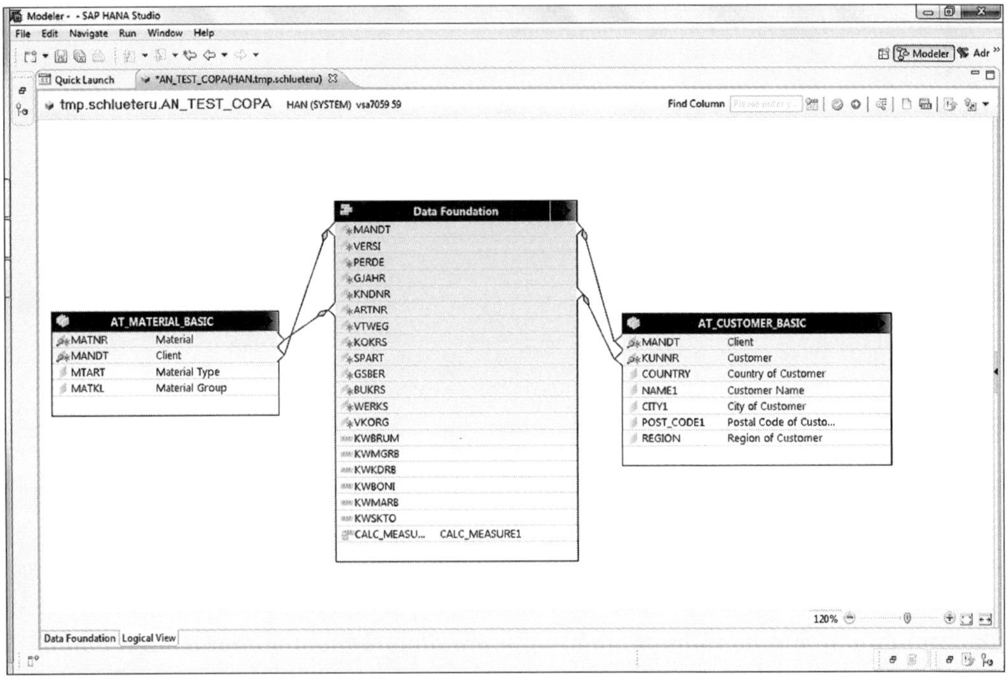

Figure 13.2 Analytical View for CO-PA Data

Using SAP HANA to Summarize on the Fly

If you've been using CO-PA for a while, it's likely that your profitability reports are set up to read summarization data or a summarization level, so the first thing to do is to change these settings to have the system select the data afresh each time you navigate to a new dimension. To implement this change, choose **Accounting • Controlling • Profitability Analysis • Information System • Define Report • Change Report** or Transaction KE32, enter the operating concern, choose a report, and select the **Options** tab shown in Figure 13.3. Choose **Read upon Each Navigation Step** and save your report. This will ensure that you are taking full advantage of SAP HANA in your profitability reporting and selecting and aggregating on the fly with each navigation step.

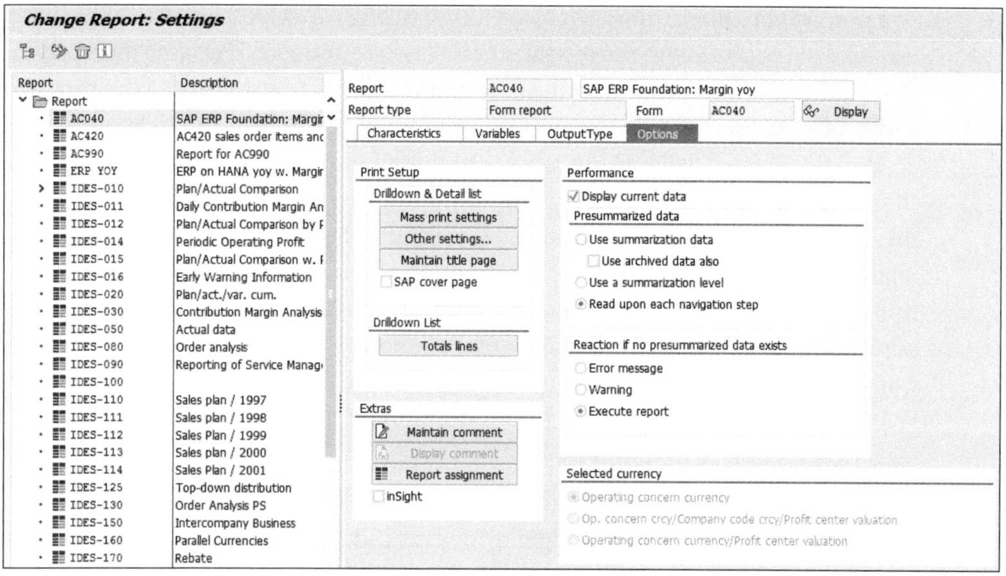

Figure 13.3 Report Settings for SAP HANA

Period-Close Improvements in CO-PA

As you saw in Figure 13.1, the CO-PA Accelerator accelerates not just profitability reporting but also allocations and top-down distribution. In Chapter 7, Section 7.1.4 we looked at how to allocate costs from cost centers to CO-PA dimensions. The best results will be for those assessment cycles that use sender rules with *variable portions*, because they select the relative data for each of the receivers before performing the allocation. In our example, we allocated R&D costs to the divisions supported based on the relative costs of goods sold in those divisions. SAP HANA would allow you to accelerate the selection and aggregation of the cost of goods sold for each division, potentially accelerating the time to run an assessment cycle (Transaction KEU5) by around 30%. This approach also can be used to accelerate indirect activity allocations that work with sender rules by using variable portions, bringing significant improvements to the runtime of Transaction KEG5. If you are unsure how much time your allocation cycles spend in the selection step, use Transaction KEDZ to analyze the performance of the read interfaces in your operating concern.

The same approach can also be used to accelerate top-down distribution (see Chapter 7, Section 7.4.2) by improving the selection of the base data used in the distribution. Imagine that you've posted the bonuses awarded to each sales manager in CO-PA.

You now want to use a top-down distribution to break down these costs to the products sold in proportion to the relative costs of these products. The same mechanisms that helped in the allocations will allow you to aggregate the costs of the products sold and improve the performance of Transaction KE28. You can achieve further acceleration by parallelizing the process so that the data for each sender (in this case the sales managers who have received a bonus) can be processed in parallel. This means that the receivers (the products to receive a share of the bonus costs) and the relative product costs are selected separately and then posted for each sender in turn, bringing further performance benefits. If you're unsure how your distributions are performing, use Transaction KE28L to find out how much time is spent on the selection of the source data and the reference data.

New User Interfaces for Profitability Reporting

You can use the CO-PA Accelerators to make your existing reports and period-close processes run faster, but you might also want to bring a new look to your CO-PA reports, especially if you're planning to bring new users online who have never learned to work with the traditional CO-PA reporting tools. Figure 13.4 shows a CO-PA report in SAP Analysis for Microsoft Office. One thing to consider in this context is how you want to set up your authorizations. SAP HANA uses the *analytical privileges* concept to determine which users can see what data, so you will have to ensure that your users have the appropriate privileges.

You may remember, however, that we discussed the use of virtual InfoProviders in Chapter 8, Section 8.3, and it's this approach that was used to create the report shown in Figure 13.4. The virtual InfoProviders become interesting in the context of SAP HANA because they allow you to continue using your existing authorizations. This is because the virtual InfoProvider translates the operating concern into an SAP BW structure that comprises InfoObjects for the characteristics and key figures that you will use for reporting but uses routines in SAP ERP to perform the data selection and check authorizations.

To create a virtual InfoProvider for your operating concern, use Transaction KEIP, enter your operating concern, then choose whether the operating concern is for costing-based CO-PA, account-based CO-PA, or both, and choose **Execute**, as shown in Figure 13.5. This will result in the generation of virtual InfoProviders with the key `/RKE/C_XXXX` for a costing-based operating concern and `/RKE/A_XXXX` for an account-based operating concern (where `XXXX` is the code of your operating concern). Our example uses two InfoProviders: `/RKE/C_SFIN` and `/RKE/A_SFIN`.

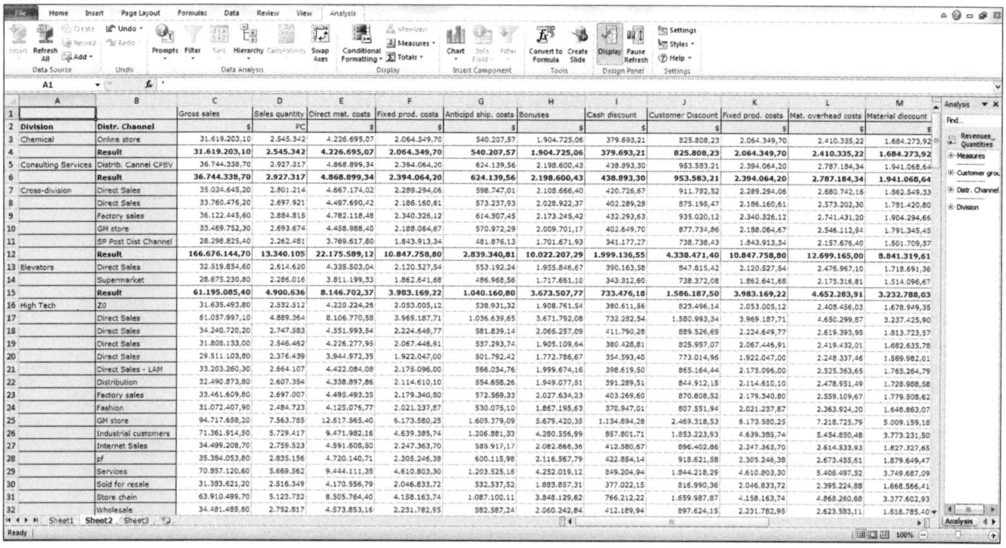

Figure 13.4 Profitability Report in SAP BusinessObjects Analysis, Edition for Microsoft Office

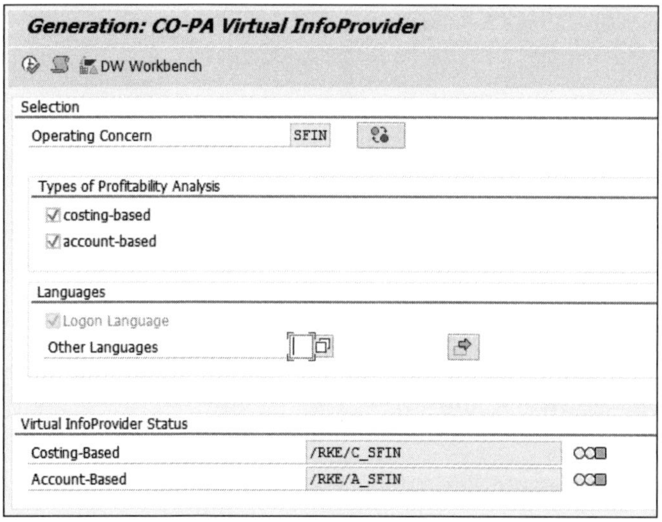

Figure 13.5 Generating Virtual InfoProvider for Your Operating Concern

To display the virtual InfoProvider you've created, choose Transaction RSA1 (in your SAP ERP system), select **InfoProvider** on the left, and **Unassigned Nodes • CO-PA • Virtual InfoProvider** on the right. Figure 13.6 shows the virtual InfoProvider we created for the costing-based operating concern SFIN. Note that the screen is the same as that for the Administrator Workbench in SAP BW that we looked at in Chapter 8, but this time we're in SAP ERP.

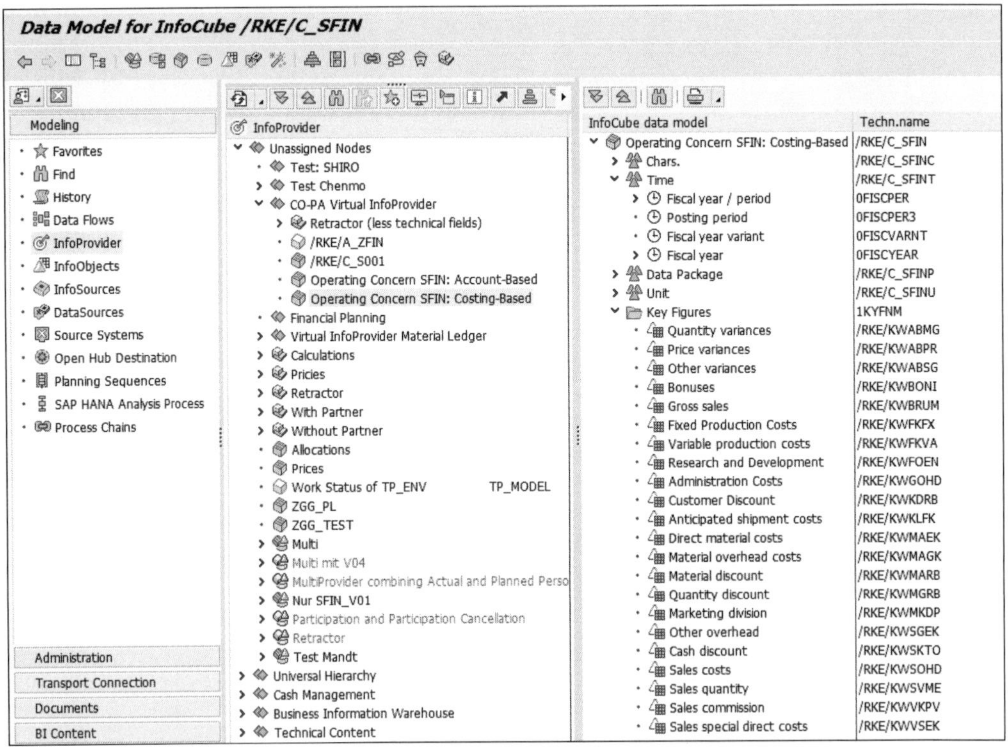

Figure 13.6 Virtual InfoProvider for Operating Concern SFIN (Generated Characteristics and Value Fields)

This virtual InfoProvider will allow you to create SAP BW queries and SAP BusinessObjects reports like the one shown in Figure 13.4.

Modernizing the User Interface for Profitability Reporting in CO-PA

You can create virtual InfoProviders for CO-PA and modernize the user interfaces, provided that your organization is using SAP ERP 6.0 or above. To check whether your organization is using a support package that includes the relevant coding, refer to SAP Note 1667584. You can use this option even if you aren't using SAP HANA.

13.1.2 Product Cost Controlling (CO-PC)

One of the main reasons to move Profitability Analysis to SAP HANA was to aggregate large amounts of data on the fly. Because the drilldown reports for Product Cost Controlling take a very similar approach, they benefit in equal measure from a move to SAP HANA. By comparison, for many years no drilldown reporting existed at all for the Material Ledger. Recently a new transaction (Transaction KKMLO) has been introduced that allows you to create drilldown reports on Material Ledger data that in turn allow you to drill down via multiple dimensions in the way you are used to doing in Profitability Analysis and Product Cost Reporting. This transaction is supported by new reporting tables designed to bring the Material Ledger data into a structure more readily useful for reporting.

Product Cost Reporting

When we looked at the product cost reports in Chapter 8, Section 8.1.3, we described how to use Transaction KKRV to collect the relevant data for summarized reporting. To see the reports that can benefit from the acceleration, run Transaction KKOO, as shown in Figure 13.7.

Figure 13.7 Product Cost Reports That Can Be Accelerated Using SAP HANA

If your organization has defined its own reports, you'll see additional reports for drill-down reporting on this screen. You'll find these reports under **Accounting • Controlling • Product Cost Controlling • Cost Object Controlling • Product Cost by Order • Information System • Summarized Analysis • With Product Drilldown.** You can also use the CO-PC Accelerator with the simplified reports shown in Chapter 2, Section 2.6.

Whereas the CO-PA Accelerator works by replicating tables CE4, CE1, and CE2 to SAP HANA, the CO-PC Accelerator selects the transactional data (actual costs, planned costs, target costs, variance categories, WIP, etc.) for each production order or product cost collector using DataSource 0CO_PC_10 (Production Costs), a technique more commonly used to transfer data to SAP BW. To display the settings for the CO-PC drill-down reporting, use Transaction HDBC and select **Product Cost Controlling • Drilldown Reporting** on the left and then the **Replication Tables** tab, as shown in Figure 13.8. The table shows the DataSource that has been transferred to SAP HANA.

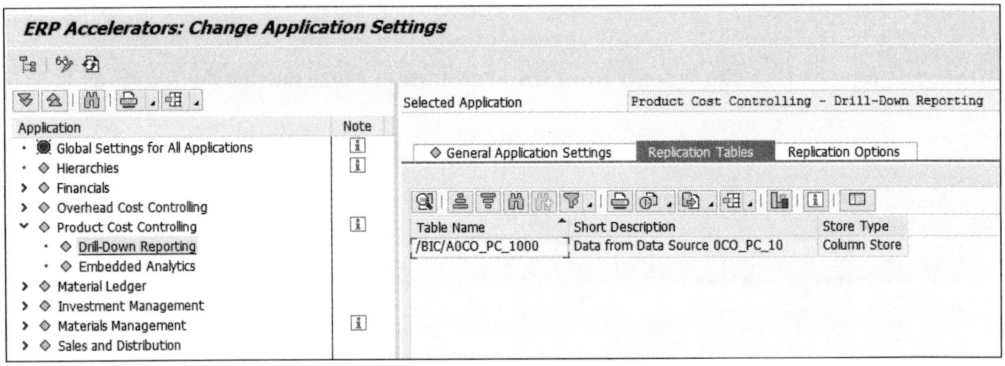

Figure 13.8 Settings for Drilldown Reporting in Product Cost Controlling

This DataSource is mapped to SAP HANA as analytic view AN_PROD_COST. Figure 13.9 shows the analytic view for product cost reporting within SAP HANA Studio. If you compare this with Figure 13.2, you'll see that it also has an analytical view containing the transactional data (this time selected from multiple tables) and several attribute views for the various master data attributes.

In the context of SAP HANA, it's also worth considering whether your reports might benefit from the inclusion of additional dimensions. You might want to consider including information such as the cost center or the activity type that is available in the CO records but wasn't accessed during summarization for the old reports. Be aware, however, that adding dimensions still counts as a modification. SAP Note 1523578 describes how to add the profit center and SAP Note 1514091 how to add the origin to your product drilldown report. If you implement these SAP Notes, you'll have to rebuild the drilldown tables for your historical data.

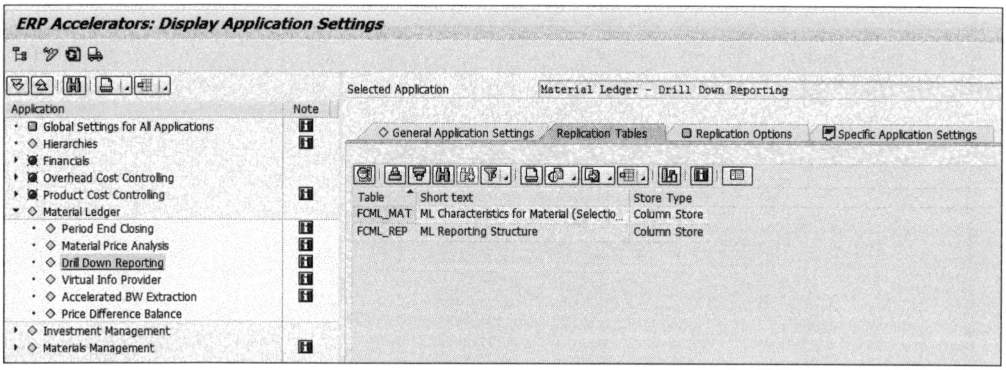

Figure 13.9 Analytic View AN_PROD_COST for Product Cost Reporting

Material Ledger Reporting

If your organization didn't move to a data warehouse, Material Ledger reporting was essentially Material Price Analysis (Transaction CKM3) and Quantity Structure Analysis (Transaction CKMQS), both of which allowed you to report on the goods movements and order confirmations for one material at a time. During Material Price Analysis (see Chapter 2, Section 2.5), the selection of the folders for each procurement alternative was reasonably quick because the procurement alternatives were preaggregated in table MLCD, but the selection of the documents assigned to each procurement alternative from tables MLIT and MLPP was often performance-intensive. Moving the line item tables to SAP HANA can dramatically improve the performance of Material Price Analysis. To find out more about this solution, refer to SAP Note 1654782 (ERP Accelerators: Material Ledger—Price Analysis).

Arguably the more significant breakthrough in the Material Ledger reporting is the introduction of drilldown reporting, in which the costs for multiple materials can be analyzed in the same report. To work with drilldown reports, choose Transaction KKMLO and select Report 01MLREPORT (the delivered drilldown report). Figure 13.10 shows the materials received and consumed within the time frame of the report together with the beginning and ending inventory. In the navigation block, notice the many material-based dimensions that you can use to aggregate your materials (we've selected the material group in the center of the screen). This report is also available without SAP HANA, but it may experience performance issues if you have substantial data volumes. To find out more about this option, refer to SAP Note

1654255 (ERP Accelerators: Material Ledger—Drilldown Reporting). To include additional characteristics in your reports, refer to SAP Note 1654225 (Derivation of Customer-Specific Fields in Table).

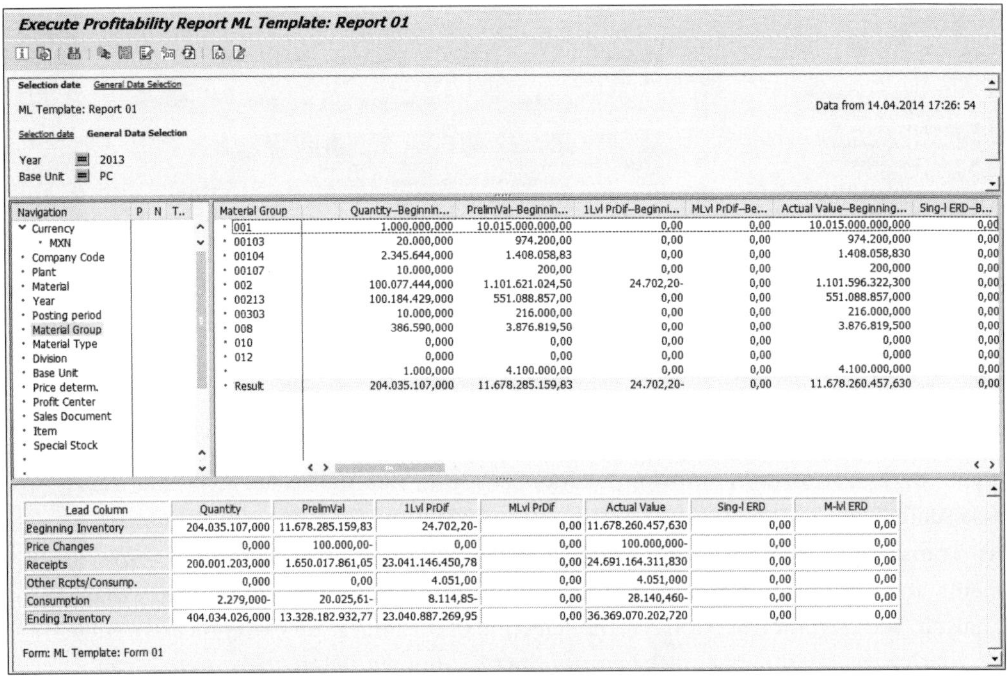

Figure 13.10 Drilldown Reporting in Material Ledger

> **Extend Your Material Ledger Drilldown Report**
>
> Once you've explored the summarized postings in the drilldown report, you will probably want to drill down to the detail in the Material Price Analysis report (CKM3) and the Quantity Structure report (CKMQS). To activate these links, follow the instructions in SAP Notes 1875113 and 1875733.

To display the settings for the Material Ledger reports, use Transaction HDBC and select **Material Ledger • Drilldown Reporting,** as shown in Figure 13.11. This time, the replication tables are the new tables `FCML_MAT` and `FCML_REP` that were introduced in the context of SAP HANA.

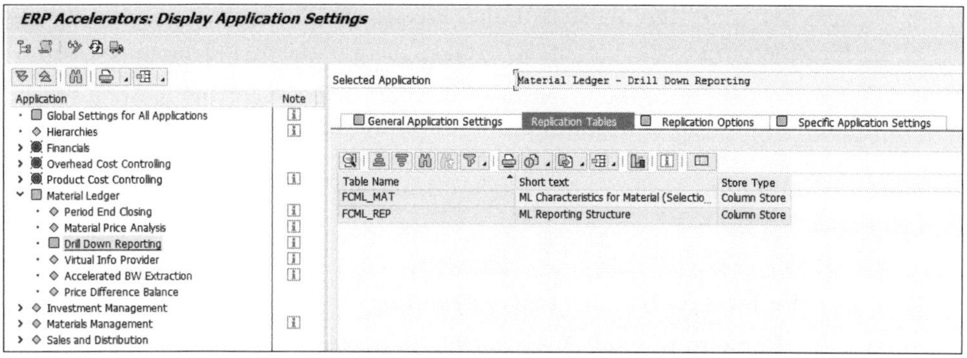

Figure 13.11 Settings for Material Ledger Accelerator: Showing New Tables

To make Material Ledger reporting more efficient, the following tables have been designed specifically for reporting with SAP HANA:

- FCML_MAT
  This table contains the materials plus reporting dimensions such as plant, product group, business area, valuation class, division, and so on. You can create derivations to include additional characteristics just as you do in Profitability Analysis.
- FCML_REP
  This table contains the procurement alternatives together with quantities and values in a condensed form. It's comparable in function with DataSource 0COPC_C02 (CO-PC: Actual Costing/Material Ledger—Cost) used in SAP BW.
- FCML_CCS_REP
  This table contains the actual cost component split data. It is comparable in function with DataSource 0COPC_C07 (CO-PC: Actual Costing/Material Ledger – Cost Component Split used in SAP BW).

Because these tables are new, you'll need to use Transaction FCML_FILL or Report FCML_FILL_REPORTING_TABLES to transfer the existing reporting data to the new tables. From then on, you can replicate to SAP HANA as each new data record is created.

Period-Close Improvements in the Material Ledger

The costing run that we looked at in Chapter 7, Section 7.3.2 can also be accelerated using SAP HANA. With this approach two steps in the costing run have been accelerated. The new options are described fully in SAP Note 1654778 (ERP Accelerators: Material Ledger—Period-End Closing):

- The *selection step*: Here those materials are selected for inclusion in the costing run for which goods movements have taken place in the period (table CKMLPP).
- The *posting step*: Here the inventory values are selected for the materials to be updated (tables MLHD, MLPP, and MLIT).

The calculation steps are accelerated in SAP S/4HANA 1610, which we will look at in Chapter 14.

New User Interfaces for Material Ledger Reporting

We discussed how to use SAP BusinessObjects Explorer for Profitability Analysis. Let's now look at how to use SAP Analysis for Microsoft Office for the Material Ledger, again using a virtual InfoProvider. To use the virtual InfoProvider for the Material Ledger, select Transaction HDBC, choose the **Virtual InfoProvider** node, click on the **Specific Application Settings** tab (as shown in Figure 13.12), and generate each of the virtual InfoProviders in turn. Note that the same constraints apply as we described for Planning in Chapter 10 and that you can only perform this step in the client that has been declared the SAP BW client for your system. To find out more, refer to SAP Note 1654843 (ERP Accelerators: Material Ledger—Virtual InfoProvider).

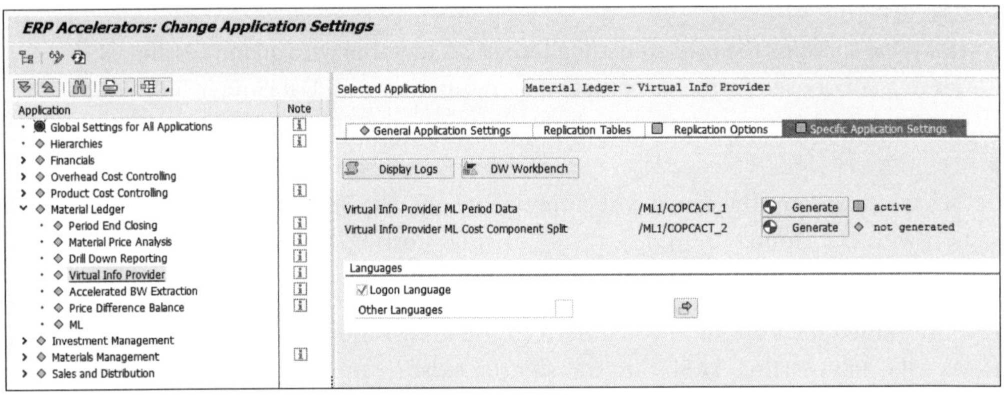

Figure 13.12 Generating Virtual InfoProvider for Material Ledger

Figure 13.13 shows a Material Ledger report in SAP Analysis for Microsoft Office. This report uses the virtual InfoProvider for the Material Ledger to convert the SAP ERP structures into SAP BW structures for reporting. As well as the transactional data, you will notice the many material-dependent characteristics that we discussed earlier available for drilldown within the **Analysis** tab.

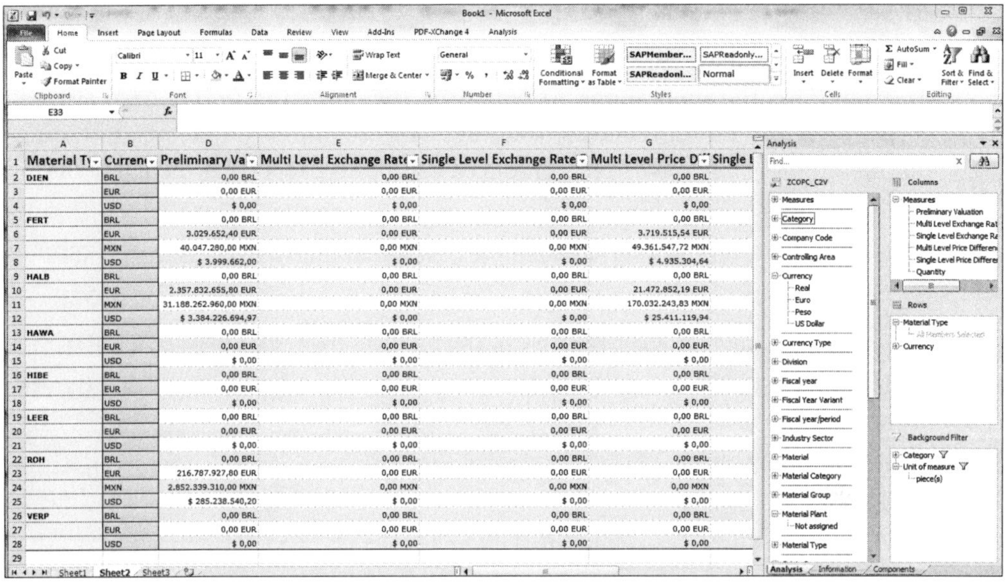

Figure 13.13 Material Ledger Reporting Using Virtual InfoProvider

Unusually, the Material Ledger accelerators also offer the chance to accelerate the extraction of your data to SAP BW. As you can see in Figure 13.14, all the Material Ledger tables are read to fill InfoSource 0CO_PC_ACT_10 (Actual Costing/Material Ledger—Cost Component Split). For full details, refer to SAP Note 1664155 (ERP Accelerators: Material Ledger—BW Extraction).

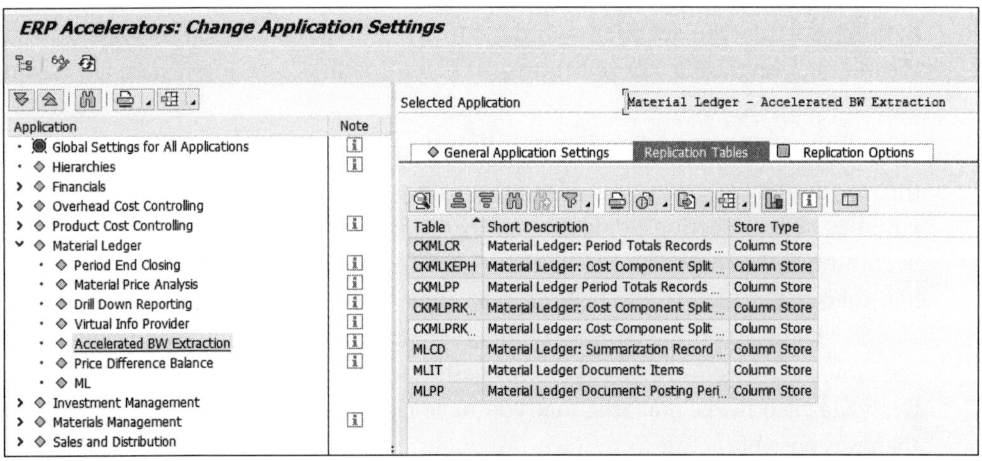

Figure 13.14 Material Ledger Tables Included in SAP BW Extraction

13.1.3 Overhead Management (CO-OM)

Although Profitability Analysis, Material Ledger, and Product Cost Reporting are the traditional big data applications in Controlling, the advent of SAP HANA has also had a positive impact on Cost Center Accounting, Order Accounting, and Project Accounting. New transactions have been introduced for line item reporting, including the following:

- Transaction KSB1N as alternative to the cost center line item transaction (KSB1)
- Transaction KOB1N as an alternative to the order line item transaction (KOB1)
- Transaction CJI3N as an alternative to the project line item transaction (CJI3)
- Transaction KSBPN as an alternative to the cost center planned line items transaction (KSBP)
- Transaction KOBPN as an alternative to the order planned line items transaction (KOBP)
- Transaction CJ14N as an alternative to the project planned line items (CK14)
- Transaction KOB2N as an alternative to the order commitment line items (KOB2)
- Transaction KSB5N as an alternative to the CO document display (KSB5)

New Line Item Reports

Let's now compare the new transactions with their older counterparts. Figure 13.15 shows the selection screen for Transaction KSB1N. Compare this with the selection screen for Transaction KSB1 shown in Chapter 2, Figure 2.3. The **Cost Center**, **Cost Center Group**, **Cost element**, **Cost element group**, and **Posting Date** fields are the same in both transactions. To get a sense of the difference between the new transaction and the old, click on the **Further Selection Criteria** button in the top-right area of the icon bar.

The **Further Selection Criteria** button allows you to select from many of the fields in the line item table (table COEP). However, with a traditional database and large data volumes such a selection would frequently result in a timeout. As we discussed at the beginning of the chapter, if you were to select by trading partner or personnel number, then the system would have to read each line item row by row to determine whether it contained the correct trading partner or personnel number. If you make the same data selection using a column-based store, then the system can select effectively via such fields, meaning that you have far more powerful querying available than was possible before.

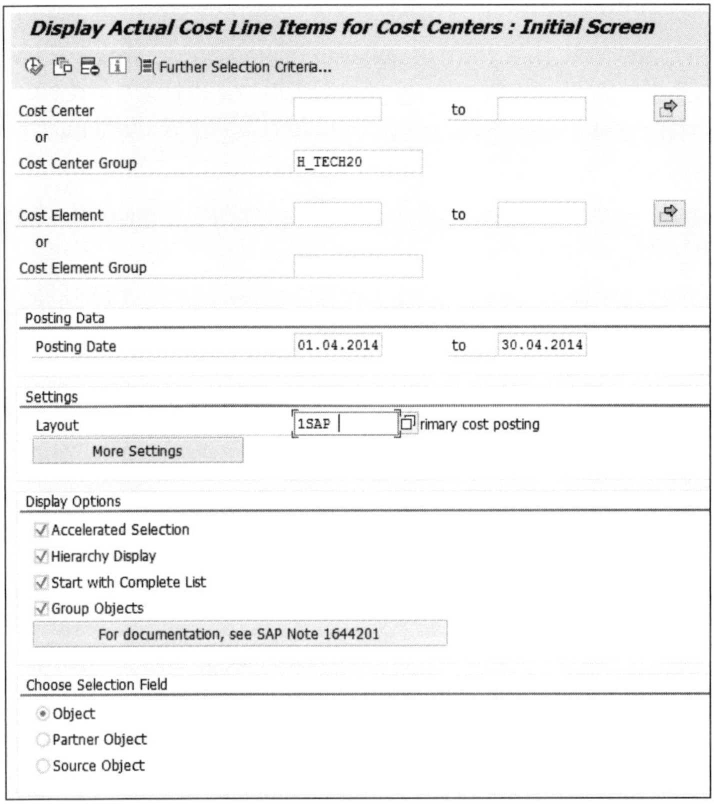

Figure 13.15 Selection Screen for Cost Center Line Item Report

Returning to the new flags, you might wonder why you need an **Accelerated Selection** option at all. The existing ABAP List Viewer (ALV) layouts described in Chapter 2 (**1SAP** to **5SAP**) were designed for the classic row store. Because fetching data from the database was performance-intensive, all fields in the layout were included.

If you use the **Accelerated Selection** option, *only* those fields included in the ALV layout are selected initially, and all the other fields are summarized. Although this will improve performance, it may result in unintended side effects, which is why the new transactions are offered as alternatives rather than a replacement for the existing transactions. You will typically have authorizations set up for individual cost centers, orders, projects, and cost elements. However, if these fields aren't included in your selection, then the authorizations won't be checked. If you haven't included the cost element field in your ALV variant, then the system selects as if you had **Authorization for Cost Element** blank and aggregates across all cost elements. This can lead to different results than in Transaction KSB1, for which the cost element is always part of the selection. Note that you can only call related documents, such as the accounting document, if all the fields are included in the selection that the report-to-report interface needs as parameters to call the relevant document. This may result in blank documents.

If you return to Figure 13.15, you'll also notice new selection options—**Object**, **Partner Object**, and **Source Object**:

- To have the report continue to behave as described in Chapter 2, Section 2.1.1, select the **Object** flag. The report will select all records for your chosen cost center(s) within the selected time frame.
- If you select the **Partner Object** flag, you'll see those records for which the cost center was not the sender but the *receiver* of an allocation. This would typically have resulted in a timeout in a classic database.
- If you select the **Source Object** flag, you'll see the origin of the postings (e.g., payroll in Brazil).

Figure 13.16 shows the result of the selection, a list of cost center line items for a group of cost centers. Of course, it's hard to show the speed of the selection in a static page.

The cost center group in the tree on the left is the result of selecting **Hierarchy Display**. In the old line item reports, if you entered a cost center group in the selection screen the results would be shown according to the individual cost centers belonging to that group. You can use this tree for navigation purposes. If you double-click on a tree node, such as **H_SERV20** in our example, then you will trigger the selection of all line items relating to cost centers in the **H_SERV20** node. To get back to the results for the full tree, simply click on the top node of the hierarchy (**H_TECH20** here). If you prefer to remove the tree from the screen, use the **Tree On/Off** button at the top right of the screen.

The ALV layouts (bottom left) are always visible. One catch is that if you create ALV layouts with only a very few fields, it's entirely possible to remove all fields containing information about the account assignments, such as texts, and this can make the report results difficult to interpret. To get around this, select the **Group Objects** flag in the selection screen. To find out more about the new options for line item reporting, refer to SAP Note 1644201 (KAEP: Functions of the New Line Item Reports). Similar functions are available for the reporting of project line items. These are described in detail in SAP Note 1698066 (CJI3N and CJI4N: Functions of the New Line Item Reports).

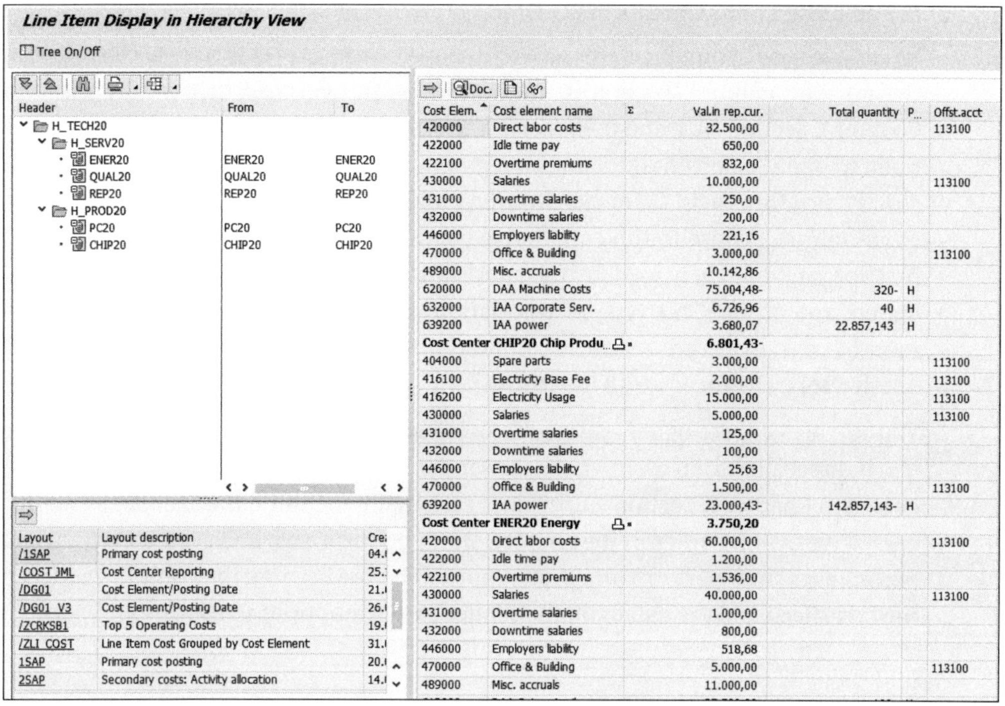

Figure 13.16 Cost Center Line Item Report with Tree and Layouts

Improvements to Report Writer Reports

The latest addition to the accelerators is the ability to accelerate the Report Writer reports for CO-OM. These work with the totals records (tables COSP and COSS), as shown in Figure 13.17.

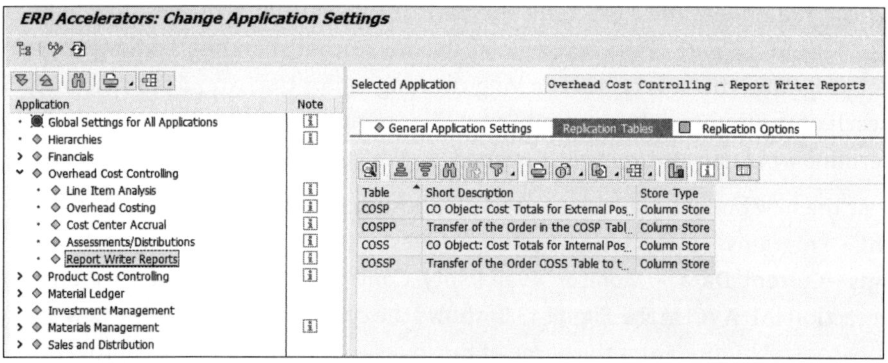

Figure 13.17 Tables Replicated for Report Writer Reports

Period-Close Improvements in CO-OM

When you move your line items to SAP HANA, you can expect further acceleration in certain transactions. The first is the calculation of overhead that we discussed in Chapter 7, Section 7.2.1, and the second is the calculation of accruals. Both use conditions to apply a percentage value to a group of costs. Provided these are run on a strictly monthly basis, there usually aren't any performance issues. However, some organizations choose to run cumulative overhead calculation, calculating overhead first for January, then for January and February, then for January, February, and March, and so on. This type of calculation can become time-critical as the final months of the year are reached. To find out more, refer to SAP Note 1658547 (ERP Accelerators: Overheads with SAP HANA).

You can also expect benefits if you're using assessment cycles, distribution cycles, and indirect allocation cycles that have sender rules that read variable drivers, as discussed in Chapter 7, Section 7.1.3. This is essentially the same mechanism as we discussed for CO-PA earlier in the chapter. Don't be surprised, however, if cycles using percentages show performance pretty much as before because they only have to read the cycle itself and the values on the sender cost center prior to allocation.

13.1.4 Investment Management (IM)

When we looked at master data in Chapter 4, Section 4.8, we looked at the way an investment program acts as an umbrella for the various internal orders and WBS elements assigned to the program. In Chapter 5, Section 5.2, we looked at how to plan and assign budget to an investment program and the associated orders and WBS elements and in Chapter 6 at how an active availability check is performed every time you post expenses to an order or a WBS element. As a controller, you need to be able to check the budget for each item, the part of that budget that has already been assigned, and the part of the budget available for further spending. For large investment programs, this was typically a long-running report that would read the budget for each of the items in the program, read the assigned orders and WBS elements to determine what had already been assigned, and calculate what budget remained.

To use the new budget availability checks, choose **Accounting • Investment Management • Programs • Information System • Investment Management Reports • Programs—Current Data • Monitor Availability Control for Investment Programs** or Transaction IM_AVCHANA. Figure 13.18 shows the selection screen for the new availability control report. Enter the name of the investment program, the approval year, and whether you're looking at overall values (multiple years) or values for a single year. Don't forget to make the appropriate settings for your status.

The result of executing the transaction is shown in Figure 13.19. A status is set for each investment program item, and you can expand the nodes of the investment program to understand where budget is running short and clarification is required. Finally, you see the internal orders that are assigned to these program items. This report responds such that it can be run in dialog mode rather than in batch mode as was common in the past. To find out more about this report, refer to SAP Note 1652021 (Monitor Availability Control for Investment Programs). In a similar vein, two new transactions allow you to monitor budget availability for WBS elements and internal orders: Transaction IM_AVCHANA_WBS for WBS elements and Transaction IM_AVCHANA_ORD for internal orders. A further transaction, Transaction IM_AVCALRT_EXEC, allows you to assign additional budget automatically when a budget ceiling is exceeded. Similarly, you can report on budget depletion using Transaction IM_AVCALRT_ORD for budget on internal orders and Transaction IM_AVCALRT_WBS for budget on WBS elements.

Figure 13.18 Selection Screen for Budget Availability Control

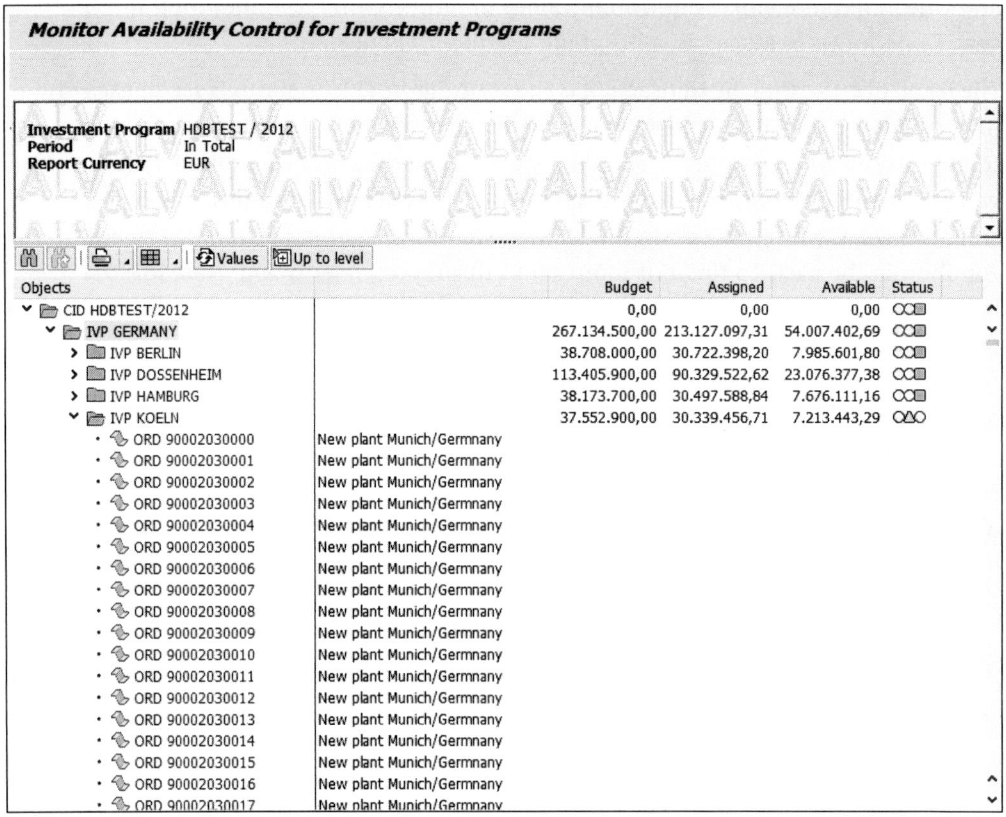

Figure 13.19 Investment Program with Status Information

13.1.5 SAP HANA Live

So far, we've looked at how to use SAP HANA to accelerate reports and period-close processes that already exist. As we discussed in Chapter 8, organizations moved to data warehouses not only for performance reasons but also for the modeling opportunities they afforded. SAP HANA Live offers a way to take the transactional data, such as the cost center and order line items, and extend the basic data included in the tables to include whatever details are relevant for your reporting needs. You can use SAP HANA Live when SAP HANA is the secondary (sidecar) database or the primary database.

The approach involves two layers: private views and reuse views. *Private views* are generally created by SAP developers and do much the same thing as the SAP BW extractors. They map the fields in the underlying tables (tables `COBK` and `COEP` in our example) into a structure that's easier for a nonprogrammer to understand and include in a report.

A simple example of what happens in this layer is the handling of the object number used to represent all cost centers, orders, projects, and so on to which costs are assigned. It takes a developer to know the syntax of the `OBJNR` field (object numbers beginning with KS are cost centers and are concatenated with the controlling area, object numbers beginning with OR are internal orders, object numbers beginning with PR are projects and internal numbers have to be converted into external numbers before display, etc.).

The reuse view is the layer that organizations and SAP partners can work with to build their reports. To find out what views exist in SAP HANA Live, you should work with the SAP HANA Live Browser. Figure 13.20 shows the various master data views used within Controlling. These are the SAP HANA equivalent of the InfoObjects for SAP BW that we looked at in Chapter 8.

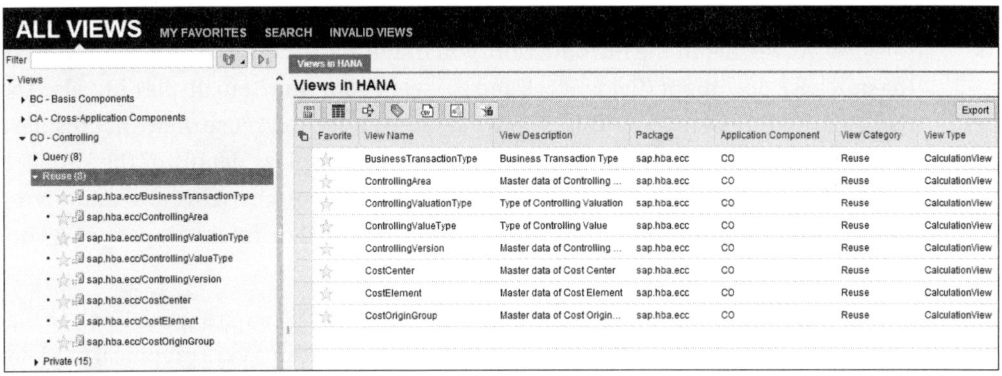

Figure 13.20 Master Data Views in SAP HANA Live

The master data views of course only make sense when combined with transactional data. Figure 13.21 shows the data structure of the cost center line item query.

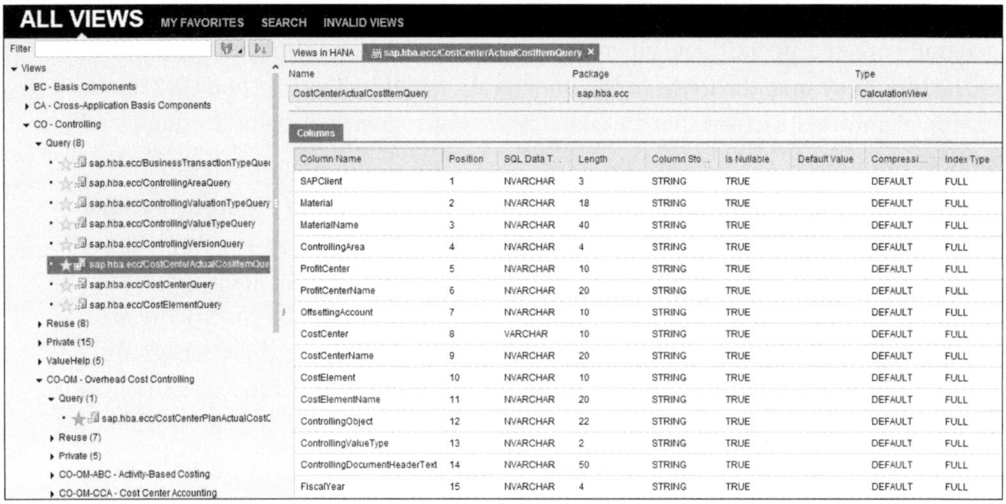

Figure 13.21 Cost Center Line Item Query in SAP HANA Live

You might wonder how this reuse view differs from the cost center line item report (Transaction KSB1N) that we discussed in the previous section. What makes this view interesting is not the fields in the delivered view, but how you can potentially extend the view. As we said in the introduction, you might want to display not just details of the purchase document (fields EBELN and EBELP) in your line item display but also the name of the supplier. To do this, you would need a second reuse view that displays the purchase document and the attribute view that displays details of the supplier. It's the potential to incorporate additional data without changing the underlying data structure or writing ABAP code that makes the view interesting from a controlling point of view.

For more complex reporting requirements, *calculation views* are used. In a calculation view, you can perform flexible join and union operations via a graphical modeler or implement coded logic via SAP's SQLScript language. One example in which SAP decided to extend the CO line item is shown in Figure 13.22.

This is the Cost Efficiency Analysis by Work Center report, in which the line item for the production order (COBK/COEP) has been joined with the confirmation document for the production order (AFRU). The dimensions listed for analysis therefore include the familiar cost center and activity type from the CO documents and the less familiar work center and operation from the confirmation documents.

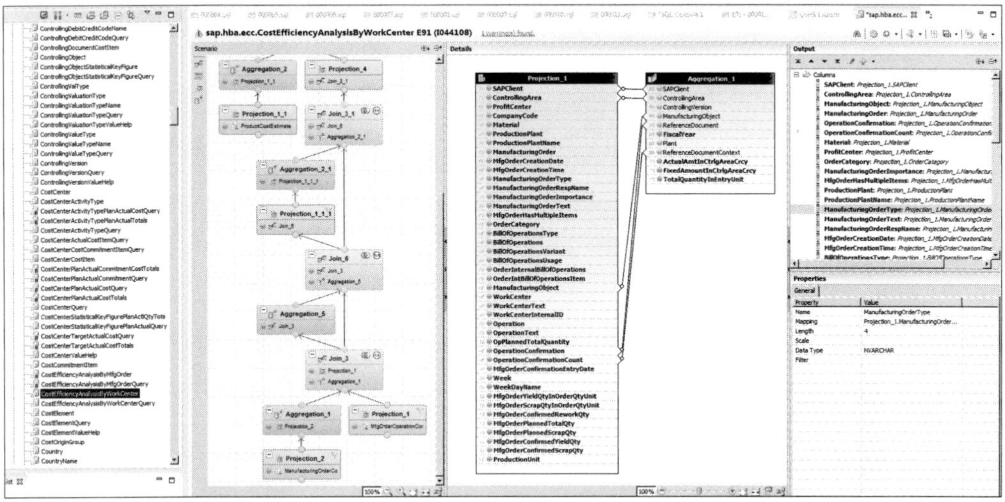

Figure 13.22 SAP HANA Live Model for Cost Efficiency Analysis by Work Center

These data models will form the basis for the analytical applications in SAP Fiori that we will look at later in the chapter. To find out more about the solution in general, refer to *http://help.sap.com/hba*.

As of the time of writing (summer 2018), the use of a data warehouse as we described in Chapter 8 should not be written off completely. As the name implies, SAP HANA Live works with *live* data and is primarily designed for operational reporting. If you've archived data or made retrospective changes (e.g., following a profit center reorganization), then you won't be able to view this data in your reports, whereas a data warehouse will allow you to store financial data in a structure that meets your requirements regardless of your archiving strategy in the source system.

SAP HANA Live shows the data according to the structures that are current in the system at the time. It doesn't support time-dependent hierarchies, so you can't simulate the effect of organizational changes on your financial data or restate your financial results based on the new structures.

SAP HANA Live allows you to merge data from multiple systems, but if you're performing significant transformations to your data, then the performance might be better in a dedicated data warehouse.

SAP HANA Live and SAP S/4HANA

SAP S/4HANA offers a simplified data model for Financials that merges the transactional tables for Financial Accounting, Controlling, Material Ledger, and Asset Accounting, and the delivered SAP HANA Live structures won't work with the new data model. Even where the data model is unchanged, SAP made a strategic decision to switch from calculation views to CDS views in SAP S/4HANA. SAP Note 2270382 (S4TWL—SAP HANA Live Reporting) explains the details.

Now that we've discussed the basic possibilities of SAP HANA, we'll look at the new user interfaces that can be built to change the daily work of a controller or the managers he supports.

13.2 SAP Fiori Applications

SAP Fiori was introduced as a new approach to user interface design, offering applications that could run on a desktop, tablet, and smartphone and deliver key information quickly to managers on the move. The connection with SAP HANA might not seem immediately obvious, but clearly a smartphone can't wait half an hour for a report to return a result. Applications need to receive results back from the server in a few seconds or the connection will time out before the response has reached the phone.

The basic tenets of SAP Fiori are that an application should be the following:

- Role-based (designed for a specific user)
- Responsive (adaptive to the device on which it is being run, whether the desktop, a tablet device, or a mobile device)
- Simple (follows the 1-1-3 design paradigm, or 1 user, 1 use case, 3 screens)
- Coherent (the applications all speak the same language)
- Of instant value (low barrier to adoption)

To check whether your devices are compatible with SAP Fiori, refer to SAP Note 1935915 (Fiori for Business Suite: Browser/Devices/OS Information).

There are three types of applications within SAP Fiori:

- *Search models* and *fact sheets*
- *Transactional applications*, such as My Spend and My Unusual Items
- *Analytical applications*, such as Net Margin Results and Profit Analysis

Assuming your organization is using SAP Fiori, you will find all these applications on your laptop, tablet, or mobile device within a launchpad that is configured for your role(s) within the organization. This launchpad offers a search function and tiles that provide access to both transactional applications, such as purchase requests or travel approval, and analytical applications, such as the financial statement or margin dashboard.

SAP Fiori Library

If you haven't worked with SAP Fiori before, you'll find basic information about every delivered application in the SAP Fiori library, which can be accessed using the following url: *https://fioriappslibrary.hana.ondemand.com/sap/fix/externalViewer/*.

In this chapter, we'll look at the early SAP Fiori applications that can be used in combination with SAP Business Suite. In the next chapter, we'll look at the SAP Fiori applications that are delivered in combination with SAP S/4HANA. Each new edition of SAP S/4HANA includes new SAP Fiori applications. Every SAP Fiori application is given an ID by development, and we'll mention this application ID with every application that we describe to make it easy for you to find out more about the product features and the technical requirements for implementation. When several versions exist, make sure to read the details for your current backend release.

13.2.1 Search Models and Fact Sheets

So far, we've looked at applications in which SAP HANA's ability to select and aggregate quickly has been in the forefront, but this ability can also be used to search quickly. Although fairly cumbersome search models in the form of F4 help and matchcodes have been around for years in SAP ERP, the SAP HANA-based search models available from EHP 7 for SAP ERP 6.0 are more dynamic, making the user experience more like using an Internet search engine. The old matchcodes required you to have a pretty good idea about what sort of business object you were searching for and what a useful restriction for the search might be.

Figure 13.23 shows the SAP Fiori launchpad for the cost manager role and the **Search** box that you'll find at the top of every SAP Fiori launchpad.

Figure 13.23 SAP Fiori Launchpad for Cost Manager with Search Box

Now, enter "47111" in the **Search** box at the top of the screen. Bear in mind that you haven't specified what type of business object you're looking for. Figure 13.24 shows the search results for 47111: several assets, a cost center, and several internal orders. This result list only contains objects from SAP ERP Financials, but search models are available for business objects in most areas of SAP Business Suite.

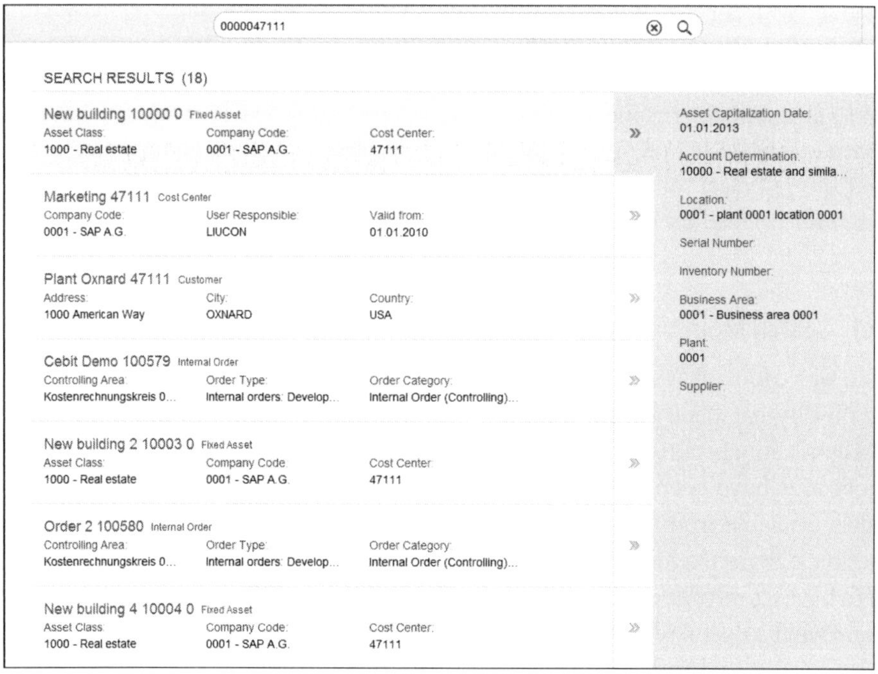

Figure 13.24 Search Results for 47111 Showing Various Business Objects

Clicking on the link for any object in the result list will take you to a simple fact sheet for the object that shows the sort of details that will help you to determine whether the object is the one you are looking for and navigate from there, if necessary, to the full display transaction. Figure 13.25 shows the SAP Fiori app for the marketing cost center 47111 (the cost center in the search result list). Technically speaking, this is the cost center fact sheet with the SAP Fiori ID F1721.

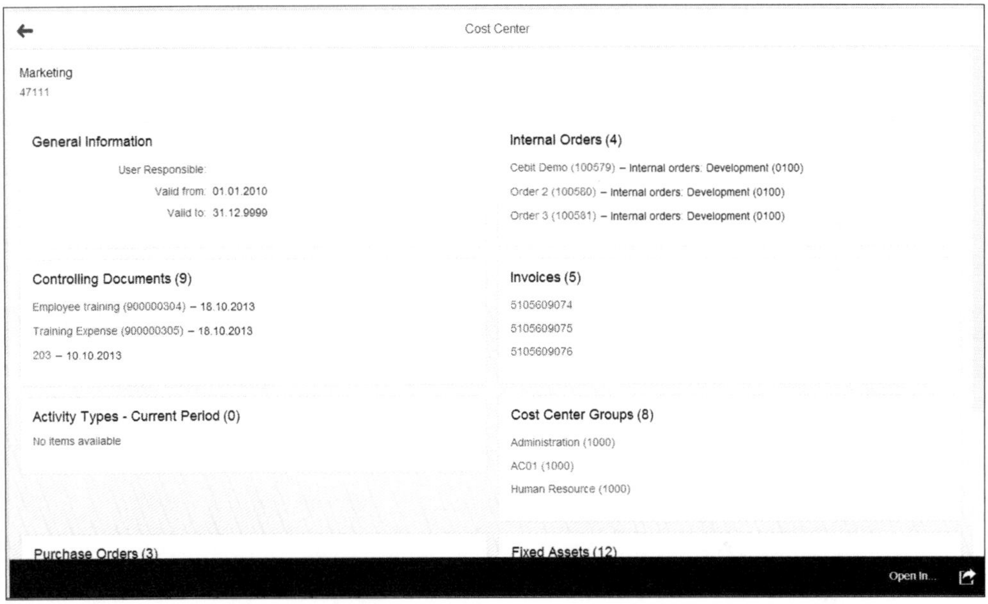

Figure 13.25 Cost Center Fact Sheet

Remember from when we looked at the controlling master data in Chapter 3 that we explained how the various master data objects are linked to each other, so cost centers are linked with fixed assets, internal orders, activity types, statistical key figures, and so on. They belong to cost center groups and are included in documents such as invoices for cost center expenses. These links are also displayed in the fact sheet by calling additional search models that establish these links dynamically. Finally, note the **Open In...** button in the bottom right-hand corner, which will navigate you to the full cost center display transaction (Transaction KS03).

This same basic approach is taken for all the fact sheets. Figure 13.26 shows the activity type fact sheet (SAP Fiori ID F1717) with the associated sender cost center and receiver cost centers, internal orders, and WBS elements and the option to navigate to Transaction KL03 (Display Activity Type).

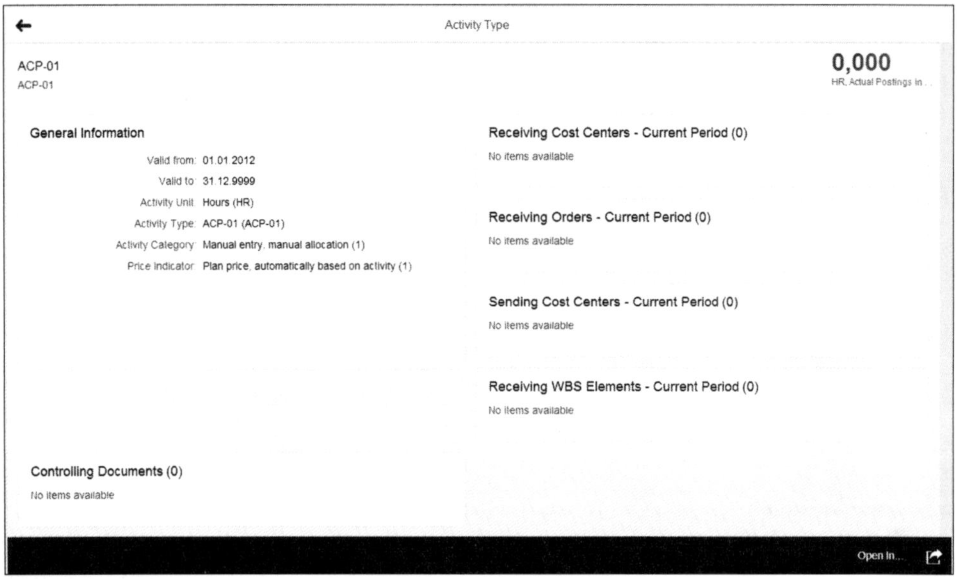

Figure 13.26 Activity Type Fact Sheet

SAP Business Suite includes search models for the following master data objects in Controlling:

- Cost centers (COST_CENTER_H)
- Cost center groups (COST_CENTER_GRP_H)
- Cost elements (COST_ELEMENT_H)
- Cost element groups (COST_ELEMENT_GRP_H)
- Internal orders (INTERNAL_ORDER_H)
- Activity types (ACTIVITY_TYPE_H)
- Statistical key figures (STAT_KEY_FIGURE_H)
- Controlling documents (CONTROLLING_DOCUMENT_H)

To learn more, refer to SAP Note 1861013 (HANA-Enabled Search Models for SAP Business Suite—Enable Fiori Search and Fact Sheet).

If you look again at the cost center fact sheet and activity type fact sheet, you can see that though the initial search delivers results in the form of one cost center or one activity type, further searches are used to deliver the links from the selected object to other objects, such as the fixed assets assigned to the cost center or the controlling documents containing the cost center.

You can navigate from the cost center fact sheet using the following search models, which are called with the parameters from the cost center selected:

- Controlling documents (CONTROLLING_DOC_H)
- Cost center groups (COST_CENTER_GRP_H)
- Cost center (COST_CENTER_H)
- Activity types in cost center (COST_CTR_ACTTYPE_H)
- Fixed assets (ASSET_H)
- Invoices (INCOMING_INVOICE_H)
- Internal orders (INTERNAL_ORDER_H)
- Projects (PROJECT_H)
- Purchase orders (PURCHASE_ORDER_H)
- Internal order quantities (SKF_INTERNAL_ORDER_H)

You can navigate from the activity type fact sheet using the following search models:

- Activity types (ACTIVITY_TYPE_H)
- Controlling documents (CONTROLLING_DOC_H)
- Receiving cost centers (RECEIVING_COSTCTR_H)
- Receiving orders (RECEIVING_ORDERS_H)
- Receiving projects (RECEIVING_PROJECTS_H)
- Sending cost centers (SENDING_COSTCTR_H)

Again, stay abreast of developments by referring to SAP Note 1930487 (Release Information Note for SAP Fiori Fact Sheets) and SAP Note 1933191 (Release Information Note for SAP NetWeaver Embedded Search in Fiori).

13.2.2 My Spend and My Unusual Items

We introduced the idea of Manager Self-Service when discussing how to set up cost centers and the idea of responsibility accounting in Chapter 3. This basic idea has recently been revisited, but with a substantially improved user interface that can be used to display the manager's budget and spending on the desktop, a tablet device, or a mobile device.

To access the My Spend application (SAP Fiori ID F1717), select the **My Spend** tile from the SAP Fiori launchpad for the cost manager role, as shown in Figure 13.27.

Figure 13.27 My Spend Tile in SAP Fiori Launchpad

Figure 13.28 shows the spending by department. The manager in the example is responsible for two cost center groups: **LoB FIN** and **LoB GRC**. These in turn comprise several cost centers. The relative size of the boxes is determined either by the budget or the spending per cost center. You can toggle between the two by using the dropdown to switch from **Budget** to **Spend**. The relative size makes it easy to see at a glance where potential problems lie.

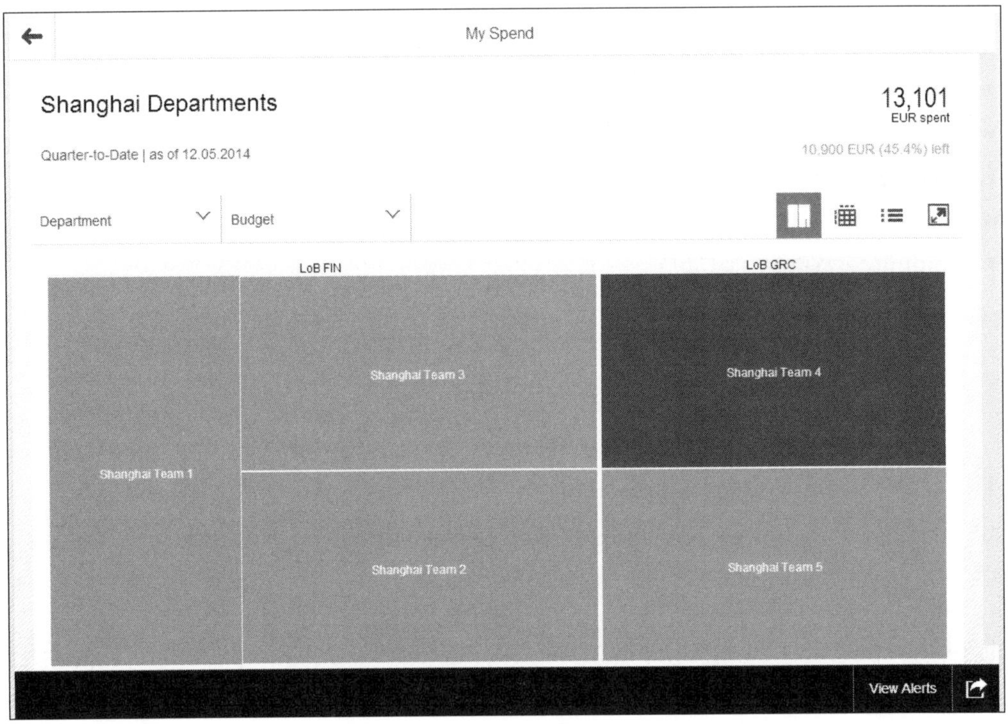

Figure 13.28 My Spend by Department (Cost Center)

The manager's cost centers are selected using the same mechanisms as are used for Manager Self-Service. My Spend uses the DIA_CC_MONITOR dialog to determine which cost centers are assigned to the manager's user. The DIA_CC_MONITOR dialog also determines which cost elements are accounted for in the application. It's important to decide whether you want managers to focus only on the primary costs that they can reasonably influence or on all costs on their cost centers.

The manager's spend can be displayed not only by department (cost center), but also by project (internal order) and expense type (cost element). Let's now use the dropdown box on the left to switch to the project view. The result is shown in Figure 13.29. This time the DIA_IOMONITOR personalization dialog has been used to preselect the relevant orders. Again, the relative size of the boxes is determined by the budget or the spending per order. As of the time of writing (summer 2018), only internal orders are evaluated; WBS elements are not.

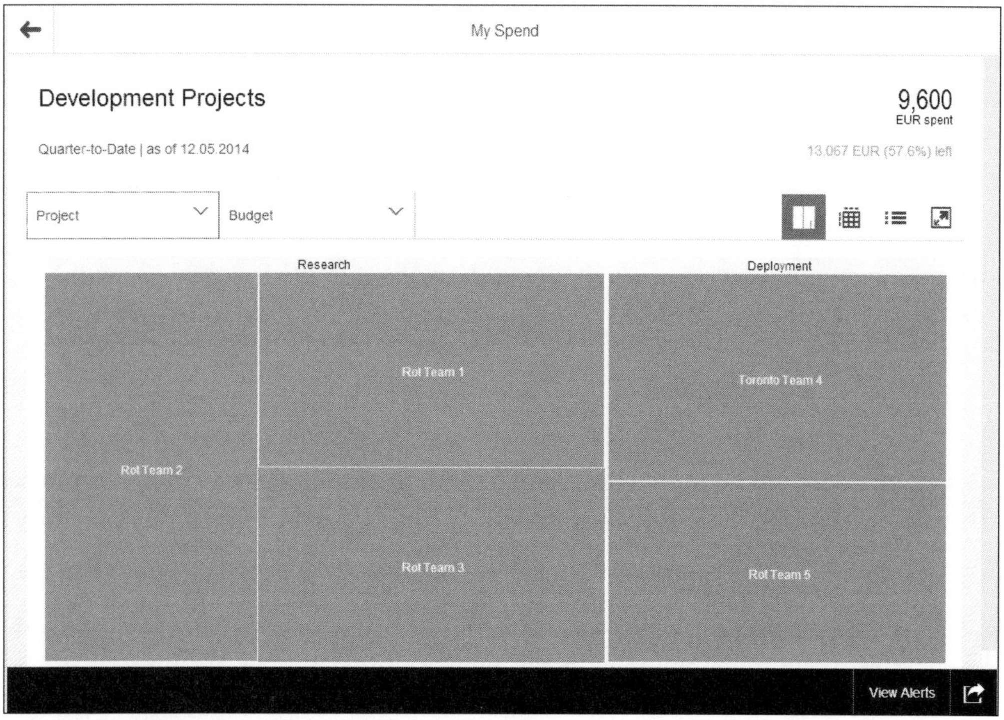

Figure 13.29 My Spend by Project (Internal Order)

Let's now use the dropdown to view the **Expense Types** (cost elements) in Figure 13.30. To make sure that this tree map is legible, you may need to reconsider the structure of the cost element group that you enter for your managers in the DIA_CCMONITOR and DIA_IOMONITOR dialogs. In our example, **Travel** and **Supplies** are the first nodes in the structure and they are the top nodes in our chosen cost element group, followed by **Travel Expenses: Entertainment**, **Travel Expenses: Other**, and so on. You want to create cost element groups that will make instant sense to your managers rather than, for example, groups that are convenient for selection in allocations.

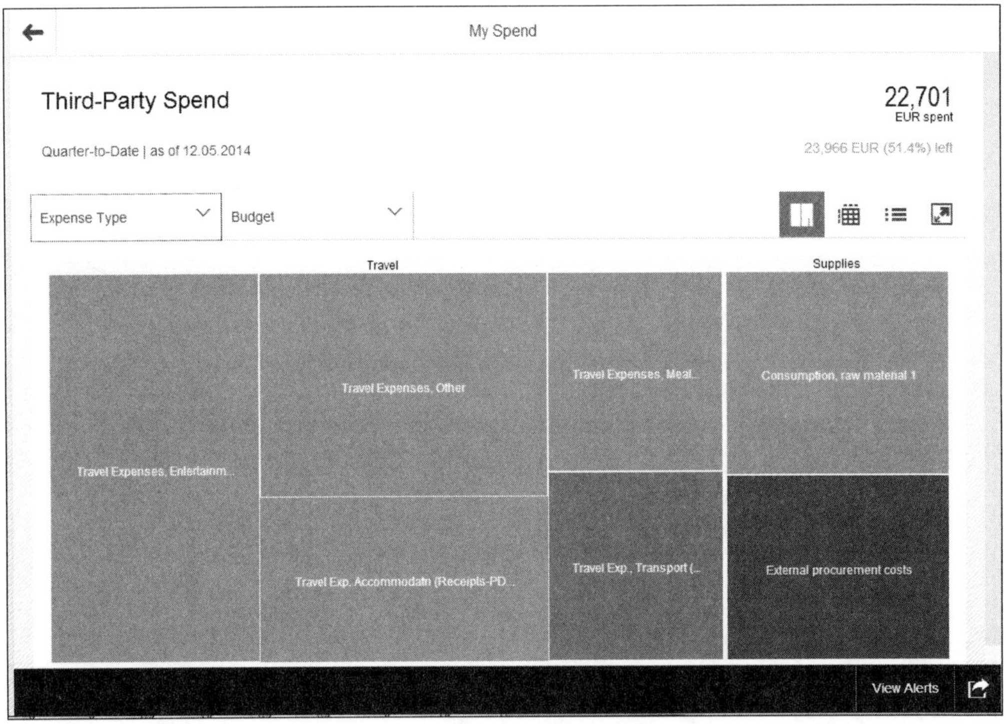

Figure 13.30 My Spend by Expense Type (Cost Element)

You can change the thresholds using the **Settings** icon in the bottom left of the screen. Here you can also change the time frame, the currency, and the scaling of the figures.

My Spend was initially delivered with Wave 1 of SAP Fiori. To work with this application, you'll need the SAPUI5 component to handle the UI on your various devices, SAP Gateway to make the connection between the mobile device and the SAP ERP backend, and the add-on for SAP Fiori that contains the code to select the costs per cost center, order, and so on. Every edition of SAP S/4HANA includes new SAP Fiori applications; we'll see more examples in Chapter 14.

Another example of this sort of application is My Unusual Items, shown in Figure 13.31 (SAP Fiori ID F0368). The unusual items are selected based on rules in SAP ERP via which any items assigned to the manager's cost center or order are treated as unusual items against various rules in SAP ERP configuration. The details for each item show the account and account assignment. To remove the item from the list, use the **Confirm** button. To forward the issue to your counterpart in the controlling department, use the red **Dispute** button.

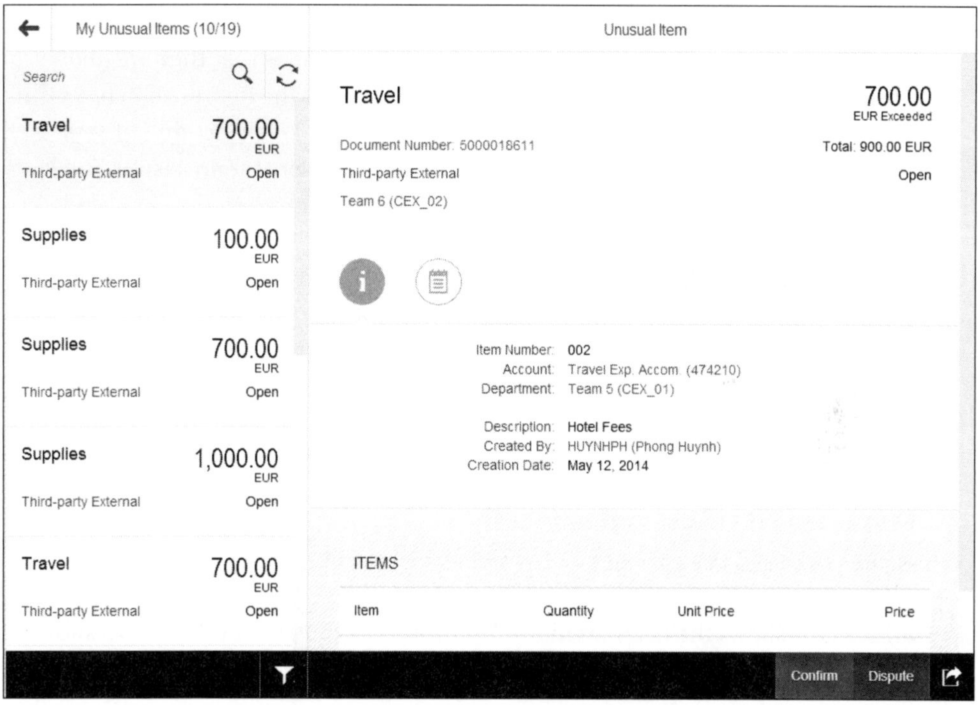

Figure 13.31 My Unusual Items

13.2.3 Net Margin Results and Profit Analysis

These applications are useful for cost center managers, but sales managers with margin responsibility need different information. The early waves of SAP Fiori offer several applications for this user group:

- Net Margin Results (SAP Fiori ID F0194) shows the net margin over time and allows you to drill down to a waterfall view of the contribution margin that shows how the total revenue is matched against the direct costs for the product and further indirect costs that result from the allocation of the various overhead blocks to the product.
- Profit Analysis (SAP Fiori ID F0684) shows the relative performance of each customer group/customer and product group/product and allows you to drill down to the detail.

Both use the information in account-based Profitability Analysis as their source (the dimensions that the sales managers are responsible for and the revenues, direct costs and indirect costs that make up the net margin).

The difference between these applications and My Spend is that they are *analytical*, meaning that instead of ABAP code being used to select the figures shown, a virtual data model like the ones we looked at for SAP HANA Live (Section 13.1.5) is used. Figure 13.32 shows how the sales manager accesses the **Net Margin Results** and **Profit Analysis** tiles from his launchpad.

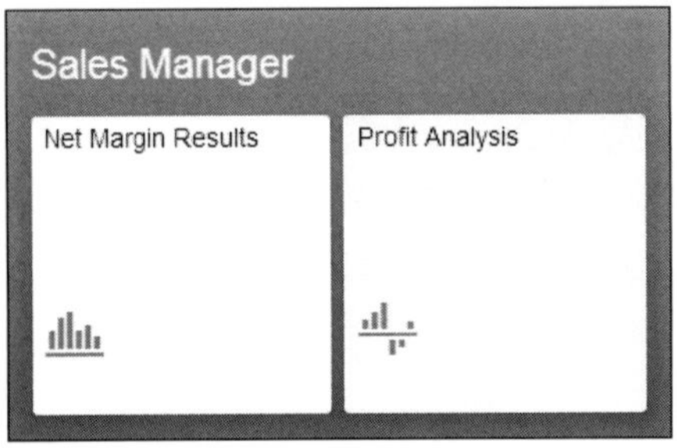

Figure 13.32 Sales Manager Role with Margin Dashboard Tiles

Figure 13.33 shows the net margin results for 2013. If you prefer to switch to show the revenue and costs for the same time frame, switch from **Net Margin Over Time** to **Revenue and Cost Over Time** in the dropdown. If you prefer to view quarters rather than months, switch from **Month** to **Quarter**.

To view the figures in detail, select a month. Figure 13.34 shows the details for March 2013. To see details, choose **View Revenue, Cost, and Net Profit**.

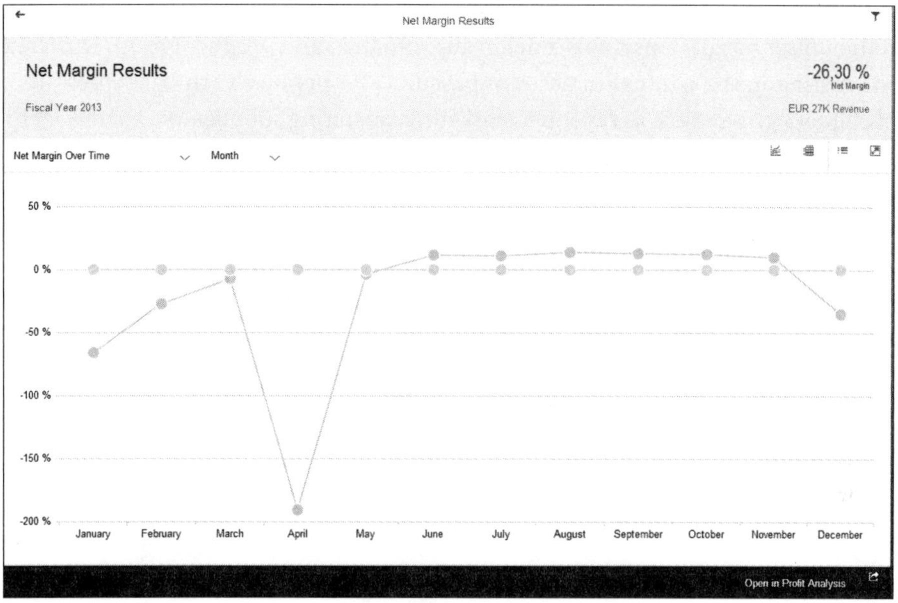

Figure 13.33 Net Margin Results over Time

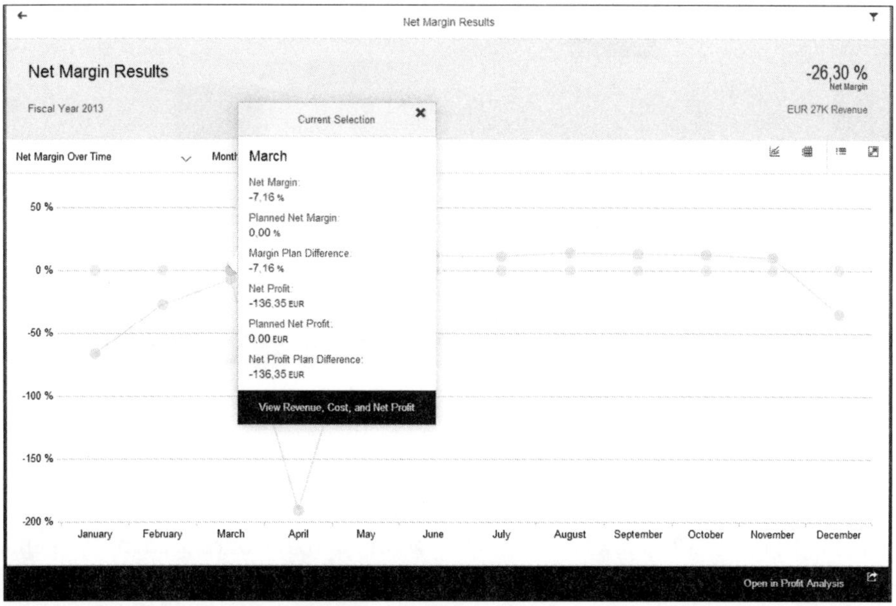

Figure 13.34 Details for March and Navigation

Figure 13.35 shows the net margin for the selected period as a waterfall graphic. You can then filter by customer, customer group, product, and product group. This view is interesting in the context of account-based CO-PA because each bar represents a cost element group, such as revenue, marketing, operating supplies, packaging, labor, and taxes. The delivered cost element group is NMA, which you should set in your user data (Transaction SU3) by entering parameter KAG and group NMA. Because your cost element groups are going to be specific to your organization, you'll need to make sure that the correct cost element groups are assigned to the **Revenue**, **Direct Costs**, and **Indirect Costs** nodes in cost element group NMA to ensure that the correct data is shown in this view.

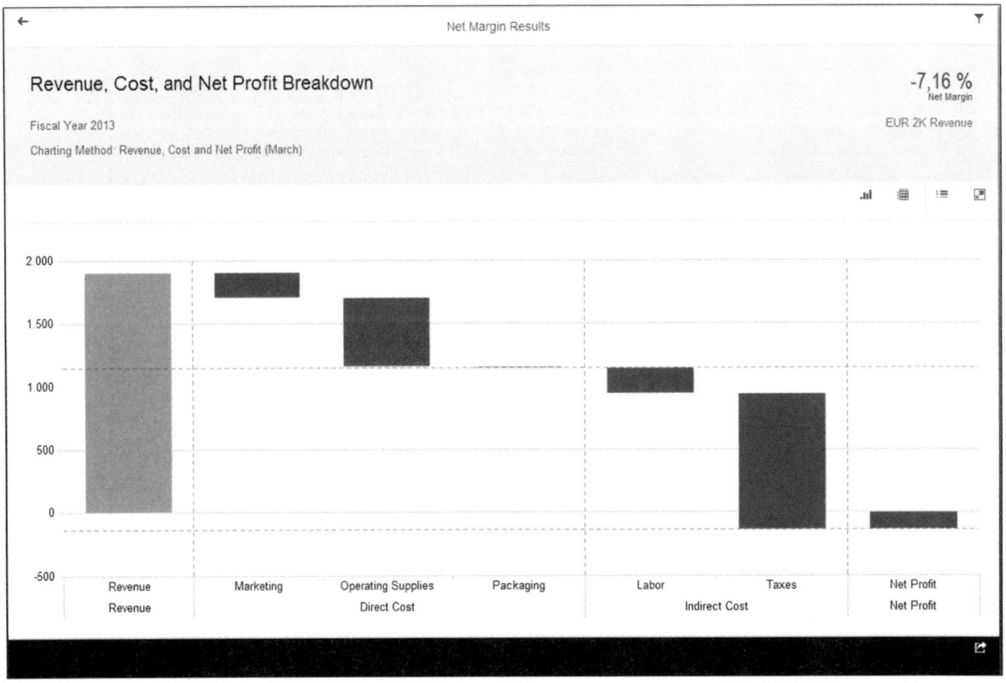

Figure 13.35 Revenue, Cost, and Net Profit Breakdown

To access the Profit Analysis app, either select the relevant tile (shown in Figure 13.32) or choose the **Open in Profit Analysis** button shown at the bottom right corner of Figure 13.34. Figure 13.36 shows a tree map view similar to the ones used in My Spend.

The product groups and customer groups in the dropdown boxes are characteristics in account-based CO-PA. Here, even more than in My Spend, you'll want to use the **Filter** icon at the top right of the screen to reduce the number of groups shown. Alternatively, you can switch between product groups and customer groups via the dropdown on the left of the screen.

Figure 13.36 Profit Analysis Application

You can then select one of the boxes and navigate to its details, as shown in Figure 13.37.

From here you can navigate to the detail for this customer by choosing **View Customers with Biggest Difference** (see Figure 13.38).

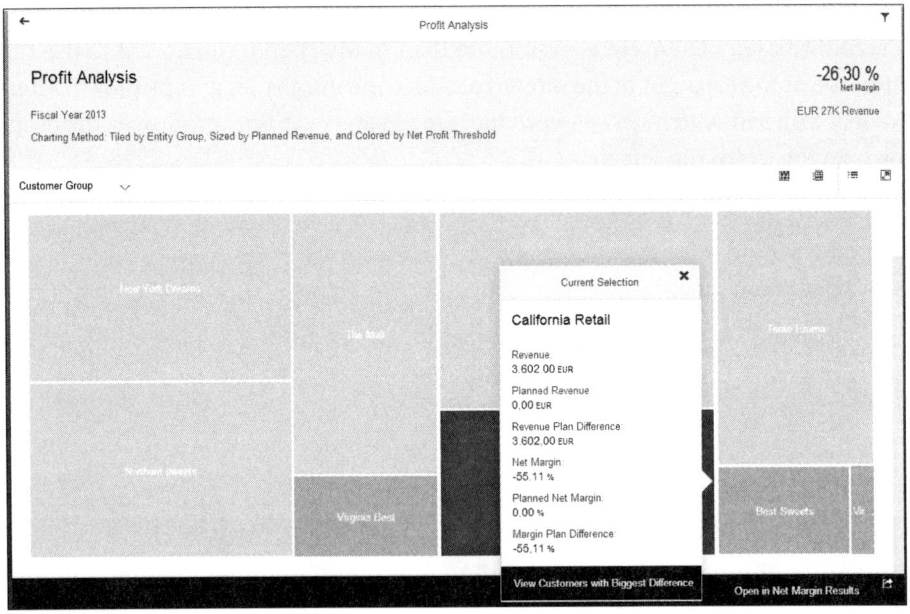

Figure 13.37 Detail and Navigation

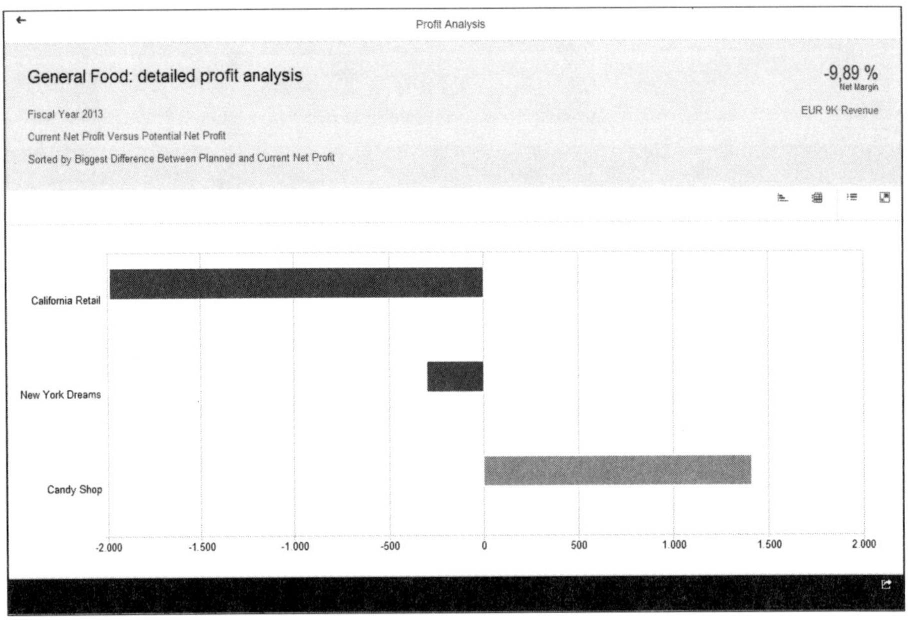

Figure 13.38 Details per Customer/Product

Net Margin Results and Profit Analysis in SAP S/4HANA

Both apps for the sales manager are built using calculation views rather than CDS views and thus will run up until SAP S/4HANA Finance 1605, but not in SAP S/4HANA 1511, 1610, or 1709.

13.3 Summary

We've now looked at the original use case for SAP HANA: the transfer of individual tables to SAP HANA to accelerate reporting and/or the period close in certain applications and the way it allows SAP to build new applications under the SAP Fiori umbrella. In the next chapter, we'll look at the more radical changes that become possible when SAP HANA becomes the primary database in the case of SAP S/4HANA.

Chapter 14
SAP S/4HANA and Controlling

This chapter walks you through the fundamental changes to Controlling with SAP S/4HANA, putting the information scattered in boxes throughout the previous chapters into its proper context. It's designed to guide you through the pending changes rather than to be a detailed guide to the conversion process.

In Chapter 13 we looked at how an SAP HANA database can accelerate the reporting and period-close activities in Controlling. In this chapter we'll look at how SAP is rebuilding the Finance applications to take advantage of the new architecture and deliver a brand-new product, SAP S/4HANA. When SAP S/4HANA was first released in March 2015, several controllers had somehow been told that CO was gone in the new world. In fact, the opposite is probably true. Controlling is very much back in the spotlight, and this chapter will guide you through what changes and what stays the same for the controller.

We began Chapter 1 by explaining how the cost elements in Controlling link with the accounts in Financial Accounting. With the introduction of the *Universal Journal* in SAP S/4HANA, this separation disappears as the cost elements are merged with the accounts, but you'll still need to know the difference between a primary cost element, a direct activity allocation, an assessment cycle, and a settlement to set up your accounts properly.

We then looked at record keeping by cost center, order, and project. The basic notion of cost assignment remains identical in SAP S/4HANA, so you won't need to change the logic of your account assignments or your workflows. What does change is that the master data assignments to company code, business area, profit center, and functional area that we looked at in Chapter 3 become the basis for multidimensional reporting out of the Universal Journal whenever a posting is made to the relevant cost center, order, or project or an allocation moves costs between these objects.

In Chapter 2 we looked at the reporting options in SAP ERP and introduced the Material Ledger and Profitability Analysis. The Material Ledger becomes compulsory in

SAP S/4HANA, but only as a way of storing inventory values in multiple currencies. Actual costing continues to be optional, along with group and profit center valuation. Profitability Analysis moves into the Universal Journal, with the CO-PA characteristics in your operating concern becoming part of the multidimensional data model that is the Universal Journal.

In Chapter 7 we walked through the steps in the period close. SAP is rethinking this process to provide real-time profitability information where possible. The first iteration for professional services companies was delivered for the SAP S/4HANA cloud project services edition and the changes incorporated into SAP S/4HANA 1610 to make these functions available to all organizations running commercial projects. This is one example of SAP's cloud-first approach, in which functions are developed first for the cloud edition and then included in the subsequent on-premise edition.

In Chapter 8 we looked at various tricks to speed up reporting in SAP ERP and the case for a move to SAP BW. With SAP S/4HANA the reporting layer becomes a *virtual data model* that brings together the transactional data in the Universal Journal, the master data attributes for the cost centers, projects, and so on, and hierarchical structures, such as the cost center hierarchies, financial statement version, cost element groups, and so on. The virtual data model can be used to prepare data for the delivered web applications, such as the trial balance and cost center plan/actual reports, but can also be used in combination with the SAP BusinessObjects tools if you prefer Microsoft Excel as your reporting frontend.

To most controllers, a report on the actual data is only useful in combination with the plan, budget, and target for that entity. With this goal in mind, SAP is rebuilding the planning applications, both for the planning processes we looked at in Chapter 5 and for the planned data on the production orders that we looked at in Chapter 6.

This chapter won't replace the many books and blogs dedicated to the various changes introduced in SAP S/4HANA, but it will hopefully help you to understand the impact of the transition and arm you for conversations about the future of controlling in your own organization.

14.1 The Universal Journal

Probably the most fundamental change for the controller is that the line item tables for Controlling (COEP), Material Ledger (MLIT), Asset Accounting (ANEP) and the General

Ledger (FAGLFLEXA) merge into a single line item table in SAP S/4HANA: the Universal Journal (ACDOCA).

The easiest way to imagine what this means is to return to the very first posting example that we looked at in Chapter 1, where an expense posting is made to a cost center. The trigger for this posting remains identical: a vendor invoice. What changes is that instead of us having a document in Financial Accounting that shows the account and the company code, plus the assignments to business area, profit center, and segment (see Chapter 1, Figure 1.4) and a separate document in Controlling that shows the cost center and the cost element (see Chapter 2, Figure 2.5), we have a single document that contains the account/cost element, the cost center, the company code, the business area, the profit center, and the segment. This document provides the basis for multidimensional reporting on all these entities, as you can see in Figure 14.1, which shows the SAP Fiori app for the trial balance (SAP Fiori ID F0966A), delivered as part of the General Ledger accountant role. The trial balance is traditionally the mainstay of Financial Accounting, but we see here a drilldown not just by company code and General Ledger account, but also by cost center. The list of available fields in the **Navigation Panel** on the left gives a sense of the new options, and we could go on to drill down by activity type, asset, business area, trading partner, or any of the other dimensions not visible in the list (alphabetical).

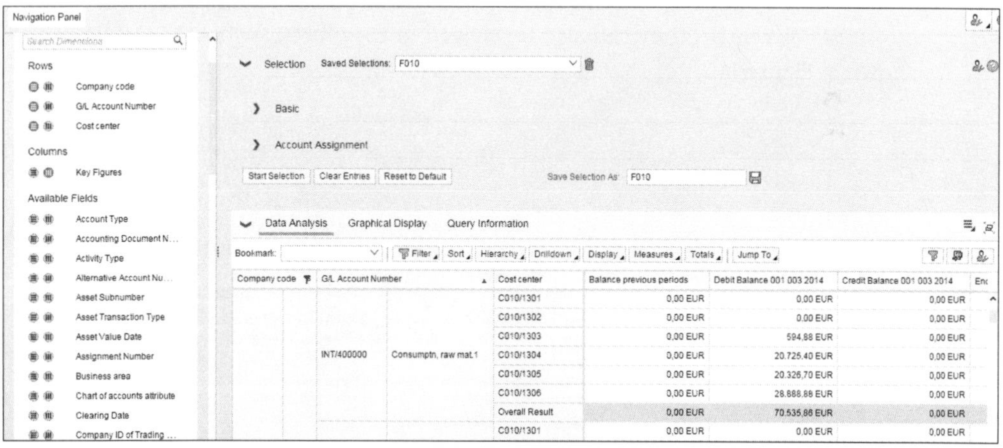

Figure 14.1 Trial Balance Showing Drilldown by Company Code, General Ledger Account, and Cost Center

What you can't see in Figure 14.1 is the different granularity between the General Ledger and Controlling. A Financial Accounting document in SAP ERP can only contain up to 999 posting lines, so many organizations summarize large documents to remove the reporting dimensions with the most variability. Therefore, the payroll document in Financial Accounting would inevitably have the cost center removed, whereas it would be included in the Controlling document. Customer invoices would typically have the material removed, but it would be included in the Profitability Analysis document. With SAP S/4HANA, the Universal Journal can have up to 999,999 posting lines, so such deliberate mismatches are no longer necessary and there is no longer any need to reconcile the *primary cost postings* that we looked at in Chapter 2 against the General Ledger. The Universal Journal is the single source of truth for such postings, and the assignment to cost center, order, or project simply extends the posting line in the General Ledger to include the account assignment.

This leaves the *secondary cost postings* for activity allocation and settlement that we looked at in Chapter 6 and for assessment, indirect activity allocation, and overhead calculation that we looked at in Chapter 7. These originate in Controlling and typically have one or more senders and one or more receivers, but a single secondary cost element that depends on the CO business transaction (assessment, settlement, and so on). From a CO point of view, little changes here in terms of how the transaction works, but the secondary cost element becomes a General Ledger account and such postings show up in all the Financial Accounting reports, though they always balance to zero. In SAP ERP, such documents would only have been visible in the CO reports, but in SAP S/4HANA they can also be viewed in FI reports, such as the trial balance, shown in Figure 14.2.

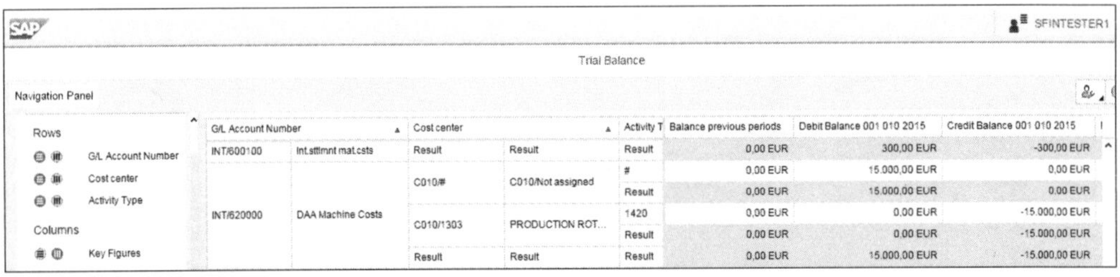

G/L Account Number		Cost center		Activity T	Balance previous periods	Debit Balance 001 010 2015	Credit Balance 001 010 2015
INT/600100	Int.sttlmnt mat.csts	Result	Result	Result	0,00 EUR	300,00 EUR	-300,00 EUR
INT/620000	DAA Machine Costs	C010/#	C010/Not assigned	#	0,00 EUR	15.000,00 EUR	0,00 EUR
				Result	0,00 EUR	15.000,00 EUR	0,00 EUR
		C010/1303	PRODUCTION ROT...	1420	0,00 EUR	0,00 EUR	-15.000,00 EUR
				Result	0,00 EUR	0,00 EUR	-15.000,00 EUR
		Result	Result	Result	0,00 EUR	15.000,00 EUR	-15.000,00 EUR

Figure 14.2 Trial Balance Showing Drilldown by General Ledger Account, Cost Center, and Activity Type

In this example, the General Ledger account is the secondary cost element for an activity allocation. The sender is production cost center 1420 and the activity type is machine hours. You can see that the offsetting entry for the cost center is # (unassigned) because the receiver was a production order in this example. Of course, we could continue by using the **Navigation Panel** to pull those production orders into the trial balance that have received machine hours from the production cost center.

Although the sender-receiver relationship in the allocation determines which lines exist in the posting, it's important to understand the assignment of the senders and receivers to company codes, business areas, functional areas, profit centers, and segments because this determines whether there is a shift among any of these reporting dimensions during the posting. In reporting this will lead to an update of the partner company code, partner business area, partner functional area, and so on. This allows you to track the way your costs move through the various functional areas within your organization until they can finally be associated with a sale or capitalized.

Plenty of accountants are excited about these changes, but there are also controllers who see no reason to go hunting for "their" data in the trial balance. If you're happy with the reporting options we showed in Chapter 2, you can carry on using transactions such as KSB1 (cost center line items) as shown in Figure 14.3. Here we see the line items for the cost centers that we looked at in the drilldown in Figure 14.1 in a classic cost center line item report. Notice that the General Ledger account has been translated back into a cost element. Behind the scenes a *compatibility view* is converting the information in the Universal Journal back into the structure of the Controlling line items (COEP) so that you can move forward gradually even as your organization makes the decision to convert to SAP S/4HANA. 14

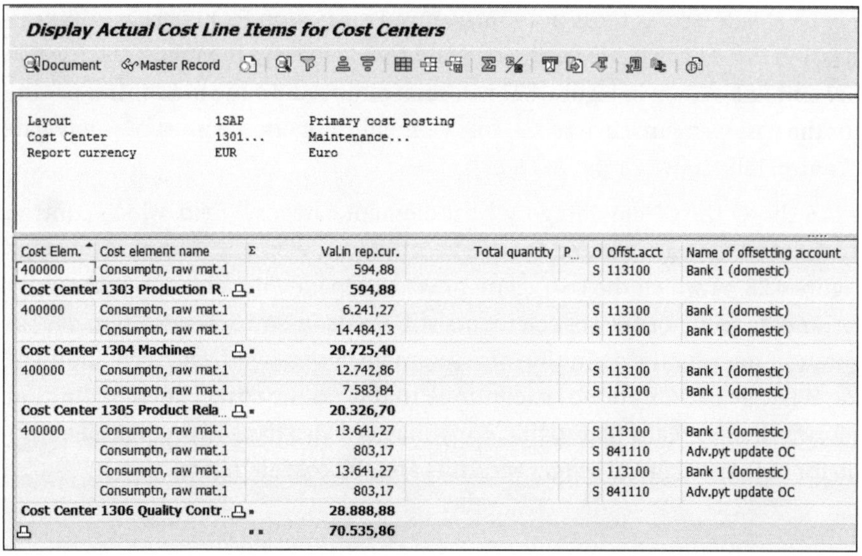

Layout	1SAP	Primary cost posting
Cost Center	1301...	Maintenance...
Report currency	EUR	Euro

Cost Elem.	Cost element name	Σ	Val.in rep.cur.	Total quantity	P...	O	Offst.acct	Name of offsetting account
400000	Consumptn, raw mat.1		594,88			S	113100	Bank 1 (domestic)
Cost Center 1303 Production R...			**594,88**					
400000	Consumptn, raw mat.1		6.241,27			S	113100	Bank 1 (domestic)
	Consumptn, raw mat.1		14.484,13			S	113100	Bank 1 (domestic)
Cost Center 1304 Machines			**20.725,40**					
400000	Consumptn, raw mat.1		12.742,86			S	113100	Bank 1 (domestic)
	Consumptn, raw mat.1		7.583,84			S	113100	Bank 1 (domestic)
Cost Center 1305 Product Rela...			**20.326,70**					
400000	Consumptn, raw mat.1		13.641,27			S	113100	Bank 1 (domestic)
	Consumptn, raw mat.1		803,17			S	841110	Adv.pyt update OC
	Consumptn, raw mat.1		13.641,27			S	113100	Bank 1 (domestic)
	Consumptn, raw mat.1		803,17			S	841110	Adv.pyt update OC
Cost Center 1306 Quality Contr...			**28.888,88**					
			70.535,86					

Figure 14.3 Sample Cost Center Line Items

You can find more details about the conversion process and how the system merges the General Ledger and the controlling documents in SAP Notes 2270333 (S4TWL—Data Model Changes in FIN), 2270339 (S4TWL—General Ledger) and 2270404 (S4TWL—Technical Changes in Controlling). SAP also offers a conversion process to migrate the separate documents created in SAP ERP to the Universal Journal. Because the shift from 999 posting lines in table BSEG to 999,999 posting lines in table ACDOCA also raises many questions, consult SAP Note 2591291 (S/4HANA—Error F5 727 when Posting via Accounting Interface) for details.

14.1.1 Merging Accounts and Cost Elements

What you see in Figure 14.1 and Figure 14.3 is the same account (400000) acting as both an account and a cost element. To display the account/cost element, use Transaction FS00 or go to **Accounting • Financial Accounting • General Ledger • Master Records • GL Accounts • Individual Processing • Centrally** (see Figure 14.4).

Accounts for Primary Cost Elements

If you compare Figure 14.4 with Figure 4.27 in Chapter 4, you'll see a new field called **Account Type** that specifies that this General Ledger account is also a primary cost element. During the conversion to SAP S/4HANA, all primary cost elements and revenue elements are merged with their sister accounts; following the conversion, you will only be able to access these accounts using Transaction FS00 because Transactions KA01 to KA03 have been deactivated and removed from the menu and the **Edit Cost Element** link shown in Figure 4.27 has been removed. To see the control parameters for the cost element, such as the cost element category, we must now navigate to the **Control** tab, shown in Figure 14.4.

Figure 14.5 shows the **CElem Category** (cost element category) field, which controls what types of posting are allowed for this account/cost element. Compare this view with Figure 4.28, in which the cost element was a separate data record. Technically, the master data table for the cost elements still exists in SAP S/4HANA because the configuration steps for the definition of assessment cycles, overhead calculation, settlement, WIP calculation, and so on continue to rely on the cost element definition. Going forward, this means that to make any master data changes you'll need authorization for both the General Ledger accounts and the cost elements.

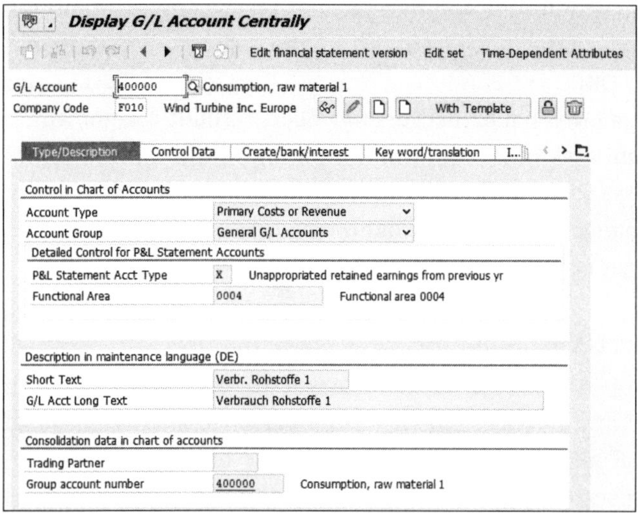

Figure 14.4 General Ledger Account for Primary Cost Element

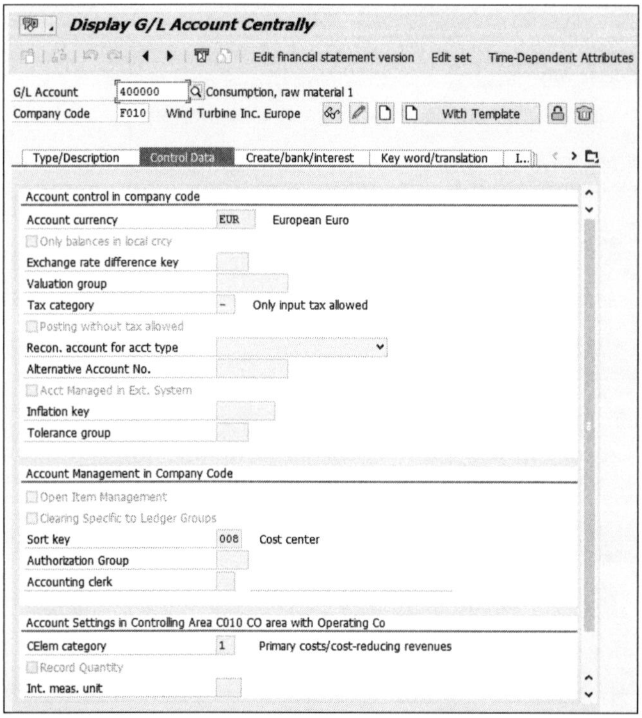

Figure 14.5 Cost Element Category for Primary Cost Elements

One change is that the old **Default Acct Assgmnt** (default account assignment) tab shown in Figure 4.28 is gone, so the only way to set up the default account assignments is to use Transaction OKB9 or follow the menu path **Controlling • Cost Center Accounting • Actual Postings • Manual Actual Postings • Edit Account Assignment**. If you included default account assignments in your cost element master data in SAP ERP, the conversion process creates entries in table TKA3A for these default assignments. The other major change is that the accounts are not time-dependent; this means that you can no longer retire cost elements by adjusting the **Valid To** date.

Accounts for Secondary Cost Elements

Figure 14.6 shows the master data for the General Ledger account we looked at in Figure 14.2. When we looked at such cost elements in Chapter 3, we said that they had no counterpart in Financial Accounting, but with the move to SAP S/4HANA an account is created for each secondary cost element during the conversion process and assigned to **Account Type**: **Secondary Costs**. Again, the only way to access this account is using Transaction FS00 because Transaction KA06 (Create Secondary Cost Element) has also been deactivated and removed from the menu.

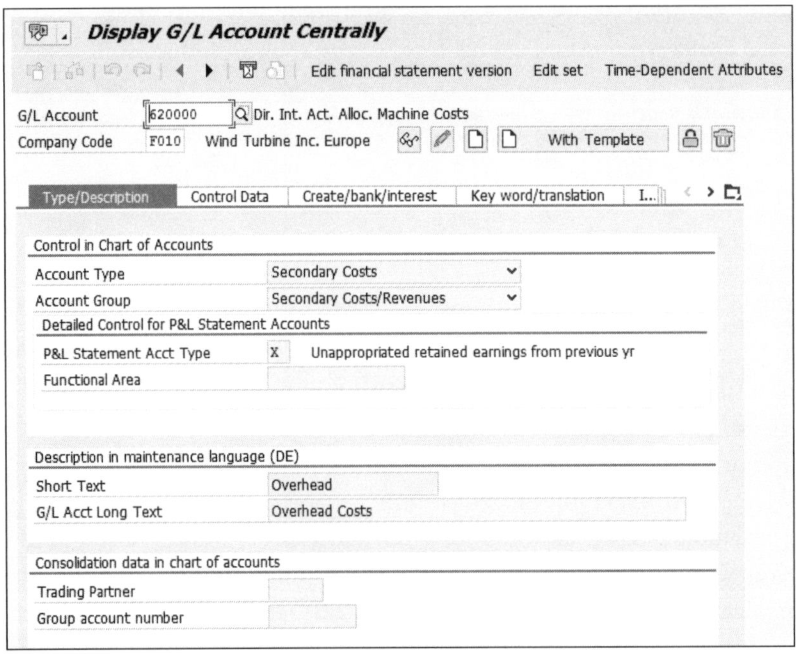

Figure 14.6 General Ledger Account for Secondary Cost Element

The **Control Data** for secondary cost elements is substantially simpler than for primary cost elements, with the focus being on **CElem Category** (cost element category). Cost element category 43 for internal activity allocation in Figure 14.7 is reassuringly familiar. What this means is that if you use a secondary cost element as part of an activity allocation (as here), an assessment cycle, a settlement, or an overhead calculation, there is no change to the basic value flow in Controlling. All that's changed is that the secondary cost element is recorded as a General Ledger account in the Universal Journal. What happens during posting is that you are creating an accounting document rather than a controlling document and you may want to have your implementation team set up a special document type for each CO business transaction, rather than having them all write a journal entry under the default document type SA (General Ledger posting). Now you will no longer need reconciliation accounts like the one we showed in Chapter 4, Figure 4.29 because all updates are recorded under the cost element/account and there is no longer a reconciliation ledger (classic General Ledger) or real-time CO-FI integration (SAP General Ledger).

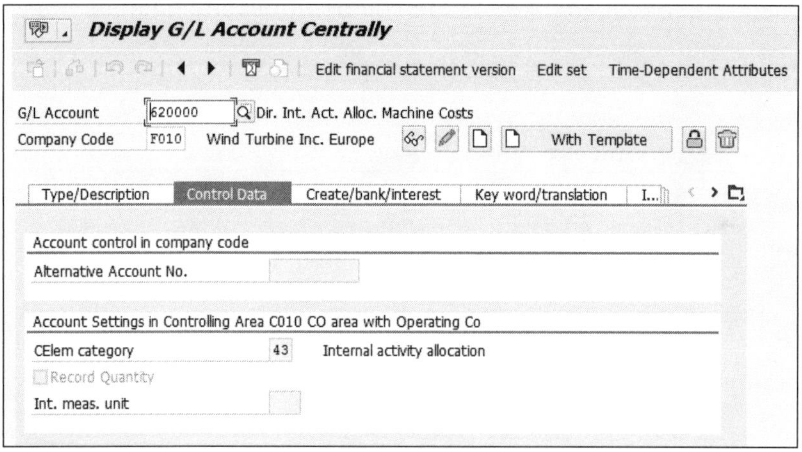

Figure 14.7 Cost Element Category for Secondary Cost Element

You can find more details about the conversion process and how the system merges the accounts and cost elements in SAP Note 2270419 (S4TWL—Account/Cost Element). Bear in mind that this is a technical note, and make sure that you also understand how your General Ledger accounts are used in consolidation, reporting, and any other applications that read accounts because they may also be affected by the conversion.

14.1.2 Cost Centers, Orders and Projects

In terms of the posting logic in SAP S/4HANA, everything we discussed in Chapter 1 and Chapter 6 continues to hold and you can leave your account assignment logic and the field status groups unchanged (except for the default account assignment that we mentioned in the previous section). You can also leave any validations and substitutions that manipulate the account assignments in the documents unchanged. The call-up points continue to be 0001 for line items from Financial Accounting (primary costs) and 0002 for internal CO postings (secondary costs). The main change is simply the way that the cost information is stored. Figure 14.8 shows the part of the Universal Journal (table ACDOCA) that includes the cost center and the elements derived from the cost center master record during posting—the profit center, the functional area, the business area, and the segment—and the partner objects derived during the secondary postings. This table provides the basis for the trial balance that we looked at in Figure 14.1. During migration these fields are filled automatically by merging what was the FI document and what was the CO document.

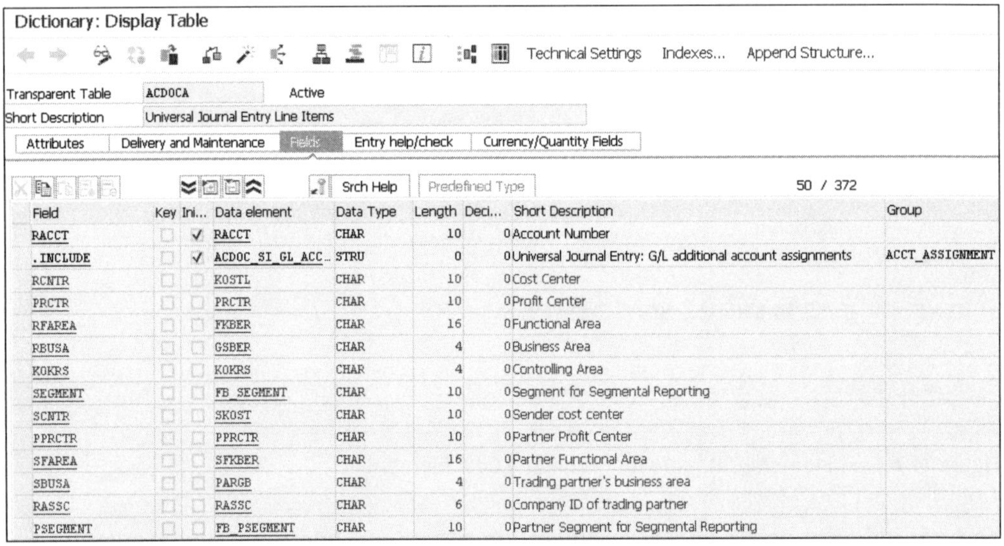

Field	Key	Ini...	Data element	Data Type	Length	Deci...	Short Description	Group
RACCT		✓	RACCT	CHAR	10	0	Account Number	
.INCLUDE		✓	ACDOC_SI_GL_ACC..	STRU	0	0	Universal Journal Entry: G/L additional account assignments	ACCT_ASSIGNMENT
RCNTR			KOSTL	CHAR	10	0	Cost Center	
PRCTR			PRCTR	CHAR	10	0	Profit Center	
RFAREA			FKBER	CHAR	16	0	Functional Area	
RBUSA			GSBER	CHAR	4	0	Business Area	
KOKRS			KOKRS	CHAR	4	0	Controlling Area	
SEGMENT			FB_SEGMENT	CHAR	10	0	Segment for Segmental Reporting	
SCNTR			SKOST	CHAR	10	0	Sender cost center	
PPRCTR			PPRCTR	CHAR	10	0	Partner Profit Center	
SFAREA			SFKBER	CHAR	16	0	Partner Functional Area	
SBUSA			PARGB	CHAR	4	0	Trading partner's business area	
RASSC			RASSC	CHAR	6	0	Company ID of trading partner	
PSEGMENT			FB_PSEGMENT	CHAR	10	0	Partner Segment for Segmental Reporting	

Figure 14.8 Universal Journal Showing General Ledger Account Assignments

If we scroll further down the table, we come to the other CO account assignments: the order number, the Work Breakdown Structure (WBS), the network, the business process, and the operation, as shown in Figure 14.9. It is at this point that some controllers will feel uneasy with the multidimensional model because in Chapter 6, Section

6.4.1 we said that any cost posting can only have one genuine cost assignment (and potentially additional statistical assignments). This rule continues to apply in SAP S/4HANA, and to ensure that the reports work correctly, the Universal Journal includes two new fields—ACCAS (account assignment) and ACCASTY (object type)—to identify the *real* postings that update the cost center, order, project, and so on. The real posting can be identified by the entry in the ACCASTY field, so a genuine posting to a cost center with an additional statistical posting to an order will update the real account assignment as ACCASTY KS (for cost center), but in the Universal Journal there will be an entry for both the cost center number and the order number. You won't find any statistical postings in the drilldowns in the trial balance or profit center and market segment reports to avoid showing the same costs twice. However, the standard reports for cost center, order, and project reporting include a flag so that you can easily identify and display statistical postings.

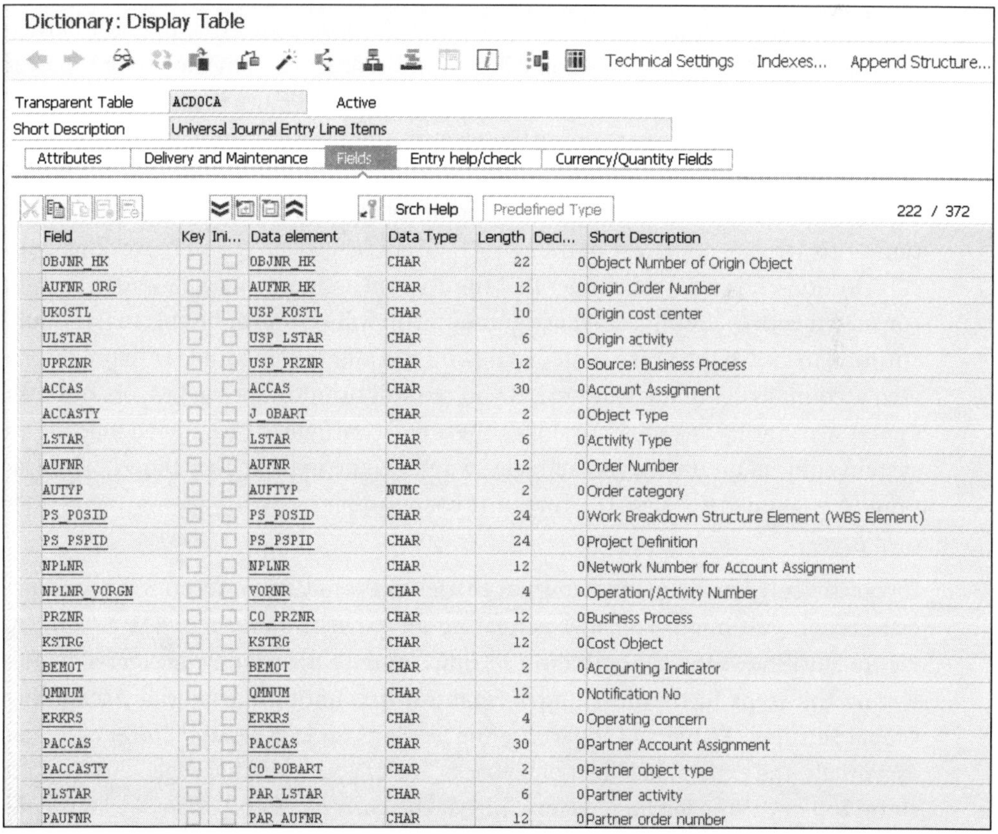

Field	Key	Ini...	Data element	Data Type	Length	Deci...	Short Description
OBJNR_HK	☐	☐	OBJNR_HK	CHAR	22	0	Object Number of Origin Object
AUFNR_ORG	☐	☐	AUFNR_HK	CHAR	12	0	Origin Order Number
UKOSTL	☐	☐	USP_KOSTL	CHAR	10	0	Origin cost center
ULSTAR	☐	☐	USP_LSTAR	CHAR	6	0	Origin activity
UPRZNR	☐	☐	USP_PRZNR	CHAR	12	0	Source: Business Process
ACCAS	☐	☐	ACCAS	CHAR	30	0	Account Assignment
ACCASTY	☐	☐	J_OBART	CHAR	2	0	Object Type
LSTAR	☐	☐	LSTAR	CHAR	6	0	Activity Type
AUFNR	☐	☐	AUFNR	CHAR	12	0	Order Number
AUTYP	☐	☐	AUFTYP	NUMC	2	0	Order category
PS_POSID	☐	☐	PS_POSID	CHAR	24	0	Work Breakdown Structure Element (WBS Element)
PS_PSPID	☐	☐	PS_PSPID	CHAR	24	0	Project Definition
NPLNR	☐	☐	NPLNR	CHAR	12	0	Network Number for Account Assignment
NPLNR_VORGN	☐	☐	VORNR	CHAR	4	0	Operation/Activity Number
PRZNR	☐	☐	CO_PRZNR	CHAR	12	0	Business Process
KSTRG	☐	☐	KSTRG	CHAR	12	0	Cost Object
BEMOT	☐	☐	BEMOT	CHAR	2	0	Accounting Indicator
QMNUM	☐	☐	QMNUM	CHAR	12	0	Notification No
ERKRS	☐	☐	ERKRS	CHAR	4	0	Operating concern
PACCAS	☐	☐	PACCAS	CHAR	30	0	Partner Account Assignment
PACCASTY	☐	☐	CO_POBART	CHAR	2	0	Partner object type
PLSTAR	☐	☐	PAR_LSTAR	CHAR	6	0	Partner activity
PAUFNR	☐	☐	PAR_AUFNR	CHAR	12	0	Partner order number

Figure 14.9 Universal Journal Showing CO Account Assignments

Along with the separate controlling document, SAP S/4HANA has also removed the totals records (tables COSP and COSS) used in Controlling. For a transition period, a core data service (CDS) view exists to read the data from the Universal Journal and present it in the structure of the old tables to ensure that existing transactions and reports continue to run, especially those written by partners and customers. SAP is gradually rewriting all programs that read from the totals records to select directly from the Universal Journal. To learn more, refer to SAP Note 579584 (Recommendations for Financial Reporting in SAP S/4HANA). You can continue to use your old reports (see Figure 14.3) immediately after the conversion, but start to put a plan in place to move to the new reports, such as the trial balance shown in Figure 14.1, to get the full benefit from the data model switch.

14.1.3 Profit Centers, Functional Areas, and Segments

The posting logic in SAP S/4HANA remains essentially unchanged, as does the derivation of the profit centers, functional areas, and segments from the related master data as we discussed in Chapter 3. What changes is the structure shown in Figure 14.8, in which the posting line containing the account and the cost center also contains the profit center, the functional area, and the segment if the master data is maintained correctly. There is no longer a requirement for separate ledgers to store this information or to activate scenarios in the SAP ERP General Ledger. If you're working with substitutions, however, remember that the account assignments will need to remain consistent with the profit center assignment. You will no longer be able to use a substitution to switch the profit center so that it is no longer compatible with the associated account assignment. However, if you are still running Special Ledgers or Profit Center Accounting as a separate ledger, these will continue to be updated following a system conversion unless you actively switch off the update. This allows organizations to migrate to the new structures and change their reporting approaches at their own pace.

If you currently create manual journal entries in Profit Center Accounting or a Special Ledger, you might consider activating an *extension ledger* in SAP S/4HANA. Figure 14.10 shows the configuration settings for extension ledger JS created by following the steps in the IMG under **Financial Accounting • Financial Accounting Global Settings • Ledgers • Ledger • Define Settings for Ledgers and Currency Types**. Essentially, the extension ledger piggybacks one of your existing ledgers, so it might sit on top of OL (the leading ledger), inherit the currencies and other settings from this ledger, and record any differences that are not considered part of this ledger, such as a reclassification of profit center expenses or top-line adjustments for consolidation. The update can be made using Transaction FBO1L (for ledger-specific postings in the General Ledger) or Transaction KB11N or KB41N (for ledger-specific CO postings).

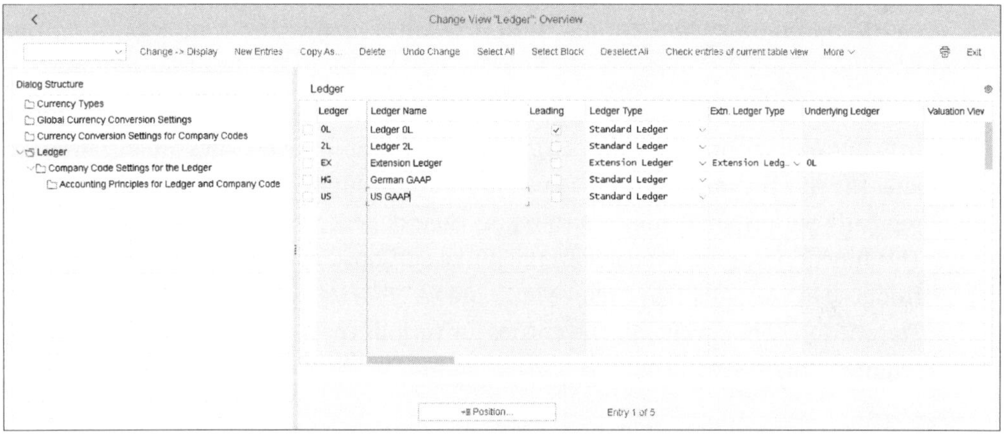

Figure 14.10 Configuration Settings for Extension Ledger

14.1.4 Profitability Analysis (CO-PA)

With SAP S/4HANA, the various characteristics in an existing operating concern become part of the Universal Journal. Controllers coming from SAP ERP still talk about account-based Profitability Analysis (CO-PA), but the correct term is *Profitability Analysis in the Universal Journal*, which gives a better impression of the way the characteristics from the operating concern are simply included in the Universal Journal, as shown in Figure 14.11. This ensures that the revenue per product or customer is determined by selecting from the same documents as the revenue per company code or profit center. Essentially, we're looking at different aggregations of the same data: the Universal Journal provides the single source of truth.

The fields in the upper part of the screen are available in every operating concern—billing type, sales organization, distribution channel, division, product, material group, and customer group—and are derived from the sales document as in SAP ERP, as is the material number, which is in a different part of the table. The fields in the lower part of the screen are specific to the sample operating concern used in this implementation; again, you can continue to use whatever derivation logic you implemented for your characteristics in SAP ERP. During conversion, the system will read the characteristics in your operating concern and create new columns in the Universal Journal for those that are specific to your organization. It makes sense to activate account-based Profitability Analysis from the word go to ensure that your revenues and costs of goods sold are being assigned to the most granular account assignments, rather than being aggregated to higher-level entities such as company codes and profit centers, because it isn't possible to split these aggregated entries later.

What the Universal Journal gives us initially is what we used to call the *as posted* view in CO-PA (see Chapter 2, Section 2.6). However, it's common for sales organizations to alter the way they segment their customers and group their products over time and regularly perform *realignments* to report their data according to the new structure. This function was not available in the initial editions of SAP S/4HANA but was reintroduced in SAP S/4HANA Finance 1605 and SAP S/4HANA 1610, so you can again use Transaction KEND to change the entries for various characteristics as your reporting requirements evolve.

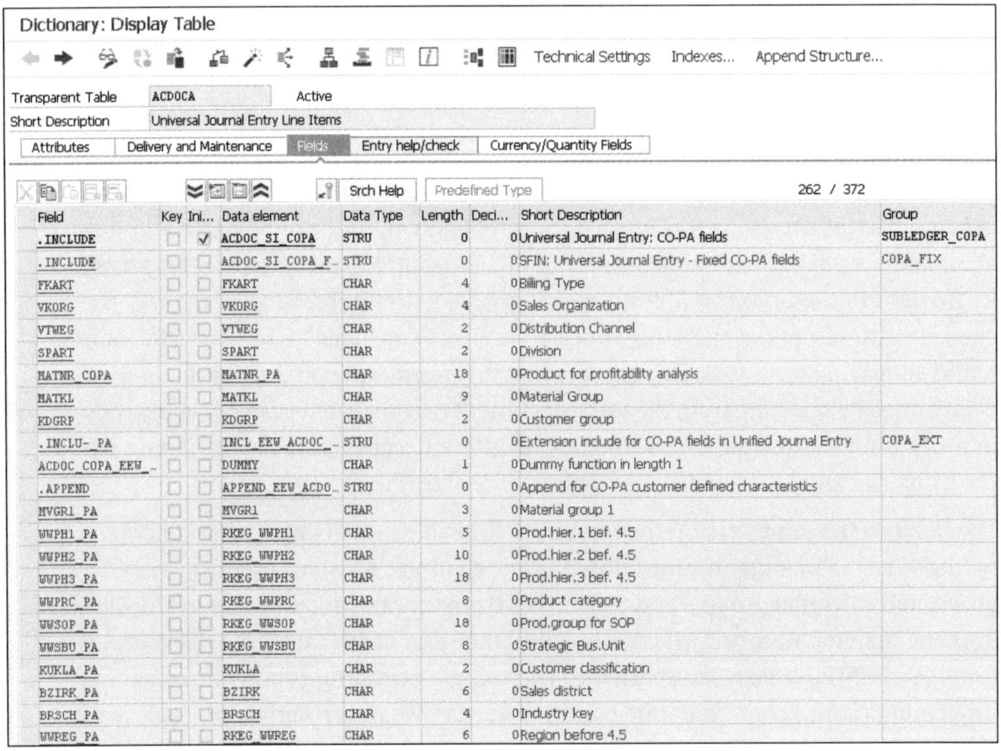

Field	Key	Ini...	Data element	Data Type	Length	Deci...	Short Description	Group
.INCLUDE	☐	☑	ACDOC_SI_COPA	STRU	0	0	Universal Journal Entry: CO-PA fields	SUBLEDGER_COPA
.INCLUDE	☐	☐	ACDOC_SI_COPA_F...	STRU	0	0	SFIN: Universal Journal Entry - Fixed CO-PA fields	COPA_FIX
FKART	☐	☐	FKART	CHAR	4	0	Billing Type	
VKORG	☐	☐	VKORG	CHAR	4	0	Sales Organization	
VTWEG	☐	☐	VTWEG	CHAR	2	0	Distribution Channel	
SPART	☐	☐	SPART	CHAR	2	0	Division	
MATNR_COPA	☐	☐	MATNR_PA	CHAR	18	0	Product for profitability analysis	
MATKL	☐	☐	MATKL	CHAR	9	0	Material Group	
KDGRP	☐	☐	KDGRP	CHAR	2	0	Customer group	
.INCLU-_PA	☐	☐	INCL_EEW_ACDOC_...	STRU	0	0	Extension include for CO-PA fields in Unified Journal Entry	COPA_EXT
ACDOC_COPA_EEW_...	☐	☐	DUMMY	CHAR	1	0	Dummy function in length 1	
.APPEND	☐	☐	APPEND_EEW_ACDO...	STRU	0	0	Append for CO-PA customer defined characteristics	
MVGR1_PA	☐	☐	MVGR1	CHAR	3	0	Material group 1	
WWPH1_PA	☐	☐	RKEG_WWPH1	CHAR	5	0	Prod.hier.1 bef. 4.5	
WWPH2_PA	☐	☐	RKEG_WWPH2	CHAR	10	0	Prod.hier.2 bef. 4.5	
WWPH3_PA	☐	☐	RKEG_WWPH3	CHAR	18	0	Prod.hier.3 bef. 4.5	
WWPRC_PA	☐	☐	RKEG_WWPRC	CHAR	8	0	Product category	
WWSOP_PA	☐	☐	RKEG_WWSOP	CHAR	18	0	Prod.group for SOP	
WWSBU_PA	☐	☐	RKEG_WWSBU	CHAR	8	0	Strategic Bus.Unit	
KUKLA_PA	☐	☐	KUKLA	CHAR	2	0	Customer classification	
BZIRK_PA	☐	☐	BZIRK	CHAR	6	0	Sales district	
BRSCH_PA	☐	☐	BRSCH	CHAR	4	0	Industry key	
WWREG_PA	☐	☐	RKEG_WWREG	CHAR	6	0	Region before 4.5	

Figure 14.11 Universal Journal Showing CO-PA Characteristics

From Value Fields to Accounts

If you are starting an SAP S/4HANA project and haven't used Profitability Analysis in the Universal Journal until now, start by looking at the value fields in your existing operating concern and understanding how you calculate contribution margins to understand what will potentially change going forward when the postings are made to accounts/cost elements rather than to value fields. The following elements are included in Profitability Analysis in the Universal Journal:

- **Revenues**
  Normally the revenues are derived from the billing document and assigned to accounts/cost elements using SD account determination. In many cases, it won't be a huge leap to switch from value fields to accounts. However, be aware that the approach for the handling of statistical sales conditions has changed and these are only supported from SAP S/4HANA 1809.
- **Cost of goods sold**
  With costing-based CO-PA, the cost of goods sold is recorded in the invoice using the valuation function, as you saw in Chapter 6. With Profitability Analysis in the Universal Journal, the cost of goods sold account becomes a primary cost element and the costs are captured at the time of delivery. It's also possible to split the cost of goods sold in accordance with the various cost components in the underlying cost estimate.
- **Order and project settlement**
  You shouldn't need to change the way you settle overhead orders and projects to Profitability Analysis initially. The main difference will be that reporting is based on the secondary cost element for settlement, so make sure that your chart of accounts provides sufficient granularity for your needs. However, later in the chapter we will introduce an option to derive the profitability characteristics at the time of posting so that you no longer need to settle. Bear in mind that this will mean that such expenses remain primary in nature (such as travel costs charged to a project).
- **Settlement of production variances**
  You will need to make minor changes if you settle production variances to Profitability Analysis because it's now possible to split the production variances in accordance with the variance categories for the production orders. You'll need new accounts to report these variances.
- **Cost center allocation**
  Likewise, you shouldn't need to change the way you allocate cost center costs to

Profitability Analysis. The main difference will be that reporting is based on the secondary cost element for assessment, so make sure that your chart of accounts provides sufficient granularity for your needs. It's also worth checking what drivers you currently use for your allocations. You may also find that for simple assessment cycles with only one receiver, you can derive the CO-PA characteristics at the time of posting.

- **Top-down distribution**
  As for assessment cycles, take a good look at the drivers you use for cost distribution. If you split bonuses based on the relative revenues for the different product groups, you won't have a problem because the revenues are attached to accounts already. If you split freight costs based on the statistical freight costs for the different products, you may have a problem because statistical costs for market segments are not yet available in the Universal Journal.

You'll find a more detailed description in SAP Note 2349278 (S4TWL—Profitability Analysis). If you find functional gaps as you draw up your list, remember that you don't have to stop using costing-based Profitability Analysis with SAP S/4HANA. Consider running the two approaches in parallel for a transition period, to give you historical data for the period immediately prior to the conversion, but don't forget that table CE1XXXX for costing-based profitability analysis typically contains millions of entries when you are sizing your SAP S/4HANA system.

Splitting the Cost of Goods Sold

When we walked through the order-to-cash process in Chapter 6, we showed the way the invoice document is transferred to costing-based Profitability Analysis and provides information on the invoiced quantity, the revenue, the total cost of goods sold, and the cost components for raw materials, fixed and variable labor costs, fixed and variable machine costs, and so on. The delivery document was not recorded in costing-based Profitability Analysis.

In SAP S/4HANA the cost of goods sold is recorded in Profitability Analysis with the delivery, meaning that it's always in sync with financial accounts, while the revenue continues to be recorded with the invoice. In SAP ERP, only the total cost of goods sold was captured in account-based Profitability Analysis, but with SAP S/4HANA you can configure the system to split the cost of goods sold in accordance with the weighting of the cost components in the standard cost estimate for the material sold.

Figure 14.12 shows the accounting document for a sales delivery, in which the initial posting was from **Finished Goods Inventory** to **Cost of Goods Sold** (the first two lines of the document). The cost of goods sold posting is then reversed (the third line of the document) and split to accounts for **COGS—Labor**, **COGS—Material**, **COGS—Overhead**, and **COGS—Others** in accordance with the relative weighting of the standard costs for each cost component.

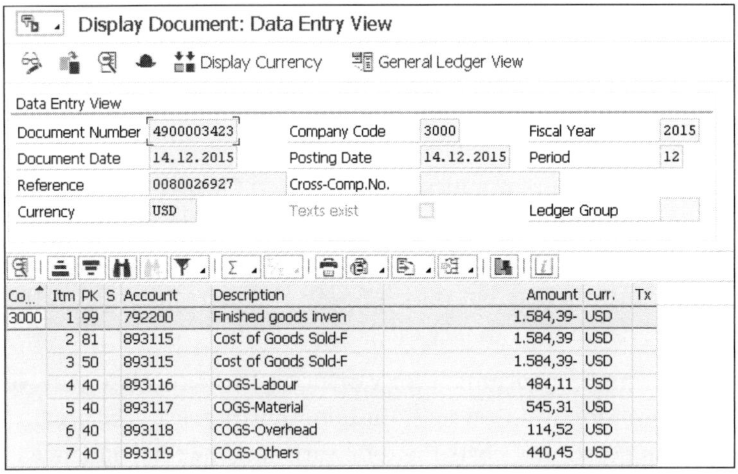

Display Document: Data Entry View

Display Currency | General Ledger View

Data Entry View

Document Number	4900003423	Company Code	3000	Fiscal Year	2015
Document Date	14.12.2015	Posting Date	14.12.2015	Period	12
Reference	0080026927	Cross-Comp.No.			
Currency	USD	Texts exist		Ledger Group	

Co...	Itm	PK	S	Account	Description	Amount	Curr.	Tx
3000	1	99		792200	Finished goods inven	1.584,39-	USD	
	2	81		893115	Cost of Goods Sold-F	1.584,39	USD	
	3	50		893115	Cost of Goods Sold-F	1.584,39-	USD	
	4	40		893116	COGS-Labour	484,11	USD	
	5	40		893117	COGS-Material	545,31	USD	
	6	40		893118	COGS-Overhead	114,52	USD	
	7	40		893119	COGS-Others	440,45	USD	

Figure 14.12 Accounting Document Showing Cost of Goods Sold Split

The standard configuration for this process takes the cost of goods sold account to which the delivery is posted (893115 in our example) and breaks out the costs in accordance with a cost-splitting profile defined in Customizing. The default cost estimate used to weight the different cost components is the standard cost estimate used for inventory valuation, but from SAP S/4HANA 1709 you can use BAdI `FCO_COGS_SPLIT_BASIS` to select a different cost estimate, such as the auxiliary cost component split if you prefer to use the primary cost component split as the basis for the weighting.

If things go wrong and the system is unable to find a cost estimate to explain the delivery, it will post only the first two lines in Figure 14.12. From SAP S/4HANA 1709 there is a reposting function that will allow you to create the additional lines later when you've fixed the error. You'll find more details in SAP Note 2512013 (Subsequent Posting of Cost of Goods Sold in S/4HANA). If you can't find what's gone wrong, use the trace functions to understand what might have gone wrong and repost if necessary, as described in SAP Note 2515707 (SAP S/4HANA Finance—Trace Function for Splitting Cost of Goods Sold).

Actual Cost Component Split in SAP S/4HANA

If you've been working with actual costing and using the revaluation function (Transaction KE27) to pull the changes to the actual costs into Profitability Analysis, please be aware that the update of the cost component split with the results of the actual costing run will be delivered with SAP S/4HANA 1809.

Splitting the Production Variances

When we looked at the settlement of production variances in Chapter 7, we showed how variance categories on the production orders can be settled to costing-based Profitability Analysis. In SAP ERP, only the total production variances were captured in account-based Profitability Analysis, but with SAP S/4HANA you can configure the system to split the total variances by variance categories.

Figure 14.13 shows the accounting document for variance settlement. Note that we have the same mechanism as for the COGS split. The initial posting clears the production order of its remaining costs and posts the total variance. The total variance is then reversed (posting line three) and then split in accordance with the relative weighting of the different variance categories (**Input Price Variances**, **Input Quantity Variances**, **Remaining Input Variances**, and **Output Variances**).

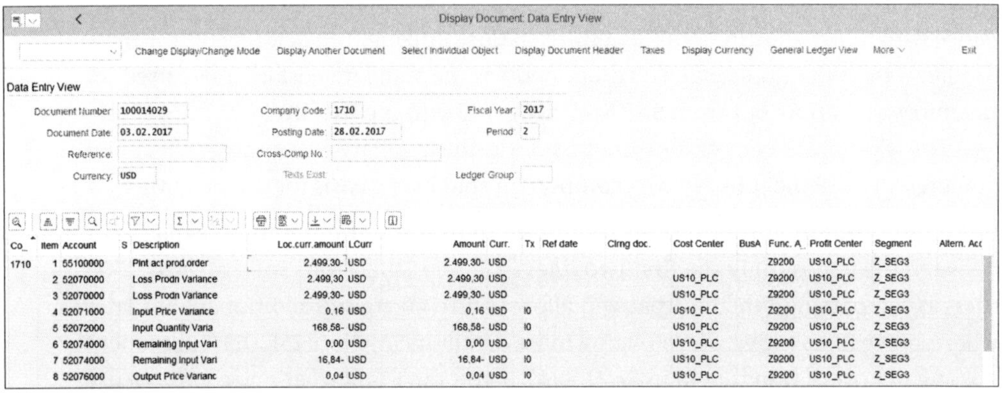

Figure 14.13 Variance Categories

Assessment, Settlement and Top Down Distribution

When we walked through the various methods of bringing costs into costing-based Profitability Analysis in Chapter 7, the receiver was always a value field and the tracing factors for assessment and top-down distribution based on selection of the relevant value fields.

Working with assessment and settlement to assign overhead costs to Profitability Analysis in the Universal Journal, you may at first miss the value fields. Because these screens were designed for costing-based CO-PA originally, you'll see that the **Segment Header** in Figure 14.14 contains the **Amount/Qty** field entry of **Total Costs** as the receiver tracing factor rather than the more specific **Value Field/Key Figure** entry **Cost of Goods Sold** that you saw in Chapter 7, Figure 7.17. After selecting **Total Costs** in the **Segment Header**, you'll have to define which cost elements are to be included in the assessment by making the appropriate entries in the **Senders/Receivers** tab.

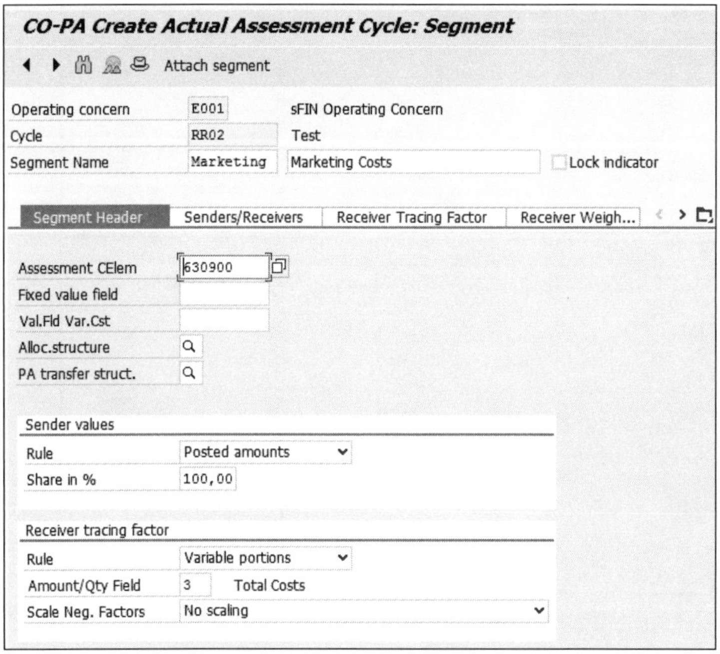

Figure 14.14 Assessment Cycle for Profitability Analysis in Universal Journal

If you're running account-based and costing-based Profitability Analysis in parallel, then the assessment cycle will credit the marketing cost center and create debit lines in both account-based and costing-based Profitability Analysis. You'll have to choose which form of Profitability Analysis should be used to determine the tracing factors for the allocation.

If you now compare the settings for top-down distribution in Figure 14.15 with Chapter 7, Figure 7.56 you'll notice the use of the **KSTAR** (**Cost Element**) field as one of the selection criteria (Transaction KE28). This means that instead of referencing a value field such as revenue or cost of goods sold, we're referencing a cost element interval as part of the selection for the top-down distribution. This won't give you all the options that you had in costing-based Profitability Analysis because you can't use statistical value fields, such as freight, to provide a basis for the distribution—but it will certainly support some of the major use cases for top-down distribution.

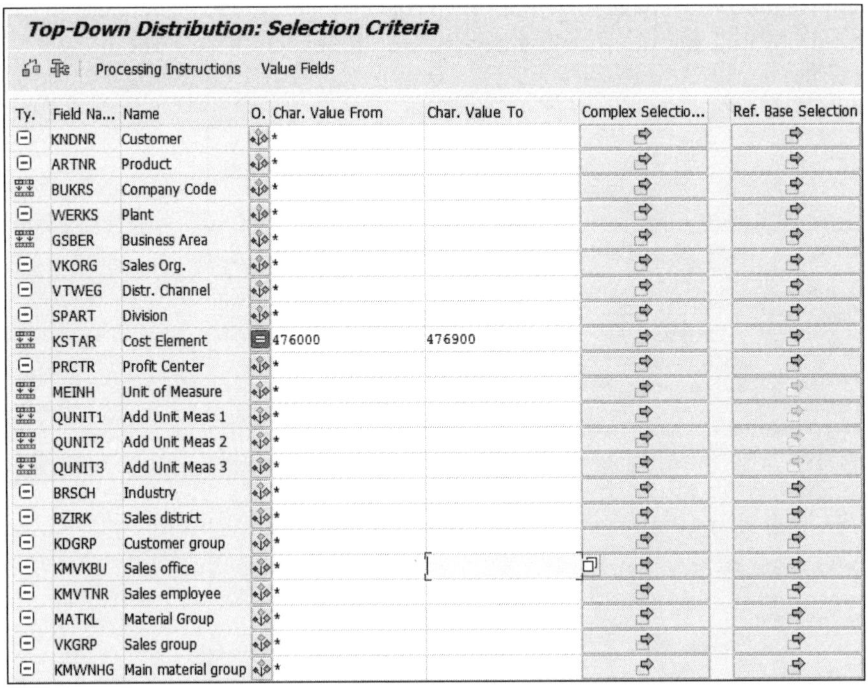

Top-Down Distribution: Selection Criteria

Processing Instructions   Value Fields

Field Na...	Name	O.	Char. Value From	Char. Value To	Complex Selectio...	Ref. Base Selection
KNDNR	Customer		*			
ARTNR	Product		*			
BUKRS	Company Code		*			
WERKS	Plant		*			
GSBER	Business Area		*			
VKORG	Sales Org.		*			
VTWEG	Distr. Channel		*			
SPART	Division		*			
KSTAR	Cost Element		476000	476900		
PRCTR	Profit Center		*			
MEINH	Unit of Measure		*			
QUNIT1	Add Unit Meas 1		*			
QUNIT2	Add Unit Meas 2		*			
QUNIT3	Add Unit Meas 3		*			
BRSCH	Industry		*			
BZIRK	Sales district		*			
KDGRP	Customer group		*			
KMVKBU	Sales office		*			
KMVTNR	Sales employee		*			
MATKL	Material Group		*			
VKGRP	Sales group		*			
KMWNHG	Main material group		*			

Figure 14.15 Top-Down Distribution for Profitability Analysis in Universal Journal

We've now seen the main elements of the Universal Journal, including how the accounts and cost elements merge and how the familiar account assignments from Controlling (cost center, order, project, etc.) and the CO-PA characteristics move into the Universal Journal to provide the basis for multidimensional reporting. We'll now look at how the Material Ledger has also been absorbed into the Universal Journal to support basic inventory valuation. We'll then look at how the actual costing functions were rebuilt in SAP S/4HANA 1610.

14.2 The Material Ledger

Until SAP S/4HANA, most controllers used the terms Material Ledger and actual costing as synonyms, simply because activating the Material Ledger in a plant generally meant that you intended to run actual costing to include your purchase price variances and production variances in the periodic unit price for each material. The **Actual Costing/Material Ledger** menu encouraged this view by lumping the two functions into one bucket.

With SAP S/4HANA we need to be cleaner in our terminology. The *Material Ledger* is active for every material from SAP S/4HANA 1511, but all this means is that you will have inventory values in your local currency, your group currency, and a third currency, such as a functional currency or index currency, depending on local legal requirements.

When we looked at intercompany goods movements in Chapter 6, you saw how to use the Material Ledger to store intercompany transfer prices, a group valuation, and a profit center price for each material. These valuations are *optional* but becoming increasingly popular as customers move towards a single instance in which the entire value chain can be captured as a single flow.

When we talk about *actual costing*, we refer to the way that we followed an integrated process flow in Chapter 6. In terms of the purchase price variances in the procure-to-pay process, the production variances in the plan-to-manufacture process, and any additional variances in the order-to-cash process to get a holistic view of the actual costs across this value chain. Actual costing continues to be *optional* in SAP S/4HANA but is becoming increasingly popular as price and currency volatility make standard costs ever more unreliable in some industries.

14.2.1 Inventory Valuation in the Universal Journal

If the Universal Journal now contains the General Ledger account assignments (see Figure 14.8), the CO account assignments (see Figure 14.9), and the CO-PA characteristics (see Figure 14.11), it also includes the fields for inventory valuation in the Material Ledger. Figure 14.16 shows that part of the Universal Journal that contains the fields relevant for inventory valuation. Notice the **Price Control Indicator** (standard or moving average price), the **Material Ledger Price Determination Control** (transaction-based or single-/multilevel), and the price units that we looked at in Chapter 4, together with all the special stock types that we discussed in Chapter 6 and the various structuring elements for material price analysis. This first architectural simplification took place in SAP S/4HANA Finance 1503. If you check the contents of SAP Note 2270333 (S4TWL Data Model Changes in FIN), you'll see that several material ledger tables—MLCD, MLCR, MLHD, MLIT, and MLPP—become redundant with the Universal Journal but are replaced by views.

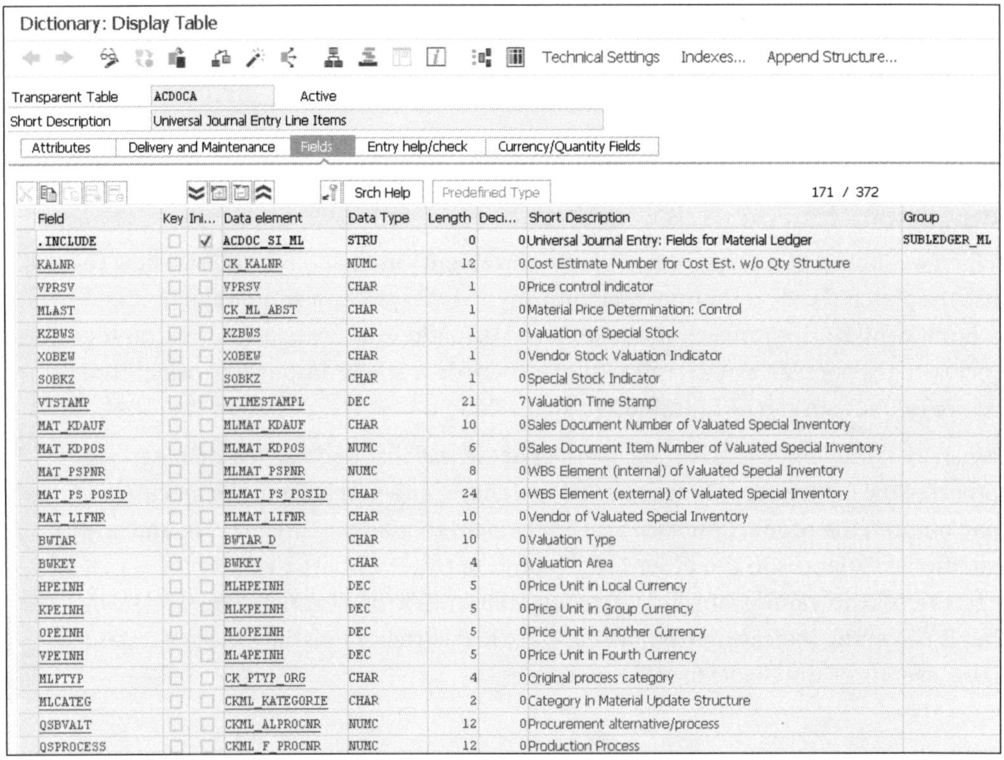
Dictionary: Display Table

Technical Settings Indexes... Append Structure...

Transparent Table: ACDOCA Active

Short Description: Universal Journal Entry Line Items

Attributes | Delivery and Maintenance | Fields | Entry help/check | Currency/Quantity Fields

Srch Help | Predefined Type 171 / 372

Field	Key	Ini...	Data element	Data Type	Length	Deci...	Short Description	Group
.INCLUDE	☐	✓	ACDOC_SI_ML	STRU	0	0	Universal Journal Entry: Fields for Material Ledger	SUBLEDGER_ML
KALNR	☐	☐	CK_KALNR	NUMC	12	0	Cost Estimate Number for Cost Est. w/o Qty Structure	
VPRSV	☐	☐	VPRSV	CHAR	1	0	Price control indicator	
MLAST	☐	☐	CK_ML_ABST	CHAR	1	0	Material Price Determination: Control	
KZBWS	☐	☐	KZBWS	CHAR	1	0	Valuation of Special Stock	
XOBEW	☐	☐	XOBEW	CHAR	1	0	Vendor Stock Valuation Indicator	
SOBKZ	☐	☐	SOBKZ	CHAR	1	0	Special Stock Indicator	
VTSTAMP	☐	☐	VTIMESTAMPL	DEC	21	7	Valuation Time Stamp	
MAT_KDAUF	☐	☐	MLMAT_KDAUF	CHAR	10	0	Sales Document Number of Valuated Special Inventory	
MAT_KDPOS	☐	☐	MLMAT_KDPOS	NUMC	6	0	Sales Document Item Number of Valuated Special Inventory	
MAT_PSPNR	☐	☐	MLMAT_PSPNR	NUMC	8	0	WBS Element (internal) of Valuated Special Inventory	
MAT_PS_POSID	☐	☐	MLMAT_PS_POSID	CHAR	24	0	WBS Element (external) of Valuated Special Inventory	
MAT_LIFNR	☐	☐	MLMAT_LIFNR	CHAR	10	0	Vendor of Valuated Special Inventory	
BWTAR	☐	☐	BWTAR_D	CHAR	10	0	Valuation Type	
BWKEY	☐	☐	BWKEY	CHAR	4	0	Valuation Area	
HPEINH	☐	☐	MLHPEINH	DEC	5	0	Price Unit in Local Currency	
KPEINH	☐	☐	MLKPEINH	DEC	5	0	Price Unit in Group Currency	
OPEINH	☐	☐	MLOPEINH	DEC	5	0	Price Unit in Another Currency	
VPEINH	☐	☐	ML4PEINH	DEC	5	0	Price Unit in Fourth Currency	
MLPTYP	☐	☐	CK_PTYP_ORG	CHAR	4	0	Original process category	
MLCATEG	☐	☐	CKML_KATEGORIE	CHAR	2	0	Category in Material Update Structure	
QSBVALT	☐	☐	CKML_ALPROCNR	NUMC	12	0	Procurement alternative/process	
QSPROCESS	☐	☐	CKML_F_PROCNR	NUMC	12	0	Production Process	

Figure 14.16 Material Ledger Fields in Universal Journal

What this means in business terms going forward is that we can include these fields in the reporting views, just as we drilled down by cost center earlier. Figure 14.17 shows the trial balance again, together with some of the fields available for drilldown in the **Navigation Panel**, including **Special Stock Type**, **SD Doc of Inventory**, **SD Item of Inventory**, **WBS Element of Inventory**, **Supplier of Inventory**, **Valuation Type**, and **Valuation Area**.

Figure 14.17 Trial Balance with Drilldown Options from Material Ledger

14.2.2 Compulsory Use of Material Ledger for Inventory Valuation

The next major architectural simplification took place in SAP S/4HANA 1511, making the use of the Material Ledger compulsory and changing the way that the inventory values were stored in the system. Let's start by looking at what happens when the Material Ledger becomes compulsory. Figure 14.18 shows the **Accounting View** of the material master for a finished product. You might want to compare this with the material master shown in Chapter 4, Figure 4.2. Following conversion to SAP S/4HANA, the screens look different, with the **Period** tabs along the top. All materials have the **ML Active** flag and the stock values are shown in local currency (USD here) and group currency (Euros here). After the conversion, both the material master (Transactions MM01-03) and material price change (Transaction MR21) support multiple currencies.

You can continue to choose between valuing inventory at standard costs or moving average price. We have chosen **Prc Ctrl** (price control) **S** for standard price control rather than **V** for moving average price in this example. You can also choose between **Price Determ.** (price determination) **2** (transaction-based; see Figure 14.18) and **3** (single/multilevel), as you saw in Chapter 4, Figure 4.3. If we use *transaction-based price determination*, the inventory value can change with every goods movement and invoice rather than remaining constant until we release a new standard price or revaluate inventory following actual costing at period close. Single/multilevel price determination is used when working with actual costing. We'll return to this option in Section 14.2.4. Your main business decisions concerning inventory valuation remain unchanged. The difference is simply that you have inventory values in multiple currencies.

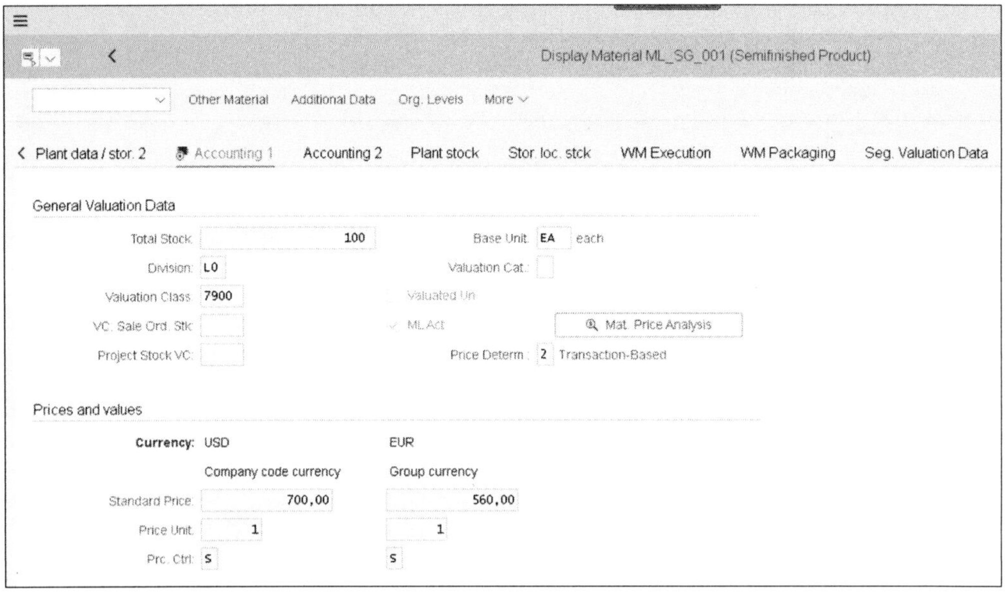

Figure 14.18 Material Master Showing Compulsory Use of Material Ledger

The inventory values shown in Figure 14.18 were previously stored in table MBEW and equivalent tables existed for sales order stock (table EBEW), project stock (table QBEW) and subcontractor stock (table OBEW). Work has been going on behind the scenes to remove these inventory valuation tables and replace them with views that calculate these values on the fly, significantly increasing the number of material movements that can be posted within a given time frame. Don't be concerned if you still find these tables in your system. They're still used to store material attribute information that doesn't change regularly, but any analysis of stock values per plant, storage location, and so on will be calculated on the fly using the new views. You'll get the fastest results if you work with standard prices, for which the price must simply be read from the material master as each movement is posted. If you work with the moving average price, then the system must briefly lock the tables with each movement to calculate the new moving average price. To find out more about the switch, refer to SAP Note 2267834 (S4TWL—Material Ledger Obligatory for Inventory Valuation).

14.2.3 Using the Material Ledger for Transfer Prices and Group Valuation

Although Figure 14.18 showed the simplest use case for the Material Ledger, allowing you to store inventory values in multiple currencies, the Material Ledger also provides the technical basis for the group valuation and profit center valuation views that we showed when we discussed intercompany goods movements in Chapter 6. In the earliest versions of SAP S/4HANA, the use of group valuation and profit center valuation wasn't supported (see SAP Note 2270414 [Transfer Prices/COGM/ABC Using Delta]), but the approach was reenabled in SAP S/4HANA Finance 1605 and SAP S/4HANA 1610.

From a Material Ledger point of view, little changed with SAP S/4HANA. The Material Ledger continued to be able to store three valuations, so you could continue to handle your intercompany transfer prices as the legal valuation, to eliminate intercompany profits in the group valuation, and to define transfer prices between profit centers as the profit center valuation. We can see what happens by looking at two views of the same material in Material Price Analysis (Transaction CKM3N).

Figure 14.19 can be compared with Chapter 6, Figure 6.79. The main difference is that Material Price Analysis now shows the figures in the **Price Determination Structure** and for the **Cost Components** on one screen. Notice that in the legal view we see the entire product costs under the **Direct Material** component because thanks to arm's-length trading the goods are being bought from an affiliate company in the same group and incur additional costs for **Freight.** The intercompany profit agreed on between the two subsidiaries is shown in a separate column: **I/C Profit**. If the supply chain involves work at several plants in different locations, the I/C profit will cumulate the intercompany markups across the whole supply chain.

Figure 14.20 can be compared to Chapter 6, Figure 6.82 and shows the material from Figure 14.19 as viewed from the headquarters in Europe. Now we can see that the product costs have been broken down into their components, **Direct Material**, **Machine Time**, **Personnel**, **Setup**, **Material Overhead**, and **Production**, and that the intercompany profits have been eliminated, leaving the **I/C Profit** column empty. What we're seeing is a management view that provides full cost transparency across the whole supply chain for this product.

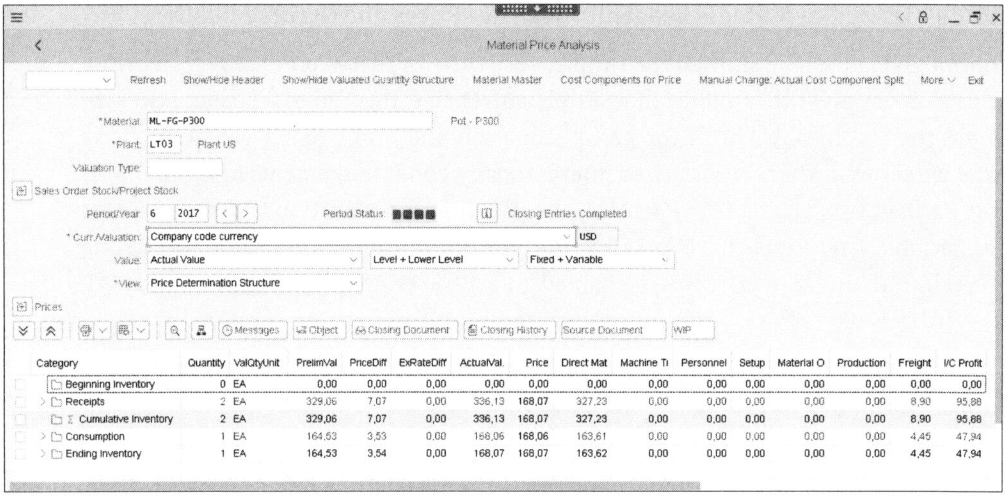

Figure 14.19 Material Price Analysis Showing Legal Valuation

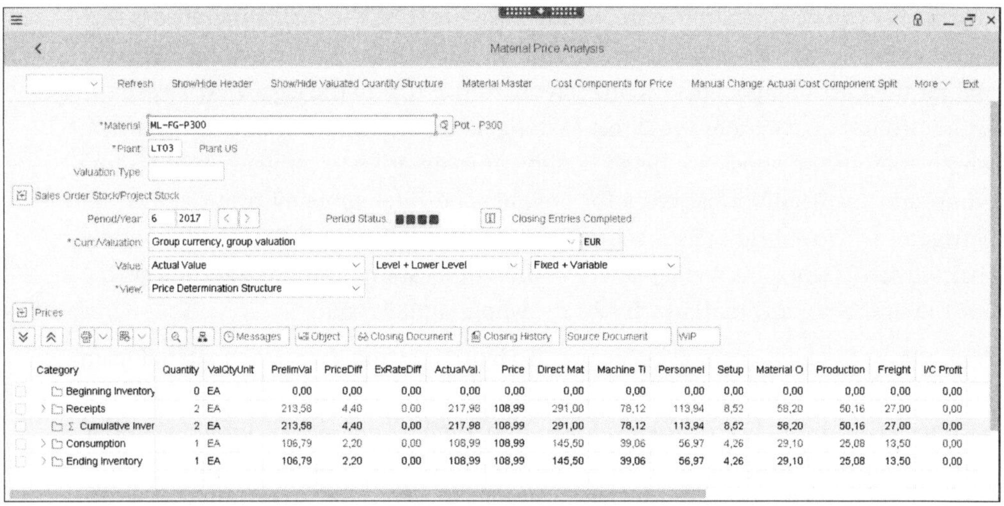

Figure 14.20 Material Price Analysis Showing Group Valuation

What did change, however, was how these additional valuation approaches are stored in the Universal Journal: the valuation views are now stored as additional columns in the Universal Journal rather than delta versions in Controlling. The main settings are made per ledger when you set up the Universal Journal (see Figure 14.21). In our example, we've set up Ledger L1 to show what happens during a migration from SAP ERP to

SAP S/4HANA. In this case, all the valuations are stored as columns in the same ledger (essentially this is also what happened in the SAP General Ledger). In a greenfield approach, you can store the different valuations in different ledgers, as we see with the examples L2 (Group Ledger) and L3/L4 (Profit Center Ledger), with the **Valuation View** assigned directly to a ledger.

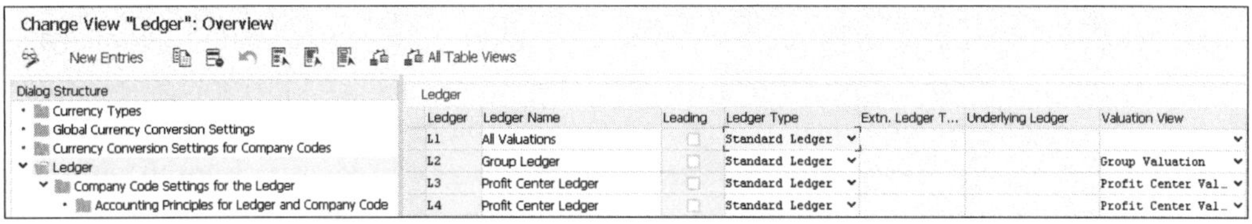

Figure 14.21 Ledger Settings for Group and Profit Center Valuation

All ledgers contain two currencies: the local currency (currency type 10) and the group currency (currency type 30). You can add additional currencies as required. These might be to meet local requirements; for example, a plant in Mexico operating mostly with the United States might need to add USD as a functional currency, and you might need to add a hard currency or an index currency to meet some local reporting requirements. Figure 14.22 gives an overview of the delivered currency types (greyed out) and examples of some of the currencies that were added in a test system.

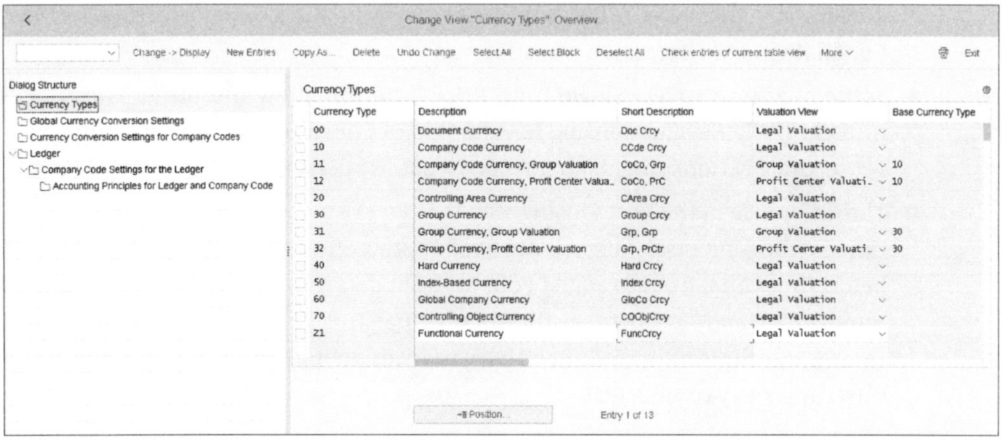

Figure 14.22 Currency Types in SAP S/4HANA

From a management reporting point of view, it's good to store the group valuation and the profit center valuation in the headquarters' currency to provide consistent corporate reporting. However, discuss these requirements with the team that runs your consolidation process. We also see organizations choosing to store their group valuation view in local currency to eliminate the intercompany profits but to convert to the group reporting currency in their consolidation tool. Whatever approach you choose, be aware that adding a new valuation view to the Universal Journal is technically done by adding a currency. At the time of writing, it isn't possible to add a new currency to the Universal Journal and convert the historical documents retrospectively, meaning that if you need these functions urgently you may want to perform a conversion in SAP ERP *before* making the move to SAP S/4HANA.

14.2.4 Architectural Changes in Actual Costing

When we looked at the costing run in Chapter 7, we mentioned that the number of steps in the costing run had been reduced. Figure 14.23 shows the new Costing Cockpit: Actual Costing transaction (Transaction CKMLCP) with only the steps **Selection**, **Preparation**, **Settlement**, **Post Closing**, and **Mark Prices**:

- There's no change in the **Selection** step. You're still choosing the plants for which actual costing will be performed. To ensure consistent valuation, you should select all the plants in a specific company code.
- **Preparation** now covers **Determine Sequence** in the periodic costing run and **Cumulate** in the alternative valuation run.
- **Settlement** now covers Single-Level Price Determination, Multilevel Price Determination, WIP Revaluation and Revaluation of Consumption. However, you'll still get separate ML documents that record what happened in each of these steps.
- The difference in the Post Closing step that you're performing inventory revaluation in the Universal Journal. Most of the account determinations remain as before, but you'll need to adjust your account determination for actual costing to remove PRV and KDV because they're no longer needed and to add new accounts for PRL, which clears any outstanding variances on the cost center and requires an offsetting entry to GBB/AUI.

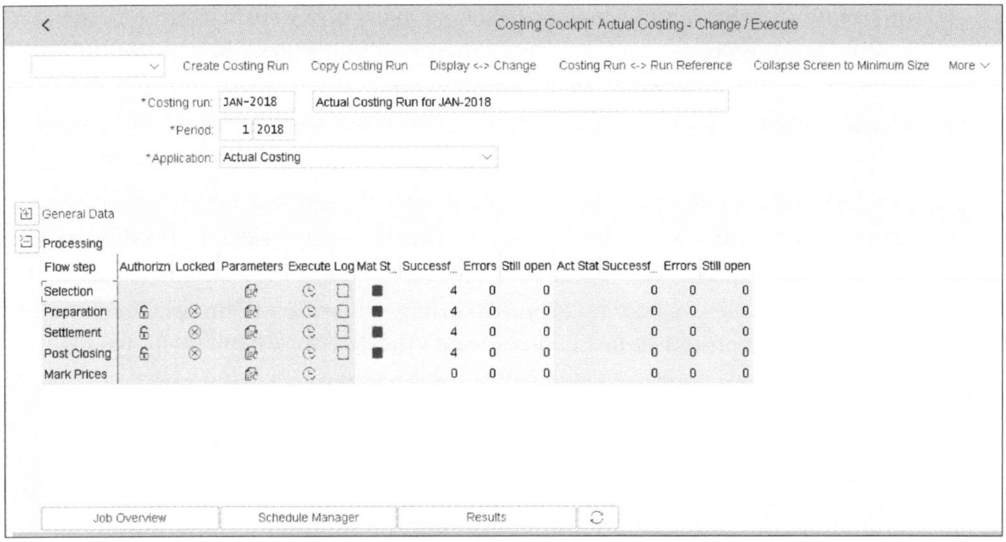

Figure 14.23 Costing Run for Actual Costing

Behind the scenes, the number of tables updated during actual costing has been radically reduced with table `MLDOC` recording the quantity structure and its valuation and table `MLDOCCCS` recording the cost component split information. Make sure that your IT team is aware of the contents of SAP Note 2352383 (S4TWL—Conversion of Actual Costing and Material Ledger) if you're planning to convert. If you aren't already running actual costing, it's possible to activate it at any time after the conversion.

We've now looked at the Universal Journal and the Material Ledger to explain how the SAP ERP world has been changed in the move to SAP S/4HANA. We'll now look at some new features that were introduced with SAP S/4HANA and that could potentially change your approach to Profitability Analysis.

14.3 Profitability Analysis

In Section 14.1.4 we looked at how the characteristics used for Profitability Analysis become part of the Universal Journal and how to make the switch from the value fields in costing-based Profitability Analysis to the accounts and cost elements in SAP S/4HANA. To do this requires virtually no changes to your existing account assignment logic. However, moving Profitability Analysis into the Universal Journal is not just a technical switch. The move can bring opportunities and a chance to do things differently as well. We've been used to seeing many of the costs relating to the revenues in Profitability Analysis as period costs that are transferred using assessment cycles and settlement at period close. The chapters in this book follow this convention, with Chapter 6 explaining how revenue and cost of goods sold are captured in real time and Chapter 7 how the remaining costs are brought into Profitability Analysis using assessment cycles, settlement, and so on at period close. In SAP ERP the matching principle is achieved for product-related costs of sales, but project-related sales costs are typically not matched until we run results analysis and settlement at period close. As we consider real-time finance, the question becomes whether some costs could be captured earlier. One way to do this is to *enrich* the posting document with more information than was available in the initial cost assignment. To imagine what this means, consider a simple example. When you post costs to a commercial project, you know which customer will be billed and so you can derive the customer as a CO-PA characteristic as you post the project costs, giving you a view of the costs per project and the costs for the customer supported. You still have the old view of the costs per project, but you have an enriched posting that also shows the customer supported and all the derived CO-PA characteristics. We'll now look at this process in more detail.

14.3.1 Derivation of CO-PA Characteristics during Cost Assignment

Instead of waiting until period close to settle orders and projects to profitability analysis, SAP S/4HANA allows you to *derive* the CO-PA characteristics on the fly as the cost posting is made. With a project billed to an external customer, you're capturing costs on the various WBS elements assigned to the project and billing based on the sales order. In SAP ERP you collected the costs on the various WBS elements and settled to Profitability Analysis at period close. This typically resulted in the shift from cost by nature to cost by function (see Chapter 2). If we rethink the business process, we realize that when we make the expense posting to the WBS element, we already know which sales order item is behind it and derive the associated profitability characteristics from either the settlement rule or the sales order item itself.

Figure 14.24 shows a very simple example in which we've posted a consultant's travel expenses to the WBS element that he's working for and then derived the product, customer, and distribution channel for that WBS element by reading the settlement rule that would normally be read at period close. In this example, the entry in the ACCASTY field (Section 14.1.2) would be PR for project and we would see the WBS element in the ACCAS field, but the system would also fill the product, customer, and distribution channel fields based on the derivation settings. There is no change in the account/cost element. If you don't settle, these costs continue to show as travel expenses. The Market Segments—Actuals SAP Fiori app (SAP Fiori ID F0943A), delivered as part of the cost accountant—sales role, reads these fields, as well as the familiar CO-PA characteristics that would be associated with an EO in the ACCASTY field. If your organization isn't yet ready to make the move to SAP Fiori, you will be able to view these characteristics in Transaction KE24N (CO-PA line items) but you won't see them in Transaction KE24 or KE30 (Drilldown Reporting), where only those fields are shown for which CO-PA was the account assignment and ACCASTY is EO (revenues, cost of goods sold, assessments, and settlement).

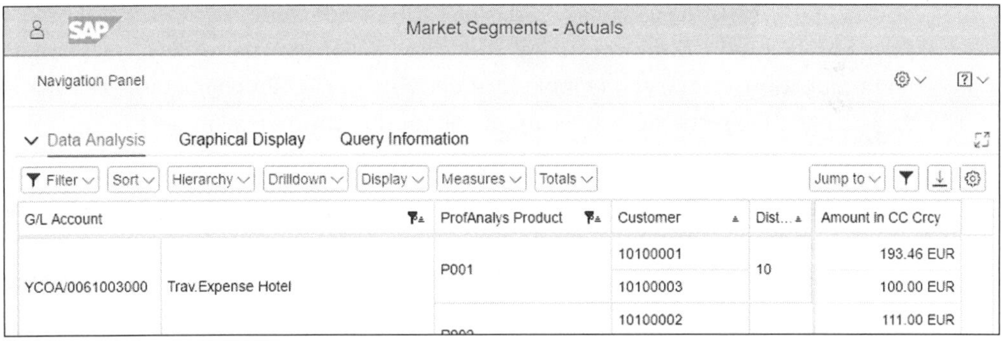

Figure 14.24 Expense Reporting by Market Segment

You can set up this logic in the IMG. Go to **Controlling • Profitability Analysis • Master Data • Activate Derivation for Items without Profitability Segment** and choose the CO account assignments that you wish to associate with CO-PA characteristics. The objective is to select those CO account assignments that are making a single-level settlement to CO-PA. In this example, we selected **Items Assigned to Projects**. You then need to decide whether you are only deriving CO-PA characteristics for P&L accounts (which would be sufficient in our travel expense example) or whether you also want to derive CO-PA characteristics for balance sheet accounts, such as work in process. Usually it doesn't make sense to activate the derivation for all project types because capital expense projects do not settle to CO-PA. You can select your commercial projects by entering the appropriate project profile.

Using derivation doesn't prevent you from settling at period close if required. In the example in Figure 14.24 we've extended the posting line to post to both the WBS element and the CO-PA characteristics. If you settle, you will credit the WBS element and write a completely new posting line containing the CO-PA characteristics with the

ACCASTY field EO (for profitability analysis). This will credit the project under a secondary cost element as before, meaning that you can still make the shift from costs by nature to costs by function. If you don't need to settle, then you should adjust your settlement profiles for the commercial projects and flag them as **Not For Settlement**.

Just occasionally, you may begin to assign costs to the WBS element before the sales order item has been assigned for billing. If this is the case, the derivation function can't access the data it needs and there will be no assignment to the CO-PA characteristics. However, once the sales order item has been correctly assigned, you can use the realignment function (Transaction KEND) to read the sales order item and make the derivation later.

You can take the same approach to derive CO-PA characteristics for internal orders, sales orders, production orders, and cost centers. For internal orders, sales orders, and production orders, you're looking at deriving the CO-PA characteristics early as an alternative to settlement as we discussed for the commercial project.

With cost centers, however, you are looking at deriving the CO-PA characteristics as an alternative to running an assessment cycle at period close. Let's briefly recall the example in Chapter 7, Section 7.1.4, where we settled the research and development costs from a cost center to multiple divisions. The function to derive CO-PA characteristics immediately extends the posting line to the cost center to add additional CO-PA characteristics, so it would be possible to assign all research and development costs to *one* region or one country at the time of posting. In this case we would have to find a way of linking the cost center with the region or country and then reading this link during derivation. However, if we need to spread the research and development costs across *multiple* regions or countries, then we must use a conventional assessment cycle to calculate the relative weighting of the different regions or countries and create new posting lines for each region or country. You can, of course, also use the two approaches in combination and make the assignment to the region or country during the initial posting and then use a traditional assessment cycle to split the costs to the many products sold in that region at period close. Of course, this approach will not work for all allocations. You will still need to allocate costs from supporting cost centers to operational cost centers using assessment or indirect activity allocation cycles or from operational cost centers to production orders, maintenance orders, and so on using direct activity allocations as before.

14.3.2 Revenue Recognition for Professional Services

As well as enriching the original posting document to add the relevant CO-PA characteristics, SAP S/4HANA also allows us to create *additional* documents that anticipate the postings previously carried out as part of the period close to ensure the matching principle. Event-based revenue recognition is one example of this approach. Recall Chapter 7, Section 7.2.5 in which we discussed the use of results analysis for valuing sales orders. In SAP ERP the costs are collected during a period and then used to calculate the revenue in excess of billings that can be recognized on account of the percentage of completion (POC) at period close. In SAP S/4HANA, every time a consultant makes a time recording to the WBS element, the revenue can be accrued *immediately*. This results in two postings being made to the WBS element based on a common reference document. Figure 14.25 shows the G/L Account Line Items app (SAP Fiori ID F2217) with all the line items associated with the reference document 300011008:

- The first line item is triggered by the time recording as we saw in Chapter 6, Section 6.3.4 and results in a credit to the cost center and a debit to the WBS element for the hour of consulting work. You can identify these postings by the business Transaction RKL (Direct Activity Allocation).
- The second line item is triggered by event-based revenue recognition and results in accrued revenues of EUR 120. You can recognize these postings by the business Transaction TBRR (Transaction-Based Revenue Recognition). In the case of a fixed-price contract, the system calculates the realized revenue using the cost-based POC multiplied by the planned revenue. In the case of a time and materials (T&M) project, the system simulates the T&M billing to calculate the revenue to be realized.

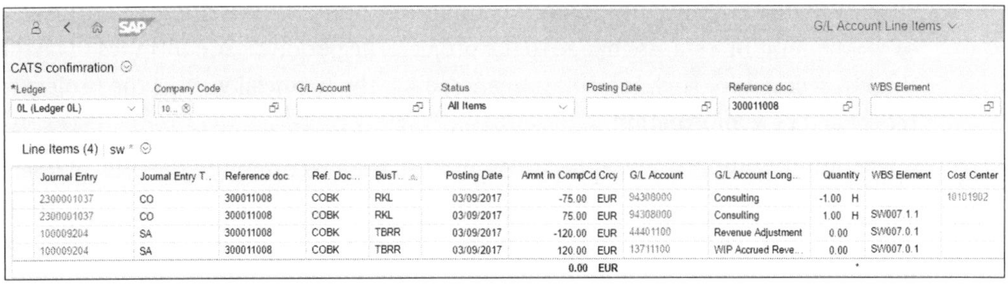

Journal Entry	Journal Entry T..	Reference doc.	Ref. Doc...	BusT...	Posting Date	Amnt in CompCd Crcy		G/L Account	G/L Account Long...	Quantity		WBS Element	Cost Center
2300001037	CO	300011008	COBK	RKL	03/09/2017	-75.00	EUR	94308000	Consulting	-1.00	H		10101902
2300001037	CO	300011008	COBK	RKL	03/09/2017	75.00	EUR	94308000	Consulting	1.00	H	SW007.1.1	
100009204	SA	300011008	COBK	TBRR	03/09/2017	-120.00	EUR	44401100	Revenue Adjustment	0.00		SW007.0.1	
100009204	SA	300011008	COBK	TBRR	03/09/2017	120.00	EUR	13711100	WIP Accrued Reve...	0.00		SW007.0.1	
						0.00	EUR						

Figure 14.25 G/L Account Line Items for Confirmation and Accrued Revenue

SAP S/4HANA includes new applications that allow users to monitor the process in more detail. Figure 14.26 shows the Event-Based Revenue Recognition—Projects SAP Fiori app (SAP Fiori ID F2129) that's delivered as part of the sales accountant role. This shows all the WBS elements that are flagged as billing elements (see Chapter 4, Figure 4.22) and that contain an appropriate revenue recognition key along with the associated revenue and cost of goods sold. To understand what happened during the calculation, select a line.

Figure 14.26 Event-Based Revenue Recognition App

Figure 14.27 shows details of the posting, including the costs assigned to the WBS element and any billed revenue, along with the adjustment postings made by event-based revenue recognition. If the project manager feels that these values do not reflect the actual situation on the project, he can enter a temporary adjustment using the links at the top right of the app.

Although event-based revenue recognition represents a huge leap forward in the move towards real-time finance, it doesn't account for any changes during a period, such as changes to the percentage of completion, hours to be written off in the case of T&M billing, or a status change to the project. The period close continues to be the time to account for such information and adjust the financial view of the project to reflect any new information.

It can also happen that errors occurred and the time recording to the WBS element was posted successfully, but the follow-on revenue recognition posting failed. There are various sources for such problems. The plan data might have been incomplete or there might have been no revenue recognition key assigned to the project at the time of billing. For this reason, you should still perform a revenue recognition run at period close to fix any inconsistencies.

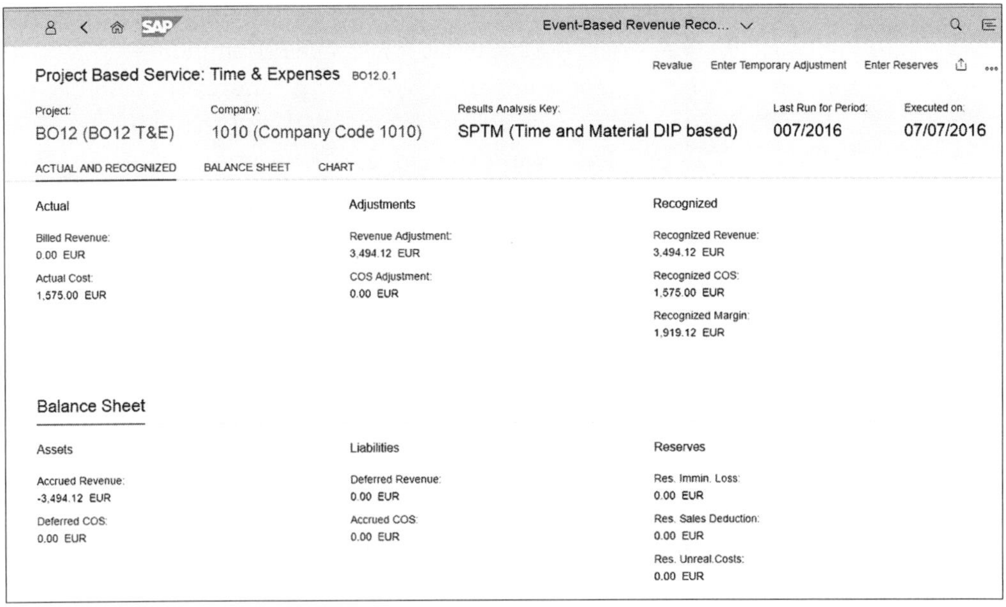

Figure 14.27 Details of Event-Based Revenue Recognition Posting

You'll find the Event-Based Revenue Recognition application (SAP Fiori ID REV_REC_COL_PRO) shown in Figure 14.28 in the sales accountant role. In the bottom part of this screen you can see whether the follow-on postings were made successfully or need to be retriggered and find details about why the posting failed. You need to ensure that errors are fixed here before you execute results analysis to recognize the proper revenue for the period. Once you've completed this step, you can run revenue recognition for the project by clicking **Execute**, shown in Figure 14.28.

Let's end this section by looking at the Project—Actuals app (SAP Fiori ID F0942A). If we compare Figure 14.24 with Figure 14.29, we see the same basic idea in that costs and revenues are assigned to both the project and various CO-PA characteristics (in this example we're showing product and customer) using the derivation function. However, we also see additional lines for the revenue and cost adjustments that have been triggered by event-based revenue recognition and these lines help to ensure that there is less work to be done at period close. Running revenue recognition at period close will make any final adjustment postings to ensure that the project result is stated correctly for the period.

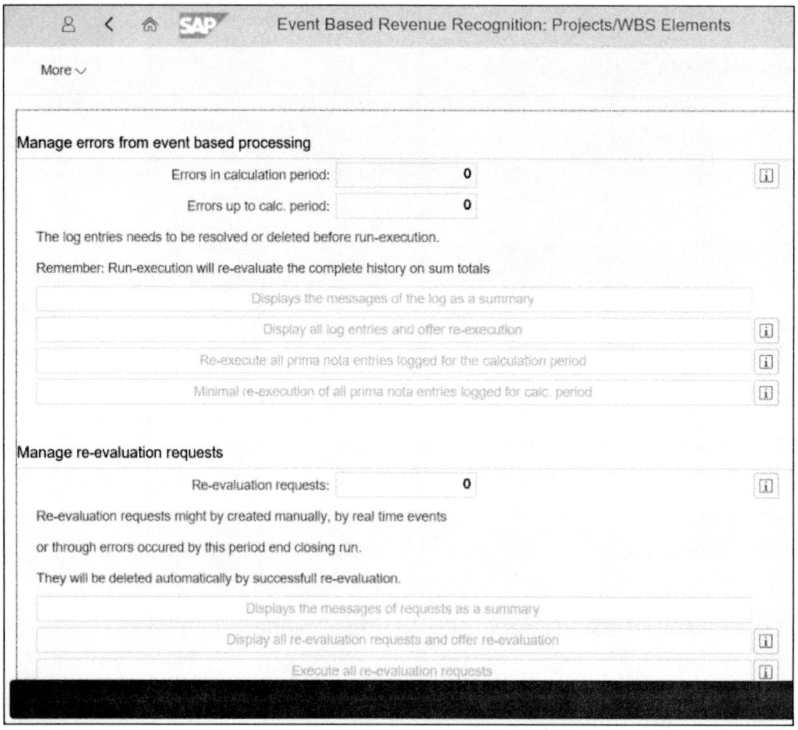

Figure 14.28 Error Correction for Event-Based Revenue Recognition

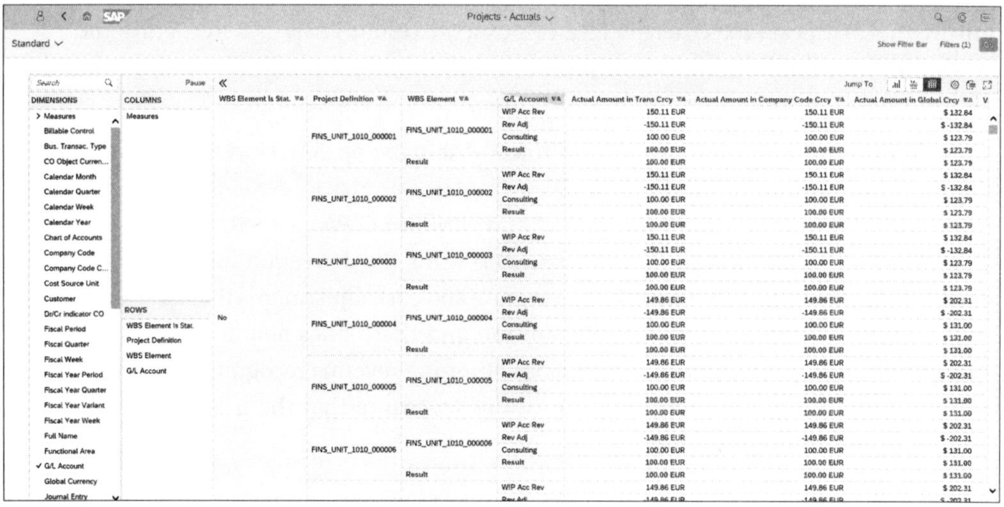

Figure 14.29 Report Showing Projects—Actuals

14.3.3 Cross-Company Resource-Related Billing for Professional Services

As organizations become more global, it is increasingly common for the consultants performing the work on a project to be assigned to a different company code from the project itself. This means that the time recording is effectively cross-company, a situation that will be familiar in any professional service organization but is also increasingly the case for many internal projects. Again, we used to have a mismatch with costs being collected in one company code and the billing performed in another. In SAP S/4HANA we can create a markup in the sending company code that reflects the intercompany billing and immediately moves the costs to the company code that will be billing the customer.

The mechanism to perform this posting continues to be time recording, but this time the cost center being credited is in company code 1710 and the project debited is in company code 1010, as shown in Figure 14.30. If you compare this with the time recording postings in Figure 14.25, you'll again see posting lines in business Transaction RKL (Direct Activity Allocation) that record the value of the hours worked. This time, however, the additional document contains an intercompany margin (the lines in business Transaction KAMV) and intercompany clearing accounts are posted for both sets of lines. You'll also notice that the document is enriched with the **Trading Partner** as a preparation for the elimination of intercompany markups during consolidation.

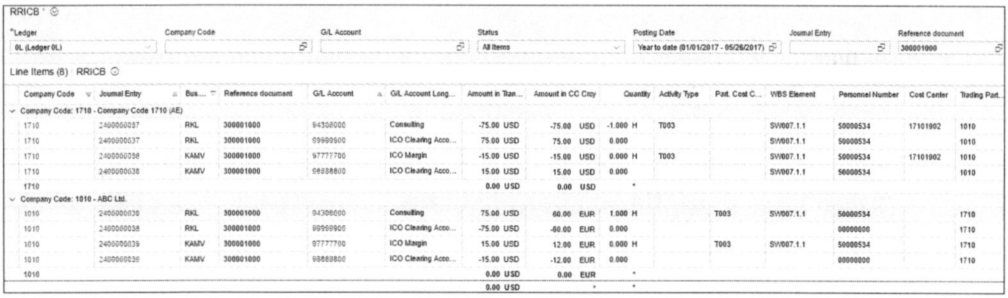
RRICB *

*Ledger: 0L (Ledger 0L) | Company Code: | G/L Account: | Status: All Items | Posting Date: Year to date (01/01/2017 - 05/26/2017) | Journal Entry: | Reference document: 300001000

Line Items (8) RRICB

Company Code	Journal Entry	Bus....	Reference document	G/L Account	G/L Account Long...	Amount in Tran...	Amount in CC Crcy	Quantity	Activity Type	Part. Cost C...	WBS Element	Personnel Number	Cost Center	Trading Part...
Company Code: 1710 - Company Code 1710 (AE)														
1710	2400000037	RKL	300001000	94308000	Consulting	-75.00 USD	-75.00 USD	-1.000 H	T003		SW007.1.1	50000534	17101902	1010
1710	2400000037	RKL	300001000	99999900	ICO Clearing Acco...	75.00 USD	75.00 USD	0.000			SW007.1.1	50000534		1010
1710	2400000038	KAMV	300001000	97777700	ICO Margin	-15.00 USD	-15.00 USD	0.000 H	T003		SW007.1.1	50000534	17101902	1010
1710	2400000038	KAMV	300001000	98888800	ICO Clearing Acco...	15.00 USD	15.00 USD	0.000			SW007.1.1	50000534		1010
1710						0.00 USD	0.00 USD	*						
Company Code: 1010 - ABC Ltd.														
1010	2400000038	RKL	300001000	94308000	Consulting	75.00 USD	60.00 EUR	1.000 H		T003	SW007.1.1	50000534		1710
1010	2400000038	RKL	300001000	99999900	ICO Clearing Acco...	-75.00 USD	-60.00 EUR	0.000				00000000		1710
1010	2400000039	KAMV	300001000	97777700	ICO Margin	15.00 USD	12.00 EUR	0.000 H		T003	SW007.1.1	50000534		1710
1010	2400000039	KAMV	300001000	98888800	ICO Clearing Acco...	-15.00 USD	-12.00 EUR	0.000				00000000		1710
1010						0.00 USD	0.00 EUR	*						
						0.00 USD	*	*						

Figure 14.30 General Ledger Account Line Items for Time Recording and Intercompany Markups

To use this approach, you'll have to activate business function FINS_CO_ICO_PROC_ENH_101 (Intercompany Process Enhancements 1). This will allow you to define activity rates that are more sophisticated than those we looked at in Chapter 5, in which the assumption was that the assembly of the pumps would take place in a single legal entity (the plant). With SAP S/4HANA 1610, we can define activity rates that depend on the legal entity of the receiving cost object. Figure 14.31 shows the Maintain Activity Cost Rates app (SAP Fiori ID CMACA02), delivered as part of the cost accountant—overhead role. In this example, services performed in the delivering company code (1710) are charged at a rate of USD 75 per hour. However, if the receiver of the service is in a different company code, in our case 1010 (the German company code), a higher charge is made that includes the intercompany markup. This results in the two lines shown in Figure 14.30, where you see a charge of USD 75 plus an intercompany charge of USD 15. As the time recording is posted, it triggers a second posting using Transaction KB15N that records the intercompany markup (the posting lines in business Transaction KAMV). You can use the same mechanisms to trigger a markup when other expenses are charged to the project (such as travel).

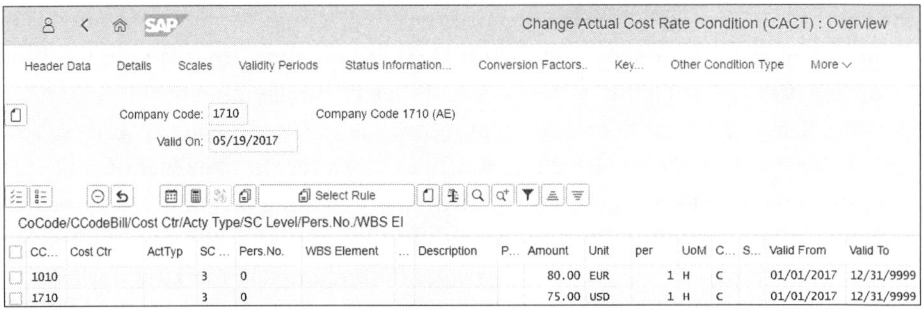

Figure 14.31 Activity Rates for Cross-Company Charging

Although the intercompany margins are being calculated and posted whenever an employee records time to the project, you won't actually want to bill the receiving company on a daily basis. Resource-related billing is triggered as in SAP ERP using Transaction DP93 (Resource-Related Billing between Company Codes). The difference is that with SAP S/4HANA you won't have any intercompany reconciliation issues because the figures shown in Figure 14.32 (the time recording and the markup in the delivering company) will be used to create the invoice for the receiving company.

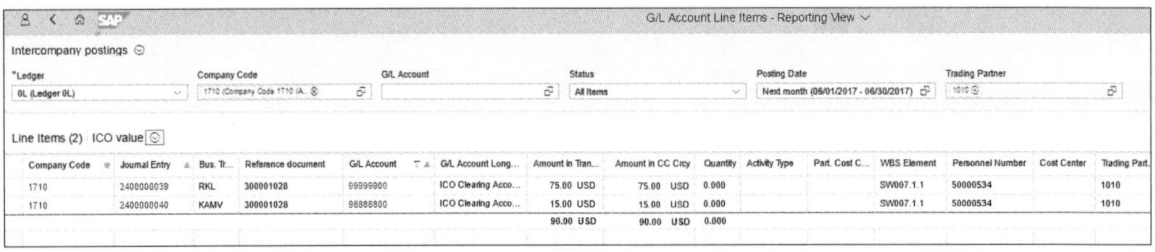

Figure 14.32 General Ledger Account Line Items to Be Used for Intercompany Billing

14.3.4 New Approaches in Cost Object Controlling

The derivation functions that we discussed in Section 14.3.1 are also available for internal orders, sales orders, and production orders that will settle to CO-PA. To this extent, it makes sense to review all your settlement processes for orders, projects, and so on to understand where the settlement might be replaced by a derivation and where you will still need a classic settlement. The derivation function simply extends the posting line to include an assignment to the CO-PA characteristics. It cannot *split* a posting line. This means that you cannot use derivations for orders and projects that settle to multiple receivers (e.g., fixed assets and cost centers) or that settle hierarchically through the WBS.

Work began in SAP S/4HANA 1610 to provide new report options for Cost Object Controlling. Figure 14.33 shows the Production Cost Analysis app (SAP Fiori ID F1780), delivered as part of the cost accountant—production role. This app offers simple exception rules to help you to quickly identify those production orders that need further analysis. The key performance indicators (planned costs, target costs, actual costs) will be familiar from Chapter 6, Section 6.1.2. The difference is that the data selection for this report is based on a *virtual data model* using CDS views to select the relevant data and calculate these key figures. This virtual data model is delivered with SAP S/4HANA. In a nutshell, the virtual data model is converting the contents of tables such as the Universal Journal into a structure that can be used in reporting, either in SAP Fiori as you see here or in SAP Analysis for Microsoft Excel as you saw in Chapter 8.

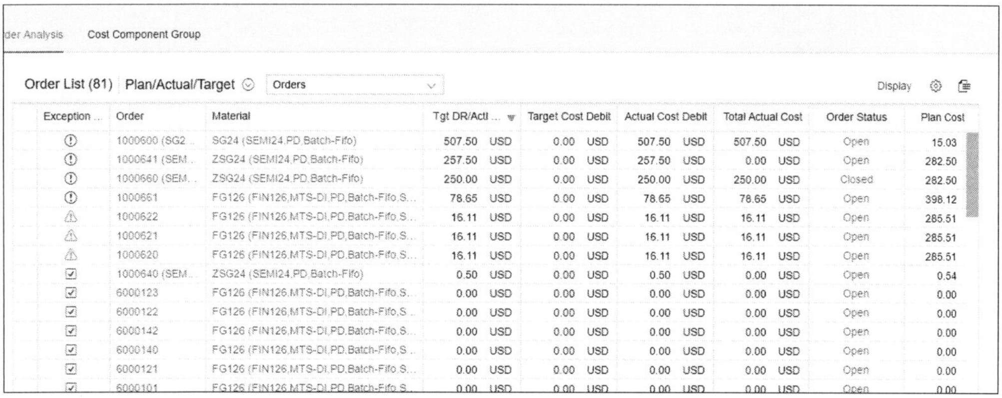

Figure 14.33 Production Cost Analysis App

However, we are not simply visualizing the information needed for production controlling in a new way. Probably the most significant change for production controllers in SAP S/4HANA is the fact that though the operations within a production order were always performed at a work center, the information about the operation and the work center were lost when the relevant document was created in Controlling because the confirmation resulted in a posting to the cost center and associated activity type (see Chapter 6, Section 6.1.2). Now the Universal Journal includes the work center and operation for every document created during confirmation. Figure 14.34 shows the costs collected on the production order by work center and operation. This is another example of how SAP is enriching the accounting documents to provide greater transparency and improve reporting. Remember, however, that though all activity confirmations are automatically linked with a work center, the material components will only be assigned to the correct work center if you have assigned them to the correct operation (see Chapter 4, Section 4.4.1).

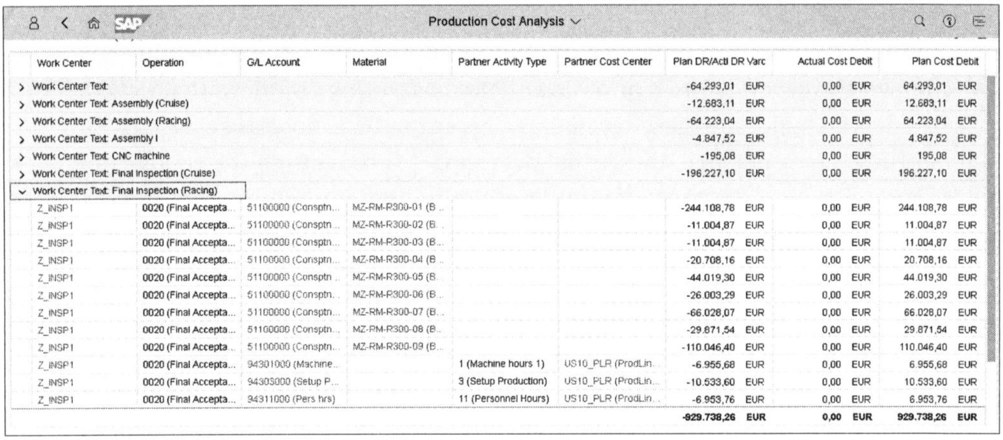

Work Center	Operation	G/L Account	Material	Partner Activity Type	Partner Cost Center	Plan DR/Actl DR Varc	Actual Cost Debit	Plan Cost Debit
> Work Center Text:						-64.293,01 EUR	0,00 EUR	64.293,01 EUR
> Work Center Text: Assembly (Cruise)						-12.683,11 EUR	0,00 EUR	12.683,11 EUR
> Work Center Text: Assembly (Racing)						-64.223,04 EUR	0,00 EUR	64.223,04 EUR
> Work Center Text: Assembly I						-4.847,52 EUR	0,00 EUR	4.847,52 EUR
> Work Center Text: CNC machine						-195,08 EUR	0,00 EUR	195,08 EUR
> Work Center Text: Final Inspection (Cruise)						-196.227,10 EUR	0,00 EUR	196.227,10 EUR
˅ Work Center Text: Final Inspection (Racing)								
Z_INSP1	0020 (Final Accepta...	51100000 (Consptn...	MZ-RM-R300-01 (B...			-244.108,78 EUR	0,00 EUR	244.108,78 EUR
Z_INSP1	0020 (Final Accepta...	51100000 (Consptn...	MZ-RM-R300-02 (B...			-11.004,87 EUR	0,00 EUR	11.004,87 EUR
Z_INSP1	0020 (Final Accepta...	51100000 (Consptn...	MZ-RM-R300-03 (B...			-11.004,87 EUR	0,00 EUR	11.004,87 EUR
Z_INSP1	0020 (Final Accepta...	51100000 (Consptn...	MZ-RM-R300-04 (B...			-20.708,16 EUR	0,00 EUR	20.708,16 EUR
Z_INSP1	0020 (Final Accepta...	51100000 (Consptn...	MZ-RM-R300-05 (B...			-44.019,30 EUR	0,00 EUR	44.019,30 EUR
Z_INSP1	0020 (Final Accepta...	51100000 (Consptn...	MZ-RM-R300-06 (B...			-26.003,29 EUR	0,00 EUR	26.003,29 EUR
Z_INSP1	0020 (Final Accepta...	51100000 (Consptn...	MZ-RM-R300-07 (B...			-66.028,07 EUR	0,00 EUR	66.028,07 EUR
Z_INSP1	0020 (Final Accepta...	51100000 (Consptn...	MZ-RM-R300-08 (B...			-29.871,54 EUR	0,00 EUR	29.871,54 EUR
Z_INSP1	0020 (Final Accepta...	51100000 (Consptn...	MZ-RM-R300-09 (B...			-110.046,40 EUR	0,00 EUR	110.046,40 EUR
Z_INSP1	0020 (Final Accepta...	94301000 (Machine...		1 (Machine hours 1)	US10_PLR (ProdLin...	-6.955,68 EUR	0,00 EUR	6.955,68 EUR
Z_INSP1	0020 (Final Accepta...	94303000 (Setup P...		3 (Setup Production)	US10_PLR (ProdLin...	-10.533,60 EUR	0,00 EUR	10.533,60 EUR
Z_INSP1	0020 (Final Accepta...	94311000 (Pers hrs)		11 (Personnel Hours)	US10_PLR (ProdLin...	-6.953,76 EUR	0,00 EUR	6.953,76 EUR
						-929.738,26 EUR	**0,00 EUR**	**929.738,26 EUR**

Figure 14.34 Production Cost Analysis App Showing Work Centers

Figure 14.34 includes planned costs as well as actual costs. We walked through the postings in Chapter 6, Section 6.1.2, but if you refer to Figure 6.17 you'll see that we only had the planned costs by cost center and activity type. Now the planned data is also written at this more granular level to include the work center and operation that are available in the routing and the BOM if the materials have been assigned to operations and stored in a new table ACDOCP. We'll look at the process of reworking planning in Section 14.5.

Although real-time revenue recognition was introduced for commercial projects in SAP S/4HANA, the ability to calculate overhead immediately as a follow-on document for secondary postings was introduced with EHP 4 for SAP ERP 6.0 and extended in SAP S/4HANA Finance to cover primary postings. Over the next editions, SAP plans to rework the calculation of work in process and the calculation of scrap and variances to provide real-time information for production controlling as soon as the relevant material document or confirmation is posted so that the people on the shop floor can act immediately as soon as variances become apparent instead of waiting until period close.

We've now looked at some of the functional changes in Controlling with SAP S/4HANA. We'll end the chapter by looking at the major changes in reporting and planning.

14.4 Reporting in SAP Fiori

We introduced the idea of the virtual data model as SAP's new approach to reporting while talking about the Production Cost Analysis app in the previous section. Nevertheless, to avoid disruption, SAP has tried to keep the existing reports running wherever possible by using *compatibility views*. These convert the data in the Universal Journal back into the old structures to allow users to continue to work with their usual reports, as you saw when we looked at the cost center line items in Figure 14.3. What's happening in these reports is that they select those fields from the Universal Journal that were available in the old tables, so in Figure 14.3 we were seeing only the data previously available in table COEP (CO line item table). This holds true for all the existing reports, so a classic financial statement will only show those fields that were available in the old table FAGLFLEXA (General Ledger line item table), a cost center report will show those fields that were in the old tables COSP (CO primary costs) and COSS (CO secondary costs), a profitability drilldown report will only select using those CO-PA characteristics available in the operating concern (table CE4XXXX), and so on. The totals records (tables COSP, COSS, FAGLFLEXA, and so on) have been removed in SAP S/4HANA, but most of the reports based on these tables will continue to work. If you recall the many financial documents that we looked at in Chapter 6, you'll find that the Document Relationship Browser also continues to work and shows what appear to be separate Financial Accounting documents, Controlling documents, and Material Ledger documents. However, the real document is the Financial Accounting document; the related Controlling and Material Ledger documents are only views on the data in the Universal Journal. Both the Controlling and Material Ledger document numbers begin with an A (for artificial) and are not real documents in the database. Again, we're seeing compatibility views that allow the system to behave as before even though the underlying architecture has changed.

These classic reports allow you to transition slowly, but you won't get the benefits of moving to SAP S/4HANA if you use these reports indefinitely. If you now compare the new reports shown in Figure 14.1, Figure 14.2, Figure 14.17, Figure 14.24, and Figure 14.29, you'll see that the SAP Fiori apps have been designed to include fields that were previously considered part of separate application components. This cross-component view of Finance should be the aim of a transition to SAP S/4HANA.

Another aspect to consider as you draw up a reporting strategy is how you plan. We'll look at planning in detail in the next section, but the existing reports continue to read from the separate planning data stores for each of the applications. So, a classic plan/actual report for a cost center reads planned data created using Transaction KP06, a plan/actual report for a project reads planned data created using Transaction CJR2, a plan/actual report for an order reads planned data created using Transaction KPF6, and so on. Again, these planning transactions allow you to plan against dimensions in the old planning layouts, so the salary costs on your cost centers will not be automatically assigned to functional areas or profit centers until you fill these fields using the plan integration functions. Compare now the views in Figure 14.33 and Figure 14.34, in which we're comparing planned data and actual data that contains details about the work center and the operation that weren't available in the old tables; the case for making the transition now becomes stronger.

Remember also that you should not think about reporting just in SAP S/4HANA but also about any data warehouses that are taking feeds from your accounting system. If you're using SAP BW, all the extractors that we discussed in Chapter 8 will continue to run because they're also using compatibility views to read data from the Universal Journal as if the old table structures were still there. There is also a new extractor (DataSource `0FI_ACDOCA_10`) that selects all the fields in the Universal Journal and transfers them to SAP BW. Again, in the long term it's worth converting your SAP BW reporting to read from the wider table.

Note

Because there is a significant mindset change between the new virtual data model and the old Report Writer structures, you may want to read the following blog to familiarize yourself with the new approach: *https://blogs.sap.com/2016/05/27/getting-started-with-s4-hana-embedded-analytics/*. SAP Note 2579584 (Recommendations for Financial Reporting in SAP S/4HANA) walks you through further elements to consider as you embark on the new reporting journey.

14.4.1 Multidimensional Reporting

When experts make the case for SAP S/4HANA, it tends to be heavy on the need for multidimensional reporting. One of my accounting friends described the Universal Journal as the pivot table that accountants have always dreamed about, with the new table providing the technical basis for almost limitless drilldowns to every reporting dimension.

To get an idea of what's available out of the box, use the SAP Fiori library to select the apps delivered for the CO-OM-IS (Controlling Information System) and FI-GL-IS (General Ledger Information System) components. Don't be put off by the conventional sound of many of the app titles, such as Cost Center—Actuals or Projects—Actuals. As you saw in Figure 14.29, the new Projects—Actuals app is much wider than its equivalent report in SAP ERP, showing not just the revenues and costs assigned to WBS elements but also the derived CO-PA characteristics (Section 14.3.1). Figure 14.35 shows the reports delivered for the sales accountant role in SAP S/4HANA 1709. Here you can see the market segment reports that you might expect to find associated with this role, but also the sales orders and projects that this controller also will be monitoring. In all cases, these reports include drilldowns by company code, profit center, and so on alongside the CO account assignments.

Figure 14.35 SAP Fiori Launchpad for Sales Accountant Role

Nevertheless, SAP still does not deliver CDS views for all the key figures that you will potentially use for Controlling. We saw target costs for production orders in Figure 14.33, but there isn't yet an equivalent view for target costs in Cost Center Accounting (see Chapter 7, Section 7.1.5). SAP has yet to build CDS views to display control costs and the various variance categories. When we think of project reporting, we also expect to see budget, commitments, and so on, but these views are still being built. The situation is changing all the time, so watch for updates to SAP Note 2349297 (S4TWL—Reporting/Analytics in Controlling) for details of any progress. You can generally assume that if SAP announces a cloud enhancement for budget or commitment reporting, it will find its way into the on-premise delivery during the next year.

14.4.2 Accounts and Key Figures

Plenty of sales controllers are delighted with the idea of a single source of truth in the Universal Journal, but many express concern about the sheer number of accounts that can show up in Profitability Analysis and how this could make reporting extremely cumbersome. For all the restrictions of only being allowed to use up to 200 value fields in the past, this limit ensured that the costing-based CO-PA reports were never struggling to present thousands of accounts in a meaningful manner.

Figure 14.36 shows the Product Profitability app (SAP Fiori ID F2765), which is currently only available in the cloud. The **Dimensions** column on the left gives a real sense of the power of the new options for multidimensional reporting; you can see many of the reporting dimensions in the Universal Journal that are available for drill-down (we've drilled down by **Product Sold Group**). The existing on-premise reports for the market segments offer these dimensions but use accounts to build the lines of the report. In this case, we've created a more classic contribution margin report by using *semantic tags* to identify the accounts for **Billed Revenue, Recognized Revenue, COGS—Variable, COGS—Fixed, Price Differences, Admin Overhead, Sales Overhead, Marketing Overhead**, and **R&D Overhead**. We've then grouped these in the report to calculate the various contribution margins and deliver a report that feels much more like the one we showed in Chapter 5, Figure 5.49. Of course, if you want to understand the assignment of the accounts to the semantic tags, choose **G/L Account** as a drill-down option from the list of dimensions on the left of the report.

The idea behind the semantic tags is that SAP can deliver applications and key figures for which the structure remains stable. So the Product Profitability app (see Figure 14.36) can be used out of the box by simply mapping your own accounts/cost elements to these tags. Again, this assignment is made in the IMG under **General Ledger**

Accounting (New) • Master Data • G/L Accounts • Assign Semantic Tags for Balance Sheet and Profit and Loss Structures. The idea is that the tags themselves should remain stable, so if you use different revenue accounts in the United States and in Brazil, you should keep one revenue tag but assign the different accounts in dependency from your financial statement version (Transaction OB58). The assignment uses the nodes of the financial statement version, but you can also assign individual accounts or combinations of accounts and functional areas to the delivered tags.

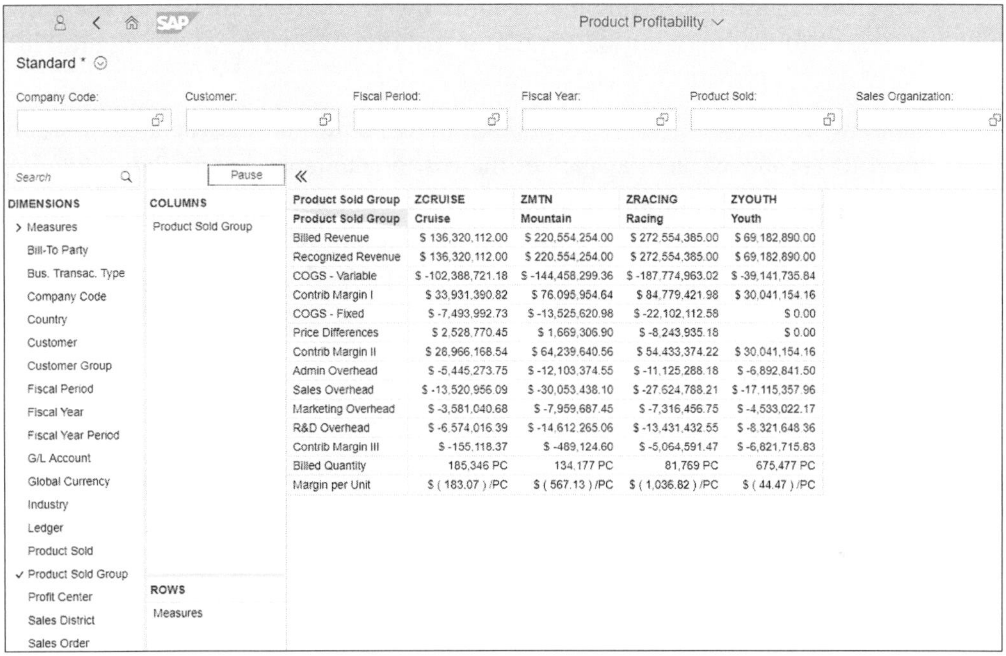

Figure 14.36 Product Profitability App

SAP delivers around 58 semantic tags for cash reporting and profitability reporting, so start your journey in the IMG under **General Ledger Accounting (New) • Master Data • G/L Accounts • Define Semantic Tags for Balance Sheet and Profit and Loss Structures** to see whether the delivered semantic tags match the value fields that you use for reporting today. You can then create further tags as required. If you create new semantic tags, you'll need to extend the CDS query to reference these tags. To learn more about this approach, refer to SAP Note 2538634 (Semantic Tagging for FSV and CDS Query Extension).

14.4.3 Hierarchies

For all the enthusiasm for multidimensional reporting from the Universal Journal, many controllers have also asked about plans for the profit center hierarchies, cost center hierarchies, cost element groups, and financial statement versions that they use to aggregate costs in their daily work. If you look back at Figure 14.1 or Figure 14.24 you'll see that the accounts are shown as a flat list but with a **Hierarchy** button above the dataset, which you can use to select the financial statement version that you would like to use to structure the accounts. If you now compare this view with the account structure in Figure 14.29, you'll see that the accounts are hierarchically structured according to the financial statement version.

One SAP Fiori app that's easy to overlook is the Replicate Runtime Hierarchy app (SAP Fiori ID F1478), delivered as part of the cost accountant and the General Ledger accountant role and shown in Figure 14.37. What this app does is to copy the financial statement versions, cost center hierarchies, and profit center hierarchies into views specifically designed for use with the SAP Fiori reports. This will not only improve the performance of your analytical apps but also ensure that you have regular snapshots of the hierarchy structure at a given time.

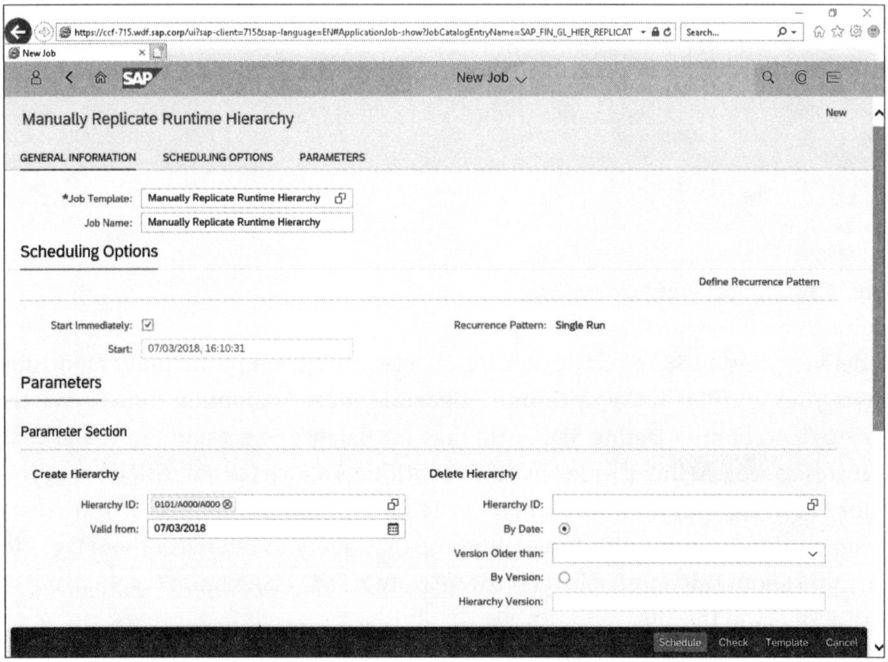

Figure 14.37 Replicate Runtime Hierarchy App

Many controllers also told SAP that they struggled to keep their cost center hierarchies and profit center hierarchies in sync because they typically kept several hierarchies in parallel to provide different views of their organization; the process of adding to or changing these hierarchies was rather cumbersome. With SAP S/4HANA 1709, SAP introduced a new SAP Fiori app called Manage Flexible Hierarchies (SAP Fiori ID F2759), delivered as part of the cost accountant—overhead role, which is designed to provide an alternative approach to this challenge.

Figure 14.38 shows the new app that can be used to manage either cost center hierarchies or profit center hierarchies (we show a profit center hierarchy in this example).

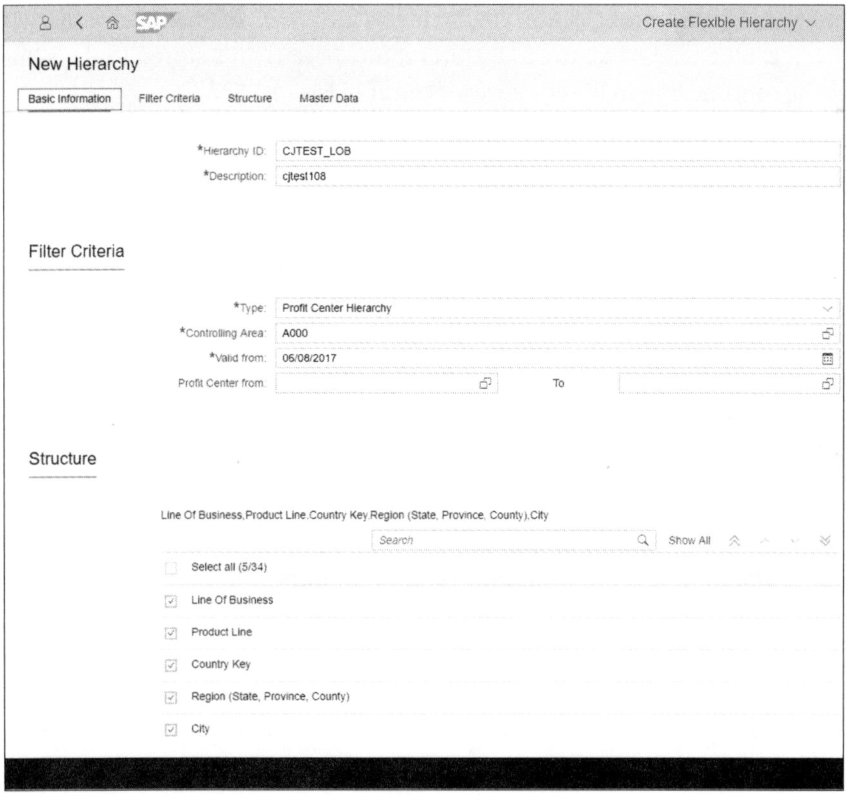

Figure 14.38 Manage Flexible Hierarchies App

Notice at the bottom of the screen a list of fields: **Line of Business**, **Product Line**, **Country Key**, **Region (State, Province, County)**, and **City**. These are the fields that will be used to generate the tree structure for profit center reporting, giving a reporting node for each line of business, product line, and so on. In fact, the idea isn't new. If you refer to Chapter 8, Figure 8.9, you'll see the same approach being used to report on production orders based on the plant and material number to which the orders are assigned. But where orders and projects provide hundreds of fields that can be used to build these kind of tree structures, cost centers and profit centers offer far fewer fields. To build these kind of structures, you will need to add new fields to the relevant master data, extending the profit center master to include custom fields that you can then use to build hierarchies. Don't get carried away with this approach and multiply out your profit centers and cost centers by all the attributes that you think you might need for reporting; instead, consider this as a useful alternative to classic cost center and profit center hierarchies. Once you've generated a flexible hierarchy, it can be read by all the SAP Fiori reports because it's stored in the same tables as the runtime hierarchies that we looked at in Figure 14.37.

14.5 Planning

The radical shift that brought about the move to the Universal Journal has also been applied to financial planning. Chapter 5 saw us selecting many different planning applications, entering figures by cost center, order, project, and CO-PA dimension, and then copying data between the different planning applications. The new financial planning applications treat profit and loss planning, cost center planning, order planning, and so on as one single model and store the data in a single table (ACDOCP), which has a structure that maps easily to the Universal Journal (table ACDOCA).

14.5.1 Simplified Planning Model for Financial Planning

Figure 14.39 shows the new planning line item table ACDOCP that was introduced in SAP S/4HANA 1610. The aim of this planning table is to have a similar structure to the Universal Journal so that you can plan against the same General Ledger account assignments (see Figure 14.8), the same CO account assignments (see Figure 14.9), and the same CO-PA characteristics (see Figure 14.11). If you add a new CO-PA characteristic, the system will update both the Universal Journal and the planning table automatically.

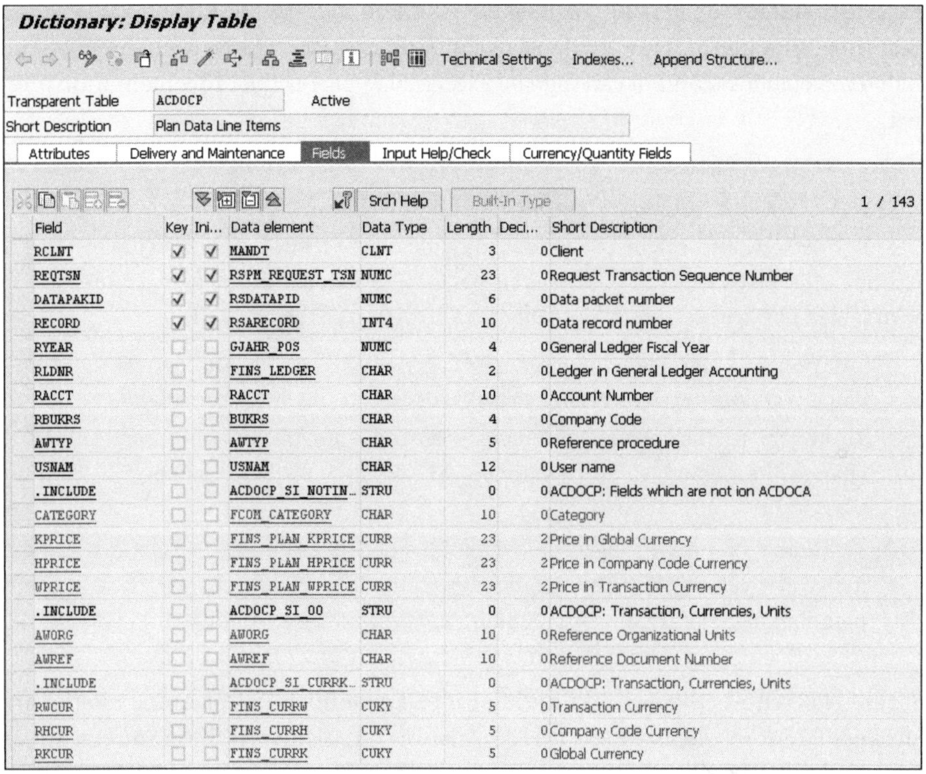

Field	Key	Ini...	Data element	Data Type	Length	Deci...	Short Description
RCLNT	✓	✓	MANDT	CLNT	3	0	Client
REQTSN	✓	✓	RSPM_REQUEST_TSN	NUMC	23	0	Request Transaction Sequence Number
DATAPAKID	✓	✓	RSDATAPID	NUMC	6	0	Data packet number
RECORD	✓	✓	RSARECORD	INT4	10	0	Data record number
RYEAR			GJAHR_POS	NUMC	4	0	General Ledger Fiscal Year
RLDNR			FINS_LEDGER	CHAR	2	0	Ledger in General Ledger Accounting
RACCT			RACCT	CHAR	10	0	Account Number
RBUKRS			BUKRS	CHAR	4	0	Company Code
AWTYP			AWTYP	CHAR	5	0	Reference procedure
USNAM			USNAM	CHAR	12	0	User name
.INCLUDE			ACDOCP_SI_NOTIN...	STRU	0	0	ACDOCP: Fields which are not ion ACDOCA
CATEGORY			FCOM_CATEGORY	CHAR	10	0	Category
KPRICE			FINS_PLAN_KPRICE	CURR	23	2	Price in Global Currency
HPRICE			FINS_PLAN_HPRICE	CURR	23	2	Price in Company Code Currency
WPRICE			FINS_PLAN_WPRICE	CURR	23	2	Price in Transaction Currency
.INCLUDE			ACDOCP_SI_00	STRU	0	0	ACDOCP: Transaction, Currencies, Units
AWORG			AWORG	CHAR	10	0	Reference Organizational Units
AWREF			AWREF	CHAR	10	0	Reference Document Number
.INCLUDE			ACDOCP_SI_CURRK...	STRU	0	0	ACDOCP: Transaction, Currencies, Units
RWCUR			FINS_CURRW	CUKY	5	0	Transaction Currency
RHCUR			FINS_CURRH	CUKY	5	0	Company Code Currency
RKCUR			FINS_CURRK	CUKY	5	0	Global Currency

Figure 14.39 Planning Line Item Table

The challenge with planning, however, is that people plan at different levels, as we saw in Chapter 5. In a top-down planning scenario, targets are set for company codes, profit centers, and so on, and then broken down to the more granular account assignments. At the same time, bottom-up planning scenarios are busy aggregating the data planned by cost center, order, project, and CO-PA characteristic to see whether these targets can be reached, and the two approaches iterate until the results converge to everybody's satisfaction. Planning is performed by controllers and managers who need to work with different planning layouts that store data to the same underlying data model, as you saw in Chapter 9.

SAP S/4HANA therefore includes a planning model based on SAP Business Planning and Consolidation (SAP BPC). This model is generated as part of the customer project and includes the workbooks, queries, and virtual InfoProviders needed to provide a basic approach to financial planning. The full title of this option is *SAP BPC optimized for SAP S/4HANA*. By default, planned data entered in these workbooks updates the real-time InfoCube S/4HANA Financials: InfoCube for Plan Data (/ERP/SFIN_R01). The delivered business content can then be extended as part of the implementation project.

How to Switch from Cubes to Tables in Planning

SAP S/4HANA also offers the virtual InfoProvider S/4HANA Financials: Plan Data from ACDOCP (/ERP/SFIN_V20). This virtual InfoProvider stores the plan data records in table ACDOCP, which has almost the same structure as table ACDOCA.

Before you start your planning cycle, you can choose to store your plan data in the virtual InfoProvider instead of the real-time InfoCube. You have two options:

1. To switch to the virtual InfoProvider centrally for all planning applications, change the default value of variable /ERP/P_0INFOPROV to value /ERP/SFIN_V20.
2. To switch to the virtual InfoProvider for specific planning applications only, assign the value /ERP/SFIN_V20 directly to the 0INFOPROV characteristic in the planning filters of the specific planning applications.

Figure 14.40 shows the new application for P&L planning. The planning queries are delivered as *workbooks* for use with SAP Analysis for Microsoft Office. You can access these by choosing **File • Analysis • Open Workbook.** This might look like an SAP BW–based application, but the master data for the account structure shown on the left and the reference data for 2015 shown in the first column are read directly from SAP S/4HANA without replication. What we're using here is embedded SAP BW on SAP S/4HANA to give us planning functions just like the ones we looked at in Chapter 10. The difference is that the new InfoProviders are designed specifically to work directly with SAP S/4HANA. To access the latest data from SAP S/4HANA, choose **Recalculate**.

The easiest way to start planning is to use the **Copy Actual to Plan** button. Behind the scenes the *Planning Application Kit* (PAK) can select millions of lines of actual data, aggregate them to the dimensions shown in the planning application, and then update the planned values. You can then plan either line by line as we did in Chapter 5 or at the node level (such as labor expenses) and use planning functions to break down the values from the node to the lines or from the year to the relevant periods.

Figure 14.41 shows the same data broken down by customer group, and Figure 14.42 shows the data broken down by cost center. As you enter data by customer group or cost center, it's automatically aggregated to the P&L view.

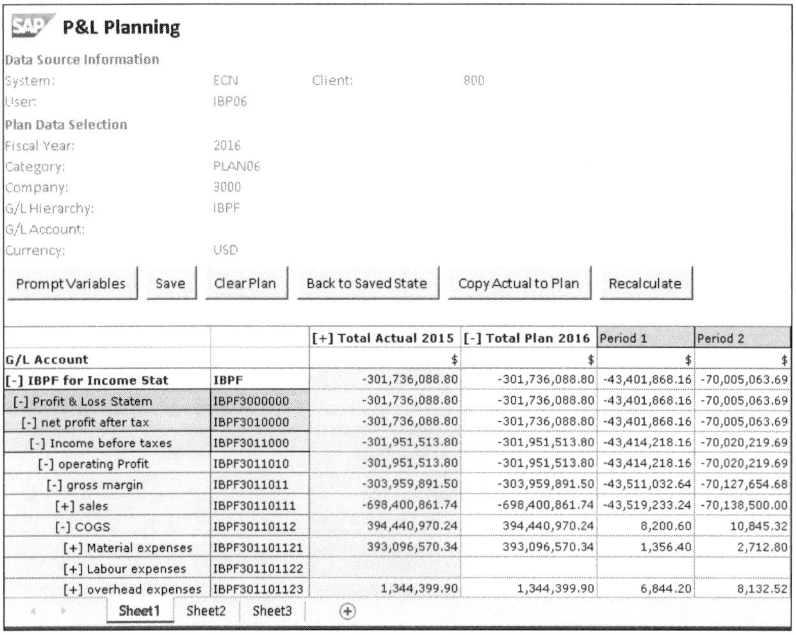

Figure 14.40 P&L Planning in SAP BPC

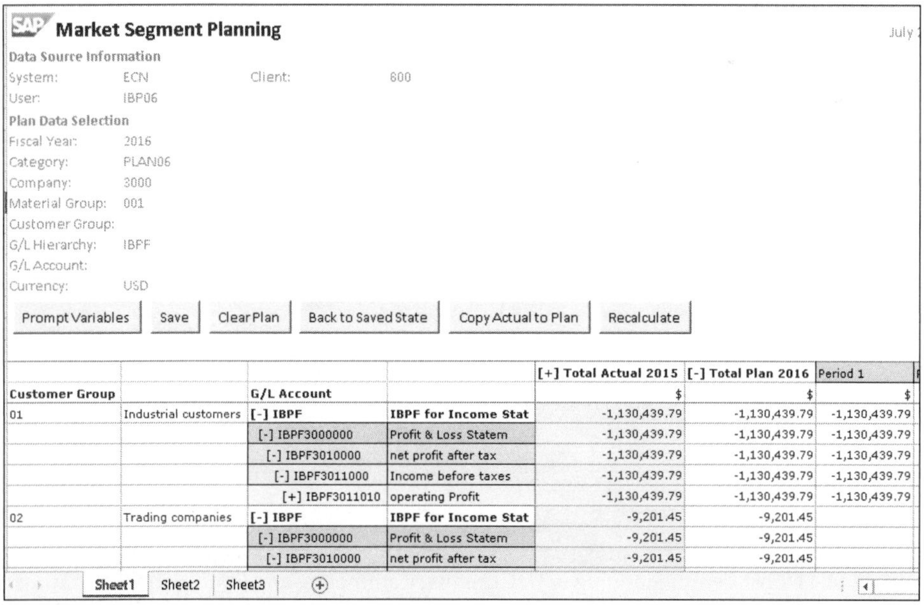

Figure 14.41 Market Segment Planning in SAP BPC

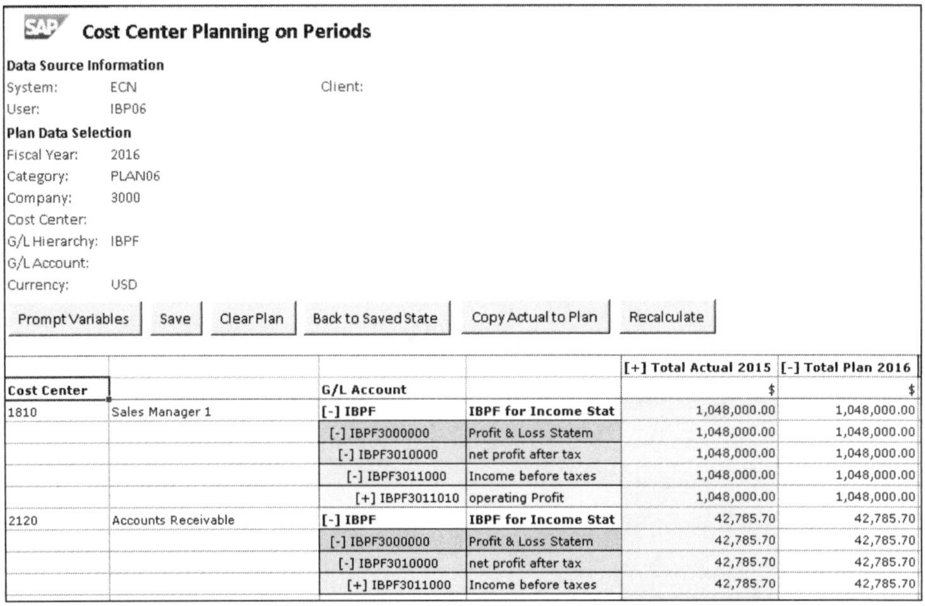

Figure 14.42 Cost Center Planning in SAP BPC

Of course, the delivered workbooks are only a starting point. Figure 14.43 shows how the planning workbooks can be extended to include graphical elements and conditional formatting. To add comments to a planning application, follow the instructions available at the following blog: *https://archive.sap.com/documents/docs/DOC-59001*.

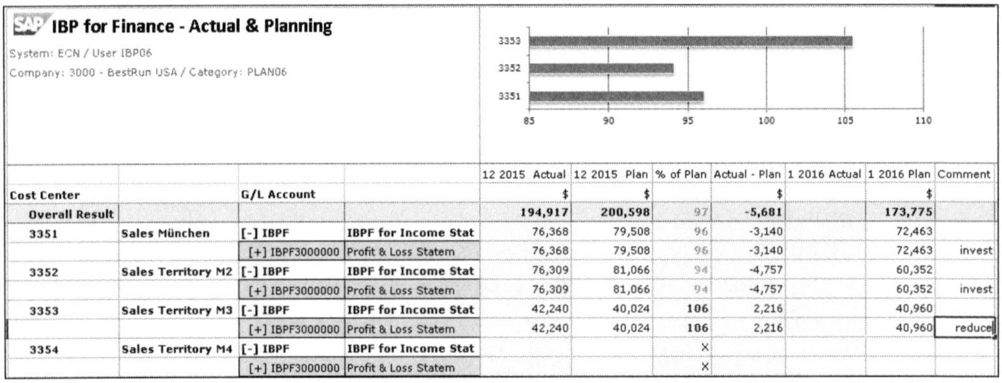

Figure 14.43 Cost Center Planning with Graphics, Comments, and Conditional Formating

Although you will be able to handle simple planning scenarios via this approach, you may need to keep some of your classic planning transactions while SAP continues to deliver on its roadmap. To find out more, refer to SAP Note 2270407 (S4TWL—Profit and Loss Planning, Profit Center Planning, Cost Center Planning, Order Planning, and Project Planning).

It's also possible to combine the two approaches. Figure 14.44 shows the same cost center planning application with buttons for two planning functions to download data planned in SAP BPC to SAP ERP (**Copy IBP to ERP**; the product was originally known as SAP Integrated Business Planning or SAP IBP) and to upload plan data from SAP ERP to SAP BPC (**Copy ERP to IBP**). Similar planning functions are available to upload/download planned data for orders and projects.

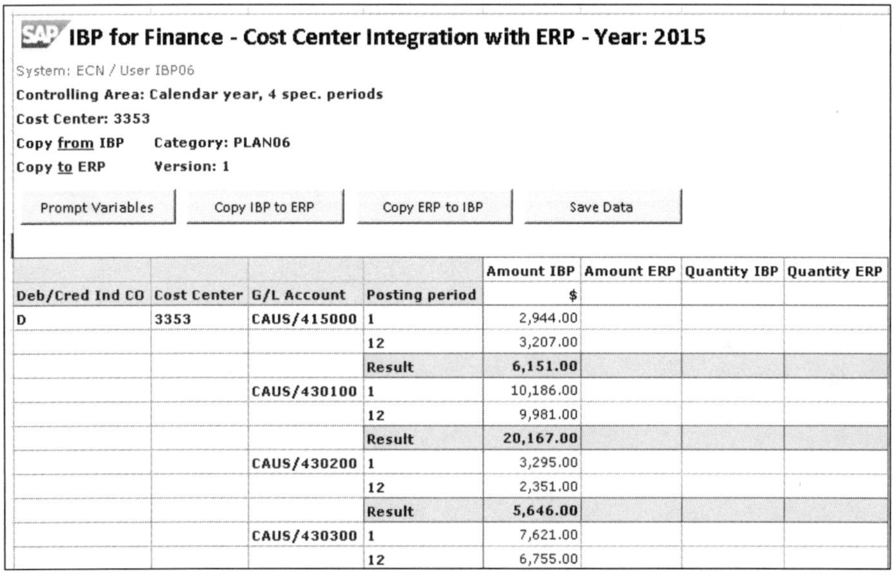

IBP for Finance - Cost Center Integration with ERP - Year: 2015

System: ECN / User IBP06
Controlling Area: Calendar year, 4 spec. periods
Cost Center: 3353
Copy from IBP   Category: PLAN06
Copy to ERP   Version: 1

Prompt Variables | Copy IBP to ERP | Copy ERP to IBP | Save Data

				Amount IBP	Amount ERP	Quantity IBP	Quantity ERP
Deb/Cred Ind CO	Cost Center	G/L Account	Posting period	$			
D	3353	CAUS/415000	1	2,944.00			
			12	3,207.00			
			Result	6,151.00			
		CAUS/430100	1	10,186.00			
			12	9,981.00			
			Result	20,167.00			
		CAUS/430200	1	3,295.00			
			12	2,351.00			
			Result	5,646.00			
		CAUS/430300	1	7,621.00			
			12	6,755.00			

Figure 14.44 Cost Center Planning with Upload/Download to SAP ERP

Complete instructions for setting up the new planning model are beyond the scope of this chapter, but you'll find the basics described in SAP Note 1972819 (Setup SAP BPC Optimized for S/4 HANA Finance and Embedded BW Reporting [aka Integrated Business Planning for Finance]).

14.5.2 Functional Expenses and Sales Costs

In the previous section our focus was on account-based planning with revenues being planned by market segment and costs by cost center and the two sides rolled up to give a P&L plan. However, cost center planning generally involves planning functional expenses and then assigning them to other cost centers and market segments using the various allocations we looked at in Chapter 5. We'll now look at how the data entered on the cost centers as functional expenses can be allocated as part of a simulative planning process. Figure 14.45 shows the primary costs for three cost centers prior to allocation. Of course, we could have built the same example using the data entered in Figure 14.42.

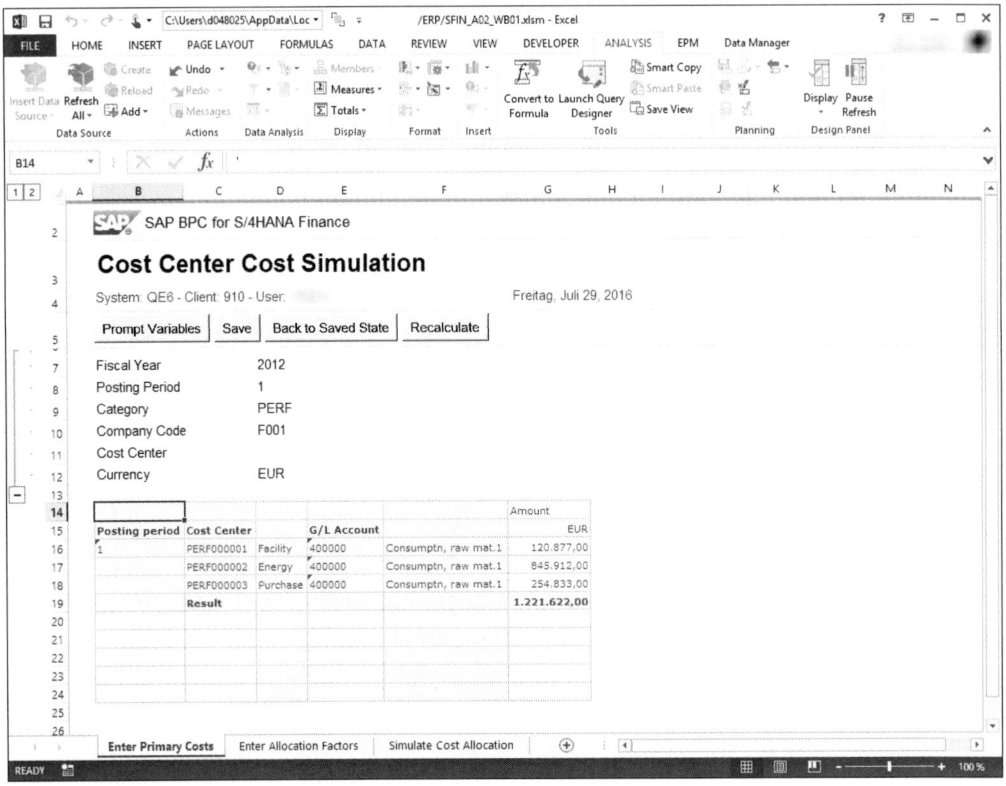

Figure 14.45 Enter Primary Costs for Simulation

The next step is to plan the drivers to be used for such an allocation. Figure 14.46 shows a planning query containing the sender cost centers from Figure 14.45, the receiver cost centers (see Chapter 5), and the account/cost element under which the allocation will be posted. For each combination we've entered the quantities that will be used as allocation factors (**Quantity** column).

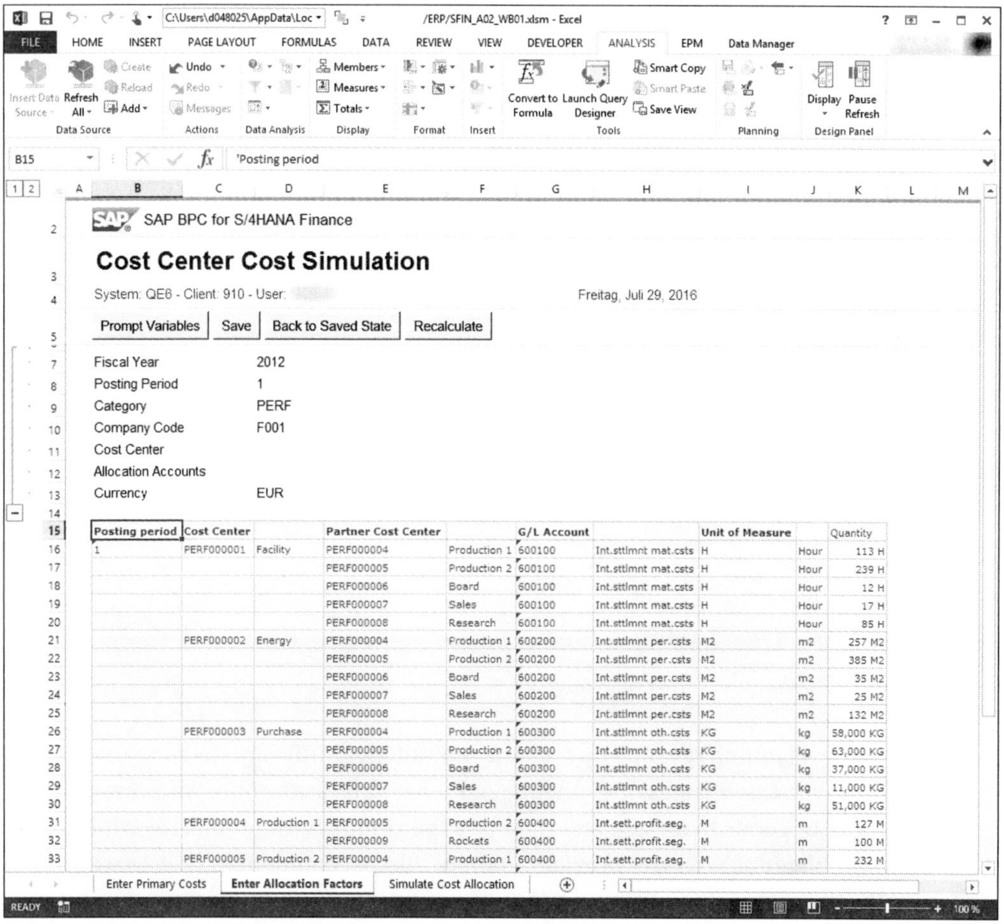

Figure 14.46 Enter Allocation Factors for Cost Simulation

Figure 14.47 shows the result of the allocation. To see what happened in the allocation, we need to use the **Deb/Cred Ind CO** (debit/credit indicator) column to understand which lines are debits (**D**) and which are credits (**C**) within the allocation.

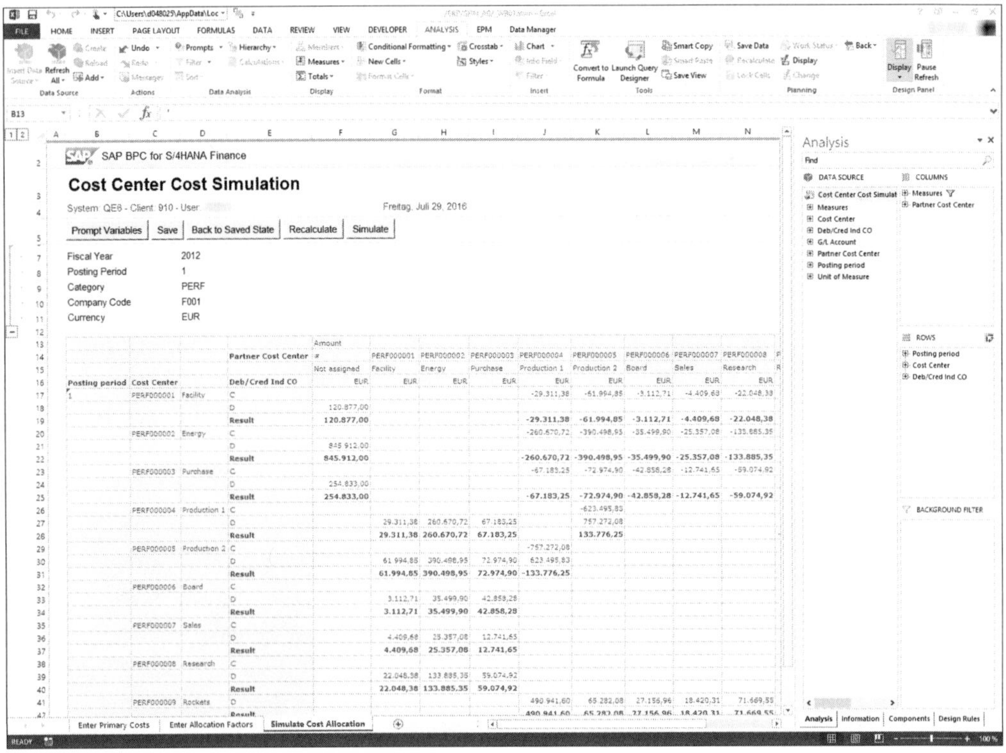

Figure 14.47 Simulate Cost Allocation

Similarly, planning revenue by account will not give sufficient detail to understand what drives the business. To understand what drives revenue, we must plan the quantity of goods to be sold and then pull the results of the standard cost estimate into the planning layout to provide details of the cost component split, as we showed in Chapter 5.

From SAP S/4HANA 1709, SAP offers a production cost planning workbook that allows you to plan the quantities of goods sold, the sales prices, and the sales deductions in dedicated queries. The cost side of the equation is filled by reading the standard cost estimates for the materials to be sold along with the standard lot size in the cost estimate. A planning function then uses the same mechanisms as we used to split the cost of goods manufactured for the delivery (see Figure 14.12) to give the result shown in Figure 14.48. Here we plan to sell a quantity of mountain bikes (material WDF07-F-0001) from plant 0001. When the user selects the **Calculate Production**

Costs button, the system uses the cost component split for the mountain bike to determine the production costs and assign them to the cost of sales accounts (**Changes in Inventory**, **Material Expenses**, and **Personnel Expenses**).

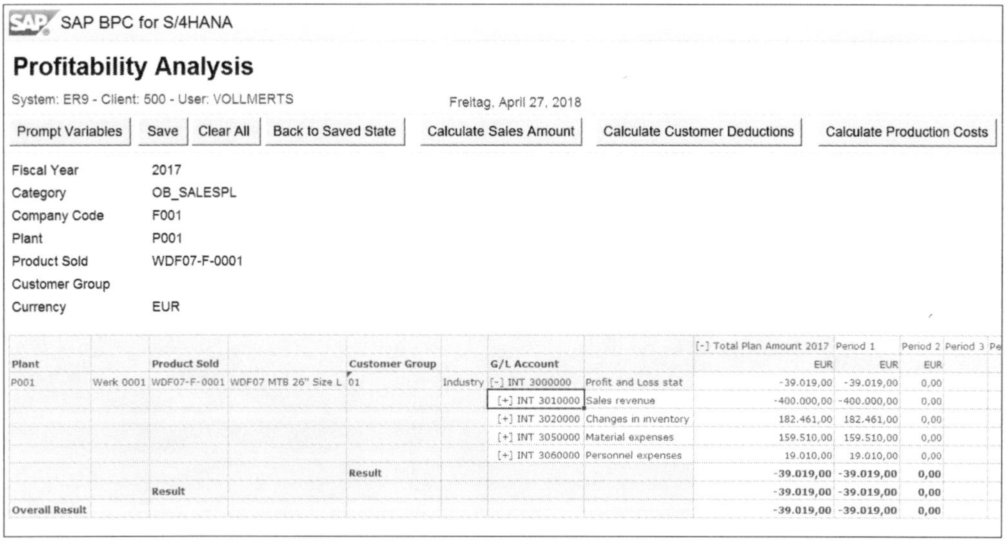

Figure 14.48 Sales Planning with Cost of Goods Sold

To understand what happened behind the scenes, we'll now look at the **Transfer Production Costs** function (see Figure 14.49). Here the system has selected the items in the cost estimate for the mountain bike. You'll remember from our discussions about the BOM in Chapter 4 that a standard cost estimate is built up in layers, creating a cost estimate for each semifinished product in turn until the final saleable finished product is reached. In sales planning, the reverse happens: the system removes any semifinished products (such as the wheels in this example) and replaces them with the components used to build these levels (so the wheels are replaced by rims, spokes, hubs, etc.). This flattened itemization for the whole bike is used in combination with the lot size to determine the costs for the quantity of bikes to be sold.

Probably the best way to summarize this section is to show a full list of all workbooks delivered for SAP BPC in SAP S/4HANA 1709 (see Figure 14.50), as this gives a sense of the range of planning queries available.

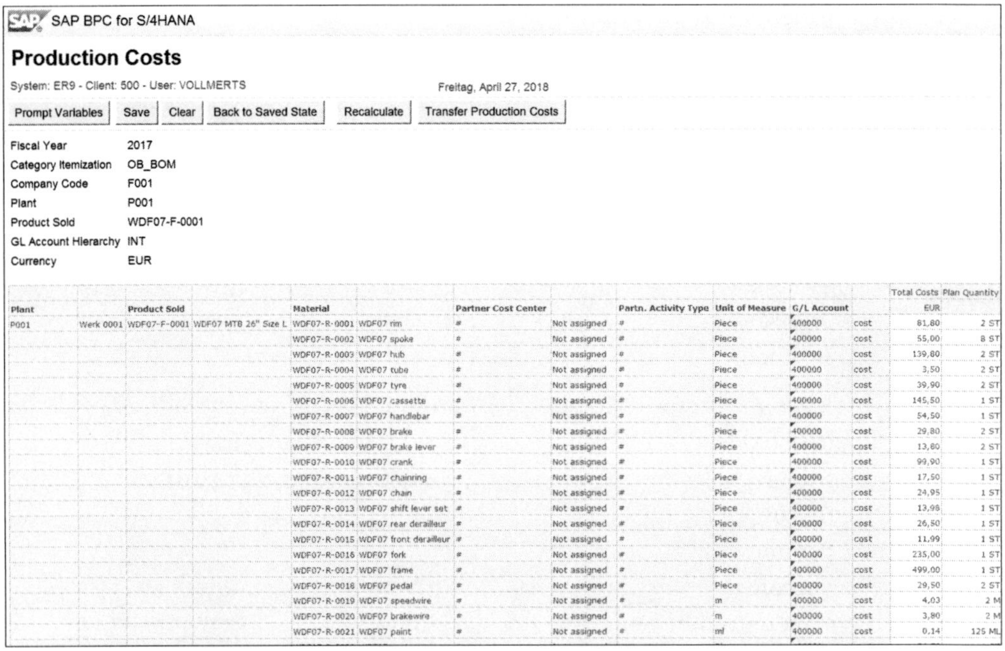

Figure 14.49 Production Costs for Inclusion in Sales Planning

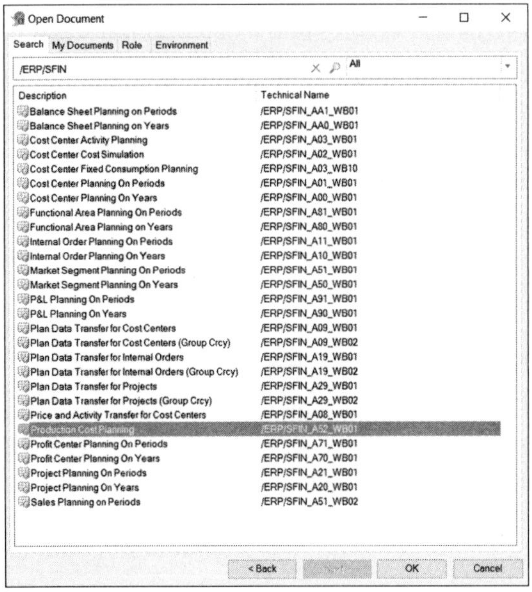

Figure 14.50 Planning Workbooks for SAP BPC Optimized for SAP S/4HANA

14.5.3 Commitments and Budgeting

In Chapter 5 we looked at budgeting and planning and in Chapter 6 at commitments, and we explained how a plan could be used to generate a budget and how the budget was checked against a combination of actual costs and commitments. Both budgeting and commitments are currently undergoing a redesign in SAP S/4HANA. In the case of budgeting, this is simply being treated as a new plan category that captures budget in the same structure as the plan. However, the point of a budget is that it represents a ceiling for spending; operative checks are made against this budget, looking at the costs incurred already and any open commitments. The newly designed availability check is planned for release in SAP S/4HANA Cloud 1808.

Commitments have undergone a more radical change. A commitment is created with each purchase order to record the amount of spending expected on a cost center, project, or order (see Chapter 6, Section 6.3.4). The commitment is then used and finally canceled as the goods and then the invoice are received for the purchase order. In SAP ERP the commitment is a one-sided posting to the CO account assignment. In SAP S/4HANA it becomes a fully fledged accounting document recording not just the expected spend in Controlling but also the relevant lines in accounts payable—and of course the due date for the delivery so that the costs can be recognized in the correct accounting period. A commitment is not yet a GAAP-relevant document, so we must separate these accounting documents from the goods receipt and invoice receipt that will come later in the business process. This is achieved technically by using an *extension ledger* (see Figure 14.10) that separates the *predictive accounting* documents from the normal GAAP-relevant documents. The notion of predictive accounting may sound strange to an accountant used to looking backwards at the data in the closed accounting periods, but it's simply a different way of looking at commitment accounting. The first commitment scenarios were delivered with SAP S/4HANA Cloud 1711 and are available with SAP S/4HANA 1809.

The same predictive accounting approach is used in reverse for incoming sales orders. These were previously captured in costing-based CO-PA (see Chapter 6, Section 6.1.3). In SAP S/4HANA the incoming sales orders also generate fully fledged accounting documents recording the expected contribution margin in Profitability Analysis and the relevant lines in accounts receivable in an extension ledger. Like the commitments, the value of the open item must also be canceled as the goods are shipped and the invoice issued later in the business process. This is a change from the old process, in which reporting/planning was simply a case of distinguishing between record types F (for invoices) and A (for sales orders). The first app for the reporting of incoming sales orders was delivered with SAP S/4HANA 1805 (SAP Fiori ID F2964), and the first predictive contribution margin scenarios are planned for delivery with SAP S/4HANA Cloud 1811.

From SAP S/4HANA 1809, it's also possible to record statistical sales conditions to an extension ledger. The basic approach will be familiar from costing-based CO-PA, but instead of updating value fields, the statistical conditions are linked with accounts, and you can create new accounts to record the costs and liabilities associated with these conditions.

14.6 Summary and Postscript

We've now shown how the Controlling application has been absorbed into the Universal Journal and discussed some of the new options for multidimensional reporting. This is probably the most significant change to SAP Controlling since the move from R/2 to R/3 in the early 1990s—and the journey is by no means complete, as SAP works with its customers to understand the changing needs of the Controlling department in organizations that have gone global since their early SAP implementations.

There has also been a shift in deployment options from the classic on-premise approach, in which the IT department at the customer site is responsible for all upgrades and maintenance, to the cloud approach, in which SAP performs these steps on behalf of the customer. You may have noted that in the last sections we were often describing functions that were being delivered for the cloud editions of SAP S/4HANA. A radical change is underway to offer a cloud solution for Finance that will be available with only minimal configuration. SAP delivers a cloud edition once per quarter and an on-premise edition once per year. Each on-premise edition includes many of the functions originally released for the cloud, so the new approach for commercial projects was originally released for the cloud edition for professional services and came into SAP S/4HANA with 1610.

When I embarked on the first edition of this book, several people asked me why it had taken me so long to start. The easy answer is that in the late 1990s I was a working mother with two small children. The real answer is that it's virtually impossible to write a book with the software changing around you and new functions being added in each release. By 2010 I thought that the world of software development had slowed down, but SAP HANA arrived before the first edition had even gone to print, and we were soon revisiting a lot of our working assumptions about Controlling in the light of SAP HANA. By the time I started work on the second edition, we were removing totals records and summarization objects and designing the Universal Journal. By the third edition, we had already developed the Universal Journal and rearchitected the Material Ledger for actual costing. So much for the idea of writing about stable software!

My role involves working with developers in Walldorf and Shanghai to create the latest versions of the Controlling software, but in parallel I'm talking to real controllers about their daily concerns and what their organizations would like them to do with ever-fewer resources. I also present (and listen) at conferences. This book is for the people who take my classes at SAP Financials or SAP Controlling in the United States or my workshops at Mastering SAP Financials in Australia and South Africa and want a little more meat than I can give them in a single session. It's for those people who would dearly love to go to one of those conferences but find themselves struggling alone with the difference between a direct or an indirect activity allocation or between the moving average price and periodic unit price.

As I finish the third edition, I would love to say that the world of Controlling is slowing down again, but it isn't. My day-to-day work involves me in coinnovations with some of SAP's biggest customers in Germany and the United States. The world where I began my career is long gone: no longer am I activating product costing in a single plant where the only currency is the Deutschmark. Instead, we're always thinking globally, which means multiple currencies, multiple accounting principles, a raft of local legal requirements, and lots of work at headquarters to make sense of that complexity and enable managers to make key steering decisions in terms of which products and customers are profitable. It's an exciting time to be in Controlling, but it's certainly not a quiet one. And on that note, I hope that this edition can help you navigate the storms of the digital transformation and make sense of the changes sweeping over the business world.

The Author

Janet Salmon is currently chief product owner for management accounting at SAP SE and has accompanied many developments to the Controlling components of SAP ERP Financials as both a product and a solution manager. She regularly works with key customers and user groups in the United States and Germany to understand their Controlling challenges and requirements. Her role is to design and implement innovative Controlling solutions with development teams in Germany and China.

She joined SAP AG as a translator in 1992 having gained a degree in Modern and Medieval Languages from Downing College, Cambridge and a post-graduate qualification in Interpreting and Translating from the University of Bath.

She became a technical writer for the Product Costing area in 1993 and a product manager in 1996. In 1998 she received an award from the Society of Technical Communication for *Functions in Detail: Product Cost Controlling*, which the judges described as "refreshingly free of fluff." She is an advisor and regular contributor to SAP Financials Expert (*https://sapexperts.wispubs.com/Financials/*) and regularly presents at Financials conferences.

Index

D

E

F

G

H

I

P

Q

R

S

T

SAP PRESS
2nd Edition
Actual Costing with the SAP Material Ledger
Vanda Reis
Rheinwerk